Intermediate Accounting

An Analytical Approach

Second Edition

Intermediate Accounting

An Analytical Approach

Second Edition

ROBERT H. CRANDALL
Professor
School of Business
Queen's University

Prentice–Hall Canada Series in Accounting

Prentice–Hall Canada Inc.,
Scarborough, Ontario

Canadian Cataloguing in Publication Data

Crandall, Robert H. (Robert Hunter), 1930–
    Intermediate accounting

(Prentice-Hall Canada series in accounting)
2nd ed.
Bibliography: p.
Includes Index.
ISBN 0–13–470345–6

1. Accounting.   I. Title.   II. Series.

HF5635.C73 1989   657'.044   C88–094670–9

© 1990 Prentice-Hall Canada Inc., Scarborough, Ontario

Prentice-Hall, Inc., Englewood Cliffs, New Jersey
Prentice-Hall International, Inc., London
Prentice-Hall of Australia, Pty., Ltd., Sydney
Prentice-Hall of India Pvt., Ltd., New Delhi
Prentice-Hall of Japan, Inc., Tokyo
Prentice-Hall of Southeast Asia (Pte.) Ltd., Singapore
Editora Prentice-Hall do Brasil Ltda., Rio de Janeiro
Prentice-Hall Hispanoamericana, S.A., Mexico

ISBN 0–13–470345–6

Production Editor: Maurice Esses
Designer: Robert Garbutt Productions
Cover Graphic: © The Stock Market Inc.
Production Coordinator: Sandra Paige
Typesetting: Colborne, Cox and Burns

1   2   3   4   5   T.H.B.   92   91   90   89

Printed and bound in Canada by T.H. Best Printing Company Ltd.

For the many Queen's students who cheerfully endured the manuscript stages of this text.

Table of Contents

5 Cash, Temporary Investments, and Accounts Receivable   *170*

6 Inventory and Cost of Goods Sold

7 Land, Buildings, and Equipment

8   Depreciation, Depletion, and Amortization   *331*

9   Intangible Assets   *369*

10   Long-Term Investments   *394*

13   Corporate Income Taxes   *488*

Preface

This book covers topics usually referred to as "intermediate accounting." Many students — especially those who have had an introductory accounting course that concentrated on techniques rather than concepts — have a hard time anticipating how these topics might be approached. Thus, here is a good place to say what this book sets out to accomplish.

First, the text covers the standard topics in intermediate accounting, with some additional coverage of consolidations and financial-statement analysis. The student who wants to be more sophisticated in using financial statements will find that the coverage in this text helps considerably. There is a genuine effort to assess the strengths and weaknesses of accounting as the topics are introduced. I believe that the definition of a true expert in accounting is someone who understands a technique but knows when it *won't* work; someone who can sense when a perfectly acceptable accounting technique is being used in an unacceptable setting.

Second, although regular reference is made to the pronouncements of the accounting regulatory bodies (the references to the Canadian *CICA Handbook* are shown in square brackets), this book is not intended to encourage the student to learn the rules of the moment of financial accounting standard-setting bodies. Because the work these bodies do is important, their role should be understood. Accordingly, attention is paid to that topic in this book. But the detailed rulings of the regulatory bodies change from time to time, and they often appear contradictory or incomplete unless examined against the conceptual problems being addressed. Therefore, this book represents a departure from many intermediate texts whose authors evidently think it necessary to cite "authoritative" rulings to support their view. Many such texts were written originally for readers in the United States, where the legal environment — with its greater danger of lawsuits — compels professional accountants to study the wording of rulings carefully. We do not have a similar situation in Canada, and there is a feeling in both Canada and the United States that such "legal accounting" is a step in the wrong direction. As one Canadian group said after a study of the situation, "We urge that an attempt to resist (detailed rules) be made, and we believe the profession can meet the challenge. If we are proven wrong, detailed rules can be drafted and adopted; but once we abandon principles for detailed rules, it may be impossible to turn back." [CICA Special Committee on Standard Setting, *Report to CICA Board of Governors* (Toronto, December 1980), p. 13.]

How does the accountant avoid detailed rules and concentrate on the underlying principles? This can be done by analysing the issues in a framework of economics, and then applying the results to the specific accounting cases. It is this aspect of financial reporting that I emphasize throughout the text. One main goal is to develop the ability to analyze and organize financial information so as to aid the person who must make essentially economic decisions. This person may be the investor deciding whether to add an item to the portfolio he or she is responsible for managing; the public servant assessing the economic impact on the private sector of government policies; the reader trying to make sense of an article in *The Financial Post* or *Report on Business*; or simply the voter trying to assess the significance of the reported financial performance of publicly owned companies such as Petro-Canada. The focus in this book is on *why* financial accounting is as we find it, and critiques are offered of existing accounting standards where appropriate to promote understanding.

It is natural for individuals to differ on the topics, and the emphasis among topics, that they consider important. For this reason, in some of the chapters I have included appendices that deal in depth with topics of a more technical nature, including bank reconciliations, the management and aging of accounts receivable, and the time value of money.

In the four years since the first edition was completed, the author has been able to compile roughly one-third more assignment material for this text, thus giving the student and instructor a wider choice of assignment material. The feedback from the users of the first edition has also made it possible to rewrite some sections in a clearer fashion and to add new topics that instructors desired. The text of the second edition has also been updated in line with the constantly changing *CICA Handbook*.

Kingston, Ontario
1989

Acknowledgments

The first edition of this book was started while the author was on sabbatical leave from Queen's University, at the National Office of Deloitte Haskins + Sells in Toronto. An early draft was reviewed by at least two of their partners who provided technical assistance, suggestions for improvement, and general encouragement. Chief among this group were the late Howard Lyons (who provided technical help in the roughest spots, interesting examples, and some pungent appraisals of the state of the art), Alister Mason, Bob Wardell, Keith McRoberts, and Denman Lawrenson. The second edition was reviewed at an early draft stage by Alister Mason and Bob Wardell. Their help was timely, extensive, and given graciously.

I also benefited from extensive talks with Ross Skinner, especially on the topics of pension and price-change accounting. He was generous in supplying me with a manuscript of *Accounting Standards in Evolution*, and I was the beneficiary of his penetrating analysis and lucid exposition.

My academic colleagues were helpful and thought-provoking. Some of them are anonymous, but some are not. I am particularly grateful to Michael Gibbins, John Parker, Barbara Trenholm, George Murphy, Dick Cheslie, Dan Thornton, Nabil Elias, John Hughes, Arnott Coish, Terry Anderson and the late David Blazouske for reviews, and to Carol McKeen and Jane Craighead for testing the material. Over three summers I had a lot of help in developing assignment material (with financial help from friends at Arthur Andersen & Co.) from Warren Bonham, Doug McIntyre, Marilyn Moreland, Scott Berry and Cyrus Madon. My collaborator on an earlier edition of this text was Joan Cohrs, now with Thorne, Ernst & Whinney.

Readers will note extensive references to the *CICA Handbook* through the text (indicated by square brackets), and I am grateful to the CICA for permission to quote (© The Canadian Institute of Chartered Accountants, Toronto, Canada). Material from the Chartered Accountants *Uniform Final Examinations* is adapted with permission and indicated as "CICA adapted." (© The Canadian Institute of Chartered Accountants, Toronto, Canada. Changes to the original questions and/or suggested approaches to answering are the sole responsibility of the author and have not been reviewed or endorsed by the CICA.) Material adopted from the examinations of the Society of Management Accountants of Canada is used with permission and indicated as "CMA adapted." Similar material from the Certified General Accountants Association of Canada is also used with their permission and noted as "CGA adapted." These professional associations were generous in their assistance.

Finally, I should thank my students at Queen's University who tolerated working with the early drafts with remarkable cheerfulness and taught me a lot about what should and shouldn't go into a text of this sort. They caught a lot of errors, but needless to say the responsibility for remaining errors and omissions is mine.

CHAPTER 1
Review of Basic Concepts

Introduction

Accounting influences our lives to a surprising degree, even though we may be unaware of it, because accounting affects decisions that have an economic impact. Does this budget work? Is that company making inordinate profits? Are we being charged too much for our telephone, electricity, or natural gas? Should we invest in this company? What is happening to the textile industry?

This chapter will examine the basic concepts of accounting. Although we will review the principal assumptions of bookkeeping as well as the central ideas and vocabulary of accounting, the emphasis will be placed on the underlying concepts rather than on the technical issues that concern the student in an introductory course. This single chapter is not intended to take the place of a good elementary accounting textbook.

Review of Basic Ideas in Bookkeeping and Accounting

THE ENTITY CONCEPT

Accounting is a method of reporting the results of the economic activities of an organization, such as an individual, a partnership, an incorporated company, or an economically related group of companies. In the public sector it may report the financial results of such organizations as clubs, universities, charities, and various levels of government. The term **entity** is generally used to describe the organization being reported on.

Most of the time it will be self-evident which activities to include as part of the entity. At other times it is not so apparent, and the accountant must be prepared to look through the form to get at the economic substance of the situation. Here are some examples:

1. In order to prepare financial statements to depict your personal financial affairs,

1

you would describe yourself as the entity and you would keep track of your personal income and expenses. If you were to draw up a balance sheet, it would show your personal assets and liabilities. Note that this financial statement would be quite distinct from the financial statements of the place where you work because, for accounting purposes, that is a quite distinct entity.

2. If you bought a house-painting business and became its owner-manager, you would have your business affairs in addition to your personal financial affairs. If you wanted to know how profitable the business was, you would want the analysis of its economic success to be kept separate from your personal finances. The business would then be one accounting entity, and your personal affairs would be a second, and very distinctly separate, entity. You could, if you wished, combine them into one entity, but you would probably prefer to keep them separate for the reason given above.

3. The financial statement of a large company, such as the Moore Corporation, would contain a number of separate legal entities that are all closely related and controlled by the parent company. In this case the accounting entity has been defined as the cluster of legal entities, and one **consolidated** financial statement (a term to be explained later) would be issued to shareholders.

4. If a business were operated through a corporation rather than an unincorporated proprietorship, then Revenue Canada would insist that it be accounted for as a separate entity because corporations are taxed separately from individuals. However, even though corporations must be regarded as separate entities for tax purposes, the accounts of several companies may be combined into a single entity for reports to their shareholders. This is an example of an entity being defined in one way for one purpose (tax reporting) and in another way for another purpose (reporting to shareholders).

The examples above help to demonstrate the following: (i) The boundaries of the entity are drawn to include those economic activities than can be most usefully grouped for the reader of the financial statements; (ii) The entity can be a person or a partnership — it does not have to be a legally incorporated company; and (iii) Although every legally incorporated company must by law report on itself to governmental authorities as a separate entity, it is quite common to group many separately incorporated companies together into a cluster forming a single accounting entity for the purpose of reporting to shareholders. Thus, what we choose to define as the entity can vary as the reporting needs vary.

Now that the entity has been identified, it is appropriate to describe the mathematics of accounting for it.

BASIC MATHEMATICS OF BOOKKEEPING

Why do accounting books balance? The answer lies in the **accounting equation** which states that for every entity the following relationship holds:

Total Assets = Total Liabilities + Owners' Equity

Assets are items of value that the entity possesses. Examples include cash, accounts receivable, inventory, and plant assets such as land and buildings. **Liabilities** are amounts owing by the entity to those outside it, such as accounts payable, bonds payable, and income tax payable. **Owners' equity** is the residual interest of the owners of the enterprise. (This is a hard concept to make clear in the early part of this text, but in general it can be thought of as the amount of financing provided by the owners. It is *not* the amount the business could be sold for as of the date of the financial statements.)

It should be stressed that the definitions given above are approximations designed to help in starting to understand the meaning of these terms — they are not formal definitions. In fact, these terms are so fundamental to accounting that it is hard to capture all the aspects of each in a single definition.

Let us assume in example (2) above that the house-painting business has total assets of $15,000 and liabilities of $10,000. Then, the owners' equity is the difference, or $5,000.

If we arrange the above equation, it is easier to understand the terms **debit** and **credit**:

$$\text{Total Assets} - \text{Total Liabilities} - \text{Owners' Equity} = 0$$

In terms of our example, this becomes:

$$\$15,000 - \$10,000 - \$5,000 = 0$$

It is a convention of accounting to refer to amounts with positive (+) balances as **debit balances**, and amounts with negative (−) balances as **credit balances**. There is no other meaning that needs to be attributed to these terms.

These two terms were adopted about six hundred years ago to represent positive and negative numbers without their authors realizing that this was what they were in effect doing. Instead of making sure that the single column of numbers added to zero, as we might do, they added the debits and credits up in separate columns and checked to see that the totals of the two were the same.

To decrease the amount of an asset balance, a negative number is added to it, or as the accountant would say, the account is credited. Crediting a liability account would make it larger, since we are adding two negative numbers together. This can be summarized as follows:

Impact on		Accounting Entry	
		Debit (+)	Credit (−)
Assets	(+)	Increase	Decrease
Liabilities	(−)	Decrease	Increase
Owners' equity	(−)	Decrease	Increase

In addition to the three main accounts shown above, accountants normally introduce temporary sub-accounts of owners' equity referred to as **nominal accounts**. The two main types are **revenue accounts** (such as sales) and **expense accounts** (such as salaries, cost of goods sold, and depreciation). The owners of an entity are naturally going to be very interested in how much their owners' equity changed over a period. The purpose of such revenue and expense accounts is to act as temporary storage for recording these items to see how much they add up to over the period. At the end of the period we transfer these amounts to owners' equity.

The basic steps in bookkeeping will be shown below by continuing the example of the house-painting business. Notice throughout how the accounting equation is used to structure the accounting entry.

First, suppose that at the beginning of the entity's existence there is a nil balance in all accounts. Thus we have:

$$\text{Assets} - \text{Liabilities} - \text{Equity} + \text{Expenses} - \text{Revenue} = 0$$
$$0 \quad - \quad 0 \quad - \quad 0 \quad + \quad 0 \quad - \quad 0 \quad = 0 \tag{a}$$

Next, assume that the owner puts $5,000 cash into the business as its initial capital. The accounting entry would be:

$$\text{Assets} - \text{Liabilities} - \text{Equity} + \text{Expenses} - \text{Revenue} = 0$$
$$5{,}000 - \quad 0 \quad - 5{,}000 + \quad 0 \quad - \quad 0 \quad = 0 \tag{b}$$

This shows the increase in an asset, cash, and the increase in owner's equity. (The 0's were shown for each of the other terms for completeness, but from now on they will be omitted for simplicity.)

If equipment were purchased for $3,000, the bank balance would decrease by that amount but the equipment account would increase. In effect, one asset, cash, is being given up to purchase another, equipment. To avoid posting a debit and credit to the same Assets account, we subdivide it into Assets (Cash) and Assets (Equip), and make the following entry:

$$\text{Assets} + \text{Assets} - \text{Liabilities} - \text{Equity} + \text{Expenses} - \text{Revenue} = 0$$
$$\text{(Cash)} \quad \text{(Equip)}$$
$$-3{,}000 + 3{,}000 \qquad\qquad\qquad\qquad\qquad = 0 \tag{c}$$

The conventional accounting journal entry for the above transaction is essentially the same:

	Debit	Credit
Equipment	3,000	
Cash		3,000

To record purchase of equipment.

Equation Format and Conventional Format Compared

There are four major differences between the equation format and the conventional accounting format: (i) the use of debit and credit in the conventional format to stand for " + " and " − "; (ii) the omission of the formal statement in the equation format that the debits and credits are equal; (iii) the placement in the conventional format of each account name and its amount in the same row, rather than in the same column; and (iv) the addition of other information in the conventional format such as the reason for the entry and the date. Except for the last item, where additional information is provided, the differences are ones of form and not of substance.

In the following chapters the conventional format will be used because it is convenient, once the basic relationships are understood, and because it is used by accountants to communicate technical accounting points to each other. The equation format is initially useful since it clearly shows that all accounting entries are based on the accounting equation. However, more columns are needed as the three basic accounts are subdivided into more detailed accounts. Thus, on the one hand, the equation format soon becomes cumbersome when one is working with paper-based accounting records. On the other hand, the equation format lends itself readily to computer processing. Most computer-based accounting systems have more similarities to the equation format than to the conventional format. The spread-sheet programs designed for personal computers, for example, lend themselves readily to the equation format.

If, in the example stated above, the house was painted and $1,000 cash was received for doing this work, the entry would be:

```
Assets + Assets – Liabilities – Equity + Expenses – Revenue = 0
(Cash)   (Equip)
1,000                                      –   1,000   = 0        (d)
```

If rent of $300 was paid in cash, the entry would be:

```
Assets + Assets – Liabilities – Equity + Expenses – Revenue = 0
(Cash)   (Equip)
– 300                              +    300            = 0        (e)
```

If there were no further transactions to record, the above entries could be combined by bringing the equations together and adding. However, before doing this, it is customary to transfer the revenue and expense accounts (the nominal accounts) created in (d) and (e) and net them out to find the income of the period. This is transferred to owners' equity as follows:

```
Assets + Assets – Liabilities – Equity + Expenses – Revenue = 0
(Cash)   (Equip)
                           –  700  –   300  +  1,000  = 0        (f)
```

Entries such as the one above are normally done at the end of each accounting period. They are often referred to as **closing entries** because they close out the nominal accounts. Compares these to accounting entries made daily in order to record activities, such as (d) and (e) above.

All the above entries can now be combined to find the net balance in each account:

```
Assets + Assets – Liabilities – Equity + Expenses – Revenue = 0
(Cash)   (Equip)
   0 +      0 –      0 –     0 +      0 –        0 = 0            (a)
5,000                 –  5,000                     = 0           (b)
– 3,000 +  3,000                                   = 0           (c)
1,000                                 –   1,000 = 0              (d)
– 300                        +    300              = 0           (e)
                             –  700 –  300 +  1,000 = 0          (f)
─────    ─────          ───  ─────      ───  ─────
2,700 +  3,000 –          0 –  5,700 +      0 –        0 = 0      (g)
```

Note that the sum of the equalities totals zero because each of them totals zero. This flows from the rules of algebra, and from the accounting rule that the accounting equation must be followed in every entry.

Line (g) above, which represents the net balance in each account, is referred to as the **trial balance**. Under the conventional paper-based accounting format, the trial balance would be arrived at by recopying the amounts from each ledger account, and the ledger accounts in turn would have been created by copying the amounts from each journal entry. In other words, (i) Journal entries are created to reflect economic events as they occur; (ii) The amounts in the journal entries are copied in the appropriate ledger accounts; (iii) After addition, the final amounts in each ledger account are copied onto the trial balance; and (iv) The trial balance forms the basis for the financial statements. The equation format makes it possible to do steps (i) to (iii) in one step. The computer treatment varies according to the results desired by the person writing the software, but once again computer processing has more similarities to the accounting equation treatment than to the conventional paper-based accounting format. The example above could be readily done on a computer spreadsheet program.

BASIC ACCOUNTING REPORTS

Four financial reports are generally provided for the reader. They are (i) the **balance sheet** (which shows the financial position of the company at a point in time); (ii) the **statement of retained earnings**; (iii) the **income statement** (which shows the net income earned in the period and gives a summary of the transactions that gave rise to it); and (iv) the **statement of changes in financial position** (which shows the changes affecting the company's most liquid assets). They will be examined in more detail later, but the bookkeeping origins of each can be shown from the example developed above.

Balance Sheet

The balances in (g) above can now be restated in balance sheet form since the nominal account has been closed out to owners' equity. The balance sheet below has not been substantially changed from (g); only the form has been changed.

BALANCE SHEET

Assets		Liabilities and Owners' Equity	
Cash	$2,700	Owners' Equity	$5,700
Equipment	3,000		
	$5,700		$5,700

Statement of Changes in Retained Earnings

The purpose of the statement of changes in retained earnings is to account for all changes in retained earnings from the beginning to the end of a given period. Usually, changes are due to (i) income earned during the period and closed out to retained earnings through entries such as (f) above; and (ii) amounts withdrawn by the owners through direct drawings (as in partnerships and sole proprietorships) or dividends (in corporations). For this simple type of case, the following new example illustrates the format:

STATEMENT OF CHANGES IN RETAINED EARNINGS

Balance, start of period	$ 0
Net income	6,000
Dividends	2,700
Balance, end of period	$3,300

Income Statement

Let us reconsider the example of the house-painting business. The income statement can be derived from (f), the entry in which the nominal accounts were closed out to owners' equity.

INCOME STATEMENT

Sales	$1,000
Expenses	300
Net income	$ 700

Statement of Changes in Financial Position

The statement of changes in financial position explains the changes in the entity's more liquid resources from the beginning to the end of the period. Let us consider an example where there are no current liabilities and only one current asset, cash. One approach to preparing the statement of changes in financial position here would be to give all the changes in the "Assets (Cash)" column in the accounting equation. One such form would be as follows:

STATEMENT OF CHANGES IN FINANCIAL POSITION

Operating:	
Sales in cash	$100,000
Expenses paid for in cash	(60,000)
Net cash from operations	40,000
Financing:	
Issue mortgage on property	500,000
Issue of shares in Company	400,000
	900,000
Investing:	
Purchase of building	(850,000)
Net increase (decrease) in cash	$ 90,000

It will be apparent that in a real situation it would be too cumbersome to analyse every account to produce this statement. Fortunately, there are short cuts that make it possible to infer what the changes must have been by examining the non-current assets and liabilities. They will be discussed later in Chapters 3 and 18.

ACCOUNTING AND BOOKKEEPING COMPARED

The algebra of accounting is, as the above examples show, deceptively simple. However, since even medium-sized firms generate thousands of accounting entries in a month, the *bookkeeping* challenge is to record these entries accurately and promptly and to process them according to the rules of accounting in order to produce financial statements at the lowest possible cost.

The *accounting* challenge is quite different. It is to make sure that numbers used in the accounting transactions that form the input to the accounting system capture the important aspects of the economic events being recorded, and that the finished financial statements that represent the output from the system do a useful job of reporting the affairs of the entity. Although the algebra is simple, the accounting is not, because the accountant has to make sure that the numbers are useful for making decisions. In general, accountants are most concerned with the input and output phases of the process, and they assume that the bookkeeping that links these two is being properly conducted. A specially trained accountant also plays the role of auditor and conducts tests of the accounting system to make sure this assumption is justified.

In this text we approach accounting issues by examining the output of the accounting process, such as the financial statements, and testing them to see if they make sense when judged against other criteria, such as economic analysis. If we become convinced they do not, then we will seek to change the input rules to make the output more acceptable.

This process can be summarized diagrammatically as follows:

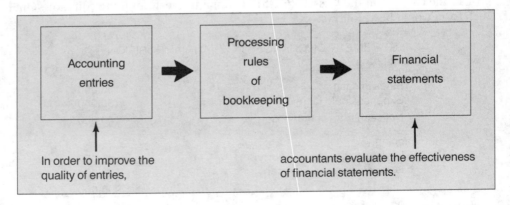

The above diagram implies, correctly, that the ultimate test of an accounting system is whether it produces effective financial statements. Because accounting reporting is based on numbers, people not familiar with the process assume that good accounting reports are produced mainly by adding up the numbers correctly — that is, by accurate bookkeeping. In fact, good accounting and reporting is more subtle and demanding. The approach used by accountants can be viewed broadly as consisting of two steps. First, accountants have a group of *heuristics*, or useful simplifications, which they employ to process the raw data in order to identify the accounting *transactions* that they will enter into the accounting system. (Examples of such transactions were illustrated above in the journal entries (a) to (f) for the example of the house-painting business.) Second, accountants have a series of tests to apply to the finished financial statements to see if they are effective in communicating relevant financial information. If the statements are found to be ineffective, then accountants revise their heuristics for the appropriate accounting treatment of transactions, in the hope of obtaining improvements.

In this text we follow the second step described above in order to understand and evaluate existing accounting reporting standards. We will start, however, by examining some general-purpose heuristics that accountants have adopted over time. They go by a variety of names such as *accounting principles, conventions, standards*, and *basic concepts*. Whatever name is used, it is important to recognize them for what they are — convenient and useful simplifications, to be modified as circumstances change. They are not fundamental statements about the nature of things, such as the laws of physics; nor are they basic premises upon which a system of logic is constructed, such as the axioms of Euclidean geometry. In this text we will usually refer to them as *conventions*, but any of the terms above are common.

Accounting Conventions

The rules given below are usually referred to as *accounting conventions* because they are assumptions that accountants normally make in their day-to-day work. In a particular case a convention should be changed if its underlying assumptions are inconsistent with the specific facts. Therefore, the person making such a judgement must be familiar with both the facts of the matter being evaluated and the assumptions lying behind the use of each convention. This is an important aspect of *professional judgement*, a term often heard in connection with the work of public accountants.

THE CONVENTION OF PERIODIC REPORTING

It is usually assumed that the financial statements should be prepared at the end of predetermined financial periods (e.g., at the end of each year) rather than at the end of each natural productive cycle of the entity. For example, de Havilland Aircraft of Canada Limited might prefer to report at the end of each market cycle of its Dash planes, or a building contractor might wish to report on financial progress at the end of each major construction project. But in practice most entities must report quarterly and annually. The underlying reason is that natural economic cycles are often much longer than a year, but financial reports are needed more frequently than that.

Corporate legislation and securities commissions usually have periodic reporting requirements. The Canada Business Corporations Act requires that shareholders be furnished annually with a financial statement; and the Ontario Securities Commission requires that full reports be issued annually, with brief unaudited reports to be issued quarterly.

The need to report at frequent intervals has three main implications for accounting reporting: (i) Because many business transactions are initiated but not completed by the end of the period, estimates must be made of the likely outcome of each; (ii) Rules or conventions must be developed for assigning "values" to assets other than cash; and (iii) Conventions must be developed for deciding upon the period in which the profits from ongoing business activities will be recognized. This desire to issue financial statements as periodic intervals motivates many of the conventions discussed below.

COST CONVENTION

The cost convention is usually stated in this way: Assets are recorded at their cost as of the time of their acquisition. This always includes (i) the amount paid the supplier for the asset; but whether it includes (ii) the costs of transporting it to the site where it will be used, (iii) any costs of installing it, and (iv) the interest costs of financing it until it is ready for use depends on the nature of the asset being acquired. Generally, current assets include only (i), whereas plant assets are more likely to include the others as well. This will be covered in Chapter 7.

Whenever possible, practising accountants like to base the accounting entries reflecting the transactions on "objective" evidence. This is usually defined as evidence that, if interpreted by two trained accountants, would result in the same or similar accounting entry being made by both. The cost principle is consistent with this desire for objectivity because it is more likely to produce similar accounting entries than, say, valuation based on more subjective criteria such as expected selling price or discounted expected value. It will become apparent later that there are important situations where the cost principle does not lead to unique accounting treatments. Thus, unfortunately, it does not always result in the objectivity desired.

Historic cost was firmly established as virtually the sole basis for accounting reporting by the late 1930s, and with it the **matching principle** (discussed later in this chapter) became firmly established as well. This principle states that the cost of an asset should be matched against the revenue it helped to earn. This seems intuitively sensible since it means that for a given period the accounting system will present us with both the revenue earned in that period and the costs of earning that revenue. With the matching principle in full use, it then becomes more difficult to influence reported income by varying the timing of cash receipts and expenditures. It will become apparent later that this is easier to state as an objective than it is to accomplish satisfactorily in all cases. Nevertheless, this is the objective.

An important result of the cost principle to keep in mind is that once the cost of an asset is determined for accounting purposes, it is not normally changed later if the price of the asset fluctuates in the marketplace. For example, if a company purchased an office building, it would record this building at the cost of acquiring it and would not normally make any entries to revalue it, even if the value of the building changed significantly.

The same convention also applies to liabilities. A liability is recorded in the accounts as of the time at which it was incurred, and no entries are normally made to reflect changes in the market value of that liability. For example, if a company issued ten-year bonds payable at $100, it would not change their value in its books even if the market value of these bonds subsequently dropped to $80 because of changes in market interest rates.

The cost convention has many attractions; but, because assets are shown at their historic cost regardless of subsequent price changes, the use of this convention means that financial statements may fail to reflect the current economic conditions facing a company. The cost convention has been severely criticized, especially in periods of rapid changes in the general price level. Alternative methods have been proposed that take into account the change in general price levels or the change in prices of specific assets or the change in both. These will be discussed in Chapter 20.

There is an exception to the cost principle, known as the **lower of cost and market rule**, which applies to current assets. It is discussed below under the conservatism convention.

RECOGNITION CONVENTION

The recognition convention states that income arising from an activity is not recognized in the accounts until (i) the bulk of the economic activity giving rise to the income has been completed and (ii) the major part of the risk connected with the activity is past.

The effect of this convention is that an entity values the goods or services it is creating at their acquisition cost up until the point of recognition, at which time it values the assets at the amount it expects their realization value to be. It is at this point that the estimated profit is reflected in the books. Thus, the accounting decision where to place this point in the production process may have an important impact on a company's reported income. A company that wanted to report net income earlier in its life would want to make the point of recognition as early as possible; a company with conservative accounting practices would tend to delay it.

The convention that revenue is earned at a distinct point in the production process should be contrasted with the economists' assumption that income is earned over the whole of the production process. The point at which the accountant would recognize the revenue as earned is, to the economist, just one of many points in the productive cycle.

Because the recognition convention is so firmly implanted in most accountants' minds, there is often debate among them as to where the "real" point of recognition is in the productive cycle. This is actually an empty question since the point of recognition is part of a *convention* developed by accountants. The recognition convention is useful in that it greatly simplifies the bookkeeping and meets the desire for "objectivity", but it is not the sole way of measuring the "real" income.

Here are some examples of the point of time when revenue is recognized.

1. A jeweller buys a watch in January from a wholesaler for $40. She checks it over and puts it in her display case, where it stays until November when it is sold on credit for $90. In December she receives payment in cash of $90. She recognizes the gross profit of $50 in November because that is the month when the main economic activity — selling — is completed. It is true that she does not actually receive the cash until December, but she will not regard payment of her bill as a particularly risky matter. If failure to receive payment were a likely possibility, potential bad debts would be dealt with when valuing her accounts receivable. It would not affect the timing of the recognition.

2. A large land developer buys a tract of raw land and does the extensive work necessary to make it suitable as a housing subdivision. He landscapes, builds roads, and installs sewers and water mains. This work makes the land more valuable, but following the cost principle he carries the land at its acquisition cost plus the cost of work done to date. It is only when the land is sold as building lots that profit, if any, will be recognized.

   There have been some instances, particularly in the United States, of land development companies having sold building lots to purchasers who made a very small down payment and gave a large mortgage for the balance. For many years the profit on such a transaction was recognized at the point of sale, but this has now been stopped on the grounds that a significant part of the risk remains with the developer. The current practice is to recognize the profit on the sale piecemeal as payments are made on the outstanding mortgage.

3. It is quite common for companies that build large objects, such as skyscrapers or jet aircraft, to take into income the percentage of profit they estimate they have earned to date. This is referred to as the **percentage-of-completion method**. We will examine it in detail in Chapter 6 on inventories. Of all recognition methods used in practice, this one comes closest to the economists' notion of when income is earned.

4. Baton Broadcasting Incorporated's air-time revenue is recognized when advertisements are aired under broadcast contracts. This seems reasonable since the economic activity for which the company is being paid is the broadcast of the advertisement.

   On the other hand, revenues from programs produced by the company under contract are recognized to the extent that services have been performed under these contracts. (For example, a company with a contract to produce twelve half-hour programs may have produced and shipped six of them to the client.) It would appear that the total contract does not have to be completed in order to recognize some of the revenue earned. Therefore it seems similar to the percentage-of-completion method.

5. Versatile Cornat Corporation recognizes ship repair and industrial engineering revenues and profits on completion of contracts, with anticipated losses provided for immediately. Another acceptable method would be to recognize revenue on a percentage-of-completion basis.

It is apparent from the examples above that there is some latitude in choosing the point at which revenue is recognized. If a company has a short production cycle, it does not make much difference where the point of recognition is set, because almost all transactions will be completed within the same year anyway. Examples of such companies would be food retailers and fast-food outlets.

If the production cycle is long but production output is steady, the choice of the point of recognition will have some impact, but amounts will tend to even out. An example would be a whisky distillery that ages the raw whisky for three or more years. If it puts roughly the same amount of raw whisky into the aging process each year, there would be no significant effect on reported income (after the initial three years of operation) if income were recognized as earned at one of several points. The distillery would probably choose to recognize income after the aging is complete and the whisky has been sold. However, if there is a ready market for three-year-old whisky, there is some argument for recognizing the revenue at the point of production. Nevertheless, in practice this is not usually done.

It is when the production cycle is long and the rate of completion is uneven that the choice of the point of recognition becomes important in its effects on reported income. Suppose, for example, that an aircraft company builds two identical planes (A and B) and recognizes the income from each plane when it is delivered to the customer. The aircraft are started in the first month of each fiscal year and take fourteen months to build. The planes turn out to be unsuccessful because a better competing plane becomes available. Consequently, production stops after plane B is delivered. The revenue recognition pattern could be summarized as follows:

Event	Effect on Revenue Recognition
First Year	
— Plane A is started and almost completed.	None. No planes are delivered.
Second Year	
— Plane A is finished and delivered.	Income from sale of Plane A.
— Plane B is started and almost completed.	
Third Year	
— No new orders come in, better planes are available.	
— Plane B is finished and delivered.	Income from sale of Plane B.

The results do not well reflect the company's activities: (i) no revenue is reported in the first year when much economic activity connected with plane building has taken place; (ii) significant income is reported in the second year when there is both productive activity and delivery of planes; and (iii) significant revenue is reported in the third year at a time when the firm had actually not done much production other than to complete existing orders.

MATCHING PRINCIPLE

The matching principle states that when revenue is recognized, the costs of earning that revenue should be matched against it in the same time period. The balance sheet can be thought of, in part, as a storage place for costs that have not yet been charged to expense because their related revenues have not yet been earned. This applies especially to plant assets. The point when revenue will be deemed to be realized is determined under the recognition convention; but once the point is recognized, then the matching principle requires that all related costs must now be charged to expense.

Two accounting procedures that follow from the matching principle merit attention here. First, when goods are bought to be resold or used as supplies, their cost is reported on the balance sheet as an asset until the period in which they are sold or used, at which time it is charged as a cost of the period. Second, when a plant asset is purchased, its undepreciated cost (i.e., purchase cost less expected disposal value) is allocated over each of the years in which is is expected to be used.

The matching principle is intuitively sensible as an objective to strive for, because matching costs with revenues seems the appropriate way to measure the income, or economic success, of the entity. However, controversial problems arise in practice. How does one identify those periods that benefit from the use of an asset? What portion of the asset costs does one assign to each of those periods? Thomas [1969] has argued that such allocations of cost are arbitrary and that therefore the resulting measures of income are arbitrary. Supporters of the allocation process have generally adopted two arguments: (i) Consistency makes up in part for arbitrariness so that if depreciation, for instance, is applied according to a consistent formula, this helps to make up for the arbitrariness of the formula itself; and (ii) At times allocation is a necessary part of the social process of deciding who will be responsible for paying certain costs. To demonstrate this second argument, consider the following example. When a telephone company allocates costs between long distance and local traffic, it is implicitly deciding how much of the total telephone operating cost will be covered through long distance charges and how much through local equipment rental charges. The essential point here is that even though such cost allocation is arbitrary, it is acceptable if most telephone users consider the division of costs to be fair.

Nevertheless, the inherent arbitrariness of many accounting allocations is troublesome. Since the rationale for accounting reporting is to aid in making good decisions, the impact of arbitrary allocation needs to be kept constantly in mind. We will examine this topic in more detail while looking at specific topics.

CONTINUITY CONVENTION

The continuity convention states that unless accountants have reason to believe the contrary, they should think of the entity as a going concern that will continue its activities into future periods.

This convention has direct implications when drawing up the financial statements. It implies, for example, that assets should be shown at cost and need not be written down to the amount that they would bring in a distress sale. It also has a more subtle implication: given that the entity is continuing into the future, there will be future shareholders or owners. In formulating accounting policies, accountants should try to ensure that they are acting in the best interests of both present and future shareholders. This will become more apparent in our discussion below of the conservatism convention.

CONSERVATISM CONVENTION

The conservatism convention applies in general to the measurement of a firm's income. It also springs from an attitude toward measurement of current assets on balance sheets. It states that if there is some doubt whether income should be recognized now or at some later date, then its recognition should be postponed. One implication is that where there is doubt about a future outcome, revenue realization should be postponed, but expense recognition should take place currently. Another implication is that if the market value of a current asset has dropped below its cost, it should be written down to the market value. On the other hand, a current asset is never restated at replacement cost if this would increase its value.

For example, if the firm is holding inventory that cost $250,000 and could now be replaced for $200,000, accounting conservatism indicates that the inventory should be valued downward to $200,000, with a consequent charge to current income of $50,000. On the other hand, if the same inventory were to have a replacement cost of $300,000 instead of $200,000, it would not be revalued upward by $50,000 to $300,000, because this figure is higher than its cost.

In preparing financial statements an accountant will often find himself having to make estimates of how things will turn out in the future. Examples include (i) the probable net realizable value of inventory, (ii) the amount of accounts receivable that will become bad debts, (iii) the functional life of plant assets, and (iv) the outcome of unsettled lawsuits. In such cases where the outcome is uncertain, accountants are following the doctrine of conservatism if they assume that the outcome will be on the unfavourable side. Nevertheless, it is not the doctrine of conservatism to be excessively gloomy about the future or to allow for all possible losses.

Accounting conservatism is generally applied to the valuation of the current assets of the firm, such as cash, accounts receivable, and inventory. It is not usually applied to the valuation of non-current assets. In this regard accounting is inconsistent. Accounting critics of conservatism argue that conservatism is itself inconsistent in the following three ways. First, it is a clear abandonment of the cost convention, but only in the downward direction and only for certain types of assets and liabilities. Second, it mainly affects the timing of the recognition of a loss or gain. To the extent that a loss is recognized in the current year, it will not be recognized in a later year. Hence, by being conservative in their statement of this year's profits, accountants are being unconservative about the profits of a later year. Third, it is not evenhanded because it has the potential to understate systematically an entity's current income while overstating its income of later years. If shareholders literally believed what the statements said, then conservatism would discriminate against current shareholders in favour of future shareholders.

RELEVANCE AND MATERIALITY

The term **relevance** is used when the information in a report provides at least some of the information readers need to know in order to make meaningful decisions. In contrast, the term **materiality** is used when a given piece of information has sufficient surprise value to make readers alter the decisions they would have made without that information. For example, the morning weather forecast supplies information that is *relevant* to a decision whether to take a raincoat. However, the news that the probability of rain has been revised to 100%, instead of the 90% given in an earlier forecast, is probably not *material*. Presumably one would have already decided to take a raincoat based on the earlier forecast. The new forecast would not affect that decision.

Note that one cannot talk meaningfully of either the relevance or materiality of information on a financial report without knowing the nature of the decision the user of the information is going to make. This has two significant implications. First, the more precisely we understand the reader's decision-making process, the better we can evaluate the relevance and materiality of a given report to his needs. Second, the information that is relevant or material (or both) to one decision-maker is not necessarily relevant or material (or both) to another.

For example, imagine a situation where a company's banker and shareholder are examining the same financial statement. The banker has a short-term loan of $85,000 outstanding to the company. The loan is secured specifically by accounts receivable and inventory. The shareholder is reviewing his portfolio and trying to decide whether to sell his shares in the company.

The banker looks first at the accounts receivable and notes it is $100,000, she then notes that the inventory — valued at the lower of cost and market — is $120,000. She estimates that at least 80% of the accounts receivable, or $80,000, is fully collectable. This leaves only $5,000 of the loan to be recovered out of inventory. She does not know what the inventory could be sold for at a quick sale (she does know that the lower of cost and market figure of $120,000 is *not* a sure indication). Nevertheless, she is not concerned because she feels certain she will have no trouble getting $5,000 out of an inventory of that size. In other words, the exact size of the inventory is not particularly material because its recovery value appears far in excess of the amount needed to cover the loan. She glances only briefly at the rest of the financial statements since their relevance is rather low. She has already answered the questions that needed answering.

On the other hand, the investor has a different decision to make. Assume that he is interested in the company's shares as one of the investments in his portfolio and that he would like to use the company's reported net income as a measure of the company's success to date. In that case he would probably concentrate on the income statement, because it is more relevant to his decision to buy or sell, and he would probably pay less attention to the balance sheet. However, since inventory valuation affects the reported net income of $80,000, it might be very material to him that the inventory was stated at $120,000 when just possibly it might have been stated as low as, say, $80,000 or as high as, say, $150,000. In other words, inventory valuation is material to him because it has a direct impact on net income.

This example helps to provide an intuitive grasp of the two terms *relevance* and *materiality*. In order to be more precise about their application, it is necessary to specify the decision-making process more exactly. There has been some work in this area (see Foster [1986] for examples); but extensive specification of the decision-making processes that are, or should be, used by readers of financial statements is still in the development stage. It has been helped by theoretical developments in finance and economics as well as by the urging of professional reports. For instance, the Trueblood Report [1973] asserted that "the basic objective of financial statements is to provide information for making economic decisions."

In addition to relevance for decision-making of the kind described above, there are two other uses made of accounting information. First, it can be used as a device for specifying the rules to be used to decide future distributions of wealth. For example, agreeing in advance to make the manager's salary a stated percentage of reported net income defines the split of profit between the manager and the shareholders. This agreement provides a workable way for them to contract with each other for the remuneration to be paid. Second, accounting information can be used by management of a company to track the results of their behaviour and see whether their activities result in "good" accounting results. This is similar to students using the results of their mid-term exams to track whether their approach to studying for courses is effective in producing the grades they want.

Basic Financial Statements: A Closer Look

The basic role of each of the financial statements has already been explained using a simple example. In this section we look in more detail at the format and objectives of these reports and explain some of the major items that appear on each. On all statements it is usual to present both the current and previous period's results. This is a general requirement for all financial statements published in Canada.

BALANCE SHEET

The general requirement for the balance sheet is that it should follow the basic accounting equation:

Assets = Liabilities + Owners' Equity

Format

The three main components shown above may be — and are — arranged in a variety of patterns for reporting to the reader. One common layout is to present the assets on one page and the liabilities and owners' equity on the adjoining page. Another method is to put all three on one page, with the liabilities deducted from the assets and owners' equity shown separately. In North America it is usual to put the assets on the left side (for side-by-side presentation) or top (for one-page presentations). However, in other countries different arrangements can be found. The important thing is to see how the accounting equation is expressed in any given situation.

Objectives of Presentation

The balance sheet is the portrayal of the affairs of the firm at a fixed point in time. It is typically used to determine the following factors: (i) the financial soundness of the firm (e.g., what current assets are available to cover its debts); (ii) the manner in which the firm is using its assets to earn income (e.g., what is the composition of its assets?); and (iii) certain key variables that will be combined with other information to assess the efficiency with which the firm is run (e.g., the ratio of accounts receivable to sales).

It is important to keep the objectives of balance sheet presentation clearly in mind because this has strongly influenced the arrangement of items on the statement itself and, to a degree, the valuations assigned to some assets. In the last century most fund-raising by corporations tended to be through debt issues (e.g., bonds or bank borrowing). Thus, there was a natural tendency for the creditor to want to know to what extent his loan was covered by current assets and what proportion of the risk of corporate failure would be borne by the shareholders. Such readers would also want to be sure that the value of the assets was not overstated. Hence, they would favour the doctrine of conservatism.

In the 1920s the method of raising capital for companies shifted toward selling shares instead of bonds. As a result, more readers of financial statements had the perspective of shareholders rather than creditors. They were interested in "proper" income measurement rather than tests for creditworthiness. As a result, they were concerned that the matching principle should be carried out consistently, even if this meant deferring costs until later periods (when it was hoped that the expected benefit would be realized). When this point of view became prevalent, the balance sheet began to show such things as *deferred charges* (i.e., charges already incurred that were being deferred to a later period when the benefit was expected to arise). Although such items helped to address the matching concept, they would have been looked at with some scepticism by the firm's creditors because these items have little salvage value.

The balance sheet can be expected to undergo other changes to suit the needs of its readers. The student should be alert to these underlying pressures for change and should concentrate on understanding the basic concepts rather than on memorizing the elusive "correct" version.

Major Items on the Balance Sheet

Even a moderate-sized company would have many hundreds of individual ledger accounts which represent assets, liabilities, and owners' equity. If the balance sheet is going to be presented on one or two sheets of paper, then these many individual ledger accounts must be aggregated into about two dozen balance-sheet accounts.

The procedures for aggregating the hundreds of accounts into a handful of balance-sheet items are usually straightforward: assets of a similar nature are added together (e.g., all similar inventories are combined and shown as one amount), as are liabilities. The owners' equity section usually does not have a lot of individual accounts, so aggregation there is less of a problem.

Assets

On a typical balance sheet the assets are shown under three headings: (1) current assets; (2) plant assets (or property or plant and equipment); and (3) other assets.

1. Current Assets: The **operating cycle** is the cycle in most companies in which (i) cash is used to buy inventory; (ii) inventory is sold in return for accounts receivable;

and (iii) the accounts receivable are paid, leaving the company once again with cash. In most companies one would expect this to take place within a year. But in some industries (e.g., distilleries that sell aged whisky) the cycle takes longer than a year. The inventory and accounts receivable connected with this longer cycle would still be considered accounts receivable. **Current assets** are those assets that are expected to be turned into cash or equivalent by the later of (i) twelve months or (ii) the end of the company's operating cycle.

It is also assumed that the assets are generally available to pay creditors and are not earmarked for a special purpose. It is useful for the company's creditors to know the total of assets that would soon be turned into cash, and originally this was what influenced this classification. There is a presumption that items classed as current assets should form a part of this revolving fund of liquid assets.

Accounts usually included under current assets are (i) cash on hand and bank balances; (ii) accounts receivable, notes receivable, and short-term mortgages receivable; (iii) inventory; and (iv) prepaid expenses.

2. Plant Assets: Assets actively used to support the productive activities of the enterprise are called **plant assets** and include land, buildings, and equipment. They usually include only tangible assets (i.e., assets that can be seen and touched). Non-tangible productive assets (e.g., computer programs or licensing agreements) are usually included as *other assets*. It is common to have plant assets shown on the balance sheet in summary form, with further detail provided in a note to the financial statements.

3. Other Assets: This catch-all term covers assets that do not fit neatly into the other two categories. Items here would include:

1. Assets that superficially appear to be current, but are not because of some restriction on their liquidity (e.g., cash on hand held for some restricted use).

2. Productive assets that are not tangible, such as franchises, purchased patent rights, deferred charges, incorporation expenses, and the purchase difference between the cost of shares of subsidiary companies and the underlying market value of their tangible assets. (These terms will all be covered in detail in Chapter 9. At this point it will suffice to have a superficial understanding of their meaning.)

3. Tangible assets that are not productive (e.g., land or buildings being held for resale or future development, but which are not at present used in the productive process).

The **other assets** category is conceptually troublesome in that it is hard to put an economic interpretation on it. The plant assets category can be compared to the capital assets of the firm in economic theory, and the current assets can be explained as the buffer stock of liquid assets necessary to the firm's operation. Introductory economic theory does not have an explanation why a firm would retain assets whose use is restricted (other assets, point (1) above), or have a separate categorization of productive assets just because they are intangible (other assets, point (2) above), or retain assets that are unproductive (other assets, point (3) above). As we shall see later in the text, real-world circumstances produce results not contemplated in the economic theory that forms much of the foundation of accounting thinking. *Other assets* can be thought of as a means of coping with these uncontemplated results.

Liabilities

On a typical balance sheet the liabilities are shown under the following headings: (1) current liabilities; (2) long-term liabilities; (3) deferred income taxes; and (4) contingencies. The objective in disclosing these items on the balance sheet is to show all those liabilities whose amounts can reasonably be determined.

1. Current Liabilities: These are liabilities due within the longer of (i) twelve months or (ii) the end of the company's operating cycle. This parallels the general test for a current asset.

Typical **current liabilities** are (i) bank indebtedness and notes payable, (ii) accounts payable and accrued liabilities, (iii) income taxes currently payable, (iv) other taxes payable, (v) dividends payable, (vi) deferred revenue expected to be realized within the year, and (vii) the portion of any long-term debt that is payable within one year.

2. Long-term Liabilities: These are liabilities whose maturity date is longer than one year or beyond the company's normal operating cycle. **Long-term liabilities** typically include (i) debentures payable, (ii) long-term bank debt, (iii) obligations under capital leases, (iv) unfunded pension liabilities, and (v) deferred revenue that is not expected to be realized within the year. (Some of these terms may not be familiar. They will be discussed in detail in Chapter 12.)

3. Deferred Income Taxes: It is quite common for governments to use the tax system to encourage certain economic activities (e.g., to urge companies to invest in new equipment). They often do this by allowing companies to claim these expenditures as tax deductions before they would normally be claimable under ordinary accounting conventions. As a result **taxable income** is often different from **accounting income** reported to shareholders. Hence the actual income tax paid is often different from the amount that the matching principle would indicate. The accountants' response to this has been to show in the income statement a tax expense based on the accounting income rather than the taxable income, and to defer on the balance sheet the difference between these two amounts. This will be covered in more detail in Chapter 13. For the moment let us simply note that it arises because of differences between the tax actually paid and the tax reported on the income statement.

4. Contingencies: A **contingent liability** is one where the company may be liable to make a payment in the future because of some existing condition that will not be resolved until some future event takes place. A typical example is a claim against the company for damages allegedly suffered by a customer. Whether the claim will have to be paid is contingent on some future event, such as a court case or the findings of an arbitrator.

In such situations it is common to disclose the nature of the contingency through a note to the financial statements, but not to make an accounting entry. To draw the readers' attention to the relevant note, a reference to it is often put right on the balance sheet.

Owners' Equity

Owners' equity is the residual amount on the balance sheet after calculating the assets and liabilities. Whether the entity is incorporated or unincorporated, the purpose is to show the following items separately: (i) the equity that has been contributed; (ii) the net equity that has been earned (or lost) through the entity's life, less payments (e.g., dividends) to the owners; and (iii) any changes arising from revaluations of assets or liabilities.

The terms used depend on whether the entity is incorporated or unincorporated. For an unincorporated entity, contributed capital is called **owners' original capital** and earned equity is called **retained earnings less the drawings account**. For an incorporated entity, contributed capital is called **share capital and contributed surplus** and earned equity is called **retained earnings**.

In unincorporated entities the owners' equity section tends to be less extensive, since by law the whole of the entity's net assets together with the owners' personal assets are available to pay any outstanding debts.

In an incorporated entity it is only in rare cases that the personal assets of the owners are available to satisfy outstanding debts. It therefore becomes important to try to ensure that the shareholders do not pay themselves dividends out of the shareholders' capital, which would impair the soundness of the company to the detriment of the creditors. It is usual for most companies' laws to make the directors personally liable if they declare dividends that impair the capital of the company. A major test of this was whether the dividends would cause the retained earnings account to go into a deficit. (This test is now little used in Canada.) Also, there are usually strict controls over the circumstances in which the shares of the company can be redeemed. For this reason, accounting for owners' equity in incorporated companies is carefully specified. This will be covered in more detail in Chapter 16.

STATEMENT OF RETAINED EARNINGS

The basic accounting equation

   Assets = Liabilities + Owners' Equity

is for the balance sheet, which is a statement of financial position as of a given point in time. Suppose we denote the balance sheet for a company as of its 19X2 year-end as

   Assets (19X2) = Liabilities (19X2) + Owners' Equity (19X2)

Further suppose that we denote the balance sheet for its equivalent 19X3 year-end as

   Assets (19X3) = Liabilities (19X3) + Owners' Equity (19X3)

Then the change in its owners' equity for the year would be equivalent to

   Owners' Equity (19X3) − Owners' Equity (19X2) = Change in Owners' Equity

Owners' equity is made up of 3 items: capital contributed by the owners, the net change in retained earnings, and revaluations of assets and liabilities. It is possible to account for changes in owners' equity by accounting for all changes in each of these three items.

1. Changes in capital contributed are disclosed by showing the details of the shares issued and redeemed for the period, as well as any changes in contributed surplus [*CICA* 3240.04].

2. Changes in retained earnings are shown through the statement of retained earnings, whose general format is as follows:

Opening balance	$ xxxx
Add: Net income for the period	xxxx
	xxxx
Deduct: Dividends declared	xxxx
Closing balance	$ xxxx

Information about net income for the period is provided by the income statement, to be described below.

3. Revaluations of assets and liabilities are uncommon in historic cost-based accounting systems. One exception consists of changes in the value of current assets because of the lower-of-cost-and-market rule for inventories. The other main exception consists of general downward valuations arising from the application of the convention of conservatism. Such current asset changes are reflected in the income statement and are *not* reported separately in the owners' equity section. Separate accounting in the owners' equity section has been proposed for accounting systems where the historic cost convention has been dropped. This will be covered in detail in Chapter 20 on price-change accounting.

INCOME STATEMENT

The usual format for the income statement can be summarized as follows:

INCOME STATEMENT

Income (usually broken into a few major categories)	$xxxx
Deduct: Costs (usually broken into a dozen or more categories)	xxxx
Income before income taxes	xxxx
Deduct: Income taxes	xxxx
Income from operations before extraordinary item	xxxx
Add or deduct: Extraordinary item (net of tax)	xxxx
Net income	$ xxxx
Earnings per share	$ x

The objectives of the income statement are to permit the reader to see how net income is arrived at and to aid the reader in judging the level of net income that can be expected in the future. In addition, selected items from the income statement may be combined with information from other sources to calculate ratios about the company's performance. (For instance, the ratio of sales to total assets may be used as a measure of the company's ability to keep its assets in use.)

Since most companies have hundreds of income and expense accounts in their ledgers, it is necessary to aggregate these to produce the brief form of income statement found in most reports to shareholders. When accounts are aggregated, some information is usually lost. Most jurisdictions have minimum disclosure rules to restrict the amount of aggregation. These will be discussed in Chapter 4 on income statements.

STATEMENT OF CHANGES IN FINANCIAL POSITION

The objective of the statement of changes in financial position (SCFP) is to show the major reasons why the company's **liquidity** has changed since the previous balance sheet. Liquidity is usually defined in terms of cash and those assets that can readily be converted into cash. Prevailing circumstances will help determine whether it is likely that an asset is convertible easily enough into cash to be included in the liquid assets. At the most restrictive it might include only cash itself; whereas at the broadest it might include all net current assets. Until 1985 the choice of assets to include in the liquid asset fund was the choice of the reporting company. Most companies used **net current assets**, the current assets minus current liabilities. In 1985, Section 1540 of the *CICA Handbook* was revised so that the only assets to be included would be cash and **cash equivalents**. Cash equivalents are temporary investments in liquid marketable securities, net of short-term borrowings. The usual format statement of changes in financial position can be summarized as follows:

STATEMENT OF CHANGES IN FINANCIAL POSITION

Operating	
Income per income statement	$ xxxx
Adjust for items which do not cause cash flow (e.g., depreciation, changes in other current assets and liabilities)	xxxx
Net from operating	xxxx
Financing	
Issue of long-term debt	xxxx
Issue of share capital	xxxx
Redemption of long-term debt	(xxxx)
Redemption of share capital	(xxxx)
Net from financing	xxxx
Investing	
Replacement of existing plant:	
Sale of plant assets	xxxx
Acquisition of plant assets	(xxxx)
Acquisition of new plant	(xxxx)
Net from investing	xxxx
Net Change in Cash and Cash Equivalents	xxxx
Balance, Start of Year	xxxx
Balance, End of Year	$ xxxx

The way in which the statement of changes in financial position is constructed can be seen by going back to the basic accounting equation:

Assets = Liabilities + Owners' Equity

Let us split assets and liabilities into two segments each, consisting of cash and cash equivalents on the one hand and non-cash and non-cash equivalents on the other hand. If we use "(cash)" to stand for "(cash and cash equivalents)", we can rewrite the basic accounting equation as follows:

Assets   +   Assets   = Liabilities   +   Liabilities   +   Owners' Equity
(Cash)   (Non-cash)   (Cash)   (Non-cash)   (Non-cash)

By transposing terms we obtain:

Assets − Liabilities = Liabilities + Owners' Equity − Assets
(Cash)   (Cash)   (Non-cash)   (Non- cash)

Recall that by definition we can write:

Cash and Cash Equivalents = Assets − Liabilities
                             (Cash)   (Cash)

If we use "(s)" to denote the position at the start of the year, we can combine the two preceding equations to obtain the following:

Cash and Cash Equivalents(s) = Liabilities(s) + Owners' Equity(s) −   Assets(s)
                                (Non-cash)   (Non-cash)

Similarly, if we use "(e)" to denote the position at the end of the year, we arrive at the following:

Cash and Cash Equivalents(e) = Liabilities(e) + Owners' Equity(e) −   Assets(e)
                                (Non-cash)   (Non-cash)

The increase in cash and cash equivalents from the start to the end of the year can now be expressed as the difference of the above two equations:

Increase in Cash and   Increase in Non-   Increase in   _   Increase in
   Cash Equivalents   =   Cash Liabilities + Owners' Equity   Non-cash Assets

This equation states that cash and cash equivalents can be increased by (i) increasing non-cash liabilities, (ii) increasing owners' equity, or (iii) decreasing non-cash assets. Similarly, cash and cash equivalents can be decreased by doing the reverse. The basic format of the SCFP given above in this section reflects these relationships.

OTHER ITEMS IN THE FINANCIAL REPORT

The other items to be found in most financial reports are (1) the auditors' report, (2) notes to the financial statements, and (3) miscellaneous supplementary reports.

1. Auditors' Report: The term **auditor** in this text means an independent professional accountant. The auditors' report is included with the annual financial statements of all public companies and is usually addressed to the shareholders. According to the *CICA Handbook*, the standard auditors' report should cover "all financial statements required for fair presentation in accordance with generally accepted accounting principles" [*CICA* 5400.04]. Normally this means the balance sheet, the income statement, the statement of retained earnings, and the statement of changes in financial position. It also includes any notes that are an integral part of the financial statements.

If the auditors are satisfied with the financial statements, they will give an unqualified report along the following lines (the format is taken from Calpin [1981]):

AUDITORS' REPORT

To the Shareholders of New World Discoveries

We have examined the balance sheet of New World Discoveries as at 31 December 19X2 and the statements of income, retained earnings and changes in financial position for the year then ended. Our examination was made in accordance with generally accepted auditing standards, and accordingly included such tests and other procedures as we considered necessary in the circumstances.

In our opinion, these financial statements present fairly the financial position of the company as at 31 December 19X2 and the results of its operations and the changes in its financial position for the year then ended in accordance with generally accepted accounting principles applied on a basis consistent with that of the preceding year.

(Signed by auditors)

Chartered Accountants

Any City, Canada
31 January 19X3.

Although minor variations in wording are permitted, it is traditional for auditors to use this uniform wording. Consequently, if a different wording is found, it is important to grasp its meaning very clearly. There are three types of reservations of auditors' opinion:

a. An opinion that the financial statements are presented fairly *except for* some matter in question. This may arise from (i) an inappropriate accounting treatment (e.g., inadequate depreciation), (ii) the failure to present a piece of information in the financial statements that the auditor considers essential (e.g., an important accounting policy), or (iii) the inability on the auditor's part to carry out an audit procedure that he considers necessary (e.g., the inability to confirm a note receivable).

b. An opinion that the financial statements are not presented fairly because of some matter in question. It is rare to find this in practice because it says in effect that the financial statements are misleading or virtually useless. In most Canadian provinces the securities commission would refuse to allow a company to file such a statement with such an opinion. The commission would suspend trading in the company's stock until the issue was resolved.

c. A denial of opinion. In this case the auditor states that he is unable to form an opinion because of some deficiency stated in his report. This too is rarely encountered in practice.

Because qualified opinions have such significance, it is worthwhile for readers of financial statements to become familiar with the unqualified auditors' report. This will help them to recognize a qualified report immediately.

2. Notes to the Financial Statements: It is quite common to find that the notes to the financial statements take up as many pages as the financial statements themselves. The notes serve several purposes. First, they set out the major accounting policies followed by the company in preparing the financial statements. Second, they provide more detailed information about items shown aggregated on the financial statements. For instance, they may show a further breakdown of the composition of plant assets. Third, the notes provide financial information that is difficult to express through the accounting system (e.g., information about contingent liabilities).

3. Supplementary Reports: Financial information that may be provided in supplementary reports would include the following: (i) financial summaries going back many years (typically five to ten), (ii) information on operations by industry segments, (iii) other information that may be required by securities commissions, and (iv) financial information based on current market values rather than historic cost (which may or may not be audited).

Accounting and Economic Models Compared

It is common to hear accountants speak of *economic reality* or of going back to economic principles in order to evaluate alternative accounting treatments of some issue. It is clear that economic analysis has a very fundamental influence on how accounting reporting is done. The purpose of this section is to review some of the basic analytical tools that economists have developed to think about the firm. The similarities and differences between the economic and accounting views of the firm help to provide insight into the strengths and weaknesses of each.

ECONOMIC MODEL OF THE FIRM

Let us consider the following basic elements of the economic view of the firm:

1. A **production function**, which explicitly describes what outputs the entity is capable

of producing from the inputs that it uses, and what this output-input relationship is. This is a statement of the technical relationship between inputs and outputs. Here is a common example. A farmer uses seed, fertilizer, and labour together with a given piece of land to produce a crop of wheat. It is nearly always assumed that the ratio in which he combines seed, fertilizer, and labour is not fixed for all time. Instead, it is usually assumed that the ratio can be varied; so that as the prices of these inputs change with respect to one another, he can search for a more cost-effective combination of inputs and outputs.

2. An assumption that the manager will have a single goal — to maximize the profits of his entity.

3. An assumption (in the simple model taught in introductory economics courses) that all inputs used in the period will be purchased in the same period. In other words, the firm does not end the period with any raw materials inventory; and any wear and tear to, or obsolescence of, the plant assets will be made good by the end of the period. The physical plant will be left functionally the same as it was when the period started.

4. A parallel assumption that everything produced will be sold; so that the firm's revenues are exactly equal to the value of what was produced, and there is no opening and closing finished goods inventory. This means that the firm has no problem of matching costs with revenue, because all benefits received (and costs incurred) in that period are the result of the economic activity of that period only.

5. A formal statement that the objective, profit, is a function of the revenue and costs of that period (that is, Profit = Revenue − Costs) and that profit should be maximized, subject to the limiting technological constraints of the production function.

At the level of introductory economics courses, this model leads to the conclusion that entrepreneurs maximize profit best if they respond incrementally by adopting the following measures: (i) shift the inputs until the contribution of each is exactly equal to their relative cost; (ii) shift the output mix until the amount received for each unit is proportional to its relative production cost; and (iii) adjust the production volume until the incremental cost of the last unit produced is just equal to the incremental revenue that it brings in.

If a firm does this and is profitable, then it attracts other firms into the industry. Competition will increase until the profit for the industry sinks to the "normal" rate. If a firm is unable to make a profit, then it uses up its stock of resources and moves to another more profitable industry. If a firm were to fail to make this move, its shareholders would tend to sell its stock, thus depressing the stock price. The raising of additional capital would then become so expensive that the firm would choose to close. In this way the productive components of society are continually shifted toward those activities that are most in demand (i.e., those activities that the shift in relative prices of commodities indicate are the most wanted).

The appeal of the economic model of the firm is that with a few basic sets of variables and a straightforward notion of optimizing something (namely, profit), it is able to fit the variables into a framework that prescribes (i) how individual entrepreneurs should adjust their production and sales policy to maximize profit (and the economic efficiency of their firms) and (ii) how society at large can have its changing needs for goods and services looked after by industries seeking the most profitable activities.

It should be pointed out that almost all societies, regardless of their political views, aim to increase the economic efficiency of their productive units and strive to aid the smooth adjustment of productive facilities to meet the changing needs of their members. Given these common objectives, the differences between societies tend to concentrate on (i) the process by which this efficiency and adjustment is to be achieved (e.g., through market mechanisms or through top-down planning and direction); and (ii) the trade-offs that must be made between two desirable goals, such as efficiency and equity. Consequently, if accounting reports can be designed to aid in economic decision-making, then they should be helpful in the conduct of affairs in a variety of economies, including the market economies of the West, and the top-down economies of the Soviet bloc.

COMPARISON OF THE ECONOMIC MODEL AND THE ACCOUNTING MODEL

Ideally, the financial information generated by the accounting system would provide inputs to the economic model of the firm that would aid the manager and investor to assess how well the firm was doing. Specifically, the generated information would provide (i) a measure of **total revenue** consistent with its equivalent economic measure, and a breakdown of it by product line; and (ii) a measure of **total expenses** consistent with its equivalent economic measure, and a break-down of it by type of expense. We would want to have (iii) a measure of the number of units of each input used; (iv) the number of units of output sold; and (v) some way of identifying the production function.

It would be reasonable to expect the accounting system to help in collecting (iii) and (iv), even though they are not, strictly speaking, accounting measures. However, the production function, (iv), is not something that could be inferred from the accounting system. The usual expectation in economics is that this is something that would be provided by someone with training in the technology of the processes in the industry (e.g., engineers).

The accountant runs into practical troubles while trying to measure (i) and (ii). They are usually not fatal problems, but they often seriously affect the usefulness of the numbers one is able to generate. We can distinguish two reasons for this:

1. The economist's notion of **total revenue** assumes that everything produced in the period will be sold and that there is no carry forward of goods or activities from one period to the next. But there are very few real world situations where this is the case. The accountant has responded to these carry-forward situations by applying the recognition convention, which usually means that income earned on work unfinished at the end of the period is left uncounted until a later period when it is deemed to be realized. (A review of the section above on the recognition convention will refresh your memory on why this is done.)

In addition, the economist assumes that total revenue can be subdivided into the revenue earned on each unit of product sold. The accountant rarely measures in finer detail than the total revenue (in the accounting sense) earned on each *product line*, rather than on the *individual products* in each line. For instance, a supermarket may know how much fresh produce it has sold in a given day, but it is unlikely to know how much each orange sold for. This is partly a practical problem: the number of individual products that most organizations sell is so huge that it is not worthwhile to keep such a detailed account of their sales. At a more fundamental level it is also a problem of definition: two oranges can be different (e.g., in size) and yet be treated as similar items for purposes of classification. On the other hand, a context may arise in which it is no longer useful to consider them the same for some purposes. It is often not clear where this transition from being the same to being different occurs.

2. The economist's definition of *total expenses* assumes that all inputs to the productive process have been purchased in the period being reported on. The accountant's problem is that, in the real world, productive activities are ongoing. Expenditures made in one period may very likely benefit that period as well as subsequent periods. Under the matching principle, the accountant tries to allocate these expenditures against the periods that will benefit from them. However, as we have already explained, the practical problems of this are enormous and usually prevent allocations from being done in a completely satisfactory manner.

The net result of these practical problems is that the measures of total revenue and total expenses are, at best, approximations of the variables in the economist's model of the firm. In some circumstances they may be good approximations; at other times they may not be much good at all. One of the skills of the thoughtful reader of financial statements is to be able to distinguish the good situation from the poor situation and then make the appropriate adjustments. One of the main purposes of this text is to help the student to acquire this skill.

The economic view of the firm can be summarized as a flow of raw material inputs (labour, raw material, services) into an organization that has the capability of turning them into finished goods, which are then sold for money. The money flows back into the firm, with some of it going out again to buy the inputs required for the next cycle. If the manager does things right, the maximum amount of money is retained from this cycle and used to pay the shareholders who have financed the assets of the firm. We can show this diagrammatically as follows:

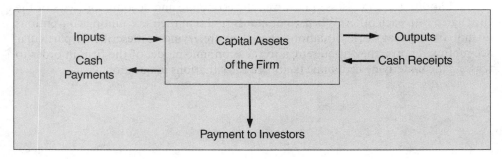

The accountant would change this model slightly by adding the buffer stocks of working capital items such as cash, inventory, and accounts receivable and payable.

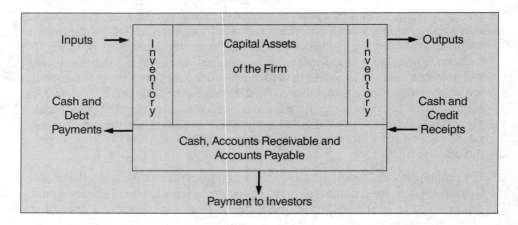

The accounting model is slightly more complex than the economic model, but it does account for the working capital items that the accountant finds in real companies. The balance sheet portrays the capital assets of the firm, together with some other assets that fit the model as well. The income statement provides information about the revenue inflows (on the right-hand side of the model above) and also about the expense outflows (on the left-hand side).

This is a highly simplified way of viewing the firm, and there are many items thrown up by the accounting system that do not fit neatly into the model above. Nevertheless, although it is simplified and lacking in realistic detail, we will find it useful. We will see the thinking reflected by this model of the firm many times as we search for ways to interpret financial statements and make accounting reports more useful.

Summary

As well as providing a quick review of material usually covered in an introductory course, the purpose of this chapter has been to highlight some of the complexities that accountants and readers of financial statements have to cope with in everyday life.

In addition, we have assessed how well the economic and accounting views of the firm agree with each other. When accountants find that their accounting conventions do not fit the real-world situations that they are trying to describe in particular accounting reports, they often return to the economic model of the firm in order to reassess the underlying economic factors of the situations in question.

QUESTIONS

Q1-1. Review the following words and make sure you understand their meaning:

a. entity	**f.** credit	**k.** recognition
b. asset	**g.** revenue	**l.** matching
c. liability	**h.** expense	**m.** relevance
d. owners' equity	**i.** cost convention	**n.** economic model of the firm
e. debit	**j.** conservatism	**o.** materiality

Q1-2. Do you agree with the following statements? Explain why or why not.

a. The Chevrolet Division of General Motors is not separately incorporated. Nevertheless it is clearly a separate entity.

b. The accounting process is normally associated with *debits* and *credits*. Yet there is no evidence of them on the financial statements.

c. The use of the terms *debit* and *credit* is a holdover from the old days. Accountants would be better off dropping them in favour of more general terms like *plus* and *minus*.

d. It is possible for the financial statements of a company to be misleading, even though the bookkeeping has been done properly and all the accounting conventions have been followed.

e. Although accounting is based on numbers, accounting reports are not very exact.

f. The cost convention makes it possible for accountants to arrive objectively at the accounting entries they make.

g. Many of the difficulties of accounting reporting could be eliminated if accountants would drop the convention of periodic reporting.

h. One of the main differences between the accountant's and the economist's view of the firm concerns the identification of the times at which income is earned.

Q1-3. Explain why accountants may change accounting conventions from time to time. Does this mean that earlier financial statements issued before the change are incorrect?

Q1-4. "Because economists generally recognize income as earned all through the productive process, a firm that uses the economists' method of income recognition would always report a higher profit." Discuss.

Q1-5. "It often does not matter where in the earning process the point of income realization is placed." Discuss.

Q1-6. Consider the following cases. For each, (i) discuss the problems that might be present at the end of each accounting year; and then (ii) evaluate the advantages or disadvantages of waiting until the end of the economic cycle before issuing a financial report.

a. A student house-painting business has its financial year-end on 31 December of each year.

b. A group of investors band together to finance a Broadway play. It is booked into a theatre for seven weeks, but the first week's reviews are so favourable that the producer is frantically trying to find a theatre that will take them after the seventh week.

c. Software Spectaculars has created a piece of business software that they are certain is the next Lotus 1-2-3. The development work is mostly done, and over the next two years they intend to market it and do the final development.

d. Titanic Mines has found a lead-zinc deposit of commercial quality in British Columbia. They intend to develop it at a cost of $20 million. They expect that the deposit will be commercially workable for seven years.

e. A Canadian-financed disaster film called *City on Fire* was made in Montreal. The critics did not like it (one of them terming it "roast turkey"). Assume that the film producer's year-end is nine months away.

Q1-7. "The recognition convention and the cost convention are contradictory, since under the recognition convention we are prepared to value accounts receivable at more than they cost." Discuss.

Q1-8. Explain why the matching principle is intuitively sensible as an objective to strive for but often hard to make work in practice.

Q1-9. A world-wide firm of public accountants issued a monograph containing the following assertion: "There is probably more than a grain of truth in the statement that so many of the problems currently facing preparers and auditors of financial statements are due to the fact that we do not have a conceptual framework, *which means we do not have a clear idea as to the basic objective of, and the reasons for preparing, financial statements*." (emphasis added) Our text suggests that there are practical problems in converting the economic model of the firm into the accounting model. Do you think the problem referred to above is due to a lack of a conceptual framework? Or is it due to the difficulty of putting the conceptual framework into practice?

Q1-10. What do accountants mean when they refer to *economic* reality? How might this differ from (i) *accounting* reality and from (ii) *legal* reality?

Q1-11. Part of the black humour among accountants is that accounting is a system of income measurement that prefers being *exactly wrong* to *approximately right*. What accounting conventions might lead in that direction? What are the corrective processes within accounting that help to guard against this?

Q1-12. What are the differences between the economic and accounting models of the firm? Evaluate their implications for the reader of financial statements.

Q1-13. Do you agree with the following statements? Explain why or why not.

a. Although the entity concept is fundamental to accounting, it is too elastic because one person could define the entity to be a corner store, and a second person could expand the definition to include the whole town in which the grocery store is located. It is confusing to have the same thing as part of two different entities.

b. The matching principle and the recognition convention are closely related. Until we have decided how to recognize costs, there is no point trying to match them to revenue.

c. A company's financial statements are an incomplete portrayal of that company's affairs. They leave out as much as they include.

d. The economist's measure of corporate income differs significantly from the accountant's measure.

e. The conservatism convention in accounting means that a company's net income is always understated.

Q1-14. What is the distinction between accounting and bookkeeping that we have made in this chapter? Do you think this distinction is overdrawn? Explain.

Q1-15. It is a convention of accounting that assets should be shown at their *cost* to the company, not at their *market value*, for instance. In the following situations indicate why the cost of the asset being acquired may or may not be hard to determine.

   a. A company purchased a car from a car dealer. The list price of the car was $13,000; but because the purchaser was a good customer, it was sold for $12,300 cash.

   b. A storage shed was refinished and turned into a small office. The storage shed had cost $5,000 to build five years before. The cost of the material to refinish it was $3,000, and 130 hours of labour were needed to do the work. Of the 130 hours, 50 were for casual hired labour that cost $300 cash; 60 were for a skilled carpenter paid $10 an hour who had to be pulled off a job where he was earning $13 an hour for the company; and 20 were for the foreman, who had a salary of $3,500 a month. The foreman did this work on an overtime basis because the office was for him and he desperately needed it to do his job efficiently.

   c. A car was purchased with a radio and tape deck. The car cost $13,000 without the radio, and the radio would have cost $600 if purchased separately. However, the two together were purchased for $13,300. What was the cost of the radio for depreciation purposes?

Q1-16. "If the production cycle is long but production output is steady, the choice of the point of recognition will have some impact but the amounts will tend to even out." Explain in your own words.

Q1-17. Explain in your own words what the matching principle and the recognition convention are. In what manner, if any, does the choice of one of them impact on the working of the other?

Q1-18. A columnist in *The Globe and Mail* reported that Bell Canada argues that it makes $1.90 for every $1.00 it spends on long distance calls and earns only $0.32 for every dollar spent on local calls. He then goes on to say that others disagree with Bell's "economics." Explain, using ideas developed for the matching principle in accounting, why there might be disagreement over Bell's figures.

Q1-19. A college pub, owned by the student body, owns the furniture in its premises, as well as glassware, uniforms, and assorted equipment. It has always reported on the assumption that it will continue as a going concern, but of late there has been some doubt as to its long-term feasibility. Explain what difference, if any, it would make to those preparing its financial statements if the assumption of a going concern were dropped and replaced by the assumption that the pub would be going out of business in the near future.

Q1-20. What are the usual objectives of a reader looking at a balance sheet? an income statement? Are these objectives similar? mutually complementary?

Q1-21. Using only plain English words and no technical accounting terms, explain the meaning of the following: (i) current assets; (ii) plant assets; (iii) assets other than current or plant assets; (iv) current liabilities; (v) long-term liabilities; (vi) owners' equity. Which term(s) do you find hardest to explain in ordinary English? Can you explain why?

Q1-22. What are the various types of auditors' opinions? What message is the reader to take away from each?

Q1-23. Alpha Ltd. issued a purchase order to a supplier for inventory costing $3,500. The supplier has sent an acceptance of the order, with the information that the items will be shipped in three weeks. What journal entry is required to record this?

Q1-24. The cost convention is sometimes criticized for being *un*conservative. Explain.

Q1-25. Explain how being a stockholder of a public corporation differs from being:

a. a partner in a business

b. the sole proprietor of a small business

(CGA adapted)

EXERCISES

E1-1. For each of the following situations explain when the revenue would normally be recognized.

a. Fitwell Shoe Store sold a pair of $100 shoes to a customer on credit. The shoes were sold with a money-back guarantee, and it knows from experience that 10% of these sales are likely to be returned.

b. C.A. Smith charges his clients $100 per hour. In January he worked 50 hours for a client; but he did not bill him until February, and the client did not pay until March.

c. In January a travel agent arranged a trip for her client that was going to cost $2,000. The travel agent knew the commission on this trip would be $150. She made out the tickets in February, and the client actually went on the trip in March.

d. Shelter Construction builds and sells family homes in the $80,000 range. The purchaser puts down $2,000 when he signs the original offer to purchase. He makes the rest of the down payment and takes over the mortgage at the time that legal title passes to him. Only one percent of those who pay the deposit and sign the offer to purchase fail to go through with the purchase.

e. In order to exert greater control over the delivery of petroleum, the Alberta Government passed a law in 1981 that as soon as oil was pumped to the surface it had to be legally sold immediately to the Government of Alberta. The equivalent oil was then sold back to the same companies when it left the province and continued on its usual distribution channels to the ultimate customer. The oil companies continued to have the same physical possession of the oil that they always had; the only difference was that for a brief period it became legally the property of the Alberta Government.

E1-2. For each of the situations below, (i) show the journal entry, if any, that the accountant would make; and (ii) explain the impact on the timing of when the gain or loss is reported.

a. The inventory that the company has on hand costs $200,000. If sold immediately, it could realize $250,000 net.

b. The situation is the same as in (a) except that the inventory has a net realizable value of $150,000.

c. A building was recently purchased for $1.3 million to be used for the manufacture of phonograph records. It has an estimated life of ten years. Because of the fall in the price of real estate, it now has a net realizable value of $0.9 million.

d. Genesplice Limited has this year spent $2 million in research on genetic engineering and has patented a technique that has the industry excited. It has been offered $3 million if it will grant an exclusive licence to use the patent to a large reputable drug firm. The $2 million had been charged to accounts receivable, and the president proposes leaving it there until next year when the $3 million arrives from the drug firm. He thinks this treatment is over-conservative, however, and asks your opinion.

E1-3. Complete the following table.

Item	Is the Item on Balance Sheet or Income Statement?	Is the Account Balance Normally Debit or Credit?
a. Accounts receivable		
b. Prepaid expenses		
c. Bond interest		
d. Cost of goods sold		
e. Premium on bonds issued		
f. Work in process		
g. Accrued wages payable		
h. Depreciation expense		
i. Accumulated amortization		

E1-4. In each of the following cases state (i) what the journal entry debits and credits would be, (ii) which of the accounts below would be increased, and (iii) which would be decreased. The accounts are:

1. Owners' equity	4. Plant assets	7. Accounts receivable
2. Cost of goods sold	5. Accounts payable	8. Bank
3. Sales	6. Inventory	9. Rental expense

a. Merchandise is sold on credit for $300.
b. The company pays an outstanding invoice of $150.
c. A cheque is issued for the monthly rent of $2,500.
d. Merchandise sold for cash is returned for a refund of $125.
e. A typewriter is purchased on credit for $950.
f. The directors declare a dividend totalling $3,000.

E1-5. For each of the accounts shown above, state whether they would be: (i) found on the balance sheet or the income statement; (ii) and if on the balance sheet, whether they would be classed as assets, liabilities, or owners' equity.

E1-6. What, if anything, is wrong with the following journal entries? If you find something wrong, then show what the right journal entry should be. (Do not make the entry that would correct the one shown below.)

a. Sales	350.00	
Inventory		200.00
Profit on sale		150.00

To record merchandise returned. It originally cost $200.00 and was sold for $350.00.

b. Depreciation expense	123,000.00	
Plant assets		123,000.00

To record annual depreciation expense.

c. Accounts receivable	56,000.00	
Cash		56,000.00

To record receipt of cash in payment of credit sales.

d. Depreciation expense	85,000.00	
Accumulated depreciation		85,000.00

To record depreciation, as follows:

Historic cost of asset	$258,000
Accumulated depreciation	120,000
Net book value	138,000
Current replacement cost	53,000
Additional depreciation required	$ 85,000

E1-7. Mr. Winston is the auditor of a small manufacturing company. After the year-end at 30 September 19X2, he reviewed the accounting records prepared by the company's accountant and he isolated for further investigation those entries that appeared to be incorrect. These entries and related information follow.

Required: Prepare the correcting journal entries that should be made by Mr. Winston before completing the financial statements.

a. 31 July 19X2

Insurance expense	3,000.00	
Cash		3,000.00

To record the payment for insurance on the buildings and equipment for the 12 months beginning 1 August 19X2.

b. 31 October 19X1

Purchases	8,000.00	
Cash		8,000.00

To record the payment of an invoice for inventory received during September 19X1. The correct accrual had been made as at 30 September 19X1.

c. 30 September 19X2

Cost of goods sold	2,120.00	
Inventory		2,120.00

To adjust inventory to actual per physical count.

Note: The company uses a perpetual inventory system. The above entry, made after the year-end count, was based on the following information:

Inventory per count	$33,450
Inventory per books	31,330
Difference	$ 2,120

d. 30 June 19X2

Inventory	4,000.00	
Cash		4,000.00

To record the purchase of office equipment. (This amount is part of the inventory per book number in part (c) above.)

e. 5 September 19X2

Cash	2,000.00	
Sales		2,000.00

To record the cash received when a customer ordered special equipment. At year-end, no work on the order had been initiated.

E1-8. During 19X1, the Watford Manufacturing Company hired a recent university graduate as their bookkeeper. The bookkeeper made a number of entries in error during the year and these were not corrected before the 30 November 19X1 year-end statements were prepared. (The company's owner is interested only in production and sales and considers all accounting requirements a nuisance.)

Required: In each case, (i) identify the financial statement(s) that is (are) affected by the error and (ii) the direction of the resulting misstatement(s). (*Hint:* Consider the impact on future statements as well as on the current income statement, balance sheet, and statement of changes in financial position.)

a. Inventory of $35,000 was received on 28 November and included in the periodic inventory count. Because no invoice had been received, no entry was made in the accounting records.

b. Depreciation of $110,000 was determined using the straight-line method for the current year. In past years, the declining-balance method was used for all assets. Last year it totalled $80,000, and it would have been $70,000 this year.

c. Routine repair expenditures to the company's service trucks were capitalized in the company's fixed asset account for vehicles.

d. Unpaid salaries for the last week in November and unpaid vacation pay were not accrued.

e. The company rents out warehouse space which they cannot presently utilize. On 1 November, rent for three months (November through January) was received, and rental revenue was credited for the full amount.

f. The inventory listing prepared from the physical count was added incorrectly (understated), and some items were omitted. The total was then used to make the year-end inventory adjustments.

g. No consideration was given to providing for possible bad debts despite a material balance in the accounts receivable account.

h. The salesmen's cars are leased by the company. The monthly lease payments were charged to miscellaneous expense instead of selling and administration.

E1-9. For each of the following items, indicate the appropriate classification (type of asset, liability, owners' equity, or item not normally appearing on a balance sheet).

   a. Furniture and fixtures

   b. Prepaid rent

   c. Cash on hand

   d. Estimated future liability under a product warranty

   e. Rental fees paid in advance

   f. Unexpired insurance

   g. Convertible preferred shares

   h. Potential settlement to be paid as a result of a pending lawsuit

   i. Unamortized excess of purchase price over fair value of net assets acquired

   j. Raw materials on hand

   k. Debentures payable

E1-10. For each of the following items indicate the appropriate classification (type of asset, liability, owner's equity, or item not normally appearing on the balance sheet).

   a. Contributed surplus

   b. Unfilled customer orders

   c. Interest due on debentures payable

   d. Mortgage payable

   e. Advances from customers

   f. Patent rights

   g. Salaries payable

   h. Notes receivable

   i. Land held for future use

   j. Work in process

   k. Organization costs

   l. Advances to employees

   m. Good credit rating

E1-11. For each of the following items, indicate if classification as a liability is appropriate under generally accepted accounting principles.

    a. A tenant's obligation to maintain a rented office building in good repair.

    b. An incompetent employee (the brother-in-law of the owner).

    c. The common shares of the company which have been authorized but are unissued.

    d. An obligation to provide a photocopier to a customer who has paid three months' rental charges in advance.

    e. Unpaid vacation pay owing to employees as a result of government regulations.

    f. The amount payable by a company for advertising brochures which have been printed and received but for which payment is not due for 30 days.

    g. The reputation of a business for not paying bills promptly.

    h. An obligation to deliver merchandise.

    i. Amounts withheld from employee pay for the company pension plan.

E1-12. For each of the following items, indicate if classification as an asset is appropriate under generally accepted accounting principles.

    a. A reputation for selling quality products.

    b. A good credit rating with the bank.

    c. A prepayment by a customer on the order of special merchandise.

    d. A vending machine in the employees' cafeteria.

    e. A sales contract with a customer who agrees to buy $10,000 worth of goods each year for three years.

    f. A patent developed by the company which improves production efficiency by 20%.

    g. The successful recruitment and hiring of a marketing specialist.

    h. Ten years of strike-free operations because of good relations with the employees' union.

E1-13. Using the format provided, determine the effects of the individual transactions listed below as well as the cumulative effects of the various entries.

Transaction	Assets	–	Liabilities	–	Owners' equity	=	0
(a)	$ + 80,000				$ + 80,000		
subtotal	80,000				80,000		

    a. Ten thousand common shares were issued for proceeds of $8 per share.

    b. Merchandise priced at $32,300 was purchased on account.

    c. Equipment was purchased with 10% down and the balance payable over three years. The invoice total was $8,900.

    d. Office supplies costing $437 were purchased. Payment was made by cheque.

    e. A 60-day promissory note was issued to the supplier of (b) for the full amount due.

    f. Payment of $1,400 was made to the owner of the building to cover the rent due for the following two months.

    g. Dividends of $8,000 were paid.

E1-14. In each of the following situations, identify the entity most likely to be reported upon. Explain.

    a. Ms. H. Hardware owns and operates three franchised retail operations in the Sudbury area.

b. H. H. Incorporated has twenty-six retail outlets in Ontario of which fourteen are operated directly and twelve are run by franchise holders.

c. A group of cottage owners band together to lobby for improved legislation to control acid rain. Funds have been raised from various sources to facilitate their efforts.

d. Two small businesses with adjacent premises agree to share the cost of a new parking lot, half of which will be located on each property.

e. A paving company and a road construction company bid together on a highway project and receive the contract.

E1-15. Fleetham Corporation acquired a much needed operational asset. The list price on the item was $37,500. Since the Corporation was short of cash, it exchanged a parcel of land it had acquired eight years earlier for $20,000. The land was assessed for tax purposes at $30,000. Two recent appraisals, each by an independent appraiser, yielded almost identical amounts: the resulting average of the two appraisals was $35,000.

Required:

a. What accounting principle should govern at the time of acquisition?

b. Record the acquisition of the operational asset in exchange for the land.

c. What accounting principle governs the recognition of depreciation on the asset?

(CGA adapted)

E1-16. The Hopton Corporation, which manufactures equipment for sale, sold five pieces of equipment in December 19X8 at 20% off the list price. The list price was $10,000 for each piece of equipment. The Corporation estimated, based on prior years' experience, that $600 would be spent during 19X9 on each of the five pieces of equipment to make good on the one-year warranty covering the sold equipment.

Required:

a. When should the warranty expense be recognized?

b. What accounting principle should govern the recognition of the warranty expense?

c. Give the journal entry (entries) to record the warranty expense for 19X8 and 19X9.

(CGA adapted)

E1-17. Manchester company acquires goods for resale (merchandise inventory) from regular suppliers for $10 per unit. However, in 19X7 the company was able to make a good deal and purchased 5,000 units for $37,500 cash. Because the deal was completed in 19X7 and the company anticipated no change in the selling price, it believed that the *windfall profit* belonged to 19X7 and consequently recorded the purchase as:

Inventory	50,000	
Cash		37,500
Extraordinary gain		12,500

Required:

a. Was any accounting principle violated in the company's recording of the purchase? If yes, identify the principle(s).

b. If you are in disagreement with the company's recording of the purchase, present the journal entry you would have made at the time of purchase (assume the perpetual-inventory system).

(CGA adapted)

E1-18. You have been hired to assist an accountant prepare analyses and working papers in preparation for a company's 31 December year-end. The accountant hands you a ledger account entitled "Mysteries!" that was under the supervision of your predecessor. "I don't know what's in there," the accountant says, "but please look up the details behind the entries and let me know what journal entries you propose to close this account out." After some work you have prepared the following annotated version of the "Mysteries!" ledger account.

MYSTERIES!

Description	Debit	Credit	Balance
i. Inventory write-down	$32,580.00		$32,580.00
ii. Prepaid insurance	5,863.00		38,443.00
iii. Interest, etc.	4,781.00		43,224.00
iv. Acme Supplies	2,514.00		45,738.00
v. Accrued interest payable		$2,806.00	42,932.00

i. After the closing inventory was counted and valued, this is the amount that had to be credited to the inventory account to reduce it to its correct value.

ii. The prepaid insurance account at the start of the year was written off to this account. When the insurance was renewed during the current year, $5,980 was charged to this year's expense and the remainder, $6,350, was charged to prepaid insurance. Your review indicates that this prepaid amount of $6,350 is correct for the current year.

iii. A bond that had been purchased at par for $100,000 was sold for total proceeds of $95,219, and the difference was charged to this account. Your examination of the broker's contract indicates that the total proceeds include $4,650 of accrued interest.

iv. Acme Supplies was paid $2,514 after invoicing the company for equipment made to special order for the Planning Department. Planning won't accept the equipment or the $2,514 charge, saying the equipment does not perform according to specifications. As an interim measure, the charge had been taken out of Planning's account and transferred here.

v. During the current year the company had a bank loan, which is now paid. At the end of the first six months the amount of $2,806 was accrued in order to get the interest expense into the first six month's expenses.

Required: Show the journal entries that would be required to close out the "Mysteries!" ledger account and transfer the entries to the proper accounts.

PROBLEMS

P1-1. In each of the cases below, identify the organizational unit that you would use as the entity for which accounting reports would be prepared. In those cases where there is a choice of entity to be used, you should identify all the choices and discuss the relative advantages of each.

a. Smith Shoes Limited has an agreement with Mammoth Department Stores that Smith will run all the shoe departments within Mammoth. Smith will hire the staff and supply the inventory, but customers will pay at the usual check-out counters of Mammoth. The clerks at the check-out counters will record all Smith Shoes' sales separately, so at the end of the day they will know how much Smith's total sales are.

b. Happy Valley Shopping Centre has forty-three stores that sell a variety of goods and services. Happy Valley rents the space to each store operator and provides such basic services as heat, garbage removal, security, and exterior janitorial services.

c. The Bank of Montreal has hundreds of branches connected to a central computer that does the basic accounting for all these branches in a few computing centres. Managers of a branch are assessed in part on their ability to attract people to use the services offered by the bank and on their ability to control costs.

d. McBunions and Bunch is a firm of lawyers. In legal form it is a partnership, with twenty of the lawyers forming the partnership. The remaining forty lawyers on the staff are paid a salary and enjoy some participation in the firm's profits.

e. John and Helen Smith are both practising lawyers as well as husband and wife. They share an office for the practice of law and split the costs of maintaining it. However, John practises under his own name, and Helen practises under hers.

f. IBM Corporation as a matter of policy operates in various countries of the world only through wholly owned subsidiaries. The individual subsidiaries are required to prepare financial statements by the taxing authorities in the country in which they operate. Yet, in many ways from an operating viewpoint, they are not thought of as separate units. It is quite common for the individual companies to specialize in the production of just a few products that are then sold world-wide.

P1-2. Below is the trial balance for Camden Limited. In addition to the trial balance, you are given the following information. It was discovered after the trial balance was prepared and it needs to be reflected in adjusting entries.

(1) There are unpaid wages of $3,100 in addition to the accrued wages shown in the trial balance.

(2) An additional $800 of finished goods inventory was discovered.

(3) A deposit for money received on the last day of the year had not been entered. It was for $3,400, of which $2,600 should have been credited to accounts receivable and $800 should have been credited to cash sales.

(4) Prepaid insurance was only $1,300 in total.

(5) An additional $8,200 of building depreciation expense needs to be entered, as well as an additional $3,500 for equipment.

CAMDEN LIMITED
TRIAL BALANCE

	Debit	Credit
Cash	$ 15,000	
Accounts receivable	35,000	
Inventory: Finished goods	32,000	
Work in process	52,000	
Raw material	15,000	
Prepaid insurance	2,400	
Buildings: At historical cost	126,350	
Accumulated depreciation		$ 57,890
Land — at historical cost	24,000	
Equipment: At historical cost	243,100	
Accumulated depreciation		19,530
Franchise — at cost	2,800	
Accounts payable		25,346
Accrued wages		2,850
Taxes payable		19,520
Mortgage payable		150,000
Deferred income tax		18,230
Preferred shares		15,000
Common shares		56,000
Retained earnings: Start of year		164,384
Dividends paid	3,000	
Sales		315,300
Cost of goods sold	189,100	
Selling and administrative expenses	78,200	
Income tax	26,100	
	$844,050	$844,050

Required:

a. Prepare a worksheet showing (i) the trial balance above, (ii) adjusting entries, (iii) adjusted trial balance, (iv) columnar balance sheet, (v) and columnar income statement. In the adjusting entries column, label each adjusting entry with the number of the above note that it reflects.

b. Give reasons to support your answers to each of the following questions:

(i) What kind of a company might have a financial statement such as this?

(ii) Given the volume of sales, are the sizes of the company's accounts receivable, inventory, and plant assets plausible?

(iii) Roughly how much would you advise a prospective buyer to pay for this company?

P1-3.   Here is the trial balance of Dresden Office Equipment Inc.

DRESDEN OFFICE EQUIPMENT INC.
PRELIMINARY TRIAL BALANCE
31 July 19X3

	Debit	Credit
Cash on hand and in bank	$35,320	
Accounts receivable	69,760	
Notes receivable	85,000	
Store supplies inventory	1,200	
Store equipment	44,000	
Accumulated depreciation — store equipment		$ 8,800
Accounts payable		39,400
Notes payable		12,000
Capital stock		150,000
Retained earnings		10,820
Sales revenue		288,680
Interest revenue		500
Interest expense	300	
Sales salaries	69,200	
Advertising	39,000	
Store supplies expense	1,480	
General office expense	4,940	
Insurance expense	2,400	
Office salaries	40,400	
Officers' salaries	80,000	
Legal and audit expense	5,000	
Telephone and telex	2,400	
Rent expense	28,800	
Dividends	1,000	

Consider the following additional information as at 31 July 19X3:

(1) Unexpired insurance: $700
(2) Store supplies on hand: $850
(3) Prepaid rent: $3,500
(4) Depreciation rate for store equipment: 10% straight line
(5) Unpaid salaries — sales: $2,000
                  — office: $1,500
(6) Net realizable value of accounts receivable: $63,760
(7) Unpaid interest on note payable: $1,200

Required:

a. Prepare the adjusting journal entries as at 31 July 19X3 for the year just ended.

b. Complete the worksheet and prepare closing entries.

c. Prepare the balance sheet, income statement, and statement of retained earnings.

P1-4. Imagine a situation in which all the bookkeeping for a company is done on its computer. One simply has to enter on the keyboard the amounts to be debited and credited along with account names. The computer does the rest instantly, posting the amounts to the correct account and preparing trial balances and financial statements that can be printed out any time they are requested. Out of habit the management of the company only ask for the financial statements at the end of each month. At the same time they also ask for a printout of the ledgers and trial balances.

Required:

a. Are the balances stored in the computer as debits and credits?

b. How long is the accounting cycle?

c. Is the real ledger inside in the computer or on the printout?

P1-5. The following information pertains to the first year of operations for Caledonia Graphics Ltd.

CALEDONIA GRAPHICS LTD.
PRELIMINARY TRIAL BALANCE
31 January 19X4

	Debit	Credit
Cash		$ 1,721
Accounts receivable	$3,875	
Plant assets: Office equipment	2,150	
Drafting equipment	1,000	
Deferred charges	3,300	
Accounts payable		1,852
Loan payable — long term		10,000
Sales revenue		11,882
Rent expense	4,000	
Office and drafting supplies inventory	6,207	
Interest expense	700	
Insurance expense	442	
Miscellaneous	3,781	

Consider the following additional information relevant at the company's year-end, 31 January 19X4:

(1) The company was incorporated on 2 June 19X3 with one common share issued to Mr. Brown for $1 and one common share to Mrs. Brown for $1. The proceeds were credited to accounts payable in error.

(2) On 1 July 19X3 the company signed a five-year lease for office and studio space in a new industrial park. Rent is $500 per month and one month's rent was paid as a deposit.

(3) On 15 July 19X3 the company borrowed $10,000 from the bank with the Brown family home as collateral. Interest at 14% is payable on the 15th of every month.

(4) Leasehold improvements were made to the rented premises. Total cost for such things as partitions, painting, and wiring was $3,000 and was charged to miscellaneous expense. The improvements are to be amortized over five years on a straight-line basis.

(5) Used drafting tables and related equipment were purchased from Mr. Brown's brother-in-law, Mr. White, for $1,000. The fair market value of the equipment was $4,000.

(6) The accounts payable subledger balance on 31 January 19X4 was $1,722. However, it was subsequently discovered that one of the subledger account cards was added incorrectly. (The balance was recorded as $250 and should have been $350; the balance therefore *should be* $1,822.)

(7) Advertising costs of $1,200 and incorporation expenses of $2,100 had been capitalized as deferred charges.

(8) Bad debts relating to the year-end accounts receivable are expected to be $350.

(9) Year-end accounting fees are estimated to be $1,800.

(10) On 1 October 19X3 Mr. Brown purchased a used car for $4,200. Although the vehicle was to be used only on company business, he used personal funds to pay for it. Consequently no entry was made in the books of the company.

(11) The company's owners decided that the following depreciation and amortization rates applied to year-end balances are appropriate.

Office equipment: 20% straight line
Drafting equipment: 20% straight line
Vehicles: 30% declining balance
Intangible assets: 10% straight line

(12) The effective tax rate for the company is 50%.

Required:

a. Prepare the adjusting journal entries required at year-end.

b. Complete the year-end worksheet. (Round all figures to the nearest dollar.)

c. Prepare all financial statements (balance sheet, income statement, statement of retained earnings, and statement of changes in financial position using *working capital* as *funds*.)

d. Comment on the viability of the company based on the accounting information provided.

e. What other factors should be considered in assessing the future profitability of the operation?

P1-6. James Donovan, the auditor for the Tupperville Cement Co., is currently examining the records of the company for the year ending 31 December 19X8. The accountant for the company had prepared the preliminary financial statements prior to the start of the audit. The balance sheet and income statement are provided below.

Mr. Donovan obtained the following information during the course of the audit:

(1) The company sold machinery with an original cost of $96,000 and accumulated depreciation of $76,800 for proceeds of $40,000. The following entry was made at the time of the sale:

Cash   40,000.00
    Gain on sale of equipment   40,000.00

(2) When examining the inventory, Mr Donovan learned from the stockkeeper that inventory recorded on the books at $50,000 was obsolete. It had a fair market value of only $5,000.

(3) Two of the company's trucks were completely overhauled in January 19X8 at a total cost of $30,000. As a result, the useful life of each truck was extended for three more years. The full amount was expensed when incurred.

(4) No recognition had been given to taxes payable for the year. Accounting income equals taxable income, and the effective tax rate for the company is 50%.

(5) A dividend of $15 per share was declared on 21 December 19X8 with a payment date of 21 February 19X9. The company is owned by three brothers who each hold 2,000 common shares. No entry was recorded at the time of the dividend declaration.

(6) One of the brothers borrowed $60,000 from the company in October 19X8. This amount was included in accounts receivable.

TUPPERVILLE CEMENT CO.
BALANCE SHEET
As at 31 December 19X8

Assets

Cash		$ 3,897
Accounts receivable		218,921
Inventory		210,432
Fixed assets	$1,239,000	
Accumulated depreciation	875,430	363,570
Other assets		32,000
		$828,820

Liabilities

Accounts payable	$284,519
Bonds payable	300,000
	584,519

Owners' Equity

Common shares	6,000
Retained earnings	238,301
	244,301
	$828,820

TUPPERVILLE CEMENT CO.
INCOME STATEMENT
For the Year Ending 31 December 19X8

Sales		$1,492,399
Cost of sales		1,120,487
		371,912
Expenses		
Selling and administration	$249,691	
Accounting and legal	21,000	
Interest	45,000	315,691
		56,221
Other income		40,000
Net Income		96,221
Retained Earnings at beginning of year		142,080
Retained Earnings at end of year		$ 238,301

Required:

a. Prepare any adjusting journal entries necessary.

b. Revise the financial statements as required.

c. Prior to the audit, the accountant had provided the bank with the preliminary statements. On this basis a loan for $250,000 was approved. This amount was deposited in the company's account in January 19X9. When making the loan decision, the bank considered the following:

(i) The amount of the loan was "covered" by 75% of accounts receivable and 50% of inventory. (The fixed assets were pledged as collateral on the bonds.)

(ii) Reasonable profitability for the current year.

(iii) A good equity position by the owners as indicated by the retained earnings figure.

How do you think the bank will react when it receives the audited financial statements?

P1-7. On 31 December 19X1, the Butler Swimming Pool Co. is closing its books. Adjusting entries are required to reflect accurately the financial position as at 31 December.

The pre-closing trial balance for the company is shown below.

BUTLER SWIMMING POOL CO.
TRIAL BALANCE

	Debit	Credit
Accounts payable		$ 24,500
Accounts receivable	$ 80,000	
Advertising expense	4,800	
Accumulated depreciation — pools		19,800
Allowance for doubtful accounts		2,500
Swimming pools	72,000	
Capital stock		127,000
Cash	25,000	
Dividends	14,400	
Fee returns	3,360	
Insurance expense	1,600	
Interest expense	2,640	
Interest revenue		840
Inventory 31 December 19X0	70,000	
Land	45,000	
Long-term investments	12,600	
Mortgage payable		37,900
Notes payable — short term		12,800
Office expense	13,400	
Retained earnings, 31 December 19X0		15,730
Revenues — pool fees		188,000
Pool supplies expense	4,200	
Taxes — real estate and other	5,430	
Purchases	30,000	
Wages	44,640	
	$429,070	$429,070

Consider the following additional information as at 31 December 19X1:
(1) The inventory on hand is $95,520 according to the physical count.
(2) The allowance for doubtful accounts should have a balance of $3,000.
(3) Swimming pools are depreciated at a rate of 4% per year (straight line).
(4) There are supplies of $800 on hand.
(5) Prepaid insurance relating to 19X2 and 19X3 totals $720.
(6) Accrued interest receivable on long-term investments is $240.
(7) Accrued real estate, payroll, and other taxes payable are $980.
(8) Accrued interest payable on the mortgage is $480.
(9) Income tax is estimated to be 40% of the income before income tax.

Required:

a. Prepare adjusting, closing, and reversing entries.

b. Prepare an eight-column worksheet.

c. Prepare the year-end balance sheet, income statement, and statement of retained earnings.

P1-8. On 31 December 19X1 the Fox Poster Company is closing its books. Adjusting entries are required to reflect accurately the financial position as at 31 December.

The pre-closing trial balance for the company is shown below.

FOX POSTER COMPANY
TRIAL BALANCE

	Debit	Credit
Accounts payable		$ 36,000
Accounts receivable	$67,200	
Advertising	4,800	
Accumulated depreciation — buildings		19,800
Allowance for doubtful accounts		1,380
Buildings	72,000	
Capital stock		180,000
Cash	24,000	
Dividends	14,400	
Freight in	3,600	
Insurance expense	1,440	
Interest expense	2,640	
Interest revenue		660
Inventory, 31 December 19X0	64,800	
Land	69,600	
Long-term investments	12,600	
Mortgage payable		48,000
Notes payable — short term		15,000
Office expense	16,080	
Purchases	138,480	
Purchase discounts		1,140
Retained earnings, 31 December 19X0		14,040
Sales		246,000
Sales discounts	5,400	
Sales returns	3,360	
Selling expense	49,440	
Supplies expense	4,200	
Taxes — real estate, payroll, and other	7,980	
	$562,020	$562,020

Additional information as at 31 December 19X1 is as follows:
(1) The inventory on hand is $90,720 according to the physical count.
(2) The allowance for doubtful accounts should have a balance of $3,000.
(3) Buildings are depreciated at a rate of $3^1/_3\%$ per year (straight line).
(4) There are supplies of $780 on hand.
(5) Prepaid insurance relating to 19X2 totals $720.
(6) Accrued interest receivable on long-term investments is $240.
(7) Accrued real estate, payroll, and other taxes payable are $900.
(8) Accrued interest payable on the mortgage is $480.
(9) Income tax is estimated to be 45% of the income before income tax.
(10) Accrued selling expenses are $3,840.

Required:

a. Prepare adjusting, closing, and reversing entries.

b. Prepare an eight-column worksheet.

c. Prepare the year-end balance sheet, income statement, and statement of retained earnings.

P1-9. On 31 December 19X1 the Loghead Breweries Co. is closing its books. Adjusting entries are required to reflect accurately the financial position as at 31 December. The pre-closing trial balance for the company is shown below.

Additional information as at 31 December 19X1 is as follows:

(1) The inventory of yeast and hops on hand as at 31 December 19X1 is $65,000 according to the physical count.

(2) The allowance for doubtful accounts should have a balance of $2,500.

(3) Buildings are depreciated at a rate of 3% per year (straight line).

(4) There are supplies of $920 on hand.

(5) Prepaid insurance relating to 19X2 and 19X3 totals $750.

(6) Accrued interest receivable on long-term investments is $380.

(7) Accrued real estate, payroll, and other taxes payable are $1,000.

(8) Accrued interest payable on the mortgage is $530.

(9) Income tax is estimated to be 50% of the income before income tax.

(10) Accrued selling expenses are $3,690.

LOGHEAD BREWERIES CO.
TRIAL BALANCE

	Debit	Credit
Accounts payable		$ 43,000
Accounts receivable	$ 63,900	
Advertising	17,690	
Accumulated depreciation — buildings		22,400
Allowance for doubtful accounts		1,700
Buildings and brewing equipment	91,800	
Capital stock		150,000
Cash	42,300	
Dividends	18,800	
Insurance expense	2,000	
Interest expense	4,300	
Interest revenue		900
Inventory of yeast and hops, December 19X0	46,740	
Land	76,000	
Long-term investments	60,060	
Mortgage payable		52,000
Notes payable — short-term		24,300
Office expense	17,080	
Retained earnings, 31 December, 19X0		28,000
Sales		239,700
Sales discounts	7,000	
Sales returns	6,400	
Selling expense	3,940	
Supplies expense	5,670	
Taxes — real estate and other	9,700	
Work in process	43,120	
Purchases	45,500	
	$562,000	$562,000

Required:

a. Prepare adjusting, closing, and reversing entries.

b. Prepare an eight-column worksheet.

c. Prepare the year-end balance sheet, income statement, and statement of retained earnings.

P1-10. The following balance sheet has been prepared under the accrual basis of accounting for the Marvel Company.

MARVEL COMPANY
POSITION STATEMENT

	31 Dec. 19X6		31 Dec. 19X7	
Assets				
Cash		$ 240		$ 400
Accounts receivable	$?		$ 560	
Less: Allowance for				
uncollectibles	(30)	?	(80)	480
Inventory		480		400
Plant and equipment	2,400		2,400	
Less: Accumulated				
depreciation	(800)	1,600	(960)	1,440
Total assets		$?		$2,720
Liabilities and Equities				
Trade accounts payable		$ 320		$ 400
Wages payable		80		170
Long-term payables		800		?
Common stock		800		800
Retained earnings		?		640
Total liabilities and equities		$2,650		$2,720

Consider the following additional information:
(1) Purchases of inventory (all on credit) during 19X7 amounted to $3,200.
(2) Wages actually paid in cash during 19X7 amounted to $1,440.
(3) Dividends paid in cash in 19X7 amounted to $80.
(4) No customer accounts were written off (no customers defaulted) in 19X7.
(5) There were no equipment retirements or write-offs during 19X7.

Required:

a. What was the dollar amount of gross accounts receivable on 31 December 19X6?

b. What is the dollar amount of wage expense for 19X7?

c. What is the dollar amount of bad debts expense for 19X7?

d. What is the dollar amount of cost of goods sold for 19X7?

e. Prepare an income statement in good form for 19X7.

f. What is the dollar amount of cash received for 19X7?

g. How much cash was paid to suppliers in 19X7?

h. Prepare a schedule showing *all* of the changes in the cash account for the period.

(CMA adapted)

P1-11. The Yarker Furniture Store has been in operation for a number of years and has been quite profitable. The company uses a perpetual inventory system. The annual accounting period ended on 31 December 19X8, and the end-of-period information processing cycle has been started. The following unadjusted trial balance was derived from the general ledger at 31 December 19X8.

YARKER FURNITURE STORE CO.
UNADJUSTED TRIAL BALANCE

Cash	$ 17,000	
Accounts receivable	36,000	
Allowance for doubtful accounts		$ 5,000
Merchandise inventory	120,000	
Store equipment	20,000	
Accumulated depreciation		8,000
Accounts payable		10,000
Note payable — long term		48,000
Capital stock		70,000
Retained earnings		12,000
Sales revenue		440,000
Sales returns and allowances	25,000	
Cost of goods sold	220,000	
Selling expenses	105,000	
Administrative expenses	50,000	
	$593,000	$593,000

Consider the following additional information:

(1) An examination of accounts receivable reveals that losses due to uncollectible accounts are estimated to be $6,000.

(2) The store equipment is being depreciated using the straight-line method over an estimated useful life of ten years with no residual value.

(3) The long-term note of $48,000 was for a two-year loan from a local bank. The interest rate is 12%, payable at the end of each twelve-month period. The note was dated 1 April 19X8.

(4) The income tax rate is 40%.

Required:

a. Prepare adjusting entries for the year ended 31 December 19X8.

b. Prepare a balance sheet in good form as at 31 December 19X8.

(CMA adapted)

BIBLIOGRAPHY

CALPIN, MARTIN. *Understanding Audits and Audit Reports.* Toronto: Canadian Institute of Chartered Accountants, 1981. Anyone who studies financial statements seriously and is not familiar with the role of auditors' reports should read this small monograph. Prepared for the non-specialist and highly readable.

FOSTER, GEORGE. *Financial Statement Analysis.* 2d ed. Englewood Cliffs, N.J.: Prentice-Hall Inc., 1986. A modern text that discusses most of the criticism to be levelled against conventional financial statement analysis.

ROSEN, L.S. *Accounting: A Decision Approach*. Scarborough, Ont.: Prentice-Hall Canada Inc., 1986. An introductory text that should be consulted by a student who finds the coverage in this chapter too brisk.

SKINNER, ROSS. *Accounting Standards in Evolution*. Toronto: Holt, Rinehart, and Winston of Canada Ltd., 1987. This book is a classic. Skinner was a partner of Clarkson Gordon, and the strength of the book is its clear analysis of accounting issues in a real-world setting.

THOMAS, ARTHUR. *Accounting Research Study No. 3: The Allocation Problem in Financial Accounting*. Evanston, Ill.: American Accounting Association, 1969. The first of several studies by the same author, all of them with the same theme; namely, that most of the cost allocations in accounting are arbitrarily chosen and are no better than quite different allocation schemes for the same costs.

TRUEBLOOD, ROBERT (chairman). *Report of the Study Group on the Objectives of Financial Statements*. New York: American Institute of Certified Public Accountants, 1973. A report to the major U.S. professional accounting group by a mixed group of professionals and academics. Its emphasis that financial statements should be useful for making economic decisions has often been cited.

CHAPTER 2
Accounting Standards

Blind compliance with standards is both unprofessional and contrary to the public interest.

*Report of
the* CICA *Special Committee
on Standard Setting,
1980.*

Without a basic accounting philosophy, or sense of fundamentals, the professional accountant is in danger of becoming a technician with inadequate depth and flexibility to meet changing conditions and expanding demands.

*Response of an ad hoc committee
of the Canadian Academic Accounting Association
to the* CICA *Special Committee
on Standard Setting,
1981.*

Introduction

Accounting standard-setting bodies wield direct or indirect influence over the actions of the managers and auditors who prepare and approve financial statements for external use. These bodies include (i) legislative bodies, such as Parliament, which influence standards through laws (e.g., the Canada Business Corporations Act); (ii) authorities created by governments, such as the provincial securities commissions; and (iii) professional accounting organizations. The one we will be examining most closely in this chapter is the **Accounting Standards Committee (AcSC)** of the **Canadian Institute of Chartered Accountants (CICA)**.

The influence of such bodies on accounting reporting can be seen by contrasting the 1946 and 1986 financial statements of Consolidated-Bathurst (Appendix 2–1). It is immediately apparent that recent financial statements have far more disclosure. Although it may not be as apparent, the recent statements are also drawn up under far more definitive accounting standards.

We have four main objectives in this chapter. First, we will explain the circumstances that gave rise to the changes alluded to in the preceding paragraph. Second, we will describe the accounting standard-setting bodies and explain how they influence the setting of standards. Third, we will investigate how these standard-setting bodies interact with each other. Fourth, we will consider and evaluate the difficulties that these bodies face. This last objective poses the most deep-seated challenges — the same challenges, in fact, that face accounting itself.

Accounting standard-setting bodies are found where there are large organizations that must report their financial results to someone who does not have immediate access to their records. We will concentrate on standard setting in Canada and the United States, but similar arrangements exist in Great Britain and, in a modified form, in continental Europe. In France, for example, the *Plan comptable général* was created by a quasi-governmental body. It contains detailed charts of accounts as well as rules for, and definitions of, accounts. Government-controlled standard-setting bodies also exist in communist countries such as Russia and China. Standard-setting bodies cannot be described accurately without reference to the rest of the institutional structure in a country or province. That is why we will proceed to treat Canada and the U.S. separately.

Development of Accounting Standards in Canada

STANDARD SETTING BEFORE 1934

Prior to 1934 Canadian companies enjoyed wide latitude in preparing their financial reports. Federal companies legislation, under which many were incorporated, had rules that said that shareholders must be given financial statements. Even though this early Canadian legislation was among the most advanced in the world, it had only modest requirements for disclosure. There were also provincial companies acts, but they were in varying stages of development. (To provide a historical context, we would point out that it was not until 1933 that a standard audit report in the U.S. first referred to *accepted principles of accounting*. See Rosenfield [1964].)

STANDARD SETTING SINCE 1934

The evolution of standard setting in Canada can be traced to three developments (i) changes in legislation that required companies incorporated under various companies acts to disclose more in their financial statements; (ii) the growth of provincial securities commissions that required more extensive financial reporting; and (iii) the development of an extensive written body of opinion on accounting standards developed by the professional accounting bodies.

Legislative Development

The collapse of the stock market in 1929 started in New York and affected financial markets all around the world. There was a widespread belief that at least part of the hardship arising from this collapse could have been avoided if investors had been more fully informed about the companies whose securities they were buying.

The response in Canada was to amend the companies acts (this was done federally in 1934) to require greater disclosure. There was a further increase in the amount of disclosure required with the passing of the Canada Corporations act in 1965 and the Canada Business Corporations Act (CBCA) in 1975. The latter made a significant change in that it no longer tried to set out the details of what should be disclosed in financial statements. Instead, it effectively required that financial statements should be drawn up in accordance with the *CICA Handbook*. This was done in Regulation 44 of the CBCA which states that financial statements must be drawn up "in accordance with the standards, as they exist from time to time, of the . . . *CICA Handbook*." We will return to this later.

For reasons that will become apparent, it is virtually impossible to draw up a set of rules which, if followed, will reliably produce useful financial statements. Yet this was what was being attempted in earlier companies acts. The CBCA neatly side-stepped this problem by using the detailed standards maintained by the CICA.

The adoption of the *CICA Handbook* by the regulatory authorities had a curious side effect. The original authors of the *Handbook* did not intend that it should set out the *only* acceptable accounting principles; for they realized that exceptional situations might conceivably require a departure from the *Handbook* in order to inform the reader properly. In these unusual cases the authors explicitly acknowledged that a departure from the *Handbook* would be quite appropriate if adequate disclosure were made. However, the CBCA said flatly that the acceptable standards were those to be found in the *Handbook*, a strictness that the *Handbook*'s creators had not intended.

Development of Provincial Securities Commissions

The Canadian constitution is unclear whether regulation of securities markets should be a provincial or federal responsibility. The provinces took the lead in establishing regulatory bodies. With the rapid development of Toronto as a major centre for securities trading, the role of the **Ontario Securities Commission (OSC)** has become pivotal. The OSC, established in its present form in 1966, has the power to forbid a company's securities to be issued or traded in Ontario. It may obtain a court order to force compliance with its orders for corporate disclosure. Very few, if any, major Canadian companies can avoid relying on the Ontario capital market.

One of the mechanisms that securities commissions use to regulate the securities markets is to require all companies trading in their jurisdiction to file audited financial statements with them by a deadline, known as the **filing deadline**, which is a preset number of weeks following the end of the companies' financial year. If the statements are not filed, or are considered unacceptable, the commission has the power to order a stop in trading of the companies' shares, and thus effectively deny them future access to the capital markets. The commission might find a set of statements unacceptable if the audit report has some reservation whether the statements conform with generally accepted accounting principles.

While in theory the securities commissions have great powers, their authority is restricted in practice. They have limited budgets and thus limited size of staff. This in turn restrains their ability to hire skilled technical people to create or interpret accounting standards. Large sums are often at stake if the commission denies a company access to the capital markets. Consequently, it is worthwhile for those opposing the commission's view to hire talented legal and accounting assistance. In addition, securities commissions are created by political processes; hence they are open to charges that they are not acting in the public's best interests, whether these charges are made in the media or privately. Therefore it is appropriate for these commissions to have an independent group provide a ready reference for good accounting reporting, such as the AcSC provides through the *CICA Handbook*. (The AcSC is independent in that it is funded almost entirely from the annual membership fees paid by chartered accountants to the CICA.)

Most provinces have similar legislation to that of Ontario. The various securities commissions, through meetings of the Canadian Securities Administrators, attempt to have similar policies in all provinces. Through the adoption of uniform **National Policy Statements**, they have created a consistent code of practice in many key areas. In 1972 they issued National Policy Statement No. 27: here they essentially adopted the *CICA Handbook* as their reference for **generally accepted accounting principles (GAAP)**; and they said that they would not accept financial statements if there were a reservation in the auditor's opinion that the statements conformed to these principles. This was challenged in 1981 by Denison Mines, Ltd., on the grounds that the OSC had no authority to delegate the setting of accounting standards to another body. However, the challenge was not successful, and the company had to comply with GAAP to maintain trading privileges.

All that remained to close the link between the securities commissions and the *CICA Handbook* was a requirement that auditors, in giving their opinions had to address any matter that was not in accordance with the *Handbook*. This remaining link was supplied by the professional conduct committees of the provincial institutes of chartered accountants.

Professional Accounting Bodies

The organization of professions in Canada is a reflection of the federal nature of the country. This is true for professional accountants, who are organized both provincially and federally. Each Chartered Accountant (CA) is a member of a provincial institute of CA's (in Quebec the term is *ordre* rather than institute) and automatically a member of the CICA. There is a similar arrangement for members of the Society of Management Accountants (CMA's) and Certified General Accountants (CGA's).

In most provinces an auditor must be licensed in order to give an audit opinion. The licensing body is concerned with both the competence and integrity of the auditor, since it is the auditor's job to give an expert independent opinion whether the financial statements conform to generally accepted accounting principles. The various forms of audit reports were summarized in Chapter 1.

Canadian Institute of Chartered Accountants

The CICA assumed the role of setting accounting standards in an agreement with the provincial institutes of chartered accountants. In 1938 the forerunner of the present Accounting Standards Committee was formed. It was known as the Accounting and Auditing Research Committee. By 1946 it was authorized by the Council of the CICA to prepare and publish reports on accounting standards under its own responsibility. It began to issue *bulletins* that were attempts to codify existing practice for the purpose of encouraging uniformity of practice. It was not until 1967 that a review committee of the CICA encouraged ". . . initiating and overseeing basic research at the frontiers of our profession rather than gathering together to record the best current practice."

Under the standards committees of the CICA, a number of research studies and other publications were commissioned. Probably the most widely used was *Accounting Principles* by Skinner [1972].

The 1967 committee made another significant recommendation — that henceforth the bulletins should be replaced by a handbook to be prepared and kept up to date under the authority of the Accounting and Auditing Research Committee. Consequently the research committee was transformed into two new committees: (i) the **Accounting Standards Committee (AcSC)**, responsible for the handbook's sections on "Accounting Recommendations" (on which this text will concentrate); and (ii) the **Auditing Standards Committee (AuSC)**, responsible for the handbook's sections on "auditing Recommendations."

The creation of a handbook setting out the AcSC's opinion about generally accepted accounting principles was a significant event: it created a major reference source, the *CICA Handbook*, which is now the standard for accounting reporting for both companies acts and most securities commissions. Because the *Handbook* has come to play such an important role in standard setting, it is important to understand the process that created it and keeps it up to date.

The Accounting Standards Committee is a standing committee of the Canadian Institute of Chartered Accountants. It has been authorized by the Board of Governors of the CICA to issue pronouncements on accounting standards without reference to the Board. This is unusual since the board normally prefers to reserve to itself the right to make final decisions. In this case an exception was made to underline the autonomous role of the AcSC. Another unusual feature of the AcSC is its composition: of the twenty-two members, up to six of them may be nominated by organizations representing financial analysts, financial executives, and other professional accounting societies such as the Society of Management Accountants of Canada. These six need not be CA's.

Another body, the Accounting Research Advisory Board, was established in 1974 to "provide a forum for a representative group of professional, business, academic, labour, and government leaders to discuss and assess the Research Department's present activities and to comment on its direction and future."

The permanent staff of the AcSC maintain a list of topics that might be dealt with by the AcSC at some future time. The topics are often suggested by a provincial securities commission, by a government body, or changes outside Canada (e.g., a new pronouncement of the comparable U.S. body, the Financial Accounting Standards Board). Because the time of the AcSC is limited, some topics may never be dealt with; but for various reasons some topics will come to the top of the list for active consideration by the AcSC.

After the AcSC formally decides to deal with a topic, the matter is first researched by the permanent staff to find out what stand the AcSC has taken on similar issues in the past, and what position, if any, has been taken by standard-setting bodies in other countries. At that point there are three options: put it before the AcSC, commission an in-depth research study, or put it on hold. If it is decided to proceed, the topic is then assigned to one of the sections (the AcSC is divided into three working groups called sections) which is asked to report to the full committee with draft recommendations. If their recommendations are accepted by at least two-thirds of the AcSC, an **Exposure Draft** is written setting out the AcSC's recommendations.

The Exposure Draft is freely circulated, and those interested are invited to comment. By this process it is hoped that problems of theory and practice will be identified, and the amount of support for the proposal can be gauged. Although the committee pays attention to the response to the Exposure Draft as a measure of acceptance, it does not feel bound by it. Once the problems identified through the Exposure Draft are dealt with, a vote is taken. If the Draft receives the approval of two-thirds of the AcSC, it is then issued as part of the *Handbook*. The material for the *Handbook* has background material and suggestions set in ordinary type, but the specific Recommendations for the accounting standard are in italic type to make them stand out.

The process rarely goes as smoothly as described above. Patient negotiation is often required to obtain consensus — both inside and outside the AcSC — for the members of the AcSC to feel comfortable in issuing a new pronouncement. At times a proposed standard fails to obtain the needed two-thirds vote; the proposal is then amended or possibly not issued at all.

In 1974 "Accounting and Auditing Guidelines" were introduced as part of the *Handbook*. They are intended to express the committees' views on existing standards; or their views on a particular issue of concern to the profession where recommendations would be inappropriate (e.g., where the scope of the coverage would be too narrow for the more broadly based *Handbook*); or their views on issues when there is insufficient time for the extended process ordinarily followed by the AcSC or the AuSC. An example is the Guideline on the audit of a candidate under the Canada Elections Act.

Provincial Institutes/Ordre

The provincial institutes/ordre have the right to discipline a member for misconduct. They can suspend or withdraw an individual's membership, thereby affecting that individual's right in some provinces to practise as a licensed professional accountant. The institutes/ordre have drawn up rules of professional conduct to which members are expected to adhere. In each of the provinces there is a rule, similar to that of the Institute of Chartered Accountants of Ontario, which states that a member may not express an unreserved audit opinion on the financial statements "if such statements depart in any material respect from the Recommendations of the Canadian Institute of Chartered Accountants as set out in the *CICA Handbook* as amended from time to time." Recall that the Recommendations are in italics; a CA is expected to be influenced by the non-italicized parts, but adherence to them is not a disciplinary matter.

Consequently, it has become a disciplinary matter if an auditor who is a member of a provincial institute/ordre of chartered accountants breaks its rules of professional conduct by failing to qualify an audit opinion if the financial statements are not in accordance with the *Handbook*. Recall that financial statements with a qualified auditors' report stating non-compliance with the *Handbook* are not acceptable to the various provincial securities commissions. It thus becomes apparent that, with few exceptions, publicly traded companies must comply with the *Handbook* in their financial reports. The exceptions are special institutions such as banks and life insurance companies that are incorporated under special acts of their own. They are essentially exempted in the *Handbook* itself.

Large CA Firms

The formal standard-setting process has been outlined above. In addition, there is an informal standard-setting process that goes on continuously, supported by the dozen or so large firms of chartered accountants. Starting in the 1960s, most of these firms have developed a specialized group at their national (head) office whose responsibility it is to prepare detailed policy statements on their firm's position on accounting issues. Such people are often referred to as the **technical staff**. They frequently are called on by their practice offices to give advice on the accounting treatment of issues on which the *Handbook* is silent or nearly so. This has encouraged the development of informal inter-firm meetings of senior technical staff from the larger firms to discuss such issues and see if an informal consensus can be reached for an appropriate accounting treatment. This has resulted in the development of a high level of expertise; and the advice of the technical staff of these firms is often sought informally by AcSC members, the securities commissions, various governmental bodies, and the CICA staff.

International Accounting Standards Committee

The International Accounting Standards Committee (IASC) is an international body supported by the professional accounting societies in most major countries of the non-communist world. Its aim is to harmonize accounting standards among developed countries and to provide a body of accounting standards for the use of developing countries. In support of this, the AcSC has a stated policy of modifying the *Handbook* to conform with the IASC position unless there is some fundamental disagreement on AcSC's part with the position taken by the IASC. Adherence to this policy has, however, been uneven.

Specialized Groups

Some organizations with specialized accounting considerations form study groups to recommend the appropriate accounting treatment for their industry. They include such diverse groups as real-estate developers, financial institutions, insurance companies, and governmental bodies. Sometimes their mandate is to develop specialized accounting standards within the general framework of the *Handbook*; but some organizations (e.g., banks and insurance companies) have in the past operated within special disclosure standards governing that industry.

Development of Accounting Standards in the United States

STANDARD SETTING SINCE 1929

The collapse of the financial markets that signalled the beginning of the Great Depression began first in New York in October 1929. The political repercussions from this collapse were evident in the U.S. election of 1932, when Herbert Hoover was defeated and Franklin D. Roosevelt was elected. There was a feeling that the U.S. capital markets had been manipulated by insiders at the expense of the general investor, and the demand for greater regulation of the stock markets was strong.

In 1932 a joint committee of the New York Stock Exchange (NYSE) and the U.S. equivalent of the CICA (known today as the **American Institute of Certified Public Accountants**, the **AICPA**) met to recommend better disclosure policies for companies trading on the NYSE. Stock exchanges were, in principle, in favour of more disclosure, but the management of companies listed on exchanges usually objected and threatened to list their securities on some other exchange. In addition, companies were incorporated under the laws of the individual states that vied with each other in the laxness of the companies legislation. An example was Delaware. This small state, the size of Prince Edward Island, is the place of incorporation of many large companies, including General Motors, Revlon, Ford, Texaco, duPont, and Colgate-Palmolive. Its companies act has no requirement for disclosure or the appointment of independent auditors. Now, however, disclosure standards are set by a federal body, so the disclosure standards of a state are no longer important. The state has continued to attract large companies by low taxation.

The joint NYSE/AICPA committee made some recommendations about accounting disclosure, but they were essentially eclipsed when the **Securities and Exchange Commission (SEC)** was established in 1934. It had broad powers to regulate the securities markets and prescribe and enforce rules of accounting disclosure for all companies whose securities were traded publicly. The SEC concentrated on disclosure requirements. In 1940 it began requiring companies to disclose information that most of them had treated as secret (e.g., how much top managers were paid) through its filing requirements (e.g., *10–K* Reports).

The AICPA was encouraged by the SEC to continue its work on setting standards of accounting measurement (e.g., how various assets should be recognized and valued), which is central to measurement of corporate income. The standard-setting work of the AICPA was rarely done without criticism. In addition to the usual complaints about the content of its standards, there was a more ominous complaint that the members of its standard-setting body, the **Accounting Principles Board**, lacked independence because of the pressure that large corporations could place on its volunteer members (who were usually partners of large auditing firms). Those close to the situation contended that this suspicion was unjustified; nevertheless, the belief was present and detracted from the authority of the Board.

It is interesting to speculate why this problem was never as prevalent in Canada. First, in the U.S., disagreements are traditionally settled in a more open forum, which makes it easier for the protagonists to play to a wider audience. This became particularly evident when members of the U.S. Congress became involved in disputes, because the process was then clearly brought into the political arena. Second, the voting record of each individual on the boards was often made public through the recording of dissenting opinions. This made it easier for interest groups to lobby in favour of their viewpoint and check up on particular board members after the vote. By contrast, the tradition in Canada since the introduction of the *CICA Handbook* has been for the members of the AcSC to settle their differences in private and then present a united front. Third, prior to 1973 it had been traditional for members on U.S. standard-setting boards to consider themselves as representatives of the firms they worked for;

whereas the AcSC tradition has been that the members should not represent their firms, but be there as individuals.

The remedy, adopted in 1973, was the appointment of a full-time salaried **Financial Accounting Standards Board (FASB)** supported by a full-time staff which now numbers over 100. It is financed by various private sector groups, including auditing firms.

The process used by the FASB to set accounting standards has been developed over the years and has many similarities to that of the AcSC. A specific accounting issue is identified as needing an authoritative accounting standard. The staff of the FASB then prepare a background paper showing the position of the FASB on this and similar issues in the past and discussing possible points of view. If the FASB decides to proceed with the issue, it then puts out an Exposure Draft and invites comment. Much of this comment will be considered at open meetings. If the FASB arrives at a decision on the matter, it will issue a *Financial Accounting Standard*. Members of the FASB who dissent from the Standard are free to record their reasons (unlike Canadian practice).

The usual Standard issued by the FASB is far more detailed than one issued by the CICA, since the CICA approach concentrates on stating the underlying principles and avoids details. The pressure in the United States has been to do the opposite. The main reason cited is the higher probability of being sued for damages in the U.S. because (i) the legal profession often bases legal fees in civil damage suits on the damages collected; and (ii) class action suits are allowed in which the defendant is sued on behalf of a class of people who may have suffered damage. There is the possibility of very high damage settlements and thus high legal fees. One way for an auditor to defend his work is to refer to a ruling of the FASB that covers the situation; hence the pressure for detailed and specific FASB rulings.

A detailed accounting standard is a two-edged sword, however. On the one hand, it is true that it makes it easier to insist on a given accounting treatment for circumstances that fit those described in the standard. On the other hand, by being detailed about when the standard does apply, it makes it easier (for those wishing to avoid the application of the standard) to change some of the circumstances so that they no longer appear to fit, and then to argue that the standard does not apply. This is the old problem of distinguishing between the word and the spirit of the law; as the words grow in number and become more detailed, it becomes difficult to refer to the spirit.

A classic example is that of accounting standards for leases. Many companies in fact were "buying" their fixed assets, but doing so via a very long-term lease. Their purpose was to avoid recording the asset and its related debt on their financial statements. In response, the FASB issued a detailed accounting standard to say that the signing of leases that met certain detailed criteria effectively constituted the purchase of an asset and the assumption of debt and therefore should be accounted for as such.

The response by those wishing to avoid the spirit of the FASB ruling was to arrange for long-term leases that had legal terms that just avoided the conditions of the Financial Accounting Standard. This in turn meant that the FASB had to issue another ruling on leases that dealt with such borderline situations, which in turn invited further modification to leasing agreements. This has been termed the **criteria dodging syndrome**. The original standard on leases was issued in 1976. By 1985 the FASB had interpreted or modified it with eight Statements, six Interpretations, and seven Technical Bulletins. The FASB treatment exceeded 230 pages; by contrast the section on leases in the *CICA Handbook* is only 32 pages.

COMPARISON OF U.S. AND CANADIAN STANDARD SETTING

There are some striking general similarities between the Canadian and the U.S. systems. Both use a mixture of government organizations (e.g., the provincial securities commissions and the SEC) and private/professional organizations (e.g., the CICA, the AICPA, and the FASB) to create and administer accounting standards. For the most part, the government organizations enforce disclosure, and the private/professional ones concern themselves with how the accounting ought to be done within the disclosure guidelines.

However, on a more detailed level, the contrasts are very pronounced:

1. Canadians have influenced their disclosure standards much more heavily through the companies acts; in the U.S. the securities commission has played a more prominent role of enforcing disclosure.

2. The standard-setting process in the U.S. has typically been a more open one; debates over issues are now usually conducted in public, and there is less tendency to smooth over dissent.

3. Once agreement is reached in the U.S., it tends to be spelled out in a detailed code, rather than stated in a briefer statement of more general principles as in Canada.

4. There has been a heavier total investment in accounting standard setting in the U.S. As a result, there is a much bigger research staff at the FASB than at the CICA, and much of the AcSC work is done by volunteers rather than full-time salaried staff.

5. Because of the greater size of the U.S. and its history of corporate innovation, U.S. standard setters tend to be the first to be faced with new problems of accounting reporting. Hence the job of pioneering a new standard is often theirs. Because multinational corporations in Canada are largely U.S.-owned, there is a tendency for the AcSC to wait until a controversial issue has been settled in the United States and then to adapt the FASB standard to Canadian conditions.

Fundamental Problems Facing Accounting Standard Setters

There are two extreme attitudes toward accounting standard-setting bodies (such as the CICA or the FASB) that should be avoided. The first is excessive deference to their pronouncements on the grounds that they are produced by experts who must understand the situation better than anyone else. The second is the belief that their views are irrelevant because they are following tired old formulas that are no longer appropriate.

The truth is that all such standard-setting boards are operating in the very difficult areas of regulating the information supplied to decision-makers and revising the terms under which many existing contracts have been drawn up. An understanding of the conceptual nature of this process should assist in understanding why these difficulties arise. While coverage of this topic is necessarily brief, it should help to explain why it is essential to try to analyse and understand the basic issues rather than simply memorizing and acting on the *CICA Handbook* or any other accounting standard.

OBJECTIVES OF ACCOUNTING STANDARDS

Rather than starting with the weaknesses of the standard-setting system, it is helpful instead to ask what would be achieved if it worked flawlessly. Here is one view:

1. Investors would get **fair game** conditions in the stock market. In other words, they might win or lose, but the accounting information provided to them would be about as good as that provided to anyone else. Disclosure would be large enough that insiders could not earn unconscionable returns with **inside information**.

2. The information provided through the accounting system would aid in the maintenance of an efficient capital market. This means that investors would get all the information that was relevant to their decision and the information would not bias the decision-making in either direction — it would be neutral. Provided investors acted rationally with the information provided, this would mean:
   a. Society's wealth would be directed toward those firms whose products were in greatest demand because they would be seen as potentially profitable. This would serve the important social purpose of seeing that society's wealth was invested in the most effective way.
   b. Investing in the capital markets would be as efficient as possible with no costs incurred because of inadequate information. For example, if investors believe a company is riskier than it really is and thus demand a higher return, then the company will be paying a higher price than it should in order to acquire the capital it needs. Similarly, a genuinely risky company should be seen as such by investors and should provide a higher yield to investors.

3. The method of informing the reader of the statements would be efficient. This supports the argument that similar situations should be reported using similar accounting standards, thus reducing the amount of explanation needed about what accounting standards were used. If there is an accepted standard, such as the *CICA Handbook*, then it is only necessary to tell the reader of the financial statements about those accounting policies that differ from the *Handbook* and those policies on which the *Handbook* is silent. The chairman of the OSC summed this up in 1982 as "maintaining an efficient capital market that operates with integrity."

4. Because many day-to-day business contracts are based on the reported accounting numbers (e.g., management remuneration and covenants on long-term debt), the

consequences of new accounting standards would be reasonably predictable. For example, a new accounting standard that resulted in reporting significantly different income would probably mean that executive compensation would have to be renegotiated (see Thornton [1984]).

While these sound like worthwhile objectives, they can never be reached completely because of the nature of information, the costs of disclosure, the difficulties of rule setting, the agency problems of motivation and incentive, and the manner in which information is used. In fact, the high goals that accounting standard setting sets itself are an inherent part of the problem.

FUNDAMENTAL PROBLEMS FACED BY THE INFORMATION PROVIDER

Let us assume a **cooperative environment**, in which the managers, readers of financial statements, and other parties to the information genuinely want to cooperate and help each other. The first problem faced by standard setters is that the person preparing the financial statements of a company rarely knows who is going to read that statement or how decisions of a particular reader might be influenced as a result of that reading. This might be thought to be advantageous because the preparer is obviously in a position to make neutral assumptions in preparing the financial statements. In Chapter 1 an example was given of a banker and a shareholder looking at the financial statements of the same company. Each one had a different type of decision to make and each evaluated the financial statement information differently. There was a good argument that they would have different preferences for how the inventory should be valued and they would have preferred financial statements tailored to their individual needs rather than ones that were neutral.

Let us construct an example that has been simplified enough that we *can* devise a suitable financial report. We will make the following assumptions: (i) There is only one person who reads the financial statement of a company, and we know who that person is: the banker who has loaned the company money on the security of its accounts receivable and inventory; (ii) We know the decision she has to make: whether she should agree to raise the bank loan from $120,000 to $180,000; (iii) We know the decision rule she will follow: she will lend the company the additional funds if the accounts receivable and inventory have a realizable cash value at least 50% higher than the amount she is asked to lend, or $270,000; and (iv) We know how important the outcome is to her: her success in lending money is tied to her annual bonus.

It then becomes possible to design financial statements for the banker. At the minimum, they would consist only of the accounts receivable and inventory portions of the balance sheet since these are the only items that affect the decision. The accounts receivable and inventory will both be stated at realizable value (rather than the lower of cost and market for inventories). This is not the financial statement that one would normally expect using GAAP, but in this case it is tailored to the banker's needs and meets the test of relevance.

Let us change the decision criterion in (iii) above so that in addition to wanting accounts receivable and inventory to be equal to 150% of the loan, the banker also wants the company to demonstrate a net cash inflow for the past twelve months. In that case we would also prepare a statement of changes in financial position to measure the net cash change. Note in this second case how the nature of the decision criteria has changed the financial statements presented to the reader.

This example could be elaborated, but it should be reasonably clear by now that we need to know some critical facts about the decision-maker before we can design the best financial report. Furthermore, for each decision it is quite possible that a different report would be needed, so the variety of financial reports that might be needed about the same company, if one is to provide the best one for each decision, is virtually infinite. This is a practical problem of enormous size for a relatively simple setting. It is not hard to imagine how the practical difficulties increase as the setting in which the decisions have to be made grows more complex.

One practical response to this is to identify classes of users (e.g., shareholders, creditors, regulatory agencies, and tax collectors) and try to identify the types of decisions they might reasonably be making and how they might use data to make them. That might give us a start in designing financial statements that would be useful to particular groups. This approach contains a problem in that there is nothing to prevent a user from making decisions that are quite different from what was expected when the statements were drawn up. It is quite possible that uses will be made of the statement that were never contemplated by the person preparing them or by the authoritative body that prepared the financial accounting disclosure standard.

Up to this point we have assumed a cooperative environment. Now let us make the assumptions more realistic by introducing **moral hazard**. This arises in situations where a person can influence an outcome where he stands to benefit from that outcome. The term arose in the insurance industry where companies are naturally watching for situations where the insured can benefit by making an "accident" happen.

The same type of problem exists with financial statements, but in this case it is the managers of companies who stand to benefit by influencing the financial statements. They might (i) withhold information that is likely to cause embarrassing questions about the quality of their management; (ii) overestimate the value of assets and/or underestimate liabilities in order to influence important decisions, such as those by a creditor; (iii) understate net income to reduce the amount of taxes payable; or (iv) overstate net income if it will increase executive bonuses. If managers manipulate information covertly, they violate at least one of the objectives of standard setting — that information be freely available to all market participants. Finance theory suggests that if shareholders, bondholders, and bankers become generally aware that the possibility of this sort of information manipulation exists, they become less interested in participating. This could lead to an increase in the cost of capital, which violates the objective of efficient operation of the financial market for society's benefit.

Moral hazard is, by its nature, impossible for a standard-setting board to eliminate. A board can try to curb moral hazard by (i) limiting the rights of insider trading; (ii) allowing managers to make some key judgements (e.g., the rate of depreciation), but then making it difficult for them to change these judgements later; (iii) getting confirmation from an outside expert (e.g., using outside actuarial consultants to confirm pension fund liabilities); (iv) making managers disclose (e.g., the SEC requirement that trading in company shares by insiders must be disclosed); and (v) imposing arbitrary judgements of the standard-making authority (e.g., research costs must be written off when the expenditure is made, even if a reasonable person would agree that the benefits extend beyond the current year). Although these approaches usually help to keep the moral hazard problem within bounds, they often impose problems of their own through the arbitrary nature of the standard imposed. In fact, some of the accounting standards that are most contentious are those of this nature. Examples are the requirement that research costs must be written off in the year they are incurred and the rule that purchased goodwill must be amortized over a period not exceeding forty years.

The formal analysis of moral hazard is beyond the scope of this text. It is being developed as part of *agency theory* in economics. When it is more fully developed, it may be appropriate to incorporate its results into standards directly.

GLOBAL VERSUS INCREMENTAL PROBLEM SOLVING

Imagine that someone is starting to play a game of checkers with a friend who has just made the first move. What move should be made in reply? One way to approach this is to list all the moves that could be made in reply, then all the moves the friend might make in reply to all these moves, and so on, until one comes to the last possible move in each combination of plays. Then these final outcomes are examined and the initial move is chosen by working backwards. The key idea is to work out the whole plan before making the first move. An approach to decision-making in which you construct a comprehensive model of the entire situation and then make your decision in the light of what is best overall is termed **global** decision-making. Its objective is **optimizing**.

The contrasting method is **incrementalism**, in which one makes the best decision possible for any given situation, but without working out the whole plan beforehand and within limits of time or money. In the checkers situation you would probably use a rule of thumb such as, "Avoid the edges of the board, and don't leave your pieces unprotected." The objective in this case is often referred to as *satisficing*. Standard setting in accounting is almost universally incremental in nature, although from time to time there is a call for a more global approach.

The checkers analogy can be carried one step further by pointing out that in checkers the computational problem of finding the best move is formidable, but at least we know what the checkerboard looks like. It was pointed out above that we cannot speak meaningfully of "proper" accounting standards unless we know quite a bit about the user or decision-maker. Our knowledge of how humans make investment decisions (or how they ought to make such decisions) is limited. This in turn places a limit (for the time being at least) on our ability to construct a global approach to standard setting.

The alternative, incrementalism, involves working out from existing solutions to try to add to our body of knowledge in the surrounding areas. This approach has been proposed as appropriate when our limited knowledge of an area means that we have to settle for partial solutions. When the AcSC or the FASB identify a problem area in accounting reporting, have it researched by the staff, and then discuss it in various committee stages, they are practising a form of incrementalism.

The great strength of incrementalism is that it allows decision-makers to muddle through to some kind of decision — admittedly not the best possible decision, but a decision nevertheless. When the AcSC or the FASB has been under pressure to eliminate an acknowledged accounting abuse, incrementalism has often allowed them to arrive at some standard.

The problem, however, is that the standard has not been arrived at by working out from some central body of theory and applying the general principles of that theory to the specific situation. As a result, it is possible to find accounting standards that are inconsistent with each other. In addition, since the accounting standards have been developed to deal with specific problems, there are holes in the published standards simply because some issues have not been pressing enough to warrant attention. The *SCOSS Report* [1980] points out, for example, that there is no requirement in the *CICA Handbook* to depreciate plant assets or to follow the matching principle. To balance this, many of the provincial institutes have a rule of professional conduct that requires its members to adhere to accounting standards that have been generally adopted by the profession.

As a result, professional accountants fall back on what they term **professional judgement** to fill in the holes left by the standard-setting bodies or to amend official pronouncements when they think they are not appropriate to the situation under consideration. To do this well, they need to have an understanding of the objectives of accounting reporting, a sympathy for the basic problems faced by the standard-setting bodies, and a good knowledge of the circumstances under which the financial statements might be used. In essence, a good accountant knows when to stick to the rules and when to break them because they are no longer appropriate. Professional judgement is developed through an education in analytical skills such as economics and an interest in evaluating the results of the application of accounting standards. That is why blind compliance with accounting standards is not in the public interest. The professional organizations in most provinces make specific provisions for departures from the *CICA Handbook* (e.g., section 1500.06 in the *Members' Handbook* of the Institute of Chartered Accountants of Ontario.)

POLITICAL OBSTACLES TO STANDARD SETTING

Because accounting standard setting is a mixture of public and private processes in most English-speaking countries, it should not be surprising that opposition to standard setting by the private sector arises from time to time in the political arena. It should be pointed out that while governments at all levels have shown an interest in passing laws to require good accounting for private sector companies, they have shown a more limited interest in promoting good accounting for that 43% of the economy controlled by governments. The annual report of the Auditor General of Canada usually provides extensive evidence of this problem.

The economic consequences of accounting standards occasionally make politicians wonder if standard setting is too important to be left to the accounting experts. The issue usually arises because some proposed accounting standard is seen as adversely affecting some government initiative, such as reducing unemployment or maintaining confidence in the banking system. The issue is not that the proposed standard will distort the facts, but that knowledge of the facts might hurt.

The investment tax credit controversy in the United States during the 1960s is such an example because it was believed at the political level that a new accounting standard was going to frustrate an economic recovery initiative by the U.S. government. The government proposed to give a tax reduction to companies that made investments that might help unemployment, and the AICPA's proposed standard would not have made the participating companies look as profitable as the government had hoped. Consequently political pressure was brought to bear and the accounting standard was weakened. A similar example, but with a different outcome, occurred some time ago in Canada. The federal government threatened in 1982 to pass legislation overruling a CICA standard for accounting for government grants under the Petroleum Incentive Program (PIP). There was a belief that the accounting standard was going to discourage investment and hinder the government initiative to find oil in the high Arctic and off the east coast of Canada. In addition, the reported financial results for the government-owned oil company, Petro-Canada, were being adversely affected. In the face of strong opposition from the CA profession, the government decided not to take action at that time.

HAS THE ROLE OF STANDARD SETTING BEEN DEFINED CORRECTLY?

Some schools of thought believe that standard setting is unnecessary or that it is necessary but has been given the wrong mandate.

The idea that standard setting is unnecessary comes from the belief that if there is a need for a certain kind of accounting report, then market forces will lead rational managers to supply it. This is hard to prove or disprove. Nevertheless, Benson [1973] has produced some evidence to support the view that standard setting is unnecessary by analysing company reporting practices prior to the founding of the SEC or in countries that do not have compulsory disclosure requirements.

The view that standard setting is necessary but has been given the wrong mandate arises from the **efficient markets** school, which asserts that while individual investors may be fooled over the manner in which accounting information is presented, the market as a whole is not fooled as long as the information is disclosed. This leads to the belief that the important role of the standard setters is to require disclosure and that the manner of disclosure is of much less importance. For example, it is argued that it does not matter whether securities are valued at cost or market value on the balance sheet as long as information on both is supplied somewhere.

RESTRICTION OF SCOPE

The emphasis throughout this chapter has been on setting accounting standards for investors and, by implication, for companies operating in the private sector. As taxpayers, however, we are all investors in governmental bodies such as our municipal, provincial, and federal governments. If they invest poorly, then ultimately we are all poorer as a result. Thus good financial accountability to the taxpayer seems central to good democratic government. Despite this evident need, accounting standards for most public organizations (governments, commissions, non-profit organizations, and crown corporations) are not as well specified as those for private-sector companies, and it is only recently that much interest has been shown in improving this situation. The solution is not one of simply doing something; there needs to be a careful evaluation of objectives. Most organizations in the public sector, for example, have a set of goals that are less well defined and more complex than those of private companies. Before one begins to report on how well an organization is doing, it is necessary to be clear about what it is trying to accomplish.

Examples from Published Reports

This section presents the 1946 financial statements of Bathurst Power and Paper Company Limited and the 1987 statements of its successor company, Consolidated-Bathurst Inc. Comparing these two statements gives an idea of the change that has taken place in financial reporting over this forty-year span.

When examining these statements, note the following:

1. The lack of supplementary information to the balance sheet and income statement in the 1946 report.

2. The absence of a statement of changes in financial position in the 1946 report.

3. An unusual presentation of the balance sheet in the 1946 report. For instance, note the use of a *Reserves* category under Liabilities, to contain the accumulated depreciation and what seem to be appropriations of retained earnings ("Contingencies").

4. The extensive use made of the *Deferred Charges* category in the 1946 statements to hold things as varied as "Prepaid taxes" (now classed as a current asset) and "Miscellaneous debits."

5. The lack of any segmented information on the various divisions of the company.

Generally, the 1946 statements are briefer and disclose less. They are also less rigorous than today's statements in classifying similar things in the same place.

Bathurst Power and Paper Company Limited: Financial Statements, 1946

CONSOLIDATED STATEMENT OF PROFIT AND LOSS
For the Year Ended 31 December 1946

Net sales, less freight allowances and discounts		$ 11,753,798.39
Cost of sales and expenses — Including manufacturing cost, general administration and selling expenses except officers' remuneration, directors' fees, legal expenses, interest on bank loans and after deducting miscellaneous operating income		9,278,006.93
		$ 2,475,791.46
Non-operating revenue — Premium on exchange and sundry non-operating income		134,067.99
		$ 2,609,859.45
Deduct:		
Officers' remuneration — including subsidiary companies	$ 131,034.05	
Legal expenses	27,696.07	
Directors' fees	8,452.01	
Employees' pension fund	50,000.00	
Interest on bank loans	65,078.92	282,261.05
Profit before depreciation, depletion and income and excess profits taxes		$ 2,327,598.40
Depreciation	$ 489,876.93	
Depletion	116,402.12	606,279.05
Net profit before income and excess profits taxes		$ 1,721,319.35
Income and excess profits taxes		795,000.00
		$ 926,319.35
Balance of reserve previously provided to meet cost of restoring pulpwood inventory		70,000.00
Net profit for the year		$ 996,319.35

CONSOLIDATED STATEMENT OF EARNED SURPLUS
For the Year Ended 31 December 1946

Earned Surplus — 31 December 1945	$ 1,561,412.12
Proportion of subsidiary company's 1945 profits transferred	3,701.13
	$ 1,565,113.25
Less: Adjustments affecting prior years	20,784.04
	$1 544,329.21
Add: Net profit for the year	996,319.35
	$ 2,540,648.56
Dividends paid on Class "A" shares	400,000.00
Earned Surplus — 31 December 1946	$ 2,140,648.56

CONSOLIDATED BALANCE SHEET
31 December 1946
Assets

Current Assets:

Cash in banks and on hand	$ 984,740.86	
Marketable securities at cost	21,617.50	
(Quoted value $ 22,552.50)		
Accounts receivable, less reserve for doubtful accounts	993,477.05	
Inventories of pulpwood, other raw materials, supplies and finished products, as determined and certified by the Management, valued at cost, by using in respect of pulpwood and basic raw materials of Bathurst Power & Paper Company Limited a "last-in first-out" inventory method, not in excess of market	2,903,173.15	
Expenditures on current season's logging operations	1,189,506.80	
Cash surrender value of life insurance policies	31,073.50	
		$ 6,123,588.86
Properties at book values as at 31 December 1934, with the cost of subsequent additions (excepting plants of container subsidiary companies valued at appraised replacement value of $ 2,080,951.58 as certified by Industrial Valuation Company Limited as at 15 March 1946) and after applying in reduction of values, capital surplus of $ 8,804,082.45 at 31 December 1935:		
Timber limits and undeveloped water powers	$ 7,491,146.97	
Land, buildings, plant and machinery, etc.	12,522,253.60	
		$ 20,013,400.57
Miscellaneous Investments		45,004.00
Refundable Portion of Excess Profits Tax		102,647.47
Deferred Charges:		
Prepaid taxes and unexpired insurance	$ 106,457.11	
Depletion on pulpwood on hand to be absorbed in future operations	60,474.52	
Deferred charges applicable to future operations and other miscellaneous debits (net)	262,679.63	
		429,611.26
		$ 26,714,252.16

Liabilities

Current Liabilities:

Bank loan (secured by pledge of outstanding capital stock of two subsidiary companies)	$ 1,400,000.00	
Accounts payable and accrued liabilities	842,825.49	
Income and excess profits taxes, less instalments paid	390,310.74	
Other taxes and stumpage dues	204,287.40	
		$ 2,837,423.63

Note: Income and excess profits taxes have been assessed to the year ending 31 December 1943, except one subsidiary company assessed to the year ending 31 December 1941. Provision for subsequent periods is stated in amounts deemed to be adequate, subject to the Government's claim for interest on arrears of Bathurst Power & Paper Company Limited under appeal and for which, to the extent of approximately $17,000, no provision has been made on the books.

Reserves:

Depreciation of buildings, plant and machinery	$ 5,101,988.44	
Depletion of timber limits	1 329,837.69	
Contingencies	29,158.95	
Insurance on bush camps	23,011.17	
		6,483,996.25

Common Stock and Surplus:

Class "A" —
  Authorized — 750 000 shares
    without nominal or par value
  Issued — 400,000 shares

without nominal or par value (Class "A" shares are redeemable at $65.00 per share upon 30 days' notice.)	$ 14,400,000.00	

Class "B" —
  Authorized — 500 000 shares
    without nominal or par value
  Issued — 300,000 shares

without nominal or par value	840,000.00	
	$ 15,240,000.00	
Earned surplus — per statement attached	2,140,648.56	
Deferred surplus — refundable portion of excess profits tax (per contra)	$ 102,647.47	
Less: Portion thereof applicable to subsidiary companies at acquisition	90,463.75	12,183.72
		17,392,832.28
		$ 26,714,252.16

Consolidated — Bathurst Inc.: Financial Statements, 1987

Distribution of Revenue* (millions of dollars)	1987	%	1986	%
Materials, supplies, etc.	$ 986	43	$ 905	45
Wages, salaries and fringe benefits	610	27	565	28
Fuel and power	195	8	194	9
Federal, provincial and municipal direct taxes	150	7	100	5
Depreciation	114	5	99	5
Dividends	65	3	45	2
Interest	47	2	55	3
Retained earnings (excluding extraordinary items)	113	5	57	3
	$2 280	100	$2 020	100

*Comprises net sales, other income and equity earnings.

Quarterly financial data

	Net sales	Earnings before extraordinary items	Earnings before extraordinary items	Dividends declared	Stock price range Low	High
	(millions of dollars)		(per common share)		(per common share)	
1986						
First quarter	$ 454	$ 15	$0.11	$0.075	$ 9	$13 5/8
Second quarter	515	25	0.21	0.075	11 1/8	14 3/8
Third quarter	523	29	0.25	0.075	10 7/8	12 7/8
Fourth quarter	526	35	0.30	0.075	$11 5/8	$15 3/8
	$2 018	$104	$0.87	$0.30		
1987						
First quarter	$ 533	$ 33	$0.29	$0.125	$14 3/8	$23 5/8
Second quarter	574	43	0.38	0.125	16 1/2	21 3/8
Third quarter	557	46	0.41	0.125	17 3/4	21 1/4
Fourth quarter	597	60	0.55	0.160	$13 1/2	$22 5/8
	$2 261	$182	$1.63	$0.535		

Financial Review

The Company's earnings before extraordinary items for 1987 were a record $181.5 million, or $1.63 per common share, representing a 75% improvement over 1986 earnings of $103.7 million, or $0.87 per share. Extraordinary items amounted to a net credit of $32.9 million, or $0.32 per share. This credit reflected gains on sales of the Company's investment in Diamond-Bathurst Inc. and of permanently closed plants in Munich, West Germany, and Burnaby, B.C., partially offset by a charge arising from the write-down of Sulbath Exploration Ltd. In 1986, there was an extraordinary charge of $54.2 million related mainly to the write-off of oil and gas investments. Consolidated-Bathurst's net earnings for 1987 were $214.4 million, or $1.95 per common share, compared with $49.4 million, or $0.34 per share, in 1986.

As a result of these improved earnings, the Company's return on common shareholders' equity increased from 12.8% in 1986 to 19.6% in 1987. Consolidated-Bathurst's net earnings margin excluding extraordinary items went up from 5.1% in 1986 to 8.0% in 1987.

Net sales in 1987 aggregated $2.261 billion, representing an increase of 12% over sales of $2.018 billion in 1986. Sales of pulp and paper products increased by 14% while those of CB Pak Inc. and Europa Carton AG rose by 7% and 11%, respectively.

Operating earnings amounted to $353.3 million, 38% higher than those of 1986. Pulp and paper operations in Canada and the United Kingdom posted substantial gains chiefly as a result of higher shipments and improved prices. These positive factors were partially offset by lower results in the packaging companies.

Cash flow from operations in 1987 totalled $360.2 million and was well in excess of capital expenditures of $260.7 million. The additional cash flow generated from the sale of the investment in Diamond-Bathurst contributed to a net increase in funds of $91 million.

The capitalization of Consolidated-Bathurst at December 31, 1987 consisted of $459 million of debt, $150 million of preferred shares and $853 million of common shareholders' equity. The debt / equity ratio of 31 / 69 at December 31, 1987 represented a considerable improvement over the ratio of 40 / 60 at the end of 1986. The Corporation's working capital improved from $339 million to $394 million in 1987; the working capital ratio, however, declined from 2.13 to 2.00 during that period. The decline was largely attributable to the increase in the current portion of long-term debt as a result of the Series I sinking fund debentures coming due on November 15, 1988 and in the accounts payable related to the capital expenditure program.

Effective January 1, 1988, Consolidated-Bathurst sold the operations of the Bridgewater Division to Bridgewater Paper Company Limited, a wholly owned subsidiary of the Corporation, and agreed to guarantee to the lessor the lease obligation related to the Bridgewater mill. This restructuring, which followed the first year of profitable operations of the U.K. newsprint operations, resulted in the designation of Bridgewater Paper Company as a self-sustaining subsidiary for purposes of translation of its financial statements in Canadian dollars. The U.K. operations were previously considered as an integrated operation of Consolidated-Bathurst. In 1988, the foreign currency translation of Bridgewater Paper Company under the current rate method will result in the deferment of the translation adjustments in the shareholders' equity section of the balance sheet.

Sales, Property and Plant, Employees, Shareholders and Shares by Country as at December 31, 1987

	Net Sales	Property & Plant – Net	Number of Employees	Number of Common Shareholders	Number of Common Shares
	(millions of dollars)				
Canada	$ 880.5	$1 023.4	11 533	11 926	85 716 970
United Kingdom	172.7	124.0	576	879	15 245 871
United States	508.7	0.1	34	377	1 001 399
West Germany	533.4	175.6	2 895	611	9 737
Other Countries	166.1	15.6	73	84	344 422
	$2 261.4	$1 338.7	15 111	13 877	102 318 399

Segmented Information   (millions of dollars)

Classes and major product lines

Sales to Customers		Inter-segment Sales		Net Sales		
1987	1986	1987	1986	1987	1986	
$ 651.8	$ 603.6	$ —	$ —	$ 651.8	$ 603.6	Canadian newsprint and groundwood specialties
196.5	157.5	—	0.6	196.5	158.1	U.K. newsprint
135.2	101.9	49.3	41.5	184.5	143.4	Market pulp
199.6	188.8	5.7	5.5	205.3	194.3	Paperboard
61.8	39.6	—	—	61.8	39.6	Lumber
1 244.9	1 091.4	55.0	47.6	1 299.9	1 139.0	Pulp and Paper
504.6	472.4	1.3	1.2	505.9	473.6	Glass, plastic and flexible packaging – CB Pak
502.6	451.3	—	—	502.6	451.3	Packaging – Europa Carton
1 007.2	923.7	1.3	1.2	1 008.5	924.9	Packaging
9.3	2.7	0.9	1.2	10.2	3.9	Oil and gas
—	—	(57.2)	(50.0)	(57.2)	(50.0)	Eliminations
$2 261.4	$2 017.8	$ —	$ —	$2 261.4	$2 017.8	Total operations

Inter-segment sales are accounted for at prices comparable to
market prices for similar products.

Producing geographical regions

Sales to Customers		Inter-segment Sales		Net Sales		
$1 562.3	$1 409.0	$ 57.2	$ 49.4	$1 619.5	$1 458.4	Canada
196.5	157.5	—	0.6	196.5	158.1	United Kingdom
502.6	451.3	—	—	502.6	451.3	West Germany/Netherlands
—	—	(57.2)	(50.0)	(57.2)	(50.0)	Eliminations
$2 261.4	$2 017.8	$ —	$ —	$2 261.4	$2 017.8	Total operations

Canadian operations had export sales to the United States of
$508.7 (1986 $482.8), to Western Europe of $79.4 (1986 $65.5)
and to other countries of $93.6 (1986 $76.8).

(millions of dollars)

	Operating Earnings		Depreciation		Capital Expenditures		Identifiable Assets as at December 31	
	1987	1986	1987	1986	1987	1986	1987	1986
	$149.5	$123.0	$ 35.4	$32.7	$ 59.3	$ 92.6	$ 669.1	$ 646.7
	29.4	(0.3)	9.3	7.4	9.7	23.0	192.0	185.9
	57.6	25.1	11.3	11.0	14.4	26.4	234.6	227.1
	41.2	28.0	8.0	7.0	69.4	10.6	199.4	133.1
	4.8	3.7	3.7	2.4	17.6	2.2	66.9	38.2
	282.5	179.5	67.7	60.5	170.4	154.8	1 362.0	1 231.0
	39.4	44.8	25.1	23.4	43.6	39.6	450.9	387.1
	28.8	30.4	19.1	14.6	39.2	27.8	328.3	276.1
	68.2	75.2	44.2	38.0	82.8	67.4	779.2	663.2
	2.6	0.4	2.1	0.6	7.5	9.0	52.7	71.7
	—	—	—	—	—	—	—	—
	$353.3	$255.1	$114.0	$99.1	$260.7	$231.2	$2 193.9	$1 965.9
	$295.1	$225.0	$ 85.6	$77.1	$211.8	$180.4	$1 673.6	$1 503.9
	29.4	(0.3)	9.3	7.4	9.7	23.0	192.0	185.9
	28.8	30.4	19.1	14.6	39.2	27.8	328.3	276.1
	—	—	—	—	—	—	—	—
	$353.3	$255.1	$114.0	$99.1	$260.7	$231.2	$2 193.9	$1 965.9

Corporate assets amounted to $70.8 in
1987 and $64.9 in 1986.

Consolidated Statement of Earnings for the year ended December 31, 1987		1987	1986
		(thousands of dollars)	
Net sales		$2 261 430	$2 017 834
Costs and expenses	Cost of goods sold	1 697 163	1 575 458
	Depreciation	114 020	99 132
	Administrative and selling	96 981	88 186
Operating earnings		353 266	255 058
	Interest expense – long-term	40 687	46 660
	– short-term	6 430	8 268
	Corporate administrative expense	22 679	20 975
	Other income (expense) (note 3)	2 200	(4 719)
Earnings before income taxes		285 670	174 436
	Income taxes (note 4)	112 898	72 430
Earnings before undernoted items		172 772	102 006
	Equity earnings (note 8)	16 608	6 720
	Minority interest	7 840	5 076
Earnings before extraordinary items		181 540	103 650
	Extraordinary items (note 5)	32 875	(54 233)
Net earnings		214 415	49 417
	Dividends on preferred shares	14 585	14 881
Net earnings attributable to common shareholders		$ 199 830	$ 34 536
Earnings per common share	Before extraordinary items	$1.63	$0.87
	Extraordinary items	0.32	(0.53)
	Net	$1.95	$0.34
Weighted average number of common shares outstanding – in thousands		102 379	102 244

Consolidated Statement of Retained Earnings for the year ended December 31, 1987		1987	1986
		(thousands of dollars)	
Retained earnings at beginning of year		$374 423	$371 882
Net earnings		214 415	49 417
Excess cost of purchasing common and preferred shares over stated value		(3 382)	(1 601)
Dividends	Preferred	(14 585)	(14 881)
	Common	(50 493)	(30 394)
Retained earnings at end of year		$520 378	$374 423
Dividends per share	Preferred		
	1966 Series	$1.50	$1.50
	Series A	5.75	5.75
	Series B	6.90	7.26
	Series C	2.04	2.04
	Common	$0.54	$0.30

Consolidated Statement of Changes in Financial Position for the year ended December 31, 1987

Funds provided (used)		1987	1986
		(thousands of dollars)	
Operating activities	Operating earnings	$353 266	$255 058
	Depreciation	114 020	99 132
	Interest	(47 117)	(54 928)
	Current income taxes	(48 561)	(30 700)
	Other items	(11 382)	(11 143)
	Cash flow from operations	360 226	257 419
	Decrease (increase) in accounts receivable	(47 827)	(15 069)
	Decrease (increase) in inventories	(11 008)	(5 640)
	Increase (decrease) in accounts payable and accrued liabilities	42 946	16 959
	Other items	463	5 490
	Net decrease (increase) in operating working capital	(15 426)	1 740
		344 800	259 159
Dividends	On common shares in cash	(50 493)	(29 200)
	On preferred shares	(14 585)	(14 881)
		(65 078)	(44 081)
Investing activities	Additions to property and plant	(260 756)	(231 230)
	Grants on additions to property and plant	10 550	2 780
	Increase in investments	(7 085)	(41 267)
	Other items – net	20 568	13 837
		(236 723)	(255 880)
Financing activities	Proceeds from sale of investment in Diamond-Bathurst Inc.	114 273	—
	Proceeds from sale of permanently closed plants	16 465	—
	Disposal of investments	14 777	1 560
	Issue of long-term debt	2 176	148 994
	Repayments of long-term debt	(94 623)	(78 988)
	Purchase of common and preferred shares	(5 109)	(2 863)
		47 959	68 703
Net increase in funds		$ 90 958	$ 27 901
Analysis of net change in funds	Increase in cash and short-term investments	$ 86 562	$ 9 281
	Decrease in bank loans and notes payable	4 396	18 620
		$ 90 958	$ 27 901

On behalf of the Board:

W.I.M. Turner, Jr.,
Director

T.O. Stangeland,
Director

Consolidated Balance Sheet as at December 31, 1987		1987	1986
		(thousands of dollars)	
Assets			
Current assets	Cash and short-term investments	$ 106 125	$ 19 563
	Accounts receivable	317 829	270 002
	Inventories (note 6)	355 554	344 546
	Prepaid expenses	6 890	5 884
		786 398	639 995
Property and plant (note 7)	Pulp and paper mills	1 538 065	1 370 239
	Packaging plants	646 535	548 249
	Woodlands	23 487	22 765
	Oil and gas properties	37 456	40 267
		2 245 543	1 981 520
	Less accumulated depreciation	906 808	790 306
		1 338 735	1 191 214
Investments	(note 8)	109 607	172 994
Other assets	(note 9)	29 929	26 582
		$2 264 669	$2 030 785

Management's Report

The consolidated financial statements have been prepared by management on the historical cost basis in accordance with Canadian generally accepted accounting principles consistently applied and conform substantially with International Accounting Standards. These statements, which necessarily include estimates and approximations, reflect information available to February 25, 1988, and have been audited by Touche Ross & Co., Chartered Accountants, whose report is included on the next page. The financial information contained throughout the Annual Report conforms with that shown in the financial statements.

Management maintains an accounting system which incorporates extensive internal financial controls. The internal audit department performs independent appraisals of the effectiveness of these internal controls and reports its findings and recommendations to management and to the Audit Committee.

The Board appoints the members of the Audit Committee which is composed solely of outside directors. This Committee reviews the consolidated financial statements with management and the external auditors prior to submission to the Board for approval, as well as any significant recommendations of the external and internal auditors for improvements in internal controls and the actions of management to implement such recommendations.

T. J. Wagg,
Vice-President, Finance

Montreal, Quebec
February 25, 1988

		1987	1986
		(thousands of dollars)	
Liabilities and Shareholders' Equity			
Current liabilities	Bank loans and notes payable	$ 3 534	$ 7 930
	Accounts payable and accrued liabilities	267 151	224 205
	Taxes payable	39 393	29 059
	Dividends payable	2 497	2 542
	Current portion of long-term debt	79 888	37 350
		392 463	301 086
Long-term debt	(note 10)	375 524	508 634
Provision for German pensions		70 315	54 422
Deferred investment tax credits		66 620	54 700
Deferred income taxes		295 834	227 932
Minority interest		61 105	41 270
Shareholders' equity	Stated capital (note 11)	452 961	454 567
	Retained earnings	520 378	374 423
	Foreign currency translation adjustments	29 469	13 751
		1 002 808	842 741
		$2 264 669	$2 030 785

Auditors' Report

The Shareholders,
Consolidated-Bathurst Inc.

We have examined the consolidated balance sheet of Consolidated-Bathurst Inc. as at December 31, 1987 and the consolidated statements of earnings, retained earnings and changes in financial position for the year then ended. Our examination was made in accordance with generally accepted auditing standards, and accordingly included such tests and other procedures as we considered necessary in the circumstances.

In our opinion, these consolidated financial statements present fairly the financial position of the Corporation as at December 31, 1987 and the results of its operations and the changes in its financial position for the year then ended in accordance with generally accepted accounting principles applied on a basis consistent with that of the preceding year.

Touche Ross & Co.

Chartered Accountants

Montreal, Quebec
February 25, 1988

Notes to Consolidated Financial Statements
December 31, 1987

1. Summary of Significant Accounting Policies

Principles of consolidation

The consolidated financial statements include the accounts of all subsidiaries. All significant inter-company items are eliminated. Acquisitions of all subsidiaries are accounted for on a purchase basis and earnings are included in the consolidated financial statements from the date of acquisition.

Foreign currency translation

For domestic companies and integrated foreign operations, assets and liabilities are translated into Canadian dollars at exchange rates prevailing at the balance sheet date for monetary items and at exchange rates prevailing at the transaction dates for non-monetary items. Income and expenses are translated at average exchange rates prevailing during the year with the exception of depreciation which is translated at historical exchange rates. Exchange gains or losses are included in earnings except for unrealized gains or losses on translation of foreign long-term debt which are deferred and amortized over the remaining term of the related obligation. Foreign debt covered by a currency exchange agreement is translated at the guaranteed exchange rate.

For self-sustaining foreign operations, all assets and liabilities are translated into Canadian dollars at the exchange rates prevailing at the balance sheet date and all income and expenses are translated at average exchange rates prevailing during the year. Foreign currency translation adjustments are deferred in the shareholders' equity section of the balance sheet.

Inventory valuation

Pulpwood, chips, expenditures on wood operations, raw materials and supplies are stated at average cost. Work in process and finished goods inventories, the cost of which includes raw materials, direct labour and certain manufacturing overhead expenses, are stated at the lower of average cost and net realizable value. Provision is made for slow-moving and obsolete inventories.

Investments

Short-term investments are stated at the lower of cost and market. Long-term portfolio investments are stated at cost less write-downs for any permanent decline in value, when appropriate. Long-term investments over which the Corporation has significant influence are accounted for by the equity method.

Property and plant, depreciation and capitalization

Mills, plants and other properties are stated at cost. On retirement or disposal of property and plant, the Corporation removes the cost of the assets and the related accumulated depreciation. Gains or losses on disposal of assets are included in earnings.

Depreciation, calculated principally on the straight-line method, is charged to operations at rates based upon the estimated useful life of each depreciable property. The following rates apply to those assets being depreciated on the straight-line method:

	Buildings	Equipment
Pulp and paper mills	2½%	6%
Packaging plants	2–5%	8–10%

Expenditures which result in a material enhancement of the value of the facilities involved are capitalized. Maintenance and repair costs are expensed as incurred.

Grants relating to property and plant additions are deducted from the cost of the assets and depreciation is calculated on the net amount. Accruals are made for the appropriate portion of the estimated total of approved grants. Grants in respect of current expenses are included in earnings.

Interest is capitalized on major additions to property and plant involving the construction of new or materially improved manufacturing facilities. The interest cost is determined using the prime interest rates of the Corporation's principal bankers.

Summary of Significant Accounting Policies (continued)

Investments in shares of oil and gas companies are accounted for as described under Investments. Oil and gas expenditures by the Corporation are accounted for under the successful efforts method whereby geological, geophysical and carrying costs are expensed and exploratory drilling costs are capitalized as property and plant. When no reserves are discovered, exploratory costs are expensed. All development costs are capitalized. The amortization of capitalized costs is based on proven reserves.

Leases

Long-term leases in which the Corporation, as a lessee, retains substantially all the benefits and risks incident to ownership are accounted for as additions to property and plant. The asset value and related obligation for such capital leases is recorded at the present value of the future lease payments, using an appropriate discount rate.

Pensions

The Corporation and its subsidiaries, with the exception of Europa Carton AG, have defined benefit pension plans which are funded, trusteed and principally contributory. Europa Carton AG has unfunded defined benefit pension plans with provision being made in the financial statements for the accrued pension cost.

The cost of the benefits earned by the employees is determined using for the most part

the projected benefit method prorated on time of service. The pension expense reflects the current service cost, the interest on the actuarial surplus or unfunded liability and the amortization over the estimated average remaining service life of the employees of (i) the actuarial surplus or unfunded liability and (ii) experience gains or losses.

Income taxes

The Corporation follows the tax allocation basis in accounting for income taxes. Deferred income taxes shown in the financial statements result principally from capital cost allowance claimed for tax purposes in excess of depreciation.

Investment tax credits relating to additions to property and plant are recorded in the balance sheet in the year in which the qualifying expenditures are made. These tax credits are amortized to income on the same basis as the related property and plant are depreciated.

Earnings per common share

Earnings per common share are calculated after deducting dividends on preferred shares and using the weighted average number of common shares outstanding during the year. Common shares issuable as dividends on the Series B common shares are included as being outstanding from the dividend declaration dates.

2. Change in accounting for pension costs

Effective January 1, 1987, the Corporation adopted prospectively the recommendations of the Canadian Institute of Chartered Accountants with respect to accounting for pension costs and obligations as described under Pensions in Note 1. In previous years,

the pension costs were charged to earnings as funded except for the German pension costs which were calculated in accordance with local legislation. The new rules had no material effect on the earnings of the year.

Notes to Consolidated Financial Statements   (thousands of dollars)
December 31, 1987

3. Other income (expense)

	1987	1986
Investment income	$ 7 136	$ 3 172
Net gain from debt retirement and disposal of property and plant	2 889	1 805
Net translation loss on long-term debt	(7 825)	(9 696)
	$ 2 200	$ (4 719)

4. Income taxes

	1987	1986
Current	$ 48 561	$ 30 700
Deferred	64 337	41 730
	$112 898	$ 72 430

The Corporation's effective income tax rate is determined as follows:	1987	1986
Combined Canadian federal and provincial income tax rate	43.7%	43.7%
Increase (decrease) in the income tax rate resulting from:		
Higher effective income tax rate on earnings of a foreign subsidiary	1.6	2.3
Federal income tax surcharge	0.7	1.3
Manufacturing and processing profits deduction	(5.2)	(4.7)
Amortization of deferred investment tax credits	(1.0)	(1.3)
Effect of tax-free dividends	(0.2)	(0.4)
Miscellaneous	(0.1)	0.6
Effective income tax rate	39.5%	41.5%

5. Extraordinary items

	1987	1986
Gain on sale of investment in Diamond-Bathurst Inc., less deferred income taxes of $15 805	$ 34 178	$ —
Gain on sale of permanently closed plants, less income taxes of $4 805	7 165	—
Write-down of investment in Sulbath Exploration Ltd., less income tax credits of $3 092 (1986 Nil)	(8 468)	(17 500)
Write-off of investment in Sulpetro Limited	—	(29 944)
Provisions for plant shutdowns, less income tax credits of $6 247	—	(6 789)
	$ 32 875	$(54 233)

(thousands of dollars)

6. Inventories	1987	1986
Pulpwood, chips and expenditures on wood operations	$ 79 674	$ 76 392
Raw materials and supplies	133 964	126 365
Work in process and finished goods	141 916	141 789
	$355 554	$344 546

7. Property and plant

(a) Paper mill equipment held under capital leases amounted to $135 002 (1986 $134 632) less accumulated depreciation of $28 218 (1986 $17 005).

(b) Interest capitalized on major additions during 1987 was $8 461 (1986 $6 288).

8. Investments	1987	1986
Portfolio:		
Sceptre Resources Limited		
Common shares (market value $7 758; 1986 $5 633)	$ 9 459	$ 9 459
Preferred shares (market value $4 464; 1986 $3 976)	6 984	6 984
Sulbath Exploration Ltd.	—	14 949
Other investments and advances	15 291	16 087
	31 734	47 479
Equity:		
Joint ventures		
MacMillan Bathurst Inc. (50% owned)	32 815	32 405
Power Consolidated (China) Pulp Inc. (50% owned)	21 844	25 257
Libbey-St. Clair Inc. (50% owned by CB Pak Inc.)	20 501	17 793
	75 160	75 455
Other investments	2 713	2 500
Diamond-Bathurst Inc.	—	47 560
	77 873	125 515
	$109 607	$172 994

Notes to Consolidated Financial Statements
December 31, 1987

(thousands of dollars)

Investments (continued)	The changes in the equity investments are summarized below:	1987	1986
	Balance at beginning of year	$125 515	$ 90 274
	Equity earnings	16 608	6 720
	Disposal of investment in Diamond-Bathurst Inc.	(47 474)	—
	Increase (decrease) in investments	(8 828)	34 739
	Dividends received	(7 948)	(2 419)
	Extraordinary item – Diamond-Bathurst Inc.	—	(3 799)
	Balance at end of year	$ 77 873	$125 515

	The combined financial statements of the equity-accounted-for companies, except for Diamond-Bathurst Inc., which was sold in 1987, are summarized below:	1987	1986
	Results of operations for the year		
	Net sales	$517 049	$382 632
	Costs and expenses	463 379	357 778
	Earnings before income taxes	53 670	24 854
	Income taxes	21 823	11 727
	Net earnings	$ 31 847	$ 13 127
	Financial position at December 31		
	Current assets	$168 149	$141 028
	Current liabilities	80 900	64 465
	Working capital	87 249	76 563
	Property and plant – net	124 754	116 230
	Other assets	2 654	3 437
	Long-term debt, other liabilities and shareholders' equity	$214 657	$196 230

9. Other assets		1987	1986
	Deferred translation loss (net) on long-term debt	$18 966	$17 387
	Advances to trustees under share option plans	4 643	4 950
	Deferred charges	4 274	2 033
	Unamortized long-term debt expense	2 046	2 212
		$29 929	$26 582

Of advances to trustees, $3 762 (1986 $4 246)
is owing to the trustees from officers, two of
whom are directors.

(thousands of dollars)

10. Long-term debt		1987	1986	1987	1986
		Foreign currencies		Canadian dollars	
		(thousands)			
Consolidated-Bathurst Inc.					
Sinking fund debentures (a)					
5.85% Series A 1988	U.S. $	367	1 332	$ 477	$ 1 839
6⅛% Series B 1988	U.S. $	146	1 146	190	1 582
8¼% Series C 1993				4 442	5 692
9% Series F 1992	U.S. $	6 107	6 107	7 938	8 431
17½% Series I 1988	U.S. $	37 000	47 000	48 093	64 884
Obligations under capital leases					
at Bridgewater (b)	£	46 116	51 733	113 082	105 877
Revolving credit (c)	U.S. $	—	100 000	—	138 050
Note issuance facility (d)	U.S. $	—	—	—	—
Consolidated-Bathurst Pontiac					
Limited					
11% first mortgage sinking fund					
bonds, Series A, 1995				5 781	6 881
CB Pak Inc. and subsidiaries					
9½% sinking fund debentures,					
Series A, 1990				9 208	9 208
Revolving credit (c)				—	20 000
5⅛% Swiss bonds, 1991 (e)	SFr.	85 000	85 000	65 724	65 724
Mortgages and other				1 571	1 709
Europa Carton AG and subsidiaries					
Term bank loans, various					
interest rates, 1988 to 1995	DM	44 562	52 694	36 879	37 802
Reclassification of short-term					
borrowings (f)				157 749	69 025
Obligations under capital leases				4 251	6 764
Other				27	2 516
				455 412	545 984
Less current portion				79 888	37 350
				$375 524	$508 634

(a) The trust deeds governing the sinking fund debentures were cancelled in May 1986 in accordance with the defeasance provisions of the trust deeds. In place of the floating charge on the Corporation's assets securing these debentures, the Corporation has arranged for two major Canadian banks to guarantee the payment obligations in respect of these debentures. Since the defeasance was carried out by means of a bank guarantee, ·the amounts outstanding under the sinking fund debentures continue to be reported as debt in the balance sheet.

Notes to Consolidated Financial Statements
December 31, 1987

(thousands of dollars)

Long-term debt (continued)

(b) Under the capital lease obligation for equipment at the Bridgewater Division, the lease payments vary until March 31, 1994, with short-term U.K. interest rates and the lessor's effective tax rate in respect of the leases. Thereafter, annual lease payments will be fixed at a nominal rate based on the total cost of the leased equipment. Effective January 1, 1988, the operations of the Bridgewater Division were sold to Bridgewater Paper Company Limited, a wholly owned subsidiary of the Corporation in the United Kingdom, which also assumed the capital lease obligation. The Corporation has agreed to guarantee this obligation.

(c) The revolving credit facilities at December 31, 1987, are summarized as follows:

	Consolidated-Bathurst Inc.	Domglas Inc.
Amount of facility	Cdn./U.S. $100 000	Cdn. $20 000
Outstanding borrowings	—	—
Secured by	Unsecured	Demand debenture, Series B
Current revolving period ends	November 28, 1989	December 29, 1989

Under the revolving credit facilities, funds can be borrowed by way of direct advances or bankers' acceptances, repaid and re-borrowed during a two-year period, renewable annually. If not renewed, borrowings can, at the borrower's option, either be repaid or converted to a term loan at floating interest rates for four years in the case of Consolidated-Bathurst Inc. and ten years in the case of Domglas Inc. Effective January 26, 1988, Consolidated-Bathurst Inc. reduced its revolving credit facility from U.S. $100 000 to U.S. $50 000.

(d) On December 17, 1987, Consolidated-Bathurst Inc. arranged a U.S. $125 000 floating rate note issuance facility with a consortium of financial institutions. Under this facility, which provides direct access to the Euro-Commercial Paper Market for a minimum term of seven years, extendable annually after the second year, funds can be raised through the issue of unsecured and unsubordinated notes of the Corporation.

(e) As a result of a currency exchange agreement relating to the SFr. 85 000 principal, CB Pak Inc. is committed for fees aggregating $13 850 which are being paid and expensed over the term of the bonds. These fees guarantee a fixed exchange rate for the repayment of the bonds at maturity.

(f) Bank loans and notes payable of $157 749 at December 31, 1987, (1986 $69 025) were included in long-term debt as the Corporation intends to refinance these borrowings under its unused long-term credit facilities.

(g) As a result of an interest rate swap, Consolidated-Bathurst Inc. has fixed the interest rate at 13.1% per annum to November 1, 1992 on U.S. $50 000 of floating rate debt.

(h) Sinking fund requirements and principal payments during the next five years, based on exchange rates at December 31, 1987, are: 1988 $79 888; 1989 $28 267; 1990 $36 816; 1991 $93 395; 1992 $33 423.

(thousands of dollars)

11. Stated capital

Preferred shares

(a) Authorized
   – 6 000 000 preferred shares of which 1 027 169 are designated as 1966 Series

– unlimited number of second preferred shares, issuable in series, of which 800 000, 700 000, and 2 000 000 are designated as Series A, Series B, and Series C, respectively.

(b) Issued and outstanding

	1987		1986	
	Shares	Stated Value	Shares	Stated Value
Preferred shares – 1966 Series	699 126	$ 17 478	741 926	$ 18 548
Second preferred shares				
Series A	800 000	40 000	800 000	40 000
Series B	700 000	42 931	700 000	42 931
Series C	1 992 100	49 802	2 000 000	50 000
		$150 211		$151 479

(c) Principal features
   (i) General
   The shares are redeemable and are non-voting unless the Corporation fails to pay, in the aggregate, eight quarterly dividends. Subject to the provisions attaching to all preferred shares, the Corporation, at its option, may effect share redemptions on 30 days' notice at specific prices plus accrued dividends thereon. Unless the market price is in excess of the redemption price, the Corporation is obliged to make all reasonable efforts to purchase annually a certain number of shares of each series.
   (ii) Cumulative dividends – payable per share and quarterly on all Series
   1966 Series – $1.50 per annum
   Series A   – $5.75 per annum
   Series B   – U.S. $5.25 per annum
   Series C   – $2.04 per annum, on or prior to December 31, 1990, and thereafter, at a rate per annum of 70% of the average prime rates of two major Canadian banks applied to $25
   (iii) Redemption
   1966 Series – at $26 per share
   Series A and
   Series B   – On January 21, 1988, the Corporation announced its intention to redeem on April 15, 1988, all Series A shares at $52 per share and all Series B shares at U.S. $52 per share.

   Series C   – at $25 per share on or after December 31, 1990
   (iv) Purchases for cancellation
   1966 Series – 38 686 shares annually at a cost not exceeding $26 per share. 42 800 shares were purchased in 1987 (38 700 in 1986) at a cost of $866 ($760 in 1986)
   Series A   – 2% per year of the shares issued at a cost not exceeding $50 per share
   Series B   – same as Series A except in U.S. dollars
   No Series A and B shares were acquired in 1987 and 1986 as the shares of each series traded above $50 per share and U.S. $50 per share, respectively, throughout this period.
   Series C   – 40 000 shares annually at a cost not exceeding $25 per share up to and including December 31, 1990 and thereafter, 80 000 shares annually
   7 900 Series C shares were acquired in 1987 at a cost of $176 (nil in 1986)
   (v) Currency election
   The holders of the Series B shares may elect to receive the U.S. dollar dividend and redemption payments in the Canadian dollar equivalent thereof.

Notes to Consolidated Financial Statements   (thousands of dollars)
December 31, 1987

Stated capital (continued)

Common shares

(a) Authorized – unlimited number of shares

(b) Issued and outstanding

	Series A		Series B	
	Shares	Stated Value	Shares	Stated Value
Balance January 1, 1987	98 623 016	$275 208	3 643 084	$27 880
Net conversions from Series A to Series B (c)	(18 447)	(62)	18 447	62
Issued as stock dividends	—	—	244 999	—
Issued under the 1984 Employee Share Option Plan (d)	36 700	266	8 000	58
Purchased and cancelled	(237 400)	(662)	—	—
Balance December 31, 1987	98 403 869	$274 750	3 914 530	$28 000

(c) Principal features
The Series A and Series B shares are voting, inter-convertible on a share for share basis, and identical in all respects with the exception that dividends on the Series B shares are paid in the form of shares instead of cash.

(d) 1984 Employee Share Option Plan
In 1984, options were granted to a number of officers and employees to purchase, until December 31, 1989, up to an aggregate of 1 174 000 common shares of the Corporation, at $7.25 per share. As at December 31, 1987, 1 115 900 shares had been issued under this Plan.

---

12. Segmented information

The classes of business of the Corporation are pulp and paper, packaging and oil and gas. Information segmented by classes and major product lines and by producing geographical regions is reported on pages 30 and 31 of this report.

---

13. Related party transactions

Power Corporation of Canada is the major shareholder of the Corporation, owning approximately 40% of the outstanding common shares. In 1987, the Corporation had transactions with certain companies in the Power Corporation group, mainly in respect of sales of newsprint and purchases of share transfer agency, trusteeship and insurance services. Such transactions were made at market prices for similar products and services and the total value was not significant in relation to the total sales and purchases of the Corporation.

The Corporation had transactions with MacMillan Bathurst Inc., a joint venture company, in respect of sales of containerboard and purchases of corrugated containers. Such transactions were made at market prices and were not significant in relation to the total sales and purchases of the Corporation.

(thousands of dollars)

14. Commitments

(a) At December 31, 1987, the future lease payments under capital and operating leases that have initial non-cancellable lease terms in excess of one year are as follows:

	Capital Leases	Operating Leases
1988	$ 29 500	$ 12 100
1989	26 800	6 900
1990	26 100	5 100
1991	26 100	3 700
1992	26 000	2 700
Thereafter	22 700	4 500
	157 200	$ 35 000
Less imputed interest	39 867	
Present value of lease payments	$ 117 333	

(b) At December 31, 1987, outstanding commitments for capital expenditures under purchase orders and contracts amounted to approximately $ 87 000.

15. Pension plans

The funded status of the pension plans of the Corporation and its subsidiaries, with the exception of Europa Carton AG, at December 31, 1987, was:

Plan assets at adjusted market values	$ 517 554
Actuarial projected benefit obligation	467 826
Plan assets in excess of projected benefit obligation	$ 49 728

16. Subsequent event

On February 15, 1988, the Corporation was advised that a company formed by two executives of CB Pak Inc. proposed to make a take-over bid for all the issued common shares of CB Pak Inc. The offer, subject to obtaining satisfactory financing and regulatory approvals, is to be $25.50 per share in cash, less a special dividend of up to $3.50 which may be paid by CB Pak Inc. The Corporation, which owns 16 000 000 shares of CB Pak Inc., has agreed to tender these shares if the bid is made not later than April 15, 1988.

Summary

Standard setting has been a growth industry since 1934 and especially since the 1960s. There seems little doubt that readers of financial statements have far more access to reliable accounting information than they used to have. This is part of a general trend in Canada, the United States, Great Britain, and many other major industrial countries. The development of the International Accounting Standards Committee, with its aim of harmonizing accounting standards among countries, is a further step in this direction.

It is a mistake to believe that the development of institutions for enforcing accounting standards is all that is required. It is also necessary to create standards that achieve the results desired. This has turned out to be a difficult task because of the complex and often little understood manner in which humans process information to make decisions. A more fundamental understanding of this process is needed.

QUESTIONS

Q2-1. Explain what the following are, stating with which country, if any, each one is identified:
   a. FASB
   b. CICA
   c. Accounting Standards Committee
   d. Auditing Standards Committee
   e. Securities and Exchange Commission
   f. OSC
   g. Financial Accounting Standards Board
   h. AICPA
   i. Accounting Principles Board
   j. National Accounting Policy Statement
   k. Exposure Draft

Q2-2. Explain the following terms:
   a. moral hazard
   b. fair game
   c. insider information
   d. global versus incremental decision-making

Q2-3. Compare and contrast the manner in which accounting standards are created in Canada and the United States.

Q2-4. Accounting has been in existence since before 1500. Explain why it is only in the past fifty years that there has been an active interest in establishing common standards within Canada.

Q2-5. Why do you think accounting standard-setting bodies are needed in communist countries? Explain. (*Hint*: Are there external investors in the state factories? Would moral hazard be present?)

Q2-6. "The need for professional judgement in carrying out a task would seem, by definition, to preclude the use of standard answers or methods." This seems to rule out standard-making bodies. Do you agree or disagree? Why?

Q2-7. "In applying professional judgement, objectivity and intellectual integrity are just as, or even more, important than skill and experience." Discuss.

Q2-8. State whether you agree or disagree with the statements below and briefly explain your position.

a. The SEC in the U.S. has the power to dictate the financial principles to be used in reports to shareholders, but has delegated most of these powers to the FASB.

b. The CICA has no legal powers to establish accounting standards, but has wide influence because the members of the Accounting Standards Committee are people who are acknowledged experts in their field.

Q2-9. Imagine that the medical profession decided to issue "Generally Accepted Principles for Treating the Common Cold" and that they decided to set up a system for doing so that was similar to that used by AcSC for deciding on accounting standards. What would this system look like? Why is such a system not used? Are the apparent differences between the two professions in setting professional standards justified?

Q2-10. "Corporate accounting standards should result in data that are useful for economic decisions provided that the standard is consistent with the national macro-economic objectives and the economic programs designed to reach these goals. . . . Because the FASB has the power to influence economic behaviour, it has an obligation to support the government's economic plans." Do you agree? Discuss.

Q2-11. We all like to give the best impression when possible, and it seems unfair to pick on managers for doing what everyone does. After all, students cram before an exam so the instructor will think they know more than they actually do. The instructor reviews his lecture beforehand so the student will think he is very familiar with the material. So why should the manager be subjected to auditors and accounting standards when he makes his report to shareholders? Do you agree with this argument? Explain.

Q2-12. "Most accounting principles are not covered in the *CICA Handbook*." Do you agree? Explain.

Q2-13. The financial statement is said to have the same neutral role in portraying a company as a map does in portraying a city. If you do not like the city, do not try to fix it by changing the map. Do you agree?

Q2-14. In each of the following independent situations outline the information needs of the decision-maker and identify the financial statement(s) that would be most relevant for making the necessary decision.

a. The loans officer (the decision-maker) at the local branch of a chartered bank has been approached by a small entrepreneur who wants to establish a $100 000 line of credit. The bank has had no previous dealings with that person's company.

b. A member of the audit staff at one of Revenue Canada's offices is reviewing the corporate tax return for an investment company to ensure that the correct amount of income tax has been paid.

c. The manager of a food processing plant must make a recommendation to the company's head office whether the plant should be expanded.

d. A lumber company is a regular supplier to a construction company. A large order has just been received, but the owner of the lumber company is concerned because this customer's account has not been paid for three months.

e. The Canadian Radio and Telecommunications Commission (CRTC) is in the process of reviewing the operations of pay TV. One of its objectives is to determine whether the current monthly charges are appropriate.

Q2-15. Until the late 1800s the main function of accounting was to provide accurate records in case management or others wanted to check some fact about the operations; thus the emphasis in accounting education was on "how to do it." Then an information communication goal was added to the record-keeping function; and at that point interest in the theory of accounting reporting grew rapidly. Explain.

PROBLEMS

P2-1. Assume that financial analysts have become highly critical of accounting disclosure because companies are publishing financial information based on different accounting interpretations of terms such as *market* in the valuation of inventories at the lower of cost and market. What objective of accounting are they saying is being violated? Describe briefly how the leading professional accounting organizations may go about formulating a recommendation to their members on the acceptable accounting treatment of this matter. What sanctions exist to compel or encourage compliance? Is there any discernible difference in the development of accounting principles in Canada and the United States?

Required: Answer the above question, confining your response to the equivalent of three double-spaced typed pages (800 words).

P2-2. Outline briefly the nature of the argument that the practice of accounting in accordance with generally accepted accounting principles is socially desirable because it assists a more efficient allocation of scarce resources among their alternative uses. Explain briefly also how the practice of auditing may complement the practice of accounting in this process.

P2-3. The president of a public corporation recently commented:

"Our auditor states that our financial statements present fairly our financial position and the results of our operations. I challenged him as to how he determined such fairness. He replied that fairness means that the financial statements are not misstated in amounts that would be considered material.

I believe that there is some confusion with this materiality concept, since different users of our financial statement may have different ideas as to what is material. For example, bankers, institutional investors, small investors and tax assessors all have different perceptions of materiality."

Required: Discuss the issues raised by the president.

(CICA adapted)

P2-4. **a.** Compare the Table of Contents of the Accounting Recommendations found in the *CICA Handbook* with the Table of Contents of this text. Identify topics found in the text but not in the *Handbook* and vice versa. How can these apparent discrepancies be explained?

b. Repeat the procedure in (a) comparing the index of the text with the index found in the *CICA Handbook*.

P2-5. Although the *CICA Handbook* standards provide general guidance, the application of these standards is dependent upon particular circumstances.

In practice, a Chartered Accountant may encounter situations where *CICA Handbook* standards do not exist or may not apply.

Since there is no substitute for the exercise of professional judgement in the determination of what constitutes fair presentation and good practice, it has been suggested that too much effort is being directed towards the development of standards.

Required: Discuss the issues raised in the above statements.

(CICA adapted)

P2-6. Obtain a copy of the annual report of each of the following companies. As a user of these statements, specify the decision(s) you are making and then review the statements thoroughly and list any relevant economic information about the company that is not provided. How would you go about obtaining the information you need in order to make your decision that is not provided in the annual financial statements? (*Hint:* Look for such things as monopoly position, technological obsolescence, cash flow problems, strikes, loss of franchise, and changing market structure.)

a. Air Canada

b. Thomson Newspapers Ltd.

c. Tele-Metropole Inc.

d. Dofasco Inc.

e. Massey-Ferguson

f. Leon's Furniture

P2-7. "Canada, like the United States, tries to protect the reader of financial statements with a mixture of public and private bodies — the public bodies have the power and do little standard setting, and the private ones set the standards and have little power."

Required: Write a brief essay responding to the above comment.

P2-8. A business-related magazine reported, in an article entitled "Accountability for the Accountants," that "an accounting firm of reputation" had expressed an unqualified audit opinion on a company's financial statements, and a few months later that company was found to be "in serious trouble." The magazine speculated that perhaps the trouble arose from the competition among auditors. It went on to suggest that as a result audit partners are often under pressure to do more than they once were to hold on to a client. "The problem is that making the extra effort may weaken allegiance to accounting principles. . . . If an audit partner insists on issuing [a qualified] opinion, the firm often gets fired for its pains."

Required: Discuss the implications of the situation as outlined in the article for (i) investors, (ii) auditors, and (iii) standard-setting bodies (both public and private). Is the situation any different between Canada and the United States?

P2-9. *The Globe and Mail* (26 May 1983) reported that the auditors of Dome Mines Ltd. said that they would have qualified the company's 1982 financial statements if they had been prepared in accordance with accounting principles generally accepted in the United States, but that the actual auditors' report, prepared in accordance with Canadian accounting principles, was not qualified.

The auditors had said that under U.S. standards their opinion would have been qualified "as being subject to the outcome of uncertainties related to Dome Petroleum Ltd. of Calgary." In notes to its financial statements, Dome Mines said "the continued existence of Dome Petroleum as a going concern and the carrying value of the company's investment in Dome Petroleum depend on the outcome of Dome Petroleum's previously reported refinancing negotiations and on a return to profitability by Cyprus Anvil Mining Corp."

Required: Write a one-page memo assessing the implications of this difference between Canadian and U.S. requirements. Your memo should include an assessment of each of the following:

(i) the merits, if any, of putting comments on the going-concern aspects of a company in the auditors' report instead of in the notes to the financial statements

(ii) the merits, if any, of having generally accepted accounting standards consistent between countries.

P2-10. *The Wall Street Journal* reported in 1983 on a dilemma faced by public accounting firms. It appeared under the heading "More Ailing Concerns Are Firing Auditors in Hopes of Keeping Bad News from Public." Senior members of accounting firms were quoted as follows:

"Independence is a state of mind. You have a responsibility to the public, but you're paid by the client."

"Once you give a qualified report you always have a cloud over you. Two years later it may happen that you're fired, but ostensibly for some other reason."

"The word 'qualification' is such an emotional word. It brings an emotional function that causes investors to stampede."

"Our firm tried to avoid, if possible, 'going-concern' qualifications because of the 'self-fulfilling prophecy' question."

Required: Write a brief essay that considers the above comments and answers the following questions.

(i) How important is "auditor independence"?

(ii) How independent are auditors in the United States and in Canada?

(iii) How should accounting and auditing regulators respond to this situation?

(iv) What is meant by "self-fulfilling prophecy"?

P2-11. Accounting standard setters must deal with the issue of how much information companies should be required to provide. An article in *Canadian Business*, entitled "Indecent Disclosure: Can There Be Too Much?", discussed this problem and concluded with the following comments from a former Toronto Stock Exchange executive: "In the end you can't regulate propriety. Strict adherence to the law doesn't guarantee anything. Those who wish to avoid disclosure will do so, no matter how stringent the reporting standards. The key to an efficient market is that the players should be honest."

Required: Answer the following questions:

a. What does the last sentence of this quote imply for standard setters and for users?

b. Is the TSE executive's comment a practical solution to the problems of good disclosure? Does the fact that some companies manage to avoid disclosure mean that reporting standards should be abandoned? Is after-the-fact punishment of those avoiding disclosure of any use? How should accounting regulators respond?

c. How should users of financial statements react?

   d. What is the view of the efficient markets school? What are the implications of this view for standard setters?

P2-12. Evaluate each of the following comments that have been made about the process for setting accounting standards that currently is in place. Do you agree with each statement? Explain.

   a. In some instances, companies purchased major assets ten years ago that are not only still in use, but are worth more in present-day dollars than their original cost. Because the firm is required under GAAP to depreciate these assets based on historic cost, it appears that the assets have cost the firm money, whereas in reality the company has made money on them.

   b. In the United States, companies whose shares are traded must show the net remuneration (salaries, bonuses, perks, etc.) of their five highest-paid officers. In Canada, one must show the net remuneration only in *aggregate* for this group of officers, plus the aggregate net remuneration of all those earning more than $50,000 annually. One person has described even the milder Canadian version as an invasion of privacy. He goes on to say that in cyclical industries such as pulp and paper, it would exert a downward pressure on executive salaries during bad economic times because it would be politically prudent to tie them to the company's financial performance. This might mean that such companies would have a difficult time keeping senior people (especially during a turndown).

   c. Banks have resisted giving details about their poor loan portfolios on the grounds that this would precipitate a run on the bank thought to have the weakest financial situation. Critics say that some of the loan exposure, particularly to foreign governments, is so huge that investors have the right to judge the risk for themselves.

P2-13. When asked what information an investor should want from a company, one experienced investment analyst said: "A detailed description of a firm's goals and objectives and a regimen of complete candour with the investor." He pointed to Canada Trustco Mortgage Co. as an example of a company that is going in the right direction: it reported the goals it had set for itself and admitted it had not achieved six out of nine.

   Required: Do you think that this is what an investor would want? Is it complete or practical? Discuss.

P2-14. "There is a lot of crucial information that you will never get through disclosure — for instance, background on a firm's principals and their previous business experience, business connections, and reputation. That knowledge comes from careful analysis and a bit of digging, something most individual shareholders don't have the time or inclination to pursue."

   Required: Answer the following questions.

   a. Is it rational behaviour for individual shareholders not to do the "careful analysis" and "digging" that the quote suggests?

   b. Does this mean they will be less well informed than those who do?

   c. Is this the *fair game* investing suggested in the text?

P2-15. In the 1870s the editor of the London *Economist* was commenting on a proposal to reduce the self-regulatory power of the Stock Exchange and create a government body to regulate it (similar to the SEC). Bagehot wrote:

   "A Commission will not show that the quasi-moral jurisdiction of the committee of the stock exchange can be advantageously transferred to the government. No government department could undertake such a jurisdiction, or exercise it. The purity of our civil service is now one of the best points in our society, but if we mix it up with stock exchange business we might easily corrupt the service without purifying the business."

Required: Assuming that Bagehot is correct, what does this imply for the SEC, FASB, and CICA?

P2-16. Complete the essay below (750 words maximum).

This essay is about the PIP accounting controversy between the federal government and the CICA. In this essay I propose to do the following:

(i) set out the major accounting issues that lay behind the controversy;

(ii) evaluate the theoretical arguments that both sides might make to support their case; and

(iii) evaluate the implications for standard setting as it exists at present if the federal government had prevailed in its desires

P2-17. It has been said that "War is too important to be left to generals" (the implication being that the important decisions should be made by politicians). It might also be said that "Standard making is too important to be left to accountants." The thinking behind both quotes is that the strategic decision-making that influences wars and standard setting is likely to be done better at the political level than by technical people such as generals and professional accountants. As a result, the advocates of this view propose that standard setters might be allowed to make proposals for changes in reporting policy but that the ultimate decision should be a political one.

Required: Write an essay (1000 words maximum) in the spirit of the above quotes, using the PIP accounting controversy as your specific example. In your essay you should

(i) indicate the nature of the accounting issues involved;

(ii) assess why the federal government and the CICA might legitimately have been seeking different objectives; and

(iii) evaluate the implications for standard setting if the ultimate decision in this case had been made at the political level

P2-18. There is a body of opinion that holds that any group that makes rules affecting society must ultimately be answerable to the people affected by those rules. It points out that accounting standards are typically made by a group like the FASB or the Accounting Standards Committee that is not answerable in any discernible way to the people affected. Accordingly, so this argument goes, the government of the day should have ultimate control over setting accounting standards.

Required: Write an essay (1000 words maximum) evaluating this view, using as your focus the PIP grant controversy between the federal government and the CICA. In your answer be sure to

(i) outline the nature of the accounting issues in the controversy;

(ii) evaluate to what extent the FASB or the Accounting Standards Committee or both are answerable (either directly or indirectly) to the people they are responsible for serving;

(iii) evaluate who are or ought to be the people they are responsible for serving; and

(iv) assess the implications for standard setting in Canada if the federal government had the power to overrule accounting standards that it did not like

P2-19. The following unrelated cases require discussion in the light of generally accepted accounting principles. Your *concise* answer should focus on the primary accounting principle, if any, that is involved. Give the recommended treatment or disclosure for good accounting treatment of the issue. You should do so by answering the following for each case: (i) What primary accounting principle has been violated, if at all? (ii) How has it been violated (if indeed it has been)? (iii) What treatment do you recommend that would be consistent with good accounting principles?

    a. Lakeshore Rail Company did not recognize periodic depreciation expense on its rolling stock on the grounds that maintenance expenditures kept the rolling stock in "just like new condition."

    b. Chicken Licken Corporation is responding to competition by embarking on a promotion campaign of its own. The campaign centres on the slogan: "Buy one Chicken Licken dinner at the regular price of $5.00 and get an additional one for 50 cents." In order to maintain the same gross margin percentage, the corporation intends to record each deal as follows:

Cash	5.50	
Advertising expense	4.50	
Sales		10.00

    c. Seabright Marine Construction Company constructed a fishing boat for Fairweather Fisheries Ltd. The terms of the sale were $1,200 cash at time of delivery and three non-interest-bearing notes of $1,200, due one year, two years, and three years from the time of delivery. Seabright recorded the sale as follows:

Cash	1,200.00	
Notes receivable	3,600.00	
Sales		4,800.00
		(CGA adapted)

P2-20. In this chapter you are given the financial statements of Bathurst Power and Paper Company Limited, and its successor company, Consolidated-Bathurst Inc. Consider these two statements as examples of how statements looked *before* and *after* systematic disclosure requirements came into place.

Required:

    a. What are the three or four most significant differences between these two sets of statements?

    b. What accounting information might an analyst of the company legitimately want that is still not found in the *modern* statements? Give two or three examples.

    c. As a potential investor in the company, which statement is the more useful to you? Explain.

P2-21. It has been said that the *Handbook* recommendations tend to follow in the footsteps of the pronouncements of the FASB. Test this proposition as follows:

    a. Prepare a listing of the FASB pronouncements of the last three years, showing date of issue. For your source you might use the *Journal of Accountancy*.

    b. Prepare a listing of the *CICA Handbook* pronouncements of the last three years, showing date of issue.

    c. Prepare a summary of the evidence that supports the view expressed above.

    d. Prepare a summary of the evidence that argues against this view. (Consider the CICA pronouncements that do not appear to be inspired by comparable FASB pronouncements.)

BIBLIOGRAPHY

BEAVER, WILLIAM H. "What Should Be the FASB's Objectives?" *Journal of Accountancy* (August 1973). A readable appraisal of the implications for standard setters of the research of the *efficient markets* school.

BENSTON, GEORGE. "Required Disclosure and the Stock Market: An Evaluation of the Securities and Exchange Act of 1934." *American Economic Review* (March 1973). A critical evaluation of the role of the SEC.

BORITZ, EFRIM. "Accounting Standard Setting: From Plato to Robin Hood." *CA Magazine* (June 1982). A discussion of implications of the resource distribution aspect of standard setting.

BRYANT, MURRAY, AND THORNTON, D.B. "Public Choice of Corporate Accounting Standards." *Proceedings of the CAAA Conference, Halifax 1981*. Revised in *Modern Accounting Research: Survey and Guide*, edited by R.V. Mattessich, Canadian CGA Research Foundation, 1984. A paper assessing the importance of predictability of accounting standards, since they are used as an important reference for business contracts.

BURTON, JOHN C. "Statement in Quotes." *Journal of Accountancy* (June 1982). The former chief accountant of the SEC describes the role of that body as a "creative irritant."

CHOW, CHEE W. "The Impacts of Accounting Regulation on Bondholder and Shareholder Wealth: The Case of the Securities Acts." *The Accounting Review* (July 1983). An examination of the proposition that increased disclosure regulation had the effect of decreasing the wealth of the shareholders of the companies.

COOPER, KERRY, and KEIM, GERALD D. "The Economic Rationale for the Nature and Extent of Corporate Financial Disclosure Regulation: A Critical Assessment." *Journal of Accounting and Public Policy* (1983). A good survey of the debate over whether accounting standards should be regulated or left to market forces.

CRANDALL, ROBERT H. "Government Intervention in Accounting Standard Setting: The PIP Grant Accounting Controversy." *Cost and Management* (September-October 1983). An account of the conflict over standard setting.

DENMAM, JOHN H. "Setting Standards for Standard Setting." *CA Magazine* (March 1984).

GERBOTH, DALE. " 'Muddling Through' with the APB." *Journal of Accountancy* (May 1972). An application of the incremental approach to decision-making.

HORNGREN, CHARLES. "Accounting Principles: Private or Public Sector?" *Journal of Accountancy* (May 1972). An evaluation of the dependent roles of the FASB and the SEC.

MURPHY, GEORGE J. "The Evolution of Corporate Reporting Practices in Canada." *The Academy of Accounting Historians Working Papers Series*, Vol. 1. Academy of Accounting Historians, 1979. Part of the growing literature on Canadian business history.

MURPHY, GEORGE J. "Financial Statement Disclosure and Corporate Law: The Canadian Experience." *The International Journal of Accounting* (Spring 1980).

ROBB, CLAYTON, and ROBINSON, CHRIS. "Theories of Standard Setting: The Simplest is Best." *CA Magazine* (April 1983). A review of the possible objectives of standard setting, with a bibliography.

ROSENFIELD, PAUL H. "The Auditors' Standard Report Can Be Improved." *Journal of Accountancy* (October 1964).

[The *SCOSS Report*]. *CICA Special Committee on Standard Setting: Report to CICA Board of Governors*. Toronto, December 1980. A report of a special committee commissioned by the CICA to evaluate the standard-setting process and make recommendations.

SKINNER, ROSS. *Accounting Principles*. Toronto: Canadian Institute of Chartered Accountants, 1972.

———— . *Accounting Standards in Evolution*. Toronto: Holt, Rinehart and Winston of Canada Ltd., 1987. An excellent reference book for the student who wants a more detailed explanation and examination of accounting issues.

STOREY, REID K. *The Search for Accounting Principles — Today's Problems in Perspective*. New York: American Institute of Certified Public Accountants, 1964. A readable account of the efforts to establish accounting standards.

THOMAS, R.D. "Setting Accounting and Auditing Standards." *CA Magazine* (September 1978). A description of the standard-setting process at the CICA, by the General Director of Research.

THORNTON, DANIEL B. "Agency Theory: A Pedagogic Note for Accountants." *CA Magazine* (November 1984 and January 1985). An excellent introductory survey of the topic.

———— . "Current Cost Disclosers and Nondisclosers: Canadian Evidence." *Contemporary Accounting Research* (Autumn 1986). An examination of the evidence that management of firms in Canada are motivated by self-interest to be selective in their reporting.

WATTS, ROSS, and ZIMMERMAN, JEROLD. "The Demand for and Supply of Accounting Theories: The Market for Excuses." *The Accounting Review* (April 1979). An application of agency theory to the standard-setting process.

ZEFF, STEPHEN A. *Forging Accounting Principles in Five Countries*. Champaign, Ill.: Stipes Publishing, 1972. Contains one of the best summaries of the evolution of accounting reporting in Canada.

———— . "Some Junctures in the Evolution of the Process of Establishing Accounting Principles in the U.S.A.: 1917–1922." *The Accounting Review* (July 1984). A capsule history.

CHAPTER 3
Balance Sheets

Introduction

In this chapter we complete our introduction to the balance sheet. We will soon be looking at balance-sheet items in more detail, as most of our chapters are arranged around balance-sheet categories. The starting point for the statement of changes in financial position is the balance sheet at the beginning and end of the period. We will, therefore, also take a brief look at the statement of changes in financial position, which we will deal with in detail in Chapter 18.

Development of the Balance Sheet

The common brief description of the balance sheet is that it is a snapshot of the firm at a particular time. From a technical point of view it performs a pivotal role in the accounting process because it is the only major financial statement that shows the financial position of a firm at a point of time. The other published statements (income statement, statement of changes in financial position, and statement of retained earnings) explain what has happened between two balance-sheet dates.

In the Middle Ages merchants produced balance sheets for themselves with virtually no accounting assistance. They simply toured their shop and made a list of all the assets they owned, wrote down what they thought they were worth, and added them up. Then they consulted their memories and records and made a list of all their debts. To find out how much they were worth they deducted one from the other. They unconsciously made use of the balance-sheet equation:

Owners' Equity = Assets − Liabilities

The present-day balance sheet uses this same equation; but it values the assets by using the historic cost convention, rather than the current values used by the medieval merchants. In Chapter 20, we will discuss a modern trend to reintroduce current-value accounting.

Present-day balance sheets are usually expressed as:

Assets = Liabilities + Owners' Equity

While this equation is algebraically the same as the preceding one, there is a subtle difference in emphasis between the two that needs to be explained. On the one hand, the first equation concentrates on the measurement of owners' equity and is used by the owner of the business to arrive at his net worth. This is called the **proprietorship** approach to thinking about the firm, inasmuch as we are standing outside the firm looking in and using a technique that indicates what the net assets are worth to the owner. Under the proprietorship concept, the firm is just an extension of its owner.

The second equation, on the other hand, can be interpreted to mean that the firm's assets are financed by debt (liabilities) and contributions from the owners (e.g., shareholders through purchased shares and retained earnings). In a sense we are inside the entity looking out and asking what the most advantageous mix of debt and owners' equity might be for the firm. The firm is not regarded as an extension of its owners, but as something at arm's length from them (e.g., shareholders are just another supplier of the capital needed by the firm). This is called the **entity** approach to thinking about the firm.

Up to the 1920s the balance sheet reigned supreme as the most important of the financial statements. This was because the worth of a business was judged by the size of its **net assets**, or the net of assets minus liabilities. Later, its position of pre-eminence was taken by the income statement, as the belief grew that earnings were more important than the information shown on the balance sheet. The balance sheet continued to be supplied to readers, but not as much attention was paid to it. However, the adverse financial climate experienced in the 1970s and 1980s increased the relative importance of a company's ability to survive financially. Therefore, interest in the information about liquidity and financial stability supplied by balance sheets increased again.

ASSETS

An **asset** is something which is expected to provide benefits to the firm now or in the future. This is the characteristic that is held in common by all the items listed in the assets section of the balance sheet. Because the test is whether the firm receives any future benefit, it is an economic, not a legal, concept. The test of whether an asset exists for accounting purposes always revolves around this question of future benefit. As a practical matter, it must be possible to make a reasonable estimate of the benefit to be conferred by the asset in order to make the journal entry. In Chapter 1 we indicated that it has been customary to classify all the firm's assets into three main groups: (i) current assets, and the two components of non-current assets, which are (ii) plant assets and (iii) other long-term assets. We will give an overview below and discuss them in detail in later chapters.

Current Assets

Current assets are those that will benefit the firm within a year or within the firm's operating cycle if this is longer than a year. For most current assets, such as accounts receivable and inventory, there is also the expectation that they can be converted into cash fairly quickly. Hence short-term creditors of the company have traditionally taken a special interest in current assets and they have influenced the conservative way current assets are valued for financial statement purposes. There is also the notion that most current assets represent a buffer stock of assets on their way to being converted to other purposes and that consequently they should be kept as low as possible consistent with the objectives of the firm. For example, cash in a current bank account has little or no earning power and is kept by the firm in order to have an asset that other firms will accept as payment. Any excess would normally be converted to short-term marketable securities, which over the long term would be used to purchase assets with greater earning power or to reduce interest-bearing debt.

A small group of current assets result from the matching process discussed in Chapter 1. They represent outlays in one period that are carried forward to the next period before being recognized as period expenses. An example is prepaid rent, which is deferred to the period for which the prepayment is made. If the company did not go through with the rental agreement, the prepayment would probably be forfeited; hence it has little realizable value, unlike most other current assets. Let us now proceed with a brief survey of the more common current assets.

Cash is the cash on hand and in the company's bank accounts, both in Canada and in foreign accounts (unless its use is restricted). Cash would not be classified as a current asset if it is specifically earmarked for some long-term purposes of the company. If it is earmarked for specific purposes it is shown separately. For example, the Royal Bank of Canada shows its cash resources as follows:

	1986	1985
Cash resources (thousands of $)		
Cash and deposits with Bank of Canada	$ 1,385,701	$ 1,406,259
Deposits with other banks	13,522,326	13,585,754
	$ 14,908,027	$ 14,992,013

The cash on deposit with the Bank of Canada is there for a specific purpose — to fulfil the Royal Bank's obligation to maintain some of its currency reserve with the central bank. Hence that cash is shown separately.

Cash that is earmarked for some non-current purpose would be classified as a non-current asset, as explained in Chapter 5.

Short-term investments are those held with the intention of converting them into cash or another current asset within a year. It is the *intention* to convert that counts; some may actually be held for longer than a year. Typical short-term securities would be (i) short-term investments at a bank or trust company; (ii) promissory notes that are traded on a public market of a government or large corporation; and (iii) shares of other corporations traded on a stock market. These are sometimes grouped with cash on the balance sheet; at other times they are shown separately.

Bell Canada Enterprises Inc. reported them combined, as follows:

	1986	1985
	(millions of $)	
Cash and temporary cash investments —		
at cost (approximates market)	$ 679.6	$ 279.5

Note how the amounts are stated in millions of dollars, accurate to one decimal place.

Accounts receivable and **notes receivable** are amounts owed to the company, usually by customers who have made purchases on credit. The difference between the two is that notes receivable are documented by a formal written promise to pay. The amount usually shown on the balance sheet is the gross amount receivable net of any allowance for doubtful accounts. This balance-sheet item is discussed further in Chapter 5.

Inventory consists of three components: (i) raw material and supplies purchased by the company for use in its productive processes; (ii) semi-processed material still being processed; and (iii) finished goods awaiting shipment to customers. It is common to find these three kinds of inventory set out in the financial statements, often in a note. Here is an example from Great Lakes Forest Products Limited.

	1986	1985
	(thousands of $)	
Inventories:		
Finished goods	$ 10,053	$ 16,033
Pulpwood and sawlogs	45,526	45,431
Materials and supplies	39,578	38,866
	$ 95,157	$ 100,330

Inventory is usually a very important current asset for most companies. It is the one whose ultimate value creditors worry about most. This important asset will be carefully discussed in Chapter 6.

A **prepaid expense** arises because a payment is made in one period that is expected to benefit a later period. Under the matching convention such payments are deferred to the period that receives the benefit and are shown on the balance sheet as a prepaid expense. Examples of prepaid expenses include rent, insurance premiums, and municipal taxes.

Usually this is not a large item on balance sheets. Normally the means of calculating the amount prepaid is simply to apportion the payment to accounting periods in proportion to the time elapsed in each period.

For example, suppose that municipal taxes are $24,000 and must be paid by 30 June of each year for a period covering the entire calendar year. If a company's year-end were 31 August, it would treat four months as prepaid. If the entire tax bill had originally been charged to tax expense, it would make the following journal entry at 31 August:

Prepaid expense — municipal taxes	8,000.00	
Municipal tax expense		8,000.00

To record four-twelfths of the municipal tax payment
of $24,000 as prepaid.

It is quite possible that a prepaid expense does not benefit the next period, but a later one. In that case it would be classed as a non-current asset.

Non-Current Assets

A **non-current asset** is one whose benefit extends beyond the year following the date of the balance sheet. It is usual that the asset also benefits the period immediately following the balance sheet date, like a current asset; but as a general rule it is treated as a non-current asset except for the current portion of long-term receivables. (This is consistent with the treatment of long-term payables.)

Non-current assets fall into two main groups: (i) **plant assets** — the tangible productive assets used to make the product or services sold by the company; and (ii) **other long-term assets**. Of the latter, the two most important sub-groups are usually (a) **long-term investments** — such as shares of other companies, mortgages receivable, bonds receivable, and notes receivable; and (b) **intangible assets** — namely, those that have no physical existence, such as patents and copyrights.

If the firm is thought of in the economic sense as a device for taking in raw inputs and creating finished products (as in Chapter 1), then there is no obvious reason for segregating non-current assets on the basis of whether they are tangible or not. They both play an equally important role in the productive process. There is a practical reason for this segregation, however: often it is very difficult to find evidence that supports the claim that particular intangible assets will provide a future benefit to the firm.

The type of non-current asset that does not fit the economic model of the firm is that of long-term investments, primarily because introductory economic theory does little to explain why one firm would buy shares in another. What logic leads a firm to buy long-term investments if its shareholders could own them directly if they wanted to? The reason is that the company buying the shares often wants to establish an association with another company through being an important shareholder; and by so doing it can exert some influence on the company whose shares it has bought. Alternatively, sometimes a firm is forced to accept a long-term investment as part payment for some other asset it wants to sell. For example, when selling a factory that is no longer needed, a company may have to take back a mortgage from the purchaser as part payment.

The matching convention requires that the cost of plant assets and intangible assets should be charged against the periods which benefit from their use. This is done by a process termed **depreciation** (for tangible assets), **depletion** (for wasting assets, such as coal mines), or **amortization** (for intangible assets). Here the net cost of the asset is charged against the periods which benefit from its use. The principles behind the application of depreciation are set out in Chapter 8.

Plant Assets

Plant assets is a general term given to land, buildings, and equipment used in the productive process. If they are not used in the productive process but are held for resale, they would not be classed as plant assets but as assets held for resale. **Productive process** is defined broadly to include the manufacturing, storage, marketing, transportation, and administrative activities of the company. This means that the factories, offices, fleets of trucks and ships, and related equipment of the company are all included in plant assets. This is consistent with the economic model of the firm set out in Chapter 1.

Usually the reader is given some detail on the plant assets of the company. For instance, a note to the balance sheet of Great Lakes Forest Products Limited reads as follows:

Fixed assets (thousands of $)	Cost	31 December 1986 Net Value	31 December 1985 Net Value
Land	$ 1,510	$ 1,510	$ 1,494
Buildings, machinery, and equipment:			
Pulp and paper	850,198	531,746	534,492
Building products	46,922	13,954	15,916
Woodlands improvements and equipment	96,340	20,973	22,933
Timber licences	3,945		
Construction in progress	900	900	9,589
	$ 999,815	$ 569,083	$ 584,424

We will discuss plant assets in detail in Chapter 7.

Intangible Assets

Intangible assets are those non-current assets that have no physical existence, such as copyrights, patents, a mailing list of subscribers for newspapers or magazines, a licence to operate a taxi, or a licence to operate a cable TV network. Although intangible, they otherwise have similarities to land, buildings, and equipment inasmuch as they play a role in the productive processes of the enterprise. The intangible assets for The Molson Companies Limited are described in a note to their financial statement as follows:

> Intangible assets include principally goodwill and hockey franchises. Goodwill is amortized on a straight-line basis over periods not exceeding forty years. Hockey franchises are not amortized as the Corporation believes there has been no decrease in their value.

We will consider intangible assets in depth in Chapter 9.

LIABILITIES

If one thinks of the firm as being financed by debt and owners' equity (the entity concept of the firm), then the common element among liabilities and equity is that they provide the source of the firm's assets. Under the proprietorship view, liabilities are a sort of negative asset, to be deducted from assets to find the net assets, or owners' equity in the firm. Since both points of view are equally valid, in our opinion, we will keep the distinction clear between liabilities and equities so as not to rule out the proprietorship view.

Just as an asset is something that brings future benefit to the firm, a **liability** is something that entails future obligation. This obligation will be discharged by the transfer of assets to creditors and/or the performance of some service. For example, an account payable is a debt owed to a supplier that will be discharged with payment of cash. A liability for prepaid subscriptions at a newspaper will be discharged by delivery of the newspaper to the subscriber in accordance with the terms of the contract. In the case where a liability is incurred to purchase an asset, the liability is not recorded unless the asset is recorded as well. If, for example, the company contracts to buy an automobile, the legal obligation to pay for the car is not recorded until the acquisition of the car is recorded. This is because the notion of a liability is an economic one — similar to the notion of a asset — and hence the obligation is not recorded until the matching benefit is recorded.

If a legal obligation exists but no transfer of resources has been made by either party to the contract, this is termed an **executory contract**. Such a contract is not recorded in the accounts. Examples of executory contracts include rental agreements where the tenant company has not moved in, has paid no rent, and has received no benefit as tenant; construction contracts where no work has taken place and no payment has been made; and employment contracts where the employee has not started work and the company has not made any wage payments.

The exception to the rule that liabilities are not recorded until at least part of the matching benefit has been received is the unusual case where the company incurs an obligation without *any* prospect of receiving a matching benefit. The most common example is losing a court case where the company has been sued. The company will be obliged to pay out funds in damages, and hence has a future obligation. However, it will not be receiving any benefit, aside from a discharge of the claim for damages. In this case the accounting convention of conservatism indicates that the liability should be recorded in the accounts as soon as it is reasonably capable of being estimated. If there is a possibility of having to pay damages but it is too soon to make an estimate, the information is not entered in the accounts of the company. Instead a note is added to the statements giving a summary of the situation. In Chapter 11 we will deal in depth with this issue.

Current Liabilities

A **current liability** is one that is expected to be discharged through transfer of a current asset or provision of goods or services within the year or within the company's normal operating cycle if this is longer. This means that a long-term liability to be discharged by the issuing of another long-term liability would not be classed as a current liability, even though due within one year.

The net difference between the current assets and current liabilities is called the **working capital, net current assets** of the firm or sometimes **funds** (a term that is going out of use). The distinction between current versus non-current assets and liabilities plays an important role in constructing the statement of changes in financial position.

One of the most common current liabilities is the debts owed to the firm's suppliers, termed **accounts payable**. In a sense they are the mirror image of the accounts receivable in current assets.

Another significant current liability is **loans** from the company's banks. This is the mirror image of the current asset, cash. It is quite common for a company to have both cash and a bank loan on its financial statements, since frequently banks require companies to borrow in round amounts, or keep compensating cash balances if they have a loan (especially in the U.S.). Another reason may be that the company has borrowed from the bank on a term loan with a fixed repayment schedule, and is not free to reduce its loan during those periods when it has excess cash. If the bank loan is for a period exceeding one year, it would normally be classed as a non-current liability.

Accrued liabilities are liabilities that are not legally payable, but are required by the matching convention. The expenses are recorded in the period which receives the benefit, which is prior to the period in which payments must be made. Therefore the credit balance arising from the amounts charged to expense are carried on the balance sheet as current liabilities. They are the mirror image of prepaid expenses.

The **current portion of long-term debt** is the portion of a long-term debt that is payable within a year. Its asset equivalent is the portion of long-term receivables due within a year. The accounting treatment is the same for both.

Other current liabilities have no equivalent current asset counterparts. **Taxes payable on income** is the tax owed to Revenue Canada or some equivalent taxing authority. **Dividends payable** are a liability to the shareholders that arises when the directors of the company declare a dividend. We will examine current liabilities in Chapter 11.

Non-Current Liabilities

Non-current liabilities are those that do not fit the definition of a current liability. They are usually referred to as **long-term liabilities**, and frequently are incurred by the company to purchase specific long-term assets. The most common examples of long-term liabilities are bonds payable, mortgages payable, and long-term bank loans. The terms of such long-term loans are often complex. To safeguard the interests of the lenders, there are frequently terms in the contract governing the loan that limit the right of the company to pay dividends, sell certain assets, or incur other debt. We will discuss this topic in Chapter 12.

An item that is usually found between long-term debt and shareholders' equity is **deferred income tax**, which arises from a timing difference between the recording of the tax expense on the income statement and the actual payment of tax. The standard-setting bodies have said specifically that this is not to be regarded as a liability; but they have not said what economic interpretation should be put on it. Present-day accounting treatment of this is not satisfactory. We will analyse this issue in Chapter 13.

SHAREHOLDERS' EQUITY

The **shareholders' equity** (owners' equity in a corporation) represents the residual after deducting liabilities from assets. It rarely represents the value of the business to the shareholders inasmuch as (i) in present-day financial statements, assets are valued at their historic acquisition cost, not their current value; and (ii) the balance sheet does not include all assets and liabilities of the company. It is important to keep this point clearly in mind because the **book value of the company**, as the financial press often calls it, is not meant to be a close approximation of the company's market value. We will explore this point in depth in Chapter 9 on intangible assets. Let us now discuss the usual components of owners' equity in a corporation.

Share capital represents the funds contributed by shareholders through the purchase of the company's shares. Companies acts permit the issuance of various classes of shares. The type of share issued is usually influenced by what, at the time, is thought to be most attractive to potential shareholders. All companies must have **common shares**, which are shares that have the residual claim on the assets of the corporation. At least some of these common shares must give the holder the right to vote at general meetings of the shareholders at which directors are elected and other important company business is ratified.

A **preferred share** is one giving the holder some preference over the common shareholders with respect to payment of dividends or claim to assets if the company is wound up. It often restricts the holder's right to vote as long as the terms of the share agreement are met. Typically, a preferred share gives the holder the right to receive a dividend of a stated annual amount before any dividends can be paid on the common shares. If it is **cumulative**, then any arrears in dividends must be paid before common shareholders can receive a dividend.

The **retained earnings** is the account to which annual net earnings of the company are transferred, and to which dividends and prior period adjustments are charged.

The shareholders' equity section of the balance sheet of Loblaw Companies Limited reads as follows:

	1986	1985
	(millions of $)	
Capital stock (note 8)		
Preferred shares	$ 168.9	$ 94.4
Common shares	104.5	104.1
	273.4	198.5
Contributed surplus	10.2	10.3
Retained earnings	347.5	294.8
Equity from foreign currency translation	24.1	17.4
	$ 655.2	$ 521.0

The *contributed surplus* will be discussed in Chapter 16. (The *equity from foreign currency translation* is not a topic that will be covered in this text.) Here is an extract from Note 8 concerning the preferred shares:

First preferred shares (authorized — 1,000,000)

First series — $2.40 cumulative dividend redeemable at $50.

Second series — $3.70 cumulative dividend redeemable at $70. In each fiscal year the Company is obligated to apply $400,000 to the purchase of these shares for cancellation, provided that such shares are available at a price not exceeding $67. During 1986, the Company purchased 8,800 of these shares for cancellation at a cost of $422,500. The premium of $132,100 on these purchases has been deducted from contributed surplus.

We will pursue the topic of the owners' equity account in Chapter 16.

FORMAT OF THE BALANCE SHEET

All balance sheets are based on some variation of the balance sheet equation:

Assets = Liabilities + Owners' Equity

If the balance sheet follows the above form without variation then the assets are listed on the left side of the balance sheet, and liabilities and owners' equity on the right, as follows:

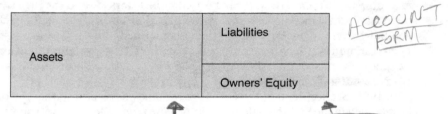

This arrangement is often called the **account form** and implies the equity concept of the firm. About three-quarters of all balance sheets published in Canada use this format.

The balance sheet can also be arranged to express the equation as

Assets − Liabilities = Owners' Equity

It is usually presented vertically to show owners' equity as the residue, consistent with the proprietorship view of the firm, as follows:

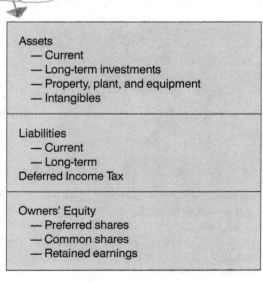

This is termed the **report form** of the balance sheet. It is often referred to as the **statement of financial position**.

The order of assets and liabilities shown above is common for most companies in North America, although utility companies such as telephone, gas, and electrical, often put plant assets first and current assets last. In Great Britain it is common to put the liabilities and equity on the left and assets on the right, with the most liquid assets last. In most North American balance sheets the assets are listed in order of descending liquidity, although exceptions can be found.

Statement of Changes in Financial Position

A statement of changes in financial position (SCFP) is one which explains the changes in a company's *liquid assets*. It can be used by investors to see if the firm is getting more or less liquid. Hence it provides some indication of management's handling of the company's resources. **Liquid assets** may be defined in a variety of ways. One of the most common is as *cash and cash equivalents* (the latter are highly liquid assets that can be quickly turned into cash). Another common definition of liquid assets is as *net current assets* (also called *working capital*).

In 1985, Section 1540 of the *CICA Handbook* was revised so that the only assets to be included in the SCFP would be *cash* and *cash equivalents*. We will now introduce the methodology to produce a statement using any definition of funds, such as working capital or cash, but the example will be with cash and cash equivalents.

A comprehensive discussion of the statement of changes in financial position and its preparation will be given in Chapter 18. The purpose of this section is to introduce the statement and show its relationship to the balance sheet.

The procedure for preparing the SCFP is as follows:

1. The balance sheets for the start and end of the period are arranged in columnar form beside each other.

2. The changes in all accounts between the start and end of the year are calculated.

3. A decision is made on the definition of *funds* (e.g., what should be included in cash and cash equivalents).

4. All changes for non-funds are segregated into other columns, and the reason for the change is investigated. It would normally be one of the following: (i) purchase or sale of a non-current asset; (ii) retirement or issue of long-term debt or share capital or both; (iii) net income less dividends declared; or (iv) change in working capital other than that defined as funds.

5. The statement of changes in financial position is prepared using (4).

Note how the balance sheet is the basic starting point for preparing the SCFP. It should also be noted that all the conventions and assumptions that go into the preparation of the balance sheet are automatically reflected in the SCFP.

Here is a simple example of how the SCFP is prepared. Hill Island Limited had the following balance sheets at the beginning and end of 19X6. The changes in balance-sheet items are also shown.

WORKSHEET FOR STATEMENT OF CHANGES

	19X6	19X5	Change
Cash	48,000	52,000	(4,000)
Short-term treasury bills	21,000	25,000	(4,000)
Accounts receivable	170,000	138,000	32,000
Plant and equipment, at cost	1,818,000	1,693,000	125,000
Accumulated depreciation	(564,000)	(506,000)	(58,000)
Bank loan	(22,000)	(19,000)	(3,000)
Accounts payable	(61,000)	(57,000)	(4,000)
Long-term liabilities	(310,000)	(220,000)	(90,000)
Share capital	(611,000)	(601,000)	(10,000)
Retained earnings, start of year	(505,000)	(505,000)	0
Net loss for year	16,000		16,000
	0	0	0

Let us suppose we are also given the following information. During the year $233,000 was spent on new plant and equipment. Old equipment was sold for $36,000, which was also its net book value. It had cost $108,000, and the accumulated depreciation was $72,000 to the time of sale. There was a net loss for the year of $16,000 and the provision for depreciation was $130,000. Long-term liabilities of $30,000 had been retired and $120,000 of new long-term liabilities were issued. Proceeds on the issue of additional shares was $10,000. No dividends were paid.

In general, the statement of changes in financial position is divided into three sections:

1. Operating
2. Financing
3. Investing

When preparing an SCFP we start with the changes in all non-cash items and adjust them in each of the above three sections. In this way we determine the net cash flow in each section. In our present example let us define cash and cash equivalents as consisting of *cash and treasury bills, net of the bank loan.*

Operating: In this section of the statement we wish to show the changes in financial position created by the normal operating activities of the company, such as selling, manufacturing, and administration. The basis for this is the income statement, which is then modified to account for those transactions that did not create an inflow or outflow of cash in the current year. It makes intuitive sense that all items which did not affect cash but did affect income should be reversed. This is what is done in the operating section. For example, depreciation decreases income, but does not affect cash in the current year; therefore depreciation is added back to the income or loss figure we started with. It is also in this section that any increase or decrease of non-cash items in working capital is recorded. An increase in the non-cash items in working capital can be thought of as a use of cash; thus a cash outflow must be recorded to show this. Similarly, a decrease in non-cash working capital represents a cash inflow. In our example, there is a loss of $16,000, depreciation of $130,000, and an increase in non-cash working capital of $28,000. The operating section would look like this:

Operating:

Loss for the year per income statement		$ (16,000)
Add (subtract) items that did not affect cash flow		
Depreciation	$130,000	
Increase in non-cash working capital	(28,000)	102,000
Net cash from operating activities		$ 86,000

Financing: The next section of an SCFP is financing. Here we want to show the effect of all financing activities on cash. We are given that long-term debt has increased by $120,000. This represents an increase in cash. Shares were issued which increased cash by $10,000; hence, this too will be added. We are told in the example that $30,000 of long-term debt has been retired. This obviously decreases cash and is therefore deducted in this section. The resulting financing section appears as below:

Financing:

Issue of long-term debt	$ 120,000
Issue of shares	10,000
Retirement of long-term debt	(30,000)
Net cash from financing activities	$100,000

Investing: The treatment of this section resembles that of the financing section, but here we show the effect of investment activity on cash flow. In the example we are told that plant assets were sold for $36,000. This increases cash and is therefore shown as an increase in this section. Note that the $36,000 is known as **proceeds**. We will always show the amount of the proceeds in this section. Plant assets were purchased for $233,000. This figure must be deducted as the purchase of the assets decreases cash. The following would be the investing section of the SCFP:

Investing:

Proceeds from sale of plant assets	$ 36,000
Purchase of plant and equipment	(233,000)
Net cash from investing activities	$ (197,000)

Let us consider further the sale of plant assets. In this example we sold a plant asset for $36,000, which is the amount of proceeds. The proceeds just happen to equal the net book value in this case. If there had been a gain or loss on the sale of the asset, it would have been included in the income or loss figure we started with under the operating section. An adjustment would then have been required to offset this gain or loss under the operating section. Just as the effect of depreciation is reversed, so would be the effect of any gain or loss on the sale of an asset.

When we combine the three sections of Operating, Financing and Investing, we have created the SCFP. For our example it would be as follows:

HILL ISLAND LIMITED
STATEMENT OF CHANGES IN FINANCIAL POSITION
For the Year Ended 31 December 19X6

Operating:		
Loss for the year per income statement		$ (16,000)
Add (subtract) items that did not affect cash flow		
Depreciation	$ 130,000	
Increase in non-cash working capital	(28,000)	102,000
Net cash from operating activities		86,000
Financing:		
Issue of long-term debt		120,000
Issue of shares		10,000
Retirement of long-term debt		(30,000)
Net cash from financing activities		100,000
Investing:		
Proceeds from sale of plant assets		36,000
Purchase of plant and equipment		(233,00)
Net cash from investing activities		(197,000)
Net decrease of cash and equivalents		(11,000)
Cash and equivalents, beginning of period		58,000
Cash and equivalents, end of period		$ 47,000

This is a very simple example. (In Chapter 18 we will demonstrate how to deal with more complex situations.) However, it is sufficient to show the basic ideas behind the funds statement. There are four important ideas to note in even this simple example.

First, we picked cash and cash equivalents as our definition of funds. Had we chosen another definition, such as working capital, this would have affected what balance-sheet items were assigned to the non-funds. It would have produced a statement in which changes in the other current assets became reasons for the change in cash flow.

Second, the change in balance-sheet amounts from the start of the year to the end is the beginning of the analysis, but only the beginning. We still have to find the reasons for the changes and prepare the SCFP accordingly. For instance, while the net change in long-term liabilities was an inflow of $90,000, it is the gross flow in both directions that we note in the SCFP. The treatment of additions to, and disposal of, plant assets is particularly interesting. We look through the accounting treatment and report the proceeds of the sale rather than the amounts of historic cost and accumulated depreciation that were written off.

The third idea to note from our example is that because the SCFP's approach is to use the balance sheet as the start of its preparation, this leads to a treatment of net income which many find confusing initially. Note that the SCFP starts with the net loss of $16,000, and adjusts it for the change in other current assets and liabilities, as well as depreciation (because it did not involve an outlay of funds), to arrive at a total funds inflow of $86,000. We would get exactly the same results if we took the income statement and split it between funds and non-funds as we did the balance sheet. This is shown below.

HILL ISLAND LIMITED
INCOME STATEMENT
For the Period Ended 31 December 19X6
Showing the Division between Funds and Non-Funds

	19X6	Non-cash		Cash
Sales	$ 1,326,000	$ 32,000	(accounts receivable)	$ 1,294,000
Cost of goods sold	923,000	(4,000)	(accounts payable)	919,000
Selling and administrative expenses	243,000			243,000
Depreciation	130,000	(130,000)		
Interest expense	20,000			20,000
Other expenses	26,000			26,000
	1,342,000	134,000		1,208,000
Net income	$ (16,000)	$ 102,000		$ 86,000

Because we have accounted for all non-fund asset changes, the other items on the income statement must have arisen from the inflow and outflow of cash and cash equivalents. For instance, the sales resulted in the inflow of cash of $1,294,000 and an accounts receivable increase of $32,000. Cost of goods sold resulted in a $919,000 cash outflow and a decrease in accounts payable of $4,000. (We assume for this example that accounts payable and receivable changed for the reasons stated. In real life this would be ascertained by examining the individual accounts, if necessary.) Depreciation expense was recorded by a journal entry of the following nature:

Depreciation expense	130,000.00	
Accumulated depreciation		130,000.00

To record annual depreciation.

No flow of cash or cash equivalents was involved. In essence, the net book value of plant assets was decreased, and so was retained earnings. Both of these are non-fund items.

The fourth idea to note from our example is that the SCFP does not show all the flow of funds. It omits, for instance, all the flows arising from operations shown in the income statement. Instead only the net inflow or outflow from operations is shown. Since most readers would be primarily interested in the net flow caused by operations, this helps to keep a lot of detail out of the SCFP. For similar reasons, it is customary to show only the net change in working capital items other than cash and equivalents.

It can be seen that the SCFP is a useful statement for anyone interested in the reasons for the change in the company's liquidity over the year. It can accommodate a variety of definitions of funds and hence answer a variety of different questions. If working capital is used as the definition, the reader is probably interested in broad issues of liquidity; but if cash is used as the definition, the reader can focus more sharply on the company's ability to pay its bills.

Examples from Published Reports

Imperial Oil Limited

Imperial Oil produces crude oil, refines it, and markets it. It also produces and markets fertilizers and petrochemicals. In addition, it has substantial interests in the mining and building materials industries. The company's statement of changes in financial position and balance sheet are shown below with excerpts from the relevant notes. Note that the company does *not* start the SCFP with *net income*, but instead uses *revenue less expenses other than exploration*. By so doing, it shows the net impact of operations directly. Also note in the balance sheet that the company has chosen a format that groups current assets and liabilities together to emphasize net working capital. It then adds all other assets to arrive at a total, *Total capital employed*. This is then balanced against the total of long-term debt and owners' equity. It is the *entity* view of the firm, not the proprietorship view, that has influenced the use of this format.

IMPERIAL OIL LIMITED
CONSOLIDATED STATEMENT OF CHANGES IN FINANCIAL POSITION
For 1985 and 1986

	1985	1986
	millions of $ inflows (outflows)	
Funds provided from operating activities		
Revenue less expenses other than exploration	$ 2,516	$ 1,895
Current taxes and levies	(1,300)	(928)
	1,216	967
Work-force reduction programs (note 10)	—	(29)
Change in operating working capital	56	391
Dividends	(268)	(262)
Total funds provided from operating activities	1,004	1,067
Investment of funds		
Capital and exploration expenditures	(1,158)	(648)
Proceeds from sale of property, plant, and equipment	50	53
Other	(37)	5
Total investment of funds	(1,145)	(590)
Inflow (outflow) of funds before external financing	(141)	477
External financing		
Long-term debt and other obligations, after repayments	7	19
Retirement of 15½ percent debentures (note 10)	—	(315)
Common shares issued (note 18)	76	23
Total external financing	83	(273)
Inflow (outflow) of funds	(58)	204

(Continued)

Increase (decrease) in funds by component

Marketable securities	(130)		213
Outstanding cheques, less cash	62		(10)
Short-term notes	10		1
Total increase (decrease) in funds	$ (58)	$	204

IMPERIAL OIL LIMITED
CONSOLIDATED STATEMENT OF FINANCIAL POSITION
As at 31 December

	1985	1986
Capital Employed:	(millions of $)	
Working Capital:		
Current assets:		
Marketable securities at cost, which approximates market	$ 519	$ 732
Accounts receivable (note 3)	984	664
Accounts receivable from Exxon Corporation and affiliates (note 17)		6
Inventories of crude oil and products	1,294	819
Materials, supplies, and prepaid expenses	143	135
Taxes recoverable		62
Total current assets	$ 2,940	$ 2,418
Current liabilities:		
Outstanding cheques, less cash	66	$ 76
Short-term notes	1	
Accounts payable and accrued liabilities (note 3)	1,100	766
Accounts owing to Exxon Corporation and affiliates (note 17)	49	
Taxes payable	42	
Dividends payable	68	65
Total current liabilities	$ 1,326	$ 907
Total working capital	1,614	1,511
Investments and other long-term assets	576	414
Property, plant and equipment at cost, less accumulated depreciation and amortization (note 6)	5,680	5,816
Total capital employed	$ 7,870	$ 7,741

(Continued)

Sources of Capital Employed:

Long-term debt and other obligations (notes 9, 17)	1,219	1,034
Commitments and contingent liabilities (note 11)		
Deferred income taxes (note 5)	1,607	1,617
	2,826	2,651
Shareholders' equity:		
Common shares (note 18)	1,400	1,423
Earnings retained and used in business		
At beginning of year	3,268	3,644
Earnings for year	644	285
Dividends	(268)	(262)
At end of year	3,644	3,667
Total shareholders' equity	5,044	5,090
Total sources of capital employed	$ 7,870	$ 7,741

Summary of Significant Accounting Policies

The company provides one and a half pages of notes on significant accounting policies. They are mainly intended to point out which of several acceptable policies the Company has adopted in particular instances. For example, inventories are carried at the lower of cost or net realizable value.

IMPERIAL OIL LIMITED
Summary of Notes to Financial Statements

3. The company engages in *swaps* of petroleum products with other oil companies and shows the net amount receivable as a result of these swaps. The amounts shipped are not treated as sales, but instead are netted out through cost of goods sold. Apparently the company does not think that the realization test has been met in these swaps.

6. This note gives details of the assets owned by the company by major category and shows the depreciation by category as well.

9. This note gives the detail on the amounts and terms of the outstanding long-term debt. This might be used by the analyst trying to forecast significant future cash flows through redemptions.

10. In 1986 the company announced plans to reduce its work force and made a charge to earnings of $90 million as a result. Since this did not result in an outflow of cash, only the actual cash portion of $29 million is shown.
   Denominated bonds in $U.S. issued at $280 million were redeemed in 1986 at a cost of $315 million, for a net charge to income of $65 million. As explained above, the funds provided by operations were shown exclusive of these non-cash charges. Therefore the full amount of the cash outflow from the redemption, $315 million, is shown here.

11. This note essentially says that there are no long-term contractual obligations and commitments and no pending lawsuits that would significantly affect the company's financial position and/or earnings.

17. Exxon Corporation is a major shareholder in Imperial Oil. Hence any dealings with Exxon fall under the *related company* category and must be reported in accordance with the *CICA Handbook*.
18. This note shows in detail the changes in shares from the beginning to the end of the year and explains the difference between the Class A and Class B shares.

Summary

In this chapter we have given an overall survey of the balance sheet and explained some of the basic ideas behind it. In general, as one goes down the asset side of the balance sheet, the assets become less liquid and our ability to put a meaningful valuation on them using the cost convention becomes weaker. We also introduced the statement of changes in financial position and showed how it was constructed by starting with the comparative balance sheets.

QUESTIONS

Q3-1. Review and be sure you understand the following terms:

a. proprietorship versus entity

b. asset

c. liability

d. owners' equity

e. cash

f. short-term investments

g. accounts receivable and notes receivable

h. types of inventory

i. prepaid expense

j. plant asset

k. long-term investments

l. intangible asset

m. depreciation versus amortization

n. executory contract

o. current liability

p. net current asset

q. accounts payable

r. accrued liability

s. deferred income tax

t. common versus preferred shares

u. cumulative preferred shares

v. working capital

Q3-2. Can you see any problems in the method used by the merchants in the Middle Ages to prepare their balance sheets? Can you see it being applied to preparing the balance sheet for an average-sized Canadian Tire store?

Q3-3. It is said of balance sheets that they leave off as much as they include. What items of economic importance might be omitted from the balance sheet of Imperial Oil Limited?

Q3-4. A company has legal title to a truck. Under what conditions would it not be included as an asset for balance-sheet purposes?

Q3-5. Explain the conditions, if any, under which the following might be treated as either a current or non-current asset:

a. a delivery truck

b. cash in the bank

c. common stock of Imperial Oil Limited

d. a television set

e. a down payment on a special order

f. a $300,000 payment to purchase a right to use a patent

Q3-6. Would communist bloc countries be more inclined to favour the entity or proprietorship approach to the balance sheet? Explain.

Q3-7. Explain how prepaid rent might be *an artifact of the matching process*.

Q3-8. Give examples of current assets that have one of the following characteristics:

a. no likely market value

b. no physical existence

c. not likely to be converted into cash or used within the next twelve months.

Q3-9. Give examples of current liabilities that have one of the following characteristics:

a. amount owed not known for certain

b. no persons can be identified to whom the liability is owed

c. not likely to be paid or otherwise discharged within the next twelve months.

Q3-10. "If shareholders' equity on the balance sheet does not represent the equity of the shareholders in the company, what is the use of having it?" Discuss.

Q3-11. It is said that the balance sheet is different from all other financial statements in that it deals with *stocks* of assets at a *point* in time, whereas other financial statements deal with *flows* of assets over a *period* of time. Illustrate this through an example by comparing the treatment of finished goods inventory in the balance sheet and income statement.

Q3-12. In the early days of its operations, the Ford Motor Company ran out of cash even though it was very profitable. How might this have happened? Could the statement of changes in financial position have helped to analyse this problem? How?

Q3-13. Many financial reports used to include a *statement of source and application of funds*. It was essentially a statement of changes in financial position that omitted any transactions that did not involve working capital directly. For instance, buying a plant asset through issuing long-term bonds would be omitted. Do you think the present statement is more useful than the statement of source and application of funds? Explain.

Q3-14. "The reason that liabilities are shown on the right-hand side of many balance sheets is because of the conservatism convention." Discuss.

Q3-15. "The purpose of adding notes to the balance sheet is to provide supplementary information that is not important enough to put in the financial statements themselves." Do you agree? Why?

Q3-16. The statement of changes in financial position is of doubtful accuracy because the amount shown as the net flow of funds depends entirely on what is chosen as the definition of "funds." Discuss.

Q3-17. The fact that a balance sheet balances is really not very impressive. It only happens because owners' equity is forced to equal the amount needed to balance the statements. Do you agree? Discuss.

Q3-18. A prepaid expense, such as prepaid insurance or prepaid taxes, usually arises in cases where the firm must prepay the expenses or suffer a financial penalty (e.g., insurance must be purchased in advance for a twelve-month period in order to get the normal quoted rates). Does the prepaid portion at the end of the fiscal year represent a future benefit to the firm? Or is it simply something created through the workings of the matching process? If the latter, should it be treated as an asset? Discuss.

Q3-19. Give examples of liabilities that are discharged by the following means:

a. payment of cash

b. providing assets other than cash to the creditor

c. providing services of the company

Q3-20. A reason frequently given for the accountant's adoption of the conservatism convention is that "it protects the reader of the statements." Evaluate this statement, indicating when the convention might protect the reader and when it might hurt the reader.

Q3-21. Compare and contrast the usefulness of a company's balance sheet and statement of changes in financial position to each of the following readers:

a. a passive investor

b. a bondholder

c. a short-term creditor such as a bank

d. the management of the company

EXERCISES

E3-1. Are the following assets, liabilities, or something else for the companies involved? Are they current or non-current? Explain.

a. A company has signed a contract to supply cars to a Middle East country. The manufacture of the cars has not yet been started because the purchaser is refusing to provide the down payment required by the contract.

b. A truck was ordered to be added to the company's fleet of delivery trucks. A deposit of $1,000 was given to the supplier, to be applied as part payment for the total purchase price of $34,000 when the truck arrives.

c. A newspaper sold a subscription to start in four weeks. The customer has paid $120, which entitles her to delivery of the paper for twenty-five weeks.

d. A company that operated a chain of fast-food stores had a program of acquiring attractive sites for future stores as the land became available. The company had no immediate plans to develop these sites and rented them to anyone who would take them on a short-term lease. As of the balance-sheet date, it had thirty such sites with a total cost of $3,000,000.

E3-2. Are the following recognized as liabilities under GAAP? If not, should they be? Explain.

    a. A reputation for being a poor employer.

    b. A reputation for not paying bills on time.

    c. A contract in which the firm must deliver merchandise to a customer next year. No deposit has been received from the customer.

    d. A contract in which the firm must deliver merchandise to a customer next year. A deposit of $300 has been received from the customer.

    e. Bond certificates on hand but not yet issued.

E3-3. Indicate whether according to GAAP each of the following is (i) an asset, (ii) a liability, (iii) owners' equity, or (iv) none of these.

    a. retained earnings   **f.** finished goods inventory

    b. accrued wages payable   **g.** patents

    c. accounts receivable   **h.** technological know-how

    d. accrued interest receivable   **i.** trade secrets

    e. accrued interest payable

E3-4. Indicate whether according to GAAP each of the following is (i) an asset, (ii) a liability, (iii) owners' equity, or (iv) none of these.

    a. delivery truck   **e.** work-in-process inventory

    b. preferred shares   **f.** franchise for a hockey team

    c. a major lawsuit about to go to trial   **g.** contributed surplus

    d. prepaid insurance   **h.** licence to operate a cable TV system

E3-5. State whether the following would be regarded for accounting purposes as (i) an asset, (ii) a liability, or (iii) neither. If it is an asset or a liability, state whether it is current or non-current. Explain your answer.

    a. Portsmouth Corporation has paid $38,000 for excavation work connected with putting up a new building. The company intends to bury large storage tanks on the property and now has three large holes in the ground.

    b. Selby Limited was owed $10,000 by Yarker Corporation. Selby received and deposited at the bank a cheque for $10,000 on the last business day of its financial year. At the time, Selby did not know that the following week the cheque would be charged back to the Selby bank account because Yarker did not have sufficient funds in its account to cover the cheque.

    c. Ace Road Construction recently acquired a bulldozer. Payment was made not with cash but by trade. Ace built an access road to Deuce Limited's storage yard and in return received a used bulldozer that Deuce was not using.

    d. Calabogie Limited has ordered a delivery van costing $18,000. They have signed a contract to purchase the van, the dealer has ordered it from the factory, and it is expected to arrive before the end of the month. Calabogie is a good customer and so was not required to make a down payment; it has no intention of backing out of the deal.

E3-6. Identify the balance-sheet items that typically require amplification in the notes to the financial statements. What extra information would you expect to find? Why is this information needed? (*Hint*: Examine some financial statements actually issued by companies.)

E3-7. Imagine that a company's balance sheet for the end of the current year is unavailable, but the balance sheet for the end of the previous year can be obtained.

    a. What could you infer about the amounts on the missing balance sheet if you had this year's (i) income statement? (ii) statement of changes in financial position (prepared on a cash bases)? (iii) statement of changes in retained earnings?

    b. What balance-sheet amounts would you probably still not be able to infer even if you had *all* of the above statements?

E3-8. It has been said that the important characteristic of an asset from the point of view of the entity using it is not whether the entity has legal title to it but whether the entity "bears the risk and is in a position to reap the rewards from possession of the asset." Evaluate whether this point of view makes sense in the following situations:

    a. A bank has $1,000 in cash in a safe-deposit box. The cash was put there by a customer who has rented the box.

    b. The same bank has $1,000 in cash in a teller's drawer. It has just been put there after a customer came in and deposited it to the customer's account.

    c. A computer company has installed a new automatic teller machine at the bank. The bank has not agreed to buy the machine, but the computer company is hoping that the bank will be so pleased with the operation of the machine that it ultimately will make the sale.

    d. The same computer company had installed computer terminals for the tellers four years ago. They had an expected life of five years and were rented to the bank on a five-year non-cancellable lease. Legal title to the machines is held by the computer company.

    e. The bank lent $1,000 in cash to a customer. Under the agreement with the customer, the $1,000 has to be returned within 30 days with interest at 16% annually.

E3-9. Shown below is a summarized 19X7 income statement for the R.E. Company.

Total revenue	$ 1,000,000
Total expenses	750,000
Net income	$ 250,000

    a. Make the necessary journal entries with respect to the following (no narratives are required):

      (i) Close the revenue and expense accounts for the year end 19X7.

      (ii) The company declared a $50,000 dividend prior to the year end.

      (iii) The company paid the dividend during 19X8.

      (iv) In 19X8, it is discovered that a prior-period adjustment is required that increases income taxes payable by $100,000.

    b. What effect do journal entries (iii) and (iv) above have on the company's 19X8 income statement?

E3-10. The following balance sheet was prepared by a person who was familiar with straightforward bookkeeping but not with standard balance-sheet presentation. How many things can you find that ought to be changed? Explain your preferred treatment of each.

TRAYMOR COMPANY
BALANCE SHEET

For the Period Ending 31 December 19X9
(in thousands of $)

Assets

Cash on hand and in bank	$ 21	
Accounts receivable	56	
Inventory, at cost	81	$ 158
Plant assets	251	
Less accumulated depreciation	124	127
Other assets		
Short-term investments	24	
Plant assets under construction	36	60
		$ 345

Liabilities

Bank loan	$ 36	
Bonds payable	58	
Income taxes payable	36	$ 130

Owners' Equity
Retained earnings
Share capital:

Preferred shares	80	
Common shares	135	215
		$ 345

PROBLEMS

P3-1. In the Middle Ages merchants used to prepare balance sheets by making a list of all their possessions and their debts. Assume that a married couple (no children, both working, twenty-five years old) spent part of last weekend doing something similar and came up with the following list.

	Cost	Resale Market Value
Car — three years old, needs new tires, but otherwise in reasonable shape	$ 7,650	$ 2,800 to 3,000
Stereo — excellent working order, but four years old and lacking some recent features	1,430	750 (?)
Cash in bank	1,235	
Cash on hand	124	
Canada Savings Bonds	400	
Owing on Visa account	350	
Contents of apartment not listed above	4,320	2,000

Required:

a. Prepare a balance sheet from the above list, making whatever assumptions are necessary to produce one according to GAAP.

b. Assess the usefulness of this balance sheet, giving reasons.

c. Describe possible methods of valuing assets and liabilities other than the one you actually used above. Assess the usefulness of the alternatives, after stating what your criteria for *usefulness* are.

P3-2. Shown below is a condensed comparative balance sheet for Stella Corporation. Assume there was no disposition of plant assets and there were no dividends.

Required:

a. Prepare a statement of changes in financial position using working capital as the definition of funds.

b. Prepare a statement of changes in financial position using *cash* as the definition of funds (i.e., cash on hand less bank loan).

c. Write a one-paragraph explanation of how the two statements prepared above might complement each other.

	19X5	19X4
Cash	$ 18,000	$ 10,000
Other current assets	98,000	65,000
Plant assets	200,000	150,000
Accumulated depreciation	(50,000)	(30,000)
Bank loan	(16,000)	(25,000)
Other current liabilities	(50,000)	(35,000)
Long-term debt	(100,000)	(80,000)
Share capital	(35,000)	(25,000)
Retained earnings	(65,000)	(30,000)
	$ 0	$ 0

P3-3. Here is a condensed statement of changes in financial position for the Marysville Corporation for the year 19X7.

Sources of Funds	
Income after taxes	$ 64,000
Add: depreciation	36,000
	100,000
Share capital issued	9,500
Sale of plant assets at net book value (historic cost was $20,000)	5,000
Long-term debt issued	16,000
	130,500
Uses of Funds	
Purchase of plant assets	65,000
Dividend paid	25,000
	90,000
Net Funds Provided During the Year	$ 40,500

Here is a condensed balance sheet for the Marysville Corporation at the beginning of 19X7.

Cash	$ 13,000
Other current assets	84,500
Plant assets	195,000
Accumulated depreciation	(39,000)
Bank loan	(32,500)
Other current liabilities	(45,500)
Long-term debt	(104,000)
Share capital	(32,500)
Retained earnings	(39,000)
	$ 0

Required:

a. Prepare the balance sheet as of the end of 19X7. Show all your calculations.

b. Prepare a statement of changes in financial position using cash as the definition of "funds." Some end-of-year balances are cash, $46,000; other current assets, $87,000; bank loan, $22,500; and other current liabilities, $50,500.

P3-4. Using the information supplied below, prepare a balance sheet in account form using the format shown for Imperial Oil Limited in the text. Credit balances are shown in parentheses.

	19X7	19X6
Retained earnings	$ (25,165)	$ (30,213)
Work in process	125,483	85,412
Accumulated depreciation	(26,897)	(25,148)
Bonds payable — due in three years	(95,000)	(89,000)
Customer deposits	(4,521)	(2,589)
Cash	12,587	8,592
Prepaid expenses	1,254	2,356
Raw materials	12,547	10,256
Property and plant	285,089	270,268
Delivery equipment	25,481	16,895
Patents	1,254	5,689
Bank loan	(56,188)	(28,094)
Finished goods	8,512	5,684
Common shares issued	(56,000)	(45,000)
Accounts payable	(128,562)	(145,256)
Accounts receivable	45,126	65,148
Mortgage payable	(120,000)	(100,000)
Preferred shares	(5,000)	(5,000)
	$ 0	$ 0

P3-5. Using the information supplied below, prepare a balance sheet in report form. Use the same convention for inserting dollar signs and underlining as shown in the text for Imperial Oil Limited. Credit balances are shown in parentheses.

	19X7	19X6
Common stock	$ (10,000)	$ (10,000)
Accounts receivable	58,192	78,136
Income tax payable	(15,128)	(14,895)
Short-term deposits	15,741	13,265
Dividend payable	(3,500)	(5,891)
Finished goods	78,152	65,123
Property and plant	85,189	78,156
Contributed surplus	(15,000)	(15,000)
Cash	18,975	13,564
Mortgage receivable — due in three months	18,000	19,000
Bonds payable — due in six months	(58,942)	(68,745)
Accounts payable	(158,268)	(145,789)
Accumulated depreciation	(15,000)	(9,411)
Supplies	1,589	2,487
	$ 0	$ 0

P3-6. Right and Left, Chartered Accountants, is a local accounting firm which services small and medium-sized clients in the community. Mr. Ed Sinclair, the owner of an auto body shop, is a new client. He arrives at the office with a large box filled with receipts and "anything he thinks looks like accounting stuff." As a student in accounts, you have been assigned by the partners the task of preparing the financial statements that Mr. Sinclair needs.

Required:

a. Using the information provided below, prepare the financial statements. If you think additional information is required, then identify this need, make a reasonable assumption, and proceed.

b. Comment on the usefulness of the accounting information available to Mr. Sinclair during the year and that available to him after Right and Left have completed their work.

c. Make practical recommendations that Mr. Sinclair can implement which will improve the usefulness of his accounting information.

Contents of Box

(i) Twenty-five customer invoice copies. Mr. Sinclair uses pre-numbered invoices and number 40 was used on 24 November. You total the invoices with the following results:

Revenue (auto body work)	$ 6,678.00
Revenue (parts)	$ 925.00
Revenue (unidentified)	$ 213.00
Sales tax charged	$ 543.00

All accounts were paid by cash or cheque.

(ii) Monthly bank statements June through November (the balance as at 30 November is an overdraft of $249.72). From these statements you determine the following totals for the period:

Deposits	$ 6,188.00
Cheques	$ 5,235.00
Cash withdrawals	$ 615.00
Bank charges	$ 87.98

(iii) Cheques returned from the bank. You group the cheques by supplier and total. Your summary is as follows:

North Industrial Supply	$ 888.00
South Landholdings	$ 3,200.00
Tom West (employee)	$ 922.00
Corporation of East City	$ 225.00

(iv) Invoices from suppliers which you summarize as follows:

North Industrial Supply	$ 1,276.00
High and Low Freight	$ 125.00

(v) Several deposit slips, only one of which is dated in November ($658 on the 25th). This includes a cheque for $390 from Mr. Downandout. There is a notice from the bank dated 4 December indicating that this cheque was returned NSF.

(vi) Retail sales tax forms indicating that a sales tax of 7% on all sales of parts is to be collected and remitted monthly to the government by the 15th of the following month.

Additional Information (obtained from a conversation with Mr. Sinclair)

(vii) The garage opened on 1 April of the current year.

(viii) Mr. Sinclair used his own funds to buy the equipment necessary to start up the business (about $1,500) but "takes cash from the register when he needs to buy groceries on the way home." He thinks depreciation should be straight line over five years.

(ix) Mr. Sinclair estimates that he spends about $50 per month of his own money on company expenses.

P3-7. Financial statements for the fiscal year 19X2 for Law Supply Corp. have just been prepared. Balance Sheets for 19X2 and 19X1 are shown below.

	19X2		19X1	
Current Assets				
Cash	$ 25,000		$ 15,000	
Marketable securities	42,000		30,000	
Accounts receivable	52,000		42,000	
Inventory	66,200	$ 185,200	61,300	$ 148,300
Land, buildings, and equipment	100,500		96,000	
Accumulated depreciation	34,000		30,000	
		66,500		66,000
Investments		32,000		35,000
Goodwill				25,000
Total Assets		$283,700		$274,300
Bank loan		$ 26,700		$ 17,200
Accounts payable		31,100		26,100
Bond Payable				50,000
Unamortized bond discount				(1,250)
Preferred shares ($100 par)				50,000
Common shares		206,000		105,000
Retained earnings		19,900		27,250
Total Liabilities and Equity		$ 283,700		$ 274,300

Suppose that you are given the following additional information:

(1) The premium on retirement of preferred shares is $1,000.

(2) Dividends of $17,500 were paid during the year. Net income was $11,150.

(3) Fully depreciated equipment which had originally cost $10,500 was traded in during the year for new equipment worth $15,000. A trade-in of $1,500 was allowed.

(4) Two hundred preferred shares of Bradshaw Aluminum Co. which had cost $20,000 were sold at a loss of $2,500 at the start of the year.

(5) The purchase of bonds of Alexis Boat Lines accounted for the rest of the change in the investment account.

(6) Common stock was issued during the year to retire the preferred shares at $102 each. An additional $50,000 of common stock was issued for cash.

(7) The outstanding bond was called during the year at a 5% premium.

(8) The discount that had been amortized to the time of the call was $250.

(9) Depreciation for the year was $14,500.

(10) The goodwill on the books in 19X1 was judged worthless and was written off.

(11) All changes in cash and cash equivalents arose from operating activities.

Required: Prepare a statement of changes in financial position using cash and cash equivalents as the definition of funds. Show all calculations.

P3-8. Stratton and Bolton are partners in the sporting goods business. They are preparing their financial statements for the year ended 31 December, 19X1. They are having trouble preparing their statement of changes in financial position.
The balance sheets for 19X1 and 19X0 are shown below.

	19X1	19X0
Cash	$ 5,800	$ 4,350
Accounts receivable	10,000	11,900
Inventory	45,000	30,000
Land, buildings, and equipment	25,800	16,000
Accumulated depreciation	(13,950)	(10,500)
Total assets	$ 72,650	$ 51,750
Accounts payable	$ 10,250	$ 11,850
Mortgage	7,000	0
J. Stratton, capital	20,550	19,550
D. Bolton, capital	34,850	20,350
Total liabilities and equity	$ 72,650	$ 51,750

You are also given the following additional information:

(1) Net income during the year was $30,000 and was put into both capital accounts equally.

(2) During the year, $9,800 of equipment was purchased. The purchase was financed with a chattel mortgage.

(3) Other changes in the capital accounts are due to withdrawals made by the partners.

Required: Prepare the statement of changes in financial position for the year ended 31 December 19X1 using cash and cash equivalents as the definition funds.

P3-9. Balance sheets for 19X1 and 19X0 for the McIntyre Poster Company are shown below. The only task now remaining is to construct the statement of changes in financial position. The following necessary information is also presented:

(1) During the year, land worth $9,400 was purchased.

(2) Buildings which had cost $48,000 originally were sold. Accumulated depreciation on the buildings amounted to $36,000, and the gain from the sale was $23,070.

(3) Depreciation for the year was $22,000.

(4) Long-term debt of $14,000 was retired during the year.

	19X1	19X0	Difference
Current Assets			
Cash and short-term investments	$ 24,000	$ 35,000	$ (11,000)
Accounts receivable	64,440	7,900	56,540
Inventories	91,500	117,120	(25,620)
Prepaid expenses	720	8,600	(7,880)
Total current	180,660	168,620	12,040
Non-current Assets			
Land	69,600	60,200	9,400
Buildings	72,000	120,000	(48,000)
Depreciation	(22,200)	(36,200)	14,000
Long-term investments	12,600	12,600	0
Total non-current assets	132,000	156,600	(24,600)
Total Assets	$ 312,660	$ 325,220	$ (12,560)
Current Liabilities			
Accounts payable	$ (41,220)	$ (49,020)	$ 7,800
Income tax payable	(12,960)	(8,100)	(4,860)
Notes payable — short term	(15,000)	(12,060)	(2,940)
Total current liabilities	(69,180)	(69,180)	0
Long-term Debt			
Total long-term debt	(48,000)	(62,000)	14,000
Capital Stock			
Common	(180,000)	(180,000)	0
Retained earnings			
Start of year	(14,040)	(11,280)	(2,760)
Net income/year	(15,840)	(6,760)	(9,080)
Dividends	14,400	4,000	10,400
End of year	(15,480)	(14,040)	(1,440)
Total owners' equity	(195,480)	(194,040)	(1,440)
Total Liabilities and Owners' Equity	$(312,660)	$(325,220)	$ 12,560)

Required:

a. Determine the proceeds from the sale of the buildings.

b. Construct a statement of changes in financial position (using cash and equivalents for funds).

P3-10. Shown below are some of the financial statements of Watts Equipment Rental. Part of the balance sheet for 19X2 was run over by a tractor and destroyed. The surviving portion is shown.

You are also given the following additional information:

(1) During 19X2, equipment which had cost $35,300 some time before was sold for $33,860. There was accumulated depreciation of $34,240 on the equipment.

(2) Bonds worth $80,000 which had been issued at par were redeemed during the year at par.

(3) Goodwill is amortized at a rate of $5,000 per year.

(4) Preferred shares with a book value of $34,000 were redeemed during the year at par.

(5) A cash dividend of $15,000 was paid during the year.

(6) The bank reconciliations showed balances of $36,000 at the start of the year and $45,000 at the end. There was no bank loan outstanding at either date.

WATTS EQUIPMENT RENTAL
Balance Sheets

	19X1	19X2
Current assets	$ 107,850	$ 123,970
Land, buildings, and equipment	878,900	
Accumulated depreciation	(481,500)	
Goodwill	30,000	
Total Assets	$ 535,250	
Current liabilities	$ 145,250	$ 106,310
Bond payable	180,000	
Mortgage payable	50,000	
Preferred shares	70,000	
Common shares	40,000	
Retained earnings	50,000	
Total Liabilities and Equity	$ 535,250	

WATTS EQUIPMENT RENTAL
Partial Income Statement
Year Ended 31 December 19X2

Gross profit	$ 310,960
Less: Expenses	
Selling and administrative	127,960
Depreciation	38,000
Goodwill	5,000
Net Income	$ 140,000

Required: Complete the balance sheet for 19X2 and prepare a statement of changes in financial position in a format consistent with GAAP.

P3-11. The following is a balance sheet for the N. Kerr Cauliflower Factory with the items listed in alphabetical order. You will have to decide which are debits and which are credits. Some account balances are missing.

THE N. KERR CAULIFLOWER FACTORY
Consolidated Balance Sheet

Accounts payable	(missing)
Accrued compensation	$ 32,204
Accumulated depreciation	(678,008)
Cash	25,420
Common stock	141,367
Earnings reinvested in the business	(missing)
Inventories	76,884
Long-term debt	(missing)
Marketable securities	94,883
Other long-term assets	(missing)
Other accrued liabilities	81,090
Other non-current liabilities	61,851
Prepaid expenses	72,402
Property, plant, and equipment	(missing)
Receivables	394,170
Short-term debt	66,594
Total assets	1,741,251
Total current assets	(missing)
Total current liabilities	306,693
Total liabilities and shareholders' equity	1,741,251
Total net property, plant, and equipment	997,386
Total non-current liabilities	(missing)
Total shareholders' equity	1,005,008

Required: Find the missing balances and prepare the balance sheet in good form.

P3-12. Michael Taylor, a merchant, kept only limited records. Major purchases including those of merchandise were paid by cheque, but most other disbursements were paid out of cash receipts. Cash in excess of $300 on hand at the end of the week was deposited in the bank. No cash journal was kept; nor was a record kept of sales. A record of accounts receivable was maintained by keeping a copy of the charge ticket. This copy was given to the customer when the account was paid.

Taylor had started business the first week of January 1984 with $50,000 cash. The first week's transactions included the rental of a suitable building at $500 per month with the first payment due on 2 January, the date of the lease. On 5 January, Taylor purchased equipment for $12,000 list price, payable in ten equal monthly instalments of $1,200 each beginning 5 February. Had Taylor paid cash, he would have received a 5% discount on the list price. Taylor estimated that the equipment would be useful for ten years, at which time it would be sold for salvage at $400. On 6 January, merchandise costing $25,000 arrived.

An analysis of the bank statements for the year showed total deposits of $290,000. This amount included the initial investment and a $10,000 loan for which Taylor signed a 12% one-year note dated 30 June. The balance on the bank statement on 31 December, 1984 was $9,400, but there were December-dated cheques amounting to $2,100 not paid by the bank until January. On 31 December 1984 the cash on hand was $300. An inventory of merchandise taken on 31 December 1984 showed $36,800 at cost. Tickets for accounts receivable totaled $8,400, but $380 of that amount is probably not collectible. Customers ordered special merchandise not carried in stock by depositing 50% of the selling price. As at 31 December, $400 of such advances by customers were outstanding. Unpaid suppliers' invoices for merchandise amounted to $8,200. Taylor paid himself, in cash, a salary of $200 per week (for 52 weeks). Other cash disbursements were as follows:

Utilities	$ 1,400
Telephone	320
Advertising	420
Sales personnel (part-time)	8,800

Analysis of the cheque stubs indicated that cheques were drawn for the following:

Monthly rental payments
Monthly payments for equipment
Merchandise purchases
Business taxes for the year, $500
Three-year insurance policy dated 1 February 1984 on equipment and
    contents. The premium for the three years was $1,800.
Delivery service, $1,100

At year-end, Taylor estimated that for December unpaid utilities amounted to $150 and unpaid delivery service amounted to $100.

Early in January 1985, the banker phoned Taylor and requested a set of financial statements. Taylor felt that he did not have the time or knowledge to prepare the requested statements in good form. He has engaged you to prepare the statements for him.

Required:

Prepare the balance sheet and income statement for the year ended 31 December 1984. (*Hint*: Set up the balance sheet and income statement formats and fill in as many of the amounts as you can determine.)

(CGA adapted)

BIBLIOGRAPHY

ALDERMAN, WAYNE; GUY, DAN M.; and MEALS, D.R. "Other Comprehensive Bases of Accounting Alternatives to GAAP?" *Journal of Accountancy* (August 1982). An examination of accounting standards that differ from GAAP.

GOURLAY, GLEN I. "Making Financial Reports More Decision Oriented." *CA Magazine* (February 1984). On designing financial reports for specific management users.

SALOLE, A.R. "Trends in Financial Reporting." *CA Magazine* (June 1982). A comparison of reporting practices of companies and the *CICA Handbook* recommendations.

CHAPTER 4
Income Statements

Introduction

An **income statement** is a financial statement summarizing the items of revenue, income, expenses, gains, and losses for an accounting period. It connects with the statement of retained earnings, which reconciles the opening and closing balance of this balance-sheet item. It is also called an **earnings statement** or **operating statement**. Because the income statement connects with the statement of retained earnings, the amount of net income or loss can be determined from the change in retained earnings from successive balance sheets, after adjusting for the impact of dividends and prior-period adjustments. The income statement can therefore be thought of as a detailed explanation of the operations component of the changes in retained earnings.

In this chapter we address the questions: What interpretations can be put on the term "income"? How should it be measured? In what ways can the calculation of income be reported on the income statement?

Measurement of income is at the heart of accounting reporting, and it is a concept that needs to be carefully evaluated.

Models of the Firm

A **model** is a simplified view of some relatively complex system that we wish to study. Usually the real system is so complex that if we studied it in its entirety, we would soon bog down in detail. Over the centuries people have learned how to make simplified models of complex relationships. These simplified models are easier to work with. By suppressing most of the detail, they permit concentration on the issues that are important for the decision at hand. Consider the following examples:

1. A road map kept in the glove compartment of most cars is a simplified model of the terrain. It does not show a lot of detail, such as hills, radio stations, or the depth of bodies of water in the region covered by the map. For a car trip it is perfectly adequate, and the additional information would simply clutter it up. However, a

person planning a bicycle trip would find the detail on hills of interest; an aviator would be interested in radio stations; and a sailor would be interested in the depth of bodies of water. For each of them there would be a specialized map, which suppresses some details in order to concentrate on others.

2. A model of the solar system concentrates on the size and position of the sun and the planets, identifying them as the key elements. It treats the mass, position, and velocity as important elements. It enables accurate predictions to be made where each of these planets will be, say, two years from now. It is a highly useful model, even though it completely ignores other very real aspects of the solar system, such as human life.

3. An organization chart of a company is a tree-like diagram that shows the reporting relationships within the organization. It can be used to predict how authority flows through the organization and what the formal communication links are. As organization theorists are quick to point out, however, it does not reflect the informal organization, with the unplanned flows of information that arise through friendships, family relationships, or sharing an adjacent office.

The point of all these examples is that ease of analysis was obtained by suppressing much of the other available detail. How much detail one ought to give up to achieve ease of analysis is a cost-benefit issue that has to be settled in each case. Working with a simplified version of the real thing is a sacrifice we make through deliberate choice. By definition, all models are "unrealistic" in that they leave out elements of the real system under study. What we ask of them is that in a given context they should be useful in (i) identifying the key elements of the system; (ii) suggesting ways of measuring these elements; and (iii) suggesting possible cause-and-effect relationships between the elements to allow us to make predictions of future outcomes.

Just as we model physical aspects of systems such as the solar system, so we can also model economic aspects of organizations such as businesses and non-profit entities. In this text we concentrate mainly on profit-seeking organizations and we use accounting as a system for identifying, measuring, and interrelating certain variables within those organizations. Like any model, accounting will measure only selected aspects of the real organization. Therefore, we should judge it for its usefulness rather than its completeness in portraying the "real" company.

If usefulness is to be the test of the quality of the accounting model, then we have to ask, Useful to whom? If we can settle that question, it will help to indicate what things can be usefully measured and what measurement standards to use. One correct answer to the question is, "Probably everyone"; but some limit has to be placed on the variety of groups to be served in order to keep the model workable. Thus, more specifically, the two most common answers are (i) the shareholders and (ii) the management. Let us now examine the differences in approaching the models that arise from these two different perspectives.

Shareholders' Perspective

Here the first assumption is that the group being reported to are the owners of the entity, the shareholders who bear the risk. This suggests that one should think of the firm as a collection of assets and liabilities, with the owners having the right to the net assets. That is,

Owners' Equity = Total Assets − Total Liabilities

Suppose we want to answer the question, Is the firm as well off at the end of the year as it was at the beginning? The test would be whether the ownership equity is as great at the end of the year as it was at the beginning. For example, suppose that the owners started the beginning of the year with $500 and borrowed another $500 from the bank to buy $1,000 in inventory. Further assume that at the end of the year the general price level was 10% higher but the inventory was worth $1,200. We could calculate the owners' equity at the end of the year as follows:

Owners' Equity = 1,200 − 500 = 700

Thus, the monetary increase in equity was $700 less $500, or $200. However, since prices had gone up 10%, there was an erosion of $50 in the purchasing power of the original equity contributed by the owners. We might summarize our analysis of this example as follows:

Profit on $500 of owners' capital invested in inventory	$ 100
Profit on $500 of money borrowed from bank and invested in inventory. (This profit goes to the equity owners because they bore the risk.)	100
Total monetary profit for ownership equity	$ 200
Less: Decline in purchasing power of investment in equity of $500	50
Real profit for ownership equity after adjustment for change in purchasing power of money	$ 150

This is known as the **proprietorship** view of the firm. (Recall our discussion at the beginning of Chapter 3.) The firm is simply regarded as an extension of its owners. The managers of the firm are ideally acting in the owners' best interests. This is frequently referred to as the **stewardship** role of management. If we ask whether the firm is any better off at the end of a year's operation, we are essentially asking the question on behalf of the equity owners.

Management Perspective

An alternative view is that the shareholders are just one of the many suppliers of capital to the firm. The creditors of the firm are the other suppliers. This is the viewpoint that might be adopted by the managers of a firm as they weigh the least-cost methods of raising capital. This approach can be expressed as follows:

Owners' Equity + Liabilities = Total Assets

While it is admitted that the equity owners bear more risk than the creditors, it is argued that this is simply a matter of degree and that creditors bear risk in varying degrees too. Under this view the firm is not regarded as an extension of the equity owners but as something at arm's length from them.

This is known as the **entity** view of the firm. (Recall our discussion at the beginning of Chapter 3.) It becomes more difficult to ask whether the firm is any better off after a year's operation, because the equity owners and the creditors might have differing views of what constitutes *better off*. In the preceding example, for instance, the equity owners seem better off by $150; but at the same time the creditors have lost $50 in purchasing power through erosion of the real value of their loan.

It matters what view of the firm one takes, because the usual working definition of income is the amount that can be paid out in dividends and still have the firm *as well off* as it was before. This implies that we need to develop some measure of how *well off* the firm is. We will do this using the *proprietorship* view of the firm since it is conceptually easier to deal with than the entity view.

Income Measurement

Income can be thought of as the amount the firm could pay out to shareholders and still be as well off as it was before. It is the maximum flow of assets that can be sent to the owners while still leaving the same amount of **stock of capital** in the firm. (Note that the word *stock* is used here in the sense of *stocks and flows*; thus the *stock of capital* is quite different in meaning from *capital stock*, which means shares of the company.)

STOCKS AND FLOWS

The connection between stocks and flows can be illustrated by the amount of gold held by the Bank of Canada at any given time. Consider the following sketch:

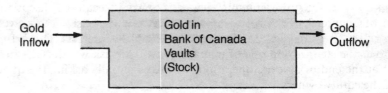

Note that if we know the opening amount of stock and can measure any two of (i) inflow, (ii) outflow, and (iii) change in stock, then we can calculate the amount of the third item. Furthermore, if we know any two of (i) the opening stock, (ii) the closing stock, and (iii) the change in stock for the period, then we can calculate the third. Which two of the three we choose to measure in each case is often based on practical considerations such as cost. For example, if the stock of gold is huge and the outflow and inflow are rather small, it would be easier to determine the amount of gold on hand by measuring the flows, calculating the change, and adding this to the opening stock. It would be more cumbersome to make frequent counts of the closing amounts of the stock — although one would want to do this periodically as a check.

Sometimes the choice is affected by what can reasonably be measured. For example, a house in winter can be thought of as a store of thermal energy that flows out to the cold outside but is replaced by a flow of thermal energy from a heat source such as a furnace. It is very difficult to measure the flow from the house outward (although not impossible); but it is relatively easy to measure the amount of the heat inflow needed to keep the level of thermal energy within the house to some set level, such as 20 degrees Celsius. For that reason we normally state a house's heat outflow in terms of heat inflow required to maintain a certain temperature (e.g., the furnace burned 2,400 litres of oil per year).

Although it is a little more difficult conceptually, it is possible to think of a firm as a *stock* of liabilities and assets. Throughout its operating life, assets and liabilities flow into and out of the firm. We can measure how economically successful the firm is by seeing whether its net stock of assets increases or decreases (after adjusting for capital additions or withdrawals by the owners). Because it is hard to show negative amounts diagrammatically, we will think of liabilities as negative assets and we will use the terms *net assets* or simply *assets* to mean assets minus liabilities. We can represent this approach by the following diagram:

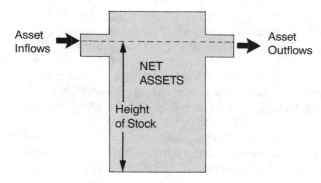

By definition we have,

Owners' equity = Total Assets − Total Liabilities
= Net Assets

Therefore, the measure of net assets shown in the diagram is *also* the measure of owners' equity. Instead of measuring the change in owners' equity directly, we can measure it indirectly by measuring the change in net assets.

In this exposition we will assume that once the original capital has been contributed by the owners, there will be no further additions or withdrawals. In other words, we will assume that change in owners' equity is the result of an income or loss experienced by the firm. It is not necessary to introduce this assumption, but it will simplify our discussion.

MEASURING THE SIZE OF STOCKS

Although the basic notion of *stocks and flows* is the same in both instances, there is a significant difference between the model of the stocks and flows of the gold of a bank and the model of the stocks and flows of the net assets of a firm. Gold is a single commodity, and the amount of the stocks and flows can be easily expressed in physical units of measurement (e.g., in ounces). The net assets of the firm are a mixture of commodities (e.g., inventory, plant assets, and accounts receivable), and there is no meaningful single physical characteristic by which they can all be measured (e.g., if you were told the firm had 3,000 kilos of accounts receivable, what would that mean?). Instead, since we are interested in reporting on the economic aspects of the assets, we assign dollar amounts to each asset according to some rule (to be discussed shortly). Once this has been done, we can add up these assigned dollar amounts.

There are several common rules for assigning dollar amounts to assets. The one chosen in a given situation depends on the definition of *well off* that is being used. The alternative measurement rules, along with the definition of *well off* served by each one, can be summarized as follows:

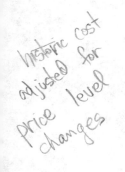

1. All non-cash assets are valued at what was paid for them and liabilities are valued at the cost of the assets that were received for them. As non-cash assets are sold or disposed, they are written off. Assets that are used up in the production process rather than held for sale (e.g., plant assets) are systematically written down over the time they are used. This is the **historic-cost** approach, which most students learn in introductory accounting. How well off the shareholders are is measured by totalling the dollar amounts assigned to the assets and liabilities in the pool according to this historic-cost rule. Income of the firm is the amount that could be taken out while still leaving the stock of net assets (as measured by this system) the same as it was at the beginning of the period. It preserves the owners' original money capital, but in times of inflation this would represent increasingly smaller amounts of purchasing power.

   For example, assume that a company bought a single asset for $1,000 with an expected life of five years. It agreed to rent it out for an annual sum exactly equal to its depreciation. At the end of the five-year period, it would have cash on hand of $1,000. Assume this was returned to the shareholders. They would get back the financial capital they invested, but it might have quite different purchasing power from what they put in five years previously.

2. The second approach is similar to the first, except that the historic costs are adjusted for the change in the purchasing power of the dollar. Income is the amount that can be taken out after the stock at the beginning and end of the period has been adjusted for changes in the value of the money unit. This approach would preserve the investor's money capital adjusted for inflation, something economists call the **real** capital of the investor.

   For example, assume that a company bought a single asset for $1,000 and held it for five years. The asset earned no income, but during a period of rising prices its value just kept pace with inflation, which was 50% over the period. At the end of five years it was sold for $1,500 and this amount was returned to the shareholders. The company used an accounting system that measured historic costs in terms of current dollars. According to this system, the historic cost of the item was $1,500 if stated in units of currency as of the sale. The shareholders got back exactly the same amount of purchasing power they put in. This could be stated as either *$1,000 in first-year dollars* or *$1,500 in fifth-year dollars* because the purchasing power of each was identical.

3. Under the third approach, all assets (liabilities) are valued at what it would cost to replace them (discharge them) as of the current date. The income of the firm is the

amount that could be taken out and still leave enough in the firm to purchase the original stock of net assets at their **current replacement** prices. In this approach, being well off is measured in terms of preservation of the equivalent of the physical stock of assets.

In the example immediately above, let us assume that at the end of the fifth year the asset now had a value of $1,800 instead of the $1,500 (in current dollars) paid for it. If the shareholders want to preserve their physical capital, they should be able to replace the machine in order to be as well off as they were at the start of the operation. The $1,500 they received is not sufficient to purchase an equivalent machine. Hence by the physical capital maintenance test, the shareholders are worse off than when they started.

4. The fourth approach is similar to the third, except that the net stock of assets is measured in terms of their current *selling* price (rather than their current *purchase* price). It is commonly described as a **net realizable value rule** for net asset valuation.

It should be apparent that there are a variety of ways of attaching dollar amounts to non-cash assets. Since non-cash assets make up the bulk of the assets of most firms, it follows that there are significantly different values that could be assigned to the owners' equity, depending on the method used for valuing *well-offness*. Accountants have traditionally used the historic-cost approach outlined above in (1). Nevertheless, alternative approaches have been explored with increasing urgency because of the marked significance of inflation in the 1970s and early 1980s. In Chapter 20 we will explore applications of these other approaches.

For the remainder of this chapter we will develop the traditional income measurement concepts associated with the historic-cost approach.

REVENUE RECOGNITION

We have modelled a firm in terms of stocks and flows of assets and we have emphasized the idea that there is no unique physical characteristic for measuring this bundle of assets. We overcame this by assigning a number to each asset that represents an economic attribute that we believe is worth knowing, such as its historic cost. If we wish to value the firm at a given point in time we could, under the historic-cost approach, make a list of all its assets and liabilities and assign dollar amounts to them on the basis of the amount paid or received, adjusted for depreciation and amortization. While this approach would give us the total dollar amount of the firm's assets and would show by how much the value had changed for the period, it would not analyse the sources of change. To do that, we have to measure and analyse the inflows and outflows that caused the change.

Inflows of assets resulting from providing goods and services to customers of the firm are referred to as **revenue** or **gross income**, and outflows are referred to as **expenses**. Because the difference between the two is the amount of the change in net assets arising from operations, the difference is the **net operating income** of the period. There are often additional items of an infrequent or unusual nature that are added to the net operating income to produce the so-called **net income** for the period.

Unlike the inflow of gold into the vaults of the Bank of Canada, there is no physical measurement for revenue, just as there is no physical measure for the assets of the firm. Furthermore, direct observation will not determine *when* the revenue flows into the firm. Consider, for example, the following tests of revenue recognition:

1. Should it be based on the flow of cash arising from the payments by customers for goods and services? This would be convenient since a cash flow can be determined by observation. However, it is quite common for customers to pay cash before the goods and services have been delivered (e.g., you may be asked to give a store a deposit if you order some special item), and it is very common for customers to pay after delivery (e.g., purchases on credit). Thus using the flow of cash to represent the flow of assets would lead to some unintended distortions.

2. Should it be based on the flow of assets outward to the customers, such as the physical flow of inventory? Although it initially seems paradoxical to measure an inflow of assets based on the outflow of other assets, there is a certain logic to it, because presumably the company would not allow an asset to flow out unless an asset flowed in as compensation. However, at times this system runs into problems for there are occasions when a company will ship inventory on consignment or make a temporary loan of goods to a customer on approval. The customer is obliged to return the same goods only if he decides not to buy them. The inflow of assets on their return is not revenue within the usual meaning of the word.

We pointed out in Chapter 1 in our discussion of the recognition convention that the usual test for revenue recognition rests on the following two conditions: (i) the bulk of the economic activity that is required to supply the goods and services to the customer has been done and (ii) the risk that the customer might not pay, or that the remaining costs cannot be reasonably estimated, is mostly past. This test is not based on the physical flow of assets, although it might be influenced by it. It can be adapted effectively to both types of examples described above.

If the point of sale (the point in time where legal title passes to the purchasers and they take possession of the goods) is taken as the midpoint, we can consider the recognition of revenue along a continuum by distinguishing the following three cases.

1. *Recognition before the point of sale.* This is not a common point of revenue recognition, but it is sometimes used if there is great certainty about the eventual outcome. For instance, the selling price may be fixed or fixable and the production costs may be known with great accuracy. We can further distinguish two types of scenarios:
   a. Some economic activity has taken place, but the flow of goods to the purchaser and/or the flow of payment from the purchaser has not been completed. Consider, for example, a long-term construction contract.
   b. One of the inflows or outflows is incomplete. For example, companies that mine silver or gold may sometimes recognize the profit earned when the costs of production have been incurred and the metal is ready for delivery, even though the metal has not actually been sold.

2. *Recognition at the point of sale.* This is the point where most revenue is recognized. The goods and services are complete when delivered to the customer, and the customer pays or agrees on the sum to be paid in the near future.

3. *Recognition after the point of sale.* The reason for the delay in recognition is that there is some major uncertainty to be resolved, such as the likelihood of being paid or a major production cost to be determined or the ultimate selling price to be set. We can further distinguish two types of scenarios:

a. One of the inflows or outflows is complete, but not the other. For example, in the sale of resort land on a long-term mortgage with a low down payment, there is uncertainty whether the purchaser will complete the mortgage payments or walk away from the deal.

b. Both inflow and outflow of resources is complete, but the economic significance is not established. For example, goods have been delivered and the customer has agreed to pay, but the ultimate selling price is contingent on some event that has not yet happened, such as the behaviour of competitors' pricing.

The flow of revenue into the firm is not a reality, like the flow of gold into the Bank, but an artificial construct of the human mind. The concept has been created because physical phenomena do not measure the economic factors that we want to incorporate in our model. Consequently, there is no point in seeking to find when the revenue was "really" earned, only in asking whether our treatment of revenue recognition is consistent from period to period and whether it conforms to the concept of *well-offness* that we wish to use. Chapter 1 gave several examples of how the timing of revenue recognition might be affected by our desire to measure well-offness in differing ways.

In 1986, Section 3400 on the timing of revenue recognition was added to the *CICA Handbook*. For the most part, this section codifies existing good practice. We can summarize the main points of this section as follows:

1. For transactions involving the sale of goods, revenue should be recognized when (i) the buyer has assumed the significant risks of ownership and (ii) reasonable assurance exists as to the measurement of the consideration that will be derived from the sale (*CICA* 3400.07). Reasonable assurance would apply to both the selling price and the probability of payment. The *Handbook* does not discuss when one should recognize instalment sales.

2. Either the percentage-of-completion or completed-contract method may be used "whichever relates the revenue to the work accomplished." This relationship appears to exist "when reasonable assurance exists regarding the measurement of the consideration that will be derived from rendering the service or performing the long-term contract" (*CICA* 3400.08).

3. The reasonable assurance rule also applies to royalties, interest income, and dividends. Royalties are to be recognized as they accrue according to the terms of the contract. Interest is to be recognized on a time-proportion basis. Dividends are to be recognized "when the shareholder's right to receive payment is established" (*CICA* 3400.09). The *Handbook* does not restrict dividends to the *legal* right to receive dividends; so presumably one may use a broader definition of when the right exists.

4. The amount of revenue earned during the period should be disclosed in the income statement (*CICA* 3400.19). This means that the net income after expenses is not sufficient; both revenues and expenses must be disclosed.

MATCHING CONVENTION

It was explained above how the timing of revenue recognition can be affected by the assumptions that are made or the conventions that are adopted. The matching convention, however, requires that once the revenue recognition method has been adopted, it should be used to control the timing of the expense recognition or the point where the outflow of assets is recognized. The usual way of saying this is that accountants want to match expenses against the revenue earned by them.

Chapter 1 indicated that the assumption that it is always possible to carry out the matching objective is not well founded. It should now be clearer why this is so. We are interested in measuring the outflow of assets in terms of the valuation rule we have adopted (e.g., valued at their historic cost of acquisition). However, while it is relatively easy to identify the historic acquisition costs of assets as they flow into the firm, it is hard to follow the costs of these assets once they enter the stock of assets within the firm. Hence, it is hard to say what their historic costs are as they flow out of the firm. Indeed, it is difficult to say when many of them actually flow out.

This problem arises for two reasons. First, some assets, such as inventory, consist of more or less identical physical units, and it is usually arbitrary which one is identified as the one being sold. Second, plant assets are consumed in the productive process and never really flow out of the firm in the way the model implies, except to the extent that their services are incorporated into the goods and services being produced and sold. To handle this problem we employ a convenient fiction, namely, that these assets depreciate according to some formula. In the historic-cost model the annual outflow is taken to be this depreciation.

Thus, the recognition convention is clearly the starting point and the matching convention comes next. The difference between the deemed inflow of assets arising from revenues and the outflow of assets arising from expenses is, by definition, the income of the company.

EVALUATION OF INCOME MEASURES

Note that we have not been able to arrive at a unique measure of income either by (i) measuring the change in stocks of assets (since there is no unique way of measuring the asset stock) or (ii) by measuring the difference between the inflows and outflows (since the flows are not physically observable phenomena but conceptual artifacts). It is possible to state as an assumption that a particular concept of income will be used, such as the historic-cost convention, but it should be noted that there are other assumptions which may be equally valid. Further, even if we select the historic-cost convention, we are still faced with some arbitrary assumptions about the way assets flow into and then out of the firm.

It is important to keep these difficulties in perspective. Despite them, an insightful and useful way of thinking about the firm has been developed in the accounting model. At the same time, the assumption that the firm can be modelled using stocks of assets and flows of revenues and expenses can only be maintained by further assumptions about how these flows take place. It should not be surprising that reasonable and well-informed people arrive at different decisions about the assumptions that are most appropriate and hence they arrive at different estimates of income.

Analysis of Revenues and Expenses

Measuring the size of the stock of assets at the end of each period (and then calculating the change in that stock over the period) is referred to as the **indirect method of income measurement**. The alternative method, measuring the inflow of revenue and outflow of expenses, is called the **direct method of income measurement**. While neither method leads to a unique measure of income, the direct method does offer the opportunity to analyse the flows. Hence it provides potential information about *why* the change in assets took place. The flow of assets into and out of the firm is generally recorded when some overt economic activity of the firm, or transaction, takes place. Therefore, it is said to be a **transactions-based system**.

REVENUE

Revenue typically arises from two sources: (i) the sale of the company's goods and services and (ii) ownership of assets that yield some form of investment income, such as bonds. **Revenue** should be contrasted with a **gain**, which is the net benefit derived from a transaction or group of transactions that are separate from the normal operating activities of the company (e.g., the gain from the sale of a factory site). Gain is a *net* concept, whereas revenue is a *gross* concept.

Revenue from sales is analysed in great detail for internal reporting purposes in most companies, although the results are greatly summarized in published financial reports (often on the grounds that detailed reporting would help the competition). For internal reporting, the sales are usually analysed by product line and by geographical region (with further subdivisions to the level of salesperson). For external reporting, however, the *CICA Handbook* requirement for public companies is that sales should be reported for each industry segment (not each product line) and for each geographical segment [*CICA* 1700]. Note that this does not require that sales for each industry segment be subdivided again for each geographical area.

Income from other sources includes investment income and government assistance. The *CICA Handbook* requires separate disclosure of income and government assistance. It also requires that investment income should be broken down into seven parts: (i) non-consolidated subsidiaries, (ii) companies subject to significant influence by the investor company, (iii) joint ventures with other companies, (iv) other affiliated companies, (v) portfolio investments, (vi) finance income from capital leases, and (vii) operating leases [*CICA* 1520]. In addition to requiring the above information, the *Handbook* also says that it would be "desirable" to disclose separately the income from contingent rentals (rental income, such as that based on percentage of sales, that is *not* based on the passage of time) and from sub-lease rentals. In later chapters, we will cover the specific issues arising from income reporting for all of the above.

EXPENSES

Conceptually, expenses represent the outflow of assets from the firm. An **expense** should be contrasted with a **loss**, which is the *net* of expense over revenue for a period. For internal reporting, it is common to find expenses broken down by (i) division, (ii) type of expense, (iii) product line, (iv) person responsible for controlling the expense, and (v) objective supported by the expense (especially common in non-profit organizations). For external reporting, the analysis is much more condensed. The *CICA Handbook* [1520] requires separate disclosure for the following expense items:

1. Amount charged for the total of depreciation and depletion of assets plus amortization of leasehold improvements. The rates and method used in computation should also be shown.

2. Amortization of property under a capital lease (explained in Chapter 14).

3. Amortization of deferred charges, with the basis of amortization disclosed.

4. Amortization of intangible assets.

5. Research and development costs.

6. Interest expense, with interest on long-term debt shown separately.

7. Interest expense related to capital lease obligations (this can be included with long-term debt).

8. Gains and losses from normal business activities "which are both abnormal in size and caused by rare or unusual circumstances."

9. Income taxes (see Chapter 13).

10. Minority interest in income or loss (see Chapter 19).

11. Extraordinary items and their related income taxes.

In addition, separate disclosure of the following is considered "desirable":

1. Other major operating expenses, such as selling and administrative expenses.

2. Operating rental expense.

3. Contingent rental expense (rental costs based on some factor other than the passing of time, such as those based on percentage of sales).

4. Foreign currency gains or losses included in income.

There is no requirement to report expenses segmented by product line and geographical area, as there is with revenue. Nevertheless, Section 1700 of the *CICA Handbook* requires operating income to be shown by segments for public companies, so that one can calculate what the total segment expenses must be.

There is no requirement that cost of goods sold should be disclosed, although the *Handbook* describes it as "desirable additional information." In 1985, only 60% of the companies surveyed disclosed this useful piece of information.

Interim Reports

In many jurisdictions, companies are required to report to shareholders with an audited financial statement annually and to furnish income statements each quarter. The latter are usually summarized and unaudited. These quarterly statements are referred to as **interim financial reports**. The purpose of such interim reports is to provide shareholders with information on a more timely basis than they would other-wise receive if they had to wait for the annual statements. Although the purpose is praiseworthy, there is an inescapable risk that arises from the relationships between stocks and flows.

This can be illustrated by going back to the example of gold flows at the Bank of Canada. Let us assume that we wanted to estimate the outflow of gold for the month of January and used the opening and closing stocks and the inflow for the period to make our estimate. Assume also that we wanted to estimate the outflow for the period 1 January to 31 December and that the amounts were as follows:

	January	Twelve months
Opening stock of gold	800,000 oz.	800,000 oz.
Inflow	2,000	24,000
	802,000	824,000
Closing stock of gold	795,000	795,000
Estimated outflow	7,000	29,000

What if there were an error in the opening inventory and it was 1% less than the amount shown, or 8,000 less? The estimated outflow for January would then be 7,000 + 8,000, or 15,000, an error of over 100%. On the other hand, the revised outflow for the whole year would be 29,000 + 8,000, or 37,000, an error of about 28%. We thus have widely differing error rates for the same absolute size of error in the measurement of the stock. Furthermore, the shorter the time period on which we are reporting, the greater the disparity is between the size of the stock and the flow, and the greater the impact of a stock measurement error is on the estimate of the size of the flow.

Recall that the stocks in accounting measurement are not usually physically verifi-able. We attribute some economic measure to them, such as historic cost, which often involves some degree of judgement. For this additional reason, the measurement of income over shorter and shorter periods must be handled with great care.

Uses of Income Measures

It has been said that if you wanted to make money on the stock market, there is no single number that you could ask to know in advance of everyone else that would be more useful to you than the amount of a company's net income. Measurements of net income as well as estimates of what this number might be in the future, therefore, appear to be pivotal to private investment decisions.

Even non-profit organizations such as universities calculate and use measures of net income. Such organizations try to maximize their effectiveness in carrying out their mission, subject to resource constraints. If they run a deficit, this is an indication they are exceeding their available resources; and if they run a surplus, it indicates they are not using the resources available. As a result, non-profit organizations usually aim for a zero net income and use income measurement to monitor their success in so doing.

There is a third type of organization where measurement of income is very useful, and that is the regulated monopoly such as a telephone system or a gas distribution utility. By definition:

Net Income = Total Inflow of Revenue − Total Outflow of Expenses

If the monopoly seller is left uncontrolled, economic theory suggests that such monopolies would pay market prices for the expenses they incur, but set rates (selling prices for their product) that would maximize their net income at the public expense. As a result, there is a public-policy argument in favour of establishing a public rate-setting body that will regulate selling prices for the monopoly, thus regulating the total inflow of revenue. To establish the selling prices that are appropriate the regulation body first decides what net income is appropriate (usually choosing a sum that will give a return on shareholders' investment that seems sufficient to attract investment in that company) and then it decides what rate structure will produce this income.

Form of Income Statements

The usual components of an income statement are shown below:

INCOME STATEMENT — CONTENTS

Sales, income from investments, government assistance
Operating expenses
Depreciation, amortization, research and development, interest expense, gains and losses that are not extraordinary items
Gain or loss on foreign exchange
Income (loss) on continuing operations before taxes
Share of income of unconsolidated or partly owned companies
Income (loss) before income taxes, minority interest and extraordinary items
Provision for income taxes on non-extraordinary items
Income (loss) before minority interest and extraordinary items
Minority interest
Income (loss) before extraordinary items
Extraordinary item (net of income tax)
Net income (loss)

The form and content of the income statement matters because the reader is usually interested in more than just net income for the period. For instance,

1. The reader may be trying to estimate the future earning ability of the company. Here the reader would want to separate out and evaluate items of revenue and expense that appear to be of a non-recurring nature. A distinction in the statement between ordinary operating income and extraordinary gains and losses may well prove helpful.

2. The reader may want to compare one company against others in the same industry, using criteria developed from individual items on the income statement (e.g., gross profit margins or fixed charges as a percentage of sales).

There is no prescribed format for the income statement, only requirements of disclosure. A review of the published income statements of various companies will show that many have given a substantial amount of thought to adapting the format to their industry and making their presentation informative. Some statements are arranged in **multiple steps**, in which the gross margin, operating income before income tax, income tax on operations, net operating income, net income after extraordinary items, and earnings per common share are all shown. By contrast, in the so-called **single-step** statement, all expenses are deducted in a single step.

Extraordinary Items

The accounting meaning of an extraordinary item is more restrictive than its usual meaning. The *Handbook* states that extraordinary items "(1) should include only gains, losses and provisions for losses which, by their nature, are not typical of the normal business activities of the enterprise, or (2) not expected to occur regularly over a period of years and (3) are not considered as recurring factors in any evaluation of the ordinary operations of the enterprise" [*CICA* 3480.05]. If gains or losses are "extraordinary" within the usual meaning of the word, but not within the one above, they would be included as part of the items making up the operating income of the firm; and if they are material, they would be shown separately regardless of size [*CICA* 3480.12]. Examples of items not considered extraordinary are losses with respect to inventory or bad debts, gains or losses from fluctuations in foreign exchange rates, and adjustments with respect to contract prices [*CICA* 3480.12]. Examples of items that are classified as extraordinary are estimated losses from discontinued operations, write-downs of long-term investments, and write-down of goodwill. Extraordinary items are more commonly found on Canadian financial statements. They have been virtually eliminated in the United States.

The accounting treatment of extraordinary items is strongly biased *against* treating an event as "extraordinary" if there were any reasonable possibility that it might have been anticipated. In other words, there is a bias toward treating all gains and losses as part of the normal activities of the company. One could surmise that the accountants' bias arises because of the temptation for management to dismiss as "extraordinary" any loss that they don't feel fully accountable for. However, such an interpretation does not apply as readily to gains.

Extraordinary items should be shown separately and their nature described [*CICA* 3480.10]. The income statement should not only include extraordinary items in income [*CICA* 3480.07], but also show income both before and after extraordinary items [*CICA* 3410.09].

Given the requirement that income be shown both before and after extraordinary items, it is natural to ask which one is more useful to the user. It has been argued that income *before* extraordinary items is the more useful measure because practice is more uniform in calculating income before extraordinary items. However, the rule of classifying an item as extraordinary or not is often difficult to apply, and the decision to classify something as extraordinary or not affects *both* the income measures. In many ways this issue is another illustration that users of this information should inform themselves about the nature of the extraordinary items, should clarify the relevance of the items to the decision they are going to make, and should decide what amounts might be material to their decision.

Adjustments to Income

Despite the accountant's bias against treating an item as extraordinary, there are two items that are regarded as deserving of special treatment: (i) prior-period adjustments and charges; and (ii) credits arising from changes in accounting policy. Both these items bypass the income statement and go directly to retained earnings.

PRIOR-PERIOD ADJUSTMENTS

A **prior-period adjustment** has been defined as "an adjustment disclosed in the current financial statements and applied to one or more prior periods resulting from a gain or loss specifically identified with and directly related to the business activities of particular prior periods. . . ." (*Terminology for Accountants* [1983]). The point about a prior-period adjustment is that for the year in which it is first disclosed, it is usually shown as an item in the statement of retained earnings, not the income statement. The reasoning behind this is that the item has nothing to do with the current year's activities and thus should be excluded. Accountants are naturally uneasy about a reporting system that allows gains and losses to be excluded from the income statement. As a result, there are very restrictive rules about what constitutes a prior period adjustment. There are also retroactivity rules that will be explained below.

For gains or losses to qualify as prior-period adjustments in Canada they must meet *all four* of the following tests [*CICA* 3600.03]:

1. They are specifically identified with and directly related to the business activities of particular prior periods.

2. They are not attributable to economic events (including obsolescence) occurring subsequent to the date of the financial statements for such prior periods.

3. They depend primarily on decisions or determinations by persons other than management or owners.

4. They could not be reasonably estimated prior to such decisions or determinations.

Items that typically meet these four tests include the settlement of income taxes payable for prior periods and the settlement of legal claims for prior-period activities. Items that do not meet all four tests must be reported on the income statement of the current year.

The retroactivity rules state that when the financial statements of the prior periods are published again they must be restated to include the prior-period adjustment. This could be, for example, on the five-year or ten-year summaries that are included in the annual reports.

If a prior-period adjustment is made, the *CICA Handbook* requires disclosure of the following: (i) a description of the adjustment, (ii) the effect on the financial statements of the current and prior periods, and (iii) the fact that the financial statements of prior periods that are presented have been restated [*CICA* 3600.08].

Here is an example of a prior-period adjustment for Gesco Industries Inc. Note that the prior-period adjustment is shown as a separate item in retained earnings because it relates to years prior to the ones reported on here. If a five-year or ten-year summary were shown, the revised tax provision would be included in the year to which they relate, and the years 1980 to 1982 would be restated.

Statement of Retained Earnings

	1984	1983
Retained earnings as previously stated	$ 8,108,793	$ 6,267,644
Prior-period adjustment, reassessment of prior year's taxes	(120,609)	(120,609)
Retained earnings, at beginning of year, restated	7,988,184	6,147,035
Net (loss) income for the year	(365,640)	1,841,149
Retained earnings at end of year	$ 7,622,544	$ 7,988,184

Notes to Financial Statements
9. Prior-period adjustment:
    As a result of income tax reassessments applicable to years 1980 to 1982, the Company paid an additional $120,609 in income taxes in the year. For comparative purposes, the prior year's figures have been restated to reflect this adjustment.

ACCOUNTING CHANGES

On occasion, accounting income can be affected by changes arising through the accounting process itself. In this regard we can distinguish the following: (i) a change in accounting policy, (ii) a change in an accounting estimate, and (iii) the correction of an error in the financial statements of a prior period. Let us now discuss the recommended treatment of each of these.

Changes in Accounting Policy

A change in accounting policy includes such things as changing the method of inventory valuation from last-in-first-out (LIFO) to first-in-first-out (FIFO) or changing the method of depreciation from straight line to diminishing balance. It would *not* include a change in the estimate of how an existing accounting policy should be applied (e.g., that the straight-line method of depreciation should be changed so that assets are depreciated over five years instead of seven); nor would it include the initial introduction of an accounting policy in response to changed events.

Any change in accounting policy is likely to have an impact on reported net income, both in the current period and for past periods. The accountant's problem is how to disclose this to the reader. There are three main choices (none of them particularly satisfactory):

1. Begin the change in the current period and ignore the effects on prior periods. This method is called **prospective application**. Thus, for example, the current period might begin with the inventory valued at FIFO and end with it valued at LIFO, which would have a distorting effect on cost of goods sold.

2. Calculate the cumulative impact that the change would make in prior periods and recognize this as a special item in the current period. This method is called **retroactive** application. For example, at the start of the current period the inventory would be revalued from FIFO to LIFO and LIFO would be used thereafter. Thus, the current year's cost of goods sold would not be distorted. The cumulative effect of the inventory adjustment from FIFO to LIFO would be recorded as either (i) an item on the income statement or (ii) a direct charge or credit to retained earnings. If put on the income statement, it would have a distorting influence on reported income; and if entered directly in retained earnings, it would be an income item that never appeared on an income statement.

3. Apply the accounting policy to prior periods, and restate financial statements for those periods. This method is called **retroactive application with restatement**. Consequently, the reader will now have more than one set of financial statements for the same year, which might be confusing. However, it would be very clear which particular prior years were affected by the change in accounting policy.

The preference in the *CICA Handbook* [1506.09] is for choice (3), retroactive application with restatement. For those items where it is not possible to identify the prior periods that would be affected, its preference is for choice (2), with the cumulative effect charged or credited to retained earnings. While these are sensible guidelines, they are essentially attempts to make the best of a messy situation. In addition, the *Handbook* [1506] requires rather extensive disclosure of the following: (i) the nature of the accounting policy change, (ii) its effect on the financial statements of the current period, and (iii) whether the change has been applied retroactively to prior periods.

Here is an example from the Saskatchewan Economic Development Corporation.

	1984	1983
Retained earnings (Deficit), beginning of year:		
As previously reported	$ (7,246)	$ 4,277
Adjustment for the cumulative effect of the change in accounting policy (2)	383	240
As restated	(6,863)	4,517
Retained earnings (Deficit), end of year	$ (15,744)	$ (6,863)

Note 2. — Change in Accounting Policy:
Retained earnings at 31 December 1983 and 31 December 1982 have been increased by $383,000 and $240,000 respectively to reflect a retroactive change in the Corporation's method of depreciation for its buildings from the straight-line method to the sinking-fund method. This change in accounting policy has been retroactively applied to the 1983 comparative figures and has reduced depreciation expense from $685,000 as previously reported to $542,000. The remainder of the change is applicable to years prior to 1983.

A change in accounting policy that arises from some changed real circumstances is not considered a change in accounting policy for purposes considered here. For example, the change in use of an asset may mean that it is now in a category where the expected functional life is shorter, and hence a different pattern of depreciation is considered appropriate. This is not a change in accounting policy because it is made in response to some change in the underlying conditions. It is sometimes hard to separate a change in accounting policy from a change in accounting estimate. Thus the change from straight-line depreciation to declining balance may be both: on the one hand it may be thought to offer a better matching of costs and revenues (a policy issue) and on the other hand it may help to compensate for the under-depreciation of prior years (an estimating issue).

Similarly, the adoption of a new accounting policy is not considered a change for our purposes if it is done to recognize some events or transactions taking place for the first time or previously immaterial. For example, imagine a company that is recognizing income on its production at the point when it is sold. Suppose that for the first time it starts to produce some product that takes several years to make. The company may decide that for this product it would be more appropriate to recognize the revenue over the lengthy period of production. The adoption of this second method of revenue recognition (the *percentage-of-completion method)* would not constitute a change in accounting policy. However, if the company had for years been making products that took a long time to make, it *would* constitute a change in accounting policy if it shifted the method of revenue recognition from the point-of-sale method to the percentage-of-completion method [CICA1506.04]. The adoption of new standards required by the *Handbook* is not considered a change of accounting policy.

Changes in Accounting Estimates

Accountants are constantly forced to make estimates about future events in order to make the accounting system work. They estimate such items as the accounts receivable not likely to be collected, the market value of the inventory, the functional life and salvage value of a plant asset, the liability on product warranties, and the economic life of a mine or oil well.

In the course of revising these estimates, it may become apparent that prior periods have been charged too much or too little. However, in the case of revised estimates the recommended practice is to have *no* retroactive adjustments, but instead to reflect all the changes in the current and future periods [CICA1506.24]. In other words, it should be accounted for prospectively.

Consider the following example. At the beginning of 19X9 a company finds that the recovery value of the accounts receivable at the end of 19X8 was overestimated by $30,000. The company further discovers that a $15,000 computer that was depreciated on a five-year straight-line basis in 19X8 is going to have a functional life of only three years. The company handles these changes correctly as follows. First, the estimation error in accounts receivable that increased the 19X8 income by $30,000 in error is not retroactively charged to that year. Instead, it is allowed to fall in 19X9, the current year. As a result, 19X8 will be overstated by $30,000, and 19X9 will be understated by the same amount. "Rare or unusual" items of this sort that affect both the current and future accounting periods should be disclosed [CICA1506.24], but normal estimating errors are not. The reader is supposed to know that normal estimating errors are not an unusual event in preparing financial statements.

Second, the company handles the estimation error in the service life of the computer by revising the estimate of the net book value that should be recorded as of the end of 19X9 and then writing off the difference in 19X9. The computation would be as follows:

Original cost	$ 15,000
19X8 depreciation (20%)	3,000
Undepreciated cost at beginning of 19X9	12,000
Undepreciated cost required at the end of 19X9:	
one more year's depreciation (15,000/3)	5,000
Depreciation recorded for 19X9	$ 7,000

If this event is material and considered to be rare and unusual, it would be the basis of a note describing the nature of the event and its impact on the current and future periods.

Correction of Accounting Errors

One would not normally expect to find a serious accounting error in the financial reports of a large company whose shares are publicly traded. Such an error is more likely in the statements of a small company where internal controls are not as strong. An accounting error is distinct from an estimating error (discussed above). It arises when there has been an error in the mechanics of preparing the statements. Examples would be (i) understating a periodic inventory because some of the count sheets were not included; (ii) overstating a periodic inventory because of fraudulent misrepresentation of the amount on hand by those doing the count; (iii) omitting a warranty liability through failing to be aware of it; and (iv) failing to accrue wages payable.

If the amounts of the errors are material, then accepted practice according to the *Handbook* [*CICA*1506.28] is to account for it retroactively with restatement. In other words, one should restate financial statements of the prior periods affected.

For example, suppose that after the 19X8 financial statements of a company were published, it was discovered that there had been a serious inventory valuation error at the end of that year. An error in filling out some of the inventory summaries had resulted in the inventory part number being taken incorrectly as the quantity on hand. A review of these records indicated that the opening 19X9 inventory was overestimated by $165,000. As a result, the 19X8 income was overstated by $165,000, and the 19X9 income will be understated by the same amount. These amounts are considered material. Because this is a material accounting error, the accepted procedure is to correct the 19X8 financial results when producing the 19X9 statements, showing that cost of goods sold is higher by $165,000. Consequently, the revised 19X8 statements will show an end-of-year balance in retained earnings that is $165,000 smaller than before. Although the financial statements for 19X8 are restated, *the books of account are not rewritten for 19X8* because by 19X9 when the error was discovered the closing entries would already have been recorded. Instead, in 19X9 the following entry is made:

Retained earnings	165,000.00	
Opening inventory		165,000.00

To record adjustment arising from overstatement of 19X8
    closing inventory through an accounting error.

This then brings the 19X9 opening balance in retained earnings to the corrected amount, thus agreeing with the financial statements.

Examples from Published Reports

General Motors of Canada Limited.

GM of Canada is the largest automotive company in the country. Although the bulk of its business is derived from car and truck sales, GM also produces diesel locomotives for companies such as Via Rail and military vehicles for the U.S. Marine Corps.

GENERAL MOTORS OF CANADA LIMITED
Statement of Income and Net Income Retained for Use in the Business
Year Ended 31 December 1986 with Comparative Figures for 1985

	1986	1985
	(thousands of $)	
Net sales	$ 18,532,562	$ 18,993,305
Costs and expenses:		
Cost of sales and other operating charges, exclusive of items listed below	17,175,166	17,192,879
Selling, general, and administrative expenses	330,891	301,433
Depreciation of plants and equipment	239,183	218,837
Amortization of special tools	90,555	122,695
Total	17,835,795	17,835,844
Operating income	696,767	1,157,461
Other income less income deductions — net	85,023	129,965
Interest expense:		
Interest on capital leases	927	2,555
Interest on long-term debt	384	—
Other interest	5,126	1,815
Total	6,437	4,370
Income before income taxes	775,353	1,283,056
Income taxes (Note 5)	356,918	570,081
Net income before share of loss of associated companies	418,435	712,975
Share of loss of associated companies	20	—
Net income for the year	418,415	712,975
Net income retained for use in the business at beginning of the year	2,156,489	1,686,557
Total	2,574,904	2,399,532
Dividends paid	249,429	243,043
Net income retained for use in the business at end of the year	$ 2,325,475	$ 2,156,489

Note 5 is a reconciliation of the company's *statutory* rate of income tax (50.8%) to the rate actually paid (46.0%). This will be explained in Chapter 13.

Note how relatively uninformative the income statement has become through grouping a large number of expenses under the general heading of *Cost of sales and other operating charges, exclusive of items listed below*. This amounts to about 17.175 out of 17.836, or 96% of all operating expenses reported as a single amount. The *CICA Handbook* sets out certain expenses that *must* be shown separately and others whose separate disclosure is considered "desirable" (the latter including cost of goods sold and major operating expenses such as selling and administrative expenses). The GM management appear to feel that separate disclosure is less desirable than the authors of the *Handbook* advocate. The GM practice is widespread in Canada.

The Seagram Company Ltd.

Compare the GM statement above with the following income statement of Seagrams.

THE SEAGRAM COMPANY LTD.
INCOME STATEMENT

	Twelve months ended 31 January		
	1988	1987	1986
Sales and other income	$ 3,815,480	$ 3,344,820	$ 2,970,669
Cost of goods	2,436,640	2,189,628	1,940,993
	1,378,840	1,155,192	1,029,676
Selling, general and administrative expenses	1,093,127	927,360	815,021
Restructuring costs	—	35,000	—
Operating Income	285,713	192,832	214,655
Interest expense	80,397	84,294	82,013
Income before income taxes	205,316	108,538	132,642
Provision for income taxes	60,801	5,715	33,417
Income from Spirits and Wine Operations	144,515	102,823	99,225
Interest expense related to share repurchase, after income taxes	—	(2,513)	(6,683)
Dividend income from E.I. du Pont de Nemours and Company	165,367	154,091	150,838
Equity in unremitted earnings of E.I. du Pont de Nemours and Company	211,206	169,057	75,694
Net Income	$521,088	$ 423,458	$ 319,074

Summary

Measures of business income are an important, and subtle, topic in accounting. In this chapter we do no more than introduce some of the basic concepts of income measurement. We will return to the topic again when discussing price-change accounting. Income measurement is an important topic in accounting theory. A thorough examination of it is beyond the scope of this text.

Despite the seeming hardness of accounting numbers, accounting is in fact a reporting system whose measurements must usually take place when some key facts are unknown or, at best, only capable of estimation. This gives rise to transactions that clearly relate to a prior accounting period, and hence prior-period adjustments are often needed. In other cases, prior estimates are later seen to be wide of the mark and must be dealt with within applicable accounting standards.

QUESTIONS

Q4-1. Review and be sure you understand the following terms:

    a. income statement

    b. earnings statement

    c. income

    d. model

    e. proprietorship view

    f. entity view

    g. stock *versus* flow

    h. revenue *versus* gain *versus* income

    i. expense *versus* losses

    j. revenue recognition *versus* matching convention

    k. interim report

    l. extraordinary item

    m. prior-period adjustment

Q4-2. John Hicks, an economist, wrote: "A man's income is the amount he can spend in a week and still be as well off at the end of the week as he was at the beginning." Is this statement helpful in defining the income of

    a. a trader at a flea market?

    b. a dentist?

    c. a student self-employed as a house painter for the summer?

    d. a university?

    e. the members of a rock group?

Q4-3. In *The Wall Street Journal* of 17 November 1982 Gates Learjet offered its Learjet 25D model for $1,995,000, but said, "There is one catch, though. This offer is good only until 17 December 1982 — and delivery must take place by the end of this year." The company's year-end is 30 April. Is this special offer likely to have any effect in moving their reported income from one year to another? If it has, is there anything improper in this? If you were considering the purchase of the company's stock, would you want to know about this special offer? Why or why not?

Q4-4. *Business Week* reported in June 1981 that Investors Diversified Services Inc. (IDS) would sell its 57-storey IDS centre in Minneapolis for $200 million to a company from Edmonton. "IDS stands to reap a pretax gain of about $95 million on the sale, but it must substantially boost its own payments as a tenant…," the magazine reported. Using the usual rules of income recognition, should IDS recognize the profit of $95 million on completion of the sale?

Q4-5. Is the direct method of income measurement any easier to understand than the indirect method? Why? Which one do you think would produce the most reliable estimate of income?

Q4-6. **a.** Explain the difference between the proprietorship and entity views of the firm.

b. Give one example why it might matter which view of the firm one adopts.

Q4-7. Explain why measuring the net *stock* of assets in a firm cannot be done directly in the same manner as one measures the stock of cars in a parking lot.

Q4-8. As long as we are careful to measure costs against revenues, why does it matter *when* we recognize the revenue as earned?

Q4-9. The error in estimating income is likely to increase as a percentage of income as the reporting period is made shorter and shorter. However, this may vary from one type of industry to the other. Evaluate in each of the cases below whether you think the estimating error for reported income is likely to go up sharply as the reporting period is reduced from one year to one month. Explain your reasoning in each case.

a. A professional hockey team

b. A toy company that sells most of its product for the Christmas trade

c. A fast food outlet

d. An airline

e. A cafeteria

f. A women's clothing store

Q4-10. *The Wall Street Journal* carried an article that began: "When Sandra Kurtzig went into business for herself 10 years ago, she operated out of a room in her home and stashed all her business funds in a shoe box. If there was more money in the shoe box at the end of the month than the beginning, her company made a profit."

a. Assuming that this was a relatively simple company that sold computer software, would the "shoe-box" test for profitability be a poor one?

b. If the shoe-box test worked when the company was small, would it work when the company had 100 employees but remained in the same line of business? Explain.

Q4-11. Do you agree with the following statements? Explain your answers.

a. A company that had not been previously unionized suffered a two-month strike. The loss arising from this strike would be considered an extraordinary item on the income statement.

b. In some very fundamental ways, the net income reported by the accounting system fails to report how much better off the company is as a result of the year's operating activities.

c. It would be easy to make an accurate estimate of a company's income if only one did not have to issue income statements for fixed periods of time, such as a year.

Q4-12. A friend challenges you to "say what this accounting concept of *revenue recognition* really means without using any accounting jargon, such as 'transaction', 'realization', 'event', etc." What is your reply?

Q4-13. Explain why errors in estimating inventory have a more serious impact on reported income as the length of the reporting period gets shorter. Are there any other assets likely to have a similar serious impact on reported profit for this same reason?

Q4-14. Explain why a body setting the monthly rate that you can be charged by the telephone company for the use of your telephone would be interested in the net income reported by the telephone company. How would this income information be used?

Q4-15. The income statement is described as connecting with the statement of retained earnings. What does this mean? What other statements, if any, does the statement of retained earnings connect with?

Q4-16. Do the following statements reflect an entity view or a proprietorship view of the firm? Explain your reasoning.

a. We did very well this year because the market value of the assets went up and most of the financing was done by debt.

b. We need to find an additional six million dollars. Probably we will finance it with debt instead of equity because on an aftertax basis it is cheaper that way.

c. The firm appears to be better off but actually it is not. We bought the inventory for $100,000 and sold it for $130,000. That looks like a profit of $30,000. The fact is, though, that replacing it will cost $130,000. By the time we have done that, we are fundamentally no better off, despite the fact we did it all on borrowed money. Now the shareholders think they should get the "profit" in their dividends.

Q4-17. In this chapter we made the distinction between things whose size we can measure directly (e.g., gold in the Bank of Canada) and those whose size we have to infer by indirect measurement (e.g., the owners' equity of a company). In each case below explain whether the measure is direct or inferred.

a. The value of Canadian cash held by the Bank of Montreal at the end of its fiscal year.

b. The value of all cash, Canadian and foreign, held by that bank.

c. The value of the bank's loan portfolio.

d. The historic cost of the plant assets.

e. The undepreciated cost of the plant assets.

f. The gross revenue of the bank.

g. The net income of the bank.

h. The retained earnings of the bank.

i. The owners' equity of the bank.

Q4-18. What are the four major approaches for assigning dollar amounts to assets for purposes of preparing financial statements? What are the advantages and disadvantages of each?

Q4-19. Name three alternatives to the point of sale for revenue realization and in each case give an example of the circumstances in which it is properly used. Justify the use of each in terms of generally accepted accounting principles.

(CMA adapted)

Q4-20. "There is no point in seeking to find when revenue is 'really' earned, only in asking if the treatment of revenue recognition is consistent from period to period and if it is in conformity with the concept of *well-offness* that we wish to use." Explain in your own words what this statement means. What reasoning lies behind it? Does this mean a company's net income can be made whatever the company wants?

Q4-21. Explain why accountants act as if the timing of expense recognition is dependent on the timing of revenue recognition.

Q4-22. It was reported that the crash of an American Airlines DC-10 had the effect of "increasing earnings per share from $1.75 to $2.63." How could this have happened?

Q4-23. Differentiate between unusual and extraordinary items and explain why a company might prefer to disclose an item as an extraordinary item.

(CMA adapted)

Q4-24. Some authors talk of the *asset and liability viewpoint*, in which the emphasis is put on the ability to give an economic interpretation to each item listed on the balance sheet (this would tend to eliminate such items as deferred charges from the balance sheet). Others stress the *revenue and expense viewpoint*, in which the matching of revenues and expenses is given emphasis even if it means that some items must be put on the balance sheet as a way of deferring them until matching can be done. One author has said: "In a world of certainty, there would be no conflict between the asset and liability viewpoint and the revenue and expense viewpoint. It is only when uncertainty enters the picture that confusion arises." Do you agree? Explain.

Q4-25. Compare and contrast the usefulness of a company's income statement and statement of changes in financial position to each of the following:

a. a passive investor

b. a bondholder

c. a short-term creditor such as a bank

d. the management of the company

Q4-26. What is the justification for the exclusion of *prior-period adjustments* from the income of the current year? State, as part of your answer, the four necessary criteria for the classification of an item as a prior-period adjustment.

(CMA adapted)

EXERCISES

E4-1. Using the stocks and flows concept, explain:

a. What problem, if any, would arise if a company adopted a financial year of exactly 52 weeks?

b. What problem, if any, would occur if a company adopted a financial year with ten "months" of five weeks each, with an additional two weeks for plant shutdown and holidays?

c. What problem, if any, would arise if a company had a variable year that was brought to an end whenever the company finished a major project?

E4-2. In each of the cases below, you are given a well-known model of some real-world activity. In each instance, (i) identify the real world that the model refers to; (ii) identify the aspect of the real world that the model is trying to capture; and (iii) identify some related aspects of that world that the model has omitted:

a. a road map of Alberta

b. a weather map such as the one commonly published in the daily newspaper

c. a globe of the world

d. indifference curves used in introductory economics

e. a balance sheet of a company

E4-3. State, with reasons, whether you think the following should have been included as (i) ordinary income or expense or (ii) an extraordinary item.

a. The Canadian Broadcasting Corporation had a major loss of TV advertising revenue in 1981 because of a lengthy strike.

b. Mammoth Mines management decided that their equipment had not been depreciated fast enough in prior years and therefore ordered that it should be written down by an extra $530,000 in the current year. If they had not made this write-off, their net income before tax would have been $640,000.

c. Ford Motor Company incurred significant costs for it had to recall autos because of faulty transmissions.

d. When Lockheed management did a re-evaluation of the sales potential of the L-1011 Tristar passenger jet, they decided on a large write-off of development costs that had to that time been shown on the balance sheet as deferred charges to be amortized against future sales (which they no longer think will develop as previously forecasted).

E4-4. In a critical article on accounting for the income of public utilities, *Forbes* Magazine cited the following practices that were justified on the grounds that the utility was a monopoly supplier and could be sure of earning the revenue allowed it by the controlling regulatory commission:

(i) A utility abandoned a power-generating plant for it was no longer economic to operate because of a shift in the relative price of fuels. Instead of writing it off immediately, the utility was allowed by the regulatory commission to write it off over the next five years. "Presto," *Forbes* commented. "The utility now has one-fifth the expense the manufacturing company would have had."

(ii) A utility that is building a new facility is allowed to capitalize the opportunity interest cost of the facility under construction and show the offsetting credit as interest income. Since this capitalized interest will be built into the charges for its power that the utility is allowed to make in the future, *Forbes* observes that "a utility can manufacture profits out of thin air by simply building a new facility."

Required: Do the above practices have merit in a regulated monopoly such as an electrical utility? Or as *Forbes* suggests, are they done to please the current consumers of electricity who might soon be going to the polls?

E4-5. It is the practice of the large U.S. auto companies such as GM and Chrysler to recognize revenue on an automobile when it is sold to the dealer — even though it has not been sold to the ultimate user. Comment on the following quotes from *Business Week* and *The Economist* magazines.

a. "Detroit makes its money selling cars to dealers, not when dealers sell cars to customers" (*Business Week*).

b. "But many observers suspect that Chrysler managed its razor-thin profit in the second quarter [of 1981] by dumping too many cars on its dealers." However, the head of Chrysler was quoted as saying, "It was real, a genuine operating profit" (/*Business Week*).

c. *The Economist* (Britain) also reported on the Chrysler improvement in reported profits, saying, "Dealers now have about 100 days' supply of Chrysler's most popular 'K-cars'... Even 70 days would be more than enough, since dealers must finance them at interest rates of around 22%." Does this change your view expressed in (b) above? Explain.

d. *The Economist* further commented, "Clever accounting also contributed to Chrysler's April-June profits. It has sought permission to spread out over a longer period a $260m payment due to be made to its pension fund this year... Without such a delay, the car company would probably have lost $35m during the past three months." Under the matching principle, should delay of the pension payment affect the reported profits? Explain.

E4-6. Your examination of the books of Dr. Marcelle Vacon, a local general practitioner, revealed that her secretary followed the cash basis of accounting in all matters with the exception of equipment. The equipment, which cost $42,000 at the time Dr. Vacon started the practice (2 January, 19X5), was set up as an asset and to date has not been depreciated. The equipment had an estimated useful life of ten years, at which time it would be sold for an estimated $2,000. Upon further examination you were able to identify relevant data as follows:

	19X7	19X8	19X9
Reported income	$ 41,000	$ 46,000	$ 39,000
Supplies on hand at year-end	500	300	1,200
Wages not paid at year-end	600	800	500
Billings to the Provincial Hospital Insurance during December for which a cheque has not been received	6,000	3,000	10,000
Miscellaneous expenses owing at year-end.	300	700	200

Required: Compute the correct net income for each year on the accrual basis of accounting by showing the effect of the given information. Use the format given below.

	19X7	19X8	19X9
Reported income	$ 41,000	$ 46,000	$ 39,000
Supplies			
Wages			
Billings			
Miscellaneous			
Depreciation			
Accrual-basis net income			

(CGA adapted)

E4-7. Adamson and Ford are partners in a successful travel agency. They are about to admit a third partner and have asked you to look at their accounts prior to that event. The partnership was formed at the beginning of 19X5 and profits and losses are shared on a 2:1 basis by Adamson and Ford respectively.

During your examination of the accounts you find the following:

(i) The inventory of tickets at 31 December 19X5 was overstated by $1,000.

(ii) The inventory of tickets at 31 December 19X7 was understated by $6,000.

(iii) On 1 January 19X7 a five-year insurance policy was acquired for $1,500 and charged to expense.

(iv) Accrued expenses of $500 for 19X8 were not recorded at year-end. These were paid in January 19X9.

(v) Accrued expenses of $800 for 19X9 were not recorded at year-end. These were paid in January of the following year.

(vi) On 1 January 19X5 an item for $5,000 was incorrectly charged to Adamson's account instead of being expensed.

(vii) The books were closed as of 31 December 19X9. Net income for January of the following year, before any adjustments required for the above items, was $30,000.

Required

a. Calculate the correct net income for the January following December 19X9.

b. Prepare journal entries for the January following December 19X9 to correct the accounts. The books have not been closed as of the end of January; they are closed only at 31 December each year.

(CGA adapted)

E4-8. The following two cases are unrelated.

(1) During May of Year 2 the following facts were discovered about the year just past that ended on 31 December.

(i) Accrued expenses of $1,100 for utilities had not been included in the adjustments for the end of Year 1.

(ii) On 3 March of Year 1, a five-year fire insurance policy was purchased for $2,000 and debited to General Expense. No adjusting entry had been made for unexpired insurance at the end of Year 1.

(iii) A mistake in the calculation of the value of the inventory at the end of Year 1 had resulted in an overstatement of Year 1's inventory by $5,500.

Required

a. Determine the net effect of the above errors on the net income of Year 1. Ignore tax implications.

b. Prepare the necessary correcting journal entries for 31 May of Year 2. Ignore tax implications. Assume the books are closed for Year 1.

(2) On 31 December 1989 Farside Company determined that heavy machinery previously thought to have a twenty-year life would actually last only fifteen years. The machinery was purchased eight years previously on 4 January 1982 for $90,000 and had an expected residual value of $10,000. The straight-line depreciation method is used. The estimated residual value remains unchanged.

Required: Prepare the necessary journal entry with regard to this asset as of 31 December 1989, the company's year-end.

(CGA adapted)

E4-9. The Fargone Company has been depreciating equipment on a diminishing balance at twice the rate of the straight-line method. The equipment had an expected life of eight years. It cost $56,000 with a residual value of $2,000. At the beginning of the fourth year, it was determined that the straight-line method of depreciation was more appropriate because the machine was maintaining its operational efficiency from year to year. The estimations of its useful life and residual value remained the same.

Required: Prepare the necessary journal entry(s) with regard to this asset, as at 31 December of Year 4.

E4-10. In 1988 *The Wall Street Journal* reported that a U.S. financial institution similar to a Canadian trust company had fired Peat Marwick Main as its auditors "after a rancorous dispute" and proceeded to retain Price Waterhouse. The issue appeared to be the company's choice of when to recognize the fee it earned for collecting the payments on mortgages. The trust company looked after mortgages owned by other people: it collected the payments when they became due and turned them over to their owners after deducting a "servicing" fee. The company reportedly wanted to "boost net income and realize projections made by management." Therefore, it sold the right to collect this fee to a third party and intended to book a profit of $12.7 million (presumably after providing for the costs of servicing these debts). In effect, it appeared to be selling its expected future profits in servicing this block of debt. The chief financial officer of the company said that instead of just selling the rights to collect the profits, they could have sold the complete servicing package to another company "and then there would have been no discussion of the quality of the earnings."

Required: Evaluate the merits of this proposal by answering the following questions:

a. Do you agree with the claim that an outright sale would have produced the same result?

b. What accounting issues do you think are central to this dispute? Discuss the merits of the two sides of the argument.

PROBLEMS

P4-1. A business earns income by continuously converting assets and resources into other assets and resources. For example, through the efforts of its work force and the use of its equipment, a business converts inventories of raw materials into receivables and cash. The value of the new assets generated may be termed *revenue*, that of the assets and resources consumed may be termed *expense*, and the increased value may be termed *income*. Therefore, it can be argued that asset valuation, revenue recognition, and matching of expenses to revenues are interrelated.

Required: Discuss in this context each of the following relationships and give examples:

a. The choice of asset valuation method affects revenue recognition.

b. The theory on which revenue generation is based affects the valuation of the related assets.

c. The timing of revenue and expense recognition relates to the nature of the transaction.

d. When the objectives of asset valuation and income recognition conflict, it becomes necessary to choose either the desired asset valuation method or the desired income recognition method.

(CICA adapted)

P4-2. If you had a choice of measuring any three of (i) opening stock, (ii) closing stock, (iii) inflow, and (iv) outflow, which would you choose in each of the following cases? Give your reasons.

a. A company that buys natural gas from Alberta and sells it in eastern Canada finds it cheaper to buy more gas than it needs in the warm weather and store it in underground chambers for later use in cold weather. Unfortunately its financial statements must be prepared when there is large amount of gas stored in the chambers.

b. A supermarket has a cash register that records all receipts and payments rung up on it. The cashier is given a fixed amount of $100 at the beginning of each shift.

c. A student-run bar has a dispensing machine that measures out all liquor sold and records the dollar amount of the sale. All liquor is sent to the bar in bottles, which are counted on the way in. The bar begins the night with $100 in cash. The managers would like to end each evening session knowing the amount of liquor and cash on hand.

d. A parking lot has 1,000 spaces. It begins the day empty and cars arrive very rapidly. As they enter they are given a serially numbered ticket. The management does not like to oversell the lot because that means angry drivers are going around the lot fruitlessly looking for a space.

e. Consider the same parking lot as in (d), but this time in the period after lunch. Some cars that arrived earlier in the day have left, and management would like to resell their space to other drivers wanting to get in to park.

P4-3. *The Globe and Mail* reported that Sydney Development Corp. of Vancouver had initiated an accounting change that would result in a "large one-time, non-cash extraordinary loss and prior-period adjustment in that period." This arose because the company had decided to make a retroactive change in its accounting policy and to charge research and development expenditures to expense in the year they occurred. Previously the company had capitalized these costs and amortized them on a straight-line basis over five years.

Required:

a. Show the format of the statement of income and the statement of retained earnings that Sydney Development Corp. would provide to its shareholders for the 31 March year-end. Draft the note to the financial statements that this accounting change and prior-period adjustment would require.

b. Why do you think the company made this accounting change?

c. How should the shareholders interpret the statements of the company?

P4-4 The Richardson Company has hired you as their accountant just as the statements of 31 December 1990 are being finalized. A review of the company's transactions reveals the following:

(i) On 31 March 1990 the company paid $100,000 in taxes, half of which was the final payment for 1989 taxes and half of which was payable due to an income tax reassessment for the 1987 fiscal year.

(ii) The company held land for future use as a long-term investment. During the current year this property was found to be contaminated by chemicals buried in the ground in past years. As a result the investment was written off at a loss of $120,000 and included in *Other expenses*.

(iii) Certain fixed asset depreciation was not recorded in 1989. This error was discovered in 1990 and the $20,000 depreciation omitted in 1989 was added to the current year's charge.

(iv) The company pays income tax at a rate of 50%, and taxable income is the same as accounting income.

One of the accounting clerks has prepared the draft income statement which follows:

THE RICHARDSON COMPANY
INCOME STATEMENT
For the Year Ended 31 December 1990

Sales		$ 1,500,000
Cost of goods sold		720,000
Gross margin		780,000
Expenses:		
Selling	$ 150,000	
Depreciation	50,000	
Interest	8,000	
Bad debts	12,000	
Other	120,000	340,000
Income before taxes		440,000
Income tax expense		280,000
Net Income		160,000
Retained Earnings at beginning of year		168,000
Dividends		145,000
Retained Earnings at end of year		$ 183,000

Required: Prepare a corrected income statement for 1990. Explain any changes made and draft the notes to the financial statements (if any) that are required.

P4-5. *The Economist* Magazine reported that there was such an oversupply of airline seats that heavy price cutting was taking place. This had the effect of reducing the demand for new aircraft, which was hard on the manufacturers trying to sell these craft. The usual tactic was for manufacturers to try to get one large airline to buy a new model in order to guarantee themselves enough volume of sales to get somewhere close to the break-even level (the volume needed was usually around 400 aircraft). *The Economist* concluded: "The simple truth sets a premium on volume, if a project is to make a profit. It puts the engine makers at the mercy of the airframe makers and the latter at the mercy of the airlines."

Required: Set out below are some real situations. In each case you should indicate (i) when the income should be recognized by the company leasing or selling the aircraft, according to generally accepted accounting principles; and (ii) any reservations you have about the usefulness of the revenue recognition convention to someone who is considering buying shares in the company.

a. McDonnell Douglas (M-D) agreed to supply American Airlines with twenty DC-9 Super 80s on a five-year lease, with an option to extend the lease for another thirteen years. Boeing aircraft company accuses M-D of offering a "very substantially subsidized lease-rate". M-D disagrees, saying the lease is essentially over eighteen years because it does not expect to get the aircraft back at the end of five years.

b. McDonnell Douglas sold thirty Super 80s to Alitalia, but agreed to buy old (but still usable) airplanes as part of the agreement. Until the Super 80s are delivered, some of the old aircraft are being leased back to Alitalia.

c. Boeing arranged for thirty-three new Boeing 737-200s to be leased to Delta Airlines by General Electric. As part of the deal Boeing agreed to buy eleven of Delta's old Lockheed L-1011 aircraft.

d. Pratt & Whitney, a competitor with Rolls-Royce for supplying aircraft engines, sold its engines to Delta Airlines on the promise that they would use 6 – 8% less fuel over a ten-year period than any engines from Rolls-Royce or General Electric. *The Economist*'s opinion was, "Pratt has given Delta an open cheque."

e. In 1979 Boeing persuaded TWA to order its 767 aircraft by promising $20,000 per year per aircraft for each percentage point the fuel consumption exceeded a maximum level guaranteed by Boeing. Says *The Economist*, ". . . its promise is likely to be expensive."

f. Airbus, the European aircraft manufacturer, sold twenty-three A300 aircraft to Eastern Airlines. Eastern wanted aircraft with 170 seats, but the A300 had 250. Airbus offered (i) the use of four A300s on a free six-month trial and (ii) a deferred payment schedule under which twelve of the planes were paid for over a period of four years as though they only had 170 seats. The remaining seats are to be paid for eventually, but for four years Eastern neither pays for them nor pays interest on that portion of the loan. (*The Economist*, 28 May and 3 June 1983.)

P4-6. F. Tobin, G.A. Prenger, and D. Wilkins are three young lawyers who formed a partnership which commenced business on 1 January 19X0. The partners agreed on everything except how to recognize revenue. Tobin thought it should be recognized as work was done. Prenger thought that the revenue should be recognized when the work was billed. Wilkins thought that the appropriate time would be when the clients paid their invoices. The three never resolved their conflict so that three sets of books were kept. The dispute eventually became so serious that they decided to go their separate ways at the end of the third year of operations. Trial balances are shown below for the beginning of operations and for each subsequent year-end.

TRIAL BALANCES

	Start	19x0	19X1	19X2
Accounts payable	($ 11,300)	($ 9,140)	($ 7,320)	($ 5,100)
Accrued wages	—	(4,200)	(3,800)	—
Accumulated depreciation	—	(1,000)	(2,000)	(3,000)
Building	40,000	40,000	40,000	40,000
Depreciation expense	—	1,000	1,000	1,000
F. Tobin, Capital	(30,000)	(30,000)	(34,350)	(47,990)
G. A. Prenger, Capital	(30,000)	(30,000)	(30,350)	(39,590)
D. Wilkins, Capital	(30,000)	(30,000)	(37,850)	(57,750)
Cash	15,110	10,440	22,180	46,630
F. Tobin, Drawings	—	8,000	15,000	25,800
G. A. Prenger, Drawings	—	12,000	19,400	30,140
D. Wilkins, Drawings	—	4,500	8,740	15,900
Interest expense	—	4,000	4,000	4,000
Land	82,300	82,300	82,300	82,300
Mortgage	(40,000)	(40,000)	(40,000)	(40,000)
Revenue	—	(172,960)	(243,800)	(274,500)
Short-term investments	—	20,000	50,000	75,000
Supplies	3,890	4,150	3,970	4,140
Supplies expense	—	5,130	7,280	5,970
Wage expense (Juniors)	—	104,380	124,200	117,050
Wage expense (Secretary)	—	21,400	21,400	20,000
	$ 0	$ 0	$ 0	$ 0

The following financial information is also available:

(1) At the end of 19X0, there was $21,800 of billings which had not been paid.

(2) The balance of unpaid billings at the end of 19X1 was $32,700.

(3) There were no unpaid billings at the end of the third year.

(4) Billings to clients are based on a rate of two times the costs of the work done by junior partners. All work done by juniors is billed.

(5) The short-term investments are non-interest bearing.

Required:

a. Decide which partner's trial balances are presented above.

b. Calculate the income for each year and for the entire three-year period, using each of the three methods in turn.

c. Comment on the effect of the method of revenue recognition chosen and suggest which method is most appropriate in this situation.

P4-7. It was suggested in this chapter that revenue was not always recognized at some invariant point in the realization process, but that it might vary depending on the circumstances. In the cases below, how soon might revenue be recognized? How late? What point would you prefer? Why?

a. A dentist examines and treats a patient on Monday. On Wednesday she sends the patient a bill for $32 and on Friday the patient pays the bill in cash.

b. A contractor and a dentist agreed that the contractor will remodel the dentist's office. This involves design work followed by actual construction when the plans are approved. The contractor estimated that the design work if billed separately would be about $1,200, and the contracting if billed separately would be $8,500. The contractor decided to quote a total price of $9,000, which was accepted. The job was started in January, the design work was finished by the end of March, and the construction was finished by the end of June.

c. An engineer undertakes to design a bridge and supervise its construction. He is to be paid 6% of the cost of the bridge as his fee, with the payments to coincide with the payments to the contractor putting up the bridge. The total fee is estimated to be $360,000. The engineer estimates his costs as follows:

i. When the design is completed and the bridge is ready to be built	$ 150,000
ii. Between step (i) and the point when the bridge is complete and ready for use	225,000
Total expected cost	375,000
Total expected fee	390,000
Expected profit on job	$ 15,000

d. A manufacturer of computers has adopted the practice of renting its computers instead of selling them outright. They are rented on a month-to-month lease, but the cost of designing the software to go with them means that the lessees rarely return a computer once it is rented. The lessees normally keep them for a long enough period that the entire cost of the computer is easily paid back.

P4-8. Several material events have occurred with respect to the Collins Company during 19X8, and you are assigned responsibility for financial statement classification of these items. The events are as follows:

(i) A major customer has declared bankruptcy, and notification has been received that an account receivable in the amount of $120,000 has very little probability of collection.

(ii) A settlement of $105,000 from a patent-infringement law suit originating in 19X5 has been awarded in favour of the company. The full amount has been received.

(iii) The company sustained a non-insured flood loss of $350,000 in April as a result of a catastrophic washout of a major hydroelectric dam.

Required: How would each of the above items be shown on the 19X8 financial statements of the Collins Company? Justify your treatment of each item, including in your commentary a full explanation of the relevant criteria that led to your decision.

(CMA adapted)

P4-9. Consider the following data about a particular company:

(i) It won a court case related to a 19X4 patent infringement. The company collected the $8,000 settlement in 19X8 and recorded the following entry:

| Accounts receivable | 8,000 | |
| Miscellaneous revenue | | 8,000 |

To record settlement of court case.

(ii) In estimating its provision for uncollectable accounts during 19X7, the company determined that 1% of sales is the appropriate amount of bad-debts expense to be charged to operations. The company had used 0.5% as its rate in 19X6 and 19X5 when the expenses had been $4,500 and $3,000 respectively. The company would have recorded $6,000 of bad debt expense on 31 December under the old rate.

Required:

a. What accounting principles or concepts, *if any*, have been violated by the company's treatment in *each* of the above cases? If a principle has been violated, explain why.

b. For each of the foregoing items, present all the necessary correcting and adjusting entries to state properly the accounts of the company as at 31 December 19X7. The books have not yet been closed for 19X7. Ignore the effects of income taxes in your analysis. If no entries are required for any of the above situations, then make a statement to that effect.

P4-10. You are engaged as auditor of the Watchorn Curtain Company in April 19X5 to examine their books for the year ended 31 December 19X4. An examination of the accounts discloses the following information:

(i) Improvements in buildings of $18,000 had been debited to expense at the end of April 19X2. The improvements are estimated to have a total eight-year life with no residual value. The company uses the straight-line method of recording depreciation. Depreciation is computed to the nearest month and nearest dollar.

(ii) The merchandise inventory did not include merchandise that was in transit at the end of 19X3 and 19X4 and to which the company had title. These shipments of $1,900 (19X3) and $2,750 (19X4) were recorded as purchases in January 19X4 and January 19X5 respectively.

(iii) The company had not recorded sales commissions payable of $2,400 at the end of 19X4. They were paid in March 19X5.

Required:

a. From the above information, calculate the effect on the *19X4* net income.

b. Record any correcting journal entries necessary in *19X5*. (Assume the 19X4 books are closed.)

(CGA adapted)

P4-11. Shaky Corporation has applied for a significant bank loan. Prior to considering the application, the bank asks you to conduct an audit for the three years the corporation has been in existence. In conducting the audit, you find the following:

(i) Reported net income for the three years:

    19X0 — $16,000
    19X1 — (4,000)
    19X2 — 24,000*

The $24,000 net income for 19X2 was picked up from the worksheet that was completed for the year. The adjusting entries as of 31 December 19X2 were journalized and posted. The closing entries have not as yet been journalized. Shaky uses the periodic inventory procedure.

(ii) Omission of earned (uncollected) revenue at year-end was $500 in 19X0, $800 in 19X1, and $600 in 19X2.

(iii) A three-year insurance policy was purchased 1 July 19X0 for $1,800. The expenditure was debited to insurance expense at the time of purchase.

(iv) Goods in transit shipped FOB shipping point had not arrived in time for the inventory count, which resulted in an understatement of ending inventory of $1,200 as of 31 December 19X1. The invoice was received and had been recorded in 19X1.

(v) Advances from customers (unearned at year-end) were included in revenue. The amounts were $600 in 19X0, $400 in 19X1, and $700 in 19X2.

(vi) On 1 July 19X0 Shaky purchased bonds as an investment at a premium of $6,000. The investment account was debited for the par amount of the bonds and the premium was written off to expense in 19X0. The bonds mature on 30 June ten years later and are intended as a long-term investment.

(vii) Shaky used the direct write-off method of bad debts rather than the allowance method which should have been used. The following data is to be used for conversion to the allowance method and adjustment of reported net income (loss). Probable losses of outstanding accounts as of 31 December 19X2 are $800 for 19X1 accounts and $2,200 for 19X2 accounts. Accounts have been written off to expense as follows:

	19X0	19X1	19X2
19X0 accounts	$ 600	$ 1,800	—
19X1 accounts	—	1,600	$ 2,400
19X2 accounts (net effect)	—	—	1,200

Required: Determine the correct net income (loss) for 19X0, 19X1, and 19X2. (Assume there was no change in income tax expense.)

(CGA adapted)

BIBLIOGRAPHY

ABDEL-KHALIK, RASHAD. "Teaching a Course in Income Determination." *CA Magazine* (September 1983). A good discussion of the concepts of income measurement.

HICKS, JOHN R. "Income." Chapter 14 of his *Value and Capital*. 2d ed. Oxford: The Clarendon Press, 1946. This is a standard reference for those wishing to understand the economic notion of income.

SKINNER, ROSS M. *Accounting Standards in Evolution*. Toronto: Holt, Rinehart, and Winston of Canada Ltd., 1987. Contains a good evaluation of the issues of income measurement. *Terminology for Accountants*. 3d edition. Toronto: Canadian Institute for Chartered Accountants, 1983. A useful compendium of definitions of standard terms.

CHAPTER 5
Cash, Temporary Investments, and Accounts Receivable

Introduction

This chapter looks at the most liquid assets most firms have; namely, cash, temporary investments, and accounts receivable. **Cash** has a broader meaning in accounting than in common usage. It includes not only currency on hand but also bank accounts in Canada and in foreign countries. **Temporary investments** are those that can be easily converted into cash and that the management intends to convert in the short run. (It should be noted that determining someone's intentions is often difficult.) **Accounts receivable** are sums owed to the company, usually by customers to whom it has sold goods on credit.

Although the distinction between cash and temporary investments seems clear cut at first, it will become apparent that at times they blur into each other. Investors' and borrowers' needs have interacted to produce a wide variety of financial instruments. The transition is a gradual one from cash on deposit in a bank to temporary investments. Although it is not usually thought of as such, a bank account is an account receivable from the bank which the bank promises to honour any time. Many temporary investments can normally be converted into a bank deposit at any time (e.g., funds on temporary deposit with a broker or short-term certificates of deposit sold by a bank). Many companies report cash and temporary investments as a single item on their balance sheets.

Because of its portability and universal acceptance, cash is an asset of the firm that must be guarded carefully against loss or theft. In addition, because cash and other liquid assets are of great interest to analysts and others assessing a firm's ability to survive, it is important for the reader of statements to be aware that there are ways to manipulate the amounts reported.

Since uninvested cash is an asset that earns little or no income, most companies try to keep it at the minimum level consistent with financial safety for the company. Cash that is in excess of requirements is usually kept in temporary investments so that some income can be earned. Maintaining the optimal balance between cash and other temporary investments is a subject that is usually covered in finance courses. We will not address it in this text.

The transition from temporary investments to accounts (and notes) receivable can also be a gradual one. Nevertheless, in most companies the bulk of receivables are those owed by customers.

In most companies more clerical effort is expended on the collection, disbursement, and control of these assets than any other assets, with the possible exception of inventory. These clerical operations are necessary in safeguarding these important assets because their liquidity makes them subject to fraud. The reader of financial statements is not normally concerned with these internal operations. For that reason they are not covered extensively in the body of this chapter; but they are examined in some detail in Appendices 5-1, 5-2, 5-3, and 5-4.

Cash

We will now look at those aspects of cash that are most likely to be of interest to the reader of the financial statements who is not involved in the day-to-day management of the company. (The reconciliation of bank accounts is discussed in Appendix 5-1.) For the general reader, it is sufficient to note that there are good reasons why the amount of money shown in the bank account is rarely the amount reported by the company on its balance sheet.

WHAT IS INCLUDED?

On a financial statement the term *cash* includes (i) currency on hand; (ii) cash funds, such as change funds and petty cash funds; and (iii) money on deposit that is available on demand. Bank overdrafts are current liabilities. The funds must not only be available for current use, but they must be available for the general use of the company and not restricted to some special purpose such as redeeming an outstanding bond issue. If they are so restricted, they are included in *Other assets*.

FOREIGN CURRENCIES

Cash may be in Canadian funds or in the funds of a foreign country, as long as there is a reasonable expectation that the latter can be converted into Canadian funds without restriction of the amount. For example, funds on deposit in U.S. funds would have a high expectation of convertibility and hence would be considered as cash. On the other hand, funds on deposit with a third-world country with a shortage of foreign exchange would not, if material, be classified as cash. (The main exception here would be the case in which a company has a foreign operation that is largely self-contained, so that any holdings of foreign cash would be used in its local operations.)

Consider the classification of cash items for foreign operations that are not self-sustaining and for deposits or temporary investments in foreign countries. The classification of these items poses difficult problems of judgement when the foreign country falls into the middle range of riskiness (as Canada does on occasion) by sometimes imposing exchange controls but ordinarily trying not to. A country can quickly shift from one end of the spectrum to the other. For example, foreign exchange difficulties arose rather suddenly in Mexico in the wake of weakening world oil prices and in Brazil following the collapse of a currency-stabilization plan.

If there are material restrictions on conversion, the funds in foreign currencies should be shown separately, with disclosure of the restrictions. They are shown translated at the rate prevailing on the date of the balance sheet, not at the cost of acquisition. Note that although this is a departure from the cost convention, it seems to be a sensible one.

Temporary Investments

WHAT IS INCLUDED?

A temporary investment of a company is one that meets two tests:

1. It should be capable of being turned into cash readily (within the current period). This usually means either that the instrument has a current maturity date or that a market exists where the owner can find another buyer quickly and make the sale without having to discount excessively the price of the asset sold.

2. It must be the intent of management to hold the investment on a temporary basis only.

Financial institutions, such as banks and trust companies, offer facilities for temporary investment through financial instruments, such as term-deposit receipts. These are typically for a term equal to any number of days the purchaser wants, with the interest rate varying according to the term and general market conditions. They can usually be cashed before the end of their term, but often at an interest penalty. Larger companies can purchase government treasury bills or promises by a government to pay a stated amount in, say, 60 days. These bills are frequently in denominations of $100,000. They are traded in financial centres such as Montreal and Toronto. As companies grow larger, the pay-off they receive from sophisticatedly managing their temporary funds grows accordingly. Hence, complex short-term investment instruments have developed. The topic of short-term investment management is usually studied in a finance course. For our purposes it is sufficient to note that such temporary investments exist.

The mere fact that investments are highly liquid or only have a short term before they mature, does not in itself indicate that they are to be classed as temporary investments for accounting purposes. It must also be management's intention to hold these securities on a temporary basis only. Thus, if they are held as part of the funding of a long-term pension, they would be considered not temporary investments but long-term assets, since they are held to meet a long-term liability. In addition, if the use of any of these investments is restricted (e.g., if they can only be sold and used to retire a maturing bond issue), the securities whose use is restricted would be shown separately and the nature of the restriction would be noted. Also, if the securities are those of an affiliated company, the *CICA Handbook* [3010.03] requires that they be shown separately. In addition, the *Handbook* [3840.13] requires that any amounts due to or from a related party must be disclosed.

VALUATION OF TEMPORARY INVESTMENTS

Under the cost convention, temporary investments would be valued at their cost of acquisition. However, we have already seen that cash held in foreign currencies is often stated at its market value, not cost. A similar argument could be made for valuing temporary investments at market value. The readers of the financial statement are interested in the amount of cash and temporary investments because they want to make some judgement about the ability of the company to pay its bills. Readers are unlikely to be very interested in the historic cost of these liquid assets. The *CICA Handbook* requirement is that the basis of valuation should be disclosed; and that if there are holdings of marketable securities, both the market value and carrying value should be shown. If market value is less, they should be carried at market value [*CICA* 3010.06]. In effect, this is the **lower-of-cost-and-market-rule** (LCM) that we will see again in the valuation of inventories.

The *Handbook* section on temporary investments [*CICA* 3010] is very brief. It does not specify *how* to apply the lower-of-cost-and-market principle. In particular it does not state which is preferable: valuing at the lower of *aggregate* cost and the aggregate market value of the securities or valuing at the lower of the *individual* cost and market value of each security separately. In contrast, the FASB explicitly prefers the less conservative of these two choices — namely, the lower of *aggregate* cost and market values.

If temporary investments must be written down to a market value below cost, then the amount of the write-down is charged to the current period's income. If the market value subsequently increases, then either of two approaches are followed: (i) The temporary investments are written up to the lower of this new value or the investments' historic cost, and the increase is taken into the current period's income; or (ii) The earlier, lower market value is taken as the new *cost*, with no upward valuation to follow market value. Both practices appear to be followed in Canada. In both cases the amount taken into current income is treated as an ordinary item.

For an example of the first approach, suppose a firm had the experience with its temporary investments as summarized below:

Security	Year purchased	Cost	Market value (31-12-19X7)	Market value (31-12-19X8)	Market value (31-12-19X9)
Thomson Newspaper	19X6	$ 3,287	$ 3,100	$ 3,250	$ 3,300
TeleMetropole B	19X6	7,600	7,700	7,800	8,500
Imasco	19X5	3,213	2,850	3,000	3,400
		$ 14,100	$ 13,650	$ 14,050	$ 15,200

At the end of 19X7 the aggregate market value is below cost, and the following entry would be made:

```
19X7
Unrealized loss on investments                                    450
        Allowance for excess of cost over market                          450

To recognize loss on short-term investments
   (14,100 − 13,650 = 450).
```

By the end of 19X8 the market value has risen, but it is still below cost. Thus, an entry would be made to recognize the increase in market value as follows:

```
19X8
Allowance for excess of cost over market                          400
        Recovery of unrealized loss on investments                        400

To record the reduction in the allowance account to
   bring the balance to $50, the amount by which cost
   exceeds market at this time (14,100 − 14,050 = 50).
```

By the end of 19X9 market value is well above cost, but the investments are not written up above cost. Therefore, the entry would read as follows:

```
19X9
Allowance for excess of cost over market                          50
        Recovery of unrealized loss on investments                        50

To record the reduction in the allowance account to
   bring the balance to nil, as market is now above cost.
```

If an investment is only partially sold, the cost attributable to the part sold should be the average cost of that particular investment [*CICA* 3050.37]. For example, assume that a company held 200 shares of Bell Canada Enterprises and that it had bought 100 shares at $35 and the other 100 at $45, for a total cost of $8,000. Suppose it then sold 100 of the shares for $50. Regardless of which certificates were actually sold, it would calculate the average cost of $40 per share, and make the following journal entry:

```
Bank                                                          5,000.00
        Short-term investments                                         4,000.00
        Gain on disposal                                               1,000.00

To record sale of 100 shares of Bell Canada Enterprises
   at an average cost of $40 per share.
```

Accounts Receivable

Accounts receivable are sums of money owing to the company that are expected to be paid within a year. If the time period is longer, they are classed as **long-term receivables** and are not included in current assets. **Notes receivable** are also sums owing that are expected to be paid within a year. They differ from accounts receivable in that here the debt if formally acknowledged in writing by a promissory note. Usually accounts receivable do not bear interest (unless the delay in payment exceeds the credit period), whereas notes receivable do bear interest from the first day. This is not a fixed rule, however.

The term **receivable** is used broadly to refer to accounts and notes receivable of various types. Receivables are often a significant item within a company's current assets. It is quite common for them to amount to 20% to 33% of total current assets.

We shall now set out to identify and explain (i) the nature of accounts and notes receivable; (ii) the process by which they are recorded and managed; (iii) issues in valuing them for financial statement purposes; and (iv) disclosure issues in financial statement presentation. Further information on the concept of *present value* is given in Appendix 5-2; accounting for long-term receivables is explained in Appendix 5-3; and the recording and managing of accounts receivable are discussed in Appendix 5-4.

Accounts receivable typically arise because a company sells its goods and services on credit. Very few companies seek to increase the amount of their accounts receivable because in most cases they are non-earning assets. It is usual for the terms of payment to specify that no interest is payable if the receivable is paid by the due date). In some cases, a **cash discount**, or reduction of the amount normally payable, is allowed if the bill is paid within a shorter time period, such as within ten days of the invoicing. This cash discount is in addition to any *trade discounts* that the buyer might receive. A **trade discount** is a reduction from the catalogue price given to certain customers.

Some accounts receivable do bear interest (e.g., VISA or MasterCard bank credit card accounts) if not paid by the due date. They may be attractive to the creditor for that reason. Typically, however, accounts receivable arise because the company has decided that selling on credit is so important to selling its product or service that it has no effective choice but to offer credit. The extensive credit facilities offered by such stores as Eaton's, Simpsons, Sears, and The Bay are evidence of this.

EXAMPLES

The types of receivables that a company has will be strongly influenced by the nature of its business. Most companies have **trade receivables** that arise from selling its product to its customers. A typical accounting entry when a sale is made would be as follows:

Accounts receivable — Smith Limited	300.00	
Sales		300.000
To record sales of merchandise to Smith Limited on credit.		
Cost of goods sold	160.000	
Inventory		160.00
To record cost of goods sold from inventory:		

Sometimes receivables arise because a company has sold some long-term assets and has not yet been paid for them. This might include the sale of equipment, buildings, trademarks, or shares in another company. These assets may have been surplus to the company's needs, as was the case with Cadillac-Fairview's 1982 sale of a block of Toronto apartments. Alternatively, the company may be selling long-term assets in order to raise money, as Pan Am did when it sold its headquarters building in New York. A typical accounting entry for the sale of such assets would read as follows:

Accounts receivable — M Limited	60,000.00	
Fixed assets — accumulated depreciation	150,000.00	
Fixed assets — trucks at cost		180,000.00
Gain on sale of trucks		30,000.00

To record sale.

Sometimes a company is eligible to receive a government grant as an inducement to build a factory in a place of high unemployment. In such an instance, the journal entry would resemble the following:

Account receivable — Government of Canada	200,000.00	
Plant asset: offset account		200,000.00

To record grant receivable from Government of Canada.

A company owning shares or bonds of another company may record the dividends and interest owed it at the end of its financial year in the following manner:

Dividends receivable	3,500.00	
Dividend income		3,500.00

To record dividends on common shares of Imperial Oil declared as of 15 December but not payable until 15 January.

A company acquiring a long-term receivable that is not interest-bearing should consider showing it at its present value instead of its gross value. (Present values tables are given at the end of this book.) For example, suppose that a company sold a factory site that had a net book value of $600,000 and received $300,000 in cash and was to receive the balance of $700,000 in 36 months' time. Assume its cost of borrowing money is 1% per month. In this case it should show the receivable of $700,00 at its present value of $489,247.46 (the present value of $700,000 at 1% compounded monthly) and treat the difference of $210,752.54 as deferred interest income. The journal entry on acquisition would read as follows:

Accounts receivable — gross	700,000.00	
Loss on sale of building	110,752.54	
Deferred interest income		210,752.54
Factory site — net book value .		600,000.00

To record sale of factory site for a gross amount of $700,000 whose present value at 1% compounded monthly is $489,247.46.

At the end of each month the company would take into income an amount equal to the interest income on the net amount of the receivable. At the end of the first month the entry would read as follows:

Deferred interest income	4,892.47	
Interest income		4,892.47

To record one month's amortization of deferred
interest income ($1/12$ of 12% of $489,247.46).

The following month the interest income would be $1/12$ of 12% of (489,247.46 + 4,892.47), or $4,941.40.

RECOGNITION CONVENTION

The recognition convention has already been covered in earlier chapters. It is especially important in the consideration of accounts receivable because the decision when to recognize revenue usually governs when the accounts receivable are created. For example, in a move to control the shipment of oil out of Alberta, that province passed a law that transferred legal title to the oil from the oil company to the Province as soon as it was pumped out of the ground. If the oil company decided to treat the oil as sold at the point of leaving the ground, the entry would be as follows:

Accounts receivables — Government of Alberta	xxxxx	
Sales — crude oil		xxxxx

To record the sale of crude oil.

On the other hand, it might be decided to ignore this transfer of title. Because the oil would have been resold to the company as it left the Province, it could be argued that in an economic sense there had been no real sale. In that case, no journal entry would be made and no receivable would be recorded.

Companies that want to increase their reported income are tempted to recognize revenue as soon as possible, which will increase their accounts receivable. As a result, a review of accounts receivable can sometimes give a clue to unusual policies of revenue recognition. Normally, this can only be done by someone with access to the company's records.

VALUATION OF ACCOUNTS RECEIVABLE

Accounts receivable are rarely shown on the balance sheet at the face amount receivable. Instead they are usually shown at something less, because of factors that reduce the face value. The calculation of this lesser amount is known as **valuation**. Valuation of accounts receivable is covered in the *CICA Handbook* in Section 3020. There are two major issues to consider in valuing accounts receivable. First, are they likely to be fully collectable? Second, even if they are paid in full, is the time of payment so far away that they are not worth their face value?

Collectability

The ultimate value of an account receivable lies in its collectability. However, the financial statements have to be prepared before that event occurs. Thus the probability of collectability must be estimated. The usual start is to age the accounts receivable or analyse each balance according to the date when it was incurred. The procedure for doing this is described in Appendix 5-4. In addition to aging, there are other valuation factors to weigh. For instance, consider the following:

1. If a debtor is in a foreign country, there is some danger that foreign exchange difficulties may make it impossible for the foreign debtor to buy Canadian funds to pay the account. For example, such foreign exchange difficulties arose in Mexico in 1982. When the financial statements are prepared, it may be necessary to make an estimate of the likelihood that these difficulties will be remedied and of the probability of payment. In these circumstances it becomes very important whether the debt is denominated in Canadian or foreign currency because of the potential shift in value between currencies.

2. If a customer is in financial difficulties, it becomes difficult for a major supplier to decide whether credit should continue to be extended. If it is cut off, there is a danger that the customer will go bankrupt through lack of supplies. Therefore at times there is a tendency to continue to supply limited additional credit as a means of delaying or perhaps preventing the bankruptcy. It is reported that in 1982 some suppliers of International Harvester found themselves in that position. In this situation aging the accounts is not as indicative of their conditions as it normally would be.

The above considerations should help to point out that judging the collectability of accounts receivable is not something that can be approached in a mechanical manner.

If at the end of a financial period the collectability of some accounts receivable is in question, an estimate of the potentially uncollectable accounts receivable should be made and this amount should be expensed in the current period. An expense is recognized in the current period, the period in which the receivable is created, in order to adhere to the matching convention. In the following period the receivable will either be confirmed as uncollectable or it will be collected. For example, suppose a firm recognizes an account receivable of $1,000 during 19X7. At the end of 19X7 the firm is uncertain about the collectability of this account. The following entry would be made:

Bad debt expense	1,000.00	
Allowance for doubtful accounts		1,000.00
To record estimated bad debts expense.		

Notice that the accounts receivable account is not credited. The account is not credited until we are completely certain that the account is uncollectable. Suppose now that in 19X8 we have determined that we will not collect this account. The following entry is then made:

Allowance for doubtful accounts	1,000.00	
Accounts receivable		1,000.00

To write off accounts receivable against the
allowance account.

If however, the receivable is paid off during 19X8, we would make the following entries:

Accounts receivable	1,000.00	
Allowance for doubtful accounts		1,000.00

To reinstate accounts receivable to reflect collection
of account considered doubtful.

Cash	1,000.00	
Accounts receivable		1,000.00

To record receipt.

Bad debt estimation is covered in Appendix 5-4. Note that bad debts expense is usually recognized and charged against income well *before* the accounts receivable is actually written off as a bad debt. This is because the matching principle indicates that the bad debt expense should be recorded in the same period as the credit sale that later created the bad debt. If the expense were not recorded until the accounts receivable were actually written off (an approach termed the **direct-write-off method**), then the matching principle would be violated.

Discounting

Suppose that a business's accounts receivable ledger showed that it was owed $100 by each of two people. The company is certain it will collect both amounts, but one will be paid in six months and the other in eighteen. Meanwhile, it has a loan at the bank that is costing 1% per month, compounded monthly; and if it had funds to invest, it could receive 0.75% per month.

Are the two accounts receivable each worth $100? The market value of the one due in six months might be estimated by finding the amount of money that would grow to $100.00 in six months if one used a *market* rate of interest such as 1% per month. This sum is $94.19. If the rate of 0.75% were used, it would be $95.62. Similarly, $100.00 due in eighteen months would have a present market value of about $83.60. (For more details see Appendix 5-2.) You will note that the present value of the debt drops as its maturity date moves further away or as the interest rate goes up.

One of the ways to make a sale more attractive to the customer is to extend the time period for repayment (since the vendor is bearing part of the cost of financing the purchase). There is a good argument that if an item is sold for $100, with payment not due for eighteen months, the entry should be:

Accounts receivable — gross	100.00	
Accounts receivable — deferred interest		16.40
Sales		83.60

To record a sale of of $100 gross, of which $16.40 is
    considered to be deferred interest.

There are three main arguments to support this treatment. First, the imputed interest income of $16.40 should be recognized as such and not be confused with the "real" selling price of $83.60, because the $83.60 is probably what the product would realize if sold on the open market for immediate payment. To do otherwise would overstate the gross margin on the income statement. It would confuse a kind of investment income (interest) with operating income from the sale of merchandise. The second argument asserts that the market value of the accounts receivable is closer to $83.60 than $100.00 since that is approximately what it would realize on the capital markets if sold right now. Therefore, the proposed method gives a balance-sheet valuation that is closer to market. The third argument points out that the realization principle indicates that income should be attributed to the period in which it is earned. Inasmuch as a portion of the $16.40 will be earned in the current period and a portion in the next financial period, it would be improper under the matching principle to include all of it in the income of the current period. That is what would happen if all the $100 were treated as sales income.

The arguments set out above are now reflected in generally accepted accounting principles. In the U.S. they have been formally set out in the Accounting Principles Board *Opinion 21* [1971]. (The APB was the predecessor body to the FASB.) There has been no similar pronouncement in Canada. Nevertheless, as we pointed out in Chapter 2, there are holes in the *CICA Handbook* coverage that have to be dealt with by analysis and judgement. In practice, the ideas in APB *Opinion 21* are often followed in Canada.

In 1982 this issue of **discounting** came to a head over the financial reports of Grandma Lee's Inc., a fast food company that sold franchises to operate under its name. The Ontario Securities Commission halted trading in the company's shares until it received more information about the company's financial results. The company had $6 million of franchise sales, but only $325,000 of this had been received to date. In addition, the OSC charged that some of the receivables carried interest below the normal rate, and that significant numbers of franchise sales took place in the final month of 1981, some of them to directors or major shareholders of the company. The low interest rate raised questions about the carrying value of the receivables. In addition, the receivables were created with a related party.

When determining the present value of receivables it is important that they be discounted at the selling company's market rate of interest, because that rate reflects the feeling of riskiness felt about the company. How does one estimate this market rate? If the company is regularly borrowing and lending in the financial markets, the task is not very difficult. If this is not the case, then the rate must be estimated on the basis of what similar companies are paying.

As a practical matter, the APB opinion is not intended to apply to receivables under one year, even though there would be some distortion of income reporting as a result.

If the interest rate is reasonably low, the amount of the discount for current receivables is not very significant, as the following table shows:

PRESENT VALUE OF $100 PAYABLE IN SIX, TWELVE, AND EIGHTEEN MONTHS

Interest Rate	Present Value		
	6 months	12 months	18 months
6%	$ 97.05	$ 94.19	$ 91.41
8%	96.09	92.34	88.73
10%	95.14	90.52	86.12
12%	94.20	88.74	83.60
14%	93.28	87.00	83.16
16%	92.36	85.30	78.79
18%	91.45	83.64	76.49
20%	90.56	82.01	74.27

When the APB issued its opinion in December 1971, the bank prime lending rate in Canada was 6%. A decade later it rose to 17%, and by that time there was increasing pressure to discount receivables with a term over one year because the amount of the discount was likely to be significant.

In the example given earlier, the discount on $100 of receivables was $16.40. Let us suppose that the sale took place three months before the company's year-end. At the end of the year an entry would be needed to take into income the portion of the $16.40 that represented interest earned in the current year. This would be as follows (see Appendix 5-2 for further explanation):

1% of 83.60 for the first month	$	$ 0.836
1% of (83.60 + 0.836) for the second month	=	0.844
1% of (83.60 + 0.836 + 0.844) for the third month	=	0.853
Total interest earned	$	$ 2.533

Accounts receivable — deferred interest	2.53	
Interest income		2.53

To take into interest income the portion of
deferred interest earned in this period.

DISCLOSURE

"Accounts and notes should be segregated so as to show separately ordinary trade accounts receivable, amounts owing by related parties and other unusual items of substantial amount." [*CICA* 3020.01] In addition, "Where assets of the business are pledged as security against liabilities, the nature and, where practicable, the carrying value of such assets should be disclosed." [*CICA* 1500.12]

The intent of the *CICA Handbook* seems to be to disclose (i) items to be shown separately on the balance sheet because of special circumstances concerning their collectability and their related-party nature; (ii) additional information to be given in the notes to the financial statements about the availability of receivables to general creditors; and (iii) special terms about the receivables that mean their payment must be delayed or otherwise altered.

SPECIAL CIRCUMSTANCES CONCERNING COLLECTABILITY

Related Party Transactions

A **related party transaction** is one in which (i) one of the parties has control or significant influence over the operating and financial decisions of the other or (ii) both parties have significant influence exercised over them by a third. An example would be a transaction between Shoppers Drug Mart and Imperial Tobacco, as both are controlled by Imasco Limited.

If a receivable arises out of a related party transaction, then the usual assumptions of an arm's length relationship do not exist and the transactions may have been entered into for other than normal business reasons. The argument for disclosing these receivables separately is that readers have the right to know of their related party nature and judge the quality of the receivables for themselves. Accordingly, the *CICA Handbook*[3020.01] requires that receivables owing by related parties be shown separately.

Unusual Items

The reader is entitled to assume that if a single amount is shown on the balance sheet for accounts receivable, it is from an accounts receivable ledger that consists of balances arising from sales in the usual course of business and whose amounts owing are roughly similar. The amount shown in the financial statements is statistically the *mean expected value* of the total receivables, and the reader is not normally told the statistical distribution around this mean.

It is possible, for example, that two companies might have an accounts receivable made up of the individual items shown below. In each case the company has made estimates that are "reasonably pessimistic" and "reasonably optimistic" and then made an evaluation of the amount to be used for financial statement purposes. Each of these estimates is shown in the table below:

COMPANY A Expected Collections			COMPANY B Expected Collections		
Pessimistic	Optimistic	Used	Pessimistic	Optimistic	Used
$ 6,000	$ 11,500	$ 10,000	$ 600	$ 1,150	$ 1,000
			600	1,150	1,000
			600	1,150	1,000
			600	1,150	1,000
			600	1,150	1,000
			600	1,150	1,000
			600	1,150	1,000
			600	1,150	1,000
			600	1,150	1,000
			600	1,150	1,000
		$ 10,000			$ 10,000

RISKIER

Although both have the same expected value of $10,000, Company A with the single receivable of $10,000 is, all other things being equal, in a riskier position because everything is riding on the one account. If we assume that there is some statistical independence among the ten receivables of $1,000, then the total receivable of $10,000 for Company B has less riskiness than the individual accounts (for the statistical reason that the mean of a group of variables has less variance than the individual items in the group). Hence, the assumption that receivables are roughly the same size and are unrelated is violated for Company A. The inherent riskiness of collecting the receivables is higher because the *portfolio* of accounts may no longer be as well diversified as it was before.

It would be possible to construct some measures of the change of riskiness of the receivables by measuring the change in diversification. However, some of the important measures are highly subjective (e.g.,the ability and willingness of important customers to pay and the covariance between each receivable account). Such measures are not required for external reporting purposes, but "unusual items of substantial amount" are required to be shown separately [*CICA* 3020.01].

Instalments Over One Year

Normally, receivables extending over one year are included under long-term receivables. Two issues are raised when the term of a receivable becomes extended. First, has the risk of not collecting it gone up? Second, has sufficient discount been allowed to reflect its expected present value? The answers to both questions frequently involve subjective evaluation — by the person preparing the statement and/or the person reading it — and it can be difficult to know how this evaluation should be shared. The *CICA Handbook*'s pronouncement on this is that the "amounts and, where practicable, maturity dates of instalment accounts maturing beyond one year should be disclosed. In some circumstances it may be desirable to give information about the terms of instalment accounts." [*CICA* 3020.02] Once this is done, part of the role of assessing the quality of the receivables falls to the reader.

Receivables Pledged as Collateral

It is quite common for a company to assign its accounts receivable to a bank or other lender as security for a loan. Let us examine three ways in which this can be done. Although the terminology varies, the nomenclature we shall introduce is widespread.

Pledging

Under **pledging**, the company must hand over the receivables to the lender in case of default. The receivables continue to be shown on the balance sheet of the borrowing company. However, they have been "spoken for" by the lender, who has established a legal right to collect the loan out of the accounts receivable proceeds ahead of all other ordinary creditors of the company.

There is no accounting entry required when accounts receivable are pledged, but the financial statements should contain a note that this has happened. Usually this is attached to the secured liability. A typical note would state: "Bank indebtedness is secured by a pledge of accounts receivable." [*CICA* 1500.12]

Factoring

In the case of **factoring**, the accounts receivable are sold to an outsider. They no longer appear in the financial statements of the company provided the purchaser cannot claim bad debts from the seller. This is known as a **no-recourse** sale of receivables. The entry for such a sale would read as follows:

Cash	10,562.00	
Accounts receivable		10,562.00

To record sale of accounts receivable on a
no-recourse basis.

If the purchaser can claim any bad debts from the company, then the company has a contingent liability until all the accounts are collected. It is common to show the amount received either in the liabilities section of the balance sheet until the amounts are collected or in the assets section as an offset to the pledged account receivable. Using the example above, the entry would read as follows:

Cash	10,562.00	
Accounts payable		10,562.00

To record sale of accounts receivable on a
recourse basis.

Assignment

In the case of **assignment**, the borrower agrees to allow the lender to collect the payments on the accounts receivable directly until the loan is repaid. The accounts receivable are legally transferred to the lender, but they remain on the books of the company. Therefore, no accounting entry is required. However, a note to the financial statements similar to that for pledging is needed. From time to time the lender informs the company of the payments it has received; and individual accounts receivable are reduced, as is the loan. Here is an example:

Loan payable	15,000.00	
Accounts receivable — Smith		1,000.00
— Jones		4,500.00
— LeBlanc		8,350.00
— Galasso		1,150.00

To record payment of accounts receivable and
reduction of outstanding loan.

Returns and Allowances

Goods are often sold on the condition that they can be returned by the purchaser. An example would be textbooks, which can usually be returned to the publisher by the college bookstore. At the date of the financial statements, there may be a significant amount of sales that might be returned in the following year. The matching principle indicates that possible returns should be estimated and charged against the current period, as follows:

Sales — estimated returns	xxxxx	
Accounts receivable — provision for returns		xxxxx

To provide for estimated returns following the date
of the financial statements.

JUSTIFIED READER ASSUMPTIONS ABOUT RECEIVABLES

The reader is entitled to being informed if *any* of the following conditions apply:

1. There are special circumstances that change the usual assumptions about the collectability of a receivable.

2. There is a material amount of imputed interest in the amount shown as receivable.

3. Even though the receivable exists as an asset of the company, it is not available to general creditors because some other creditor has a prior claim to it.

Generally accepted accounting principles do try to ensure that the reader gets this information where it would be material. However, it is not intended that all the subtleties of the risks of collectability or value be communicated to the reader. If there is reason to think there are special circumstances that need to be evaluated with respect to a company's receivables, then one has to go beyond the information normally supplied according to usual reporting standards. For example, if there were a rapid increase in both sales and accounts receivable from the previous comparable period, this might indicate that the company had adopted a more generous policy of revenue recognition. Alternatively, the company might have speeded up sales that would otherwise have taken place in the next period. Yet another possibility is that the company might have arranged to sell inventory to a friendly firm.

Financial Statement Manipulation

Financial statement manipulation refers to the deliberate arrangement of a company's financial transactions to create a potentially misleading impression with the reader of the statement. It is also called **window dressing**. Usually, it is intended to make the company appear more profitable or more financially sound than it really is. Familiarity with this text will disclose other areas besides cash, temporary investments, and accounts receivable where this is possible, but probably the most clear-cut examples are in these areas. Let us now investigate manipulation contrary to GAAP and manipulation within GAAP (but not necessarily ethical).

MANIPULATION CONTRARY TO GAAP

Certain types of financial statement manipulation are clearly contrary to GAAP. They would not be allowed by the company's auditors if they were detected (and the auditor has procedures for detecting them).

A **cut-off error** is one where a transaction is entered in the incorrect accounting period. Such errors can be knowingly used for manipulation. For example, suppose that for its year-end of 30 June 19X3, a company wished to increase the amount shown for cash on its balance sheet and was willing to allow its accounts receivable to be reduced accordingly. This would make it look more liquid, and the lower accounts receivable would make it look as if it had been doing a good job collecting amounts owed on receivables. It could create this impression by "forgetting" to close off the cash receipts journal at the end of June and then including as June business those receipts received in the first week of July. Assume it collected $23,567.09 in that week. If it were detected, the correcting entries would be:

30 June 19X3
      Accounts receivable   23,567.09
            Cash   23,567.09

        To correct cut-off error. Cash receipts in the first week
          of July were included in June's business in error.

1 July 19X3
      Cash   23,657.00
            Accounts receivable   23,657.00

      Cash receipts in the first week of July were included in
        June's business in error. This reinstates the
        amounts eliminated at the year-end.

Other examples of the manipulation of financial statements contrary to GAAP would include the following:

1. Leaving open the sales journal past the year-end, so that sales and accounts receivable are both overstated.

2. Closing off the purchase journal early, so that incoming shipments are not set up as payable. This would understate both inventory and accounts payable.

3. Issuing and mailing cheques to suppliers, but not entering them into the cheque register until the following year. This would overstate both cash and accounts payable.

All of the above would normally be detected by an audit and then corrected if material. A person reading unaudited statements should be aware that such misleading techniques exist. However, to detect them, one usually needs access to the company's records.

MANIPULATION WITHIN GAAP

Any manipulation of financial statements intended to mislead the reader is improper. However, sometimes it can be done without apparently breaking any specific accounting standards. This is best explained through examples.

As a first illustration, let us consider a company that has the following current assets and liabilities on its balance sheet:

Cash	$ 3,600
Accounts receivable	4,500
Inventory	8,000
Total current assets	$ 16,100
Bank loan	$ 20,000
Accounts payable	7,000
Total current liabilities	$ 27,000

Management calculates the (current) ratio of current assets to current liabilities as $16,100/27,000 = 0.60$. Suppose management wants to increase this. They note that if they borrow another $10,000 from the bank and put it into temporary investments at the same bank their current ratio will be $26,100/37,000 = 0.71$. In fact, the more they borrow, the closer they can bring their current ratio to 1.00. However, the rate of interest charged by the bank on the loan is likely to be higher than the yield on the temporary investments. Consequently the company would actually be worse off, although the ratio would look better.

Does this type of financial statement manipulation violate any generally accepted accounting principles? This is a hard question to answer. On the one hand, no specific GAAP is violated inasmuch as the company does possess the current assets shown and does owe the liabilities reported. On the other hand, a general principle of financial statement presentation states that the reader should not be misled. Management's response to this would probably be that the reader is not being misled: the facts reported are correct, and if the reader chooses to act on the basis of the simplistic use of the current ratio test, then the fault is with the reader. Management might also assert that there were genuine business reasons why it was in the company's interest to borrow money and buy term deposits. Normally this is hard for someone outside the management to refute.

As a second example, let us consider a company that has a disappointing year in 19X1 because its sales are below expectations. To increase the sales reported for 19X1, it makes an agreement with a customer to give a special discount if the customer will place an order and take delivery in 19X1 instead of in the first month of 19X2. The order would have totalled $23,000 at the normal price, and the marginal cost of it to the company is $10,000; so the contribution margin is $13,000. In order to persuade its customer to take the order in 19X1 the company has to give a discount of $2,000. As a result of this deal, the company will report in 19X1 additional sales of $21,000 and an additional contribution margin of $11,000. However, in 19X2 its sales will be lower by the same amount, and its contribution margin will be $13,000 lower. Over the two years the company is $2,000 worse off.

No GAAP was violated in this example because the order was placed and the goods were delivered in 19X1. In other words, the tests of the income recognition convention have been met. One could question the good judgement of a management that offers a discount of $2,000 just to be able to deliver the merchandise a month earlier. However, it would normally not be difficult for the management to give a plausible reason for doing what they did (e.g.,it was necessary because they believed a competitor was about to do the same thing).

Financial statement manipulation is a troublesome issue to deal with. At one extreme, any simplistic use of financial statements is potentially misleading to the reader regardless of how hard those who prepare the statement try to avoid it happening. At the other extreme, even sophisticated readers of financial statements may be misled if they ask the wrong questions or make plausible (to them) but mistaken assumptions. As this section has demonstrated, certain kinds of manipulation are clearly intended to mislead. On the other hand, other kinds do not arise from misleading accounting so much as from misleading activity on the part of management.

Examples from Published Reports

Stelco Inc.

Stelco Inc. is a producer of steel with plants in Ontario, Quebec, and Alberta.

	1986	1985
	(thousands of $)	
Current Assets:		
Cash	$ 4,073	$ 7,604
Short-term investments, at cost		
(approximates market value)	177,271	204,943
Accounts receivable	309,805	332,282
Inventories	677,559	738,045
Prepaid expenses	8,123	12,418
Total Current Assets	$ 1,176,831	$ 1,295,292

This is an example of temporary investments where market value approximates cost. Consequently only one value is disclosed.

Bell Canada Enterprises Inc.

Bell Canada Enterprises Inc. is primarily a provider of telecommunications services.

	1986	1985
	(millions of $)	
Current Assets:		
Cash and temporary cash investments, at cost (approximates market)	$ 679.6	$ 279.5
Accounts receivable — principally from customers, including $31.9 (1985 — $27.0) from associated companies, and less $69.6 (1985 — $59.2) for provision for uncollectibles	2,802.2	2,458.4
Inventories (note 7)	1,043.8	1,219.9
Other (principally prepaid expenses)	163.4	147.2
Total Current Assets	$ 4,689.0	$ 4,105.0

segregated related parties

Under accounts receivable, the company has segregated the amount owing from associated companies. The uncollectable provision is also disclosed.

Mobil Corporation

Mobil Corporation is an American oil exploration and refining company.

	1986	1985
	(millions of $)	
Current Assets:		
Cash	$ 341	$ 593
Marketable securities, at cost (approximating market value)	1,241	953
Accounts and notes receivable	3,949	4.930
Inventories	4,555	4,902
Prepaid taxes and other current assets	783	1,152
Total Current Assets	$ 10,869	$ 12,530

Note how the accounts and notes receivable are grouped together. This implies that both groups of receivables are considered similar in terms of liquidity.

TransAlta Utilities Corporation

TransAlta Utilities Corporation is a utilities company based in Alberta.

	1986	1985
	(millions of $)	
Current Assets:		
Cash and term deposits	$ 26.3	—
Accounts receivable	91.6	108.8
Materials and supplies at average cost	42.6	37.0
Total Current Assets	$ 160.5	$ 145.8

In this case cash and term deposits are combined. This is acceptable if the term deposits are readily convertible into cash and if it is management's intention to do so within one year.

Thomson Newspapers Limited

Thomson Newspapers Limited is a Canadian newspaper publisher with over 150 newspapers in circulation.

	1986	1985
	(thousands of $)	
Current Assets:		
Cash and term deposits	$ 67,389	$ 114,357
Trade accounts receivable	115,569	115,101
Other accounts receivable	3,005	6,156
Inventories	13,387	12,368
Prepaid expenses	1,922	1,622
Total Current Assets	$ 201,272	$ 249,604

Accounts receivable are broken into *Trade* and *Other* as is required under Section 3020.01 of the *CICA Handbook*.

Summary

Cash and temporary investments are the most liquid assets on the balance sheet. Included in both are Canadian and foreign currencies, with the latter converted at the exchange rates as of the date of the financial statements. If the temporary investments have a market value, then this is shown and the investments are written down to market if this is lower.

Accounts and notes receivable are a significant asset on the balance sheets of many companies. The reader is entitled to assume that the amount shown is the net amount estimated to be collectable; and that any material conditions such as a few large debtors, related party transactions, extended time payments, or debt denominated in a foreign currency will be disclosed.

Although there are good theoretical reasons for showing all accounts receivable at their present value, this is rarely done for receivables due in less than one year. In times of high interest rates, however, even a relatively brief waiting period can have a significant impact on the value of receivables.

QUESTIONS

Q5-1. Review and be sure you understand the following terms:

    a. cash

    b. temporary investments

    c. lower-of-cost-and-market rule as applied to short-term investments

    d. financial statement manipulation

    e. window dressing

    f. accounts receivable

    g. notes receivable

    h. operating cycle

    i. trade receivables

    j. recognition convention

    k. related party transaction

    l. factoring

    m. assignment

    n. pledging of accounts receivable

    o. cut-off error

Q5-2. When a supplier's invoice arrives at firm M. Inc., a cheque is immediately made up to pay it, and the cheque is entered in the cheque register. However, the firm has adopted the custom of signing and holding each of the cheques until the last possible date before payment is due. It is then mailed to the supplier at this last date.

At the year-end there are cheques on hand of $63,400. The company accountant wants to make the following entry:

Bank	63,400.00	
Accounts payable		63,400.00
To record receipt.		

However, his boss is not so sure. He points out that although the cheques are still on hand, they have been signed and entered in the accounts. He argues that "making the entry suggested would be no different from making an entry to recognize the cheques that have been mailed but not yet returned to our bank." With whom do you agree? Why?

Q5-3. Some people argue that the term *cash* on the balance sheet is misleading since it implies that there is currency on hand, whereas most of it is money owed to the company by its bankers and should be regarded as a kind of accounts receivable. Do you agree? Can you suggest a more appropriate term?

Q5-4. In each of the cases below, state whether you think the funds of a Canadian company on deposit should be included as *cash*. If not, indicate the accounting treatment that you think would be appropriate.

Foreign currency	Place of deposit	Special conditions
U.S.	New York	None, other than usual exchange fluctuations.
Britain	London	None at the moment, although in the past the country has a long history of exchange controls.
Australia	Melbourne	Has formal exchange controls in place, but foreign investors usually experience no difficulty in converting their local funds to Canadian.
Country A	Country A	Has not usually had significant exchange controls; but its main foreign exchange earnings are from oil, and the currency has experienced severe devaluation when there was a drop in oil prices. Severe inflation now prevails.
Country B	Country B	Formal exchange controls are in place, but foreign investors have usually been able to take earnings out easily (with some greater difficulty in repaying capital invested). Main source of foreign exchange earnings is gold. Under heavy political pressure from other countries because of racial policies.
Country C	Country C	A Soviet bloc country that has had a good record for paying foreign debts.

Q5-5. Explain whether, in a bank reconciliation, each of the following would be (i) timing differences (ii) adjustments or (iii) neither. (See Appendix 5-1.)

a. Cheques that have been fully completed, signed, and entered in the cheque register but not yet mailed.

b. Cheques that have been sent to the creditors and returned to the company's bank, but through an oversight had not been entered in the cheque register.

c. A charge for a credit report requested from the bank. It was charged for by the bank, but not yet entered in the books of the company.

d. A cheque issued to a creditor and through an oversight not entered in the books of the company. However, it is still outstanding.

e. Cash receipts taken in at a branch of the company and remitted to the head-office bank. However, the remittance was too late to be entered into the head-office bank account by the close of the accounting period.

f. A cheque written by another company on its account and charged to this company's account by the bank in error.

Q5-6. State whether each of the following are short-term investments and give reasons.

a. Funds on deposit in a bank savings account. The bank has the legal right to demand ninety days' notice in advance of withdrawal, but has never insisted on this right.

b. Bonds of Ontario Hydro due in ten years' time. Management believe these bonds to be easily saleable in the Toronto bond market. They are being held to earn interest until the company decides the timing is right for a large purchase of equipment.

c. Bank term deposits that mature in seventy days. They will be used to redeem a mortgage that comes due on that date, although there is no formal requirement that the company must use them for that purpose.

d. Funds owed to the company by a major customer. The customer has offered to pay interest at the rate of 2% above the rate the company could get on other short-term investments. The customer also states that she will repay the loan on three days' notice.

e. A promissory note from a company that is a regular customer. The note bears interest and is due in fifty days. The company took the note when it became concerned that the customer's accounts receivable were larger than usual. The customer offered the note in lieu of immediate payment.

Q5-7. Evaluate the merits of the lower-of-cost-and-market rule when applied to individual items in the short-term portfolio as contrasted with applying it to the portfolio as a whole.

Q5-8. For each of the following, indicate (i) whether you think it constitutes financial statement manipulation; and (ii) if you do, whether you think it is being done within GAAP. Explain your reasoning.

a. A publishing house that was for sale had a large inventory of reference books that were not selling well. It sold them to another company with the written assurance that they could be returned for full credit at any time.

b. A small private company had no purchase journal. To make sure that all the purchases were entered for the month, it would make up cheques for all payable invoices and enter them in the cheque register. However, the cheques were not released for payment until the invoices were due.

c. A company had a year-end of 31 December. In order to keep its cash balance on the balance sheet as large as possible it dated all its cheques for early in January and entered them in the January cheque register. However, these cheques were mailed to the suppliers in December.

d. Customers of a store were offered a special discount if they made their purchase prior to the end of the company's year-end and paid cash.

e. Company A sold a piece of vacant real estate to Company B (an unrelated company) for $1,225,000 on the last day of its fiscal year. It was paid by an ordinary cheque, which it deposited. The day following the year-end it purchased a similar — but not the same — property from Company B for the same amount of money.

Q5-9. On the financial statements of some companies the outstanding cheques are shown separately on the balance sheet as a current liability. Discuss the merits of this treatment.

Q5-10. Defend the argument that the "real" bank balance that ought to be shown on the balance sheet is the amount actually in the bank and not the balance in the company's general ledger account. How might this "real" balance be shown on the balance sheet and still have it balance?

Q5-11. A company has an overdraft at Bank A. How should the overdraft be shown on the balance sheet under each of the following circumstances? Explain fully.

a. The overdraft is in the company's sole bank account.

b. The company has money in a different bank that exceeds the amount of the overdraft in Bank A.

    c. The company has money in another account at Bank A that exceeds the amount of the overdraft.

    d. The overdraft arises because of a bank error. The company has money in another account at Bank A which should have been transferred to the account with the overdraft.

Q5-12. What is the justification for discounting receivables whose term is greater than one year but not discounting those with a lesser term. Do you agree? Explain.

Q5-13. Explain why the allowance for doubtful accounts should not have a debit balance at the end of the year. Are there circumstances under which it might have a debit balance through the year?

Q5-14. "Accountants report bad debt expense ahead of time because they report bad debts expense well before the accounts are written off." Discuss.

Q5-15. A company had been using the percentage-of-sales method for estimating its provision for bad debts expense. (See Appendix 5-4.) As a result, during the current year it had credited $12,000 to the allowance for doubtful accounts. At the beginning of the year the balance in the allowance for doubtful accounts had been a credit balance of $3,000. Bad debts written off against this account were $5,500. A review of the accounts receivable at the end of the fiscal year indicated that the balance in the allowance for doubtful accounts should be $8,000. What journal entry is required? Is this journal entry *backwards*? If so, why?

Q5-16. Accounts receivable are sometimes referred to as one of the quick assets, meaning that they are assets that can be converted into cash quickly and whose value is known. You are asked to challenge both these assumptions, anticipating the counter-arguments that might be made and dealing with them fairly.

Q5-17. An example was given in the text of a company whose accounts receivable would contain a *provision for returns* to reflect the fact that merchandise that had already been billed out might be returned. Give examples of other types of companies that might have similar items on their financial statements, indicating in addition how you would try to estimate the size of the account.

Q5-18. Set out below are some examples of possible receivables. For each, state (i) where they should be shown on the balance sheet, (ii) whether the face amount of the debt should be shown at its present value, and (iii) whether any additional note should be supplied.

    a. Fenelon Furniture specializes in selling furniture to young couples. They offer a "starter set" for $3,000, with a $300 down payment and the remainder payable in equal instalments over 27 months with no additional payment of interest.

    b. When Sue Smith started into professional practice, the condition for receiving a bank loan was that she complete a form (that the bank manager described as "routine") in which she agreed to assign her accounts receivable to the bank for collection should the bank ever demand it. She has had a successful practice and has never come close to her borrowing limit. She has borrowed $5,000 from the bank and is owed $30,000 from her clients as follows:

        $ 10,000: less than 30 days old
          15,000: 30 or more days but less than 60
            4,000: 60 or more days but less than 90
            1,000: over 90 days

    c. Hot-Shot Records sells mostly through TV spot advertisements in which the customer is promised "Your money back if not satisfied within 10 days." As a matter of policy the firm gives a full refund if the record is returned within a month, although it believes it has no legal liability to do so. At its year-end it is owed $120,000, and normally it would expect to have about 10% of the records returned. However, unfortunately the last record promoted was a dog, and the preliminary indications are that as many as 20% may be returned.

Q5-19. What factors affect the quality of each of the following receivables? How would the information affect an investor's assessment of the company involved? What disclosure is appropriate in the financial statements in each case?

    a. A company records a significant receivable from a newly incorporated subsidiary that resulted from the transfer of tangible assets to the new company. Both consolidated and unconsolidated statements are prepared.

    b. A Canadian manufacturer sold a large piece of equipment to a Mexican construction company in late 1981. Shortly thereafter the Mexican peso was significantly devalued. The sales contract required a payment on delivery and three annual payments. All amounts are denominated in pesos.

Q5-20. Agree or disagree with each of the following statements. Give your reasons.

    a. On financial statements *Cash in bank* is a form of accounts receivable and should be grouped with the other accounts receivable.

    b. In reconciling a bank account, outstanding cheques and outstanding deposits are timing differences whereas bank service charges and loan interest are permanent differences that require an adjustment in the books of the company. (See Appendix 5-1.)

Q5-21. The London *Economist* claimed that "neither new laws nor good auditing will stamp out the practice of *window dressing*." Do you think this is an excessively gloomy view of this problem? Discuss.

Q5-22. "The reason window dressing is hard to stamp out is because it is perfectly legal." Discuss.

Q5-23. A company sold a truck to a customer for $45,000. As part of the deal the company agreed to allow the customer to pay over three years ($15,000 per year) with no interest charges. Nevertheless, under proper accounting principles, the company would report interest income arising from the transaction. Do you agree? Explain.

Q5-24. The bad debts expense on the income statement is very rarely the same as the actual accounts recognized as bad and written off in that year. Do you agree? Explain.

Q5-25. In each of the following situations, identify at least two points in time when the revenue might be recognized. Do you think one of the points is preferred over the others for purposes of reporting to (i) shareholders? (ii) internal management? Explain.

    a. A firm of professional engineers undertakes to design the system and supervise the contractors during the installation of water mains for municipalities. Its fee is a percentage of the total cost of the work. A typical job will take about three years. The firm receives an initial retainer fee when the consulting contract is signed. Thereafter it receives an interim payment approximately every three months. Three months after the end of the job the final payment is usually received.

    b. An integrated wood-products firm makes particle board for use in constructing dwellings. The company has its own timber lands. The trees are felled, hauled to the mill, and converted into a number of products, of which one is particle board. The whole process takes about a year from the time the tree is felled until the product is sold. There is a ready market for the intermediate products, such as felled trees ready to be milled.

c. Exxon Corporation buys oil from a number of suppliers and also pumps some of its own. The oil is shipped to the company's refineries in its own or leased ships, where it is refined into finished products. These products are then sold at retail through the company's own outlets or sold to others wholesale.

d. A large dairy buys most of its milk from independent farmers, but some of its milk is produced at farms that it owns. The milk is converted into finished products such as ice cream and yogurt. Most of it is sold at wholesale to retail stores, but some is retained and sold in company-owned stores.

e. Coastal Wines produces a red wine of high quality from grapes grown in its own vineyards. After the grapes are crushed, they are fermented for about a week and then the fermented juice is transferred to large casks for aging. The company could sell its wine after a few months; but it prefers to hold the wine for about four years before putting it on the market because its quality improves steadily over that period and the price at which it can be sold goes up steadily.

Q5-26. What is the lower-of-cost-and-market rule in accounting? Name those current assets to which this rule is commonly applied. Are any current assets omitted? Explain.

Q5-27. The text implies that all or most of the assets covered in this chapter are really accounts receivable in some form. Do you agree? If so, why are they not all shown as accounts receivable in one lump sum on the balance sheet?

Q5-28. A company sold a truck for $15,000 that had cost it $25,000 three years ago and now has a net book value of $12,000. The company will receive $5,000 in each of three equal annual instalments. It is estimated that the current cash price of the truck is $10,000. Given that it is accepted practice to show assets on the books of the company at cost, which of the above amounts, if any, should the company use to record the accounts receivable with respect to the truck? Justify your choice by demonstrating, if relevant, that the amount chosen is the appropriate cost to use.

Q5-29. Under the matching principle the costs of earning revenue should be recorded in the same period as the revenue itself is recognized. Suppose that a company knew that on average it had bad debts expense equal to 1.5% of credit sales. Should it record as its bad debts expense a sum equal to 1.5% of each period's credit sales? If your answer is "yes," what would your response be if at the end of the year, the allowance for doubtful accounts appeared to be too large or small when compared to the collectability of the accounts receivable? Can you think of an argument for sticking with your original figure and not adjusting it?

Q5-30. Give examples of each of the following:

a. Cash is in a bank and is available any time the company wants to withdraw it. Nevertheless it is not considered a current asset.

b. Cash is in a bank and is intended to be used for current purposes. It can be withdrawn at any time, but is not treated as a normal current asset.

c. One thousand shares of Bell Canada Enterprises are treated as a current asset, while another five thousand shares are treated as a non-current asset.

d. An account receivable due in thirty days is segregated into a special category on the balance sheet.

e. An account receivable for $1,800 considered to be fully collectable is nevertheless shown on the balance sheet at a net of $1,500.

Q5-31. A very successful owner of a moderately large business claimed that he had one sure way of knowing how well he was doing. He just called up his bank and asked how much money he had in his account. Under what conditions would the amount of money in the bank actually be a good indicator of profitability?

Q5-32. A company sells small kitchen utensils through heavy TV advertising in which the viewer is given a toll-free number and invited to call to place the order. There is usually a rush of phone orders immediately after the advertisement is shown. The order is taken over the phone, and the goods are shipped within two weeks. The customers may either charge the purchases against their credit cards or have them sent C.O.D. All purchases may be returned within one month of receipt if not satisfactory. About 15% of all orders are returned. Discuss the appropriate methods(s) for timing the revenue recognition of these sales.

Q5-33. Under what circumstances, if any, might each of the following occur:
  a. A debit balance in the allowance for doubtful accounts half way through the accounting period.
  b. Temporary investments shown on the financial statements at cost, which is in excess of market value.
  c. A balance sheet showing both cash in bank (an asset) and a bank loan (a liability).
  d. A credit balance in accounts receivable at the end of the accounting period.
  e. All accounts receivable classified as non-current.
  f. A credit balance in the temporary investments account.
  g. A short-term note classified as a temporary investment whose face value is less than the amount shown on the balance sheet.

Q5-34. At the beginning of the year a company had a balance in the allowance for doubtful accounts of $13,000. During the year it decided to write off accounts receivable considered uncollectable. They totalled $15,000 and were charged to the allowance for doubtful accounts. At the end of the year the accounts receivable were reviewed and it was decided that the allowance for doubtful accounts should be $18,000. What would the amount of bad debts be for the year on the income statement? Is this really the amount of the year's bad debts? Explain.

Q5-35. A company had accounts receivable of $100,000 as of 31 July 1985. It was its custom to offer a cash discount of 2% if customers paid their accounts within ten days of receipt of the invoice. A study of the cash receipts in August indicated that $80,000 of the $100,000 had been paid within the discount date. Hence net receipts had been $1,600 less than the gross shown at the end of July. Under the matching principle should the $1,600 have been attributed to the period before or after 31 July? What issues are relevant to making this decision?

EXERCISES

E5-1. Which of the following would you expect to find on the balance sheet of a Canadian company under the heading *Cash*?
  a. Money received on the last day of business but not yet put into the bank.
  b. Money kept in a Swiss bank in British pounds.

c. Funds on deposit with the Bank of Montreal in New York, payable in Canadian dollars.

d. Funds on deposit with Canadian Tire as prepayment on a special order that has not yet come in.

e. A petty cash fund held in the company's business office to pay for small purchases (under $25). This fund is nominally $300, but at the year-end there had been purchases of $3.50 for envelopes and $25.00 for an accounting journal.

E5-2. State whether each of the following items should be (i) an adjustment to the books of the company, (ii) a bank error that the bank should correct on its books, (iii) a timing matter, or (iv) none of these items. Explain your reasoning. (See Appendix 5-1.)

a. A cheque for $89.56 was issued by the company, but it was not cashed at the year-end.

b. A cheque for $36.00 was received by the company and entered in its books, but it was not put into the bank until after the year-end.

c. A cheque for $13.25 was issued by the company and certified by the bank prior to the year-end, but it was held uncashed until after the year-end.

d. A cheque was issued for $13.97 by the company, but it was entered in its books as $19.37. State the difference in treatment, if any, if it were cashed or uncashed at the year-end.

e. A cheque for $356.00 was received by the company before the year-end and was deposited. It was returned by the bank after the year-end because it was found to be post-dated.

E5-3. For each of the following, state (i) whether you disapprove of the practice; (ii) what might have motivated management to use it; and (iii) what correcting journal entries, if any, are needed.

a. Invoices totalling $15,600 were held back from their usual payment just prior to the end of the fiscal year. There was sufficient money in the bank to pay them on time.

b. Just prior to the end of its financial year, a life insurance company sold a large block of its portfolio to a financial house with which it often did business. At the same time it negotiated to repurchase these same investments just after the end of the year at the same price as it sold them. The finance house received a nominal commission on both trades.

c. A computer manufacturer mainly leased its machines to customers, and the usual mark-up on the sale was taken into revenue over the five-year life of the lease. Recently it sold a large number of computers instead of leasing them. The company that bought them was not owned by the computer manufacturer, but had been especially created by a friendly arrangement with a company with whom the computer company often did business. The computer manufacturer undertook to take back with full refund any machines that the newly founded company was unable to lease.

E5-4. Canten Corporation acquired the following short-term investments during 19X5.

Shares	Number	Unit cost	Unit market value		
		19X5	19X6	19X7	19X8
Bluechip Co.	100	$ 23.58	$ 21.50	$ 22.00	$ 24.00
Hitech Co.	50	$ 41.20	$ 45.00	$ 49.00	$ 32.00
Flybynight Co.	1200	$ 2.60	$ 1.85	$ 2.62	$ 4.20

Required: What is the balance sheet presentation for short-term investments under each of the following valuation alternatives?

a. cost

b. market

c. lower of cost or market (on an aggregate basis)

d. lower of cost or market (on an individual basis)

e. GAAP

E5-5. Rosie's Department Store is reconciling its bank balances for the year ending 31 December 19X4. Consider the following items:

(i) Receipts of 31 December totalling $5,680 have not been deposited (this total includes a cheque dated 20 January 19X5 in the amount of $230).

(ii) The December bank statement showed charges on 31 December for $15 (service charge) and $35 (safety deposit box rental).

(iii) A customer cheque for $185 was returned NSF in December resulting in a $5 charge to the company. The company was unaware that the cheque had bounced until the statement arrived.

(iv) A $2,000 bank draft deposited on 10 December was collected by the bank on 28 December.

(v) The bank charged the firm's account in error for a cheque in the amount of $93 issued by Rosie's competitor.

(vi) Cheque #98 was issued on 4 December to a supply company in payment for goods totalling $253. A "stop payment" was placed on the cheque when it was determined that the cheque had been lost in the mail. No entry was made at the time. A new cheque (#109), issued and recorded on 28 December, is still outstanding.

(vii) Additional outstanding cheques as at 31 December are as follows:

> #110 — $ 489.00
> #102 — $ 74.00 (incorrectly recorded in company's books as $47.00)
> #103 — $ 192.00 (certified 18 December)

Required:

a. The company wants to determine the correct cash balance to be shown on the financial statements. To this end, state whether each of the items above should be added (or deducted) from either the balance per the bank statement or the balance per the general ledger.

b. The unadjusted book balance is $31.00, and the bank balance is $(4,940.00). Prepare the bank reconciliation.

E5-6. Set out below are a number of unrelated cases. You are provided with some of the account balances at the end of the companies' financial year and asked to fill in the blanks.

| | Provision for Bad Debts | | Allowance for Doubtful Accounts | |
	Actual Balance	Desired Balance	Actual Balance	Desired Balance
a.	12,000 Dr	25,000 Dr	10,000 Cr	
b.	8,000 Dr		2,000 Dr	18,000 Cr
c.		93,000 Dr	2,500 Cr	83,000 Cr
d.	24,000 Dr	36,000 Dr		10,000 Cr

E5-7. Set out below are some unrelated situations where the recognition of income has been affected by either a change in accounting methods and/or a change in circumstances affecting the company. In each case you should (i) identify the factors that appear to be pivotal to the decision when to recognize income as earned; (ii) identify a group of investors or creditors who might be interested in the information provided; and (iii) evaluate how their decision might be affected, if at all, by the method used for recognizing income.

  a. Florida Developments Inc. bought a large tract of land in a swampy area near an established resort. It drew up plans for streets, parks, golf courses, and building lots for houses and condominiums. It advertised these lots heavily during the winter in the northern part of North America, offering to sell them for a down payment of $1,000 and a mortgage of $30,000 with 30 years to maturity at an interest rate of 5% instead of the usual interest rate of 12%. At the time that a down payment was received and a sale was legally executed, it made the following journal entry:

Mortgage receivable — 5%	30,000	
Cash	1,000	
Sales		31,000

  To record sale.

  b. Ace Machining Limited was a machine shop that did custom machine work for a variety of customers. It had a financial year-end of 30 June. The manager was discussing the plant scheduling with his shop foreman in the early part of June and said: "I've promised our bank manager that we'll make $50,000 this year. We can do it, too. Just pull the job from Baker Company out of the regular schedule. We can't get it done until after the end of the year anyway, so we won't be able to bill it. We've got enough little jobs that can be finished and out the door by the end of June to replace the Baker work, so let's get going on those things that we can get done before our financial year-end." (*Hint*: Is there anything wrong from an accounting point of view with what the manager proposed to do? If not, and you were the bank manager, would you like to know they had made this switch in jobs? If so, why?)

  c. IBM has an accounting policy of recognizing the profit on a computer at the time it is sold. If it rents the same computer instead of selling it, it then apportions the profit over the expected economic life of the lease. One analyst of IBM said that the company had not done as well as expected, the main reason being that "the company is going to have to earn its money over the approximately five years of the lease, instead of right away through sales".

  d. Stella Furniture was ready to ship its major shipment of furniture in mid-December just before its year-end of 31 December. Stella's region of the country was hit by a freak ice and snow storm that, combined with year-end holidays, resulted in the shipment not leaving the loading dock of the company until 3 January. The company's controller decided to include the shipment in December's business because she felt it had met all the usual tests for recognizing the profit in December instead of January.

E5-8. For each of the following, state (i) how the items should be classified on the balance sheet of the company; (ii) what adjusting journal entries should be made; and (iii) what explanatory notes, if any, should be included with the financial statements. Assume all receivables were outstanding at the end of the company's financial year.

  a. The company had on hand $13,285 of credit-card charge slips which it deposited on the first day of the new fiscal year, receiving $12,620 from the bank.

b. The trade accounts receivable ledger had a balance of $85 263. On examination it was apparent that $60 000 of this was due from the federal government. The company's experience is that payment is received about four months after the invoice is mailed.

c. When it arranged its bank line of credit, the company signed a document giving the bank the right to have all payments on accounts receivable sent directly to the bank to be applied against any loan the company might have. The company has no bank loan outstanding at the moment.

d. The company sold $45,000 of its accounts receivable for $40,000 to a factoring company, which accepted the receivables "as is" and has no right to charge the company for any uncollectable accounts.

e. A small sailboat-manufacturing company has adopted the practice of sending its boats to its dealers under an agreement in which the dealer does not have to pay for the boat until twelve months have passed from the time of delivery or until it is sold (whichever comes first). During the twelve-month period the boat can be returned for full credit. The company's practice is to invoice the dealer for the price of the boat when it is shipped and to charge it to a special accounts receivable account termed *Consignment*. At the end of the year the company's consignment receivable account was $123,000. It is estimated that $23,000 of this will be credited to the account in the new year for returned boats. The company estimates that its cost for the boats represented in the receivables of $123,000 is about $73,000.

E5-9. Here are some excerpts from the financial statements of various companies. State what the reader seems to be entitled to assume about the receivables with respect to (i) length of term, (ii) material differences between face value and present value, (iii) unusual items contained within the accounts receivable, and (iv) restricted availability to satisfy the debts of general creditors.

a. Current Assets

Accounts receivable (note 1)	$ 210,000
Other (note 2)	103,000

Note 1 — Bank indebtedness is secured by accounts receivable.
Note 2 — Included in accounts receivable — other is a non-interest-
  bearing loan of $10,000 due from a shareholder

b. Current Assets

Accounts receivable:

Trade less allowances	$ 310,000
Parent company	213,000
Affiliated companies	83,000

c. Current Assets

Accounts receivable:

Trade	$ 540,000
Government assistance	26,000
Other	51,000

d. Current Assets

Accounts receivable	$ 524,165

E5-10. Ivy Lea Sailboats noted that its sales pattern was highly seasonal, with 40% of its sales in each of April and May, and 10% in each of June and July. It sold one type of boat with a list price of $2,000. All boats were purchased in January. It was going to adopt a new policy of selling all its boats at list price but not requiring payment until December, when the full amount had to be paid. The boats cost Ivy Lea $1,000 plus $50 a month to store. The bank charged 12% on any outstanding loans. Its financial year-end was 30 September as that was the end of the active boating season.

a. Which is the most profitable month for the company to sell a boat prior to the policy change? Show your calculations.

b. Suppose that as a result of its new policy it sold boats in the following months at list price:

February — 20
March — 30
April — 50
May — 800
June — 500
July — 10
August — 0

What would its accounts receivable be at the end of the year?

c. In the context of the company's new policy, give a critique of the accounting standard that accounts receivable due within one year need not be discounted. In your answer indicate the approximate amount of income that would be shifted to the following year if discounting were used.

E5-11. In each of the two cases below, show the journal entry that would be required.

a. In July 19X3 the D Corporation extended credit to Mr. Unknown. By the end of August, he had made credit purchases totalling $2,360.99, but he had not paid anything on account. On 30 November 19X3, the company's year-end, it was learned from the local police that Mr. Unknown had been reported missing on 6 September. The authorities had made little progress in their investigation of the case. A journal entry must be made as of 30 November to reflect the amount of the expected payment.

b. On 14 January 19X4 Mr. Unknown reappeared from nowhere and made a cash payment of $1,500 on account. What journal entry would now be required?

E5-12. The accounting practice of writing off uncollectable accounts without the use of an allowance account (the *direct write-off method*) is not commonly used despite being a very objective approach. Outline other methods of calculating bad debt expense and the reasons for their acceptance in current practice.

E5-13. "The idea behind the estimation of the provision for doubtful accounts is to come as close as possible to estimating now what the future losses will turn out to be. I think you can get a better long-run estimate of this by using a percentage of sales rather than estimating the accounts receivable directly, since the latter tend to emphasize particular cases rather than look at the long-term trade." Explain how this difference in approach to financial statement formulation is reflected in the alternatives in accounting for bad debts expense.

E5-14. Decide whether each of the following requires (i) an adjustment to the company's books which would increase the bank balance; (ii) an adjustment to the company's books which would decrease the bank balance; (iii) an adjustment to the bank's books which would increase the account balance; or (iv) an adjustment to the bank's books which would decrease the account balance.

a. A NSF cheque returned by the bank to the company.

b. A charge made by the bank for services rendered.

c. Cheques written by the company not yet received by the bank.

d. Money received by the company and entered in the books but not yet deposited in the bank.

e. A cheque erroneously charged to the company account.

f. An error made in transcribing the amount of a cheque, issued to a supplier, into the company's books. It was entered as an amount greater than that on the face of the cheque.

g. An outstanding cheque on which payment has been stopped.

h. A cheque which has been forged and then cashed. The company will bear the ultimate loss.

i. An outstanding cheque which has not yet been cashed but has been certified.

j. A transfer of funds between two separate bank accounts.

k. Interest earned and credited on a bank account.

E5-15. For each of the following unrelated journal entries, state the transaction that most likely gave rise to it.

a. Cash 250.00
  Accounts receivable   250.00

b. Bank 250.00
 Accounts receivable 850.00
  Sales   1,100.00

c. Cash 3,350.00
  Temporary investment   3,000.00
  Interest income   350.00

d. Temporary investments 3,500.00
 Interest receivable 125.00
  Bank   3,625.00

e. Bank 3,000.00
 Loss on temporary investment 2,486.00
  Accrued interest income   486.00
  Temporary investments   5,000.00

f. Accounts receivable 15,000.00
 Accumulated depreciation 9,500.00
 Loss on disposal 1,500.00
  Fixed assets   26,000.00

g. Accounts receivable 1,200.00
  Accounts receivable deferred interest   157.00
  Sales   1,043.00

h. Cash 25,000.00
  Accounts receivable   25,000.00
 (Note: Total company receivables = 26,000)

i. Accounts receivable 1,389.00
  Allowance for doubtful accounts   1,389.00

j. Inventory 450.00
  Accounts receivable   450.00

k. Bank 1,079.00
  Notes receivable   1,000.00
  Interest income   79.00

E5-16. Given the following unrelated events, show the required journal entries. If none is required, state the reason why.

a. Cash of $250 received from sales is deposited in the company's chequing account.

b. Goods which sold for $43 and cost $29 to make were returned for cash.

c. A petty cash fund of $300 was established by drawing a cheque on the general bank account. A month later a check of the fund revealed $23 cash, $166 in postage receipts, and an IOU from an employee for $75. The fund was replenished from the chequing account.

d. The sum of $900 was paid into a special account used to pay for repair work done under warranty. There is no legal obligation to use the money in this fund for the stated purpose.

e. The sum of $1,000 was transferred from the general account to a trustee for a sinking fund that was established to retire a bond.

f. Fifteen hundred shares of Porcupine Mines was acquired at $2.23 a share. The company intends to sell the shares as the need for cash arises. The shares were paid for by cheque out of the company chequing account.

g. A service charge of $25 was instituted by the bank on the company for allowing the chequing balance to fall below $1,000.

E5-17. The College Anarchy Society treasurer, Peter Kerpotkin, has been handling the society's books for the last year. His friend John Rousseau was checking the accounts when he came across the following journal entries:

a. Accounts receivable 1,000.00
      Cash 1,000.00
    To record deposit into a term deposit at a trust company.

b. Long-term investments 2,000.00
      Bank (chequing) 2,000.00
    Bought an outstanding issue bond which matures in nine
      months.

c. Cash 625.00
      Sales 625.00
    Sales of pamphlets in Bermuda, funds received in Bermuda $.

d. Accounts receivable 350.00
      Rental income 350.00
    Rent owed by Queen's Apathy Society, a subsidiary society,
      for rental of space.

e. Accounts receivable 25,000.00
      Land 25,000.00
    Sale of land on credit, terms are five payments over ten
      years.

f. Accounts payable 1,500.00
      Accounts receivable 1,500.00
    Pledging of accounts receivable for loan.

g. Temporary investments 162.00
      Investment income 162.00
    To write up temporary investment to market.

h. Cash 855.00
      Accounts receivable 855.00
    Sales in July entered in books as sales occurring during June.

Required: For each of the transactions give the proper accounting treatment that should have been entered on the initial transaction. If the current entry is correct, explain why. The following information may be helpful: the interest rate in Canada is 12%; $1 Bermudian = $1.37 Canadian; the original cost of the land was $20,000; the interest rate in Bermuda is 15%; and pi = 3.14159.

E5-18. The Great Lakes Real Estate company, which sells property along the shore of Lake Superior, has the following temporary investments:

Stock	Amount	Unit cost	Unit market value 1985	Unit market value 1986
Vestgran	300	$ 17.50	$ 10.50	$ 11.50
Roxy A	1,000	$ 3.10	$ 1.60	$ 1.40
Canada Trust	200	$ 18.00	$ 46.25	$ 49.00
Chrysler	250	$ 30.50	$ 39.50	$ 37.00
Amco A	500	$ 39.00	$ 12.00	$ 18.00
Walker Resources	400	$ 20.25	$ 27.75	$ 19.00
IBM	100	$ 140.00	$ 180.00	$ 185.00
Parlake	10,000	$ 0.20	$ 0.25	$ 0.50

Required:

a. Show the valuation of the portfolio at the end of 1985 under each of the following assumptions:
   (i) Cost
   (ii) Market
   (iii) Lower of Cost and Market — Aggregate
   (iv) Lower of Cost and Market — Individual

b. If in 1986 all of the portfolio is sold at the given market prices, show the investment income for each of the valuation alternatives applied at the end of 1985.

E5-19. Moonpath Expeditions Ltd. is a company that runs trips to exotic locations. Mr. R. Rogers, the company treasurer, is a marginal outdoorsman and an even worse accountant. Because of his extreme apathy towards accounting, he has not bothered to classify any of the current assets. He has merely thrown them all into one account. The following is a list of what was found in the company current asset account.

   (i) A deposit receipt of $15,000 in a special bank account for the company pension fund.

   (ii) An account receivable of $14,000 from Marcie Ltd., a company that is owned by a numbered company which also owns Moonpath. The receivable arose out of sales to Marcie Ltd.

   (iii) Prepaid insurance of $100.

   (iv) Income tax recoverable of $8,000 and a grant receivable of $3,000, both due from the federal government.

   (v) A 180-day time deposit of $17,000 with the Heletian Trust Co.

   (vi) The sum of $11,500 in receivables due from customers for goods sold, of which $1,300 is deemed to be uncollectable.

   (vii) A $30,000 note due from a company which just bought land from Moonpath. The payments will take place over a period of five years.

   (viii) Dividends of $910 receivable from M.K.K. Corporation.

Required: Separate out the current assets into the appropriate accounts and explain their balance-sheet classification. Present the current asset portion of the balance sheet. Be sure to explain what each category includes and add a note to the statement if necessary.

E5-20. Big Nose Inc. is a company that makes party novelties and specializes in false nose and glasses sets. The company president, Ms. Cameron, has found the following list of goodies in the asset account:

(i) The sum of $12,000 in cash which will be used to replace fixed assets lost in a fire.

(ii) A $500 advance to an employee.

(iii) A $5,000 promissory note paying 14% interest from a small customer of the company.

(iv) A $10,000 bankers' acceptance note bearing 10% interest from a large multinational corporation.

(v) Deposits of $15,000 (Cdn.) in a British bank.

(vi) A five-year $22,000 house mortgage given to an employee.

(vii) An account receivable of $3,000 from a company that is at present undergoing bankruptcy proceedings. It is expected that 90 cents on the dollar will be paid, but not for another nine months. The receivable arose out of ordinary sales.

(viii) An account receivable of $16,000 which has been pledged to cover an outstanding debt. The receivable arose from the selling of fixed assets.

(ix) The sum of $10,000 (Cdn.) received from sales in Poland. It was part of the sales agreement that this money be left in a local bank in Warsaw.

Required: Separate out the current assets into the appropriate accounts and explain their balance-sheet classification. Present the current asset portion of the balance sheet. Be sure to explain what each category includes and add a note to the statement if necessary.

E5-21. On 31 December 19X2 the portfolio of temporary investments of Harbour Company comprised the following:

Security	Quantity	Cost	Unit market price
Higrade Corporation $1,000 bonds bearing 12%	4	$ 3,900	$ 101
Simco common stock	100	$ 2,800	$ 21
Lasco common stock	100	$ 3,600	$ 37

Assume that lower-of-cost-or-market is applied to all temporary investments as a single portfolio and that an allowance account is used. At 1 January 19X2 the allowance account had a zero balance.

Required:

a. Show the correct disclosure and balances under the temporary investments section of the balance sheet.

b. How would the effect of lower-of-cost-or-market valuation be reflected on the income statement?

(CGA adapted)

E5-22. Westbank Limited started business in 19X0. The aggregate cost and aggregate market value of the portfolio of temporary investments held by Westbank Limited at year-ends are shown below:

Year-end	Aggregate cost	Aggregate market value
31 December 19X0	$ 190,000	$ 170,000
31 December 19X1	$ 220,000	$ 235,000
31 December 19X2	$ 180,000	$ 170,000
31 December 19X3	$ 240,000	$ 230,000

Westbank uses the lower-of-cost-or-market method of recording temporary investments.

Required:

a. Prepare the journal entry required at the end of each accounting period to reflect the proper value of temporary investments. The accounting period is the calendar year.

b. Show how the temporary investments would be reported on the balance sheet on 31 December 19X1 and on 31 December 19X2.

(CGA adapted)

E5-23. Eastend Enterprises Limited had only one stock investment in its temporary investment account. It had bought 5,000 shares of the stock on 12 November 19X3 for $82,000. The market values of the stock at year-end were as follows:

31 December 19X3	$ 80,000
31 December 19X4	$ 77,000

On 15 March 19X5, during a market rally, Eastend Enterprises sold 2,000 shares of the stock for $34,600. Eastend uses the lower-of-cost-or-market method to value temporary investments.

Required: Prepare the journal entries to record the sale of the shares on March 15 and the year-end adjusting entry if the market value is $50,000.

(CGA adapted)

E5-24. Indicate whether each of the following items should be included in *Cash* on the balance sheet. Indicate how the item should be reported if not as cash.

a. Cash left in cash registers each day to serve as a change fund.

b. Cash set aside in a specific savings account to accumulate funds in order to replace equipment as it wears out. The firm is *not* legally obligated to use the funds for this purpose.

c. Cash set aside in a bond-sinking fund to accumulate funds in order to retire the debt when it becomes due. The firm *is* legally obligated to use the funds for this purpose.

d. A money order received from a customer.

e. IOU's from officers of the company.

f. Cheques which have been prepared by the company to be sent to suppliers, but which have not yet been mailed at the end of the accounting period.

(CGA adapted)

E5-25. The Queen's-Comm Company has been in business three years and has applied for a significant bank loan. Prior to considering the application, the bank asks you to conduct an audit for the last three years. Concerning accounts receivable, you find that the company has been writing off receivables when they finally prove uncollectable and have been treating them as expenses at the time of write-off. Your investigation indicates that receivable losses have approximated (and can be expected to approximate) 2% of net sales. Until this first audit, the company's sales and direct receivable write-off experience was as shown below:

| Year of sales | Amount of net sales | Accounts written off in | | |
		19X1	19X2	19X3
19X1	$ 300,000	$ 1,500	$ 4,000	$ 400
19X2	$ 400,000	—	$ 2,000	$ 4,800
19X3	$ 500,000	—	—	$ 3,000

Required:

a. Indicate the amount by which net income would increase or decrease each year if the company had used the more acceptable allowance method rather than the direct write-off method.

b. Prepare all the journal entries for each of the years 19X1 and 19X2 that would have been made if Queen's-Comm Company had used the allowance method from the start of the business. Closing entries and narratives are not required.

c. Which of the entries in part(b) are year-end adjusting entries?

(CGA adapted)

E5-26. Downside Company holds a note receivable from one of its customers for $3,000. This is a six-month, 9% note dated 15 September 19X4 and due 15 March 19X5. Downside discounts the note at the local bank on 15 November 19X4 at an 11% discount rate. (Use months, not days, in all calculations.)

Required:

a. Prepare the journal entry for the discount transaction.

b. Show how notes receivable may appear on the balance sheet of Downside Company on 31 December 19X4. Other notes receivable (not including the discounted note) were $18,000 on 31 December 19X4.

(CGA adapted)

E5-27. Ellerbeck Limited has hired you to assist the accountant for the summer in cleaning up some "difficult" accounts that were left behind by a recently-departed employee. "I don't know what you're likely to find there," the accountant says, "but here is the account with some notes I made about the entries. Please write up the journal entries that you think would be needed to close the account out completely and let me see them when you're through. If you think my notes are incomplete, let me know what's missing and what else you think needs to be done to clear them up."

Sundry Current Asset Items, 19X9

Description	Dr.	Cr.	Balance
Smith, Stephen (note 1)		68.25	(68.25)
Foreign exchange (note 2)	35.29		(32.96)
Short-term treasury bills (note 3)	80,000.00		79,967.04
Apricorn Industries Inc. (note 4)		3,514.58	76,452.46
Kathryn Woods (note 5)	3,584.22		80,036.68
Victoria Industries Inc. (note 6)	35,872.45		115,909.13

Notes:

(1) Smith's account was written off against the allowance for doubtful accounts three months ago as uncollectable. When he unexpectedly paid, we put the money in this account.

(2) We purchased a bank draft in $ U.S. to pay a U.S. supplier $7,058. However, we found that the goods were defective and sent them back. When we redeposited the bank draft we only got $7,002.71. To balance the bank account we put the difference in this account.

(3) We don't normally purchase treasury bills as a way of short-term investing, so they got charged here.

(4) This is a refund from a supplier. We paid this bill in the prior fiscal year, but we can't credit it back to the original account, Supplies Inventory, because that account was closed out at the start of this year.

(5) Woods is our V.P., Marketing. She got an expense advance before leaving on a major trip. This is what she owes us after deducting all authorized travel expenses to date.

(6) Victoria is a subsidiary company of ours. We sometimes lend them our inventory when they run out; and when they get their supply in, they return the inventory to us. To keep track of it we invoice them in the usual manner as if they had bought it, and then we credit this account when they return it.

Required: Prepare the journal entry and notes, if any, as requested by the accountant.

PROBLEMS

P5-1. You are a bank loan officer and have been asked to review the unaudited financial statements of a small privately owned company. The size of the loan will hinge on the company's ability to show that it has good collateral to cover the loan. Hence you are especially interested in the short-term investments on the balance sheet, totalling $40,629. You ask for supplementary information about this item and are given the following analysis of the total:

(i) Two hundred shares of Bell Enterprises Inc. (market value is $19.00 per share). Valued on books of company at cost.	$ 2,300.00
(ii) Promissory note from Nabob Construction Inc. Given on the purchase of construction equipment and due in two months. (Nabob is a customer of the bank and is regarded as a reasonable credit risk.)	8,000.00
(iii) Sixteen ounces of gold — purchased as an interesting speculation by the company. Market value is $495 U.S. Valued on the books at cost.	10,329.00
(iv) Term deposit purchased from Royal Trust. The certificate had a two-year term when purchased. It is now due in nine months with accrued interest of $5,600. (A certificate of deposit is a form of promissory note issued by a trust company.) Valued on the books at historic cost.	20,000.00
Total	$ 40,629.00

Required

a. State how each of these items should be valued according to GAAP and indicate whether they are properly classified as short-term investments.

b. Does valuing these assets according to GAAP provide the most useful information to you as a bank loan officer? Explain.

c. If the above items were properly classified according to GAAP, would this provide a more useful classification to you in your role as a bank loan officer? Explain.

P5-2. A friend who has accepted the job of Treasurer for the Kingston Historic Foundation asks for your help. "I've just got the cancelled cheques and the statement from the bank for November", he says, "and all I have to do now is figure out why the bank thinks we have $3,106.59, while our books say we have $1,861.75! I've already checked off the cancelled cheques against the Foundation's cheque register, and the following have not yet found their way to our bank account:

Public Utilities Commission	$ 154.87
Receiver General — for taxes withheld	1,100.00
Sears — for air conditioner	890.00
Rent	961.72

In addition, there was a deposit included in our books at the end of November that we didn't get to the bank until December. I've marked off all the cheques against the bank statement to see if that accounted for all the charges to our account. I found that they charged us service charges of $3.50 and $4.50. I called them about these, and the $3.50 was a mistake they will correct, but the $4.50 is a proper charge to us. In addition, we ran a bank overdraft at the start of the month, and they charged us $89.50 in interest. The final thing is rather embarrassing. I had to have a cheque for $128.65 certified in order to buy more postage for our meter, but I forgot to put it in the cheque register. I guess a few mistakes are to be expected from a volunteer treasurer!"

Required:

a. Draw up a schedule explaining how the bank account could have $3,106.59 in it while the books of the Foundation showed $1,861.75.

b. Make journal entries to enter into the books of the Foundation those items that should be entered properly.

P5-3. You have been hired as a loan analyst by a bank. Your boss gives you the audited financial statement of Portland Plumbing, a moderate-sized plumbing distributor that is owned by three of its senior managers. Your boss says: "I've looked over their balance sheet and the thing I'm still not happy about is their accounts receivable. Here is their aged accounts-receivable trial balance. [These type of balances are discussed in Appendix 5-4]

Summary of Aged Accounts Receivable

		Days outstanding			
Customer	Total	0 – 30	31 – 60	61 – 90	Over 90
A Limited	$ 10,320.00	$ 9,180.00			$ 1,140.00
B Limited	3,821.00	3,700.00			121.00
C Limited	2,650.00	1,200.00	$ 800.00	650.00	
D Limited	2,780.00		2,780.00		
All Others	16,532,00	13,000.00	1,250.00	1,310.00	972.00
Total	$ 36,103.00	$ 27,080.00	$ 4,830.00	$ 1,960.00	$ 2,233.00

I know all the major customers and I don't normally look on any of them as significant credit risks. I've talked to the controller and she tells me that the control account for accounts receivable is $37,832.00, and that they've had some upheaval in the credit section and haven't done a credit review for two months. I'd like you to clarify the situation for me."

Required:

a. Give a preliminary assessment based on the available evidence.

b. What other information do you think is needed for the bank to make a sound decision?

P5-4. Set out below are a number of errors made by Napanee Novelty Distributing (NND). You are asked to prepare the journal entry that would correct each error. The company arrives at its inventory position by physical count, and the books for 19X0 are still open for final adjustment of the type you are about to make. Assume all errors are material and that they were made in 19X0.

    a. The company failed to record a sale of balloons which had sold for $125.00. They cost $80.00 and were not counted in the ending inventory.

    b. The cashier had mistakenly included as part of December's business a group of cash payments received from credit customers in the first week of January totalling $1,532.00.

    c. Goods costing $63.00 were sold to a customer for $122.00 in November. He paid by cheque. His cheque was charged back to NND's account in December marked NSF. However, this was not detected by NND's accountant until January 12 when she was reconciling the December bank statement.

P5-5. Mod Corporation agreed to sell a warehouse with a book value of $200,000 to Big Corporation for $500,000. Payment terms required a $10,000 deposit when the sale agreement was signed, a payment of $90,000 at closing, and four annual payments of $100,000. Assume a 10% interest rate.

Required:

    a. How should this transaction be recorded on the books of Mod Corporation? Show your calculations.

    b. Would your answer change if Mod Corporation and Big Corporation were related? Explain.

P5-6. Local Department Store Ltd. calculates its bad debt expense on an interim basis using a percentage of sales (0.02%). At its year-end, 31 December 19X1, the receivable balances are analysed, and the final balance required in the allowance for doubtful accounts is calculated by valuing the accounts receivable directly. The results are as follows:

31 December 19X1

	Preliminary balances	Final balances
Accounts receivable	$ 250,000	$ 250,000
Allowance for doubtful accounts	40,000	28,000
Total	$ 210,000	$ 222,000

At the end of the first quarter of the following year, it became apparent from the actual collection experience that the allowance for doubtful accounts for the accounts outstanding at the year-end should have been $41,250.

Required:

    a. Explain what this discrepancy can be attributed to.

    b. Explain what effect this will have on the bad debt expense recorded in the second year.

    c. What is the appropriate accounting treatment of under- and over-accruals? Why?

P5-7. Ms. Steeves, the accountant for Moncton Productions Inc., is preparing the year-end adjustments necessary to complete the financial statements. The unadjusted trial balance indicates a balance of $6,329.99 debit for accounts receivable and $321.00 credit for the allowance for doubtful accounts. The accounts-receivable clerk has provided the aged trial balance with a commentary as shown below.

MONCTON PRODUCTIONS INC.
ACCOUNTS RECEIVABLE AGED TRIAL BALANCE
December 31, 19X6

Name	Total Amount	0 – 30 days	31 – 60 days	61 – 90 days	91 and over
Alexander & Sons	$ 1,256.89	$ 1,256.89			
Boisvert Ltd. (note 1)	932.56			$ 932.56	
Chung Manufacturing	412.81	412.81			
Hutchins Equipment (note 2)	2,323.90	652.90			$ 1,671.00
Lepage Industries (note 3)	100.72				100.72
O'Conner Company (note 4)	841.00		200.00	641.00	
Solomon Dept Store	312.12		312.12		
Wilson Storage (note 5)	149.99			149.99	
Total	$ 6,329.99	$ 2,322.60	$ 512.12	$ 1,723.55	$ 1,771.72

Notes:
  (1)   History of slow payment.
  (2)   Invoice in dispute.
  (3)   In receivership.
  (4)   Instalment payment arranged for full amount.
  (5)   History of slow payment.

Past history indicates that, in general, the following allowances are appropriate:
    Greater than 90 days — 75%
    61 to 90 days — 50%
    31 to 60 days — 25%

Specific circumstances concerning an account, however, may require deviation from the general rule. The auditors, who arrive on Monday, will review the accounts receivable and the related allowances in detail. Ms. Steeves will have to justify her decisions with respect to the allowance.

Required:

  a. Ms. Steeves wants to maximize the reported net income of the company. What journal entry will she probably make at the year-end to adjust the allowance? Show all calculations and explain the reasoning she can use to justify her decisions.

  b. As the auditor, what decisions made by Ms. Steeves would you want to examine most closely? Why?

P5-8. Quality Clothes is an independent retail store which provides credit to its customers by accepting major credit cards. This results in a commission charge to the store of 4% of credit sales. Charge slips are deposited with the bank on a weekly basis, and the commission is paid at that time. (See Appendix 5-4.)

Required: Using journal entries, indicate the appropriate accounting treatment for each of the following transactions pertaining to the first week of May 19X2.

a. Credit card sales for the week totalled $42,986.

b. Returns of merchandise, originally purchased on credit, totalled $2,651 for the week.

c. A sale of $1,234 was incorrectly recorded on the charge slip as $1,324. The error was determined by the credit company following a complaint by the customer.

d. A sale for $122 was made during the week. No credit authorization was received from the credit company, and the card number was not checked against the list of invalid card numbers. When the charge slips were deposited at the end of the week, the store was informed that the card was stolen.

e. Charge slips were deposited at the end of the week as usual.

P5-9. The following is a list of unrelated transactions which have yet to be entered in the books. For each transaction, present the necessary journal entry (entries). If none is required, state the reason why.

a. A bank charge of $75 for use of a 24-hour deposit service.

b. A cheque received from a current customer for $131, deposited in December 19X4, was returned NSF in January 19X5. The cheque bounced because of an oversight on the part of the customer.

c. A cheque received from a past customer for $131 deposited in December 19X4 was returned NSF in January 19X5. The president, treasurer, and only member of the customer corporation has since left for Paraguay, and no legal action can be taken against him unless he returns.

d. There was a transfer of $1,000 from the company chequing account to a 30-day term deposit. The deposit is redeemable on demand with loss of interest. There was a $4.75 service charge on the transfer.

e. An employee forged a cheque for $1,700. The cheque was negotiated and cashed before payment could be stopped. The president does not want to press charges because of a series of embarrassing photographs in the possession of the employee.

f. A cheque was given in November 19X4 to the federal government for the amount of $1,500 and was subsequently cashed later in the month. The amount of the cheque should have been $15 and was entered in the books as such. The government has promised to return the cheque "promptly" within the next six months.

P5-10. United Fishmongers is a small fish-packing company in Atlantic Canada which specializes in smoked oysters and pickled herring. The company's treasurer Major Opus (ret.) has just received the bank statement for the month of August. Much to his relief, the amount in the bank statement and the amount on the company books as per the bank balance are exactly the same at $4,000. However, the following transactions took place during August:

(i) There was $925 in outstanding cheques at month's end. Of these $50 worth had had payment stopped on them, whereas another $100 worth were postdated to 1 November. All $925 had been entered in the company's books for August.

(ii) A cheque received for R48.00 had been deposited in the bank after being duly entered in the company's books. This cheque was from a Russian trawler captain who bought a quantity of herring in order to fulfill his quota. The cheque was drawn on the First People's Co-op of Stalingrad. The bank notified United that it was holding the cheque and not crediting payment until money was actually received. The Commerce Bank of Nova Scotia official, A. Murray, stated that it was very unlikely that the cheque would be honoured by the "communist heathen." (1R = approximately $1.50.)

(iii) A cheque written by United Fishmongers for $533 had been mistakenly charged to the company account.

(iv) Gratuities received by the company totaling $275 had been entered in the company's books, but they had not yet been deposited in the bank.

(v) A cheque for $275 had been entered in the books as $75.

(vi) A note receivable for $175 was collected by the bank on behalf of United and deposited into the chequing account. There was a $15 charge for collecting the note. The collection of the note has not been recorded in the company's books.

(vii) The bank had mistakenly deposited $1,027.36 into the company account, but later rectified the error by withdrawing the money. The bank then charged the company $5 for withdrawing more than $1,000 without giving three days' notice. The company is contesting the charge.

Required:

a. Reconcile the bank statement and the company bank balance. Show all journal entries. If an item is not included in the reconciliation, explain why it was left out.

b. Prepare all adjusting journal entries.

P5-11. Steve Ardill, co-founder of the Queen's Calendar Corporation Ltd., was a happy man. Having had great success with the initial entrant into the calendar market, "The Ladies of Queen's," the company had brought out such biggies as "The Gentlemen of Queen's" and "The Professors of Queen's." The latest calendar, "The Small Flightless Water Fowl of Queen's," had skyrocketed. With the increased cash flow, Steve had taken to investing the company's spare cash in short-term investment instruments between calendars. The following is a list of investments made by Steve:

3 January — Bought a 90-day guaranteed investment certificate (GIC) for $1,000 yielding 12%.

16 January — Bought 100 shares of Labatts at $21.75.

30 January — Bought 150 shares of Molson A at $16.50.

8 February — Bought 500 shares of Molson A at $15.

19 February — Bought 50 shares of Labatts at $20.

27 February — Bought a $1,000 note issued by Beta Inc. It paid $950.00 for the note plus $37.50 in accrued interest. Interest of 10% is payable on October 1, the due date.

3 March — Bought a three-year bond of Mitel Corporation with a face value of $5,000. The company acquired the bonds at $97.50. It is management's intention to sell the bonds within the next six months. The bonds pay 11% semi-annually.

26 March — Sold 75 shares of Labatts at $24.50.

3 April — Received money from GIC including interest. Bought 300 shares of Alpha Petroleum at $2.90.

15 April — Labatts declared a $0.25 dividend payable 30 April.

28 April — Sold 50 shares of Labatts at $25.00.

1 May — Received 10% stock dividend from Molson.

15 June — Bought a $1,000 bond of Unicorp Canada at $104. The bond pays 13% semi-annually on 31 July and 31 January.

30 June — Year-end. Liquidated all holdings of Molson at $13.50.

Required:

a. For each transaction, give the appropriate journal entry. Assume a weighted-moving-average method of valuing the stocks is used. Show all your calculations.

b. The unit market prices of the investments as of 30 June are as follows:

Labatts — $21.25
Alpha Petroleum — $3.20
Mitel — $98.75
Beta Inc. — $94.75
Unicorp — $97.25

Show the value of the short-term investments that would appear on the balance sheet using each of the following methods:

(i) LCM on an individual basis
(ii) LCM on an aggregate basis

P5-12. Candyman Ltd. is a small candy manufacturer specializing in quality confectioneries. The Jellyroll division manager, Philip Lesh, has been reviewing the company books and has found the following:

(i) Included in the long-term investment account are 1,000 shares of IBM stock. This stock has a market value of $102,030. Mr. Lesh feels the stock should be put into the temporary investment account because it is highly liquid and could quickly and easily be sold.

(ii) Included in the notes receivable is an interest-bearing promissory note for $11,000 from a large customer, Sugar Magnolia Inc. The note is due in six months. Phil argues that this too should be included in the temporary investment account because it bears interest, can be sold if the need arises and will only be held for a short term.

(iii) Also included in the notes receivable account is an $8,500 demand note receivable from another large customer, the Cumberland Corp. Phil believes that this note might be included in the cash account because payment can be demanded at any time. He further argues that since the corporation which drew the note is a large one, there is little chance of the note being dishonoured.

(iv) Included in the temporary investment account are $25,000 in a 90-day term deposit. The money can be withdrawn on 14 days' notice with loss of interest. It is Phil's contention that this should be included with cash because it can be withdrawn on demand and the 14 days is a mere formality.

(v) Included in the other assets account are $50,000 in an account set up as a contingency fund for use should the company lose the court battle it is now engaged in. Phil argues that the contingency fund should also be included with cash because it is available on demand and there is no legal restriction on the use of the money.

Phil's newly hired assistant, Roberta Weir, was responsible for the original classifications. She defends her original position as being the correct one.

Required:

a. State the arguments Weir would use to defend her position on each of the accounts. Explain which you think is the more correct view.

b. Show the different evaluations of the various accounts following each of the arguments and explain what effect each might have on the users of financial statements.

P5-13 Eighth Dimension Corporation has accumulated over the past year a number of temporary and long-term investments. Given below is the present configuration of the two accounts.

TEMPORARY INVESTMENTS

Stock	Amount	Unit cost	Unit market value
Noranda	100	$ 22.00	$ 16.00
Datatech	2500	$ 1.80	$ 0.60
Falconbridge	200	$ 16.00	$ 46.75
Algoma	150	$ 17.50	$ 24.25

LONG-TERM INVESTMENTS

Stock	Amount	Unit cost	Unit market value
Lytton	250	$ 30.00	$ 144.00
Seagram	300	$ 39.00	$ 59.00
Denison	400	$ 19.00	$ 11.00

Buckeroo Banzai, the company president, wishes to enhance both the balance sheet and the income statement before year-end, which is only one month away.

Required:

a. Show how this might be accomplished under each of the following conditions:

(i)   The company were allowed to carry temporaries at market and long-terms at cost.

(ii)   The company were allowed to carry temporaries at lower of cost and market only and long-terms at cost.

b. Which of the above treatments is more consistent with GAAP? How does this open the door to financial statement manipulation?

P5-14. Mike Sheehan is the president and owner of Cheap Shot Photographic Ltd. Unfortunately, on 21 February 19X5 someone burglarized his office and broke into the locker in which the company cash ledger was kept and burned it. Thus all records of cash transactions that had occurred since the end of 19X4 have been lost. However, Mike, being a C.A. (convicted arsonist), realizes that all is not lost. He knows the ending company cash balance, before reconciliation, for 31 December 19X4 was $6,332. He also has the following information from the bank statement for March 19X5:

(i) Beginning balance was $4,805.

(ii) Deposits for January totalled $23,816, of which $1,200 were outstanding from December.

(iii) There was a service charge of $27 for chequing privileges for January, and there were year-end charges of $175 pertaining to 19X4.

(iv) NSF cheques totaling $350 were returned, of which $152 originated in December 19X4.

(v) The bank collected a $250 note receivable for the company for a $25 charge.

(vi) The ending bank balance was $9,521.00.

From various other sources Mike was able to ascertain the following:

(vii) Cash from sales in January totalling $750 had been deposited on 2 February.

(viii) He had received cancelled cheques totalling $19,100 from the month of January.

Required:

  a. From the given information, assist Mr. Sheehan in determining the cash balance as per the company books.

  b. As Mike is a tad behind on his accounting practices, can you reassure him that this is the correct balance?

P5-15. Pat Pitblado is the controller of a sporting goods chain called Run & Jump Limited. She admits to you, a C.A., that she got the job under false pretenses and that she knows nothing about accounting. She asks you to examine the current assets section of the balance sheet. On viewing this section, it becomes apparent to you that she must have received her degree in phys.ed. There is a $60,790 *Cash* balance under current assets as of 31 December 19X7. An examination of the books reveals that *Cash* includes the following:

  (i) a current deposit of $16,330 at the Royal Bank
  (ii) a term deposit of $5,000 which cannot be withdrawn until after 1 May 19X9
  (iii) customers' cheques for $500, not yet deposited
  (iv) a customer's NSF cheque for $200
  (v) a demand deposit of $9,185 that is unavailable, being in a bank in a foreign country which is at war
  (vi) advances of $1,675 to officers of the company
  (vii) a pension fund of $28,000 for employees
  (viii) a petty cash fund of $200, of which $65 is cash, $45 is in the form of employees' IOU's, and $90 is supported by receipts for expenses paid out of the fund
  (ix) an overdraft of $300 at the Commercial Bank

Required:
Aside from suggesting to Pat that she should study for another degree, indicate how the items in the *Cash* balance should be reported on the balance sheet of Run & Jump Limited. Give the proper classification, account name, and amount for each item.

(CGA adapted)

P5-16. When examining the accounts of Single Account Company you focused on an account called Receivables which had a balance of $133,000. Your analysis of the details of this account revealed the following:

Accounts receivable — customers	$ 60,000
Loans receivable — officers	25,000
Prepayments made to suppliers for orders	4,000
Expense advances to salespersons	2,000
Common stock subscriptions receivable	82,000
Overpayment of accounts payable	1,000
Overpayments of accounts by customers	(3,000)
Accounts payable — purchases of merchandise	(38,000)
Net receivables	$ 133,000

Required:

  a. Give the necessary journal entry (entries) to reflect the correct treatment of each of the above items.

  b. Present the partial balance sheet to show how the above items would be reported.

(CGA adapted)

P5-17. Gibson Company's portfolio of temporary investments is appropriately included in current assets. The portfolio has performed as follows:

On 31 December 19X7

Stock	Cost	Market	Unrealized gain (loss)
Anchor Co. Ltd.	$ 10,000	$ 10,000	Nil
Keller Inc.	20,000	15,000	$ (5,000)
Peltier Co. Inc.	25,000	26,000	1,000
Total	$ 55,000	$ 51,000	$ (4,000)

On 31 December 19X6

Stock	Cost	Market	Unrealized gain (loss)
Anchor Co. Ltd.	$ 10,000	$ 12,000	$ 2,000
Keller Inc.	30,000	26,000	$ (4,000)
Peltier Co. Inc.	20,000	24,000	4,000
Total	$ 60,000	$ 62,000	$ 2,000

Required:

Disregard income tax considerations. What amount should be reported as an unrealized gain or loss (indicate which) in Gibson Company's 19X7 income statement? Why?

(CGA adapted)

P5-18. Your assistant prepared the following bank reconciliation statement. Obviously the statement is unacceptable. The task of preparing a proper reconciliation falls upon you.

BEVERLY HILLS COMPANY
BANK RECONCILIATION
(Prepared by Assistant)

31 October 19X7

Balance per books as of 31 October		$ 6,000
Add: Note collected	$ 1,000	
Interest on note	110	
Deposit in transit	2,900	4,010
		$ 10,010
Deduct: Bank charges	$ 10	
NSF cheque from Mr. Axel Foley	100	
Outstanding cheques	1,500	
Error in cheque No. 78 issued for $872 and recorded in the books as $827 (cheque was debited to accounts payable)	45	$ 1,655
Indicated bank balance		$ 8,355
Balance per bank statement		5,555
Discrepancy		$ 2,800

Required:

a. Determine the true cash balance of Beverly Hills Company as of 31 October 19X7.

b. Prepare the necessary journal entries for 31 October 19X7 that would result from the proper bank reconciliation.

(CGA adapted)

APPENDIX 5-1
Reconciliation of Company and Bank Balances

Most companies have at least several bank accounts that may be used for specialized purposes such as payroll, routine payment to suppliers, and general banking. Unless special arrangements are made, a bank normally issues a statement of a commercial customer's account monthly and returns the cancelled cheques at that time. If a company operates an active bank account, the bank balance shown in the ledger of the company is almost never the same as the balance shown in the bank statement as of the same moment. There are two general reasons for this. First, **timing differences** arise because the same entries were posted by the company and the bank in two different accounting periods. Second, **adjustments** usually need to be made by either the company or the bank, but not both.

One main *timing difference* concerns **outstanding cheques**; that is, cheques issued by the company and entered in its books, but not yet recorded in the company's bank account, and hence outstanding. They arise because the cheques are still in the mail to the creditor or have not yet been returned through the banking system from the creditor's bank. Another main timing difference concerns **outstanding deposits**, that is, deposits entered in the company's books but not yet recorded by the bank. The use of electronic funds transfers has reduced both these items to some extent, but for most companies they are still an important consideration.

Typical *adjustments* include (i) bank service charges which the company has not entered in its books, and (ii) bank interest. These have to be entered in the books of the company. Adjustments that would need to be made by the bank, but not the company, would be cheques charged against the company's bank account in error or disputed service charges which the bank agrees to reverse.

Mainly as a result of timing differences, the amount actually in the bank is often much different from the balance in the company's books. Normally the bank will show the company as having a larger balance than the company itself will show. A handful of companies (e.g. Leon's Furniture) show the outstanding cheques as a liability, probably to emphasize the point that the actual bank balance is not as low as the financial statements would otherwise show.

An important step in the control and management of cash is the **bank reconciliation**, a document that explains the difference between the balances in the books of the company and the bank statements by calculating the effect of each timing difference and adjustment. Here is an example of a simplified bank reconciliation:

A HYPOTHETICAL BANK RECONCILIATION

	Balance per bank	Balance per company
Balance on hand, per records	$ 3,356.18	$ (2,356.87)
Bank adjustment needed: cheque of another company charged to our account in error	100.00	
Bank balance after bank error is adjusted (1)	3,456.18	
Time Differences:		
Deposits received at the end of the month, but not taken to the bank until the following day (2)	854.76	
Outstanding cheques (list of these cheques would normally be attached) (3)	(6,788.51)	
Adjustment needed in company books for:		
Cheque deposited, but returned NSF (4)		(8.50)
Credit report requested from bank (4)		(22.50)
Interest on overdraft (4)		(89.70)
Balance in both books when corrections are made and timing differences have cleared	$ (2,477.57)	$ (2,477.57)

The timing differences (items 2 and 3) do not give rise to any accounting entry because the bank will process these transactions in due course. Item (1) will be adjusted in the books of the bank. The company adjustments (item 4) are entered in the books of the company as follows:

Accounts receivable — NSF cheque	8.50	
Credit report expense	22.50	
Interest expense	89.70	
Bank		120.70

To record charges made by bank that had not yet been
  entered in the books of the company.

If the above entry contained material items, it would be entered in the books of the company before the financial statements were prepared.

A bank reconciliation is an internal working document for management. There are two important goals to be accomplished. First, any differences between the balance in the company's books and the bank should be explained. Second, entries that need to be made in the company's books for items such as service charges should be identified and entered. Therefore, the form of the reconciliation does not matter as long as it does the job. An alternative format is as follows:

HYPOTHETICAL BANK RECONCILIATION — ALTERNATIVE FORMAT

Balance, per bank	$ 3,356.18
Bank adjustment needed: cheque of another company charged to our account in error	+ 100.00
Deposits received at the end of the month, but not taken to the bank until the following day	+ 854.76
Outstanding cheques (list of these cheques would normally be attached)	(6,788.51)
Corrected balance (overdraft)	$ (2,477.57)
Balance in company books before making adjustments	$ (2,356.87)
Adjustment needed in company books for:	
Cheque deposited, but returned NSF	(8.50)
Credit report requested from bank	(22.50)
Interest on overdraft	(89.70)
Corrected balance (overdraft)	$ (2.477.57)

APPENDIX 5-2
Present Value and Imputed Interest

This Appendix gives a brief introduction to the concepts of **present value** and **imputed interest** for those who have not studied it before in a course such as Mathematics of Investment. For those who have already studied this subject, it should provide a quick refresher course.

IMPUTED INTEREST

One can think of **interest** as the *rent* that is charged by people for letting someone else temporarily use their money. The amount of money lent is referred to as the **principal**. The rental charge is usually quoted as a function of (i) the interest rate, or the fraction formed by dividing the total amount of the interest by the amount borrowed (e.g., if one lent $100 and asked $24 in interest, the rate would be 24/100 or 24%); and (ii) the length of time over which the money is borrowed (thus, if in the preceding example the money were borrowed for one year, then the rate would be 24% for one year). If the length of time is not quoted, then the convention is that the rate is for one year (e.g., 8% would mean $8 for every $100 borrowed for one year).

The **compounding period** is the elapsed length of time before interest is calculated and payable or compounded. If it is not paid, then the amount of interest is added to the principal, and interest thenceforth is calculated on both the principal and the accumulated interest. For example, if $100 were borrowed at an annual rate of 12% compounded half-yearly, then at the end of six months the interest would be calculated as follows:

$$100 \times 12/100 \times 6/12 = 6.00$$

If the interest of $6.00 is not paid, then it is added to the principal. Hence $106.00 is owing for the second six months, and the interest for the second six months would be as follows:

$$106 \times 12/100 \times 6/12 = 6.36$$

In other words, it is $0.36 higher than for the first six months. This can be explained as $6.00 interest on the principal plus $0.36 interest on the unpaid interest of $6.00. **Compound interest** occurs when interest is charged on the unpaid accumulated interest. Note that the amount of interest would increase with each passing period as long as the interest rate is greater than zero.

How is the rent or interest established? The usual answer is that it is established by competition in the marketplace in such money-market centres as Toronto or New York. The government-owned banks such as the Bank of Canada and the Federal Reserve Board heavily influence the interest rate as part of their activity in influencing the country's overall finances. The rate that an individual company has to pay is then related to the rate that one of these banks pays. The interest rate paid is usually thought of a being composed of three elements: (i) a premium to the investor for bearing a risk that repayment might not be forthcoming; (ii) a portion to compensate the investor in times of inflation for the loss in purchasing power of money between the time of investment and the time of repayment; and (iii) the "pure" interest, or the amount the investor would receive in a riskless, inflation-proof world.

Another major influence on the interest rate that an individual or a company pays is the perceived riskiness of that borrower. The riskier the borrower, the higher becomes the "insurance premium" that the lender wants built into the interest rate, and hence the higher the interest rate itself becomes.

PRESENT VALUE

The **present value** of a future payment is the amount of that payment discounted to the present using some rate of interest. If there are to be multiple future payments, one would calculate the present value of each to find the present value of all the payments. (Present value tables are given at the end of this book.)

In the preceding section we implicitly assumed that the borrower either (i) pays the interest at the end of each period or (ii) allows the interest to be added to the principal and pays off both at some later date. The arrangements for payment that a borrower can make — in theory — are completely flexible. Even assuming a fixed interest rate, it is possible to arrange an infinite variety of repayment schedules that will repay all principal and interest over the life of the loan. Let us examine four particular methods. We will illustrate each method with an example. In each instance, let us suppose that $100 is borrowed on 1 January with interest at 1% payable monthly. Let us further assume that the principal is due in two years.

Method 1.   Under this method, interest is paid at the end of each period, and the principal is paid when it is due.

In our example, at the end of each month the borrower pays the lender 1% of $100 or $1.00. The borrower does this at the end of each of the first 23 months; at the end of the 24th month the borrower pays the principal plus one month's interest, or $101.00.

This type of payment arrangement is typically found if money is borrowed from the bank on a personal loan. The bank lends the money and then charges the borrower's bank account each month with that month's interest.

Method 2.   Under this method, interest is paid at the end of each month, and the principal is retired by small monthly repayments. The combined payments for interest and principal retirement are the same each month.

In our example, at the end of January a payment of $4.71 is made. This is sufficient to pay the interest of $1.00 and contribute $3.71 toward repaying part of the principal. At the end of February another payment of $4.71 is made. Here the interest cost is 1% of (100.00 - 3.71 = 96.29) = 0.96. Thus the capital repayment is $3.75, slightly higher than the month before. Payments of $4.71 continue for 24 months in all. Each month the interest cost drops, and hence the capital repayment part goes up. A summary is given below:

Month	Principal owing	Interest	Monthly payment	Repayment of principal	Month	Principal owing	Interest	Monthly Payment	Repayment of principal
1	100.00	1.00	4.71	3.71	13	52.95	0.53	4.71	4.18
2	96.29	0.96	4.71	3.75	14	48.77	0.49	4.71	4.22
3	92.54	0.93	4.71	3.78	15	44.55	0.45	4.71	4.26
4	88.76	0.89	4.71	3.82	16	40.28	0.40	4.71	4.31
5	84.94	0.85	4.71	3.86	17	35.97	0.36	4.71	4.35
6	81.08	0.81	4.71	3.90	18	31.62	0.32	4.71	4.39
7	77.18	0.77	4.71	3.94	19	27.23	0.27	4.71	4.44
8	73.24	0.73	4.71	3.98	20	22.79	0.23	4.71	4.48
9	69.26	0.69	4.71	4.02	21	18.31	0.18	4.71	4.53
10	65.24	0.65	4.71	4.06	22	13.78	0.14	4.71	4.57
11	61.19	0.61	4.71	4.10	23	9.21	0.09	4.71	4.62
12	57.09	0.57	4.71	4.14	24	4.59	0.05	4.71	4.66

Note how the interest cost drops from $1.00 in the first month to $0.05 in the 24th month and how the capital repayment portion rises correspondingly. The principal repayment of $4.66 differs from the principal owing of $4.59 only because we have rounded off the figures. For precision, the actual monthly payment would have to be fractionally higher than $4.71.

This repayment method is often termed **blended principal and interest** since in arriving at the fixed monthly payment both interest charges and principal repayment are taken into account. It is commonly used to repay mortgages on houses, where the householder pays a constant amount each month over the life of the mortgage. It is also commonly used by retired people who have built up a sum of money in a pension fund and who want to withdraw it over a stated period of years at a fixed amount each month. The pension application will be discussed later in Chapter 15.

Method 3.   Under this method, the debtor does not pay any interest or principal until the principal is due. Each month's interest is calculated and added onto the principal amount. The combined amount then forms the base for calculating the next month's interest. Clearly, the interest cost will keep rising each month.

In our example, the first month's interest would be 1% of $100.00, or $1.00. The second month's interest would be 1% of (100.00 + 1.00), or $1.01. Each succeeding month's interest would be slightly bigger. The interest grows at a faster rate with each passing month.

Month	Principal	Interest	Month	Principal	Interest
1	100.00	1.00	13	112.68	1.13
2	101.00	1.01	14	113.81	1.14
3	102.01	1.02	15	114.95	1.15
4	103.03	1.03	16	116.10	1.16
5	104.06	10.4	17	117.26	1.17
6	105.10	1.05	18	118.43	1.18
7	106.15	1.06	19	119.61	1.20
8	107.21	1.07	20	120.81	1.21
9	108.29	1.08	21	122.02	1.22
10	109.37	1.09	22	123.24	1.23
11	110.46	1.10	23	124.47	1.24
12	111.57	1.12	24	125.72	1.26

At the end of the 24th month the debt would be repaid by a sum of (125.72 + 1.26), or $126.98; the person owed the money would get back the $100.00 plus interest of $26.98.

Let us consider this pattern by asking the following question: "If you thought the market rate of interest was 1% per month and if someone offered to enter into a contract to pay you $126.98 at the end of 24 months, then how much should you be willing to offer to pay for this contract at the beginning of the 24 months?" The calculation above indicates that you would be willing to pay $100 for such a contract because $100 compounded at 1% will equal the amount promised, or $126.98.

Although most tenants would not realize it, if the landlord asks for the last month's rent as a deposit and promises to pay interest on it, he is getting a loan of this sort, The principal of the loan will be repaid by allowing the tenant to use the apartment during the last month of the lease, and the interest will presumably be paid by cheque.

An example that is of most interest to us would be a purchase by a customer of an item at a price of $126.98 payable at the end of 24 months. Such a purchase would be regarded as made up of two items: (i) the purchase of an item whose present value is $100 and (ii) a loan of $100 payable in 24 months with accumulated interest of $26.98. The accounting reporting issue is whether it should be recorded as:

(A) Accounts receivable		126.98	
Sales			126.98

or

(B) Accounts receivable		126.98	
Sales			100.00
Accounts receivable — deferred interest			26.98

Method 4. Under this method, some equal sum is paid at the end of each interest period; but it is not equal to the interest due and not sufficient to retire the capital by the end of the loan period.

In our example, suppose that the monthly payment is $1.185. At the end of the first month the interest due would be $1.00. With a payment of $1.185 the amount of capital repaid wuld be (1.185 − 1.00) or $0.18. (The arithmetic below is shown for $1,000 instead of $100 to make it easier to show fractional amounts.) At the end of the second period the interest would be 1% of

$(100.00 - 0.185 = 99.815) = \$0.998$. Thus capital repayment would be $1.185 - 0.998 = \$0.187$. The history of the repayment over 24 periods is shown below.

Month	Principal owing	Interest	Monthly payment	Repayment of principal	Month	Principal owing	Interest	Monthly Payment	Repayment of principal
1	1,000.00	10.00	11.85	1.85	13	976.54	9.77	11.85	2.08
2	998.15	9.98	11.85	1.87	14	974.45	9.74	11.85	2.11
3	996.28	9.96	11.85	1.89	15	972.35	9.72	11.85	2.13
4	994.39	9.94	11.85	1.91	16	970.22	9.70	11.85	2.15
5	992.49	9.92	11.85	1.93	17	968.07	9.68	11.85	2.17
6	990.56	9.91	11.85	1.94	18	965.90	9.66	11.85	2.19
7	988.62	9.89	11.85	1.96	19	963.71	9.64	11.85	2.21
8	986.65	9.87	11.85	1.98	20	961.50	9.61	11.85	2.24
9	984.67	9.85	11.85	2.00	21	959.26	9.59	11.85	2.26
10	982.67	9.83	11.85	2.02	22	957.01	9.57	11.85	2.28
11	980.64	9.81	11.85	2.04	23	954.73	9.55	11.85	2.30
12	978.60	9.79	11.85	2.06	24	952.42	9.52	11.85	2.33

At the end of the 24th period, the capital outstanding would be $95.24 - 0.24 = 95.00$. Hence a payment of $95.00 at the end of the term would retire the debt.

A common example would be a bond with a redemption value of $95.00 at the end of the 24 periods. Attached to the bond are 24 coupons that can be detached and cashed at the end of each month, each worth $1.185. If the market rate of interest were 1% per month, then a person would be willing to pay $100 for this bond at the beginning. As we have shown, the $100 investment would be regained over the 24 months of payments. We will discuss this case further in Chapter 12 on long-term bonds.

Note that if the market interest rate rose above 1%, then less of the capital would be repaid at the end of each month. Consequently, one would want either (i) a higher repayment at the end of the term or (ii) a lower purchase price at the beginning of the term. Because the terms of repayment at the end are normally fixed when the bond is originally sold, the only variable is usually the purchase price at the beginning. Thus, we have the following rule: as the interest rate goes up (down), the price at which fixed rate bonds can be purchased goes down (up).

SUMMARY

It can be seen from the above that there are four essential ingredients to interest calculations: (i) the **present value**, or the amount at the beginning of the loan; (ii) the **future value**, or the amount at the end of the loan; (iii) the **payment** each period; and (iv) **interest rate** used to calculate the periodic interest charge. It should also be noted that if any three are known, the fourth can be calculated. In real business situations the present value usually is not known and cannot be calculated precisely; for often one has to estimate what the interest rate should be.

There are many common examples where the exact amount of interest is not paid at the end of each compounding period. In fact, the periodic payment may be greater or less than the amount of interest due; the amount paid at the end of the term of the loan will make up the difference.

In a typical business transaction where a sale has been made on extended terms, it may not occur to those involved that the extension of the terms has decreased the present value of the accounts receivable. It, therefore, may not occur to them to show the accounts receivable at their present value instead of their future value.

APPENDIX 5-3
Accounting for Long-Term Receivables

Some people find the accounting for long-term receivables confusing. The purpose of this Appendix is to explain the general concept through an example.

Suppose that Florida Developments Inc., having bought a large tract of land in a swampy area near an established resort, sold lots for a payment of $1,000 down and a $30,000 mortgage due in 30 years at an interest rate of 5%. Suppose also that at the time the deal for one sale was concluded the market interest rate was 19%.

Leaving aside accounting entries for the moment, let us see what the economic substance of the deal was. If one believed that the market rate of interest of 19% was going to last for the next 30 years, then our knowledge of the time value of money would tell us that the market value (i.e., present value) of the mortgage could be calculated as follows:

The present value of $30,000 discounted at 19% for 30 years	$ 162.45
The present value of an annuity of $1,500 per annum (5% of 30,000) discounted at 19%	7,851.99
Total present value of above mortgage	$ 8,014.44

In effect, the company has sold its land for cash of $1,000 and a 30-year mortgage worth $8,014.44 if 19% is taken as the market rate of interest.

If the market value of the mortgage is recognized, the accounting entry on the sale of the land would be as follows:

Mortgage receivable	30,000	
Cash	1,000	
Discount on mortgage receivable		21,985.56
Sales		9,014.44
To record sale of lot. Proceeds were $1,000 in cash and a 30-year mortgage at 5% whose present value at the market rate of 19% was $ 8,014.44.		

The **discount on mortgage receivable** here is the difference between the face value of $30,000 and the present value of $8,014.44. In effect the company has decided to engage in two activities: (i) land development, in which it will realize a profit of $9,014.44 less the costs of development; and (ii) financing its customers in the purchase of its product, in which it can expect to make $21,985.56 in financing income over the 30-year life of the mortgage.

How much financing income does it make in a given year? One way of calculating this would be to reason as follows. In calculating the discount on the mortgage we assumed a discount rate of 19% over the next 30 years. This is another way of saying that we assumed an earning rate of 19% on the asset on hand for each of the years. At the end of the first year we would, therefore, assume an earning of 19% of our investment of $8,014.44, or $1,522.74. On receipt of the payment due under the mortgage, the accounting entry would be as follows:

Bank	1,500.00	
Discount on mortgage receivable	22.74	
Interest income		1,522.74
To record receipt of annual payment of $1,500 (5% of $30,000) and to record interest income of 19% of the discounted value of $8,014.44.		

At the end of the second year we would be carrying a net investment of $8,037.18. Thus the interest income booked for that year would be 19% of 8,037.18, or $1,527.06. Note that the interest income steadily rises because the company is earning interest on its investment but does not get paid for it in full until the end of 30 years. If the company were to ignore the time value of money, it would make the accounting entry as follows:

Mortgage receivable — 5%	30,000.00	
Cash	1,000.00	
Sales		31,000.00
To record sale.		

Note that the revenue of $31,000 it would book is exactly equal to the revenue shown above of $9,014.44 on sale of land and $21,985.56 of interest income. The difference in treatment is not how much is taken into income, but in what year and how it is described. Is it recorded entirely as revenue from land sales or is it split into interest income and income from interest on a mortgage investment?

APPENDIX 5-4
Recording and Managing Accounts Receivable

The recording of accounts receivable is, by volume of transactions, one of the largest segments of most companies' accounting systems, since at least one ledger account must be kept for each customer, with a posting for each credit sale and each payment. Because the value of a receivable lies only in the likelihood of its being paid, this asset can quickly "disappear" if the company fails to keep accurate records of who owes it money. In addition, it is usual to have staff within the company who are responsible for credit management. They must approve credit sales and review each of the accounts in order to follow up those not paid within the company's credit terms. In assessing the quality of the company's accounts receivable, it is common to assess the quality of the record keeping and credit management. In this section we will review the most important features.

ACCOUNTING FEATURES

For financial statement purposes it is essential to know the *total* amount of accounts receivable, whereas for credit review and collecting purposes one needs to know how much is owed by each *individual*. The manner in which these two needs are served varies in detail, but the usual plan is to keep a detailed ledger account for each customer and prepare either (i) a summary trial balance of the individual general ledger accounts receivable or (ii) a summary general ledger account for all customers. The difference is that under the first method the general ledger keeps the individual accounts separate. In practice, the first method is commonly found with non-computerized accounting systems, and the second usually restricted to computerized systems.

We can illustrate the two methods by means of a simple example. Let us assume that there are only the following journal entries:

January 19X0

Accounts receivable — Sam Jones	15.00	
Accounts receivable — Mary Smith	38.00	
Sales		53.00
To record credit sales.		

February 19X0

Cash	45.00	
Accounts receivable — Sam Jones		10.00
Accounts receivable — Mary Smith		35.00
To record cash receipts.		

If method (i) were used, the individual accounts would be found in the general ledger as follows:

GENERAL LEDGER
ACCOUNT RECEIVABLE — SAM JONES

Date	Description	Debit	Credit	Balance
January	Sales	15.00		15.00
February	Cash		10.00	5.00

GENERAL LEDGER
ACCOUNT RECEIVABLE — MARY SMITH

Date	Description	Debit	Credit	Balance
January	Sales	38.00		38.00
February	Cash		35.00	3.00

the section of the general ledger trial balance dealing with accounts receivable would show at the end of February 19X0 the following:

Accounts receivable — Sam Jones	5.00
Accounts receivable — Mary Smith	3.00
Total accounts receivable	8.00

If method (ii) were used, the same individual accounts receivable would be kept, but not as part of the general ledger. Instead, in the general ledger would be one accounts receivable account, termed a **control account**. The individual accounts would be in a **subsidiary ledger**. That ledger exists in addition to the general ledger and balances to the control account. To the control account would be posted all the entries affecting the individual accounts. Thus for our example it would read as follows:

GENERAL LEDGER
ACCOUNT RECEIVABLE — CONTROL ACCOUNT

Date	Description	Debit	Credit	Balance
January	Sales — Sam Jones	15.00		15.00
	Sales — Mary Smith	38.00		53.00
February	Cash — Sam Jones		10.00	43.00
	Cash — Mary Smith		35.00	8.00

In practice, only the totals of the debits and credits would be posted above. Notice that the final balance in the general ledger control account as produced under method (ii) is the same amount, $8.00, as the trial balance of the individual accounts kept under method (i). Both methods produce the same end result. Which one is chosen usually depends on some external factor, such as the organizational arrangements in a given company or the economic costs in a given situation.

CREDIT MANAGEMENT

Credit management helps to ensure that accounts receivable are paid on time, thus reducing the company's investment in this asset that produces no revenue and also reducing the probability that the account will turn out to be a bad debt. There are many facets of credit management that are beyond the scope of this book. Nevertheless, let us focus on one of the basic factors, which is for the person responsible to keep informed about how much each customer owes and whether they are paying their bills on time. The main source of information for this is the accounts receivable ledger accounts. Credit departments are usually placed where they can get information from this ledger either physically or, for computer-based systems, with inquiry terminals.

Each ledger account will be aged so that the company can analyse which invoices have been paid and hence which unpaid ones make up the balance owing. If the company requires payment within, say, thirty days of invoicing, the clerk will watch for those over thirty days that have not been paid. Typically there are three causes of overdue accounts. First, the customer may be short of cash. The company may then have to decide whether to cut off further shipments to the customer until payment is made or perhaps require the customer to pay on delivery. The second cause is that an invoice may be in dispute for some reason. For example, a customer may be disputing that he received the goods or he may claim that he has returned them. Such disputes need to be settled quickly, while the evidence is still fresh. The third cause is that there may be some accounting mistakes. For example, the payment may have been received, but credited to some other account in error.

Suppose that the credit clerk has aged an accounts receivable trial balance and it reads as follows:

Customer	Total amount owing	Current 30 days or less	31 to 60 days	61 to 90 days	Over 90 days
Apple, Frank	$ 24,813.81	$ 23,567.43	$ 678.56	$ 0.00	$ 567.82
Baker, H.W.	412.74	356.87	0.00	55.87	0.00
Campbell, J.D.	869.43	123.45	356.86	389.12	0.00
Dingbat, A.W.	356.85	356.85	0.00	0.00	0.00
	$ 26.452.83	$ 24,404.60	$ 1,035.42	$ 444.99	$ 567.82

This is called an **aged trial balance**. In the left column is the regular trial balance, and the columns to the right of it show the *age* of the total amount showing. Frank Apple, for instance, owes a total of $24,813.81. Of this amount, $567.82 has been owing for over 90 days, $678.56 has been owing for over thirty days but less than sixty-one days, and $23,567.43 has been charged in the past thirty days. It is the credit clerk's responsibility to know the customer and his paying habits. On the whole it looks as if Frank Apple's account is current. The disturbing amount is $567.82 that has been overdue for more than ninety days. This seems out of character with his overall payment history and seems to imply that the amount is in dispute. On the other hand, it looks as if J.D. Campbell is a reliable but slow payer.

It can be seen that an aged trial balance is not the last word on the collectability of the accounts receivable. However, when it is combined with other knowledge that a credit clerk should have about customers, an aged trial balance provides a powerful tool for surveying the accounts. It also provides a useful way for an outsider, such as a bank, to make a quick evaluation of the quality of the accounts receivable if it is asked to lend money on the receivables as security for the loan.

BAD DEBTS EXPENSE

Bad debts are a fact of business life, even with a good credit department. The accounting treatment of them has to reflect the fact that the company may suspect an account is at least partly uncollectable long before it is willing to write the account off formally. The usual approach is to avoid showing the write-off in the individual's account (Because the individual would usually receive a copy of the account, showing the write-off might well reduce the likelihood of payment). Instead, a separate *Allowance for doubtful accounts* is opened, and the credit balance in that account reflects the estimate of the total uncollectable individual accounts.

When it is decided that an individual account should be written off, a typical entry would read as follows:

Allowance for doubtful accounts	5.00	
Accounts receivable — Sam Jones		5.00

To write off the portion of Jones's account estimated to be uncollectable.

A company starting out in business would find by the end of its financial year that write-offs of individual accounts into the allowance for doubtful accounts had left the latter account in a debit balance. It should never be in a debit balance at a year-end inasmuch as its function is to offset those debit balances in accounts receivable that are considered doubtful. Thus a debit balance is remedied by making the following journal entry:

Bad debts expense	xxxxxxxx	
Allowance for doubtful accounts		xxxxxxxx

To adjust the allowance for doubtful accounts to estimated amount.

How is the amount of the above journal entry arrived at? By working backward and deciding first how big the closing balance should be in the allowance for doubtful accounts. This is done by reviewing the accounts receivable, by aging, and by other means. Then the above entry is made to "force" the allowance for doubtful accounts to be the amount desired.

For example, let us assume that at the year-end the balance in the allowance for doubtful accounts was a debit of $2,300.00. After reviewing the accounts receivable, it was decided that $4,560.00 of them were estimated to be uncollectable. Therefore the balance in the allowance for doubtful accounts should be a credit of $4,560.00. To attain this, the journal entry would be as follows:

Provision for bad debts expense	6,860.00	
Allowance for doubtful accounts		6,860.00

To set up the year-end balance in the allowance for doubtful accounts.

The above example has been kept as simple as possible to show the basic principle. Many companies would not want to wait until the end of the year to recognize the bad debts expense. Because they issue interim financial reports, they would want each period to be charged with its estimated bad debts expense. There are two common methods for doing this. Under the first method, they can review the accounts receivable at the end of the financial period. They can then make the appropriate entries (such as the one above) at the end of each period. A typical entry would read as follows:

Provision for bad debts expense	150.00	
Allowance for doubtful accounts		150.00
To provide for estimated bad debts after a review of the accounts receivable ledger.		

Under the second method, the company can estimate what the amount of the bad debts expense would be (e.g., by estimating it as a percentage of sales). They can then make a monthly adjusting journal entry, with a final adjustment to the allowance for doubtful accounts at the end of the fiscal year after the individual accounts have been reviewed. The journal entry would be similar to the one above. The difference does not lie in the form of the journal entry, but only in the manner in which the amount of bad debt is estimated.

Making adjustments through the year adds slightly to the complexity of the accounting. But if one keeps in mind that the ultimate step is to force the allowance for doubtful accounts to be the balance that seems appropriate, in the light of review of the individual accounts, and to charge this amount to bad debts expense, then the preliminary steps that might take place before this will seem less confusing.

Note that the decision about the appropriate size of the allowance for doubtful accounts is a judgement call. One cannot know the actual amount of bad debt contained in the accounts receivable until well after the year-end, when the final outcome becomes clear.

CREDIT CARDS

Many retail stores and restaurants accept bank credit cards such as VISA or MasterCard. These do not become the accounts receivable of the business that accepts them in payment, because they can be immediately deposited in the bank for cash (less commission of 3% to 6%).

For example, suppose a VISA card is used to purchase an item in a store costing $10.85. The accounting entry would read as follows:

Account receivable — VISA	10.85	
Sales		10.85
To record credit card sale.		

When the charge slips were deposited with the bank, the store would make the following entry:

Bank	10.45	
Commission paid	0.40	
Account receivable - VISA		10.85
To record assignment of VISA charge slips to the bank.		

Technically, the merchant is selling his charge slips to the bank. There are circumstances under which the bank might later demand repayment (e.g., if the credit card was out of date or if the merchant had not got prior permission for a sale over a preset amount, such as $75). However, such charge-backs are not likely to be major if the merchant has been careful to follow the procedures of the credit card company. A typical journal entry for a charge-back would be the following:

Account receivable — R.J. Smith	125.03	
Account receivable — VISA		125.03
To record VISA charge slip charged back because it was not authorized by phone. Charged to general accounts receivable for direct collection by store.		

BIBLIOGRAPHY

ACCOUNTING PRINCIPLES BOARD. *Opinion No. 21: Interest on Receivables and Payables*. New York: American Institute of Certified Public Accountants, 1971. This opinion issued by the predecessor body to the FASB contains an extensive discussion of the discounting issue.

TRITES, G.D. "A New Approach to Accounting for Portfolio Investments." CA Magazine (April 1984). A discussion of a study on accounting for portfolio investments commissioned by the CICA.

CHAPTER 6
Inventory and Cost of Goods Sold

Introduction

For many companies, inventory is one of their most significant assets. By its very nature, inventory usually presents a greater problem to the accountant than do most other current assets for three main reasons. First, verifying its physical existence can be time-consuming and the results are often subject to error. Second, within the historic-cost convention, there are a variety of methods for arriving at the *cost* of the inventory, each producing a different answer. Third, the convention of conservatism has led to the practice of writing inventory down to market if this is less than cost, thus making it necessary to develop measures for both cost and market as well as ways of applying the cost-and-market test.

Types of Inventories

Inventories are like accounts receivable; they are owned by a company to achieve a purpose. They are not desirable in themselves unless the company considers one of its roles to be commodity speculation and seeks gains through holding the inventory over a period of rising prices. If it does not seek the spectacular role, then it has two possible reasons for holding inventory: (i) to provide buffer stocks to avoid hand-to-mouth ordering of inventory and possible inventory shortages; and (ii) to provide **work in process**, also called **work in progress**, in which semi-manufactured goods form a necessary part of the manufacturing process.

For example, a company that manufactures chocolate bars would have raw material stocks of sugar, cocoa, various oils, flavouring, nuts, and wrapping materials. Although it could order these items on a day-to-day basis if needed, it would usually find it cheaper and more convenient to have at least a few days' supply of each on hand. On any given day when it is manufacturing chocolate bars, its manufacturing equipment will be fed the raw material. A walk through the plant would show chocolate bars in various stages of manufacture on their way to being wrapped and boxed.

When the chocolate bars are wrapped and boxed they would be transported from the plant to the finished goods warehouse, where they would be used to fill customer orders.

If a manufacturing company is thought of as a unit for converting raw material, labour, and services into a finished product, then the flow of material through the company can be shown as follows:

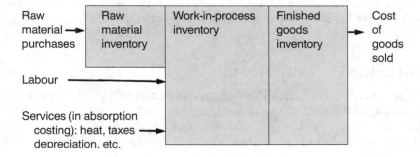

In the diagram the raw material inventory and the finished goods inventory fulfill the buffer stock function, whereas work-in-process inventory arises because the manufacturing process takes place over time.

Establishing Inventory Quantities

Unless a company wishes to purchase inventory as a speculative commodity, it will try to keep its inventory as low as possible consistent with its buffer-stock and manufacturing objectives. This means that strict attention must be paid to the size of the various types of inventories. Then quick action can be taken when the inventories get too high or low because of falling demand for the finished product or over-ordering of buffer stocks.

For example, in a retail store the control of inventory is crucial to the store's success. Not only must the merchandise match the customers' tastes, but quantities must be at an appropriate level. If this level is too low, the customers will not be able to find the goods they want; and if it is too high, the store must bear the cost of interest for the financing, storage, obsolescence, and possible deterioration of them.

While it is usually in the company's overall best interest to keep inventories low, the incentive at lower levels within the organization may be the reverse. If a plant supervisor or head of a retail store department is criticized for running out of stock and not rewarded for keeping it as low as practical, then that person will naturally tend to overstock. Thus the *natural* level of inventory will often be higher than the *best* level; and inventory will remain too high unless management takes special steps to counteract this. Sometimes management can accomplish the goal by a periodic review of inventories or by watching the inventory turnover ratios. Some inventories are so large and complex that informal control approaches become ineffective and more formal inventory control techniques become appropriate. These inventory optimizing approaches, addressing the issue of calculating the *best* level, can be found in texts on managerial finance or operations research.

Regardless of the control system used, the maintenance of careful records of inventory movements and levels is usually at the heart of the system. Inventories are accounted for separately by inventory types (raw material, work in process, and finished goods) and are often broken down by geographical location (e.g., a separate inventory control for each supermarket in a grocery chain).

PERPETUAL INVENTORY SYSTEMS

A perpetual inventory system is one in which the inventory records show at all times the amount of physical inventory that should be on hand. The record that provides this information is similar to a ledger account, except that the entries are for physical quantities of inventory and can also include dollar amounts. A typical arrangement is the following:

1. When the goods are ordered, a notice is sent to the receiving department to say they are expected.

2. When the goods arrive they are inspected and counted. Then a notice describing the inventory item and showing the amount received is sent to the department maintaining the perpetual record.

3. The notice of receipt, usually called a **receiving report,** is posted as incoming inventory to the appropriate perpetual inventory ledger card.

4. Before an item of inventory may be taken out of the raw material inventory stores, an authorized **requisition** (a document authorizing the release of the goods) must be received by stores. If the shipment is from finished goods stores to a customer, the authorizing document is usually called a **shipping order**. A copy of these documents is sent to the perpetual inventory clerk, where it is recorded as outgoing inventory.

5. The perpetual inventory records are kept updated to show the amount that should be on hand. They are used for
   a. identifying inventory levels that are below or above the optimum level;
   b. preparing lists of inventory on hand to aid in valuing inventory for financial statement purposes; and
   c. detecting thefts or misplacement of inventory through periodic comparison of the perpetual records and actual inventory counts.

6. Actual inventory counts are undertaken from time to time to help validate the perpetual inventory records.

An example of a perpetual inventory ledger card in a manual system is shown below. Such a ledger might be maintained by an appliance dealer.

Item: Refrigerator: white, 1.250 cubic m.				
Part #: 2016-857Z				
Date	Description	Physical Quantity		
		In	Out	Balance
1990				
14 Feb	Appliance Manufacturer Ltd.	25		25
20 Feb	R.C. Smith		2	23
3 Mar	K.W. Hospital		4	19
5 Apr	Student Residences		6	13

It is essential that these records be well kept and verified periodically by physical count to check the reliability of the system. In particular, a reliable system requires that the following three rules be observed. First, incoming shipments into inventory need to be tightly controlled to ensure that all of them are recorded in the perpetual inventory record and that the entry is made to the correct account. Second, shipments out of inventory should only be made on receipt of proper shipping documents that are closely connected to the perpetual inventory system and the company's invoicing system. Third, the perpetual inventory records must be kept properly. Many companies have started perpetual inventory records but failed to observe the above rules. Thus they have ended up with expensive but essentially worthless records. Often those originating the receiving and shipping advices are stockroom clerks with little interest in what is for them a boring and pointless procedure. Yet the system is critically dependent on the reports they generate. If the perpetual inventory system is well maintained, then the preparation of financial statements without actually doing a physical inventory count each time is easily feasible.

The development of reliable computer methods for recording receipts and shipments has made it possible to keep perpetual inventory records in settings where previously it would have been too expensive and cumbersome. For example, it is now commonplace to see in retail and grocery stores electronic scanning devices that read the inventory number from a tag attached to the item and then ring up both the quantity and part number for later processing into the perpetual inventory system. Similarly, libraries can keep their inventory of books in a computer file and record "shipments" and "receipts" through a similar electronic scanning process.

In addition to improving the recording of inventory movements, electronic processing has helped in maintaining perpetual inventory ledgers more cheaply and accurately.

PERIODIC COUNT METHOD

If a perpetual inventory system is not used, the company must fall back on estimating the amount of inventory (to be explained later) or making a physical count of the inventory as of the date of each financial statement. The latter system is referred to as the **periodic count** method. Anyone who has worked on a physical count of inventory usually finds the work is boring, hard, and often dirty. Counts of inventory arrived at under these conditions are often subject to error. Items of inventory get miscounted, missed, or counted twice in error, so that inventories based on "actual count" are not necessarily as accurate as the phrase implies.

Whether a company chooses the periodic count over the perpetual method is usually a question of cost-effectiveness. Some of the factors that influence the choice are shown below.

PERPETUAL METHOD VERSUS PERIODIC COUNT	
Factor	Influence on choice
Ease of recording shipments and receipts	Easy, reliable recording favours perpetual method (e.g., electronic cash registers that read the part number and transmit it to computer record).
Value and number of individual inventory items	Because it is expensive to keep a perpetual ledger, inexpensive inventory items are not as suitable for a perpetual system.
Ease of doing a physical count	Some inventory is relatively easy to count physically (e.g., cars in a dealer's lot); other inventory is impossible to measure directly (e.g., natural gas stored in an underground well).
Need for up-to-date information on inventory status	If the inventory is not easy to observe directly and knowledge of how much is available is crucial to sales (e.g., unsold seats in an airline), the pressure for a perpetual inventory is strong.
Ease of physical control	If inventory cannot easily be kept within a warehouse or compound, but may be lent to customers on approval or moved around the company, a written record of its location becomes more desirable.

Although at first it seems paradoxical, a careful physical count of inventory does not in itself always produce an accurate listing of the physical amounts on hand that should be in the company's inventory. The physical presence during a count of items looking like the company's inventory can be misleading. Not all items counted during a physical count should be included as part of the company's inventory, and some inventory not physically present should be included. This happens for two reasons:

1. Inventory may be on **consignment,** a situation where the inventory has been physically moved to the premises of someone not the owner while legal title is still retained by the original owner. For example, some ski shops will undertake to display used equipment on a consignment basis. The original owner retains title to the equipment until it is sold, and the ski shop simply takes a commission out of the proceeds of sale and remits the difference. If a physical count is being made of the

ski shop inventory, the inventory on consignment should not be included. However, if the ski shop has some of its own inventory on consignment elsewhere (e.g., out being repaired), then it should be included even though it is not physically present with the other inventory.

2. There may be **cut-off errors**, or errors of inconsistent treatment over a financial year. There are two main causes of cut-off errors. First, an item may have been shipped from the finished goods inventory before the year-end and not included in inventory, but it might not have been invoiced until after the year-end and not included in accounts receivable (or the opposite might have happened). Second, an inventory item may have been received before the year-end and included in inventory, but the invoice might not have been included in accounts payable until after the year-end (or the opposite might have happened). A more complete treatment of this problem will be found in Appendix 6-1.

An issue that has some similarities to the problem of *when to recognize a sale* is the question of *when to recognize a purchase of inventory*. When the company sends a purchase order to the supplier, it is legally bound to complete the transaction it has started. However, it has not yet received any benefit from the transaction, so no accounting entry is made. The usual point at which the purchase is recognized is when the goods are received and/or the company has legal title. If an invoice has not been received, it may be necessary to estimate the amount. From a reporting point of view, the important issue is that a company should *consistently* use whatever convention it has adopted for recognizing the purchase.

Establishing Inventory Valuations

Once the physical existence of inventory has been established, the next step is to assign dollar values to the individual items so that these values can be aggregated to arrive at the total inventory valuation on the financial statements. The large majority of Canadian companies value their inventory at the lower of cost and market. About 5% of the companies value it at market only. The *CICA Handbook* [3030.10] allows a choice, requiring only that the method of valuation should be shown.

ESTABLISHING COSTS

The two major issues in establishing the costs of inventory can be summarized as follows:

1. Should a cost of acquiring the inventory be treated as a *cost of inventory* or as a *period cost*? If treated as an inventory cost, then it is added to inventory and carried forward to the period in which the inventory is sold. If treated as a period cost, it is expensed immediately.

2. What process should be established for assigning the costs to each item in the inventory? The process must be such that cost of goods sold can be appropriately charged as the items themselves are sold.

Let us now examine these issues in more detail.

Measurement of Purchase Costs

Under the matching concept the costs to be assigned to the inventory account should be the purchase or manufacturing cost of the inventory plus the costs of bringing it physically to the warehouse. In other words, the inventory account would be charged with (i) the market cost of the inventory (usually the amount paid the supplier for purchased inventory) or the costs of manufacturing the item (to be discussed later); and (ii) additional costs of purchasing the inventory such as customs duties and transportation from the supplier to the warehouse.

At the same time, the inventory account should be credited with any trade discounts given the purchaser. A **trade discount** is one given by the supplier in expectation of further significant purchases from the buyer: it is based on an expectation of volume. By contrast, a **cash discount** is one given to the buyer if he pays the account before a stated date. Both types of discounts are usually treated as deductions from the cost of inventory. There is at least an argument, however, that cash discounts should be treated as a revenue item inasmuch as the company has given up investment income (or incurred higher interest costs) by paying the bills earlier than required. If the supplier pays the transportation costs to the customer's location, it is referred to as **FOB destination**; if the customer pays the transport costs, it is referred to as **FOB shipping point.**

It is not customary to include in the cost of inventory the other costs of keeping the inventory available for use or sale, such as the interest cost of financing it, the cost of insuring it, or the costs of storing it. These are normally treated as period costs, probably for reasons of expediency and custom. However, under the matching principle there seems to be a good reason for including them in the cost of inventory. The *CICA Handbook* encourages adding in storage charges in cases where storage is an integral part of the manufacturing process (e.g., aging whisky). "In a few cases" the *Handbook* also encourages adding in carrying charges.

Land development companies carry an inventory of land, which may range from undeveloped land, purchased to make sure some is available when needed, to developed land that is ready for sale. Aside from the construction costs incurred to put in such services as water and drainage, other major costs would be the costs of holding the land (such as interest on the money borrowed to finance the project and municipal taxes). In principle all the costs incurred to get the land to the point of sale would be inventory costs. Like other inventory, however, an inventory of land would be subject to the lower-of-cost-and-market rule.

Selection of Cost Flow Assumption

Once the inventory has been acquired, it will either be held past the financial year-end (and be treated as closing inventory) or be sold during the current period (thus forming the major portion of cost of goods sold). How should this division of costs between inventory and cost of goods sold be made? In this section we will outline some common methods for doing this.

It may be helpful to visualize the various forms of cost flow by picturing a bucket for each inventory category. Into this bucket the costs of acquiring the inventory flow. As long as no inventory is sold, the costs remain in the bucket as the cost of the inventory. It is when some inventory is sold and some remains that the problem of allocating the costs between inventory and cost of sales arises. Let us assume that three identical items of inventory were purchased in a series of separate purchases, one after the other. Suppose item A cost $4.00, item B cost $5.00, and C cost $6.00. The total cost of the inventory is $15.00. The problem of selecting the cost flow assumption arises when the first inventory item is sold. We must then decide what cost to attribute to the item in order to arrive at the amount of cost of goods sold. Here are some possibilities:

1. We could assume the item sold was the first item purchased that was still in inventory. This is the **first-in-first-out (FIFO)** assumption of determining the cost of goods sold. In that case we would use $4.00, since that is the cost of item A. Because it takes some time for the costs to flow through the inventory under FIFO, the *cost of goods sold* tends to represent costs of an earlier period. On the other hand, because the oldest cost in the inventory is the next cost to be expensed, *FIFO-valued inventory* often tends to represent fairly current prices.

2. We could assume the item sold was the last item purchased. This is the **last-in-first-out (LIFO)** assumption of determining the cost of goods sold. In that case we would use the cost of item C, or $6.00. Because the costs of the earliest items purchased are the ones left in inventory, a *LIFO-valued inventory* usually is not representative of current market values. On the other hand, the *cost of goods sold* tends to be more representative of current market prices.

3. We could use the **average cost** of the inventory, dividing $15.00 by 3 to get an average cost of $5.00.

4. We could decide to use the actual cost of the **specific item** we picked out and sold. Since A,B, and C are identical, we could choose any one of them, thus having a choice among costs of $4.00, $5.00, or $6.00, depending on which item was chosen.

5. We could pick a unit cost that seemed to represent the **standard cost**, or usual cost, of the item and we could then enter all purchases into inventory at that amount. The standard cost of an item is a preset cost, usually determined as part of a standard cost accounting system, that represents what the ideal cost of the item would be under normal conditions. There is a presumption that any differences between the actual and standard costs represent some unusual aspect of the actual purchase that should not be taken into account when costing the inventory. Any difference between the standard cost and the actual cost, termed a **purchase difference**, would be posted to a separate account. Suppose in our example that $4.00 was chosen as the standard cost. Then when item B was purchased for $5.00, it would be put into inventory at $4.00 (as that is the standard cost), and the purchase difference of $1.00 would be charged to a purchase difference account.

Which of these methods should be chosen? The disturbing answer is that if the individual inventory items are similar in their economic worth to the firm (and often this is the case), then a defence can be made for using any of the above cost flow assumptions. In this sense the choice of assumption is arbitrary. This means that the split of cost between inventory and cost of goods sold — which depends in part on the cost flow assumption adopted — is an arbitrary choice as well. Thus the accountant's objective of matching costs with revenues is at least partially frustrated. The accountant's response to this is to insist that once a cost flow assumption has been adopted by a firm, it should stick to it (unless real economic events change the wisdom of using the current method, in which case the impact on inventory valuations should be disclosed).

In Canada, LIFO is not acceptable for tax purposes and hence it is seldom used. In the U.S., LIFO is acceptable for tax purposes and its use is common. In a period of rising prices the use of LIFO will tend to state inventory at a lower value than would other inventory valuation methods, and taxable income will be lower as a result. From an administrative viewpoint, LIFO is a difficult system. As the inventory is increased, the LIFO costs of it can be imagined as being built up in layers: the most recent layers are assigned to cost of sales as the inventory is run down, and the oldest layer of cost is assigned to the cost of the last to be taken out of inventory. If a company kept its inventory steady or rising over a period of years, the LIFO costs assigned to it would become very old and might well be far less than the current cost of the same items. In 1983 many companies tried to reduce their inventories because of slow sales and financial pressures. Using LIFO they found they were assigning some of the old layers to cost of sales. Since these costs were much under current costs, the reported gross profit margins tended to be larger than they had been in the immediately preceding years when inventory was steady or rising. To the extent that the level of inventory is a management decision, the possibility for income manipulation exists.

The specific-item method deserves specific mention, because intuitively it seems to offer conceptually the most attractive way out of the dilemma of arbitrariness. Under this method the cost of each item of inventory is calculated, and the cost of sales is taken to be the cost of the item actually sold. There is no prior *assumption* of cost flow as in FIFO or LIFO. This method does indeed seem to be conceptually the best one when the individual items in inventory are each unique and not easily substituted for each other. For example, this method might be adopted by a used-car dealer inasmuch as each car in the lot has individual characteristics that mean it could not usually be substituted for any other. Such a dealer might keep one inventory ledger card for each car and record on it the purchase cost of the car and the cost of any further work done on it. However, the specific-item method would not be defensible for a manufacturer of new cars if one car could readily be substituted for the other. This is because the manufacturer could manipulate costs to increase reported profits by choosing for sale the vehicle with the lower cost. It is a mistake to assume, as many students first do, that the specific-item method is the "real" method of inventory costing and that all other methods are approximations of it. The specific-item method does *not* usually get rid of the arbitrariness of inventory costing *if* it permits management to manipulate costs by arbitrarily choosing which inventory item they will sell and which they will keep. Unfortunately, many inventories are of this nature.

If inventory is manufactured within the company, there is a question of which manufacturing costs should be attached to the inventory and which should be treated as expenses of the period. There is little dispute that the cost of direct raw material and labour should be included. The controversial issue is whether to include indirect and fixed costs of manufacturing, such as depreciation, insurance, and salaried staff. If only direct material, direct labour, and variable overhead are included, then we have a **variable cost** approach to inventory valuation. If indirect and fixed manufacturing costs are included as well, then we have an **absorption cost** system. Details about these two approaches will be found in a cost accounting textbook. For our purposes it is sufficient to note that these differences in approach exist and that the variable (or direct) cost approach will tend to produce the lower inventory valuations. Regardless of which approach is used, the choice of cost flow assumption still has to be made for the finished goods inventory. Absorption costing is required by the *CICA Handbook* [3030.06].

LOWER-OF-COST-AND-MARKET RULE

So far we have been assuming that inventories will be valued at cost and we have been focusing on the question of choosing the cost flow assumption. Now let us turn to the question of valuation. It is possible that the cost of the inventory will be higher than its current market value. In that case the convention of conservatism requires that the inventory be written down to market. This is referred to as the **lower-of-cost-and-market (LCM) rule**. Market value may be less than cost for a variety of reasons. First, the product may be becoming obsolete and might have to be sold at a lower price or be reprocessed at extra cost (e.g., personal computer software that has been eclipsed by newer versions). Second, the raw material from which the product is made may have fallen in price (e.g., copper plumbing when the price of raw copper falls). Third, general economic conditions may have caused a drop in demand that has depressed prices in the industry (e.g., the drop in demand for air travel in the early 1980s meant that fewer aircraft were purchased, thereby depressing the selling price of both new and used aircraft).

There are at least two market values that might be calculated. These are (i) the current cost of replacing the existing inventory, called the **replacement cost**; and (ii) the net proceeds that would be realized if the inventory were sold, called the **net realizable value**. For example, the market value of a used car in a car lot might be calculated by seeing what it would cost to purchase a similar car (the current cost) or by estimating the cost of repairing it to make it fit for sale, and deducting this cost from the estimated selling price (net realizable value). We would expect the two market values to be reasonably close together in this case, but it is possible to think of other cases where they might be quite far apart. For example, the net realizable value of a custom-made piece of jewellery might be considerably less than its replacement cost.

The choice of valuation method is usually dependent on the type of inventory being valued. Raw material is usually valued at replacement cost, since it is at the start of the production process and replacement cost is usually readily obtainable. In contrast, manufactured finished goods are at the end of the productive process and hence are usually valued at net realizable value. Purchased finished goods might be valued at either replacement or realizable value.

When calculating net realizable value, should one deduct the profit one would normally make on the sale? For example, consider the following for an inventory item:

Cost	$ 5.60
Expected selling price	$ 7.40
Expected selling costs	2.00
	$ 5.40
Less: Normal profit expected	0.80
Net after normal profit	$ 4.60

If $5.40 is chosen as the net realizable value, then the inventory would be written down by $0.20 (since cost is $5.60), and in the period in which it was later sold there would be no gain or loss (assuming it sold for a net of $5.40 as expected). On the other hand, if $4.60 is used as the net realizable value, then the inventory would be written down by $1.00, and in the period in which it was later sold a profit of $0.80 would be recorded. Whether one chooses the first or second method appears to be a function of how conservative one wishes to be.

The preferred practices in the *CICA Handbook* are rather general, but there is a requirement for clear disclosure of the basis used for valuation of inventories. Preference for the lower-of-cost-and-market rule is implied [CICA 3030.11]; and if the valuation method produces a number which does not differ materially from recent cost, the simple term *cost* may be used. If costs are not stated at historic cost, the valuation method should be explicitly indicated (e.g., net realizable value, or net realizable value less normal profit margin).

We have yet to deal with the valuation of work in process, that is, the inventory in the middle of the production process and the one furthest away from the commodity markets at either end. The replacement cost of an item can be estimated by adding together the purchase cost of all the items of raw material, direct labour, and overhead that have gone into making it. The net realizable value can be estimated by calculating the cost of finishing the item and deducting this from the net realizable value of the finished item. Calculating both the replacement cost and net realizable value precisely can be a difficult job in most situations. One often has to judge what needs to be done to complete the item and estimate what its ultimate selling price will be.

There is one further issue in applying the cost-and-market rule: should it be applied to each item of inventory or to the inventory as a whole? Consider the following example where there are just two items in inventory.

	Cost	Market	Lower of cost and market
Item A	$ 4.50	$ 8.00	$ 4.50
Item B	8.00	4.00	4.00
	$12.50	$12.00	$ 8.50

If the cost-and-market rule is applied item by item, then the figures shown in the right-hand column would be used and the inventory would be written down to $8.50. If we simply used the lower of total market-and-cost, then we would use the middle column and write the inventory down to $12.00. The item-by-item method will always yield the lower valuation. In practice, the item-by-item method is rarely used.

PERCENTAGE-OF-COMPLETION METHOD

The usual assumption of historic-cost-based accounting is that inventory will be valued at the lower of cost and market. However, under the **percentage-of-completion method** this assumption is relaxed. As we explained in Chapter 1, the revenue recognition convention (of valuing inventory at cost and not recognizing profit until the item is sold) is a convenient one that works well when the individual inventory items are small in relation to the company's total annual sales. For example, a company making wine may choose to value the bottles of wine at cost and not recognize the profit on the manufacture of each bottle until that bottle is sold. An economist would maintain that each step in the wine-making has increased the value of the bottle of wine and thus would accept the accountant's practice of delaying the recognition of this increase in value until the point of sale only on the grounds of conservatism and simplicity of information processing. However, an economist would object to the argument that the income was not really earned until the point of sale.

The percentage-of-completion method goes a long way to meeting this objection. Under it, the income earned on a project is recognized as the project is completed. This is done by using some proxy for the percentage completed, such as (i) the ratio of cost incurred to date over expected total cost, (ii) the ratio of direct hours worked to date over total expected hours, or (iii) the ratio of some measure of physical production to the total expected output (e.g., for the construction of a dam one might use the tons of cement poured to date over the total expected). The effect is that the company recognizes the expected revenue and expenses of the project on a piecemeal basis, rather than all at once at the point of completion. However, in those cases where the company realizes it will suffer a loss on the overall project, the principle of conservatism requires that *all* the loss be recognized in the period in which the company becomes aware of it. The loss is *not* distributed among several time periods, as an expected profit is.

In principle, the percentage-of-completion method has a lot to recommend its use on large projects whose construction takes place over several financial periods. Its weakness lies in the requirement to estimate (i) total cost to complete, (ii) percentage of completion, and (iii) final price (where the customer must pay for later charges). Each of these factors has a potentially large impact on the amount of income recognized in any one year. In many cases the group most able to make a knowledgeable estimate is the management of the company — the very group whose performance is being reported on in the financial statements. Thus, once again, the possibility of income manipulation arises. In Appendix 6-2 we shall examine the percentage-of-completion method in more detail.

Inventory Estimating Methods

The inconvenience and expense of making a physical count of inventory, a requirement of the periodic inventory method, has already been noted. In addition, there are circumstances where the maintenance of a perpetual inventory record is too costly. However, it is often desirable to produce financial statements even when physical counts or perpetual records cannot supply the amount of inventory on hand. In such cases one must use estimates of the inventory. The two most commonly used inventory estimating methods are the **gross profit method** and the **retail inventory method**.

Both methods make use of the relationship between cost of goods sold and sales; and both assume that this relationship, or some variant of it, can be used to estimate inventory. The gross profit method, as its name implies, assumes that the gross profit from one period to another is reasonably stable and that the cost of goods sold can be estimated: hence the closing inventory can be calculated. The retail method uses relationships in the current period between the cost of goods made available for sale and their retail selling price to infer the amount of the closing inventory. A more detailed comparison between these two methods will be made after they are explained.

GROSS PROFIT METHOD

The **gross profit**, or **gross margin**, is the difference between the sales and cost of sales. The **gross profit percentage** is the gross profit as a percentage of sales. Thus we have

$$\text{Gross Profit Percentage} = \frac{\text{Gross Profit}}{\text{Sales}} \times 100$$

Note that this is calculated on sales, not cost of goods sold. We will see in both estimating methods that percentages are expressed on *sales*. The *gross profit method* estimates the value of inventory by assuming that the relationship between sales and gross profit is sufficiently predictable that one can make a reliable estimate of gross profit (and hence cost of goods sold) if one knows the total sales. If one knows the opening inventory and the cost of goods sold, then the closing inventory can be calculated directly. In addition to its use in preparing interim financial statements, the gross profit method is frequently used to check the reasonableness of inventory amounts calculated by other methods. It is also used to estimate inventories in cases of fire loss, where the inventory can no longer be counted and the supporting records may have been destroyed.

For example, assume that a company had the following financial results in 19X5:

	Amount	Percentage
Sales	$10,000	100%
Cost of sales:		
Opening inventory	2,500	
Purchases	4,800	
Subtotal	7,300	
Closing inventory	1,600	
Net	5,700	57%
Gross profit	$ 4,300	43%

Assume that the company had a stable record of earning about 43% on sales over the past several years. In 19X6 it had a fire in which the inventory and inventory records were destroyed. The inventory is insured and the insurance company wants to be given reasonable proof of the value of the destroyed inventory. The company knows that its sales for the end of 19X5 to the time of the fire were $7,500, and its purchase records show that inventory costing $5,175 had been purchased since the end of 19X5.

Assuming that the gross profit percentage remained at 43% during 19X6, we could estimate that it would have been 43% of $7,500, or $3,225. This means that the cost of goods sold would be $7,500 minus $3,225, or $4,275. We can now reconstruct an estimate of the financial results from the end of 19X5 to the time of the fire:

	Amount	Percentage
Sales	$ 7,500	100%
Cost of sales:		
Opening inventory	1,600	
Purchases	5,175	
Subtotal	6,775	
Closing inventory	?	
Net	4,275	57%
Gross profit	$ 3,225	43%

The only item missing is the closing inventory, and it is apparent from the above that it must be $2,500.

The gross profit method is a quick and convenient method for estimating inventory provided one knows (i) the dollar amount of sales, (ii) the dollar amount of purchases since the last accounting period, and (iii) the probable gross profit percentage in the current period.

This estimation method can also be used as a means of checking the reliability of other methods, such as physical counts or perpetual inventories. If the gross profit percentage seemed out of line with expectations when one of the latter two methods of deriving the inventory were used, then one might well suspect a miscount, poorly kept perpetual records, or a mistake in inventory valuation.

RETAIL INVENTORY METHOD

The **retail inventory method** is a method of estimating the lower-of-cost-and-market value of inventory once its total *retail* value is established. Its use is popular in situations where the inventory does have a retail value and where the small value and large number of inventory items make a perpetual inventory system cumbersome and costly (e.g., clothing stores, hardware stores, or groceries).

Before explaining the retail method it is helpful to introduce some terms with respect to retail prices. Since the original retail price plays an important role as a reference price, the following vocabulary has been developed to describe changes above and below it.

The **list price** of an item is the price that the customer is normally asked to pay. If the price is raised above list, it is called a **mark-up**. If the price is dropped below list, it is called a **mark-down**. A **mark-up cancellation** takes place when the asking price is dropped, so long as the price remains above list. A **mark-down cancellation** takes place when the asking price is raised, so long as the price remains below list. These terms are illustrated in the following diagram:

The retail inventory method can be broken down into four steps:

1. A continuing record is kept of the value of inventory at its *retail* price, or the inventory is counted and priced at retail.

2. A record is kept of the purchases at both cost and retail. The cost of the purchases is calculated in the usual manner (i.e., purchase discounts are deducted).

3. A record is kept of all mark-ups, mark-downs, and any cancellations.

4. The closing inventory at the lower of cost and market (LCM) is estimated using the following formula:

Inventory at LCM = Total inventory priced at retail × Estimating Ratio, where

$$\text{Estimating Ratio} = \frac{\text{Opening inventory at cost} + \text{Purchases at cost}}{\text{Opening inventory at retail} + \text{Purchases at retail} + \text{Adjustment}}$$

and Adjustment = Mark-ups + Mark-up cancellations (but *not* mark-downs or mark-down cancellations).

The *Adjustment* term is used to revalue the inventory down to market should this be below cost. (The reason for this will become apparent in the following example.)

Here is an example that has been kept rudimentary in order to illustrate the principles. Assume that a sports store purchased only two pairs of skis during the whole year. The cost to the store was $100 a pair, and the original *list price* put on them was $180. One pair sold at this price early in the season. The manager noted that the price of her skis was significantly less than that charged by the competition. Accordingly, she marked up the price on the remaining pair to $210, so the *mark-up* was $30. However, the skis did not sell, so she cancelled the mark-up and brought the price down to $180, thus producing a *mark-up cancellation* of $30. The item still did not sell, so she made a *mark-down* of $18 to $162. At the end of the fiscal year the skis are counted in inventory at a retail price of $162. They are thus priced below the usual list price of $180, which implies that net realizable value after the usual profit percentage is less than cost.

A summary of the year is shown below.

	Retail	Cost
Opening inventory	$ 0	$ 0
Purchases — two pairs of skis	360	200
Goods made available for sale	$ 360	$ 200
Mark-up	30	
Mark-up cancellation	(30)	
	360	
Sales	180	
Skis on hand — at original list price	$ 180	
Mark-down	(18)	
Skis on hand — at actual retail price	$ 162	

Because the skis are now priced below the "normal" retail price, the store is not going to make its usual profit on their sale. We can estimate their reduced market value by the relationship between the new retail price of $162 and the original retail price of $180. If we apply this ratio to the original cost price, we obtain the following result:

162/180 × 100.00 = 90.00

The same result can be obtained by the formula already given:

162.00 × (200.00/360.00) = 90.00

The estimated net realizable value of the skis is therefore $90.00, which is less than the cost of $100.00. Therefore, for their LCM we would use $90.00. In effect, the skis are written down to preserve the same relative gross margin in the period when the skis are sold. If they were to sell in the following period for $162 as expected, then the gross margin would be $72 (i.e., 162.00 − $90.00), which represents a gross profit percentage of 44% (i.e., (72/162) × 100). This is the same as the ratio of the original expected gross margin ($360.00 − $200.00) over the expected retail value ($360.00).

Let us now consider the reason for excluding mark-downs and mark-down cancellations from the estimating ratio. If they had been included, then the *Adjustment* referred to above would include both net mark-ups and mark-downs and thus would be a deduction of 18 (i.e., 30 − 30 − 18 = − 18). Consequently the net realizable value of the inventory would be as follows:

Purchases at cost / (Purchases at retail + Adjustment)

$$= 162 \times \frac{200}{360-18}$$

= 94.74

The result is a higher estimate than the $90 produced above and hence it would not have preserved the gross profit percentage of 44%.

Note that the *market* being estimated here is one that will preserve this gross profit percentage. It is *not* the retail price of the goods (as some students mistakenly assume), but an estimate of the net realizable value.

Let us change the example slightly and assume instead that the skis were marked up to $210.00, but not marked down by the time the inventory valuation was made because it was believed they would sell at that price.

We can find the lower of cost and market in one step, regardless of whether the merchandise is now above or below list. We will use the two examples already given where the final retail price in the first case was $162 and in the second case was $210. (The capital letters following key numbers in the table below will simply serve as abbreviations.)

	Final retail price = $162		Final retail price = $210	
	Retail	Cost	Retail	Cost
Opening inventory	$ 0	$ 0	$ 0	$ 0
Purchases	360	200	360	200
Goods made available for sale	$ 360	$ 200(B)	$ 360	$ 200(B)
Mark-ups	30		30	
Mark-up cancellation	(30)			
	$ 360(A)		$ 390(A)	
Mark-down	(18)			
Sales	(180)		(180)	
	$ 162(C)		$ 210(C)	
Closing inventory — actual	$ 162		$ 210	

In both cases, we calculate as follows:

Estimate of inventory at lower of cost and market = C × B / A

1. For final price = $162:   162 × 200/360 = 90.00

2. For final price = $210:   210 × 200/390 = 107.69

In the first case the inventory was priced at retail below its normal list, so the $90 is an estimate of market (net realizable value) rather than cost. In the second case the price of $210 is above normal market, so we should use cost instead of the net realizable value of $116.67 (i.e., (210/180) × 100). Note that we have an estimation error because the real cost is $100 and not $107.69. The error arises because the cost of the item in inventory is estimated by using the ratio of the *total* cost of goods made available for sale to the retail price, net of mark-ups, of the same goods. This approximation is not completely accurate and hence produces the estimating error.

This example was designed so that only one item was left in inventory at the end. This was done to make it possible to judge the effectiveness of the retail inventory method in estimating the lower of cost and market. In a real retail situation one would not be able to identify individual items with the inventory at hand. In fact, it is unlikely that the estimated inventory at the lower of cost and market would agree with an inventory developed from a physical count, even if there were no physical shortages. The reason for this is the manner in which mark-ups and mark-downs are used in the estimating process. By including mark-ups but excluding mark-downs in the estimating percentage, we are making the assumption that the ending inventory will contain about the same proportion of marked-down and marked-up items as do the total goods made available for sale. However, perhaps all the marked-down items were sold and the inventory contains only items at original list price or above. If this were the case, then by the ordinary rules of accounting the inventory should be priced at cost. But information about the mark-downs or mark-ups for items in inventory is not normally available. Therefore, the inventory value is estimated using the normal retail formula, and the resulting value will be below cost if there were any mark-downs during the period.

Consequently, even if there is a physical count at the fiscal year-end, the retail method is capable of producing lower-of-cost-and-market estimates that are different from those that would be produced by an orthodox periodic inventory method. Such differences are accepted as part of the cost of using an estimating method.

The major differences between the gross profit and retail inventory methods of estimation are given in the following chart:

GROSS PROFIT (GP) VERSUS RETAIL INVENTORY (RI)

Factor	Difference
Knowledge about closing inventory	GP — All that is known is the estimated dollar cost derived by the calculation method. RI — The retail value that should be on hand can be calculated directly for each department or inventory segment.
Critical assumptions	GP — Assumes that the gross profit percentage for the current period can be estimated using historic data because the relationship is reasonably steady. RI — Assumes that the relationship between cost and retail of goods made available for sale in the current period provides the basis for converting the closing inventory at retail to the lower of cost or market. Also, it assumes that the normal mark-up percentages should be used to calculate the net realizable value.
Ability to provide estimates of lower of cost and market	GP — Not done overtly, but may be reflected in the percentage of gross profit from prior periods. RI — Done overtly by excluding mark-downs in the denominator of the ratio of cost to goods made available for sale.
Normal use	GP — Not normally used as the primary source of inventory valuation except for interim reports. Used as a supplementary source to cross-check other valuation methods, such as periodic count. RI — Frequently used as the sole source of inventory valuation when backed up by a physical count at retail performed on a regular basis. Most appropriate when inventory items are small in value and large in number.

Comparison of Inventory Methods

We have now examined four methods of measuring inventory. Their strengths and weaknesses can be summarized as follows:

INVENTORY METHODS

Method	Main Features	Advantages	Disadvantages
Periodic count	Every item in inventory is counted.	If done carefully, it confirms the amount of inventory.	Often slow and costly. Must be done carefully.
Perpetual	Inventory is derived by measuring inflows and outflows.	If well maintained, it can produce inventory results quickly. Sometimes physical count is impractical or impossible.	Needs accurate and low-cost way to measure flows.
Gross profit	Closing inventory is derived by estimating cost of goods sold.	Quick — often used to double-check other methods.	Must estimate gross margin — the factor that management is most often in doubt about.
Retail	Derive inventory priced at retail, then estimate LCM by applying the markup ratio to inventory priced at retail.	Gives good control over losses. May or may not be combined with physical count.	Limited applicability.

Disclosure Requirements

Requirements for disclosure of inventory information are set out in Section 3030 of the *CICA Handbook*. Four major points are discussed:

1. The basis of valuation should be clearly stated [*CICA* 3030.10]. It seems clear that the lower of cost and market is the preferred valuation, although this is not a requirement.

2. The cost flow assumption must be disclosed if the cost figure resulting is materially different from recent cost. Presumably this means that some cost flow assumptions, such as FIFO and average cost, need not be disclosed, whereas others, such as LIFO, would have to be [*CICA* 3030.11].

3. Any change in the basis of valuation should be disclosed, together with the effect on net income [*CICA* 3030.13].

4. The "laid-down cost" (undefined) should be used for raw material and material purchased for resale [*CICA* 3030.05]. Work in process and finished goods should be valued at the laid-down cost of material and direct labour plus "the applicable share of overhead expense properly charged to production" [*CICA* 3050.06]. This last phrase means that absorption costing should be used, not direct costing. How one is to determine (if ever) precisely what part of indirect costs are "applicable" or "proper" is not set out in the *CICA Handbook*.

These disclosure requirements are not extensive. For example, companies are not required to segment their inventory by major categories (raw material, work in process, finished goods), product line, or geographical area.

Examples from Published Reports

Minnesota Mining and Manufacturing Company (3M)

This innovative U.S. firm manufactures and sells technologies in a variety of fields such as computer diskettes, transparent fastening tape, and adhesives.

	1986	1985
	(millions of $)	
Current Assets:		
Cash and securities	$ 545	$ 192
Accounts receivable — net	1,442	1,344
Inventories	1,654	1,622
Other current assets	320	315
Total current assets	$3,961	$3,473

Accounting policies — Inventories: Inventories are stated at the lower of cost or market, with cost generally determined on a first-in, first-out basis and market based on the lower of replacement cost or realizable value.

	1986	1985
	(millions of $)	
Inventories:		
Finished goods	$ 860	$ 854
Work in process	447	434
Raw materials and supplies	347	334
Total inventories	$1,654	$1,622

Inventories are the largest part of the current assets for this company. The breakdown of inventory by type is not required by the *CICA Handbook*. However, the information is provided here and is useful to the reader wanting more information about this asset (e.g., to evaluate liquidity or calculate inventory turnover ratios).

Canadian Occidental Petroleum Ltd.

Canadian Oxy is a diversified energy and chemicals company.

	1986	1985
	(thousands of $)	
Current Assets:		
Cash	$ 25,054	$ 29,360
Accounts receivable	108,306	122,134
Inventories and supplies (Note 5)	37,471	34,280
Prepaid expenses	1,984	4,558
Total current assets	$172,815	$190,332

Accounting policies — Inventories: Inventories and supplies are stated at the lower of cost and net realizable value. Cost is determined using the first-in — first-out and average cost methods.

Note 5. Inventories and Supplies

	1986	1985
	(thousands of $)	
Finished products	$ 10,022	$ 5,002
Work in process	6,459	8,469
Field supplies	20,990	20,809
	$ 37,471	$ 34,280

Note the three very different types of inventory represented above. The *field supplies* would be those raw materials needed to make drilling and exploration possible, and the *finished product* would be the crude or refined oil that had been produced as a result of the company's activities.

BP Canada Inc.

BP is a natural resources company whose prime activities are the exploration for and the production of oil and gas as well as the exploration for and mining of minerals.

	1986	1985
	(thousands of $)	
Current Assets:		
Cash and short term investments	$172,834	$ 90,514
Accounts receivable	54,864	84,719
Inventories (Note 3)	9,376	10,650
Prepaid expenses and deposits	279	377
Total current assets	$237,353	$186,260

Accounting policies — Inventories: Inventories of products are valued at the lower of cost and net realizable value. Materials in process, raw materials, and supplies are valued at the lower of cost and replacement cost. Cost is determined on a first-in — first-out basis.

Note 3. Inventories

	1986	1985
	(thousands of $)	
Oil and gas:		
Materials and supplies	$ 5,805	$ 7,409
Sulphur	397	568
	$ 6,202	$ 7,977
Mining and minerals:		
Materials and supplies	3,174	2,673
	$ 9,376	$10,650

This company and Canadian Oxy are in a similar line of business. Note the similarities and differences between the presentation and analysis of inventory in each case.

Summary

Inventories are an important asset with most companies. Establishing the quantity of inventory on hand can be done by a variety of methods, such as physical count, perpetual records, or estimating techniques. Inventories are usually valued at the lower of cost and market. The cost flow assumption that one adopts to establish the cost of the inventory can produce widely varying results in practice; and if this cost is significantly different from current cost, then the costing method (but not the difference from current cost) must be disclosed.

QUESTIONS

Q6-1. Review and make sure you understand the following terms:

    a. raw material *versus* work in process *versus* finished goods

    b. perpetual *versus* periodic inventory methods

    c. receiving report *versus* shipping order *versus* requisition

    d. consignment

    e. cut-off errors

    f. trade discount *versus* cash discount

    g. LIFO *versus* FIFO *versus* average cost *versus* specific item methods

    h. standard cost

    i. variable costing *versus* absorption costing

    j. net realizable value

    k. lower-of-cost-and-market rule

    l. percentage-of-completion method

    m. gross profit method *versus* retail inventory method

    n. mark-up *versus* mark-down

    o. list price

Q6-2. Which kind of inventory system — periodic or perpetual — would be more suitable for each of the following? Explain.

    a. a neighbourhood hardware store

    b. an expensive ladies' dress boutique

    c. a used car dealer

    d. the bar in a student pub

    e. Loblaws

    f. a student house-painting business

    g. a Canadian Tire dealer

Q6-3. "Because inventory tends to be valued higher with FIFO than with LIFO, the former measure is to be preferred in each of the following cases: (i) you want to impress your bank manager with the size of your current assets, (ii) you want to improve your funds flow, and (iii) you want to improve the ratio of current assets to current liabilities." Do you agree in each case? Explain why.

Q6-4. The *CICA Handbook* says that the cost flow assumptions used in valuing inventory should be whatever method most fairly represents the matching of costs against revenues "regardless of whether or not the method corresponds to the physical flow of goods." Explain why the CICA is prepared to disregard the real flow of goods when attributing cost flows to inventory charges.

Q6-5. You are the vice-president finance of a large oil company that has been accused of making "obscene" profits during a period of rising oil prices.

    a. Could your choice of cost flow assumption have influenced the profit your company reported? Explain.

    b. If the company uses LIFO, under what circumstances in the future might it report even more "obscene" profits even though oil prices are falling? Explain.

Q6-6. State whether you agree or disagree with the following statements, and explain why.

    a. Deposits paid to vendors for goods to be delivered in the next period should be recorded by a debit to the merchandise purchases account and a credit to cash.

    b. Under the percentage-of-completion method of income recognition, entries will be made periodically throughout the period in which the contractor is engaged in the construction work. The entries will be of the following general nature:

        Dr. — Contract work in progress
        Cr. — Estimated income on contract work

    c. The failure to record merchandise purchases in the period in which goods are received will have no effect on the financial statements as long as the goods in question are also excluded from the valuation of closing inventory.

    d. Deposits for machinery to be produced for the company should be classified as current assets provided the machinery will be delivered in the following accounting period.

Q6-7. If inventories are not desirable in themselves, why did they form such a large part of the total assets of the three companies reviewed at the end of the chapter?

Q6-8. Explain the basic differences between a periodic count and a perpetual inventory approach to establishing the quantity on hand. Explain how either method might be used to help increase the accuracy of the other.

Q6-9. The sardonic term "garbage-in-garbage-out" has been used to describe some perpetual inventory systems. Explain how this term might have come about. Would keeping the perpetual stock ledger on a computer instead of manually help this situation? Explain.

Q6-10. Explain whether the following items would normally be included as part of the cost of inventory. If you think normal treatment is inconsistent with the matching concept, explain why.

    a. Freight charges for delivering the inventory from the manufacturer to the receiving dock.

    b. Insurance charges while the items were in transit from the manufacturer.

    c. Stealing of inventory while it is in transit at the docks. Such stealing is so commonplace that the purchaser expects it and bears the cost of it.

    d. Costs of storing whisky to improve its flavour. Would your answer be different if it were being stored because demand for it had dropped, yet its taste was improving nonetheless?

    e. Costs of storing gin, whose flavour is not improved with aging.

    f. Costs of taking inventory out of the shipping containers they arrived in and repacking them into individual cartons.

    g. Costs of drying out inventory after a water pipe broke in the storage shed.

Q6-11. "There is no acceptable method for valuing inventory." Do you agree? Explain.

Q6-12. "The percentage-of-completion method may be conceptually superior, but in practice it is inferior. In fact, it is the method most open to income manipulation." Assess the validity of this statement.

Q6-13. Does the amount taken into income in any given year under the percentage-of-completion method reflect only the income earned through completion of the project in that year? Explain.

Q6-14. Could the gross profit method and retail inventory method both be used to estimate a store's inventory? Are they likely to give the same answer? Explain.

Q6-15. Does the gross profit method estimate the inventory in terms of (i) cost, (ii) market, or (iii) lower of cost and market? Explain.

Q6-16. Explain what the "market" value is that the retail inventory method tries to estimate. Explain *how* that method tries to estimate market.

Q6-17. Evaluate the disclosure requirements for inventory in the *CICA Handbook*. If you could make three changes for additional disclosure, what would they be? Explain how these might be beneficial.

Q6-18. Four students shared a rented house and split the cost of groceries. They allowed a friend to stay over one weekend, but they insisted that he pay for the extra cost of the food. One of the ways in which the friend kept the cost of food low was to examine the price label on each of the cans in the storage cupboard. If there were more than one can of the same thing, he chose the can with the lowest sticker price on it. Was this the right way to calculate the cost of food? Would another way have been fairer? Explain.

Q6-19. Assuming no beginning inventory, what can be said about the trend of inventory prices if cost of goods sold using FIFO exceeds cost of goods sold using LIFO?

Q6-20. "A firm that wishes to stay competitive should shift from FIFO to LIFO because that would lower the cost of goods sold." Do you agree? Why?

Q6-21. "In a period of rising prices, FIFO is better than LIFO since it gives a more realistic estimate of cost of goods sold, although it is inferior in valuing inventory for the balance sheet." Do you agree? Why?

Q6-22. Give examples where raw materials inventory in one company might be finished goods industry in a second company and fixed assets in a third.

Q6-23. "The lower-of-cost-and-market rule for inventory is so conservative it will always understate a firm's reported income." Do you agree? Explain.

Q6-24. Explain each of the following:
   a. the principal features of the percentage-of-completion method.
   b. what other methods of revenue recognition might be used instead.
   c. in what situations the percentage-of-completion method might be preferred to the others.
   d. how the annual income under percentage-of-completion is calculated.
   e. what the annual income amount represents here.

Q6-25. What are the circumstances under which a company would choose to use an inventory estimation method? What other inventory valuation methods are more accurate? Why would they not be used instead?

Q6-26. "The retail method of inventory valuation is just the gross profit with an extra feature to bring in an estimation of market as well as cost." Do you agree? Explain.

Q6-27. What would be the inventory of a video rental shop? Which of the following inventory methods would you recommend: (i) physical count, (ii) perpetual method, (iii) retail inventory method, or (iv) gross profit method. Discuss each and give reasons. Explain how the inventory could be valued at the lower of cost or market.

Q6-28. Assume the following costs are all related to (i) acquiring inventory, (ii) getting it to the place where it is needed for resale or manufacturing, and (iii) having it ready at the right time:

Payment to supplier — $890

Freight from supplier to company — $87

Cost of fuel to heat warehouse to prevent inventory spoilage — $35

Insurance on shipment — $35

Insurance while stored in warehouse — $45

Labour to unload truck and store inventory in warehouse — $30

Shipping cost from company to customer — $25

Which of the above costs would normally be included as cost of inventory and which as costs of the period?

Q6-29. When calculating the net realizable value of inventory, the "normal" profit associated with the item may or may not be deducted. What are the arguments in favour of including or excluding this item and what is the effect on the timing of revenue recognition? Construct an example to illustrate your points.

Q6-30. "When estimating the market value of inventory under the retail inventory method, the resulting market value is usually significantly less than the retail market value of the same inventory." Explain.

Q6-31. The use of the lower-of-cost-and-market rule has been attacked for years on the grounds of inconsistency. It has been suggested that to be completely consistent, all assets, including inventory, should be valued at all times at their cost. This proposal in turn has met with a lot of hostility. What are the arguments on both sides of this controversy?

Q6-32. If you wanted to be able to manipulate your reported income, which inventory valuation method would you prefer in each of the following occupations: (i) a jeweller selling sterling-silver table settings; (ii) a used-car dealer; and (iii) an owner of a video rental store? How successful would you expect to be with your choice of inventory valuation method?

Q6-33. It has sometimes been suggested that as a general rule the expenditures included in the cost of inventory should be those that increase its ultimate value, whereas any expenditures that simply maintain its value should be treated as period cost. Cite particular costs that are already treated in accordance with this approach. Cite examples of costs whose treatment contradicts this approach.

Q6-34. "The main reason I am opposed to the use of LIFO is the way we would have to make our inventory shipments. It would mean that the first goods we had ever bought would still be in our inventory. They would be so deteriorated that they would not be worth anything, and yet we would probably be showing them on the balance sheet at their original cost." Comment on this quote.

Q6-35. "FIFO means that our customers can be sure of getting fresh stock because FIFO guarantees a constant and even turnover." Do you agree with this quote? Explain.

Q6-36. In this chapter we suggested periodic counts and the maintenance of a perpetual inventory system. Each serve to provide information about the physical quantity of goods on hand. Explain how the perpetual inventory system might be extended to provide up-to-date information on the cost of the inventory on hand.

Q6-37. Under a periodic count system the cost of goods sold cannot be determined until the inventory has been counted and valued. In particular, it is not possible to charge cost of goods sold every time an item is sold. Would it be possible to extend the perpetual inventory method set out in this chapter to provide enough information to charge cost of goods sold each time an item is sold? If so, what are the merits of this approach as opposed to calculating cost of goods sold at the end of each accounting period?

Q6-38. Would you recommend the use of periodic count or perpetual inventory method in each of the following situations? Explain.

   a. a video cassette rental shop

   b. a shop in a plaza that makes and sells fresh bread and rolls

   c. a Burger King

   d. a store that sells classical records

   e. a Radio Shack retail store

   f. a Radio Shack store selling only computers

   g. a fuel oil dealer who has his own storage tanks

Q6-39. Where, if at all, would you report each of the following items on the balance sheet?

   a. goods in your showroom on consignment

   b. goods in your workshop to be repaired for a customer

   c. goods on consignment in a customer's showroom

   d. an inventory of small tools used in the manufacturing process

   e. goods in transit from a customer which are being returned as unsatisfactory

Q6-40. In period of economic downturn, it is common for manufacturing and mining companies to build up their inventories. It has been said that they might be motivated to do this in order to keep their profits up. Explain the conditions under which this might happen.

Q6-41. Inventory may be in transit either (i) from a supplier or (ii) to a customer. For each case give an example of how the item in transit might be included in inventory. For each case, give an example of how the item might be excluded from inventory. Explain.

Q6-42. A firm has an inventory of memory chips that are used in micro-computers. The chips do not deteriorate physically over time. They are shipped in small boxes so that they are very easy to count. It is therefore simple to establish the physical quantities on hand at any given time. However, because of rapid technological change, the replacement cost of the chips has been steadily dropping. In addition the rapid change in the design of personal computers has resulted in a constant shift in the type of memory chip demanded. If the company wished to value its inventory at the lower of cost and market, how might it go about establishing the market price?

Q6-43. What would be the impact on (i) cost of goods sold and (ii) net income of each of the following?

   a. Opening inventory was understated because some items were missed in the physical count.

   b. Closing inventory was understated because of a pricing error.

   c. Purchases and closing inventory were understated because an item in transit to the company had not been included in purchases and had not been included in closing inventory.

   d. Purchases were understated but closing inventory was stated correctly because an invoice for an item that had been received was not entered in the purchase journal.

e. An item on hand at the start of the year had been correctly included in opening inventory but incorrectly entered as a purchase of the present year.

f. An item purchased in the current period was damaged in the warehouse and written off as worthless.

Q6-44. A department store used the retail inventory method to estimate the lower-of-cost-and-market value of inventory in the kitchen wares department. The store arrived at an amount of $150,000. As a cross-check, it also estimated inventory by using the gross profit method. This produced a result of $135,000. The discrepancy was disturbing enough to the manager that he had a physical count done. This produced a lower-of-cost-and-market value of $140,000. Aside from mistakes in counting or calculating the amounts, what other factors could have caused the differences?

Q6-45. What would be the effect, if any, if cash discounts on inventory purchases were treated as a revenue item instead of being deducted from the cost of inventory?

Q6-46. Work-in-process inventory is commonly valued at replacement cost for items near the start of the production process and at net realizable value for items near the end. It has been argued that this means that the profit margin to be recorded at the time of sale has been left in the items valued at replacement cost but squeezed out of items valued at net realizable value. Do you agree? If so, is this treatment consistent?

EXERCISES

E6-1. Battersea Novelties has a varied inventory and does not use a perpetual inventory method. Instead it relies on a physical count at the end of its fiscal year. At the end of 19X1 it counted and priced its inventory and calculated it to be $81,000. However, the following errors had been made:

(i) The owner's nephew had been hired to help in the count, but he was not told that Battersea was storing merchandise for another novelty company while its building was under alteration. The goods he mistakenly included in his count were included in the inventory at a value of $9,000.

(ii) A shipment of ski posters was counted in inventory and valued at $350. The goods had been ordered by Battersea and were received a week before the end of the fiscal year. However, the bookkeeper had misread the date on the invoice and did not enter it in the books of the company until after the year-end.

(iii) A shipment of paper cups arrived in the last week before the year-end. Because of crowded storage, it was put in a lunchroom where it was overlooked during the count. It was later discovered that the invoice for the shipment, totalling $125, had not been entered in the books until 19X2.

(iv) Goods on consignment with a retailer were overlooked in the count. They cost $350 and had an estimated market value of $500. The customer holding the goods had been invoiced for $500, but the invoice had never been entered in the books of the company.

Required: Prepare journal entries to correct each of the above for both the 19X1 and 19X2 financial years. Assume that journal entries may still be made with respect to the 19X1 year.

E6-2. Penrose Manufacturing Inc. purchased its raw material on terms that entitle it to a cash discount of 2% if it pays the invoice within ten days of the invoice date. The company has sufficient funds to pay its accounts promptly. The major owner of the company feels that the management should take advantage of all available purchase discounts.

    a. Explain how an accounting system might be designed to report to the owner the kind of information she considers important in this respect.

    b. Would it make any difference to the determination of a cost figure for year-end inventory if merchandise purchases are recorded throughout the year at their net price after the cash discount, instead of at full invoice price? Explain.

(Prepared by J.E. Smyth)

E6-3. A company whose prime activity is writing software for other companies to use with their computers has followed the practice of treating this software as work-in-process inventory until it is completely developed and the customer has accepted it. They do not use the percentage-of-completion method for recognizing income. Critics of this approach think expeditures on software should be considered as an expense since "it is just a pile of (computer) tapes and ring-bound books." However, the president of the company is strongly in favour of the current accounting practice. He points out that "the key distinction between our spending on this software and equivalent spending on research and development is recoverability. We are developing something we know we can sell. We have a backlog of orders to prove it. To expense it would be misleading."

Required: Do you agree with the president? Discuss the merits of his view about capitalizing the expenditures, disregarding all you know about the treatment required by the *CICA Handbook* or the FASB.

E6-4. A new retail operation that sells one product has completed its first year of operations and is trying to decide which method of inventory valuation to adopt. They provide you with the following information for 19X5 (31 December year-end).

Sales:	11 units	
Purchases:	1 January	3 @ $ 300
	1 March	5 @ $ 360
	18 August	2 @ $ 360
	8 November	8 @ $ 330

On 28 December an order for ten units at $324 each was placed with the wholesaler. This order was filled on 10 January 19X6.

Required:

    a. From the above information, calculate the cost of the closing inventory using each of the following cost flow assumptions: (i) FIFO, (ii) LIFO, and (iii) average cost.

    b. Determine the lower-of-cost-and-market value for each case in (a).

    c. Disregarding everything you know about the requirements of the *CICA Handbook*, set out the balance-sheet presentation and valuation method you prefer. Discuss the advantages and disadvantages of your approach and of the alternatives.

E6-5. Given below are several unrelated situations where errors have been made in recording a company's inventory. If the errors were caught and corrected in the year in which they occurred, how would this affect (i) the current year's income?, (ii) next year's income?, and (iii) this year's total assets on the closing balance sheet?

    a. Shipping charges of $600 relating to the inventory on hand at the end of the year were expensed during the year.

b. The clerk who priced the year-end inventory on hand was using an outdated price list and consequently undervalued the ending inventory by $350.

c. On the last day of the fiscal year the company purchased inventory costing $200. The purchase was not recorded but the items were included in the year-end physical count.

d. During the year-end physical count, errors were made which resulted in an under-statement of the inventory on hand by $250.

e. The company holds goods on consignment. The ending inventory included such goods with a value of $400.

f. On the last day of the fiscal year the company purchased inventory costing $500. The purchase was not recorded, and the actual goods were not included in the year-end physical count.

g. On the last day of the fiscal year the company made a cash sale of merchandise worth $300. The sale was not recorded, and the goods were not included in the year-end physical count.

E6-6. Consider the following three jobs. Note that amounts are billable based on the engineer's estimates of the stage of completion of the job (e.g., "10% complete, 10% billable").

Year	Contract price	Length of project (months)	Estimated costs (total)	Months done	Costs to date	Total billable	Total received
			JOB #1				
1	$1,400,000	18	$1,150,000	3	$ 230,000	10%	$ 20,000
2	1,400,000	21	1,250,000	18	1,086,000	70%	90,000
3	1,400,000	0	1,210,000	21	1,210,000	100%	1,200,000
			JOB #2				
1	$ 750,000	14	$ 650,000	7	$ 500,000	30%	$ 20,000
2	900,000	14	809,500	14	809,000	90%	50,000
			JOB #3				
1	$6,000,000	36	$5,200,000	4	$1,400,000	10%	$ 60,000
2	$6,000,000	36	6,200,000	16	2,800,000	35%	1,100,000
3	$6,000,000	36	6,000,000	28	5,000,000	65%	2,500,000
4	$6,000,000	36	5,800,000	36	5,800,000	85%	4,200,000

Required:

a. For each job, calculate the income for each year, by using (i) the percentage-of-completion method and (ii) the completed-contract method.

b. For Job #1 only, prepare the necessary journal entries for each year to record income earned to date, accounts receivable, and payments on account. Use the percentage-of-completion method.

E6-7. Construction Company Ltd. uses the percentage-of-completion method for recording income on its contracts. It is engaged in the following three projects:

    (i) Project 1: Contract price is $750,000 for a project that will take 16 months to complete. Total costs were expected to be $650,000. Costs incurred in Year 1 were $75,000. At the end of Year 2, fifteen months of work had been finished and an entry was recorded for a loss of $32,000. The estimates at the end of Year 2 accurately forecasted the actual results of Year 3.

    (ii) Project 2: On a 40-month project with an original contract price of $12,500,000 and an expected profit margin of 11.5%, the following amounts were recorded as income or loss by the company:

Year 1 (after 8 months)	$ 400,000
Year 2 (after 20 months)	$ 300,000 (job is 50% complete)
Year 3 (after 32 months)	$(900,000)
Year 4 (after 44 months)	$ 350,000

(iii) Project 3: On a 27-month project, the following estimates of total costs were made by management:

Year 1 (initial and after 3 months)	$ 920,000
Year 2 (after 15 months)	$1,456,565
Year 3 (after 27 months)	$1,220,500

Actual costs at the end of Year 1 totalled $100,000 and a profit of $30,435 was recorded. In Year 2 a loss of $287,000 was recorded. In Year 3 the company managed to increase the contract price by 10% by negotiating with the client on the basis of design changes made during the construction period.

Required:

a. What was the original estimate of total profit for Project 1?

b. What was the income or loss recorded at the end of Year 1 and Year 3 for Project 1?

c. For Project 2, determine the total estimated costs for each year.

d. What was the original contract price for Project 3?

e. What was the income or loss recorded at the end of Year 1 and Year 3 for Project 3?

E6-8. Scylla Ltd. and Charybdis Inc. are two companies both working on the same projects. Scylla uses the percentage-of-completion method of recognizing income, whereas Charybdis uses the completed-project method. Given below is a summary of various contracts the companies are working on. (All costs are given in thousands of $.)

(i) A five-year, $7.5 million project.

	Year				
	1	2	3	4	5
Scylla					
Projected completion cost	$5,000	$6,500	$6,000	$4,800	$5,200
Contract price	$7,500	$7,500	$7,500	$7,500	$7,500
% complete	10%	30%	50%	85%	100%
Charybdis					
Completion cost					$5,200
Contract price					$7,500
% complete					100%

(ii) Five one-year, $1.5 million projects.

	Project				
	1	2	3	4	5
Each company					
Completion cost	$1,300	$ 900	$ 800	$1,200	$1,000
Contract price	$1,500	$1,500	$1,500	$1,500	$1,500
% complete	100%	100%	100%	100%	100%

Required: For each of the six projects above, show the incomes for each company for each year.

E6-9. For each of the following projects give a reasonable standard on which the percentage of completion might be based:

a. The construction of an eight-lane superhighway from Wawa to Kapuskasing.

b. The construction of a 110-storey highrise in downtown Smooth Rock Falls.

c. Writing a computer software program designed to balance the national budget.

d. The construction of a bridge to connect Labrador to the main island of Newfoundland.

e. A project to convert 100 Canadair executive jets into fighters for the armed forces.

f. A project to decentralize the government by moving the members of the official opposition to Moose Jaw.

E6-10. H-Two-0 is a small retail store which specializes in water-related products, including dehydrated water, bottled water from the glistening waters of Lake Ontario, and soft water made especially for water beds. The company books reveal the following for the year ending 31 December 19X6.

	Cost	Retail
Inventory, 1 January	$ 3,000	$15,250
Purchases	18,000	59,000
Purchase discounts	1,900	
Sales (gross)		53,000
Sales returns		6,500
Sales discounts		1,250
Freight in	1,300	
Mark-ups		1,750
Mark-up cancellations		1,250
Mark-downs		1,000
Mark-down cancellations		750

Required:

a. Estimate the ending inventory using the retail inventory method according to GAAP.

b. Estimate the ending inventory using the gross profit method, given that the gross margin in the past has been 75%.

c. Why are the two numbers calculated above different? Which would reflect more accurately the value of the inventory?

E6-11. Tuktoyuktuk Pleasure Crafts Ltd. is a small yacht distributor servicing the Northwest Territories. During 19X6 sales hit an all-time high; they finally sold a boat. Given below is information pertaining to the 19X6 fiscal year.

	Retail	Cost
Inventory, 1 January	$155,000	$105,500
Purchases	200,000	126,500
Sales	202,000	
Freight in		15,000
Mark-ups	25,000	
Mark-up cancellations	23,000	
Mark-downs	30,000	

Required:

a. Calculate the ending inventory using the retail inventory method according to GAAP.

b. Evaluate the retail inventory method as a method of estimating inventory.

E6-12. Hot Wheels Ltd. is a company which does a high volume in buying used cars, refinishing them, and transporting them to another province where they are then sold. On auditing the company books at year-end, you find the following has been charged to inventory:

(i) Freight costs of $15,000 to bring the cars to the company warehouse in Témiscaming.

(ii) $10,000 to store the cars before being shipped.

(iii) $5,000 to insure the warehouse and its contents.

(iv) $2,000 to fix a car that had been stolen from the company warehouse and driven into a moose.

(v) $1,550 in heat and electricity bills

(vi) $45,000 in paint used to repaint all the cars.

(vii) $50,000 in labour costs, of which $15,000 went to pay for a night watchman.

(viii) $5,000 in grinding materials to clean off the engine blocks on which someone had inscribed a series of numbers and letters.

(ix) $150,000 in purchases of used cars.

Required: Separate out those items that should be expensed during the period. Calculate the value of the year-end inventory, given that there was no beginning inventory and no sales as of yet.

E6-13. Green Cheese Inc. is a real estate developer currently developing land on the moon. Examination of the company books reveals the following items have been included in inventory:

(i) $100,000 to fill in a crater.

(ii) $55,000 to cover the land and instal an atmosphere.

(iii) $1,500,000 for transportation of supplies and workers to the worksite.

(iv) $10,000,000 in interest costs to cover the first year's interest payment.

(v) $4,750,000 to build a solar collector to supply electricity to the area.

(vi) $3,500,000 in advertising costs to entice people to buy land on the moon.

(vii) $5,600,000 to repair several buildings hit by meteors.

(viii) $2,500,000 in taxes on the land.

Required: Separate out those items that should be expensed during the period. Calculate the value of the land inventory at year-end. Be sure to explain why each item has been expensed or included in inventory.

E6-14. Examine the report on inventories of Minnesota Mining and Manufacturing Company, Canadian Occidental Petroleum Ltd., and B.P. Canada Inc., all found in this chapter. For each company answer the following questions regarding their inventory.

a. To what extent does the inventory include those items usually found in inventory?

b. What would be the most likely method used to establish the market value of the inventory?

c. Would the company carry the inventory below the market value?

d. Given the nature of the industry, describe the degree of natural error that would likely occur in trying to establish physical inventory on hand, finding its cost, and estimating market value?

E6-15. The coast of British Columbia has become the site of "salmon farms," where the fish are bred and raised in captivity in salt-water pens. This is a big operation, and the shares of some of the companies are publicly traded. The press reported that one of the companies had encountered an inventory shortage that resulted in a write-down of $1.4 million because the number of fish that seemed to be in the pens was considerably less than the records had originally indicated.

Required:
Comment on the probable cost/reliability tradeoff of each of the following methods for estimating the actual inventory:

  a. Scuba divers check the pens several times a week to make sure that there is no undetected predator damage, unexplained mortality, or cannibalism.

  b. A video camera costing $100,000 is used. It is lowered in the water to do sample counts in various parts of the pen.

  c. Sonic equipment is used to bounce sound waves off the fish. This yields an estimate of the relative density of fish in an area.

  d. The fish are physically counted. It is estimated that fish can be counted at the rate of 4,000 per day, but that the counting process itself causes stress for the fish and contributes to their mortality.

E6-16. It is said that the retail inventory method is unsatisfactory because it leads to systematic *overvaluation* of inventory for two reasons:

  (i) Turnover distortion — Goods carrying a high margin tend to be slow to sell; therefore at the year-end, the inventory carries proportionately more of these items.

  (ii) Future mark-downs — The selling price on the items at the time of the inventory count does not reflect their ultimate selling price inasmuch as some of them will later be marked down to sell.

Required: Evaluate the merits of these complaints for a specific kind of retail store, namely, a jewellery store. To the extent that these charges have merit, can you think of any way to compensate for them?

E6-17. In Year 1 a jeweller had an item in inventory which had cost $1,000. It was held in inventory and sold for $1,800 in Year 4. Its market value at the end of each year was as follows: Year 1, $1,000; Year 2, $800; and Year 3, $1,200. The jeweller followed the practice of valuing inventory item by item using the lower of cost and market.

Required:

  a. What would be the reported profit for this item in each of the four years?

  b. Describe the disadvantages of the lower-of-cost-and-market rule beginning as follows: "The lower of cost-and-market rule is capable of valuing inventory at an amount which is neither cost nor market...." Use this example to illustrate your points.

  c. What response do you think a fair-minded person who supported historical-cost accounting would give to your critique?

  d. Suppose the company used the lower-of-cost-and-market rule, but compared the *total* cost of the inventory to its *total* value. Is it possible that individual items could, in effect, be written up from a lower market value of a previous year?

E6-18. The inventory of Traymoor Nurseries has all been counted and costed from suppliers' invoices. The final figure is $87,543, and the net income for the year is $35,822. You have been assigned the task of reviewing the inventory valuation. You discover the following items had not been taken into account when the company calculated the above inventory valuation of 30 September, the company's fiscal year-end.

(i) A supplier's invoice for 200 evergreens for $6,000 was dated 3 October and was not included in accounts payable for September. However, the inventory count sheets show that the 200 trees must have been included in the 30 September count.

(ii) When investigating another supplier's invoice for $5,432 you were unable to find the items in the inventory list, but the invoice had been entered prior to 30 September and charged to Purchases. On further investigation you find that the items had been received prior to 30 September but had been left off the count in error because they were still in the receiving area.

(iii) Thirty ornamental cedars were mispriced at $325.00 each (instead of the correct $32.50), and twenty blue spruce were mispriced at $65 (instead of the correct $165).

(iv) Four hundred bags of fertilizer were omitted from the count because the people counting were unaware of the shed where the bags were stored. The invoice, which had not been entered by 30 September because of a processing error, showed that the bags had cost $2.10 each.

(v) Thirty lawn ornaments had been included in the count at $25 each, the amount shown on the invoice. When you tried to trace the invoice to the purchase journal, you were unable to find where it was entered. You were told that the ornaments were at the nursery on a consignment basis and that the invoicing was just a formality to keep track of how many had been shipped to the nursery for possible sale.

(vi) Shrubs and trees to the value of $3,500 were being planted at a site where the nursery had a landscaping contract. They were not included in the inventory. The job had just been completed by 30 September; but the invoice was not prepared and sent until 10 October, since it was the company's custom to wait ten days after the job before invoicing to see if the customer had any complaints or wished any additions or alterations. The labour on the job had cost $2,800, and the customer was ultimately invoiced for $7,500.

Required: Using the above information, prepare the following:

a. A schedule showing the changes that must be made to revise the closing inventory and the net income for the year.

b. The journal entries needed to correct inventory, accounts payable, accounts receivable, and cost of sales.

PROBLEMS

P6-1.   Records for the Enterprise General Store disclose the following:

	Cost	Retail
Merchandise inventory, 1 January 19X0	$ 15,000	$ 30,000
Purchases, 1 January to 31 December 19X0	90,000	
Sales, 1 January to 31 December 19X0		102,000
Sales returns, 1 January to 31 December 19X0		2,000
Freight in, 1 January to 31 December 19X0	6,200	
Purchase discounts taken, 1 January to 31 December 19X0	1,000	
Physical inventory, 31 December 19X0		60,000

Required: Calculate the estimated cost of the ending inventory using (i) FIFO and (ii) LIFO. Assume there was no theft or breakage.

P6-2. Records for the Big Time Department Store disclose the following:

	Cost	Retail
Inventory, 1 January 19X0	$ 19,200	$ 24,000
Purchases	118,000	160,000
Sales		140,000
Mark-ups		12,000
Mark-up cancellations		3,000
Mark-downs		6,000
Freight in	5,690	
Sales discounts		4,000
Purchase discounts	2,000	
Physical inventory, 31 December 19X0		40,000

Required: Estimate the value of inventory on hand at 31 December 19X0 using the retail inventory method. Also calculate the inventory loss.

P6-3. The Wallace Company expects a price decline for its major raw material immediately after the first of the year. They expect that the purchase price of this material, which is now $5 a pound, will drop by 10% to $4.50 per pound. The company uses the LIFO method of valuing its inventory. At present the company has on hand its normal year-end stock of 100,000 pounds, priced at an average of $2 per pound. The company expects to sell 75,000 pounds of this stock before the end of the year. The purchasing agent argues that the company should place an order for delivery immediately after the first of the year at the new lower prices. The controller argues that they should place an order for the immediate delivery of 75,000 pounds of the material even though it will cost 50 cents per pound more.

Required:

a. What, if any, is the difference in income for the current year between the two proposals? Who is right?

b. What, if any, will be the difference in income for the coming year, assuming an inventory at the end of the coming year of 100,000 pounds?

c. What, if any, is the difference in the cash required for the two alternatives, assuming the income tax effect is the same.

P6-4. You are the person who has just been appointed to design and keep the perpetual inventory records in a company that sells only personal computers. On your arrival at work the first day you find out the following:

(i) There are three basic computer models, A, B, and C. It is possible for each model to have additional features, such as disk drives, special screens, or additional memory, so that at the extreme there could be as many as sixty submodels for each of the basic models. Probably, however, the company will never actually have on hand more than twenty different submodels, and among some of them the differences in cost will be slight, although the technical features may be significantly different.

(ii) No perpetual inventory exists at the moment. Therefore you do a physical count and find the following (the retail price of each feature is shown below the feature number):

Model	Feature attached? (Yes/No)					
	1 ($30)	2 ($1,400)	3 ($3,000)	4 ($80)	5 ($120)	6 ($25)
A	N	Y	Y	N	N	Y
A	Y	N	Y	N	N	Y
A	N	Y	N	N	N	Y
A	Y	Y	Y	Y	N	Y
B	N	Y	Y	N	N	Y
B	Y	N	Y	N	N	Y
B	N	Y	N	N	N	Y
B	Y	Y	Y	Y	N	Y
C	N	Y	N	N	N	Y
C	Y	Y	Y	Y	N	Y

Required: Discuss how you would organize the record keeping for a perpetual inventory system in this company. In particular,

a. Would you keep the records for the three basic computer models or for the sixty submodels of each of the three? Evaluate the advantages and costs of each approach.

b. Show a sketch of the manual ledger card you would use. It need not be of high drafting quality, but the essential features should be there.

c. How well would the purposes of a perpetual inventory be served by the approach you recommend? Your assessment will be graded as much for your ability to perceive the weaknesses of your approach as for your skill in recommending the system of your choice.

P6-5. Prepare journal entries for the following unrelated events at Portsmouth Hardware Store. Assume it has no retail inventory system and relies on periodic counts for inventory valuation. Be sure to explain your journal entries.

a. The store ordered five wheelbarrows from a supplier, and they arrived in good order. The invoice arrived shortly afterwards for $89.54, with a note indicating there was a cash discount of 2% if the bill was paid within 20 days.

b. The above bill was paid within fifteen days of the invoice date.

c. A bill arrived from the trucking company that had delivered the wheelbarrows from the supplier. The bill was for $15.87 and was paid.

d. The wheelbarrows were originally priced at $38.00 and three were sold at that price.

e. Because the season was coming to an end, the retail price was then reduced to $28.00.

f. At the financial year-end, only one of the two wheelbarrows was counted (because of a counting error), and the inventory was set up accordingly.

g. After the financial statements had been prepared, the error was found and corrected on the inventory count sheet.

P6-6. An investor had the following activity in shares of Bell Canada:

Date	Activity	Number of shares	Balance on hand	Unit price
19X3				
1 May	Buy	200	200	$20.00
10 May	Buy	200	400	25.00
15 May	Sell	100	300	30.00
8 Nov	Buy	200	500	22.00
20 Dec	Sell	300	200	25.00

Required:

a. Calculate the cost of the shares sold on 15 May and 20 December using each of the following methods of inventory valuation: (i) FIFO, (ii) LIFO, and (iii) weighted average cost. Show all your calculations.

b. If the sale on 15 May had been for 400 shares and the purchase on 8 November had been for 500 shares, would this have affected the LIFO valuation at the end of the calendar year? Discuss.

P6-7. A friend is thinking of buying a small business, located in a shopping plaza, that rents video games. On examining the financial statements you see that the sales appear to be entirely on a cash basis and that the inventory of cassettes appears to be the major asset. Your friend asks your advice about how she might go about keeping adequate control over this inventory.

Required: Write your friend a memo on the topic, making sure you cover the following points:

a. The relative merit of using periodic or perpetual inventory in that particular business.

b. How she might generate monthly reports without having to do physical counts.

c. The merits of the retail inventory method in this case.

P6-8. Oakleaf Corporation is a wholesale distributing company. Its balance sheet as of 30 June 19X8 included the following items:

Accounts receivable	$85,500
Merchandise inventory, at cost	82,500
Trade accounts payable	70,000

The company's income statements for the past three years (with year-end at 30 June) have included the following data:

	19X6	19X7	19X8
Sales	$690,000	$735,000	$800,000
Cost of goods sold	517,500	529,200	624,000

On 9 October 19X8 a fire occurred in the company's main warehouse. The fire completely destroyed the contents of the building including all the merchandise on hand and the company's accounting records for sales, purchases, and cash.

After the fire, the company managed to salvage a box containing cheques issued to suppliers and since returned paid and cancelled by the bank. An analysis of these vouchers revealed payments to suppliers of inventory items in the amount of $245,000 during the period 1 July to 30 September 19X8. The bank produced further cheques issued to suppliers and paid in the period from 1 October to 9 October 19X8 totalling $30,000.

Letters were sent to all suppliers requesting a statement showing details of amounts owing to them as of 9 October 19X8. Replies indicated that balances due at the time of the fire aggregated $77,500.

The bank reported the details of all deposits received for the company's account during the period from 1 July to 9 October. These deposits totalled $420,000. The only deposit in this total that could be identified as other than a deposit of remittances received from customers on account was a deposit of the proceeds from the sale of a machine in August for $52,000.

An analysis of copies of sales invoices and of deposits reported by the bank indicated amounts receivable of $67,500 as of the date of the fire.

Required:

a. For the period 1 July to 9 October 19X8, calculate each of the following: (i) an estimate of sales, (ii) an estimate of purchases, and (iii) an estimate of cost of goods sold. Compare your estimates with available figures from the previous three years.

b. For insurance purposes, calculate an estimate of merchandise inventory cost as of 9 October 19X8.

(Adapted from J.E. Smyth)

P6-9.   Abbott Shoe Stores lost much of their inventory in a fire on 4 October 19X5. Fortunately some company records were salvaged, including the previous year's financial statements and the other information provided below:

ABBOTT SHOE STORES
BALANCE SHEET
As at 31 December 19X4

Assets:	
Cash	$ 1,568
Accounts receivable	8,915
Inventory	38,962
Fixed assets (net of depreciation)	60,743
Total Assets	$110,188
Liabilities:	
Bank loan	$ 10,000
Accounts payable	9,657
	19,657
Owners' Equity:	
Capital stock	40,000
Retained earnings	50,531
	90,531
Total Liabilities and Owners' Equity	$110,188

ABBOTT SHOE STORES
INCOME STATEMENT
For the Year Ending 31 December 19X4

Sales		$551,980
Cost of goods sold		386,386
		165,594
Expenses		
Selling and administration	64,055	
Legal and audit	4,100	
Interest	1,200	
Other	1,895	71,250
Net income before taxes		94,344
Provision for income taxes		23,586
Net Income		$ 70,758

The other salvaged information consists of the following:
(i) For the period 1 January to 4 October 19X5:

Sales	$325,680
Purchases	282,100
Purchase Returns	16,850
Sales Returns	1,430
Freight in	418

(ii) Merchandise with a selling price of $8,800 was undamaged in the fire.

(iii) Other merchandise with an original retail value of $4,300 was partially damaged and now has a net realizable value of $1,350.

Required: Calculate the inventory loss to Abbott shoes due to the fire.

P6-10. On 22 August 19X4, the inventory and fixtures of Makie's Furniture Store were completely destroyed by fire. The company has always carried fire insurance on its inventory. According to the terms of the policy, they can make a claim based on 80% of the loss.

The partial records for the current year which were salvaged from the fire disclosed the following data:

Sales salaries	$ 25,500
Sales	578,800
Purchases	303,980
Sales discounts	21,565
Freight in	1,210
Purchase returns	3,150
Sales returns	5,485
Purchase discounts	965

The income statement for the year ending 31 December 19X3 was found at home by the accountant (who took work home from the office on a regular basis). This statement included the following selected information:

Purchases	$415,315
Net sales	898,220
Purchase returns	4,160
Cost of goods available for sale	538,690
Freight in	2,020
Cost of goods sold	448,930
Total selling and administration expenses	101,538

Required: Calculate the amount that Makie's Furniture can expect to collect from the insurance company.

P6-11. In 1983 Revenue Canada appeared to have selected Vancouver artist Toni Onley as a test case of how artists must treat expenses for tax purposes. On 15 October 1983 *The Financial Post* reported that at issue was the travel expenses he incurred while creating artistic works. The artist felt that such travel expenditures should be charged as expenses in the year in which they were incurred ("like any other businessman"). However Revenue Canada felt that they were a cost of producing finished works of art and therefore should be treated as inventory costs. Revenue Canada argued that the expenditures should not be treated as expenses until the art is sold.

Required:

a. Write a brief essay justifying the position of Revenue Canada.

b. Similarly, make the case for Toni Onley.

c. Do generally accepted accounting principles help you resolve this problem?

P6-12. On 8 June 1983 *The Globe and Mail* reported on Canadair's accounting practices. Canadair Ltd. of Montreal, like many other companies, had followed the "program" method of accounting, which was designed to recognize the unique nature of the industry. Background notes to the company's financial statements said Canadair had "treated all costs which were in any way related to the Challenger program as costs of the program." Such costs showed up on the balance sheet as work-in-progress inventory. In 1982, the company reported a sudden billion-dollar write-off of program costs and a change in its accounting policy for these expenditures. One of the stated reasons was the recognition that the company "could never reasonably hope" to recover all the expenses it had included in the program inventory.

Required:

a. Evaluate the accounting policy followed by Canadair before 1982.

b. Prepare a proposal for Canadair outlining a new accounting policy for the company to follow and clearly explain your reasoning.

P6-13. McKinnon General Store is a small store servicing a nearby village. Their accounting system is not very complex. Therefore inventory is counted using the retail inventory method. Records indicated the following for the period ending 31 December 19X4:

	Cost	Retail
Merchandise inventory, 1 January 19X4	$ 30,480	$ 44,670
Purchases for the year	102,370	168,900
Sales		175,680
Sales returns		1,080
Mark-ups		10,400
Mark-up cancellations		4,000
Mark-downs		2,500
Freight in	5,700	
Purchase discounts taken	10,240	
Physical inventory, 31 December 19X4		36,890

Required:

a. Estimate the value of the inventory on hand as at 31 December 19X4 using the retail inventory method to estimate the lower of cost and market.

b. State whether you think this is an appropriate way to calculate the value of the inventory for this store. Give reasons.

P6-14. Johnson One-Stop is a small store servicing a large rural area. They estimate their inventory using the retail inventory method. This year, some of their records have been lost, and they have asked you to help them reconstruct some of their statements. The surviving information is shown below:

(i) Inventory at the start of the year was $19,200 at cost and $24,000 at retail.

(ii) During the year, there were mark-ups of $12,000 and mark-up cancellations of $3,000. As well, there were mark-downs of $6,000.

(iii) Sales for the year were $140,000.

(iv) Because of cash flow problems, the company was not able to take advantage of purchase discounts.

(v) The terms with the suppliers are FOB destination.

(vi) The ending inventory count is $40,000 at retail.

(vii) The estimate of ending inventory at lower of cost and market is $28,435.

(viii) The estimate of ending inventory at cost is $29,947.

(ix) Purchases were $160,000 at retail, but no figure is available for purchases at cost.

Required: Johnson One-Stop needs to know the amount of purchases at cost that were made during the past year. Without this amount, it will be impossible to construct the income statement. Derive the figure from the above data and show all your calculations.

P6-15. Biederbecke Department Store values its inventory using the retail inventory method. It is now year-end for the company, and the following data have been compiled for the year's operations.

	Retail	Cost
Inventory, 1 January 19X3	$ 21,318	$ 10,225
Physical inventory, 31 December 19X3	18,880	
Purchases for the year	132,670	67,990
Purchase discounts taken		1,200
Sales	128,545	
Mark-ups	10,560	
Mark-up cancellations	3,400	
Mark-downs	1,557	
Freight in		5,600

Required: For the year-end 31 December 19X3, estimate the value of the closing inventory at lower of cost and market using the retail inventory method.

P6-16. Armstrong Jazz Supplies is preparing its year-end financial statements. They require an estimate of their closing inventory. The following data are presented to you:

	Cost	Retail
Inventory as at 1 June 19X0	$ 54,300	$ 78,920
Physical count of inventory, 31 May 19X1	57,890	84,565
Sales		248,900
Purchases	187,650	263,000
Purchase discounts taken	11,280	
Mark-ups		10,320
Mark-up cancellations		8,990
Mark-downs		3,270
Freight in	3,090	

Required: Estimate the lower-of-cost-and-market value and the historic-cost value of the inventory at the year-end 31 May 19X1.

P6-17. Two accounting students are sitting around one Sunday afternoon discussing the merits of the different methods of accounting for long-term contracts.

Student #1 boasts that his uncle, the owner of a construction company, can produce whatever income number he wants. He can manipulate the figures to suit the current situation (e.g. for credit purposes to show the bank or for tax purposes to submit to Revenue Canada). Consequently, Student #1 feels very strongly that as an investor or banker he would prefer the completed contract method because of its objectivity.

Student #2 is morally outraged at the type of actions described by Student #1. However, as a closet economist, she states that since the percentage-of-completion method best approximates the economic process of earning income, it should be the preferred method for financial reporting.

Required: Write a short essay reconciling the opinions of the two students. Clearly outline the advantages and disadvantages of both methods and state which method you prefer.

P6-18. Yarker Novelties was an agent for a line of inexpensive and colourful "fun" umbrellas, carrying custom-printed messages, that were sold at football games and other student events for $10. Its records showed the following for the fiscal year ending 31 October:

	Cost	Retail	Number
Inventory at start of year	$ 8,000	$15,000	1,500
Purchases — invoiced from supplier	25,000		5,500
— shipping	3,000		
— insurance	500		
	$28,500		
Sales to agents		$65,000	
Cash received from agents for all sales to date:		$60,000	

The owner of Yarker told you: "It's getting near the end of the season, and I'm going to authorize the selling agents to reduce the price of umbrellas to $8 from $10. Although I hold them responsible for the unsold umbrellas they hold in stock, they can return them to me for full refund at the end of the season, so I control their selling price."

Required:

a. Should the umbrellas in the selling agents' hands be treated as part of Yarker's inventory? What is the other main alternative? Discuss the *two* possible treatments and their effect, if any, on Yarker's reported income for the year.

b. Suppose Yarker considered the umbrellas in the agents' hands to be part of its inventory, but did not want to do an inventory count at 31 October. Show how the inventory might be estimated at the lower of cost and market for the purposes of financial statements. Show all your calculations.

P6-19. Gibb Co. wants to estimate its purchases for the upcoming year 19X5. They will get significant savings if they forecast their needs right now such that they only order their inventory at one time. They have a good sales department, and demand has been fairly easy to predict in the past. As well, Gibb Co. likes to maintain closing inventory at a fairly constant percentage of estimated yearly sales.

	19X2	19X3	19X4	19X5
Sales	$50,000	$62,000	$89,000	$94,000
Opening inventory	8,000	9,500	11,875	?
Purchases	27,500	34,615	51,315	?
Less: closing inventory	(9,500)	(11,875)	(16,910)	?
Cost of sales	$26,000	$32,240	$46,280	?

Required: Use past results to estimate purchases for the 19X5 fiscal year, given the sales estimate of $94,000. Make any reasonable assumptions and state what they are.

P6-20. You are given the following information for Upton Co. with respect to its five items (*A*, *B*, *C*, *D*, and *E*) of inventory for the year 19X3:

	A	B	C	D	E
Number	50	200	95	470	25
Cost per unit	$4.80	$2.00	$1.95	$5.35	$ 9.85
Replacement cost	4.70	2.10	2.00	5.10	11.00
Estimated selling price	7.20	4.50	5.25	8.75	14.30
Estimated cost to finish	2.50	2.70	2.50	3.65	2.25
Normal profit	0.45	0.60	0.80	0.40	1.00

Required:

a. Estimate the value of inventory, using the lower of cost or market rule, in each of the following ways: (i) on an individual basis and (ii) on a portfolio basis. Note that Upton Co. has the practice of using the lower of replacement cost and net realizable value less normal profit margin when estimating inventory at market.

b. What are the main issues that arise from the fact that there are different ways to value inventory? Discuss the issues as they relate to Upton Co. and as they relate to companies in general.

P6-21. Ferris Co. uses the percentage-of-completion method for projects that are expected to take longer than twelve months. The following information is available for the building they have been constructing:

Year	Total price	Estimated total costs	Actual costs to date	Percent billed and complete
1	$400,000	$360,000	$ 80,000	20%
2	400,000	410,000	205,000	45%
3	400,000	395,000	325,000	80%
4	400,000	390,000	390,000	100%

Required:

a. Prepare the journal entries for the above project each year.

b. Prepare the journal entries using the completed-project method (i.e., where revenue is recognized only at the completion of the project).

P6-22. Defense Contractors Inc. has been awarded a contract to build a hammer for the United States Navy. At the beginning of the project, the projected completion cost (PCC) is $250,000. Outlined below is a summary of the project through to completion.

	Year 0	Year 1	Year 2	Year 3
PCC	$250,000	$300,000	$200,000	$250,000
Contract price	$275,000	$275,000	$275,000	$275,000
% complete	0%	20%	60%	100%

Required:

a. Show the appropriate journal entries for each year to record the annual income and the changes in work in progress and accounts receivable.

b. What would the difference have been if the company had had perfect information as to the cost of the project all the way through?

P6-23. X, Y, Z are all divisions of Alpha company and are all working on an equal portion of a contract for the phone company. In accordance with the new Charter of Rights and Freedoms, the phone book must be completely randomized so that the A Aardvarks of this world no longer have the great advantage of having their names first in the phone book. Each division is using the percentage-of-completion method to recognize income. However, since they are autonomous divisions, each is using a different standard to measure the percentage completed. X is using the total cost incurred to date, Y is using the labour hours to date, and Z is using the lexicographer's estimate.

The following data is available. (All costs are given in thousands of $.)

	Year 0	Year 1	Year 2	Year 3
Projected completion cost	$ 500	$ 550	$ 600	$ 525
Contract price	$ 650	$ 650	$ 650	$ 650
Cost to date	$ 0	$ 110	$ 350	$ 525
Projected labour hours	1,200	1,100	1,150	1,175
Labour hours to date	0	300	900	1,175
Lexicographer's estimate	0%	25%	65%	100%

Required:

a. Show the reported net income of each division in each year.

b. Which division reported the highest net income in the first year? In the last year? Was this difference in income a good indicator of real performance? Explain.

P6-24. Wilson Bros. Inc. and Patronage Unlimited Ltd. are both working on projects for the Canadian government to attempt to establish a national identity. It is expected that the projects will take three years to complete. Both companies bid $1.5 million for the contracts. However, the companies have differing views of how much it will cost them to complete their projects, as shown below. (All costs are given in thousands of $.)

WILSON BROS. INC.

	Year 0	Year 1	Year 2	Year 3
Projected completion cost	$1,000	$1,100	$ 900	$1,300
Contract price	$1,500	$1,500	$1,500	$1,500
% complete	0%	40%	70%	100%

PATRONAGE UNLIMITED LTD.

	Year 0	Year 1	Year 2	Year 3
Projected completion cost	$1,400	$1,600	$1,700	$1,300
Contract price	$1,500	$1,500	$1,500	$1,500
% complete	0%	40%	70%	100%

Required:

a. Show how much income each company would report in Years 1, 2, and 3.

b. Which of the companies was more profitable at the end of Year 2? Year 3?

c. Suppose the companies had perfect information from the beginning that was available only to the company management. Explain why each company might still have chosen to project their costs as shown above.

P6-25. Lex Moser is the owner of Rocks on Rocks Ltd., a small company that sells exotic gravel and other precious stones. Lex has run the company out of his own home for the past eight years and keeps a wide and varied inventory scattered about the house. Lex has decided to move and must sell his inventory. Mabel Miller, a local geologist, has agreed in principle to buy the rocks if a suitable price can be established.

Mabel, using the gross profit method and knowing that the cost of goods sold in 1988 amounted to $5,850, has established a price of $2,800 for the inventory. By contrast, Lex, using the retail inventory method, has established a figure of $3,800. Given below is some information pertaining to the business over the past few years. (All amounts are given in hundreds of $.)

	1988		1989		1990	
	Retail	Cost	Retail	Cost	Retail	Cost
Beginning inventory	$150	$ 37	$158	?	$190	?
Purchases	$270	$ 50	$280	$ 40	$230	$ 57
Purchase discounts		$ 4		$ 3		$ 5
Sales	$240		$250		$290	
Sales returns	$ 6		$ 7		$ 9	
Freight in		$ 10		$ 8		$ 12
Mark-ups	$ 20		$ 15		$ 25	
Mark-up cancellations	$ 18		$ 12		$ 9	
Mark-downs	$ 30		$ 8		$ 12	

Required: State what you think is the appropriate price to be paid for the rocks. Show all calculations.

P6-26. High Digger Ltd. is a store that sells ditch-digging equipment. Given below is information relating to the new "Dasein" shovel.

	19X4		19X5		19X6	
	Units	Value	Units	Value	Units	Value
Beginning inventory	0	0	13	?	23	?
Sales	30	$1,200	44	$1,892	57	$2,736
Cost of goods sold		?		?		?
Purchases (in order of acquisition)	20 @ $22.20		12 @ $23.50		23 @ $27.00	
	5 @ $23.00		11 @ $24.30		12 @ $28.65	
	4 @ $25.00		5 @ $26.00		4 @ $30.90	
	6 @ $22.50		15 @ $24.00		8 @ $30.10	
	8 @ $24.75		11 @ $28.00		13 @ $31.00	

Required:

Calculate the gross margin for the product each year using each of the following methods. (*Hint*: This problem can be efficiently done on a computer spreadsheet program.)

a. LIFO

b. FIFO

c. average cost

P6-27. Torie Video Inc. is a company that manufactures realistic video games. The company has just finished manufacturing 100 of its new video game called "Sellout," the object of which is to sell the entire country to the Americans before the next election. It is approaching year-end and the company president, Brian Baloney, is wondering how to value this inventory. Given below are some of the facts to be taken into consideration.

(i) In order to make the machines, the company had to use twenty labour hours at $20 per hour and $1,400 worth of parts.

(ii) Variable overhead runs at approximately $10 per labour hour per machine.

(iii) There is fixed overhead of $1,000 per week while the machines are being made.

(iv) Because of inflation, supplies will cost 10% more in the future and labour will cost $25 per hour.

(v) If each machine was now sold, it would bring approximately $2,900 FOB destination.

(vi) Transportation costs average $200 per machine.

(vii) If the machines were not sold, but kept and leased to arcades, they would bring in $8 per day each for thirteen months. (Assume a 30-day month.) Maintenance would cost $500 per machine per year. At the end of thirteen months they could be converted into other games and thus would have a salvage value of $400.

Required:

a. Evaluate the inventory using each of the following:

(i) Net present value (assume the interest rate = 10%)

(ii) Current replacement cost

(iii) Historic cost

(iv) Net realizable value

b. Which of the above methods is the least prone to forecasting error? Which should be used for financial statements purposes? Give your reasons.

P6-28. Gina Carlson is President and owner of Time Warp Corporation, a company which manufactures time-saving devices. Gina is thinking of expanding and is considering acquiring Weird and Wonderful Devices Inc. (WWDI), a company that designs and manufactures revolutionary new products. WWDI uses a year-end periodic physical count for inventory control. Based on the following information, Gina believes that the company would be a good buy, as it seems very profitable.

WWDI

BALANCE SHEET

As at 31 December 1989

Assets		Liabilities and Owners' Equity Liabilities	
Cash	$ 2,000	Accounts payable	$ 20,000
Accounts receivable	25,000	Notes payable	13,000
Inventory:		Long term debt	50,000
Raw materials	10,000	Total liabilities	83,000
Work in progress	25,000		
Finished goods	90,000	*Owners' equity*	
Temporary investments	4,000	Common stock	20,000
Fixed assets (net)	32,000	(4,000 outstanding)	
		Retained earnings	85,000
		Total owners' equity	105,000
		Total liabilities and	
Total assets	$188,000	owners' equity	$188,000

WWDI
INCOME STATEMENT
For year ending 31 December 1989

Sales		$ 95,000
Cost of goods sold		35,000
Gross margin		60,000
Expenses:		
Selling	5,000	
Depreciation	2,000	
Interest	4,000	
Bad debts	1,000	
Other	500	12,500
Income before taxes		47,500
Income tax expense		23,750
Net Income		$ 23,750
Earnings per share		$5.94

Required:

a. What errors, both factual and judgemental, might have crept into the valuation of inventory? Assuming a 20% over-evaluation error of finished-goods inventory, how would this affect the net income and earnings per share of WWDI?

b. WWDI has just changed its method of evaluating its inventory from the LIFO method to the FIFO method. What effect would you expect this change to have on the balance sheet and on net income?

P6-29. For each of the following journal entries, state the event that most likely led to its occurrence.

a. Work-in-progress inventory	50,000.00	
Loss on work under construction		50,000.00
b. Raw materials inventory	980.00	
Accounts payable		980.00
Nine days later:		
Accounts payable	980.00	
Cash		960.40
Cash discounts		19.60
c. Accounts receivable	1,200.00	
Sales		1,200.00
Cost of goods sold	876.00	
Finished goods inventory		876.00
d. Loss on value of inventory	293.00	
Inventory		293.00
e. Costs of goods sold	51,770.00	
Work-in-progress inventory	8,230.00	
Sales		60,000.00

P6-30. Comrade James Ayers, the leader of the United Student Society of Revolutionaries, was examining the books of the previous student government. He and his band of revolutionaries had overthrown the bourgeois preppies and had established themselves in an effortless, bloodless and somewhat unexpected coup. The books revealed that the previous administration had 2,000 painter hats in inventory to be sold to naive unsuspecting frosh. The hats normally sold for $5.00, with a gross margin of 50%. However, because of the outdated style of the hats, they could only be sold to frosh who couldn't read. Even then they could only be sold for $2.50. The inventory had been written down to a total value of $5,000 and was presented on the balance sheet as *lower of cost and market*. Comrade Ayers was indignant that the inventory had not been marked down further so that his government might realize some profit when the hats were sold. James called for his predecessor, Kimberley Sue, to be brought out of solitary confinement in the newspaper office to explain her actions.

Required: State how Ms. Sue might defend her actions and give the probable intentions behind her actions. What counter-arguments would you expect?

P6-31. Hospital Giftshop is a charity run by volunteers with one paid employee. It has a small retail shop in a major hospital that sells gifts and toys, mainly to people who want something to take to a patient they are visiting. The Giftshop buys items from normal trade sources (e.g., boxes of candy), but also accepts items on consignment from local artisans (e.g., earthenware pots) as well as handicrafts made and donated by its members. When items are put into the shop they are repackaged, wrapped for resale, and priced at retail. If the retail price is subsequently changed, a record is kept of the change. At the end of the year the inventory is counted and priced at retail. The following information is available for the year ended 30 November 19X5.

	Cost	Retail
Opening inventory	$ 1,050	$ 2,500
Goods received on consignment	7,750	19,375
Packaging material	1,395	
Wrapping material	279	
Total goods made available	10,474	21,875
Mark-ups		250
Mark-up cancellations		(25)
Mark-downs		(340)
Mark-down cancellations		40
Subtotal		21,800
Sales		(19,110)
Calculated inventory on hand		2,690
Actual inventory on hand		2,500
Shortage at retail		$ 190

Required:

a. What is the actual inventory at the lower of cost and market using the retail method?

b. What is the estimated cost of the missing inventory?

c. In 19X4 the gross profit percentage was 43%. What is the estimated gross profit for 19X5? Explain clearly what might account for the difference, if any, in the gross profit percentage of the two years?

d. Explain whether the treatment of mark-downs and mark-down cancellations in computing the lower-of-cost-and-market ratio in the retail method is sensible.

e. After the above inventory was prepared, one of the Board members pointed out that some of the inventory had been accepted on consignment from the local artisans. Although the cost of these items had been included in the statement above, the

Giftshop was not the legal owner of these items and could return them at any time. Suppose that the consignment inventory on hand was $900 at cost and $1,400 at retail and that there had been no accounting entry on receipt of the goods. What would be the likely misstatement on the balance sheet? on the income statement?

P6-32. The records of Philips company as of 31 December 19X7 show the following:

	Net purchases	Net income	Accounts payable	Inventory
Balance per company's books	$186,000.00	$15,500.00	$19,500.00	$39,000.00
(1)				
(2)				
(3)				
(4)				
(5)				
Correct balances				

(1) Merchandise that cost $3,500 was included in the ending inventory. The related purchase has not been recorded. The goods were shipped FOB destination and arrived 30 December 19X7. However, the invoice had not arrived.

(2) Damaged goods that cost $1,200 were segregated on the loading dock ready for shipment back to the vendor. The damaged goods were included in the year-end inventory count. The goods had been recorded as part of a large purchase early in December and the entry for their return had been made on 28 December 19X7.

(3) Merchandise in transit that cost $2,500 was excluded from inventory because it had not arrived. The invoice had arrived and was recorded on 29 December 19X7. The goods were shipped FOB destination.

(4) Merchandise that cost $2,200 was specially ordered for a customer. The goods were shipped FOB customer's place of business, but had not arrived by 31 December 19X7. The invoice had arrived, but it was not recorded; nor was the sale of the goods for $3,300 recorded.

(5) Merchandise that cost $1,600 was segregated in a corner of the warehouse. Because a large SOLD tag was placed on the merchandise, it was exluded from the year-end inventory count. The merchandise was segregated because of a customer's interest to buy it. The customer asked for a few days to arrange financing. The sale for $2,400 was not recorded.

Required:
Using the format provided above, show separately each required adjustment and the correct amount for net purchases, net income, accounts payable, and inventory for Philips company as at 31 December 19X7.

(CGA adapted)

P6-33. Upon the death of her Aunt Frances, Gail Jones inherited a significant amount in cash and readily marketable securities, which she intends to use to realize a long-standing dream of going into business for herself. After considerable searching, she located the Nu-Vogue Company which was just what she wanted. Before deciding to purchase Nu-Vogue Company, Gail asks you for advice.

She is rather concerned about the fluctuations in the reported net income during the five years Nu-Vogue has been in operation — especially the decline in net income during the last two years. The statements of Nu-Vogue show the following net incomes:

Year	Reported net income
19X1	$ 22,500
19X2	36,800
19X3	43,700
19X4	34,600
19X5	29,900
Five-year total	$167,500

You agree to look into the matter and are given full access to the accounting records. Your preliminary examination indicates a stability both of selling prices and cost of merchandise. You are surprised, therefore, that there is such a considerable year-to-year variation of the gross margin. However, in your examination of the supporting inventory records, you discover numerous errors in quantifying inventory values. You assemble the following list of corrections:

Date	Reported inventory value	Corrected inventory value
19X1 January 2	$ 0	$ 0
19X1 December 31	30,200	38,600
19X2 December 31	34,500	39,300
19X3 December 31	42,700	36,400
19X4 December 31	44,800	38,100
19X5 December 31	43,800	43,800

Your examination of all other net income determinants reveals only very minor errors. Therefore, you conclude that you can complete your task by using the corrections to inventory value to adjust the net incomes.

Required:

a. Calculate the corrected net income for each of the five years.

b. Total the five years of net incomes as you have determined them.

c. Is your total different from the total of the originally reported net incomes? Why or why not?

(CGA adapted)

P6-34. Beta company buys and sells product Zed, for which the following data is available for the year 19X8.

	Units	Unit cost
Purchases:		
January	200	$60.00
February	100	60.50
March	900	61.00
April	200	61.50
November	200	62.00
December	100	63.00
Sales:		
January	100	
February	200	
May	400	
June	200	
November	100	
December	400	
Sales returns	100	
Inventory on hand:		
January 1, 19X8	210	59.00
December 31, 19X8	600	

Required:

a. Determine the inventory value at 31 December 19X8 under the periodic inventory system using each of the following methods:

    (i) FIFO

    (ii) LIFO

    (iii) weighted average

b. Which method will produce the highest net income? Why?

c. Determine the cost of units lost based on the weighted-average method.

    (CGA adapted)

P6-35. The Hong Kong Trading Company lost most of its inventory in a fire in December 19X0 just before the year-end physical inventory was taken. The company had no insurance. The company has had an average yearly gross margin of 20%. The company's books disclose the following data for the year 19X0:

Beginning inventory	$ 15,000
Purchases for the year	490,000
Freight-in	10,000
Purchases returns	30,000
Sales	520,800
Sales returns	48,000

After the fire, undamaged merchandise with a selling price of $25,000 was on hand. In addition, there was fire-damaged merchandise on hand which had an original selling price of $18,000 and a salvage value of $7,000.

Required:

Compute the amount of loss as a result of the fire.

    (CGA adapted)

P6-36. The Sunnyside Manufacturing Company Limited computes its inventory on 31 December. You are given the following information:

Item	Cost	Replacement cost	Sales price	Cost of completion	Normal profit
A	$1.75	$1.80	$2.25	$0.30	$0.17
B	0.68	0.65	1.00	0.30	0.04
C	0.29	0.27	0.50	0.15	0.05
D	0.83	0.83	1.05	0.24	0.05
E	0.79	0.74	0.90	0.11	0.07
F	1.19	1.15	1.25	0.13	0.07

Required:
For each of the items listed above, state the unit value that should be employed for inventory pricing under the lower-of-cost-and-market method. Give your reasons.

(CGA adapted)

P6-37. Textone Electronics suffered a break-in on 1 July, and all their stereo equipment merchandise was stolen. Their records showed the following data concerning the merchandise:

	At cost	At selling price
Inventory, 1 January	$12,000	$ 20,000
Purchases (net), 1 January – 30 June	60,000	100,000
Additional mark-ups		16,000
Mark-up cancellations		11,000
Mark-downs		10,000
Mark-down cancellations		2,000
Sales (net)		91,000

Required:
  a. Calculate the inventory value that would be reported to the insurance company using the retail method and average cost (excluding LCM).
  b. Calculate the inventory value using the retail method and FIFO cost (excluding LCM).

(CGA adapted)

P6-38. At the end of the annual accounting periods, the inventory records of Scott Company reflected the following:

	19X2	19X3	19X4
Ending inventory at FIFO	$35,000	$33,000	$39,000
Ending inventory at LIFO	32,000	35,000	34,000

Required:
  a. Give appropriate journal entries for each year to convert from the FIFO method to the LIFO method for purposes of external reporting.
  b. Indicate how the inventories should be shown on the 19X2, 19X3, and 19X4 comparative balance sheet for purposes of external reporting.

(CGA adapted)

P6-39. The Great-Northern Company accounts for product X using LIFO and periodic procedures. Data about product X for the year ended 31 December 19X3, are as follows:

Inventory, 1 January 19X3 — 4,000 units @ $8

TRANSACTIONS DURING 19X3

Date	Purchases	Sales
1st quarter	8,000 units @ $10	5,000 units @ $16
2nd quarter	20,000 units @ $12	16,000 units @ $18
3rd quarter	16,000 units @ $15	18,000 units @ $20
4th quarter	8,000 units @ $16	12,000 units @ $22

Required:

a. Compute the gross margin on sales of product X for 19X3.

b. Repeat part (a) assuming that 4,000 rather than 8,000 units were purchased @ $16 in the 4th quarter.

c. Repeat part (a) assuming that 12,000 rather than 8,000 units were purchased @ $16 in the 4th quarter.

d. Solve parts (a),(b), and(c) using the FIFO method rather than the LIFO method of inventory valuation.

e. Which inventory valuation method (FIFO or LIFO) permits more manipulation of net income?

f. Which inventory valuation method emphasizes the balance sheet?

g. Which inventory valuation method emphasizes the income statement?

h. Which inventory valuation method matches current costs with current revenues?

i. Which inventory valuation method results in a procession of costs in the same order as they occurred?

j. Which inventory valuation method costs inventory at approximately replacement cost?

(CGA adapted)

APPENDIX 6-1
Accounting for Inventory Cut-Off Errors

Several types of cut-off errors can occur with inventory. In this Appendix we will examine how these errors affect the financial statement. Let us start by distinguishing the following types of errors:

1. Count Errors:

    a. The goods should have been included in inventory but were left out in error. (For example, they were missed during the count because they were on consignment somewhere else or simply because the counter missed them.)

    b. The goods were included in the count when they should not have been. (For example, inventory belonging to someone else was mistakenly included in the count.)

2. Entry Errors

    a. An entry was put through too late to record (i) a purchase of raw materials inventory or (ii) a sale of finished goods. (For example, an invoice for raw material was entered in the purchase journal in 19X2, but it should have been entered in late 19X1. This type of error would also occur if an item was sold in 19X1, but was not entered in the books until early 19X2.)

b. An entry was put through too early to record (i) a purchase of raw materials inventory or (ii) a sale of finished goods. (For example, an item was invoiced in 19X1 and entered in the sales journal of 19X1 although it did not actually leave the company's shipping dock until the first week of 19X2 and was therefore included in their closing inventory.)

3. Combined errors

It is not uncommon for count errors and entry errors to be linked. (For example, inventory items were omitted from the count — a type 1(a) error — and their purchase was not included in the books — a type 2(a) error.) Combined errors are often less disastrous than single errors because the errors tend to compensate each other.

Examples of Correct Accounting Treatment by Type of Error

For each type of error we will now show the journal entries that should be put through prior to the end of the financial year to correct the mistake. In each of the examples below we have assumed that there is still time to make the correcting entry in the current year because the company's books have not yet been closed.

Correcting Error 1(a)

In counting the inventory of OneA Limited, the clerks failed to count inventories of shoes worth $2,500 because they did not notice that they were stored behind another inventory item. Because of this error, the ending inventory has been understated by $2,500. Assuming that purchases and the change in inventory have been closed out to cost of goods sold, this means that cost of goods sold has been overstated by $2,500. To correct the error requires the following journal entry:

Inventory	2,500.00	
Cost of goods sold		2,500.00
To correct error.		

Correcting Error 1(b)

In counting the inventory of OneB Limited, the staff doing the count were not aware that some of the inventory included in the count was material on consignment to OneB that should have been excluded from the count. On checking the inventory sheets after the error was discovered, it was determined that inventory had been overstated by $24,000. This is the reverse of the preceding example. Here the correcting journal entry would be as follows:

Cost of goods sold	24,000.00	
Inventory		24,000.00
To correct error.		

Correcting Error 2(a)

TwoA-1 Incorporated had a new bookkeeper who neglected to enter an invoice for the purchase of goods that had arrived just before the company's year-end. The goods totalled $3,870. If this had been entered properly, it would have been charged to purchases and hence to cost of goods sold when purchases were closed out at the end of the year. The correcting entry would therefore read as follows:

Cost of goods sold	3,870.00	
Accounts payable		3,870.00
To correct error.		

TwoA-II Limited sold and shipped a TV set at a price of $650 in 19X1. However, by error, the invoice was dated January 19X2 and it was entered in the 19X2 sales journal instead of the 19X1 journal. The correcting entry would read as follows:

Accounts receivable	650.00	
Sales		650.00
To correct error.		

It would also be necessary here to make an entry in 19X2 that reverses the erroneous 19X2 entry.

Correcting Error 2(b)

TwoB-I Limited got an invoice dated December 19X1 for three sets of Nordic skis priced at $500 in total. They entered it in their books at that time as an accounts payable. However, it was later discovered that the skis had not arrived until mid-January. As a result they had not been included in the December inventory. Because the goods should not have been included in December business, the correcting entry would be as follows:

Accounts payable	500.00	
Cost of goods sold		500.00
To correct error.		

TwoB-II Inc. shipped a set of speakers costing $500 and retailing for $850 to a customer in July, the month immediately after their June year-end. The clerk preparing the invoice mistakenly dated it as June and it was included in the June sales journal. the correcting entry would be as follows:

Sales	850.00	
Accounts receivable		850.00
To correct error.		

Correcting Error 3

As we mentioned earlier, combined errors tend to compensate each other. Thus, suppose that in our example under Correcting Error 1(a), the purchase entry had been omitted as well. Then we would have needed a second correcting entry, as follows:

Cost of goods sold	2,500.00	
Accounts payable		2,500.00
To correct error.		

The two correcting entries nets out to the following entry:

Inventory	2,500.00	
Accounts payable		2,500.00
To correct error.		

Generally, combined errors with respect to inventory purchases result in misstated amounts on the balance sheet with little or no impact on the income statement. The results are more serious, however, when there are combined mistakes with respect to sales. Reconsider our second example under Correcting Error 2(b). The correcting entry with respect to the billing was:

Sales	850.00	
Accounts receivable		850.00
To correct error.		

If the goods had been mistakenly left out of the inventory count as well, then another correcting entry would be required:

Inventory	500.00	
Cost of goods sold		500.00
To correct error.		

Thus, here both the income statement and the balance sheet would be affected to the same degree. In the income statement the net decrease on net income would be as follows:

Sales	$850
Cost of goods sold	($500)
Net decrease on net income	$350

In the balance sheet the net impact on current assets would be as follows:

Accounts receivable	$(850)
Inventory	500
Net decrease on current assets	$(350)

APPENDIX 6-2
The Percentage-of-Completion Method

The percentage-of-completion method is typically used when the item being manufactured is very large relative to the company's total inventory. One example would be a construction company putting up a large office complex under a fixed-price contract with the owner. Another example would be a computer-software house writing a large custom-designed program for a customer. A third example would be a construction company putting up a bridge, expected to take thirty months to complete, under contract with the Highways Department. If a company does not use the percentage-of-completion method under these circumstances, but instead recognizes the total income only when the project is completed, then there is some opportunity for income manipulation by speeding up or slowing down the official completion if it happens to occur close to a financial year-end. The percentage-of-completion method is also open to manipulation — but of a different sort — through the estimates that must be made.

Here is an example. A company won a contract to build a $30-million office complex. The project is expected to take twenty-five months and stretch over three calendar years. It is estimated that the total cost to the builder is $26 million, and the expected profit on the job is $4 million. During the life of the project the contract price did not change, but the total estimated cost did. A summary of the key information is provided below.

	Start	Year 1	Year 2	Year 3
Contract price	$30,000,000	$30,000,000	$30,000,000	$30,000,000
Estimated cost to complete	26,000,000	26,300,000	30,000,000	31,500,000
Total expected profit (loss)	$ 4,000,000	$ 3,700,000	$ 0	$(1,500,000)
Cost to date	$ 0	$ 2,800,000	$23,000,000	$31,500,000
$\dfrac{\text{Cost to date}}{\text{Total estimated cost}}$	0%	10.65%	76.67%	100%

Note that the company's estimate of the total cost to complete changed over each of the years. The company began expecting to make a profit, then estimated a break-even situation at the end of Year 2, and finally estimated a loss at the end of Year 3. If the company used the ratio of *cost incurred to date* to *total expected cost* as its measure of percentage completed, it would report its revenues and costs for each period as follows:

	Start	Year 1	Year 2	Year 3
Cost to date				
———————	0%	10.65%	76.67%	100%
Total estimated cost				
Total profit earned to date (based on percentage of cost)	$ 0	$393,916	$ 0	$(1,500,000)
Earned to start of period	0	0	393,916	0
Earned in current period	$ 0	$393,916	$(393,916)	$(1,500,000)

In Year 1 the company would report an income of $393,916 because that is 10.65% of the total expect profit of $3,700,000. By the end of Year 2 the total expected profit is nil; therefore, the income of the previous year has to be reversed in the current period. By the end of Year 3 a total loss of $1,500,000 has been incurred. If this loss had been anticipated earlier, say at the end of Year 2, then the doctrine of conservatism would have required that *all* the loss be provided for (not just 76.67% of it!).

Now let us work through the journal entries for this example year by year.

Year 1

During Year 1 the company incurs costs totalling $2,800,000 and makes payments for them. Thus the company would make journal entries equivalent to the following:

Work in process inventory	2,800,000.00	
Bank (or accounts payable)		2,800,000.00
To record costs incurred to date.		

Because the company is using the percentage-of-completion method based on the ratio of costs incurred to total estimated costs, it would also make the following journal entries:

Contract value of work in process: unbilled	3,193,916.00	
Revenue from contract work		3,193,916.00
To record revenue earned to date		
(10.65% of $30,000,000 = $3,193,916.00)		

Construction expense: long-term contract	2,800,000.00	
Work-in-process		2,800,000.00
To record expense incurred to date		
(10.65% of the total estimated cost of $26,300,000)		

If the company is entitled to receive a progress payment from the customer, the payment is often based on the certificate of an architect or equivalent. Suppose that in this case a certificate were issued in Year 1 entitling the company to receive $3,000,000, of which 90% was receivable immediately, and the balance after ninety days when all subcontractors' bills had been paid (such a delayed payment is referred to as a **holdback**). The entry would be as follows:

Accounts receivable: short-term	2,700,000.00	
Accounts receivable: holdback	300,000.00	
Contract value of work in process: unbilled		3,000,000.00
To record progress billing to customer on the basis of architect's certificate.		

Note that the architect's estimate of how much has been completed need not agree with the company's estimate based on the ratio of costs.

Year 2

In Year 2 a re-estimate of the total cost to complete indicates it will be $30,000,000. Therefore the expected total profit is nil. The journal entries would be as follows:

Contract value of work in process: unbilled		19,806,084.00	
Revenue from contract work			19,806,084.00
To record revenue earned to date			
(76.67% of $30,000,000)	$23,000,000.00		
Less: portion recorded to start of			
year (10.65% of $30,000,000)	3,193,916.00		
Net	$19,806,084.00		

Construction expense: long-term contract		20,200,000.00	
Work-in-process			20,200,000.00
To record expense incurred to date			
(76.67% of $30,000,000)	$23,000,000.00		
Less: portion recorded to start of			
of year (10.65% of $26,300,000)	2,800,000.00		
Net	$20,200,000.00		

Note that the net income for the project for Year 2 will be $19,806,084 less than $20,200,000, or a net loss of $393,916. The loss in the current year arises because of an estimating error in the previous year. At that time it was thought that a profit would be earned on the project, and some income was recognized accordingly. The amount taken into income each year is therefore the sum of the estimated income earned in that year plus the carry-forward effects of revising the prior years' estimates. It is likely that before the project is completed the present estimate will have to be revised again.

The journal entries for recording the expenditures on work in process and setting up the receivables in Year 2 would be similar to those of Year 1.

Year 3

For the journal entries of Year 3, we proceed as we did in the previous year:

Contract value of work in process: unbilled		7,000,000.00	
Revenue from contract work			7,000,000.00
To record revenue earned to date			
(100.00% of $30,000,000)	$30,000,000.00		
Less: portion recorded to start of			
year (76.67% of $30,000,000)	23,000,000.00		
Net	$ 7,000,000.00		

Construction expense: long-term contract		8,500,000.00	
Work-in-process			8,500,000.00
To record expense incurred to date			
(100.00% of $31,500,000)	$31,500,000.00		
Less: portion recorded to start of			
year (76.67% of $30,000,000)	23,000,000.00		
Net	$ 8,500,000.00		

Therefore the net income for the project for Year 3 will be $7,000,000 less $8,500,000, or a net loss of $1,500,000.

In general, under the percentage-of-completion method there are two possible ways of indicating on the income statement how the income is earned: (i) show both estimated revenues and expenses for the period or (ii) show only the net of revenues and expenses as a single item. In its section on revenue, the *CICA Handbook* [3400.19] states: "The amount of revenue recognized during the period should be disclosed...." Therefore the first way described above seems preferable.

BIBLIOGRAPHY

BUNTON, B. JAMES, and SYCAMORE, ROBERT J., "What's Wrong With the Retail Method." *CA Magazine* (October 1981). An examination of some potential estimating errors inherent in the retail method.

DAVIS, HARRY ZVI. "History of LIFO." *Journal of Accountancy* (May 1983). Traces the history of LIFO as an outgrowth of the base-stock method.

DESMARAIS, ALAIN. "Accounting for Long-term Contracts: A Long-time Problem." *CA Magazine* (March 1983). A critique of the AICPA *Statement of Position* entitled "Accounting for Performance of Construction-Type and Certain Production-Type Contracts."

DROZD, F. ANNE. "When Should Customers Pay for Construction Work in Progress in Regulated Utilities?" *CA Magazine* (November 1984). An example of how inventory accounting interacts with utility rate regulation.

CHAPTER 7
Land, Buildings, and Equipment

Introduction

The asset side of balance sheets can generally be split into major sections:

1. current assets

2. tangible, long-term, productive assets such as land, buildings, and equipment

3. assets held as long-term investments

4. intangible assets

   In this chapter we examine land, buildings, and equipment, often known collectively as *plant assets*, *fixed assets*, or *long-lived assets*. Since the criteria for assessing them are primarily economic, we start by reviewing the economist's notion of productive capital and relating that to the accountant's concept of a plant asset. We will then review the life of a plant asset, starting at the time of acquisition, going on to its productive period, and ending with its disposal. Finally, we will assess the implications of fixed asset accounting for the readers of financial statements.

The Nature of Plant Assets

Plant assets are the (i) tangible, (ii) long-term, (iii) productive assets of the company. (Like all good definitions, this one is fuzzy at the margin.) Typically, they consist of land, buildings, and equipment used in the productive process.

   If assets are long-term, productive, but not tangible, they are classed as **intangible assets**. A computer software program or a patent right would fall into this category. Intangible assets are discussed in Chapter 9.

   If assets are tangible, long-term, but not used in the productive process, they are classed as **long-term investments**. A common example would be the shares of another company. Long-term investments are covered in Chapter 10.

   Some examples of plant assets typically found in a *manufacturing* setting are (i) factory buildings used for production; (ii) the equipment in those buildings; (iii) the land the buildings stand on; (iv) computer installations (but not the software); (v) office buildings, the land they stand on, and the equipment and furniture inside; (vi) trucks and cars (but not for auto dealers, where they would be inventory); (vii) costs of improving land for later use (e.g., costs of landscaping, grading, and improvements such as sewers, water mains, and electrical services); and (viii) costs of making alterations and improvements to leased property (even if the company has no legal title to the assets).

Some examples of plant assets that might be found in a *retail* setting such as Canadian Tire are (i) stores and distribution warehouses; (ii) the land the buildings stand on; (iii) display cases; (iv) computer equipment; (v) equipment used in car repair shop; and (vi) delivery trucks and highway tractor-trailers.

Some plant assets such as aircraft, ships, and highway construction equipment, have no fixed place of business.

Plant Assets and the Economic Model of the Firm

THE ECONOMIC MODEL

Accounting for plant assets is one of the more challenging problems in accounting and it is clearly one where an unthinking application of rulebook techniques is inappropriate. In the body of conventions that they have built up for accounting for plant assets, accountants are seeking to approximate an underlying economic phenomenon. The conventions are merely attempts to capture this. Thus it is important to understand the basic underlying concepts because they will help to explicate the conventions and indicate what should be done when the conventions are inappropriate or inapplicable.

Recall from Chapter 1 that the economist thinks of the firm as a mechanism for taking in raw material, labour, and services and turning out the finished goods and services that society wants. Exactly what the physical process is that converts the raw input into the finished product is not something that economists are concerned with. Nevertheless they do acknowledge that the process typically requires land, buildings, and machinery (which are confusingly called **capital**). These items cost money. In introductory economics one usually supposes a fixed amount of starting capital and asks how it can best be utilized by varying the inputs and outputs to make the firm as profitable as possible. The conversion process is shown in the diagram below.

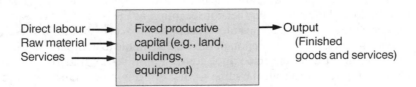

It can be seen in the above diagram that the economist makes a clear distinction between (i) those assets (such as raw material, services, and direct labour) that are transformed by the production process into finished goods and services and (ii) the capital assets that are used to convert those assets into finished goods and services that are only consumed indirectly in the productive process. Many of the accounting issues regarding plant assets arise from trying to make this distinction in real life between *capital* versus *non-capital* items. It will become apparent that this distinction has important implications for income measurement.

RETURN ON INVESTMENT

Having made the distinction between capital and non-capital expenditures, it is useful to form the following ratio:

Net income/Net investment = Return on investment

Return on investment (ROI) can be used to make comparisons between companies since it represents an overall measure of performance. In general, the higher the ROI, the more attractive the company is. Note that the ROI can be raised either by increasing net income or by decreasing net investment. Because plant assets are a major item in most companies' net investment, their effective and efficient utilization is reflected in the ROI or its equivalent.

The **effectiveness** test of the acquisition of plant assets is whether the assets purchased are appropriate for achieving the objectives of the company. This is a question of strategy. The **efficiency** test is whether, once they have been acquired, the assets are being operated at least cost. Thus, the British/French decision to build the supersonic airliner, Concorde, turned out to be not very *effective* from a profitability viewpoint. Because of its high-speed design, the aircraft is not fuel efficient; and because oil prices rose and passenger demand fell off, large losses resulted. Even if the airliner were run very *efficiently* by cutting fuel and other operating costs, it would still be unprofitable because of the earlier strategic decision to build a small supersonic aircraft with inherently high fuel consumption per passenger-mile.

Although ROI in its many forms is a useful measure of effective or efficient use of plant assets, it does not directly distinguish between effectiveness and efficiency. This must be inferred using more extensive analysis. In examining financial statements, the individual appraisal of effectiveness and efficiency of plant assets is usually attempted — at least implicitly. However, useful ROI measures are not easily derived from the financial statements, and the reader needs to be aware of what is — and is not — available from them. For example, the Concorde would show a low return on investment. From an examination of the financial statements, however, it would not be apparent that the attempts to operate efficiently are swamped by the original strategic decision to build a plane with high fuel consumption as the price of having it go very fast. In other words, the financial results reflect the impacts of both the effectiveness and efficiency factors. It is only if enough data are available to compare, say, its actual fuel consumption with its expected fuel consumption — to find that actual and expected consumption are about the same — that one might begin to suspect that the low ROI is due to the original strategic decision.

DISTINCTION BETWEEN CAPITAL AND EXPENSES

There are many occasions in real life where the decision must be made between treating an expenditure as a capital item or a non-capital item. The general rule is to treat an expenditure as a capital item if the following two conditions hold: (i) it is acquired for use in the company's production, not for resale; and (ii) the benefit from the expenditure will extend beyond twelve months.

Consider the following example. A company that sells furniture purchased on the same day (i) a workbench to be used in the maintenance shop, (ii) a table to be sold in its retail store, and (iii) a can of furniture polish to keep the furniture in the store looking good. The company would capitalize the workbench since its benefit is expected to exceed one year and it is used indirectly in the productive activity of the company. It would charge the table to inventory since it will ultimately be sold and was not acquired for use. The can of furniture polish would be charged to expense. It could be argued that its benefit might extend beyond one year, but as a practical matter small items of this sort are normally charged directly to expense to simplify bookkeeping. Most companies have policies that expenditures below a certain dollar amount (e.g., $500) are expensed automatically.

However, many situations lie in the grey zone. Here is an example. Suppose a company has a ROI of 10%, calculated as follows:

Net income/Net investment = 10,000/100,000 = 10%

In arriving at the net income, the company had to decide how to treat an expenditure of $1,000 for small tools, such as hammers, electric drills, screwdrivers, tape measures, files, and electric sanders. At the time the tools were purchased, it was estimated they would have a useful life of two years. Thus it was decided to depreciate them 50% in one year and 50% in the second. Accordingly, the company made the following journal entries:

Equipment — small tools	1,000.00	
Accounts payable		1,000.00
To record purchase of small tools.		

Depreciation expense	500.00	
Accumulated depreciation		500.00
To record first year's depreciation.		

By the end of the first year it was apparent that the decision to capitalize the expenditure and depreciate it over two years was a mistake. The electrically powered tools had been given such continuous use that they were no longer worth fixing, and many of the screwdrivers, tape measures, and other small items had disappeared. On checking with other companies in a similar position, this turned out to be a common experience. In retrospect the company saw it should have made the following entry:

Small tools expense	1,000.00	
Accounts payable		1,000.00
To record purchase of small tools.		

Had it done so, it would have charged $1,000 to the current year instead of $500. Consequently, the reported net income would have been $500 lower, or $9,500, and the

ROI would have dropped to 9.5%. Yet at the time of purchase, the decision seemed a reasonable one. This illustrates the point that a decision whether to capitalize has to be made right at the start of the asset's life — at the time of purchase — and in deciding on the accounting entry one simply has to make the best estimate of what the future will bring.

If one examines the income statement of most companies, one finds that the decision whether to capitalize is likely to have a significant impact on reported income. Since plant assets are, by their nature, assets whose value to the firm depends very much on future events, the policy to be followed in deciding how much of the expenditure to capitalize is essentially a judgement call. The preceding example illustrates that the decision can have a significant impact on reported net income. As we explained at the beginning of this section, the guiding principle for the accountant is to try to approximate the economic model of the firm.

Calculating the Cost of Plant Assets

When a person goes into a store to buy a consumer item, such as a book or a radio receiver, that person expects to be given, in return for money, an item that is immediately usable. Furthermore, one can readily check whether the price is reasonable by finding out what others are charging for similar merchandise. An economist would say that there is an **efficiently operating market** for these items and therefore the amount paid is probably close to the market price.

For most companies, the acquisition of a plant asset is not usually as simple as the purchase described above. Here are some ways in which it may differ:

1. The purchaser may find it more convenient or cheaper to have all or part of the work needed to acquire the asset done by the firm's own employees. This raises the problem of costing self-constructed assets.

2. Part or all of the purchase price may have to be paid months before the asset is available for use, and the purchaser may incur interest costs on the money borrowed to finance the purchase.

3. The purchaser may have to incur expenses to transport the asset to the firm's premises, prepare the foundations to hold it, and instal it.

4. Some of the acquisition cost may be paid by third parties, such as governments, as an incentive to the company to make an investment it would otherwise avoid.

5. The asset may be acquired as part of a package (e.g., of land and buildings) with no division of the purchase price among the component parts.

6. The assets may be acquired as part of a barter deal in which no money changes hands.

Let us now investigate the accounting treatment of each of these cases.

GENERAL PRINCIPLES

The accountant's task is to reflect as faithfully as possible the economic essentials of acquisitions of plant assets. The basic idea is that the accountant tries to bring the plant assets on the books at the equivalent of their cash price as if paid at time of delivery. We will describe some of the major issues in estimating the acquisition cost of plant assets under these conditions. (The distinction between capital and expense items has already been illustrated above.) In any exchange, the accountant records the transaction based on the fair market value of the asset given up or the fair market value of the asset acquired, whichever appears to be the most reliable.

Here is a simple example of how one may have to look through the form of a transaction to get at its economic substance. O Ltd. traded in a truck on a new one whose list price was $18,000. It received a trade-in on the old truck of $5,000 and paid the difference of $13,000 in cash. Had it sold the truck on the used car market, it would have received $3,000 cash. The old truck had cost $10,000 and had accumulated depreciation of $6,000. The journal entry should be as follows:

New truck — at cost	16,000.00	
Old truck — accumulated depreciation	6,000.00	
Loss on sale — old truck	1,000.00	
Old truck — at cost		10,000.00
Cash		13,000.00

To record purchase of new truck at an estimated market
value of $16,000. Payment was $13,000 cash and a
used truck with a market value of $3,000.

Note that the **list price** of the new truck is not reflected in the transaction because it is evidently not the market value of the truck if the truck agency was willing to sell it for assets worth a total of $16,000. Therefore, the fair market value of the assets *given up* is used to value the exchange in this case.

SELF-CONSTRUCTED ASSETS

A **self-constructed asset** is one where the company uses its own equipment and work force to produce the plant asset instead of purchasing it. Examples would be a construction company that builds its own employee parking lots or a home-building company that puts up its own office building. Even in the case where the asset is purchased, there is often preparation work that needs to be done on the site, such as pouring concrete foundations for machines or moving the equipment in and setting it up. This is often done by the company's own employees.

What costs incurred by the company to instal or construct plant assets should be treated as an expense of the period and what costs should be treated as a capital item? In theory, it should make no difference in accounting treatment whether the asset was purchased outright or acquired through self-construction inasmuch as the economic results are similar. There is, however, a problem of **moral hazard** because it is possible to manipulate income through the decision to capitalize the costs of self-construction.

For example, consider a company that could have bought a tool shed for $60,000, payable when the shed was complete and ready for use. It chose self-construction, however, since making the tool shed with its own staff was well within its competence. The expenditures were as follows: (i) material — $30,000, (ii) hourly labour — $15,000, and (iii) supervisory staff — $5,000. If it were building the same structure for a customer, it would charge $60,000 and expect to make a gross profit of $10,000 over the above costs that would cover the interest costs during construction and contribute to the other fixed costs of the company.

Assume for simplicity that if it had not put the building up itself, it would have avoided the material cost of $30,000 and the hourly wages of $15,000, but would not have been able to avoid supervisory labour of $5,000. By putting the building up itself, what amount should be capitalized?

There is no "right" answer to this question. It is helpful to use economic analysis in approaching the problem. In addition to recording out-of-pocket costs, we should try to establish the **opportunity cost** of the building to the firm, or the cost of the things it had to give up in order to construct it. The out-of-pocket costs are the funds to purchase the material and direct labour, a total of $45,000, and there is no controversy about including them as part of the asset cost. However, did the supervisory labour "cost" $5,000? If it was a cost that had to be incurred anyway and if the supervisors had nothing else to do, then no opportunity was lost by occupying them in putting up the building. Similarly, if times were slack, then using the work force in this manner would not mean that a construction profit of $10,000 had been lost through not being able to do similar work elsewhere. Hence the economic cost of putting up the building was just the cost of material and hourly wages, or $45,000. In that case the journal entry would be as follows:

Building — at cost	45,000.00	
Hourly wages		15,000.00
Material inventory		30,000.00
To record out-of-pocket costs of a self-constructed building.		

On the other hand, if the firm had been busy with profitable work, then the supervisory staff could have been charged out to outside work and the firm could have expected to make its usual profit of $10,000. The opportunity cost in that case would be the out-of-pocket costs of material and labour plus the opportunity costs of the supervisory labour plus the profit that was forgone by diverting the work force from outside jobs. There would then be a good argument for making the journal entry as follows:

Building — at cost	60,000.00	
Hourly wages		15,000.00
Materials inventory		30,000.00
Supervisory wages		5,000.00
Net income on self-constructed building		10,000.00
To record the opportunity and out-of-pocket costs of a self-constructed building.		

In practice, an entry such as the one above is rarely, if ever, made. The reason appears to be the problem of moral hazard. It is difficult, if not impossible, to provide objective evidence to support the kind of reasoning that led to the above journal entry. For example, how does one provide good evidence that the profit forgone by making the building oneself is $10,000? If the company is not busy, this is the time when the management wants to find ways of making the financial statements look better. It is also the time when the company has the spare capacity to engage in self-construction. As a result, there could be a temptation to generate "profits" through self-construction.

Recall from Chapter 2 on standard setting that in the case of moral hazard, the accountant has several reactions, three of which are disclosure, enforced consistency from one period to the next, and arbitrary rulings. There are no definitive Canadian or U.S. rulings on the issue of self-constructed assets; thus one has to fall back on fundamental analysis and general practice. It is understood that in Canada the opportunity cost of the $10,000 profit would never be included in the cost. Whether the $5,000 of fixed cost would be included would depend on the circumstances. In addition to the economic analysis outlined above, one would also consider the consistency of treatment from one year to the next and whether during that year most such judgement calls within the company all happened to fall in a similar direction. For example, if most such judgement calls fell in the direction of favouring profits by capitalizing such items, then the external auditor would likely react negatively.

INTEREST COSTS

General Principles

In Chapter 5 on accounts receivable it was explained why customers would expect to pay higher prices as they delayed payment and lower prices as they advanced them. For similar reasons, purchasers of plant assets would expect the price to vary according to the terms of their payment. The general accounting principle is that the amount recorded as the cost of the asset should *not* reflect the timing of the payment and that differences between the actual payment and the recorded cost arising from timing of the payment should be treated as interest costs.

The basic assumption is that the price of a plant asset should be its price at the point where the asset becomes usable. If payments are made before that point, then there is an implicit financing discount in the cost of the asset. The amount of this discount can be approximated by the financing cost to the purchaser of borrowing the funds to make the advance payment. These interest costs should, therefore, be added to the cost of the plant asset.

Examples

Assume that a company purchased a truck for $80,000 for delivery on 1 November. Under the terms of the purchase, it had to pay $60,000 on the prior 1 June and the balance of $20,000 on delivery. It borrowed the $60,000 at the bank, paying 1% per month for the five months, or $3,000. On payment of the deposit the entry would be as follows:

Advance on purchase of plant asset	60,000.00	
Bank loan		60,000.00
To record payment of advance on purchase		

When the truck was delivered the entry would read as follows:

Truck	83,000.00	
Advance on purchase of plant asset		60,000.00
Bank		20,000.00
Deferred interest		3,000.00
To record purchase of truck.		

Each month the bank interest would have been charged to the interest account. If this were the company's only bank borrowing, the $3,000 credit above would just offset the $3,000 debit.

In the above example the $60,000 was borrowed from the bank, and hence the interest cost of the advance payment was easy to see. The issue becomes more difficult if the company does not borrow the $60,000 specifically for this purpose, but instead gets the funds through a mixture of loans incurred for this and other purchases. In that case we might estimate the **weighted average interest rate** and use that, although it has some unsatisfactory aspects. The nature of this problem is difficult to explain unless the *cost of capital* issue has been studied in finance, but a few more examples help to illustrate some aspects of it.

The company might have borrowed in the past for low-risk investments and paid a low interest rate as a result. However, suppose the proposed addition to plant assets is regarded as large and risky. Borrowers would then want a higher rate of interest on all their loans to the company. Should the incremental cost of interest arising from this new addition be regarded as the interest cost attributable to it? If so, how should it be calculated?

As another example, suppose that when interest costs were high in 1981, the company borrowed on a long-term bond. The company could borrow at a lower rate now because overall interest costs have dropped, but the high-interest bonds are non-redeemable. Should interest on purchases of plant assets be calculated at this high rate?

A final problem is presented by the use of funds provided by shareholders. Assume in the initial example that instead of borrowing the $60,000 from the bank, the company had issued additional shares for $60,000. If it were to make the entries shown above, the $3,000 of interest would turn up as interest income since there would be no offsetting payments to the bank. In effect, we would be recognizing the interest that was "earned" by lending the shareholders' own funds to the supplier of the truck.

Issues Raised by Capitalization of Interest

Recall that when a company *sells* an item and receives a long-term receivable in payment, it splits the proceeds into two parts: (i) an amount representing the present value of the long-term receivable and (ii) the deferred interest to be earned on the receivable over its life. The reason for this is that the company is playing two roles. First, it acts as the supplier of the equipment (and for this it should count as revenue only the cash-equivalent price). Second, it acts as the financier for its purchase (for which it records interest income). Similarly, when a company *buys* an item and pays for it in advance, one could argue that it should bring the asset on its books at the cash-equivalent price and treat the difference as interest income arising from its activities as a financier.

However, there has been a reluctance to do this on the part of many companies and auditors. Why? There are theoretical as well as practical reasons:

1. There are many situations where it is not clear which loan is financing which activity of the company. Thus attributing the interest cost of a given loan to a given plant asset acquisition is often arbitrary. For example, a plant asset may be purchased for $300,000 just at the time that a bond issue for $300,000 at 8% has come due and a new one for the same amount, but at 14%, has to be issued. Is the new issued "caused" by the purchase of the plant asset? Or would the issue have been made anyway? There are enough arbitrary decisions of this sort in accounting, the critics say, without adding more.

2. The capitalization of interest potentially leads to income manipulation since a company with idle funds can create interest income by purchasing plant assets and paying for them before they are ready for use. This assumes that the idle funds could not be invested in some straightforward short-term investment yielding as much as the imputed interest on the asset purchase.

3. In the case of plant assets constructed within the company, the question of how much should be capitalized does not have a satisfactory practical answer (as demonstrated above). Because the amount capitalized forms the base on which the interest should be calculated, it follows that there is no satisfactory way of calculating the interest costs.

The issues raised above are troublesome. Yet to ignore imputed interest costs of a capital acquisition appears to raise other problems just as troublesome. Many companies are capital-intensive, and their plant assets take a long time to build. An outstanding example is electrical utilities, where it takes years to design and build a generating plant (fourteen years is typical). The annual interest costs of financing such a project in its construction stages can be very large. If they are charged as an expense of the period, the impact on net income is usually significant.

This problem can be reduced to a more human dimension by noting that the amount paid monthly for electricity is set by some government body, and the charge is calculated to be sufficient to cover the cost of producing the electricity (including interest and other capital costs). Assume that somewhere in the electrical utility serving you, there is a generating plant under construction. Should you be asked to pay for the interest costs of financing that generating plant — assuming that it will not be producing electricity until four years from now? Your reaction probably is that you are not deriving any benefit from this plant under construction and that the costs of it should be paid by those who benefit from it. Accordingly, the costs of interest during construction should be considered to be part of the construction cost. Hence they should be capitalized.

In fact, most utilities do capitalize such interest costs of plants under construction, for the reason stated above. This has been done for some time; it is the comparable treatment for non-utilities that has been slow to develop.

Current Accounting Treatment

The only major pronouncement on this subject has come from the United States where the FASB issued Statement of Financial Accounting Standards No. 34 in October 1979. It contains two main points. First, interest shall be capitalized on assets constructed or otherwise produced for a company's own use or for resale or lease (e.g., ships). Assets not used in the earning activity of the company (e.g., land held for later use) should not be included. Second, the amount of interest is that amount that would have been avoided if the expenditure for the asset had not been made. This refers only to the interest expenditures on borrowed funds and does not include the lost interest income from invested funds. Whether interest cost is capitalized, therefore, depends on how the construction is financed, which seems contrary to most accounting treatments.

For example, if Company A builds a factory and finances it by selling enough investments to cover the cost, then no interest would be capitalized because although interest income was forgone, no interest expense was incurred. On the other hand, if Company B built the same factory but financed it by borrowing instead of selling investments, then it would capitalize the interest it actually paid out. The FASB was apparently reluctant to capitalize the opportunity cost of interest forgone. It has been criticized for this reason. However, FASB No. 34 does require disclosure of the total amount of interest cost incurred during a period and the amount that has been capitalized. Hence readers have some information to aid in reconstructing the accounts in a manner they think might be more appropriate.

Until 1987 the *CICA Handbook* was silent on the issue of capitalizing interest costs. However, in that year a section was added to the *Handbook* [3850.03] that required disclosure of the amount of interest capitalized in the period. But it did not set out any criteria for making such a capitalization; nor did it express any views on its desirability. Boersema and van Helden reported that nearly half of Canada's largest companies capitalize interest. They further noted a lot of diversity in the manner in which the policy was applied and in the amount of information disclosed. The authors opposed capitalization on the grounds that it provided no useful information. The following differences between Canadian and U.S. practice are noteworthy:

1. It is common in Canada to capitalize interest on plant assets held for later use (e.g., land held for later development) provided that the capitalized value does not exceed the net realizable value.

2. Canadian practice generally is to capitalize only the interest on funds specifically borrowed to construct the asset; the U.S. practice is somewhat broader in that it does not limit interest to specific borrowings.

3. The FASB requires that interest be capitalized if the tests are met. Since there is no specific standard in Canada, no such requirement exists here.

In general, the issue of capitalizing interest has not been brought to a satisfactory state. The only standard in existence, FASB No. 34, is conceptually inconsistent.

COSTS PAID BY OTHERS

It may seem unlikely that plant assets would be "donated" to companies, but it happens regularly. A common example is a subsidy paid by some level of government to assist in the acquisition of a plant asset, such as a factory, in an area of Canada that is thought to be in need of economic stimulation. By providing the factory at less than cost and hence subsidizing the project through lower capital costs, the government hopes that the project will be economically viable and that the company will be better able to cope with the higher operating costs that probably kept other firms out of the area in the first place.

An example, and one that is hard to identify, might be the "dumping" of plant assets by a foreign parent company to its Canadian subsidiary to make that subsidiary profitable. This might consist of specialized equipment provided to the subsidiary at a price that is less than market but more than out-of-pocket construction costs.

Once again it is helpful to use economic analysis to deal with this issue. Presumably the donation of the assets is intended to provide an incentive to offset some adverse factors that would otherwise deter the company from making the investment. It is thus intended to make the project competitive with a similar investment made elsewhere. The accounting problem is to identify those adverse factors and then to match them against the favourable impact of the subsidy. While the concept is easy to state, it is hard to implement.

The *CICA Handbook* position [3800] is that the subsidies should be used to reduce the cost of the plant assets that were subsidized and hence reduce the depreciation expense over the life of those assets. This is not exactly the same as the objective set out above in the preceding paragraph. The life of the subsidized assets may not be the same as the period of disadvantage, and the pattern of amortizing the grant benefit may not match the pattern of the adverse factors that the company has to face. It probably does at least rough justice, however. An ideal system would be hard to implement in practice.

ACQUISITION BY BARTER

Sometimes assets are acquired by **barter**, or a transaction in which payment is made in something other than money. For example, in 1982 the Russian government made a barter deal with a number of Western European countries to supply gas from Russia in return for the pipeline equipment needed to bring the gas to Western Europe. Another example would be a company issuing its own shares in return for plant assets. This is common when one company acquires another as a going concern.

In theory, no new problem is introduced by a barter transaction: the aim is always to reflect in the accounts the amount that would have been entered had the transaction taken place in a free market with payment in cash on delivery. The problem here is a practical one of approximating what that price would be.

Sometimes it is difficult to find the market price of the asset being acquired but less difficult to find the market price of the asset being given. In that case the value of the item given is used as the proxy for the cost of the item received. For example, if a company acquired a large tract of undeveloped land, it might have difficulty narrowing down the current market value. But if it gave as payment an asset whose value was reasonably ascertainable, such as shares of a company traded on the stock market, then the value of the shares could be used as the proxy for the value of the land. What usually happens is that the company issues its own shares in payment for the asset. The question may then arise whether the current market price of the shares is a good proxy — especially if the amount issued is a significantly large part of the total shares outstanding or if the issued shares have some restriction that makes them less desirable than the shares traded on the market.

For example, M Ltd. acquired all the assets of S. Ltd., which consist of shopping centres and undeveloped land suitable for shopping centres. In return M Ltd. gives S. Ltd. 1,000,000 common shares of a special issue that are similar to those trading on the stock market at $30. There are 20 million of these publicly traded shares. The only differences between the two issues are that the special issue does not give the holder any voting privileges and they may not be sold until five years have passed.

The restriction of voting privileges would have a downward influence on the value of the shares. Therefore they would probably be worth something less than $30 — although the exact amount will not be knowable until they can be traded in a reasonably open market. Assuming it were estimated that the shares were worth $28 each, the journal entry on the books of M. Ltd. would be as follows:

Land, buildings, and equipment	28,000,000.00	
Share capital		28,000,000.00
To record acquisition of shopping centres and undeveloped land in return for the issue of 1,000,000 special common shares (without voting rights and not tradeable until five years from issue) with an estimated market value of $28 each.		

There is an assumption lying behind the recording of all accounting transactions that they were made **at arm's length**; that is, between two well-informed people who were acting in their individual best interests and not at the expense of some third parties. If a true arm's length transaction occurs, the accountant does not normally try to look behind it to see if the terms need to be somehow altered before being recorded in the books. However, if the deal is not at arm's length, the general rule is to disclose the nature and extent of the transaction and a description of the relationship [*CICA* 3840.16].

LUMP-SUM ACQUISITIONS

Often a group of plant assets is purchased for a single price, and no attempt is made at the time of purchase to break down the purchase price among the component parts. For example, it is common to pay a single price for the building and the land it sits on. After the purchase, however, it is frequently necessary or desirable to break the single amount down among the component parts (because they may have differing rates of depreciation, for instance).

Once again, there is no difficulty in theory inasmuch as the aim is to enter each item on the books at its equivalent market cost. The difficulties are practical ones: (i) knowing the market prices of the various assets, and (ii) dealing with any differences between the total estimated value of the individual items and the actual price paid for the whole group.

The usual approach to estimating market prices is to obtain, if possible, an outside evaluation from specialized appraisers. In the unlikely event that the appraised values total less than the price paid, the difference should be written off. On the other hand, if the appraised values exceed the price paid, the cost principle would indicate that the lower price (i.e., the purchase price) should be used. The common treatment is to allocate the lump-sum purchase price among the assets in proportion to their individually appraised values.

For example, suppose an apartment building was purchased for $110,000, including the cost of the land. One method for splitting the cost between land and building would be to use the tax assessor's appraisal if a fair-market-value appraisal was not available. The amount arrived at in a tax assessor's appraisal is often different from a fair-market value appraisal, but the relative amounts assigned to land and buildings are often similar in each. Assume the tax assessor's appraisal was as follows:

Land	$ 32,000
Building	68,000
	$ 100,000

Then the journal entry would be

Land	35,200.00	
Building	74,800.00	
Bank		110,000.00

To record purchase of land and building for $110,000 and split the lump-sum purchase price between the two on the basis of their assessed values. This is calculated as follows:

        Land — 32/100 of 110,000 = 35,200
        Building — 68/100 of 110,000 = 74,800

LEASEHOLD IMPROVEMENTS

When a company rents an office or factory space it is common to find that the space is not suitable for its needs until alterations or additional construction has taken place. For example, companies renting store space in shopping centres usually get a space with no display cases, special lighting, or partitions, and they must bring it up to their standards at their own expense. Depending on the terms of the lease, all such improvements may belong to the owner of the building at once or revert to him at the end of the lease. Legally, anything attached to a building becomes the property of the landlord in the absence of agreement otherwise. Such expenditures made to leased property are called **leasehold improvements**. They are capitalized and written off over the lesser of the term of the lease or the useful life of the improvements.

There is nothing unusual in the day-to-day accounting for leasehold improvements that makes it different from other plant assets. The same tests for capitalization are used, for instance. What is interesting is that the company is including as plant assets items to which it has no legal title, although it does have the legal right to their use over the term of the lease. We have emphasized that the accountant is interested in portraying economic benefits (and costs). Thus, here is an illustration of the accountant's willingness to overlook the fact that the company does not technically own the assets.

Expenditures During the Life of an Asset

It is common to make expenditures on a plant asset during its life. The question arises how much of the expenditure is capital in nature and how much non-capital. For example, suppose that after purchasing a personal computer for $5,000, one spent $800 to have its memory expanded, $120 to replace a defective keyboard, and $2,000 to add new disk drives for an expanded memory and faster operation. With these improvements, one hopes to increase its useful life by a few more years.

The general principle here is that an expenditure that simply keeps the asset functioning the way it was intended to function does not increase its productivity. Hence it is regarded as an expense of the period — that is, as a necessary cost of keeping the equipment doing what it was intended to do. As a result, the $120 spent to replace a defective keyboard would be a period expense. An expenditure made to keep equipment in the operating condition for which it was intended is referred to as **maintenance**. *expense*

By contrast, an expenditure made to increase the productivity of the equipment or prolong its expected useful life represents an increase in the capital stock (in the economist's sense) of the company. Hence the expenditure would be capitalized. Thus, the $800 spent to expand the computer memory would be a capital expenditure since a rational person would not make the expenditure without expecting to receive at least $800 of value in return.

The troublesome expenditures are those in between, where the expenditure makes the asset more productive than it would have been but at the same time takes the place of a regular maintenance expenditure. Such expenditures are often referred to as **betterments**. For example, by adding the new disk drives at a cost of $2,000 one expects that the equipment will be more useful and have a longer useful life, thus meeting both of the tests for capitalization. On the other hand, if some routine maintenance costs on the old disk drives have been avoided, then some non-capital expenditures have been eliminated. Thus it appears that at least part of the expenditure was related to cost reduction for the current year — that is, at least part of it was a non-capital expenditure.

How does one split such an expenditure between plant assets and expenses? In those rare cases where the pattern of expenditure for the lifetime of the asset is known at the time the asset is purchased, it could be argued that the total cost of owning the asset is the present value of all expenditures to be made to keep the asset operating, including original cost, maintenance, subsequent additions to the asset, betterments, and the costs of financing the expenditures. Presumably a company would purchase such an asset if the present value of the expected revenue exceeded the present value of the expected expenses. The company would then have the accounting problem of allocating the present value of the expected expenses over the time periods that benefited from the use of the asset. The problem of accounting for betterments would simply be a subset of this more general accounting problem. For a more extensive explanation see Appendix 7-1.

The conceptual problem becomes more difficult when expectations change after the asset is purchased. If it is found that the betterment is forced on the company because of technological changes not anticipated when the asset was purchased, should the cost of the betterment be capitalized or not? For example, during the 1980s personal computers developed so fast that some components such as disk drives approached obsolescence within a few years after their introduction. New drives with more attractive features became available at little more than the original cost of the old ones. As a result, many companies felt they had to replace their disk drives simply to stay competitive. If the impending development in disk drives had been anticipated, the company would have waited a little while longer in order to get them at about the same price as the less efficient ones. It would seem in this case that the apparent "betterment" is an improvement in a technological sense; but in an economic sense the company is no better off. There would therefore be a good economic argument for treating the cost of the new drives as an expense on the grounds that a capitalized expenditure has to make the company better off *in an economic sense*, not just in a technological sense.

In practice, the same expenditure on a betterment receives a wide variety of treatments by companies because it is so difficult to assess the additional economic benefit to be derived from such an expenditure. In general, if a payment on a plant asset simply maintains the company's existing economic position, then it will be treated as an expense of the period. If it also improves that position, then a portion of the expenditure will be capitalized.

For example, assume it is company policy to do a major maintenance overhaul on its truck engines at 120,000 kilometres. Further, suppose that this overhaul is normally done every twelve months, usually costs $600, and is charged directly to expense. During one of the normal engine overhauls, it was decided to convert the engine from gasoline to propane in order to save in operating costs. To do the conversion separately at another time would have cost $2,400, but together the conversion and overhaul cost $2,600.

In this situation the issue is how much of the $2,600 should be treated as a capital item and how much as an expense. If done alone, an overhaul would cost $600, and converting the engine to propane would cost $2,400. Done together, they cost $2,600. There is no right way, even in theory, to apportion the $2,600 between the two items. At the most, $600 should be charged to expense; and at the most, $2,400 should be capitalized. A logical approach would be to apportion the $2,600 between the two in the ratio of the costs if done independently, which would total $3,000. If that were done, the journal entry would read as follows:

Engine repair expense	520.00	
Plant asset — equipment betterment	2,080.00	
Account payable		2,600.00

To record overhaul and conversion of truck engine.
(Total cost is apportioned as 600/3,000 x 2,600 = 520 for regular overhaul and 2,400/3,000 x 2,600 = 2,080 for propane conversion.)

Disposal of Plant Assets

TECHNICAL ISSUES

When a plant asset is sold or otherwise disposed of the following accounting entries must take place:

1. the cost of the asset is removed from the plant assets account

2. the accumulated depreciation to date for the asset is removed from that account

3. the amount, if any, received on disposal of the asset is recorded

4. the remaining difference (i.e., amount received - (cost of asset - depreciation)) is entered as a **gain on disposal** or a **loss on disposal**

For example, K Ltd. bought a typewriter for $800 at the beginning of 1986. It depreciated the typewriter on a straight-line basis at 20% a year and then sold it at the beginning of 1989 for $200. By the beginning of 1989 the company had depreciated it for three years. Thus the accumulated depreciation would be 3 x 0.20 x 800 = $480.00. The entry would be as follows:

Accounts receivable	200.00	
Loss on sale	120.00	
Accumulated depreciation	480.00	
Equipment — typewriter		800.00
To record sale of typewriter.		

Note that the *loss on sale* has a very special meaning: it is the difference between the net book value of the asset and the proceeds from its sale. Suppose the company had decided to depreciate the typewriter at 30% a year. Then the accumulated depreciation would have been $720.00, the net book value of the asset would have been $80.00, and there would have been a profit on the sale of $120.00. The profit or loss on sale of a plant asset is, therefore, a function of several factors: (i) how good a bargain the asset was when bought originally; (ii) how much depreciation has been charged to expense already; (iii) how much the market price of the asset has changed over the years it has been owned; and (iv) the skill of the management in selling it.

IMPLICATIONS FOR INCOME REPORTING

It was shown above that the income reported on the sale of a plant asset is the result of a number of factors, some of them stemming from decisions made long before the asset was disposed of (such as the purchase price and the depreciation policy). In brief, a gain on disposal is not in itself an indication that the management have done a good job. In addition, the time when a plant asset is disposed of is frequently at the discretion of management, and the profit or loss on disposal is often significant in relation to the reported operating profit. Given these factors, it is often possible for the management of a company to affect the net income significantly by a decision to sell — or not sell — some of the plant assets. This also can work in reverse. Management may think it would be prudent to sell some plant assets; but realizing that doing so would result in a large reported loss on disposal, they may choose not to sell in order to avoid adverse criticism.

This situation was given a new twist in the fall of 1982 when Cadillac-Fairview sold 11,000 apartment units at $270 million for a substantial gain on disposal. Normally one would have expected a favourable shareholder response. However, there was extended press coverage of an immediate resale of the same assets at an apparently higher price, and some of the company's shareholders expressed displeasure that the gain to Cadillac-Fairview had not been higher.

BARTER AND MULTIPLE DISPOSALS

When assets are disposed of by barter the accounting treatment is symmetrical with that of acquisition by barter. The general objective is to estimate the market price received on disposal.

Disposal of a group of plant assets for a single amount is also symmetrical with the equivalent treatment of a purchase of a group of assets. The amount received is allocated to the individual items. It is hoped that the basis of allocation can be based on some criterion established outside the firm, such as real-estate assessment or independent appraisal.

IMPACT OF DISPOSALS ON FUNDS FLOW

It is a common mistake to assume that a Gain on Disposal is the equivalent of a funds inflow to the firm and that a Loss on Disposal means an outflow of funds. Some examples showing the gain or loss on the sale of two filing cabinets should help to illustrate why this is not true. The facts are summarized below.

	Cabinet #1	Cabinet #2
Proceeds of sale	$ 30	$ 30
Historic cost	100	80
Less: accumulated depreciation	80	40
Net book value	20	40
Gain (loss) on sale	$ 10	$ (10)

For simplicity, assume that these were the only transactions in the period. How much was the cash inflow from each? Common sense says it was $30 for both. This can also be demonstrated by eliminating the non-cash transactions, as follows:

	Cabinet #1	Cabinet #2
Gain (loss) on sale	$ 10	$ (10)
Add or subtract accounting entries made in calculating gain (or loss) that did not arise from a flow of cash:		
— write off historic cost of assets	100	80
— write off accumulated depreciation	(80)	(40)
Net non-cash entries	20	40
Cash inflow from sale	$ 30	$ 30

These examples demonstrate that the (i) original historic cost and (ii) the accumulated depreciation — in other words, the items forming the net book value of the asset — have no impact on the funds or cash inflow arising from the sale. You should modify these examples in other ways to convince yourself of the general validity of this proposition. Our examples also illustrate that the gain or loss on the sale is not a reliable indicator of the funds generated by it.

Changing the Valuation of Plant Assets

Under generally accepted accounting principles, the general rule for valuing assets on the financial statements is to value them at their **cost of acquisition** (generally referred to as **historic cost**). There are two major exceptions to this rule. First, *current* assets are valued at their market value if this is lower than their cost. Second, *plant* and other *long-term productive* assets are valued at their acquisition cost with a deduction for periodic write-offs to revenue, referred to as **depreciation**, **depletion**, or **amortization**. These write-offs are intended to allocate the historic cost of the asset against the periods that benefit from their use.

The point to observe with plant assets is that they are *not* normally written down to market value if this should be less than net book value (historic cost less depreciation). Instead they are simply shown at net book value for as long as they are in use. There are a number of reasons for this. The chief ones are as follows:

1. The basic methodology of GAAP is to record assets at their acquisition cost, not market. The treatment of current assets (i.e., lower of cost and market) was developed for the benefit of creditors. It is not consistent with the general methodology of GAAP and should not be extended to other assets unless there is some clear advantage to the reader in doing so.

2. Finding the current market value for plant assets is expensive, and there is little likelihood of experts agreeing on a figure. The core of the problem is that to ask for the market value of an asset assumes the existence of a well-developed market for that item; but such a market may not exist, especially for long-term assets. The price depends on the assumptions made by the assessors, and these may differ for quite legitimate reasons. For example, an asset such as a car may have different market values depending on whether one values its individual parts or the whole car.

3. The benefit derived from the information should exceed the cost of getting it. In most cases the process of valuing plant assets is expensive, and the benefits have rarely been convincingly demonstrated. To allow it to be done only when management felt it to be appropriate would invite manipulation of the financial statements.

The arguments in favour of the historic-cost versus the current-value approach are controversial, and this controversy is quite prominent in the accounting literature. In Chapter 20 we will discuss accounting systems based on current value.

One should be clear what the implications are for plant assets of valuation based on historic cost. First, the amounts shown on the balance sheet for plant assets do not, and do not attempt to, show the current market values for plant assets. In particular, current market values may be less than the book values shown. It is, therefore, dangerous to use net book value as a proxy for market value. Second, because the net book value shown on the balance sheet may be significantly different from the disposal value, it is possible for the management to trigger either gains or losses on disposal by deciding to sell one plant asset and not another. Third, strategic successes or blunders in the acquisition of plant assets are not shown as such in the financial statements. If a particularly brilliant move is made to acquire a plant asset, the benefits to the firm show up over the life of that asset through depreciation charges that are less than the benefits that the asset confers to the firm — in other words, in higher-than-normal profits over a number of years. Poor strategic decisions with respect to plant assets show up similarly through a negative impact on profits.

Because of the carry-over impact of strategic decisions with respect to the acquisition of plant assets, it is possible for new management to be blamed or credited for financial results that are due in part to the decisions of prior managment. One method for eliminating the negative carry-forward effects is for the new management to write down the plant assets to their present market value, thus taking one "big bath" instead of repeated charges to income over the depreciable life of the asset.

For example, assume that at the beginning of 1985 a company built a special-purpose plant in Ontario for making consumer electronics. It cost $30,000,000 and was judged at the time of construction to have a functional life of ten years, with no salvage value and with straight-line depreciation to be charged. The annual depreciation would, therefore, be $3,000,000. By the beginning of 1989 the company acknowledged that the construction of the plant was a strategic error. Because of changing technology and competitive labour costs from newly industrialized countries, the profitability of the plant had dropped to the point where the operating margin after operating costs, but before deducting depreciation, was only $300,000 per year. If things were to continue unchanged, the loss on operation of the plant after operating and depreciation costs would be $2,700,000 per year for the next six years.

A newly appointed general manager of the plant might be inclined to point out that the market value of the plant just taken over was far less than its net book value of $18,000,000 and hence that the annual depreciation of $3,000,000 was unreasonably high. Since the plant is now capable of generating income before depreciation of only $300,000 per year for the next six years, the manager might feel that its value should be related to what it could earn. If it were written down, the depreciation charge would be closer to the real opportunity cost of using it. The accounting question is essentially whether the loss in earning power of the plant should be recognized at once in a large write-down and charged to this year's income or instead left to be worked out over the remaining six years in large depreciation charges.

It is also possible for the opposite to happen. The market value or earning value of plant assets may be considerably more than the amount at which they are carried on the company's books. In that case the annual depreciation charge would be less than the economic opportunity costs of using the assets, and the operation would tend to look more profitable. In this case, might the newly appointed manager have a motive to insist that the assets be written up to market value so that more realistic depreciation could be recorded? Probably not. There appears to be a moral hazard in management's decision to revalue plant assets. As a result, a company's auditors are usually reluctant to agree to such a revaluation unless there is some major change in the company's affairs, such as a significant sale of plant assets or a major reorganization.

The *CICA Handbook* [3060] notes the preference for using historical cost and says that fixed assets should not normally be written up. (The *Handbook* is silent on write-downs.) In all cases the basis of valuation should be disclosed. In those extraordinary instances where plant assets are not recorded at cost, the following particulars should be disclosed: (i) the date of appraisal, (ii) the name of the appraiser (if made within five years of the statement date), (iii) the basis of valuation, and (iv) what accounts were affected by the appraisal adjustment. In addition, depreciation should be based on the revised new amounts.

Examples from Published Reports

The Royal Bank of Canada

The Royal Bank of Canada is Canada's largest bank. It has over 1,400 branches and more than 1,100 banking machines throughout the country.

ROYAL BANK OF CANADA
BALANCE SHEET

	31 October 1986	31 October 1985
	(thousands of $)	
Land, buildings and equipment (note 6)	$ 1,168,247	$ 1,028,192

Note 6. Land, Buildings and Equipment

	Cost	Accumulated depreciation	Net book value, 1986	Net book value, 1985
Land	$ 135,953	$ —	$ 135,953	$ 130,112
Buildings	710,358	158,190	552,168	475,968
Computer equipment	386,011	180,603	205,408	171,738
Furniture, fixtures and other equipment	387,257	252,926	134,331	122,950
Leasehold improvements	235,185	94,798	140,387	127,424
	$ 1,854,764	$ 686,517	$ 1,168,247	$ 1,028,192

Depreciation expense for the year ended 31 October 1986 was $116,189,000 (in 1985 it was $97,867,000).

Plant assets are often shown in a highly condensed format in the balance sheet with more detail shown in a note.

Summary

The common treatment of plant assets under generally accepted accounting principles is to show them at their depreciated historic cost, regardless of current market values. Occasionally they are revalued at current market values; but this is rare and is usually precipitated by some unusual event such as a company reorganization.

As a result, it is not uncommon to find that the net book value of the plant assets on the financial statements is significantly different from their market value. As a result, when plant assets are disposed of there is often a significant gain or loss on disposition. Since management is often in a position to decide which plant assets to sell, they have some influence on the reported net income for that year.

Plant assets are often purchased under terms that are far from payment on delivery. Consequently, the interest costs incurred prior to use can become a significant factor. In addition, assets may be acquired by barter, by self-construction, or as part of a lump-sum purchase; and after their purchase, significant sums of money may be spent to improve them. The general principle guiding the accounting treatment here is that it should try to approximate the entry that would have been made had the asset been purchased in a competitive market for cash on delivery.

QUESTIONS

Q7-1. Make sure you are familiar with the following terms:

a. fixed asset
b. ROI
c. effectiveness *versus* efficiency
d. capital *versus* non-capital expenditures
e. efficiently operating market
f. moral hazard
g. opportunity cost
h. barter
i. lump-sum purchase
j. betterment
k. maintenance
l. loss on disposal
m. list price
n. arm's length transaction
o. leasehold improvement

Q7-2. In the following examples, state whether you think the acquisition costs should be classed as plant assets. If they should, then indicate whether they should be classed as (i) land, (ii) buildings, (iii) equipment, or (iv) something else. Explain your reasoning.

a. The cost of painting an office when the building is first put up.
b. The cost of an original painting purchased as part of the interior decorating of the president's office.
c. Land purchased for a new building. The architect for the building has been hired; but because of delays in getting planning permission and financing, it is expected that the building will not be in use for another twenty-four months.
d. A party given by the owner of a newly constructed building for the purpose of attracting tenants to his unrented offices.

      e. The fees of an interior decorator hired in connection with furnishing a new office suite.

      f. An "Employees Only" sign purchased to attach to a door.

      g. A fee of $300 for a building permit in connection with a new office building.

Q7-3. "Patents should be classed as plant assets because they meet all the tests. The patent agreement is tangible evidence that you've a right to it; it allows you to be more productive; and it has a life longer than one year." Do you agree? Give reasons.

Q7-4. Imagine a world where the current value of plant assets could be obtained without cost, where appraisers had all undergone the same training, and where as a result, all appraisers produced the same appraised values for given plant assets. Would there then be an overwhelming argument in favour of using current values instead of historic cost in financial statements?

Q7-5. The text cautions against using "rulebook" techniques in accounting for plant assets. Describe some circumstances under which this is particularly valid advice. Explain.

Q7-6. "The economist does not think about assets as an accountant does, in terms of how long they might last. Instead the economist classifies them by the role they play in the productive process." Do you agree? Explain.

Q7-7. Explain why ROI is not a directly usable measure of effectiveness or efficiency considered separately.

Q7-8. What are some of the common ways in which the purchase of a plant asset differs from the standard assumption of a payment on delivery? What impact does each deviation have on how the accounting for the purchase is done?

Q7-9. Explain the stand of the FASB toward capitalization of interest. What have its critics said about it?

Q7-10. The CICA's position on government grants given to subsidize the acquisition of plant assets is that they should be used to reduce the cost of that asset and hence reduce the annual depreciation.

      a. Often the position of governments in Canada and the United States has been the opposite of the CICA and FASB position. They would like the grant to be treated as income of the period in which it was given. Can you explain why? (*Hint*: Why would they have given such a grant in the first place?)

      b. Give a critique of the CICA position.

Q7-11. There is an argument that when assets are donated by the shareholders to a company, the assets should be placed on the books at their market value, and the offsetting credit should be to owners' equity instead of as an offset to the asset as the CICA recommends. If this were done, what might be the impact, if any, on reported income?

Q7-12. "A gain on disposal of a plant asset is not in itself an indication that the management have done a good job". Explain.

Q7-13. Explain why a gain or loss on disposal may or may not be a good indicator of (i) the company's cash flow and (ii) profitability. If the asset is fully depreciated, is your answer the same? Explain.

Q7-14. What are the circumstances under which a plant asset might, under generally accepted accounting principles, be restated at current market value? If this is done, will it eliminate the problem of moral hazard? Explain.

Q7-15. In the text you were given the arguments in favour of stating plant assets at their historic cost. What arguments might be made in valuing them at their current value? Assess the merits of each.

Q7-16. Two companies not related to each other agreed to sell each other some land. Suppose that the details were as follows:

	Company A	Company B
Date of purchase	1 January 19X1	11 February 19X2
Date of sale	29 December 19X3	29 December 19X3
Purchase price	$ 130,000	$ 180,000
Selling price	$ 250,000	$ 250,000

When the auditor of Company A was told of this transaction, she told the officials of Company A about the man who was so pleased because he had sold his elderly dog for $1,000. When a sceptic asked to see the $1,000, the man said, "I don't have any folding money, but you should see my two $500 canaries." What point about the sale of the land was the auditor making with her story?

Q7-17. "A company that wants to increase its reported profit can do so by searching out those fixed assets whose market value is greater than net book value and selling them." Do you agree? Why?

Q7-18. "While accountants use the lower-of-cost-and-market rule with no hesitation for valuing inventory, they refuse to use it for valuing plant assets on their balance sheet." Do you agree? Why?

Q7-19. A computer trade publication reported the following in a section devoted to trade gossip: "We hear that the used-computer market dealers are paying kickbacks to data processing managers to sell their firms' used equipment to the dealers for less than book value." Explain how the writer of this might be confused, and why.

Q7-20. Gamma Limited decided to put up a storage building on land it already owned. It signed a contract with a builder to construct the building for $350,000 and gave the builder a $25,000 deposit under the terms of the contract. By the end of its fiscal year it has also incurred legal fees (unpaid) of $2,300 and paid a landscape architect $3,500 to prepare plans for the site on which the building is located. Show the journal entries to record these transactions.

Q7-21. "No asset except land lasts forever." Do you agree? Discuss.

EXERCISES

E7-1. In each case below, write the journal entry that would be required by the purchaser at the time the expenditure was made or the asset acquired. Be careful to indicate what items, if any, should be capitalized.

    a. A typewriter was purchased for $1,200 and a typing table was purchased for $350.

    b. A personal computer was purchased for $2,500. Instead of buying a new piece of furniture to place it on, the company brought an old desk in from dead storage, had it refinished at a cost of $80, and used that.

    c. A storage shed and the hectare of land it stood on were purchased for $80,000. Because the real estate market was sluggish, the purchaser was able to pay for it with a non-interest-bearing promissory note due in 364 days, thus avoiding payment of the market rate of interest of 12%.

d. An automobile was purchased for one of the the company executives. Included in the purchase price of $21,000 was a two-year "everything" guarantee that covered all costs of repairs and maintenance — even oil changes — arising in the course of normal use. It is estimated that the present value of this additional guarantee would be worth $500 if the company had to pay for it at normal rates. However, the company has found out that the cost to the automobile dealership is only $200 because they will use their own staff at no extra cost to them.

E7-2. In each situation below (i) list the factors you think are relevant to the decision about how much to capitalize; (ii) indicate which items you think should be capitalized; and (iii) defend your decision.

a. Ace Machinery rented construction equipment for building roads and repaired the equipment in its own machine shop. It was not happy with the scoops it bought to attach to its bulldozers to lift sand and other similar material. Therefore it started designing and building its own scoops. The original cost of designing them was $3,000, of which $500 was for materials and $2,500 was for hiring a freelance draftsman. The out-of-pocket cost of the special-purpose equipment it made to build the scoops was $1,200. That equipment is estimated to be useful as long as scoops of this design are made (about eight years is the estimate). The out-of-pocket costs of each scoop is $8,000 each. Of this amount, $4,000 is for material and $3,000 is for the hourly labour. The remainder is for wear and tear on the general-purpose machinery that was originally bought solely for repairing purchased rental machinery.

b. Each year Suicide Ski Hills hires a local contractor to start work in the late spring on the ski slope. He helps pull out rocks that have caused trouble during the winter; he may improve some of the runs by a moderate amount of grading with his bulldozer; and he diverts small streams that have caused ice to form on the trail. He usually charges around $8,000 for his work. He does not open up any new trails.

E7-3. State whether you would expect to find each of the following classified under the heading *Property, Plant, and Equipment* on the balance sheet. If not, state where, if at all, you would expect to find it on the balance sheet.

a. Land that has been purchased for a new factory site, but has not yet been developed.

b. A deposit with Boeing by Air Canada for an aircraft being built to Air Canada's specifications.

c. A payment to the city for putting in sewers and water mains to a plant site. Although the city does not have legal title to the sewers and water mains, it requires payment of their cost if the lines have to be specially laid for that one use.

d. A warehouse that is still in use, but has been put up for sale.

E7-4. State whether each of the following should be capitalized. Be sure to give your reasons with reference to the economic model of the firm discussed in this chapter.

a. A painting bill for $1,800 in connection with the remodelling of one floor of a former warehouse to make it suitable for office space.

b. The purchase of software costing $800 to do accounts receivable on a mini-computer.

c. A pencil sharpener costing $35 and expected to last five years.

d. A bill for $2,000 from a local contractor who was hired to move a large machine into a difficult position in the factory. He estimates that $500 of the cost is for a large crane used to lift the machine from outside into the factory and that $1,500 is for cutting and later repairing a hole in the roof to drop the machine through.

e. A legal bill of $2,400 in connection with a lawsuit over office space you are renting. You were not getting the air conditioning services promised by the owner, and you have successfully sued to have the rent reduced by $1,000 a year for the next five years.

E7-5. Explain whether each of the following expenditures meet the test of a plant asset.

    a. Land purchased for a building to be started immediately.

    b. A down payment of $10,000 in May on a factory building to be purchased in November. The company's year-end is 30 June.

    c. Car radio for a company car.

    d. Payment of $180 for a magnetic disk that contains a computer program. A blank disk would cost about $5.

    e. A restaurant buys a five-year supply of paper serviettes.

E7-6. Flippo Windsurfing School asked you to be their accountant. When you arrived you found they had already made the following expenditures:

(i) Two windsurfing boards, complete with sails	$ 3,200
(ii) Five sets of training manuals for students to read	250
(iii) Three outdoor patio chairs for waiting customers	240
(iv) Wages of students hired to help distribute advertising pamphlets	90
(v) Advertising pamphlets	180
(vi) One portable wharf	1,200
(vii) Life jackets	260

Which ones would you decide to capitalize? Explain why.

E7-7. Here are some examples of expenditures made during the life of each of the assets. Decide whether each is a maintenance item or a betterment. Justify your decisions. What practical problems, if any, would arise in making the journal entries?

    a. After SwiftAir had bought a fleet of jet aircraft in 1972, the actions of OPEC caused a sharp rise in oil prices that convinced them to replace the engines in their present fleet with more fuel-efficient engines. The replacement was expensive, but it also reduced the cost of maintenance.

    b. Sigma Trucking had a policy of stripping down its truck engines after 200,000 kilometres and rebuilding them. This reduced the maintenance and fuel costs and extended the useful life of the engine about 100,000 kilometres beyond what would normally be expected.

    c. Delta Consultants had a large thick rug in their reception area. One wintry day a client walked across it with such dirty shoes that it had to be sent out to be cleaned well before they expected to do it.

E7-8. Sonja set up a professional accounting practice in a small town and bought a microcomputer for $5,000 on 31 January. She decided to depreciate it at the rate of $100 a month. On 31 October she came into her office in the morning to find that her equipment had been stolen. The insurance company paid her $4,100 on her claim. She did not buy the identical equipment because she had more experience and knew her needs better. Instead, for $5,500 she bought equipment that did her work faster than before.

    a. Show the journal entries to record the above transactions.

b. Leaving aside the results shown by the accounting records, evaluate the results from an *economic* rather than an *accounting* viewpoint. Is Sonja better or worse off as a result of the theft? Do the accounting records show this? Discuss.

E7-9. Rental Cars Ltd. was in the business of renting cars on two- or three-year leases. It had ordered six new cars with an average cost of $15,000 and leases arranged to start on 1 April. It ordered the cars in early January, asking for late March delivery. Instead, the cars arrived in late January. In accordance with the custom of the business, they had to be paid for on delivery. The company financed the cars with a firm that specialized in financing automobiles for 80% of their cost at a rate of 1.5% per month. To save money, Rental Cars Ltd. kept the cars on its lot unlicensed until 1 April. How much of the interest to 1 April, if any, should be capitalized?

E7-10. Air Canada purchased new Boeing 767 aircraft with delivery starting in 1982. Unlike the jets they replaced, these aircraft required only two pilots instead of three. The pilots' union refused to fly the aircraft until they received increased rates of pay. While negotiations were going on, the aircraft sat on the ground — usable but unused. Assuming the aircraft were financed individually at 90% of their purchase price, should Air Canada have capitalized the interest while the pilots refused to fly them? Would your answer have been any different if all the planes had been financed through one bank loan? What if they had been financed by the company's sole shareholder, the federal government?

E7-11. Ontario Hydro was unable to operate a new generating station at more than 60% of full power because a transmission line that was intended to connect it with the provincial grid had been delayed because of objections from people in the area it was intended to pass through. Consequently, Ontario Hydro had to obtain electrical power from an older generating station with higher operating costs. Should it have capitalized interest on the part of the generating capacity that was unused?

E7-12. When putting up high-rise office buildings it is common to finish and rent the lower floors before the upper floors are even constructed. Should interest be capitalized on the portion that is not rented, but not on the rest? Explain.

E7-13. A subdivision developer normally proceeds as follows after purchasing a tract of undeveloped land. First, an urban planner is paid to develop a subdivision plan, showing the location of streets, parks, schools, churches, house lots, etc. Then, a contractor grades the land, instals sewers and water mains, and builds roads to municipal specifications. Finally, the housing lots are sold to individual home-building contractors. The land and development costs are normally financed by a mortgage. Assume that the mortgage covers 90% of the costs of land and development and that the rest is supplied by the developer. What principles should be followed by the developer in capitalizing each of the above expenditures?

E7-14. An oil company has developed and patented a superior technology for making fertilizer from oil or gas. It agrees with a Soviet-bloc country to supply the key equipment needed to build such a plant in that country. In return it will be paid in fertilizer produced at the new plant, which it will then sell outside the Soviet bloc. It is estimated that the sales of this fertilizer will fetch $20 million per year for the next five years if prices hold at their present level. However, the risk of price changes is to be borne by the oil company. Explain how you would account for this sale of plant assets in the books of the oil company.

E7-15. In a farming community a farming family's barn was constructed by the neighbours. All the family had to pay for was the building materials plus food and refreshment for the families who helped. At the same time, they knew such a favour from the neighbours placed them under a real obligation to donate their own time should help be needed. Should the donated time be capitalized when keeping the books for the farm? Justify your answer.

E7-16. A lawyer does legal work for a plumber. In return, the plumber supplies labour at no charge for installing a washroom in the lawyer's offices. How should this be recorded in the books of the lawyer? What problem, if any, arises?

E7-17. A small firm of professional accountants agreed to do work to the value of $5,000 for a retailer of small computers in return for a machine that listed at $5,000. The partners of the accounting firm felt that they could have purchased the same machine for $4,500 if they had paid cash; but they felt it was a good deal since their work was done at a time of year when they had little else to do. How should this transaction be entered on the accountants' books. If the accounting firm had had to do their work at a busy time of year, how would your answer differ?

E7-18. How would (i) effectiveness and (ii) efficiency be affected in each of the following cases? Explain your answers.

    a. The cost of educating university students can be greatly reduced by doubling the size of classes.

    b. Many airlines are considering the replacement of their present fleet of aircraft. The new ones will have engines that make them more fuel-efficient and will be of a size that better fits their projected passenger flows.

    c. Many companies owning fleets of cars and vans are converting their engines so they will burn propane instead of gasoline. An engine burning propane costs more; but propane costs less per mile than gasoline, although it is not as generally available.

E7-19. *The Globe and Mail* reported that a "short cut" taken by a boiler manufacturer had added $850 million to the cost of the Pickering power plant near Toronto. Because of the short cut, the boilers had to be rebuilt. This was one of the contributing factors in the total cost of the plant rising from $2.176 billion to $3.9 billion. This increase of $1.724 billion was estimated to be caused as follows:

	Millions of $
(i) In 1976 it was decided to postpone completion for a year, leading to increases due to inflation and interest on the work done to date	$ 115
(ii) Difficulty in finding staff for the plant	183
(iii) Design changes insisted on by the Atomic Energy Control Board	120
(iv) Increased charges for heavy water (needed to moderate the fusion reaction when the plant is operating)	300
(v) Boiler rebuilding	850
(vi) Other factors — mainly higher than expected interest and inflation rates	156
	$ 1,724

It is estimated that without these factors the plant's cost would not have been "much above" the original estimate of $2.176 billion. Which of the above expenditures should be regarded as expenses of the period in which they were incurred and which should be capitalized? Give reasons.

E7-20. Suppose a sale of depreciable assets results in a loss. Indicate which of the following accurately describes the proceeds from the sale:

(i) less than current market value

(ii) greater than cost

(iii) greater than book value

(iv) less than book value

E7-21. In 1985, W Company purchased a word processing unit for its main sales office in Vancouver. It was considered functionally obsolete by 1989. Consequently, it was fully depreciated on the books by that time. The unit was replaced by the latest model and the original machine was moved to the sales office in Victoria. At what value should the transfer of the asset be recorded? (*Hint*: Consider more than one treatment.)

E7-22. Company Y purchased three extruding machines on 8 July 19X2 for $6,200. Freight and installation costs were $742 per machine. At that time they anticipated that major overhauls would be required every three years to maintain the operational capacity of the equipment. These overhauls would each cost between $1,500 and $3,500 depending upon the condition of the machines. According to the manufacturer's estimates, the useful life of each machine, if properly maintained, is eight to ten years. What accounting entries are required in the year of purchase? How should the scheduled maintenance costs be accounted for ? State all your assumptions.

E7-23. Assume that a company follows the policy of capitalizing the interest cost of a plant asset prior to the point in time when it is put into service. They ask you to write them a memo giving your views on the capitalization policy that should be followed in each instance below regarding a manufacturing plant they plan to build.

a. The plant will be built in stages and is not expected to be in full production for three years. However, at the end of the first year it is expected that 20% of its production capacity will be available. Should interest on the 20% completed no longer be capitalized?

b. At the end of the second year an additional 30% of the plant will be fully installed and ready to operate. However, the output of this part of the plant is an intermediate product that can only be used by the part of the plant not yet completed. Thus it is functionally ready, but there is no point in operating it until the rest is done. Should we stop capitalizing interest on the grounds that this section is substantially complete, or should we keep capitalizing it on the grounds that it is not capable of operating at a reasonable level of capacity?

E7-24. Select the *best answer* for each of the following unrelated items. Select only one answer and briefly justify your choice.

a. Prairie Company exchanged high-volume inventory items that cost $15,000 and normally sold for $20,000 for a new truck with a list price of $21,000. At what amount should the truck be recorded on Prairie's books?

(i) $15,000

(ii) $20,000

(iii) $21,000

(iv) $20,500

b. Good Deal Company received $10,000 in cash and a used computer with a market value of $90,000 from Harvest Corporation for Good Deal's existing computer having a market value of $100,000 and an undepreciated cost of $80,000 on its books.

How much gain should Good Deal recognize on this exchange, and at what amount should the acquired computer be recorded respectively?

(i) Zero and $70,000

(ii) $2,000 and $72,000

(iii) $10,000 and $80,000

(iv) $20,000 and $90,000

c. A Company exchanged 100 shares of B Corporation stock, that A was holding as a long-term investment, for a machine from F Company. B Corporation stock, which had been purchased by A Company for $60 per share, was selling on the market at $68 per share at the date of exchange. The machine had a recorded amount on F's books of $6,200. What journal entry should A Corporation make to record this exchange?

(i) Equipment	6,000.00	
Investment in B stock		6,000.00
(ii) Equipment	6,200.00	
Investment in B stock		6,000.00
Gain on disposal of B stock		200.00
(iii) Equipment	6,800.00	
Investment in B stock		6,800.00
(iv) Equipment	6,800.00	
Investment in B stock		6,000.00
Gain on disposal of B stock		800.00

d. Video Theatre Corporation recently purchased the Roxy Theatre and the land on which it is located. Video plans to demolish the building and to build a new modern theatre on the site. How should the cost of the Roxy Theatre be treated?

(i) Written off as an unusual loss in the year the theatre is demolished.

(ii) Capitalized as part of the cost of the land.

(iii) Depreciated over the period from the date of acquisition to the day that the theatre is to be demolished.

(iv) Capitalized as part of the cost of the new theatre.

e. Time Plan Company purchased a machine for $10,000 cash on the date of purchase and signed three $10,000 non-interest-bearing notes, with one note due at the end of each of the next three years. The company can obtain financing at 15%. At what amount should the machine be recorded on Time Company's books?

(i) $10,000

(ii) $40,000

(iii) $32,830

(iv) $28,550

(CGA adapted)

E7-25. The bookkeeper for Beaver Canada Inc. is unable to record entries with respect to the following transactions in 19X7. The company's year end is 31 December 19X7.

(i) 31 December 19X7

Purchased equipment with a list price of $14,000 by making a down payment of $4,000 with the balance of $5,000 payable on 31 December 19X8 and $5,000 on 31 December 19X9. The company's borrowing rate is 10%.

(ii) 1 July 19X7

Acquired land and building for a lump-sum payment of $100,000 with a view to building a new plant. At the time of acquisition the appraised value of the land was $120,000 and the appraised value of the buildings was $5,000. The old building was demolished at a cost of $2,000 cash, but $1,000 cash was recovered through the sale of salvaged building material.

(iii) 31 December 19X7

Exchanged an old truck for a drilling machine. The relevant data is as follows:

Purchased truck on 1 January 19X1	$ 8,000
Accumulated depreciation on the truck as of 1 January 19X7 on	
a straight-line basis	4,800
Fair value of the drilling machine	2,800

Required: Prepare the necessary journal entries to record each of the above transactions and briefly give reasons to justify your entries.

(CGA adapted)

E7-26. Garbo Company purchased a machine to be used in its operation on the following terms: $10,000 cash payment at the time of purchase plus a non-interest-bearing note requiring payment of $10,000 on each of five anniversary dates subsequent to the purchase. Assume that Garbo can borrow funds at 15%.

Required:

a. Record the purchase of the machine.

b. What accounting principle dictates the amount to be set up as the machine cost at time of purchase?

c. What accounting principle governs accounting for the machine in subsequent years?

(CGA adapted)

E7-27. Companies A, B, C, and D, all listed companies, each acquire a machine with a list price of $14,000. The transactions are unrelated.

(i) Company A paid $2,000 down and agreed to pay $4,600 per year in three instalments starting one year from now. The company usually pays 12% interest on such loans.

(ii) Company B issued 1,000 shares of common stock in payment. The stock has a book value of $12 per share and is currently selling on the market at $12.75.

(iii) Company C exchanged an old machine which had originally cost $18,000. It has a book value of $8,000 and a market value of $11,000. Company C also paid $2,000 in cash.

(iv) Company D paid $14,000 for the machine and received a government grant of $5,000 as part of an industrial assistance program.

Required: State the value at which each machine would be recorded on each company's books at the date of acquisition.

(CGA adapted)

E7-28. In this chapter we emphasized that profitability and return on investment (ROI) can be affected by both the *effectiveness* and the *efficiency* of the use of a plant asset. In each of the following scenarios indicate which of the following best describes ROI:

(i) most affected by effectiveness

(ii) most affected by efficiency

(iii) affected equally by effectiveness and efficiency

(iv) not affected by effectiveness or efficiency

a. A rock star smashes up his equipment at each show. Yet he still makes a high ROI despite having to buy new equipment for each show.

b. An airline is able to design an engine which is far more fuel-efficient than that of its competitors. The company cuts its prices in half, and its ROI increases.

c. Chrysler Corporation was losing money to the point that it almost filed for bankruptcy. It changed its strategy to that of producing fuel-efficient cars at a low cost and for the widest market possible. Consequently its ROI increased dramatically.

d. A company makes snowmobiles at a cost far greater than that of its competitors. It proceeds to sell them in Florida and experiences negative ROI.

E7-29. Depreciation has been described as an arbitrary cost-allocation process. Support this by using as an example the depreciating of an automobile. Indicate three areas where estimates must be made in order to calculate the automobile's depreciation. Which of these estimates is arbitrary?

E7-30. You have recently been hired to help straighten out the accounts of Sydenham Inc. after its accountant had departed because of a dispute with the Controller over technical competence. Your senior assigns you the task of reviewing an account called "Plant asset suspense" which he suspects contains some dubious entries. Your senior asks you to prepare whatever journal entries are needed to clear out this account and transfer the items to the correct account in preparation for the 31 December year-end. After looking up the details about these postings, you have prepared a note for each account entry. The given account and your set of notes read as follows:

Plant Asset Suspense Account

Date (19X9)	Description	Dr.	Cr.	Balance
A. 3 January	Machinery Supply	25,874.00		25,874.00
B. 15 February	Alwington Salvage Inc.		1,256.00	24,618.00
C. 28 February	Allied Insurance Limited	1,263.42		25,881.42
D. 15 March	Bank of Montreal	95.00		25,976.42
E. 9 April	A-1 Machine Shop	3,685.12		29,661.54
F. 30 June	Data Supplies Inc.	8,521.36		38,182.90
G. 8 July	Gore Landscaping Ltd.	6,591.20		44,774.10
H. 18 August	Mowatt Equipment Inc.	5,622.14		50,396.24

Notes

A. Purchase of replacement part for milling machine.

B. Proceeds of sale of scrapped equipment. According to the ledgers, it originally cost $36,872 and was fully depreciated on a straight-line basis. Both the cost and the accumulated depreciation are still in the ledger.

C. Insurance coverage during shipment of replacement part for milling machine.

D. Bank service charges for handling payment of equipment purchase in foreign funds.

E. Rebuilding machine to put it back in good working condition. Machine had slowly deteriorated until it reached the point where it could still produce the work, but it was unreliable and often inaccurate.

F. Purchase of personal computer for use in Production Planning. According to the invoice, the hardware originally cost $5,200 and the software needed to run the equipment for the desired tasks originally cost $2,100. The remainder of the cost was for a prepaid service contract in which Data Supplies guaranteed to be available to help instal the software and maintain the equipment for the first twelve months.

G. Grading, planting, and removal of an excess fill from the landscaping of a new building site. The work had been done for the new home of the new Vice-President, Marketing. The Company had arranged the work because the new VP had just moved in from out of town. The bill had been sent to the Company and they had paid it by mistake.

H. Charges for use of a crane and other moving equipment, together with charges for ninety hours of staff time. These charges were for moving equipment from one part of the factory to another as part of a general plan to introduce new production techniques in order to cut costs.

Required: Prepare the journal entries requested by your senior. If you have to make assumptions, be sure to state what they are.

PROBLEMS

P7-1. Jarmila got the concession to sell ice cream at a football stadium for the season. She purchased the following:

1 used insulated cart to hold ice cream for vending	$1,100.00
3 new uniforms for herself and two helpers	550.00
4 signs advertising ice cream for sale	200.00
1 game's supply of ice cream	800.00
1 used freezer to hold the ice cream	500.00

Required: Prepare the journal entry or entries that would be needed for these purchases. What important assumptions, if any, did you make when preparing the journal entries.

P7-2. Perfect Painters Inc. started up in business in April 19X3 and purchased the following:

3 stepladders	$ 250.00
4 plastic sheets to catch paint spatters	45.00
3 buckets	30.00
paint thinner and brush cleaner	18.00
6 paint brushes	120.00
3 putty knives	36.00
sandpaper	40.00

Required: Assume that they purchased the material on credit. Prepare a journal entry or entries showing how you would account for each of the above.

P7-3. Serge trades in his taxi under the following terms. The car dealer will take his present taxi and give him a trade-in allowance of $8,000. In addition, the dealer will give Serge $300 off the list price of $13,000 for the new taxi. Serge thinks he could get $6,000 net cash for his old taxi if he sold it privately. The historic cost of his old taxi is $10,000 and the accumulated depreciation is $5,000.

Required: Show the journal entry that Serge should make to record the acquisition of the new taxi. Explain your reasoning.

P7-4. Audio Distortions is the name of a group of students who provide sound systems for student events such as dances. Their business has expanded and they decide to acquire another sound system. The prices quoted to them are as follows:

amplifier	$ 500
tape deck	500
microphones	100
speakers	800

The component business is heavily competitive, and they were not surprised that after some bargaining, they were able to get the components above for a package price of $1,500 cash.

Required: Show the journal entry they should make to record the purchase of each asset. Explain your reasoning.

P7-5. Ennui Resorts Inc. is a company that owns a resort hotel in the lake country near a major city. It had an average annual income before depreciation of $70,000. In a period of rapidly rising land prices, its owners paid $1,000,000 for it. The building and equipment were estimated to be worth $600,000, and the land $400,000. The purchasers believed that an increase in popularity of resorts in that area should, within ten years, make it possible to raise the rates enough to bring in an average annual return of $150,000. Two years after the purchase you have been asked to take over as manager of the resort. You find that although rates have gone up, the costs of energy and labour have gone up just as fast, and the resort still earns on average $70,000 a year. It is proposed to pay you a modest salary with a substantial bonus based on profitability. The expectations for the future are now less optimistic. Furthermore, it is estimated that the market value of the building is $400,000, and the land $200,000. The buildings are being depreciated at 5% per annum on a straight-line basis.

Required: Write a memo to the management in which you explain why you would like them either (i) to write down the value of the land and buildings or (ii) to have a formula for adjusting the reported annual income before using it to calculate your bonus.

P7-6. The Fisher Corporation purchased a machine on 1 November 19X0 for $74,000. At the time of acquisition, the machine was estimated to have a useful life of ten years and an estimated salvage value of $2,000. Fisher has recorded monthly depreciation using the straight-line method. On 1 July 19X9 the machine was sold for $6,500.

Required:
Which of the following should be the loss recognized from the sale of the machine? Explain.
  (i) $0
 (ii) $2,500
(iii) $5,100
(iv) $6,500
  (v) none of the above

P7-7. On 1 December 19X1 Spacesaver Limited leased office space for ten years at a monthly rental of $15,000. On that date Spacesaver paid the landlord the following amounts:

Rent deposit	$ 15,000
First month's rent	15,000
Last month's rent	15,000
Installation of new walls and offices	96,000
	$ 141,000

Required:
Spacesaver charged the entire $141,000 to rent expense for the year ended 31 December 19X1. Which of the following is the correct amount that Spacesaver *should* have charged to rent expense for that year? Explain.
  (i) $15,000
 (ii) $15,800
(iii) $30,800
(iv) $96,000
  (v) $141,000

P7-8. Mr. X operates a home renovation business. The operation has been very successful during the last two years and, as a result, Mr. X feels that he should improve the company offices. His own staff removes the existing partitions, instals a new permanent wall, paints the entire office (including the new wall), removes part of the rear wall, and builds an addition to be used as a storeroom. Mr. X also purchases new office furniture. Mr. X is concerned with the accounting treatment of these expenditures because the income tax position of the company will be affected.

Required:

a. How should each of the above transactions be recorded?

b. How does your answer to part (a) change if the work was done in the off season? (*Hint*: Consider incremental costs.)

c. Since Mr X. is more concerned with income tax implications than good accounting, how will he want to account for these expenditures?

P7-9. College Haircuts, an established hairstyling business, moved to new premises on 1 October 19X9. The following transactions occurred prior to opening:

(i) A five-year lease on the premises was signed, and a deposit of $800 for one month's rent was paid.

(ii) Special electrical installations were necessary to accommodate existing equipment. The invoice from the contractor totalled $2,100.

(iii) Hair dryers with an estimated life of three years were purchased. The cost of the dryers, including delivery and installation, was $9,420.

(iv) Plumbing with a useful life of seven years was installed at a cost of $3,129.

(v) Special fire detection equipment was required because of the nature of the business. Under the fire regulations the landlord was responsible for installing this equipment. As a result, the rent for the first month included an additional charge of $1,200.

Required: Show the journal entries to record each of these transactions.

P7-10. Suppose the Canadian government introduces a plan to reward companies that build manufacturing plants in areas of high unemployment. The reward consists of a deduction from taxes ordinarily payable of 7% of the purchase cost of the manufacturing plant. Section 3800 of the *CICA Handbook* says that such assistance to purchase plant assets should be deducted from the cost of the asset (with a corresponding reduction made in depreciation) or should be deferred and amortized to income on the same basis as the depreciation of the related assets. This means that the assistance would not be recognized as income in the period in which it was received.

Required: Write a short essay discussing the merits and drawbacks of the CICA position.

P7-11. Here are two excerpts quoted from the financial press:

"The fire aboard an Air Canada DC-9 jetliner on June 2 that claimed 23 lives ironically helped the airline record a modest $10.3-million profit for the second quarter of 1983."

"A fire that destroyed a Pacific Western Airlines Corp. plane will show up on the airline's books in the form of a profit estimated at $6-million."

Required:

a. Explain how it is possible for companies to suffer disasters as significant as the ones above and yet have them create higher profits.

b. What does this imply that readers of financial statements should be wary of?

c. Should a new accounting standard be developed to handle such situations? What should such a standard require?

P7-12. Three companies each contract to buy an identical piece of equipment for $1,000,000 payable immediately. The equipment will not be ready for delivery until one year after full payment is received. The All-Debt Company issued $1,000,000 in 12% bonds and $5 in common shares (to provide working capital!). All-Preferred Company issued $1,000,000 in 8% cumulative term-preferred shares, redeemable at the option of the holder at the end of the term of two years from date of issue, and $5 in common shares. All-Common Company issued 1,000 shares for $1,000,005 cash. These were the only transactions conducted by the three companies for one year after making full payment.

Required:

a. Show the balance sheets for each of the three companies at the end of the first one-year period. Assume that bond interest and preference dividends were paid and that the cash was provided by a bank loan.

b. Compare the cost of the plant asset at the end of the first year as shown by each of the three companies. Which of the costs most closely approximates the opportunity cost to the company of acquiring the plant asset? Explain.

P7-13. On 1 January 19X8 Landsdown Company decided to purchase a new piece of manufacturing equipment. The manufacturer's list price is $24,500. The agreed arrangements are that the manufacturer will allow a trade-in of Landsdown's old equipment at $4,500. Landsdown will pay the manufacturer $8,000 and will sign a finance contract. The finance contract calls for eighteen monthly payments of $500 plus 1% interest per month on the outstanding balance. The used equipment had originally cost Landsdown $16,000 and has been depreciated on a 25% declining-balance basis for three full years. Recent transactions indicate that this used equipment could sell for $3,500 in the second-hand market.

Required:

a. Compute the book value of the old equipment.

b. Prepare the journal entry to record the purchase of the new equipment and the trade-in of the old.

c. Prepare a journal entry to record the first payment on the finance contract.

(CMA adapted)

P7-14. At a bankruptcy sale on 2 January 19X0 the Davis Company purchased for $50,000 cash a parcel of land, a building, and a large machine. The company treats these purchases as follows:

	Land	Building	Machine
Appraised value	$ 20,000	$ 30,000	$ 50,000
Salvage value	—	$ 4,500	$ 6,000
Useful life	—	20 years	10 years
Depreciation method	—	Straight-line	20% declining-balance

In 19X0 the company took the following steps:

2 January: The building roof was repaired at a cost of $1,000, and the machine was installed at a cost of $750.

| 5 January: | A new concrete chimney was added to the building at a cost of $800. |
| 30 September: | The machine was oiled and inspected at a cost of $50. |

In 19X1 the following events took place:

2 January:	Major renovations were completed on the building at a cost of $6,000, extending its useful life by three years.
15 April:	The building was painted at a cost of $1,500.
30 June:	The machine and building were completely destroyed by fire. The insurance company paid Davis Company $20,000 for the building and $30,000 for the machine.

Required: Prepare all the necessary journal entries with dates for the years 19X0 and 19X1. The company's fiscal year-end is 31 December.

(CMA adapted)

APPENDIX 7-1

Fixed Asset Accounting and Interest Costs

When assets are purchased the accountant may include interest as part of the capitalized cost of the asset. The accountant does not take explicit account of interest costs otherwise. The purpose of this Appendix is to show the impact of this omission on financial statements.

Let us work through the following simple example. A company considers buying a single asset costing $10,000 at the beginning of Year 1. It will finance the purchase by borrowing $10,000 at 10% on a mortgage repayable at the end of three years. Other than interest payable annually, it is expected that the only further payments will be maintenance, a betterment, and a capital addition. Yearly sales are known and will be received in cash. The amount and timing of expenditures and sales is shown below (see Statement A). Suppose that the asset is purchased at the start of Year 1 but that all other transactions take place at the end of each year. Assume that any cash surplus can be invested at the same rate as the mortgage, or 10%. (This has the same effect as assuming that the bond can be paid off at the end of each year as cash is available.)

STATEMENT A — TIMING OF PAYMENTS AND RECEIPTS

	Start	Year 1	Year 2	Year 3	Total
Purchase asset	$ 10,000				$ 10,000
Loan	(10,000)			$ 10,000	0
Maintenance		$ 1,000	$ 2,000	3,000	6,000
Betterment			1,000		1000
Capital addition		500			500
Total expenditures	$ 0	1,500	3,000	13,000	17,500
Sales receipts		6,000	8,000	6,000	20,000
Net before interest		4,500	5,000	($ 7,000)	2,500
Interest on loan — 10%		(1,000)	(1,000)	(1,000)	(3,000)
Interest income — 10%			350	785	1,135
Net cash receipts		$ 3,500	$ 4,350	($ 7,215)	$ 635
Cumulative		$ 3,500	$ 7,850	$ 635	

The company decides to proceed as follows. The asset is to be depreciated over three years on a straight-line basis. The maintenance is to be treated as a period expense when incurred. Two hundred dollars of the betterment is to be deferred to the next year and the balance of $800 is to be treated as an expense in Year 2. The capital addition is to be charged equally to Year 2 and Year 3. A condensed accounting statement would then read as follows:

STATEMENT B — ACCOUNTING TREATMENT

	Year 1	Year 2	Year 3	Total
Depreciation	$ 3,333.33	$ 3,333.33	$ 3,333.33	$ 10,000.00
Maintenance	1,000.00	2,000.00	3,000.00	6,000.00
Betterment		800.00	200.00	1,000.00
Capital addition		250.00	250.00	500.00
Total expenses	4,333.33	6,383.33	6,783.33	17,500.00
Revenue	6,000.00	8,000.00	6,000.00	20,000.00
Net before interest	1,666.67	1,616.67	(783.33)	2,500.00
Interest on loan	(1,000.00)	(1,000.00)	(1,000.00)	(3,000.00)
Interest income		350.00	785.00	1,135.00
Net income	$ 666.67	$ 966.67	$ (998.33)	$ 635.00

Notice the two interest items near the bottom of Statement B. The interest on the loan is the annual payment of 10% of $10,000. The interest income is the yield, at 10%, on the accumulated cash receipts. You should verify from Statement A that this is the proper amount. Also note that the total net income of $635 in Statement B is the same as the amount of cash that would be on hand at the end of the three years in Statement A.

Another way of evaluating this would be to calculate the present value of the proposed purchase by calculating the present value of each of the cash flows connected with it. See Statement C below.

STATEMENT C — PRESENT VALUE OF EXPECTED CASH FLOWS

	Start	Year 1	Year 2	Year 3
Cash outflows:				
Payment of loan	$ 7,513.14			$ 10,000.00
Maintenance	4,815.92	1,000.00	2,000.00	3,000.00
Betterment	826.45		1,000.00	
Capital addition	454.55	500.00		
Total expenses	13,610.06	1,500.00	3,000.00	13,000.00
Cash inflow: Sales	16,574.00	6,000.00	8,000.00	6,000.00
Net before interest	2,963.94	4,500.00	5,000.00	(7,000.00)
Interest on loan	(2,486.85)	(1,000.00)	(1,000.00)	(1,000.00)
Interest income	879.04		350.00	785.00
Net Income	$ 1,356.13	$ 3,500.00	$ 4,350.00	$ (7,215.00)
Cumulative		$ 3,500.00	$ 7,850.00	$ 635.00

The first column in Statement C shows the present value at the start of Year 1 of each of the cash inflows and outflows that are expected to take place because of the asset purchase. For example, at the end of Year 3 the $10,000 loan has to be repaid. This represents a cash outflow that is three years away from the present, and we would find the present value of it by discounting $10,000 by three years at 10%, the assumed rate. This would be equal to (100/110)x(100/110)x(100/110) of $10,000, or $7,513.14. Finding the present value of the maintenance is slightly more complex because we have to find the present value of each of the three payments and then add them together. According to the present value analysis, the asset, if purchased, should bring in a cash flow with a net present value of $1,356.13.

Statement C illustrates a new way to look at plant asset expenditures. It indicates that in buying a plant asset one also buys the whole package of maintenance, betterment, and capital addition, which together total $13,610.06. With the addition of the interest cost of $2,486.85, the total investment is $16,096.91. It can be argued that it is this whole sum of $16,096.91 whose cost should be allocated over the three years, not just the cost of the asset alone. If we did that, then we could, for instance, balance off the cost of the betterment against the reduced maintenance and also make adjustments for additional maintenance done to prolong the life of the asset.

In theory this is an appealing way to proceed; but in practice it is never done. There are two main reasons. First, when an asset is purchased, it is usually not possible to know with any certainty what the pattern of betterments and capital additions will be. Hence estimates of the present value are hard to establish. Second, it is often impossible to predict what the interest rates and hence the interest costs will be. In the body of this chapter we have already discussed these practical difficulties.

Although we do not use this approach, we still have the difficulty of dealing satisfactorily with betterments. We tend to be asked to decide on the capitalization of a betterment within the context of a single year, the year in which the funds were spent. By their nature betterments often arise from decisions made in the past, and they will certainly affect future costs. Unless we use an approach that integrates the results of a number of years — such as the one illustrated here — our decisions will continue to tend to be ad hoc in nature.

BIBLIOGRAPHY

BOERSEMA, JOHN, and VAN HELDEN, MARK. "The Case Against Interest Capitalization." *CA Magazine* (December 1986). A survey of Canadian practice, the article presents an argument against capitalizing interest on the grounds that it obscures information about cash flows caused by interest payments.

BRENNAN, JOHN W., and SILVESTER, W. HAROLD. "Accounting for Interest Cost." *CA Magazine* (October 1981). Published in the "Research" section of this magazine. Good coverage of this issue.

CLARKSON GORDON. "Capitalization of Interest Costs." *Accounting Developments* (December 1981). This monograph is part of an occasional series on current topics.

FINANCIAL ACCOUNTING STANDARDS BOARD. *Statement of Financial Accounting Standards No. 34: Capitalization of Interest Cost*. Stamford, Conn., 1979. The most extensive and authoritative (though controversial) coverage of this issue by a standard-setting body.

CHAPTER 8
Depreciation, Depletion, and Amortization

Introduction

Over the life of a plant asset a periodic charge is made against each year's revenue to record the cost of the use of that asset. Plant assets have long lives, and the purpose of depreciation, amortization, and depletion is to match the original cost of these assets against the periods that are thought to benefit from their use. Thus, as used at present, they are methods of cost allocation. They do not measure the economic cost of using a given asset; nor do they ensure that sufficient funds are set aside to replace the asset at the end of its life. Both these other goals are important at times, but they are not served through the accounting methods now in use.

Definition of Terms

Depreciation is the allocation of the historical cost, less residual value, of some producing asset to the periods benefiting from its use. (See Chapter 7 for the meaning of *producing asset*.) **Depletion** is a similar concept, but it is used with natural resource assets such as ore bodies in mines. **Amortization** is yet another similar concept, but it is used for allocating the costs of intangible assets. We will discuss amortization in Chapter 9. It is important to note that in everyday use the term *depreciation* implies a decline in the market value of the asset, which is different from the accounting meaning. The everyday meaning refers to value, whereas the accounting meaning refers to apportionment of historic cost. Since most of the principles of depreciation accounting also apply to depletion, it can be assumed that in this chapter when we refer to depreciation, we are also including depletion unless stated otherwise.

Nature of Depreciation

Recall that plant assets are valued at their historic cost and that it is rare for them to be revalued to their current market value. It is, therefore, consistent to treat depreciation as a method for allocating the historic cost of a plant asset over time periods. There is no attempt to measure, for instance, the economic opportunity cost of using the asset. If the latter is wanted, it has to be estimated outside the framework of generally accepted accounting principles.

THE MATCHING PRINCIPLE AND THE CHOICE OF ALLOCATION METHOD

One of the basic ideas of cost-based accounting is that costs incurred to earn revenue should be matched against the revenue received within the same time period in order to arrive at a measure of net income. Since plant assets are necessarily used up in the productive process, the matching principle would indicate that the cost of these assets should be charged against the income of each period in which the asset is used. By the time the asset comes to the end of its useful life, it should be fully depreciated against the revenue of those years. Furthermore, the charge against each year should match the benfit received from the asset in that year. The matching objective is rarely achieved in a completely satisfactory manner; nevertheless, this is the objective being sought.

The reason it is not achieved satisfactorily arises from a fundamental unsolved problem in accounting termed the **allocation problem**. Let us illustrate the allocation problem by means of an example.

To provide themselves with summer employment, two students opened a lawn maintenance business in which they would contract to fertilize, mow, and do weed control for homes in their neighbourhood. They purchased two heavy-duty lawn mowers costing $900 each. They estimated that each mower would have a functional life of two seasons. At the end of the first season they wished to calculate how much they had "really" earned. One of the issues to be decided was how much of the cost of the lawn mowers should be considered to be part of the first season and how much a part of the second season. They knew the accounting principle was that the cost should be allocated to each of the years in proportion to the benefit received; but as they thought about it, they developed various possibilities:

1. They should charge each year $450 for each lawn mower because they expected them to last two seasons.

2. In the second year the maintenance costs were likely to be higher and the machines less dependable. Thus the first season should be charged more, say, $550.

3. The machines' lives depended on the number of hours they were used and the care they received, not on the number of months they were owned. The students should estimate the total number of service hours available from them and charge each season at the average cost per hour used. This would help to compensate for any

change in the rates of grass growth between summers owing to different weather conditions.

4. Since they contracted to keep the lawns maintained for a fixed sum per month, the students should first estimate the total revenue to be earned over the two seasons. Then they should allocate the cost of the lawn mowers on the basis of revenue earned, using revenue as a proxy for "benefit received" from the equipment.

It will be appreciated that each of the above methods would produce a different depreciation charge for the first season of operation. Unless we are able to demonstrate that one is logically preferable to the others, it follows that we are unable to say that one measurement of income for the season is the "true" measure. Each of the above methods is systematic and rational; yet they produce different results. This is the allocation problem. It can be shown that in most real-world situations there are a variety of acceptable methods of allocating depreciation costs to periods, each as defensible as the other. The accountant's problem is not the lack of a good depreciation method but the existence of too many methods that are equally valid.

The matching principle with respect to depreciation can be honoured as a general guideline to be followed. However, it is not a principle that leads to one right answer in the choice of depreciation method.

As we have already stated, an allocation method should be chosen that reflects the benefit conferred by the asset to the periods in which it is used. This is different from a method that would approximate the decline in usefulness. Let us reconsider our earlier example of lawn mowers. Suppose that the lawn mowers were fully usable for two years and then disintegrated overnight. If depreciation were based on the decline in usefulness, then no depreciation would be charged until the night the mowers disintegrated. However generally accepted accounting principles require instead that allocation be based on the benefits conferred. Thus, the cost would be allocated over the two years because the benefit was conferred over that period.

It would be a rare case for the benefit to be exactly equal to the cost of the asset inasmuch as assets are normally purchased with the expectation that their benefits will be greater than their costs. There is no way, even in theory, for showing the "right" way to allocate this surplus. In addition, a newly purchased plant asset is usually used in combination with other assets, and it is then not possible to identify the contribution of that single asset with any precision. In other words, there lacks a definitive theory for allocating depreciation costs of assets to the periods that benefit from them. As we have said above, this is called the *allocation problem*. It has been given extensive coverage in accounting literature [Thomas, 1969].

Lacking a theoretical concept to guide them, accountants have fallen back on allocation methods that look "reasonable" in the light of the performance of a given asset over time. The method chosen by a given company is, within broad limits, at the discretion of that company. However, once chosen it should not be changed unless there is some material change in the company's circumstances. (such as going from a single-shift to a double-shift operation in response to rising demand for the product). A consistent approach is especially important because the choice of depreciation method is to a large degree arbitrary. Later in this chapter we will discuss some common allocation methods.

PHYSICAL AND FUNCTIONAL DECLINE IN PLANT ASSETS

Regardless of the allocation scheme used, there is no question that the asset should be depreciated to its expected salvage value by the time it is no longer useful for the purpose for which it is intended.

An asset experiences a **physical decline** when it is no longer capable of performing the job for which it was designed. For example, a car tire is physically obsolete when it wears out and is not repairable. A wharf may become silted in by river currents so that ships can no longer get to it. A road may become unusable because the pavement has been broken up by frost action.

An asset experiences a **functional decline** when it is no longer worthwhile to use it for the purpose intended, even though it may still be in good operating condition. A car tire may still have adequate tread on it and yet be discarded to purchase a radial tire that has better road-holding abilities and fuel economy. A wharf may be as usable as ever and yet be passed by because ships have become bigger and need a wharf with greater capacity. A road may still be in excellent physical condition and yet suffer a functional decline because it leads to a mine that has now been abandoned.

Electronic calculators and computers provide an excellent example of functional decline. You may have a hand calculator that still does the simple arithmetical calculations for which you bought it; yet you may end up leaving it in a drawer unused because it is bulky and uses up batteries too fast. It is physically still operational but functionally obsolete. Computer companies may have older models that still perform according to their specifications; but the older models may no longer be in demand if there are newer models that are faster, smaller, run cooler, and are far more flexible in their application. Air Canada replaces its DC-8 jets with newer 767 models because the latter are more fuel-efficient in a period of expensive energy costs.

In brief, a plant asset may be functionally obsolete while still in good physical shape and able to do the job for which it was designed. Because the asset's period of benefit to the company ends when it is functionally obsolete, it is the period of functional usefulness that we are interested in for purposes of charging depreciation and depletion. "All machinery is on an irresistible march to the junk heap, and its progress, while it may be delayed, cannot be prevented by repairs" [Hatfield 1927]. This statement can be interpreted to mean that physical decline can be slowed by repairs, but functional decline is unrelated to physical condition and cannot be prevented.

Technical Issues

The methods for charging depreciation and depletion to the periods benefited by the asset are varied, but the general pattern is the same. First, the acquisition cost must be established. Second, the functional service life of the asset must be estimated. Third, the estimated residual (or salvage) value at the end of the asset's life must be determined. Fourth, a method must be decided for allocating the **net depreciable amount** (i.e., acquisition cost minus residual value) to each of the time periods.

ESTABLISHING THE ACQUISITION COST

In Chapter 7 we set out the principles for finding the historic cost of an asset. In the present context it is important to note that depreciation is based on various characteristics of the asset, such as the expected functional service life. Therefore, assets with different depreciation characteristics should be kept separate, or alternatively a composite rate should be established with these different characteristics in mind. Thus, because land itself is not depreciable, land improvements should be capitalized in a separate account to facilitate the calculation of depreciation.

Let us consider another example. When a truck is purchased it is estimated that the engine and drive train should be good for 300,000 kilometres, and the tires for 60,000 kilometres if recapped at 30,000 kilometres. The frame and cab should last six years. It is estimated that the truck will be driven 600,000 kilometres, and a projection of the company's business indicates that this will be reached in four years from the date of purchase. The truck will cost $80,000. One possible way of handling depreciation here would be to apportion the purchase price among the various components named above. One could then depreciate each as follows: (i) engine and drive train and tires — on the basis of number of kilometres driven; and (ii) frame and chassis — over four years because it is judged uneconomic to extend their lives by putting in more than one replacement engine and drive train.

Although such a breakdown of total asset cost over a variety of components is possible, it is not commonly done because of the record-keeping burden it imposes on the company. Instead, there is a practical incentive to classify the plant assets into groups with roughly the same depreciation characteristics. Thus, in our example, the entire truck might by depreciated as one unit for simplicity.

ESTIMATING THE SERVICE LIFE

The **service life** of a plant asset is the length of time it is expected to be functionally useful. This obviously is an estimate since one cannot know with certainty at the time an asset is purchased how long it is likely to be kept in service.

Estimating the probable physical life gives an outer limit to the functional life. Sometimes one can feel reasonably confident about estimating the functional life of some assets, especially if there is a history of stable use and there is no replacement for them looming on the horizon (e.g., tables). Estimates of the functional life of some assets, however, are necessarily difficult to make, especially if the technology on which they are based is changing rapidly. Examples of service lives that would be difficult to estimate are (i) micro-computers, (ii) automatic bank teller machines, and (iii) pilot plants for genetic engineering processes.

ESTIMATING SALVAGE VALUE

The amount of historic cost to be charged as depreciation expense over the life of the asset is the net amount after deducting the estimated salvage value from the original cost. The **salvage value** is the net amount that is received for the asset after it has been removed and the site has been put back into its original shape. This is often a difficult estimate to make because the event is in the future and the amount to be received is influenced by factors not entirely knowable at the present.

Frequently, for simplicity, a zero salvage value is assumed, perhaps with the working hypothesis that the asset removal charges will be covered by the proceeds of the sale of the plant asset. It is contemplated that disposal of the asset will not cover its demolition costs, then provision for this must be made at the beginning through a negative disposal value in the depreciation calculations. This will increase the annual depreciation charge. The issue of using negative salvage values arises, for instance, with nuclear electric generating plants. Some people argue that such plants are more costly than stated because the cost of clean-up at the end of their life has been underestimated. Thus they conclude that the annual depreciation expense has been understated. The potentially heavy restoration costs at the end of a logging program, or after open-pit mining, would furnish similar arguments in favour of using negative salvage values.

GAIN OR LOSS ON DISPOSAL

The accounting entries needed to record the gain or loss on disposal have been outlined in Chapter 7 on plant assets. However, we have not yet discussed whether the gain or loss should be calculated (i) on an individual basis, as each asset is disposed of or alternatively (ii) on a pooled, or *group reserve*, basis. The arguments in favour of each are essentially the same as those found in accounting for inventory by (i) identifying cost with the individual item sold (the specific identification method) or alternatively (ii) by identifying cost with a group of similar inventory items (which leads to the LIFO, FIFO, or average cost methods). There is no definitive argument in favour of one method over the other. The best approach depends on the circumstance of the individual company. Generally, one would expect to find fewer groups of similar plant assets than groups of similar inventory.

Allocation Methods

In this section we examine some of the common methods for allocating the historical costs of plant assets over their useful lives. As discussed above, the choice of method is essentially an arbitrary one. However, under certain circumstances, one might feel intuitively that a particular method approximates the benefit conferred by the asset more closely than other methods do.

STRAIGHT-LINE METHOD

Under the **straight-line method**, the net amount to be depreciated is divided by the expected functional life, and an equal amount is charged to each of the years in which the asset is used. If the net amount to be depreciated is denoted as "n" and the number of years as "y", then under this method we have the following:

Annual depreciation = n/y

This would produce a straight line if graphed.

For example, Perth Warehouse recently completed a new storage building costing $350,000 and estimated that the building would last twenty years with a final salvage value of $10,000. It it decided to use the straight-line method, the annual depreciation charge would be $17,000 (i.e., 340,000/20).

The straight-line method is easy to understand and simple to use. It is the method most commonly used in practice by large public companies.

DECLINING-BALANCE METHOD

Under the **declining-balance method** (or diminishing-balance method), the rate of depreciation stays fixed, but the rate is applied each year to the remaining undepreciated book value. Thus, the dollar amount of depreciation declines steadily year by year without ever reaching zero, no matter how long the asset lasts. The balance remaining undepreciated slowly approaches the expected salvage value. In an attempt to reflect the expected cost pattern, this method is often used for assets whose benefit decreases over time or whose required maintenance increases over time.

The method for calculating the depreciation rate is to use the nth root as follows:

Rate = 1 − (Residual value/Original Cost)$^{1/n}$
where n is the number of years of expected functional use.

For example, Odessa Trucking bought a new truck for $60,000. It is expected to last five years and have a salvage value of $25,000. The rate to use would be as follows:

Rate = 1 − (25/60)$^{1/5}$
     = 1 − 0.84
     = 0.1606

Therefore, the depreciation pattern would be as follows:

Year	Depreciation	Balance Remaining
1	$9,637	$50,363
2	8,089	42,273
3	6,790	35,483
4	5,699	29,784
5	4,784	25,000

This method is popular in Canada because a variation of it is required by Revenue Canada to calculate the depreciation permitted for income tax purposes. In calculating taxable income (which is nearly always different from income for accounting purposes), the depreciation charged by the company in its books of account is ignored. Instead, Revenue Canada requires that the capital cost allowance be calculated. For simplicity, many smaller, privately held companies use Revenue Canada's method of depreciation in their own external financial statements as long as the result is not materially different from generally accepted accounting principles. The Revenue Canada method has some variations that are designed to ease administration, but these variations can run counter to good accounting reporting. An introduction to capital cost allowance as used by Revenue Canada is given in Appendix 8-1.

USAGE METHOD

Under the **usage method**, an estimate is made of the total amount of product that a given plant asset will produce over its life. This method is also known as the unit-of-production method. The annual depreciation charge is then based on the ratio of actual usage for that year to the total estimated usage.

For example, Verona Construction bought a bulldozer for $60,000 with an estimated remaining work-life of 1,600 hours. During 1989 the bulldozer worked for 400 hours. Therefore, the depreciation charge for that year would be 400/1,600 x 60,000 = $15,000.

The usage method appeals strongly to our intuition since the annual depreciation charge appears to be closely related to the amount of productive capacity used. However, this appeal is deceptive because the ultimate accounting test is benefit, not usage. Moreover, unfortunately in many instances, it is not at all apparent how many units of capacity a given asset may provide (e.g., what is the productive capacity of a building?). Even when it is apparent, there is often a question whether the units of output produced toward the end of the asset's life yield the same benefit as the ones produced at the beginning of its life. For example, if the estimated life of a rental car is 80,000 kilometres, would a person be willing to pay the same daily rental for one that was three years old (but still within the 80,000 kilometre limit) as for one that was almost new?

INTEREST METHODS

The important thing to remember about all depreciation allocation methods is that they allocate the same total amount of depreciable cost over the same number of time periods; they differ only in the pattern of allocation to each year. This is easy to forget while studying the interest methods of allocation because the arithmetic is more complex.

The two most common types of interest methods are the annuity method and the sinking-fund method. Under the **annuity method**, the depreciation allocation over the life of the asset is the same as it would have been if the company had (i) financed the asset 100% by debt due at the end of the asset's service life, (ii) arranged to repay the debt in equal annual instalments of blended principal and interest (i.e., in the pattern of an annuity), and then (iii) charged as its annual depreciation an amount equal to that year's principal repayment. Note that there is no requirement that the company actually finance the asset in this manner; it is simply a way of allocating the depreciable cost.

For example, suppose that a plant asset is purchased for $10,000. Further suppose that it has an estimated service life of five years and an expected salvage value of $2,000. The amount to be depreciated is, therefore, $8,000 over five years. Under the annuity method this would be the same pattern as if the company had borrowed $10,000 at the beginning of the five-year period and then made equal annual instalments of principal and interest to bring the debt down to $2,000 at the end of five years. Assume the interest rate is 10%. The schedule of debt repayment is shown in columns *A* to *D* below, and the resulting depreciation pattern is shown in column *E*. An annual payment of $2,310.38 (column B) is required under these assumptions. For our purposes it is sufficient to note that this amount can be calculated using interest tables designed for this purpose or by other methods using numerical analysis that are outside the scope of this text. It is common to find pocket calculators that contain the program to calculate this amount directly. Note that the total depreciation charged for the five years is $8,000, which is the amount desired. However, unlike most other methods of depreciation, the annual depreciation rises from Year 1 to Year 5.

ANNUITY METHOD

Year	A Starting balance	B Annual payment	C Interest cost	D Capital repayment	E Depreciation expense	F Accumulated depreciation	G Net book value
1	$10,000.00	$ 2,310.38	$1,000.00	$1,310.38	$1,310.38	$1,310.38	$8,689.62
2	8,689.62	2,310.38	868.96	1,441.42	1,441.42	2,751.80	7,248.20
3	7,248.20	2,310.38	724.82	1,585.56	1,585.56	4,337.36	5,662.64
4	5,662.64	2,310.38	566.26	1,744.12	1,744.12	6,081.47	3,918.53
5	3,918.53	2,310.38	391.85	1,918.52	1,918.52	8,000.00	2,000.00
Total		$11,551.90	$3,551.90	$8,000.00	$8,000.00		

The entry to record the depreciation expense in the first year would be as follows:

Depreciation expense	1,310.38	
Accumulated depreciation		1,310.38
To record annual depreciation expense using the annuity method.		

Under the **sinking-fund method,** the annual charge is the same as it would have been if the company had (i) decided to have a sum of money on hand at the end of the asset's life that was exactly equal to what was originally paid for it; (ii) arranged to pay into a special fund, in equal annual instalments, an amount sufficient to accumulate to the sum it needed at the end of the asset's life; and then (iii) charged as its annual depreciation expense an amount equal to that year's payment into the fund plus the interest earned on the fund that year. Once again, there is no requirement that the company actually act in this manner; it is simply a way of allocating the depreciable cost.

A schedule showing such a scheme, using the same example as in the annuity method, is shown below. The balance that would accumulate in such a fund is shown in column A, and the annual build-up of interest earnings on the fund together with the annual payment into the fund is shown in column D. Note that the depreciation expense in column E is equal to the annual payment of $1,310.38 into the fund together with the interest earnings of that year. Note also that the annual charge against income is exactly the same whether the annuity or sinking fund method is used.

SINKING-FUND METHOD

Year	A Starting balance	B Annual payment	C Interest income	D Capital accu-mulation	E Depre-ciation expense	F Accu-mulated depre-ciation	G Net book value
1	$ 0.00	$ 1,310.38	$ 0.00	$1,310.38	$1,310.38	$1,310.38	$8,689.62
2	1,310.38	1,310.38	131.04	1,441.42	1,441.42	2,751.80	7,248.20
3	2,751.80	1,310.38	275.18	1,585.56	1,585.56	4,337.36	5,662.64
4	4,337.36	1,310.38	433.74	1,744.12	1,744.12	6,081.47	3,918.53
5	6,081.47	1,310.38	608.15	1,918.52	1,918.52	8,000.00	2,000.00
Total		$6,551.90	$1,448.10	$8,000.00	$8,000.00		

The usual end result of interest methods is that when both depreciation and interest costs of a plant asset are added together the total cost remains the same from year to year. The increase in depreciation costs is compensated for by falling interest costs. This method is used most often by real estate developers, who finance their developments using mortgages in which they pay a constant sum per month that combines interest and principal repayment. (We explained such an arrangement above in Appendix 5-2 under *Present Value, Method 2.*) Because the debt is being slowly repaid, the annual interest cost declines. If interest and depreciation together are to remain constant, then the annual depreciation must increase proportionately over the life of the asset.

It is difficult to think of many situations where the benefit conferred by a plant asset increases as it ages. Yet the interest method outlined above implies that this is what happens. The impact becomes more pronounced as the assumed life of the asset is lengthened. Some Canadian land development companies assume a service life of fifty years or more. This has the effect of charging little depreciation to the early years, which does not seem to fit with one's intuitive ideas about depreciation patterns of buildings. This approach seems more justifiable with regulated utilities, whose rates are set by public authorities on the basis of their accounting costs; for here it would have the effect of levelling out the rates charged over the life of a major asset because depreciation and interest will total a constant amount annually.

A counter-argument that might be given by a real estate company is that depreciation of real estate assets with long lives is not a very meaningful concept anyway.

Historically, the combined price of land and buildings has tended to increase over time — not decrease — as the value of the land has risen. It is arguable, however, how much increase there would have been in the price of the buildings had there not been significant inflation. As we will discuss in Chapter 21 on price-change accounting, accountants are relunctant to reflect the impact of inflation in a piecemeal fashion. Hence a defence based on deflation effects is unlikely to have much support. Interest methods for allocating depreciation are not used in the United States because of SEC disapproval.

SUM-OF-THE-YEARS DIGITS (SOYD) METHOD

The **sum-of-the-years digits (SOYD)** method is widely used in the U.S. but is uncommon in Canada. It produces results similar to the declining-balance method, except that the undepreciated balance actually reduces to the expected salvage value at the end of the depreciation span. Let us illustrate this by modifying the Odessa Trucking example we presented above in the section on the declining-balance method.

Suppose that instead of using the declining balance method, Odessa Trucking had decided to use the sum-of-the-years digits method. Here is a summary of the facts concerning the new truck:

Cost when new	$60,000
Expected salvage value	25,000
Total amount to depreciate	$35,000
Expected life	5 years

The sum of the digits that represent each of the years is $(1 + 2 + 3 + 4 + 5) = 15$. Thus the annual depreciation would be as follows:

Year	Depreciation		
1	5/15 times $35,000	=	$11,667
2	4/15 times 35,000	=	9,333
3	3/15 times 35,000	=	7,000
4	2/15 times 35,000	=	4,667
5	1/15 times 35,000	=	2,333
Total			$35,000

GROUP DEPRECIATION

Group depreciation refers to the practice of grouping assets with a similar life and calculating depreciation on the entire group rather than on the individual assets. It is usually done for convenience and in the belief that the results will not be much different from calculating depreciation on an individual basis. Because capital cost allowance regulations under the Income Tax Act are a form of group depreciation, the adoption of group depreciation for the accounts allows a company to calculate depreciation in a manner similar to that of Revenue Canada.

When one asset is disposed of, there are two possible approaches. One can calculate the depreciation that can be attributed to the asset and record the gain or loss on disposal. Alternatively, one can credit the entire proceeds to the undepreciated asset account (as the Tax Act does). If the latter choice is made, there is a danger that the undepreciated cost of the group of assets will not be reasonable given their original cost and remaining service lives. In other words, there is a danger that the matching principle will not be adhered to.

For example, suppose that a company purchased two cars for $20,000 each and decided to use straight-line depreciation over three years. The estimated salvage value of each car at the end of the three years was $5,000. At the end of two years one of the cars was sold for $6,000. As explained above, the company can now use one of two approaches. Here is a summary of both:

	Individual basis			Group
	Car A	Car B	Total	
Purchase	$20,000	$20,000	$40,000	$40,000
Depreciation: Year 1	(5,000)	(5,000)	($10,000)	(10,000)
Depreciation: Year 2	(5,000)	(5,000)	($10,000)	(10,000)
Net book value: end of Year 2	10,000	10,000	20,000	20,000
Disposal of car		(10,000)	($10,000)	(6,000)
Net book value after sale	10,000		10,000	14,000
Depreciation: Third year	(5,000)		($5,000)	(9,000)
Net book value: time of disposal	$ 5,000		$ 5,000	$ 5,000

The main difference between the two approaches is that with the individual basis the loss on the sale of the car of $4,000 (proceeds of $6,000 less not book value of $10,000) was recognized when it was sold at the end of the second year. Under the group method the proceeds of $6,000 were credited to the group account and the annual depreciation was revised to reduce the net book value to the salvage value of $5,000 at the end of the third year. One could argue that the matching principle is not being adhered to in the group method because the net book value under the group method at the end of the second year is $14,000, which is unreasonably large for a car that is two years old.

CHANGES IN DEPRECIATION

A company may make a change in its depreciation *policy* or in its depreciation *estimates*. The consequent accounting treatment will depend on what type of change has been made.

If a change in accounting policy results in a material change in depreciation charges, then this requires a retroactive application with restatement of prior periods' financial statements. Such a change might take place, for example, if one company were purchased by another that wished to have uniform accounting policies across all its subsidiaries. If a change is made in an accounting estimate related to depreciation, such as service life or salvage value, then the amount of the change is charged to present and future periods, with no retroactive application to prior periods.

For example, Lyndhurst Limited bought a heavy truck in 19X7 costing $80,000. The company decided to use straight-line depreciation. The salvage value of the truck was estimated at $10,000 at the end of its estimated seven-year service life. Suppose that in 19X8 the company decided that it should have used the declining-balance method at 20%. It would then make the following comparison:

	19X7	19X8
Depreciation under straight-line method	$10,000	10,000
Depreciation under new declining-balance method	16,000	12,800
Difference	$ 6,000	$ 2,800

Because the company has changed its depreciation policy, the 19X7 financial statements would be restated to show depreciation as $6,000 higher. As a result, the reported net income for 19X7 would be $6,000 less. The journal entry in the 19X8 books would be as follows:

Retained earnings	6,000.00	
Accumulated depreciation		6,000.00

To record charge against retained earnings arising from a change in depreciation policy.

Note that if some change in the use of the truck had led the company to switch to the declining-balance method, this would *not* constitute a change in accounting policy. Instead, the company would take the net book value at the start of 19X8 as a given and change depreciation methods at that point. For example, it would take the net book value as $70,000, and apply the 20% declining-balance rate to that, producing a total depreciation for 19X8 of 20% of $70,000, or $14,000.

Let us change this example and assume that the company was content with the straight-line method of depreciation. Suppose that in 19X8 the company decided that the service life of the truck was five years instead of seven. This means that annual depreciation should have been $70,000/5, or $14,000 a year from the start. The company could then make the following comparison:

	19X7	19X8
Depreciation under seven-year assumption	$10,000	10,000
Depreciation under five-year assumption	14,000	14,000
Difference	$ 4,000	$ 4,000

Since this is a change in an accounting estimate, there is *no* retroactive application to 19X7. Instead, the usual practice is to take the remaining depreciable amount of $70,000 (i.e., 80,000 - 10,000) and depreciate it over the revised estimated life of four years from the beginning of 19X8. The revised annual charge would then be 70,000/4 = 17,500.

Evaluation of Depreciation Methods

We have already explained why it is pointless to seek the "correct" depreciation method in any particular instance. Instead, the accountant should look for allocation schemes that seem to do rough justice to the aim of cost allocation. The straight-line method is preferred for its simplicity and is the most popular. Accordingly, unless there is some clear reason to the contrary, it seems desirable to use straight line. The 1987 edition of *Financial Reporting in Canada* indicated that about half of the reporting companies used straight line, and another third used it in combination with the usage or declining-balance methods.

The use of the declining-balance method was encouraged by the adoption of that method by Revenue Canada in 1949. Declining balance is often used with assets whose benefits decline over time, such as rental cars, automotive equipment, computing equipment, and aircraft.

We have already discussed the virtues, or lack of them, of depreciation methods (such as interest methods) that allocate heavier costs to the later part of an asset's life. Such methods seem to be confined to real estate development companies.

Whichever method is chosen, accounting standards generally require that it not be changed over the life of the asset except under unusual circumstances. The *CICA Handbook* does not give guidance on this point. The *Handbook* does call for disclosure of the amount of depreciation, the methods of calculation, and the rates used. If the adoption of a depreciation method involves a change in accounting policies, then the *Handbook* [1506] requires disclosure of (i) a description of the change and (ii) the effect of the change on the financial statements of the current and prior periods.

Depletion and Accounting for Mineral Exploration

ALLOCATION METHODS

When a mine has been developed or an oil well proved, the matching principle requires that the cost of the mine or well should be charged against accounting periods in a manner that matches the cost against the revenue reported from the sale of the mineral wealth. Accordingly, the usual procedure is as follows:

1. An estimate is made of the total amount of mineral or oil that can be economically recovered. This is usually less than the total amount in the ground since some may not be worth recovering (e.g., it is too deep to be economical to recover).

2. An estimate is made of the total expected revenue from the sale of the mineral or oil.

3. The capitalized cost of the developed mine or oil field is then written off as a function of the mineral or oil taken out. This may be calculated in terms of the physical quantity removed or in terms of the revenue income of that year compared to the total expected revenue. The second method opens up the possibility for income manipulation because of the need to estimate future revenue.

FULL COSTING VERSUS SUCCESSFUL EFFORTS

Depletion costs are normally associated with the extractive industries like mining and oil drilling. A mine or well is costly to find and, once found, costly to develop up to the point where the mineral is brought to the surface and transported to the place where it can be processed. There are two major issues to be addressed that are not covered adequately under the general topic of depreciation. First, what is the "cost" of finding and developing a mineral deposit or oil well? Second, how should this cost be written off against revenues through depletion allowances?

In this section let us focus on the costing of oil wells. (The costing of mineral deposits is similar in some ways.) The essential problem with oil drilling is that a company may suspect that an area contains oil, but may have to drill many unsuccessful wells before finding out how well-founded its beliefs are. Many years after exploration starts — after the oil field has been discovered, developed, and pumped dry — the company would be able to calculate precisely how successful it had been in that particular field. At any time between the beginning and the end of the field's life, however, the company cannot be sure of the final outcome.

Accountants face the problem that often they must prepare financial statements when the oil company is in the middle of exploring for oil, rather than when the exploration is completed. Accountants can calculate easily enough the financial outlay made to date in the drilling program; their problem is to decide what part of this outlay represents an expense that should be written off and what part should be capitalized. The general principle is that any expenditure that confers a benefit on the company extending beyond the current year should be capitalized. It is recognized from the start that the company will frequently drill dry holes in its attempt to find oil. The accounting problem is whether to treat the cost of drilling the dry holes as an expense of the period or as a necessary capital investment to find the productive ones.

There have been two rather different accounting methods adopted to deal with this problem: the **successful-efforts method** and the **full-costing method**. Successful efforts makes the decision on each well individually. A well is drilled and if it turns out to be a dry hole, it is written off to expense. If oil is found, the cost of that well is capitalized and depletion is charged as the oil is pumped out.

Full costing, on the other hand, assumes that the whole drilling problem in some broadly defined geographical area is the basis for cost allocation. The costs of the entire exploration program are accumulated, and dry holes are capitalized up to the total expected value of the resources found to date. These costs are charged as depletion as the oil is pumped from the wells. The charges are made in terms of the production of the whole area, not the individual wells. If the whole area produces nothing but dry holes, then all costs would be written off when the area was abandoned.

Full costing will tend to defer the write-off of dry holes until a later period. It has traditionally been favoured by the smaller oil companies, perhaps because it makes their income statement look better in the early days of an exploration program. It has been used in Canada by such companies as Norcen Energy Resources, PanCanadian, Husky Oil, and Dome Petroleum. By contrast, successful efforts have been favoured by the larger integrated oil companies such as Imperial Oil, Texaco Canada, and Gulf Canada.

Let us work through an example. Suppose that Successful Efforts Inc. drilled two wells. The costs of developing these wells and the success of each are shown below:

	Parcel A	Parcel B	Total
		(in millions)	
Acquisition costs	$10	$ 6	$ 16
Exploration costs	24	24	48
Development costs	40		40
Total costs	$74	$30	$104
Estimated barrels of recoverable oil	16	0	16

Using the method suggested by its name, the company would capitalize only the $74 million from the successful A Parcel. It would charge to expense the $30 million from B Parcel as soon as it was decided to abandon the well. It would amortize the $74 million over the 16 million barrels of oil. Therefore it would charge as amortization $4.625 for each barrel of oil pumped from the well.

On the other hand, Full Costing Inc., following the method suggested by its name, would treat this scenario differently. It would capitalize the costs of both Parcel A and Parcel B, for a total of $104 million. It would then amortize the cost over the 16 million barrels, for a cost per barrel of $6.500.

Let us continue with this example by adding more information. All the exploration took place in Year 1. Eight million barrels were produced in Year 2 and another 8 million in Year 3, after which the well was exhausted. The oil sold for $15 per barrel. The relevant parts of the income statement for each company would then read as follows:

	Year 1	Year 2	Year 3	Total
		(millions of $)		
Successful Efforts Inc.				
(Revenue) @ $15 per barrel	$ 0	$(120)	$(120)	$(240)
Costs written off	30			30
Costs amortized @ $4.625 per barrel		37	37	74
(Gain) or loss before other expenses	$30	$ (83)	$ (83)	$(136)
Full Costing Inc.				
(Revenue) @ $15 per barrel	$ 0	$(120)	$(120)	$(240)
Costs written off				0
Costs amortized @ $6.500 per barrel		52	52	104
(Gain) or loss before other expenses	$ 0	$ (68)	$ (68)	$(136)

Note that the total income over the three years is the same for both companies, but Full Costing Inc. has better-looking results in the first year.

The merits of successful efforts and full costing have been heatedly debated. The *CICA Handbook* has never taken a stand in favour of either. In 1986 the CICA issued an *Accounting Guideline* setting out suggested procedures for full costing, but explicitly refraining from either recommending or discouraging its use. The proponents of full costing tend to be smaller oil companies that argue that the financial markets will treat them less favourably if they use the successful-efforts method.

We should emphasize that neither method is particularly satisfactory. The core of the problem is that the original cost of acquiring oil assets through exploration usually bears little relationship to the eventual market value of the assets acquired. Hence there is a violation of the usual assumption that the purchase price of the asset bears some resemblance to its market value as at the point of acquisition. Consequently, a third method of reporting has been proposed in an attempt to solve the problem. The SEC in the U.S. has experimented with requirements that the company should also disclose the expected net value of the expected future output of oil from the field. This approach is termed **reserve-recognition accounting**. This experiment does not appear to have been successful because of the difficulties in arriving at satisfactory estimates, both of the probable amount of oil that will be recovered and its sale price at the time of recovery. The SEC specifies that the estimates should be made on the basis of current economic conditions with respect to price, costs, and competitive conditions. However, history has shown that current conditions are imperfect indicators of the later conditions under which the oil might actually be recovered.

In conclusion, there are at least three widely different approaches used to arrive at the basis of valuation of an oil field, and none of them is particularly useful for the reader of financial statements. It is reported that oil industry analysts tend to make their own estimate of the value of a company on the basis of the expected present value of its oil assets.

Common Mistakes Made by Readers of Financial Statements

By now the rather limited objective of accountants in their accounting for depreciation should be apparent. It is easy for a reader of financial statements to be misled by misuse of this information. Some common mistakes are set out below. They arise in part from a misunderstanding of the term **net book value**. (i.e., historic cost minus accumulated depreciation).

EQUATING NET BOOK VALUE WITH MARKET VALUE

One mistake is to assume that net book value of the plant assets is a reasonable approximation of their market value. This assumption often leads to the false conclusion that a company's stock is over- or under-valued if it differs materially from the book value. In other words, the false conclusion is that with proper accounting the net book value of the plant assets should approximately equal the market value of those assets. However, accountants have no intention of making net book value equal to market value — they are pursuing an entirely different objective, that of cost allocation. Thus, it would be sheer accident if net book value and market value happened to be similar.

It is common to find articles in the financial press comparing a company's net book value and stock price. If there is a discrepancy, the articles often imply that something is wrong with the company. This false conclusion seems to arise from a lack of familiarity with the meaning of the accounting term *net book value*.

MAKING DECISIONS ABOUT ASSET DISPOSAL ON THE BASIS OF BOOK VALUE

It was pointed out in Chapter 7 that the gain or loss on disposal is the result of a variety of factors and that great caution should be used in interpreting it as a measure of management expertise. Sometimes the decision to keep or sell an asset is based on whether the company would record an accounting gain or loss on the sale. Leaving tax considerations aside, the gain or loss to be booked on the sale should not be a material consideration because this amount is simply a reflection of (i) the depreciation policy adopted by the company and (ii) the change in relative prices for that piece of equipment since it was purchased. The decision whether to keep the equipment should be an economic one. In other words, it should be based on whether the company would benefit more from the use it can make of the proceeds of sale than it would from keeping the asset. The gain or loss on disposal is *not* a good indication of the merits of that economic decision.

EQUATING DEPRECIATION WITH CASH FLOW

There is a common mistaken assumption that a large depreciation charge per year always means that the company has a good positive cash flow. Let us look at an example where this is true.

Quality Brewers has a very steady trade in its established brands. Being highly mechanized, it has a high annual depreciation charge as this equipment is depreciated. Its plant was purchased at the end of 19X1. Its first operating year is 19X2. A condensed income statement is given below.

QUALITY BREWERS
19X2 INCOME STATEMENT
(millions of $)

Sales — all in cash	$25
Cost of goods sold	
Depreciation	10
Everything else — paid cash	10
Total	$20
Net income	$ 5

Assume that all balance sheet changes have been caused solely by the results reported on the income statement above. A simple comparative balance sheet is given below:

	19X2	19X1
	(millions of $)	
Cash	$15	$ 0
All other net current assets	10	10
Subtotal	25	10
Plant assets — cost	$80	$80
— depreciation	10	0
— net book value	70	80
Total assets	$95	$90
Owners' equity — share capital	$90	$90
— retained earnings	5	0
— total	$95	$90

Note how the cash balance increased by $15 million even though the net income was only $5 million. Why the difference? The common (misleading) explanation is that "depreciation provided $10 million more cash flow." This actually reverses the interpretation of what happened. The explanation should be: "We had cash sales of $25 million and cash outlays of only $10 million; so we had a net cash inflow of $15 million. The difference between the $15 million of cash inflow and the $5 million reported profit was a depreciation charge of $10 million, which did not involve an outflow of cash; it was a partial write-off of plant assets to reflect the cost of their benefit to the operations of 19X1." The second explanation is much longer than the first and — although more accurate in describing what happened — harder to understand. We will deal with this later in Chapter 18 on the statement of changes in financial position. At present, it is sufficient to remember that depreciation has no direct impact on the flow of cash into the firm.

Examples from Published Reports

Eastman Kodak Company

Eastman Kodak is a U.S. company that is primarily engaged in the manufacture of photographic products. The company is also active in a wide variety of technologies research. Some idea of the size of the company's plant assets can be judged by noting that their cost would purchase the equivalent of over 100,000 three-bedroom bungalows!

EASTMAN KODAK COMPANY

	1986	1985
	(millions of U.S. $)	
Properties		
Land, buildings, and equipment at cost	$12,919	$12,047
Less: Accumulated depreciation	6,643	6,070
Net properties	$ 6,276	$ 5,977

Major Accounting Policies

Depreciation: Depreciation expense is provided based on historical cost and the estimated useful lives of the assets. The provision for depreciation is calculated generally by accelerated methods [such as the declining-balance method or sum-of-the-years digit method] for assets in the United States and by the straight-line method for assets outside the United States.

Property retirements: When assets are retired or otherwise disposed of, the cost of such assets and the related accumulated depreciation are removed from the accounts. Any profit or loss on retirement, or other disposition, is reflected in earnings.

The following note is provided to give detail on the properties and accumulated depreciation.

Note

	1986	1985	1984
	(millions of U.S. $)		
Properties:			
Balance at beginning of year	$12,047	$10,775	$10,049
Additions	1,438	1,495	970
Deductions	(566)	(223)	(244)
Balance at end of year	$12,919	$12,047	$10,775
Made up of:			
Land	$ 215	$ 202	$ 190
Buildings and building equipment	2,440	2,332	2,156
Machinery and equipment	9,810	9,090	8,033
Construction in progress	454	423	396
Total as above	$12,919	$12,047	$10,775
Accumulated depreciation:			
Balance at beginning of year	$ 6,070	$ 5,386	$ 4,801
Provision for depreciation	956	831	758
Deductions	(383)	(147)	(173)
Balance at end of year	$ 6,643	$ 6,070	$ 5,386

Stelco Inc.

Stelco Inc. manufactures steel products in Ontario, Alberta, and Quebec. Note how the briefest of information is given on the balance sheet, with the notes used to provide the detail.

STELCO INC.
BALANCE SHEET

	1986	1985
	(thousands of $)	
Fixed assets (Note 6)	$1,603,181	$1,492,535

Significant Accounting Policies: Fixed Assets and Depreciation
Fixed assets are recorded at historical cost less investment tax credits and include construction in progress. Depreciation is provided using the straight-line method applied to the cost of the assets at rates based on their estimated useful life and beginning from the point when production commences.

The following annual depreciation rates are in effect:

Buildings	2$1/2$ to 5%
Equipment	6 to 7$1/2$%
Automotive and mobile equipment	10 to 20%
Raw material plants and properties	4$1/2$ to 5%

Note 6.   Fixed Assets

	1986	1985
	(thousands of $)	
Raw material plants and properties	$ 220,058	$ 221,979
Manufacturing plants and properties	2,598,041	2,515,819
	2,818,099	2,737,798
Manufacturing plants and properties under capital lease	50,000	50,000
Less deferred gain	8,763	9,437
	41,237	40,563
	2,859,336	2,778,361
Less accumulated depreciation	1,537,600	1,452,826
	1,321,736	1,325,535
Construction in progress	281,445	167,000
	$1,603,181	$1,492,535

Summary

Plant assets less accumulated depreciation are often one of the largest amounts on balance sheets. Because they are valued at historic cost, the amounts given may represent the purchases of earlier periods when the dollar had a quite different value. In addition, the accumulated depreciation represents the end result of an allocation process whose objective is the matching of the cost of an asset to the periods benefiting from its use. Unfortunately, there is usually no method preferable to others. The choice of method is often arbitrary. It follows that as a general rule the precise significance of the numbers provided decreases as one goes down the balance sheet from current assets to plant assets.

Under generally accepted accounting principles the objective of depreciation and depletion is to allocate the historic cost of a plant asset, net of estimated recovery value, to the periods that will benefit from its use. There are a variety of methods used to do this. Any one of them is acceptable provided it does a plausible job of achieving the objective.

QUESTIONS

Q8-1.   Make sure you are familiar with the following terms and can distinguish between them:
   a. depletion
   b. depreciation
   c. amortization
   d. the allocation problem
   e. physical decline *versus* functional decline
   f. service life
   g. salvage value
   h. straight-line method
   i. declining-balance method
   j. usage method
   k. interest methods
   l. sum-of-the-years digits method
   m. group depreciation
   n. successful efforts *versus* full costing *versus* reserve recognition
   o. net book value

Q8-2.   In the 1800s, when railroads were being built on this continent, their managements were reluctant to depreciate such assets as the roadbed. They argued that it would never wear out. Has time proved them right? Explain.

Q8-3.   "An asset, once created, begins its inevitable march to the scrapheap." What view of obsolescence is implied by this statement? Is it a complete enough view to describe the need for depreciation?

Q8-4. What is the accountant's declared objective in depreciation accounting? How well do the commonly accepted methods of depreciation accomplish this objective?

Q8-5. In each case below indicate (i) how you would estimate the service life, (ii) approximately how many years you think it would be, and (iii) which of the various methods of depreciation you think would be most appropriate. Give your reasons.

　　a. A canvas canopy purchased by a student society for rental to other student societies at social functions such as formals.

　　b. Electronic game machines purchased for use in a downtown games store frequented by teen-agers.

　　c. An automated dispensing machine for measuring liquor sold at a bar.

　　d. A microwave oven purchased by a catering company for use near dispensing machines in a student dining area.

　　e. Light fixtures purchased for use in a restaurant.

Q8-6. "The distinction between depreciation and depletion is a wholly artificial one and should be abolished." Discuss.

Q8-7. Imagine that you are trying to help a friend who has started a small business to understand his financial statements. He has taken economics but not accounting. He asks you to answer the following questions:

　　a. "To what extent does the annual depreciation charge represent the opportunity cost to me of keeping those fixed assets for another year?"

　　b. "What use can I make of the depreciation figures on my financial statements?"

Q8-8. Some advocates of "cash only" accounting argue that depreciation should be eliminated entirely as an accounting concept. They argue that the whole idea is so shot through with problems that it is better to drop it. It is not hard to list the problems depreciation fails to overcome. Can you think of any benefits from retaining its use? (*Hint*: Consider how assets would be charged as an expense if depreciation were eliminated.)

Q8-9. "None of the methods of accounting for oil exploration is particularly satisfactory." Explain.

Q8-10. M. Ltd. decides to stop production in one of its plants because of poor demand for the product manufactured there. Management believe the stop will be temporary, and they intend to maintain the plant in working order. They propose to suspend charging depreciation while the plant is temporarily shut. They ask your opinion. What would it be?

Q8-11. Assume that in the final year of use of a plant asset the company failed to charge depreciation. Would this alter the reported net income of that year? Explain.

Q8-12. "Depreciation as it is calculated under the usual historic cost basis using GAAP is an example where the attempt to match costs with revenues has been completely frustrated." Do you agree? Explain.

Q8-13. "The accountant's concept of depreciation reflects the triumph of economic reasoning over technological reasoning." Do you agree? Explain.

Q8-14. Explain in your own words the nature of the *allocation problem* in accounting.

Q8-15. "The accountant's problem is not the lack of a good depreciation method but the existence of too many methods that are equally valid." Explain the nature of this problem. Could the problem be solved by arbitrarily choosing one of the methods and requiring everyone to use it?

Q8-16. For each depreciation method covered in this chapter, supply the following:

    a. Explain how the annual depreciation charge is calculated.

    b. State whether over the life of an asset the annual depreciation charges would be (i) constant, (ii) rising, (iii) falling, or (iv) free to fluctuate.

    c. Give an example where the method is commonly used.

Q8-17. In the period when railroads were virtually the only method of hauling freight long distances, some customers complained that the railroads charged them too much and that other customers were being charged too little. The railroads' response to the regulatory authorities was that their charges simply covered their cost. How might the railroads have been taking advantage of a weakness in depreciation accounting to make sure that the "right" customers had relatively little cost assigned to them?

Q8-18. In 1985 TransCanada PipeLines Ltd. announced a write-down of oil and gas assets by $70 million. A company official said the write-downs arose "from a decision to adopt a country-by-country accounting method instead of a global method." The company uses full costing, not successful efforts. Would the write-down have been even higher if the company had adopted a province-by-province accounting method? Explain the factors that would influence the amount of the write-down.

Q8-19. A carpenter's hammer has an expected life of two years or 5,000 nails hammered in, after which it is of no use. A discussion arose about the method(s) of depreciation that would most properly fulfill the matching convention for the hammer. Ms. A thought that half the cost should be charged to each year, so that each year would be charged for the time period in which the hammer was owned. Ms. B thought that the most accurate way (although perhaps impractical) would be to allocate the cost in terms of the number of nails driven in each year. Ms. C disagreed, saying: "If the hammer is in perfect condition at the end of year one, why charge anything to that year? The hammer should have an indefinite life. If it breaks in Year 2, it will be because of misuse. In that case, Year 2 should be charged all of the cost."

    Required:

    a. Suppose the hammer costs $45. Show how the cost would be allocated between the two years under each of the depreciation methods suggested above. What general differences emerge?

    b. Which method do you think best fulfills the accounting objective of "allocating the cost of the asset to the periods that benefit from its use"? Explain.

EXERCISES

E8-1. What would you estimate the functional service life of each of the following to be? What factors would you have to take into consideration in arriving at your estimate?

    a. a three-bedroom bungalow in a suburb of a large city

    b. the hand calculator you now own

    c. Air Canada's purchase of the Airbus to replace its fleet of Boeing 737s

    d. Ontario Hydro's nuclear generating station at Darlington, Ontario

    e. A university's purchase of a new IBM computer to replace the present Burroughs equipment

E8-2. Which seems the best depreciation method for each of the following? Explain.

    a. a heavy-duty dump truck used by a construction company

    b. a micro-computer used by a professor to write textbooks

    c. computer software the company has purchased

    d. a car used as a taxi

    e. an office building

    f. a factory built in Detroit to manufacture GM cars

E8-3. In each of the following situations calculate (i) the net amount that should be depreciated, (ii) the estimated service life, and (iii) the first year's depreciation charge.

    a. CKSS, a teen-age rock radio station, bought a new transmitter for $60,000. It had an estimated service life of 15 years. The salvage value would normally be $5,000, but CKSS as a matter of policy gives the transmitter to a local campus radio station when it is fully depreciated. They plan to use straight-line depreciation.

    b. On 3 January 19X1 Chaffey's Locksmith Limited bought a new machine for cutting keys at a cost of $2,500 net, after trading in its old machine as part of the deal. The old machine would have sold for $300 cash on the open market, but as a trade-in the company was allowed $500. It is estimated that the new machine will cut 100,000 keys before needing major overhaul, and it is decided to depreciate it on the basis of the number of keys cut. By the end of the first financial year, 31 December, 3,000 keys had been cut.

    c. Godfrey Trucking Corporation bought a new truck. The truck cost $54,000, and additional accessories cost another $15,000. The expected resale value of the truck in five years is $22,000. The company will use the declining-balance method at a rate of 20%.

E8-4. A housing co-operative owned and run by a student group has a policy that the fees charged to its members who live there should be based on "cost", which is defined to include depreciation on the co-operative's buildings. They recognize that the method of depreciation chosen is going to result in differing charges in each of the years in which the housing is used. They ask you to explain to them what the various methods of depreciation are and to judge each method in terms of its fairness to those living in the co-operative now and to those who will be living there, say, ten years from now.

E8-5. In each of the following situations, calculate the missing numbers. (For part (g) a computer spreadsheet program is required.) NBV stands for net book value.

	Estimated life	Rate method	Original cost	NBV at beginning of year	Depreciation for this year	NBV at end of year
a.	6 years	20% declining balance	$ 40,000	$ 25,600	?	?
b.	5 years	?	?	?	$ 10,000	$ 10,000
c.	5 years	30% declining balance	$ 20,000	?	$ 2,940	?
d.	?	SOYD	$25,000	?	$ 4,762	?
e.	8 years	?	?	$ 52,000	?	$39,000
f.	?	straight line	$65,000	?	?	$ 36,112
g.	7 years	10% annuity	?	$ 11,680	?	?

E8-6. In each of the following situations (i) identify an appropriate depreciation/depletion method and defend your choice and (ii) calculate the charge for depreciation or depletion for the first year. (Make any assumptions that are necessary to carry out the calculations.)

    a. A company drilled a successful oil well and capitalized $4.8 million as the cost of this particular well. Reserves are estimated to total 100,000 barrels. During the first year 5,000 barrels were removed from the ground and 4,200 were sold.

    b. A manufacturing company purchased a machine for use in its plant at a cost of $850,000 plus $53,000 for delivery and installation costs. They expected to process 450,000 units of the company's product through this machine before it required a major overhaul. This overhaul would cost $400,000 and allow a further 275,000 units to be processed before the equipment was sold for $40,000. It was expected that the overhaul would be required in Year 3 and that the equipment would be sold in Year 5.

    c. A truck with an expected life of five years was purchased for $65,000. Because maintenance costs were expected to increase significantly over the life of the truck, the company wanted to use a method of depreciation which took this into account.

    d. An asset was purchased for $85,000 and was expected to benefit the company increasingly as it was used over its projected life of seven years. As a result, the controller thought that the depreciation policy should somehow reflect this benefit pattern. (The fact that he liked to play around with computer spreadsheet programs had nothing to do with his decision.)

E8-7. The McColm Oil Company undertook an exploration program in a region of Texas. Oil was found when the seventh hole was drilled. While costs for the whole program totalled $8,555,000, the costs for Well 7 were only $980,000 with reserves originally estimated to be 150,000 barrels. Thereafter, no further exploration was carried out in this area. The actual production pattern is as follows:

Year	Barrels
1	6,000
2	38,000
3	48,000
4	42,000
5	29,000

At the end of Year 5 it was considered uneconomical to continue operating the well.

Required: Calculate the annual depletion charge under both the full costing and the successful efforts methods of accounting for such assets. Evaluate the results from the point of view of the investor.

E8-8. A company purchased a major piece of equipment with a cost of $300,000, an expected life of six years, and an estimated salvage value of $30,000. The company decided that straight-line depreciation was appropriate. In Year 3, the company revised its estimate of the expected life to four more years (i.e., to a total of seven years) and the salvage value to minus $10,000. What effect would these changes in estimates have on the financial statements in Year 3?

E8-9. Allison Corporation is switching to a composite depreciation rate for its vehicles at each plant location this year. Given the following information, outline a rational depreciation policy for each plant.

	Vehicle	NBV at beginning of this year	Estimated life	Salvage value	Usage pattern
Plant 1	1	10,000	5	1,000	even
	2	20,000	3	5,000	declining
	3	5,000	2	0	declining
	4	12,000	5	1,000	even
Plant 2	1	80,000	4	5,000	usage
	2	120,000	3	10,000	declining
	3	10,000	5	1,000	even
	4	5,000	2	0	declining
	5	12,000	5	1,000	even
Plant 3	1	120,000	6	10,000	declining
	2	10,000	5	1,000	even
	3	5,000	2	0	declining

E8-10. The Blakely Corporation purchased a machine in Year 1 for $100,000 with an estimated useful life of seven years. The company uses the declining-balance method of depreciation for assets of this type. In Year 4 an overhaul to the machine at a cost of $40,000 extends the expected life to ten years. Calculate the depreciation charge for Years 3, 4, and 5.

E8-11. The Goodcitizen Mining Corporation acquired a piece of land with recoverable reserves of 3.5 million tons at a cost of $7.8 million. A condition of the purchase contract requires the company to restore the land after the mining operation is completed so that the property will be suitable for recreational use. The restoration costs are estimated to be $1.05 million, and the land should sell for about $800,000 when the restoration is complete. If the company carries no inventories, what should be the charge to depletion expense per ton of extracted material?

E8-12. The Davies Delivery Corporation purchased a vehicle for $39,000 in Year 1. The company's policy is to sell such vehicles after five years, and in this case it should receive $8,000 on the sale. The expected mileage for this vehicle is 180,000 kilometres. Compute the depreciation for Year 2 under each of the following methods: straight-line, declining-balance, usage, and sum-of-the-years digits.

E8-13. Savy Corporation acquired a machine for use in its business. It cost $25,000 and had an expected service life of ten years with a residual value of $3,000. Consider the following three independent scenarios regarding the asset:

(i) At the end of the fifth year (prior to adjusting entries), it was discovered that no depreciation had ever been recorded for the machine. Assume straight-line depreciation.

(ii) At the end of the fifth year (prior to adjusting entries), the estimated life was changed from ten years to fifteen years. Assume straight-line depreciation.

(iii) At the end of the third year (prior to adjusting entries), the company changed from straight-line depreciation to the declining-balance method at double the straight-line rate.

Required:
Suppose that in each scenario Savy Corporation asked you to provide the following information. (Disregard tax effects.)

a. Identify the type of accounting change.

b. Give the necessary entry to reflect the above change. (If no entry is required, state the reason.)

c. Give the entry to record the depreciation for Year 5 in scenarios (i) and (ii) and for Year 3 in scenario (iii).

(CGA adapted)

E8-14. The following cases are unrelated.

a. On 2 January 19X2 Sloppy Corporation purchased an operational asset that cost $24,000. At the date of the purchase the full amount was debited to expense. The item was discovered during an audit of the books in 19X8, prior to closing the books. The operational asset has an estimated ten-year service life and no residual value. The corporation uses straight-line depreciation on similar assets. Give the necessary journal entry or entries with regard to the asset as of 31 December 19X8, the company's year-end.

b. On 2 January 19X2 Cakebread Company purchased an operational asset that cost $24,000. At the date of the purchase the full amount was debited to the asset account Plant and Equipment. The amount was being depreciated on a straight-line basis over a ten-year service life, with no residual value. During 19X8 an engineering study was conducted that concluded that the operational asset would have a total life of fourteen years rather than the ten years originally assumed. Give the necessary journal entry or entries with respect to this asset as of 31 December 19X8, the company's year-end.

c. On 2 January 19X2 Extreme Corporation purchased an operational asset at a cost of $40,000. At the date of the purchase the full amount was debited to the Plant and Equipment Account. The asset was being depreciated over a ten-year life, with no residual value, using the straight-line method. During 19X4 an engineering study was conducted that concluded that the use of the diminishing-balance method at twice the straight-line rate would provide a better matching of revenues and expenses. Consequently the corporation decided to change to the diminishing-balance method. The estimated useful life was not changed. Give the necessary journal entry or entries with respect to this as of 31 December 19X4, the company's year-end.

(CGA adapted)

E8-15. On 2 January 19X0 Spadina Corporation acquired a specialty machine used in producing a new line of products. The machine cost $38,000 and was being depreciated on the basis of an estimated service life of ten years and $3,000 salvage value. During the fifth year of use, in 19X4, the company revised its estimates as a result of its experience of the previous four years. The company now estimated that the machine will be useful for only three more years (including the current year) and will have no salvage value. The company uses the straight-line method of depreciation.

Required:

a. Identify the nature of the accounting change

b. Prepare the journal entry pertaining to the specialty machine for 31 December 19X4, the company's year-end.

(CGA adapted)

E8-16. On 2 January 19X1 Northern Corporation purchased a machine at a cost of $30,000. Freight and installation of $9,000 were incurred and debited to repairs expense. The machine was being depreciated on a straight-line basis with estimated service life of six years and no salvage value. The company year-end is 31 December.

Required:

a. By how much was income understated or overstated in 19X1?

b. By how much was income understated or overstated in 19X2?

c. Prepare all journal entries on 31 December 19X4, the date of discovery of the error. Assume that the books have not been closed and that the adjusting entry to recognize *depreciation expense for 19X4* has not been recorded. No narratives are required.

(CGA adapted)

E8-17. In reviewing the books of Livingston Inc. you find an account termed *Miscellaneous Accumulated Depreciation*, which reads as follows:

MISCELLANEOUS ACCUMULATED DEPRECIATION (19X9)

Description	Dr.	Cr.	Balance
A. Balance from equipment account	8,500.00		8,500.00
B. Equipment		7,500.00	1,000.00
C. Group equipment account	1,600.00		2,600.00
D. Transfer from sundry equipment account	2,365.00		4,965.00

On investigating this account, you find the following explanations of the above entries:

A. When equipment costing $34,560 had been sold for $12,340, the following journal entry had been made:

Equipment — accumulated depreciation	13,720.00	
Miscellaneous accumulated depreciation	8,500.00	
Bank	12,340.00	
Equipment — cost		34,560.00

B. Equipment costing $45,000 with no residual value had been depreciated on a 10-year straight-line basis for the past five years. In the current year it was decided that its life would total fifteen years and that the annual depreciation should have been $3,000 per annum instead of $4,500. The following calculation was made:

Total accumulated depreciaiton to date	— actual	22,500.00
	— should be	15,000.00
	Excess:	7,500.00

C. The company had operated a group depreciation account for its electrical hand tools. A review of the account indicated that the market value of the equipment in the group was well below its net book value. The amount need to decrease the net book value to market value was charged to the Miscellaneous Depreciation Account.

D. When the Miscellaneous Equipment Account was found to contain just one remaining asset, it was decided to close it out to a sundry account and this one was chosen. The entry was as follows:

Miscellaneous accumulated depreciation	2,365.00	
Miscellaneous equipment — accumulated depreciation	3,527.00	
Miscellaneous equipment — cost		5,892.00

Required: Use journal entries to explain the treatment that should be given each of the above items. Explain any assumptions you make.

PROBLEMS

P8-1. One weekend a close friend asks you to come over to see him. You know he has been the owner-manager of a ski rental and repair store at a local ski resort for the past three seasons. When you arrive he hands you a set of condensed financial statements, given below. He provides you with the following explanation:

"Here are the financial statements I just got from the accountant I hired to come in and do my books and prepare the financial statements. She's a pretty good bookkeeper, but I find she's not much help in explaining what the figures on the statements mean. My business has been very steady for the three years I've been open, and yet my net income has gone up steadily. It's obvious because my depreciation expense has gone down. Yet when I look around the shop it seems to me that the equipment is wearing out, and it's soon going to be time to replace it. Perhaps with the increasing income I should be thinking of higher depreciation. Anyway, the whole thing doesn't seem to tie together. What's your advice?"

FRED'S SKI RENTALS AND REPAIRS
Income Statement

	19X3	19X2	19X1
Income			
Repairs	$ 2,500	$ 2,500	$ 2,500
Rentals	42,000	42,000	42,000
	44,500	44,500	44,500
Expenses			
Wages	20,000	20,000	20,000
Rent	6,000	6,000	6,000
Other	11,000	11,000	11,000
Depreciation and amortization:			
Equipment	2,000	2,000	2,000
Rental skis	2,560	3,200	4,000
Leasehold improvements	1,600	1,600	1,600
Total Expenses	43,160	43,800	44,600
Net Income	$ 1,340	$ 700	$ (100)

FRED'S SKI RENTALS AND REPAIRS
FIXED ASSET SCHEDULE AS OF JUNE 30

	19X3	19X2	19X1
Equipment — cost	$ 10,000	$ 10,000	$ 10,000
Accumulated depreciation	6,000	4,000	2,000
	4,000	6,000	8,000
Rental Skis — cost	20,000	20,000	20,000
Accumulated depreciation	9,760	7,200	4,000
	10,240	12,800	16,000
Leasehold Improvements — cost	8,000	8,000	8,000
Accumulated depreciation	4,800	3,200	1,600
	3,200	4,800	6,400
Total	$ 17,440	$ 23,600	$ 30,400

Required: Write a memo of about 250 words to your friend addressing the questions he has raised.

P8-2. A friend has asked you to review the financial statements of a medium-sized nursery specializing in plants to be sold to suburban home owners. Your friend is thinking of buying the nursery, and its earnings ability is one of the key factors that will influence her decision. She notes that over the past three years the company has recorded significant income from sale of plant assets, as follows:

	19X3	19X2	19X1
Profit on disposal of:			
Land — proceeds	$ 350,000	$ 200,000	$ 100,000
Land — cost	120,000	80,000	35,000
	230,000	120,000	65,000
Buildings — proceeds	123,000	80,000	120,000
Buildings — net book value	18,000	10,000	35,000
	105,000	70,000	85,000

Required: Write a memo to your friend not exceeding 500 words in which you evaluate this component of reported net income. Suggest two important questions to which she should find the answer when she next talks to the owners of the business.

P8-3. A company has installed an elevator costing $10,000. It is expected to last ten years and to have a salvage value at the end of that time of $1,200. The company is thinking of depreciating it on one of the following bases: (i) straight-line; (ii) declining balance at an annual rate of 19%; (iii) sum-of-the-years digits; (iv) the annuity method using 12% interest and an annual equal repayment amount at the end of each year of $1,701.46; (v) the sinking fund method using 12% interest and an equal annual repayment amount at the end of each year of $501.46; or (vi) usage. The usage would be based on the estimated number of thousand trips that the elevator would make in each year, as shown below.

Year	Usage	Year	Usage
1	25	6	65
2	25	7	40
3	30	8	20
4	40	9	10
5	80	10	5

Required:

a. Calculate the depreciation that would be charged in Year 1 for each of the six methods above.

b. Do the same for Year 10.

c. In Year 10 which method would create the highest depreciation charge?

d. In Year 10 which method would create the lowest? By how much would it be lower?

e. Which method do you think is most appropriate in this case? Explain.

P8-4. In each of the following unrelated transactions, evaluate how the purchase of plant assets should be shown in the accounts of the company for purposes of applying some group rate of depreciation. If you think part of the purchase should be classed as a separate asset for depreciation purposes, give your justification.

a. Evergreen Nurseries decided to expand. For $80,000 it purchased one of the pieces of land adjoining its existing operation. On the land was a house that Evergreen intended to use for two years and then tear down when it expands its greenhouse on to the new land. The appraised value of the land was $70,000 and the house was $10,000.

b. Audio Fantastics Inc., a company providing sound for public events, purchased the following items:

Item	Estimated life in years	Cost
Outdoor speakers	3	$ 1,200
Amplifier	4	450
Tape decks	2.5	450
Tapes	0.75	120
Truck	4.5	10,000

c. Yacht Rentals purchased a fibreglass sailboat hull for $50,000. With proper care it should last twenty years. The sails cost an additional $8,000 and were expected to last three years. The electronic gear such as depth gauge, ship-to-shore radio, and direction finder cost an additional $15,000 and had an expected physical life of ten years, although developments in technology had been limiting the functional life to an average of five years. Additional interior fittings such as extra bunks, a chart table, and a microwave oven cost $2,000 and were expected to last for the life of the ship.

P8-5. The public utilities commission of a small city installed sewers in a new subdivision to service approximately 450 new homes. The net cost to the city (after grants from other governments) was $2 million. The cost of the sewers is to be recovered from the home owners through their monthly water bills over the next five years.

Required:

a. Outline four alternative methods available to the commission for calculating the monthly charge.

b. Which of these proposals would the commission prefer? Which would the home owners prefer? Why?

c. Which proposal would you recommend?

P8-6. A local telephone utility completed a major program to change its residential customers' service by installing telephone jacks in their homes. Previously, the monthly customer charges were based on all operating costs including depreciation on all lines and equipment including telephone receivers. Under the new system, billings will include a charge for the use of the telephone line and a charge for the rental of the actual telephone for those customers who do not purchase their own. Central switching equipment and other such common costs will be allocated to these two customer charges.

Required:

a. How should the various charges be determined? What is the impact of the depreciation policies chosen? Does you proposal lead to fair charges to the different customers?

b. The utility is gradually replacing the rotary dial telephones in its inventory of rental telephones with touchtone. Should the valuation of the rotary phones be affected by this change? Should the depreciation policy be affected? Explain.

P8-7. Crawford Mines acquired a new mine which was expected to produce three million tons of ore over ten years. The following costs were incurred in the first year.

Property	$ 1,200,000
Buildings and equipment to be used to mine the ore	850,000
Labour and operating costs	440,000

In Year 1, 400,000 tons of ore were mined and 300,000 shipped. The company expects to sell the land for $50,000 when it is no longer feasible to mine the ore body.

Required: Compute the cost of goods sold for Year 1 and show your calculations. Explain any assumptions you make.

P8-8. Hutchinson Manufacturing installed a new automated production line at a cost of $1,750,000. The company anticipated that after ten years the line would be dismantled and parts with a fair market value (at that time) of $200,000 would be used elsewhere in the plant. The company chose to use straight-line depreciation for this equipment. At the end of Year 4, a review of the company's production facilities revealed that the line would be in operation for only three more years and that its usefulness to the company would steadily decline during that period.

Required:

a. Is this a change of accounting estimate or accounting policy? Explain.

b. Show the journal entry (entries) that should be made in Year 4 with respect to this equipment.

P8-9. In 19X6, the Cooper Co. hired you as its new accountant. While preparing the financial statements for the year ending 31 December 19X6 you notice that the current year's operating expenses are significantly less than those of the previous year. A review of the operating expense account for 19X5 reveals that the purchase of a piece of equipment (that was in use as of 15 September 19X5) was not capitalized but charged as an expense of the period. The invoice price is $45,000 and similar equipment is depreciated on a straight-line basis over ten years. The company's financial statements (without adjustment for the above) include the following information:

	19X5	19X6
Net income	$ 60,000	$ 110,000
Retained earnings	$ 200,000	$ 280,000
Dividends paid	0	$ 30,000

Required:

a. What accounting change is required? Show your calculations.

b. Prepare the journal entry or entries you would make to record this change.

c. Prepare the statement of changes in retained earnings for 19X5 and 19X6.

d. What is the effect of the change on the other financial statements?

P8-10. Doyle Inc. purchased an asset in Year 1 for $300,000 with an estimated useful life of eight years and an expected salvage value of $40,000. The company initially decides that the declining-balance method of depreciation is appropriate for this asset. In Year 3, the company changes its estimate of useful life to ten years and expected salvage value to

$20,000. In Year 5, based on actual usage, the company decides that straight-line depreciation better reflects the benefit the company receives from the asset. In Year 8, the asset is sold for $10,000.

Required: Prepare the journal entries for Years 1 to 8 for this asset. Doyle Inc. has a policy of recording a half-year's depreciation in the year of acquisition and a half in the year of disposition.

P8-11. The C.A. firm for whom you are employed audits the accounts of the McGirr Manufacturing Co. You have been assigned the task of reviewing the fixed asset and depreciation accounts. A review of the company's records reveals the following information:

(i) The company's depreciation policy is as follows:

Buildings and land improvements — 5% straight line

Equipment — 10% straight line

A half-year's depreciation is taken in both the year of acquisition and the year of disposition.

(ii) The company parking lot was paved and fenced. The work cost $35,000 and was charged to the land account.

(iii) A machine with an original cost of $250,000 and accumulated depreciation of $150,000 was sold. The proceeds of disposal were credited to the asset account as follows:

Bank	85,000.00	
Equipment — historic cost		85,000.00
To record receipt of proceeds of disposal.		

Depreciation was recorded for the year at the normal rate of 5% on the asset balance as follows:

Depreciation expense	8,250.00	
Accumulated depreciation		8,250.00
To record annual depreciation on equipment at 5% of (250,000 − 85,000).		

No other entries affecting these accounts were made.

(iv) Land with a fair market value of $50,000 and buildings with a fair market value of $120,000 were donated to the company by the city. Because there was no payment required, no entry was made in the books to record the acquisition.

(v) During the year company personnel constructed a building at a cost of $58,000 (consisting of $25,000 direct labour, $17,000 materials, $9,000 allocated management salaries, and $7,000 for other overheads). Prior to construction, the company had sought bids for the work. Since the lowest bid was $65,000, this was recorded as the cost of the building. The difference was credited to income as follows:

Building	65,000.00	
Direct labour expense		25,000.00
Materials inventory		17,000.00
Management salaries		9,000.00
Overhead expense		7,000.00
Gain on construction of own building		7,000.00
To record construction of own building at an estimated value of $65,000.00.		

(vi) The equipment account includes a machine, with an original cost of $76,000 and accumulated depreciation of $45,600, that was classified as surplus during the year and put up for sale. No entry has so far been made to reflect this reclassification.

Required: Prepare the adjusting entries to be made at the end of the year. (The company's books have not been closed.)

P8-12. East Co., West Co., North Co., South Co., Left Ltd., Right Ltd., Front Ltd. and Back Ltd. have all recently purchased large shopping centres. They were all able to lease out the centres, on operating leases, for the next twenty years for identical amounts of $120,000 per year. This was the only source of income for each firm. Each company paid $500,000 for its shopping centre. The companies obtained mortgages with different interest rates. Moreover, the companies used different methods for depreciating the shopping centres and different estimates of the functional lives of the shopping centres. These differences are shown below.

	Life	Interest	Depreciation
East Co.	10 years	10%	Annuity
West Co.	10 years	20%	Annuity
North Co.	10 years	10%	Straight line
South Co.	10 years	20%	Straight line
Left Ltd.	20 years	10%	Annuity
Right Ltd.	20 years	20%	Annuity
Front Ltd.	20 years	10%	Straight line
Back Ltd.	20 years	20%	Straight line

The companies that use the annuity method of depreciating their centres use the interest rate on their mortgages as the rate for calculating their yearly depreciation charges.

Required: Show how the various methods of treating the purchase of a shopping centre affect the net income firgure of the eight different firms over the next twenty years. Assume that other expenses for each firm are negligible. (*Hint*: Use a computer spreadsheet program to calculate and tabulate the various amounts. This will be especially helpful with the annuity method.)

P8-13. Harrowsmith Printing Inc. purchased a special-purpose press on 1 January 19X5 for $200,000. This machine was expected to have a ten-year life with $20,000 salvage value. The company initially chose to depreciate it using the declining-balance method. In late 19X8 the company decided to change the method of depreciation to straight line. While preparing the necessary entries, the accountant determined that the depreciation entry for 19X6 had been omitted.

Required: (Assume all amounts are material. Disregard tax effects.)

a. What disclosure is necessary as a result of the above events? Include in your explanation a description of the required accounting changes and the necessary correction process. Show your calculations.

b. Prepare the necessary adjusting journal entries as of 31 December 19X8 with respect to the above events.

(CMA adapted)

P8-14. Smythe Inc., whose fiscal year end is 31 December, paid $3,000 and traded in an old milling machine in order to acquire a *similar* piece of new equipment. The acquisition of the new equipment occurred on 1 October 19X7. The fair market value of the new equipment on that date was $6,000. The old machine had been acquired on 1 January

19X2 at a cost of $9,000. Since that time it had been depreciated using the straight-line method. The company had estimated that the old machine would have no residual value at the end of its estimated useful life of ten years.

Required:

a. Using the most conservative method, prepare the necessary journal entries on the books of the company with respect to the disposal of the old machine and the acquisition of the new equipment.

b. There are three factors that enter directly into the calculation of depreciation using the straight-line method. Explain what these factors are and how they interrelate in the determination of the appropriate charge for depreciation.

(CMA adapted)

P8-15. The records of Lowbrow Co. include the following information:

(i) Lowbrow purchased a truck on 1 January 19X3 for $10,000. The truck has a $1,000 salvage value and a six-year life. At the time of the purchase the company debited delivery expense and credited cash. The error was discovered in 19X7.

(ii) During 19X7 Lowbrow changed from the straight-line method of depreciation for its building to the declining-balance method. The following calculations show the depreciation under each method:

	19X7	19X6	19X5
Straight-line	$ 80,000	$ 80,000	$ 80,000
Declining-balance	90,000	70,000	60,000

(iii) In January 19X2 Lowbrow purchased a piece of equipment at a cost of $9,000 with an estimated salvage value of $1,500 and a five-year life. Early in 19X5 Lowbrow decides that the piece of equipment will be usable until 31 December 19X8 and will have a salvage value of $750. To date, Lowbrow has been using straight-line depreciation for the piece of equipment.

Required:

a. What accounting principles or concepts, *if any*, have been violated by the company's treatment in *each* of the above cases? If a principle has been violated, explain why. If no principle has been violated, then say so.

b. For each of the foregoing cases, present all the necessary correcting and adjusting entries to state the accounts of the company properly as at 31 December 19X7. The books have not yet been closed for 19X7. Ignore the effects of income taxes in your analysis. If no entries are required for any of the above cases, then say so.

(CMA adapted)

P8-16. Explain why the matching principle is "intuitively sensible as an objective to strive for" but often hard to make work in practice. In your answer you should refer specifically to difficulties that arise *with respect to matching* in each of the following areas:

(i) matching the cost of inventory to the period in which the inventory is sold

(ii) matching the cost of a plant asset to the period that benefits from its use

(iii) calculating the "actual" gain or loss on the sale of a short-term security

(iv) calculating the cost of bad debts that should be matched to the sales for the same period

In each area you should explain briefly the nature of the difficulty and the problems this might cause for the reader who wants a reliable measure of the firm's income.

APPENDIX 8-1
Capital Cost Allowance for Tax Purposes

The purpose of this Appendix is to explain how depreciation is calculated in Canada for federal income tax purposes. It will become apparent that the method used by Revenue Canada for the purpose of taxable income has some significant differences from the usual accounting method. The following description concentrates on the elements necessary for a general understanding of the procedures. We will leave out complexities.

The approach used by Revenue Canada is as follows:

1. Any depreciation claimed on the financial statements as a deduction from income is disallowed. It must be added back to reported income. Depreciation is then calculated using the rates set out in the Regulations to the Income Tax Act. It is termed **capital cost allowance (CCA)**.

2. When an asset is purchased it must be assigned to a class in accordance with the Regulations to the Act which state the kind of asset that must be in each class. There are 35 classes, but some of them are rarely used. For example, Class 30 (40% depreciation) is "an unmanned telecommunication spacecraft designed to orbit above the earth." Equipment for marine or aircraft use that is not designed for electrical generation goes into Class 8 at 20%. For each class an account is set up that pools together the costs of the assets in that class. The rate stated in the Regulations is the maximum allowed in each class. The balance in the account for each class is called the **undepreciated capital cost (UCC)**.

3. When an asset is disposed of, all the proceeds of disposal are credited to the UCC of that class up to the total amount of the original cost. Any excess is classed as income of the period and generally treated as a capital gain. This differs from the usual accounting practice of treating the difference between net book value and the proceeds as a gain or loss of the period. No attempt is made to identify and remove from the UCC the original cost and the CCA accumulated to date on that asset.

4. At the end of each tax year, the taxpayer applies the rate of each class to the UCC of that class to find the maximum amount of CCA allowed. Only half the usual rate is allowed in the first year that an asset is purchased, regardless of when in the year the purchase was made. Note that the rate is applied to a balance consisting of the historic cost minus proceeds of sale (or cost of the assets sold if that is less) minus CCA claimed to date. Thus the system is essentially a declining-balance method applied to a pool of costs.

5. The taxpayer then decides how much CCA he will claim, up to the limit allowed in each class. There are some instances (e.g., where the company would incur a tax loss) where it is in the taxpayer's interests not to claim the maximum, but to reserve some CCA for future. This differs from the usual accounting treatment, where the amount claimed is not discretionary.

6. The amount of CCA that the taxpayer decides to claim is deducted from the UCC to establish the closing balance of UCC at the end of the taxation year.

7. The balance in a class may not be claimed as a deduction for income tax purposes until the last item in that class is disposed of. Only then may the remaining UCC be written off against taxable income. Thus, if a group of assets have been sold for less than their individual UCC's, the differences representing the loss on disposal would have been left to build up in the UCC account until charged against income via the capital cost allowance system or until the last item was disposed of. Thus it is quite possible for the UCC to be larger than the cost of the last item remaining in that class.

Although the rules adopted by Revenue Canada seem to be inconsistent with the usual accounting treatment, they do have real virtues from the tax collector's point of view. They are easy for the tax collector to administer because the amount of information needed is relatively small. Although the rules do not make much attempt to allocate the depreciation cost to the proper year, they do a reasonable job over the life of the asset. If too much capital cost allowance is permitted, it is recovered after the asset is sold through the requirement that all proceeds up to the cost of the asset must be credited back to the asset class.

Let us consider a simple example. A company had the following purchases and disposals of office equipment that all fell within Class 8, whose maximum allowable rate of CCA is 20%.

Year purchased	Purchase cost	Year sold	Proceeds on disposal
19X1	$ 2,400	19X2	$ 700
19X2	$ 1,600	19X3	$ 2,400
19X2	$ 3,700		still on hand

The company's schedule of UCC and CCA is summarized below:

Year	Balance of UCC at start of year	Additions	Disposals	One-half of additions less disposals	Amount available for CCA	CCA	Balance of UCC at end of year
19X1	$ 0	$2,400	$ 0	$1,200	$1,200	$240	$2,160
19X2	2,160	1,600	700	450	2,610	500	2,560
19X3	2,560	3,700	1,600	1,050	3,610	722	3,938

In 19X1 the company claimed the full CCA of 20% of one-half the cost of additions, or $240. In 19X2 it would have been entitled to claim 20% of $2,610, or $522, but it elected to claim only $500 for reasons of tax strategy. In 19X3 it sold for $2,400 an asset that had been purchased for $1,600. Because the purchase price is less than the proceeds of sale, only the purchase price is credited to the pool (the rest is taxed as a capital gain). Since one asset is left in the pool at the end of 19X3, the account cannot be closed out. However, note that the closing balance of $3,938.00 is different from 80% of the cost of the one remaining asset (80% of $3,700), or $2,960. This is because the gains and losses on the sale of the assets bought in Years 1 and 2 are still being included and depreciated in the asset pool.

BIBLIOGRAPHY

CANADIAN INSTITUTE OF CHARTERED ACCOUNTANTS. *Financial Reporting in Canada*. Toronto, 1987. A standard reference on disclosure and format of financial statements.

HATFIELD, HENRY RAND. *Accounting: Its Principles and Problems*. New York: D. Appleton & Co., 1927. Despite its age, this book is a classic.

PRICE WATERHOUSE, *The Canadian Real Estate Industry: 1981 Survey of Annual Reports*. A useful survey of existing reporting practices.

THOMAS, ARTHUR. *Accounting Research Study No. 3: The Allocation Problem in Financial Accounting*. Evanston, Ill.: American Accounting Association, 1969. Argues that most of the allocations in accounting are arbitrarily chosen and are no better than different allocation schemes for the same costs.

CHAPTER 9
Intangible Assets

"The only reason for recording intangibles on the balance sheet
is to avoid having the debits on the income statement."
A practising accountant

Introduction

An **intangible asset** is one that (i) has no physical existence and (ii) is not specifically identified somewhere else on the balance sheet. There are other assets, such as accounts receivable and prepaid expenses, which also have no physical existence, but they are not usually referred to as intangible assets because they are specifically identified on the balance sheet (where they are usually classified as current assets). For convenience, we will include deferred charges among intangible assets.

When accountants say that an asset has no physical existence they mean that any physical object that may be thought of as representing the asset is only symbolic of the asset's value. Thus, the accounts receivable ledger cards represent the fact that people outside the company will pay the sums of money shown in the ledger. It is the fact that debtors will pay that is of value; the ledger cards are simply a record of this debt. Similarly, a patent licence certificate is symbolic of the legal right to use the process or object described in the patent. The patent document itself would not be used in the process. In contrast, plant assets, for example, are valuable in their own right because their intrinsic physical properties allow the company to make something valuable.

The accounting notion of an asset is so fundamental that there has never been a fully satisfactory definition of what it is. Generally, the notion of an asset is an economic one — assets are things that provide future economic benefits to the person possessing them. There is in principle no requirement that these benefits should flow only from assets that have a physical existence. Hence there is in principle nothing unusual about recording on a company's balance sheet assets that have no physical existence as long as they provide future economic benefits to the company. The nature of many intangible assets makes it difficult to assess their likely economic benefits. The accounting response is to treat some of them as assets and capitalize them but to treat others as expenses and charge the cost of acquiring them as period expenses.

The accounting treatment of intangible assets appears inconsistent and contradictory. We set out this treatment — which in some ways differs between Canada and the United States — and discuss the reasons for present-day accounting standards in this area. When the accounting treatment appears confused, there is often a difficult conceptual problem lurking in the background. In this chapter we will bring such problems to the fore.

Types of Intangible Assets

An important distinction can be made between **identifiable intangible assets**, whose separate existence can be clearly identified, and **non-identifiable intangible assets**, where the accountant is confident that an intangible asset exists but cannot identify any particular asset as being it.

The other major distinction is whether an intangible asset has been created within the company (**internally developed**) or purchased in a completed state (**purchased**). This distinction is useful because the market value of most intangible assets is hard to establish. If they have been purchased, there is clearer evidence of their value.

The four categories arising from these two distinctions are shown below, with examples of each.

	Identifiable	Non-Identifiable
Purchased	Patent rights and copyrights Mineral rights Fast food franchises	Goodwill — excess of purchase price of a group of assets over the cost of identifiable net assets
Internally developed	Research and development Aircraft design cost Organization costs Internally developed patent rights	Goodwill — potential excess of worth of a company as a going concern over market value of assets

INDENTIFIABLE INTANGIBLE ASSETS

If an asset is identifiable, it is likely that its useful asset life is reasonably determinable. Then it is often possible to amortize the cost over that useful life, as will be discussed later. For example, the life of a patent right is normally determined by the contract assigning the patent to the purchaser. On the other hand, the inability to identify an intangible asset also means that one cannot usually specify its useful life. In that case the period over which it is amortized must be chosen arbitrarily. Let us now consider various examples of identifiable intangible assets.

A **patent** is the legal right to the exclusive use of a process, design, product, or plan and the right to permit others to use it under licence, generally for seventeen years with certain rights of renewal. Some patent rights can become very valuable (e.g., the patents on gene-splicing), but most patents are not put into commercial use and have no value. If the patent right is purchased, its market value at date of purchase is thereby established, and the remaining problem is how its purchase cost will be amortized. Often, a patent may be most useful in its early years before competitors develop something similar. Therefore it is a mistake to assume that the amortization pattern should necessarily be straight line. Nevertheless, because of the difficulty of measuring the economic decline in intangible assets, the universal custom is to use straight-line amortization. If the patent arises from work done within the company, its market value is usually less clear.

A **trademark** is a distinctive word, mark, or symbol (e.g., Walt Disney) that helps producers to distinguish their products or services from those of others. Since the licence for it can be renewed as long as it is used, it has in effect an indefinite life. It may be licensed to other manufacturers for a specific use and time period, as is the "Pierre Cardin" trademark. For someone purchasing such trademark rights, the market value and the useful life are clear, and the main issue left is deciding the pattern of amortization.

A **copyright** is the right to publish material such as books, records, tapes, and computer programs. An individual and an individual's estate can hold a copyright for that person's lifetime plus fifty years. A firm can hold it for seventy-five years from first publication. The issues of valuation and useful life are similar to those of patents.

A **franchise agreement** gives the purchaser the right to operate under the name of the franchisor, usually in a specified territory for a stated period of time and subject to certain specific conditions. Examples would be fast-food franchises such as McDonald's, Wendy's, and Burger King. Franchises are also found in real estate (Century 21), hardware stores (Home Hardware), and hotels (Holiday Inn). The purchaser of the franchise is assuming that its possession will provide some special advantage that will benefit future periods for an amount at least as great as the amount paid. The accounting problem is to match the cost of the franchise against the periods that benefit from it. The purchase price of the franchise and its terms would normally be the basis for the annual amortization.

In addition to these particular types, there are many other identifiable intangible assets. For example, a mailing list may be developed with the company or bought from another company which has developed such a list and is willing to sell it. Depending on its nature, the list could then be used for selling consumer items by direct mail (such as magazines, radios, or travel) or for soliciting funds for a charitable organization. If the list is purchased, the cost would then be amortized over its useful life.

A company may defer the costs of developing a major product until the point at which it comes on the market. For example, Canadair deferred the costs of developing its Challenger executive jet, intending to amortize these costs over the aircraft produced and sold. Lockheed Aircraft did the same thing with its Tri-Star, or L-1011, passenger jet. In both cases the management ultimately decided that the sales forecast had been too optimistic, and they consequently made large write-offs of these deferred costs.

With the rapid spread of cable TV, municipalities invited competitive bids from cable TV companies. To acquire the franchises, the companies incurred large expenses. Sometimes the companies bought the franchises from existing owners, paying substantial sums for the customer base (in the same manner as the purchaser of a magazine pays a significant amount of the purchase consideration for the developed mailing list).

A catch-all term, **deferred charges**, is sometimes used to describe assets of an intangible nature. It literally means a charge (debit) that has not yet been classed as a period expense. This is not a very helpful description for the reader, and its use is gradually fading in favour of more informative titles. One cannot tell from the term itself whether the asset is identifiable. Long-term deferred charges usually arise from the matching process. It is often hard to give them an economic interpretation. For example, the initial costs of organizing the company might be classed as a deferred charge, as might deferred debt discount or deferred income taxes. The *CICA Handbook* recommends that major items within deferred charges should be disclosed separately [*CICA* 3070.02]; that they should not be classified as current assets [*CICA* 3070.01]; and that if amortization has been deducted, this fact should also be disclosed [*CICA* 3070.03].

Prepaid expenses represent expenditures made in a current or prior period for items that are expected to benefit a future period. Examples would be an insurance premium for a policy expected to last longer than a year, prepaid rental expenses, or interest paid in advance. If the benefit is expected to be received by the end of the next period, it is classed as a current asset. Otherwise, it is classed as a non-current asset. A prepaid expense fits the general description of an intangible asset: it has no physical existence (and often no market value); but if material, it is usually shown as a separate item on the balance sheet.

NON-IDENTIFIABLE INTANGIBLE ASSETS

As suggested in the chart at the beginning of this section, non-identifiable intangible assets are generally referred to as **goodwill**.

How is it possible for a company to have an asset that it cannot identify? Further, if it cannot identify such an asset, how does the convention of conservatism allow it to be recorded on the books of the company? To understand this, it is necessary to understand why there is usually a difference between the value of the individual assets that make up the firm and the total that a purchaser would be willing to pay for the firm as a whole.

Consider, for example, a successful firm of chartered accountants. Except under exceptional "distress" circumstances, the going concern value will usually be more than the value of the individual assets because some assets disappear if a business is broken up and sold off as individual assets. Such assets include the firm's reputation in the business community, the spirit of teamwork built up among the management group of the partnership, and the shared expertise of its technical staff.

If we wanted to establish the total value of the *individual assets* of a company, we would establish market values for the following: (i) physical assets such as inventory, land, buildings, and equipment; (ii) legal rights to collect money, such as accounts receivable and bonds; and (iii) legal rights to enjoy benefits not available to the public at large, such as patents, copyrights, royalties, franchises, trademarks, and trade names. Adding up the individual values would give the total value of the individual assets.

If we wanted to calculate the value of the company as a *going concern*, however, we would take a different approach and estimate the future benefits the firm would bring to its owners. This might be estimated by calculating the expected present value of the future earnings, as follows:

1. List the expected financial benefits that will flow to the owners from each year's future ownership.

2. Find the present value of these benefits.

3. Sum the individual present values to find the total expected value of the firm.

Playing a definite but hard-to-define role in influencing a valuation of the firm as a whole would be such things as (i) the evaluation of the management skills of the company's executives and whether they would stay after the purchase; (ii) how loyal the company's customers are and how much advertising one would be able to avoid by the purchase of this customer base; (iii) the technical expertise one would be able to inherit by keeping on the technical staff of the company; (iv) the organizational start-up costs to be avoided by buying a company that had already paid legal fees of incorporation and the initial cost of finding financing; and (v) any special advantages that would be enjoyed because of barriers, such as government regulations or zoning laws, that discourage or prevent others from entering that business.

The assets referred to above are intangible assets of a special type. They are generally lumped together under the label of goodwill, which is another name for a non-identifiable intangible asset. Although it is usually not possible to put a valuation on goodwill directly, we can infer its total value as follows:

1. Place a valuation on the business as a going concern, as above.

2. Place a valuation on the identifiable assets if sold individually.

3. Deduct (2) from (1) to get an estimate of goodwill. Usually the amount will be positive, although negative goodwill is not unknown.

Note that the total valuation placed on the shares of a company in a public stock market is rarely the same as the net market value of the assets owned by the firm. The difference arises for two main reasons. First, the firm has assets that have no value once the firm has been broken up (as discussed above). Second, a firm's shares have a day-to-day value that is influenced by general factors in the stock market such as overall interest rates, the standing of the industry the company is in, and attitudes toward risk. The price of the individual assets may be only indirectly influenced by these factors and at a much slower rate.

It is possible that a firm is worth more if it is broken up and its individual assets sold off. If in addition a break-up seems unlikely, the shares would have a market value below the total value of the individual assets.

Let us work through an example of how to estimate goodwill. Here is the condensed balance sheet of Battersea Corporation, showing both the book value and the market value of its net assets.

BATTERSEA CORPORATION
CONDENSED BALANCE SHEET
As at 31 December 19X5

	Book value	Market value
Cash	$ 1,500.00	$ 1,500.00
Accounts receivable	12,568.00	11,250.00
Inventory	24,583.00	22,150.00
	38,651.00	34,900.00
Plant assets	25,000.00	
Accumulated depreciation	(14,890.00)	
Net	10,110.00	5,600.00
Total Assets	$ 48,761.00	$ 40,500.00
Current liabilities	$ 27,590.00	$ 27,590.00
Owners' equity	21,171.00	12,910.00
Total	$ 48,761.00	$ 40,500.00

This summary indicates that if the individual assets of the firm were sold, they would realize a total of $40,500; and when the current liabilities of $27,590 were discharged, there would be $12,910 left for the owners. Now let us assume that the business is going to be sold ten years hence and that the proceeds on sale will be paid out as a liquidating dividend. Let us further suppose that dividends are to be paid out at the end of each year, starting in 19X6, for ten years. These future dividends are estimated to be as follows:

Year	Dividends		Year	Dividends
1	$ 3,500.00		6	$ 6,000.00
2	$ 3,500.00		7	$ 6,000.00
3	$ 4,500.00		8	$ 6,000.00
4	$ 5,500.00		9	$ 6,000.00
5	$ 6,000.00		10	$ 25,000.00

The expected present value of these future dividends can be found by totalling the present value of each. Suppose the discount factor is 10%. Then, the expected value of the first year's payment of $3,500 is calculated as follows:

Present value = 3,500/1.10 = 3,181.82

Similarly, the present value of the payment of $3,500 in the second year is calculated as follows:

Present value = 3,500/1.10/1.10 = 2,892.56

In the chart below we show the present value of each of the ten payments. Thus the total present value of this stream is the sum, or $38,385.40.

Year	Dividends	Present value		Year	Dividends	Present value
1	$ 3,500.00	$ 3,181.82		6	$ 6,000.00	$ 3,386.84
2	$ 3,500.00	$ 2,892.56		7	$ 6,000.00	$ 3,078.95
3	$ 4,500.00	$ 3,380.92		8	$ 6,000.00	$ 2.799.04
4	$ 5,500.00	$ 3,756.57		9	$ 6,000.00	$ 2,544.59
5	$ 6,000.00	$ 3,725.53		10	$ 25,000.00	$ 9.638.58

Continuing with our example, let us assume that another company, Verona Inc., wanted to buy Battersea's assets and business and assume responsibility for its liabilities. Battersea was willing to sell for the present value of the expected receipts, or $38,385.40. Suppose the sale was transacted at that price. The journal entry in Battersea's books would be as follows:

Co. Sold

Cash	38,385.40	
Plant assets — accumulated depreciation	14,890.00	
Current liabilities	27,590.00	
Cash		1,500.00
Accounts receivable		12,568.00
Inventory		24,583.00
Plant assets		25,000.00
Gain on sale		17,214.40

book Value

To record sale to Verona of all assets and assumption of the debt of this company.

Note that if one valued Battersea by adding up the value of its individual assets, it is worth only $12,910; but the earning power of the company produces a price based on expected value of $38,385.40. The difference of $25,475.40 represents the value of the goodwill, or the excess of the value of the whole firm over the sum of its individual assets. It is normally never recorded except when the firm is sold, as in this example.

The journal entry in Verona's books to record the purchase would read as follows:

Co. buying

Cash	1,500.00	
Accounts receivable — gross	12,568.00	
Inventory	22,150.00	
Plant assets	5,600.00	
Goodwill	25,475.40	
Allowance for doubtful accounts		1,318.00
Current liabilities		27,590.00
Cash		38,385.40

market value

To record purchase of the assets and assumption of the liabilities of Battersea Corporation. Tangible assets are recorded at their market value as of the date of the purchase, and the difference between the total purchase price and net tangible assets is goodwill.

Note that the tangible assets are brought into the books of Verona at their market value as of the time of the purchase. The historic cost of the assets to Battersea is not relevant to Verona. In addition, although Verona is satisfied that the business is worth $38,385.40, it is only able to identify assets with a total net market value of $12,910.00.

The difference is the excess earning power of Battersea as a going concern, which we have labelled goodwill.

There seems to be ample evidence that goodwill, despite its intangible and non-identifiable nature, is an asset that purchasers are willing to pay for. Once it is purchased, should it be amortized over its useful life? The answer in principle is yes. Differences of opinion arise over estimating the useful life of something that is both intangible and non-identifiable. Some argue that the goodwill they have purchased has an indefinite life and should not be amortized. However, in both Canada and the United States the standard-setting bodies have stated that goodwill should be amortized over a period not exceeding forty years. It is common to find the forty-year period chosen in published reports. To circumvent the requirements of the standard-setting bodies, companies also commonly decide that they have not purchased goodwill at all, but some identifiable intangible asset that has an indefinite estimated life.

Before the introduction of the *CICA Handbook* requirement in 1974 to amortize purchased goodwill, there must have been a temptation for the management of some companies to treat as much as possible of the purchase price as goodwill. At that time goodwill would not have been depreciated whereas most plant assets would have been. Thus, assigning a large portion of the purchase price to goodwill would have significantly reduced the amount of the annual fixed charges for depreciation and amortization.

Note that the purchase of goodwill has been recorded on the books of the buying company. In Chapter 19 on consolidated financial statements, we will be examining *goodwill on consolidation*, which would arise if Verona had purchased the shares of Battersea instead of its assets. It will become apparent that goodwill on consolidation has some similarities to the goodwill explained here, although it is not recorded as a separate item on the books of the producing company.

Present Accounting Treatment

The *CICA Handbook* gives scant attention to the accounting treatment of intangibles in general [*CICA* 3080] and more attention to research and development costs [*CICA* 3450]. Section 1580 deals with goodwill on consolidation. In the United States, the Accounting Principles Board, and later the FASB, have issued pronouncements on accounting for intangible assets, and these have influenced Canadian practice. In general, the differences in accounting treatment between the two countries have turned on whether the asset is (i) identifiable and (ii) purchased, not internally generated. The Canadian standards for the treatment of intangibles are as follows:

1. Identifiable intangible assets such as patents, copyrights, royalties, franchises, and trademarks may be carried on the financial statements as assets provided they have been purchased from an outsider. They should be amortized over their useful life, but in no case can this exceed forty years. The *Handbook* requires separate disclosure of major items making up the intangibles, both identifiable and non-identifiable [*CICA* 3080.01]. It also requires disclosure of the basis of their valuation [*CICA* 3080.02]. If amortization has been deducted in arriving at the valuation, this must be disclosed as well [*CICA* 3080.03].

2. Identifiable intangible assets that have not been purchased but were created by the

company's own staff can be considered to be either a period cost or a capital addition, with the exception of research and development costs. In practice, such assets are nearly always expensed except for development costs. **Research costs** are defined as "part of a continuing activity required to maintain an enterprise's business and its competitive position" [*CICA* 3450.15]. **Development costs** are those "normally undertaken with a reasonable expectation of commercial success and of future benefits arising from the work, either in increased revenue or from reduced costs" [*CICA* 3450.17]. It is the *Handbook's* view that research costs cannot be readily matched to the periods expected to benefit from them, whereas under certain conditions development costs can be so matched and should be deferred to those periods that benefit from them. Deferral is justified if *all* of the following conditions are met for the the product or process in question: (a) it is clearly defined and the costs in question can be identified; (b) technical feasibility is established; (c) management has indicated it intends to go ahead with the project; (d) the future market and/or internal usefulness has been established; and (e) the company has adequate resources to complete the project [*CICA* 3450.21]. If these conditions are not met in the year of the expenditure, then the expenditure must be charged as an expense of the period in which it is made. Even if evidence later comes to light that would have justified capitalization, it cannot be done retroactively [*CICA* 3450.25]. (By contrast, in the U.S. development costs may not be deferred even if the above criteria are met. This is set out in the FASB's *Statement of Accounting Standards No. 2*.)

3. Intangible assets that cannot be individually identified, such as customer goodwill and monopoly rights, are never capitalized if they were created by the company itself, even if they were created at heavy expense.

4. However, if non-identifiable intangible assets are purchased from outsiders, capitalization is then permissible and the maximum amortization period is the useful life of the asset purchased, within the forty-year limit.

The Canadian standards for the accounting treatment of intangibles are summarized in the chart below.

	Identifiable	*Non-Identifiable*
Purchased	Capitalize outlays	Capitalize the excess of purchase amount over identifiable assets purchased
Internally developed	May be capitalized or expensed, except for research and development. Under certain circumstances, development may also be capitalized. (In the U.S. both research and development must be expensed.)	Expense

EVALUATION AND CRITIQUE
OF PRESENT ACCOUNTING STANDARDS

Why are present accounting standards sometimes arbitrary and inconsistent in their treatment of intangible assets? The reason appears to be the inability to find objective evidence to verify the economic value of most intangibles. Readers of financial statements expect the external auditors of a company to satisfy themselves that assets do have economic potential before including them in the statements. The auditors (who heavily influence the setting of accounting standards) find themselves in a very uncomfortable position facing the reporting of intangibles. They may feel that intangibles do in fact exist; but auditors are sceptical that evidence of their economic worth can be found, apart from the assertions of the company's management. Since the financial statements are, in effect, a report on management, auditors never like to be in the position of relying almost exclusively on the opinion of management about the value of some asset.

The problem of reporting on intangibles can therefore be viewed as a problem of missing evidence. The ultimate value of any asset is its ability to confer benefits in the future; and with most intangibles, the evidence is hard to find, except in the form of management testimony. Usually accountants look to the market outside the company to satisfy themselves that a valuation of a given asset on the financial statements is not unreasonable. By their nature, intangible assets that cannot be individually identified are not often traded; consequently the market test is not available. Thus, it is possible for a company to create at great cost a valuable intangible asset, like customer goodwill, but have difficulty establishing its value through any usual market test. The accountants' response to this difficulty in reporting has been the rather arbitrary set of rules that we have explained above in this section.

IMPLICATIONS FOR THE READER OF
FINANCIAL STATEMENTS

Many of the implications for the reader of financial statements will now be apparent. The reader should be very aware when reading financial statements that there has been no attempt to capitalize intangible assets that have been generated within the company if they cannot be individually identified. If they can be individually identified, then intangible assets may be capitalized, but at their historic cost. With most assets, their purchase cost, if reasonably recent, is often a useful proxy for their market value. However, this is unlikely to be true for intangible assets because of their very nature. Hence the amount shown on the balance sheet is not likely to be informative about the value of intangible assets.

Critics have pointed out that managements that are concerned with their bottom line will have an incentive (i) not to make expenditures for non-identifiable intangible assets and (ii) to purchase their research and development rather than produce it themselves. According to present rules, if management creates the asset themselves, it must be charged to expense as incurred; but if they purchase the asset, they can amortize the expense over its useful life.

Examples from Published Reports

Examination of the balance sheets of many companies indicates that they show no significant intangible assets. For example, The Minnesota Mining and Manufacturing Company shows just a small amount of intangible assets in its balance sheet. This does not mean that 3M does not have any significant intangible assets. In fact the patents it holds over various types of innovative products, such as transparent sealing tapes, audio and video tapes, and the popular yellow "stick-on" notes, are clearly very valuable. The balance sheet simply demonstrates that for accounting purposes the historic cost or the market value (or both) of these brand names has not been capitalized.

The financial statements of 3M were chosen to illustrate a company that does most of its own research and development. The company charges it all to current expense because of U.S. regulations. On the other hand, the financial statements of Baton Broadcasting were chosen to illustrate a company that has purchased a significant amount of intangibles, as a result of its purchases of existing radio and television stations.

Minnesota Mining and Manufacturing Company

Minnesota Mining and Manufacturing Company (3M) is an innovative U.S. company, best known for its *Scotch* brand of transparent tapes and stick-on labels. It does a lot of in-house research and presumably has a number of valuable patents. However, as the second accompanying note below indicates, very little of this research is included in "Other Assets" on the balance sheet.

BALANCE SHEET
(millions of $)

	1986	1985
Other assets	$ 200	$ 182

Accounting Policies
Intangibles: Goodwill, patents and other intangibles are included in other assets. Goodwill is generally amortized on a straight-line basis over 10 years. Other intangibles are amortized on a straight-line basis over their estimated economic lives.
Research and Development: Research and development costs are expensed as incurred and totaled $564 million in 1986, $507 million in 1985 and $457 million in 1984.

Observe that research and development are expensed as incurred. Had this been a Canadian Company, some of the development costs may well have been capitalized.

Baton Broadcasting Incorporated

Baton Broadcasting is a communications company that holds broadcasting licences across Canada.

CONSOLIDATED BALANCE SHEET

	1987	1986
Broadcast licences (note 6)	$ 36,369,507	$ 34,420,187
Goodwill (notes 4 and 6)	25,446,291	24,213,549

Note 1. Change in Accounting Policy

During the year the Company retroactively changed its policy in accounting for the excess of the purchase price over the estimated fair value of net assets acquired whereby the amount paid for broadcast licences of $36,369,507 is segregated from the amount paid for goodwill. Broadcast licences are not amortized but will be written down if it is determined that a permanent impairment in value has occurred. The effect of this change in accounting policy on retained earnings at September 1, 1986, and on net income for the year ended August 31, 1986, is not significant. As a result of this change, amortization for 1987 has been reduced by approximately $770,000. Accordingly, net income has increased by $770,000 or 2.8 cents per share.

Note 4. Goodwill

Goodwill is comprised of:

	1987	1986
Goodwill acquired before April 1, 1974		$ 489,828
Goodwill acquired on or after April 1, 1974 (net of accumulated amortization of $1,442,461 in 1987 and $776,491 in 1986)	$ 25,446,291	23,723,721
	$ 25,446,291	$ 24,213,549

Note 6. Acquisition

On February 27, 1987, the Company purchased the 10% minority interest in the television operations of CKCK-TV serving Regina, Saskatchewan, Canada. This acquisition has been accounted for by the purchase method and earnings therefrom are included from the date of acquisition. Assets acquired and consideration given are as follows:

Net assets acquired	$ 564,226
Broadcast licence acquired	2,126,000
Goodwill acquired	2,388,544
Consideration given	$ 5,078,770

Observe the splitting of goodwill between that acquired before and after 1 April 1974. According to the *Handbook*, goodwill acquired after that date must be amortized. The company has used the maximum amortization period of forty years, which gives it the maximum deferral in writing off this asset. The company does not explain why it has two policies for amortization. Moreover, the company does not amortize its licences and goodwill depending on whether they were acquired before or after 1 April 1974. This approach is not conceptually logical. However, 1 April 1974 was the date the

Handbook acquired a new section, 3080.05, that said goodwill arising from a business combination should be accounted for in accordance with the provision of Section 1580 on business combinations. Section 1580.58 in turn says: "The amount reflected as goodwill at date of acquisition should be amortized to income by the straight-line method over the estimated life of such goodwill; however, such period should not exceed forty years. The period of amortization should be disclosed." The *Handbook* does *not* require retroactive changes to new accounting standards.

On occasion the introduction of a new accounting standard can cause difficulties because of pre-existing contracts. For example, requiring that a company start amortizing goodwill will mean that their reported income will be lower than expected. Pre-existing legal arrangements with respect to executive remuneration or debt covenants may be based on the income reported under generally accepted accounting principles. A new standard may effectively change the terms of these contracts.

Note that the company has adopted the forty-year amortization period. This term, coupled with the policy of not amortizing acquisitions prior to 1 April 1974, will give the minimum annual amortization costs. It is hard to be overly critical of the substance of this arrangement because the value of goodwill and broadcast rights may very well last indefinitely.

The company policy of making write-downs "if it is determined that a permanent impairment in value has occurred" is not particularly satisfactory for the reader because the criterion is highly subjective. It is reminiscent of the practice around the turn of the century of depreciating fixed assets at an amount chosen annually at management's discretion. The *Handbook* recommendation of 1 April 1974, while arbitrary, at least moved the process of amortizing onto a more consistent base.

The amount paid by the company for broadcast licences is a good example of the purchase of an identifiable intangible asset. Broadcast licences are issued by the Canadian Radio and Television Commission (CRTC). There are a limited number of licences issued for a given city. The holder of a commercial radio licence then has the right to broadcast commercial messages in return for a fee. It is the fee from advertising revenues that make the licence valuable. The CRTC rarely cancels a licence once it is issued. Therefore, the owner of a station is effectively able to sell its licence along with its broadcast facilities. In calculating the purchase price, the buyer and seller would first make an estimate of the earning power of the radio station. Then they would consider the amount by which the purchase price exceeded the market value of the tangible assets to represent the broadcast licence, an identifiable intangible asset.

Summary

Most firms have many intangible assets, but only certain of these assets appear on the balance sheet. Most of the ones shown are those purchased ready-made, particularly those that are identifiable intangible assets.

Goodwill on balance sheets usually arises when the assets of an existing business are purchased and it becomes apparent from the price paid that the value of the business as a going concern is worth more than its individual indentifiable assets.

While generally accepted accounting principles for the treatment of intangible assets are fairly clear, they are often hard to apply because of the various kinds of intangible assets. In addition, critics say that the application of the standards leads to results that are inconsistent for similar items.

QUESTIONS

Q9-1. Review and be sure you understand the following terms:
  a. intangible asset
  b. identifiable *versus* non-identifiable intangible assets
  c. patent
  d. trademark
  e. copyright
  f. franchise agreement
  g. deferred charge
  h. goodwill
  i. going-concern value of a business
  j. research costs
  k. development costs

Q9-2. Explain in your own words why a company might be worth more than the market value of its individual assets. Give examples. What is the proper accounting treatment for this excess?

Q9-3. Explain whether each of the following are intangible assets within generally accepted accounting principles. If not, do you think they should be classed as intangible assets? Explain.
  a. The cost of training the staff at the start of a business.
  b. The initial advertising campaign when a sport store opens up in a college town.
  c. The cost of doing the major redesign of an existing model of a car.
  d. The cost of developing a new jet engine. It is expected to take three years from the start of development before the first sale is made.
  e. The purchase cost of a mailing list. It is expected to have a useful life of eight months if not kept updated, but the company has plans for the updating.

Q9-4. The editor of *Harrowsmith* Magazine was quoted as saying that the magazine's auditors look on his mailing list as a liability since it represents the subscribers who have paid but are still owed magazines. However, the editor said that he regarded the list as an asset. Who is right? Explain.

Q9-5. Explain the apparent reason that accountants are willing to capitalize assets created by research if they are purchased (e.g., through buying a patent right) but not if they are developed within the company. Do you agree with this treatment? Explain.

Q9-6. Exxol Corporation paid $150,000 for the right to use a patented process that would reduce its manufacturing costs. The right to use this patent lasts for five years, and in that time the company expects to process six million gallons of product using the patented process. A newly hired accounting student suggested that the $150,000 cost should be amortized annually on the basis of the actual number of gallons processed versus the total expected gallonage over the life of the patent agreement. The chief account disagreed, saying, "You could have been right a few years ago, but GAAP now states that research and development costs should be expensed as incurred, and all we've done is buy someone else's research and development." Which, if either, is right? Explain.

Q9-7. Company A developed a manufacturing method that saved it $10,000 a year. It cost $75,000 to develop. You overheard the comment: "The $75,000 will not be shown on the balance sheet. Therefore the company's financial statements will never reflect the financial benefit the company is receiving from its money-saving development." Do you agree? Explain.

Q9-8. In a biography of Sir Alexander Korda, a flamboyant movie producer and director of the 1930s and 1940s, his nephew, Michael Korda, told how his uncle improved the reported financial results for his studio, London Films, by "a simple matter of accounting" using the following devices:

(i) He carried on the books as assets unfinished films, finished films that were too bad to release, and scripts and literary properties that could never be made into films. Thus, his nephew reports that "every disaster could be used to improve the balance sheet, and the larger the disasters, the rosier the prospects of the company would seem." This "basic principle of accounting" was exploited even further by Korda, who bought up foreign films, which were left in the vaults and "carried on the books for year after year as assets."

(ii) He bought up screen rights for published works, hoping that the sale of these rights would be a later source of profit. In addition, "they could be carried as assets, provided nothing was ever done with them."

Required:
a. Describe under what conditions, if any, the above would have worked as described.
b. Would the "simple matter of accounting" described above be consistent with GAAP as they are understood today?

Q9-9. The assets of S Ltd., a going concern, were purchased by M Ltd., which paid for the assets by issuing 10,000 of its shares to S Ltd. The market value of the individual identifiable assets of S Ltd. was $300,000 and their book value was $450,000. On the day of the sale the shares of M Ltd. were traded on a public stock exchange for $50, but on the day the agreement was signed they were trading for $60. How much goodwill, if any, should be recorded on the books of M. Ltd. with respect to the purchase of S Ltd.?

Q9-10. A newspaper chain purchases a small-town newspaper for a sum that is $350,000 in excess of its assets other than circulation and goodwill. Discuss how this purchase difference might be split between these two asset categories.

Q9-11. The financial press reported that Abitibi paper company had closed a plant in Chicago. Because the plant was in existence when new anti-pollution laws had come into effect, it was granted what amounted to a licence to add a certain amount of pollution to the Chicago air. Furthermore, this licence could be sold. Imagine that you are the controller of the company that has recently bought this licence and that you paid $1,200,000 for it. Where, if at all, would you put it on the balance sheet? If you do consider it to be an asset, what amortization policy, if any, would you recommend?

Q9-12. "Generally accepted accounting principles for intangible assets are an inconsistent mess." Do you agree? Explain.

Q9-13. A practising accountant was quoted as saying "The only reason for recording intangibles on the balance sheet is to avoid having the debits on the income statement." Explain in your own words what might have been meant by this statement. What would be so wrong with "having the debits on the income statement"?

Q9-14. In Ontario, wineries are permitted to have a limited number of retail stores in which they sell their product direct to the consumer at the same markup taken by the provincial liquor stores. As a result these retail stores can be very profitable. Should the manager of such a store be paid an extra-generous salary because of this profitable operation? If not, who "deserves" to get this extra income? Justify your answer in terms of who has contributed the most valuable earning assets to the operation.

Q9-15. It has been suggested that the present accounting treatment of research and development will have a "feedforward" effect in that managers will not want to make expenditures for "assets" that are not treated as assets on the financial statements. Why might this be so?

Q9-16. "Capitalizing the goodwill on the purchase of a radio station is nothing but the capitalization of the licensing body's unwillingness to cancel a licence once it is given." Do you agree? Explain.

Q9-17. *The Financial Times* of Canada carried a lengthy article on the inconsistent treatment of "research and development" expenses. It emphasized the following points:

(i) Many company executives believe that "the high-technology industry is too unpredictable to assume that deferred costs will ever be recovered from future product sales."

(ii) There is "no consistent treatment" of capitalizing research and development costs. For example, of thirteen publicly traded "high-tech" companies, seven write off all research and development costs while the others have chosen various forms of capitalization.

(iii) Existing standards allow "total management discretion" in deciding if the "highly subjective" criteria for capitalizing research and development costs are met. Outside auditors are "simply not qualified to police management's deferral decision."

(iv) Newly established companies find that deferral of development costs "makes the company more attractive to investors" and thus helps them to raise necessary capital.

Required: Comment on the validity of the points listed above.

Q9-18. In Canada there is no requirement that *all* intangible assets should be amortized, only certain specified ones such as goodwill. As a result it is possible to classify a purchase difference as an intangible such as "circulation list" or "customer base" and then choose to leave it unamortized. In the U.S., however, all purchased intangible assets must be amortized over not more than forty years. Which practice do you think allows the better opportunity to fit the amortization policy to the economic facts in a given case? Which is more open to moral hazard? Discuss.

Q9-19. The only labour services that are routinely classed as assets instead of expenses are those of factory labour (which may be included in inventory). According to some people, it is "not completely logical" that a company should set up a wages liability for the services it has received from its supervisory staff without also considering whether their services might have created a long-term asset which might also be recorded. Do you agree? Explain.

Q9-20. One of the strong practical arguments for expensing instead of capitalizing research and development is that the projects frequently take place over several years and one cannot tell which, if any, will turn out to be economically worthwhile. Suppose that a friend says, "This sounds very similar to the problem of accounting for oil well drilling, but in that industry they are willing to assume that drilling dry holes is a part of finding holes with oil in them. Wouldn't it be possible to develop some kind of 'full costing' approach to research and development?" Give a thoughtful reply.

Q9-21. Imagine that a Canadian company bought a machine tool for $180,000 for the sole purpose of using it in a project that was considered, for accounting purposes, to be for development (not research).

Required:

a. According to Canadian accounting standards, should the asset be classified as a plant asset, with depreciation charged to a Development Account (where it would be capitalized and later amortized)? Or should the total cost of the equipment be charged directly to the Development Account?

b. What would be the accepted accounting treatment if the company were in the U.S.? Should the company include the machine tool with plant assets, but charge the depreciation to expense annually? Or should it immediately expense the machine tool at the time it is purchased?

Q9-22. A company recently acquired two assets: a new car and a patent for an improvement in a machine tool that it manufactured. Are the balance sheet figures equally representative of market value for each asset? Would your answer be any different if the company had purchased the patent right instead of doing the development work itself? Explain.

PROBLEMS

P9-1. Look up in the business press the accounting history of *one* of the following companies with respect to accounting for intangible assets. (For a Canadian company, use a Canadian source such as *The Financial Post*, *The Globe and Mail Report on Business*, or *The Financial Times*; for a U.S. company, use a U.S. source such as *The Wall Street Journal*.)

  (i) Canadair Limited

 (ii) Thomson Newspapers Limited

(iii) Minnesota Mining and Manufacturing Company

(iv) Rogers Cablesystems Inc.

 (v) Mitel Limited

(vi) Lockheed Aircraft Corporation

Required:

Write an essay of around 400 words that focuses on one accounting problem in the treatment of intangibles of the company you have chosen. Organize your essay around the following:

a. State the nature of the accounting problem that caused the press coverage.

b. Indicate whether the accounting appears to have been done according to GAAP.

c. Discuss any special circumstances that probably made the accounting problem particularly difficult.

d. Consider how GAAP might be changed in future to remedy such a problem.

P9-2. A friend is interested in buying a florist business and he asks your advice about a small business he has located that might be for sale. He shows you the following balance sheet:

	Book value	Market value
Cash	$ 1,250.00	$ 1,250.00
Inventory	5,600.00	5,000.00
Fixtures (net)	1,200.00	3,500.00
Truck	9,800.00	8,500.00
Total assets	$ 17,850.00	$ 18,250.00
Accounts payable	$ 5,500.00	$ 5,500.00
Equity	12,350.00	12,750.00
	17,850.00	18,250.00

"I know it's not very large," he says, "but I think I would look on owning it as a learning experience, and I would expect to sell it and move to something a little more challenging at the end of three years. I estimate that I can take home $2,250 in excess of my normal wages at the end of the first year, $3,890 at the end of the second, and at the end of the third year I can sell it for $15,890. (I know those figures look over-precise, but that's the way the forecast came out when I did it on my personal computer!) The cost of money to me is about 12%, and I have calculated the present value of these three years of additional earnings to be worth $16,420 now. When I purchase the business I want the inventory, fixtures, and truck, and the right to carry on business under the florist's name. I don't want the cash and I want the owner to pay the accounts payable himself, so I have adjusted the third year recovery value of $15,890 accordingly."

Required:

a. What is the maximum price you would advise your friend to pay for the business? Show your calculations. Explain your reasons.

b. Assuming he got it for the maximum price you recommend, show the journal entry to record on his books the acquisition of the business assets. Assume he pays cash.

P9-3. You are approached with an offer to buy an existing franchise to sell programs and soft drinks at a football stadium. The market value of the assets and liabilities to be turned over to you are given below:

Cash	$ 4,850.00
Accounts receivable	11,560.00
Inventory	3,280.00
	$ 19,690.00
Accounts payable	$ 8,950.00
Net value	10,740.00
	$ 19,690.00

The franchise has five more years to run, at which time it lapses and is put out for tender again. Thus, it has no resale value at that time. Ignoring taxes, you estimate that the cash earnings, in addition to normal wages, that can be taken out at the end of each year are as follows:

Year	Earnings
1	$ 2,450.00
2	$ 2,450.00
3	$ 2,890.00
4	$ 3,680.00
5	$ 4,590.00

Required:

a. What is the present value of the projected earnings, assuming that the interest rate is 10%?

b. Show the journal entry to record the purchase of the business assets, assuming it was purchased for the present value of its earnings.

c. What would be the present value of the same earnings if you assumed an interest rate of 15%? Would you still recommend buying the business? Explain.

P9-4. Assume that the CICA Accounting Standards Committee is adamant about putting a section in the *CICA Handbook* saying that companies should value all identifiable intangible assets on their balance sheets at their current market value. They ask you for assistance. Write a supporting memo of no more than 500 words in which you (i) state the general principles to be followed in valuing all assets; (ii) state how the new standard differs from present standards; and (iii) assess the practical problems of implementing the proposed standard.

P9-5. In 19X6, an investor is considering the purchase of a local franchise outlet. She obtains the following information for three possible acquisitions:

	Franchise 1	Franchise 2	Franchise 3
Market value of			
Assets	$ 240,000	$ 450,000	$ 500,000
Liabilities	140,000	300,000	400,000
Cash flow from operations			
19X1	$ 20,000	$ 40,000	$ 20,000
19X2	20,000	40,000	40,000
19X3	20,000	30,000	10,000
19X4	20,000	30,000	0
19X5	20,000	20,000	30,000
Liquidation value at end of			
19X5	$ 50,000	$ 100,000	$ 70,000
Required rate of return	15%	15%	10%

Required: Calculate the amount that the investor should be willing to pay for each franchise. Prepare the journal entry to record the acquisition at that price.

P9-6. Many companies develop computer software to sell or lease to users of computer systems. Activities range from the development of concepts for new software to routine improvements of existing products.

Required:

a. Prepare a report of no more than 250 words to the owner of such a company setting out accounting policies for the treatment of costs incurred to arrive at their end product. (*Hint:* What constitutes "research," "development," and "production"?)

b. As an investor, what treatment would you prefer for these costs? What response would you expect from the accounting standard-setting bodies? Is this likely to differ between the U.S. and Canada?

P9-7. The Fargo Corp. received an offer from a large competitor for 100% of the company at a price that was three times the book value of its tangible assets. For various reasons the deal was never completed. Later that year, Fargo approached the bank for a loan and was turned down because its assets were insufficient as collateral.

Required: What arguments and information could Fargo Corp. submit to the bank to try to persuade it to change its decision? Be as specific as possible. (*Hint*: Consider the types of conditions that would explain the competitor's offer earlier in the year.)

P9-8. The Bright-Ideas Group Ltd. discover and patent a new device. They are immediately offered $2 million for the patent rights, which they decline. Unfortunately, the patent process used all the company's cash reserves. Therefore, they approach the bank to borrow an amount sufficient to set up the production facilities. Their request is turned down because they have insufficient asset collateral.

Required: What arguments and information could Bright-Ideas submit to the bank to try to persuade it to change its decision?

P9-9. On 1 January 19X1 a group of friends formed a new company to develop, manufacture, and market a revolutionary new product to be used in electronics manufacturing. The initial design work had been done by one of the individuals in a garage. By 31 December 19X1, production of the new product had not begun, but a working prototype was being tested. In that first year, the company had incurred the following costs:

Design and engineering studies	$ 150,000
Market research	$ 50,000
Administration expenses including salaries, interest on bank loans, etc.	$ 200,000
Design equipment with an expected useful life of four years	$150,000
Manufacturing equipment for the prototype and the final product with an expected useful life of eight years	$ 350,000

At the end of the first year, the company projected that sales would be as follows:

19X2	50,000 units
19X3	100,000
19X4	150,000
19X5	100,000

Required:

a. Outline the practical and conceptual reasons for the conclusions arrived at by the standard-setting groups in Canada and the U.S. for accounting for research and development.

b. According to the *CICA Handbook*, how shoud the costs outlined above be accounted for in 19X1?

c. In 19X2, 60,000 units were produced and 25,000 were sold. What journal entries are required with respect to the costs listed above? Assume depreciation is based on units of production.

P9-10. In recent years there have been a number of cases reported in the financial press where a company makes an offer for the *shares* of another company and the price bid exceeds the trading price of the target company's stock. Assuming rational behaviour on the part of the management of the bidding company, what issues raised in this chapter might explain this situation?

P9-11. A company whose prime activity is writing software for other companies to use with their computers has followed the practice of treating this software as work-in-process inventory until it is completely developed and the customer has accepted it. They do not use the percentage-of-completion method for recognizing income. Critics of the company's approach think expenditures on software should be considered as an expense since "the software is just a pile of computer tapes and ring-bound books." However, the president of the company is strongly in favour of the current accounting practice, saying, "the key distinction between our spending on this software and equivalent spending on research and development is recoverability. We are developing something we know we can sell. We have backlog of orders to prove it. To expense it would be misleading."

Required: Do you agree? Discuss the merits of the present's view about capitalizing the expenditure, disregarding all you know about the treatment recommended by the *CICA Handbook* or the FASB.

P9-12. *The Wall Street Journal* reports that the owner of Falstaff Brewery, the "senior citizen of the brewing industry," bought near-bankrupt breweries and ran them profitably "his own way". He managed them tightly, reducing their advertising budgets and selling prices. Also, he was not reluctant to go to court over a dispute (e.g., he refused to move one of his breweries in Los Angeles with the result that the Santa Ana Freeway has to take "a rather significant bend" around it). A beer consultant who has studied his strategy says, "Sure, his market share is falling but the rate of decay is about the same as before he took over." Despite the falling market share, however, the breweries he controls have survived because of his extensive cost-cutting.

Required:
a. Evaluate whether the value of the goodwill is rising or falling in this firm.
b. Do you think the accounting goodwill is positive or negative? Explain.
c. How might an investor evaluate the worth of this company? Explain.
d. How might the financial statements be misleading as to the profitability of the company?

P9-13. The president of Sparkle Ltd. asks your advice concerning the appropriate accounting treatment for the acquisition of a patent right. He gives you the following background information. "The company that we bought the patent rights from charged us a flat fee of $24,000 for the use of the patent that allows us to put a protective finish on our product. There are other types of such finishes around, but we thought this one would make our product more competitive. We have the rights for a total of five years, but our competition will introduce a technologically superior product in about four years. We have decided we do not have the resources to keep up technically. So when sales drop to the point where the product is not selling well enough to contribute to our bottom line, we will drop this particular line. In addition to the $500 fees from our lawyer for advising us on the terms of the contract, we have incurred travel expenses of $1,200 and used up about $2,000 of executive time. We will also have to put about $3,000 worth of direct labour into modifying our equipment to apply the new finish. Furthermore, a problem has arisen with the head of our finishing department, who will be retiring in about a year. She has a bonus that is based on her ability to control her cost budget. She is claiming that it would probably be unfair to her if some of the above items were treated as period expenses in her final year."

Required:

In a memo of about 400 words, set out the proper accounting treatment that should be followed for the acquisition of the patent right. In your memo, be sure you do the following:

a. Identify those expenditures, if any, that should be capitalized. Give your reasons.

b. Explain the amortization policy that should be followed.

c. Consider the objection raised by the head of the finishing department and recommend the appropriate treatment of the above costs in the company's internal accounting reports.

P9-14. Consider the following unrelated cases:

(i) Mammoth Newspapers Inc. buys the assets of the sole newspaper in a small town. Mammoth pays $1,200,000 more than the market value of the tangible assets. It attributes $800,000 to goodwill and the difference to circulation. It is the management's private view that the circulation of the newspaper will increase about 3% annually compounded, that newspapers in some form will be in demand indefinitely in that town, and that they have the technological ability to keep abreast of any changes.

(ii) A software company has spent $350,000 developing a custom package that will allow funeral homes to keep their accounts, inventory records, and funeral scheduling on a micro-computer. They have been encouraged to do this by an association of funeral directors that set up a committee that worked very closely with the software developers. A prototype has been used for six months by two funeral homes, and the response to the final product has been enthusiastic. It is proposed to market the software through the association for an annual fee. The income from the annual fees is expected to be $80,000 in the first year and $95,000 thereafter. It is expected that changes in such things as income tax law and funeral regulations will require an annual update of the software at a cost of about $20,000. It is also expected that the software can be used without a major revision for about five years.

(iii) A company that specializes in coating paper for food packaging has paid $15,000 for five-year rights to use a patent that will permit them to expand their range of coatings. When the process was first put into use, it was found that under certain winter conditions it would peel. Consequently, the company spent an additional $10,000 adapting the coating to Canadian conditions. It has patented this adaptation and hopes that the original patent owner will buy the rights for use in other cold climates.

Required:

For each of the three cases above, provide the following:

a. The capitalization and amortization policy according to the recommendations of the *CICA Handbook*.

b. The capitalization and amortization policy that gives the best approximation of net income for the purposes of analysis, regardless of GAAP.

c. The reasons for the differences, if any, between (a) and (b).

P9-15. In anticipation of negotiations for the sale of a particular business, the following projections were made in order to estimate the potential value of goodwill.

Average annual earnings projected (four-year basis)	$ 45,000
Fair value of average net assets expected (exclusive of goodwill)	$ 220,000
"Normal" rate of return on net assets for the industry	15%
Rate of return expected on excess earnings	20%
Expected recovery period for excess earnings	4 years
Year's purchase of average excess earnings	4 years

Required:

a. Calculate the average excess earnings.

b. Estimate goodwill under each of the following independent approaches:

  (i) Goodwill is equal to the capitalized average annual excess earnings as computed in (a) above.

 (ii) Goodwill is equal to the total annual excess earnings, as computed in (a), in the four years following purchase.

(iii) Goodwill is based on present value of average annual excess earnings as computed in (a) above.

(CGA adapted)

P9-16. Examine the financial information provided above in this chapter for Baton Broadcasting Incorporated. Suppose that as an analyst you would like more useful information about Baton's intangible assets. In a one-page memo (300 words maximum), set out any changes in accounting treatment and reporting that you would like to see in their statements.

P9-17. The radio and television regulating authority in Canada awards the licence to broadcast with restrictions on the licensee regarding broadcast policy. There is only a nominal charge for the licence, and it is rare for the licence to be cancelled once it is issued. Suppose that the regulatory authority took a tougher line and cancelled more licences because of non-performance; or alternatively suppose that the regulatory authority put the licence up for auction to the highest bidder every ten years. Write a one-page memo (300 words maximum) setting out the changes, if any, that would have to be made to existing accounting policies of such companies as Baton Broadcasting, Standard Broadcasting, or Tele-Metropole. (Your university library probably has the financial statements of these companies, either in their original or condensed form.)

P9-18. *The Globe and Mail* reported that Rogers Cablesystems Inc. "turns loss into profit by changing accounting rules." It did this by (i) reducing its depreciation costs by $1.6 million, (ii) reducing by $1.1 million "the cost of amortizing goodwill associated with the purchases last year of two cable companies," and (iii) transferring $3 million of franchise costs "to the balance sheet from the income statement." Rogers pointed out that newspapers capitalized new subscribers when buying another paper. Rogers claimed that it was just doing something similar.

Required: Under what circumstances might these three changes be made within generally accepted accounting principles? Explain.

P9-19. *The Economist* Magazine reported that speculation over the demise of Harold Ballard, a 79% owner of Maple Leaf Gardens, had nearly quadrupled the value of his shares. *The Economist* continued as follows: "Leading the speculators is Dr. Morton Shulman, a

Toronto physician who has written a book on how to make a million and writes a column in a Canadian stock tipsheet. Dr. Shulman asked a property specialist to appraise the value of Maple Leaf Gardens' real estate, and spiced it with an evaluation of Mr. Ballard's life expectancy. His conclusion: an octogenarian diabetic who won't follow his diet has a short future."

Required: Look up the financial statements of Maple Leaf Gardens. Write a brief memo on the informativeness of these financial statements, assuming they had been prepared according to GAAP. In your memo you should use *and underline* the following phrases: (i) historic cost, (ii) *market value*, (iii) identifiable intangible assets, and (iv) non-identifiable intangible assets.

P9-20. As a staff accountant of Fine Printing Inc. you are responsible for analyzing the Intangible Assets Account in the general ledger. After your examination you have determined that the entries which have been made to that account during 19X0, the first year of operations of the company, are as follows:

	Debit	Credit
Incorporation fees	$ 9,000	
Printing of stock certificates	2,500	
Stock promotion expense	4,000	
"Start-up" advertising campaign	43,400	
Operating loss during initial three months	25,000	
Computer software (life: 3 years)	18,000	
Research costs	14,900	
Development costs related to specific marketable patents	12,000	
Internally generated goodwill	9,000	
Proceeds on sale of patent		$ 10,000
Accounts payable: research department		6,400

Required:

a. Explain as fully as possible the meaning of the accounting term *goodwill*. Discuss the accounting treatment for recognition of goodwill.

b. Differentiate between *research costs* and *development costs* and give an example of each. What accounting treatments are normally used for each of these types of costs? Justify the accounting treatment of *research costs* in terms of generally accepted accounting principles.

c. Prepare a general journal entry to update the appropriate asset, liability, and expense accounts of Fine Printing Inc. as of 31 December 19X0, the end of its current year. Where appropriate, the company records a full year's amortization in the year of acquisition of assets. Show all your calculations.

(CGA adapted)

P9-21. Give the journal entries that would be needed, as of 31 December 19X1, to correct the accounts for the following unrelated events in Diversified Industries. The company's year-end is 31 December.

a. On 1 June 19X1 a five-year contract was signed giving the company the use of a special patented chemical process that is essential in the production of a new product line. The terms of the contract required the company to pay $60,000 on signing the contract and a further $10,000 1 June for each of the following four year of the contract. The $60,000 was charged to Intangible Assets.

b. On 1 January 19X1 the company purchased Acme Trucking as a going concern, acquiring the assets and assuming the liabilities. Acme had been operating as a sole proprietorship, and the owner-operator agreed to stay on and manage the business. The tangible assets were valued at $350,000 (with an estimated ten-year life with no residual value), and the liabilities at $80,000. The company paid $360,000 for the company. It estimated that the trucking franchise owned by the company was worth $30,000 and the remainder of the amount paid was for goodwill. The company has the policy of depreciating or amortizing all assets using the straight-line method. The franchise has a total expected life of six years. The payment of $360,000 was charged to long-term investments.

c. Computer software that the company expects will save it $35,000 a year in labour costs was licensed for five years for the company's use at an annual fee of $18,000. The company paid the annual fee at the start of the contract on 1 September 19X1, charging it to Software Licence Costs, a charge against current income. It also paid the software company an additional $50,000 on 15 December for its staff to come and adapt the software to the special needs of the company. This was also charged to Software Licence Costs.

d. On 31 July the Company signed a licensing agreement for the use of the logo of a popular baseball team on a line of sports clothing it intended to promote. The agreement called for an initial payment of $125,000 and a royalty of 5% of gross sales on the product line. The payment of $125,000 was charged to Franchises, a balance-sheet item. The licence was to last for five years from the date of signing. As of the end of the current year none of the product line with the logo had been sold.

BIBLIOGRAPHY

EBER, VICTOR I. "The Valuation of Closely Held Corporations." *Journal of Accountancy* (June 1984). Valuation in this situation is especially tricky since there is no external stock market to provide a valuation.

STIVERS, BONNIE P.; KERTZ, CONSUELO L.; and BEARD, LARRY H. "What's Proper Accounting for Software Development?" *CA Magazine* (January 1985). A critique of the existing standards for research and development as applied to computer software.

WISE, ROBERT M. "Some Valuation Concerns in Buy-Sell Agreements." *CA Magazine* (February 1985). Consideration in the valuation of goodwill.

CHAPTER 10
Long-Term Investments

Introduction

Long-term investments is a term reserved for assets that will be held as investments for a period longer than a year. Typically, they consist of shares in other companies, bonds, mortgages, and life insurance policies that have a cash surrender value. A company may own long-term investments for any of the following reasons:

1. **Passive investment:** A company may own the assets for the same motives as a small investor, with the intention of earning income and possible capital gains.

2. **Funding:** A company may own certain assets because it is required to purchase and keep them under the terms of an agreement. For example, a company may be required to build up a fund of liquid assets to redeem a long-term debt that is coming due.

3. **Influence:** A company may hope to influence the policies of another company whose shares it has bought. The goal might be to get more of that company's business, to influence its dividend policy, to gain access to more favourable borrowing rights, to obtain technical expertise, or to ensure a supply of a critical raw material.

4. **Control:** A company may seek control of another company by buying a majority of its voting shares.

The accounting treatment adopted in a particular instance is influenced by the circumstances set out above. Let us now discuss the accounting treatment according to the categories in this list.

Passive Investments

Passive investments (also called **portfolio investments**) are those in which the owners do not expect to influence the policies of the investee company. Examples of passive investments are small shareholdings in other companies, bonds, and mortgages. For example, a person holding one hundred shares of a large corporation does not expect to be able to demand a seat on the board of directors or in any way influence the policies the board adopts. Owners of bonds and mortgages do not normally have voting power on the board except under exceptional circumstances connected with default. In particular, the passive investor does not expect to be able to influence the size of the dividends that are declared. The usual test to determine if an investment is a passive one is whether the investor owns a sufficiently high percentage of the outstanding voting shares to be able to exercise "significant influence" on the policies of the company [*CICA* 3050.21]. We will return to the issue of *significant influence* later.

INCOME RECOGNITION

Income from an investment is a reward for putting money at someone else's disposal for a period of time. Under the matching convention it is the passing of time, rather than receipt of the funds, that influences income recognition. If the income is from a debt investment such as a bond, the income is recognized as a function of the passage of time [*CICA* 3400.09]. If income is considered earned but has not been received, it is *accrued*.

For example, suppose that on 1 July Sunbury Limited bought a $10,000 bond paying 15% interest on 1 July and 1 January of each year. By its next fiscal year-end, 31 December, Sunbury would have received no interest payment, but it would accrue the bond interest as follows:

Bond interest accrued	750.00	
Interest income		750.00

To accrue bond interest for six months, calculated as 1/2 of 15% of $10,000, or $750.00.

The effect of this practice is that the timing of the interest payments does not affect the timing of the income recognition. Income from mortgages would be treated similarly.

If the investment income is material, it should be accrued at the end of each period for which financial reports are issued. This means it should be accrued at least annually, and perhaps as frequently as monthly.

Income from shares, called **dividends,** are not treated the same way as income from a contractual obligation such as a bond. There is no contract between the company and its shareholders that they will be paid dividends over the long term. A dividend is not legally payable until declared by the directors of the company, and they normally do not do this until shortly before the payment date. At the time the dividend is declared, they indicate (i) the rate of the dividend per share, (ii) the date they will close their shareholder list to prepare the dividend cheques (the **record date**), and (iii) the date on which the dividend will be paid (the **payment date**).

The *CICA Handbook* states that the revenue should be recognized "when the shareholder's right to receive payment is established" [*CICA* 3400.09]. This appears to imply it would be appropriate to accrue the dividend from the record date onward. However, it is a common practice to wait until payment is received before considering it to be income.

For example, assume that Sunbury Limited also owned 100 shares of Alpha Limited that has regularly paid dividends of $1.50 per share as of 1 July and 1 January. It would not accrue the dividend unless the directors had met and declared the dividend to be payable. Assume that a dividend of $1.50 per share was declared payable on 1 January to shareholders of record of 11 December. On 31 December Sunbury could accrue the dividend for the amount declared as follows:

Dividend receivable	150.00	
Dividend income		150.00
To accrue dividend payable 1 January to shareholders of		
record of 11 December.		

Although such an entry is quite proper, for expediency a common practice is to wait until the dividend is received and then make the following entry:

Cash	150.00	
Dividend income		150.00
To record dividend received.		

Passive investments are accounted for using the **cost method** [*CICA* 3050.28], in which earnings from these investments are recognized only to the extent they are received or receivable. If dividends on shares are greater than the company's share of post-acquisition income, then any excess is treated as a reduction of the amount of the investment [*CICA* 3050.03 (d)].

Before explaining the revenue recognition rules for bond interest, it is helpful to explain a few key terms. Recall that bonds are simply a contract to pay the holder a fixed amount of money at a specified date and to pay periodic amounts of interest at a rate specified in the bond contract. Let us illustrate the technical terms with a bond that is for $1,000 payable in the year 2000 and that makes interest payments of $50 each six months on 1 June and 1 December:

Maturity date: the date on which the amount owed under the bond becomes due and payable to the holder of the bond. In this case it is the year 2000.

Coupon date: the date when the interest payments under the bond are due. Generally, this would be every six months. In this case it is 1 June and 1 December.

Coupon rate: the interest rate at which the amount of the annual interest payment is calculated. In this case there are two payments of $50 per year. Therefore the coupon rate is $(50 + 50)/1,000$, or 10% payable semi-annually.

Face amount: the amount payable at maturity. In this case it is $1,000. The face amount is also referred to as the **face value** or **par value.**

Market value: the amount that would be paid for the bond in a market where they are traded. The price paid depends on investors' views about the adequacy of the coupon rate compared to the going market rate, its riskiness, etc. If the bond is selling above its face amount, it is said to be selling at a **premium:** if the bond is selling below its face amount, it is said to be selling at a **discount.**

Yield rate: the yield to maturity that an investor can expect if the bond is purchased at its market value.

Purchase date: the date on which the investor enters into a contract with a bond dealer to buy or sell a bond.

Settlement date: the date on which the investor and bond dealer exchange cash for the bond. Some time usually elapses from the purchase date to the settlement date.

Bonds are normally quoted in units of $100. Thus, if a $1,000 bond were selling on the open market for $958, it would be quoted as trading at $95.80. It is understood that the purchaser will, in addition to the quoted price, pay the vendor of the bond for all accrued interest from the last coupon date to the date of settlement. Therefore the accrued interest is not quoted in the price of the bond. Here is a quote from *The Globe and Mail* for bonds of Imperial Oil:

	Coupon	Quote	Yield
15 August 1994	10.63	84.63	13.46%

This means that a bond of $100 face value can be bought for $84.63 and that it will have annual interest payments totalling $10.63. If held to maturity it will yield 13.46% in combined interest and discount between the face amount and the market price. Under the matching concept, if one purchased such a bond with a premium or discount, this difference between face value and market price would be amortized to income over the remaining life of the bond.

The yield of a bond is set by market forces and fluctuates daily. The coupon rate is set when the bond is issued and is not subject to fluctuation. Therefore, it is the current purchase price of the bond that rises or falls in response to the change in the yield demanded by the market. As the yield demanded by the market rises, the price of the bond falls. In other words, the purchaser will pay a smaller premium or be given a larger discount to compensate for the fixed coupon rate. The opposite happens when the market yield falls.

For example, assume that on 1 April 19X6 Sunbury purchased a 15.5% bond with a face value of $1,000 for $1,142.53 to give a yield of 11% computed half yearly. The bond matures in 48 months and pays interest at the end of September and March. Sunbury bought the bond with the intention of holding it until maturity. With a coupon rate of 15.5% the semi-annual interest payments would be $77.50. This means that Sunbury could expect to receive that amount for seven payments, and on the eighth payment it would receive $77.50 plus the face amount of $1000. The journal entry to record the purchase would be as follows:

Long term investment — bond	1,142.53	
Cash		1,142.53

To record purchase of a bond at a premium of $142.53.

The income earned on the bond in each period is the interest payment of $77.50 less a portion of the amortization of the bond premium. There are two main approaches to amortizing the premium: (i) writing it off on a straight-line basis; or (ii) writing in amounts that will produce a constant yield of 11% over the period it is held (termed the **effective-interest method**).

Under the straight-line method the premium is written off in even amounts over the four years. If the company recorded its interest income every six months when the interest payment was made, the entry would be as follows:

Bank	77.50	
Amortization of bond premium		17.82
Interest income		59.68
To record receipt of interest payment and amortization of		
bond premium of $142.53 on a straight-line basis over the		
eight payments of interest.		

Under the effective-interest method the amount taken into income is always equal to 11% of the face value of the bond plus its unamortized premium. This should be contrasted with the straight-line method where the sum taken into income is always the same *amount*, rather than the same *rate*. The calculation using the effective-interest method over the life of the bond is shown below. Note that although the income falls from $62.84 to $56.18, it remains a constant 11% of the amount shown in the "Total" column. Under the effective-interest method, the premium to be amortized is that amount which, when added to the face value times the market interest rate, equals the actual interest payments. So, as we amortize the premium, the face value falls. Thus, over the life of the bond, larger amounts of the premium are amortized and interest income is reduced.

Months elapsed	Face amount of bond	Unamor-tized premium	Total	Income at 11%	Interest payment	Premium amortiza-tion
6	$1,000	$142.53	$1,142.53	$ 62.84	$ 77.50	$ 14.66
12	$1,000	127.87	1,127.87	62.03	77.50	15.47
18	$1,000	112.40	1,112.40	61.18	77.50	16.32
24	$1,000	96.08	1,096.08	60.28	77.50	17.22
30	$1,000	78.87	1,078.87	59.34	77.50	18.16
36	$1,000	60.70	1,060.70	58.34	77.50	19.16
42	$1,000	41.54	1,041.54	57.28	77.50	20.22
48	$1,000	21.33	1,021.33	56.18	77.50	21.32
				$447.47	$620.00	$142.53

Although the effective-interest method is superficially more impressive because of its complexity, it rests on the questionable assumption that the yield to the company should remain at a constant 11% over the life of the investment. Because the amortization of a premium or discount over several time periods is an arbitrary allocation, there is little to choose between the two methods. In Canada there is no *CICA Handbook* requirement that a company should use one over the other, whereas in the U.S. the effective-interest method is strongly preferred by standard setters. However, the straight-line method is more commonly used in Canada.

VALUATION OF LONG-TERM PASSIVE INVESTMENTS

Valuation is similar to the **lower-of-cost-and-market rule** for inventories. Recall that a decline in market value is immediately recognized with inventories if this value falls below cost. With long-term investments the Canadian custom is to defer recognizing such a loss if it is thought to be temporary. However, companies with long-term portfolio investments that have a market value must also disclose this [*CICA* 3050.46] in order to enable the reader to evaluate the potential loss of such securities.

It is hard to find a conceptual justification for ignoring losses that are thought to be temporary, especially for those investments where the reader is not given the current market value. The defence of this practice probably rests on the difficulty of valuing securities that do not have a well-established market value. For example, a company may own shares in another company whose shares are not publicly traded. Placing a valuation on these shares would involve a process similar to that described in Chapter 9 for valuing a business. In other words, it would involve making estimates of future outcomes, and the people most expert in making such judgements are the management of the company — who usually have an interest in how the financial report looks.

For non-portfolio investments the requirement is only that the basis of valuation should be disclosed [*CICA* 3050.43]. There is no requirement that the basis should be at cost, for instance. We have seen in Chapter 6 on inventories that "cost" can produce a variety of results, so the *CICA Handbook* requirement is probably not as weak as it appears. However, the reader of financial statements needs to recognize the difficulty that accountants have in this area.

If it becomes apparent that an investment's market value is going to remain well below its historic cost, Canadian accounting standards require that it should be written down permanently to that new value [*CICA* 3050.33]. This treatment is reserved for severe cases, such as a prolonged period during which the quoted value of the investment is less than its carrying value in the investor's books. In this respect its accounting treatment is consistent with that of plant assets [*CICA* 3060].

Investments Held for Specific Funding Purposes

Sometimes a company will be required under the terms of an agreement to keep assets in a separate fund to be held for a specific purpose. In effect, assets are shifted from one category on the balance sheet, such as short-term investments, to the long-term investment category where they are earmarked for a specific use. The potential confusion in the accounting treatment of such funds is that the assets usually must be shifted from one category to another to match the liability.

For example, purchasers of a company's mortgage may want a means of assuring themselves that when the mortgage comes due the company will have sufficient liquid assets to pay them off. Typically, the agreement for specific funding will require the company to purchase marketable securities of a stated type annually (e.g., bonds of the Government of Canada). If the funding agreement is carried out by the company, then at the maturity of the mortgage there should be sufficient liquid assets on hand to pay for the mortgage retirement. Since the funding requirement starts well before the maturity of the mortgage, such an agreement provides an opportunity for the mortgage holders to see that these preparations for repayment of their debt are being carried out. Without a funding agreement, the creditors would have to rely on the good intentions of the company's management to have sufficient funds assembled by the time the mortgage comes due. With a funding agreement, the specific means by which funds will be assembled are spelled out.

Sometimes the terms of the funding agreement require the company to deposit the securities with a trustee who ensures that the securities are used only for the purposes stated in the agreement. It would depend on the terms of the agreement whether handing the securities over to a trustee discharged the company's obligation or whether the company was still ultimately liable. Funds that are earmarked to retire some debt in the future are often referred to as *sinking funds*.

Let us work through an example. Crosby Marine borrowed $300,000 under a 20-year 15% mortgage. Under the terms of the mortgage there is to be no repayment of principal until the end of the 20th year. However, each year the sum of $10,000 is to be set aside in cash, Canadian government bonds, or guaranteed investment certificates so that over the period of the mortgage a portfolio will be built up that can be cashed and used to pay off the mortgage. The first year's entry would be as follows:

Long-term investment — mortgage fund bank account	10,000.00	
General bank account		10,000.00
To record transfer of funds from general bank account to special mortgage fund bank account in accordance with mortgage agreement.		

When securities are purchased the entry would resemble the following:

Long-term investment — mortgage fund securities	4,500.00	
Long-term investment — mortgage fund bank account		4,500.00
To record purchase of bonds for mortgage fund account.		

Any income earned on these mortgage fund investments would usually be added to the mortgage fund bank account and used for additional investments. The entry for such a transaction would resemble the following:

Long-term investment — mortgage fund bank account	350.00	
Investment income		350.00
To record receipt.		

Note that although the cash goes into the special bank account, the investment income in this example is still considered to be part of the company's investment income. The main purpose of this agreement is to ensure that a growing pool of liquid assets is kept to retire the mortgage when it comes due. The mortgage holders do not own the investment fund and have no claim on the income it earns unless the agreement states otherwise.

In other situations the company may, in effect, be a trustee for other people. The funding requirement may exist to make sure that the funds held for others are invested in marketable securities and not mixed in with the company's own affairs. In that case the investment income accrues to the benefit of others and should be credited to a separate liability account.

For example, Glenburnie Furniture Manufacturing set up a supplementary retirement fund for its senior employees. Under this plan the employees would contribute 2% of their salaries, and the company would match it. The funds so generated would be kept separate: earnings on the fund would accrue to the benefit of the employees and be used to increase the retirement benefits. At the end of the first month Glenburnie had withheld $850 under the 2% withholding plan, matched it with $850 of its own, and put the money in a separate fund.

The journal entry for the withholding from employees would be as follows:

Wages expense	850.00	
Long-term liability — pension retirement fund		850.00
To record sums withheld from wages for pension retirement		
fund.		

The journal entry for the matching contribution would be as follows:

Pension expense	850.00	
Long-term liability — pension retirement fund		850.00
To record company's contribution to fund.		

Up to this point, the company has recorded its liability to its employees via the supplementary retirement fund account, but it has not created the separate asset fund. It would do this with the following entry:

Long-term investment — pension-fund bank account	1,700.00	
General bank account		1,700.00
To record transfer of funds from general bank account to		
special pension-fund bank account.		

In this case let us assume that the revenue earned on the investments would accrue to the benefit of the employees. It would then be recorded in the following manner:

Long-term investment — pension-fund bank account	350.00	
Long-term liability — pension retirement fund		350.00
To record receipt of income on investments of pension		
retirement fund.		

Investments Held to Influence Management Policy

It is possible for one company to purchase a large enough percentage of the voting shares of another company and thus be able to influence the policies of that company. For example, Brascan bought a significant number of the shares of Noranda and then asked to have some of its representatives on Noranda's board of directors. The Canada Development Corporation purchased a majority of the shares of Acquitaine of Canada. Several large Canadian corporations bought significant shareholdings in Royal Trust at the time that Campeau Corporation sought to gain control. In many instances, the purchasing company initially buys less than a majority of the voting shares. It is often sufficient to have a significant block of shares — often less than a majority — to start to influence the company's board of directors.

EQUITY METHOD OF ACCOUNTING

When a corporation buys shares in another company and through these shareholdings and other means, is able to exercise **significant influence** on the policy making of the second company, then the usual accounting rules change. In particular, dividends are no longer treated as investment income, and the company owning the investment recognizes as investment income an amount based on the reported net income of the company that is being influenced. This is termed the **equity method** of income reporting, and the companies involved are often referred to as **associated companies.** This method is to be contrasted with the **cost method** used above for passive investments, where the company recognizes income only to the extent it receives dividends.

For example, assume that Lyndhurst Corporation purchased 10,000 of the 50,000 outstanding common shares of Morton Corporation when it was first incorporated. In 19X8 Morton paid a divided of $1.20 per share and had a net income after tax of $90,000. If Lyndhurst used the cost method of reporting its income, it would make the following entry on receipt of the $12 000 in dividends:

Bank	12,000.00	
Earnings of affiliated company		12,000.00
To record receipt of investment income.		

However, if Lyndhurst used the equity method, it would make the following entry on receipt of the dividends:

Bank	12,000.00	
Investment in Morton Company		12,000.00
To record receipt of dividend.		

Note that the investment account is reduced by the receipt of dividends. In effect, the investment in Morton is being partly liquidated by the receipt of its cash. As we see below, the investment in Morton is increased when that company earns income.

At the end of the year the corporation would examine the financial statements of Morton to establish the net income and make the following entry:

Investment in Morton Corporation	18,000.00	
Earnings of affiliated company		18,000.00

To record as investment income our 20% share in the reported net income of Morton Corporation.

Under the cost method, the investment recorded on the financial statements is the following:

Investment recorded = historical acquisition cost

By contrast, under the equity method, the investment recorded is as follows:

Investment recorded = Historical + The firm's share − Dividends
cost of the investee's received from
net income (loss) the investee

Before the equity method was required by GAAP, companies were free to use the cost method even if they exercised significant influence. If A Limited owned enough shares of B Limited to be able to influence its dividend policy, it would then be able to influence its own reported profit simply by influencing B to raise or lower its dividends. The folklore of corporate life prior to the 1930s contains stories of corporations taking control of other corporations, boosting dividends to an unsustainable level in order to make the income statement of the acquiring corporation look good, and leaving the acquired company as a shell stripped of its assets.

The original intent of the equity method appears to have been to make reported income insensitive to dividend policy and to allow the earnings of the underlying asset to be reflected in the books of the company owning the shares. We can summarize the essential features of the equity method as follows:

1. When a dividend is received from a company over which the investing company has significant influence, the dividend is credited to the long-term investments account on the balance sheet.

2. At the end of each accounting period the company exercising significant influence obtains the financial statements of the other and takes into its income a sum equal to the net income of the owned company multiplied by its proportion of ownership.

3. If shares are purchased at a price different from the net book value (which would nearly always be the case), an examination is made of the reason for this difference, and it is attributed to the difference between current market value and recorded book value of each of the purchased company's tangible assets. If there is a difference still unaccounted for, it is classified as goodwill. These additional amounts are all amortized by the owning company in calculating its investment income as if it owned the assets directly. Goodwill is amortized over a period not exceeding forty years.

Let us illustrate this third point by means of an example. B Limited had a book value of $120,000 as of the date A Limited purchased 25% of its shares for $40,000. A's carrying value for B's shares is 120,000/4 = 30,000 at the time of purchase. The purchase difference is $40,000 minus $30,000 = $10,000. A Limited decided to pay the additional $10,000 for the 25% interest because it believed that B was worth $40,000 more than its book value. A Limited calculated as follows:

	Amount on B's books	Estimated market value	Excess of market over book
Net current assets	$ 20,000	$ 20,000	$ 0
Buildings — depreciation rate of 5%	70,000	90,000	20,000
Equipment — depreciation rate of 20%	30,000	46,000	16,000
Subtotal	$120,000	$156,000	$36,000
Goodwill	0	4,000	4,000
Grand Total	$120,000	$160,000	$40,000

The purchase difference in this example of $10,000 (25% of $40,000) has to be depreciated or amortized and deducted from A's share of B's income. Therefore A Limited would make the following journal entry:

Investment income	1,075.00	
Investment in B Limited		1,075.00

To record the amortization of the purchase difference of $10,000 in accordance with its allocation over B's assets as shown below.

Item	Excess of market over book	Percent purchased	Net purchased	Rate	Deprecia- tion or amor- tization
Buildings	$20,000	25%	$ 5,000	5.0%	$ 250
Equipment	16,000	25%	4,000	20.0%	800
Goodwill	4,000	25%	1,000	2.5%*	25
	$40,000		$10,000		$1,075

* Forty-year amortization.

The reasoning behind amortizing purchase differences will be explained more thoroughly in Chapter 19 on consolidated financial statements. Briefly, it is to prevent A from showing an inflated income from B through a failure to record depreciation or amortization on B's assets that it has, in effect, bought. You can see this best by assuming that A owns 100% of B and comparing the impact on its net income of (i) continuing to own B through ownership of its shares versus (ii) collapsing B and taking over its assets directly. The economic substance of both arrangements is the same, and the accounting should therefore be set up to produce the same results. If the policy explained above is followed, this goal is accomplished.

MEANING OF SIGNIFICANT INFLUENCE

When does a company exercise sufficient *significant influence* to adopt the equity method? The position of the FASB's predecessor body, the APB [Opinion No. 18], was that ownership of 20% or more of a company's shares creates a presumption of significant influence. This appears to have encouraged a fixation with achieving the 20% level, sometimes at the expense of examining the more substantive issue of whether significant influence really exists. However, the *CICA Handbook* and the FASB (Interpretation No. 35) clearly emphasize that one should not become preoccupied with the 20% level of voting interest. They both say one should examine other material things such as representation on the board of directors, participation in policy-making processes, material inter-company transactions, interchange of personnel, and provision of technical information. Moreover, "substantial or majority ownership by another investor would not necessarily preclude an investor from exercising significant influence" [*CICA* 3050.21].

The intent of the *Handbook* seems to be to emphasize that judgment about the substantive issues should be used, not a simplistic rule like 20% of the voting interest. The FASB has illustrated situations where a company might own 20% or more of the shares of another company (the investee) and still be unable to exercise significant influence. For example, (i) the company is being sued by the investee, (ii) the company has agreed to surrender significant rights as a shareholder, (iii) the company has been refused the data it needs to do equity accounting, (iv) the company is unable to get representation on the board of directors, or (v) another company has control.

CURRENT USE OF THE EQUITY METHOD

The original purposes of the equity method were to prevent the manipulation of income through influence over the investee's dividend policy and to reflect the earning of the investor's underlying investment. This aim has been accomplished, but a curious side effect can be seen today. Since most companies pay dividends that are substantially less than their annual earnings, a company that increases its shareholdings enough to exercise "significant influence" and hence shift from the cost method to the equity method will find that its reported income from investments has been increased substantially by the change in method.

As a result, there has been a preoccupation with purchasing enough shares to be considered to have significant influence in order to achieve this cosmetic effect on the financial statements. It is also common to find the financial press erroneously reporting that if a company gets 20% of the shares of another company, "it will earn more income."

Investments Held for Control

A **parent corporation** is one that has control over the affairs of another, termed a **subsidiary,** through its power to elect the majority of the subsidiary's board of directors. Normally the parent acquires this control through purchasing voting shares.

In the case of control it is usual for the financial affairs of the two companies to be reported in consolidated form to outside investors. In other words, one financial statement will be prepared for both companies to treat them as a single economic entity. For example, see the report from Consolidated Bathurst Inc. given above in Chapter 2. The method for preparing consolidated statements is reserved for Chapter 19, but the general approach will be discussed here.

There are many examples in accounting of a willingness to look through the legal form to try to get at the economic substance of events or corporate arrangements. Consolidated financial statements provide one such example. When two corporations are closely linked through share ownership and it is more meaningful to think of them in economic terms as one unit, consolidated financial statements seem to make sense.

For example, IBM sets up local companies in most of the countries in which it operates. It is IBM policy that these companies should be 100% owned by IBM. It attempts to achieve economies of scale in manufacturing by having local companies specialize in the equipment they manufacture. From an economic point of view it is easy to think of IBM as one worldwide entity in which local incorporation should be ignored for purposes of reporting to shareholders (but not to the local taxing authorities!). This is done through the preparation of consolidated financial statements which include all IBM companies that are part of the same economic group.

For many years it was acceptable practice in both the United States and Canada *not* to consolidate subsidiaries whose economic activities were very different from the parent. For example, in the past Sears did not consolidate the financial statements of its insurance subsidiary with those of its retail store operations. However, the U.S. practice changed in 1987 when the FASB [*Statement of Accounting Standards No. 94*] required that *all* subsidiaries should be consolidated if they were controlled by the parent.

Where consolidation is not used, the *CICA Handbook* requires that the equity method of accounting for the revenue of the subsidiary must be used for the same reasons it is used when there is significant influence. In addition, the financial statements of the unconsolidated subsidiaries would be supplied in condensed form [*CICA* 3050.14].

Under the usual rules of accounting for investments, a company owning more than 20% but less than 50% of a joint venture would normally use the equity method. If it owned more than 50%, it would consolidate the joint venture into its own financial statements. Under certain conditions it *may* use proportionate consolidations, but this is not required. The conditions that allow for proportionate consolidation are two in number: (i) the venturers conduct a significant portion of their business activities through joint ventures and (ii) the earnings of the joint venture are likely to accrue to the venturer. If a company has controlling interest but does not use consolidation or proportional consolidation, then it should use the equity method [*CICA* 3055.11]. However, if condition (ii) does not hold, then it should use the cost method.

Examples from Published Reports

Minnesota Mining and Manufacturing Company

Excerpts from the reports of the 3M Company have been given above in Chapters 6 and 9.

BALANCE SHEET

	1986	1985
	(millions of $)	
Investments	$433	$344

Notes to Financial Statements
Consolidation: All significant subsidiaries are consolidated. Subsidiaries outside the United States are consolidated on the basis of their fiscal years ended October 31. Unconsolidated subsidiaries and affiliates are included on the equity basis.

INVESTMENTS

	1986	1985
	(millions of $)	
Equity in unconsolidated affiliates	$326	$275
Other investments — at cost	107	69
	$433	$344

The total assets of the company are $7,348 million. Therefore, unconsolidated affiliates are relatively small.

Exxon Corporation

Exxon Corporation is a large multi-national integrated oil company.

BALANCE SHEET

	1985	1986
	(millions of $)	
Investments and advances	$2,311	$2,778

Note 3. Investments and advances
Components of investments and advances were:

	1985	1986
	(millions of $)	
In less than majority-owned companies		
Carried at equity in underlying assets:		
Investments	$1,379	$1,997
Advances	45	46
	1,424	2,043
Carried at cost or less	105	154
	1,529	2,197
Long-term receivables and miscellaneous investments at cost or less	782	581
Total	$2,311	$2,778

Exxon appears to use the equity method for some company holdings and the cost method for others, which is acceptable if the underlying conditions warrant it.

Summary

Long-term investments may be held to earn income (passive investments), to meet the terms of a contract (the portfolio built up to pay debt when it comes due), to influence the policies of another company, or for outright voting control. While the matching convention is adhered to for purposes of income recognition, the special circumstances with respect to each holding indicate different rules for each. Valuation of these investments follows the lower-of-cost-and-market rule in general; but temporary declines are not recorded, and the equity method departs from this rule in order to reflect the earnings of the investee corporation.

QUESTIONS

Q10-1. Review and be sure you understand the following terms:
  a. passive investments
  b. dividend
  c. record date
  d. coupon rate of bonds
  e. face value of bond
  f. premium on bond purchase
  g. discount on bond purchase
  h. yield rate of bonds
  i. settlement date
  j. straight-line method *versus* effective-interest method of amortization
  k. lower-of-cost-and-market rule for investment valuation
  l. equity method *versus* cost method of accounting for income
  m. significant influence
  n. parent corporation

Q10-2. What are a company's possible objectives in holding long-term investments? If you were the manager of the company, how would you evaluate how successful you were in achieving those objectives?

Q10-3. Compare the accounting treatment and disclosure requirements for marketable securities held as current assets with (i) long-term investments and (ii) inventories. Are the differences, if any, desirable?

Q10-4. State whether you think significant influence exists in the following situations. Give your reasons.
  a. A Limited owns 20% of B Limited. The management of A Limited have told the financial press that they purchased the shares in B "solely for investment purposes." They have not requested a place on the board of directors of B, although the financial press has been openly speculating that they will do so soon. There are no other large shareholders of B Limited.

b. D Limited owns 19% of E Limited and has been angrily demanding a seat on the board of E, but to no avail. The management of D Limited make it clear that if elected to the board of E they would sharply increase dividends, which have been far under E's annual earnings for the past ten years. The present management of E are clearly nervous about their position because they have recently declared "special" generous dividends.

c. F Limited owns 20% of G Limited, and the officers of F have a place on the board of directors of G Limited. F uses the equity method of accounting for G's income. F owns 10% of H Limited, and G recently bought another 15%. Neither F nor G has a place on the board of H, and the management of H is openly hostile to what they regard as an unfriendly purchase.

Q10-5. "The equity method was designed to prevent flagrant income manipulation through dividend manipulation. It has resulted in more subtle income manipulation by companies seeking the 'benefit' of switching from the cost method to equity method." Discuss.

Q10-6. "Under the matching convention, it is the passing of time, rather than the receipt of funds, which influences income recognition for passive investments." Discuss whether this is true for the recognition of dividend income, and how this differs from the treatment of mortgage income.

Q10-7. In each of the cases below, state whether you would expect the bond to be trading at a premium or discount to its face value:

	Market rate	Coupon rate
a.	12%	10%
b.	13%	13%
c.	10%	12%
d.	12%	14%
e.	12%	12%

Q10-8. Explain how it might be proper for a company to segregate marketable securities in a special fund under an agreement with long-term creditors, such as bond holders, and yet credit the income earned on those bonds to its own investment income account.

Q10-9. Do you agree with the following statements? Give your reasons.

a. The equity method is to be preferred to the cost method when dividends are greater than net income because it makes the company more profitable.

b. The only way long-term creditors such as bond holders can be sure they will get repaid is to make the company build up a fund of marketable investments prior to the redemption date.

c. Passive investments are so named because the investor does not do anything about them once they have been purchased.

Q10-10. Explain the basic difference in (i) income reporting objectives and (ii) accounting treatment between the equity method and the cost method.

Q10-11. Company P had had a 40% interest in Company S for the past five years and had accounted for it on the equity basis. This past year Company S had run a substantial loss. It was so severe that the bond holders had appointed a committee that insisted that dividends be stopped and the company take drastic measures to reduce its costs. The company agreed. The management of Company P are delighted, saying "Our significant influence no longer exists, and we can stop using the equity method that has been contributing to our loss this year. But we will still keep the retained earnings we have built up by using the equity method in the past."

a. Do you agree that they should stop using the equity method? Give your reasons.

b. Given that they will stop using the equity method, should they retain in retained earnings the income they have recorded in excess of dividends in the preceding five years? Or should they make some retroactive adjustment? Justify your answer.

Q10-12. Company J owned a significant percentage of the shares of Y Limited and accounted for Y on the equity basis. Y is a publicly traded company whose shares traded in the $30 to $50 range. When Y began to be unprofitable, J paid a dividend to its shareholders in the form of all of its shares of Y. The management commented, "Our shareholders are no worse off than they were before, and J is a lot more profitable." Explain how, under the equity method, J could give away valuable shares and be "a lot more profitable." Do you agree that J's shareholders are "no worse off than they were before?"

Q10-13. "A company that wished to show the best possible income from a bond in its early years would prefer the effective-interest method over the straight-line method". Do you agree? Explain.

Q10-14. Evaluate the merits and weaknesses of the equity method. For example, if all companies were required to use the cost method, would the reader of financial statements be seriously misinformed? Under all conditions?

Q10-15. It is reported that some companies have virtually complete control over other companies without owning any shares in that company. They do this through one of the following: (i) being the sole purchaser of the other company's product (thus they can dictate production volume, price, and quality); (ii) owning the patents on which the other company is completely dependent for the product it makes; (iii) being the sole supplier of a vital component in the product that the other company makes (e.g., supplying a few high-technology parts that are essential to the manufacture of a turbine engine for an aircraft). Assuming that one of these conditions exists to give Company A virtual control over Company B, should Company A use the equity method with respect to B? Explain.

Q10-16. Evaluate the merits of combining the equity method with the market rule to show an investment at the lower of cost (as determined by the equity method) and market value.

Q10-17. In 1982 Bell Canada owned 33.8% of the shares of Maritime Telegraph and Telephone Company, Limited and had a close working relationship in technical co-operation. However, under a statute passed by the Nova Scotia Legislature, not more than 1,000 shares may be voted by any one shareholder. Should Bell Canada use the equity method in accounting for Maritime T & T? Explain.

Q10-18. Some companies have the practice of not recording the loss on long-term investments if this loss is thought to be temporary. Is this consistent with the convention of conservatism? Discuss.

Q10-19. What are the similarities in the treatment between plant assets and long-term investments when the market value is less than the unamortized historic cost? What is the justification for this similarity in treatment? Do you think it is appropriate?

Q10-20. As treasurer of a neighbourhood improvement association, you have been asked to lend $1,000 on a three-year loan to a local group for the purpose of buying lawn-mowing equipment that will be used on a rental basis within the neighbourhood. It is expected that the equipment will provide a steady annual rental income and that its functional life will be about three years. You have some doubts about the financial sophistication of the group that wants to borrow the money. Thus, you would like to design a funding method for them so that when the $1,000 comes due in three years they will have the cash on hand for repayment. Describe a simple funding method they might follow and the function of any new accounts that would be created in their books.

Q10-21. "The equity method is not just a method of making reported income insensitive to dividend policy, it is also a useful way of reporting income that reflects a number of factors not often reflected in dividends. In fact, it should be used by passive investors as well as those with significant influence." Do you agree? Discuss.

Q10-22. **a.** Give an example of each of the following situations: (i) a company owns 90% of the voting stock of another company, but accounts for it on the equity basis; (ii) a company owns less than 20% of the voting stock of another company, but accounts for it on the equity basis; and (iii) a company owns more than 20% of another company, but accounts for it on the cost basis.

b. Is it likely that a company might own 90% of the voting stock of another company, but account for it on the cost basis? Explain.

Q10-23. Under the following unrelated circumstances should the real estate be considered (i) a long-term passive investment, (ii) a short-term investment, (iii) a plant asset, or (iv) a current asset? Justify your answers.

a. A house builder was also a land developer. He would buy a farm in a developing area, put in roads and utilities, and then sell the individual building lots to his own construction company or to other builders.

b. A company bought a parcel of land adjoining a factory site. It ultimately would sell the land or use it to build an addition to the factory, depending on later developments. Meanwhile it had levelled the land and was renting it to a company that ran it as a parking lot.

c. A company purchased more land than it actually needed because it seemed economically attractive. The part not needed is now up for sale, and all necessary permission has been obtained to sell it separately.

d. A company does not actually own a piece of land, but it holds an option to purchase that originally cost $23,000. The company intends to exercise this option within the year.

EXERCISES

E10-1. In the following unrelated situations indicate what income you think should be reported for the accounting period. Show all calculations.

a. Interest of $1,250 on a mortgage was paid monthly on the 15th. The company that held it as an investment had a year-end of June 30 and had owned the mortgage since 15 January of that year.

b. A bond with a face value of $1,000 was purchased as of 1 July for $1,135.56 plus accrued interest of $33.33. It paid interest on 1 September and 1 March of each year at a coupon rate of 10%. It would mature ten years from the date of purchase. The company's first year-end after the bond purchase is 31 December.

c. O Limited had owned one hundred shares of P Inc. for the past two years. On 10 December the directors of P Inc. declared a dividend of 90 cents a share payable on 1 January to shareholders of record of 20 December. O's year-end is 31 December.

d. K Limited purchased one hundred shares of L Inc. on 8 December 19X4 for $8,900 for settlement on 15 December. On 10 December the directors of L Inc. declared a dividend of 90 cents a share payable on 1 January to shareholders of record of 20 December. K's year-end is 31 December.

e. J Limited had owned two hundred shares of S Inc. for three years. It sold them on 24 September for settlement on 1 October. The directors of S Inc. had declared a $0.90 dividend per share on 19 September payable on 30 October to shareholders of record of 2 October. Although J Limited delivered the shares on time on 1 October, they were not transferred to the new owner's name until after 2 October. Hence, J Limited received the dividend payable 30 October.

E10-2. Stonehouse Corporation purchased a bond for a long-term investment. The bond traded at $116.25 with a yield of 11% and a coupon rate of 14%. Its face value was $10,000. It matures ten years from the date of purchase.

Required:

a. What would be the first twelve months' amortization using the straight-line method?

b. Explain in words the objective of the effective-interest method. Then show how it is calculated here for the first twelve months' amortization.

c. Explain in words why the income generated by the effective-interest method is larger (or smaller) than that generated by the straight-line method.

d. Would the choice of method affect the annual cash flow? Explain.

E10-3. Complete the following table comparing the effect of the cost and equity methods of accounting for investments in other companies. The first line has been completed as an example. Assume that the net book value of the shares at the time of purchase was equal to the purchase price.

	Dividend received	Total net income of investee	Percentage of shares owned by investor	Income reported Cost method	Income reported Equity method
a.	$15,000	$180,000	10%	$15,000	$18,000
b.	$20,000	$180,000	10%		
c.	$25,000	$180,000	20%		
d.	$35,000	$180,000	20%		
e.	$50,000	$180,000	20%		

E10-4. A company has the following long-term investments:

	Historic cost	Market value
Investment A	$35,000	$40,000
Investment B	35,000	20,000
	$70,000	$60,000

Required:

a. Explain how under the lower-of-cost-and-market rule the company could value these investments at either $55,000 or $60,000.

b. Explain what journal entry, if any, would be made under each of the following:
 (i) It was decided that the decrease in value was temporary.
 (ii) It was decided that the decrease in value was permanent.

c. What is the minimum information you would expect to find disclosed if the company adhered to the recommendations in the *CICA Handbook?*

E10-5. On the first day of its financial year, Singleton Corporation purchased 25,000 shares for $750,000, representing 30% of the voting shares of Higley Inc. The purchase price of the shares was $400,000 more than their book value at that time. In that first year Higley had a net income of $250,000 and paid dividends of $100,000.

Required:

a. Explain the accounting treatment of the above purchase difference under (i) the cost method and (ii) the equity method of accounting. What would the reported income be under the cost method?

b. Why do two methods exist for treating a purchase difference, as given in (a) above. What are the justifications for having two methods?

c. Assume that Singleton decided to apportion the purchase difference as follows:

Asset	Depreciation rate	Amount
Plant assets	10%	$300,000
Equipment	20%	100,000
		$400,000

What would the reported income be under the equity method? Show all your calculations.

d. Assume instead that Singleton decided to apportion the purchase difference as follows:

Asset	Depreciation rate	Amount
Plant assets	10%	$50,000
Equipment	2.5%	350,000
		$400,000

What would the reported income be under the equity method? Is it different from what you calculated in (c)? By how much? Which treatment (if any) is preferred by GAAP? Explain.

E10-6. Describe the appropriate financial statement treatment for each of the following. Show journal entries if they help to describe the appropriate treatment.

a. The Kingston Antiquarian Society, a registered charity, agreed to accept a donation of $30,000 in Bell Canada stock "to be held in trust with the income therefrom to be used to promote the importance to the Kingston area of regaining its architecturally interesting historic buildings." You are the Treasurer and have to include the donation and the income earned on it in the financial statements.

b. Enterprise Lumber Yard had a customer, Fred Smith, who wanted an expensive window that was not normally stocked. Enterprise agreed to order it if Smith would give a deposit of $200 to be credited to his accounts receivable to offset the $800 charge when the window was delivered.

c. The employees of Tichborne Industries agreed to have 50 cents per week deducted from their pay. This was to be retained by the employer, with interest accumulating at 15%, and used to buy flowers for those away ill. Tichborne Industries would not agree to set up a separate bank account to hold the funds because of the additional work involved. It had a balance of $351.24 in the account at the end of its fiscal year.

E10-7.   Parham Industries owned 25% of the common shares of Godfrey Canning and used the equity method for reporting. When it had purchased Godfrey it paid $100,000 for the shares, even though its share of the net book was only $80,000. The $20,000 purchase difference was attributed as follows: land — $8,000; buildings — $5,000; and goodwill — $7,000. Parham's depreciation rate for buildings was 10%, and it elected to write off the goodwill over 40 years. The straight-line method was to be used in each case. In the financial year following the year of acquisition, Godfrey reported a net income of $12,000 and paid dividends of $6,000.

Required:
Prepare the journal entries in Parham's books to reflect the events set out above.

E10-8.   In 19X4 Charleston Corporation paid dividends of $80,000 and had a net income of $100,000. During the entire period Donaldson Limited owned some of Charleston's shares. The total net book value at the time of purchase was $1,000,000. Any difference between book value and cost of shares is considered to be goodwill and will be amortized at 10% a year.

Required: What income would Donaldson report from Charleston in each of the following scenarios? Show all calculations.

a. It owns 20% of the shares for which it paid $200,000. It uses the cost method.

b. It owns 20% of the shares for which it paid $200,000. It uses the equity method.

c. It owns 40% of the shares for which it paid $200,000. It uses the equity method.

d. It owns 40% of the shares for which it paid $300,000. It uses the equity method.

E10-9.   A Ltd. owns all the cumulative preference shares of B. Ltd. The preference shares are non-voting as long as B Ltd. pays regular dividends on them, but they become voting if two successive dividends are omitted. B Ltd. has missed one regular dividend on the preference shares, and independent observers doubt that it will be able to pay the next one. A Ltd. has already announced that it will not be using its right to vote the preference shares "because B Ltd. is reporting a loss and we don't want to use the equity method of accounting for it."

Required:
What is the most appropriate accounting treatment for A Ltd. to use to account for its investment in B Ltd.? Justify your choice.

E10-10.   The Carcross University Student Co-op is a housing co-operative which provides reasonably priced housing to students. The co-op is managed by a member of the co-op who is elected by all members for a period of one year. Like most previous managers, she is an upper-year student who will only stay in the position for one year before graduating. The co-op houses have fallen into disrepair, because previous managers wanted to avoid controversy with their fellow members, and were unwilling to charge more than required to cover the immediate costs of the year. Thus, over time the furnace has received only enough repairs to make it through each winter, and the leaks in the roof have been fixed by temporary patches. One fall the fire department inspected the furance and condemned it as being unsafe. The co-op had only sufficient funds to cover the temporary repairs. It decided to turn to the university for additional funding to replace the furnace.

As we enter the scene we find Dr. George Carmacks, president of the University, talking to Petra Tesla, present manager of the co-op.

Tesla: Well sir, we need to borrow $3,000 to replace the furnace, and we thought the University was the obvious place to start.

Carmacks: Yes, well we'll lend you the money only if we can come up with some way to ensure that there will be money in the future to replace or make major repairs to equipment and buildings. The University can't, and doesn't want to, meddle in your financial affairs, but as a creditor we've got to be assured yearly that our loan is going to be repaid. We might consider making a loan to be repaid at the end of ten years. Submit a proposal by which you can send me your annual financial statements and I can see from them that you are on track for paying the loan when it comes due.

Required:

As co-op manager write a memo to the President proposing a funding plan consistent with these loan requirements.

E10-11. On 2 January 19X2 Lakeside Company purchased 2,000 of the 10,000 outstanding common shares of Riverview Corporation for $30 per share. At that date, the following data were available for Riverview Corporation:

	Book value	Market value
Assets not subject to depreciation	$100,000	$100,000
Assets subject to depreciation with remaining life of 10 years	220,000	240,000
	$320,000	
Liabilities	$ 70,000	70,000
Common stock	150,000	
Retained earnings	100,000	
	$320,000	

At the end of 19X2 Riverview reported net income of $50,000 and declared dividends of $20,000 to be paid in January 19X3. Any goodwill is to be amortized over a five-year period.

Required:

a. Prepare all the necessary journal entries arising from the investment in shares of Riverview Corporation assuming the use of (i) the cost method and (ii) the equity method.

b. Under what conditions should the cost method be used? Under what conditions should the equity method be used?

(CGA adapted)

E10-12. While examining the accounts of Sundance Company Ltd. as of 31 December 19X3 before the accounts are closed, you find the following long-term investment account balance. All transactions have been debited or credited to cash, and the balancing entry has been recorded in the investment account.

Account: Investment in Longacre Steel

11% bonds — maturity date: 1 April 19X7
    — yield: 10%
    — interest payable: 1 April and 1 October

Date	Item	Debit	Credit	Balance
19X3				
1 Jan.	Bonds, $100,000 par value; acquired at			
	103.5 plus accrued interest	106,250		106,250
1 Apr.	Interest received		5,500	100,750
1 Oct.	Interest received		5,500	95,250
1 Oct.	Amount received on call of bonds,			
	$20,000 par, at 101		20,200	75,050

Required:

a. Prepare the journal entries that *should* have been made in this account, including any adjusting entries that would be made on 31 December, the end of the fiscal year. Bond premium amortization is by the straight-line method. Round amounts to the nearest dollar.

b. Compute the correct balance for the investment account *and* for the interest revenue account for the year ended 31 December 19X3.

E10-13. On 1 January 19X4 Investor Ltd. acquired 40% of the outstanding common shares of Investee Ltd. for $8,000 cash. Investor Ltd's year-end is 31 December.

  The net income for 19X4 for Investee Ltd. was $2,000. Investee Ltd. declared and paid a cash dividend of $1,000 during the year. Goodwill arising on acquisition is to be amortized over the maximum period allowed according to accounting standards in Canada. Tangible fixed assets are to be depreciated over ten years. The following figures are made available:

INVESTEE LTD.
BALANCE SHEET
as at 1 January 19X4

	Book value	Fair value
Current assets	$ 4,000	$ 4,000
Tangible fixed assets	8,000	13,000
	$12,000	
Current liabilities	$ 2,000	$ 2,000
Common shares — no par 1,000 outstanding shares	4,000	
Retained earnings	6,000	
	$12,000	

Required:

a. Determine the amount of goodwill paid by Investor Ltd. on 1 January 19X4 on the acquisition of 40% of the common shares of Investee Ltd.

b. Under the equity method, determine (i) Investor Ltd.'s equity in the 19X4 earnings of Investee Ltd. and (ii) the account balance at 31 December 19X4 of the investment in Investee Ltd. that would appear in the books of Investor Ltd.

c. Under the cost method, determine (i) Investor's investment income for 19X4 from Investee and (ii) the investment account balance as at 31 December 19X4 that would appear in the books of Investor Ltd.

d. Determine the book value and fair value per share of Investee Ltd. at 1 January 19X4.

(CGA adapted)

E10-14. On 1 January 19X3 Bolson Inc. purchased 40% of the shares of Plymouth Inc. for $600,000 and charged this purchase to Long Term Investments. By Bolson's year-end of 31 December it had received $30,000 in dividends from Plymouth and credited it to Investment Income. Assume that at the end of the year it was decided that Bolson should use the equity method in reporting its investment income from Plymouth.

Required:
In each of the scenarios below, indicate by how much the reported income of $30,000 should be *increased* or *decreased*.

a. Plymouth's reported net income after tax was $160,000 for the twelve months ending 31 December, 19X3.

b. At the time of the purchase Plymouth Inc. had owners' equity of $1,200,000, which Bolson estimated was approximately equal to the market value of its tangible net assets. Any purchase difference is to be amortized straight-line over 10 years.

c. Bolson had shipped goods to Plymouth and invoiced Plymouth for $38,000. This was still unpaid by 31 December, although Plymouth had sold all the goods.

d. Although Plymouth had only paid $30,000 to Bolson in dividends by the end of the year, it had actually declared, but not yet paid, additional dividends of which $10,000 was due to Bolson. Bolson had not recorded these dividends as receivable or accrued the dividend income of $10,000.

PROBLEMS

P10-1. Prepare journal entries for each of the following unrelated events.

a. Mortgage interest of $1,256.87 was paid monthly on the 15th. The company that held it as an investment had a year-end of 30 June. Show the journal entry to record the payment of interest and the accrual of interest at the end of the month.

b. A bond with a face value of $10,000 was purchased as of 1 July for $11,135.56 plus accrued interest of $333.33. It pays interest on 1 September and 1 March of each year at a coupon rate of 10%. It will mature ten years from the date of purchase. Show the journal entry for 30 June, the end of the company's financial year, assuming that straight-line amortization and accrual are done monthly.

c. Vega Limited has owned one hundred shares of Oakleaf Inc. for the past ten years. On 10 December the directors of Oakleaf declared a dividend of 90 cents a share payable on 1 January to shareholders of record of 20 December. Vega's year-end is 31 December. What journal entry, if any, is needed at the year-end?

d. K Limited purchased one hundred shares of L Inc. on 8 December 19X4 for $8,900 for settlement on 15 December. On 10 December the directors of L Inc. declared a dividend of 90 cents a share payable on 1 January to shareholders of record of 20 December. K's year-end is 31 December. What journal entry, if any, is needed?

e. J Limited had owned 200 shares of S Inc. for three years. It sold them on 24 September for settlement on 1 October. The directors of S Inc. had declared a dividend on 19 September of $1.00 per share payable on 30 October to shareholders of record of 2 October. Although J Limited delivered the shares on time on 1 October, they were not transferred into the new owner's name until after 2 October. Hence J Limited received the dividend payable 30 October. What journal entry, if any, is needed in J's books when it receives the dividend cheque?

P10-2. Webster Lake Corporation owned 20,000 shares of Soperton Limited. On 2 February 19X6 Soperton announced that it had a net income of $1,200,000 for the twelve months ending 31 December 19X5. During the same period it had paid dividends of $600,000 equal to $6.00 per share. Webster Lake had purchased the shares in 19X4 for $6,000,000, paying $4,000,000 more than their book value. It had attributed all of the purchase difference to goodwill, to be amortized over forty years.

Required:

a. Show the journal entry in Webster Lake Corporation's books for the receipt of investment income in 19X5, assuming it used the cost method.

b. Show the journal entry in Webster lake Corporation's books for the receipt of investment income in 19X5, assuming it used the equity method.

c. Calculate by how much Webster Lake Corporation's income would increase or decrease if it attributed the purchase difference to plant assets with an average depreciation rate of 10%.

P10-3. Show the journal entries that would be required in each of the following unrelated cases. If you think no journal entry is required, then explain why:

a. As part of the condition of selling a bond issue, a company enters into a contract with a bond trustee to purchase a minimum of $80,000 in marketable securities each year. The securities are to be lodged with the trustee for safekeeping as evidence that the terms of the contract are being fulfilled. In the first year, rather than sell marketable securities that it already owned in order to purchase similar ones, the company simply took its own short-term marketable securities and delivered them to the trustee.

b. A bank was nervous about a company that owed it money. Therefore, it persuaded the debtor to agree that its inventory should be under the charge of a bank nominee who would take over the administration of the warehouse in which the inventory was stored. The debtor could remove inventory only after the bank had approved the terms of sale. When the nominee took over for the bank, there was inventory with a cost of $258,000 and an estimated market value of $180,000. What journal entry, if any, would be required when the assets are taken over by the nominee?

c. Killenbeck Limited's coin vending machines for fast food are operated by a concessionaire under an agreement that any profits will go into an employee benevolent fund. A committee oversees the fund to buy gifts in case of employee sickness, deaths, and weddings. The first month the following events take place:

(i) A cheque for $2,512.58 is received from the concessionaire. It is deposited in the company bank account.

(ii) A member of the committee points out that there is no interest paid on this bank account. Because most of the expenditures will be around Christmas, he suggests it would make sense to invest $2,000.00 of this money in a term deposit at the bank that will mature on 15 December. The rest agree, and this is done by the company on their behalf.

(iii) A payment of $35.87 for flowers is made out of the account.

    d. The sum of $25,867.25 is deducted from employees' wages in February as part of their compulsory income tax deductions. It is payable to Revenue Canada by the 15th of the following month. The employer is regarded as a trustee for Revenue Canada, but is not required to keep the funds in a separate trustee bank account.

P10-4. In 1981 a group headed by Robert Campeau attempted to gain control of Royal Trusco (known to most people for its ownership of Royal Trust). As part of the rescue operation from the Campeau group, Olympia and York (developers of a number of city complexes such as First Canadian Place) agreed to purchase some Royal Trusco shares. *The Globe and Mail* reported that a spokesman for Olympia and York had "expressed interest in buying shares if Olympia were invited to buy up to 20 per cent and given assurances that two representatives would be allowed to sit on Royal Trusco's board of directors and executive committee." He said in a later interview that "the 20 per cent level was selected because it held certain equity accounting advantages" because "he can often account for his percentage share of the profits . . . even if he does not hold control."

Required:

As a member of the CICA, you are asked to write a memo to Olympia and York outlining the considerations that would determine whether Olympia and York would be entitled to use the equity method if it purchased roughly 20% of Royal Trusco. You are instructed (i) to write a clear and well organized memo of about 250 words and (ii) to apply the general principles of equity accounting to the particular facts of this case. You are not expected to go beyond the information given above.

P10-5. In 1978 *The Economist* of London reported that Lonrho Ltd. (described by a U.S. business magazine as "a high-flying multinational") wanted to use the equity method in accounting for House of Fraser, a company that owned a group of stores that included Harrods in Knightsbridge. Lonrho holds 19.43% of the House of Fraser's voting shares and just under 30% of another company called Scottish and University Investments (SUITS) that in turn owns 10.29% of House of Fraser. It is calculated that Lonrho's indirect holding of House of Fraser through SUITS adds approximately 3% more and brings the total shareholding in House of Fraser to over 20%.

    The auditors had agreed to the equity method for Lonrho. *The Economist* commented acidly that the auditors had said that this "complied with 'established accounting practice' — a seeming admission that anything goes provided it has been done before." Lonrho has two directors out of fourteen on House of Fraser's board of directors. *The Economist* quoted one of the directors of Lonrho as saying of House of Fraser: "To me it's someone else's company and it's their business to make it profitable."

Required:

    a. Explain why Lonrho might be motivated to include the House of Fraser as an associated company.

    b. Evaluate the merits of using the equity method in this instance. Make sure that you apply the general concepts to the facts of this particular case.

P10-6. In August 1984, *The Globe and Mail* reported: "For the second time this year, Ivaco Inc. has raised its stake in the country's second largest and most profitable integrated steel producer, Dofasco Inc. of Hamilton. And for the second time this year, the Montreal-based steelmaker's actions have raised questions about its intentions."

Required:

Ivaco's holdings of Dofasco after this purchase total 11% of the voting stock. Outline the "intentions" that Ivaco might have for their investment in Dofasco. Could accounting requirements affect their plans?

P10-7. In each of the following situations, prepare the journal entry to record the acquisition described. Show goodwill and excess of market over book separately.

a. Co. B reported an income of $100,000. Co. A purchased 30% of the outstanding shares of Co. B for $66,000. The net book value of B's net assets is $143,000, and the market value of the fixed assets is $30,000 greater than book value. Co. A regards itself as having significant influence.

b. Co. C acquired 18% of the common shares of Co. D for $50,000 and plans to buy additional shares some time in the future.

c. Co. E bought the assets of one of the divisions of Co. F for $100,000. The book value of the net tangible assets was $40,000, and the market value was $65,000.

d. Co. G acquired 80% of the issued shares of Co. H for $450,000. The net assets of H had a book value of $437,500 and a market value of $562,500.

e. Co. I bought 70% of the issued shares of Co. J for $300,000. The net assets of J had a book value of $500,000 and a market value of $600,000.

P10-8. For each of the following journal entries, state what event most likely brought them about.

a. Long-term investments	5,000.00	
Bond discount		617.85
Bank		4,382.15
b. Long-term investments	15,000.00	
Accrued interest	416.75	
Bond premium	3,804.00	
Bank		19,220.75
c. Bank	22,325.00	
Loss on disposal	3,800.00	
Long-term investments		25,000.00
Interest receivable		1,125.00
d. Interest receivable	75.00	
Amortization of bond discount	16.00	
Interest income		91.00
e. Earnings of affiliated company	9,000.00	
Investment in X company		9,000.00
f. Investment in B Ltd.	8,075.00	
Investment income		8,075.00

P10-9. For each of the following unrelated events, given the appropriate journal entry (or entries) for Iota Company. Show all your calculations.

a. Iota buys a $50,000 5-year bond at 104.75 on 9 September 19X4. The bond will mature on 1 January 19X8. It pays 13.75% per annum, and interest is paid semi-annually on 1 July and 1 January. Show the entry for the purchase.

b. On 5 November Iota company receives a stock dividend from Upsilon company of 10%. Iota owns 10,000 shares of Upsilon.

c. On 26 June Iota purchases 15,000 shares of Omicron Ltd. for $5 per share. Omicron has a book value of $300,000. On 15 July Omicron declares a total of $150,000 in dividends at $0.50 per share. Iota will attribute any purchase difference of this investment to goodwill over a 40-year amortization period.

d. Iota sets up an unfunded retirement plan, run by the company, whereby 5% of the employees' wages are withheld for the fund and this amount is matched by the company at year-end. In 19X5 the company pays $165,000 in wages distributed evenly over the year. The company year-end is 31 May. There have been no entries pertaining to the fund during the month of May. Show the journal entries required for May 19X5.

e. Iota buys 10,000 shares of Lambda Ltd. at $15.00 per share on 18 May. On 1 June Labda declares a stock split of 3:1. On 1 September Lambda declares a $1 dividend payable on 30 September to holders of record on 13 September. On 19 September Iota sells at its shares of Lambda for $167,000.

f. On 19 February 19X5 Iota sells 10,000 shares of Gamma Ltd. for $150,000. Prior to the sale, Iota had a 30% interest in Gamma, but now owns only 10% of the outstanding stock. They had acquired all the shares five years earlier for $250,000 when Gamma had a book value of $850,000. They had attributed all of the purchase difference to goodwill to be amortized over 20 years. Over the last five years Gamma has had earnings in excess of dividends of $30,000.

g. On 2 March 19X5 Iota purchased 1,000 shares, amounting to 44% of Rho Inc., for $750,000. At that time Rho has a book value of $1.6 million. Iota decides that the purchase difference can be attributed as follows: 50% to assetes with a 10-year life, 40% to buildings with a 20-year life, and the remainder to goodwill with a 40-year life. All of the purchase difference will be allocated on a straight-line basis. On 1 April Iota receives a $0.98 per share dividend from Rho. Rho has a net income in 19X5 of $78,000. Given a 31 December year-end, show all journal entries required for 19X5.

h. On 1 January 1975 Iota acquired a 30-year, $100,000 bond of Epsilon Ltd., paying 5% per annum at the end of each calendar year. Since that time Iota has been carrying the bond at its face value. At the 1990 year-end, 31 December, Iota decides to write down the investment to market. At that time the interest rate for a bond of similar quality to Epsilon is 13%. Give the journal entry required to write down the investment.

P10-10. On 13 August 19X0 the Pi-Meson Corporation Ltd. acquired 50,000 shares of Quark Inc. for $1 million. This amounted to 25% of the outstanding shares. At that time Quark had a net book value of $3.5 million. The excess paid for the shares could be attributed 80% to equipment that had a 5-year life span, 10% to buildings that had a 10-year life span, and the remainder to goodwill, all of which would be amortized using the straight-line method. However, because 51% of Quark was owned by Charm Ltd., Pi-Meson chose not to use the equity method to account for income from Quark.

At the end of the 19X0 fiscal year Quark reported a net income of $60,000 and paid out $80,000 in dividends. In 19X1 Charm sold all of its holdings of Quark to assorted investors. At the end of 19X1 Quark reported a net income of $80,000, all of which was paid out in dividends.

Required:

a. Should Pi-Meson switch to using the equity method after Charm sells its interest in Quark? Discuss.

b. Suppose that Pi-Meson does switch to the equity method in 19X1. Show all journal entries for Pi-Meson arising from the above transactions.

c. Which year's investment income for Pi-Meson from Quark would a financial analyst consider to be more representative of "real" income? Explain.

P10-11. On 6 June 19X2 Knesset Ltd. acquired 45% of the outstanding shares of the Panamanian-Liberian Oil Corporation Ltd. in a not entirely successful takeover attempt. It acquired 1.5 million shares at a price of $150 million.

The book value of Panamanian-Liberian was $300 million at the time of acquisition. Mr. Solomon, who headed the takeover attempt, felt that any purchase difference could be attributed to the buildings owned by the oil company, which had an expected life span of 5 years. In fiscal 19X3 Panamanian-Liberian reported a net income of $50 million; in fiscal 19X4, $75 million; and in fiscal 19X5, $40 million. Both companies have year-ends of 30 May. Ignore any partial year differences.

Required:

a. For each of the following situations give the required journal entries from 19X3 to 19X6.

(i) In each year Panamanian-Liberian pays out all of its earnings as dividends, and in fiscal 19X6 Knesset sells all of its shares in the company for $310 million.

(ii) In each year Panamanian-Liberian pays out only $10 million in dividends, and in fiscal 19X6 Knesset sells all of its shares in the company for $310 million.

b. Interpret the income (loss) made on the disposal of the shares in a(ii). How would the stock market likely react?

P10-12. Yarker Ltd. acquired 10,000 shares of Barcelona Inc. for $200,000 on 1 January 19X2. This amounted to 25% of the outstanding shares. At that time Barcelona had a net book value of $700,000. The excess paid for the shares could be attributed as follows: 60% to equipment that had a 5-year life span, 20% to buildings that had a 10-year life span, and the remainder to goodwill with a 40-year life span. All of the purchase difference was to be allocated on a straight-line basis. However, because restrictive legislation prevented Yarker from voting its shares, it chose not to use the equity method to account for Barcelona's income.

At the end of the 19X2 fiscal year, Barcelona reported a net income of $25,000 and paid out $20,000 in dividends. At the beginning of 19X3 the restrictive legislation that had prevented Yarker from voting its shares was repealed over objections from the opposition party, which threatened to introduce it again if elected. At the end of 19X3 Barcelona reported a net income of $20,000, all of which it paid out in dividends.

Required:

a. Should Yarker switch to using the equity method after the repeal of the restrictive legislation? Discuss.

b. Suppose that Yarker does switch to the equity method in 19X3. Show all journal entries arising from the above transactions for 19X3 for Yarker. Assume that Yarker does not make any retroactive applications.

c. Comment on the general merits of the equity method of accounting for long-term investments. How well does it serve the original purposes for which it was developed?

P10-13. On 1 March 19X7 the Moore Company paid $8,400 plus accrued interest to purchase 12% bonds of Kraus Inc. with a face value of $8,000. Interest on the bonds is paid semi-annually on 31 May and 30 November. Moore received cash of $3,200 on 1 October 19X7 when it sold a portion of these bonds with a face value of $3,000. The temporary investment was quoted at 90 as of 31 January 19X8.

Required:

a. Prepare all necesary dated journal entries to record the transactions relating to this temporary investment during the fiscal year ending 31 January 19X8. Show all your calculations.

b. Show how these accounts would appear on the balance sheet of the Moore Company at 31 January 19X8. Show all your calculations (*T-accounts* may be useful for your analysis.)

c. The above transactions were based on the assumption that the bonds were treated as a temporary investment. How, if at all, would their accounting treatment have differed if they had been considered to be a long-term investment? Explain.

(CMA adapted)

BIBLIOGRAPHY

APB (ACCOUNTING PRINCIPLES BOARD). *Opinion No.18*. "The Equity Method of Accounting for Common Stock". New York: AICPA, 1971.

FASB. *Interpretation No. 35*. "Criteria for Applying the Equity Method of Accounting for Investment in Common Stock." Stamford, May 1981. An interpretation of an earlier pronouncement of the Accounting Principles Board.

FASB. *Statement of Accounting Standards No. 94*. "Consolidation of All Majority-Owned Subsidiaries." Stamford, 1987. An amendment to A.R.B. No. 51 of the Committee of Accounting Procedures of the AICPA issued in 1959. This new standard requires consolidation of a majority-owned subsidiary even if it has "nonhomogeneous" operations, a large minority interest, or a foreign location.

LLOYD, MICHEL, and WEYGANDT, JERRY. "Market Value Information for Non-subsidiary Investments." *Accounting Review* (October, 1971). An examination of the usefulness of providing readers with the stock market valuation of shares in associated companies.

O'CONNOR, MELVIN C., and HAMRE, JAMES C. "Alternative Methods of Accounting for Long-Term Non-Subsidiary Intercorporate Investments in Common Stock." *Accounting Review (April, 1972)*. The authors develop an extensive matrix of possible ways of accounting for associated companies.

CHAPTER 11
Current Liabilities

Introduction

In this chapter our discussion shifts from assets to liabilities. The general definition of a **liability** is that it is a *sacrifice* one must suffer in the *future* for some *benefit* one has already received in the *past (CICA* 1000.25).

Some relationships between an asset and a liability that help to show their similarities and differences are set out below:

Characteristic	Applied to assets	Applied to liabilities
Benefit (sacrifice)	Relates to future benefits	Relates to future sacrifices
Existence on financial statements suggests the firm probably has legal ownership (liability)	The firm usually has legal title to the assets on its books, but not necessarily (e.g., leasehold improvements are not legally owned by the firm showing them on its books)	The firm usually has a legal obligation to pay the liabilities on its books, but not always (e.g., a liability may accrue for estimated warranty expenses that exceeds the amount for which the company is legally liable simply because it is the company's custom to be generous regarding customer complaints)

Characteristic	Applied to assets	Applied to liabilities
Legal ownership (liability) often means the existence of an asset (liability)	Legal ownership of something usually means that it is treated as an asset of the firm, but not necessarily (e.g., goods sold under a contract where the vendor keeps legal title until completely paid are not shown on the vendor's books after the point of sale)	Legal obligation to pay does not necessarily mean that a liability exists (e.g., outstanding purchase orders are not usually treated as liabilities for accounting purposes)
Physical form	Assets usually have physical existence, but not necessarily (e.g., intangible assets have no physical existence)	Liabilities usually are payable to a specific person or firm, but not necessarily (e.g., warranties are treated as estimated liabilities for accounting purposes, even though only the category of persons is known to whom the estimated amounts will likely be paid)

Definition of Liabilities

Although it is difficult to produce a definition of the term *liability* that suits all occasions, it is still possible to develop a working definition. It should satisfy the following three criteria:

1. A liability should involve some future sacrifice on the company's part to provide services, cash, or goods. Note that it is the probability of the sacrifice occurring some time in the future that matters, not the legal necessity to make it. A company that voluntarily fixes defective merchandise in order to preserve its good name in the marketplace — even though it is not legally required to make the repairs — would still record this future sacrifice as a liability. Thus it is possible to have a liability for accounting purposes even when none exists legally.

2. A liability should relate to events that have at least in part already occurred. For example, a company that ordered material would not consider its purchase price to be an accounting liability until the goods had been delivered by the supplier or at least until some substantial progress had been made in manufacturing them. The company is usually legally liable when it issues a purchase order that is accepted by

the supplier, but the accountant waits until some substantive step has been taken by the supplier to deliver the goods before recording the acquisition of inventory along with the acquisition of the liability. Thus it is possible to have a legal liability that is not recorded for accounting purposes. The term **executory contract** is used to refer to a contract that has been executed and is legally binding, but none of whose terms has yet been performed. Normally, executory contracts are not reflected in the accounts (although there are some exceptions, such as leases, to be discussed later). For example, a company issues a purchase order to a supplier for three personal computers. The supplier sends an invoice indicating the goods have been shipped via a truck line on 3 April. The invoice arrives on 5 April. The goods arrive on 6 April at the shipping dock and are sent to the department that ordered them. That department checks out the computers to make sure they fit the specifications of the order. It does not return the receiving report acknowledging receipt until it is satisfied that the shipment meets the order (say, 10 April). The earliest point of recognizing the liability would be when the computers are transferred to the shipping company by the supplier (3 April). The latest point would be when the receiving department sends in the receiving report (10 April). Under routine circumstances it would be the latter point in most companies.

3. A liability should be capable of being measured with reasonable accuracy in terms of amount and time of settlement. Note that it is sufficient to be able to arrive at *estimates* of the probable amount and time of settlement. It is not necessary to know the exact numbers beforehand. Moreover, it is not necessary to know to which individuals or companies the settlement will be made. Thus a manufacturer of mini-computers that warrants its product for one year need not know which of its units will have to be repaired under warranty or how much the repair of each will cost. It is sufficient for the manufacturer to know that (i) there is an identifiable group for whom warranty work will likely have to be done, (ii) the total warranty cost can be estimated, and (iii) the date when the work is likely to be done can be estimated. The motivation for creating a liability under these circumstances arises from the matching principle. If goods are sold with a promise of future repairs to be done at the vendor's expense, the matching principle indicates that the cost of these future repairs should be considered a cost of the period in which the goods were sold, not the period in which payment is made. Thus, it is possible to have an accounting liability without knowing precisely who is to get the future benefit. On the other hand, suppose a company is being sued and it is likely that it will have to pay damages to a particular individual. Whether this is treated as a liability depends on whether the ultimate cost can be reasonably estimated.

A liability is a **current liability** if either (i) it is due within a year or (ii) it is payable with a current asset or by the assumption of another current liability within the normal operating cycle of the company. Recall that the **operating cycle** is the length of time it takes the company to pay for raw material, convert it into finished product, sell it, and collect the funds from the sale. We use a similar test to distinguish current and long-term assets (see above, Chapter 1). Hence, if the operating cycle test is applied, it should result in a similar treatment of classifying current assets and current liabilities.

For instance, if the operating cycle is longer than a year, and for this reason certain inventory is classified as current, then comparable accounts payable longer than a year should also be classed as current.

By contrast, it is possible for a liability to be payable within a year and yet not be classed as current. This occurs when a long-term debt is nearing maturity. If the company intends to redeem the debt out of general funds, then it will be classed as current following the normal rules. However, if there is a firm commitment to replace it with another long-term debt instrument, then it is left as long-term debt even though it is due within the year. If this were not done, the company would show a sharp, transitory increase in its current liabilities during the year in which the debt came due.

A distinction has been made between contractual obligations on the one hand and equitable obligations and constructive obligations on the other hand. This distinction is useful when considering liabilities. A **contractual obligation** is one that arises out of an explicit legal agreement between parties, of which one is the entity being accounted for. For example, when an employee is hired his salary payment is usually expressly agreed upon, and payment of it would become a contractual obligation for the employer. An **equitable obligation** arises from ethical or moral considerations; the company undertakes it because of feelings about fairness and justice. For instance, even though there is no contractual reason to do so, some companies undertake to increase benefits paid under a pension fund if some retired employees have experienced significant erosion of their purchasing power through inflation. A **constructive obligation** arises from the facts of a particular situation, frequently by the past behavior of a company. For instance, a company that regularly gave its employees more paid holidays than the employment contract required would have incurred a constructive obligation to do the same in the future. Similarly, if they had built their good reputation with customers by being generous in accepting returned goods or in making repairs beyond the warranty period, they would find it difficult to adopt more restrictive policies without a customer backlash. This kind of obligation can be summed up in the aphorism "No good deed goes unpunished"!

Liabilities of Known Amount and Maturity

The most common type of current liability is one where the company knows the amount to be paid and when this payment must be made. Common examples will be discussed below.

ACCOUNTS PAYABLE

Accounts payable are those debts to suppliers that arise from the normal purchasing activities of the company. The purchasing process normally begins when the purchasing department chooses the supplier and agrees on the terms of the purchase. It then sends a **purchase order**, or a formal acceptance of the supplier's offer to enter into a contract to supply the goods or services. After the acceptance has taken place, there usually exists a legal contract between the two parties. A copy of the purchase order is normally sent to the receiving department to provide details about the incoming shipment. When the goods arrive the receiving department checks them and sends a **receiving report**, or a document acknowledging receipt of the goods. Most companies recognize the liability at the point when the goods are delivered according to the contract. The supplier sends an **invoice**, or his bill for the goods supplied, and this provides the evidence of the amount needed to discharge the liability.

Let us now consider some typical journal entries. A liability is set up by making an entry such as the following:

Inventory	23,456.82	
Accounts payable		23,456.82
To record accounts payable on receipt of goods for inventory.		

When the liability is discharged the entry would read as follows:

Accounts payable	23,456.82	
Bank		23,456.82
To record payment of accounts payable.		

To reduce the volume of bookkeeping, many companies do not record invoices as payable when they are received. Instead they make the following entry at the time of payment:

Inventory	17,564.72	
Bank		17,564.72
To record payment of invoice for goods.		

This cuts the number of accounting entries in half and produces exactly the same result, provided the liability is incurred and payment is made within the same accounting period. To pick up those cases where this has not happened, the unpaid invoices are totalled at the end of the accounting period, and the following type of entry is made:

Inventory	5,892.10	
Accounts payable		5,892.10
To record accounts payable at the end of the period. [A list of unpaid invoices would be attached or referenced.]		

This second method is popular with smaller companies. A person examining the unaudited financial statements of such companies should be on guard that the use of this system has not resulted in an understatement of accounts payable.

It is common for a purchaser to be allowed a **purchase discount**, or a reduction from the regular list price of the article being purchased. In such cases the net amount of the purchase, not the list price, is charged to the account. It is considered unacceptable to charge the list price to the regular account and to treat the discount as a form of income of the period. There are two main reasons for this. First, accounting entries are normally based on the *market price* of the article being purchased. The net amount after purchase discounts is closer to market than to list price. Second, there is a reluctance to approve of a method which allows an item affecting current income, purchase discounts, to be created simply by the purchase of goods and services, some of which would normally not be charged to the current period.

NOTES PAYABLE

A **note payable** is a legal document in which the company undertakes to make payment to a person named in the document (who may be *the bearer* of the note) of a stated sum at a stated time (which may be *on demand*). A note is often preferred by the creditor to an accounts receivable because it makes legal action for collection easier. A bank usually demands a note as a condition for a bank loan. Although the term *bank loan* or *bank advance* is often used, the reader is expected to understand that the company has given the bank a promissory note as a condition of the loan. Some firms combine bank loans and notes payable into one balance-sheet category, *Bank advances and notes payable*.

Large companies are able to sell their promissory notes in the open market. They find this a cheaper way to borrow for short terms than from the bank. Such promissory notes are often called **commercial paper.**

ACCRUED WAGES AND INTEREST

An **accrued liability** is one that is not legally payable as of the date of the financial statement, but will become payable later. In order to match the related expense to the proper time period, both the expense and liability are accrued in the period in which the expense should be recorded. Accrued liability is therefore a conceptual tool arising from the matching principle.

Accrued wages arise because employees' wages are payable to them after the accounting period in which they worked. If the wages were not accrued, then the cost of the partial pay period prior to the end of the accounting period would not be recorded until the next one. For example, suppose that employees are paid on the lst and 15th of every month. Further suppose that an accounting period ends on the 20th of a month. Although as of the 20th the employees have not been paid for 5 days that they have worked (16th-20th), that expense should somehow be reflected in the accounts. Therefore, the wages earned by the employees would be calculated for those four days, and a journal entry such as the following would be made:

Wages expense	15,851.92	
Accrued wages payable		15,851.92
To record wages earned in the five-day period prior to the end of the accounting period.		

The same problem occurs with bond, mortgage, or loan payments that span two adjoining accounting periods. If an accrual were not made, then all the interest expense would fall into the period in which the payment was made. For example, assume that a company with a year-end of 30 June had $180,000 in bonds outstanding that paid interest at the rate of 10% at the end of February and August. At its year-end, four months would have elapsed since the last interest payment. To record the interest in the appropriate period, it would make the following journal entry:

Interest expense	6,000.00	
Accrued interest payable		6,000.00
To record interest expense accrued from the end of February		
(4/12 of 10% of 180,000).		

Note that the interest is not legally payable until the end of August. Thus here we have a case of recording an accounting liability that is not at that time a legally payable debt.

CURRENT PORTION OF LONG-TERM DEBT

It is quite common for a company to issue long-term debt in which some portion comes due each year. This makes it more attractive to market since individual purchasers of the debt can pick the maturity date they prefer. It may also allow the company to pay off its debt as funds are generated by using the assets purchased. With such a type of debt, a portion of it becomes a current liability each year. This portion is reclassified for the balance sheet from long-term debt to current liabilities.

CUSTOMER DEPOSITS AND ADVANCE PAYMENTS

A **customer deposit** is a payment received from a customer as security that the customer will complete the purchase. Examples are deposits made to guarantee the return of some asset, such as a reusable container holding the company product or an item rented to the customer. Damage deposits are sometimes required of tenants.

A customer **advance payment** is one made before the customer takes delivery of the goods they have ordered. For example, airlines normally receive payment for their tickets in advance. Air Canada's funds on hand from advance ticket sales are over 25% of their total current liabilities. Advance payment is sometimes used in the retail trade for customers who place an order for an item that has to be custom-made (e.g., tailored clothing) or especially ordered (e.g., a new car that the dealer does not have in stock). Advance payments are also common for very large items such as jet aircraft, but here the customer normally contracts to pay stated amounts at various stages of construction. These are usually referred to as **progress payments**.

Suppose that an item is ordered that cost $85,000 and that an advance payment of $10,000 is required when it is ordered. The entry on receipt of payment would read as follows:

Bank	10,000.00	
Advance payments		10,000.00
To record receipt of advance payment in accordance with		
the terms of the sales contract.		

When the item is finished and the revenue is recognized, the following entry would be made:

Accounts receivable	75,000.00	
Advance payments	10,000.00	
Sales		85,000.00
To record sale.		

INCOME TAX WITHHELD
AND SALES TAXES COLLECTED

All companies are involuntary tax collectors because by law they must collect the bulk of the taxes levied by governments against individuals through income tax withholdings and sales tax collections. In addition, employers are expected to make withholdings from employees' salaries for a variety of other reasons, such as union dues and medical benefits. The author has seventeen different categories of withholding from his monthly salary. We will deal here only with income taxes as an important type of withholding from employee wages. The accounting treatment for the other types of withholding is similar.

Income taxes are collected by withholding part of employees' wages and remitting them to the government. Let us assume that an employee is owed $800.00 in salary and that $250.00 in income taxes must be withheld. The entry on payment of the salary would be as follows:

Salary expense	800.00	
Income tax withholding liability		250.00
Bank		550.00
To record payment of salary of $800.00 with tax withholding of $250.00.		

The tax withheld must be remitted to the taxation authority at regular intervals. In our example entry would be as follows:

Income tax withholding liability	250.00	
Bank		250.00
To record payment of Revenue Canada of tax withheld.		

Sales taxes are collected at the point of sale and then remitted to the taxation authority. The entry to record the sale of an item with the related tax collection would resemble the following:

Accounts receivable	432.00	
Sales		400.00
Sales tax liability		32.00
To record sale.		

Estimated Liabilities

Frequently it is not possible to know at the date of the financial statements what the amount of a liability is because it will be affected by events in the future. The accountant's response to this is first to estimate and record the liability in the period called for by the matching principle and then to make correcting entries when the actual amounts are known. Since the correcting entries may not be made until a later accounting period, such estimates may produce earnings estimates that later turn out to be in need of adjustment. Nevertheless, despite the uncertainty of the estimates, this is an area where the accountant prefers to be approximately right by recording the liabilities rather than precisely wrong by omitting them altogether.

ESTIMATED INCOME TAXES

Income taxes are an important estimated liability for most companies. The need for estimation arises because the taxation authorities retain the right to reassess the taxpayer if they disagree with the company's estimate of tax payable, and the taxpayer has the later right to appeal the assessment through the courts. Since these procedures may take place many years after the taxation year, the tax expense related to any given year is necessarily an estimate.

At the end of each financial year the company makes an estimate of the taxes payable with respect to that year. (The procedure for making this estimate will be addressed briefly in Chapter 13). The entry would take the following form:

        Tax provision (expense)
        xxxxx
                Taxes payable (liability)

        xxxxx
        To record estimated taxes payable with respect to the
            current year.

Corporations are required to make monthly instalment payments based on the lesser of their prior year's tax and their estimated current year's tax. When these payments are made, the entry would take the following form:

        Taxes payable (liability)
        xxxxx
                Bank

        xxxxx
        To record monthly instalment.

If subsequent events show that the tax provision was incorrect, the adjustment is shown on the income statement of the year in which the re-estimate was made. If material, it is shown separately as a prior-period adjustment [*CICA* 3600, and 1506.25].

WARRANTIES

A **warranty** is an undertaking by a vendor to maintain and repair an item sold according to the terms of the warranty agreement. For example, a new car is usually sold with a warranty that the manufacturer will pay for repairs within some distance limit (e.g., 20,000 kilometres) and some time limit (e.g., twelve months). A warranty is a method for making the article more salable. Hence, according to the matching principle, the cost of the warranty should be charged to the period in which the profit on the sale is recognized. Usually much of the warranty work is done in accounting periods following the sale. Thus, the cost of the warranty must be estimated in the year of the sale and the corresponding liability recorded. When the warranty work is actually done it is charged against this liability account. Periodically the warranty costs need to be re-estimated, and the liability account is revised at those times.

For example, a nursery sells evergreen trees under the slogan, "If it doesn't grow, we replace it free." They estimate that the probability of having to replace a tree is as follows:

In the first year	5%
In the second year	2%
In the third year	1%

The average cost of replacing a tree is estimated to be $80.00. At the end of each accounting period, the number of evergreen trees sold is determined and the following type of entry is made:

Warranty expense	25,600.00	
Estimated warranty liability		25,600.00

To record estimated warranty liability arising from sale of evergreen trees, as follows:

Number of trees sold		4,000
Estimated cost of replacement:		
first year	4000 × 0.05 × 80 =	16,000
second year	4000 × 0.02 × 80 =	6,400
third year	4000 × 0.01 × 80 =	3,200
Total estimated liability		$ 25,600

When a customer is provided with a replacement tree, the cost is accumulated and charged to the liability account in the following manner:

Estimated warranty liability	98.00	
Inventory — evergreen trees		45.00
Wages expense		38.00
Transportation expense		15.00

To record replacement of evergreen tree under warranty.

The above entry shows that wages and transportation were charged to expense accounts when the original expenditure was made and that it is now necessary to reallocate the expenditure to the warranty liability account. This will reduce the balance in this account. Note that the cost of replacing this tree is $98, or $18 higher than the estimated average cost. If replacement costs continue to be this high, by the end of the year the balance in the liability account will be inadequate.

At the end of the first warranty year, a re-estimate must be made of the company's warranty experience in order to revise the estimated liability. At that time one might find that two parameters turned out differently from their original estimates: (i) the estimated cost of fulfilling the warranty and (ii) the probability of warranty work having to be done. If, in the preceding example, the trees had been very healthy and the weather had been unusually good, the claims under the warranty program might have been smaller than predicted. The liability account would then have been larger than necessary to pay the remaining warranty costs. In that case the revising entry would have been as follows:

Estimated warranty liability	xxxxx	
Warranty expense		xxxxx

To reduce estimated warranty liability because of lower-
than-expected claims in the first year.

The company will not know if its estimates are correct until the warranty finally ends. In our example, for instance, it may turn out that in the next year the growing conditions are particularly bad and the percentage of trees replaced is much higher than previous experience would have suggested. The company would know after the event that it should not have reduced its estimated liability by as much as it did; but by that time its financial report would have been long since published.

PREMIUMS AND TRADING STAMPS

A **premium** is an item of value that is supplied to a purchaser in consideration of that purchaser buying some product. Sometimes the premium is included in the product (e.g., boxes of breakfast food may contain premiums such as flower seeds, toys, or foreign coins of small value). Sometimes, however, a certificate is given that entitles the customer to obtain the premium later. For example, some breakfast cereal manufacturers promise purchasers a premium if they send in a stated number of box tops. Similarly, certificates are sometimes sold with personal computer software that entitle the holder to a reduced price on a later version of the software when it comes on the market.

A **trading stamp** is a specially designed stamp or coupon that is given by a retailer to a customer as an incentive to make further purchases in the future. The customer can later redeem such stamps or coupons for merchandise. An example is the Canadian Tire "money" given to customers who pay in cash. At any given time, a larger number of unredeemed stamps or coupons will be in the hands of customers, and the company will have to estimate this liability.

Certificates of the type described above usually have an expiry date beyond which they have no value. This not only encourages their quick use, but also helps to simplify the calculation of the company's liability, especially if expiry occurs one or two months prior to the company's year-end.

The accounting principles for both premiums and trading stamps are similar to those for warranties. Here we will illustrate the procedure for premiums. The matching principle requires that the expense should be recorded when the merchandise is sold. In this instance, one must estimate (i) the probability that the premium will be claimed and (ii) the cost of the premium.

For example, Kiddies Cookies marketed biscuits for children that contained a coupon in each box. Ten such coupons could be redeemed for a bag of balloons that cost the company $0.80 to buy and $0.40 to package and send. It is estimated that 70% of the coupons will be redeemed. During its first year the company sold 40,000 boxes of cookies. The entry to record the estimated liability would be as follows:

Premium expense	3,360.00	
Estimated premium liability		3,360.00

To record estimated expense of premium offer in cookies, as follows:

Sales — in boxes	40,000
Ratio of coupons to premium	10:1
Total number of premiums redeemable	4,000
Estimated percentage redeemed	70%
Estimated cost of premium	$1.20
Total estimated cost	$3,360

During this first year 20,000 coupons were actually redeemed. The entry to record the redemption would read as follows:

Estimated premium liability (2,000 × 1.20)	2,400.00	
Inventory — balloons (2,000 × 0.80)		1,600.00
Bank — for packaging and mailing costs (2,000 × 0.40)		800.00

To record 20,000 coupons redeemed for balloon premium.

The balance in the estimated premium account at the end of the financial year would be (3,360 − 2,400), or $960. It would be necessary at that time to make another estimate of the probability of the remaining coupons being redeemed and to adjust the liability account accordingly. For example, if it was estimated that 450 more coupons would be redeemed and that these outstanding coupons would cost the company $540, then the following entry would be made:

Estimated premium liability	420.00	
Premium expense		420.00

To revise estimated expense of premium offer in cookies from $960 to $540.

CONTAINER DEPOSITS

It is quite common for the deposits required by some companies on their reusable containers to give rise to an estimated liability. For example, a company ships its product in reusable containers and requires a refundable deposit of $60.00 per container. When the customer is invoiced for the product the deposit is added on. Suppose the product itself cost $300.00 per container and the customer bought three containers. The company would make the following entry:

Accounts receivable	1,080.00	
Sales		900.00
Deposits payable		180.00

To record sale of three containers of product at $300 each,
and charge for deposit on three containers at $60 each.

If the containers were returned, the entry would read as follows:

Deposits payable	180.00	
Accounts receivable		180.00

To record receipt of containers and return of deposit.

The need for estimation arises because not all containers are likely to be returned. In effect the customer has "bought" the containers for $60.00 each. Periodically the company makes an estimate of the container deposits that are expected to be returned and adjusts the liability account accordingly. If, for example, the books showed a balance of $23,850.00 in the customer deposit account, and the company estimated that only $18,000.00 are likely to be returned, it would make the following entry:

Customer deposits payable	5,850.00	
Sales — containers		5,850.00

To write down customer deposits account to $18,000, the
amount estimated as still outstanding.

At the same time it would be necessary to revise the estimate of the container inventory and write off any shortage, as follows:

Cost of sales — containers	xxxxx	
Inventory — containers		xxxxx

To record revised estimate.

Valuation of Liabilities

The valuation of liabilities is similar to the valuation of receivables. There is a presumption that the liability will be shown at its present value if the difference between its present value and face amount is material. This is most likely to occur if the liability extends beyond one year and interest payments are significantly different from the market rate of interest.

For example, A Ltd. purchased a piece of equipment on 1 April for $100,000. Under the terms of the purchase it did not have to make payment for eighteen months and was not obliged to make interest payments. The rate of interest it would normally have had to pay is 12% compounded monthly. When it recorded this transaction it would calculate the implicit interest cost of the loan by finding the present value of a payment of $100,000 due in eighteen months at 12% discounted monthly. The calculation would yield the following:

$$100,000 / (1.01)^{18} = 83,601.73$$

Hence the company would make the following journal entry:

Equipment	83,601.73	
Deferred interest expense	16,398.27	
Loan payable — face amount		100,000.00

To record purchase of equipment for $100,000 payable in eighteen months, discounted at 12% compounded monthly.

If the company's year-end was 30 June, it would treat a portion of the deferred interest expense as an expense of the period. In the U.S. the company would be expected to use the interest method for allocating this expense. Hence it would calculate the expense as 1% of the outstanding balance at the end of each month, as follows:

Month	Capital	Interest at 12% / 12
April	83,601.73	836.02
May	84,437.75	844.38
June	85,282.12	852.82
		2,533.22

Another approach would be to use the straight-line method. In the U.S. this is an acceptable alternative if the results are not materially different. The difference would be as follows:

Straight-line (16,398.27 × 3/18)	2,733.05
Interest method (see above)	2,533.22
Difference	199.83

Unless one evaluated all other factors, such as the total amount of interest expense, it is not possible to say whether the above difference is material or not. Initially, at least, it does not seem to be material.

The treatment shown here is part of the developed accounting standards in the United States. In Canada there is no specific standard set out in the *CICA Handbook*.

Contingent Liabilities

A **contingent liability** is one where the occurrence or non-occurrence of some future event will strongly influence the amount or timing (or both) of the payment of the liability. A classic example is a lawsuit that will be settled some time after the company's year-end. At the time the financial statements are prepared, one may know the damages that the plaintiff is asking; but the outcome of the case may be uncertain enough that one cannot know for sure whether the case will be won or lost, and if lost, what the damages are likely to be. This may ultimately give rise to a prior-period adjustment.

It is useful to compare contingent liabilities with estimated liabilities such as premiums, where there is also some uncertainty about the ultimate amount that has to be paid. In our example above illustrating premiums, it was believed that 70% of the premiums would be redeemed. If one were to ask the decision-maker for more detail about this belief, the response might be that 70% was the average expectation and that this was calculated by estimating the probability of all possible redemption rates. See Columns A, B. and C below.

Possible redemption rates A	Probability of each redemption rate occuring B	Expected redemption C	Cost at redemption rate shown D	Estimated liability E
0.50	0.03	0.015	$2,400	$ 72.00
0.60	0.13	0.078	2,880	374.40
0.70	0.65	0.455	3,360	2,184.00
0.80	0.19	0.152	3,840	729.60
	1.00	0.700		$3,360.00

The costs resulting from these different rates are shown in Column D. They are calculated by multiplying the estimated cost of $4,800 if all coupons are redeemed (4,000 premiums at $1.20) by the redemption rate shown in Column A. Column E is calculated by multiplying the expected redemption rate (joint probabilities in column C) by the total possible liabilities ($4,800), or alternatively by multiplying Column B by Column D. This analysis shows that the expected redemption cost might be as high as $3,840 or as low as $2,400 (Column D), but the average expected cost is $3,360 (total of Column E). Since all the expected outcomes tend to cluster around the average, the accountant can feel reasonably comfortable in using the estimate of $3,360 to make the journal entry.

In the case of a lawsuit, however, a similar analysis might show the following:

Possible outcomes of lawsuit	Probability of each outcome occurring	Cost to settle each outcome	Expected liability
Lost nothing	0.30	$ 0	0
Lose costs = $3,000	0.50	$ 3,000	1,500
Pay damages = $30,000	0.18	$ 30,000	5,400
Pay damages = $300,000	0.02	$300,000	6,000
	1.00		$12,900

Although the procedure is the same as the calculation of the estimated premium liability, the accountant may feel very uncomfortable in showing an estimated liability of $12,900 on the balance sheet when the loss might be as high as $300,000. The basic problem here is that the expected loss of $12,900 is not very useful in giving a picture of the outcome because there is such a wide spread between the best outcome (losing nothing) and the worst (losing $300,000). In this situation the accountant's solution is to give more information about the situation so that the reader can make an evaluation of the likely outcomes.

The *CICA Handbook* distinguishes three categories of situations [*CICA* 3290.15]. The first category is **likely**, where the probability is high that a given event will occur or not occur. This is the case with the estimated warranty and premium liabilities. The second category is **unlikely**, where the probability of occurrence is slight. This is the case with the lawsuit ending up with a settlement of $300,000 in the example above. The third category is **not determinable**, where the decision-maker is unable to estimate the probabilities of the various outcomes occurring — or perhaps cannot even predict the possible outcomes.

For the *likely* category the *Handbook* [3290.12] recommends that the liability should be estimated and entered in the books (as shown above in our example of premiums). For the *unlikely* category and the *not determinable* category, the Handbook [3290.15] requires disclosure in the notes to the financial statements. For these two categories the *Handbook* [3290.22] further specifies that the following information should be provided: (i) the nature of the contingency; (ii) an estimate of the amount of the contingent loss, or a statement that such an estimate cannot be made; and (iii) whether the ultimate settlement will be treated as a prior-period adjustment or included in the income of the period in which the settlement occurs. The *Handbook* [3290.23] also states it is desirable that contingencies be noted on the face of the balance sheet.

Subsequent Events

Sometimes a significant event occurs after the end of the fiscal year but before the auditors express their opinion. Such an event may either (i) throw new light on the valuation of an asset or liability on the financial statements of the prior year or (ii) significantly alter the financial affairs of the company subsequent to the end of the fiscal year.

An example of the first type would be a bankruptcy of a significant customer, whose accounts receivable is now seen to be worth significantly less than was estimated at the time the financial statements were prepared. Another example of the first type would be an estimated warranty liability that is seen to be understated because of a rash of product defects that came to light after the year-end. An example of the second type would be significant damage to the company's plant arising from some event such as a flood, fire, or earthquake.

The *CICA Handbook* [3820] specifies how to deal with such events. For the first type of significant event, the accepted practice is to revise the financial statements before they are issued to show the corrected amounts. For the second type of significant event, the accepted practice is to disclose the existence of the event and to give a description and an estimate, where practicable, of the financial effect.

Contractual Obligations

A company can enter into contractual arrangements that will have a significant effect on the company's future but that do not at the time give rise to any transaction that would be recorded as an accounting liability. Arrangements of this sort would include the following: commitments with a high degree of speculative risk that are not in the ordinary course of business (e.g., an undertaking by a Canadian manufacturer of restaurant equipment to do land development in the Bahamas); commitments that are not risky but are abnormal (e.g., an agreement to make a large plant asset purchase); commitments to issue shares; and commitments that will "govern the level of a certain type of expenditure for a considerable period of time" (e.g., the employment contracts that professional hockey and baseball teams enter into with their star players). If obligations of this type exist as of the date of the financial statements, the *CICA Handbook* [3280.01] requires disclosure.

Examples from Published Reports

Here we present examples of U.S. companies because the legal situation in that country makes the likelihood of damaging lawsuits much higher. Hence, disclosure with respect to liability is especially significant there.

Minnesota Mining and Manufacturing Company

Excerpts from the financial statements of 3M have been given above in Chapters 6, 9, and 10.

BALANCE SHEET

	1986	1985
	(millions of $)	
Current Liabilities:		
Accounts payable	$ 519	$ 411
Payrolls	271	220
Income taxes	254	169
Other current liabilities	368	320
Short-term debt	411	459
Total current liabilities	$1,823	$1,579
Balance-Sheet Information		
Short-Term Debt:		
Commercial paper and equivalents	$215	$301
Long-term debt — current portion	112	13
Other borrowing	84	145
Total short-term debt	$411	$459

The liability side of this company's balance sheet looks quite straightforward. The note on litigation and claims reads as follows:

> Various legal actions, government proceedings and other claims are pending against the company and certain of its subsidiaries. In some cases, these actions seek damages as well as other relief which, if granted, would require sizable expenditures.
>
> Although the total amount of liability at December 31, 1986, with respect to such matters cannot be ascertained, it is the opinion of counsel for the company that any resulting liability will not materially affect the financial statements of the company.

The equivalent note for General Motors of Canada says something almost identical:

> There are various claims and pending actions against the company with respect to product liability, warranties and other matters arising out of the conduct of the business. The amounts of liability on these claims and actions at December 31, 1986 were not determinable but, in the opinion of management, the ultimate resulting liability will not materially affect the financial position or results of operations of the company.

The Dow Chemical Company

Dow is a large multi-national company that makes chemicals and plastics.

BALANCE SHEET

	1987	1986
	(millions of $)	
Current Liabilities:		
Notes payable	$ 129	$ 221
Long-term debt due within one year	50	58
Accounts payable:		
Trade	1,085	901
Other	498	276
United States and foreign taxes on income	511	346
Accrued and other current liabilities	1,182	1,135
	$3,455	$2,937

Note I — Notes Payable
Notes payable consisted primarily of obligations due banks with a variety of interest rates and maturities. There was no commercial paper in notes payable at December 31, 1986, or at December 31, 1987.

Note P — Commitments and Contingent Liabilities (All amounts are in millions of dollars)
The Company and its subsidiaries are parties to a number of claims and lawsuits

arising out of the normal course of business with respect to commercial matters including product liabilities, government regulation including environmental matters, and other actions. Certain of these actions purport to be class actions and seek damages in very large amounts. All such claims are being contested. The amounts of ultimate liability thereunder are not determinable at December 31, 1987. The Company is also party to several lawsuits arising out of insurance policies issued to the Company and its subsidiaries. These lawsuits involve the recoverability under these insurance policies of certain losses and expenses incurred by the Company. In the opinion of management, resolution of these matters will not materially affect the consolidated financial position or results of operations of the Company and its subsidiaries.

As a general partner of several partnerships, the Company may be liable for any deficiencies which may arise in meeting the terms of loan obligations incurred by the partnerships. Assets of the partnerships which have been pledged as security for these loans are currently in excess of the loan obligations.

The Company has various purchase commitments for materials, supplies and items of permanent investment related to the ordinary conduct of business. Such commitments are not at prices in excess of current market. While certain of these commitments are for quantities in excess of the Company's present requirements, they are not expected to have any material adverse effect on the consolidated financial position or results of operation of the Company.

At December 31, 1987, pursuant to an agreement with Royal Trustco Ltd., the Company had an indemnity of $14 on loans with face value of $49. A Canadian subsidiary has entered into two 20-year agreements to purchase substantially all the output of an ethylene plant (Plant No. 1) and 40% of the output of a second ethylene plant (plant No. 2) upon its completion. The purchase price of the output is determined on a cost-of-service basis which, in addition to covering all operating expenses, provides the owner of the plants with a specified return on capital. [The note continues with details of other financial commitments.]

Extensive information is given on lawsuits against the Company. A *class-action lawsuit* is one where a plaintiff sues the company on behalf of all other possible plaintiffs in the same class. If successful, such a suit can be very costly to the company because it must pay damages to all the defendants, not just the one who started the suit. Class-action lawsuits are virtually unknown in Canada. Moreover, in most parts of the U.S. lawyers are permitted to base their fee on the amount of damages collected ("contingent fees"). Thus the plaintiff would not pay a legal fee unless the lawyer were successful. This tends to encourage more people to engage lawyers and sue. It also encourages lawyers to seek large amounts in damages on behalf of their clients. By contrast, in Canada the legal fee is based on the amount of time it takes the lawyer to argue the case. Thus an unsuccessful plaintiff must still pay legal fees.

Observe that extensive information is also given about commitments the company has entered into that have not yet reached the stage of being considered liabilities for accounting purposes.

Summary

Current liabilities are those due within one year or within the company's operating cycle if this is longer. Discharge of liabilities may be either by payment of a current asset or by discharge of services. Most liabilities represent legal debts of the entity, although this is not necessary for an accounting liability to be so recognized. Not all legal obligations are recognized as accounting liabilities because an accounting liability requires one of the parties to the contract to have made some payment or provided some of the services or product required by the contract. In addition, if the liability cannot be reasonably estimated, it is not included in the books of the company. Instead, disclosure is made through the notes to the financial statements.

QUESTIONS

Q11-1. Review and be sure you understand the following terms:

    a. accounting liability *versus* legal liability

    b. current liabilities *versus* long-term liabilities

    c. operating cycle

    d. contractual obligation *versus* equitable obligation and constructive obligation

    e. accounts payable

    f. purchase order

    g. receiving report

    h. invoice

    i. note payable

    j. commercial paper

    k. accrued liability

    l. customer deposit

    m. advance payment

    n. progress payments

    o. estimated liability

    p. warranty

    q. premium

    r. trading stamp

    s. contingent liability

    t. likely *versus* unlikely *versus* not determinable outcomes for contingencies

Q11-2. "The role of accounting reports is to reflect the economic reality of the company. For that reason there should be no hesitation in ignoring the legal arrangements with respect to liabilities." Discuss.

Q11-3. State, giving reasons, whether you would expect to find each of the following classified as current or non-current liabilities.

    a. A company has issued $100,000 in bonds. $10,000 come due at the end of each of the ten years that the bonds will be outstanding.

    b. Mammoth Construction is putting up a building that will take three years to build. Under the terms of its purchase agreement with certain suppliers it will not be obliged to pay them for the material supplied, costing $150,000, until after the building has been certified by the customer as acceptable. This is not expected to happen for another eighteen months.

    c. Odessa Manufacturing has an agreement with a firm that supplies a large component that goes into its finished product that Odessa will not be asked for payment until the product is finished and Odessa itself is paid. The completion time of the product is not exactly certain at this point, but the best guess is that it will take another twenty months to complete it and bill the customer.

Q11-4. "Accounting should come into the 20th century. Instead of trying to cram all information about a liability into just one number, accountants should be prepared to give probability distributions about (i) the likelihood that the amount will be paid and (ii) the amount to be paid." Discuss.

Q11-5. "Unfortunately for the readers of financial statements, some very important liabilities never appear on the balance sheet. They are left off because accountants cannot be completely certain what the ultimate amount payable is likely to be." Do you agree? Discuss.

Q11-6. Imagine an accounting system in which the company's liability was set up as soon as a purchase order was issued, instead of when the goods were received. What significant changes, if any, would this make to the balance sheet of a typical retail clothing store? Would the statements be more useful or less useful? Why?

Q11-7. Give three examples of each of the following:

    a. liabilities shown on the financial statements where the company has no legal liability to make payment or provide services

    b. legal liabilities of the company that are left off the financial statements according to generally accepted accounting principles

    c. assets shown on the balance sheet that have no physical existence

    d. assets shown on the balance sheet that the company does not own

    e. assets owned by the company that are not on the balance sheet

Q11-8. Is it possible for a company to record as an asset something to which it has no legal title by incurring a liability it has no legal obligation to pay? Explain.

Q11-9. State, giving reasons, whether each of the following would be treated as current liabilities for accounting purposes. In each case the company's year-end is 30 July.

    a. A bond issued by the company pays interest at the end of June and December.

    b. A rental agreement is signed on 3 July in which the company agrees to rent office space from 1 September of that year at the rate of $2,000 a month. The company gives a deposit of $1,500 on signing the lease.

    c. A retail store sold a suit to a customer who brought it back and pointed out that it did not fit. The store sent it to the tailor for alterations on 15 July. At July 30 it had not yet been returned.

d. A house-painting firm painted a house in May. The customer complained about the workmanship, and the painting crews returned twice in response. At the end of July the customer was still unhappy and was threatening a lawsuit. The company believes the complaints are petty, but is thinking of sending a painter around in August to make one more try.

e. A neighbourhood car repair garage is accused by a customer of failing to instal the brake system properly after a repair job. The customer had an accident that she claims arose from this brake failure and her insurance company has notified the garage that it will be held responsible for any damage settlement. The owner of the garage has read his own insurance policy and does not think it covers him for this situation.

Q11-10. Explain how the matching principle leads accountants to set up liabilities when they do not know to or for whom the payment or service will ultimately be provided. Give three examples.

Q11-11. Would the following be short-term liabilities, long-term liabilities, neither, or both? Explain.

a. Money is borrowed on a promissory note due in two years. It is intended to finance the inventory of wine, which needs to be aged for at least two years.

b. Money is borrowed on a promissory note due in two years. It is needed for general financing purposes of the company, but mostly to finance the accounts receivable that have been building up as the company has grown.

c. An agreement is made with the company's bank to borrow $85,000 starting in two weeks. As part of the documentation in preparation for the loan, the company treasurer signs a demand promissory note for $85,000 that is left with the bank.

d. A company sells a bond issue with a face value of $2,000,000 and a maximum term of ten years. Each year one-tenth of the bonds become due. Thus in the tenth year only $200,000 is outstanding.

e. A company borrows $300,000 from the bank under terms in which it is informally understood between the bank and the company treasurer what the terms of repayment will be. Nevertheless, under bank regulations the company is required to give the bank a promissory note payable on demand for $300,000. The main purpose of the note is that the bank can demand immediate payment if the informal agreement is not adhered to.

Q11-12. Beta Inc. had a warranty policy under which it guaranteed for two years the washing machines that it sold. It had had a dispute with a customer over the performance of one of its machines in its 19X3 fiscal year, and the customer had sued the company prior to the year-end. Beta had estimated its probable loss when sued would be $800. Therefore, it had included this amount as an estimated short-term liability on its 19X3 balance sheet. Subsequent to that date negotiations with the customer had been successful in persuading the customer to take a new machine in full settlement of the claim. The new machine is now being shipped to the customer and a journal entry is needed to record the shipment and cancel the estimated liability. The new machine is in the company's inventory at $450. Show the journal entry to record this.

Q11-13. We began this chapter by defining liabilities according to certain characteristics and criteria. By referring to this material, explain whether each of the following should be considered a liability:

a. A company that "packages" tours for travel agents is completely sold out on a "gala train trip" to Moosonee. It plans to stage a "welcome aboard" party which it estimates will cost $750. Those people going on the tour are unaware of the planned party, which will take place at the start of the trip two weeks from today. The company has the practice of recognizing revenue on each trip package when the tour is completed.

b. Would your answer to (a) have been any different had the company adopted the practice of recognizing the income on each package when it was sold out or completely committed to take place? Explain.

c. A week before the tour started the manager of the company was asked what liabilities she had incurred in connection with it. She replied: "We have $30,000 in customer deposits, with about $42,000 yet to come. We have unpaid advertising costs of $4,000, and then we'll owe about $9,000 to the railway and about $10,000 to the bus companies. These costs are due within ten days of the start of the trip."

d. After the trip was completed the company received a letter from a passenger's lawyer. It stated that the client had suffered a dislocated shoulder because of an unsafe stairway which the group had been directed to take. The client was asking damages of $1,200. On enquiring about the details of the accident from the tour staff, it was learned that one of the passengers had suffered a slight fall on returning to the hotel after a party. The company believes it has no liability, but is referring the letter to its own lawyer.

e. The company has a promotion in which all of those taking one of its package trips automatically become eligible for a "double it up" draw at the end of the year. If the passenger's name is drawn, the full amount of the trip is returned, and the passenger is given a credit on the next trip equal to the amount paid on the previous one. The company expects to sell 2,000 trips during the year. Given that the company will select a winner from all the passengers, each individual trip-holder would have a 0.05% chance of winning.

Q11-14. In this chapter we caution against treating as current period income the purchase discounts on the purchase of inventory. What reasons are given? Explain how a company could create current income by this method. What would the journal entry be for this?

Q11-15. Accrued liabilities are described as "a conceptual tool arising from the matching principle." What does this mean?

Q11-16. Companies occasionally make the news because they have gone bankrupt "owing the tax collector millions of dollars." Cite two types of debts that might be owing Revenue Canada by a bankrupt corporation.

Q11-17. Consider the following independent scenarios:

(i) Champ printers sells a line of dot-matrix printers for home computers. Each printer is shipped with a warranty card that the purchaser has to fill out and return in order to validate the warranty. This gives the purchaser the right to free repair of the printer for one year. Although the printer is a new model, the company estimates that the frequency-of-repair record will be about the same as its previous model. The repair work is done by authorized dealers who then bill the company for the work done, using predetermined costs for labour hours. Parts are supplied by the company.

(ii) Nifty Trust is a trust company that conducts a promotion to encourage the use of its savings accounts. Customers who deposit money into their account are given one coupon for each $100 deposited. They are invited to fill out their name and address on each coupon and deposit them into a drum prominently displayed in each office.

At the beginning of each month the coupons so deposited are mixed and one is drawn. The person whose name is drawn is entitled to receive a new car if successful in answering a skill-testing question and if agreeable to having his or her name and photo used in subsequent company promotions.

(iii) Frontenac Quilters is a society whose members are interested in producing, displaying, and encouraging the appreciation of fine quilts as works of fibre art. They are about to finish a quilt that will either be sold or given away at a lottery. They have already held a silent auction among their members and the highest a member is willing to bid for the quilt is $1,500. Under the terms of the auction that member is committed to offer $1,500 to the person who successfully wins a lottery, to be held when the quilt is finished. At the close of the group's fiscal year they have sold 1,000 lottery tickets for a total of $1,000. They expect to sell 1,000 more before the lottery on the quilt is held.

Required:
For each of the above, answer the following:

a. Explain how the warranty (or trading stamp or premium) expense might be calculated in the period of sale.

b. Explain how the related outstanding liability might be calculated at the end of each fiscal period.

Q11-18. This chapter includes an example of a company that gives a warranty on each tree it sells. We mentioned one possible scenario in which the company realizes well after the end of the fiscal year that it should not have reduced its estimated liability by as much as it had. In this scenario, should the company in the following year(s) treat the adjustment of the estimated liability as a prior-period adjustment? Explain.

Q11-19. It has been suggested that the point at which a liability is recognized should be influenced by the type of benefit the company receives when incurring the liability. If the benefit will yield cash in the near term (e.g., from an inventory purchase), it is not particularly urgent to recognize the liability until the inventory arrives. On the other hand, if the liability is being incurred to purchase something with cash inflows that will take place long after the liability is discharged, then it is more important that the liability be recognized in advance of the cash flows. What considerations do you think might have led to this suggestion? Discuss.

Q11-20. There are two golf clubs reasonably close to each other outside the same city. They both charge their members a one-time fee of $2,000 when they first join. Club One holds the fee as long as the person stays a member, but returns it if the person quits (but not if the person dies). Club Two treats the fee as non-refundable. What accounting policy should each club follow on receipt of the fee? Justify your position by reference to good accounting treatment of liabilities.

Q11-21. The following note appeared in the financial statements of General Motors of Canada Limited for 31 December 1986.

Subsequent Event
On January 8, 1987 General Motors Corporation signed a letter of intent for the sale of its North American transit bus business. As part of the sale, the company will sell its St. Eustache, Quebec bus plant and service parts inventories relating to its transit business. The purchase price and resulting gain or loss on the disposal of this segment of the business has not yet been determined but is not expected to have a material effect on the company's financial statements.

Required: What type of subsequent event does this appear to be? Explain.

EXERCISES

E11-1. Explain whether each of the following events would increase the estimated liability, decrease it, or leave it unchanged. In one or more instances, there may be insufficient information to allow for a conclusion. If that is so, explain what additional information you would need to be able to determine the direction of change.

   a. A manufacturer of TV sets finds that the sets are distinctly more reliable than was predicted when making the warranty estimate.

   b. A house-painting company has had trouble with paint peeling on the finished work. Therefore, it has been doing repairs at its own expense to keep customer goodwill. It hopes to regain the cost of this work from the paint supplier because the supplier has acknowledged that the paint is defective.

   c. A supplier of video games warrants them for twelve months. The games have turned out to be more defective than was thought at the time of sale. In the meantime, new games have come on the market that are so much better that the purchasers of the original games have lost interest in them. Thus it appears that few of the original games will be returned.

   d. A milk company uses heavy-duty plastic crates for its milk bottles and charges a deposit for them. Recently the crates have become popular with the college set to store their possessions, and the company finds that fewer of them are being returned.

   e. A supplier of nuclear electrical generating stations offered its plants for sale with a guarantee lasting for seven years that if the price of uranium fuel went up beyond a stated level, it would pay the difference in cost. The guarantee was designed to absorb most of the risk for the purchaser and to make the purchase more attractive. Unfortunately, the price of uranium went up well above the stated level after five years.

E11-2. Indicate whether each of the following should be (i) estimated and entered in the books of the company or (ii) left out of the books and shown in the notes to the financial statements. Give your reasons.

   a. A chemical company has manufactured an agricultural pesticide under licence from the inventor for the past five years. The pesticide had been approved for agricultural use on the basis of safety tests carried out by a licensed independent laboratory. Recently doubt has been cast on the reliability of a number of tests carried out by that laboratory, and there is some suspicion that the pesticide may be responsible for birth defects. The company has recently received a letter from a lawyer threatening a lawsuit if her client does not receive payment for alleged damages.

   b. Manville Corporation, a large U.S. supplier of asbestos products, commissioned a health-data research firm in Boston to provide an estimate of its probable losses through lawsuits for workers who had used its asbestos products. The firm estimated that the company faced 32,000 new lawsuits and that the average cost of disposing of each case was $40,000. The company has a net worth, before deducting probable cost of lawsuits, of $1.2 billion.

   c. In September 1975 Westinghouse Corporation told its customers that it would be unable to fulfil its contract to supply them with 80 million pounds of uranium at a price not exceeding $10. It held only 15 million pounds at the time, and the current market price for uranium was between $40 and $45 per pound. It thus had a potential liability of about $2.275 billion.

   d. A corporation that was the object of takeover bids from other corporations found it difficult to attract or hold senior executive officers. Therefore, it entered into a contract with them termed a "golden parachute" in which it offered to make a very generous cash settlement with them if the company was taken over and they were forced to leave. It is estimated that the company could face a maximum payment under this agreement of $3.5 million. At the moment there is no threatened takeover of the company.

E11-3. Ace Oil Limited has a promotional deal with a grocery chain that permits the chain to give its customers who buy $20 or more in groceries "One Dollar Off" coupons that entitle the holder to one dollar off the purchase of a tank of gasoline. Ace sells coupons to the grocery chain for $0.65 each. At the end of its 19X3 fiscal year Ace sold coupons for a total of $65,000. Of these, coupons with a face value of $50,000 had been redeemed on gas purchases by the middle of the year. Ace estimates that an additional face value of $30,000 will be redeemed by the end of the fiscal year, when the coupon expires. The gasoline subject to rebate is being sold at its normal price. Calculate the gain or loss that Ace should report on the coupon deal.

E11-4. For each of the following independent situations, indicate how the Baird Company should treat the liability on its year-end financial statements.

    a. Baird has adopted a policy of self-insurance for certain types of liability claims. The premium for the alternative, a policy from an independent insurance company, would total $2,500. There have been no claims for this type of liability in the current year.

    b. The union that represents Baird's production employees is threatening to strike unless the company agrees to certain job security commitments. The current contract expires in May of the following fiscal year.

    c. Subsequent to the current year-end but prior to the issuance of the financial statements, Baird enters into a contract that will probably result in a material loss for the company.

    d. A government contract completed in the current year is subject to renegotiation. Baird expects to have to refund $50,000 to the government because of quality control problems, but understandably it does not want to publicize the situation.

    e. A lawsuit for patent infringement which asks for token damages is pending against Baird.

E11-5. For each of the following independent situations, indicate how the Black company should treat the liability on its financial statements for the year-end 31 December 19X6.

    a. A machine that Black sold three years ago and that is no longer under warranty blew up and caused $200,000 in damages. Although no suit had been filed against Black as of February 19X7, it appears that one will be filed in the next few months.

    b. Black sold service contracts on its products in 19X6 for the first time. (Total service contract revenue was $40,000.) Future service is required only if the products do not function correctly. Thirty percent of the time covered by the contracts had expired by 31 December 19X6. Actual costs under the contracts to that date totalled $8,500.

    c. Black has received a payment of $40,000 from a customer as a deposit on a machine with a total invoice price of $97,000 and a delivery date in March 19X7.

    d. A fire destroyed one of Black's warehouses on 18 January 19X7, resulting in an uninsured loss of $750,000.

    e. Black has guaranteed debts of $70,000 incurred by its vice-president, who is a 20% shareholder.

E11-6. Examine the current liability section of The Dow Chemical Company given near the end of this chapter. Classify each liability as either known, estimated, or contingent. If a liability is contingent, give a plausible scenario that might turn it into an estimated or known liability.

E11-7. For each of the following liabilities (assets), give the analogous asset (liability) if one exists:

a. accounts payable

b. notes receivable

c. customer deposits

d. temporary investments

e. taxes payable

f. interest payable

g. inventory

h. cash

E11-8. The principal types of current liabilities are as follows: (1) known liabilities of a definite amount; (2) known liabilities of an amount dependent on operations and (3) known liabilities of an estimated amount.

Required:

a. Classify each of the following liabilities as type (1), (2), or (3).

(i) guarantee and warranty obligations

(ii) rent received in advance

(iii) sales tax collected

(iv) bonus liabilities

(v) cash dividends payable

b. Define the term *contingent liability* and explain how it differs from the three types listed above, if at all.

c. Give an example of a contingent liability.

(CGA adapted)

E11-9. Consider the following independent scenarios:

(i) In Year 1 a customer walks into a computer store and selects a type of microcomputer that the store does not normally stock. A price of $3,800 is agreed on, and the customer makes a deposit of the full amount, expecting next-day delivery. However, there is a long delay in shipment, and delivery does not take place until Year 2. The cost of the computer to the store is $3,200.

(ii) In Year 1 a customer walks into a computer store and selects a type of microcomputer that the store does not normally stock. A price of $3,800 is agreed on, and the customer makes a deposit of the full amount. The computer is delivered at the very end of Year 1. It is sold under a 90-day warranty agreement. The manager of the store estimates that the average cost of such a warranty is $90 in labour and parts. However, if the same work was not being done under warranty, the customer would have been charged $120.

(iii) A computer software house contracted with a customer to supply software for the ordering, billing, and inventory-control functions. The customer agreed to make make deposits and payments as shown below. It is the company's practice to recognize the profit on each stage as it is completed.

Stage	Initial deposit	Payment on completion	Total price	Estimated cost to company	Year of completion
Initial feasibility study	$ 1,000	$ 2,000	$ 3,000	$ 3,200	1
Program up and running	6,000	3,000	9,000	6,000	2
Final adjusting and documentation	1,000	1,000	2,000	1,500	2
Total	$ 8,000	$ 6,000	$ 14,000	$ 10,700	

Required: For each of the three scenarios described above, indicate in which period the profit margin on the work would normally be recognized. Discuss any inconsistencies you perceive in the treatment.

E11-10. For competitive reasons, airlines introduced "mileage" schemes under which passengers got credits for the number of miles flown and then could use these credits to get "free" tickets. The schemes were subsequently extended so that cooperating hotels and car rental companies gave equivalent credits. The credits thus earned could be used interchangeably for "free" airline tickets, hotel rooms and car rentals. Passengers who converted these credits into tickets tended to choose already popular routes, such as those to Europe or the Far East.

Required:
Imagine that you have been hired as an accounting consultant by one of the airlines. The Vice-President Operations asks you the following questions. Give well-reasoned responses to each.

a. "We're giving these credits to encourage people to use our airline, and although we don't hand out coupons or anything, and don't have too good an idea what percentage of the credits will be used, it seems to me that we should accrue a liability. What do you think? Passengers flying free now amount to only two to three percent of our total traffic."

b. "Suppose we do charge the current period for the credits earned. How should we calculate the amount to charge to expense? I can tell you exactly how many credits have been earned in this period, and we can make some guesses about how many might be used later. But what is the cost to us going to be when the credits are turned into free tickets? Should we use the average cost per passenger mile? the marginal cost? the average revenue per passenger mile? the revenue lost from any passengers that might have been displaced?"

c. "We are thinking of restricting the use of free tickets to low seasons. Would this affect the amount of the liability we should accrue?"

PROBLEMS

P11-1. Delta Manufacturing Ltd. sells industrial chemicals in returnable containers. When the customer buys the product, there is a charge of $18 per container. This is refunded when the containers are returned. In 19X3 the following events took place:
  (i) A customer buys merchandise at a total price of $1,356.00 plus the cost of five containers.
  (ii) Three containers are returned by a customer.
  (iii) The company buys 8,000 containers at $15 each and puts them into its container inventory.
  (iv) At the beginning of the year it is estimated that 10,000 containers are in customers' hands. During the year a total of 30,000 containers are billed to customers and 25,000 are returned for credit. At the end of the year the number still in customers' hands are likely to be returned is estimated to be 12,000. The company wants to make the journal entry to set up the estimated liability at the end of the year and to adjust for the containers in the customers' hands.

(v) At the beginning of the year a physical count of the containers in the inventory indicates that 2,000 are on hand. During the year a total of 10,000 are purchased at $15.00 each. A physical count at the end of the year shows that 2,000 are on hand in the warehouse. The company wants to make the year-end journal entry to record the closing inventory. Assume that it uses the periodic count method and that the balance in the account at the beginning of the year, $30,000 has not been adjusted since.

Required: Show the journal entries to record each of the above transactions.

P11-2. Ace Tire Company sells its car tires with "Road Hazard Guarantee" under which the purchaser can return the tire for credit and purchase a new one if the tire is damaged through normal use within the first twenty-four months of purchase. The amount of credit given to the customer is directly proportional to the tire tread remaining, which is expressed as a percentage of the original tread depth. The company loses the most if the tire is damaged soon after being purchased because the remaining tread is large; similarly, the company loses very little toward the end of the tread's life. It estimates that the probability of damage and the average cost of the credit given to the customer are as follows:

Elapsed months from date of sale	Probability of tire damage	Average credit given customer	Elapsed months from date of sale	Probability of tire damage	Average credit given customer
1	0.005	$ 8.00	13	0.01	$ 3.92
2	0.005	7.66	14	0.01	3.58
3	0.005	7.32	15	0.01	3.24
4	0.005	6.98	16	0.01	2.90
5	0.005	6.64	17	0.01	2.56
6	0.005	6.30	18	0.01	2.22
7	0.005	5.96	19	0.01	1.88
8	0.005	5.62	20	0.01	1.54
9	0.005	5.28	21	0.01	1.20
10	0.005	4.94	22	0.01	0.86
11	0.005	4.60	23	0.01	0.52
12	0.005	4.26	24	0.01	0.18

Required:

a. What is the estimated cost of the warranty for each tire? Show your calculations. Ignore discounting for this problem.

b. Up to the end of the company's fiscal year 1 it had sold 58,000 tires. Show the journal entry to set up its estimated liability at the end of Year 1.

c. By the end of Year 2 a total of $85,600 had been credited to the warranty liability account for Years 1 and 2, and there had been total claims for the two years of $25,000. At the end of Year 2 it is estimated that the warranty liability should be $55,000. Show the journal entry to revise the warranty liability account at the end of Year 2.

P11-3. Chantry Gas Bar and Hardware gives away discount coupons to customers who pay cash to purchase gasoline or diesel fuel at its gas bar. Each coupon equals 5% of the cost of the fuel to the customer. The coupons may be used instead of money for purchases in the hardware store. The following is a summary of transactions for the fiscal year 19X9:

Sales of gas and diesel		$ 1,650,000
Discount coupons:	issued	$ 49,500
	estimated outstanding at start of year	$ 3,500
	redeemed at store	$ 45,325
	estimated outstanding at end of year	$ 4,000

Required: Show the summary journal entries to record the transactions in discount coupons.

P11-4. Many companies utilize a marketing campaign in which they distribute coupons that consumers may present to retailers for "cents off" on the purchase of certain products. The retailers are reimbursed when the coupons are returned to the manufacturer. Other companies provide a warranty on their products to encourage sales.

Required:
In each of the following independent cases calculate the amount of the liability to be reflected on the financial statements for the current year (19X6) and prepare the related journal entries. (All companies have year-ends at 31 December.)

a. On 1 May 19X6, Co. A issued $10,000 worth of coupons. Based on past experience, it expects that 30% of the coupons will be redeemed before the expiry date of 31 May 19X7. As of 31 December 19X6, $2,000 has been paid to retailers.

b. During 19X6, Company B issued two sets of coupons for two different products. Based on past experience, it expects 40% of the coupons to be redeemed before the expiry date. The coupons were as follows: Coupon 1 — issued 1 February 19X6, expiry date of 31 December 19X6, total value of $15,000, and $9,000 paid to retailers by year-end; Coupon 2 — issued 1 November 19X6, expiry date of 1 August 19X7, total value of $13,000, and $4,000 paid to retailers by year-end.

c. Company C began selling a new product in 19X6 which carried a three-year warranty against defects. The company estimates that the warranty costs will be 2% of dollar sales in 19X6, 4% in 19X7, and 6% in 19X8. In 19X6 sales of the new product totalled $147,000.

P11-5. In 1983 U.S. government safety authorities urged Chrysler Corporation to recall up to 1.8 million of its cars and trucks to replace a carburetor part. Chrysler acknowledged that a rubber part in the carburetor did deteriorate, but insisted that "the condition does not represent an unreasonable risk to motor vehicle safety." Although the federal government had the authority to require Chrysler to replace the part, for a period of time it did not reach a decision about what to do. It was estimated that replacing the part would have cost Chrysler about $55 per car. In 1983 the company had 115,165,532 common shares outstanding, and earnings per common share were estimated to be $3.25.

Required: Using only the information given above, explain how this potential liability should have been treated in the financial statements of Chrysler Corporation for 1983 if the statements had had to have been issued before the federal authorities had decided whether recall was necessary. Apply the principles of liability disclosure as given in the *CICA Handbook*. Begin by considering the question of materiality.

P11-6. Blaster Sounds was a store that sold high fidelity sound equipment (mainly tape decks, tuners, record players, and receivers) in a college town. It gave a six-month warranty on all equipment and expected to get back roughly half the cost of replacement parts from the manufacturers. It estimated that the probability of an item being returned in the months following a sale was as follows: 5% for Month 1, 1.5% for Month 2, 0.5% for Month 3, 0.5% for Month 4, 0.5% for Month 5, and 0.5% for Month 6. The average cost of a repair (expressed as a percentage of the selling price of the item returned for repair) was 10% for parts (half of which cost was reclaimed from the manufacturer) and 20% for shop labour. Its sales for the six months preceding its 30 November year-end were as follows:

June	$ 65,000
July	63,000
August	55,000
September	120,000
October	85,000
November	73,000

Required:

a. The person who did the repairs under the warranty was paid a monthly salary that averaged $10 an hour. This constituted the "shop labour" costs quoted above. On reviewing the year-end financial situation, the owner of the shop pointed out that when this same person made custom equipment for the shop it was not considered appropriate to capitalize his labour costs as part of the cost of the equipment. The owner therefore asked whether it was appropriate to include these same costs when estimating a liability. What is your advice? Explain.

b. What journal entry should be made in July to record the warranty expense for that month? Assume labour costs are included in the estimated cost.

c. The balance in the account "Liability for Warranties" stood at $4,000 at 30 November. Show the adjusting entry required to bring it to the appropriate amount, assuming the company included both parts and labour in the estimate. Be sure to show all your calculations.

P11-7. From 1966 to 1973 Westinghouse Electric company offered its utility customers a supply of uranium at a fixed cost so as to induce purchase of Westinghouse nuclear reactors. In total Westinghouse had a commitment to supply 80 million pounds of uranium at an average cost of $10 per pound. The commitment would being in 1976 and run for 20 years. By September 1975 the price of uranium on the open market was up to $45.00 per pound At that time Westinghouse told its suppliers that it would not honour its contract for the uranium. Hence legal proceedings were commenced by 29 utilities against Westinghouse. Within four years Westinghouse had accumulated $721.2 million in extraordinary losses, and it was estimated that unsettled suits would amount to a further $228 million.

Required:

a. State the point at which Westinghouse should have recorded each of the following:
   (i) a contingent liability
   (ii) an estimated liability
   (iii) a known liability.

b. Describe the disclosure of information required in financial statements for each of the above.

P11-8. Collom Chalk Ltd. is a small company that grinds chalk into a fine power talc. The owner Mr. F. Collom personally grinds the chalk using the latest in calcite technology. The talc is used by surveyors for field markings and by gymnasts for their hands. It also makes a nice light snack. The talc is sold in special watertight containers, and when the product is sold there is a $5.00 refundable deposit on the container. At the beginning of 19X5 the company had 556 containers in inventory, and it estimated that 1,500 were in the hands of customers. During the year, 5,000 containers were billed to customers and 5,800 were returned for credit. In 19X5 the company purchases 500 containers at $10.00 per container under a fixed-price contract it has had since its inception. At year-end it estimates that 400 outstanding containers will likely be returned.

Required:
Suppose that at the 19X4 year-end the company estimated the number of containers that would be returned to be either (i) 800 or (ii) 1,500. In each case show all journal entries required to set up the accounts payable account for 19X5. Assume that the appropriate entry was made at the time of each sale and that only the year-end adjusting entries need to be made. Show all calculations.

P11-9. University Hi-Fi (UHF) buys most of its audio equipment with a one-month warranty by the manufacturer to the ultimate purchaser. As part of its sales promotion, UHF gives the customer a three-month warranty, covering the additional two-month warranty itself. For the first month after sale, the repair costs are covered by the manufacturer and repair costs to UHF are negligible. For the next two months after sale, UHF pays all repair costs. For each of these two months, the repair costs average 1.75% for each $1.00 of sale. Thus if a set sold for $500 in March, there is no warranty expense for March (because that is covered by the manufacturer) and an average of $8.75 (i.e., 1.75% of $500) for April and $8.75 for May. Sales for the four months prior to the end of UHF's 19X0 fiscal-year are shown below.

Month	Sales
9	$ 22,950.00
10	$ 21,250.00
11	$ 28,000.00
12	$ 42,500.00

Required:
a. Sales in the twelve months prior to the 19X0 year-end are $300,000. What net warranty expense to UHF should be recorded?

b. Sales in the four months prior to the 19X0 year-end are as shown above. What is the estimated liability at the end of the twelfth month? Assume that all units are treated as if they were purchased at the beginning of each month. Show your calculations.

c. At the beginning of 19X0 the balance in the "Estimated Warranty Liability" account was $1,200. Assume that the year-end warranty liability and the expense for the year were as you calculated them above. Suppose that the company had to write up the liability account by $800 in order to make that account equal to the estimated liability. What must the actual charges to the liability account have been for the year?

P11-10. The accounting staff of Valhalla Ltd., a pharmaceutical company, is busy preparing the 19X5 financial reports. The staff is aware that a lawsuit has been filed against the company by a farmer, alleging that one of Valhalla's products has caused birth defects in several of his lambs. The farmer seeks damages in the amount of $250,000. One of three outcomes is possible: First, the farmer will win, and the courts will assess the full $250,000 against the company. Second, the farmer will win, but the courts will award some amount smaller than $250,000 (unfortunately, it is impossible at the present time to estimate the amount more precisely). Third, the suit will be without merit and will be thrown out of court. The accounting staff is concerned with the correct reporting and disclosure of this lawsuit.

Required:

a. Define the term contingency.

b. Assume that the necessary preconditions exist for the first possible outcome. Explain how the financial statments would be affected. Provide full details and journal entries if required.

c. Assume that the necessary preconditions exist for the second possible outcome. Explain how the financial statements would be affected. Provide full details and journal entries if required.

d. Assume that the necessary preconditions exist for the third possible outcome. Explain how the financial statements would be affected. Provide full details and journal entries if required.

(CGA adapted)

BIBLIOGRAPHY

ACCOUNTING PRINCIPLES BOARD. *Opinion No. 21: Interest on Receivables and Payables.* New York: American Institute of Certified Public Accountants, 1971. This sets forth the idea that receivables should be shown at their discounted value.

FINANCIAL ACCOUNTING STANDARDS BOARD. *Statement of Financial Accounting Standards No. 15: Accounting by Debtors and Creditors for Troubled Debt Restructuring.* Stamford Conn.: FASB, June 1977. "Troubled" debt is that whose payments are likely to go in arrears.

MILLER, JERRY D. "Accounting for Warrants and Convertible Bonds." *Management Accounting* (January 1973).

STEPHENS, MATTHEW. "Inseparability of the Valuation of Convertible Bonds." *Journal of Accountancy* (August 1971).

CHAPTER 12
Long-Term Liabilities

Introduction

The accounting treatments of short-term and long-term liabilities have much in common. On the other hand, there are three main differences. First, because of the greater length of time from inception of the debt to its maturity, the market price of a long-term debt is much more sensitive to the impact of interest rates. Second, there is a well-developed market for trading long-term debt instruments; thus accounting results may be affected by trading on this market. Third, the legal arrangements for long-term debt are usually much more formal; hence greater attention must be paid to the specific legal terms of a given issue of debt.

Accounting for long-term debt has parallel features with accounting for plant assets. When a debt is issued, accountants take care to look through the legal form of the arrangement to get at its economic substance. They record the market value of the debt as of the date of its issue, just as they record the market value of plant assets as of their date of acquisition. From that point on, they do *not* attempt to revalue the debt to reflect changes in its market value, just as they do not revalue plant assets. As a result, the annual interest cost recorded in the books does not reflect any outside changes in the borrowing costs to the firm, just as depreciation does not reflect the changing opportunity costs to the firm caused by changing market prices for that asset.

Definition of Terms

Long-term liabilities are liabilities whose due date is more than a year away from the date of the financial statements. For reasons explained in the preceding chapter on current liabilities, there are a few exceptions. Thus, some liabilities due in more than one year may be treated as current (e.g., those due within the company's normal operating cycle, even though longer than one year). Moreover, some liabilities due in less than a year may be treated as long-term (e.g., former long-term debt due within the next twelve months that will be replaced by more long-term debt).

A company typically incurs a long-term liability in order to raise funds for some specific purpose (e.g., to build a new plant or to make a long-term investment in the shares of another company). If it wants to develop a specific piece of real estate by putting up an office or factory building, it may finance this with a **mortgage,** which is a loan specifically secured by a pledge of the land and building for which the money is loaned. It is common for interest on a mortgage to be paid monthly and for the monthly payments to include blended principal and interest, so that the mortgage is retired over a set period of time, say twenty-five years. Mortgage financing is especially popular with small organizations that may not have ready access to the larger financial markets or that do not want to incur the cost of a public offering of their securities.

Larger companies often issue a **bond,** which is a legal contract containing a promise to repay, at some specified date, the funds loaned together with periodic payments of interest. A typical bond might be for a term of ten years and pay interest at six-month intervals. We have already discussed bonds in the context of long-term investments, above in Chapter 10.

It is also possible for a company to **lease** assets instead of purchasing them. In so doing, it has the use of the asset in return for a rental payment. These leases can be for a long time-period, often not much shorter than the economic life of the leased asset. If one looks through the legal form of the arrangement, it becomes apparent that the lease is similar in substance to a purchase of the asset combined with the assumption of a long-term debt. Since accountants are inclined to look through legal form to get at economic substance, it can be expected that they give special treatment to such leases. Long-term leases will be dealt with in Chapter 14.

Many companies have a long-term liability to pay a **pension** to their employees when they retire. Pensions are covered in Chapter 15.

Mortgages

In Canada a typical commercial mortgage is for five years, during which time the interest rate is fixed by mutual agreement. Mortgage financing is often used by smaller organizations to raise funds for the purchase or construction of a specific building. The source of this funding is usually a trust company, bank, insurance company, or the vendor of the property. The specific security for the mortgage is the land and building itself. The lender (the **mortgagee**) has the right, subject to certain conditions, to take the property if the borrower (the **mortgagor**) defaults. In addition, the lender has the usual legal rights available to any creditor. Thus, a mortgage on the right-hand side of the balance sheet indicates that some significant plant assets are pledged specifically to the holder of the mortgage and are not available to other creditors until the debts of the creditor with the specific pledge have been satisfied.

Technically, in Ontario, the lender gets legal title to the land when he or she lends the funds, and the lender returns title to the borrower only when he or she is repaid. Note that although legal title has passed from the borrower to the lender, we do not treat this as a sale. The economic substance of the transaction is that the land is simply pledged as security for the loan. In most other provinces legal title does not change hands; a mortgage is simply legally registered against the property.

It is possible to put more than one mortgage on the same piece of real estate. The mortgage with the senior, or first, claim against the property is known as the **first mortgage,** the next is the **second mortgage,** and so on. Because the debt owed on the first mortgage must be satisfied in full before any other mortgage holders' claims are entertained, it will be apparent that the risk to the holder of a second or third mortgage is usually greater than the risk to the first, and hence the interest rates are higher.

The following is an example of the accounting treatment of a straightforward mortgage arrangement. Morton Mills Limited wanted to enlarge its warehouse. It was able to secure a mortgage of $250,000 with interest at 12% per annum payable monthly, with a term of five years and no repayment of principal until the end of the term. The mortgage was to be issued as of 15 December 19X1 and become due on 15 December, 19X6. To satisfy the trust company lending the funds that it could give good title to the land, Morton had to have the land surveyed (at a cost of $2,000) and incurred legal fees of $1,000. As it pays out the funds for these expenses, the journal entry would be as follows:

Mortgage issue — deferred charges	3,000.00	
Bank		3,000.00
To record payment of legal and survey fees.		

When the mortgage is approved and the funds are received, the following entry would be made:

Bank	250,000.00	
Mortgage payable		250,000.00
Record receipt of funds advanced on mortgage.		

Each month, interest payment would be made and recorded as follows:

Interest expense	2,500.00	
Bank		2,500.00
Payment of mortgage interest.		

In addition, a monthly entry would be made to amortize the issue cost of the mortgage, $3,000, over 60 months:

Interest expense	50.00	
Mortgage issue costs — deferred charges		50.00
Amortize mortgage issue costs of $3,000 over the 60 months of the mortgage.		

At the company's year-end, 30 June, the interest for half a month would be accrued in the following manner:

Interest expense	1,275.00	
Accrued interest payable		1,250.00
Mortgage issue costs — deferred charges		25.00

Accrue interest for one half month ($250,000 × 0.12 × 0.5 × $^1/_{12}$, or 1,250.00) and one-half month's amortization of issue costs ($3,000 × $^1/_{60}$ × 0.5, or 25.00)

Bonds Payable

GENERAL

A bond is a legal document giving evidence of a contractual obligation by a company, starting at a time referred to as the **inception date**, to (i) redeem the bond for a stated amount (the **face amount** or **par value**) at some stated time in the future called the **maturity date** and (ii) make periodic interest payments during the term of the bond. These interest payments are normally stated as a percentage of the face amount, and this percentage is termed the **coupon rate** (or **stated rate**). The length of time between the inception and maturity dates is known as the **term** of the bond. Bonds may be secured by the pledge of specific assets of the company, such as land and buildings, in which case they are referred as **mortgage bonds**. If there is no pledge of specific assets but rather a general charge against all assets, the bonds are referred to as **debentures**.

Many bonds are actively traded in financial centres such as New York or Toronto, but the trading takes place over the telephone between bond traders representing banks, trust companies, and security dealers. The current prices of actively traded bonds are quoted in the *The Globe and Mail Report on Business, The Financial Post,* and *The Wall Street Journal.*

The legal terms of the bond are very important because the sums borrowed are often very large (e.g., $25 million). Moreover, as any given issue is often widely held, renegotiation of the terms is usually expensive and difficult. The terms of the bond issue are set out in a **trust indenture,** which is a legal agreement between the issuing company and a trust company acting on behalf of the bondholders. The trust company is referred to as the *bond trustee.* It is the bond trustee's duty to see that the issuing company lives up to the terms of the trust indenture and to take whatever steps are necessary to protect the bondholders (e.g., seize the assets given as security for the bond issue).

Here is an example of a straightforward bond issue. On 1 July, 19X1, Delta Corporation issued bonds with a face value of $500,000 and a coupon rate of 16%. The bonds pay interest annually on 1 July and are due in five years. They were sold through an underwriter, who took a commission of 3% of face value. If the bonds were sold for their face amount, they would be selling at **par value**; if less than their face amount, they would be selling at a **discount**; and if more than their face value, they would be selling at a **premium**. To understand why they might not sell at their face value requires an understanding of some financial concepts. Let us suppose that the people who bought the bonds believed that 16% represented the rate that was appropriate for a company of this type. They would value the bonds by finding the present value of the total cash stream that the bonds would generate. The first payment to be received would be 16% of $500,000, or $80,000, on 1 July, 19X2. The present value of this payment, discounted to the present at 16%, would be $80,000/1.16 = $68,966. The calculation for all payments is shown below. The notation "1/1.16" indicates that the discount factor is 1 divided by 1.16, which is 0.862.

Payment Date	Amount	Discount factor	Present value
1-7-19X2	$ 80,000	$1/1.16 = 0.862$	$ 68,966
1-7-19X3	80,000	$1/1.16^2 = 0.743$	59,453
1-7-19X4	80,000	$1/1.16^3 = 0.641$	51,253
1-7-19X5	80,000	$1/1.16^4 = 0.552$	44,183
1-7-19X6	80,000	$1/1.16^5 = 0.476$	38,089
1-7-19X6	500,000	$1/1.16^5 = 0.476$	238,056
			$ 500,000

We can make the same calculation by using present-value (PV) tables or a hand calculator with the appropriate functions. The PV tables given at the end of this book are accurate to three and four decimal places. For this example, in order to reduce differences due to rounding, let us use more powerful PV tables that are accurate to six decimal places, as follows:

PV of interest payments ($80,000 × 3.274300)	$ 261,944
PV of principal amount ($500,000 × .476112)	238,056
Total present value of principal and interest	$ 500,000

Note that the present-value factor applied above to the interest payments (i.e., 3.274300) is equivalent to the total of the discount factors shown earlier for the payment dates of 1 July 19X2 to 1 July 19X6 inclusive (i.e., 0.862 + 0.743 + 0.641 + 0.552 + 0.476).

The journal entry to record the issuing of the bonds would read as follows:

Bond issue costs (deferred charges)	15,000.00	
Bank	485,000.00	
Bonds payable		500,000.00

To record issue of bonds with a face value of $500,000 at par. Coupon rate is 16%. Bond issue costs are 3% of face value.

Note that the reason the present value equals the face value is that the coupon rate is exactly equal to the market rate that investors are demanding at the inception date for this kind of borrower. Note that the market rate is in the denominator in the detailed calculation above. Hence, as the market rates goes up, the discount factor will get smaller and the present value will decline. *Thus, as the market interest rate rises above (descends below) the coupon rate, the market value of the bond will go down (up).*

For example, suppose the prevailing rate happened to go up to 17% just before the above issue was brought to the market. From what we have just said, we would expect the bonds to sell at a slight discount. We can demonstrate this by calculating the present value of the payments discounted to the present at 17%:

Payment date	Amount	Discount factor	Present value
1-7-19X2	$ 80,000	0.855	$ 68,376
1-7-19X3	80,000	0.731	58,441
1-7-19X4	80,000	0.624	49,950
1-7-19X5	80,000	0.534	42,692
1-7-19X6	80,000	0.456	36,488
1-7-19X6	500,000	0.456	228,056
			$ 484,003

We arrive at a total present value of $484,003 instead of $500,000. Thus, if the company decided to proceed with the issue, it would have to sell the bonds at a discount of $500,000 − 484,003 = $15,997. In such a case, the journal entry would be as follows:

Discount on bonds payable	15,997.00	
Bond issue costs (deferred charges)	15,000.00	
Bank	469,003.00	
Bonds payable		500,000.00

To record sale of bonds payable with a face value of $500,000 at a discount of $15,977. Underwriters' fees are 3% of $500,000, or $15,000.

The portion of the bond issue costs not written off would be classified as deferred charges, a long-term asset on the balance sheet. In the United States the discount on bonds payable is linked with the bonds payable on the balance sheet and is shown as a deduction from this long-term liability. The *CICA Handbook* is silent on this issue. In Canada the discount may be treated as in the U.S. or included with deferred charges on the asset side of the balance sheet. The U.S. practice seems preferable and is gaining acceptance in Canada.

AMORTIZATION OF PREMIUM OR DISCOUNT

A bond discount arises because the company has gone to the financial markets with a bond issue carrying a coupon rate that is less than the going market rate demanded. Since the coupon rate is not a sufficient discharge of the annual interest charge demanded by the market, the borrower is, in effect, forced to prepay the insufficient interest by accepting a discount on the bonds sold.

The matching principle indicates that the discount should be matched against each of the periods benefited by the bond issue — in other words, against the entire term of the bond. The net effect of this would be to charge to each period, as interest expense, an amount that approximates the market interest rate. It would then remain to be decided what allocation scheme to use to amortize the discount (or premium) over the life of the bonds. The common methods are the straight-line method, in which the total amount is allocated to each year equally, and the effective-interest method of amortization. We have already discussed these methods in Chapter 10.

The effective-interest method has an allocating effect similar to the sinking fund and annuity methods for allocating depreciation (see above Chapter 8). If the bond is sold at a discount, it makes a lower charge for interest expense in the earlier periods and a higher charge in later periods. If the bond sells at a premium, the higher interest charge is in the early years. Although the effective-interest method appears more sophisticated, both it and the straight-line method are essentially arbitrary allocation schemes. In other words, not even in theory is there a single best way to allocate bond discounts to the periods in which the bond is outstanding. As a result, there is little point in discussing the relative conceptual merits of these two approaches.

Let us work through an example. Lindsay Inc. sold a ten-year bond with a face value of $100,000. It paid interest semi-annually at a 12% coupon rate (i.e., 6% every six months). The market interest rate at that time was 11% if paid semi-annually. Consequently, the bonds sold at a premium of $5,975.19. The journal entry at the time of issue would be as follows:

Bank	105,975.19	
Bond premium		5,975.19
Bond payable		100,000.00
To record issue of bond at a premium of $5.97519.		

If the company were using the straight-line method of amortization, it would make the following entry at the time of the first coupon payment:

Interest expense	5,701.24	
Bond premium	298.76	
Bank		6,000.00
To record payment of coupon and amortization of bond premium on straight-line basis ($1/20$ of 5,975.19).		

If it were using the effective-interest method, the entry would read as follows:

Interest expense	5,828.64	
Bond premium	171.36	
Bank		6,000.00
To record payment of coupon and amortization of bond premium using the effective-interest method (5.5% of 105,975.19).		

In effect the effective-interest method treats the company as if it had borrowed $105,975.19 at 11%, the market rate. It neutralizes any effect of issuing the bond at a premium or discount. At the next payment period, the interest expense would be calculated as 5.5% of (105,975.16 − 171.36). Thus the interest expense would be slightly lower at $5,819.21. When a bond is sold at a premium, the effective-interest method has the effect of showing higher interest expense in the early periods and lower expense toward maturity, as compared with straight-line. It has the opposite effect when the bond is sold at a discount.

It should be noted that regardless of the method of amortization used, the effect is to move the carrying value of the bonds (the face amount plus unamortized premium or minus unamortized discount) toward the maturity value or toward the face amount.

The *CICA Handbook* has little to say on the relative merits of these allocation schemes. In practice, the straight-line method is more popular in Canada. By contrast, the Accounting Principles Board in the U.S. has favoured the interest method over the straight-line method; but they have said that the straight-line method could be used if the results were not materially different. The APB [Opinion No. 21, 1971] was therefore taking a clear stand in favour of the interest method although there is little theoretical justification for it, aside from conservatism.

SERIAL BONDS

A company may sell bonds that come due at various dates between the time of issue and the due date of the longest term bond. Such issues are referred to as **serial bonds.** The following would be an example. On 1 April, 19X2 a company issues $300 000 in bonds. $100,000 are due on each of 1 April, 19X4, 19X6, and 19X8. It is quite common to have a different interest rate for each of the maturity dates.

There is nothing conceptually different about accounting for serial bonds. Nevertheless, it will be apparent that the details are more complex, such as the allocation of bond premium or discount to each maturity date and the calculation of accrued interest at each year-end. Serial bonds are not common in Canada.

CALL PROVISIONS

Bonds may be sold with the provision that some or all of them may be **called**, that is, subject to forced redemption at the option of the company. The terms of the call provision are usually printed on the face of the bond, where the call price at any given date is indicated. If bonds are called, it is quite likely that the call price paid will differ from the net amount at which the bonds are carried on the company's books, and this will give rise to a gain or loss on redemption.

For example, on 1 September, 19X3 bonds maturing on 1 September, 19X9 were issued with a face value of $300,000 at 95.00. Interest of 15% was payable semi-annually on 1 September and 1 March each year. They could be called at the following prices:

```
1 September 19X3 — 31 August 19X4 =   95.50
1 September 19X4 — 31 August 19X5 =   96.50
1 September 19X5 — 31 August 19X6 =   97.50
1 September 19X6 — 31 August 19X7 =   98.50
1 September 19X7 — 31 August 19X8 =   99.50
1 September 19X8 — 31 August 19X9 = 100.00
```

On 1 September, 19x5 the company called for the redemption of bonds with a face value of $10,000. It has been using the straight-line method to amortize the bond discount. The journal entry would read as follows:

Bonds payable	10,000.00	
Loss on redemption	83.33	
Bank		9,750.00
Bond discount		333.33

To record calling of bonds with a face value of $10,000 and write-off of the applicable remaining bond discount at $2/3$ (i.e. 4 years/6 years) of 5% of 10,000 = 333.33.

Call provisions permit the issuer to redeem bonds at the issuer's option. Issuers usually do so when the market rate of interest drops below the coupon rate of the bonds. Because bond redemption acts to the detriment of the bondholder, bonds with call features are neither popular nor common.

SINKING FUND BONDS

Purchasers of a bond issue are naturally concerned that when the bonds become due, the company will have on hand sufficient liquid assets to be able to redeem them. One way to ensure that the company will have sufficient liquid assets is to make it a condition of the trust indenture that a fixed amount be put aside each year into a separate fund and invested in marketable securities. Such a fund is termed a **sinking fund**. The securities in the fund are only cashed for the purpose of reinvestment or redeeming the bonds. Income earned on these purchased securities may be added back into the sinking fund or kept by the company, depending on the terms of the trust indenture.

For example, S Ltd. issued $500,000 in five-year 12% sinking-fund bonds on 1 April, 19X1. Interest was payable semi-annually on 1 April and 1 October. Under the terms of the trust indenture the company had to put $100,000 at the end of each twelve months into a sinking fund that could be used to purchase bonds of the company or some other company in the market. S Ltd. was allowed to use for general purposes any income earned by the securities purchased with sinking-fund money. Its financial year-end was 31 December.

At the end of the first financial year S Ltd. would make no journal entry except to accrue interest. On 1 April 19X2 it would transfer $100,000 into a separate bank account and make the following entry:

Bank — sinking fund	100,000.00	
Bank — general account		100,000.00

To record transfer of $100,000 into sinking-fund bank account as required by terms of bond trust indenture.

If bonds were purchased with these funds, the entry would read as follows:

Sinking fund — bonds	100,000.00	
Bank — sinking fund		100,000.00

To record purchase of bonds in accordance with trust indenture.

When interest is earned on the bonds, it would be put into the company's general bank account because under the terms of this indenture, the company can use such cash receipts for its own general purposes. Suppose that in 19X3 this income amounted to $14,000. The entry would be as follows:

General bank account	14,000.00	
Investment income		14,000.00
To record receipt of income on sinking fund investments.		

In other instances, the trust indenture may require that the cash received from investment income be credited back to the sinking-fund account instead of being put in the company's general bank account. If this were the case in the above example, then the entry would be as follows:

Sinking fund — bank	14,000.00	
Investment income		14,000.00
To record receipt of investment income and deposit in sinking-fund bank account in accordance with terms of trust indenture.		

Note that the proceeds are still credited to the investment income of the company. The sinking-fund provision of a trust indenture simply says that the company must keep a certain amount of its assets in liquid form. The income earned on these assets continues to belong to the company.

If the cash received from sinking-fund investments is put back into the sinking-fund bank account in the example above, then the sinking-fund would eventually equal $500,000 plus the accumulated earnings — or more than is ultimately needed. As a result, it would be possible to put less than $500,000 into the account and let the accumulated earnings make up the rest. Exactly how much would depend on the assumption one makes about the earning rate of the sinking-fund assets and the timing of the deposits into the sinking fund. The mathematics for this type of calculation are found above in Appendix 5-2.

The term *sinking fund* may also describe a bond issue where periodic payments are made to a trustee for the purpose of purchasing a portion of the company's own outstanding bond issue for cancellation. While such issues appear to be more common than true sinking funds, there is no actual sinking fund established, except for the purpose of bond redemption. If the bonds are selling below their redemption price, the trustee would probably purchase them on the open market and cancel them. If their market price is above the price at which they can be called, the trustee would then elect to call the necessary number of bonds (usually choosing the ones to be redeemed by lot) and cancel them. The terms of each issue tend to vary, and the accounting must be adapted to each case.

CONVERTIBLE BONDS AND BONDS SOLD WITH SHARE WARRANTS

Bonds may be sold in a package consisting of bonds and **share warrants,** or rights to purchase shares of the company at the price stated on the warrant. Such a package may be attractive to the purchaser because it provides the security of a bond with the right to purchase equity in the company later at a fixed price. The purchaser can sell the warrants separately without relinquishing the bonds.

Normally the bonds and warrants are traded separately on the market once they are issued. Thus it is possible to infer what part of the total proceeds received by the company is for the bonds and what part is for the warrants. Although this aspect of bonds and warrants is not covered in the *CICA Handbook,* an example of acceptable practice is shown below.

Perth Inc. sold $500,000 in ten-year bonds with a coupon rate of 14%. With each $1,000 of bonds the purchaser received fifty warrants entitling the owner to purchase one-tenth of a share in the company at a price of $60 per share throughout the next year. Thereafter, the price escalated by $5 per share per year in each of the following four years. At the end of the four years the purchase rights lapsed. Perth Inc. received $1,100 for each package of $1,000 bond and 50 warrants. When trading started, the bonds were selling at $970, and the warrants were selling at $2.50; thus the package had a total market value of 970 + (50 x 2.50) = 1095.00. To allocate the proceeds between the bonds and warrants, we would use the relative market value of each as follows:

Value assigned to bonds per $1,000 face value
= Total issue price × (market value of bonds/total market value)
= $1,100.00 × 970.00/1,095.00
= $974.43

Bond discount per $1,000 face value
= $1,000 − 974.43
= $25.57

Value assigned to the groups of 50 warrants
= Total issue price × (market value of warrants/total market value)
= $1,100.00 × 125.00/1,095.00
= $125.57

The journal entry for the issue at $550,000 face value would therefore be as follows:

Bank (500 × 1,100)	550,000.00	
Bond discount (500 × 25.57)	12,785.00	
Common stock warrants (500 × 125.57)		62,785.00
(balance-sheet item — contributed surplus)		
Bonds payable		500,000.00

To record issue of bonds and share warrants in units of
$1,000 bonds and 50 common share warrants for $1,100
per unit. Proceeds were allocated on the basis of market
value at the opening of trading.

The justification for crediting the proceeds of the share warrants to contributed surplus (i.e., to a part of owners' equity) is that the proceeds represent a value placed on the warrants by the investors — namely, the value of the right to buy shares in the future at a price that they hope will be less than market.

Some bonds are sold with a provision that the bondholders may, at their option, convert the bonds into shares of the company at a price stated on the face of the bonds. These are referred to as **convertible bonds**. The use of such bonds may be motivated by a variety of reasons: the company desire may be to make the bond issue look more attractive or purchasers may want to hedge their investments by converting the bond into shares if the shares go up in price. Usually the price that bondholders must pay for shares through conversion goes up the longer they wait.

Let us work through an example. Devon Limited sold $500,000 ten-year bonds at a discount of 5% with the following conversion privilege: the holder of each $1,000 in bonds was entitled to convert it into common shares at a conversion price of $200 per share for the first five years and $300 per share thereafter. At the end of the first year, bonds totalling $50,000 were tendered for conversion. This was in the period where shares could be obtained at $200 each. Therefore on submission of the bonds, the company issued 50,000/200 = 250 shares. The unamortized bond discount was 9/10 of 5% of $50,000, or $2,250, and this would have had to have been reflected in the conversion transaction. Assume that the shares were trading on the stock market for $205. One acceptable entry would have been the following:

Bonds payable	50,000.00	
Loss on conversion of bonds payable	3,500,00	
Bond discount - unamortized		2,250.00
Share capital		51,250.00

To record the issue of 250 common shares under the
conversion provision of the bond indenture, which allows
each $1,000 to be converted into five common shares
as of this date. Share capital was valued at its current
market value of 250 × $205 = 51,250.

Note that the new issue of shares is recorded at the market value of the shares, not the "official" share price of $200. This is not the only value that might be considered. Other reasonable choices would include (i) the market value of the bonds as of the date of conversion or (ii) the carrying value (i.e., the book value) of the bonds as of the date of conversion. Each method is likely to give a different answer, but usually any difference will not be material. Using the market value of either the bonds or the shares should give approximately the same answer under most conditions. There is no theoretical reason for preferring one method over the other. In the U.S. the practice is to make all conversions at the book value of the debt. By contrast, Canadian accounting standards are silent on this issue.

In most of their essential characteristics convertible bonds are similar to a unit consisting of non-convertible bonds and warrants. However, in the sale of bonds and warrants the separate values of the bonds versus the warrants is recognized, whereas with convertible bonds the market price of the convertible feature is not kept separate in the accounting reports. Since the convertible feature is introduced to make the bonds more attractive to the market and since this feature represents a potential dilution of the interest of the existing holders of equity, there is a strong conceptual argument that a portion of the proceeds should be recognized as a contribution to shareholders' equity in a manner similar to that for warrants sold with bonds. The counterargument is based on practicality: the market price of any single feature of a bond issue, such as the conversion privilege, is impossible to value separately.

The practical result for readers of financial statements is that they should be aware of the implications if a convertible bond appears on the balance sheet. First, the convertible feature was probably used to make the bond issue more attractive, and hence lower the interest rate that had to be paid. Second, no attempt was made to measure and amortize the discount that was avoided by the use of the conversion privilege and to reflect it in the interest expense. Hence, interest expense is understated. The cost of the conversion feature will ultimately be paid by someone. If the price of the shares goes up, the conversion feature will be exercised by the bondholders, and the existing shareholders will have their equity diluted. If share prices fail to go up, the conversion feature will have turned out to be worthless, and the bondholders will lose. We will develop this feature further in Chapter 17 on earnings per share.

SWAPS

An **interest-rate swap** takes place when two borrowers issue bonds (or other forms of debt) and then agree, for a payment, to be responsible for certain features of the other's issue. Swaps are normally arranged by an intermediary financial institution, and payments are made through that intermediary. For example, Company A might issue fixed-interest bonds, and Company B might issue bonds whose interest rate floats according to some index such as the London Interbank Offered Rate (LIBOR). They might agree, for fees received or paid at the start of the swap, to undertake to pay each other's interest obligation. The reason such swaps are worthwhile for both companies is said to be that they can take advantage of differences in how investors perceive each company.

At the start of the swap, any fee received (or paid) is credited (or charged) to a deferred interest account. It is then amortized over the life of the swap to reduce the annual interest expense. At the time of each interest payment, each company pays the interest on its *own* debt, but makes or receives a payment to the other through the intermediary for the difference caused by the swap. This payment or receipt is treated as part of interest expense.

For example, Company A agreed to a swap with Company B through an intermediary, S Brothers Inc.. Company A had issued $500,000 of ten-year fixed-rate bonds with a 12% annual coupon rate at par, and Company B had issued $500,000 ten-year floating-rate bonds with an annual coupon, also at par. Company A received a fee from the financial intermediary of $2,500 for agreeing to the swap, and Company B had to pay a fee of $1,000. At the time of the first annual coupon payment the floating rate was 12.5%. Company A would pay its bondholders as usual and would make the following entry:

Interest expense	60,000.00	
Bank		60,000.00
To record payment of 12% interest on fixed-rate bonds.		

Similarly, Company B would also pay its bondholders and would make the following entry:

Interest expense	62,500.00	
Bank		62,500.00
To record payment of 12.5% interest on floating-rate bonds.		

In accordance with the swap agreement, Company A would make the following payment to Company B through the intermediary:

Interest expense	2,500.00	
Bank		2,500.00

To record payment to S. Brothers Inc. due under interest-rate
swap agreement.

On receipt of the funds, Company B would use them to reduce its interest expense. Each company would then amortize the up-front fee over the life of the bond issue, using either the interest or straight-line method. For example Company A might amortize the fee as shown below. Company B would do likewise.

Deferred interest expense	250.00	
Interest expense		250.00

To record amortization of $1/10$ of the initial fee received at
the start of the swap.

Financial Statement Manipulation

The reader of financial statements should always be aware of the often unintended distortions that can be produced within the accounting measurement system. Here are some common distortions arising from long-term debt.

TRIGGERING A GAIN BY REDEEMING A DEBT

Long-term liabilities share a common characteristic with assets having long lives: often the market value starts to differ materially from the value at which the asset or liability is carried in the books of the company. We have seen with fixed assets that a company's management can make reported net income look better by selling off those fixed assets whose carrying value is substantially less than market value. This allows them to record a gain on disposition of the asset. It is possible to do a similar thing with long-term liabilities by purchasing and retiring those whose market value is less than the carrying value.

For example, Verona Manufacturing issued $100,000 of twenty-year debentures on 1 January 1970 with a coupon rate of 10%. Interest was payable at the end of each year. Because of inflation, the market rate that Verona would have to pay had increased to 18% by 1 January 1981. Verona's bonds still had nine more years to go, but the present value of these bonds was now only $65,576, or $34,424 less than face value. In effect, the $34,424 (i.e., the present value of nine payments of $18,000 minus $10,000 discounted at 18%) represents the present value of the interest Verona does not have to pay because it was astute enough to issue its bonds when interest rates were 10%. By redeeming these bonds Verona is reflecting in the income of a single year the good fortune it might otherwise have enjoyed over the remaining term of the debt. The entry upon redemption would read as follows:

Bond payable	100,000.00	
Cash		65,576.00
Gain on redemption		34,424.00
To record redemption of bonds and resulting gain.		

There is nothing improper in Verona redeeming its bonds if it believes that makes good economic sense. However, the reader of financial statements should realize that such a gain on redemption is similar to the gain on disposal of assets. To a large degree the recognition of both can be triggered at a time that suits management's convenience, and the reported gain is often the result of fortuitous events beyond the influence of management (such as changed interest rates).

Sometimes the terms under which bonds are issued do not permit them to be cancelled before maturity. Hence, the option of cancelling debt by purchases on the open market is not open to a company's management. One response to this was to purchase the bonds and lodge them with a trustee who was given instructions to hold them to maturity and then cancel them. This act has been termed **defeasance**, or rendering the bonds legally null and void. The question arose of when the bonds should be considered cancelled and the gain reported. For example, if the company cannot purchase the bond issue it wants to cancel, would it be sufficient to purchase another similar issue and lodge it with the trustee, with the proceeds on maturity being used to discharge the bond issue in question?

The FASB concluded in 1982 that "debt is extinguished when the debtor's obligation to the creditor is satisfied and there is no continuing or contingent recourse to the debtor with respect to the debt." It then softened its stand in 1983 to approve "in substance" defeasance under circumstances in which cash or other "qualifying" monetary assets are placed in a trust to be used solely for satisfying the scheduled payments of interest and principal on the debt.

It should be recognized that a definition of when a bond is cancelled is a creation of cost-based accounting. In a fundamental economic sense, the real gain or loss has already taken place, and the argument is over when it should be recognized in the accounts.

RESCHEDULING "TROUBLED" DEBT

Imagine that a bank lends money on 1 November 19X0 to a company that wants to develop a ski hill. Unfortunately, after the lifts are built the resort area has a mild winter and few people ski there. The builder had borrowed $3,000,000 at 18% repayable on 1 March 19X5, with interest payable each 1 November. On 1 November, 19X1 he informs his creditor that although he owes interest of $540,000, he does not have the cash to pay. Furthermore, if the creditor puts him into bankruptcy, this will ruin the glamorous image of the ski area and make the loan collateral worth even less. The builder offers to give the bank the ski lifts as repayment, but the bank has no desire to become actively involved in the ski business.

Instead of foreclosing on the security for the loan and perhaps trying to sell the lift equipment, the bank might decide its own best interest lies in allowing the operator to continue in business with the hope that ultimately he will be able to pay off most of the principal of the debt, if not the accumulated interest. Because he has been unable to meet the first interest payment, the bank might forgive the unpaid interest but write a new agreement in which he has to make payments according to the following schedule:

1 November 19X2	$ 300,000
1 November 19X3	400,000
1 November 19X4	500,000
1 November 19X5	3,600,000

Suppose the market rate of interest was still 18%. Then, the present value of the new loan could be calculated as follows:

Date	Payment	Years to discount	Discount factor	Present value
1 November 19X2	$ 300,000	1	0.8474576	$ 254,238
1 November 19X3	400,000	2	0.7181844	287,274
1 November 19X4	500,000	3	0.6086309	304,315
1 November 19X5	3,600,000	4	0.5157889	1,856,840
	$ 4,800,000			$ 2,702,667

An observer of this event might say that the borrower had defaulted on his loan and that the bank had been forced to settle for a less attractive arrangement because it felt it had no other option. The observer might then go on to say that the market value of the new debt should be determined and the bank should write the loan down to this value. Such a journal entry would read as follows:

Loss on loan	297,333.00	
Loan receivable		297,333.00
To record reduction in value of loan		
($3,000,000.00 − 2,702,667.00)		

For the same reason, the builder would make a corresponding entry in his own books:

Loan payable	297,333.00	
Gain on reduction of loan		297,333.00
To record reduction of loan payable.		

Canadian procedure, as evidenced by the *CICA Handbook,* is silent on the proper treatment of **"troubled" debt,** but it is understood that good practice would require a write-down to present value. In contrast, the FASB was quite clear in Statement No. 15 [1977] that the change in market value should not be recognized except to the extent that the total payments to be received are less than the face amount of the loan. In the preceding example the revised payments total $4,800,000, which is greater than the $3 000 000 of the original loan. Therefore no write-down would be made.

It is a mistake to become too literal in making rules about when a debt should be written down; for the creditor may be in a position to make the debtor agree to repayment terms that cannot be met but that at the same time produce a present value which is at least equal to the amount of the debt. For instance, the creditor may preserve the present value of the loan by having the debtor agree to a large payment at the end of the term of the loan.

When the FASB was looking at this issue during the late 1970s the U.S. banks had extensive loans out to the real estate industry and they objected to recognizing the loss implicit in troubled debt. The stated reason was that bank regulators would then be forced to treat them differently, to the detriment of the U.S. economy. The recommendation issued by the FASB in its Statement 15 was controversial. Opponents raised two questions. First, if the investing public was already aware of the basic problem from other sources of information, would they not have acted on this already? Second, if the public were not aware, was it proper to leave them uninformed because it was "good" for them?

CICA Handbook Disclosure Requirements

The disclosure requirements of the *CICA Handbook* for long-term liabilities are not extensive. They are limited to one page. The main thrust of the requirements is to provide the reader with the basic details of each bond or mortgage issue outstanding. Thus, the following should be disclosed for each issue outstanding [*CICA* 3210]:

1. Title of the issue

2. Interest rate

3. Maturity date

4. Amount outstanding

5. Existence of sinking fund and the aggregate amount required in the next five years to meet its provisions

6. Existence of conversion or redemption provisions

7. Currency in which debt payable, if a foreign one

8. Whether debt is secured

9. Carrying value of security, if practical

10. Details of default, if any, on outstanding debt

There are two further requirements. The balance sheet should show the long-term debt that is payable within a year. The income statement should distinguish between (i) interest and amortization on debt incurred for a term of more than one year and (ii) other interest.

Examples From Published Reports

The usual approach to disclosing long-term debt in the financial statements is to give a very brief account in the balance sheet, with the details of the individual issues in the notes.

Loblaw Companies Limited

Loblaw is a grocery chain that finds itself owning real estate on which to place its stores and financing the assets with long-term debt.

CONSOLIDATED BALANCE SHEET

		1986	1985
		(millions of $)	
Long-term debt (note 7)		$ 430.9	$ 250.7
Note 7. Long-Term Debt			
Debentures:			
Series 1, 12$\frac{1}{2}$%	due 1990	$ 35.0	$ 35.0
Series 2, 12$\frac{1}{4}$%	due 1994	35.0	35.0
Series 3, 11$\frac{5}{8}$%	due 1992	50.0	50.0
Series 4, 11%	due 1995	40.0	40.0
Series 5, 10%	due 2006	50.0	
Series 6, 9$\frac{3}{4}$%	due 2001	75.0	
Series 7, 10%	due 2001	75.0	
Term loans:			
LIBOR plus $\frac{3}{8}$% to $\frac{3}{4}$%, due 1992 (U.S $13.0)		18.1	17.3
Repaid in 1986 and 1985			15.0
Mortgages at a weighted average interest rate of 10.1%, due 1988–2004 (including U.S. $5.2)		25.5	28.5
Other long-term debt at a weighted average interest rate of 8.9%, due 1987–2014 (including U.S. $20.9)		39.5	45.0
		443.1	265.8
Less payable within one year		12.2	15.1
		430.9	250.7

This is a rather complex debt structure. A good analyst would go over it carefully to see if there are any particularly "expensive" or "cheap" issues outstanding whose ultimate redemption will affect the company. The term loan above is at a floating rate of $\frac{3}{8}$% to $\frac{3}{4}$% above the London Interbank Offered Rate (LIBOR), which is commonly used as a floating rate on which to base such loans. Observe that as it is in $U.S., the company bears the foreign-exchange risk.

Dofasco Inc.

Dofasco Inc. is a large and successful Canadian steel company.

Debt		1987	1986
Sinking fund debentures:			
6½%	due May 15, 1987		$ 17,100
9%	due February 1, 1991	$ 24,444	25,087
10%	due June 1, 1994	25,730	28,911
10⅞%	due May 15, 1995	33,888	38,100
10⅜%	due March 15, 1996	36,700	40,557
9⅜%	due February 15, 1997	57,722	61,480
13½%	due November 1, 2000	42,240	45,120
		220,724	256,355
Notes payable:			
9.95% repayable by November 30, 2003		240,655	129,099
Total long-term debt at 31 December		461,379	385,454
Less: current requirements		2,280	18,180
		459,099	367,274
Accrued liability for relining blast furnaces beyond one year and other long-term liabilities		76,743	68,335
		$ 535,842	$ 435,609

The term "current requirements" above refers to the portion of the debt due within one year that will be reclassified as a current liability. Additional information supplied in the note provides repayment requirements of long-term debt within the next five years, as well as information about additional credit available to the company should it wish to use it. Probably the most unusual item is the last one, which concerns relining the blast furnace. The notes on the company's accounting policies state that repair and maintenance costs are expensed as incurred except for the estimated cost of relining blast furnaces "which is accrued over the period between relines." From the information available, it would appear that there is a good argument for putting this item on the asset side of the balance sheet and treating it as accumulated depreciation or amortization.

Summary

Long-term payables typically consist of that portion of bonds or mortgages which will not mature for more than one year. The accounting convention is to record the amount received for them at the time of sale as a liability. Any discount or premium over the face value is amortized over the life of the bond, but no adjustment is made for changes in the market value of the liability over its term. Thus, it is possible to trigger a gain or loss on a debt by redeeming it before it is due.

QUESTIONS

Q12-1. Review and make sure you understand the following terms:

a. long-term liability	**k.** bond premium
b. mortgage	**l.** amortization of bond premium
c. bond	**m.** serial bond
d. lease	**n.** call provision of bond
e. first mortgage *versus* second mortgage	**o.** sinking fund for bonds
f. debenture	**p.** convertible bond
g. trust indenture	**q.** share warrants
h. coupon rate	**r.** "troubled" debt
i. market rate of interest	**s.** defeasance
j. par value of bond	**t.** interest-rate swap

Q12-2. What are the exceptions to the general rule that long-term liabilities should be those whose maturity is greater than one year? As a reader of financial statements, in which industries would you expect to find these exceptions?

Q12-3. Morton Mills had a $250,000 mortgage due on 15 December 19X6. Its financial year-end is 30 June. On its balance sheet for 30 June 19X6, should it show the mortgage as a current liability instead of a long-term liability?

Q12-4. "There is little point in discussing the relative conceptual merits of the straight-line method and the interest method for amortizing bond discount." Discuss, explaining the APB stand on this issue.

Q12-5. "The management of a company can always manipulate the reported net income by redeeming a bond whose market value is below par." Do you agree? Why?

Q12-6. What is the APB's stand on the discounting of receivables whose term is longer than one year? Is this consistent with the FASB position on the valuation of "troubled" debt? Explain.

Q12-7. One supporter of the FASB's stand on "troubled" debt has said that if the discounted present value had been used instead of the method actually adopted, the banks would have been tempted to rewrite the terms of the debt to show heavy repayments that the debtors could not possibly have met. Explain.

Q12-8. When interest rates rise dramatically, it is common to see a company's bonds trading well below their face value or issue price. Consider each of the following scenarios.

    a. X Inc. had issued $100,000 in ten-year 10% bonds at par in 19X2. In 19X4 they were trading at $83.50. In that year, X Inc. purchased $30,000 face value and cancelled them. What journal entry would be required?

    b. Y Inc. had circumstances identical to X Inc., but it had a clause in its bonds saying that they could not be cancelled until maturity. In 19X4 Y Inc. purchased $30,000 face value and sent them to a trust company under a written agreement that the trust company would hold them until maturity and then destroy them. What journal entry would be required? Explain.

Q12-9. "The significant weaknesses under GAAP in accounting for long-term debt are simply a mirror image of the equivalent problems with plant assets." Do you agree? Explain.

Q12-10. Explain in your own words why a bond premium can be thought of as interest to be paid in arrears and a bond discount can be thought of as prepaid interest. Is the usual accounting treatment consistent with your explanation?

Q12-11. The following may be thought of as alternative methods to assure bondholders that the issuing company will ultimately redeem the bonds:

    (i) periodically set aside funds to create a sinking fund equal on redemption to the face value of the issue outstanding (with any earnings on the sinking fund investment to accrue to the general company account)

    (ii) annually purchase part of the outstanding issue for redemption and cancellation

    (iii) annually purchase part of the outstanding issue to be kept in a sinking fund.

What would be the effect on the company's balance sheet and income statement if methods (ii) or (iii) were used in place of (i)?

Q12-12. "Triggering a gain by redemption of bonds payable trading at a discount is another example of the inherent weakness of cost-based accounting." What does this statement mean? Do you agree? Explain.

Q12-13. A student-owned housing co-operative bought kitchen equipment on terms under which they made five annual payments of $2,000, payable at the start of each year. The estimated functional life of the equipment is five years. The dealer who sold them the equipment told them that their "credit rating was so good that no interest has to be paid." Members of the co-op must pay annual fees equal to the "cost" of operation. Is it "fair" or "unfair" to include imputed interest in the annual fees? Discuss and show your calculations.

Q12-14. Give a critique of the present disclosure requirements of the *CICA Handbook* for long-term liabilities. Set out those things that you would like to know about a company's long-term debt that are not required by the *Handbook*. *(Hint:* Use the examples given from published statements given in this chapter and see how many questions remain unanswered when you try to analyse their debt position.)

Q12-15. What are the main features that differentiate short-term and long-term debt?

Q12-16. Explain how a company in financial difficulties might be able to report an unusual gain on its long-term debt. Explain in non-accounting terms what this "gain" to the company represents.

EXERCISES

E12-1. The January 1980 issue of *Business Week* reported that the French resort operator Club Med, the corporation that "pioneered the merchandising of 'sun, sand, and sex'," had sold $8 million in sixteen-year bonds to finance the construction of another vacation village in the Caribbean. The bonds were in units of $1,000 each. They would pay 10% interest while the 700-bed village in Haiti was being constructed and 8.5% interest thereafter. The bonds had special bonus features that allowed Club Med to pay less than the 12.5% interest that was required at the time of other companies with similar credit ratings.

    The first bonus feature was that once the occupancy rate of the new village reached 65%, Club Med would put additional money into a special pool in proportion to each paying guest. This was to be distributed among the bondholders. As the occupancy rate rose, additional sums would be put into the pool. If the occupancy rate reached 85% — which was not unusual in that area — the bondholders would divide up $357,700 additional interest for that year.

The second bonus feature was that for every 1% increase in the average price charged on the six other villages in the Caribbean the bondholder would get 28 cents per year per $1,000 bond. For example, if prices increased by 10%, then each bondholder would get $2.80 per year for each $1,000 bond, or 0.28% more.

Required:

a. Assume that the bonds are shown on the balance sheet with minimum information and that for details the reader is referred to the notes to the financial statement. Write an appropriate note to explain the bonds.

b. Suppose that in the first year of operation the village in Haiti had 85% occupancy and the six other villages in the region had raised their rates an average of 12%. Show the journal entry that would be required to record the interest expense and payment.

c. It seems likely that Club Med will be paying out much higher amounts on these bonds as the years pass. This is something like a bond with low coupon rates in the early years and much higher rates in the later years of this issue. If it were considered to be such a bond, would it be appropriate to charge as interest expense in each year only the amount paid out? Discuss.

E12-2.   *The Financial Post* reported that the following "wrinkles" are being used to help raise capital.

(i) Bonds are being issued with a feature that allows the holder to participate in the profits of the project being financed by the bonds. For instance, if the bonds are used to finance a shopping centre, the bondholder would participate in any profits of that centre.

(ii) Bonds have interest paid every quarter instead of every half year.

(iii) Bonds are being issued with no fixed coupon rate. Instead, the interest will be indexed to some floating rate, such as the prime rate charged by the Canadian chartered banks.

(iv) The call option is being eliminated on some bonds so that investors know that they can hold the bonds to maturity.

(v) Sinking-fund provisions are being eliminated and replaced with a provision that a portion of the bonds outstanding must be purchased by the company each year if the bonds are trading below the issue price.

Required:

For each of the above "wrinkles," answer the following:

a. Write an appropriate note to indicate the essential information in the notes to the financial statements.

b. Discuss whether the "wrinkle" is likely to have an adverse impact on the company's interest expense in the long-run that the reader of the financial statements should be aware of.

E12-3.   S Limited issued $250,000 of first mortgage twenty-year bonds at 98.00 on 1 March 19X0. Costs of the issue, other than bond discount, were $7,500. On 1 March 19X4, it redeemed $30,000 face value of these bonds at 87.00. Give the journal entry (or entries) that would be required on 1 March 19X4 to account for the redemption. Show all your calculations.

E12-4. T Limited issued a five-year 12% mortgage for $500,000 on 1 June 19X4, with interest payable annually on 1 June. The mortgage was secured by a first charge against all real estate of the company, and annual principal repayments of $100,000 were due on 1 June of 19X5 to 19X9.

Required:

a. Assuming the company's year-end is 31 May, show the information that would be required in the financial statements for 31 May 19X5.

b. The holder of the mortgage agreed with T Limited to retire the mortgage on 1 December 19X7. The agreed redemption price was 95% of the principal outstanding. Give the journal entry that would be required on redemption. Show all your calculations.

E12-5. In each of the following unrelated cases, you are asked to fill in the blanks for the missing information with respect to a company's bonds payable. Column E is the market price of the bond at present. Column G asks whether the market rate of interest is above the coupon rate at present. Column H asks whether there would be a gain or loss on disposal if the bond were redeemed by the company (assume straight-line amortization of bond discount or premium). Column I asks whether the interest cost reported on the income statement would be greater or less than the coupon rate of the bond.

Case (a) has been completed as an illustration with the answers in italics. If the market price is lower than the par value, the the market rate of interest must be higher than the coupon rate; hence the answer to column G is *yes*. If the bond were to be redeemed now, the carrying value would be 98 ($^3/_{10}$ of 2) = 98.60. Because the market price is 99.50, there would be a loss on redemption of $0.90; hence the answer to column H is *loss*. The annual interest expense in the financial statements would be 12% plus the bond discount; hence the answer to column I is *yes*.

A	B	C	D	E	F	G	H	I
						Market rate above coupon rate?	Gain or loss on redemption?	Interest expense greater than coupon rate?
	Years since		Coupon	Market	Issue			
Case	issue	Term	rate	price	price			
a.	3	10	12%	99.50	98.00	*Yes*	*Loss*	*Yes*
b.	8	16	8	84.50	100.00			
c.	1	5	16	101.25	105.00			
d.	4	5	9	87.50	96.00			
e.	6	15	11	83.50	98.20			
f.	2	4	13	97.50	99.00			
g.	9	10	12	102.00	100.00			

E12-6. On 25 November 1981 CSM Inc. issued $500,000 12% convertible redeemable sinking-fund debentures and 200,000 share warrants. These two securities were offered as a unit of one debenture in the principal amount of $500 and 200 share warrants for a price of $550. Each debenture is convertible, at the option of the holder, at any time up to 23 November 1991 into fully paid common shares on the basis of 250 common shares for each $500 principal amount of debenture, without adjustment for accrued interest on the debentures or dividend on shares issued upon such conversion. Each share warrant entitles the bearer to purchase one common share at a price of $1.50 at any time up to 25 November 1986. Thereafter the warrants will be void.

Required:

a. Show the journal entry that would be required when the shares were issued.

b. Show the financial-statement disclosure that would be required according to the *CICA Handbook* as set out in this chapter. If the *Handbook* does not require disclosure of an item that you think should be included anyway, indicate what this is and give your reasons.

c. In no more than 100 words, write a critique of the *CICA Handbook* requirements for bonds and mortgages.

E12-7. In an article entitled "Innovative options reduce capital costs," *The Globe and Mail* reported that the devices listed below are "adding vigor to standard securities, like adding a turbocharger to an old car." This "new conceptual spin" is reported to be able to "save the corporate issuer large sums in its borrowing costs." The devices are as follows:

(i) Bonds are being sold that allow the investor to be repaid with a choice of currencies.

(ii) Some bonds being sold give the investor an option to purchase at a later date another issue of bonds with a "sharply higher" interest rate.

(iii) Some bonds are being sold with a "floating" interest rate that is tied to some market index so that the rate paid on the debt goes up or down with the market interest rate. These bonds generally sell for a lower initial interest rate.

(iv) Some of the bonds described in (iii) are sold with a *cap,* which sets an upper limit to the interest rate that will be paid. Bonds sold with caps generally have to pay a somewhat higher initial interest rate because the investor is not fully protected against rising interest rates.

(v) Some companies that sell bonds with caps in turn "resell" these cap rights to other borrowers for an up-front fee. Suppose Company A has a cap on its debt of 13% and sells its cap to Company B for a fee. Then every time A's debt would have gone above 13% (but for the cap), it must pay the difference in interest to B.

Required:

For each of the above devices, answer the following:

a. Explain why, if at all, the investor is prepared to accept an initial rate of return that is apparently below the market rate.

b. Suggest where and when an analyst might expect that the company would have increased costs of capital as compared with the relatively low cost at the outset.

E12-8. Answer the following unrelated questions:

a. $100,000 of eight-year, 8% term bonds, sold to yield 6%, are issued at $108,530. Would the amortization of the bond premium in the first year of the bond be the same under the effective-interest method and straight-line method of amortization? Explain your conclusions and use the given data to illustrate them.

b. Five-year bonds dated 1 May 19X7 were sold on 1 August 19X7 at a discount of $20,000. Interest is paid semi-annually on 1 May and 1 November. The straight-line method of discount amortization is used by the issuing company. Show how you would calculate the amount of the bond discount to be amortized for the year-end adjustment at 31 December 19X7.

c. When bonds are refunded through a new bond issue prior to maturity, there can be a gain or loss on redemption. State the alternatives available in accounting for the gain or loss and indicate the appropriate presentation on the income statement in each case.

(CMA adapted)

E12-9. Give the journal entry that would be required for each of the following unrelated transactions. Show all your calculations.

a. On 30 June 19X9 Hanover Ltd. borrowed money on a mortgage to build a warehouse. The amount received was $350,000, and the face amount of the mortgage, due in five years, was $380,000. Interest at 12% on the mortgage was payable at the end of each month. It is now 31 July, and Hanover pays interest of $3,800.

b. Mowatt Inc. pays $25,000 interest on bonds payable on 1 April 19X9. The bonds, with a face value of $500,000, bear interest at 10% payable semi-annually. They were issued on 1 January 19X5 at $93 and had a ten-year term.

c. Livingston Limited redeems bonds with a face value of $850,000 as of 1 July 19X8 for a total of $885,000. They were issued nine years previously at par with a coupon rate of 10% payable semi-annually on 1 September and 1 March. They were due to mature ten years from the date of issue.

d. Under the terms of its trust indenture, each 30 September Traynor Inc. was obliged to repurchase 11% of the outstanding bonds payable with a face value of $100,000. It could either purchase them at market or redeem them at a price of $102 plus accrued interest. It is now 30 September, and the market price is $101.50. The coupon dates are 30 June and 31 December.

e. Ellerbeck Inc. entered into a swap arrangement by which it swapped its floating-rate bond interest on a $1,000,000 ten-year bond issue for a fixed-rate interest of 12%. It paid its bank a fee of $50,000 for underwriting this swap. It is now the first semi-annual interest anniversary date, and the floating rate interest is 11.5%. Ellerbeck pays its bondholders $57,500 in interest and is making the appropriate settlement with the underwriter. Assume the company's year-end is three months away.

PROBLEMS

P12-1. On 1 July 1981 Landsdowne Marine borrowed $300,000 on a five-year first mortgage. The interest rate was 16% payable monthly, and no repayment of principal was required until maturity. The legal and surveying work required by the lender cost Landsdowne $3,600. The company's financial year-end is 31 December.

Required: Prepare the journal entries for Landsdowne's books for the month of December 1981, showing (i) payment of mortgage interest, (ii) accrual of interest, and (iii) amortizing of borrowing costs for the period from the start of the loan to the end of the year.

P12-2. Elgin Limited sold $300,000 ten-year bonds with a coupon rate of 13%. Interest was payable annually at the end of each year. The normal interest rate that Elgin would expect to pay is 18%, but it managed to sell its bonds with just a 5% discount from face value by offering a conversion feature: each $1,000 bond could be converted into 20 common shares of the company at the bondholder's option.

At the same time Delta Limited sold $300,000 ten-year bonds at 13% as part of a package where each unit consisted of one $1,000 bond and 20 warrants to purchase common shares. It too managed to sell its units at 95% of the face value of the bonds. After the issue was sold, trading began in the bonds and warrants: the bonds were trading at $77.53 per $100, and the warrants at $11.24.

Required:

a. Prepare journal entries to record the issue of bonds by Elgin and Delta. Use GAAP. Be sure to explain each entry.

b. In about 150 words write a critique of the accounting treatment used in GAAP. Try to anticipate the counterarguments by a fair-minded person who favoured present GAAP.

P12-3. For each of the following unrelated transactions, prepare all the journal entries that would be required to record them. Also prepare the notes, if any, that would be required for the financial statements.

a. A company purchased a piece of land for $110,000, and the vendor agreed to take back a five-year mortgage for $80,000 at 12% as part of the payment. Legal fees were $3,000. A survey was needed to define the land to be sold. The survey cost $2,400 and was paid for by the purchaser, but it was to be split between the purchaser and the vendor.

b. Bonds with a face value of $250,000, a term of ten years, and a coupon rate of 12% payable semi-annually were issued on 1 January 19X3 at a price of 98.50. The bonds could be called at the following prices:

> After 1 January 19X5 — 99.00
> After 1 January 19X7 — 99.50
> After 1 January 19X9 — 100.00

The underwriter charged the company $5,000 and there were legal fees of $3,000. Journal entries are needed both for the purchase and for the amortization of bond issue costs at the company's year-end, 30 June 19X3.

c. Bonds with a face value of $50,000 were called on 1 July 19X5 for cancellation. They had a call price of $99.25.

d. The company that issued the bonds in (b) above purchased the same bonds on 1 January 19X8 at a price of 84.00 for a face value of $60,000 and then cancelled them. Journal entries are needed both for the interest payment and the redemption of the bonds.

e. Bonds with a face value of $300,000 were issued in units of one warrant and $100 face value of bond. The warrants entitled the holder to purchase one share of the company for $30 and five warrants at any time within five years of the date of issue. The package of bonds and warrants was sold for $298,000, and the warrants started trading almost immediately for $1.20. Show the journal entry required at the time of issue.

P12-4. JWC Limited issued $300,000 in twenty-year bonds at par on 1 October 19X0 with a coupon rate of 15%. The proceeds were used to purchase a shopping centre for $300,000. The bonds are now trading at 83.00, and the shopping centre has a net book value of $250,000. JWC Limited has a firm offer to sell it for $400,000.

a. If the company did sell the shopping centre and used the proceeds in part to purchase the bond issue and cancel it, what would the journal entries be?

b. A potential purchaser of the company has shown you the financial statements of JWC for the year in which the above transactions took place and has asked you for an evaluation of the reported net income. Write a one-page memo in reply.

P12-5. SC Inc. issued $1,500,000 ten-year sinking-fund debentures on 1 November 19X3 at 100.00 with a coupon rate of 15%. Under the terms of the sinking-fund indenture the company was required to deposit with the trustee each year the sum of at least $100,000. If the bonds were trading below par, the sinking funds were to be used to purchase and redeem the bonds in units of $1,000, up to the amount of funds available. If the bonds were trading at par or above, the sinking funds were to be used to redeem them by lot from among the outstanding certificates.

Required: Show the journal entries that would be required in the books of the company for the following transactions. Assume that the company keeps the trust, bank, and other accounts in its own books.

a. On 1 November 19X4 the company deposited $100,000 with the trustee. The bonds were trading at 95.00, and the trustee bought the full amount with the money available.

b. On 1 November 19X5 the company deposited another $100,000 with the trustee. The bonds were trading at 102.00, and the trustee exercised the right under the trust indenture to call as many bonds as funds permitted for cancellation at par.

c. On 1 November 19X6 the company sent $50,000 to the trustee with a covering letter saying that it expected to send the remaining $50,000 within six months. Because of concern about the financial stability of the company, the bonds were now trading at 75.00, and the trustee purchased as many as possible.

P12-6. On 1 February 19X2 MWW Ltd. issued $350,000 convertible debentures at par with a coupon rate of 12%. Under the terms of the issue the bonds could be converted into shares at the prices shown below.

From 1 February 19X2 to 31 January 19X3 — $100 of face value of bond per share
From 1 February 19X3 to 31 January 19X4 — $125 of face value of bond per share
From 1 February 19X4 to 31 January 19X5 — $150 of face value of bond per share
From 1 February 19X5 to 31 January 19X6 — $175 of face value of bond per share

Thus, for example, between 1 February 19X2 and 31 January 19X3 a bond with a face value of $1,000 could be converted into ten shares.

On 1 March 19X3 debentures with a face value of $30,000 were tendered for conversion into common shares. At that time the market price of the common shares was $145, and the market price of the bonds was $120.00.

Required:

a. Give the journal entry to record the conversion of the bonds into shares, assuming that the market price of the bonds was used to value the shares issued. Show all calculations.

b. Explain what other ways of valuing the shares might be used. What are the merits, if any, of these approaches?

P12-7. On 1 July 19X7 Head SunTan Products issued a ten-year, $100,000, 8% bond with annual payments at the end of each twelve months. The bond sold such that the proceeds resulted in an annual return of 10% for the investors. No issue costs were incurred.

Required:

a. Present a year-by-year comparison of the expenses related to this bond issue using both the straight-line method and the interest method to amortize the discount. (*Note:* The yearly interest expense for the interest method is 10% of the present value of the total debt.)

b. Compare the results and state which method is preferable.

P12-8. Malcolm Parker Ltd. issued a five-year, convertible, $50,000 bond with semi-annual interest payments at 5%. The bond was convertible at a rate of 20 shares for each $1,000 face value of bonds. There were only two investors, and each bought one-half of the issue. After two years, one decided to convert. On that day, the market price per share was $42.25. The bonds had been priced to yield 8% per annum.

Required:

a. Calculate the issue price of the bonds.

b. Show journal entries to record (i) the interest expense of the first half-year and (ii) the conversion of bonds in Year 2 using the straight-line method to amortize the premium.

P12-9. Jackson Tobacco Ltd. issued a five-year $250,000 bond with semi-annual interest payments of 4%. There was a sinking-fund requirement that Jackson set aside a constant amount of money at the end of every year so that at the end of the period enough money would be set aside to retire the bonds. The bond fund was expected to earn 11% annually. It was held by the company, not a trustee.

Required:

a. Present a yearly summary of the cash flows of the sinking fund for this firm. Comment on their pattern and the implications for the company's annual funds flow.

b. If the fund earned 11% in every year except Year 5 in which it earned 14%, what entry would Jackson make (i) to record the redemption of its bonds payable out of its sinking funds assets and (ii) to record receipt of excess earnings out of the sinking fund after retirement of the bonds payable?

P12-10. On 27 August 1984 *The Globe and Mail* reported in an article entitled "Accounting Hides Provincial Debt" that the *CICA Handbook* would be requiring Canadian companies to amortize any unrealized gains or losses that arose because they had issued bonds denominated in some foreign currency that had since changed in value with respect to the Canadian dollar. Because of this ruling, a portion of the unamortized gain or loss would be recognized as an income item each year.

At the time, provincial governments that had issued bonds denominated in U.S. dollars, West German marks, Swiss francs, or Japanese yen were not required to recognize any unrealized loss because of changes in the exchange rate. The lack of recognition by provincial governments of such losses meant that the provinces were delaying recognition of the consequences of having borrowed in foreign currency.

Required:

a. What are the arguments in favour of amortizing gains and losses on foreign debt over the life of that debt? What are the arguments against it?

b. How would the adoption of the CICA method affect the financial statements of the provincial governments? Do you think this would be an improvement? Explain.

P12-11. On 12 April 1984 an article apeared in *The Wall Street Journal* reporting that National Westminster Bank PLC in England had issued debt to the public that had no maturity date, so that the bank could go on paying interest indefinitely if it wished. The owners of such notes could sell them to other investors, but had no assurance the bank would ever redeem them. On the other hand, the bank could redeem them in five years if it wished.

The bank had to pay 0.375 of a percentage point above the six-month London Interbank Offered Rate (LIBOR). In contrast, a recent offering of twenty-year floating-rate notes by Barclay's Bank PLC, Britain's largest bank, pays only 0.13 of a percentage point above LIBOR. Therefore it appears that the special terms of the Westminster loan incurred an interest penalty.

Required:

a. What should the bank's journal entry be on issue? (*Note:* Because the maturity date is infinitely far away, the present value of the liability is zero.) Discuss.

b. How should the acquisition of such a note be recorded by the purchaser?

P12-12. It was reported by *The Wall Street Journal* on 28 February 1983 that the Export Development Corporation (EDC), a Canadian government agency, had been able to borrow in London, England, at a rate of 10%, which appeared to be even less than the U.S. government could borrow at. Normally, one would expect that the rate would have been about 0.5% above the U.S. government rate.

What made this funding coup possible was that each of EDC's $1,000 notes carries a detachable, six-month warrant that can be used to buy a similar $1,000 note at par. "If interest rates decline sufficiently by the time the warrants expire on 15 September, the warrants can be sold at profit to those wishing to acquire more Export Development notes at a 10% yield." During trading in the issue, the warrants were detached and sold separately for as much as $16.

Required:

a. Why would investors and speculators be willing to buy this issue that has a rate of interest less than they would normally demand?

b. What would be the proper accounting treatment for both the purchaser and the seller of such an issue? What is the usual treatment?

P12-13. *The Financial Post* reported that in 1980 Canada's corporate treasurers had been busily coming up with innovative ways to raise capital in an often unreceptive bond market and a very hectic stock market. Companies were being forced to offer new and attractive features to ensure the success of their forays into the capital markets. The wishes of the investor were key in deciding the terms, structure, size, and pricing of all financings.

Required: Using your imagination and a little research into the financial press, give other examples of the "wrinkles" used by treasurers for raising capital. For each example indicate an appropriate accounting treatment and outline the implications for the investor in the bond or stock.

P12-14. The use by several major companies of the method of defeasance has caused a great deal of controversy in recent years in both the United States and in Canada.

Required:

a. Define the term *defeasance*. Briefly explain how and why it is used by companies.

b. Identify the accounting problems associated with the use of defeasance.

c. What are the implications for investors in companies that use this method?

P12-15. Far Plains Limited purchased equipment on 1 April 19X4 with a list price of $80,000. They paid $22,000 down and gave a $75,000 non-interest-bearing note to be paid in annual instalments of $15,000 each, starting on 1 April 19X5. The company usually had to pay interest of 10% on such loans for equipment. The equipment had a life expectancy of ten years with a residual value of $6,800. The company uses diminishing balance at twice the straight-line rate for depreciation.

Required: Prepare all the journal entries necessary for the equipment and the note on the following four dates: 1 April 19X5, 31 December 19X4, 1 April 19X5, and 31 December 19X5. Use the interest method for amortization of the note and take all amounts to the nearest dollar. The company always reverses any adjusting journal entries it made at the end of the prior year.

(CGA adapted)

P12-16. On 2 January 19X5 a company sold 5% bonds with a face value of $100,000. Bond maturity is five years, and interest is paid semi-annually on 30 June and 31 December. The bonds were sold for $95,735 to yield 6%.

Required:

a. Prepare *all* the journal entries which the company must record for the first year of the bonds. (The firm uses the effective-interest method of amortization.)

b. Under what circumstances would a corporation record (i) a bond premium? (ii) a bond discount? Explain fully.

c. "The interest method of amortization of bond premium and discount is superior to the straight-line method." Discuss.

(CGA adapted)

P12-17. On 30 June 1989, Jason Corporation purchased $100,000 par value, 8% bonds as a long-term investment. The total cash outlay for the bonds was $86,000. The ten-year bonds were dated 31 December 1986, with interest payable annually.

Required:

a. Prepare the journal entries to account for the investment in the bonds for the years ending 31 December 1989, 1990, and 1991. (*Note:* Use the straight-line amortization method.)

b. Suppose that Jason Corporation debited the bond investment account for $86,000 and recognized interest revenue on the cash basis, that is $8,000 in each of the years 1989, 1990 and 1991. Prepare the correcting journal entry (or entries) for the investment in bonds as of 1 January, 1992.

(CGA adapted)

P12-18. Harriot Corporation issued $140,000, 10%, ten-year convertible bonds. Interest is paid at 5% semi-annually on 30 June and 31 December. Each $1,000 bond is convertible into 10 shares of common stock (par $50) at any interest date after three years from issuance. The bonds were sold at 98 to Oliver Corporation as a long-term investment on 31 January 1989. The issue date was 1 January 1989. There is no ready market for Harriot Corporation bonds.

Required:

a. Give the journal entry for the issuer at the date of sale. Show all calculations.

b. Give the journal entry for the investor at the date of sale. Show all calculations.

c. Give the journal entry for the issuer, assuming that the conversion privilege is subsequently exercised by Oliver Corporation immediately after the end of the third year. Assume that at the date of conversion the common stock was selling at $125 per share. Use the book-value method.

d. Give the journal entries for the investee, assuming the same conditions prevail as in part (c). Here, use the market-value method.

(CGA adapted)

BIBLIOGRAPHY

ACCOUNTING PRINCIPLES BOARD. *Opinion No.21: Interest on Receivables and Payables.* New York: American Institute of Certified Public Accountants, 1971. This sets forth the idea that receivables should be shown at their discounted value.

FINANCIAL ACCOUNTING STANDARDS BOARD. *Statement of Financial Accounting Standards No. 15: Accounting by Debtors and Creditors for Troubled Debt Restructuring.* Stamford, Conn.: FASB, June 1977. "Troubled" debt is that whose payments are likely to go in arrears.

MILLER, JERRY D. "Accounting for Warrants and Convertible Bonds." *Management Accounting* (January 1973). A readable account of the controversy over the differing treatment of warrants and the conversion privilege for bonds.

STEPHENS, MATTHEW. "Inseparability of the Valuation of Convertible Bonds." *Journal of Accountancy* (August 1971). More on the controversy of the warrants versus conversion issue.

CHAPTER 13
Corporate Income Taxes

Introduction

Income taxes are a significant element of reported net income, often equal to after-tax net income. In this chapter we will assume that income taxes are an expense of doing business and that the problems of matching this expense against the related revenue are essentially the same as the problems of any other business expense. (This controversial point will be discussed later in the chapter). We will also examine several issues regarding the amount of the tax expense to be reported on the income statement.

The issue of **intraperiod allocation** addresses the problems of matching tax expense within a year to the category of income or loss to which it is related. The issue of **interperiod allocation** addresses the problem of matching tax expense between different years.

The treatment of tax losses arises because a company that experiences a loss may, under certain circumstances, recover taxes paid in other years or eliminate taxes payable in future years.

The appropriate accounting treatment for interperiod allocation has been, and continues to be, highly controversial. At the time of writing (1989), significant changes are being proposed to existing treatment in both Canada and the United States, and these changes are being widely contested. We will deal with these proposed changes later under the appropriate sections.

The tax a company actually pays, termed the **effective tax rate**, is often an average of different rates. There is now a requirement for publicly traded companies that their financial statements should tell readers how the effective rate is determined. Many governments have used the income taxation system as a means of encouraging investment. The tax reductions that have arisen from these incentive systems have raised accounting issues that we will also discuss here.

In Canada the provinces as well as the federal government have the right to tax corporations. However, except in Ontario, Quebec, and Alberta, this corporate tax is collected for the provinces by the federal government, applying the same rules for the calculation of taxable income that it uses to collect federal income tax. For simplicity in presentation we will stick to the federal tax rules in this chapter.

Intraperiod Tax Allocation

Intraperiod tax allocation is the matching, within financial statements, of the total income tax expense for that year with (i) ordinary operating income, (ii) extraordinary items, and (iii) prior-period adjustments and other items included in *retained earnings*.

Suppose that Portland Corporation's income statement originally appeared as follows:

Income before tax on continuing operations	$ 80,000
Less: Inventory loss resulting from fire	35,000
Total income before tax (net)	$ 45,000
Tax provision at 46%	20,700
Net income after tax	$ 24,300

The purpose of intraperiod allocation is to match the tax provision (expense) of $20,700 against the two major sources of income and loss, thereby allowing the reader to see what the after-tax earnings are for both ordinary and extraordinary income. The tax provision is split up and matched to each, as follows:

Net income before tax on regular operations		$ 80,000
Provision for income tax at 46%		36,800
Net after income tax		$ 43,200
Inventory loss resulting from fire	$ 35,000	
Recovery of income tax at 46%	16,100	
Net inventory loss		18,900
Net income after tax		$ 24,300

Note that the net income after tax is unchanged from the first example to the second; the only difference is that the tax provision has been allocated within the same income statement and within the same reporting period. Thus we use the term *intraperiod* tax allocation.

The journal entry to record the above expense would read as follows:

Provision for income tax — regular operations	36,800.00	
Recovery of tax — fire loss		16,100.00
Tax payable		20,700.00

To record tax expense on regular operations and tax reduction due to fire loss. The net of $20,700 is the tax payable for the year.

The *CICA Handbook* [3470.34] requires that the tax related to extraordinary items be shown with these items and not as part of the regular provision for income taxes. In addition, if there is income tax attributed to an item included in retained earnings, then that tax should also be included in retained earnings [*CICA* 3470.35].

Permanent Differences between Reported and Taxable Income

In this book we use the term **statement income** to refer to the income before taxes as reported on the financial statements of the company. Some of the revenue reported on those statements is never taxed, and some of the expenses reported are never allowed for tax purposes. Therefore statement income has to be adjusted if we want to arrive at **accounting income**, or the income on which the **tax provision** (the tax expense shown on the income statement) is based. Items that create differences between statement income and accounting income are called **permanent differences**. Some examples are listed below.

1. Certain types of income are considered to be capital gains for tax purposes and are taxed at less than the full rate.

2. Certain types of assets (e.g., goodwill) are eligible capital expenditures for tax purposes. Only one-half may be amortized for tax purposes.

3. Dividends received from tax-paying Canadian corporations are not taxed in the hands of the receiving corporation if it too is a taxable Canadian corporation.

4. Certain types of expenses may be recognized for accounting purposes but not for income tax purposes. These include political contributions, most fines imposed by the courts, and bribes. These may be considered normal business expenses, although they are not allowed as deductions for tax purposes. (For example, *The Globe and Mail* reported that the President of Schenley's Distillery had testified at an influence-peddling trial that his company paid the Nova Scotia Liberal Party 50 cents for each case of Schenley products sold by the provincial liquor commission between 1970 and 1978.)

5. Certain expenses may be allowable for tax purposes, but not recognized for accounting purposes. For instance, research and development costs may be charged for tax purposes at an amount greater than 100% of the actual expenditure.

The above items are added to or subtracted from the statement income to arrive at the *accounting income*. The tax expense for the year reported on the income statement is then calculated using this accounting income.

For example, suppose the following is an abbreviated income statement for Crosby Corporation, a publicly listed, tax-paying Canadian corporation:

Income from operations	$ 450,000
Dividend income from tax-paying Canadian corporations	300,000
Total income	$ 750,000
Provision for income tax @ 40%	180,000
Net income after tax	$ 570,000

Why is this company's income tax so low? Because it is in receipt of dividends of $300,000 from other taxable Canadian corporations, and such income is not subject to tax under these circumstances. (This is not philanthropy on Revenue Canada's part. It has already collected the tax from the corporation paying the dividend.) This is an example of a permanent difference between statement income and accounting income for purposes of tax calculation. The dividend income will never be taxed in the hands of Crosby Corporation.

The journal entry to record the payable tax would be as follows:

Tax provision	180,000.00	
Tax payable		180,000.00
To record tax provision at 40% of accounting income of $450,000.		

The ratio of tax expense to statement income (180,000/750,000, or 24% in this case) is termed the **effective rate**. This is distinct from the rate charged on the *taxable income* (40% in this case), which is termed the **statutory rate**. Where permanent differences may materially distort the effective tax rate the *CICA Handbook* requires disclosure. We will discuss this later in the chapter.

Timing Differences between Reported and Taxable Income

Some items of revenue and expense are recognized for accounting and tax purposes, but in different time periods. Matching often requires the recognition of estimated expenses for accounting purposes, but in general estimated expenses are not deductible for tax purposes. For example, warranty expenses are commonly estimated for accounting purposes, and the actual expenditure is later charged against this estimated liability. However, the relevant tax deduction is limited to the amount actually incurred. The result is a **timing difference** because the estimated warranty expense is likely to precede the claims by customers. Under *interperiod* tax allocation (discussed in the next section), timing differences give rise to *deferred income taxes*. By contrast, permanent differences impact on the *tax provision*.

It should be noted that permanent differences affect the total amount of tax actually paid. This should be contrasted with situations where the *timing* of the tax payments and the recognition of tax expense may be affected, but *not the ultimate amount*. Let us now consider such situations in the following section on interperiod tax allocation.

Interperiod Tax Allocation

Interperiod tax allocation is an accounting technique that regards income tax as an expense and attempts to match it in the same time period to the income that gave rise to the tax. Its use is required by the *CICA Handbook* [3470.13 and 3470.20]. The technique was developed in the 1950s in response to changing circumstances with respect to the calculation of taxable income. The alternative view, that taxes are not an expense but simply a compulsory sharing of income with the taxing authorities, was rejected at that time.

Until the 1950s the income reported to shareholders and the income calculated for tax purposes were roughly the same. It was the custom then to consider the tax expense for the year as the amount of tax actually payable on the income earned in that year. However, during the 1950s, taxable income and financial-statement income started to diverge significantly. The taxing authorities at that time introduced methods of calculating depreciation for tax purposes (termed **capital cost allowance** in Canada — see above, Appendix 8-1) that differed significantly from the depreciation shown on the books of the company for financial-statement purposes. Generally, the depreciation allowed for tax purposes was a form of the declining-balance method, and the one commonly used for financial statements was the straight-line method. Consequently, in the early life of an asset, the capital cost allowance was higher than the depreciation charged, and hence taxable income was lower than reported income. Although the total of the two depreciation charges would be the same over the life of the asset, the distribution of the two charges over the life of the asset would be different.

The proponents of interperiod allocation argue it should be adopted for two main reasons. First, they assert that corporate income tax should be regarded as an expense of doing business. Second, they maintain that the tax expense for any given year should be based on the timing of income and expenses reported for *accounting* purposes, not tax purposes. Although the total tax expense reported over the life of the company would be unchanged, there could be significant variations in *when* this tax expense would be reported. In effect, proponents of interperiod allocation argue that one should look through the timing changes introduced by the income tax acts and then match tax expense to particular periods according to *when the income and expense were recognized for accounting purposes*. Within the context of the conventional accounting model that has developed over the years, it is hard to refute this method, termed **comprehensive tax allocation.** The governing concept is the matching principle.

In the preceding section we discussed the permanent differences between *statement income* and *accounting income*. Now let us introduce a third type of income — namely, **taxable income**, or the income as defined by the tax authorities for the purpose of calculating the income tax payable. Taxable income may be different from both statement income and accounting income.

The concept of interperiod tax allocation may appear to be complicated at first. Accordingly, let us begin with a simple example. In 19X0 Yarker Limited sold merchandise under warranty, and in accordance with generally accepted accounting principles, it accrued the estimated warranty expense of $10,000. It expected that $6,000 of this amount would be paid in the following year (classed as a current liability) and $4,000 in the year after that (classed as a long-term liability). The amount and timing of the warranty payments turned out to be exactly as estimated. The following are the abbreviated income statements of the company:

	19X2	19X1	19X0
Net income before deducting warranty expense	$ 80,000	$ 80,000	$ 80,000
Warranty expense			10,000
Statement and accounting income	$ 80,000	$ 80,000	$ 70,000
Tax provision at 30%	24,000	24,000	21,000
Net income after tax	$ 56,000	$ 56,000	$ 49,000

Here the statement income is equal to the accounting income. However, the tax Yarker actually paid was $24,000 in 19X0, $22,200 in 19X1, and $22,800 in 19X2 — amounts quite different from the tax provisions shown above. Why? Because for accounting purposes the *tax provision* is based on the *accounting income*, whereas the *tax payment* is based on the *taxable income* (that is, the income as redefined by the tax authorities for the purpose of calculating the income tax payable). Since Revenue Canada does not allow the warranty expense as a deduction for tax purposes until the payment is actually made, accounting income and taxable income are different here. The tax payable is calculated as follows:

	19X2	19X1	19X0
Statement and accounting income	$ 80,000	$ 80,000	$ 70,000
Add: Provision for warranty expense			10,000
	$ 80,000	$ 80,000	$ 80,000
Less: cash outlays re warranty	4,000	6,000	
Taxable income	$ 76,000	$ 74,000	$ 80,000
Tax payable at 30%	$ 22,800	$ 22,200	$ 24,000

The appropriate journal entries are shown below. In accordance with the *CICA Handbook* [3470.24], the deferred income tax is classified as current or long-term according to the classification of the asset or liability to which it relates.

19X0

Tax provision: current portion (30% of 80,000)	24,000.00	
Deferred income taxes: long-term (4,000 × 30%)	1,200.00	
Deferred income taxes: current (6,000 × 30%)	1,800.00	
Tax provision: deferred portion		3,000.00
Tax payable (80,000 × 30%)		24,000.00
To record taxes for 19X0.		

19X1

Tax provision: current portion	22,200.00	
Tax provision: deferred portion	1,800.00	
Tax payable		22,200.00
Deferred income taxes: current (6,000 × 30%)		1,800.00
To record taxes for 19X1		
Deferred income taxes: current	1,200.00	
Deferred income taxes: long-term		1,200.00
To reclassify deferred income taxes because the related liability has changed from long-term to current.		

19X2

Tax provision: current portion	22,800.00	
Tax provision: deferred portion	1,200.00	
Tax payable		22,800.00
Deferred income taxes: current (4,000 × 30%)		1,200.00
To record taxes for 19X2.		

The *CICA Handbook* [3470.29] requires that the deferred component of the current income tax provision be disclosed. Furthermore it requires that there should be reasonable assurance that a deferred income tax debit will *reverse* before the last entry above is made. We will explain this shortly.

TIMING DIFFERENCES AND TAX DEFERRAL

In the preceding example, the treatment of warranty costs produced a timing difference. In general, timing differences arise from differences in income measurement between Revenue Canada and GAAP regarding when an expense or revenue item should be recognized. For the purpose of calculating taxable income, taxpayers normally like to claim expenses and defer revenue (even if they have not treated them this way in their books) because this allows them to delay payment of their tax. Although there are many individual expense and revenue items that can give rise to these timing differences, in practice the item that is mostly responsible is *depreciation* — in particular, the difference between the depreciation used for accounting purposes and the capital cost allowance used for tax purposes. (See Appendix 8-1 for an explanation of capital cost allowance.)

The principles of accounting measurement (primarily, the recognition convention and the matching principle) decide timing questions for accounting purposes, whereas the income tax acts decide timing questions for tax purposes. If the Tax Act is silent on a particular timing issue, then the usual accounting standards are used. For that reason, both tax considerations and accounting standards can help determine the adoption of a particular accounting policy.

Let us now list in somewhat more detail the types of scenarios that can give rise to timing differences:

1. Revenue may be recognized *earlier* for accounting purposes than for tax purposes. For example, instalment sales are normally recognized for accounting purposes when the sale is made, but for tax purposes they are delayed until payment is due.

2. Revenue may be recognized *later* for accounting purposes than for tax purposes. For example, unearned profits on certain types of construction contracts may fall into this category. (Thus a customer prepayment may be considered to be revenue for tax purposes, but not revenue for accounting purposes until the normal revenue recognition requirements have been fulfilled.) Alternatively profits on sales between closely related companies will be taxed when the sale occurs, but for accounting purposes they will be treated as inventory profits and not recognized until the goods are sold outside the entity.

3. Expenses may be recognized *earlier* for accounting purposes than for tax purposes. Examples include warranty expense (as illustrated above), depreciation in excess of that claimed for tax purposes, and write-downs of inventory in excess of that allowed for tax purposes.

4. Expenses may be recognized *later* for accounting purposes than for tax purposes.

For example, capital cost allowance claimed for tax purposes may exceed the depreciation claimed in the period for accounting purposes; oil exploration costs may be claimed immediately for tax purposes, but deferred to later years for accounting purposes; and accounting and legal costs for a bond issue must be claimed immediately for tax purposes, but may be written off over the term of the loan for accounting purposes.

We can now summarize the relationship between *statement income, accounting income,* and *taxable income* as follows:

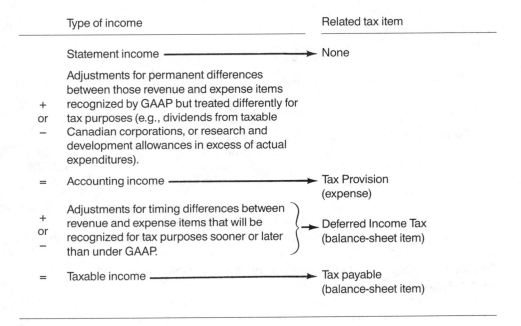

Type of income	Related tax item
Statement income ————————————▶	None
+ or − Adjustments for permanent differences between those revenue and expense items recognized by GAAP but treated differently for tax purposes (e.g., dividends from taxable Canadian corporations, or research and development allowances in excess of actual expenditures).	
= Accounting income ————————————▶	Tax Provision (expense)
+ or − Adjustments for timing differences between revenue and expense items that will be recognized for tax purposes sooner or later than under GAAP.	Deferred Income Tax (balance-sheet item)
= Taxable income ————————————▶	Tax payable (balance-sheet item)

Observe that the tax provision (expense) is the statement income adjusted for permanent differences multiplied by the current statutory tax rate. Thus, we have the following equation:

Tax provision = (Statement income ± Permanent differences)
         × Current statutory tax rate

This formula is valid except when there is a timing-difference reversal *and* a difference between the current statutory rate and the rate at which deferred taxes are accumulated.

Timing differences give rise to deferred taxes. Let us work through a simple example. M Ltd. had a statement income of $100,000, which included $20,000 of dividends from a taxable Canadian corporation. Also included were $40,000 of instalment sales, of which only $15,000 was due by the end of the year. The corporate tax rate was 45%. The income tax calculations would be as follows:

	Income	Tax at 45%
Statement income	$ 100,000	
Permanent difference:		
Dividend	– 20,000	
Accounting income	$ 80,000	$ 36,000 (Tax provision)
Timing difference:		
Instalment sale		
— GAAP	– 40,000	
— Taxable	15,000	
Net	– 25,000	– 11,250 (Deferred income tax)
Taxable income	$ 55,000	$ 24,750 (Taxes payable)

Accordingly, the journal entry would read as follows:

Tax provision (80,000 × .45)	36,000.00	
Deferred income tax (current) (25,000 × .45)		11,250.00
Taxes payable		24,750.00
To provide for taxes for the current year.		

When the time comes here that both the GAAP and tax treatment of instalment sales are treated the same again, the deferred income tax related to instalment sales disappears, or **reverses**. All deferred income tax items will ultimately reverse, although at any given time it is likely that some items will be outstanding. Hence it is likely that the balance in the deferred income tax account will never be nil throughout the life of most companies.

Note that in the preceding example the amount of the deferred income tax balance is directly related to the income being deferred to a later year for tax purposes. It is calculated using the *current* year's tax rate, even though it may well be that the rate will be different at the time the item reverses. When instalment accounts receivable are paid, then the receipts will be considered to be taxable income and the deferred income tax will reverse. If the tax rate changes by the time the reversal takes place, the reversal should be calculated at the old rate so that the original amount is exactly cancelled in the account balance. As a practical matter, an average rate is usually used to eliminate the need for voluminous record-keeping of the items and tax rates that make up the balance in the deferred income tax account.

Note also that each timing difference can be related directly to the difference in accounting and tax treatment of an asset or liability. The deferred income tax that arises from *current* assets or liabilities is classed as a *current* item on the balance sheet and shown net. The remaining deferred income tax is shown net as a *long-term* item [*CICA* 3470.24]. For example, the difference between depreciation and capital cost allowance gives rise to a long-term item of deferred income tax because it relates to plant assets. On the other hand, if the balance arises because of a difference in timing in the treatment of a current liability (such as a warranty expense), it should be classed as a current item of deferred income tax.

Deferred income tax balances on the balance sheet do not meet the criteria for liabilities or assets for two main reasons. First, the amounts are not calculated using the rates expected to be in effect when the item reverses. Second, there is no discounting to recognize any long-term aspects. Deferred income tax balances on the balance sheet are explicitly referred to in the *CICA Handbook* [3470.24], not as liabilities, but as "accumulated allocation credits and/or debits." Critics have called them "dangling credits/debits" since they cannot be given an economic interpretation. This is an issue we will return to shortly.

ALTERNATIVES TO DEFERRAL

Are accountants making things too complicated by recognizing timing differences with respect to income taxes? Even if they should recognize timing differences, is the deferral approach the most useful way of doing it?

The basic defence for recognizing timing differences is that it is fundamental to the matching principle. If income taxes are regarded as an expense of doing business, then the tax expense should be matched in the same period with the income that caused it. The timing of the actual tax payments, it is argued, is affected by a number of factors that are related to tax policy decisions, which should not be allowed to influence the matching principle any more than the date of the payment of any expense affects the date when that expense should be matched to its corresponding income item.

In addition, if two firms have identical attributes, with the exception that one has greater tax-reducing potential than the other (e.g., one has claimed more capital cost allowance than the other), then it is at least arguable that they should be given a different accounting treatment because their assets have a different after-tax value. Recognizing timing differences is a way of doing this.

Critics of comprehensive deferred income tax accounting have proposed three alternatives: the taxes payable method, the tax liability method, and partial allocation. Let us now examine each in turn.

Taxes Payable Method

The **taxes payable method** denies the need for tax allocation. Under the taxes payable method the amount of tax actually paid in a year is taken as the tax provision, or expense, for the year. In our last example the taxes payable are $24,750. This would be taken as the tax provision, and the entry would simply read as follows:

Tax provision	24,750.00	
Taxes payable		24,750.00
To record taxes for the year on a taxes		
payable basis.		

The supporters of this approach argue that taxes are part of the division of profits between the shareholders and the government doing the taxing and that the amount of tax extracted each year is the profit share that the government demands. Hence, they conclude that the matching concept should not be applied inasmuch as it applies only to allocation of costs, not division of net income. Once the initial premise is accepted that taxes are a division of profits, this argument is difficult to refute. As a practical matter, the possibilities under this approach for manipulating the amount of taxes payable, and hence the tax provision, should not be overlooked. This might be done, for example, by changing the amount of capital cost allowance claimed in a given year.

Tax Liability Method

Under the **tax liability method** (or **tax accrual method**), an estimate is made of the amount of the tax that will be payable when the reversal takes place. The income tax so calculated is treated as an estimated liability, using an estimate of the tax rate *at the time of reversal*, not the rate at the time of accrual. A straightforward method is to use the *current* tax rate as the most objective basis for this estimated rate. However, a subsequent change in the tax rate can have a significant impact on the after-tax income of the year in which the change takes place because then all of the effects of the rate change will be recognized and taken into income immediately. Nevertheless, this approach is advocated in a revision draft to the *CICA Handbook* proposed in 1989.

If it is expected that the time of reversal is not likely to be soon, in theory it would be appropriate to treat this amount in the same way as any long-term liability and show it at its discounted present value. But the conceptual and practical problems of choosing an appropriate rate of discount are daunting. For that reason no country that uses the tax liability method has adopted discounting. Moreover, discounting under the tax liability method is specifically ruled out in the changes to the *CICA Handbook* proposed in 1989.

As an example of the accounting treatment using the proposed CICA method let us modify our last example. Suppose that at the time of the instalment sale the tax rate was 40%. In the year of the sale the entry would be as follows:

Tax provision (80,000 @ 40%)	32,000.00	
Income tax liability (25,000 @ 40%)		10,000.00
Taxes payable (55,000 @ 40%)		22,000.00
To record taxes.		

Suppose that in the next year the income tax rate dropped to 30%, and the only tax liability was from the prior year. The income tax liability would then be recalculated at the new rate: $25,000 x 30\% = \$7,500$. The following entry would be used to record the reduced liability with respect to the prior year:

Income tax liability	2,500.00	
Tax provision		2,500.00
To record change in tax liability because of		
the reduction of the tax rate from 40% to 30%.		

The main criticisms that can be made against the tax liability method using the discounted estimated tax concern (i) the assumptions one must make about the future tax rates at the time of reversal and (ii) the difficulty of selecting an appropriate discount rate. Note that the changes proposed to the *CICA Handbook* in 1989 deal with the first issue by stating that the *current* rate must be used, and with the second issue by stating that the discount rate shall be nil. Clearly, both these "solutions" introduce other problems.

Partial Allocation

Under **partial allocation** some of the timing differences between taxable income and financial-statement income are recognized as being appropriate for recognizing deferred income tax; but other timing differences are regarded as *not* giving rise to deferred income tax.

Advocates of partial allocation argue that there are certain times when tax allocation methods meet the matching objective and other times when they do not.

For example, if a company sold a building in Year 1, but did not have to pay the tax on the gain until Year 2, most accountants would accept that the tax should be matched to the gain in Year 1, that is, in the same period in which the gain is reported. On the other hand, suppose a company pays lower taxes because of the shelter provided by capital cost allowance (depreciation) on its plant assets, and it appears that for various reasons this timing difference will not reverse in the foreseeable future. Then the argument for recognizing a tax cost in the present period becomes much weaker.

The proponents of partial allocation maintain that their method gives a more realistic appraisal of the company's actual tax situation than other methods do. Beechy [1985] cites the case of Wardair's pre-tax profit of $1.039 million dropping to an after-tax loss of $9.661 million because of the comprehensive tax allocation required by the *CICA Handbook*. Beechy adds: "The really frustrating part of this exercise, from Wardair's point of view, was that it had not been paying income taxes in the past and was highly unlikely to begin doing so in the foreseeable future."

The form of partial allocation that has received the most acceptance is the one adopted in Britain. Under this approach deferred taxes are calculated for all short-term timing differences, but not on longer-term ones unless they will be drawn down (i.e., reversed) within "the foreseeable future" (defined as three years). This means that the following timing differences, for example, would *not* give rise to long-term deferred taxes:

1. Capital cost allowance versus depreciation:
   In most cases this would not give rise to deferred income tax because the timing difference is typically not drawn down for a number of years. (According to Beechy [1985] this caused 67% of all timing differences in a sample of 35 Canadian companies.)

2. Exploration expenditures (in the extractive industries) versus amortization of development costs:
   Companies in the extractive industries are normally allowed to write off develop-

ment costs for tax purposes sooner than they are charged to expense for financial-statement purposes. They are not likely to be drawn down quickly and would not give rise to deferred income tax under the partial allocation method. (According to Beechy [1985] this caused 10% of the timing differences in his sample.) However, deferred taxes would continue to be required for other timing differences.

3. Warranty costs:

A long-term warranty extending beyond, say, three years, would not give rise to deferred income tax. Nevertheless, many warranty costs that are recognized in the financial statements according to GAAP, but claimed for tax purposes as the expenditure was made, would be considered a short-term timing difference that would give rise to deferred income tax.

4. Taxes on gains:

These would be recognized in the period in which the gain was reported.

The accounting literature indicates that comprehensive allocation has never won the acceptance that has been found, say, for lease accounting. It should be recognized that in comparison with the other methods, partial allocation requires more judgement from management whether a timing difference is likely to reverse in the foreseeable future. Hence there is an opportunity for management to have greater influence over the reported after-tax income.

EVALUATION OF THE DEFERRED INCOME TAX APPROACH

Deferred income taxes seem to be a classic case of a good idea that is hard to make work. In their wish to adhere to the matching concept on the income statement, accounting standard setters have created a balance-sheet item, deferred income taxes, that has little meaning to the layperson and, in its present form, little conceptual foundation. It does not have the usual characteristics of an accounting liability (see Chapter 11) and is not accorded the same treatment as a liability for such things as discounting. An approach which produces results that can be given an economic interpretation, such as the tax liability method, seems clearly preferable.

Why then was the deferred income tax approach adopted by the CICA? Skinner [1987] attributes it to historical causes: the reporting situation prior to adoption of the existing standard was "near chaos," and diametrically opposed positions had developed between those who favoured some form of tax allocation and those who did not. The new standard is a distinct improvement over what then existed. It is also possible that the tax liability basis, with its defining of deferred income tax as a liability, would have created a significant new liability on the balance sheets of many companies. Since trust indentures on debt often have financial stability requirements couched in terms of ratios that include liabilities (such as the debt/equity ratio), the accrual method might have put some companies into technical default on their indentures — purely through the introduction of a new accounting standard. (The same sort of consideration will arise in our discussion of leases in Chapter 14.) Also, at the time the standard was issued, tax rates had shown little change, and interest rates were much lower than they were subsequently.

The inability to put an economic interpretation on the deferred income tax item on the balance sheet of most companies has had some political repercussions in Canada. In the 1984 federal election campaign the leader of the New Democratic Party was able to convince himself that the existence of deferred income taxes on corporate balance sheets provided evidence that Canadian corporations had been given inordinately generous tax breaks. This became the "corporate welfare bums" plank in the NDP platform.

As of 1989 the question of tax allocation is under review in both the U.S. and Canada. It seems likely that some changes will shortly be made to the present system of comprehensive allocation.

TREATMENT OF INTERPERIOD ALLOCATION OUTSIDE CANADA

The treatment of interperiod allocation of income taxes in other major industrial countries varies in some cases from the Canadian treatment. The U.S. treatment is virtually identical in approach to the Canadian one. Comprehensive tax allocation has been mandatory there since the APB Opinion No. 11 was issued in 1967. The approach has been attacked in the United States as unsatisfactory for much the same reasons as in Canada.

The treatment in England acknowledges the argument that some deferred income tax items will take a long time to reverse. The Statement of Standard Accounting Practice No. 15 (1978), issued by the Institute of Chartered Accountants of England and Wales, recognized that certain timing differences will continue indefinitely into the future or be replaced by new timing differences as they expire. Although it required deferred tax accounting for short-term timing differences, it did not require them for the long-term ones we have discussed. Presumably the accrual concept was unattractive because changes in the tax rates would cause significant changes in the tax expense for the year of the change. In England the convention is to use the current tax rates with no discounting. One argument for using current rates is the practical one that it is rarely known what future tax rates will be. Another argument is that when tax rates undergo a sharp change, the liability method implies that the tax liability will be recalculated at the new rates with the offsetting adjustment included in the income statement of the year of the change. This could cause sharp swings in the amount charged to taxes in years when tax rates change. There is in principle nothing wrong with such sharp swings when the circumstances warrant them. The reluctance to adopt this approach is simply another example of the preference for income smoothing.

In 1979, the International Accounting Standards Committee (IASC) issued *Accounting for Taxes on Income* in which they approved both the deferral method and the *liability* method. The latter is essentially the accrual method discussed above, although the IASC made no mention of discounting long-term liabilities. (In other words, discounting was neither recommended nor discouraged.)

EXAMPLES FROM PUBLISHED REPORTS

Deferred income taxes have become a significant item on the balance sheets of many companies, and they continue to grow.

Bell Canada

BALANCE SHEET

	1986	1985
	(millions of $)	
Deferred credits: Income taxes	$ 1,929.0	$ 1,765.5

The owners' equity at the end of 1986 was $8,366.1 million. Thus the deferred income taxes formed 23% of owners' equity. Since the telephone industry is capital-intensive, such a high ratio is not surprising.

Thomson Newspapers Limited

INCOME STATEMENT

	1986	1985
	(thousands of $)	
Income Taxes:		
Current	$ 128,326	$ 95,033
Deferred	27,664	34,203
	$ 155,990	$ 129,236

Thomson's balance sheet indicates that the company has only long-term deferred income tax, presumably arising mostly from the difference between depreciation and capital cost allowance. It might have had a short-term deferred income tax if, for instance, it had used a method of recognizing newspaper subscription income that was different from that used for tax purposes.

Tax Losses

Instead of having statement income, accounting income, and taxable income, a company may have negative values for these in a **statement loss, accounting loss,** and **tax loss**.

In this section we will show the accounting treatment when the company incurs a tax loss. There are three basic ideas to keep in mind:

1. The Tax Act does not provide that a company automatically receives a tax refund when it experiences a tax loss. Instead, it sets an upper limit to the amount that can

be claimed, which is related to the amount of taxable income the company has earned in the years preceding and following the loss year.

2. The matching principle in accounting interprets a tax refund as being "earned" by a tax loss. Hence the refund should be shown as an offset to the loss in the year in which the loss occurred. The problem this poses for accounting is that one must conjecture about the likelihood of taxable income in future years when trying to estimate the amount of tax refund that will ultimately be recoverable. If the tax refund is treated for accounting purposes as an asset, or an offset to tax liability, then it must meet the usual tests of being a probable future benefit. If the probability of this benefit being received is not strong, then there are grounds for not recording the future refund as an asset until the probability increases significantly.

3. The taxpayer has some ability to influence the amount of the taxable income or loss — and hence the amount of tax refund claimed — by the amount of capital cost allowance (depreciation) claimed in any tax year. The accounting problem is that the tax recovery shown on the income statement should not be affected by this discretionary management decision about how much capital cost allowance to claim.

EXAMPLE SHOWING TAX RECOVERY

Suppose that in 19X7 M Ltd. had a statement income of $124,000 in its first year of operation, and that this was also the same as its accounting income and taxable income. Assume a tax rate of 30%. The journal entry to record the tax provision would be as follows:

19X7

Tax provision (124,000 × 30%)	37,200.00	
Taxes payable		37,200.00
To record taxes for the current year.		

Suppose that in the following year M Ltd. had a tax loss of $80,000 and that this was also the same as its accounting loss and statement loss. Assume the tax rate was unchanged at 30%. M Ltd. can recover 30% of its loss of $80,000 from the taxing authorities because it paid taxes in excess of $24,000 last year. The journal entry would read as follows:

19X8

Tax refund receivable (balance-sheet item)	24,000.00	
Tax recovery (income-statement item)		24,000.00
To record taxes for the year: a recovery due to a tax loss of 30% of $80,000.		

The tax recovery would appear on the income statement in place of the usual tax provision. It would be shown as a negative tax expense in the year in which the loss occurred because of the matching principle. A point that should be emphasized is that the Tax Act requires the company to file an *amended* tax return for 19X7 in order to report and recover the tax loss for 19X8. For accounting purposes we are concerned with matching the tax recovering to the appropriate year, not with the process used for collecting the tax recovery from Revenue Canada.

It is also quite possible for a company to have a mixture of incomes and losses as it progresses from its statement income (or loss) to its taxable income (or loss). Consider the following example:

		Income	Tax at 30%
Statement income		$ 10,000	
Deduct: Dividend from taxable Canadian corporation: included above but not taxable		30,000	
Accounting (loss)		(20,000)	(6,000)
Add: Depreciation included in above	50,000		
Less: Capital cost allowance	15,000	35,000	10,500
Taxable income		$15,000	$ 4,500

Given this data, the following journal entry would be made:

Deferred income tax (balance-sheet item)	10,500.00	
Tax recovery (income-statement item)		6,000.00
Tax payable (balance-sheet item)		4,500.00
To record taxes for the year.		

Note that the deferred income tax above is a debit. This assumes that taxable income in subsequent years will be sufficient to permit this item to reverse. This will be covered in more detail below.

LIMITS TO TAX RECOVERY

The main difficulty with accounting for losses arises from the rules of the taxing authorities with respect to refunds. The Tax Act will only permit refunds to the extent that taxable losses can be matched against taxable income earned by the company within a limited period. Revenue Canada has the following rules for claiming a refund for a tax loss:

1. The loss from operations must first be applied against any taxable income of the immediately preceding three years. An amended return, claiming the loss as an offset, should be filed for those years to which the loss has been applied. Capital losses (usually losses that arise from the sale of assets) may be applied only against capital gains.

2. Once the loss has been applied against the earliest eligible year or years, any

remainder is applied against the next eligible year sequentially, up to a total of seven years following the year of tax loss. (There is no seven-year limit for capital losses.)

Let us illustrate these rules by means of an example. Suppose a company had a tax operating loss of $10,000 in Year 4 but had a taxable income of $5,000 in Year 1. It would file an amended return for Year 1 and offset $5,000 of the tax loss against the equivalent taxable income of Year 1. Assume that it had paid tax at the rate of 45% in Year 1. By filing a return amended by the loss carryback of Year 4, it would get a refund of the tax it paid, or $2250. Even if the rate had risen by Year 4, it still would get only the rate that applied in Year 1. Although the refund mechanism requires that an amended tax return be filed with respect to Year 1, for accounting purposes the refund is considered to be part of Year 4. The entry in Year 4 would be as follows:

Tax refund receivable	2,250.00	
Tax provision		2,250.00

To record tax recoverable by filing an amended return for Year 1, equal to 45% of $5,000. Under the matching principle this is a tax recovery in Year 4 because the loss was incurred in Year 4.

After applying its Year 4 loss against Year 1 there was still a loss of $5,000 remaining unapplied. For simplicity suppose that the company broke even for tax purposes in Years 2 and 3. Assume that in Year 5 the tax rate was 30% and the taxable income before carryforwards was $3,000. Then $3,000 of the loss (for a refund of $900) could be carried forward and applied against the taxable profit of $3,000. The company would pay no tax in Year 5 and would still have $2,000 of tax loss to carry forward to Year 6. The journal entry that would be made at the end of Year 4 would depend on whether there was *virtual certainty* that the company would have taxable income in a later year.

INCOME TAX RECOVERABLE

The problem for accountants is that they do not know with any certainty that a tax loss will be recoverable in future. Thus, in the preceding example, the accountant does not know at the time the journal entry is made, at the end of Year 4, whether the company will have taxable incomes in the subsequent years that will be sufficient to ensure realization of the tax benefit with respect to the loss in Year 4. If it is assumed that the company will have such income, then the following entry would be made at the end of Year 4.

Deferred tax benefits (balance-sheet item)	1,500.00	
Tax recovery (income-statement item)		1,500.00

To record tax recovery expected from taxable income of Years 5 to 11 (30% of $5,000).

The above entry assumes that sufficient taxable income will be earned in the next seven years to permit the tax loss to be recovered. Recall that the concept of an asset includes the idea of a "reasonable" probability of future economic benefit being received. It is possible to imagine situations where it seems so certain that the necessary taxable income would be earned that, the convention of conservatism notwithstanding, the above entry should be made. When this situation is thought to exist, one says that there is **virtual certainty**.

The *CICA Handbook* [3470.43] lists three conditions necessary for virtual certainty to exist:

1. The loss results from an identifiable and non-recurring cause (e.g., an unusually long strike).

2. A record of profitability has been established over a long period by the corporation, and in the past any occasional losses have been more than offset by income in subsequent years.

3. There is assurance beyond any reasonable doubt that future taxable income will be sufficient to offset the loss within the carryforward period prescribed by the tax laws.

Note that these are rather severe tests and must be carried out each year.

Here is an example of a tax-loss accounting problem. Collins Inc. had a tax loss in 19X4 of $50,000. The previous year, 19X3, it had had a taxable income of $10,000. Subsequently it had a taxable income of $20,000 in 19X5 and $30,000 in 19X6. For simplicity we will assume that the statement incomes and loss are the same as the taxable ones and that the tax rate is 40% in all years.

In 19X4 Collins Inc. would file a tax return showing a loss of $50,000. In the same year it would also file an amended return for 19X3, for a refund of 40% of $10,000, or $4,000. When it filed the 19X5 return, the company would report $20,000 as the taxable income for that year, but it would apply $20,000 of the 19X4 loss carry-forward, thereby netting out the taxable income to nil. In 19X6 the company would report a taxable income of $30,000, but reduce it by the remaining loss carryforward from 19X4 of $20,000. This example is summarized in the chart below.

	19X3	19X4	19X5	19X6
Taxable income (loss)	$ 10,000	($ 50,000)	$ 20,000	$ 30,000
Loss carried back in 19X4 to 19X3 — amended return	(10,000)	10,000		
Loss carried forward in 19X5 from 19X4 when filing 19X5 return		20,000	(20,000)	
Loss carried forward in 19X6 from 19X4 when filing 19X6 return		20,000		(20,000)
Ultimate taxable income (loss)	0	0	0	$ 10,000

The company was fortunate in being able to apply the loss from the year 19X4 before the time limitations of the Tax Act expired. If a company incurs a string of tax losses, for example, it is not unknown for it to lose the right to claim a refund from the tax authorities for those losses arising in the earlier years. The real possibility that tax losses may never be claimable explains the stringency of the virtual certainty doctrine.

The federal law states that capital losses can only be claimed against capital gains. The virtual certainty doctrine applies to them in a similar manner [*CICA* 3470.44].

If virtual certainty does not exist, then asset recognition (deferred tax benefits) of the loss carryforward is denied. The readers of financial statements should find the existence of any such carryforwards in the notes. The *CICA Handbook* [3470.54], for instance, requires disclosure of (i) the amount of the carryforwards; (ii) their expiration date, and (iii) timing differences that would have resulted in a debit to the deferred income tax account on the balance sheet if the accounting entry had been made. Such items may have significant potential economic impact if the company later earns taxable income.

If it later develops that a loss carryforward can be utilized in a subsequent year, then it will ultimately turn up on an income statement of the company, but it will not be matched in time to the loss that gave rise to it. If this should happen, the *Handbook* [3470.56] requires that it be shown as an extraordinary item.

It may be possible to eliminate a tax loss by postponing the claim for certain expenses such as capital cost allowance (CCA). For example, if a company had a tax loss of $1,000 after claiming the maximum available capital cost allowance of $2,500, it could reduce the CCA claim to zero and report a taxable income of $1,500. The motive for so doing might be to generate a taxable income to make it possible to claim a tax loss of a prior year. Alternatively, the company might reduce its CCA claim to $1,500, thus reducing the tax loss to nil and avoiding the possibility that such losses would not be utilized prior to the expiry of the carryforward period. There is no time limit for claiming CCA, whereas there is a time limit of seven years for claiming a benefit from a tax loss carryforward.

REASONABLE ASSURANCE

There is one further issue concerning deferred income taxes that arises out of the virtual certainty doctrine. As explained above, there are some expenses allowable for tax purposes, such as capital cost allowance, that a company may claim immediately or defer to any later year. A company that is experiencing a loss year may choose to defer these or other taxable expenses over which it has control and thus claim *less* for tax purposes than is shown for accounting purposes. Hence, it is likely that there will be a debit to deferred income taxes in loss years. Consider the following situation (assume a tax rate of 40%):

	19X8		19X9	
	Income	Tax	Income	Tax
Accounting income (Loss)	$ (25,000)	$ (10,000)	$ 25,000	$ 10,000
Capital cost allowance in excess (deficit) of depreciation	(25,000)	(10,000)	25,000	10,000
Taxable income (loss)	$ 0	$ 0	$ 0	$ 0

For this example the journal entry in 19X8 might be as follows:

Deferred income taxes (balance-sheet item)	10,000.00	
Tax recovery (income-statement item)		10,000.00

To record accounting loss for year that was converted to a nil taxable income through charging capital cost allowance that was $25,000 less than the depreciation charge on the books of the company.

The income statement for 19X8 would then read as follows:

Net loss before tax recovery	$ 25,000
Tax recovery	10,000
Net loss after tax recovery	$ 15,000

In 19X9 the following journal entry might be made:

Tax provision (income-statement item)	10,000.00	
Deferred income taxes (balance-sheet item)		10,000.00

To record tax provision for year and reversal of deferred income taxes through charging $25,000 of capital cost allowance more than depreciation.

The treatment shown above would only be acceptable if there were **reasonable assurance** (not defined in the *CICA Handbook*) of having sufficient taxable income in a later year to charge enough capital cost allowance to reverse deferred income tax. If there were no reasonable assurance, the journal entry for 19X8 shown above would not be made, and no tax recovery of $10,000 would be shown on the income statement. Hence the reported loss after tax recovery of nil would be $25,000 and the tax recovery would not be recorded in 19X8 [*CICA* 3470.52].

If there was not reasonable assurance in 19X8 but there turned out to be taxable income in 19X9, the entry would be as follows in 19X9:

Tax provision (income-statement item)	10,000.00	
Extraordinary item — tax recovery		10,000.00

To record tax recovery from tax loss in 19X8 out of taxable income in 19X9. Treated as an extraordinary item under section 3470.56 of the *CICA Handbook*.

The *CICA Handbook* [3470.46] indicates that the amounts of expected tax recoverable should be shown separately, and that any portion arising from the failure to claim allowable tax deductions should be classified as deferred income tax.

It is also possible to have a situation in which a company believes it has reasonable assurance and accrues the tax recovery, only to fail to produce accounting income in a later year. The reasonable assurance that was felt to exist at the end of the first year has now evaporated. In such a case the deferred income tax already existing on the balance sheet would be written off as an extraordinary item [*CICA* 3470.50]. Note that even though this is a change in an accounting *estimate*, it is treated as an extraordinary item.

Investment Tax Credits

The tax system is frequently used by government as an incentive to encourage investment in productive assets. A common approach is to permit a direct reduction of taxes payable if a business will invest in either (i) a certain type of productive asset or (ii) productive assets in a part of the country with high unemployment. For example, the taxpayer might be allowed a direct reduction of taxes payable equal to 10% of the purchase price of qualified investments. (Thus, on qualified investments purchased for $150,000, the taxpayer would be granted a tax reduction of $15,000.) This should be contrasted with an indirect reduction in taxes payable by allowing additional claims (e.g., accelerated depreciation) that reduce the taxable income.

The accounting issue is how to account for these direct reductions of taxes payable. Are they a reduction of income tax expense, or are they a reduction of the cost of the asset that gave rise to the tax credit? While the issue is not a particularly weighty one in terms of accounting theory, it has given rise to sharp political controversy. Using the **flow-through approach**, the reduction is simply treated as a reduction of that year's income tax expense, and the introduction of an investment tax credit scheme would immediately create higher reported incomes for companies with taxable incomes. Alternatively, using the **cost-reduction approach**, the tax credit is treated as a reduction of the acquisition cost of the asset, and it would affect income as the asset cost is depreciated or amortized.

Generally, accounting standard-setting bodies have favoured the cost-reduction approach. By contrast, politicians have chosen the flow-through approach; not surprisingly, because they often introduce investment tax credit schemes at a time when governments want to encourage investment by making it be — and appear to be — more profitable. In the U.S. one of the sharpest conflicts between standard setters and governments occurred over this issue during the 1960s. In Canada a similar conflict erupted between Ottawa and the CICA in 1982 over accounting for oil exploration grants (Petroleum Incentive Program, or PIP, grants). In 1984 the *CICA Handbook* [3805.12] made the cost-reduction method the sole acceptable standard in accounting for tax credits.

Effective Tax Rates

A company may have a rate of tax that is different from the usual corporate tax rate. This may occur for a variety of reasons. For example, the company may qualify for the tax reduction reserved for small privately-owned businesses. Alternatively, the company may have a foreign subsidiary that pays a lower effective tax rate than the parent pays. The rate of tax actually payable on the taxable income of the company is termed the **statutory rate** of tax. This is distinct from the **effective rate**, or the percentage of reported accounting income actually paid out as corporate income tax. The *CICA Handbook* [3470.33] requires publicly traded companies and all life insurance enterprises to disclose the components of any variation from the basic income tax rate.

Where there is a significant variation from the expected relationship between income tax expense and pretax financial-statement income, the reader can expect to find an explanation for this variation. An example is given below:

BELL CANADA

Note 4. Income Taxes
A reconciliation of the statutory income tax rate to the effective income tax rate is as follows:

	1986	1985	1984
Statutory income tax rate in Canada	49.8%	48.5%	47.6%
i. Allowance for funds used during construction, net of applicable depreciation adjustment	(0.2)	(0.1)	(0.1)
ii. Reduction of Canadian federal taxes applicable to manufacturing profit	(0.9)	(0.5)	(0.8)
iii. Equity in net income of associated companies	(1.3)	(2.8)	(2.9)
iv. Tax incentives on research and development expenditures	(2.9)	(4.2)	(2.7)
v. Inventory credit	—	(0.4)	(0.3)
vi. Difference between Canadian statutory rates and those applicable to foreign subsidiaries	(0.7)	(0.5)	(0.8)
vii. Other	(1.6)	(0.3)	—
Effective Income Tax Rate	42.2%	39.7%	40.0%

For our purposes in this book, it is not necessary to understand the tax reasons underlying the adjustments shown above. What you should know is why such an explanation exists in most financial statements and what the general reasons are for the possible differences between the effective and statutory income tax rates.

Proposed Changes to the CICA Handbook

In 1989 the CICA issued an exposure draft proposing significant changes to the *Handbook* with respect to accounting for income tax. This paralleled a change in the United States where the Financial Accounting Standards Board had issued *Accounting for Income Taxes* (Statement of Accounting Standards No. 96) in 1987. The significant changes from existing practice proposed in the Canadian exposure draft are as follows:

1. The deferral method of income tax accounting would be dropped in favour of the tax liability method. As a result, the following procedures would be used:
   a. To calculate the amount to be shown on the balance sheet, one would use the tax rates *currently* in effect, not the past rates that used to be in effect when the timing difference first arose and the amount was initially calculated. When a change in

tax rate occurs, the tax liability would be recalculated, and any difference would be a charge or credit to the income tax expense of the year in which the change occurred.

b. The amounts shown on the balance sheet would be treated as assets and liabilities (not deferred charges and credits) and would be subject to the usual tests for assets and liabilities. As discussed earlier, however, tax liability would be calculated at the current rate, even if different from the expected future rate, and it would *not* be discounted in a manner similar to other long-term liabilities.

2. Income tax loss carryforwards would *not* be recognized as assets in the current period except to the extent that timing differences that have given rise to income tax liabilities can be reversed in the carryforward period. This appears to be more restrictive than the virtual certainty doctrine.

3. When tax assets arise from timing differences (e.g., when accounting depreciation is higher than that claimed for tax purposes), they would be subject to the same recognition criteria applied to other assets. Presumably this means that such tax assets would be subject to the usual tests of valuation, which include the likelihood of recovery.

4. A tax recovery resulting from the carryforward of a loss of a prior year would *not* be treated as an extraordinary item unless the source of the loss could be clearly identified as an extraordinary item.

There are some differences between the proposed new *Handbook* section and the standards of the FASB. Nevertheless, in 1989 both the FASB No. 96 and the CICA exposure draft have provoked considerable controversy, and both may undergo change in the future. This again illustrates the point we emphasized earlier in the chapter that income tax accounting is a good idea that is hard to make work.

Summary

The matching principle has led accountants to base income tax expense on the year's accounting income, not on its taxable income. In North America the accounting standard setters have chosen to calculate that expense using the rate of the current year, with no discounting to reflect the estimated delay before the deferral reverses. Thus the deferred income tax on the balance sheet cannot be given an economic interpretation because it is not an asset or liability within the usual meaning of those words. The conceptually preferable method is to treat the amount as an asset or liability, with the usual treatment accorded such items. The whole issue of income tax accounting was under review in both Canada and the U.S. during the late 1980s.

The matching principle also applies to tax refunds arising from a loss year; for the refund is considered to be related to the loss that generated the refund, not to the taxable income of other years to which it has been applied. The restrictions created by the tax authorities over the terms of the refund often make it uncertain whether a refund will actually take place. Consequently, the journal entries vary, depending on the particular circumstances.

QUESTIONS

Q13-1. Review and be sure you understand the following terms:

    a. intraperiod tax allocation

    b. interperiod tax allocation

    c. permanent differences

    d. timing differences

    e. accounting income *versus* statement income *versus* taxable income

    f. tax provison *versus* tax payable *versus* deferred income tax

    g. comprehensive tax allocation

    h. reversal of timing differences

    i. taxes payable method of accounting

    j. tax liability method of accounting

    k. partial allocation

    l. tax loss

    m. loss carryforward

    n. virtual certainty

    o. reasonable assurance

    p. statutory *versus* effective tax rates

    q. investment tax credit

    r. flow-through *versus* cost-reduction approach for investment tax credit

Q13-2. State whether you would classify each of the following as a permanent difference or a timing difference. Give your reasons.

    a. A company uses straight-line depreciation of 5% for its buildings for financial statement purposes, but it is able to use a 10% declining-balance rate for tax purposes. As a result, in 19X0 the depreciation charged on the financial statements is $67,000, while the capital cost allowance claimed for tax purposes is $87,000.

    b. A company accidentally exceeded provincial pollution control limits and was fined $50,000 by the courts.

    c. In 19X0, a company sold TV sets with a two-year warranty. According to GAAP the estimated warranty expense was $25,000, and the company provided for this in its financial statements. However, only $12,000 was allowed for tax purposes in that year.

    d. A company received dividends of $12,000 from Canadian corporations and $8,000 from U.S. corporations.

Q13-3. Suppose that a company failed to use intraperiod tax allocation.

    a. Would the net income after tax be affected?

    b. Would readers of the statement be provided with as much information as they would have had if intraperiod tax allocation had been used? Explain.

    c. Assume that it takes extra work and money to calculate the intraperiod tax allocation. What benefit might the reader receive that would make this extra cost worthwhile?

Q13-4. Explain why actions that are clearly illegal, such as bribery, might be considered proper business expenses for accounting purposes but not for tax purposes. Is this a consistent stance?

Q13-5. Explain why some income is never subject to tax. Does this mean that some people unfairly escape the tax burden carried by others?

Q13-6. In conducting an inventory count a sizeable segment of inventory was overlooked. As a result the closing inventory was understated, and the cost of sales for the year was overstated. The error was never discovered. Did this result in a permanent difference? A timing difference? Explain.

Q13-7. Timing differences arise for reasons having to do with the advance or delay of expenses or revenue for tax purposes. In each of the cases below, indicate whether (i) the timing difference is an advance or delay; (ii) it affects expense or revenue; and (3) it would result in a debit or credit to deferred income taxes on the blance sheet.

   a. In constructing a jet airliner a company recognizes revenue on a percentage-of-completion basis, but it is not taxed on it until it receives payment for the customer. The agreement with the customer is that payment will be received on a percentage-of-completion basis, but with a 15% holdback.

   b. Would your answer to (a) be different if the company did not recognize profit on each job until it was completed? Explain.

   c. A company decided that it had a significant amount of obsolete inventory of personal computer software recorded at $564,000 in a subsidiary company it had just purchased. It went through the inventory thoroughly and made write-downs of $240,000, with which its auditors concurred. This meant that the cost of sales that year was particularly high relative to sales. The tax department allowed only $180,000 of the write-down.

   d. In putting up a hotel a company found that it could charge immediately as tax deductible expenses certain costs such as landscaping that it wished to depreciate for accounting purposes over ten years.

Q13-8. What are the alternatives to using the deferred income tax approach to interperiod tax allocation? What are the relative merits of each?

Q13-9. Under the taxes payable method, "the possibilities for manipulating the amount of taxes payable, and hence the tax provision, should not be overlooked." Explain.

Q13-10. How does the assertion that taxes are a cost of doing business lead to a justification of the use of interperiod tax allocation? What is the alternative view? What are the implications of accepting the alternative view?

Q13-11. Why are deferred income taxes not a liability within the accepted meaning of that word?

Q13-12. Explain how companies could have been put into technical default if deferred income taxes had been considered to be a liability? Evaluate the merits of avoiding such a technical default by treating deferred taxes as "deferred credits."

Q13-13. "The concept of deferred income taxes has a great deal of merit. But the essential problem at the moment is that they are not discounted to recognize the length of time before they are likely to reverse." Do you agree? Give your reasons.

Q13-14. In a federal election campaign, Canadian corporations were referred to as "corporate welfare bums" because it was said that their financial statements showed they were being allowed to put off paying taxes that individuals had to pay immediately. Evaluate the merits of this charge.

Q13-15. "The doctrine of virtual certainty is far too restrictive and makes financial statements overly conservative." Do you agree? Explain.

Q13-16. Explain the circumstances under which income tax items can turn up on income statements as extraordinary items.

Q13-17. Assume that the bulk of a company's income is tax-exempt because it is from dividends from taxable Canadian corporations. Does the disclosure requirement on effective tax rates ensure that this will be shown?

Q13-18. Are deferred income taxes "interest free loans from the government"? Explain.

Q13-19. What are the relative merits of the deferral, accrual, partial allocation, and taxes payable methods of income tax allocation?

Q13-20. Can a company have both current and non-current deferred income tax on the same balance sheet? Both debit and credit amounts on the same balance sheet? All four of the above? Would your answer be the same under the accrual method of income tax allocation?

Q13-21. Several respected accounting authorities have disputed the appropriateness of the deferral method of accounting for income taxes. What arguments could a fair-minded person make against the present generally accepted accounting principles for deferred income taxes? What alternative method would you propose to meet these criticisms?

Q13-22. Give three examples of situations that result in timing differences between taxable and accounting income.

Q13-23. Sometimes it is not possible to recognize the benefit of a loss carryforward in the year of the loss. In such instances one treats any subsequent tax recovery as an extraordinary item. Is this procedure consistent with the usual tests used for extraordinary items? Discuss.

Q13-24. In most jurisdictions, a company is required to explain its effective tax rate (as shown in this chapter). What is the purpose of this? Do you think the example given in the chapter accomplishes this purpose? Explain.

Q13-25. What are the common approaches that have been used in accounting for the investment tax credit? What are the strengths and weaknesses of each? Explain why professional accounting bodies and government policy makers tend to disagree over the appropriate accounting method.

EXERCISES

E13-1. Rewrite the income statement of Alpha Limited to reflect the notions of intraperiod income tax allocation. Assume all items are taxed at the same rate.

INCOME STATEMENT

Net operating income before taxes	$860,000
Extraordinary items:	
Write-off of goodwill on unexpected cancellation of foreign sales concession (non-deductible for tax purposes)	200,000
Inventory fire loss	150,000
Tax provision — at 60%	306,000
Net income after tax	$204,000

E13-2. In each of the following unrelated situations, give the journal entry that would be required to convert from a taxes payable basis to a deferred income tax basis. Assume a tax rate of 40%.

    a. Capital cost allowance is in excess of depreciation in accounts by $20,000.

    b. Revenue of $8,000 booked for accounting purposes has been deferred for income tax purposes.

    c. Warranty expenses for tax purposes are $23,000, but only $10,000 for accounting purposes.

    d. Depreciation of $8,000 was charged for accounting purposes; but because the company had a tax loss, no capital cost allowance was claimed.

E13-3. Shown below are some of the common items that are treated differently for accounting and tax purposes. In the first empty column you are asked to indicate with a "P" or a "T" whether the items are *permanent* differences or *timing* differences. In the second empty column you are asked to indicate with a "DR" or "CR" whether the originating difference will result in a *debit* to deferred taxes or a *credit*. The first item has been completed to show you what is required.

	P or T	DR or CR
a. Charitable contributions in excess of tax limitations for that year. Must be carried forward.	T	DR
b. Fine for polluting. Not allowed for tax purposes.		
c. Expenses of repairing roof. Treated as expense for accounting purposes, but required by Revenue Canada to treat as a capital item.		
d. Excess of capital cost allowance over depreciation shown on financial statements.		
e. Tax-exempt dividend income.		
f. Amortization of goodwill. Not allowed for tax purposes.		
g. Estimated future warranty costs. Proper expenses for financial-statement purposes, but not allowed for tax purposes until incurred.		
h. Prepaid advertising expense. Deferred in the books, but deducted as an expense this year for tax purposes.		
i. Instalment sales income for book purposes this year exceeds the amount that must be reported for tax purposes.		

E13-4. In each of the following unrelated situations, explain whether there are sufficient grounds to assume "virtual certainty" in order to carry forward the tax loss.

    a. The loss arose because of a sharp drop in the price of pepper, which was a big item in the company's inventory. The price of pepper had been controlled by the four major countries producing it, and until now it had been relatively steady. The company is normally profitable.

    b. The loss arose because of a severe mechanical breakdown in the company's main factory that curtailed production during the peak selling season, severely limiting sales. Investigation has shown that the breakdown took place because of the inexperience of a new maintenance supervisor. The company has normally been profitable.

c. The company publishes a series of small-town newspapers and is usually profitable. The loss arose because a weekend supplement that was included in each paper failed to attract the advertisers expected. It has now been discontinued.

d. The company's main source of income in the past has been the mining and smelting of a metal that is heavily used in automobiles and house construction. The shift to smaller cars and a drop in housing construction has reduced demand for the metal, and its selling price has dropped as a result. The company has been marginally profitable even under these circumstances, but has suffered a loss because of a lengthy strike by its mining and smelting employees.

E13-5. Four unrelated situations are given below. The incomes shown in each are for Year 1. Assume a tax rate of 50% in Year 1 and 40% in all subsequent years. Assume a discount rate of 10%.

Situation	Statement income	Accounting income	Taxable income	Year in which difference will reverse
(i)	$ 25,000	$ 20,000	$ 23,000	3
(ii)	13,000	25,000	30,000	2
(iii)	50,000	50,000	20,000	8
(iv)	84,000	81,000	16,000	9

Required:

For the four situations above, calculate the tax expense using each of the following methods:

a. deferral method

b. taxes payable method

c. tax accrual method

E13-6. Consider the following five unrelated situations. Assume a tax rate of 45% in Years 1 and 2, 50% in Years 3 and 4, and 48% in Years 5 and 6.

Situation	Year 1	Year 2	Year 3	Year 4	Year 5	Year 6	Virtual certainty
(i)	$ 5,000	$ 3,000	$ 1,000	$ (10,000)	$ 8,000	$ 2,000	No
(ii)	(5,000)	(1,000)	3,000	2,000	4,000	(1,000)	No
(iii)	4,000	2,000	(9,000)	6,000	5,000	3,000	Yes
(iv)	4,000	2,000	(9,000)	6,000	5,000	3,000	No
(v)	(2,000)	(3,000)	(5,000)	8,000	6,000	(3,000)	Yes

Taxable income is shown for Years 1 through 6.

Required:

For the five situations above, calculate the following at the end of each year:

a. the tax expense or recovery that would be recorded for that year

b. the tax recovery, if any, with respect to prior years

c. the net income tax ultimately payable with respect to that year (i.e., after loss transfers from other years)

E13-7. Consider the following five unrelated situations. Assume a tax rate of 48% in Years 1 and 2, 45% in Years 3 and 4, 50% in Year 5, and 46% in Year 6.

Situation	Year 1	Year 2	Year 3	Year 4	Year 5	Year 6	Virtual certainty
			Taxable income				
(i)	$ 5,800	$ 2,100	$ 500	$ (8,000)	$ 8,000	$ 2,000	No
(ii)	(3,000)	(2,500)	4,500	3,200	3,650	(2,000)	No
(iii)	3,500	1,500	(7,500)	4,500	2,000	1,000	Yes
(iv)	2,500	1,000	(9,000)	4,000	5,000	3,000	No
(v)	1,500	(4,500)	(2,300)	7,500	6,000	(3,000)	Yes

Required:

For the five situations above, calculate the following at the end of each year:

a. the tax expense or recovery that would be recorded for that year

b. the tax recovery, if any, with respect to prior years

c. the net income tax ultimately payable with respect to that year (i.e., after loss transfers from other years)

E13-8. The following table shows the taxable and accounting income of Inverary Inc. for the fiscal periods ending 31 December each year.

Year	Taxable income	Accounting income
19X1	$ 90,000	$?
19X2	91,000	120,000
19X3	110,000	80,000
19X4	70,000	90,000

The balances in the deferred income taxes account at 1 January 19X1 and 19X5 are credits of $32,400 and $40,000 respectively. The corporate tax rate for this company is 40%.

Required:

a. Calculate the balances in the deferred income taxes account for each of the years ended 31 December 19X1 to 19X4.

b. What is the accounting income for the year 19X1?

(CMA adapted)

E13-9. Clearly explain the difference in meaning of the terms in each of the following:

a. income tax recovered from Revenue Canada *versus* the "tax recovery" item shown on the income statement

b. depreciation *versus* capital cost allowance

c. interperiod *versus* intraperiod allocation

d. virtual certainty *versus* reasonable assurance

e. long-term *versus* short-term deferred income tax

f. deferral *versus* accrual *versus* flow-through treatments

E13-10. In each of the situations below, prepare journal entries to record the handling of taxes for the year. Assume a tax rate of 45% and virtual certainty. Also assume that depreciation creates long-term deferred income tax and that warranty expense creates short-term deferred income tax.

a. Accounting income (loss)	$(5,000)
Add depreciation	4,000
Less capital cost allowance	(2,000)
Taxable income	$(3,000)

b.

Statement income	$17,500
Less dividend from taxable Canadian corporation	(3,500)
Add fines levied for overdue taxes	2,000
Less ½ of capital gain	(1,500)
Accounting income	14,500
Timing differences:	
Add depreciation	3,000
Less capital cost allowance	(4,000)
Add warranty expense in excess of expenditures	1,000
Taxable income	$14,500

c.

Statement income	$22,500
Less dividend from taxable Canadian corporation	(2,000)
Amortization of good will	3,500
Accounting income	24,000
Timing differences:	
Add depreciation	5,000
Less capital cost allowance	(6,000)
Less warranty costs incurred	(3,000)
Taxable income	$20,000

d. The credit balance in the long-term deferred income tax account was $24,000. The balance resulted from timing differences between the claiming of cost of capital allowance and the recording of depreciation. Over the years the amount of cost of capital allowance claimed exceeded depreciation by $50,000.

Accounting income	$50,000
Add depreciation	20,000
Less capital cost allowance	(10,000)
Taxable income	$60,000

E13-11. Shown below are the taxable income figures for four different companies over 5 years. Figures in brackets are losses. Assume that the tax rate was 45% and that there were no timing differences.

Company	19X1	19X2	19X3	19X4	19X5
A	$(3,000)	$(1,000)	$2,000	$1,000	$ 0
B	3,000	(4,000)	(1,000)	1,000	1,000
C	(2,000)	1,000	(1,000)	(1,000)	3,000
D	(1,000)	3,000	2,000	(5,000)	2,000

Required:

a. For each company and each year, show the current tax cost and prior-period recovery under each of the following assumptions:
  (i) virtual certainty exists
  (ii) virtual certainty does not exist

b. Explain why the assumption about virtual certainty affects the tax cost each year.

E13-12. Shown below are journal entries for six independent tax situations. Describe the scenario that most likely gave rise to each journal entry.

a.

Tax refund receivable	3,200.00	
Tax recovery		3,200.00

b. Tax provision   20,000.00
   Deferred income tax: long-term   17,000.00
     Tax payable   37,000.00

c. Income tax recoverable   11,000.00
   Deferred income tax: long-term   1,700.00
     Tax recovery   9,300.00

d. Tax provision   9,000.00
   Deferred income tax: current   350.00
     Deferred income tax: long-term   1,200.00
     Tax payable   8,150.00

e. Tax provision   2,700.00
     Extraordinary item—tax recovery   2,700.00

f. 19X6
   Deferred income tax long-term   6,750.00
     Tax recovery   6,750.00

  19X7
   Tax provision   6,750.00
     Deferred income tax: long-term   6,750.00

E13-13. Provided below are the accounting-income figures for four different situations over a five-year period. In each year assume that the capital cost allowance (CCA) that can be claimed must be between $6,000 and $11,000. The company postpones CCA claims to reduce taxable losses where possible, and the company claims the maximum CCA where it will reduce taxable profits. In each situation, there was no deferred income tax balance as of the start of 19X1. Assume a tax rate of 45% and no virtual certainty.

Situation	19X1	19X2	19X3	19X4	19X5	Reason- able assurance	Annual depreciation expense
(i)	$(1,000)	$3,000	$(3,000)	$3,500	$11,000	no	$7,000
(ii)	(1,000)	3,500	(3,000)	3,500	11,000	yes	$7,000
(iii)	1,000	(4,000)	3,000	1,000	(2,000)	no	$8,500
(iv)	1,000	(4,000)	3,000	1,000	(2,000)	yes	$8,500

Required:

a. For each situation and each year, calculate the tax expense or tax recovery; the prior-year tax recovery (if any); and the year-end deferred income tax balance.

b. In what years would the net operating income (i.e., the income before extraordinary items) differ between situations (i) and (ii)? Explain why.

c. Would the net operating income also differ in any years between situations (iii) and (iv)? Explain why.

E13-14. State whether each item below is a timing difference or a permanent difference or neither. If it is a timing difference, explain (i) whether a deferred debit or credit would arise; and (ii) whether the deferred amount would be treated as long-term or short-term.

a. Warranty expenses reported for accounting purposes exceeded actual warranty expenditures by $85,000. The company treats its warranty liability as short-term.

b. A company receives dividends of $350 from General Motors Corporation and $250 from Dofasco Inc.

c. Parking fines totalling $650 incurred by employees and reimbursed by the company were disallowed by Revenue Canada as unacceptable charges against taxable income.

d. Goods sold on long-term instalment contracts totalled $318,000 in the current year, but for tax purposes only $123,000 had to be declared as revenue.

e. A parent company accounted for its subsidiaries using the equity method. It had thus reported investment income of $350,000. Actual dividend receipts during the year from these associated companies were $35,000 from a taxable Canadian corporation and $80,000 from a subsidiary in the U.S.

f. Legal costs of $35,000 in connection with a bond issue were claimed in the current year for tax purposes, but the costs were amortized over the five-year life of the bond for accounting purposes. As a result, only $7,000 was charged to the current year's expenses.

PROBLEMS

P13-1. Amherst Corporation had differences between its taxable income and its accounting income as shown below. The items listed were the only causes of the differences. Amherst's income before tax for accounting purposes was $342,000. Assume the tax rate is 55%.

Item	Allowed for purposes of	
	Tax	Accounting
Depreciation charged	$30,000	$50,000
Fine for violation of income tax	0	5,000
Self-insurance expense	50,000	3,000
Premium expense on coupon promotion	0	2,300

Required:

Prepare the journal entry to record each of the following. Show all calculations.

a. tax expense

b. taxes payable

c. deferred income tax

P13-2. In each of the last three years the taxable income reported by DIT Limited for income tax purposes has differed from the income before taxes reported on its income statement. The record is as follows:

Year	Statement income	Taxable income
1	$170,000	$125,000
2	90,000	105,000
3	85,000	100,000

Included in net income as reported on the income statement in Year 1 was $20,000 of income that is not subject to income tax at any time. Also during Year 1, $25,000 of deductions were taken for income tax purposes that will not be reported as expenses on the company's books until later years. In Year 3, the company incurred an accounting loss of $8,000, which is reflected on the income statement; for income tax purposes, only $3,000 of this loss is deductible. In all other respects income reported on the income statement is ultimately subject to income taxes. Assume that the company is subject to a combined federal and provincial income tax rate of 45% on all taxable income.

Required:

a. For each of the three years, prepare the journal entry (entries) to record income taxes and the interperiod allocation using the deferral method. Show all calculations.

b. Assume that all income taxes due (as reported on the company's tax returns) were paid during the year following their accrual. What are the balances at the end of Year 3 in the company's tax-liability accounts (both current and deferred)?

P13-3. The KA Company prepared the following reconciliation between taxable and accounting income for 19X9.

Income as per tax return	$2,750,000
Add: Excess of capital cost allowance over depreciation	200,000
	2,950,000
Deduct: Extraordinary gain on early extinguishment of debt	150,000
Deduct: Estimated expenses of future warranties not allowed for tax	
purposes until expenses are actually incurred	100,000
Deduct: Revenue advance taxable in period of receipt	50,000
Reported accounting income before income tax and extraordinary	
items	$2,650,000

Required:

a. Prepare the journal entries to record the income tax liability at 31 December 19X9. Assume a tax rate of 40%. Show all calculations.

b. Prepare the lower portion of the income statement starting with "Reported accounting income before income tax and extraordinary items."

c. What tax balance(s) will be shown on the balance sheet?

P13-4. The figures below are extracted from the income statement of Premium Breakfast Cereal Corporation Limited for the year ended 30 November 19X0:

Income for the year before deducting or including the undernoted items		$325,000
Deduct: Estimated premiums expense	$12,000	
Deduct: Depreciation of plant, equipment, and office		
buildings	75,000	87,000
		238,000
Add: Share of earnings of UCFM Ltd., in which the		
company owns 25% of the voting common		
shares		22,000
		$ 260,000

You are given the following additional information related to the year ended 30 November 19X0:

(1) According to the separate files that the company maintains for tax purposes, undepreciated capital cost of the plant, equipment, and office buildings was $900,000 as of the end of the prior year (after deducting capital cost allowance for the year then ended). There have been no subsequent additions to, or disposals of, these assets.

The company is entitled to claim maximum capital cost allowance of 10% based on the prevailing undepreciated capital cost of these assets. Its policy is to claim the maximum allowance available.

(2) The company distributes coupons in the boxes of its cereal. Twenty of these coupons may be redeemed by retail purchasers for one premium in the form of a colouring book and box of crayons for children. The company is entitled to claim for tax purposes the cost of premiums actually sent to customers in return for coupons redeemed during the year. This cost was $10,000.

(3) The company uses the equity method in accounting for revenue from its investment in UCFM Ltd., a Canadian corporation. During the year ended 30 November 19X0, UCFM Ltd. reported a net income of $88,000 and paid dividends on its common shares of $60,000. To avoid double taxation of companies, the Tax Act exempts from corporation income tax both the receipt of dividends and the recognition of share of earnings when the affiliated company is another Canadian corporation.

(4) The applicable corporation tax rate is 45%.

Required:

a. Calculate income tax payable by Premium Breakfast Cereal Corporation Ltd. as of 30 November 19X0. Assume that there were no other permanent or timing differences than those noted above and that the Company has not prepaid any part of its tax liability. Show and where necessary explain all calculations.

b. Show for each timing difference the debit or credit to the deferred income tax account required by the deferred income tax method.

c. Show the journal entry required to record income tax expense for the year ended 30 November 19X0 as required by the deferred income tax method.

d. Complete the final part of the company's income statement, commencing with the item "Income for the year before income tax."

P13-5. In 1983 *The Wall Street Journal* reported that the Aetna Life and Casualty Co. had reported earnings of $372.4 million in the first nine months of 1982. Of this amount, $203 million comes from expected tax recoveries when losses are carried forward to future years. The *Journal* noted, "The company says that generally accepted accounting principles allow it to recognize these credits ahead of time so long as Aetna's management is convinced 'beyond any reasonable doubt' that future taxable income will be sufficient." The SEC became interested, and Aetna expected the SEC to rule on whether this tax treatment as acceptable. Aetna reported that "investor worry about a possible adverse ruling" from the SEC was partly responsible for recent weakness in the price of its stock.

Required:
Assume you are asked to write an evaluation of this situation for an intelligent reader of Aetna's stock who does not understand accounting jargon. You are asked to write a two-page memo in which you (i) set out the accounting implications of a favourable or adverse ruling by the SEC; and (ii) comment on whether there is any substance to the "investor worry" over the SEC's decision. Assume that Canadian accounting standards apply here.

P13-6. Borodin Limited, a taxpaying Canadian corporation, provides you with the following information:

	Year 1	Year 2	Year 3	Year 4
Net income before tax (loss)	$19,100	$(67,600)	$49,200	$93,500
Depreciation charged	16,000	19,000	15,000	11,000
Capital cost allowance claimed	13,000	11,000	18,000	31,000
Dividends from other taxable Canadian corporations (excluding Millsfalls Limited)	2,300	1,000	1,800	15,000
Investment income from Millsfall Limited, a company over which Borodin has significant influence	3,800	6,200	3,400	2,000

Required:

Answer the following questions. Do not assume virtual certainty with respect to loss carryforwards.

a. Calculate the taxable income for Borodin Limited for each of Years 1 to 4.

b. Calculate the income tax payable with respect to each year. Assume a tax rate of 55%.

c. Calculate the provision for income tax that should be shown on the income statement of each year.

d. Assuming that the deferred income tax was zero at the beginning of Year 1, calculate the deferred income tax at the end of each of Years 1 to 4.

P13-7. The following information is obtained from the records of Yovill Company Ltd.:

Year	Pretax accounting income	Capital cost allowance over (under) book depreciation	Taxable income	Tax paid at 46%
19X1	$25,000	$20,000	$ 5,000	$ 2,300
19X2	70,000	20,000	50,000	23,000
19X3	127,000	100,000	27,000	12,420
19X4	288,000	120,000	168,000	77,280
19X5	82,000	(60,000)	142,000	65,320
19X6	36,000	(200,000)	236,000	108,560
	$628,000	0	$628,000	$288,880

Included in pretax accounting income is a deduction for interest on overdue income taxes of $5,000 (19X1) and $3,000 (19X3). The company was eligible for an inventory allowance of $8,000 (19X4), $12,000 (19X5), and $6,000 (19X6).

Required:

Complete the schedule below for each of the years 19X1 to 19X6.

Income tax expense	Income tax payable	Increase (decrease) in deferred tax	Balance in deferred tax

P13-8. Gordon Co., which is a company in its second year, had a poor year financially in 19X4. The relevant information is shown below:

Net income before taxes	$(25,000)
Depreciation	15,000
Capital cost allowance	20,000
Dividends received	8,000
Tax rate in 19X3 and 19X4	45%
Tax payable in 19X3	14,000

One of your friends suggests there is virtual certainty, whereas another friend suggests there is not.

Required:

a. State the issues involved in the dispute between your friends.

b. Calculate the tax payable, tax provision, and amount of deferred income tax under each of the following assumptions:
   (i) virtual certainty exists
   (ii) virtual certainty does not exist

c. Show the tax entry and the bottom of the income statement for the year ended 31 December 19X5 under each assumption. The net income before tax was $50,000. The tax rate is 45%, and there were no permanent or timing differences for 19X5.

P13-9. Alwington Limited had a $105,000 net operating loss during the first year of operations, when the applicable tax rate was 40%.

Required:

a. Suppose that the corporation is *not* virtually certain it will have future earnings against which it can offset the loss carryforward. Prepare the entries for income taxes in the year of loss and in the succeeding year (assume a $135,000 pretax income and a 40% tax rate in the succeeding year).

b. Suppose that the corporation *is* virtually certain of earnings in the succeeding periods to cover the loss. Prepare the entries for income taxes in the year of the loss and in the succeeding year (assume a $135,000 pretax income and a 40% tax rate in the succeeding year).

c. For both the loss year and the succeeding year, present the lower portion of the income statement (i.e., beginning at "Pretax accounting income or loss") under each of the following assumptions:
   (i) virtual certainty exists
   (ii) virtual certainty does not exist

P13-10. The accountant for Doyle Ltd. has asked you to finish preparing the income statement and balance sheet for the year ended 31 December 19X0. You are given the following information:

Statement income	$70,000
Add/(Subtract) permanent differences:	
Membership fees in the tennis club	2,000
Dividends received	(14,000)
Accounting income	$58,000
Add/(Subtract) timing differences:	
Depreciation	16,400
Capital cost allowance	$(23,500)
Warranty expense as per GAAP	4,500
Warranty claim for tax purposes	(2,100)
Taxable income	$53,300

The tax rate for the year 19X0 is 45%.

Required:

a. Show the journal entry that would be needed at year-end to record taxes.

b. Prepare the lower portion of the income statement starting with "Net income before income tax."

c. Suppose 19X0 is the first year of operations for Doyle Ltd. How would the amounts in the journal entry appear on the balance sheet?

P13-11. MacClaren Tomato Products owns large tomato fields in Southern Ontario. The crop was recently destroyed by a freak midsummer frost. The write-down of company assets following the storm resulted in an extraordinary loss of $180,000 (tax deductible) for 19X3. MacClaren also cans and sells tomatoes in the Canadian market. Inside the label of one of their brands they include coupons allowing people 30 cents off their next purchase. You are given the following additional information for 19X3:

Dividends received from other Canadian firms except for those firms accounted for using the equity method	$12,000
Income from firms over which MacClaren exerts significant influence	14,500
Membership fees for the local golf club	3,000
Statement income	62,000
Depreciation	17,000
Capital cost allowance	21,800
Coupons expense as per GAAP	7,200
Coupons actually used by customers	3,250
Tax rate	50%

Required:

a. Prepare the journal entry to record the income tax provision and income tax payable for 19X3.

b. Show the lower portion of the income statement starting with "Net income before tax provision and extraordinary items."

c. Show how deferred income tax would appear on the balance sheet if there was a zero balance for this account from previous years.

P13-12. Fox Poster Co. has yearly income before depreciation of $15,840. Depreciation is calculated on a straight-line basis over twelve years. The original cost of depreciable assets was $72,000. All the depreciable fixed assets fall into Class 15 for tax purposes. Therefore the rate used to calculate CCA is 15%. Assume that this is the first year of operations and that the tax rate is 45%.

Required:

Show the effect on the bottom line (i.e., on net income after taxes) for each year over the next ten years of the taxes payable method versus the deferred income tax approach. How much would reported income differ between the two methods over the ten-year period? Why does the difference, if any, exist? (*Hint:* Using a computer spreadsheet program will reduce the routine work needed to make the calculations.)

P13-13. The net income before taxes for Platonic Limited was $16,245 in 19X0. The following items were included in calculating this income:

(1) Platonic had received a dividend of $214.50 from an associated company. However, because Platonic is considered to exercise significant influence over this associated company, it used the equity method and took $300.00 into income. Neither the

dividend nor the amount taken into income are considered taxable in Platonic's hands.

(2) Platonic had reported a warranty expense of $918.00, but actual payments under their warranties had been $660.00.

(3) Platonic had received dividends totalling $1,480.00 from stocks held in its investment portfolio. All were from taxable Canadian corporations, and it did not exercise significant influence over any of them.

(4) Depreciation had been calculated for statement purposes using straight-line depreciation. The total for 19X0 was $1,770. The total amount of capital cost allowance used for tax purposes was $2,690.

As of the first of the year Platonic had a tax liability of $2,000. During the 19X0 fiscal year, Platonic made payments of $9,500 on account of income tax. Assume the tax rate was 60%.

Required:

a. Calculate the amount of tax payable by Platonic for the year 19X0.

b. Calculate the amount of income tax expense that should be shown on the financial statements.

c. Calculate the balance in the tax liability account as of the end of 19X0.

d. Suppose that Platonic had a balance of $300 credit in its deferred income taxes at the start of 19X0. Calculate the closing balance.

e. Discuss to what extent deferred income taxes are a long-term liability and whether the accounting treatment of this item is consistent with that of long-term liabilities.

P13-14. Anomalies Ltd. had income before tax of $70,000 in its first year of operation. This included a deduction of $2,000 for an interest penalty on overdue income taxes. Depreciation expense of $10,000 had also been recorded. The corporation deducted capital cost allowance of $15,000 for tax purposes. The tax rate was 48%

In its second year Anomalies suffered a financial-statement loss before tax of $90,000. Depreciation of $10,000 had been recorded. For tax purposes no capital cost allowance was claimed. The tax rate in that year was 45%. The company does not have virtual certainty or reasonable assurance of using the tax loss in the future, but it can at least recover taxes from the first year.

Required:

a. Using the tax allocation method, give the journal entry to record the income tax at the end of the first year. Show all calculations, including the reconciliation between financial-statement income and taxable income.

b. What entry or entries would the company make at the end of the second year if it had paid its taxes in full for the first year?

c. What loss carryforward remains at the end of the second year for tax purposes? Show your calculations.

d. What significant tax-related information would remain unrecorded in the accounts of the company at the end of the second year?

(Adapted from Jane Craighead)

P13-15. During 19X0 Calderon Co. had only one timing difference between its accounting income and taxable income. At 31 December 19X0 the net book value of its depreciable assets ($900,000) was $140,000 in excess of undepreciated capital cost ($760,000). The income tax rate has been 40% since the start of the company. Assume that only 50% of capital gains must be included in taxable income.

The 19X1 accounts contain the following information:

(1) The income statement shows income before taxes in the amount of $500,000.

(2) The following items have been included in arriving at income before income taxes:
  — non-taxable dividends received in the amount of $20,000
  — gain on disposal of depreciable assets of $70,000, of which $50,000 is a true capital gain for tax purposes (sale price, $110,000; original capital cost, $60,000; net book value, $40,000). (*Note*: This gain is not to be treated as an extraordinary item.)

(3) The following items have been deducted in arriving at income before taxes:
  — interest of $5,000 for government fines
  — depreciation of $90,000
  — provision for repairs to fixed assets of $40,000

(4) Capital cost allowance claimed in 19X1 was $140,000.

Required:

Calculate each of the following using the deferred income tax method:

a. the taxable income for 19X1.

b. the financial-statement net income or loss for 19X1.

c. the balance in the deferred income tax account as at 31 December 19X1.

(CMA adapted)

P13-16. a. Two methods of accounting for interperiod tax allocation are the accrual method and the deferred method. Describe each of these methods fully.

b. Some accountants argue for *partial income tax allocation*. Others prefer the *comprehensive allocation* approach. Explain what is meant by each of these terms and state the major differences.

P13-17. Provided below are the statement income figures for a firm over a five-year period:

	19X1	19X2	19X3	19X4	19X5
Statement income (loss)	$(3,000)	$6,000	$(2,000)	$6,000	$8,000

There was no opening balance in the deferred income tax account. In each year the maximum allowable capital cost allowance claim was $20,000. Depreciation expense claimed each year totalled $15,000. There were no permanent differences and no timing differences other than those created by depreciation and capital cost allowance claims. The tax rate for each year was 40%.

Required:

a. Suppose that virtual certainty exists. Calculate the following for each year:
  (i) tax expense or recovery
  (ii) net income after tax
  (iii) the year-end deferred income tax balance

b. Suppose that virtual certainty does not exist but that reasonable assurance does exist. Calculate the items listed in part (a). Assume that the company deferred capital cost allowance to the extent that the taxable loss was reduced to nil where possible. The company will claim a minimum of $12,500 in each year. The deferrals were reversed as soon as possible, subject to the maximum allowable claim outlined above.

c. Suppose there is neither virtual certainty nor reasonable assurance. Calculate the items listed in part (a). Assume the company will claim a minimum of $12,500 of capital cost allowance.

d. Would it be possible to have a situation where virtual certainty existed but reasonable assurance did not? Explain.

P13-18. Preston Ltd. and Boyce Inc. experienced similar results both in 19X1 and 19X2. Shown below are partial income statements for the two companies.

	Preston		Boyce	
	19X1	19X2	19X1	19X2
Sales	$98,444	$106,430	$89,944	$95,678
Costs of goods sold	47,554	56,455	43,633	51,365
Gross profit	50,890	49,975	46,311	44,313
Selling and administrative	44,890	35,975	40,311	30,313
Depreciation	7,500	7,500	7,500	7,500
Statement income	$(1,500)	$ 6,500	$(1,500)	$ 6,500

You are given the following additional information:
- (i) Boyce decided to limit its taxable loss in 19X1 by only claiming $6,000 of capital cost allowance (CCA) in 19X1 rather than the maximum allowable of $10,000. It did claim the maximum allowable ($10,000) in 19X2.
- (ii) Preston claimed $10,000 CCA in 19X1 and $6,000 in 19X2.
- (iii) The tax rate was 50% in each of the two years.
- (iv) There were no permanent differences between income recognition for accounting and tax purposes in either year.
- (v) There were no timing differences other than that between CCA and depreciation.
- (vi) The opening balance in each company's deferred income tax account was zero.

Required:

Illustrate the differences in financial-statement items that result from the different handling of CCA by completing the table below for each company and for each of the following assumptions:

a. virtual certainty exists

b. reasonable assurance exists but virtual certainty does not

c. neither reasonable assurance nor virtual certainty exist

	19X1	19X2	Total
Accounting income			
Taxable income			
Tax expense			
Net income			
Tax receivable/payable			
Tax recovery			
Deferred income taxes			

P13-19. Edisons Electronics, Bytes Computers, and Abacus Business Machines miraculously ended up with identical results in each of the past three years. However, each company handles the interperiod tax allocation in a different manner. Edisons uses the deferred tax method, Bytes uses the taxes payable method, and Abacus uses the tax accrual method. The tax rate in each of the three years is 45%. Given below is a worksheet which shows the accounting income and taxable income figures common to the three companies.

	19X1	19X2	19X3
Statement income	$57,344	$63,333	$74,590
Permanent differences:			
Less dividends from taxable Canadian			
corporations	(3,500)	(3,500)	(4,000)
Amortization of goodwill	1,200	1,200	1,200
Accounting income	55,044	61,033	71,790

(Continued)

Timing differences:			
Add depreciation	14,000	14,000	14,000
Less capital cost allowance (CCA)	(17,500)	(14,000)	(10,500)
Add warranty expense	1,000	500	600
Less warranty costs incurred	(500)	(1,300)	(300)
Taxable income	$52,044	$60,233	$75,590

Required:

a. Complete a table in the form shown below for Edisons Electronics and Bytes Computers for each year using the interperiod allocation method that the particular company employs.

	19X1	19X2	19X3
Taxable income			
Tax expense			
Tax receivable			
Tax liability			
Tax recovery			
Deferred/accrued income taxes:			
Current			
Long-term			

b. Calculate the tax liability, tax expense, and accrued income tax in each year for Abacus Business Machines by completing the following table. Assume a 10% discount rate and an expected tax rate of 45%.

	19X1	19X2	19X3	Total
Taxable income:				
Taxable in current year				
Taxable next year				
Depreciation/CCA:				
Taxable in current year				
Taxable next year				
Taxable in two years				
Warranty:				
Taxable in current year				
Taxable next year				
Accounting income				
Summary:				
Taxable in current year				
Taxable next year				
Taxable in two years				
Accounting income				
Tax liability:				
Taxable in current year				
Taxable next year — Gross				
— Discount				
Taxable in two years — Gross				
— Discount				
Total — Gross				
— Discount				
— Net				

P13-20. Shown below is a worksheet showing the calculation of accounting and taxable income for Tolstoy Inc. over a three-year period. The tax rate for each year is 45%.

	19X1	19X2	19X3
Statement income (loss)	$ (3,238)	$21,243	$13,929
Permanent differences:			
Less dividends from taxable Canadian corporations	(5,000)	(5,000)	(5,500)
Amortization of goodwill	1,000	1,000	1,000
Accounting income	(7,238)	17,243	9,429
Timing differences:			
Add depreciation	7,500	7,250	10,250
Less capital cost allowance	(10,000)	(10,000)	(5,000)
Add warranty expense	1,200	500	1,000
Less warranty expenditures	(1,000)	(850)	(850)
Taxable income (loss)	$ (9,538)	$14,143	$14,829

Required:

Complete a table in the form shown below for each year and for each of the following allocation methods. In all instances, round to the nearest dollar.

a. deferred tax method (assume virtual certainty exists)

b. taxes payable method

	19X1	19X2	19X3
Tax expense			
Tax receivable			
Tax liability			
Tax recovery			
Deferred income taxes:			
Current			
Long-term			

P13-21. Using the figures provided in the previous problem, calculate the tax liability, tax expense and the accrued taxes for each year that would be recognized if the tax accrual method were used. Assume that the discount rate is 10% and that the current tax rate is used to estimate the liability. Your solution should be presented in the form shown in the following table:

	19X1	19X2	19X3	Total
Taxable income:				
Taxable in current year				
Taxable next year				
Depreciation/CCA:				
Taxable in current year				
Taxable next year				
Taxable in two years				
Warranty:				
Taxable in current year				
Taxable next year				
Accounting income				
Summary:				
Taxable in current year				
Taxable next year				
Taxable in two years				
Accounting income				

	19X1	19X2	19X3	Total
Tax liability:				
Taxable in current year				
Taxable next year — Gross				
— Discount				
Taxable in two years — Gross				
— Discount				
Total — Gross				
— Discount				
— Net				

P13-22. Provided below are worksheets used to calculate the 19X1 taxable income of four companies. They also contain the deferred income tax balances for each company as at the beginning of the year. Assume that the past and present tax rate is 55% and that virtual certainty does not exist.

	Company A	Company B	Company C	Company D
Balance in Deferred income tax account (credit)	$(15,000)	$ 0	$ (500)	$(11,000)
Statement income	(1,000)	0	(3,000)	1,780
Capital gain: non-taxable portion		(2,000)	(3,000)	
Accounting income (loss)	(1,000)	(2,000)	(6,000)	1,780
Depreciation	8,500	9,000	7,000	7,150
Initial capital cost allowance claim	(10,000)	(12,500)	(10,000)	(11,750)
Taxable income	$ (2,500)	$(5,500)	$(9,000)	$ (2,820)

Required:

a. Prepare the journal entries for each company under each of the following assumptions:

  (i) Reasonable assurance exists. Suppose that capital cost claims can be postponed up to a maximum of $5,000 and that claims are postponed to the extent that taxable losses are reduced to nil where possible.

  (ii) Reasonable assurance does not exist.

b. For each company and each year, calculate the after-tax net income for the year under each of the two assumptions regarding reasonable assurance given in part (a). Explain any differences that arise because of the assumption chosen.

P13-23. Provided below is the 19X1 income statement of Rip-off Rentals. The junior accountant completed the statement but failed to segregate the interperiod and intraperiod tax allocation. The tax rate for the year was 55%.

		19X1
Rental income		$485,934
Maintenance and depreciation on rental equipment	$275,834	
Selling and administrative	59,349	
Depreciation	18,500	
Warranty expense	1,250	354,933
Operating income		131,001
Dividend income		5,000
Net income before taxes		136,001
Tax expense		72,051
Net income		$63,950

You are also given the following additional information:
 (i) The company claimed the maximum allowable capital cost allowance of $25,000.
 (ii) The dividend income came from another Canadian corporation.
 (iii) Actual warranty costs incurred were $700.
 (iv) The sales figure includes an instalment sale of $7,500 which is not considered taxable until 19X2.
 (v) The maintenance and depreciation figure includes an extraordinary loss of $50,000 resulting from the theft of some uninsured equipment.

Required:
Prepare an income statement showing both the intraperiod and interperiod tax allocation for the year.

P13-24. Shown below is the information required to produce the income statements and calculate the deferred tax position for Weller Inc. for the years 19X1, 19X2, and 19X3. Assume a tax rate of 45% for each of the three years. Round all calculated figures to the nearest dollar.

	19X1	19X2	19X3
Statement income	$80,394	$83,109	$96,814
Depreciation	22,500	19,875	23,450
Warranty expense	2,500	750	
Dividends from taxable Canadian corporations	5,000	5,000	5,500
Capital cost allowance	25,000	22,500	22,500
Instalments due			9,750
Warranty expenditures		90	1,750
Instalment sales (received and taxed in the next year)		9,750	

Required:
a. Prepare the journal entries to record the tax liability for each year. Show all calculations in a worksheet form.

b. For each year, calculate the year-end balance in the short-term and long-term deferred income tax accounts. The deferred tax balances at the start of 19X1 were zero.

BIBLIOGRAPHY

ACCOUNTING PRINCIPLES BOARD. *Opinion No. 11: Accounting for Income Taxes.* New York: AICPA, 1967.

BAINES, R.A.; DIETOR, R.; and STEWART, JOHN. "Tax Allocation Revisited." *CA Magazine* (March 1984). An argument in favour of discounting under some circumstances.

BEECHY, THOMAS H. *Accounting for Corporate Income Taxes: Conceptual Considerations and Empirical Analysis.* Toronto: Canadian Institute of Chartered Accountants, 1983. A study commissioned by the CICA.

———. "Partial Allocation: Variations on a Theme." *CA Magazine* (March 1985). An excellent review of the types of partial allocation possible.

BERESFORD, DENNIS R.; BEST, LAWRENCE C.; and WEBER, JOSEPH V. "Accounting for Income Taxes: Change is Coming." *Journal of Accountancy* (January 1984). An American assessment of the factors that led to FASB Opinion No. 96.

BROUARD, NATHALIE, and LEGAULT, MICHEL. "Another Perspective on Deferred Income Taxes." *CA Magazine* (May 1984). A controversial view that sees taxes payable in the future as revenue.

DRUMMOND, CHRISTINA, and WIGLE, SEYMOUR L. "Let's Stop Taking Comprehensive Tax Allocation for Granted." *CA Magazine* (October 1981). Two members of Price Waterhouse advocate dropping deferred income taxes in favour of a partial allocation approach.

FINANCIAL ACCOUNTING STANDARDS BOARD. *Statement of Financial Accounting Standards No. 96: Accounting for Income Taxes.* Stamford: FASB, 1987. This U.S. pronouncement favours the tax liability method over the deferral method.

INSTITUTE OF CHARTERED ACCOUNTANTS OF ENGLAND AND WALES. *Statement of Standard Accounting Practice No. 15: Accounting for Deferred Taxation.* London, 1978. An examination of the partial-allocation approach.

INTERNATIONAL ACCOUNTING STANDARDS COMMITTEE. *Accounting for Taxes on Income.* London, England, 1979. The publication in which the Committee approved both the deferral method and the liability method of accounting for income taxes.

KLIGMAN, JONATHAN. "Investment Tax Credits: Some Key Issues." *CA Magazine* (October 1983). An appraisal of the accounting aspects of the investment tax credit.

MILBURN, J.A. "Comprehensive Tax Allocation: Let's Stop Taking Some Misconceptions for Granted." *CA Magazine* (April 1982). A reply to the Drummond-Wigle article. It defends tax allocation in principle, but not the deferred income tax approach currently in use.

NAIR, R.D., and WEYGANDT, JERRY J. "Let's Fix Deferred Taxes." *Journal of Accountancy* (November 1981). A review of the state of tax allocation, ending with a recommendation in favour of the liability method.

ROSENFIELD, PAUL, and DENT, WILLIAM C. "No More Deferred Taxes." *Journal of Accountancy* (February 1983). A case against interperiod tax allocation and for letting reported taxes follow the tax return.

SKINNER, ROSS. *Accounting Standards in Evolution.* Toronto: Holt, Rinehart, and Winston of Canada Ltd., 1987. Chapter 15 presents a comprehensive review of the evolution of income tax accounting and an evaluation of the merits of the various approaches.

THOMAS, ALAN R. "New R & D Incentives Challenge Conventional Accounting." *CA Magazine* (May 1984). Discussion of the accounting implications of new research and development tax incentives.

CHAPTER 14
Leases

Introduction

A **lease** is a legal contract in which someone who owns an asset, the **lessor,** agrees to allow someone else, the **lessee,** to use it for a specified time in return for specified payments called **rent**.

Here are three examples:

(1) A student leases a room in the university residence for an academic term. The student is the lessee, and the university is the lessor.

(2) The Skydome in Toronto is rarely used by its actual owners. Instead it is leased for short periods to promoters of sporting and entertainment events. The owners of the Skydome are the lessors, and the groups putting on the events are the lessees.

(3) Air Canada and other airlines rent many of the aircraft bearing their colours. The airline maintains the aircraft and bears virtually all the expenses and risks of actual ownership, but it does not legally own them.

Until the mid 1940s, most leases were the kind in which the lessee contracted to rent an asset for a period much shorter than the asset's expected life, as in example (1) above. By the late 1940s, however, lease arrangements were being worked out in which the lessee agreed to rent the asset for substantially all its useful life and to assume most of the risks of ownership, such as maintenance or property tax increases. The role of the lessor became much more passive: the lessor supplied the financing but did little else.

Essentially, the lessor had become merely the person who financed, and perhaps supplied, the asset. We might say that the lessor's "debt" was repaid in instalment payments termed rental payments. The effective owner had become the lessee inasmuch as that person now assumed most of the risks and duties of ownership. Although the substance of such a rental arrangement is essentially similar to the purchase of a capital asset and the assumption of its related debt, until the late 1970s the Canadian accounting treatment of these leases varied widely. Under the accounting standards of that time, the lease payments could be shown as expenses, and then no asset or liability in connection with this asset acquisition would be shown in the balance sheet.

This posed a new problem for accountants, because substantially similar financial arrangements for the acquisition of capital assets were being reported very differently in the financial statements of the affected firms, depending on whether the legal form of the acquisition was that of a lease or an outright purchase. Part of the background to this accounting problem was that accountants had been very careful not to reflect in the accounts any **executory contracts,** or contracts in which neither party had yet performed any of the terms. For example, an agreement for a company to purchase merchandise is an executory contract because the supplier has not yet furnished the goods and the purchaser has not yet paid for them. It is not recorded in the accounts until one of the parties to the contract has fulfilled at least some of the terms, such as delivering the merchandise or making a payment.

Executory contracts should not be confused with **executory costs,** which are the non-financing costs of maintaining an asset being leased. These would include such things as municipal taxes on the asset, maintenance, and heat. Either the lessee or lessor may be responsible for executory costs, and the terms of the lease would provide the details. In the case of a lease contract, all that the parties undertake to do is to provide the use of an asset and to make rental payments for it — all things that are to happen in the future. Under accounting standards in Canada prior to 1978, the expense and revenue related to that asset would be recorded when the services were provided, not when the asset came into first use. To give accounting recognition to the signing of such leases and treat signing as the equivalent of acquiring a capital asset was a major shift in accounting conventions. This shift can be interpreted as the growing influence of the view that, in representing events through accounting, priority should be given to interpreting the *economic* substance of the transaction rather than reflecting the *legal form* in which it was transacted.

This shift started in the United States in the early 1950s, but it took over two decades to develop into its present form. In 1953 a predecessor body to the FASB made a tentative suggestion that a lease that appeared to be the economic equivalent of a purchase should be treated as such for accounting purposes. This was reinforced in 1964; but it was not until 1976, when the FASB issued its Standard No. 13, "Accounting for Leases," that the present treatment came into clearer focus. Once such a lease was signed, the transaction would be treated for accounting purposes as if the company had purchased an asset and assumed an instalment debt. There have been over half-a-dozen subsequent pronouncements from the FASB on leases, but they have all been for the purpose of clarifying the original FASB stand of 1978. The *CICA Handbook* section on leases [Section 3065] was issued in 1978. In it the conditions for capitalization adopted by the FASB were set out as guides. In other words, the *CICA*

Handbook emphasized the need to look at the economic substance of lease arrangements. Prior to 1978 some Canadian companies followed the U.S. pronouncements inasmuch as there was no definitive Canadian practice.

Issues of Financing

A company that decides to acquire a long-lived asset often has the choice between buying it outright or leasing it. Such long-lived assets would include cars, computers, photocopiers, trucks, aircraft, and ships. If the company purchases the asset outright, it will frequently finance the acquisition through the supplier. For instance, if the company purchased a truck, it would likely finance the purchase through a finance company affiliated with the truck manufacturer, such as General Motors Acceptance Corporation.

The choice between leasing and outright purchase frequently depends on such issues as (i) the relative cost of borrowing, (ii) the availability of funds for each choice, (iii) income tax considerations, and (iv) the relative risk borne by the company acquiring the assets. The decision whether to finance the purchase by a long-term debt or by a long-term lease should be influenced by financing issues of the sort just listed. The choice should *not* be influenced by the accounting treatment it will receive, although this appears to have occurred prior to the accounting changes described above in the preceding section.

Issues of Accounting

The impact of the different accounting treatments can be shown by an example. Suppose Tichborne Trucking has purchased its trucks, each costing $90,000 and lasting three years. It finances them by giving the supplier a promissory note at 15% interest and making monthly payments of blended principal and interest of $3,119.88 to retire the debt in thirty-six months. (The $3,119.88 was determined using interest-annuity tables and could have been found using a pocket calculator that had a built-in function for determining the monthly payment needed to retire $90,000 at 15% over thirty-six months.) The entry for the purchase would read as follows:

Fixed asset — truck	90,000.00	
Note payable		90,000.00
To record purchase of truck.		

At the end of the first month the entry to record depreciation (using the straight-line method) would be as follows:

Depreciation expense	2,500.00	
Accumulated depreciation		2,500.00

To record depreciation for month (90,000/36).

The entry to record the monthly payment on the promissory note would be the following:

Note payable	1,994.88	
Interest expense	1,125.00	
Cash in bank		3,119.88

To record monthly payment on note payable, as follows:

Payment	$3,119.88
Interest — 15% on 90,000 for one month	1,125.00
Repayment on note payable	$1,994.88

Therefore, the total costs for the month of depreciation and financing would be as follows:

Interest	$1,125.00
Depreciation	2,500.00
	$3,625.00

Now suppose that Tichborne enters into a different kind of agreement with the truck supplier. Instead of buying a truck, it leases it for three years. Tichborne agrees to cover all costs of operating the truck, keeping it insured and well maintained, and generally making sure that the lessor has to bear no costs other than financing. At the end of the thirty-six months the lessee can buy the truck for a nominal amount. The lessor agrees to the same financing terms as those in the purchase. The lessor is essentially in the same position as the holder of the promissory note in the preceding example. We will assume that the monthly rental rate would be the same as the monthly payment under the promissory note. In other words, Tichborne would pay $3,119.88 monthly.

Before the Canadian accounting standards were issued in 1978, the entry to record the monthly rental payment might have been as follows:

Lease expense	3,119.88	
Cash in bank		3,119.88

To record lease payment expense for month according to the terms of the lease contract.

Compare this with the cost of $3,625.00 that would have been recorded in the books for the first month if the company had purchased the truck. Of course, over the three years of the rental period, the amount paid under the lease arrangements above would add up to exactly the total cost of depreciation and interest, but in the early years of use the lease expense is less. It only becomes greater in the later years. This is shown in

Table 14-1 below. (For an explanation of the basic mathematics of leasing, see Appendix 14-1.)

TABLE 14-1: TICHBORNE TRUCKING
COMPARISON OF MONTHLY RECORDED COST OF PURCHASING AND OF LEASING

Month	(A) Principal outstanding	(B) Interest expense at 15%	(C) Monthly depreciation	(D) = (B) + (C) Purchasing cost	(E) Leasing cost	(F) = (D) − (E) Difference between purchasing and leasing
1	$90,000.00	$1,125.00	$2,500.00	$3,625.00	$3,119.88	$505.12
2	88,005.12	1,100.06	2,500.00	3,600.06	3,119.88	480.18
3	85,985.30	1,074.82	2,500.00	3,574.82	3,119.88	454.94
4	83,940.24	1,049.25	2,500.00	3,549.25	3,119.88	429.37
5	81,869.61	1,023.37	2,500.00	3,523.37	3,119.88	403.49
6	79,773.10	997.16	2,500.00	3,497.16	3,119.88	377.28
7	77,650.39	970.63	2,500.00	3,470.63	3,119.88	350.75
8	75,501.14	943.76	2,500.00	3,443.76	3,119.88	323.88
9	73,325.02	916.56	2,500.00	3,416.56	3,119.88	296.68
10	71,121.70	889.02	2,500.00	3,389.02	3,119.88	269.14
11	68,890.85	861.14	2,500.00	3,361.14	3,119.88	241.26
12	66,632.10	832.90	2,500.00	3,332.90	3,119.88	213.02
13	64,345.12	804.31	2,500.00	3,304.31	3,119.88	184.43
14	62,029.56	775.37	2,500.00	3,275.37	3,119.88	155.49
15	59,685.05	746.06	2,500.00	3,246.06	3,119.88	126.18
16	57,311.23	716.39	2,500.00	3,216.39	3,119.88	96.51
17	54,907.74	686.35	2,500.00	3,186.35	3,119.88	66.47
18	52,474.21	655.93	2,500.00	3,155.93	3,119.88	36.05
19	50,010.25	625.13	2,500.00	3,125.13	3,119.88	5.25
20	47,515.50	593.94	2,500.00	3,093.94	3,119.88	− 25.94
21	44,989.57	562.37	2,500.00	3,062.37	3,119.88	− 57.51
22	42,432.05	530.40	2,500.00	3,030.40	3,119.88	− 89.48
23	39,842.58	498.03	2,500.00	2,998.03	3,119.88	− 121.85
24	37,220.73	465.26	2,500.00	2,965.26	3,119.88	− 154.62
25	34,566.11	432.08	2,500.00	2,932.08	3,119.88	− 187.80
26	31,878.30	398.48	2,500.00	2,898.48	3,119.88	− 221.40
27	29,156.90	364.46	2,500.00	2,864.46	3,119.88	− 255.42
28	26,401.48	330.02	2,500.00	2,830.02	3,119.88	− 289.86
29	23,611.62	295.15	2,500.00	2,795.15	3,119.88	− 324.73
30	20,786.89	259.84	2,500.00	2,759.84	3,119.88	− 360.04
31	17,926.84	224.09	2,500.00	2,724.09	3,119.88	− 395.79
32	15,031.05	187.89	2,500.00	2,687.89	3,119.88	− 431.99
33	12,099.06	151.24	2,500.00	2,651.24	3,119.88	− 468.64
34	9,130.42	114.13	2,500.00	2,614.13	3,119.88	− 505.75
35	6,124.67	76.56	2,500.00	2,576.56	3,119.88	− 543.32
36	3,081.34	38.52	2,500.00	2,538.52	3,119.88	− 581.34
		$22,315.66	$90,000.00	$112,315.66	$112,315.66	$ 0.00

In the table, observe how the monthly total of interest and depreciation (Column D) exceeds the amount of the monthly lease payment (Column E) in the early periods, then gradually drops below it. The difference between the two is shown in Column F. For the three-year period the totals of Columns D and E are identical; the timing is different, but the total amounts are the same. For a company that wanted to show low costs in the early period of asset ownership, the shift offered by leasing in the timing of the expense recognition would appear attractive. The reported income would be higher in the early years. In addition to yielding a higher *reported* income in the earlier years, the lease method would make the balance sheet appear more attractive. (For instance, the ratio of debt to equity would be more attractive if the long-term liability with respect to the lease is omitted.) If the asset were leased, no fixed asset and no promissory note would appear on the balance sheet. The monthly cash flow would be the same under both arrangements. In our example the term of the loan, the term of the lease, and the life of the asset were all made the same to make comparisons easier, but the same principles would still apply had they been different.

Under these circumstances it is hardly surprising that it became very popular to finance the purchase of fixed assets through long-term leases and to treat rental payments as expenses. There was increasing concern, however, that this so-called **off balance-sheet financing** meant that readers of financial statements would not be aware of the impact of lease financing on financial stability and reported income. This led to a two-pronged development: First, a movement arose to give similar accounting treatment to either the purchase or long-term lease of an asset if the economic circumstances were essentially similar — even if the legal arrangements were different. Second, there was a growing demand that the notes to the financial statements show more details about the commitments of the company for such items as lease contracts. Once again, this illustrates the classic contest in accounting reporting between *legal form* and *economic substance.*

Types of Leases

CAPITAL LEASES

A lease which is treated for accounting purposes as if the lessee had bought an asset and assumed a debt is frequently referred to as a **capital lease**. We can identify three distinct roles that are played under such a lease:

1. The **supplier** provides the item being leased, but does not necessarily finance it. In the case of a leased aircraft, for example, the supplier would be a manufacturer such as Boeing or McDonnell Douglas.

2. The **user** takes physical possession of the item being leased and uses it for some productive purpose. In return for having the use of the item, the user makes periodic payments to a third party, the financier. The user does not have legal ownership of the item during the term of the lease. With an aircraft the user would be the airline that has the right to use the aircraft and paint its insignia on the fuselage.

3. The **financier** provides the funds to finance the purchase of the item being leased. The financier is paid back over time by the user. The financier has legal ownership of the leased item, but no rights to its physical use so long as the terms of the lease are adhered to. With aircraft the financier is often a company specifically in the leasing business, such as General Electric Credit Corporation.

Sometimes two of the above roles are played by the same company. In general we can distinguish three types of capital leases, depending on how the roles are filled: (i) direct-financing lease (three organizations), (ii) sales-type lease (two organizations — the supplier is also the financier), (iii) sale-and-leaseback (two organizations — the supplier is also the user). Each type demands its own special accounting treatment, as explained below.

Direct-Financing Lease

Under a **direct-financing lease** all three roles are played by three separate organizations. The supplier provides the item to be leased and is paid for it by the financier, who then provides the item to the user under a lease contract. The financier then becomes the lessor, and the user the lessee. The supplier makes a normal trading profit, and the financier's income is solely the interest income arising from the lease. The lessee simply pays the going rate for the financing and use of the asset.

An example would be a fast-food outlet that was built to the specifications of the franchiser (such as Wendy's, McDonald's, or Burger King) by some contractor (the supplier), sold to an investor willing to provide the financing (the financier/lessor), and then leased long-term to some franchisee (user/lessee) who operates the outlet.

The accounting treatment here is for the lessor to record the purchase of the item from the supplier and its subsequent sale at its cost to the lessee in return for a long-term receivable arising under the lease. The lessee accounts for the transaction as if it had purchased the item and assumed a long-term debt. The supplier accounts for the transaction like any sale of merchandise, which in fact it is.

Sales-type Lease

Under a **sales-type lease**, the role of supplier and financier are played by the same company. In its supplier role the company manufactures or obtains the item and perhaps installs it for the customer. In return, the company receives the selling price of the item, which it matches against its cost of goods sold to derive its trading profit. Then, in its financier role the company provides the funds to finance the asset for the user. In return the company earns interest income. The lessee simply pays the going rate for the financing and use of the asset.

An example would be a contractor who puts up buildings (such as banks or fast-food-franchises) for long-term lease to tenants and continues to own them through the term of the lease. In this case the contractor as supplier would record a profit from the construction and "sale" of the building, and the contractor as financier/lessor would record the interest income implicit in terms of the lease.

The accounting treatment here is for the company to separate its two roles of supplier and financier, by recording a trading profit from its supplier role and interest income from its financier role. When the lease begins, the financier/lessor has a long-term receivable with respect to the lease on its books, and the user/lessee has a plant asset and a long-term lease obligation payable on its books.

Sale-and-Leaseback

Under a sale-and-leaseback, the role of supplier and user are played by the same company. In its supplier role the company provides the item to be leased (frequently one of its own buildings); whereas in its user role the same company continues to use the asset, but now as a lessee instead of owner. The financier provides the funds and in return gets the interest income implicit in the lease.

An example of this occurred when Bell Canada Enterprises purchased a downtown Toronto office building from what is now Canada Trust. The trust company as supplier received a large payment from Bell (the financier). In return, Canada Trust passed its legal title to the building to Bell, but it now continues to use the building as a lessee.

The accounting treatment here is to regard the actions of the lessee as follows: it "sold" the building to the lessor (financier), purchased it back at the new price implied by the lease, and assumed a long-term debt under the lease. Depreciation is based on this new price, and any gain or loss on the "sale" is amortized over the life of the lease in a pattern that matches the depreciation pattern.

OPERATING LEASES

An **operating lease** is any lease which does not meet the tests of a capital lease (to be discussed in detail shortly). The roles discussed above become unimportant since no sale and purchase of an asset is deemed to take place.

Examples can be found in many types of short-term leases: renting an apartment for a year; renting a car for a week or renting equipment for a weekend (to clean rugs or till the garden or mix cement).

The accounting treatment here is for the lessor to continue to show the leased assets on its books, and for the lessee to show no acquisition of a capital asset and no assumption of long-term debt. Lease payments are treated as an expense of using the asset.

DISTINGUISHING BETWEEN TYPES OF LEASES

The accounting treatment for each kind of lease discussed above is clearly different. Hence it is important to understand the criteria that are used to distinguish between the various types of leases. First, let us clarify the conditions that make a lease a capital lease. For lessees, the main question is whether property rights have passed to them with the signing of the lease; that is, whether they have obtained the benefits and risks of ownership.

According to the *CICA Handbook* [3065.06], this is assumed to have happened if *any one* of the following conditions are met:

1. The lease transfers ownership (**legal title**) of the property to the lessee by the end of the lease term.

2. The lease contains a **bargain purchase option** (i.e., the right to buy the asset at less than market value at the end of the lease).

3. The lease term is of such a duration that the lessee will receive substantially all (usually 75% or more) of the economic benefit expected to be derived from the use of the leased property over its life span.

4. The lessor is assured of recovering the investment in the leased property and of earning a return on the investment as a result of the lease agreement. This is assumed to exist if at the beginning of the lease, the present value of the total of all the minimum lease payments is equal to substantially all (usually 90% or more) of the fair value of the leased property. Costs related to the operation of the leased property (e.g., maintenance) are not to be counted as part of the minimum lease payment. The discount rate to be used in calculating the present value for the lessor is the rate that makes the annual rental payments (less the portion representing operating costs) plus the residual value equal to the fair value of the property at the start of the lease [*CICA* 3065.03m]. For the lessee it is the lower of the lessee's pretax incremental borrowing rate and the lessor's rate (if known). Note that using the lower rate tends to increase the amount of the asset and the liability capitalized.

If any of the above have occurred, then the lease is considered to be a capital lease. Conditions (1) and (2) are designed to identify those circumstances in which the regular payments under the lease (plus the bargain purchase price at the end) have covered essentially all the original costs plus the financing charges. In other words, here the lessee has paid for the asset by the time the lease is over. Condition (3) identifies those leases where the asset has been largely used up during the original term of the lease. Condition (4) has been described as the one that has been hardest to get around for those wishing to make a capital lease look like an operating lease. If the lessor is willing to draw up a lease in which less than 90% of his capital and depreciation costs are covered, then he or she is willing to assume more risks than most lessors writing capital leases.

For the lessee, the only distinction that has to be made is between operating and capital leases. For making that distinction the above test is used. If the lessee is also the supplier and if there is a sale-and-leaseback arrangement, then the profit deferral arrangements also apply.

For the lessor, there are two additional issues. First, there may be greater uncertainty than usual about (i) the ability to collect the anticipated rent or (ii) the ability to contain future costs of the lease within the estimated amounts. In both cases the lessor would not have sufficient assurance to capitalize the expected lease payments. Therefore the lessor would treat the lease as an operating one (even though the lessee would treat it as a capital lease) [*CICA* 3065.07]. The second issue is whether the lessor makes a trading profit. If the lease is a capital one and the lessor makes a trading profit, then it is treated as a sales-type lease. Otherwise it is treated as a financing lease.

These ways of distinguishing between the various types of leases are summarized in the diagram below.

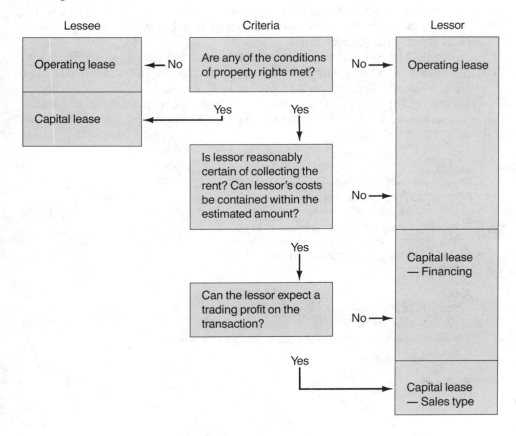

Once the decision has been made which type of lease is being accounted for, the accounting treatment should follow the general principles already outlined. We will now illustrate these principles in detail.

Accounting for Operating Leases

Accounting for operating leases is straightforward when the lessor provides the lessee with assets that are immediately usable without alteration or addition and when there is no charge except the periodic charge for the asset's use (e.g., renting a car for the day). Operating leases become more complex, however, when they are for an extended term such as five years and the lessee is required to make alterations or provide leasehold improvements at his or her own expense. Complexity also can arise when the pattern of payments is uneven. For instance, the tenant may be required to provide a deposit to be applied against the last month's rent.

In such complex cases the accountant's main concern is to match the total cost of the lease against the periods that benefit from it. Thus the cost of leasehold improvements or other initial costs would be spread over the total number of months during which the lease is in existence. Similarly, deposits against future rents would be carried as assets and expensed at the appropriate time.

For example, Ms. Able starts up her own CA practice and rents an office in August. The office is rented to her on an "as is" basis for five years for $500 a month starting 1 September. She is required to provide a deposit of $800, which will be used to pay the last month's rent of $500 and any necessary cleaning on her moving out. She makes some alterations costing $2,400 before moving in. The journal entries would read as follows:

August

Prepaid rent — September (balance-sheet asset)	500.00	
Rent deposit (balance-sheet asset)	800.00	
Cash in bank		1,300.00

To record payment of September rent of $500 and deposit to be applied to last month's rent of $500 and to possible clean-up costs of $300.

August

Leasehold improvements	2,400.00	
Cash in bank		2,400.00

To record expenditures for leasehold improvements prior to moving in.

September

Rent expense	540.00	
Prepaid rent		500.00
Accumulated amortization		40.00

To record monthly rental of $500 and write-off of 1/60 of $2,400 leasehold improvements.

Note that the main feature of accounting for operating leases is to make sure that the matching principle is adhered to.

Accounting for Capital Leases

The general principle in regard to capital leases is that they are treated as if they constituted the purchase (or sale) of a capital asset that has been financed with instalment debt effective on the date the first lease payment is due (or the date the lessee gets possession). Since the lease does not usually indicate the capitalized value of the asset and debt, the present value of the lease payments is capitalized. Let us work through a detailed example.

Glenora Manufacturing Limited arranged with Tweed Computers to lease a computer from Tweed for five years. The computer cost Tweed $1,400,000; but the retail cost in calculating the lease payments was taken as $1,800,000, and the interest rate used in calculating the monthly payments of $43,773 (rounded off from $43,772.50 for simplicity) was 16%. All *executory costs* (i.e., those future costs related to the operation of the leased property such as insurance and maintenance) were to be borne by Glenora, the lessee. The useful life of the computer was judged to be about five years, and it was thought to have no salvage value at the end of that time. It would thus be a capital lease (because condition 3 above is met). Hence Glenora should treat the transaction as the purchase of a plant asset, and Tweed should treat it as a sale.

LESSEE

The lessee, Glenora Manufacturing Limited, does not necessarily know the wholesale and retail costs of the computer. Therefore it would calculate the imputed cost as the present value of the lease payments. What interest rate should it use for this discounting? if it used the interest rate implicit in the lease, 16%, then the journal entry would be as follows:

Equipment under capital lease — computer	$1,800,000.00	
Obligation under capital lease		$1,800,000.00

To record acquisition of computer on a capital
lease. Cost is calculated as the present value
of 60 monthly payments of $43,773
discounted at 16%.

Suppose, however, that Glenora could borrow money at 15%. In that case the present value of the stream of payments represents a greater cost to Glenora, namely $1,839,980. The accepted accounting treatment is to require Glenora to use the lower of the two rates, thus increasing the amount capitalized. This will increase the total annual amortization, but lower the total imputed interest expense. Since the allocation of interest costs tends to be heavier in the early periods, this approach will tend to even out the combined amortization and interest charge. The upper limit on the amount capitalized is the fair market value of the asset. Because we have assumed here that the cost of the asset to Glenora would have been $1,800,000 on an outright sale, we would continue to use this amount in the journal entry above.

If the lease had contained a bargain purchase option, the capitalized amount of the lease would contain this payment as well.

As our example stands, bargain purchase option would not be possible simply because the computer is thought to have no commercial value at the end of the lease. If, however, it did have an expected commercial value of say $1,000, then any term in the lease giving the lessee the right to purchase the computer at the end of the lease for any amount significantly below $1,000 would be regarded as a bargain purchase option.

Let us return to our original example. At the end of the first month Glenora would make the following two journal entries:

Interest expense	24,000.00	
Obligation under capital lease	19,773.00	
Cash in bank		43,773.00

To record payment of obligation under lease.
   Interest expense is $1/12$ of 16% of $1,800,000.

Amortization expense	30,000.00	
Accumulated amortization		30,000.00

To record amortization (on a straight-line basis) over
   expected five-year life — $1/60$ of 1,800,000.

In general, assets acquired under capital leases are shown as a separate group on the balance sheet [*CICA* 3065.21]. Similarly, separate disclosure is made of lease obligations [*CICA* 3065.22].

LESSOR

Tweed Computers may have one of two relationships as a lessor of the computer to Glenora. First, Tweed may simply be acting as a source of financing in the purchase of the computer and not be expecting any profit from the transaction except a return on the funds invested in the lease transaction. In this case Tweed would presumably get the computer from a supplier. This is a direct-financing lease. Second, Tweed may be a manufacturer or dealer of computers, and it may be using leasing as a means of selling its product. It would then expect both a profit on the sale as well as financial income over the life of the lease. This is a sales-type lease. In our example, it appears that Tweed expects a gross margin of $400,000 on the computer. Hence the initial entries would reflect a sales-type lease as follows:

Cost of goods sold	1,400,000.00	
Inventory — computer		1,400,000.00

To record cost of computer sold to Glenora
   Manufacturing on a sales-type lease.

Instalment note receivable	1,800,000.00	
Sales		1,800,000.00

To record sale of computer to Glenora
   Manufacturing on a sales-type lease.

Note that the gross margin of $400,000 would be reported as income in the period when the computer was delivered — that is, on the same basis as if it had been sold outright. The usual realization test applies here for recognizing income.

At the end of the first month when the payment is received, the following entry would be made:

Bank	43,773.00	
Interest income		24,000.00
Instalment note receivable		19,773.00

To record monthly payment on lease. Interest is
1/12 of 16% of $1,800,000.

If there had been initial direct costs connected with the lease, such as legal or engineering fees, these would be written off in the first period and the net income earned on the sale would be reduced accordingly [*CICA* 3065.48].

For example, suppose Tweed had costs at the inception of the lease of $100,000 (in the form of legal fees and financing fees). It would then charge these costs as expenses of the period in which the sale occurs. It would not defer them to later periods, as it would with a financing lease (to be explained below).

The accounting treatment of items for the lessor and the lessee is quite symmetrical. Thus, the computer is no longer an asset on the lessor's books, but it is an asset on the lessee's. Similarly, the lessor has an instalment note receivable, and the lessee has a similar note payable. But there are two features that may prove to be exceptions to this symmetrical treatment. First, the lessor and lessee may in some circumstances use different rates of capitalization. Second, if the lessor is unable to estimate costs and revenues connected with the lease with reasonable certainty, the lessor may not capitalize the lease, whereas the lessee will. This second feature is another example of the realization principle at work: if the lessor cannot estimate costs with reasonable certainty, then the transaction does not meet the realization test of having the major uncertainties in the past.

If Tweed had entered into a direct-financing lease, then it would have capitalized any up-front costs instead of treating them as period expenses. This would have spread the up-front costs over the life of the lease. (By contrast, under a sales-type lease, any up-front costs are expensed immediately as part of cost of sales.) The following procedure is used to effect this cost spreading. First, the cost of the asset and all up-front costs (such as legal fees) are added together to arrive at the total investment. Second, the **effective yield** (i.e., the interest rate that equates cash inflow with cash outflow) is calculated by comparing the total investment with the total cash flow generated by the lease. Finally, the annual yield of the lease is taken to be the effective yield multiplied by the total investment.

In order that the amount of up-front costs under direct-financing leases be disclosed, the *CICA Handbook* [3065.40] requires that they be shown as both income and expense items in the year of initial financing. This has no effect on the reported income of the year. Let us illustrate cost spreading under a direct-financing lease by modifying our original computer example. Suppose Tweed purchased the computer from a third party for $1,800,000 and supplied it to Glenora on the same terms as outlined above (i.e., to be paid for at $43,773.00 per month to yield 16%). Further suppose that Tweed incurred up-front costs of legal fees and financing fees totalling $100,000. Now, Tweed's *effective yield* is not 16%; for the $100,000 installation fee must be added on to the $1,800,000 for a total cost to Tweed of $1,900,000. In fact, the effective yield is now 13.555% instead of 16%. (This could be calculated using interest tables, a pocket calculator, or a personal computer spreadsheet program.)

TABLE 14-2: TWEED COMPUTERS
RECOGNIZING INCOME UNDER A DIRECT-FINANCING LEASE WITH INITIAL COSTS OF $100,000

Schedule of Loan Payments
(Monthly payment = $43,772.50)

Schedule of Effective Revenue Earned

Month	A Capital owing	B Interest at 16%	C Repayment	D Capital owing	E Interest at 13.555%	F Repayment	G Revenue recorded
1	$1,800,000.00	$24,000.00	$19,772.50	$1,900,000.00	$21,462.08	$22,310.42	$121,462.08
2	1,780,227.50	23,736.37	20,036.13	1,877,689.58	21,210.07	22,562.43	21,210.07
3	1,760,191.37	23,469.22	20,303.28	1,855,127.15	20,955.21	22,817.29	20,955.21
4	1,739,888.08	23,198.51	20,573.99	1,832,309.86	20,697.47	23,075.03	20,697.47
5	1,719,314.09	22,924.19	20,848.31	1,809,234.83	20,436.82	23,335.68	20,436.82
6	1,698,465.78	22,646.21	21,126.29	1,785,899.14	20,173.22	23,599.28	20,173.22
7	1,677,339.49	22,364.53	21,407.97	1,762,299.86	19,906.65	23,865.85	19,906.65
8	1,655,931.52	22,079.09	21,693.41	1,738,434.01	19,637.06	24,135.44	19,637.06
9	1,634,238.10	21,789.84	21,982.66	1,714,298.57	19,364.43	24,408.07	19,364.43
10	1,612,255.45	21,496.74	22,275.76	1,689,890.50	19,088.72	24,683.78	19,088.72
11	1,589,979.69	21,199.73	22,572.77	1,665,206.72	18,809.90	24,962.60	18,809.90
12	1,567,406.91	20,898.76	22,873.74	1,640,244.12	18,527.92	25,244.58	18,527.92
13	1,544,533.17	20,593.78	23,178.72	1,614,999.54	18,242.77	25,529.73	18,242.77
14	1,521,354.45	20,284.73	23,487.77	1,589,469.81	17,954.39	25,818.11	17,954.39
15	1,497,866.67	19,971.56	23,800.94	1,563,651.69	17,662.75	26,109.75	17,662.75
16	1,474,065.73	19,654.21	24,118.29	1,537,541.94	17,367.82	26,404.68	17,367.82
17	1,449,947.44	19,332.63	24,439.87	1,511,137.26	17,069.55	26,702.95	17,069.55
18	1,425,507.57	19,006.77	24,765.73	1,484,434.31	16,767.92	27,004.58	16,767.92
19	1,400,741.84	18,676.56	25,095.94	1,457,429.74	16,462.88	27,309.62	16,462.88
20	1,375,645.90	18,341.95	25,430.55	1,430,120.12	16,154.40	27,618.10	16,154.40
21	1,350,215.34	18,002.87	25,769.63	1,402,502.02	15,842.43	27,930.07	15,842.43
22	1,324,445.71	17,659.28	26,113.22	1,374,571.95	15,526.94	28,245.56	15,526.94
23	1,298,332.49	17,311.10	26,461.40	1,346,326.38	15,207.88	28,564.62	15,207.88
24	1,271,871.09	16,958.28	26,814.22	1,317,761.76	14,885.22	28,887.28	14,885.22
25	1,245,056.87	16,600.76	27,171.74	1,288,874.48	14,558.91	29,213.59	14,558.91
26	1,217,885.13	16,238.47	27,534.03	1,259,660.89	14,228.92	29,543.58	14,228.92
27	1,190,351.10	15,871.35	27,901.15	1,230,117.31	13,895.20	29,877.30	13,895.20

Period							
28	1,162,449.95	15,499.33	28,273.17	1,200,240.01	13,557.71	30,214.79	13,557.71
29	1,134,176.78	15,122.36	28,650.14	1,170,025.22	13,216.41	30,556.09	13,216.41
30	1,105,526.64	14,740.36	29,032.14	1,139,469.13	12,871.25	30,901.25	12,871.25
31	1,076,494.49	14,353.26	29,419.24	1,108,567.88	12,522.20	31,250.30	12,522.20
32	1,047,075.25	13,961.00	29,811.50	1,077,317.58	12,169.20	31,603.30	12,169.20
33	1,017,263.75	13,563.52	30,208.98	1,045,714.28	11,812.21	31,960.29	11,812.21
34	987,054.77	13,160.73	30,611.77	1,013,753.99	11,451.20	32,321.30	11,451.20
35	956,443.00	12,752.57	31,019.93	981,432.69	11,086.10	32,686.40	11,086.10
36	925,423.08	12,338.97	31,433.53	948,746.29	10,716.88	33,055.62	10,716.88
37	893,989.55	11,919.86	31,852.64	915,690.67	10,343.49	33,429.01	10,343.49
38	862,136.91	11,495.16	32,277.34	882,261.66	9,965.88	33,806.62	9,965.88
39	829,859.57	11,064.79	32,707.71	848,455.04	9,584.01	34,188.49	9,584.01
40	797,151.86	10,628.69	33,143.81	814,266.55	9,197.82	34,574.68	9,197.82
41	764,008.05	10,186.77	33,585.73	779,691.87	8,807.27	34,965.23	8,807.27
42	730,422.33	9,738.96	34,033.54	744,726.64	8,412.31	35,360.19	8,412.31
43	696,388.79	9,285.18	34,487.32	709,366.44	8,012.89	35,759.61	8,012.89
44	661,901.48	8,825.35	34,947.15	673,606.83	7,608.95	36,163.55	7,608.95
45	626,954.33	8,359.39	35,413.11	637,443.28	7,200.45	36,572.05	7,200.45
46	591,541.22	7,887.22	35,885.28	600,871.23	6,787.34	36,985.16	6,787.34
47	555,655.94	7,408.75	36,363.75	563,886.07	6,369.56	37,402.94	6,369.56
48	519,292.18	6,923.90	36,848.60	526,483.14	5,947.07	37,825.43	5,947.07
49	482,443.58	6,432.58	37,339.92	488,657.70	5,519.80	38,252.70	5,519.80
50	445,103.66	5,934.72	37,837.78	450,405.00	5,087.70	38,684.80	5,087.70
51	407,265.88	5,430.21	38,342.29	411,720.20	4,650.72	39,121.78	4,650.72
52	368,923.59	4,918.98	38,853.52	372,598.42	4,208.81	39,563.69	4,208.81
53	330,070.07	4,400.93	39,371.57	333,034.73	3,761.90	40,010.60	3,761.90
54	290,698.50	3,875.98	39,896.52	293,024.14	3,309.95	40,462.55	3,309.95
55	250,801.98	3,344.03	40,428.47	252,561.59	2,852.89	40,919.61	2,852.89
56	210,373.51	2,804.98	40,967.52	211,641.98	2,390.67	41,381.83	2,390.67
57	169,405.99	2,258.75	41,513.75	170,260.15	1,923.23	41,849.27	1,923.23
58	127,892.24	1,705.23	42,067.27	128,410.88	1,450.51	42,321.99	1,450.51
59	85,824.97	1,144.33	42,628.17	86,088.89	972.45	42,800.05	972.45
60	43,196.80	575.70	43,196.80	43,288.84	483.66	43,288.84	483.66
End	0.00			0.00	(0.00)		0.00
		$826,350.00			$726,350.00		$826,350.00

The accounting treatment in this case would proceed in the following manner. Because the annual yield is calculated as 13.555%, the total yield over the entire period is $100,000 less than it would have been with the 16% rate. Examine Table 14-2. Columns A to C show the schedule of loan payments. The regular monthly payments of $43,772.50 for the retirement of the capital of the note receivable reduce it to nil at the end of sixty payments. Columns D to F show that the effective yield is only 13.555% when the initial capital rises to $1,900,000 from $1,800,000 and the monthly payments remain unchanged. Note that the total of column E is $100,000 less than the total of Column B.

In the year in which the expenses of $100,000 are incurred, an equal amount is shown as lease income and expense. Therefore the net after expenses is unchanged by the timing of the $100,000 expenditure. The amount of revenue each month is shown in Column G. Note that it totals to the same income as Column B, but the timing of the income recognition is different. In our example the $100,000 is incurred in the first month. Thus $100,000 of the total income is moved into the first month to offset the initial expenses. Nevertheless, the net income in each period remains at 13.555% of the unretired balance of capital.

The four journal entries in the first month would be as follows:

Instalment note receivable	1,800,000.00	
Cash in bank		1,800,000.00
To record purchase of computer that was supplied to Glenora on a capital lease.		
Rental installation expense	100,000.00	
Cash in bank		100,000.00
To record installation expense.		
Instalment note receivable	100,000.00	
Rental income		100,000.00
To set up rental income as an offset to installation expense, thus effectively capitalizing the installation expense.		
Bank	43,773.00	
Rental income		21,462.08
Instalment note receivable		22,310.92
To record first payment on lease and income on balance of investment of $1,900,000 at effective rate of 13.555% = 21,462.08.		

(margin note: direct financing type lease)

Because the $100,000 of expenses have already been charged to income for the period, the net effect on income is $21,462.08. The net result is that each period is credited with income equal to the effective rate of 13.555% multiplied by the amount of the investment still unretired.

Leases on Land

A potential anomaly arises if all of a lease for both buildings and land is treated as a capital lease, because then the capitalized value of the lease related to the land will be taken as the purchase price of the land. If the lessee has either legal title to the land at the end of the lease or a bargain purchase option, then the capitalized value of the land plus the payment under the bargain purchase option could be considered its purchase price. If the lessee has neither a bargain purchase option nor the right to renew the lease, then the lessee would lose the right to use the land at the end of the lease. Does this make the land a depreciable asset that should be amortized over the life of the lease? It is unusual to amortize land. Nevertheless, in principle there does not seem to be any reason why one should not recognize a limited service-life for land, as for any asset. If one were to do this, then the annual costs under the lease would be the amortization of the land and the implicit interest costs. Unless one used the interest method of amortization the combined annual costs would be higher in the earlier years of the lease and lower toward the end.

The *CICA Handbook* [3065.73], however, requires that land should *not* be capitalized at all. Instead, the land portion of the lease should be treated as an operating lease if the amount is significant. To do so, the lessor and lessee should allocate the minimum lease payment between land and buildings according to their market value. Then, the portion of the lease attributed to the building should be treated as a capital lease, and the portion attributed to the land should be treated as an operating lease.

Accounting for Sale-and-Leasebacks

A company that wishes to generate cash will sometimes sell one of its assets to another company and at the same time agree to lease it back. The accounting treatment for this arrangement depends on whether the substance of the transaction indicates that it is effectively a sale from the lessee to the lessor. This is determined by the same tests used for other leases. As already discussed, the distinguishing feature of the sale-and-leaseback is that the role of *supplier* of the leased asset and the role of *lessee* are combined.

Let us work through an example in detail. On 1 March 19X3 Movies Limited sells a motion picture theatre that it owns to Investor Limited for $580,000. The land is estimated to be worth $250,000, and the building $330,000. At the same time the two parties enter into an agreement under which Movie Limited agrees to rent the theatre for thirty years at an annual rental of $61,282.50 payable at the end of each year. Movie Limited agrees to pay all taxes, maintenance, heat, and other operating costs. At the end of the lease Investor Limited can sell the site at market price and keep the proceeds. The theatre building has a historic cost of $200,000 and accumulated depreciation of $117,000 at the time of sale. The land has a book value of $50,000. The residual value of land and buildings at the end of the lease is estimated to be $40,000 once the demolition costs of the theatre are subtracted.

The first step is to decide whether the lease should be capitalized. This lease does not transfer ownership of the property back to the lessee and it does not contain a bargain purchase option. Without more information it is hard to decide if the lessee will obtain substantially all the economic benefit of the site (although it appears likely that it will). The fourth test for a capital lease (as described earlier in this chapter) is whether the lessor is likely to recover the investment and get a return on the investment.

The test can be applied to our example as follows:

1. Determine the yield rate that makes the present values of the following cash inflows and outflows equal for the lessor:

   Outflows
   — the cash outflow when purchasing the asset $580,000.00
   Inflows
   — the cash inflow from the thirty annual rental
   payments $61,282.80
   — the expected cash inflow when the asset is sold
   in 30 years $40,000.00

   Although such a yield rate can be calculated manually, it is complex and tedious to do. Usually the interest rate that equates the cash flows can be determined using interest tables or a suitable pocket calculator. Here, either would show that the yield is 10%. (The mathematics of leasing is discussed further in Appendix 14-1.) The schedule of repayments is shown in Table 14-3 below. Note that the final year's payment includes both the annual payment of $61,282.80 and the expected recovery value of $40,000.00.

2. Find the present value of the lease payments using the yield rate determined above. The present value of $61,282.80 for thirty years discounted at 10.00% is $577,707.71. The difference between this amount and the $580,000 amount of the lease to the lessor is $2,292.29. This difference represents the present value of the residual value of the land, $40,000, discounted at 10% for thirty years.

3. Compare the present value derived in (2) with the current market value. If it is over 90% of the current market value, one presumes that the lease is a capital lease. In this case it is $577,707.71/$580,000, that is, over 99%.

Having established that the lease in our example is a capital one, let us turn to the journal entries that should be made. In the books of the lessor (Investor Limited) the

TABLE 14-3: MOVIES LIMITED AND INVESTOR LIMITED
LEASEBACK

Year	Principal: Start of year	Payment	Interest at 10%	Repayment	Principal: End of year
1	$580,000.00	$61,282.80	$58,000.00	$3,282.80	$576,717.20
2	576,717.20	61,282.80	57,671.72	3,611.08	573,106.12
3	573,106.12	61,282.80	57,310.61	3,972.19	569,133.93
4	569,133.93	61,282.80	56,913.39	4,369.41	564,764.53
5	564,764.53	61,282.80	56,476.45	4,806.35	559,958.18
6	559,958.18	61,282.80	55,995.82	5,286.98	554,671.20
7	554,671.20	61,282.80	55,467.12	5,815.68	548,855.52
8	548,855.52	61,282.80	54,885.55	6,397.25	542,458.27
9	542,458.27	61,282.80	54,245,83	7,036.97	535,421.29
10	535,421.29	61,282.80	53,542.13	7,740.67	527,680.62
11	527,680.62	61,282.80	52,768.06	8,514.74	519,165.88
12	519,165.88	61,282.80	51,916.59	9,366.21	509,799.67
13	509,799.67	61,282.80	50,979.97	10,302.83	499,496.84
14	499,496.84	61,282.80	49,949.68	11,333.12	488,163.72
15	488,163.72	61,282.80	48,816.37	12,466.43	475,697.30
16	475,697.30	61,282.80	47,569.73	13,713.07	461,984.23
17	461,984.23	61,282.80	46,198.42	15,084.38	446,899.85
18	446,899.85	61,282.80	44,689.98	16,592.82	430,307.03
19	430,307.03	61,282.80	43,030.70	18,252.10	412,054.94
20	412,054.94	61,282.80	41,205.49	20,077.31	391,977.63
21	391,977.63	61,282.80	39,197.76	22,085.04	369,892.59
22	369,892.59	61,282.80	36,989.26	24,293.54	345,599.05
23	345,599.05	61,282.80	34,559.91	26,722.89	318,876.16
24	318,876.16	61,282.80	31,887.62	29,395.18	289,480.98
25	289,480.98	61,282.80	28,948,10	32,334.70	257,146.27
26	257,146.27	61,282.80	25,714.63	35,568.17	221,578.10
27	221,578.10	61,282.80	22,157.81	39,124.99	182,453.11
28	182,453.11	61,282.80	18,245.31	43,037.49	139,415.62
29	139,415.62	61,282.80	13,941.56	47,341.24	92,074.38
30	92,074.38	101,282.80	9,208.42	92,075.36	0

transaction is treated as if the company had made a long-term loan to be repaid in instalments. The initial entry on 1 March 19X3 would read as follows:

Instalment note receivable	580,000.00	
Bank		580,000.00

To record purchase of theatre on a lease-back from Movies Limited. This is recorded at the present value of the annual lease payments of $61,282.80 payable in advance over thirty years discounted at 10% plus the present value of the expected recovery of $40,000.

At the end of the first year when the first lease payment is received, the following entry would be made:

Bank	61,282.80	
Interest income		58,000.00
Instalment note receivable		3,282.80

To record receipt of first instalment payment
according to the terms of the lease. Interest is
calculated as 10% of long-term loan of
$580,000.00.

The interest income represents one year's interest on the instalment note receivable, which is imputed to exist on the lessor's books because of the capitalization rules of lease accounting. A rate of 10% is used since that is the imputed rate of return indicated by the lease.

In the books of the lessee the transaction would be treated as if the company had sold the asset and then repurchased it. However, the conservatism convention acts to prevent a recognition of the profit on the "sale". Observe that the determination of the selling price of the asset leased is a function of the rental terms that the same company is prepared to pay as lessee. Within limits, the vendor/lessee can increase the amount the purchaser/lessor is willing to pay in purchasing the property by offering increased rental payments. In view of this, accounting standards [*CICA* 3065.68 and 3065.69] require that any profit on disposal of the asset should be amortized on the same basis as the acquired asset. If this is done, then the additional amortization arising as a result of the increased selling price is offset by the annual amortization of the profit on disposal.

In the case of the sale-and-leaseback of land which is not to be depreciated, the requirement is that the profit on disposal should be amortized on a straight-line basis over the term of the lease. The realization principle indicates that the profit should not be recognized until the land is effectively sold. Thus, to be consistent with the realization principle, the profit should not be amortized at all until both (i) the end of the lease and (ii) disposal of the land. For unexplained reasons, the *CICA Handbook* [3065.68] sanctions taking the profit into income through the amortization method.

In our example, the journal entries to record the sale-and-leaseback on the books of the lessee (Movies Limited) would be as follows:

Bank	580,000.00	
Building — accumulated depreciation	117,000.00	
Land — historic cost		50,000.00
Building — historic cost		200,000.00
Deferred profit on sale of land		200,000.00
Deferred profit on sale of building		247,000.00

To record sale of land and building to Investor
Limited.

Land — leaseback	249,011.94	
Building — leaseback	328,695.76	
Liability — capital lease		577,707.70

To record acquisition of previously owned land
and buildings on a sale-and-leaseback with
Investor Limited. The present value of the
lease is apportioned over land and buildings
in the ratio of their market values.

At the end of the first year when the first lease payment is made, the following entry would be made:

Liability — capital lease	3,512.03	
Interest expense	57,770.77	
Bank		61,282.80

To record first annual payment under terms of lease. Interest expense is calculated as 10% of 577,707.71, the initial value of the lease obligation to Movies Limited.

Note that the interest expense of $57,770.77 recorded by Movies Limited is $229.23 less than the interest income of $58,000 recorded by Investor Limited. This difference is related to the $2,292.29 present value of the $40,000 expected residual value of the land that Investor Limited will receive in thirty-years time. Investor's investment of $580,000 can be divided as follows:

Expected value of lease payments from Movies Limited	$577,707.71
Expected value of land at end of lease	2,292.29
Total investment	$580,000.00

Each year Investor Limited calculates the interest on this expected value and takes it into income. In the first year it would calculate as follows:

Interest on the expected value of land (10% of 2,292.29)	$ 229.23
Interest from Movies Limited lease	57,770.77
Total interest income	$58,000.00

As the lessee, Movies Limited has to depreciate the building. Suppose that Movies Limited depreciates its buildings on a straight-line basis and that it records depreciation monthly. Then at the end of the first month, Movies Limited would make the following entries:

Provision for depreciation — building	913.04	
Accumulated depreciation — building		913.04

To record one month's depreciation on building ($328,695.76/360).

Deferred profit on sale of land	555.56	
Deferred profit on sale of building	686.11	
Profit on disposal of land and buildings		1,241.67

To record amortization of deferred profit on disposal of buildings and land, as follows:
Land: 200,000/360 = 555.56 (straight-line amortization)
Building: 247,000/360 = 686.11 (to correspond with rate of amortization of leased buildings)

If the implied market price for the leased assets is less than their former net book value, then the loss on disposal would be recognized at the time the sale-and-leaseback was made. Recognition of the loss is consistent with the convention of conservatism.

Disclosure Issues

The two parties to a lease have entered into an agreement that usually has implications extending well into the future. Some future elements have been captured by the step of capitalizing the asset and liability, but information about the continuing lease commitment would also be helpful. To aid the reader, the *CICA Handbook* [3065] requires the following disclosures for the lessee and the lessor:

1. The gross amount of capital leases and related accumulated amortization should be shown by both the lessor and the lessee [*CICA* 3065.21].

2. Obligations related to leased assets should be shown separately from other long-term obligations by both the lessor and the lessee. In addition, both should show the particulars of the lease obligations (such as interest rates and expiry dates) as well as any significant restrictions placed on the lessee as a result of the agreement. Obligations due within a year should be shown as current liabilities [*CICA* 3065.22].

3. The net investment in the lease should be shown separately by the lessor, as should the financing income arising from it [*CICA* 3065.54].

4. The total of future minimum lease payments (with a deduction for executory costs and imputed interest) should be shown in total by the lessee. Minimum lease payments for each of the next five years should also be shown by the lessee. This applies for both operating and capital leases [*CICA* 3065.23 and 3065.32].

5. Amortization of leased property should be shown separately or included with other depreciation and amortization costs by the lessee. The method and rate of amortization should also be shown. [*CICA* 3065.25].

6. Interest expense from leasing should either be disclosed separately or included with similar expenses of other long-term debt by the lessee [*CICA* 3065.26].

The main effect of these requirements is to ensure that the expenses arising from the capitalization of leased assets are either (i) included as amortization or interest or else (ii) shown separately. In addition, the requirements mean that some indication of the company's lease commitments will be given.

Critique of Lease Accounting

Given the desire to maintain the integrity of historic-cost-based accounting, we can conclude that the development of lease accounting has been rather successful. The incentive to choose leasing as a form of financing simply for its cosmetic impact on the financial statements has been significantly diminished, although not eliminated. In addition, with a few exceptions, the leased assets will turn up on either the lessor's or the lessee's balance sheet. In other words, the rules for lessor and lessee are symmetrically consistent: if one party treats the leased item as a plant asset, the other does not. There are, however, some criticisms to be made of the present approach.

One criticism that has been made repeatedly in the United States is that the rules are so complex that they invite those who wish to avoid capitalization to do so by finding an arrangement that is just outside the capitalization rules. However, perhaps this is not a criticism of lease accounting in itself. As pointed out in Chapter 2, one could argue that this criticism is actually directed against the trend of trying to codify the details of accounting reporting instead of properly stating general principles.

A second criticism is that lease capitalization is unnecessary. Some critics believe that the investors ought to be told the material facts about a company's leases and then be left to decide for themselves how to adjust the company's financial statements. Research has provided evidence that when the SEC required companies to disclose lease information in 1973, the price of the shares of the affected companies reacted in a way that indicated investors were quite capable of absorbing the information without having to have the leases capitalized for them (Ro[1978]).

Finally, some people point to the practical problems of implementation. The present-value calculations that lie at the heart of lease accounting rest on the assumptions about the discount rate to use and the portion of the lease payment to consider available for retirement of debt.

Examples from Published Reports

Eastman Kodak Company

This company is a diversified technologies company, although it is best known for its photographic products. Excerpts from its financial statements have been given above in Chapter 8.

RENTAL AND LEASE COMMITMENTS

	1986	1985
	(millions of $)	
Rental expense consists of		
Gross rentals	$101	$89
Deduct: Sublease income	8	8
Total	$93	$81

The approximate amounts of noncancelable lease commitments with terms of more than one year, principally for the rental of real property, are as follows:

MINIMUM RENTAL COMMITMENTS

		Sublease (millions of $)	
Year	Gross	Income	Net
1987	$66	$ 3	$63
1988	57	2	55
1989	43	1	42
1990	34	1	33
1991	28	1	27
1992 and beyond	128	2	126
Total	$356	$10	$346

Imasco Limited

Imasco is a major Canadian products and services corporation which owns businesses such as Shoppers Drug Mart and Canada Trustco.

Note 9. Capital lease commitments

The corporation has commitments with respect to property in the Restaurant and Drug Store segments recorded under capital leases expiring on various dates through the year 2007.
The minimum annual commitments under such leases are approximately as follows:

	(thousands of $)
1988	$ 6,295
1989	6,090
1990	5,787
1991	5,291
1992	4,705
1993 and thereafter	12,450
Total minimum commitments	40,618
Imputed interest at 12.3%	(16,587)
Payments due within one year	(2,566)
Long-term obligations under capital leases	$21,465

Presumably the annual payments include both an interest and a capital repayment component inasmuch as there is a deduction of $16,587 for imputed interest.

Summary

Lease accounting is a good example of new accounting standards being developed to meet changed conditions. In this case the changed conditions were a shift to the use of long-term leases as a means of financing the effective purchase of a plant asset.

A clear distinction is made between capital and non-capital leases on the basis of whether property rights have passed to the lessee. If the lease is judged to be non-capital, then the issues are mainly those of matching the costs over its life to the periods deemed to benefit from it. On the other hand, if the lease is judged to be a capital lease, then the asset is treated as if it had been sold from the lessor to the lessee, and an instalment debt is deemed to have been created between them.

In a sale-and-leaseback the original owner of the assets sells them to the new lessor on the understanding that the original owner will now lease them. If it is a capital lease, then for accounting purposes the sale is treated as if it had not taken place. Instead, the transaction is treated by both parties as if the lessee had borrowed money from the lessor on an instalment loan. However, on the lessee's books the assets are restated to their lease value, and any gain on the sale is taken into income over the life of the lease.

In all cases there are rules for disclosure through the notes that are intended to give the reader additional information about the commitments of the lessee.

QUESTIONS

Q14-1. Make sure you are familiar with the following terms:
   a. lease
   b. rent
   c. lessor
   d. lessee
   e. executory contracts
   f. executory costs
   g. financing *versus* accounting issues in leases
   h. supplier
   i. user
   j. financier
   k. capital lease
   l. sales-type lease
   m. direct-financing lease
   n. sale-and-leaseback
   o. operating lease
   p. off balance-sheet financing
   q. bargain purchase option
   r. effective yield

Q14-2. It is reported that some leases written in Canada contain the following clause: "Nothing in this lease shall be construed to make it a lease within the meaning of section 3065 of the *CICA Handbook*." Discuss the effect of this clause in influencing whether a lease should be considered to be an operating or capital lease.

Q14-3. One of the major arguments in favour of the lease accounting that has been explained in this chapter is that without it "off balance-sheet financing" would make it possible to mislead the reader of financial statements.

   a. What important financial-statement relationships are changed in the shift away from off-balance sheet financing?

   b. Using "off balance-sheet financing," what information might be disclosed in the notes to the financial statement that would act as a substitute for the present practice of treating capital leases as an acquisition of an asset and debt?

Q14-4. One of the major sources of opposition to the present system of lease accounting came from companies that used long-term leases extensively as a means of financing. One of their arguments was that the proposed changes would make their financial statements look so unfavourable that some sources of finance would be closed to them. Evaluate the impact of lease capitalization on each of the following.(Assume that sinking-fund depreciation is not used to offset the impact of capitalizing the leases.)

   a. retained earnings

   b. ratio of current assets to current liabilities

   c. return on investment (defined as the ratio of net income to total assets)

   d. net income per year over the life of the lease

   e. cash flow

   f. interest expense

Q14-5. Design an experiment to test if capital lease information need be shown directly on the financial statements instead of only set out in the notes to the financial statements.

Q14-6. Aleph Limited enters into an agreement to lease an office building over a thirty-year period and is required to treat it as a capital lease. In the same year Aleph enters into an agreement with a contractor to buy a building to be built on a cost-plus basis (i.e., Aleph pays all the costs of construction plus an additional amount to provide the contractor with a profit). In both cases Aleph is assuming similar risks of ownership. Yet in the second case no accounting entry is made except for periodic payments to the contractor. Explain.

Q14-7. Yarker Enterprises has to pay 18% to borrow money. Hence it would have to pay $10,281.25 at the end of each month to amortize a $350,000 loan over four years. Assume it has purchased an asset costing $350,000 with a four-year life and no salvage value through a capital lease.

    a. What would be the monthly lease payments?

    b. What would be the monthly depreciation using the straight-line method? Using the declining-balance method at 40% per year?

    c. What would be the first month's interest cost?

    d. What would be the last month's interest cost?

    e. Assuming the straight-line depreciation, what would be the total cost of depreciation and interest for the first month? for the last month?

Q14-8. In each of the following cases, state whether the lease should be classified as an operating lease or a capital lease in the books of the lessor and lessee. Give your reasons.

    a. Mammoth Oils is a large integrated oil company. It enters into an agreement to lease an oil tanker from XX Ltd., a private company whose sole asset is the oil tanker and whose sole owner is a trust company with whom Mammoth regularly does business. The lease Mammoth has is for roughly half the expected economic life of the tanker. At the end of this lease term, Mammoth must either sign a second lease for the same length of time or buy the tanker for its book value. The operating costs are paid by Mammoth.

    b. Executive Suits Limited (ESL) is a clothing company that specializes in renting expensive suits to executives, whose companies pay the rental fees. The rental cost is 5% of the suit's cost per month. Insurance on the suit is paid by ESL. At the end of two years the suit must be returned to ESL, who then put it in their "sale room" and sell it for what they can get for it. The sale room's existence appears to be known to a rather limited set of customers, who appear to consist mainly of ESL's rental customers.

    c. Superior Taxi company signs a rental agreement with Jackson Motors. Superior agrees to rent its fleet of cars from Jackson under the term that Jackson will open up a "cost ledger" card for each car and charge Superior with the cost of the new car and all maintenance Jackson has to do on the car that is not covered under the warranty. Superior agrees to make monthly rental payments on each car that are estimated by Jackson to be enough to cover its maintenance and other out-of-pocket costs, with enough left over to write down the amount in the cost ledger to the approximate market value of that car at the end of the rental period. Superior is required, at Jackson's option, to buy the car at the end of the lease period (three years) for the amount shown in the cost ledger. However, for an additional $50 per month Jackson is willing to enter into a lease in which the option to buy rests with Superior, not Jackson.

d. Debbit and Creddit are the partners in a fast-growing firm offering custom software services to clients who have bought mini-computers. They are short of capital and have arranged with a local office-supply firm to supply them with office furniture and equipment. The equipment will be new and will be ordered in specially for this purpose. The lease is for two years and may be extended for another two at Debbit and Creddit's option. They have no residual rights to the furniture and equipment at the end of the four years, although they estimate that most of the furniture and equipment has a functional life of at least ten years. They had considered buying the furniture; but they believed that although leasing it was somewhat more expensive, it was worthwhile because it helped their cash flow problems. Besides, the company renting the furniture and equipment to them was a client. They expected that before the lease ran out they would have enough money to buy it outright, and they thought they would be able to get a favourable deal.

Q14-9. Some have argued that the property rights tests for distinguishing between capital and operating leases could be rendered unnecessary if instead the future cash flows in all executory contracts for leases were capitalized. In other words, as soon as a lease was signed, the present value of all future cash flows would be capitalized in a manner now used for capital leases, even if the agreement would be classed as an operating lease according to present criteria. What are the strengths and weaknesses of this proposal?

Q14-10. What depreciation method might be adopted by a company that wanted to make its reported income the same whether or not it capitalized its leases? Explain.

Q14-11. Under what circumstances would the same plant asset be carried on the books of both the lessor and lessee? Do you approve of this? Explain.

Q14-12. Explain the differing accounting treatments of a sales-type lease and a direct-financing lease in the books of the lessor. Are the differences justified? Explain.

Q14-13. "Whether or not a lease is capitalized has no effect on the reported income of the lessor; the effect is entirely on the lessee's reported profit." Do you agree? Explain.

Q14-14. A company entered into a long-term lease contract for a warehouse and capitalized it under generally accepted accounting principles. At the same time it signed a contract to rent a large computer. Under the terms of the contract for the computer, the lease could be cancelled on three-months notice; accordingly, the company treated this as an operating lease. The company's controller says to you: "I'm not sure we're doing the right thing in capitalizing one and not the other. Now that we've agreed to go with that computer manufacturer we're as bound to keep renting their equipment as if we'd signed a long-term lease. It's the economics that count. Once we've paid for all the software that can only be run on that brand of computers and trained our staff how to get it to work, there is a very low chance we will ever switch to another brand. If you accountants are interested in economic substance instead of legal form, why don't you insist that both be capitalized?" What is your response?

Q14-15. Under what circumstances might the interest income on a long-term lease be different in the lessor's books from the interest expense on the same lease in the lessee's books? Could it be higher? Lower? Either?

Q14-16. Explain the different accounting treatment accorded to initial lease costs (such as legal fees) under a sales-type lease and a direct-financing lease. Is the difference in treatment consistent with the accounting objective of matching costs and revenues?

Q14-17. Under what circumstances might the capitalized value of a lease be higher on the lessee's books than on the lessor's? Is this consistent with the accounting convention of conservatism?

Q14-18. Is it possible to frustrate the intentions of lease accounting by using the annuity method of depreciation? Explain.

Q14-19. Explain in non-technical language how the effective yield is calculated on a direct-financing lease that has initial lease costs, such as legal fees.

Q14-20. What is the economic substance of a sale-and-leaseback? Explain how the accounting standards might be designed to frustrate an attempt at income manipulation through a sale-and-leaseback. How successful have accounting standards been in this respect?

Q14-21. Under what conditions is it possible for a lease to be treated as a capital lease by the lessee and an operating lease by the lessor? Can the reverse happen? Explain.

EXERCISES

E14-1. Swiftsure is a student-run wood processing service that was started in January 19X5. On signing the two-year lease for the site, they had to provide a cheque for the following: (i) $410.00 for last month's rent deposit, (ii) $410.00 for the first month's rent, and (iii) $600.00 to pay the landlord for making renovations and decorating to meet their special requirements.

Required:

a. Show the entry needed when the above cheque was issued.

b. Show the entry that would be appropriate to record rent expense for the second month of operation.

E14-2. In each the following unrelated situations, explain (i) whether the journal entry is that of the lessor or lessee; (ii) whether the lease is a capital lease or an operating lease; and (iii) if it is a capital lease, whether it is a sales-type or a direct-financing one.

a. Instalment note payable	3,500.00	
Interest	1,200.00	
Bank		4,700.00
b. Long-term note receivable	130,000.00	
Sales		130,000.00
c. Instalment note receivable	5,000.00	
Legal fees		5,000.00
d. Cost of goods sold	3,200.00	
Legal fees		3,200.00
e. Lease expense	18,000.00	
Leasehold improvements		18,000.00

E14-3. Grafton Inc. purchased a machine for $30,000 and leased it to Lessee Inc. for three years. Under the terms of the lease three payments of $6,756 had to be paid to Grafton, one at the end of each year. At the end of the lease, the equipment, whose residual value is estimated at $19,350, must be returned to Grafton.

Required:

a. Should this be treated as a capital lease or an operating lease? Explain.

b. What rate of interest is implicit in the lease?

c. Would you choose to capitalize the lease under each of the following unrelated circumstances? If so, what interest rate would you use?

(i) Lessee is required to purchase the equipment at the end of the lease for $19,350.

(ii) Lessee is not required, but has the option, to purchase the equipment at the end of the lease for $19,350.

E14-4. Milburn Ltd. is a manufacturer of special-purpose construction equipment. Its year-end is 31 December. Milburn manufactured an item for $35,000 and put it in its display room priced at $45,000. Because it did not sell, on 1 July Milburn leased it to a customer for $875 a month for two years on an operating lease. The functional life of the equipment is estimated to be six years, at the end of which time it will have no residual value. It is depreciated on a straight-line basis.

Required:

a. Show the entry in the books of the lessor for the first month.

b. The company is wondering if the monthly rental of $875 implies that the equipment has declined in value and should be written down in the current year. What would your advice be? (Assume that Milburn's borrowing rate was 10%.)

E14-5. Lessee Corporation leased equipment from Lessor Inc. on 1 May 19X5. Annual payments of $200,000 are due at 1 May 19X6 and each year thereafter. The lease is considered by Lessor Corporation to be a sales-type lease. The equipment cost Lessor $600,000 to make. The lease is for five years, and the equipment is expected to have no residual value. Lessee Inc. uses straight-line depreciation, and its fiscal year-end is 30 April. The equipment cost Lessor $5,000 to install. The indicated rate of interest is 11%, and the present value of a $1,000 annuity paid in arrears for five periods at 11% is $3,695.90.

Required:

a. What income or loss before taxes should Lessor Corporation show in the first year as a result of the transaction? Show your calculations.

b. What expenses should Lessee Inc. record with respect to the lease for the period ending 30 April 19X6? Show your calculations and all required entries.

E14-6. The annual payment in advance to retire a loan of $100,000 at 10% over eight annual payments is $17,040.36. Suppose a company leased an asset for $100,000.

Required:

a. What rent expense would the company record for the first twelve months if the annual rental payment was $17,040.36 and if it had treated the lease as an operating one?

b. If a company had a capital lease of $100,000 with rental payments of $17,040.36 payable in advance, what would the interest and depreciation expenses be in Year 1? in Year 8? Assume straight-line depreciation over eight years and an implicit interest rate in the lease of 10%.

c. What is the ratio of lease expense in (b) over that in (a) in Year 1? in Year 8?

E14-7. The Hadfield Corporation entered into a lease for manufacturing equipment from Crosbie Corporation on 1 January 19X2. The terms of the lease provided for yearly payments, in advance, of $27,500 for ten years. The yearly payments include $2,500 maintenance costs. At the end of the lease Crosbie plans to reclaim the equipment, which is expected to last one more year. Crosbie estimated the residual value at $17,000, but did not disclose this information to Hadfield. Crosbie purchased the asset at its fair market value. The interest rate implicit in the lease is 10%, and Hadfield's incremental borrowing rate is 12%. The present value of ten annual payments of $1,000 in advance is $6,759.02 at 10% and $6,328.20 at 12%. The present value of a single payment of $1,000 ten years from now is $385.54 at 10%.

Required:

a. Provide the journal entries required to account for the lease in the accounts of Hadfield in 19X2. Assume adjusting journal entries are made only at the year-end.

b. Calculate the current and long-term portion of the lease liability of Hadfield at 31 December 19X2.

(CGA adapted)

E14-8. Select the *best* answer for each of the following unrelated scenarios. Select only one answer for each. Justify your choice.

a. On the first day of its fiscal year, Lessee Inc. leased certain property at an annual rental of $100,000, receivable at the beginning of each year for ten years. The first payment was made immediately. The leased property, which is new, has an estimated useful life of thirteen years and no residual value. Lessee's borrowing rate is 8%. The present value of an annuity due of $1 payable at the beginning of the period at 8% for ten years is $7.24689. Lessee had no other costs associated with this lease. Lessee mistakenly treated the lease as an operating lease. By doing so, what was the effect on Lessee's net earnings during the first year of the lease?
  (i) no effect
  (ii) understated
  (iii) overstated
  (iv) none of the above.

b. A company constructed an office building at a cost of $500,000. It sold this building to Jones at a material gain and then leased it back from Jones for a stipulated annual rental. How should this gain be treated by the company?
  (i) recognized in full as an ordinary item in the year of the transaction
  (ii) recognized in full as an extraordinary item in the year of the transaction
  (iii) amortized as an adjustment of the rental cost, an ordinary item, over the life of the lease
  (iv) deferred and amortized over the estimated life of the building
  (v) none of the above

c. The appropriate valuation of leased assets under an operating lease on the statement of financial position of the lessee is as follows:
  (i) the absolute sum of the lease payments
  (ii) the sum of the present values of the lease payments discounted at an appropriate rate
  (iii) the market value of the asset at the date of the inception of the lease
  (iv) zero
  (v) none of the above

d. What are the three types of period costs that a lessee experiences with capital leases?
  (i) lease expense, interest expense, and amortization expense
  (ii) interest expense, amortization expense, and executory costs
  (iii) executory costs, interest expenses and lease expense
  (iv) none of the above

e. When measuring the present value of future rentals to be capitalized in connection with a lease, one should treat identifiable payments that cover taxes, insurance, and maintenance as follows:

(i) include them with future rentals, which will be capitalized

(ii) exclude them from future rentals, which will be capitalized

(iii) capitalize them, but at a different rate and in a different account than those used for future rentals

(iv) capitalize them, but at a different rate and in a different period than those used for future rentals

(v) none of the above

f. Generally accepted accounting principles require that certain lease agreements be accounted for as purchases. The theoretical basis for this treatment is that a lease of this type has the following characteristics:

(i) it is an example of form over substance

(ii) it provides the use of the leased asset to the lessee for a limited period of time

(iii) it incorporates a relationship of cause and effect that must be recorded in this manner

(iv) it effectively conveys all of the benefits and risks incident to the ownership of the property

(v) none of the above.

(CGA adapted)

E14-9. Consider each of the four cases below.

(i) University X has decided to sell its library collection to Lessor and lease it back for ten years. At the end of that period the library collection reverts to the University. The selling price is $20 million. Payments of $275,500 at the end of each month are calculated to be sufficient to retire the principal amount over ten years yielding 11%. The University's normal borrowing rate is 10.5%.

(ii) Lakeland Software has entered into a contract with Acme Manufacturing that it will adapt one of its existing software packages and license Acme to use it for a period of ten years. During that period Lakeland will be committed to change the software as needed to respond to changing conditions, such as new government regulations and union contracts. At the end of the period the revised software will remain with Lakeland, although Acme will have the rights to sell it elsewhere if it can find a customer. Acme estimates that there is a 60% chance of such a sale, and that if it takes place it will be worth a total of $95,000. The annual charge of the lease to Acme will be $85,000, payable at the start of each year, of which $35,000 is estimated to be the cost to Lakeland of keeping the software updated. The remaining $50,000 per annum is expected by Lakeland to have the equivalent present value of $316,412 (i.e., Lakeland assumes a 12% discount rate). Acme does not know the rate of interest implicit in the lease, but is aware of the software's current market value. Acme's normal borrowing rate is 11.5%.

(iii) Kensington Foods Inc. purchased the Nova Scotia rights to a fast-food franchise and decided to open a unit near the junction of two busy roads. It selected the site, found the contractor, and made arrangements to have a building constructed and equipped to their specifications. The land was to cost Kensington $100,000 and the building $350,000. Rather than buying the land and building, Kensington made the following arrangement with the contractor. Kensington would rent the land for $1,000 a month and the building for $4,200 a month, both payable in advance. The lease was for fifteen years. The estimated residual value of the land at the end was estimated to be $230,000, and that of the building was estimated to be nil. The rate of interest implicit in lease was 12%, although Kensington had been paying 11.75% on similar arrangements. The land had cost the contractor $65,000 three years ago, and the cost of constructing the building was $375,000.

(iv) After the lease in (iii) was signed, the contractor sold the entire package to a local investor for $500,000. After paying legal and survey fees, the investor calculates that his yield will be 11.8%.

Required:
For each of the four cases above, answer the following:

a. Explain whether the lessor should treat the lease as a direct-financing lease or a sales-type lease.

b. Specify the rate of interest the lessee should use in capitalizing the lease payments.

c. Indicate whether the residual amount at the end of the lease should be included in the capitalized amounts by the lessee.

PROBLEMS

P14-1. Swiftsure WP Limited is a service bureau that types student essays at a fixed charge per page. On 1 January 19X4 it acquired two word processors on a five-year lease at an annual rental of $3,600 payable in advance yearly with the first payment due on 1 January 19X4. Maintenance and supplies are extra, and the monthly rental is intended to cover only depreciation and financing costs. The lease is based on a purchase cost of $15,000 and an assumed residual value of $820.44, which is the expected salvage value on 1 January 19X9. Swiftsure's accountant points out that because the terms of the lease have not been finalized, it might be possible to modify the terms so that the lease will be considered either as an operating lease or as a capital lease for tax purposes. If Swiftsure had purchased the equipment, it would have depreciated the word processors over five years on a straight-line basis and borrowed the funds at 12% (the same rate that is implicit in the lease terms).

Required:
Show for each of the five years the difference in reported income if the company treated the lease as an operating lease instead of a capital lease.

P14-2. Consider the following five unrelated situations.

(i) Warehouse Construction Limited (WCL) constructs warehouses to suit the needs of its customers, and then it leases them on twenty-year leases. For a recent sale, the present value of the rental payments at the implicit interest rate in the lease is $560,000, and the cost of the building to WCL was $480,000.

(ii) Leasehold Investments Limited (LIL) agreed to buy a building and a parcel of land that Happy Burgers (HB), a fast-food franchise, was about to open as a new outlet. The building had been built to HB's specifications by a local construction company that had given HB an option to purchase the building for $350,000. HB assigned this option to LIL. HB was to lease the building from LIL for 15 years, with an option to renew for another fifteen years and with the right to purchase the building for $1 at the end of the thirty years.

(iii) At another site Happy Burgers was unable to find suitable land to purchase. Therefore, HB entered into a rental agreement with Building Limited, the owners of an existing building. The lessor agreed to supply the space on an "as is" basis. A lease was signed for five years, with an option to renew for another three years. HB spent $30,000 on renovations and built-in equipment which is expected to last for the life of the lease.

(iv) Ace Shoes Inc., a retail store that owns the building its store is in, wants to raise money to expand. Therefore it decides to sell its building and then rent it from the new owners. The land and building had cost $20,000 and $80,000 respectively, and the building was now fully depreciated. The building was sold to Leasing Limited for $350,000, and Ace signed a twenty-year lease with the right to renew for another twenty years at terms to be negotiated at renewal. If Leasing Limited decides to sell the building, Ace has the right to meet the best offer that Leasing Limited gets. The land has a current market value of $100,000.

(v) Hobbies and Models Ltd. (H & M) owned a small building in a popular shopping area. In 19X9, H & M agreed to sell the building for $250,000 to a developer who undertook to build a larger building in which a store would be rented to H & M at an agreed rent of $1,000 a month for the first five years. Thereafter the rent was negotiable. H & M had originally paid $25,000 for the land and $60,000 for the building, which was now fully depreciated. In 19X9, after signing the agreement, H & M sold the building and moved to temporary quarters supplied by the developer. H & M then spent $8,000 on renovations in their temporary quarters. They expected to move to their new store at the end of two years.

Required:

For each of the above situations, do the following:

a. Decide whether the lease should be capitalized or not. Give your reasons.

b. Make any journal entries that might be required in the first year of the lease for both the lessor and the lessee to reflect any initial lease capitalization.

P14-3. Crunchy Fries Inc. is an independent fast-food outlet. They have been in business for three months in a building rented on an annual basis at $70,000 per annum payable at the start of each year from Invest Ltd., a local property developer who constructed it at a cost of $500,000. The fast-food operation is so successful that it attracts a new competitor, Tasty Fries Ltd. This competitor sets up shop across the street in a similar building that is also rented from Invest Ltd., but on a ten-year lease that is considered to constitute a capital lease. This building also cost $500,000 to build, and the rental is also $70,000 per annum payable in advance. An interest rate of 10% was used by Invest Ltd. in calculating the annual rent.

Required:

a. By how much is Crunchy Fries' reported income greater or less than that of Tasty Fries for each of the ten years because of their rental arrangements. What is the overall difference? Show all your calculations.

b. Suppose that Crunchy Fries and Tasty Fries each had a debt of $100,000 and equity of $50,000. For simplicity, assume that this remained unchanged (except for the lease liability, which is not included in the $100,000 debt) over the ten-year period. What would the debt/equity ratio of each company at the end of Year 1? Year 10?

c. Do you think the real financial circumstances between the two companies are reflected in their financial statements prepared according to GAAP? Explain.

P14-4. Hot Tapes Inc. is a chain of stores renting video cassettes. They rented space in a new shopping centre on a "bare walls" basis. They had to put in their own fixtures, rugs, cabinets, light fixtures, and interior walls. The shopping centre refuses to give a lease any longer than five years, with a renewal option of another five. Hot Tapes has not been in this business long, but the proprietor has been in a variety of retail operations and has had long experience in dealing with the management of the shopping centre. She feels confident that Hot Tapes will be there in operation for at least ten years and wants you, as her accountant, to agree to a write-off of the leasehold improvements over ten years at a minimum. What are your views? Support your conclusion by discussing both sides of the issue in a memo of about 150 words.

P14-5. Osbaldeston Cheese Limited (OCL) has been told by the Department of Health that it must replace its cheese-making equipment or shut down. Because of the concern over the possible loss of jobs, the elders of a local church have offered to help finance the purchase of the new equipment as follows. An appraiser will be hired to value the land and buildings, and then the church will buy them at market value. OCL will then enter into a lease agreement to rent the building for ten years at an annual rental of $31,069.52, payable at the beginning of the year, that will be sufficient to yield the church 10% and repay its initial investment. At the end of the ten years OCL is to have the right to repurchase the land and building for $1. The land originally cost OCL $40,000, and the building cost $180,000. The accumulated depreciation is $45,000. The appraiser gives a current market value of $120,000 for the land and $90,000 for the building. OCL and the church proceed with the suggested proposal.

Required:

a. What should be the journal entry (entries) in OCL's books for the sale of the land and building?

b. What is the proper entry for OCL at the beginning of the second year when it makes the second rental payment?

P14-6. Flawless Gems Ltd., a retailer of fake jewellery, is expanding by opening four stores in different shopping centres. The lease for each store is described in the chart below. The cost of borrowing is 10%, and each store costs $300,000 to buy outright. The expected recovery value at the end of each lease is nil.

Shopping centre location	Annual lease payment	Lease term
Oxnard Mall	$33,000	20 years
Sofar Mall	37,000	15 years
Tanbury Mall	37,000	12 years
Bluesea Mall	53,000	8 years

Required: Using only the information given above, decide whether each lease should be treated as an operating lease or a capital lease. Give your reasons.

P14-7. Investor-Owner Limited (IOL) set up a chain of video-game shops near high schools. The owner put in $50,000 of his own money and borrowed another $80,000 on the basis of a written agreement that he would keep the debt-to-capital ratio at no more than 2:1. His basic approach is to rent premises on a short-term lease and to rent his video games under a separate rental agreement. Because these games become obsolete so quickly, he is given only two options. First, he could sign a three-year lease with an annual rental of $1,904.25 per machine (payable in advance) and with an option to buy machines at the end of that time for $1 each. This lease is based on a cost per machine of $5,000 at a 15% interest rate. Alternatively, he could rent each machine on a short-term basis for $2,100 annually with the option to cancel the rental on six months' notice. He thinks he will keep the machines for three years at least. However, he is concerned that if the three-year lease is considered to be a capital lease, he will violate his agreement with respect to his debt-to-capital ratio. Prior to signing any rental agreement, his debt-to-capital ratio is $80,000/$50,000 = 1.6:1. (For the purposes of this problem, assume that the debt-to-capital ratio will be affected only by the lease chosen.)

Required:

a. If IOL chooses to sign the three-year lease and it is considered to be a capital lease, how many machines will he be able to lease before reaching the limit imposed by the debt-to-capital ratio?

b. What would his debt-to-capital ratio be immediately after signing the three-year lease? Calculate the ratio under each of the following assumptions:
   (i) the lease will be capitalized
   (ii) the lease will not be capitalized

c. Can he make significant changes in his debt-to-capital ratio by choosing the kind of lease he signs? If so, is GAAP protecting the reader of financial statements as it was intended to?

P14-8. Tenant Limited signed a fifteen-year lease with Owner Limited to rent a warehouse at an annual rental payment of $61,525.96 payable at the end of each year. Owner has purchased the building for $580,000 and the land for $20,000 from a third party about a year before the lease was signed. Tenant was required by the lease to pay for maintenance, taxes, and general upkeep. The lease was so arranged that both sides expected that Owner would incur no annual expenses other than any interest costs for money borrowed to finance the original purchase of the building. At the end of the fifteen-year term Tenant had the option to renew for another fifteen years at the same rent; and if she did not renew, she was required to move immediately, leaving the building and fixtures in good condition. At the end of the second fifteen-year term Tenant had the option to purchase the building at the going market price, which was expected to be $100,000. As of the date the lease began, the service life of the buildings was estimated to be around thirty years, and the market value of the land and buildings was estimated to be unchanged at $600,000. The rate of interest implicit in the lease was 10%. The present value of thirty years of annual payments of $61,525.96 was calculated to be $580,000; for the first fifteen years the present value was calculated to be $467,971.34.

Required:

a. If Tenant treated this as a capital lease and assumed it was for a thirty-year term, show (i) the journal entry that would be required as of the start of the lease and (ii) the journal entry that would be required on payment of the rent at the end of the first year.

b. If Tenant treated this as an operating lease, show the journal entry (entries) that would be required during the first year.

c. In your opinion should the lease be treated by Tenant as an operating lease or a capital lease? Justify your conclusion by specific reference to the tests set out in the text.

d. Show the journal entry (entries) in Owner's books at the time the lease came into effect, assuming that Owner treated it as a capital lease over a thirty-year term.

P14-9. Hardy and Moore Corp. is in desperate need of cash. They purchased a small office building exactly five years ago. They depreciated the building using the straight-line method and an estimated life of twenty years. Today, Hardy and Moore Corp. has a chance to sell the building to Dimitri Ltd. for $500,000 in cash. They would then lease the building back from Dimitri for fifteen annual payments of $84,457.68. The first payment would be due one year from today, as part of a fifteen-year non-cancellable lease. The rate of interest applicable to this transaction is 15%. The building has a fair value of $550,000. Assume the residual value will be the same as the first estimate made by Hardy and Moore Corp. The book value of the building today is as follows:

Cost five years ago	$600,000
Accumulated depreciation	137,500
Net book value	$462,500

Required:

a. What entries would be made by the lessor and the lessee when the initial sale is made?

b. What entries would they each make one year from now when the first payment is made?

P14-10. You are planning to operate an ice-cream truck during the upcoming summer. You are fairly certain that the revenue you will earn over 80 days will be $400 per day. You are also fairly sure that variable costs will be 50% of expected revenue. You have three options with respect to the ice cream truck:

(i) Rental: you can rent the truck for 100 days for $150 per day. Minimum rental period is 100 days.

(ii) Purchase: you can purchase the truck outright for $50,000. The terms are five year-end payments at 15% annually with principal to be repaid at the end of Year 5. Assume a seven-year life with straight-line depreciation.

(iii) Lease: you can sign a seven-year lease with year-end payments of $12,018.02. Title is transferred to you at the end of the lease period.

Required:

a. Which of the three methods would produce the highest expected income in the first year? In the first seven years? Show all your calculations.

b. What are some of the advantages and disadvantages of each method?

P14-11. You are planning to lease some new equipment from Scriver Leasing Corp. Scriver is in the business of leasing and does not manufacture or sell the equipment that it leases. Your incremental rate of borrowing is 15% and the rate implicit in the lease is 12%. You cannot determine Scriver's rate. However, the present value of the minimum lease payments is between 90 and 100 per cent of the fair value of the equipment, regardless of the rate used.

The lease extends for four years, which is exactly half the expected life of the equipment. You do not plan to purchase the equipment at the end of the four-year period. It is expected that Scriver will take it back and then lease it to another company. One further condition of the lease is that you are to pay all executory costs directly. This means that Scriver will be certain of the costs it will incur.

Required:

a. With respect to Scriver Leasing Corp, the lessor:

(i) What type of leasing arrangement is this? Give reasons.

(ii) What entry will be made when payments are made each period? Do not use numbers, but explain in words how the amounts would be calculated.

(iii) Describe how this lease would be disclosed on the company's financial statements.

b. With respect to you, the lessee:

(i) What type of leasing arrangement is this? Give reasons.

(ii) How should you calculate the amount to be recorded for this lease?

(iii) What will be the effect on your net income each year as a result of this leasing arrangement?

(iv) Describe how this lease would be disclosed on your financial statements.

P14-12. Lessor entered into a lease arrangement with Lessee for a building that it had recently purchased for $350,000. Under the terms of the lease, Lessee paid $58,190.07 at the end of each of ten years. The interest rate implicit in the lease was 10.5%. However, Lessee's borrowing rate was 14%. The present value of a ten-year annuity of $58,190.07 paid in arrears is $350,000 at a 10.5% interest rate and $303,526.08 at an interest rate of 14%. The expected residual value of the building is nil. Both Lessor and Lessee treated the arrangement as a capital lease.

a. Show the journal entry (entries) Lessor would make at the start of the lease.

b. Show the journal entry (entries) Lessee would make at the start of the lease.

c. Show the journal entry (entries) Lessor would make on receipt of the first payment.

d. Show the journal entry (entries) Lessee would make on issuing the first payment.

P14-13. Machinery Inc. was a manufacturer and financer of specialty equipment. It signed a five-year rental agreement with Producer Ltd. that had the following terms. Monthly payments of $13,346.67 were to be made at the end of each month for sixty consecutive months. Machinery Inc. would reclaim the machine at the end of the sixty-month period. The machine was not expected to have any residual value. Producer Inc. would pay all costs for such things as maintenance and supplies. The present value of sixty monthly payments in arrears is $600,000 at a nominal annual rate of 12% and $573,600.06 at 14%. The rate of interest implicit in the lease was 12% and Producer's normal borrowing rate was 14%. The cost of the machinery on Machinery's books at the time of leasing was $525,000. Lessee does not know the implicit rate in the lease.

Required:

a. Show the journal entry (entries) Machinery Inc. would make at the start of the lease.

b. Show the journal entry (entries) Producer Ltd. would make at the start of the lease.

c. Show the journal entry (entries) Machinery Inc. would make on receipt of the first payment.

d. Show the journal entry (entries) Producer Ltd. would make on issuing the first payment.

e. Compare the lessor's first-month interest income with the lessee's first-month interest expense. Explain in non-technical language the reasons for any difference in the two amounts.

P14-14. Bidwell Computers rented $50,000 worth of equipment to Office Systems on a three-year lease under which Office Systems paid $1,613.36 per month. The equipment had been purchased by Bidwell for $40,000, but they had to spend another $1,000 to move it to the proper site and instal it. The present value of an annuity of $1,613.36 paid in arrears for thirty-six months is $50,000 at a nominal annual interest rate of 10% (0.10/12 per month) and $51,000 at a nominal annual interest rate of 8.645%. Bidwell regards the transaction as a sales-type capital lease. Office Systems' borrowing rate is 10%.

Required:

a. Show the journal entry (entries) Bidwell would make at the start of the lease.

b. Show the journal entry Office Systems would make at the start of the lease.

c. Show the journal entry Bidwell would make on receipt of the first payment.

d. Show the journal entry Office Systems would make on issuing the first payment.

P14-15. Answer parts (a) to (d) of P14-14 above if Bidwell had purchased the equipment for $50,000, paid the same initial costs of $1,000, and treated the transaction as a direct-financing lease. Explain the reason for the difference, if any, between Bidwell's first-year interest income under a direct-financing lease and a sales-type lease.

P14-16. Investor Ltd. was a company whose business was financing small temporary industrial buildings. It entered into a rental agreement with Lessee Ltd. to provide a building at a monthly rental of $3,985.71 payable at the end of each month for thirty-six months. In addition to purchasing the building for $120,000, Investor also incurred site preparation and legal costs of $5,000. At the end of the three-year period Investor is required to remove the building from the site. It is estimated that the removal and site-clearing costs will approximate the salvage value of the building; thus the expected net recovery value is nil. The present value of thirty-six payments in arrears of $3,985.71 is $120,000 at a nominal annual rate of 12% and $125,000 at a rate of 9.184%.

Required:

Show the journal entries for each of the following:

a. capitalizing the lease in Investor's books

b. recording the $5,000 of initial costs

c. recording the first lease payment in Investor's books

d. recording the first lease payment in the Lessee's books

P14-17. Lessee entered into an agreement with Lessor to rent a new heavy-duty truck that had a market value when new of $75,000. For a period of four years Lessee agreed to make rental payments of $5,300.80 each calendar quarter, payable in advance, starting as of the date the lease began. Lessee wanted some additional radio equipment in the truck. Because Lessor refused to provide the radio equipment, Lessee purchased it outright for a cost of $1,200. The truck and radio equipment are expected to have a functional life of six years, after which time the residual value of the truck is expected to be $8,000 and that of the radio equipment is expected to be nil. Under the terms of the agreement Lessee must purchase the truck from Lessor at the end of the four-year lease period for $10,000 (its expected market value at that time). Lessor must sell it for that price. Straight-line depreciation was selected. The interest rate that is implied by these terms is 12%. However the rate at which Lessee normally borrows is 13%, which implies a present value of $73,641.55 for the truck under terms of the lease. Lessor (who is a passive investor) incurred legal and other costs of $1,400.00 that reduced its effective yield to 11%. (All the interest rates quoted above are nominal annual rates; the quarterly rate equals one-quarter of the annual rate.)

Required:

a. Should this agreement be recorded as a capital lease or an operating lease? Explain.

b. Show the journal entry in Lessor's books at the time the truck was turned over to Lessee in accordance with the terms of the lease. Assume the lease is a capital one.

c. Show the entry in Lessor's books when it receives the second payment under the lease.

d. Show the entry in Lessee's books when it makes the second payment under the lease and records its depreciation for the quarter.

P14-18. Automotive Equipment Limited (AEL) is a supplier to the smaller auto dealers. It normally sells its equipment to its customers, but occasionally it will rent. At the moment it has agreed to rent a car hoist to a customer on a ten-year lease with annual payments in arrears of $5,592.70. The installation costs, to be paid by AEL, are $2,800.00. The asset is not expected to have any disposal value at the end of the lease. The present value of the lease payments at 12% is $31,600, and the present value at 9.9761% is $34,400. The rate of interest implicit in the lease is 12%. The cost of the asset when AEL purchased it two years ago was $36,000.

a. Show the journal entry (entries) AEL would make when it supplies the equipment to the lessee under the lease.

b. Calculate what the difference would be in income for the first year of the lease between treating it as a direct-financing lease and treating it as a sales-type lease.

c. Comment on the difference in accounting treatment for initial costs such as installation between direct-financing and sales-type leases. Be sure to explain (i) the effect on the allocation of the expense over time periods and (ii) the difference, if any, in the way the matching principle is applied.

P14-19. In a search for funds to modernize their show room and expand inventory, University Sports Supply (USS) have found an investor who is willing to finance them through a sale-and-leaseback arrangement on their land and building. Three years ago, the land had originally cost them $80,000, and the building had cost them $100,000. Under the terms of the leaseback, Investor will buy their land and building for $235,000 and lease both back to them on a ten-year lease for a total annual payment of $32,758.73, arrived at as follows:

Total value of land and buildings:		$235,000.00
Of which — land:	$120,000.00	
— building:	$115,000.00	
Expected disposal value of building in ten years:		$35,000.00
Term of lease: 10 years		
Lending rate of lessor: 12%		
Operating lease for land		
(annual payment = 12% of market value of $120,000):		$14,400.00
Rental of building based on $115,000:		18,358.73
Total annual payment at the end of each year:		32,758.73

The building has a total expected life of 13 years, and its disposal value has always been estimated at $35,000. The annual rental on the building was calculated to be sufficient to reduce the amount owed on the building to $35,000, its estimated disposal value. At the end of the lease the lessee, USS, was required to buy the land and building for

$35,000 + $120,000 = $155,000$. The repayment schedule on the building portion of the leaseback was calculated as follows:

Year	Capital	Interest at 12%	Payment	Repayment
1986	115,000.00	13,800.00	18,358.73	4,558.73
1987	110,441.27	13,252.95	18,358.73	5,105.78
1988	105,335.49	12,640.26	18,358.73	5,718.47
1989	99,617.02	11,954.04	18,358.73	6,404.69
1990	93,212.33	11,185.48	18,358.73	7,173.25
1991	86,039.08	10,324.69	18,358.73	8,034.04
1992	78,005.04	9,360.61	18,358.73	8,998.12
1993	69,006.92	8,280.83	18,358.73	10,077.90
1994	58,929.02	7,071.48	18,358.73	11,287.25
1995	47,641.77	5,717.01	18,358.73	12,641.72
1996	35,000.05			

Required:

a. Show the entry (entries) in the books of University Sports Supply when they receive the payment of $235,000 and when they assume the capital lease under the sale-and-leaseback. Assume their borrowing rate is 13%.

b. Show the entry in the books of Investor when it makes the payment of $235,000.

c. Show all the entries in the books of USS at the end of the first year when they make the first payment of $32,758.73 and when they record income and expenses with respect to the lease. Assume that USS used straight-line depreciation for the building.

d. If USS had raised the money by mortgaging the building for $235,000 at 12% interest instead of using a sale-and-leaseback, would their reported expenses at the end of the first year have been higher, lower, or unchanged? Explain. (Assume straight-line depreciation in each case.) Show all your calculations.

P14-20. Seaspray Marine charters sailing yachts on a weekly basis to clientele that rents them for vacation relaxation. The yachts in question sell for $80,000 each on the retail market; but since Seaspray is a dealer and volume purchaser, it obtains them for $70,000 each. It finances the yachts by "selling" them to wealthy investors who then lease them back to Seaspray at an annual rental in arrears of $16,104.23, which at 12% is sufficient to retire a debt of $80,000 in eight years. The wealthy investors get preference for the dates on which they can charter "their" boat, but otherwise they receive no other special favors. At the end of the eight years Seaspray has the right under the lease to purchase the yacht for $1.

Required:

a. Should Seaspray consider the $10,000 margin between its purchase price of the yachts and rental price as a profit of the period in which it is "sold"? Or should it amortize the profit over some longer period, such as the term of the rental period? Discuss.

b. Assuming that Seaspray decides to recognize the $10,000 margin in the year the yacht is first financed under the lease, show the journal entry (entries) Seaspray should make when the title to the yacht passes to the lessor and Seaspray receives its cheque for $80,000.

c. Assuming that Seaspray decides to amortize the $10,000 profit over the life of the lease, show all the entries Seaspray should make at the end of the first year.

d. Show the entry the lessor would make when issuing the cheque for $80,000 to Seaspray.

P14-21. At a recent meeting of management at Yoland Inc's head office, the President abruptly cut in on a statement being made by the Vice-President, Finance. The meeting had been called to clarify company accounting procedures. Just prior to the point of interruption, the discussion had turned to the question of accounting for the many equipment and property leases that the company has with various issuers. the V.-P., Finance, was reviewing the criteria set out in the *CICA Handbook* for capitalizing leases when the President interrupted. "Look. We're living and working in the real world. If I don't want to capitalize a lease and show it on the balance sheet, then I won't. There is usually enough flexibility in interpreting *Handbook* criteria to present a lease as either an operating lease or a capital lease. I believe that our Controller can exercise her professional judgement on this issue. The *Handbook* is a set of guidelines, not a set of very strict rules, and I believe we should be prepared to interpret when appropriate. In fact, why should we report the lease as an asset and a liability on the balance sheet? It seems ridiculous to record an asset when we don't own it. Similarly, why show a liability for the amount of the lease contract when the real cash consequences that affects the firm's working capital position is only the full amount of next year's lease payments?"

Required: Do you agree with the President? Analyze his comments in a critique not exceeding 500 words.

(CMA adapted)

P14-22. Lessee Inc. leased equipment from Lessor Inc. The classification of the lease makes a difference in the amounts reflected on the balance sheet and income statement of both companies.

Required:

a. List the criteria, any one of which suffice, that must be met by the lease for Lessee to classify it as a capital lease.

b. What additional criteria must be met by the lease for Lessor to classify it as a capital lease (either as a direct-financing lease or a sales-type lease)?

c. What is the major distinction between a sale-type lease and a direct-financing lease for Lessor?

d. State two items that must be dislosed by Lessee in the financial statements with respect to capital lease transactions.

(CMA adapted)

P14-23. On 1 January 19X4 Colebrook Inc. contracted with Marlbank Leasing Inc. to lease some personal computers and related equipment. The lease covered a four-year period and was not cancellable. However, it was renewable at the end of the lease on terms which were expected to represent fair market value at the option date. No additional costs were to be incurred by Marlbank.

The following information is provided about Marlbank:

    (i) The book value of the computers and related equipment was $31,000. When they were purchased, they had been charged to the inventory account.

    (ii) The fair value of the leased equipment at the inception of the lease was $31,000.

    (iii) The estimated useful life of the leased equipment is five years.

    (iv) The interest rate implicit in the lease was 1.5% per month. This was known to Colebrook.

The following information is provided about Colebrook:

(i) Monthly lease payments (due on the first of each month) were $825 beginning 1 January 19X4.

(ii) Colebrook guaranteed a residual value of $5,000 to Marlbank at the end of the 48-month lease. If there was any excess over the $5,000 guarantee, Marlbank was to receive the excess. The present value of $5,000 payable at the end of 48 months is $2,446.81 at a monthly rate of 1.5% and $1,932.69 at a monthly rate of 2%.

(iii) All assets were depreciated on a straight-line basis.

(iv) Colebrook's incremental borrowing rate was 2% per month. The present value of $1,000 paid at the start of each month for 48 months is $34,553.19 at a monthly rate of 1.5% and $31,286.58 at a monthly rate of 2%.

(v) Colebrook was in sound financial condition and assumed executory costs.

The rentals were fair, and the estimated residual value was assumed to be the amount that would be realized at the conclusion of the lease. The lease terminated on 31 December 19X7 and was not renewed. Marlbank sold the leased equipment on 31 December 19X7 for $4,850. The amount by which the residual guarantee exceeded the proceeds was paid by Colebrook.

Required:

a. Show the journal entry (entries) that the lessor would make at the beginning of the lease on 1 January 19X4 to set it up as a capital lease. Include the first lease payment.

b. Show the journal entry (entries) that the lessee would make at the beginning of the second period when the second payment is made. Also show the depreciation of the asset for the period.

c. Prepare the required journal entry (entries) for Marlbank at the termination of the lease on 31 December 19X7.

(CMA adapted)

APPENDIX 14-1
Some Basic Mathematics of Leasing

In this Appendix we will use some basic mathematics of leasing in a simple example to demonstrate the following important points:

1. The difference in treatment betwen operating and capital leases shifts income between periods.

2. The choice of the interest rate used to capitalize a lease affects the allocation of costs between time periods.

3. The difference between the capital lease and operating lease method of accounting has no impact on funds or cash flow.

Assume that at the beginning of 19X0 Kafka Corporation entered into a capital lease for an asset with a useful functional life of two years. Under the terms of the lease it had to pay $100 a year at the end of each year. The appropriate amortization method was judged to be straight line. Had the lease been treated as an operating lease, Kafka would have made the following entry at the end of each year when it made the payment:

Rental expense	100.00	
Bank		100.00
To record annual rent.		

If the lease were judged to be a capital lease, then it would be necessary to find the present value of the annual payments. Assume that the interest rate implicit in the lease was 20%. Then the present value would be calculated as follows:

Present value of the payment at the end of 19X0: 100/1.20	$ 83.33	
Present value of the payment at the end of 19X1:		
100/1.20/1.20	69.44	
Total present value of the payments discounted at 20%	$152.77	

If this were accepted as the capitalizing rate, then Kafka would make the following entry at the start of the first year:

Leased assets	152.77	
Obligations under capital leases		152.77
To capitalize lease payments of a capital lease.		

At the end of the first year the entries would read as follows:

Interest expense (20% of 152.77)	30.56	
Obligations under capital leases (100.00 − interest expense)	69.44	
Bank		100.00
To record payment of annual rental amount of $100 and allocate it over interest expense and lease repayment.		
Amortization expense	76.38	
Accumulated amortization		76.38
To record annual amortization of plant asset acquired under a capital lease (50% of $152.77).		

Note that the amount charged to expense here is $30.56 + $76.38 = $106.94. At the end of the second year Kafka would make the following entries:

Interest expense (20% of (152.77 − 69.45))	16.67	
Obligations under capital leases (100.00 − interest expense)	83.33	
Bank		100.00
To record payment of annual rental amount of $100 and allocate it over interest expense and lease repayment.		
Amortization expense	76.39	
Accumulated amortization		76.39
To record annual amortization of plant asset acquired under a capital lease (50% of $152.77).		

Note that the amount charged to expense here is $16.67 + $76.39 = $93.06. Therefore the total amount charged to expense over the two years is $106.94 + $93.06 = $200.00, or the same amount that would have been charged over the two years had the company treated the lease as an operating lease. The difference lies in how much was charged to each year, not in the total amount. Thus we have illustrated point 1 above.

Now let us assume that Kafka's own interest cost was 15% rather than the 20% implicit in the lease. The present value of the two payments of $100 would therefore be as follows:

Present value of the payment at the end of 19X0: 100/1.15	$86.96	
Present value of the payment at the end of 19X1: 100/1.15/1.15	75.61	
Total present value	162.57	

If this amount did not exceed the market value of the asset, it would be used by Kafka to make the following entry at the start of 19X0:

Leased assets	162.57	
Obligations under capital leases		162.57

To record acquisition of assets acquired under a capital lease. Equal to the present value of two payments of $100 discounted at 15%.

At the end of 19X0 Kafka would make the following two entries:

Interest expense (15% of 162.57)	24.39	
Obligations under capital lease	75.61	
Bank		100.00

To record payment of annual rental amount of $100 and allocate it over interest expense and lease repayment.

Amortization expense	81.28	
Accumulated amortization		81.28

To record annual amortization of plant asset acquired under a capital lease (50% of $162.57).

At the end of 19X1 Kafka's entries would read as follows:

Interest expense (15% of (162.57 − 75.61))	13.04	
Obligations under capital lease	86.96	
Bank		100.00

To record payment of annual rental amount of $100 and allocate it over interest expense and lease repayment.

Amortization expense	81.29	
Accumulated amortization		81.29

To record annual amortization of plant asset acquired under a capital lease (50% of $162.57).

Let us now compare the impact on each year, and in total, resulting from the differences in treatment. We can summarize our example as follows:

Accounting treatment	19X0	19X1	Total
Operating lease	$100.00	$100.00	$200.00
Capital lease at 20%:			
Amortization	$ 76.38	$ 76.39	$152.77
Interest	30.56	16.67	47.23
Total	$106.94	$ 93.06	$200.00
Capital lease at 15%:			
Amortization	$ 81.28	$ 81.29	$162.57
Interest	24.39	13.04	37.43
Total	$105.67	$ 94.33	$200.00

Observe that in all three cases the total costs for both years are $200. However, there is a slight difference in how the costs are allocated between the years. Under both treatments of the capital lease, the costs in the first year are higher than if the lease were treated as an operating lease. Note further that the capital lease with the higher interest rate allocates the highest costs to the first year. We have thus illustrated point 2 above.

Let us now turn to point 3 above, the impact of accounting methods on cash flow. It seems intuitively sensible that the choice of accounting method should have no impact on funds or cash flow. We can illustrate this conclusion by using our example as follows:

COMPARATIVE STATEMENT OF CHANGES IN FINANCIAL POSITION

	Operating lease method	Capital lease at 20%	Capital lease at 15%
Net income before deducting the following	$100.00	$100.00	$100.00
Rental expense	100.00		
Amortization of leased property		76.38	81.28
Interest		30.56	24.39
Net loss shown on income statement	$ 0.00	$ 6.94	$ 5.67
Add: Expenses that do not involve an outlay of funds — amortization of leased property		76.38	81.28
Less: Retirement of long-term lease obligation		69.44	75.61
	0.00	$ 6.94	$ 5.67
Net change	$ 0.00	$ 0.00	$ 0.00

BIBLIOGRAPHY

AMERICAN INSTITUTE OF CERTIFIED PUBLIC ACCOUNTANTS. COMMITTEE ON ACCOUNTING PROCEDURE. *Accounting Research Bulletin No. 43: Restatement and Revision of Accounting Research Bulletins.* New York, 1953. A codification of existing bulletins that contain sections on accounting standards for leases.

———. ACCOUNTING PRINCIPLES BOARD. *Opinion No. 5: Reporting of Leases in Financial Statements of Lessee.* New York, 1964. A successor body to the Committee on Accounting Procedure tries to narrow down the acceptable procedures for reporting leases.

BRAULT, REJEAN, and MCMAHON, DANIEL. "A Superior Approach to Accounting for Sales-type Leases." *CA Magazine* (April 1983). A critique of the *CICA Handbook's* treatment of sales-type leases on the books of the lessor.

FINANCIAL ACCOUNTING STANDARDS BOARD. *Statement of Financial Accounting Standard No. 13: Accounting for Leases.* Stamford, Conn.: FASB, 1976. The FASB also tries to narrow down the acceptable procedures for reporting leases.

RO, B.T. "The Disclosure of Capitalized Lease Information and Stock Prices." *Journal of Accounting Research* (Autumn 1978). This research study was done before the FASB had issued FAS No. 13. It studies the impact of an SEC disclosure ruling on the prices of shares of companies likely to be affected by disclosure of long-term leases. It found that the disclosure did appear to affect the price of shares. This sort of evidence might be used by those who believe that capitalization of leases is not needed as long as the reader of statements is informed in some way.

WILKINS, TREVOR, and ZIMMER, IAN. "The Effect of Leasing and Different Methods of Accounting for Leases on Credit Evaluations." *The Accounting Review* (October 1983). A field experiment to see if credit analysts' decisions are affected by the capitalization of leases.

CHAPTER 15
Pensions

Introduction

A **pension plan** is a formal arrangement to provide post-retirement income to employees after retirement. An employee's pension is usually determined by that individual's years of employment and earned income. Hence, a pension can be regarded as a form of delayed compensation. Under the matching principle the expense of this delayed compensation should be recognized in the period in which the benefit, the employee's labour, is received, and a corresponding long-term liability should be recognized. The core problems facing the accountant here are as follows:

1. How to allocate the pension expense to time periods in accordance with the matching principle.

2. How to estimate pension liability when the point of retirement is many years away and the factors that will ultimately govern the size of the pension are not yet established.

3. How best to present this information to the readers of financial statements.

In all societies some people age to the point where they are no longer able to support themselves. Until this century, not many people reached retirement because accidents or disease killed them first. Life was described by Thomas Hobbes in the 1650s as "nasty, brutish and short." The few people who lived into their later years were expected to be cared for by their families. However, in the 20th century, this informal system of caring for the elderly has been supplemented by formal systems of medical and financial support, of which pensions are a major element. The pension plans we will evaluate in this chapter are those offered by private sector companies to their employees as part of their total remuneration package. We will exclude those plans offered by various levels of government, such as the Canada Pension Plan or Old Age Security.

In Canada it is only since the 1950s that such pension plans have grown to a significant size. Accounting for the pension liabilities of companies is a relatively new problem. The growth of such pension plans was spurred by union pressures and special inducements offered through the federal Income Tax Act. Companies that set up their pension plans in accordance with minimum terms established by the federal government were allowed to treat their pension contributions as tax deductions. In addition, there was a general trend in most of the Western world toward providing old age security. Encouraging private sector pension plans was part of this trend.

Virtually all private Canadian pension plans are **funded**, which means that assets are specifically segregated and kept separately to be available to discharge the pension liability. These pension assets are normally held under the control of a third party, such as a board of pension trustees or a trust company acting as custodian. The annual amounts put into the pension fund by the employer are usually the amounts recommended by an actuary hired to give this advice. The fact that the pension assets are held by a third party who administers them does not relieve the company of the responsibility for seeing that the pension is paid according to its terms. The annual amount put into the fund is not necessarily the annual cost of the pension that would be indicated by the matching principle of accounting. At present, however, most companies are treating the amount paid into the fund annually as the cost of the pension, thus potentially overstating or understating their pension cost for that year.

Explanation of Pension Terms

This section sets out some technical terms connected with pension plans. It is important to understand these terms and become familiar with the jargon in order to make some basic distinctions between different types of pension plans. Unfortunately, there is no standardized terminology in the field and variations in usage can become quite confusing.

The *CICA Handbook* [3460.03a] defines a **pension plan** as "any arrangement, contractual or otherwise, by which a program is established to provide retirement income to employees." It would exclude payments made on an informal gratuitous basis, but it *would include* arrangements outside the legal pension plan contract if these arrangements resulted in payment of specific amounts after retirement. This is an important point, because employers may at times increase pension benefits for moral or business reasons, even though they may not be legally required to do so under the terms of the pension contract.

In effect, we are encountering the distinction between contractual, equitable, and constructive obligations which we discussed briefly in Chapter 11. The employer may have a **contractual obligation** to provide only the benefits set out in the plan. However, if the plan was started before 1970, then there has been both a severe inflation (that has eroded the pension's earning power) and extraordinarily high earnings on the pension portfolio (that provide the capability of paying higher pensions). For these reasons some may feel that the employer has an **equitable obligation** to raise existing pensions above the contractual amount. In fact, laws may be passed to turn this perceived equitable obligation into a contractual one. In addition, an employer's generous treatment of retiring employees in the past (e.g., providing "past service" benefits to increase their pension on retirement) may create an expectation of continued generous treatment. In this case the employer would have a **constructive obligation**. The accountant must consider all three types of obligations when estimating the pension liability.

Pension plans are long-term arrangements between the employer and employee. It is unlikely that the assumptions that had to be made at the start of the plan (such as investment yields, the rate of inflation, taxation, and expected life spans) will work out as planned. A basic question that must be settled at the start of the plan is how the potential positive and negative outcomes over the life of the plan will be shared between the employer and employee. At one extreme the employee may assume all the risks and enjoy all the benefits: this is called a **defined contribution plan**. At the other extreme the employer takes the risks and enjoys the benefits: this is called a **defined benefit plan**. Let us explain these terms in more detail.

A defined contribution pension plan is one in which the *yearly contribution of the employer* to a pension fund is defined at the start of the plan. The contribution is not usually defined as a fixed sum of money, but as a formula that will be used each year to calculate the employer's contribution. The ultimate pension that this contribution produces cannot be known in advance, for it depends on such factors as the investment income earned on the contributions. In such a plan the employee bears the ultimate risk of gain or loss due to changes in later circumstances. The employer's obligation under the plan is discharged when the employer's contribution to the plan has been made. About 50% of Canadian pension plans are of this type. But they cover only 10% of all plan members because defined benefit plans are usually much larger. One example of a defined contribution plan would be where the employer puts a sum equal to 6% of each employee's gross pay into a pension fund each year. Another example would be where a coal company agrees with its union to put a fixed amount of money into the pension fund for every ton of coal mined. In such cases the formula for the contribution to the pension plan is agreed upon at the outset, but the ultimate pension that will be provided from these contributions cannot be known in advance.

A defined benefit pension plan is one in which the pension *benefits to be received by the employee* on retirement are defined at the start. These benefits may be defined in such terms as (i) a fixed payment per year that is related to the number of years worked, (ii) the gross salary earned during the employee's working career, or (iii) a formula that is related to years of service and salary just prior to retirement. The contribution needed from the employer to provide the pension cannot be estimated with any certainty until the employee approaches retirement, and it cannot be completely known until the pension beneficiary dies. One example of a defined benefit plan would be where on retirement an employee receives an annual pension of 2% of his or her average career earnings multiplied by the number of years worked. Thus here, if a male employee worked thirty years and averaged $40,000 over his career with the company, he would receive $30 \times 2\% \times 40,000$, or $24,000 per year until he died (regardless of intervening changes such as portfolio gains or losses). The size of pension payments that the employee will receive is settled at the start. What is not known until near the employee's retirement is what the approximate cost will be to the employer. In such plans the employer bears the risk of gain or loss.

The difference between these two types of plans can be summarized as follows:

Feature of plan	Defined benefit	Defined contribution
Pension received by employee	A fixed amount defined by the terms of the plan	An undefined amount that depends on what the contributions to the plan have accumulated to
Contributions made by employer	Whatever is needed to provide the later benefits defined under the plan	A predetermined amount each period, according to the terms of the plan
Party that bears the risks and gets the benefits of future events	Employer	Employee

Although these are the two basic types, some plans are blends of the two. Therefore, it is important to be aware of potential variations in existing plans.

It is common that employees may not join a pension plan until after they have worked at a company for several years. Once they join, their rights to receive pension benefits may be contingent on their remaining in the employ of that company for a certain number of years. Pension benefits are said to **vest** when this contingency no longer applies. It is in an employee's interests to have pension rights vest as soon as possible. On the other hand, delaying the vesting right reduces the employer's pension costs inasmuch as employee turnover helps to reduce the number of persons eligible for pension benefits. The maximum waiting period before vesting is frequently controlled by legislation.

A pension that is **portable** is so designed that if employees change jobs, their pension rights can be transferred to another employer's pension plan with no loss of pension benefits. Otherwise, if employees have vesting rights but no portability, they will retire with two pension plans — one at the old employer and one at the new.

Employees are **locked in** to a plan if they are ultimately entitled to the pension benefits of the plan, but before reaching a certain age they are not free to take out any of the funds. In most Canadian plans the assets are locked in for persons between the ages of 45 and 55.

An **actuary** is a professional who, among other things, studies the key factors (such as expected interest rates, pensioner life expectancy, and staff turnover) that determine the company's pension obligation. By estimating these factors, an actuary calculates the approximate amount needed to fund the pension plan.

The **funding** provisions for a plan describe the manner in which the employer will provide the money needed to pay the pension benefits. At one extreme the employer might put no specific funds aside and instead simply pay the pension benefits to the retired employee out of the general funds of the company. At the other (highly unlikely) extreme the employer might set aside all the funds required on the first day the employee reported to work. The usual arrangement is for the employer to set aside some funds during each year of the employee's working career. Under the matching principle, the period in which funds are set aside should have no influence on the timing of the recognition of pension expense.

In a typical plan the employer may contract with an insurance company to make periodic payments into a pension fund to be held by the insurance company. Alternatively, the employer may put money into a separate pension fund under the control of a pension trustee. The employer usually contributes for each year that the employee is eligible for pension benefits. Thus the money flows into this fund for many years before the employee retires. The calculation of the periodic payment into the fund that will accumulate to the desired amount on retirement is usually done by an actuary. Unfortunately the actuary refers to this periodic payment into the fund as the "cost". Hence, the pattern of funds flow for the period preceding retirement is termed the **actuarial cost**. Although the term "cost" is used by the actuary, the method is really a means for providing the money needed by the pension plan; the term does *not* have the same meaning as the accounting concept of costs.

The main objective of a funding plan is to ensure that there will be sufficient assets in the pension fund to provide the agreed pension benefits when employees retire. There are an infinite number of payment patterns that will accomplish this goal. The two most common patterns are the following:

1. **Accrued benefit cost method** — the amount put into the pension fund in a given year is the increase in the expected present value of the pension benefits earned to date under the terms of the pension plan. This amount will increase with each passing year.
2. **Projected benefit cost method** (also called the **entry age normal method**) — a constant contribution (either a constant amount or a constant percentage of salary) is made to the pension fund from one year to the next, based on an estimate of the total prospective benefits to be paid to the pension beneficiaries.

Both these methods are intended to produce the same amount of funds at the point of retirement. The only difference between them is the timing of the payments into the fund. Let us use an example to compare the yearly funding pattern of an accrued benefit and a projected benefit cost method.

Suppose that a company calculated it would need $34,439 at the date of an employee's retirement, thirty-five years from now, in order to purchase at that time the life annuity needed to provide that person's retirement pension. The company believed that any funds it put aside for investment would earn 5%. How much should it plan to put aside in each of the thirty-five years the employee worked for the company? For simplicity let us suppose that the employee earned the same amount in each of those years. Thus, the amount that has to be accumulated with respect to each year is 34,439/ 35 = $983.97.

If the company used accrued benefit funding, then in the first year it would calculate the amount that had to be set aside in order to accumulate to $983.37 in thirty-five years at 5% per annum. This is $983.37 / (1.05)^{35} = 178.28$. The following year it would contribute slightly more, or $983.37 / (1.05)^{34}$.

If the company used projected benefit funding, then it would calculate the *constant* amount of money that could be put in each of the thirty-five years that would accumulate to $34,439 at the end. The amount turns out to be $381.32. (The method of calculating it is beyond the scope of this text.) A comparison of the two funding patterns is shown in Figure 15-1.

FIGURE 15-1. COMPARISON OF ANNUAL PAYMENTS UNDER PROJECTED AND ACCRUED BENEFITS PLANS YIELDING THE SAME OVERALL TOTAL

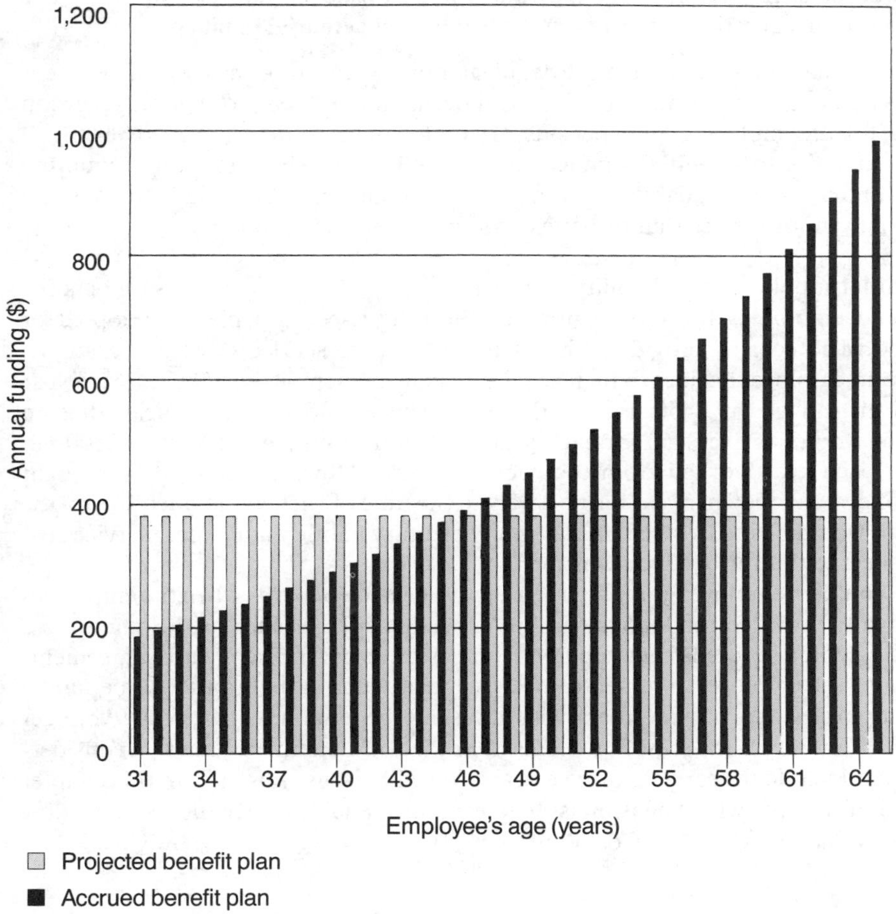

□ Projected benefit plan
■ Accrued benefit plan

In addition to recommending a funding pattern, actuaries also compute the commitment that the employer is assuming when a pension plan is introduced. This is called the **actuarial liability**. It is *not* the same as an accounting liability. Actuaries include pension benefits that have not yet been earned in their calculations, whereas an accounting liability must reflect an obligation assumed for a benefit already received. In effect, the actuary is saying to the employer: "If you introduce this plan and if your employees stay in your work force as expected, then ultimately you are going to have to provide the following sums in pension benefits." Various types of actuarial liabilities are calculated in order to answer the following possible questions from the employer:

1. What is the total pension commitment under the proposed or present plan? The answer to this question is the amount called the **gross actuarial liability**.

2. Of the total commitment, how much is not already covered by funds put into the pension fund to date? The answer to this question is the amount known as the **unfunded actuarial liability**.

3. Of the total commitment, how much additional contribution into the pension fund (beyond present commitments and funds on hand) do we have to plan for? The answer to this question is the amount called the **net actuarial liability**.

We will explain these terms in more detail later once an example has been developed.

Let us first consider one additional issue. It occurs when an employer grants pension benefits for an employee's past periods of employment, that is, retroactively. Such benefits give rise to an **initial supplementary liability**, which is both an accounting liability and an actuarial liability. It is a pension commitment (making it an actuarial liability) given for service that has already been performed (making it an accounting liability).

An initial supplementary liability is the expected present value of pension benefits granted to employees for service prior to the time a pension plan is adopted or modified. The cost of providing this is termed a **past service cost**. For example, suppose an employer decides to increase future pension benefits to $500 for each year worked instead of the $450 used in the past. This would normally mean that an employee would receive $450 for each year worked up to the present, then $500 per year for each year worked from that point onward. However, an employer might decide to give the $500 per year retroactively to the time of first employment. If so, the employer would be incurring an initial supplementary liability and a past service cost with respect to this retroactive adjustment.

Why would an employer grant such **retroactive pension benefits** when the employees have already provided the labour without expecting such an increase? Sometimes a bargaining union succeeds in gaining this concession as part of a collective agreement. Sometimes the employer enters into the agreement voluntarily in order to be fair to older employees and provide them with the same benefits now earned by younger employees. Whatever the reason, it seems clear that the decision is based on considerations that include the services of past years. We will discuss this later in this chapter when we subject the whole pension issue to economic analysis. (See the section below entitled "What Does Pension Cost Represent?")

Example of a Pension Plan

Let us work through an example. (The following is adapted from an example presented by T.R. Archibald.) Sam Jones started to work on 1 January, which was also his 30th birthday. The company had a pension plan that guaranteed him an annual payment of $500, commencing at age 65, for each year he worked. All pension rights vested in him immediately. (One way of thinking about this is to imagine that at the end of each work-year his employer would give him a certificate entitling him to receive $500 a year for life on reaching age 65. If he worked 35 years he would have 35 such certificates). He would retire on reaching age 65, and the pension would be paid to him at the end of each retirement year, that is, on his 66th and subsequent birthdays.

For example, if he worked for 35 years to age 65 he would receive 35 times $500, or $17,500, on his 66th birthday and on all subsequent birthdays as long as he lived. This might be shown diagrammatically as follows:

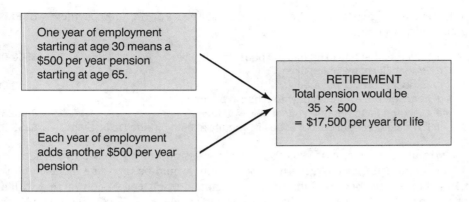

ENTRIES DURING EMPLOYMENT

To estimate the cost of the employee's pension in our example, an actuary might make the following assumptions:

1. There is a 100% probability that Jones will reach his 65th birthday and still be with the company.

2. The probability that Jones will be alive at the birthdays following his 65th are as shown below:

   66th birthday — 70%
   67th birthday — 60%
   68th birthday — 50%
   69th birthday — 30%
   70th birthday — 10%
   71st birthday — nil

3. The interest rate to use is 5%.

Suppose that on Sam's 65th birthday, at the point of his retirement, the company wished to purchase a contract from a third party (such as a life insurance company) to pay this life annuity. The estimated cost of this contract would be equal to the expected present value of the annual payments of $500 each. The values are shown in the table below:

EXPECTED COST ON 65TH BIRTHDAY OF $500 LIFE ANNUITY

Birthday	Pension payable	Probability of having to pay it	Years after retirement	Discount factor	Expected present cost at 65th birthday
66th	$ 500	0.70	1	0.95238	$ 333.33
67th	500	0.60	2	0.90703	272.11
68th	500	0.50	3	0.86384	215.96
69th	500	0.30	4	0.82270	123.41
70th	500	0.10	5	0.78353	39.18
71st	500	0.00	6		0.00
					$ 983.99

In the first year, for instance, the expected present cost of the $500 payment would be calculated as follows:

a. Payment that has to be made if pensioner is alive	$500.00
b. Probability of his being alive	70%
c. Expected cost of payment (a × b)	$ 350.00
d. Years before expected payment has to be made	1
e. Discount factor for one year at 5% = 1/1.05	0.95238
f. Expected present cost of $500 life annuity at 66th birthday (c × e)	$333.33

The total expected cost of $983.99 rests on the assumptions stated above. Disregarding any administrative charges, the expected cost would be the same if the employer planned to pay the pension himself when it came due, instead of contracting with an insurer to pay the $500 life annuity for a one-time payment (of $983.99) on Sam's 65th birthday. The only difference would be that then the employer rather than the insurer would bear the risks and enjoy the benefits or losses of the actual outcome.

On the day before Sam's 31st birthday, the end of the first employment year, the employer records his long-term liability with respect to the $500 life annuity Sam has earned. The employer is committed to provide a sum equal to $983.99 in 34 years. The present value of this liability is that amount discounted for 34 years at 5%, or $983.99 × 0.19035 = $187.31. Therefore the employer *might* make the following journal entry at the end of the first year (we will discuss other viewpoints about this later):

Pension expense	187.31	
Pension liability		187.31
To record pension liability for employee's first		
year of work. This is a life annuity of $500 per		
year, payable in 34 years.		

At the end of the second year, the second life annuity of $500 is payable in 33 years. Thus, the discount factor has risen from 0.19035 to 0.19987, and the journal entry would be as follows:

Pension expense	196.67	
Pension liability		196.67
To record pension liability for employee's		
second year of work. This is a life annuity of		
$500 per year, payable in 33 years.		

At the same time it is also necessary to record the increase in the first year's liability. Shown at its discounted present value, that liability increases because the time of payment is one year closer. The entry would read as follows:

Interest expense	9.36	
Pension liability		9.36
To record increase in pension liability with respect		
to Year 1 pension rights (187.31 × .05).		

Note that the increase in pension liability is considered to be an interest expense. This is because a pension benefit can be thought of as deferred compensation to the employee. In other words, the employee is willing to accept some of the remuneration after retirement, rather than in the year in which it was earned. This deferred remuneration becomes a long-term liability for the employer, and interest accumulates on it annually to reflect the benefit conferred on the employer through the use of the employee's funds.

Suppose the employer does not have the use of the funds, but instead pays them to a third party as trustee. Then no interest expense would be recorded because the income on the funds would be collected by the trustee and considered part of the pension fund. Most real-life pension plans are trusteed, and hence this interest expense is not normally recorded by the company.

Let us return to our example. At the end of the third year the discount factor would be for 32 years at 5% or 0.20987. Thus the entry would be as follows:

Pension expense	206.50	
Pension liability		206.50

To record pension liability for employee's third
year of work. This is a life annuity of $500 per
year, payable in 32 years.

In addition, the pension liability for the past two years is now one year closer to payment. The interest cost on this can be calculated as follows:

Year 1 pension benefit	187.31	
Interest accrued in second year at 5%	9.36	
	196.67	
Interest accrued in third year at 5%	9.83	
Accumulated liability to end of third year		$ 206.50
Year 2 pension benefit	196.67	
Interest accrued in third year at 5%	9.83	
Accumulated liability to end of their year		$ 206.50

It can be seen above that the interest accrued in the third year is $9.83 for each of Year 1 and Year 2, or a total of $19.66. The entry would read as follows:

Interest expense	19.66	
Pension liability		19.66

To record interest on pension liability with
respect to the first and second years.

In each of the succeeding years similar entries would be made to record pension liability and interest. By the employee's 65th birthday the final entry would create a total liability to him of $34,439.65 (i.e., 35 times $983.99, the cost of each individual $500 annuity). See Table 15-1 for a complete summary of all the calculations for this example. We have also included the annual numbers for the projected benefit method. (Disregard minor differences due to rounding.) Note that Table 15-1 includes the data given in Figure 15-1 above.

TABLE 15-1: PENSION CALCULATIONS OF GIVEN EXAMPLE

A. *Assumptions*
1. Discount rate = 5%
2. Years worked = 35
3. Annual pension after 35 years of work = $17,500.00
4. Probability that employee will be alive at 66th birthday = 70%
    at 67th birthday = 60%
    at 68th birthday = 50%
    at 69th birthday = 30%
    at 70th birthday = 10%
    at 71st birthday = nil

B. *Calculation of Expected Present Value at Age 65 of One Year's Pension Benefit*

Age	A Payment	B Probability of living to receive pension	C = A × B Expected cost	Discount to age 65	Expected present value at age 65
66	$ 500.00	0.70	350.00	0.9524	$ 333.33
67	500.00	0.60	300.00	0.9070	272.11
68	500.00	0.50	250.00	0.8638	215.96
69	500.00	0.30	150.00	0.8227	123.41
70	500.00	0.10	50.00	0.7835	39.18
71	500.00	0.00	0.00		0.00
					$ 983.98

Total expected cost of 35 years' service = 35 times $983.98 = $34,439.41

C. *Illustration of Accrued Benefit and Projected Benefit Funding*

| | Accrued Benefit Plan | | | Projected Benefit Method | | | | |
| | A | B | C | D | E | F | G | H |
Years of age	Annual payment	Interest credited	Accumulated balance	Annual payment	Interest credited	Accumulated balance	Present value of expected benefits	Present value of col. "D"

Age								
31	$ 187.31	$ 0.00	$ 187.31	$ 381.32	$ 0.00	$ 381.32	$ 6,555.71	$ 6,174.68
32	196.67	9.37	393.34	381.32	19.07	781.71	6,883.49	6,102.09
33	206.50	19.67	619.51	381.32	39.09	1,202.11	7,227.67	6,025.88
34	216.83	30.98	867.32	381.32	60.11	1,643.54	7,589.05	5,945.85
35	227.67	43.37	1,138.36	381.32	82.18	2,107.03	7,968.50	5,861.82
36	239.06	56.92	1,434.33	381.32	105.35	2,593.71	8,366.93	5,773.59
37	251.01	71.72	1,757.06	381.32	129.69	3,104.71	8,785.28	5,680.95
38	263.56	87.85	2,108.47	381.32	155.24	3,641.27	9,224.54	5,583.68
39	276.74	105.42	2,490.63	381.32	182.06	4,204.65	9,685.77	5,481.55
40	290.57	124.53	2,905.73	381.32	210.23	4,796.20	10,170.05	5,374.30
41	305.10	145.29	3,356.12	381.32	239.81	5,417.33	10,678.56	5,261.70
42	320.36	167.81	3,844.28	381.32	270.87	6,069.52	11,212.48	5,143.46
43	336.37	192.21	4,372.87	381.32	303.48	6,754.31	11,773.11	5,019.32
44	353.19	218.64	4,944.71	381.32	337.72	7,473.35	12,361.76	4,888.96
45	370.85	247.24	5,562.79	381.32	373.67	8,228.34	12,979.85	4,752.09
46	389.40	278.14	6,230.33	381.32	411.42	9,021.08	13,628.85	4,608.37
47	408.87	311.52	6,950.71	381.32	451.05	9,853.45	14,310.29	4,457.47
48	429.31	347.54	7,727.56	381.32	492.67	10,727.44	15,025.80	4,299.03
49	450.77	386.38	8,564.71	381.32	536.37	11,645.13	15,777.09	4,132.66
50	473.31	428.24	9,466.26	381.32	582.26	12,608.71	16,565.95	3,957.97
51	496.98	473.31	10,436.55	381.32	630.44	13,620.47	17,394.24	3,774.55
52	521.83	521.83	11,480.20	381.32	681.02	14,682.81	18,263.96	3,581.96
53	547.92	574.01	12,602.13	381.32	734.14	15,798.27	19,177.15	3,379.74
54	575.31	630.11	13,807.55	381.32	789.91	16,969.50	20,136.01	3,167.40
55	604.08	690.38	15,102.01	381.32	848.48	18,199.30	21,142.81	2,944.45
56	634.28	755.10	16,491.39	381.32	909.96	19,490.58	22,199.95	2,710.35
57	666.00	824.57	17,981.96	381.32	974.53	20,846.43	23,309.95	2,464.55
58	699.30	899.10	19,580.36	381.32	1,042.32	22,270.07	24,475.45	2,206.46
59	734.26	979.02	21,293.64	381.32	1,113.50	23,764.90	25,699.22	1,935.46
60	770.98	1,064.68	23,129.30	381.32	1,188.24	25,334.45	26,984.18	1,650.92
61	809.53	1,156.46	25,095.29	381.32	1,266.72	26,982.50	28,333.39	1,352.14
62	850.00	1,254.76	27,200.06	381.32	1,349.13	28,712.95	29,750.06	1,038.43
63	892.50	1,360.00	29,452.56	381.32	1,435.65	30,529.92	31,237.56	709.03
64	957.13	1,472.63	31,862.31	381.32	1,526.50	32,437.74	32,799.44	363.16
65	983.98	1,593.12	34,439.41	381.32	1,621.89	34,440.94	34,439.41	

ENTRIES AFTER RETIREMENT

Suppose that Sam has reached his 65th birthday and retires. During each of his years of employment the company has credited a liability account with the present value of the pension benefits earned in that year, together with interest at 5% on the pension liability brought forward from prior years. With the $34,439.65 the employer could have purchased a life annuity from a third-party insurer (assuming the insurer would purchase the contract at its expected present value). However, in our example we have assumed that the employer pays the pension himself and bears the risks of the actual outcome. (Recall that the amounts recorded reflect Sam's life expectancy.) This allows us to show the employer's accounting entries.

During Sam's first year of retirement the employer would need to record the payment to him as well as the interest cost on the accumulated pension liability. The journal entries would be as follows on the employee's 66th birthday:

Pension liability	17,500.00	
Bank		17,500.00

To record payment of first year's pension to
Sam, which is 35 times $500, or $17,500.

Interest expense	1,721.98	
Pension liability		1,721.98

To record interest expense on Sam's
accumulated pension liability. This is 5% of
$34,439.65

At this point the pension liability account has changed as follows:

Opening balance, on 65th birthday	$ 34,439.65
Interest added during subsequent year	1,721.98
	36,161.63
First year's pension payment on 66th birthday	17,500.00
Balance	$ 18,661.63

Let us now suppose that Sam died immediately after receiving his first pension cheque. Thus no further pension benefits will be paid. Because the original estimate of Sam's life expectancy turned out to be incorrect, the company charged too much to its pension expense in the prior years. Therefore, the remaining liability of $18,661.63 should now be cancelled. The difference between what the actuary estimated the pension to be and what the actual payments turn out to be is referred to as the **experience gain** or **experience loss**. (In this case it is a gain since Sam's life is shorter than expected.)

In our simple example the experience gain might be taken into income as follows:

Pension liability	18,661.63	
Experience gain on pension		18,661.63

To write off pension liability on premature death
of Sam.

The example has now illustrated four basic accounting elements of a pension plan: (i) the pension benefit to be paid on retirement, (ii) the probability that the employee will reach retirement and receive the benefit, (iii) the employee's life expectancy after retirement, and (iv) the interest rate used to calculate the present value of the expected pension benefits.

In the example we have implied that the increase from year to year in the expected value of the pension benefits is the measure of the pension costs for the year. Thus the pension costs in the first year of the plan were $187.31 and in the second year they were $196.67. It will become clearer later why this is *not* necessarily the case. For the time being, however, it is a convenient place to leave the calculation of pension expense and liability in order to turn to funding issues.

FUNDING THE PLAN

So far we have introduced accounting for a pension plan on the assumption that the employer would show the pension liability on his own books. However, most real-life pension plans are funded, with the pension assets administered and held by a third party, termed a **pension trustee**. Fund accounting was introduced in Chapter 10, and the basic ideas are similar when applied to pension funding. There are three levels of funding possible, with differing implications for the recording of interest expense and income. They are as follows:

1. The company could choose not to fund the plan at all. It could record the pension as a long-term liability, but not set aside any assets specifically to match this liability. In that case interest would be accrued on the long-term pension liability, as shown in the example above. Plans of this type are uncommon, but simplest to understand.

2. In addition to recording the pension as a long-term liability, the company could fund the plan by purchasing and setting aside within the company investment assets that are specifically designated for the pension fund. The interest earned on these assets would normally be credited to the pension liability, and the company would normally show neither interest expense nor income with respect to the pension plan or the plan assets. Plans of this type might be found with non-profit organizations, but they would also be uncommon.

3. The company could appoint a pension trustee or insurance company to administer the pension plan and its assets. The company would make periodic payments to the trustee who would invest the assets. The pension liability or assets are not shown on the company's books, but will usually be referred to in the notes to the financial statements. Plans of this type are the most common in practice.

Under the third arrangement set out above, the employer makes regular contributions to a trusteed pension fund as shown in the diagram below.

THE FLOW OF PENSION FUNDS

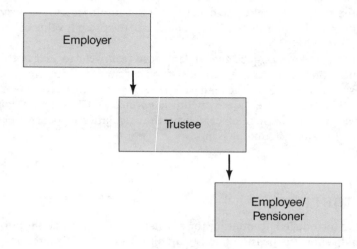

In effect, the money needed to fund the plan flows from the employer to the trustee and, when the employee retires, to the employee who will benefit under the plan. Having the pension funds held by a trustee is mainly for the protection of the ultimate pension beneficiaries. There could easily be a thirty-year lag before the money paid by the employer to the trustee is handed over to the former employee. It is not surprising, therefore, that employers have tended to think of the annual payment to the trustee as the expense of the pension plan for that year. However, if the pension plan is of the defined benefit type, then the employer must always be prepared to add additional amounts to the trustee's fund if the existing amounts prove insufficient. This is so even if the employer's annual contributions have been in accordance with the actuary's recommendation.

If the actuary responsible for recommending the funding pattern for Sam's pension uses the accrued benefit cost method, then the annual sum put into the fund will equal the present value of the benefits earned to date (as shown in the journal entries above). The journal entry for Sam's first year under a trusteed pension plan would be as follows:

Pension expense	187.31	
Bank		187.31

To record payment to pension trustee of the amount due under the accrued benefit cost method.

Contrast this entry with the one on page 588 where the company did not use a trustee, but kept the pension funds and recorded a long-term liability. When the funds have been handed over to a trustee for investment, the company records neither the liability nor related interest costs.

When receiving the funds, the trustee would make the following entry:

Bank — pension account	187.31	
Pension trust fund — contributed by employer		187.31
To record receipt of funds from Sam's employer.		

Suppose the trustee invested the funds immediately and earned 5% on them, or $9.36, during the second year. Then on receipt of the income, the trustee would make the following entry:

Bank — pension account	9.36	
Pension trust liability — investment income		9.36
To record receipt of investment income.		

Table 1, Part C, shows how the pension fund would be expected to grow if the accrued benefit plan were used (columns A, B, and C).

Instead of using the accrued benefit method for funding, the actuary might use other funding patterns. A common one is the *projected benefit method*. Here the actuary determines the equal amounts that, if put into the plan each year, would accumulate to the same amount at age 65 as under the accrued benefit method (i.e., $34,439.41). The annual amount needed can be found from tables or by using a pocket calculator. It is approximately $381.32 per annum. The application of the projected benefit plan to our example is shown in Table 1, Part C, columns D, E, and F. Note that both methods accumulate to the same amount at age 65 (ignoring small differences due to rounding).

If the pension plan is funded with a trustee, the employer would not make any entries in his books to record the increase in pension expense and liability of $9.36, as was shown earlier. By handing the funds over to the trustee, the employer has lost the opportunity to earn income on the $187.31 sent to the trustee. Hence the employer does not incur the expense of $9.36. For the time being at least, the employer has discharged his liability for the pension with respect to Sam's first year by making his payment to the trustee.

It should be emphasized again, however, that under a defined benefit plan the employer bears the long-term risk of providing the pension benefits promised. He has not discharged them by paying to the trustee the expected present value of the pension benefits. He has only made a kind of down payment.

For example, suppose that instead of earning 5% on the pension investments the trustee instead lost 2%, or $3.75, because the bonds in which he invested went down in price during the year. The employer would be obligated to make an additional payment to the trustee because of this experience loss. Should the employer recognize this loss immediately? Or should he use some smoothing technique to spread such experienced gains or losses over a period of years? This is a controversial issue. If portfolio losses are recognized immediately, there would be a parallel argument for recognizing gains immediately. Thus with a rising stock market the employer's obligation to contribute to the pension fund might fall sharply, only to rise sharply if economic conditions worsened.

Role of the Actuary

An actuary plays an important role in most considerations of pension accounting. An actuary's duties include the following: (i) estimating the amount and timing of probable outlays for any given pension plan, (ii) reflecting the impact of estimated interest earnings and costs in pension payments, and (iii) advising on the appropriate pension benefit formula for a given company and the manner in which it should be funded.

Explanation of Actuarial Terms

Actuaries have devised some technical terms that have a special meaning to them. We have already introduced these terms briefly. Unfortunately, the words are very similar to key accounting terms, although they have very different meanings. Let us re-examine the most important terms:

Actuarial cost is the amount put into a pension fund each year on the advice of the actuary. In the example above the actuarial cost for the first year of Sam's employment would have been $187.31 if the actuary had recommended the accrued benefit method. The actuarial cost would have been $381.32 if the actuary had recommended the projected benefit method. In the unlikely event the actuary had recommended that the pension be funded only when Sam retired, the actuarial cost for all years of work but his last one would have been nil, and in his final year of work it would have been the expected present value of his pension benefits, or $34,439.65. Note that the actuarial cost refers to a pattern for financing the pension plan. It is a measure of cash flows. It is *not* similar to the accountant's meaning of cost, with its concern for matching costs and benefits.

Actuarial liability is the commitment to the pension plan that the employer bears. This can be given a variety of interpretations, as we show in this chapter. In the example above, the actuary would calculate the gross actuarial liability as the present value of the amount that would be needed to provide the expected value of Sam's full pension. It was calculated that at the point of Sam's retirement the present value of his expected benefits was $34,439.65. When Sam started work at the age of 30, the present value of this amount would have been $34,439.65 discounted at 5% for 35 years, or ($34,439.65 × 0.18129) = $6,243.57. Note that this does *not* match the accounting concept of a liability because Sam has just started his working career and has not yet done anything to earn any of his pension benefits. The accounting concept of a liability requires that the company incur some future outlay for a benefit already received, but at this point the company has not received any benefit. The actuarial liability at each age of Sam's working career is shown in Column G of Table 1 above.

Net actuarial liability is the actuary's valuation of the benefits earned to date, based on the actuarial cost method the actuary has decided to adopt. It can also be thought of as the amounts that would be on hand if the actuarial assumptions for the plan had turned out to be exactly correct. The actuarial valuation depends on the actuarial cost method adopted (e.g., accrued or projected benefit methods). Thus again it is not the same as an accounting liability.

The net actuarial liability may increase if the employer offers additional pension benefits that are not matched by additional contributions. For example, if Sam's employer agreed to give him a pension of $600 for each year worked instead of $500 but failed to increase the annual funding into the plan accordingly, then the net actuarial liability would increase. In the 1970s such promises were made to employees because of steep inflation. This has given rise to concern over the increase in the net actuarial liability.

Unfunded actuarial liability is the difference between the net actuarial liability and the amount of assets actually in the pension fund. Such a difference could arise for the following reasons:

1. The employer failed to put money into the plan in accordance with the actuarial cost method adopted.

2. There have been experience gains or losses (see below).

3. The actuary has changed the actuarial cost method.

Once again, *unfunded actuarial liability* has a meaning quite different from the usual accounting meanings of a liability, both in the concept of what a *liability* is and of what *funding* consists of.

An **experience loss** or **gain** refers to differences between actual events that affect the pension plan and the estimates of them originally made by the actuary. This would include changes in such factors as (i) the income earned on the pension fund investments, (ii) the mortality of the employees in the plan, (iii) the employee earnings base on which the pension is calculated. On the basis of such an experience gain or loss, the actuary might revise the estimates of the actuarial liability and recommend a change in contributions to the pension fund.

Suppose in our example that instead of offering a pension of $500 for each year worked, Sam's employer made the pension equal to 2% of the average of the best five years' earnings multiplied by the number of years worked. Suppose further that in his best five years Sam earned an average of $30,000. His pension would therefore be 2% of 35 times $30,000, or $21,000, which is more than the $17,500 used earlier. During Sam's early work years the actuary could not know what Sam's best five years of earnings might be, but as the day of retirement draws closer the actuary would be able to make a better estimate. Presumably in this example the actuary would revise upward the estimate of the actuarial liability because of the experience loss. Similar examples could be developed for changes in estimates of the interest rate or of employee turnover.

Experience gains and losses pose challenging accounting questions because the period that should be charged or credited is not at all clear. For example, an actuary may decide, after examining the latest mortality statistics, that people are living longer and hence that the company's defined benefit pensions are going to be more expensive. Should the additional cost be charged entirely to the period in which the actuary changed the estimate of mortality (as it would be if it were treated as a change in an accounting estimate)? The immediate answer seems to be yes. Yet professional opinion about the meaning of census data tends to change slowly, and consequently actuarial evaluations are usually only made every several years. Thus answering the above question in the affirmative would lead to erratic charges to earnings. Similar questions also arise. For example, if the pension portfolio experiences a sudden increase in value because of a rising stock market, should the employer immediately decrease his contributions? Or should the employer use some averaging method over several years? These are unresolved issues for which there is no standard treatment.

Major Accounting Issues

So far we have dealt mainly with straightforward accounting issues. We have glossed over potential problems in order to explain the technical issues as simply as possible. Let us now consider more complicated issues.

HISTORY OF ACCOUNTING PRONOUNCEMENTS

Because extensive pension plans are a development that took place mainly after World War II, it is not surprising that accounting pronouncements on the subject are to be found after that date. Apparently accountants considered the technical problems of pensions to be novel ones. It seems that accountants mistakenly assumed that since actuaries used terms like "cost" and "liability," the actuaries should be the ones to indicate how the matching of costs against periods should be done. As a result, there was a tendency to equate actuarial cost with accounting cost and to accept the actuaries' recommended funding plan as the appropriate pattern for matching pension costs to accounting periods.

By 1966 both the United States and Canada had issued pronouncements on accounting for pension plans.

The common features of these pronouncements included the following:

1. The legal form of the plan should be looked through to get at its economic substance. For instance, the fact that an employer can legally cancel a plan does not release the employer from the obligation to record a pension expense.

2. Pension costs should be assigned to the period in which the employee works. Any systematic method that does so and that is consistent with an actuarial cost is acceptable.

3. "Actuarial cost" and "accounting cost" are clearly distinct. The funding pattern chosen by the actuary should not govern the accounting costs.

4. Retroactive pension benefits (e.g., costs of pension benefits given for service prior to the adoption of the plan) are considered to have been given in recognition of future expected benefits. Hence they are defined to be costs of present and future periods.

The FASB issued a new accounting standard in 1985, and the CICA issued one in April 1986. Both standards made significant changes to the manner in which most companies must report their pension costs and liabilities. Although basically similar in thrust, the two standards have some material differences that will be outlined later.

First, however, it is useful to examine the basic issue of the accounting cost created by a pension plan.

WHAT DOES PENSION COST REPRESENT?

Recall that the main reason that pensions have become an accounting issue is that such a large part of our society is expected to live to an age when they will no longer be self-supporting. In response to this, governments offered to make pension contributions tax deductible if the employer would create a pension plan that met certain general criteria laid down by the government to suit its social objectives.

Does the cost borne by the corporation represent a deferred payment to the employee? If it does, is it reflected somehow in the wages it has to pay? For instance, in our example Sam's total remuneration in his first year — in other words, the total cost of Sam's first year of employment — might be considered to be the wage he was paid plus the pension contribution from his employer of $187.31. The argument would be that in a perfect labour market if he were not paid this amount through a pension plan, he would demand and get $187.31 more in wages. The following year his total remuneration would include the $196.67 of his employer's pension contribution. Similarly in his final year his total remuneration would include the $983.99 payment of that year.

Using this approach, the employee's wages and pensions could be thought of as a combined total remuneration package that fully compensated the employee for the services rendered in that year. Both employer and employee would consider themselves fully compensated by the deal they had worked out for that year. There would be no feeling on either side that there were future promises to make good on, such as an implied promise of continued employment.

In the unlikely event that the value of employees to their employer remained constant over their working career, we could expect in a competitive labour market that the salary component of their remuneration would go down year by year by an amount equal to the increase in the cost of their pension benefits. If employees were not willing to accept this, they would be replaced because they would be uncompetitive with younger employees whose pension costs were lower.

Is that what actually happens? It is hard to say because the conditions that would allow us to verify this do not exist. Everyday observation does show us people who are staying in jobs they do not like in order to reach pensionable age, and there are stories of employees being fired as their pension contribution goes up. Nevertheless there is no systematic evidence to support the competitive wage theory outlined above.

An alternative view of the labour market is that although employees are not hired for life, there is an implicit understanding that if they do an adequate job they will not be fired simply because they have grown older. Such an understanding is made explicit in many union agreements and in many anti-discrimination laws forbidding employers to allow age to be a factor in their employment choices. The Charter of Rights and Freedoms disallows unequal pay due to age, although its implications are still not clear for the issue of compulsory retirement due to age.

In the extreme case in which employees are hired for life, the amount they are paid in any given year cannot be viewed as a measure of what they are worth to their employer.

There may be trade-offs between the amount employees are paid in the current year and the amount they are paid in other years. For instance, employees might be willing to accept a lower income in their early years in return for a higher one in their later years. The same argument holds for pensions: employees might be willing to accept small pension contributions in their early years in return for larger ones in their later years.

If we accept some version of the lifetime-employment concept, then the hiring of an employee is similar to purchasing a plant asset that is not easily resold. In each case we can calculate the total expected present value of the costs of acquiring the productive resource. We can try to assign this cost to the periods that benefit from it, but we can rarely know, even in theory, whether we have achieved this objective.

Recall that with plant assets the accountant's response is to make sure that the cost is assigned to time periods in some manner that seems to do rough justice to the objective. Once a method is chosen, however, the accountant expects it to be left unchanged unless a new circumstance arises that makes a change seem sensible. (See Chapter 8.) The major proposals for accounting standards for pension expense tend to follow this same pattern.

Nevertheless, a close comparison with accounting for plant assets reveals that pension accounting is even more complex. In the case of plant assets we can usually establish their acquisition cost, and the main concern thereafter is how to depreciate this cost. In the case of pensions it could be argued that the same cost allocation issues exist. However, the cost can only be approximately determined since the pension payments are often based on factors that can only be estimated (such as future earnings). It is little wonder that a study on pension accounting was subtitled: "The problem of equating payments tomorrow with expenses today" [Skinner, 1980].

This problem has significant implications for the measurement of pension expense and liability. It is no longer considered appropriate to calculate pension costs on a year-by-year basis through the calculation of the increase in the expected present value of the pension commitment, as was done earlier in the example. Other ways of allocating pension costs over the employee's total working career are seen to be equally defensible. No single method is clearly preferable. It has been argued that it would be useful if all companies adopted the same method for allocating pension costs because then one would be able to make comparisons more easily.

Present Accounting Presentation

The section on pensions in the *CICA Handbook* was thoroughly revised in 1986. It has the following main features:

1. Annual pension expense should be based on the accrued benefit cost method for defined benefit plans [*CICA* 3460.22 and .28]. If the pension is to be based on factors not yet determined, such as the employee's salary just before retirement, then projections should be used to estimate the ultimate pension [*CICA* 3460.28]. Previously the requirement had been only that the method chosen should be consistently applied and based on "realistic" assumptions. Thus the new rule intro-

duces a degree of uniformity in calculating pension expense. The annual pension expense for defined contribution plans is the required contribution [*CICA* 3460.65].

2. Adjustments arising from "plan initiation or amendment or changes in assumptions" should be amortized in a "rational and systematic" manner, which would normally extend over the average remaining service life of the employee group covered [*CICA* 3460.43]. Similarly, experience gains and losses should also be amortized in this fashion [*CICA* 3460.52], as should gains or losses arising from changed plan assumptions (e.g., on expected lifespans of the pensioners) [*CICA* 3460.46]. It will already be evident that there is no unique "rational" method for this amortization. Therefore variations can be expected. The *Handbook* was previously less clear about the preferred treatment. It primarily called for disclosure of the method adopted.

3. When a plan is terminated or "curtailed," gains or losses should be recognized in the period of termination [*CICA* 3460.54]. For example, if a division was shut and the employees laid off, it might be possible to contract with a third party (such as a life insurance company) to assume the pension liability. In such a case the company might have a surplus left in the pension fund, and it is this surplus that would be taken into income. To the extent the *Handbook* had dealt with this issue before, it was to encourage disclosure.

4. Pension fund assets should be valued at "market related values," which is market value itself or a gradual adjustment to market [*CICA* 3460.34]. This is an acceptance of the concept of treating changes in the market value of the fund portfolio as possibly temporary fluctuations that will ultimately return to some "normal" value. The *Handbook* had previously been silent on the subject of portfolio valuation.

5. For defined benefit plans, the actuarial present value of accumulated pension benefits should be disclosed, as well as the value of pension fund assets [*CICA* 3460.60]. This can be done as footnote disclosure (since the *Handbook* is silent on the subject). But it is controversial whether footnote disclosure is sufficient. It can be argued that although the assets are held by a trustee for the benefit of the pension plan members, the company is nevertheless liable for the full pension benefits and therefore should record both the pension liabilities and pension assets in its accounts.

6. For defined contribution plans, the present value of required future contributions to past service benefits should be disclosed [*CICA* 3460.74]. For defined benefit plans the actuarial present value of these past service benefits must be disclosed [*CICA* 3460.60], and the additional cost amortized to income "in a rational and systematic manner" [*CICA* 3460.71]. Once again, there are those who argue that disclosure in footnotes should not be sufficient and that the liabilities should be recorded in the company's books.

7. Management, not the actuary, is ultimately responsible for the estimates used for calculating pension liability and expense [*CICA* 3460.17]. The *Handbook* provides little guidance how this should be done. Yet there are some significant decisions to make. For example, the future yield on the pension portfolio must be estimated.

Note that each change of 1% in the interest rate means roughly a 20% change in the estimated pension cost of the period.

Making management responsible for the assumptions used in the estimate is an interesting and welcome development because management is in the best position to know of future company plans that might impact on the pension plan. The separation of the measurement of pension expense from the annual payment into the plan is also a welcome development because there had been no logical reason for connecting the two. The adoption of the accrued benefit method as the means of allocating pension costs does *not* mean that the allocation problem has been "solved"; it simply means that every company will now use the same arbitrarily chosen allocation method (which in itself is probably an improvement, but not a solution). Non-regular costs (past service benefits, or gains and losses arising from experience or change of assumptions) are to be allocated over a long period related to "the expected average remaining service life of the employee group covered by the plan." Although this would likely make the acceptance of the pension standards more acceptable to the company issuing the statements, there does not seem to be any theoretical reason why this approach is better than expensing these items immediately (inasmuch as most of the expenses are related to *past* periods, but were not recognized as expenses at the time). Similarly, the requirement that the pension assets should be valued at market is blurred by the discussion in the *Handbook* that states this might be "a value which is adjusted to market over a period not to exceed five years." This new section in the *Handbook* marks a significant move toward more disclosure, although it falls short of the proposals resulting from a study by Ross Skinner, to be discussed below.

The main point to notice about the *CICA Handbook* up to its 1986 revision was how little disclosure was required. Skinner [1980] has suggested that disclosure should meet three minimum tests. First, it should promote reader understanding of the factors that have influenced the results shown in the financial statements. Second, it should indicate to the reader the possible impact of alternative accounting policies. Third, it should inform the reader of the most important judgements or estimates made in arriving at the figures shown. To do all this, Skinner suggests disclosure should include the following:

1. Basic information about the plan: the nature of the plan, the extent of coverage, the important benefits, and the bases of determination (e.g., what is the pension benefit based on? are there early retirement rights? is there vesting? is there portability?).

2. The present financial status of the plan: in particular, a comparison of the accrued actuarial liability with the assets in the pension fund.

3. An analysis of pension plan assets to indicate the investment risk by showing the types of investments in the portfolio.

4. Disclosure of the actuarial cost method employed to determine pension expense.

5. The interest rate used to calculate the present value of obligations.

6. How the initial supplementary liability is determined, and how it is being charged off, as well as the company policy for granting increases to retired employees that might increase it in the future.

7. Significant aspects of the basis for calculating experience gains and losses, particularly the approach to valuing assets in the pension fund; and how such gains or losses are charged to operations.

8. Nature and effects of any significant changes in accounting policies.

9. The most significant judgements made in arriving at accounting estimates (e.g., employee turnover, early retirement, and wage escalation).

This is a significantly greater amount of disclosure than present *CICA Handbook* requirements. Consider these nine points when examining the financial statement given in the following section.

Examples from Published Reports

Bell Canada Enterprises

Excerpts from the financial statements of Bell Canada Enterprises have been given above in Chapters 5 and 13. Bell Canada has done a good job of financial reporting in the area of pensions. Here are its notes on pensions.

> BCE and most of its subsidiary companies have non-contributory defined benefit plans which provide for service pensions based on length of service and rates of pay for substantially all their employees.
>
> The policy is to fund pension costs through contributions based on various actuarial cost methods as permitted by pension regulatory bodies. Such costs are funded as accrued and reflect actuarial assumptions regarding salary projection and future service benefits. The provision for pension costs was $278.5 million for the year ended December 31, 1986 (1985 — $296.0 million, 1984 — $271.3 million).
>
> In compliance with the United States Financial Accounting Standards Board's *Statement No. 36*, the disclosure of the following information is required to exclude actuarial asumptions regarding salary projection and future service benefits. A comparison of accumulated plan benefits and plan net assets is provided as follows:

	Dec. 31, 1985	Dec. 31, 1984
	(millions of $)	
Actuarial present value of accumulated plan benefits:		
Vested	$ 3,246.2	$ 2,921.9
Non-vested	512.8	452.9
	$ 3,759.0	$ 3,374.8
Net assets available for benefits — at market value	$ 5,547.5	$ 4,415.1

> The weighted average assumed rate of return used in determining the actuarial present value of accumulated plan benefits was 7.3% for 1985 and 7.2% for 1984.

In addition to pension benefits, BCE and its subsidiary companies provide certain health care and life insurance benefits for retired employees. The costs of such benefits, excluding life insurance, are paid out of current income, as benefits are received, and in 1986 amounted to $12.4 million (1985 — $11.6 million, 1984 — $9.3 million). Life insurance for retired employees is largely funded during their working lives.

Summary

The accountant's desire to match the cost of a pension to the benefits conferred on the company by the employee's labour is a difficult one to achieve. The core problem is that the total remuneration paid to an employee in any one year is implicitly related to the remuneration of other years and that pension benefits are a part of this total remuneration. Because of this interdependence between years, one cannot claim that the amount needed to fund the pension benefits of a given year is the cost of the pension benefits for accounting purposes. This is conceptually similar to the problem of allocating the cost of plant assets over their useful life. Interdependence between years creates a similar problem in stating the amount of pension liabilities.

In addition, many defined benefit plans are based on events that have not yet happened (such as the employee's future earnings) and that can be estimated with only limited reliability. This means that the ultimate total pension cost can only be estimated in a rough manner. In this respect the pension accounting problem is even more difficult than accounting for plant assets.

The present requirements for disclosure are a distinct improvement over those in existence before 1986. The disclosure standards suggested by Skinner and others have not yet been met, but the new standards are clearly an improvement.

QUESTIONS

Q15-1. Review and make sure you understand the following terms:

    a. pension plan *versus* pension fund

    b. defined contribution plan

    c. defined benefit plan

    d. pension portability

    e. vesting

    f. role of actuary *versus* role of accountant in pensions

    g. funding

> **h.** actuarial costs
>
> **i.** accrued benefit cost method
>
> **j.** projected benefit cost method
>
> **k.** initial supplementary liability
>
> **l.** pension trustee
>
> **m.** gross actuarial liability
>
> **n.** net actuarial liability
>
> **o.** unfunded actuarial liability
>
> **p.** experience gain (loss)
>
> **q.** contractual obligation *versus* equitable obligation *versus* constructive obligation

Q15-2. "I don't get a dog and then do my own barking, and I don't see any point in a company hiring an actuary and then estimating its own pension liability." Discuss.

Q15-3. "In a defined contribution plan the employer's obligation is discharged when the employer makes the agreed contribution to the plan." Discuss.

Q15-4. "Accounting for pensions only has serious problems with respect to defined benefit plans." Do you agree? Explain.

Q15-5. A company that previously had no pension plan decided to introduce one in which each employee would get a life annuity on retirement equal to 2% of the total amount that the employee had earned over his or her career with the company. The funds for this plan would be completely provided by the company, but benefits did not vest in the employee until he or she had been in the pension plan for five years. Should the company record any pension expense in the first year of the plan's operation? Explain.

Q15-6. Should the recognition of a pension as an expense be delayed until the pension rights vest in the employee? Explain.

Q15-7. It was common in the financial press during the 1970s to see articles about the "hidden red ink in companies' books arising from unfunded pension liabilities." What did this refer to? Was the concern justified?

Q15-8. In the time of Charles Dickens it was uncommon to grant pensions to employees, if only because few of them lived to a pensionable age. Nevertheless, some employers did grant pensions. Should they have been considered an expense of the period in which the employee worked? Or the period in which the employee was paid the benefits? Or should the pensions have been considered an expense at all?

Q15-9. It has been suggested that an employer pension plan is a way of getting long-term financing from the employee. Explain under what circumstances this might be true.

Q15-10. Explain how an actuary can change the amount of a company's unfunded actuarial liability without any change in the economic substance of the existing plan.

Q15-11. Explain under what circumstances the employer bears the pension risks of a pension plan even though the pension contributions have been handed over to the trustee in strict accordance with the actuary's funding plan.

Q15-12. What would be the merits of showing on the employer's balance sheet the complete accounting of pension assets and liabilities — even when most of the assets are held by the pension trustee?

Q15-13. "Actuaries are in danger of being placed in the same category as real estate appraisers when it comes to reliance on them for financial reporting purposes." Assuming that there has been disagreement over the reliance to be placed on real estate appraisers for the valuation of plant assets, evaluate the fairness of this comment.

Q15-14. In 1983 the FASB proposed that if a company offered its employees an option of retiring earlier than their pension agreement had provided, then the cost of this earlier retirement had to be charged to the year in which the employee retired. One executive critical of the FASB's stand was quoted as saying: "The accountants are ignoring the future cost savings of not having these employees on the payroll. If the goal of accounting is to match costs and benefits for the year incurred, it seems more appropriate to spread the cost of the early retirement program over future years." Discuss.

Q15-15. According to *The Financial Times* of Canada, Chrysler Canada Limited's pension fund trustees in 1982 "saved . . . the auto maker $40 million in the deal" because they discovered that Chrysler had "laid aside more money for pensions than was needed." The trustees were thus able to buy annuities from a third party to "cover its obligation to retired workers and pocket the overpayment — an estimated $40 million." We know that inflation has pushed up interest rates at that time, and thus the cost of buying annuities had gone down. Was the "saving" to Chrysler at anyone else's expense? Explain.

Q15-16. *The Financial Times* of Canada reported that the pension trustees of Massey-Ferguson had "broken with tradition" and thus "saved the farm equipment manufacturer another $30 to $40 million." The tradition that was broken was the assumption that yields on investments should never be estimated as higher than 7%. The usual reason for this is that inflation may force the employer to pay higher-than-expected pensions (often on a retroactive basis), and yields higher than 7% presumably contain a heavy inflationary-expectation component. Hence, the actuary hopes to build in "compensating errors" by conservative estimates on income in the hope that they will match estimates of final pension payments that may be proved by inflation to be too low. By assuming a future yield of 17%, M-F could reduce the expected value of the pension liability and hence "save $30 to $40 million." How might this saving come about? Is it at anyone else's expense?

Q15-17. It has been suggested that selecting a pattern for matching pension costs and benefits has many similarities to selecting the method for depreciating plant assets. Comment on the similarities and differences between the two.

Q15-l8. What are the main accounting issues created by the introduction of pension plans? Explain why the introduction of pensions has given rise to each of these issues.

Q15-19. Explain what accounting issues have been created by the practice of having pension assets held by a trustee.

Q15-20. In this chapter we mentioned the possibility that employers might increase pension benefits above the level to which they are legally committed. In the situations below, explain how an employer might be led to do this. In each case explain whether the cost to the employer would go up.

   a. In union negotiations it is argued that the pension for present retirees is inadequate because of a period of rapid inflation.

   b. The government has a competing pension plan and is hinting at expanding it at the expense of private plans "because of inadequate provisions for vesting, portability, and women's rights" in the private plans.

c. A company wishes to expand the existing defined benefit pension plan to offer a pension of 2% of total career salaries instead of 1.8%, starting in the new year. A group of employees about to retire point out that this means they retire on a pension based almost entirely on 1.8%.

d. Because of changes in legislation, the company has been required to use "unisex" life expectancy rates for its defined contribution plan. This ensures that for the same amount of funds on retirement, each employee gets the same monthly pension payment regardless of sex.

Q15-21. In a defined benefit plan how would the following changes affect the employer's costs (if at all)?

a. Employees live longer than expected after retirement.

b. Return on pension investments rises.

c. Staff turnover increases in the period prior to vesting.

d. Staff turnover increases in the period after vesting.

e. The vesting period decreases from five to two years.

f. An unusually high number of employees reach retirement age within the current year.

g. The percentage of females in the workforce increases.

Q15-22. What are the similarities and differences between each of the following pairs?

a. Accounting liability and actuarial liability.

b. Accounting pension cost and actuarial pension cost.

Q15-23. An employee who had worked for the same employer since the age of 25 as a member of a defined contribution plan wanted to retire at 55 instead of 65. This meant she would have been in the plan for 30 years instead of 40 years. Could she expect to get 30/40 of the pension she would have got at age 65? Explain.

Q15-24. Suppose an industry that had a mandatory retirement age of 65 dropped this requirement. As a result, on average its employees remained at work three years longer than previously. Would the cost to the employer likely increase, decrease, or stay the same under (i) a defined benefit plan? under (ii) a defined contribution plan?

Q15-25. On retirement an employee insisted that his pension be in the form of a life annuity that stopped at his death. One month after retirement he dropped dead. Would the pension fund suffer an experience gain or loss?

Q15-26. The CICA now requires that the annual cost of a pension plan be calculated using the accrued benefit cost method.

a. Explain what this method is and how it affects the allocation of pension cost over the working lifetime of an employee.

b. It has been objected that this method will not produce uniform results between companies inasmuch as the actuarial assumptions used by each company will vary. Evaluate the merits of the objection.

Q15-27. One of the major problems in accounting for pension plans is that of determining how the costs (past service and current service) should be allocated to accounting periods. Discuss.

EXERCISES

E15-1. Suppose that a company has a defined benefit pension plan. For each of the following unrelated events, indicate whether immediately after the change is recognized, the effect on each of the items is to increase it, decrease it, or leave it unaffected: (i) accounting liability,(ii) gross actuarial liability,(iii) accounting pension expense,(iv) market value of pension fund investments,(v) unfunded actuarial liability.

    a. Employees are living longer after retirement than was contemplated when the pension plan was originally drawn up.

    b. Not as many employees are staying until the end of the vesting period; hence a smaller percentage is getting vesting rights than expected.

    c. The earnings of the pension fund assets are higher than expected, but the portfolio market value is the same.

    d. The company's actuary has increased the amount of money to be put into the plan in the future.

    e. As a result of the most recent collective bargaining settlement, the existing retirement benefits have been increased by 5%.

    f. The pension fund portfolio has experienced a sharp increase in value because of a general rise in the stock market.

E15-2. An employee was hired at age 50 with the understanding that on reaching age 65 she would be given a lump sum retirement benefit of $142,569. This would be funded by the company putting aside $6,000 per annum into a separate fund that was expected to earn 5%. The fund would be kept and managed by the company and shown in its books. The expected history of this fund is shown below.

Employee's age	Annual payment	Interest at 5%	Year-end balance
50	$ 6,000.00	300.00	$ 6,300.00
51	6,000.00	315.00	12,615.00
52	6,000.00	630.75	19,245.75
53	6,000.00	962.29	26,208.04
54	6,000.00	1,310.40	33,518.44
55	6,000.00	1,675.92	41,194.36
56	6,000.00	2,059.72	49,254.08
57	6,000.00	2,462.70	57,716.78
58	6,000.00	2,885.84	66,602.62
59	6,000.00	3,330.13	75,932.75
60	6,000.00	3,796.64	85,729.39
61	6,000.00	4,286.47	96,015.86
62	6,000.00	4,800.79	106,816.65
63	6,000.00	5,340.83	118,157.49
64	6,000.00	5,907.87	130.065.36
65	6,000.00	6,503.27	142,568.63

Required:

    a. Show the journal entry (entries) required to record interest earnings, pension payment and expense when the employee is age 57. Explain and justify the amounts you use.

    b. Assume that the employee reached age 65 and was paid the amount of $142,569 as agreed. Show the journal entry to record the payment.

    c. Show the journal entry to record the interest of $2,885.84 at age 58.

E15-3. A company has a defined contribution pension plan in which it contributes 7% of employee earnings into a trusteed pension fund expected to earn 5%. In practice, the investment experience of the fund portfolio turns out to be better than expected. It earns 10%, with the results shown below for an employee hired at age 40 who is expected to retire at age 65, at which time he or she will be paid in a lump sum.

Age of Employee	Earnings	Company contribution (7%)	Interest earned at 5% Earned each year	Interest earned at 5% Closing balance	Interest earned at 10% Earned each year	Interest earned at 10% Closing balance
40	$ 25,000.00	$ 1,750.00	$ 0.00	$ 1,750.00	$ 0.00	$ 1,750.00
41	27,000.00	1,890.00	87.50	3,727.50	175.00	3,815.00
42	29,000.00	2,030.00	186.38	5,943.88	381.50	6,226.50
43	31,000.00	2,170.00	297.19	8,411.07	622.65	9,019.15
44	33,000.00	2,310.00	420.55	11,141.62	901.92	12,231.07
45	35,000.00	2,450.00	557.08	14,148.70	1,223.11	15,904.17
46	37,000.00	2,590.00	707.44	17,446.14	1,590.42	20,084.59
47	39,000.00	2,730.00	872.31	21,048.45	2,008.46	24,823.05
48	41,000.00	2,870.00	1,052.42	24,970.87	2,482.30	30,175.35
49	43,000.00	3,010.00	1,248.54	29,229.41	3,017.54	36,202.89
50	45,000.00	3,150.00	1,461.47	33,840.88	3,620.29	42,973.18
51	47,000.00	3,290.00	1,692.04	38,822.93	4,297.32	50,560.49
52	49,000.00	3,430.00	1,941.15	44,194.07	5,056.05	59,046.54
53	51,000.00	3,570.00	2,209.70	49,973.78	5,904.65	68,521.20
54	53,000.00	3,710.00	2,498.69	56,182.46	6,852.12	79,083.32
55	55,000.00	3,850.00	2,809.12	62,841.59	7,908.33	90,841.65
56	57,000.00	3,990.00	3,142.08	69,973.67	9,084.16	103,915.81
57	59,000.00	4,130.00	3,498.68	77,602.35	10,391.58	118,437.40
58	61,000.00	4,270.00	3,880.12	85,752.47	11,843.74	134.551.13
59	63,000.00	4,410.00	4,287.62	94,450.09	13,455.11	152,416.25
60	65,000.00	4,550.00	4,722.50	103,722.60	15,241.62	172,207.87
61	67,000.00	4,690.00	5,186.13	113,598.73	17,220.79	194,118.66
62	69,000.00	4,830.00	5,679.94	124,108.66	19,411.87	218,360.53
63	71,000.00	4,970.00	6,205.43	135,284.09	21,836.05	245,166.58
64	73,000.00	5,110.00	6,764.20	147,158.30	24,516.66	274,793.24
65	75,000.00	5,250.00	7,357.91	159,766.21	27,479.32	307,522.56

Required:

a. Show the journal entries in both the company's books and the trustee's books to record pension cost and interest income with respect to the company's pension plan when the employee is age 61. Explain and justify the amounts you use.

b. Given that the fund ended up worth $307,522.56 instead of $159,766.21 as planned, what journal entries, if any, would be needed at age 65 to record the payment to the employee? Explain fully.

E15-4. Plausible Pastimes Inc., a travel agency for the college set, had a policy that the pension benefits in its defined contribution pension plan vested in employees completely at the end of two years, but until then employees had no vested rights in the plan. The company's contribution was 10% of each employee's earnings for each year the individual worked. To keep the problem simple, assume that all employees began work at the start of the first year, that those who left did so at the end of the year, and that no new employees were hired to replace the ones who had left.

The company estimated its expected pension expense and made monthly entries during the first year for it. The company predicted that by the end of the first year only

70% of its employees would be on hand and that by the end of the second year, only 80% of the remainder would be on hand.

During the first year of the plan the company's payroll was $100,000. Using the 70% and 80% estimate above, Pastimes calculated that only 70% of 80% = 56% of its employees would be working at the end of two years and hence eligible for pension rights. Accordingly, each month in the first year it made a journal entry charging pension expense for 56% of 10% of gross payroll for the month and crediting pension liability with the same amount. The gross payroll was $100,000 in each year.

Required:

a. At the end of the first year Pastimes found that 80% of its employees were still on hand instead of the 70% estimated. Show (i) how it might recalculate its pension expense for the first year; and (ii) the journal entry it might make to record the experience gain or loss.

b. At the end of the second year Pastimes found that 75% of those employees entering the second year were still employed at the end of the year. Show (i) how it might recalculate its pension expense for the second year; and (ii) the journal entry it might make to record the experience gain or loss.

E15-5.   Hot Pursuits Inc. is a dating bureau with a defined benefit pension plan offering employees $3,000 per year for each year worked. The company estimates that the expected present value, at age 65, of the $3,000 per annum is $6,088.93 if a 5% discount rate is assumed. This is shown below.

Age of employee	Probability of reaching this age	Benefit to be paid	Expected value	Discount factor to age 65	Expected present value at age 65
66	0.65	$ 3,000.00	$ 1,950.00	0.9523809	$ 1,857.14
67	0.55	3,000.00	1,650.00	0.9070295	1,496.60
68	0.45	3,000.00	1,350.00	0.8638376	1,166.18
69	0.35	3,000.00	1,050.00	0.8227025	863.84
70	0.30	3,000.00	900.00	0.7835262	705.17
71 +	0.00	3,000.00	0.00		
					$ 6,088.93

The company has an employee who is 50 years old and expects to retire at age 65, or in fifteen years. At 5% the discount factor for fifteen years is 0.4810171; so $2,928.88 invested at age 50 would accumulate to $6,088.93 at 5% interest rate. This employee has put in twenty years of service already. Therefore, at age 50 the present value of his accumulated pension benefits is twenty times $2,928.88, or $58,577.62.

Required:

a. The company increased its pension benefits to $4,000 for each year of service in order to compensate for inflation. It made this increase retroactive for the above employee as of age 50. By how much is the present value of his pension benefits increased? Show your calculations.

b. What accounting treatment is recommended by the *CICA Handbook* for the scenario described in part (a)? Discuss how appropriate you think it is in this example. What would be a reasonable charge for the current period? Can you give an economic interpretation to any amounts that would be treated as deferred charges because they were unabsorbed in the current period?

E15-6. A company uses the projected benefit cost method to fund the pension plan of an employee hired at age 50. The company assumes a 5% interest rate in calculating the expected balance in the plan at age 65. It believes the balance in the fund at age 65 will be $59,144 as shown below.

Age of of employee	Contribution	Interest earned	Balance, end of year
50	$ 2,500.00	$ 0.00	$ 2,500.00
51	2,500.00	125.00	5,125.00
52	2,500.00	256.25	7,881.25
53	2,500.00	394.06	10,775.31
54	2,500.00	538.77	13,814.08
55	2,500.00	690.70	17,004.78
56	2,500.00	850.24	20,355.02
57	2,500.00	1,017.75	23,872.77
58	2,500.00	1,193.64	27,566.41
59	2,500.00	1,378.32	31,444.73
60	2,500.00	1,572.24	35,516.97
61	2,500.00	1,775.85	39,792.82
62	2,500.00	1,989.64	44,282.46
63	2,500.00	2,214.12	48,996.58
64	2,500.00	2.449.83	53,946.41
65	2,500.00	2,697.32	59,143.73

Required:

a. Assuming that the company administered the pension fund through its own books and did not put the pension funds into a separate account, what journal entry (entries) would be required at age 59? Explain your reasoning.

b. If the company administered the funds itself but kept then separate from its other funds, would the journal entry (entries) at age 59 be any different from the answer to (a)? Explain.

c. Assume instead that the company used a pension trustee who administered the fund. Would the journal entry (entries) at age 59 be any different from the answer to (b)? Explain.

E15-7. It was reported in the financial press that a financially troubled company was seeking permission to take "all or most" of its pension fund assets and make them available to the company for operating purposes. The president of the company reported that "it would be like producing a life raft out of nowhere for a near-shipwrecked crew."

Required: Suppose that the pension fund sold its investment assets and bought bonds of the company where its employees worked.

a. Why are pension regulatory authorities reluctant to allow pension trustees to invest in the securities of the company where the employee works? (A common upper limit for such investments is 10%.)

b. Who would gain by this proposed arrangement? Who would lose?

c. How should this be shown on the balance sheet of the company? Of the pension fund?

d. Should this be regarded as a funded and trusteed plan? Explain.

E15-8. Sterling Inc. a financially sound firm, has decided to adopt a funded pension plan. The firm has been in operation since 1 July 19X3. The plan, which becomes operational on

1 July 19X9, will fund for past as well as current services. The actuary has determined that the present value of the past service pensions is $243,459. In order to accumulate enough to provide for these past service costs, the company must pay into the fund $49,009 at the end of each year for eight years. It must also pay an additional $30,000 per year for current-service costs. The discount rate is set at 12%, and the past-service costs are to be amortized over eight years on a straight-line basis. The company year end is 30 June.

Required: Prepare all the journal entries relating to the above pension plan that the company would have to record for the first year. It has been decided to capitalize past service costs in the first year as a deferred charge.

(CMA adapted)

E15-9. Sweet Tooth, Inc. adopted a pension plan on 1 June 19X8 and the prior service costs were established at $300,000. Payment of these costs plus interest at 10% will be over a fifteen-year period. The company will amortize the prior service costs plus interest of 10% on the unfunded portion over a twenty-year period. Funded current service costs for 19X8 and 19X9 are $50,000 and $54,000 respectively.

Required: Prepare journal entries for the first two years to record each of the following items. Show all your calculations.

a. the pension expense

b. pension contributions to the fund

(CMA adapted)

E15-10. Borodin Inc. has just started a funded pension plan for its employees several years after incorporation. The past service cost was estimated by the actuary as $306,000. The company will amortize the past (prior) service cost over four years and fund it over three years. The company's discount rate was set at 12%. Current service (normal) cost is expected to be $75,000 in each of the first two years.

Required:

a. Prepare the necessary journal entries for the first year of the pension plan.

b. What amount(s) concerning the pension would be shown on the financial statements at the end of the first year of the plan? Illustrate, using proper statement headings and classifications, where this disclosure would appear.

(CMA adapted)

E15-11. You have been recently hired, and your boss sends you the following memo: "Here is a list of some of the questions I get asked about pensions. Please send me your suggestions about what my answer should be."

Required: Provide your boss with appropriate answers for each of the following:

a. I'm told that the actuarial liability is greater than the fund assets. Should we be required to put money in to make up the difference?

b. Because of stock market performance, the pension fund assets are significantly greater than what is needed to cover the existing pension liabilities under our defined benefit plan. Is it morally proper to take out the excess funds?

c. Are actuarial pension costs and accounting pension costs the same thing? If not, how do they differ in concept?

d. I'm told that even though we put into our pension fund whatever money the actuary tells us, we are still liable to the pension fund if things don't work out as the actuary estimates. Why should our company be responsible for the honest mistakes of someone else?

e. Why aren't the pension plan assets and liabilities shown on the company's balance sheet?

PROBLEMS

P15-1. In 1983 *Business Week* reported that Eastman Kodak Co. had announced a "stunning" early retirement offer to most of its 93,000 employees, allowing them to retire as early as 55 without suffering any loss of pension benefits. Kodak announced that the impact on 1983 earnings would be minor. However, the magazine commented that "if the nation's accounting rule-makers prevail, companies that offer such incentives may be in for a shock" because the FASB is proposing that the cost of such early retirements should be recognized immediately "even though most of the cash payments may not be made for many years."

Required:
Write an analysis of not more than 500 words discussing the merits and disadvantages of charging the costs of early retirement to the year in which it takes place. Make specific reference to the Kodak proposal.

P15-2. Construct a comparative figure table: in the left column show the nine disclosure recommendations of Ross Skinner and in the right column show the present *CICA Handbook* requirements that match the Skinner recommendations. What seems to be missing from the present *Handbook* requirements? Evaluate present disclosure requirements.

P15-3. In 19X4 Gamma Inc. was informed by its actuaries that it should deposit $325,000 into its trusteed pension fund to meet the actuarial cost under the accrued benefit plan. The company made this payment. The company was also informed that the plan had earned $125,000 and had made payments to pensioners of $169,000.

Required:
a. What journal entries, if any, would be needed in the books of the company with respect to the above transactions?

b. What journal entries would be needed in the books of the pension plan to reflect the above facts?

P15-4. Assume that a company had a defined benefit pension plan with only one employee who was to receive $25,000 per year on retirement. The plan was unfunded during the employee's lifetime, but on her retirement the company put into a separate fund a sum equal to the expected present value of her pension benefits. The sum was not paid to a pension trustee; instead, it was put into a separate fund under the company's control. It was carried on the company's books as a long-term asset, and the pension liability was also shown as a liability.

According to the company's calculation it had to have on hand by the time of the employee's retirement the sum of $105,000 to fund the expected pension benefits. An interest rate of 5% was used to calculate the expected earnings of the fund set aside for the pension. Benefit payments were to be made at the end of each year of retirement, with the first payment starting one year after retirement.

Required:

a. Assuming that the fund earned 5% during the first year of retirement, what journal entries should be made to record the income earned on the pension fund and the payment of the pension benefit?

b. If 8% was actually earned on the pension fund, what entries, if any, should be made to record this favourable earnings experience? Justify your decision.

P15-5. Explain the significance for accounting reporting of the assumption that an employee's employment contract for a given year is unrelated to any other employment year. What alternative assumption could be made? Which one comes closest to your own experience? Explain.

P15-6. Consider the following presentation of a company's pension as it appears in its financial statements.

Retirement Plans

The Company and its subsidiaries maintain non-contributory retirement plans which cover substantially all salaried and hourly paid employees.

During the year, upon the recommendation of the actuaries, the actuarial bases of the retirement plans were reviewed and modified to reflect current economic factors. The effect was to reduce the present value of benefit obligations by approximately $1,300,000. The resultant surplus of plan assets over liabilities was used to upgrade certain benefits in Division A at an estimated cost of $970,000.

The approximate costs of the plans were as follows:

	19X7	19X6	19X5
Current service portion	$ 220,200	$ 125,000	$ 139,000
Past service cost	26,800	178,000	159,000
Total	$ 247,000	$ 303,000	$ 298,000

The unfunded past-service liability with respect to all the plans at January 1, 19X7, was approximately $130,000, and is being funded and amortized over periods generally not exceeding fifteen years. All vested benefits were fully funded as at January 1, 19X1.

Required:

a. How well does the above presentation meet the disclosure requirements of the *CICA Handbook?*

b. How well does it meet the disclosure requirements recommended by Skinner?

P15-7. In a mythical land named Shronk the people started their productive work life on their 25th birthday and stopped it on their 65th. They worked for the same employer all this time, and there were no deaths until after age 65. Thereafter the mortality was completely predictable, as follows:

Age	Probability of dying at that age
66	0.10
67	0.20
68	0.70
69	1.00

All workers in Shronk were guaranteed a pension of $100,000 per year on reaching 65, which was paid at the beginning of each retirement year. Thus, when a typical worker, Odon, reached age 65 he would retire and immediately receive $100,000; then if he reached 66, he would receive another $100,000; if he reached 67, he would receive another $100,000; and if he reached 68, he would receive another $100,000 (which would, of course, be his final one since the longest anyone lived was up to the day before his or her 69th birthday). The interest rate in Shronk is magically set at 10% and is never expected to changed. Magically, also, there has never been and will never be inflation.

Required:

a. Calculate the amount that would be needed to provide a life annuity of $100,000 to an individual worker at age 65.

b. Odon believes he has both a defined benefit and a defined contribution pension plan. Is this possible? Explain.

c. When worker Odon reaches his 64th birthday, how much must be set aside to provide the present value of the pension rights he has earned in the year just past? Show your calculations.

d. Explain why accountants are troubled about assuming that the amount you calculated above should be regarded as the pension expense for that year.

e. The mythical world in this question has been invented to make the situations simple and certain enough to allow some calculations. List and discuss some of the troublesome real-world issues faced by accountants in accounting for pension plans.

P15-8. A partnership wishes to provide a pension plan for its sole employee whose age is 63 as of 1 March, 19X4 and who will retire on 1 March 19X6. Should she be alive at her retirement date, they propose to give her a pension consisting of an annual life annuity of $10,000 for each year worked, with the first payment to her being on 1 March 19X6, and the payments thereafter at yearly intervals. After studying the issue they decide on the following:

(i) The probability of her being alive at the pension payment dates is as follows:

First pension payment — 80%
Second pension payment — 50%
Third pension payment — 20%
Four and subsequent — nil

(ii) The appropriate discount rate to use is 5%.

Required:

a. What is the expected present value of this pension as of the employee's retirement date? Show your calculations.

b. Suppose the company funded this using an accrued benefit plan. Assume payments are made into the fund at the end of each work year.
   (i) What would be the payment into the fund for the year starting 1 March 19X4?
   (ii) What would be the payment into the fund for the year starting 1 March 19X5?

c. When the partners make the required payment into the fund on 1 March 19X5 they ask you for advice on the journal entry. Show the journal entry (entries) you would recommend.

d. Justify the amount you chose to represent the pension expense for that year. What would a thoughtful critic say of the process by which acountants decide on the amount of pension expense in any given year. (*Hint:* Consider both theory and practice.)

P15-9.   A company had a pension plan offering a life annuity of $600 payable at the end of each retirement year for each year worked. It calculated that the probability of an employee being alive to receive payment at each year past retirement was follows:

Year	Probability of being alive to receive pension
1	0.80
2	0.40
3	0.20
4	0.20

It also believed that a discount rate of 5% should be used.

Required:

a. An employee who had been covered under the pension plan had completed 35 years of service.

   (i) What pension would he receive yearly?

   (ii) What is the expected present value of his pension as of the date of his retirement?

b. Another employee has put in thirty years of service under the pension plan. She has fifteen years to go to retirement.

   (i) What annual pension payment on retirement has she earned so far?

   (ii) What would be the expected present value of (i) at the point of retirement?

   (iii) What would be the expected present value of (i) as of now?

   (iv) If her employer wanted to increase her pension benefits retroactively to the start of employment to $720 per year worked instead of $600, by how much would this increase the expected present value of the pension as of now?

   (v) Discuss and evaluate the various accounting methods that might be used with respect to the increased present value calculated in (iv).

P15-10.   Palmer Co. started a pension plan as at 1 January, 19X1 for its employees. An actuary estimated the prior service costs as being $4,000,000. The prior service costs are to be funded over ten years with equal year-end payments of $518,018.30. The interest rate used by the actuary is 5%.

Required:

a. What is the unfunded prior service cost as at 31 December 19X1?

b. How do you think the prior service cost should be expensed? Discuss the accounting issues involved.

c. Show the required entries for 1 January 19X1 and for 31 December 19X1.

P15-11.   Salem Electric started a pension plan on 1 January 19X0 for all its employees. The actuaries estimated the prior service costs to be $10,000,000. It was decided to amortize and fund this amount over twenty years. The interest rate used was 8%. In 19X8, it was discovered that the fund was returning significantly more than 8%; in fact, the fund was now two years ahead of schedule. Salem Electric currently has a cash shortage and plans to omit the payment this year.

Required:

a. Do you thin it is acceptable for Salem Electric to omit this payment? Explain.

b. If Salem does omit payment, what will be the expense related to this situation that will appear on the income statement?

c. Discuss the accounting issues raised by this scenario.

P15-12. New Company has recently commenced operations and wishes to start a pension plan for its employees. All ten employees have just turned 45. The company proposes to give each employee a pension consisting of a $10,000 life annuity for each year worked. The first payment will be received by each employee upon turning 65. The following actuarial estimates are available:

(i) The probability of the employees being alive following retirement is given below.

Time of the first payment — 100%
Time of the second payment — 80%
Time of the third payment — 50%
Time of the fourth payment — 10%
Fifth and subsequent payments — 0%

(ii) The actuarially determined discount rate is 8%.

Required:

a. What is the expected present cost of this pension plan at the employees' point of retirement?

b. Suppose the pension is an accrued benefit funding plan and that payments are made at the end of each year. What would the payment into the fund be (i) in the first year of the plan? (ii) in the twentieth year of the plan?

P15-13. The *CICA Handbook* requires that the accrued benefit method be used to calculate the annual cost of a pension plan. In about 300 words evaluate this requirement. In your critique you should do the following: (i) indicate another allocation pattern that would have been a likely candidate for adoption; (ii) discuss the connection, if any, between the choice of the allocation pattern and the funding pattern chosen by the actuary; (iii) list the differences in objectives, if any, between the accountant and actuary; and (iv) discuss the merits, if any, in singling out a single funding pattern to be used as a basis for pension cost allocation.

P15-14. Destin Corporation had a pension plan that was funded by the annual purchase of a zero-coupon bond whose maturity value was exactly equal to the pension liability incurred in the current year. (A *zero-coupon bond* has no periodic interest payments. It is sold at a discount to produce an interest yield.) In 1986 Destin incurred a future pension liability of $100,000 that would mature in 2006. Therefore they purchased for $14,864.36 a zero-coupon bond whose value in twenty years would be $100,000 at a yield rate of 10%. Destin decided to amortize the bond on an annual basis. Thus in 1987 they amortized $4,256.78 of the purchase difference, revaluing the bond on their books at $19,121.14. However the market rate of interest dropped to 9% in 1987, and the market value of the bond increased to $19,448.97.

If the actuary revalued the pension liability at the end of 1987 at the market rate of 9%, the liability would be $19,448.97, or $327.83 higher than the amortized value of the bond.

Required: State which of the policies below you would recommend to the company. Give your reasons.

a. The company should recognize an experience loss of $327.83 and write this off against current income.

b. The pension liability should be calculated using 10%, the rate in effect when the pension liability was first calculated. The bond should be valued at its amortized value. There will then be no experience gain or loss.

c. The pension liability should be calculated using 9%, the market rate. The bond should be valued at its market value. There will then be no experience gain or loss.

BIBLIOGRAPHY

ARCHIBALD, T. ROSS. *Accounting for Pension Costs and Liabilities.* Toronto: Canadian Institute of Chartered Accountants, 1981. A report arising from a study done for the CICA.

CALLARD, ROSALIND M. "Accounting for Pension Costs and Obligations." *CA Magazine* (February 1985). The CICA accounting research manager in charge of the "Section 3460 project" writes about the issues.

CUTTEN, J. ANDREW. "The Benefits of Pension Plan Reform." *CA Magazine* (October 1983). The interaction between pension legislation and accounting standards.

DALEY, LANE ALAN. "The Valuation of Reported Pension Measures for Firms Sponsoring Defined Benefit Plans." *The Accounting Review* (April 1984). An example of the use of security price behaviour to infer the significance of types of reported pension costs.

DEWHIRST, JOHN. "A Conceptual Approach to Pension Accounting," *The Accounting Review* (April 1971). An article comparing the allocation problem in plant assets to that in pensions.

EZRA, D. DON. *Understanding Pension Fund Finance and Investment.* Toronto: Pagurian Press Limited, 1979. A good introduction to pension plans.

———. *The Struggle for Pension Fund Wealth.* Toronto: Pagurian Press Limited, 1983. A readable examination of the policy implications of pension funding.

FINANCIAL ACCOUNTING STANDARDS BOARD. *Statement of Financial Accounting Standard No. 36: Disclosure of Pension Information.* Stamford, Conn.: FASB, 1981. An influential pronouncement that has been widely followed in other countries.

GERBOTH, DALE. "Accounting Scholasticism: The FASB's Preliminary Views on Pension Accounting. *Journal of Accountancy* (January 1984). A critical evaluation of the FASB's proposed position on pensions.

HICKS, E.L. *Accounting Research Study No. 6: Accounting for the Cost of Pension Plans.* New York: American Institute of Certified Public Accountants, 1965. A comprehensive examination of the issues. Although somewhat dated, it is still a useful reference source.

LUCAS, TIMOTHY S., and MILLER, P.B.W. "Pension Accounting: Impacting the Financial Statement." *Journal of Accountancy* (June 1983). An assessment of the FASB's Preliminary Views document on this subject.

MILBURN, J. ALEX. "Pension Accounting Leaves Too Much to Interpretation." *CA Magazine* (June 1987). A thoughtful appraisal of the leeway for interpretation of the new *CICA Handbook* requirements. Makes it clear that essentially similar pension situations can still be reported in a significantly different manner.

PESANDO, JAMES, and CLARKE, CAROL. "Economic Models of the Labour Market and Pension Accounting." *The Accounting Review* (October 1983). An economic evaluation of the pension issue in terms of labour economics.

SKINNER, ROSS M. *Pension Accounting: The Problem of Equating Payments Tomorrow with Expenses Today.* Toronto: Clarkson Gordon, 1980. A monograph on the accounting issues of pension plans.

CHAPTER 16
Owners' Equity

Introduction

DEFINITION AND MEASUREMENT

Owners' equity is the residual net interest in the assets of the company. It is measured for balance-sheet purposes from the basic accounting equation, as follows:

Owners' Equity = Assets − Liabilities

Owners' equity cannot be measured by direct observation. It must be arrived at indirectly by assigning values to the assets and liabilities and finding the net amount. We have already discussed the fact that, under generally accepted accounting principles, no attempt is made to measure and include all the assets of the company or to provide a market value for those that are included (for example, see Chapter 9). It follows that the amount shown for owners' equity in the balance sheet does not represent a valuation of the owners' interests, but is simply an amount arrived at under the GAAP rules. Thus, while the owners' equity section of the balance sheet is of interest to the reader, it rarely represents the value of the enterprise to the owners.

STATED CAPITAL

Many of the complexities in accounting for owners' equity arise from (i) the introduction into companies acts of **limited liability** (creditors of the company may only expect to sue the company for recovery of their debts and cannot seek recompense from the company's shareholders) and (ii) the endeavours, through companies legislation and securities legislation, to strike a balance between the interests of the creditors and shareholders. In return for the privilege of limited liability, at least one of the classes of shareholders is required to accept limitations on their right to withdraw from the company any capital already put in — in effect, their money must be left in the company unless certain tests for the protection of creditors are met. The desire to make sure that the company's capital is not reduced below a level that would jeopardize the company's creditors can be detected in many of the accounting issues to be discussed in this chapter.

In Canada there is a companies act in each of the provinces and a federal act called the Canada Business Corporations Act (CBCA). The latter has recently been revised, and many of its terms can be found in other recently written acts such as the Ontario Business Corporations Act (OBCA). In this chapter we will refer mainly to the federal act with occasional reference to provincial acts.

Both the CBCA and the OBCA use the term **stated capital**, instead of similar terms such as **issued capital**, **paid-up capital**, or **legal capital**. With certain exceptions, the stated capital is the full amount paid to the corporation for shares, whether payment is in cash, property, or past services. The stated capital can be reduced by the directors of the company, under certain conditions to be described, by redeeming or repurchasing and cancelling the company's shares.

The directors are personally liable if they agree to certain actions (of which the most important are the payment of dividends and the redemption or purchase of the company's own shares) when there are reasonable grounds for believing that their actions would make the corporation unable to pay its liabilities as they come due or would make the *realizable value* of the assets less than the corporation's liabilities and stated capital. The acts do not say how realizable value is to be computed, but they do say that directors will not normally be personally liable if they rely in good faith on the officers of the company or on a report from an outsider, such as a lawyer, accountant, appraiser, or engineer, whose profession lends credibility to their statements.

Earlier companies acts in Canada tried to protect creditors by prohibiting actions that make the total balance in the owners' equity account less than the stated capital. They thus relied heavily on the accounting model's measurement of owners' equity and implicitly accepted the historic-cost basis for valuation of assets. The rule was that owners' equity had to be at least as great as stated capital after a payment such as a dividend.

Most Canadian companies acts now take a different approach. They go back to the fundamental accounting equation:

Assets = Liabilities + Owners' Equity

They measure the realizable value of assets and then substitute *stated capital* for *owners' equity*. The directors are proscribed from actions that would reduce the net realizable value of assets below the liabilities and stated capital. This means that if the directors believe the value of the assets is greater than the amount shown in the financial statements, they can use this market valuation when applying the test.

Canadian corporations can be incorporated under the laws of any of the provinces or under the federal law. While these laws have similarities, they can also have material differences. In addition, because they are revised from time to time, it is important to consult an up-to-date legal source before taking action. The objective of this chapter is to introduce the general principles of companies legislation and their impact on accounting for owners' equity.

SHAREHOLDERS' RIGHTS

One would hope that companies' legislation would be designed to discourage one group of shareholders from exploiting another group of shareholders within the same company. Generally, unless they specifically agree to the contrary when the shares are issued, shareholders have the right to vote to elect the board of directors and to receive financial reports at least annually. However, the needs of shareholders as investors differ, and it is common to find more than one class of shares within the same corporation. A common reason for creating different classes of shares is to give a group of shareholders greater security of annual income by giving them a preference in receiving dividends. In return for this security, they generally accept some limitations on the size of that dividend or on their voting rights or on both. Another more contentious reason is to restrict the rights of some of the common shareholders to permit another group of shareholders to maintain control of the company.

It is quite common, for example, for Canadian companies to have common shares that are divided into those with full voting privileges and those whose voting privileges are restricted or non-existent. Frequently the voting shares are held by the founders and/or executives, whereas the shares with limited or non-existent voting rights are widely held by the public.

The manner in which the various shareholders' rights are distributed among the classes of shareholders will be crucial in determining each of the following:

1. The amount of influence a shareholder has in electing the board of directors, and hence influencing company policy.

2. The relative amount of risk with respect to receiving dividends.

3. The relative share of total dividends distributed.

We will discuss these factors in more detail in this chapter and in the following chapter.

Owners' equity may arise from the purchase of shares. Alternatively it may originate from earnings retained within the business or from various sources other than the purchase of shares or earnings.

Major Divisions of Owners' Equity

The major divisions of owners' equity usually found on balance sheets are as follows:

1. **Share capital**, representing the stated capital of the outstanding shares of the company.

2. Contributed surplus not represented by outstanding shares.

3. Retained earnings.

While the details of disclosure standards vary for each item, the intent is the same for all. First, any changes from the beginning of the year should be accounted for. Second, any material matters that are not captured within the accounting system should be reported in the notes to the financial statements. This includes such items as unpaid dividends on cumulative shares and outstanding options to purchase company shares.

Share Capital

Historically, companies had **common shareholders**, or those entitled to elect the board of directors, and **preferred shareholders**, who were entitled to receive a dividend of a stated minimum amount before any dividends were paid to common shareholders. The voting rights of preferred shareholders were usually minimal or nil unless they failed to receive a dividend, at which time their voting rights increased according to the terms under which the shares were issued. In effect, the preferred shareholders had to play a more passive role, but their dividend and rights on the winding-up of the company were better protected.

This simple distinction between common and preferred shareholders has been blurred over time, as companies have developed classes of common shareholders with differing rights between them. The CBCA now makes no distinction between common and preferred shares, but allows for different classes whose rights, privileges, restrictions, and conditions must be set out in the articles of incorporation of the company. However, at least one of the classes of shares must contain (i) the right to vote at all meetings of that class of shareholder and (ii) the right to dividends and distribution of assets when the company is wound up. These are the traditional rights of common shareholders. Thus, in effect the act requires that at least one class of shares must have the minimum attributes of common shares. For convenience we will refer in the text to this class of shares as common shares.

DIFFERENCES BETWEEN CLASSES OF SHARES

The *CICA Handbook* [3240] requires that the following six types of differences between classes of shares be disclosed:

1. *Dividend preferences*: It is common for some classes of shares to have a predetermined annual dividend (e.g., $1.38 per share) that must be paid before any dividends can be paid on the common shares or any other class of shares ranking lower in preference. While there is no legal requirement that any dividend should be paid until the directors actually declare it, the provision that it be paid in preference to common shareholders' dividends would normally put pressure on the directors to declare a preferred dividend. In addition, the dividend may be made **cumulative**, so that any arrears in preferred dividends must be paid before any dividends can be paid on common shares.

2. *Redemption, call, and retraction privileges*: Certain classes of shares may be issued on the condition that they can be redeemed at the option of either the shareholder or the company (depending on the terms of issue). If redeemable at the option of

the shareholder, they are often called **retractable shares**. If redeemable at the option of the company, they are usually referred to as **redeemable preferred shares** or **callable preferred shares**. The price at which they are redeemable may change over time, and the *CICA Handbook* [3240.01] requires that the redemption price be shown. For example, Thomson Newspapers Limited had the following note in its financial statements regarding share redemptions: "The company has issued preference shares which are designated at 6 3/4% cumulative redeemable preference shares, Series A, redeemable at $51 per share."

Some preferred shares have redemption and other privileges that so strongly favour the holder of the share that they have many of the attributes of a debt security. If the redemption date is indicated at the time of issue, they are often referred to as **term-preferred shares**. Although there is no special *CICA Handbook* disclosure requirement, there is an Accounting Guideline (December 1977) stating that the "unique characteristics" of term-preferred shares should be disclosed. This might include the terms of redemption and the amounts required in each of the next five years to meet the redemption provisions.

3. *Voting privileges*: The voting privileges set out in the articles of incorporation may eliminate or restrict the right of certain classes of shares to vote to elect directors, thus keeping the bulk of the power to influence company affairs in the hands of the common shareholders. However, in certain circumstances, the shares with restricted voting rights may have these restrictions changed to increase their voting power. Typically, this happens when dividends have not been paid on these shares for a period of time, such as two years. The *CICA Handbook* does not specifically require that voting privileges should be disclosed, although the general requirement that a brief description should be given of each class of share seems to suggest that any unusual restrictions on voting rights should be disclosed.

4. *Conversion privileges*: The articles of incorporation may provide that holders of a particular class of share have the privilege of converting their shares into shares of another class. Typically, this would be the right to convert shares with a fixed annual dividend into common shares or to convert voting (but non-marketable) shares into non-voting (but marketable) shares. For example, Thomson Newspapers Limited had the following note in its financial statements regarding conversion privileges: "Class A participating shares are convertible into Class B participating shares, and vice versa, on a one for one basis at the option of the shareholder." We will discuss conversion privileges in more detail later in this chapter in the section on convertible shares.

5. *Preference on redemption*: The following excerpt from the statements of Texaco Canada Inc. illustrates preference on redemption:

> In the event of a distribution of the assets of the Corporation among its shareholders for the purpose of winding up its affairs, the holders of the Second Preferred Shares shall be entitled to receive an amount equal to $100,000 per share plus all accrued and unpaid dividends thereon, the whole to be paid before any amount is paid or any assets of the Corporation are distributed to the holders of the Common Shares, or the shares of any other class ranking junior to the Second Preferred Shares.

6. *Par value or no par value*: The **par value** of a share is the fixed price which is deemed to constitute the *stated capital* in those jurisdictions that allow par value shares. If a share is **no par value**, then the entire proceeds are deemed to constitute the stated capital. Par value shares are not permitted under the Canada Business Corporations Act and are now rare in Canada, but they are still common in the U.S. If a company sells par value shares for a sum greater than their par value, then the excess is termed **contributed surplus**, and it is held in a different owners' equity account from the share capital. Under the Canada Business Corporations Act and most provincial acts no contributed surplus can arise from the sale of no par value shares. However about one-third of Canadian balance sheets may still show some from the era in which companies were allowed to issue par value shares. Contributed surplus is dealt with in more detail later in this chapter.

The privileges, rights, and responsibilities assigned to a given class of share is a result of the following five items: (i) the restrictions laid down by the act under which the company is incorporated; (ii) the requirements of the securities commissions; (iii) the rules of the stock exchanges; (iv) the wishes of the company management and dominant shareholder group; and (v) the underwriter's desire to make the share issue attractive enough to the potential shareholders so that they will be willing to pay a good price for the shares.

The intent of the companies acts to maintain a minimum shareholder capital as protection for the creditors has already been discussed. Securities commissions, such as the Ontario Securities Commission, are charged with maintaining a fair and orderly capital market. They discourage the issue of securities that they think run counter to this objective, such as shares with the attributes of common shares but not the right to vote. Stock exchanges have similar concerns; for example, the New York Stock Exchange will not permit the trading of any shares of a company that has a class of non-voting common shares. On the other hand, common shareholders who control a significant block of a company's common shares sometimes try to persuade other passive investors in these common shares to convert their holdings to non-voting common shares. This gives the former a larger percentage of the voting common shares and hence a better opportunity to consolidate their control of the company.

Shares can be thought of as "product" that is packaged and sold by the financial community with the features that are thought to be most attractive to the investor and of the least cost to the company. It is reasonable to expect continuing innovation in the features that various issues of shares hold. Thus, it is important for the reader to look behind simplistic labels such as "common" or "preferred" shares to see what the actual features of the issue are. As we discussed above, it is also possible for shares to take on many of the attributes of debt securities. The general thrust of accounting standards is to make sure that the significant features are disclosed to the reader.

DILUTIVE SECURITIES

A company share is essentially a right to a proportionate share in the benefits of common share ownership. A **dilutive security** is one that actually or potentially decreases this proportionate share. These securities vary in form, but the essential feature is the same: the person owning the dilutive security has the right to acquire shares at less than the current market price.

Most companies acts have a general provision that requires the company to offer new shares to its existing shareholders in proportion to their interest in the company. This is termed a **preemptive right**, and it is designed to permit existing shareholders to retain their interest in the company. For example, suppose that you owned 10,000 shares that represented a 10% interest in the company. If the company issued 100,000 additional shares of the same class to someone else, you would then have only a 5% interest. The preemptive rights may be overridden if the company has obtained specific rights to issue contracts to purchase shares on terms more favourable than those available on the open market. Such contracts may be in the form of options, warrants, or conversion features attached to other securities. Examples are discussed below.

Employee Options

An **employee option** is a contract between a company and one of its employees that permits the holder of the option to purchase a certain number of a specified class of shares at a stated price up to the expiry date from the person giving the option. For example, the option might have the following features:

1. The holder of the option could purchase the common shares of the company at the following prices:
   - $35 from date of issue to the end of the first 12 months
   - $40 from the end of 12 months to the end of 24 months
   - $45 from the end of 24 months to the end of 36 months.

2. After 36 months the option expires.

Suppose that the common shares of the company were trading at $30 at the date of issue of the option. The option holder would have no incentive to exercise the option since he or she could buy shares more cheaply on the market. If, however, the common shares traded at more than the option price during any of the thirty-six months during which it was valid, then the holder would have an incentive to exercise the option or sell it to someone else. If, for example, the price of the shares rose to $60 during the period between the twenty-fourth and thirty-sixth months, the option would probably be exercised. The option holder would then get a share for $45, whereas someone buying an equivalent share on the open market would have to pay $60. It is for this reason that the option is referred to as a *dilutive* security when the issuer of the option is the company itself.

It is common for security traders unrelated to the company to buy and sell options in that company's shares. These are traded in options markets operated in a similar manner to stock markets. They are *not* the type of option being discussed here. The options under consideration in this section are between the company and its employees, and they may carry restrictions on the right to sell them to others.

Options are frequently given to senior executives of a company as a form of delayed compensation. The options are usually not transferable, and employees frequently lose some of their existing options if they go to another company before retirement. Presumably this is intended as an incentive to work hard and stay with the company.

Here is an example of an employee share option plan from the financial statements of Baton Broadcasting Incorporated:

> The Company has reserved 700,000 common shares under its 1984 Employee Share Option Plan. At August 31, 1986, 696,000 options were outstanding of which 671,000 were granted in prior years at an option price of $15.00 per share and an additional 25,000 were granted during the current year at an option price of $22.50 per share. These options are exercisable at various specified dates until expiry 10 years from the date granted.

Warrants

A **warrant** is a certificate issued by the company and sold to outsiders. It entitles the bearer to purchase from the company a stated number of shares of a stated class of the company's share at a specified price up to an expiry date. We can summarize the differences between warrants, share options, and employee options as follows.

Warrants	Share options	Employee Options
— Created by the company and sold to outsiders	— Created and traded by third parties unrelated to the company	— Created by the company for its employees
— Usually traded on organized markets	— Traded on organized markets and fully transferable	— Usually *not* traded and *not* transferable
— To convert them into something of value, the holder hopes to exercise the rights in the warrants to purchase the shares *from the company* at a price less than market	— To convert them into something of value, the holder hopes to exercise the rights in the options to purchase the shares *from a third party* at a price less than market	— To convert them into something of value, the holder (employee) hopes to purchase the shares *from the company* when the terms of the options permit

Warrants are illustrated in the following note to the financial statements of Unicorp Canada Corporation:

> On December 9, 1983, the Board of Directors authorized the issuance of: warrants to purchase 60,000 Class II Preference Shares, Series A for a price of $12.00 per share, exercisable on or before December 31, 1985; and warrants to purchase 100,000 Class II Preference Shares, Series A for a price of $12.00 per share, exercisable on or before December 31, 1985, after which date, the holders of these warrants may purchase 100,000 Class A Non-Voting Shares at a price of $12.00 per share until December 31, 1986.

The terms of these warrants are slightly unusual in that the holder may purchase one class of share up to 31 December, 1985 and another class thereafter. Usually, the warrants only give the right to purchase one class of share. In addition, no expiry date is mentioned.

Convertible Shares and Bonds

A **conversion privilege** is a right attached to a class of share or to a bond that permits the holder to convert the security into another class of security of the company at a stated price during a stated time period. The conversion privilege is often attached to bonds or preferred shares to permit the holder to convert them into common shares of the company. This is usually done to make the bonds or shares more attractive to the investor at the time of issue or, at a later date, to encourage shareholders and creditors to shift their investment into common shares.

For example, the Class D shares of Hiram Walker Resources Limited had the following conditions: 7.5% cumulative, voting, first series, convertible into common shares at $28.00 per share up to 31 December 1989, redeemable at varying premiums reducing from $1.875. The conversion price of $28.00 remains unchanged during the life of this conversion privilege. Often, however, the price increases. If the shares were redeemed, the conversion privilege would lapse. But note that the sooner the shares are redeemed, the higher the premium that has to be paid to the shareholder. This share might be attractive to an investor who wanted the prospect of a relatively secure (but fixed) dividend, with the ultimate option of converting into common shares if the latter's price exceeded $28 before the end of 1989.

The existence of potentially dilutive securities has significant implications for existing shareholders because it means that the benefit they will enjoy from the company's success will be reduced as the holders of dilutive securities exercise their rights to acquire shares. In particular, the dividend paid per share is not likely to be as high as the number of shares increase through the exercise of dilutive rights. As we shall see in the next chapter, this has significance for the calculation of earnings per share. The *CICA Handbook* [3240] requires disclosure of (i) the existence of conversion provisions, (ii) the number of shares reserved to meet rights outstanding under conversion or share option privileges and, (iii) the prices at which such rights are exercisable and the dates of expiry.

ISSUING SHARES

A corporation is authorized to issue shares by the legal documents under which it is incorporated, which may restrict the number of shares of each class that can be issued. (The CBCA and the OBCA have no such restrictions, however.) Even though not issued, the shares may be committed in the sense that holders of dilutive securities or share subscribers may have the ultimate right to obtain them. On issue they may be paid for in cash, services, or other assets. All the proceeds may be treated as the stated capital, or (in some jurisdictions in the U.S. and under special circumstances in Canada) only part of the proceeds may be so treated. When the shares are issued, it is unlikely that the corporation will receive all the proceeds because it will incur issuing costs. Finally, the issued shares may be owned by the corporation itself or by others.

Each of these factors gives rise to accounting issues that will be discussed in this section. These issues are as follows:

1. disclosure of the number of shares of each class that are authorized, issued, and committed

2. treatment of outstanding subscriptions to shares

3. treatment of stock purchases made with non-cash assets or services

4. identification of the part of the proceeds that form part of the stated capital

5. treatment of the costs connected with the issue

Authorized and Issued Shares

Under the CBCA and some of the more recently revised provincial acts, there is no limit to the number of shares of each class that may be issued unless a maximum number is specified in the articles of incorporation. Some acts of incorporation do set out such limits, and it may be important to the reader to be aware of this. The existence of dilutive securities may mean that the actual shares outstanding plus the commitments to issue additional shares have become equal to the total authorized number of shares.

The *CICA Handbook* disclosure requirements [3240.01-.04] are as follows:

1. The number of shares authorized for each class should be shown, stating the par value, if any, and giving a brief description.

2. The issued share capital should be shown, including the number of shares issued and the amount received or receivable for each class. (There would be no amounts receivable for companies incorporated under the CBCA; this provision would apply only to those companies incorporated under acts that do permit such receivables.)

3. The number of shares of each class issued since the last balance sheet date should be indicated, together with the value attributed to them.

Share Subscriptions

A **share subscription** is a contract between the company and another party stating that the company will sell, and the other person will buy, a stated number of shares at a stated price. It is different from an option in that both sides are committed to proceed. The CBCA does not permit shares to be issued until they are paid in full. Therefore any amounts received as a subscription should be treated as a liability, not as part of owners' equity.

If Portsmouth Limited entered into a share subscription contract with Mr. Smith to issue him 100 shares for a cash payment of $25,000 on 1 January 19X4, it would make no entry as a result of the contract. If Smith paid $10,000 in advance, the entry would be as follows:

Bank	10,000.00	
Current liability — deposit		10,000.00
Record receipt of funds.		

When the remaining $15,000 was received on 1 January 19X4, the following entry would be made:

Bank	15,000.00	
Current liability — deposit	10,000.00	
Common share capital		25,000.00

Issue of share capital on receipt of payment in full.

Since the CBCA does not permit shares to be issued until fully paid, it would not be appropriate to show the amounts still due from share subscribers as an accounts receivable, with an offsetting credit to share capital.

The *CICA Handbook* [3240.02] requires that if any shares are not fully paid for, disclosure should be made of the amounts that have been called or are otherwise due.

Issue of Shares for Non-Cash Consideration

A company may purchase a major asset, such as a block of shares in another company, by issuing its own shares. In principle, this is no different from issuing the shares for cash, but there may be the practical problem of placing a valuation on the assets received and thus determining the value of the shares issued.

A further complication arises when the parties to the transaction are **related parties**. This situation arises where "one party has the ability to exercise, directly or indirectly, control or significant influence over the operating and financial decisions of the other. Two or more parties are also considered to be related when they are subject to common control or significant influence" [*CICA* 3840.03].

If the shares are traded on a stock exchange, and the company and the seller of the assets are not related parties, then it can usually be inferred that the value of the assets received is equal to the value of the shares issued in exchange.

Shopping Centres Inc. purchased an existing shopping centre from its former owners by issuing 60,000 of its Series A shares. These shares traded on a stock exchange for $25 at the time of issue. Thus the inferred value of the asset received is $1,500,000. Assuming the management of the company and the owners of the shopping centre were dealing at arm's length, it seems reasonable that the purchasers valued the centre at $1,500,000 on the basis of real estate appraisals, capitalization of expected earnings, etc.

Difficulties arise when the buyer and seller are related parties or when there is no well-established market to provide a value for the assets received in consideration of the shares. Consider the following example. A Ltd., a publicly traded company, issued 10,000 Series A shares, then trading at $25 a share to purchase a shopping centre from B Ltd., a company which exercised significant influence over A Ltd. through representation on its board of directors. It is quite possible that A is paying an inflated price for the shopping centre under pressure from B; and as a result the stated capital is overvalued, and the interest of the existing shareholders has been diluted.

A related-party transaction is often not easily distinguished from a non-related party transaction (i.e., an arm's-length transaction). It would not be surprising to find the people involved in the transaction ready to dispute any assertion that the transaction was between related parties. The main protection for the reader of financial statements is disclosure of the circumstances under which shares were issued. The *CICA Handbook* [3240.04] requires that disclosure be made of the value attributed to new shares issued during the period, distinguishing between shares issued directly or indirectly for services and shares issued directly or indirectly for other considerations. While this is not a completely satisfactory solution, it is difficult to think of a stronger requirement that would be workable. The section on related-party transactions [*CICA* 3840] requires a description of (i) the nature and extent of transactions, (ii) the nature of the relationship, and (iii) amounts due to or from related parties and, if not apparent, the terms of settlement.

Identification of the Part of Proceeds That Forms the Stated Capital

In those jurisdictions where par-value shares are permitted, it is possible for a company to sell its shares for more than their par value. If the par value is the stated capital, the excess amount received may be considered to be something other than the legal capital. For this reason it is credited to a separate owners' equity account termed **contributed surplus** or simply **capital in excess of par**. If this is in excess of stated capital, and if the incorporating act, company by-laws, regulatory commissions, and restrictive covenants on bonds permit it, it is conceivable that this paid-in capital might ultimately be returned to the shareholders. However, this would be rare except when the corporation purchases, redeems, or somehow acquires its shares. At that time it might reduce the contributed capital that matched the shares being redeemed.

U.S. Inc. is a company incorporated in a jurisdiction in the United States that permits the issue of par value shares. It issues 10,000 shares with a par value of $80 for $95 cash net. The entry on issue would be as follows:

Bank	950,000	
Share capital		800,000
Capital in excess of par		150,000
To record issue of 10,000 shares of $80 par value at a price of $95 net.		

Most jurisdictions that permit par-value shares will not permit them to be sold for less than par value since this would mean that the consideration received was less than the stated capital.

The CBCA does not permit the issue of par-value shares. It requires that the stated capital be equal to the full amount paid for the no-par-value shares (except under special circumstances where the shares are issued in a transaction that is not at arm's length). Thus, the issue of contributed surplus does not arise with companies incorporated under that act. Most provincial companies acts from Quebec west have similar provisions, as they have been revised and standardized with the CBCA.

Costs of Share Issue

When a company sells shares to the public it can either do so directly or use an **underwriter** (a company that specializes in evaluating the kind of security that could be most advantageously offered investors) and then sell them to investors. Costs will be incurred for legal and accounting services, printing, advertising, and other activities connected with the issue of the shares. If the shares are sold through an underwriter, he or she may absorb some of these costs but charge a fee for services, often in the form of discounting the proceeds of the sale of shares. The usual accounting treatment is to charge the costs of issuing shares against retained earnings, but to treat the discount charged by the underwriter as a charge against share capital.

Yarker Corporation arranged with an underwriter to sell 10,000 Series A shares. The shares would be sold to the public at $25, and the underwriter would remit $24.50 per share to Yarker, keeping $0.50 per share as commission. Yarker incurred legal fees of $50,000 and additional audit fees of $40,000. (Disregard tax effects.) On payment of the professional fees, the following entry would be made:

Retained earnings (legal fees)	50,000.00	
Retained earnings (audit fees)	40,000.00	
Bank		90,000.00
Payment of legal and audit fees re issue of new shares		

When the proceeds of the issue were received from the underwriter, the entry would be as follows:

Bank	245,000.00	
Share capital — Series A		245,000.00
Record receipt of funds from underwriter on issue of 10,000 series A shares at a price to the public of $25.00 each and $24.50 net to the company.		

ACQUISITION OF COMPANY'S OWN SHARES

The acquisition of a company's own shares by redemption or purchase on the open market may potentially represent a reduction of the stated capital of the company. The incorporating act usually has provisions to prevent this happening if there is a likelihood it would adversely affect creditors of a class of shareholder. For example, the Canada Business Corporations Act (Section 32) allows a company to purchase any of its class of shares unless there are reasonable grounds for believing

a. the corporation is, or would after the payment be, unable to pay its liabilities as they become due; or

b. the realizable value of the corporation's assets would, after the payment, be less than the aggregate of its liabilities and stated capital.

As any class of share is redeemed or cancelled, its stated capital is reduced by the amount of the proceeds originally received for those shares. Under some circumstances it now seems possible, at least in theory, for a company to retire virtually all its shares.

Redemption of Redeemable Shares

Shares may be issued with a **redemption feature** under which the company or the shareholder may require that the share be redeemed at a stated price at the option of either side. Sometimes the company is required under the terms of issue of the shares to redeem a certain number of the shares per year until all are retired. Section 34 of the CBCA states that "a corporation may purchase or redeem any redeemable share issued by it at prices not exceeding the redemption price stated in the articles or calculated according to a formula stated in the articles."

For example, Dofasco Inc. had the following note in its financial statements for its Class B preferred shares:

> The Corporation is obligated to make all reasonable efforts to purchase 24,000 shares per quarter commencing in 1984 (12,000 per quarter prior to 1984) at a price not to exceed $25 per share. At December 31, 1983 the Corporation is in compliance with the terms of its obligation, and has purchased for cancellation an aggregate of 132,200 shares for $ 2,725,000 . . . These preferred shares are redeemable by the Corporation after October 15, 1985 at $25 per share plus accrued and unpaid dividends.

It would appear that the provision requiring the company to purchase a minimum number of shares per quarter commencing in 1984 is intended to give shareholders a floor price of $25 if they wish to redeem up to 24,000 shares per quarter. After October 15, 1985, the Corporation has the option of redeeming the shares at $25 per share. Presumably if the Corporation does not wish to redeem at $25 and the shareholder does not want to sell at that price, some shares could remain outstanding indefinitely.

When shares are redeemed the accounting entry is to reduce the share capital account by the stated capital of the shares. Such a reduction is generally permitted under company law if the shares are issued subject to redemption and if the redemption price does not exceed the stated capital of the shares.

Purchase of Common Shares

It is possible to imagine a doomsday scenario in which a company uses its cash to purchase all its outstanding shares and hold them as one of its assets, usually termed **treasury shares**. If the company were later unable to pay its creditors, it would be found that the shareholders had taken their funds out of the company indirectly through the tactic of having the company buy their shares on the open market. The creditors would find the now-worthless shares among the company's assets, and their ability to recover their debts would thus be reduced.

This should be contrasted with the redemption of redeemable shares, where the creditors know beforehand what the redemption features of the shares are, and the price and timing of the redemption is stated. The purchase of a company's non-redeemable shares on the open market can conceivably be done secretly, to the possible disadvantage of creditors and other classes of shareholders.

It is not surprising that companies acts, regulatory authorities, and stock exchanges have rules governing how the purchase of a company's non-redeemable shares can be done and that accounting authorities require extensive disclosure. The CBCA only permits it under the general conditions for acquiring shares stated above, and regulatory authorities and stock exchanges generally require advance notice from the company before such a purchase takes place.

The major accounting issues here are as follows:

1. Whether shares that have been purchased should be treated as assets of the company (e.g., in the same manner as the purchase of other company's shares) or as a deduction of owners' equity.

2. If shares are purchased at a price different from their issue price, how the difference should be treated.

The CBCA prohibits a company from owning either its own shares or those of its parent company, if any, except under special circumstances when acting as trustee for a third party or when taking security for a loan. Although it may purchase its own shares, it must cancel them, thus reducing its stated capital. Practice may vary from one jurisdiction to another, depending on the requirements of the governing companies act.

Classification on Balance Sheet

There is general agreement among accountants that if a company purchases its own shares, they should not be treated as assets but as a reduction of shareholders' capital. The reasoning is that a company cannot own part of itself; at the extreme its "assets" might consist entirely of its own shares, whose underlying value consists of a company whose assets are those same shares.

Purchase at Price Different From Issue Price

It is almost inevitable that shares purchased on the open market will not have the same purchase cost as the original issue price. Does this mean that if the shares are purchased for less than their issue cost, the company makes a "profit" on the purchase (or a "loss" under the opposite circumstances)? Since a company that is not doing well is likely to have a depressed price for its shares, it seems likely that unprofitable companies would be able to report a profit simply by purchasing their own shares. To prevent such a transaction, the standards in both Canada and the U.S. require that if shares are purchased for more than their original price, the difference should first be charged to contributed surplus (to be explained below), if part of the original proceeds of issue had been credited to that account, and only to the amount that was originally credited per share, i.e. pro rata. Any excess is to be charged entirely to retained earnings [*CICA* 3240.15].

Eastport Corporation issued no-par-value shares at $10 five years ago. It has now redeemed 1,000 of these shares at $12. The original issue of the shares did not create any contributed surplus, and therefore the entire difference must be charged to retained earnings, as follows:

Share capital	10,000.00	
Retained earnings	2,000.00	
Bank		12,000.00
Record purchase of shares at $12. Original price was $10.		

If shares are purchased at less than their original issue price, the difference should be credited to contributed surplus (not retained earnings). For example, Westport Corporation originally issued 30,000 no-par-value shares for a consideration of $10 per share. It recently purchased 1,000 on the open market for $8. The entry would be as follows:

Share capital	10,000.00	
Bank		8,000.00
Contributed surplus		2,000.00
Record purchase of 1000 shares at $8. Original issue price was $10.		

Note that any "profit" on redemption is treated as contributed surplus, whereas any "loss" is charged against retained earnings [*CICA* 3240.17]. In Canada this has no implications with respect to payment of dividends under most companies acts, but it does have an implication in those jurisdictions where payment of dividends is related to the balances in the shareholders' equity accounts.

Contributed Surplus

Contributed surplus (or **contributed capital**) represents equity in the firm that is not represented by capital stock or retained earnings. It is relatively uncommon in Canada, although there is a substantial residue from prior companies acts. Contributed surplus can also arise from the restructuring of "troubled" debt when the creditors agree to reduce their claim against the company.

EXCESS OF PROCEEDS
OVER PAR VALUE OF SHARES

If the proceeds on sale of par-value shares exceed the par value, the excess amount is referred to by terms such as *contributed surplus*, or simply *capital in excess of par value*. Since the Canada Business Corporations Act and most provincial acts now permit only shares without par value, the creation of new contributed surplus in a Canadian company would be uncommon. However, some Canadian companies have contributed surplus remaining from the era when par-value shares were permitted. Par- value shares are permitted in many U.S. jurisdictions.

Adam Centre Corporation, a company incorporated under legislation permitting par-value shares, sold 1,000 shares of $100 par value for $125. The journal entry would be as follows:

Bank	125,000.00	
Share capital		100,000.00
Contributed surplus		25,000.00
Record issue of 1,000 shares of $100 par value for $125.		

If the company later redeemed 500 shares at $160, it would reduce the contributed surplus by the amount related to the 500 shares and then charge the difference to retained earnings, as follows:

Share capital — 500 × 100	50,000.00	
Contributed surplus — 500 × 25	12,500.00	
Retained earnings — 500 × (160 − 125)	17,500.00	
Bank — 500 × 160		80,000.00

To record redemption of 500 shares at $160.

DONATED CAPITAL

Although it may seem mind-boggling that donations would be made to a corporation, there are occasional circumstances where this might be in the donor's interest. Examples might be (i) a shareholder of a family-owned company donates a fixed asset or (ii) a municipality or other government body donates a factory building on the condition that the company create employment in that area.

In the second case this is not normally treated as contributed capital, but as a reduction in the cost of the asset acquired [*CICA* 3800].(See above, Chapter 7.) The rationale for this treatment is that the economic substance of the gift is to offset some other, economically unattractive, aspect of the agreement that produced the gift. This might be higher labour or transportation costs, for instance. The net result of this treatment is that the benefit, if any, of the donation ultimately is reflected in a higher net income, and hence retained earnings, instead of contributed capital.

Alpha Corporation entered into an agreement with a municipality in which it received land and buildings worth $500,000 in return for certain commitments to operate in that municipality for a minimum of ten years without reducing its work force. If the grant were treated as a contribution to capital (not accepted as good accounting practice in Canada), the company would credit contributed surplus on receipt of the funds. However, this is not acceptable practice under section 3800 of the *CICA Handbook*, which requires that it be treated as an offset to the cost of the asset donated. The proper entry in Canada would be as follows:

Land and buildings	500,000.00	
Land and buildings — offset account		500,000.00

Record donation of land and buildings, with offset asset account.

The following entry would be an acceptable alternative:

Land and buildings	500,000.00	
Deferred government assistance		500,000.00

Record donation of land and buildings, with offset to deferred (balance-sheet) account.

The offset or deferred accounts would, in each case, be amortized (with the resulting increase in reported income) and shown as an income item or deducted from depreciation expense.

The accounting significance between the treatments approved in *The CICA Handbook* and treating the donation as a contribution to capital is as follows. If the receipt is credited to contributed surplus (the unacceptable method), both the asset account and owners' equity increase by the amount of the grant. The depreciation charges would be higher over the depreciable life of the asset, and thus the reported net income would be lower by the amount of the credit to contributed surplus. By contrast, if the methods approved in the *Handbook* are used, there is no immediate increase in owners' equity and no net increase in annual depreciation as a result of the grant.

Disagreement over which method to use can be interpreted as a disagreement over the economic substance of the gift. The method not approved by the *Handbook* implies that it was in fact a gift, and the company's owner's equity is that much larger as a result. The approved treatments imply that it was not a gift at all, but a kind of up-front payment to induce the company to incur other costs that it would not otherwise have been willing to bear.

DEFAULTED SUBSCRIPTIONS

It is possible that under the terms of a share subscription the subscriber must pay the additional amounts due or forfeit the amounts already paid in. In such a forfeiture, the amounts already received (and held in a liability account) would be transferred to a contributed surplus account. Situations that would give rise to defaulted subscriptions are uncommon in Canada.

PURCHASE OF OWN SHARES

The case has already been discussed where the company might repurchase its own shares at a price that was less than the original issue price. In such cases, any difference between the original issue price and the purchase price would be treated as contributed surplus.

Has the original shareholder really contributed any capital to the company by agreeing to sell his shares back to the company at a price that was less than the issue price? Probably not, especially if the shares were purchased on the open market. The lower price indicates the public think that the company is worth less than when the shares were issued and that the shares purchased have simply been a bad investment. Classifying this difference as contributed capital seems mainly intended to prevent it from being credited to retained earnings.

Retained Earnings

Retained earnings is the term given to the amount on the balance sheet that is the net of the following:

1. Accumulated annual income and/or losses — The annual net incomes or losses since the formation of the company.

2. Restatements of the gains or losses of prior periods — Prior-period adjustments not included in net income for the period of the adjustment.

3. Decreases due to dividend payments — These payments may be in cash or other assets of the company.

4. Decreases because a part of retained earnings has been appropriated to another owners' equity account.

5. Other capital transactions charged directly to retained earnings (e.g., share issue expenses).

The retained earnings account does not, of course, represent the amount available to the shareholders to take out of the company any time they like. There are two reasons for this. First, whether the company has sufficient and suitable assets to pay dividends is something that can only be determined by analyzing the asset side of the balance sheet. Second, the net incomes and/or losses that have been included in the retained earnings account each year are the end result of an accounting measurement process that has been discussed at length in this text. The usual historic-cost-based accounting system does not attempt to portray the current market values of the assets, and hence (since retained earnings is the ultimate balancing figure on the balance sheet) the balance in retained earnings does not represent the net market value of the assets available to shareholders.

Despite these limitations, the balance in retained earnings has been used as a test of the propriety of some important management actions. It is common to find in the restrictive covenants in bond indentures that the company may not pay a dividend if this would reduce the retained earnings below some threshold level. For example, in 1969 Steep Rock Iron Mines made an extraordinary write-down of deferred exploration costs. This did not affect the company's cash flow, but it did reduce the balance of retained earnings below a predetermined level set out in one of their bond covenants. As a result, the company was potentially prohibited under the covenant from paying a dividend on common shares.

ANNUAL INCOME OR LOSS

The **annual income or loss** that is included in retained earnings will be the amount that is arrived at using the generally accepted accounting principles under which the company operates. Thus, the amount is the result of both the economic activities of the company and the accounting measurement system used. Since a thoughtful reader of financial statements can usually see the possibilities of reporting a range of net income numbers for the same company in the same year, the reader needs to be even more cautious in attaching a meaning to the accumulation of such income numbers over a number of years. It is usually more productive to start by asking a more general question, such as "How much is each common shareholder likely to receive if the company were broken up and assets sold on the open market?" To answer such a question, for example, one might make estimates of the current market value of the assets and deduct from this the estimated amount necessary to pay off the creditors. In making such an estimate, however, one virtually ignores the retained earnings number on the balance sheet.

PRIOR-PERIOD ADJUSTMENTS

A **prior-period adjustment** is a gain or loss specifically identified with the activities of a particular prior period. It is shown directly in the statement of retained earnings instead of the income statement. This has already been discussed in Chapter 4 on income statements.

DIVIDENDS

A **dividend** is a payment to a shareholder following a formal vote of the board of directors of the company. The **declaration date** is the day on which the motion declaring the dividend is passed at a meeting of the board of directors. Before declaring such a dividend the directors would, if in doubt, seek assurance that the payment of the dividend was in accordance with the company's act of incorporation. For companies incorporated under the federal and most provincial acts, for instance, they would want assurance that the payment of the dividend was not likely to make the company incapable of paying its debts as they come due and that the net realizable assets would not be less than the stated capital. Otherwise, the directors may find themselves personally liable for the debts of the company.

At the declaration date the dividend becomes a legal liability of the company to the shareholders, and a journal entry is made to record this. The resolution of the board of directors will include the **record date**, or the day on which it will examine its shareholders' record to see who is registered as a shareholder as of that date. It will also include the **payment date**, or the day on which the actual payment is made.

On 30 April 19X0 at a meeting of the board of directors of Bartok Limited, a resolution was passed as follows: "It is hereby declared that a dividend of 20 cents per share shall be paid on June 30 on all Class A shares of the company to shareholders of record as of May 31." Suppose there are 10,000 Class A shares outstanding. The following journal entry would be made as of 30 April, the declaration date:

Retained earnings — dividends	2,000.00	
Dividends payable		2,000.00
Record declaration of dividend payable 30 June		
to shareholders of record 31 May; 20 cents per		
share on 10,000 shares.		

Up to 31 May the company would continue to record changes in the names of shareholders arising from trades on the stock exchange. On that date, however, it would prepare the dividend cheques based on the names in the shareholder record. If a shareholder purchased the shares before 31 May, but was unable to record this in the shareholder record before the record date, he or she would have to claim this dividend from the seller of the shares. Shares listed on a stock exchange sell "cum dividend" up to a few days prior to the dividend record date. The buyer of the shares is entitled, up to this date, to receive this dividend. Shares are sold "ex dividend" after that date, and purchasers buying such shares are not entitled to the current dividend. On that date the price of the share can be expected to drop by an amount approximately equal to the expected dividend.

On 30 June Bartok Limited would make the following entry:

Dividends payable	2,000.00	
Bank		2,000.00
Record payment of dividend.		

Manner of Payment

Most dividends are paid in cash, as illustrated above. However, on some occasions they may be paid in shares of the company (to be discussed below) or in assets other than cash. Sometimes, for example, the company will dispose of a subsidiary by giving its shares in the subsidiary to its shareholders as a dividend. The question then arises whether the dividend should be recorded at the carrying value of the asset given as a dividend or at its market value.

If the dividend is recorded at the market value of the asset disposed of, and if this market value is different from its original cost, then there will be a gain or loss on disposal, generally recorded as of the date the dividend is declared. If the dividend is recorded at the carrying value of the asset, then there would be no gain or loss on disposal.

The directors of M Limited declared a dividend to their Class A shareholders consisting of 2,000 shares of the company's subsidiary, S Limited. The declaration date was 1 December 19X8, the record date was 15 January 19X9, and the payment date was 15 February 19X9. The shares had originally cost $30 each and were now estimated to have a market value of $50 each. If the company recorded the dividend at the carrying value of the shares, the entry on 1 December 19X8 would be as follows:

Retained earnings — dividend	60,000.00	
Dividend payable		60,000.00
Record declaration of dividend — 2,000 shares of S Limited payable to holders of Class A shares on 15 February 19X9.		

By contrast, if the company valued the dividend at the market vlaue of the assets paid as dividends, the entries on 1 December would be as follows:

Retained earnings — dividend	100,000.00	
Dividend payable		100,000.00
Record declaration of dividend — 2,000 shares of S Limited payable to holders of Class A shares on 15 February 19X9.		

Investment in S Limited	40,000.00	
Gain on disposal		40,000.00
To record gain on disposal of 2,000 shares at $50 with an original cost of $30 each.		

The reason for recording the gain on disposal at the time of the declaration of the dividend is that it appears to have met the usual realization test for disposal, although the circumstances are rather different from the usual sale of an asset. Because the valuation of the asset being disposed of is usually made by related parties, there is need for care in assessing the implications of the valuation chosen. The net effect on retained earnings is the same, since any changes in calculation of the gain on disposal and dividend would offset; but the reported net income could be increased by generous valuations of the assets disposed of. If carrying value is used, the possibility is opened for management to dispose of assets whose market value has dropped below book and to avoid reporting the loss on disposal on the income statement.

Canadian practice shows the use of both carrying value and market value, although carrying value is more common. In the U.S. the use of market value is mandatory. In theory, market value appears preferable.

Share Dividend

A **share dividend** is a dividend paid in any class of shares of the company's own shares to holders of the same class of shares. Usually it is paid to common shareholders in common shares. The shareholders' proportionate share in the equity of the company has not changed after the dividend. They are essentially in the same position as before — they simply have more share certificates to represent the same interest in the company. Nevertheless, it is common to capitalize a portion of the retained earnings which is thought to represent the value of the new shares that have been issued, thus reducing the retained earnings available for cash dividends. This is particularly the case with par-value shares, since the articles of incorporation may prohibit issuing them for less than their par value or fair market value.

The Canada Business Corporations Act requires that shares must be issued for their fair market value. Thus the issue of such shares would increase the stated capital and decrease the retained earnings correspondingly.

Farrow Inc., a company incorporated under the CBCA, declared a share dividend of one Class A share for each 100 Class A shares held. There were 100,000 shares outstanding before the declaration of the dividend, and their market value at the time the dividend was declared was $15 each. The entry at the time the dividend was declared would be as follows:

Retained earnings	15,000.00	
Share dividend distributable		15,000.00
To record declaration of share dividend		
(100,000/100 × 15).		

The account "Share dividend distributable" is a temporary owner's equity account. When the shares are distributed on the distribution date, the following entry would be made:

Share dividend distributable	15,000.00	
Capital stock — Class A shares		15,000.00
Record distribution of share dividend.		

A share dividend should be distinguished from a **share split**, which is an increase in the number of existing shares outstanding. A share split if often used to decrease the price at which the company's shares are traded on the stock market, often with the intention of increasing their appeal to a wider group of small investors. Under a share split there is no increase in the stated capital of the company, only an increase in the number of shares outstanding.

Accumulated Preferred Dividends

Dividends on shares that have a cumulative dividend right are not legal liabilities of the company until declared by the directors. Nevertheless, dividends are said to be **in arrears** if they are cumulative and have not been paid. The existence of arrears is of interest to the reader of financial statements because it could mean that dividends on more junior shares may be omitted. The *CICA Handbook* [3240.02] requires disclosure of any dividends in arrears.

APPROPRIATION OF RETAINED EARNINGS

An appropriation of retained earnings is intended to indicate to the reader that at least some portion has been restricted regarding dividend payments. The reasons may be any of the following:

1. The company has entered into an agreement with respect to a bond issue that the retained earnings must be above a stated amount before a dividend can be paid.

2. Under the act incorporating the company, a portion of retained earnings must be set aside to maintain the stated capital. For example, this is sometimes required on the redemption of redeemable shares.

3. The directors may decide to designate a portion of retained earnings as unavailable for dividends, often because they want to indicate that future events should be anticipated. These might be inventory declines, self-insurance losses, or expansion plans requiring assets to be kept for internal financing. The creation of such appropriations does not ensure that sufficient cash will be available when needed, but it does reduce the cash paid out to the extent that cash dividends have been restricted.

For cosmetic reasons, company managements in the past were sometimes tempted to reduce reported income by making charges to the income statement so that amounts could be credited directly to some other owners' equity account (e.g., provision for contingencies) in order to report a lower income in good years. In later years, when it was felt that the reported income should look higher, expenses for that period would be charged to this special retained earnings account and excluded from the calculation of annual income. This potentially deceptive practice is now prohibited by the *CICA Handbook* [3260], which states that such appropriations should only be created by charges to retained earnings (i.e., after the calculation of net income), and any reductions in such an account should be returned to retained earnings and not used to "relieve the income account of charges that should properly be taken into account in determining the net income of the period." An example of a company that used to have a contingency reserve was given in Chapter 2 in the 1946 statements of the predecessor company to Consolidated-Bathurst Inc.

Examples From Published Reports

Because of the influence of companies legislation and accounting standards that require almost all gains or losses to flow through the income statement, the owners' equity section of most published Canadian reports tends to be uncluttered and straightforward.

General Motors of Canada Limited

Excerpts from the financial statements of GM have been given above in Chapter 4.

SHAREHOLDERS' EQUITY

	1986	1985
	(thousands of $)	
Authorized:		
An unlimited number of common shares		
Issued:		
703,250 shares	$ 70,325	$ 70,325
Contributed surplus (Note 3c)	36,325	3,212
Net income retained for use in the business	2,325,475	2,156,489
Total shareholders' equity	$2,432,125	$2,230,026

Note 3.   Equity in Net Assets of Associates: (c) On September 30, 1986 the net book value of the assets of Motors Holding of Canada Limited were donated to the company by its parent company. The donation amounting to $33,113,000 has been reflected as *Contributed surplus.*

This is an interesting example of a large corporation receiving assets as a donation and crediting them to contributed surplus. Presumably Motor Holdings of Canada Limited is completely owned by General Motors Corporation, as is General Motors of Canada Limited itself.

Great Lakes Forest Products Limited

Great Lakes Forest Products is a major Canadian producer of paper and paper products.

SHAREHOLDERS' EQUITY

	1986	1985
	(thousands of $)	
Common shares (19,537,420 shares issued)	$ 54,649	$ 54,649
Retained earnings	287,587	265,353
	$342,236	$320,002

RETAINED EARNINGS
Consolidated statement for years ended December 31

	1986	1985
	(thousands of $)	
Retained earnings at beginning of year	$265,353	$273,929
Net earnings	30,049	216
	295,402	274,145
Dividends declared	7,815	8,792
Retained earnings at end of year	$287,587	$265,353

Note 4 — Dividend Restriction
Certain of the indentures relating to the company's long-term debt contain covenants limiting dividends. The most restrictive of these requires that, after any dividend is declared, working capital (which for these purposes is before the deduction of the current portion of long-term debt) must be over $10 million and shareholders' equity must be over $50 million.

Note the restriction on dividend payments that is related to both working capital and shareholders' equity. As we have explained in this chapter, the shareholders' equity is not a very "hard" number, and it would be frustrating to the company to have dividends restricted because owners' equity was too low.

Summary

The main classes of owners' equity are share capital and retained earnings, but the provisions and requirements of the acts incorporating companies vary widely, especially in Canada and the United States. Canadian companies acts tend to be relatively uniform and to parallel the Canada Business Corporations Act. In most Canadian acts, par- value shares are not allowed and the stated capital is equal to the proceeds received for the shares. Dividends can be paid and shares may be redeemed or repurchased or cancelled as long as the realizable assets will be at least as great as the total of liabilities and stated capital after the act is done, and as long as the company can meet its liabilities as they come due.

Under some jurisdictions par-value shares may be issued, and their issue can give rise to contributed surplus. There are some other minor reasons why contributed surplus may be created.

Owners' equity balances do not, and are not intended to, represent the worth of the company to the shareholders.

QUESTIONS

Q16-1. Review and be sure you understand the following terms:

    a. owners' equity

    b. stated capital

    c. limited liability

    d. common shareholders *versus* preferred shareholders

    e. classes of shares

    f. redeemable preferred shares

    g. share capital

    h. retractable shares

    i. term-preferred shares

    j. par value

    k. dilutive securities

    l. preemptive rights

    m. employee option

    n. warrant

    o. conversion privilege

    p. issued share capital *versus* authorized share capital

    q. share subscription

    r. related parties

    s. underwriter

    t. contributed surplus

    u. treasury shares

    v. retained earnings

    w. share dividend

    x. share split

Q16-2. Explain the purposes of defining the stated capital of a company. Can you think of alternative ways of accomplishing the same objective?

Q16-3. Many companies acts make the directors personally liable for certain acts, such as declaring a dividend that results in the company's insolvency. Discuss how effective a deterrent this is to the directors taking such acts. How much protection does it give the creditors of the company?

Q16-4. Explain some of the ways in which one group of shareholders might exploit another group of shareholders within the same company. To what extent might the provisions of companies acts serve to deter this?

Q16-5. The Canada Business Corporations Act and most provincial acts do not allow a company to issue par-value shares. One reason for this is the belief that par-value shares might create a false impression in the investors' minds that they are worth at least their par value. Discuss how valid such an assumption is and what its implications are.

Q16-6. Give three examples of dilutive securities and explain how you would find evidence of their existence through examining the financial statements.

Q16-7. Explain the differences, if any, between a warrant and an option.

Q16-8. The Canada Business Corporations Act does not permit a share to be issued until it is fully paid for. Any funds received on partly paid shares are normally credited to a liability account. The alternative treatment would be to treat the unpaid amount as a receivable from a shareholder and to credit the full amount of the subscription price to some account in owners' equity (such as "share capital subscribed but not issued"). Discuss the merits of these two approaches.

Q16-9. Many companies acts require that when shares are issued for non-cash assets the value of the assets must be confirmed by the board of directors. What are some possible reasons for this? (*Hint:* Do you think this helps to alleviate any problems of moral hazard?)

Q16-10. It has been argued that any amounts of share capital in excess of par created when par-value shares are sold should be regarded like voluntary contributions by the shareholders and should not form part of the stated capital of the company. Do you agree? Give your reasons.

Q16-11. A company loaned $50,000 to a shareholder in the normal course of business and took as security its own shares that had a market value of $80,000. Suppose that the shareholder was unable to pay and the company took the shares in lieu of payment. Further suppose that the shares represented 100% of the outstanding shares of the company. If you were the chief executive of the company, what journal entry (entries) would you want to make to record this event? Give your reasons.

Q16-12. A prominent accountant recently referred to the retained earnings account as a "garbage can." What did he mean by this reference? Do you agree? Explain.

Q16-13. Explain why the valuation placed on non-cash assets paid as dividends has no ultimate effect on the balance in retained earnings.

Q16-14. Company A paid a stock dividend equal to one share for each share outstanding. Company B had a stock split of two shares for each share outstanding. Would they both have the same number of shares outstanding afterwards? The same stated capital? The same retained earnings? Explain.

Q16-15. A company has issued redeemable preferred dividends to its bank in return for cash. The dividends are equal to one-half the prime bank rate plus 1%, and the dividends are cumulative. At the same time as the company issued the shares, it was required to execute a promissory note in favour of the bank for the same amount as the funds received for the shares. The bank agreed to tear up the promissory note when the shares were redeemed. The company accountant wanted to accrue the dividends the same way she would accrue bond interest, arguing that the economic substance was that the company had to pay the dividends or the bank would call the promissory note. However, the usual practice is not to show the dividend as payable until it has actually been declared payable by the directors. What do you think should be done in this case?

Q16-16. Explain the circumstances in which directors might want to appropriate part of retained earnings and transfer it to a separate account.

Q16-17. It is argued that stock options given to executives in lieu of other compensation should be treated as an operating expense of the period in which the executives earned the option. Do you agree? If so, how would you value the options? What account should be charged? What account credited? Explain.

Q16-18. "If you could actually make the dollar amount shown as owners' equity equal the value of the business to the owners, then you would have solved most of the fundamental measurement problems facing accounting." This statement implies that the owners' equity amount on the balance sheet is not a measure of owners' equity. Do you agree? If so, what does it measure?

Q16-19. Earlier companies acts used to prohibit the payment of dividends if such a payment would make the owners' equity on the balance sheet negative. Modern companies acts use a different test. Explain the difference between the two tests. Which do you think is better? Explain.

Q16-20. Give seven examples of features a share might have that would make the holders' rights better or worse than those of the common shareholders.

Q16-21. The financial press often has a section showing the prices of options in certain shares similar to those for the companies' shares. Are these options the ones discussed in this chapter? Explain.

Q16-22. What provisions, if any, do the companies acts and *CICA Handbook* contain to protect minority shareholders against related-party transactions in the issue of shares? Comment on their adequacy.

Q16-23. A Canadian public utility has announced that henceforth one of its issues of preference shares will be classed as a liability instead of as owners' equity. Further, the company's auditors have stated that they agree with this treatment. What might the special terms of this share issue be that would suggest this unusual treatment? Do you think the conditions are ever special enough to treat a share issue as a liability? What does the CICA have to say on this matter?

Q16-24. Securities with "debt characteristics" are said to be those in which payments (including return of principle) to the security of holders are specified at stated amounts at more or less stated times. By contrast, securities with "equity characteristics" provide no firm promise of payment, but hold out the promise of gain to the holder if the security issue prospers. Using this distinction, into which of the two categories would you classify securities giving ownership to each of the following? Justify your choices.

  a. treasury bills

  b. common shares

  c. precious metals

  d. real estate

  e. preferred share without the right to participate in profits beyond a fixed amount

  f. a preferred share as in (e), but with a significant provision as to mandatory redemption

  g. a convertible bond

  h. life annuities

EXERCISES

E16-1. Morden Limited has two classes of shares, A and B. There are 20,000 A shares and 15,000 B shares outstanding. The differences between them are as follows:

  Voting rights: Class A shareholders have one vote per share at all shareholders' meetings. Class B shareholders have no vote unless the cumulative dividend of 37 cents per share has not been paid for four consecutive quarters. In that event they have two votes per share.

Dividends: B shares are entitled to 37 cents per share per quarter, and they share equally with A shares when the dividend on the latter exceeds 80 cents per share.

Redemption rights: B shares may be redeemed at the shareholders' option for $15 per share plus accrued dividends after 1 January 19X8. Before that date they may be redeemed at the company's option for $20 per share plus accrued dividends.

Required:

a. Assume that the dividend on the B shares has not been paid for the past three quarters. What disclosure, if any, should be made in the notes to the balance sheet?

b. Because the shares can be redeemed at the shareholders' option at a price that includes accrued dividends, should the dividends be accrued as if they were similar to interest?

c. Explain how the relative power of the two classes of shareholders might shift if the next dividend is not paid on the B shares.

E16-2. Assume that the holders of each of the following dilutive securities exercised their right to secure common shares with them. In each case explain what effect, if any, this conversion would have on each of the following: (i) stated capital, (ii) company bank balance, (iii) retained earnings, and (iv) owners' equity.

a. warrants

b. options

c. convertible preferred shares

d. convertible long-term bonds

E16-3. For each transaction in E16-2 above, explain what disclosure of the change should be made in the financial statements.

E16-4. Consider the following two parties: (i) an investor who has bought 100 redeemable cumulative preferred shares of Company X for $100 each, paying $2.50 per share per calendar quarter and (ii) a firm that is a regular supplier to Company X and is owed by them $100,000 on trade debts. Compare their rights and privileges under each of the following unrelated circumstances:

a. Company X has decided to defer payment of trade debts and dividends for three months because of a cash shortage.

b. Company X is being wound up, and the net realizable value of assets is greater than the total of liabilities and stated capital.

c. Company X is being wound up, and the net realizable value of assets is less than the total of liabilities and stated capital.

E16-5. What should the journal entry (entries) be for each of the following related events?

a. 1 January — The company was incorporated under the Canada Business Corporations Act. When issued, the shares are to be traded on a public stock exchange.

b. 6 January — The company issued 2,000 A shares for $100 cash each.

c. 7 February — The company issued 1,000 A shares for a warehouse. By resolution the directors valued the assets acquired at $100,000.

d. 9 March — The company issued 1,000 B shares, redeemable at $50 and cumulative with a dividend of $4.50 paid annually. The shares were paid for with land, which the directors by resolution valued at $50,000.

e. 3 April — The company purchased 500 A shares for $100 each.

f. 16 May — The company purchased 500 A shares for $150 each.

g. 19 June — The company redeemed 500 B shares for $50 plus accrued dividend.

E16-6. What should the journal entry (entries) be for each of the following related events?

a. 1 January — The company was incorporated under the Canada Business Corporations Act. When issued, the shares are to be held privately.

b. 6 January — The company issued 5,000 A shares for $100 cash each.

c. 7 February — The company issued 1,500 A shares for a warehouse. By resolution the directors valued the assets acquired at $300,000.

d. 9 March — The company issued 3,000 B shares, redeemable at $50 plus accrued dividend and cumulative with a dividend of $4.50 paid annually. The shares were paid for with shares of another company, which the directors by resolution valued at $150,000.

e. 3 April — The company purchased 500 A shares for $100 each.

f. 16 May — The company purchased 500 A shares for $150 each.

g. 19 June — The company redeemed 500 B shares for $50 plus accrued dividend.

E16-7. What capital transaction, if any, does each of the following unrelated journal entries represent? Explain.

a. Bank	40,000.00	
Preferred share capital		40,000.00
b. Preferred share capital	30,000.00	
Common share capital		30,000.00
c. Contributed surplus	10,000.00	
Common share capital		10,000.00
d. Long-term debt	5,000.00	
Preferred share capital		5,000.00
e. Contributed capital	1,000.00	
Bank	15,000.00	
Common share capital		16,000.00

E16-8. In each of the following unrelated circumstances, would the securities be dilutive if the right to acquire common shares were exercised? Explain.

Type of security	Current market price of common share	Acquisition right	Original issue price
a. convertible preference share	$30	Four common shares for each	$100
b. option	30	One common share for each option plus $40	10
c. convertible bond	30	Three common shares for each bond submitted	100
d. warrant	30	One common share for each warrant plus $35	5

E16-9. Here is the owners' equity section of Yolanda Limited, a company incorporated under the Canada Business Corporations Act.

OWNERS' EQUITY

Common share capital		$350,000
Preferred shares		180,000
Retained earnings, 1 January 19X2	$350,000	
Loss, 31 December 19X2	(480,000)	
		(130,000)
Total owners' equity		$400,000

You are given the following supplementary information:

(i) The stated capital as defined under the CBCA is $530,000.

(ii) The net realizable value of the company's assets is $800,000.

(iii) A covenant of an outstanding bond issue of the company contains a clause to the effect that no dividends can be paid on any class of shares if the dividend would reduce the retained earnings below their level as of 1 January 19X2.

Required:

a. The company wanted to pay a dividend of $50,000. Could it legally do so under the CBCA? Explain.

b. The company wanted to pay a dividend of $50,000. Is it permitted under the terms of the company's bond covenant?

c. Evaluate the relative merits of the dividend restriction under the bond covenant and the dividend restriction under the CBCA, with respect to protecting the interests of creditors of the company.

E16-10. Prepare journal entries for each of the following unrelated events:

a. On 31 December the company issued 1,000 options to its chief executive. These entitle her to purchase 1,000 of the company's common shares at $59, the price at which the shares were trading that day.

b. On 30 June the chief executive exercised her option and purchased 1,000 shares. They were trading that day at $68.

c. On 1 March the company issued at par $2,000,000 10% ten-year bonds with 10 warrants attached to each $1,000 bond. Each warrant entitled the purchaser to buy one common share for $60 cash. The shares were trading on the date of issue at $56.

d. On 1 August a total of 5,000 warrants were exercised. The shares were trading that day at $63.

e. On 3 September the company received $30,000 in part payment of 1,000 shares to be issued at $67 for a total amount of $67,000.

f. On 3 October the company received the remaining $37,000 of the $67,000 total owed on the shares.

g. On 14 November the company purchased for cancellation 1,000 of its common shares at a price of $53. They had originally been issued at $49.

PROBLEMS

P16-1. Coyne Corporation, a company incorporated under the Canada Business Corporations Act, issued 10,000 Class A shares for $80 each. These were sold through an underwriter who remitted $75 net to the company after deducting his fee. In addition, the company incurred other costs in connection with the issue. These were legal costs of $30,000, audit costs of $15,000, and printing and advertising costs of $5,000.

Required: Show the journal entries that would be required to record the issue of shares and account for the issue costs.

P16-2. N Ltd., incorporated under the Canada Business Corporations Act, had issued and outstanding 10,000 redeemable Class B shares that could be converted to Class A (common) shares at the following ratios:

> 6 Class A shares for 5 Class B shares up to the end of 19X3
> 5 Class A shares for 5 Class B shares up to the end of 19X5
> 4 Class A shares for 5 Class B shares up to the end of 19X7
> 3 Class A shares for 5 Class B shares up to the end of 19X9

Twenty thousand Class A shares had originally been issued for $45 each, and the Class B for $45. They had traded for the following prices:

Date	Class A	Class B
End of 19X3	$58.00	$49.00
End of 19X5	68.00	65.00
End of 19X7	58.00	69.00
End of 19X9	45.00	75.00

Required:

a. At which of the above four year-ends would you expect the holders of Class B shares to convert to Class A? Explain.

b. Show the journal entries that would be required if 1,000 Class B shares were converted at the end of 19X5, and 1,000 were converted at the end of 19X9.

c. Indicate the section of the financial statements that accounts for this change. Be sure to indicate which part of the financial statements you are referring to.

P16-3. Chesly Inc. issued 1,000 options to key employees giving them the rights to purchase one Class A share for each option held at a price of $35. These options were issued on 1 January 19X3. They were valid until 1 January 19X8 or until the employee left the company, whichever came sooner. On 31 December 19X5, 500 options were exercised, and the rest were still outstanding.

Required:

a. Show the journal entry to record the exercise of the options as of 31 December 19X5.

b. Assume the company's year end is 31 December. Show the note that would be required to the financial statements with respect to the options.

P16-4. Apsley Limited sold $500,000 convertible long-term bonds that gave the owner the right to convert within a five-year period from the date of issue to Class A shares at a conversion price of $50 per share. On 23 June, when the Class A shares were trading for $65 per share, the holder of five $1,000 bonds converted them to Class A shares. At that time the bonds were trading for $1,350 per $1,000.

Required:

a. Show the journal entry to record the conversion.

b. Discuss the merits of valuing the newly issued shares at the conversion price of $50 versus the market price at the time of conversion of $65.

P16-5. Show the journal entry (entries), if any, that would be required for each of the following unrelated events:

    a. 40,000 options were issued for a consideration of $10 each, permitting the holder to purchase Class B shares at $50 each until 1 January, 19X8.

    b. 35,000 options were issued to company executives as part of their compensation for the year.

    c. After a company was organized, the prospective shareholders signed a stock subscription agreement under which they agreed to pay $50 per share immediately and $50 per share in six months for 10,000 shares. The company is incorporated under the Canada Business Corporations Act, and the first cash instalment has been paid.

P16-6. Show the journal entry (entries), if any, that would be required for each of the following unrelated events:

    a. The company legally issued 1,500 additional Class C shares for real estate valued by an appraiser at $150,000. The shares had a par value of $80 each.

    b. The same situation as in (a) except that the company was incorporated under the Canada Business Corporations Act.

    c. Class B shares were outstanding that had been sold for $37 and were redeemable at the company's option at a price of $37 plus accrued dividends. The dividends of $1.00 per quarter, payable at the end of each calendar quarter, had not been paid for two consecutive quarters. At 31 March 19X9, 10,000 shares were redeemed.

P16-7. For each feature listed below, find an example in the financial statements of a company incorporated in Canada. Photocopy the relevant page, circle the item, identify the company, and comment briefly on the face of the photocopy about the treatment of the feature.

    a. redeemable shares

    b. shares with cumulative dividend rights

    c. options outstanding

    d. restrictions on dividend payments due to a bond covenant

    e. two or more classes of shares

    f. convertible shares

    g. a share issue in the year of the financial report

    h. a charge or credit to retained earnings that did not arise from an annual profit (or loss) or from the payment of a dividend.

P16-8. Grosco Corporation (GC), a public company manufacturing farm equipment, was federally incorporated in 1926. Its common shares and bonds are widely held. The company's year-end is 31 December. The bond indentures contain the following covenants:

    (i) At the end of any quarter, if the debt to equity ratio exceeds 2.5:1, dividends may not be declared.

    (ii) At the end of any quarter, if the debt-to-equity ratio exceeds 3:1, the bond principal becomes due and payable.

    GC has experienced severe financial difficulties in the past four years and has sought refinancing to remain solvent. On 1 May 1989 it issued a new class of preferred shares bearing a cumulative annual dividend of 12%. The shares are retractable on demand commencing one year from the date of issue. As a result of the issue, the debt to equity ratio reported by management decreased from 2.7:1 to 2.2:1. By the end of 1989, the ratio had increased to 2.4:1 because of increased bank borrowings.

It is now April 1990. You are the CA in charge of the audit of GC. The 1989 financial statements have just been drafted and will soon be ready to be issued. The 1990 first quarter financial statements have just been compiled by management and reveal a debt-to-equity ratio of 2.8:1.

Required: Discuss the accounting reporting issues.

(CICA adapted)

P16-9. Bolingbroke Corporation issued 5,000 non-transferable stock options to its senior executives on 31 December, 19X3 as part of their compensation package. Each option gave the holder the right to purchase one Class A share for $50 after 31 December 19X5 and until 31 December 19X7 provided the holder was still employed by the company. At 31 December 19X5 the market price of the company's shares was $85.

Required:

a. Prepare the note for the financial statements that would be appropriate to disclose the existence of the options.

b. Explain in ordinary English whether the options could be regarded as dilutive securities. Under what conditions would they not be dilutive?

c. Should the issue of shares be recorded as an executive compensation expense? Discuss the merits and disadvantages of this approach.

P16-10. On 31 March Hartington Industries Limited issued for $85 per share 1,000 Class B convertible shares, redeemable at $85 plus accrued dividends of $2.00 payable on the first day of each calendar quarter. One Class B share can be converted into 0.5 Class A shares at the option of the shareholder. On 1 September when the Class A shares were trading for $200, all the outstanding Class B shares were converted.

Required: Show the journal entry (entries) that would be required on the date of conversion.

P16-11. On 30 September Kaladar Corporation issued 1,000 cumulative redeemable Class B shares for a price of $100 for one share and one warrant. The shares were redeemable at $100 and had a dividend of $2.50 per quarter. Each warrant entitled the owner to purchase one Class A share for $20 for the next two years. Immediately after the issue, the shares traded for $98 without the warrant, and the warrant itself traded for $5.

Required: Show the journal entry (entries) to record this issue. Show your calculations.

P16-12. Show the journal entry (entries) that would be required in each of the following unrelated circumstances:

a. A Ltd. redeemed 10,000 of its own no-par-value shares for $3.00 per share. They had originally been issued for $4.00 per share.

b. Same as (a) except that the shares had originally been issued for $2.50 per share.

c. A Ltd. redeemed 10,000 of its own $2.50 par-value shares for $3.00. They had originally been issued for $4.00 per share.

d. Same as (c) except that the shares had originally been issued for $2.50 per share.

P16-13. Show the journal entry (entries) that would be required in each of the following unrelated circumstances for the period up to 31 December for Beta Ltd. Assume in each case that the company has 1,000 common shares outstanding.

  a. The directors declare a dividend on 1 December of 20 cents per share payable on 31 January to shareholders of record as of 15 January.

  b. The directors declared a dividend on 1 November of 20 cents per share payable on 31 December to shareholders of record as of 1 December. The cheques were dated 31 December and mailed on 15 December. As of 31 December they are all outstanding.

  c. The directors declared a dividend on 1 December of one share of Alpha Inc. for each common share of Beta. The dividend is payable 31 December to shareholders of record of 15 December. Alpha Inc.'s shares have been held by Beta as an investment. By resolution of the directors the shares of Alpha are to be valued at $10 each for purposes of the dividend. They had originally cost $6.

  d. The directors declared a dividend on 1 December of one-tenth share of Beta for each common share held. The dividend is payable 31 December to shareholders of record of 15 December. By resolution of the directors the value of the shares is declared to be $8.00, which is the market value of the shares as of the date of declaration.

  e. The directors failed to declare a dividend on 2,000 "cumulative $3.75 preferred shares." Under the terms of the issue of the shares, a dividend of $3.75 would normally be paid each 31 December. If the company failed to pay such a dividend, then no dividends may be paid on the common shares until all dividends in arrears on the preferred shares have been paid.

P16-14. The following events relate to Parham Inc. during the first year of its corporate existence. The company is incorporated under the Canada Business Corporations Act. Show the journal entry (entries) that would be appropriate for each event.

  a. 1 April: 2,000 Class A shares were issued for equipment and buildings valued by the directors at their first meeting at $240,000.

  b. 1 July: 3,000 Class B shares were issued at a net price to the company of $50. Each share entitled the holder to receive a dividend, when declared, of $0.65 per quarter. Unpaid dividends were cumulative and were to be paid in preference to any dividends on the Class A shares. The shares were redeemable at the option of the company at $62.50 after three months from the date of issue.

  c. 30 July: A dividend of $0.65 was declared for each Class B share payable 30 September to shareholders of record of 10 September.

  d. 30 September: An additional 3,000 common shares were issued for $150 cash each.

  e. 30 November: The company purchased, for cancellation at $130, 1,000 of the Class A shares it had originally issued on 1 April.

  f. 1 December: The company redeemed and cancelled 1,000 Class B shares at the predetermined price.

P16-15. *The Globe and Mail* carried an announcement that a company had issued $50,000,000 "Floating rate cumulative redeemable retractable senior preferred shares, series 1." A note in the announcement said that the shares were "retractable at the option of the holder on 15 October in each of the years 1989, 1990, and 1991, at $25 per share plus accrued and unpaid dividends." The shares had no par value, but 2,000,000 had been issued for $50,000,000.

Required:

a. Show the journal entry that would be made on the books of the company on receipt of the proceeds of issue.

b. Make the best argument you can that these shares should be shown as liabilities of the company rather than as share capital.

c. Assuming that it was agreed to show them as liabilities, how would you respond to the argument that starting in 1988 they should be shown as current liabilities? Discuss.

d. Make the best argument you can that the dividends should be accrued at the year-end in a manner similar to interest.

P16-16. Show the journal entry (entries) that would be required in each of the following unrelated circumstances. Assume in each case that the company has outstanding 2,000 Series A shares and 5,000 Series B shares. The holders of Series A shares have the right to elect the board of directors. The holders of Series B shares have no right to vote in the election of the board of directors unless the board has failed to declare a dividend of $2.50 per share at the end of four consecutive quarters. Series B shares are convertible into series A shares at any time at the option of the holder at the ratio of one for one, and they are retractable at the option of the holder for $102.50 plus accrued dividends starting in the current year. The Series B shares were originally issued for proceeds equal to $100 per share. The company is incorporated under the Canada Business Corporations Act.

a. The company issued on 1 June 1,000 additional Series A shares as payment for the purchase of an existing business that the company was taking over. By resolution of the board of directors the tangible and intangible assets of the acquired business were valued at $100,000.

b. The company declared a cash dividend on 30 October of $2.50 per share on the Series B shares payable on 31 December to shareholders of record of 28 November.

c. The company issued 300 Series A shares on the conversion of 300 Series B shares. On 28 September, the day of conversion, the Series A shares were trading for $125 per share.

d. The company received $50 per share as a subscription to 500 Series B shares on 17 July. The balance of $50 is due on 30 September.

e. The holders of 100 Series B shares presented them for redemption on 31 August.

P16-17. Three companies each contract to buy an identical piece of equipment for $1,000,000 payable in twelve months. The equipment will not be ready for delivery for an additional twelve months after full payment is received. The All-Debt Company issued $1,000,000 in 12% bonds and $5 in common shares (to provide working capital!). All-Preferred Company issued $1,000,000 in 8% cumulative term-preferred shares, redeemable at the option of the holder at the end of a term of two years from date of issue, and $5 in common shares. All-Common Company issued 1,000 shares for $1,000,005 cash. The companies invested the $1,000,000 in a one-year bond bearing interest at 10%. At the beginning of the second year they made a $1,000,000 payment for the plant asset, and at the beginning of the third year the plant asset starting yielding revenue, which was $130,000 for the entire third year.

Required:

a. Calculate the balance in the retained earnings account that All-Debt, All-Preferred and All-Common each would report at the end of each of the three years (assume no income taxes).

b. How do you explain the differences between reported income between the three companies in Year 1? Year 2? Year 3? Leaving aside existing accounting pronouncements, *should* these differences exist? Explain your views.

P16-18. Camden Company was formed on 1 January 19X7 by issuing 100,000 shares of no-par-value common stock for $500,000 and 10,000 shares of 12% preference stock redeemable at $10 issued at $12 per share. The preference stock is convertible into 20,000 shares of common stock at any time, with a provision to adjust the conversion ratio for any stock dividends or splits.

On 31 December 19X7 Camden reported net earnings for the year of $200,000. Cash dividends totalling $50,000 were paid out to preference and common shareholders. On 31 July 19X8 Camden declared a 20% stock dividend on its common stock. The market value of the common shares was $8 per share on 30 July 19X8. All of the preference stock was converted on 15 October 19X8. The market price of the preference shares was $12 per share at that time.

Required:

a. Prepare the journal entries to record the issue of shares on 1 January 19X7.

b. Calculate the basic earnings per share for the year 19X7.

c. Prepare the journal entry to record the declaration of the stock dividend.

d. Prepare the journal entry to record the conversion of the preference shares.

e. How many shares of common stock were issued to preference share holders when converted?

f. What is the amount of the change in Shareholders' Equity in 19X8 as a result of the stock dividend and the conversion of the preference stock? Explain.

g. What is the change in an individual shareholder's position as a result of the stock dividend being received? Explain.

(CMA adapted)

P16-19. As of 31 December 19X0 Flinton Limited had only one class of capital stock, which consisted of 1,000,000 authorized shares of common stock. Several years previously 300,000 shares had been issued. The shareholders' equity section of the balance sheet on 31 December 19X0 consisted of the following items:

Common stock	$4,500,000
Retained earnings	4,100.000

The following transactions with respect to shareholders' equity took place during 19X0:

1 June — The company declared a cash dividend of $1.50 per share payable 1 July to shareholders of record of 15 June.

1 August — A 3-for-1 stock split was authorized and completed.

1 November — The company declared a 5% stock dividend payable 1 December to shareholders of record of 15 November.

Net income for the fiscal year ending 31 December 19X0 amounted to $2.4 million. Stock market prices at selected dates during 19X0 were as follows: 1 June, $30; 15 June, $31; 1 July, $32; 1 August, $33; 1 November, $12; 15 November, $13; 1 December, $13.

Required:

a. Show the dollar change in total shareholders' equity as a result of each of the following: (i) the 5% stock dividend and (ii) the 3-for-1 stock split. Explain.

b. By how much was retained earnings increased or decreased as a result of the 5% stock dividend? Show all calculations.

c. Prepare dated journal entries to record the transactions relating to shareholders' equity for 19X0. Show all calculations.

(CMA adapted)

BIBLIOGRAPHY

WASSERMAN, MARTIN R. "A New Business Corporations Act for Ontario." *CA Magazine* (September 1981). An excellent article by a lawyer on the implications for accountants of the Ontario Business Corporations Act.

In addition, you will find it useful to read the relevant sections of a recent copy of the *Canada Business Corporations Act* and the corporations act of your own province.

CHAPTER 17
Earnings per Share

"The root of the difficulty [in calculating an earnings per share number that means something] lies in the attempt to reduce complicated matters to a simple statistic."

ROSS SKINNER

Introduction

Earnings per share (EPS) is a statistic that measures the earnings available to those shares entitled to participate, beyond a fixed dividend, in the earnings of the company. It is calculated by dividing the *earnings available* by *shares entitled to participate* (to be explained later). For reasons that will become apparent, a variety of interpretations can be used to measure the earnings available and the number of shares entitled to participate. Furthermore, in the detailed application of EPS calculations, there are some significant differences between Canadian and U.S. interpretations. The objective of this chapter is to illustrate EPS calculations and explain the background of the subject.

Earnings per share is a financial-statement ratio. It has not been common in the past for bodies that set accounting standards to concern themselves with how ratios are calculated. Yet, in both the United States and Canada, accounting standard setters have set out extensive guidelines for the calculation of earnings per share. There seem to be three main reasons for these actions:

1. Investors have shown great interest in the EPS figure because it normalizes reported income for the number of shares outstanding and helps in comparing the company's performance with the value of its shares or with the performance of similar companies.

2. A variety of methods had developed to calculate earnings per share, and this statistic was often prominently displayed in the financial statements. Hence, standard-setting bodies felt they could not disassociate themselves from the manner in which it was calculated.

657

3. The determination of the figure is usually based on a number of assumptions of which the readers of financial statements may not be aware.

Heightened awareness of reasons (1) and (2) above, particularly starting in the 1960s, led accountants to become increasingly concerned over reason (3). In the U.S. the Accounting Principles Board issued Opinion No. 15 in 1969.

In Canada the CICA issued a standard in 1970, but in some respects it differed significantly from its U.S. counterpart.

It is common for investors to compare companies by looking at the **price-earnings ratio**, or the ratio of market price to earnings per share. A higher-than-average ratio, or **multiple**, indicates that investors find the shares relatively attractive. One reason may be that investors believe earnings per share will be even higher in the future, and they are willing to pay a premium for the shares now in anticipation of better things to come. At the same time, companies with high multiples are also in an advantageous position to acquire the shares of other companies by issuing their own shares in trade. Thus, if a company can demonstrate that its earnings per share are good and getting better, then it is in a good position to acquire other companies.

For example, imagine that Company A and Company B each had 10,000 outstanding shares, earnings of $30,000, and hence an earnings per share of $3. Suppose they used *pooling- of-interest accounting*, a usual practice at one time. (Pooling of interest is a method of combining the accounts of two or more companies in such a manner that the income for the year and other key measures appear in a very favourable light. We will discuss this method in Chapter 19.) Their shares traded on the stock market at $60, and thus had a total market value of $600,000 for each company and a multiple of 20 (60/3). However, the next day beliefs changed, and it was thought that A would soon have an EPS of $6. With a multiple of 20 this would mean it should be worth $120 instead of $60. If A's shares went to $120, then it would be able to offer the holders of B's shares 5,000 of its own shares in exchange for the 10,000 shares of B (because the stock-market value of A's 5,000 shares would be identical with that of B's 10,000 shares). If the exchange were accepted, A would then have 15,000 outstanding shares, but would have acquired B and its earning power and would report an income of $60,000. Its earnings per share would be $4 (60,000/15,000) instead of $3, and the belief that it was a growth company would have become *self- fulfilling*.

There were several accounting techniques that were possible to use in order to produce good earnings per share figures. Two such techniques were as follows:

1. Net income could be stated as high as possible within the GAAP of the day. This could be done by the income-influencing techniques already discussed in this book. For instance, one might allow favourable extraordinary items to appear on the income statement, but charge unfavourable ones directly to retained earnings. Alternatively, assets might be depreciated over as long a period as possible to reduce annual fixed charges. Yet another possibility would be for the company to use the pooling method instead of the purchase method to account for business combinations.

2. The number of common shares actually outstanding could be kept as small as possible; but by issuing dilutive securities with legal benefits normally reserved for

common shareholders, the company might be able to entice lenders to supply capital. For instance, the company might issue bonds that are convertible into common shares at some future date. Such bonds would require a lower interest rate than bonds without the conversion feature. This would allow the company to raise funds, have a lower than normal interest cost, and not increase the number of common shares outstanding. The point with any dilutive security is that the person acquiring it is prepared to forgo benefits from the company in the present period in order to acquire potential benefits in a future period by obtaining the company's shares at a price below market.

Technique (1) above has been addressed within GAAP by changes in a number of accounting standards. For example, there are now (i) limitations on capitalizing assets such as research and development; (ii) severe limitations on what can be classed as an extraordinary item; (iii) severe limitations on the pooling method of accounting for business combinations (a method that does not recognize the annual fixed charges for amortization and depletion and that includes earnings prior to the date of acquisition); and (iv) the restrictions on what can be charged or credited to retained earnings that were set out in Chapter 16. In general, the growing accounting standards about what may or may not be capitalized, together with parallel rules about how items must be shown in the financial statements, have been directed at technique (1). They will not, of course, solve the problem completely, since income measurement is inherently such a difficult task at both the practical and the conceptual levels.

Technique (2) above, which affected the number of shares used in the denominator of the EPS calculation, was something with which accounting standard-setting bodies did not actively concern themselves until the late 1960s. Since that time both the Accounting Standards Committee and the equivalent U.S. body have issued standards for computing earnings per share.

Their basic approach has been to provide a standardized definition of

(i) income attributable to shareholders entitled to participate and

(ii) the number of shares to be included in the EPS ratio. Let us now turn to these items.

Income Attributable to Holders of Shares Entitled to Participate

The purpose of the calculation of **income attributable to holders of shares entitled to participate** is to arrive at the gross amount that is attributable to common shareholders for (i) income before extraordinary items and (ii) net income after extraordinary items. We will assume that the income statement has been prepared in accordance with GAAP and that a proper distinction has been made between ordinary income and extraordinary items.

The income attributable to shareholders entitled to participate is calculated as follows [*CICA* 3500.17]. First, deduct from both (i) and (ii) above any dividends paid or declared on shares that have a preference as to dividends. Then, deduct any dividends that would normally have been payable on **cumulative preferred shares**, (discussed in Chapter 16) regardless of whether they have been declared or not. (No deduction is made for **non-cumulative preferred shares** unless the dividend has been declared.) Finally, add or deduct prior-period adjustments if the results of that prior period have been restated.

Consider the following example. The income for Washburn Limited was $40,000 before extraordinary items and $45,000 net after extraordinary items. Dividends of $5,000 were paid on common A shares, and dividends of $10,000 were paid on non-participating preferred B shares. By contrast, dividends of $5,000 have accumulated on cumulative preferred C shares: they were not paid and are now in arrears. Given all this information, we would calculate the income attributable to common shareholders as follows:

	Income before extraordinary items	Add: Extraordinary gain	Net income
Reported income	$ 40,000	$ 5,000	$ 45,000
Dividends on preferred B shares	10,000		10,000
Accumulated dividends on cumulative C shares	5,000		5,000
	15,000		15,000
Attributable to common shareholders	$ 25,000	$ 5,000	$ 30,000

Earnings per share is normally calculated for all classes of shares that have the right to participate beyond a fixed dividend. For example, a company might have preference shares with a fixed dividend but with the right to participate in additional dividends once the dividends on common shares reach a stated amount. In such cases, earnings per share would be calculated separately for both classes of shares (where participation rights are identical) [*CICA* 3500.12].

Calculation of the Number of Shares Outstanding — Simple Capital Structure

A **simple capital structure** is one in which no potentially dilutive securities are outstanding. Suppose that a company has only common shares; or that it has other shares, but none of these other shares has any participating rights in the company's equity. Suppose further that no one has any right to acquire its common shares except by open market purchases (e.g., no one can require the company to issue common shares). Then the calculation of the **weighted average number of shares** outstanding is straightforward: it is the number of shares outstanding each month (or day) weighted by the number of months (days) they have been outstanding [*CICA* 3500.20].

The purpose in calculating the weighted average number of shares outstanding arises from the basic function of the EPS statistic as an indicator of the earning power of the company's equity. If this capital has changed during the period, then the company's asset base has been increased or decreased, and its potential earning power has changed. Using the weighted average of the amount of capital outstanding is intended to compensate for this.

Continuing the above example, assume that Washburn Limited had 2,000 common shares outstanding at the beginning of its fiscal year, 1 January, and that on 1 September it issued an additional 1,500 shares. The weighted average of shares outstanding for that fiscal year would then be as follows:

2,000 × $^{12}/_{12}$	2,000
1,500 × $^{4}/_{12}$	500
Weighted average number of shares outstanding	2,500

This weighted average would be used to calculate the EPS, as shown below:

	Income before extraordinary item	Income
Net income per income statement	$ 40,000	$ 45,000
Dividend requirement on preferred shares	10,000	10,000
Earnings applicable to common shares	$ 30,000	$ 35,000
Weighted average common shares outstanding	2,500	2,500
EARNINGS PER SHARE	$ 12.00	$ 14.00

The preference shares in this example are non-cumulative, and dividends are not deductible unless declared or paid. The earnings applicable to common shareholders could fluctuate from year to year simply because a preference dividend was declared in one year but not in the next. The *CICA Handbook* [3500.15] points this out and says it would be "desirable" (but not necessary) that the fact of non- declaration be disclosed.

Complex Capital Structures

A **complex capital structure** is one where, in addition to common shares, the company has outstanding contractual rights that allow others to acquire common shareholders' equity at prices that might be different from market price. If they were to exercise those rights, then the equity of the existing common shareholders might be diluted because the earnings per share could go down without compensation to the existing shareholders. There is a danger that earnings per share will be overstated unless this potential dilution is taken into account. The purpose of calculating earnings per share on a fully diluted basis is to show the maximum dilution of current earnings that the existence of outstanding dilutive securities might create. In some cases the exercise of such rights by the holder would be **antidilutive** (i.e., if the rights were exercised, the share in the company of the common shareholders would increase); but the calculation of EPS omits such possibilities. The calculation is a conservative one also because it includes all dilutive securities, even though it may be apparent that some or all of the holders of them have no intention of exercising their dilutive rights.

Before exploring this further, let us briefly review some of the more common types of securities or rights that might dilute the equity of existing shareholders. As explained in Chapter 16, a common feature of all of them is that the holder is given the right to acquire common shares, at his or her option, at fixed prices that may differ from market prices. Dilutive securities include convertible preferred shares, stock options, warrants, and convertible bonds.

Although the financial instruments described above may have looked attractive to the investor when they were issued, it is quite possible that market circumstances have changed so much since they were acquired that the likelihood of the rights being exercised is negligible. If that is the case, it becomes a matter of judgement how much the existing shareholders' interests are likely to be affected by the existence of such financial instruments.

It is common to make a distinction between **common shares** and **senior shares.** The meaning of common shares in this case is different from the one normally used (the meaning discussed in Chapter 16). Common shares in this case represent those shares with a residual equity in the earnings of the company; as a result, such a category would include some classes of preferred shares where there was no upper limit to their participation in earnings. All other types of shares (i.e., those with a fixed annual dividend) are senior shares. Thus it is possible for a company to have one class of preference share that is classed as common and another classed as senior.

CALCULATION OF
NUMBER OF FULLY DILUTED SHARES

If the rights under a dilutive security were to be exercised, the earnings per share of the existing shareholders would be diluted. To show the possible impact, both undiluted (**basic**) and diluted earnings per share are reported [*CICA* 3500.30]. The maximum potential dilution that can take place is referred to as the **fully diluted** earnings per share. The reader of the statements is thus given an upper and lower estimate of earnings per share (i.e., basic and fully diluted). Let us briefly describe the calculation of fully diluted earnings per share. The numerator would be as follows:

Income = NI + ADJ
where
NI = net income available to common shareholders (as calculated above)
ADJ = dividends on convertible senior shares + interest (after income taxes) on convertible debt + imputed interest (after tax) on assets that would have been received had options, warrants, and rights been exercised [*CICA* 3500.37]

The purpose of the above redefinition of income is to add back to the numerator of the EPS ratio the amounts related to the dilutive factors that are included in the denominator. For the denominator of EPS we use the following:

Full diluted shares = COM + CON + W + OPT

where

COM = common shares outstanding

CON = the common share equivalent of all convertible preferred shares and bonds

W = the common shares that would be issued if all outstanding warrants were exercised to purchase common shares

OPT = the common shares that would be issued if all outstanding options were exercised to purchase common shares

When doing these calculations, the following exceptions are usually made:

1. Conversion rights that do not become effective within ten years are not included [*CICA* 3500.33].

2. Conversions, etc., that would increase earnings per share (i.e., be anti-dilutive) are ignored.

It is apparent from the above equations that the calculation of *fully diluted earnings per share* can be based on many assumed, rather than real, events. Conversions of shares and debt, as well as the exercise of warrants and options, are assumed regardless of whether the holders will choose to convert or exercise them.

EXAMPLES OF CALCULATION
OF EARNINGS PER SHARE —
COMPLEX CAPITAL STRUCTURES

Examples will be given of the calculation of fully diluted earnings per share when convertible debentures, warrants, and options are outstanding. The treatment of convertible preference shares is similar, but slightly easier, because dividends are not deductible from taxable income as expenses for tax purposes. Hence there is no after-tax calculation to make.

Convertible Debentures

This example is based on Case Study C in the *CICA Handbook* [3500]. With a complex capital structure it is necessary to calculate both basic and fully diluted earnings per share. The usual procedure is as follows:

1. Start with the common shares at present outstanding.

2. Add on the effect the dilutive rights would have if exercised.

3. Add back to the reported income the annual carrying costs (after tax) of the dilutive securities included in (2).

There are both non- convertible preferred shares and convertible debentures outstanding in this example. In the calculation of fully diluted earnings per share we can see how earnings must be restated for the hypothetical impact of the conversion of the debentures.

Assume the following for the year being illustrated:

1. There were 1,000 common shares outstanding throughout the year. (This eliminates the need to calculate the weighted average number of common shares outstanding.)

2. An issue of 6% convertible debentures with a principal amount of $10,000, due in two years, has been outstanding for a number of years. Each $100 debenture is convertible into four common shares. None of the debentures were converted during the year under study or previously.

3. An issue of 4% cumulative redeemable preferred shares in the amount of $5,000 has been outstanding for a number of years. There was no change in the preferred share capital during the year under study. As of the end of the year, the 4% cumulative dividend was in arrears for two years, but it was declared and paid the following year.

4. The income tax rate is 45%.

For this example the calculation of earnings per share is as follows:

	Common shares	Income before extraordinary items	Net income
Basic earnings per share			
Earnings per income statement		$ 3,400	$ 2,980
Dividend requirement on preferred shares (4% of $5,000)		200	200
Earnings attributable to common shares	1,000	$ 3,200	$ 2,780
BASIC EARNINGS PER SHARE		$ 3.20	$ 2.78

	Common shares	Net income before extra-ordinary items	Net income
Fully diluted earnings per share			
Earnings applicable to common shares (above)	1,000	$ 3,200	$ 2,780
Effect of assumed conversion of all 6% convertible debentures (after income taxes) (55% of 6% of $10,000 = $330, and $10,000/ 100 × 4 = 400)	400	330	330
Totals for calculating fully diluted earnings per share	1,400	$ 3,530	$ 3,110
FULLY DILUTED EARNINGS PER SHARE		$ 2.52	$2.22

Note in this example that none of the holders of convertible debentures had chosen to convert into common shares, implying that the common stock did not look attractive enough for them to convert at the ratio of four shares for each $100 debenture. Since the debentures are due shortly, the probability of their being converted does not look high. Yet we make the fully diluted calculation on the pessimistic assumption that the debentures will be converted.

Note also that in calculating the totals for fully diluted earnings per share we added back the interest cost that would have been saved had the debentures been converted. The tax on this saving has been deducted ($100\% - 45\% = 55\%$) because interest is allowed as a deduction for tax purposes, whereas dividends are not.

The preferred shares are not convertible, and they do not affect the calculation of fully diluted earnings per share except for the deduction of the dividend. Although the dividend has not been paid, it is cumulative and is deducted anyway.

A small change in the example will illustrate an anti-dilutive security. Assume that the debentures were convertible into common shares on the basis of one-half share for each $100 debenture instead of the four shares in the original example. The number of common shares that would be issued on full conversion would therefore be 50 instead of 400, and the total number of shares on full conversion would be 1,050 instead of 1,400. This means that the earnings per share would be $3530/1050 = \$3.36$, which is more than the basic earnings per share of $3.20. Because this security is anti-dilutive it would be omitted from the calculations, and the fully diluted earnings per share would be given as $3.20.

In the original example the debentures were outstanding from the start of the year. Had they been issued through the year, then we would have had to calculate the weighted amount from the date of issue.

Warrants and Options

When a warrant or option is exercised the company receives assets (usually cash) equal to the price at which the shares can be purchased. Presumably the company will be able to earn income on these assets. Its income will therefore be higher if the option or warrant has been exercised. Unlike a convertible bond, where one knows the interest expense avoided, the income that might be earned on the assets in this case must be estimated.

Assume in our preceding example that instead of convertible debentures, the company had issued 400 warrants, each entitling the holder to purchase one common share at $25 each. If all the warrants were exercised, the company would receive $10,000. If it assumed it could earn 10% on these funds, then the before-tax income would be $1,000, and the after-tax income $550.

The fully diluted net income per share would be calculated as follows:

Earnings applicable to common shareholders	$ 2,780
After-tax income assumed if warrants were exercised	550
Total for calculating fully diluted earnings per share	$ 3,330
Number of shares outstanding	1,400
Fully diluted earnings per share	$ 2.38

The calculation of earnings per share for options is similar to that illustrated here for warrants.

Splits and Reverse Splits

If a company's shares are **split**, there is an increase in the number of shares outstanding with no change in its stated capital. As a result the earnings per outstanding share are decreased. A **reverse split** occurs when the number of outstanding shares is decreased with no change in stated capital. As a result earnings per share are increased.

Both splits and reverse splits receive the same treatment [*CICA* 3500.25]. First, earnings per share are restated to recognize the split or reverse split as if it had existed from the beginning of the fiscal period (even if it occurs after the company's year-end but before the financial statements are issued). Second, the split or reverse split is also applied retroactively to the earnings per share of the preceding period. A note to the financial statement would indicate that the EPS had been calculated with the stock split or reverse split taken into account.

Adjusted Basic Earnings per Share and Pro Forma Earnings per Share

If common shares have been issued on the conversion of debt or senior shares, the practice is to calculate the **adjusted basic earnings per share**, which is the earnings per share *as if* the conversion had taken place at the *beginning* of the year of the reporting date [*CICA* 3500.28]. Presumably the purpose is to show basic earnings per share that might be expected after the conversion. On the other hand, if common shares have been issued through the year as a result of a stock dividend on senior issues (i.e., on issues other than common shares), then the common shares are recognized only from the date of issue [*CICA* 3500.26].

If an issue of shares, as the result of conversion of debt or senior shares or reorganization, takes place *after* the period being reported on, and it is material, then **pro forma earnings per share** are calculated using the newly altered capital structure [*CICA* 3500.39 and .40]. The term *pro forma* is used in accounting to indicate a calculation or financial statement that incorporates some special assumption. In this case, the assumption is that the results should look as if the shares were issued *before* the end of the reporting year.

Differences between Canadian and U.S. Reporting Practices

Canadian and U.S. practice diverge in the calculation of the *basic* earnings per share for companies with complex capital structures. In contrast to the Canadian practice, which is to divide the earnings available for common shareholders by the weighted number of common shares, the U.S. practice is to treat some of the dilutive securities as the equivalent of common shares (**common stock equivalents**) and to calculate the primary earnings per share *as if* these shares had already been issued. The U.S. practice also treats warrants differently in computing fully diluted EPS. The U.S. rules for this are complicated and will not be explained here.

Examples From Published Reports

It is usual to find the earnings per share at the bottom of the income statement in the financial statements or in a note cross-referenced to the income statement [*CICA* 3500.09]. The earnings per share is part of the financial statements and is subject to audit opinion along with the rest of the financial data presented.

The Royal Bank of Canada

Excerpts from the financial statements of the Royal Bank have been given above in Chapter 7. The EPS is found at the bottom of the income statement:

	October 31 1986	October 31 1985
Income per share (note 3)		
Basic	$ 4.05	$ 4.28
Fully diluted	$ 3.74	$ 3.91

Note 3.   Income Per Share
Basic income per share is after deducting preferred dividends of $75,851,000 (1985 — $71,780,000) and has been calculated on the average number of common shares outstanding. The average number of common shares outstanding for the year ended October 31, 1986 was 102,110,394 (1985 — 97,321,503).

Fully diluted income per share has been calculated on the average number of common shares which would have been outstanding in each year assuming conversion of all convertible securities and exercise of all warrants outstanding as at the beginning of each year or date of issue if later. For purposes of this calculation, adjustments have been made for the after-tax interest on convertible debentures, the dividends on convertible preferred shares, and an imputed after-tax return on additional funds of $41,997,000 which would be received on the conversion of the second preferred shares series A.

Observe the complexity of this calculation, based as it is on imputed interest and the assumption of full conversion of convertible shares.

Mobil Corporation

Excerpts from the financial statements of Mobil Corporation have been given in Chapter 5.

	1986	1985	1984
Net income per share	$ 3.45	$ 2.55	$ 3.11

Note 14.   Capital Stock
At December 31, 1986, 30,000,000 shares of $1.00 par-value preferred stock were authorized, of which 6,000,000 shares of series A Junior Participating Preferred Stock were authorized for issuance upon exercise of certain preferred stock purchase rights; none were issued or outstanding. At December 31, 1986, 600,000,000 shares of $2.00 par-value common stock were authorized and 429,984,265 shares were issued, including 21,252,400 held in the treasury. There were 408,731,865 shares outstanding at year-end.

Summary

Earnings per share is a widely used statistic because it appears to capture in one number a useful measure of the firm's success for a given year. It is a figure that management cannot help but pay attention to, and it is one that has been open to manipulation. It is now included as part of the audited financial statements and its calculation has been standardized. Both the basic (undiluted) and diluted EPS are shown in the financial statements, although data supporting the calculation are often incomplete.

There are some important differences between Canadian and U.S. practices in how the basic earnings per share is calculated. In the U.S., common stock equivalents are included as part of the common shares outstanding.

Is the measure of earnings per share a useful one? As in so many important questions in accounting the answer is "It depends." If the company's accounting income is a good indicator of its economic success for that year, then this is a good start. If its share capital structure is not unduly complex, and particularly if one can make some estimates of the potential dilutive effect, then the EPS figure can be potentially very useful. To the extent the above assumptions are less realistic, one should start to be wary about making important decisions based on the EPS figure.

QUESTIONS

Q17-1. Explain the following terms in non-technical language:
   a. basic earnings per share *versus* fully diluted earnings per share
   b. price-earnings ratio
   c. multiple
   d. income attributable to shareholders entitled to participate
   e. simple capital structure *versus* complex capital structure
   f. weighted average number of shares
   g. common shares *versus* senior shares
   h. convertible debenture
   i. share option
   j. cumulative *versus* non-cumulative preferred shares
   k. convertible versus non-convertible preferred shares
   l. dilutive *versus* antidilutive securities
   m. common stock equivalents
   n. split *versus* reverse split
   o. adjusted basic earnings per share
   p. pro forma earnings per share

Q17-2. State whether you agree with each of the following statements. Be sure to explain your reasoning.

    a. *"Basic earnings per share* is a misnomer. It is simply a number obtained by dividing the earnings left for the common shareholders by the number of shares outstanding — and that could be quite different from the earnings divided by the number of common shares."

    b. *"Fully diluted earnings per share* is such a pessimistic figure that it is almost meaningless."

    c. "A company can increase its reported earnings per share by buying up its own shares for cancellation."

    d. "The EPS figure is too misleading to be useful. What is needed is more disclosure of the underlying data."

Q17-3. As a potential investor, how might you use earnings per share information to evaluate a company's stock?

Q17-4. A common criticism levelled against the EPS figure is that it attempts to crowd too much information into one figure. One suggested alternative is to have a multi-column presentation, in which the left column would show the basic earnings per share. Then in successive columns to the right the impact of the potential conversions would be set out, one security issue to each column, until the final right-hand column would show the impact of full dilution.

    Required: Evaluate this proposal, assessing its strengths and weaknesses.

Q17-5. It is a requirement of the accounting standard-setting bodies in both Canada and the U.S. that earnings per share should be shown on the financial statements and be subject to the auditors' opinion. What advantages, if any, do you see in this?

Q17-6. Explain how existing shareholders' interests are adversely affected if bonds are sold with warrants attached that allow the holder to purchase common stock at a price significantly below the market price. What has this got to do with calculating earnings per share?

Q17-7. The *CICA Handbook* requires that if common shares are issued on conversion of debt in the middle of the fiscal year, the basic earnings per share should be calculated as if the shares had been issued at the start of the year with adjustment to income for the bond interest paid. What is the purpose of this? (*Hint:* What are the alternative treatments? How useful are they?)

Q17-8. In calculating the basic *earnings available to holders of common shares,* which of the following would enter into the calculation? Would the item increase or decrease the *earnings available?*

    a. Dividends paid on non-cumulative non-participating preference shares.

    b. Unpaid dividends on non-cumulative non-participating preference shares.

    c. Outstanding options to purchase company shares at $50. The company's after-tax interest income is 6%, and the present EPS is $5.

    d. Unpaid dividends on non-participating cumulative preference shares.

    e. Unpaid dividends on non-cumulative preference shares entitled to participate on an equal basis with common shares.

Q17-9. Would your answers to Question 17-8 change if you were calculating fully diluted EPS? Explain.

Q17-10. In this chapter we suggested that a good EPS was a high one in most cases, and that it was possible to use techniques within GAAP to keep the EPS high. Give three examples of these techniques. For each, indicate (i) whether in your view it is possible or desirable to restrict its use by modifications of existing GAAP and (ii) whether this is a timing effect, which will have a reverse effect on EPS at some later date, or a permanent effect.

Q17-11. Supporters of the *efficient markets* school argue that there is widespread evidence that sophisticated investors are not fooled by the manner in which information is presented. Therefore, they maintain that one should concentrate on making sure investors have the basic information, rather than on the form in which it is presented. If one accepts their basic argument, does this present a convincing reason for dropping accounting standards for EPS and allowing companies to calculate and report their EPS as they wish? Explain.

Q17-12. What is the reason for using a weighted average of the number of shares outstanding when calculating the EPS? Under what circumstances would it be just as effective in the calculation to use something easier, such as a simple average of the opening and closing balances?

Q17-13. The practice for calculating EPS in Canada is to present the reader with two extremes, the basic EPS and the fully diluted EPS. In this chapter we gave an example where conversion of potentially diluted securities was assumed in calculating the fully diluted EPS, even though the scenario indicated it was highly unlikely that the holders of these securities would ever choose to use their conversion privilege. Do you think it is useful to keep using these extremes when the evidence indicates the assumption of conversion is not likely? Discuss.

Q17-14. In the United States potentially dilutive securities such as convertible bonds are divided into two categories: (i) *common stock equivalents* and (ii) *other potentially dilutive securities.* A security falls into group (i) if its principal value arises from the fact it can be converted into common stock. A potentially dilutive security that falls into group (i) must be added to the common shares outstanding when calculating the *primary earnings per share.* This is in contrast to Canadian practice, where the basic EPS does not include such potentially dilutive securities. Under what circumstances are there likely to be big differences between the Canadian basic EPS and the United States equivalent? Under what conditions would a change in the prime interest rate affect primary earnings per share? Is this desirable? Explain.

Q17-15. The quotation at the start of the chapter implied that reporting on the affairs of a corporation was in nature too complex to be compressed into a single number such as EPS. Yet a corporation's EPS is widely quoted and frequently cited as a basis for an opinion on the worth of that company's stock. How do you resolve this apparent paradox?

Q17-16. A company had two convertible bond issues outstanding: (i) $100,000 17% bonds trading at 130 with the right to convert each $100 of bonds into two shares; and (ii) $100,000 8% bonds trading at 125 with the same conversion rights. The company had an EPS of $5, a tax rate of 50%, and could earn 10% on invested money. Which of these bond issues, if any, would be included in the calculation of fully diluted EPS? Would it be more informative for the reader of financial statements to include both in the fully diluted EPS?

Q17-17. Some companies have provisions in the terms of their outstanding bonds payable that limit the companies' ability to pay dividends under certain adverse conditions (e.g., if their working capital falls below a certain level). What relevance might this have for the investor? Should this limitation on payment of dividends be evaluated in conjunction with the evaluation of EPS? Discuss.

Q17-18. Potentially dilutive securities can be looked on as a lottery in which the holders get the right to an above-average return if certain events take place, usually at the expense of the common shareholders. For each of the following events, explain if it would likely give rise to a return for the holders of convertible bonds that would be (i) in excess of what they could have expected had they purchased non-convertible bonds instead, (ii) less than expected, or (iii) no change.

   a. The price of the common shares goes up.

   b. The EPS goes up.

   c. The market rate of interest goes down.

   d. The conversion rate changes from three shares per $100 to two shares per $100, in accordance with the original conversion terms of the bond.

Q17-19. "In calculating fully diluted EPS for convertible bonds you add back the after-tax cost of the interest to compensate for including the equivalent number of shares in the denominator. The calculation of the dilution effect of executive stock options should be done similarly; we should add back to income the after-tax savings the company has achieved by giving executives stock options in lieu of immediate remuneration." Do you agree? Discuss.

Q17-20. It has been said that the EPS figure has replaced the net income figure on the income statement as the true bottom line. What does this mean? Discuss whether the statement seems appropriate.

Q17-21. It has been pointed out that a rising EPS from one year to the other is not necessarily a sign that a company is doing well; the rise may be due instead to other factors. Give three examples to illustrate such factors.

Q17-22. It has been suggested that return on investment (ROI) is preferable to EPS as a measure of company performance and that what is needed is a standard for computing ROI similar to that now developed for EPS. Discuss the merits of this proposal.

EXERCISES

E17-1. Identify which of the following are common shares and which are senior shares for purposes of calculating earnings per share. Assume in each case that there are A shares that participate fully as to dividend but rank after all others in preference as to dividend.

   a. B shares are non-cumulative with preference as to dividend. The dividend is fixed at $0.35 per quarter.

   b. B shares are as in (a) above, but the dividends are cumulative.

   c. B shares have preference as to dividend and are cumulative up to $0.35 per share per quarter. They participate fully with the A shares once the dividend on the latter reaches $0.35 per quarter.

   d. B shares are as in (c) above, but the dividends are non-cumulative.

E17-2. Compute the basic and fully diluted earnings per share in each of the following situations. Where applicable, the B shares can be converted into A shares on the basis of two A shares for one B share.

	A shares issued	B shares issued	Net income before extra- ordinary income	Extra- ordinary income	Dividend on B per share	Dividend declared?	Cumula- tive?	Convertible?
a.	10,000	0	$ 50,000	0	n.a.	n.a.	n.a.	n.a.
b.	10,000	5,000	50,000	0	$ 10	no	no	no
c.	10,000	5,000	50,000	0	10	yes	yes	no
d.	10,000	5,000	50,000	20,000	10	yes	no	no
e.	10,000	5,000	50,000	20,000	10	yes	no	yes
f.	10,000	5,000	50,000	20,000	10	no	yes	yes

E17-3. Compute income available to common shareholders for both basic and fully diluted earnings per share in each situation below. The company has one class of shares outstanding and an issue of $100,000 convertible 10% long-term debentures that can be converted for each $1,000 bond on the basis shown in each case. The number of common shares issued in each case is 10,000. The net income is $50,000, and there are no extraordinary income items. The tax rate is 40%. The conversion rates for each case are as follows:

a. 15 shares for each $1,000 bond

b. 13 shares for each $1,000 bond

c. 11 shares for each $1,000 bond

d. 9 shares for each $1,000 bond

E17-4. The data given below refers to the shares of Brecht Ltd. The company's fiscal year ends on 31 December, and the company has only one class of shares.

1 January	— outstanding shares:	10,000 common
1 February	— issued for cash:	1,800 common
1 April	— issued for land and buildings:	3,200 common
1 July	— purchased and cancelled:	1,000 common
31 December	— 2 for 1 stock split	

Required: Calculate the weighted average number of shares for the year.

E17-5. Petroff Ltd. began the year with 10,000 (common) (A) shares and 1,000 cumulative redeemable convertible preference (B) shares with a fixed dividend of $1.25 per quarter. These latter shares are convertible into common shares on the basis of two common shares for each preference share. The following transactions took place during the year.

		Shares	Class
1 February	— issued A shares for cash	1,200	A
1 May	— B shares converted to A	450	B
1 June	— B shares redeemed	100	B
1 October	— A shares purchased and cancelled	900	A
1 December	— B shares converted to A	60	A

Required: Calculate the weighted average shares on both a basic and fully diluted basis for the year ended 31 December.

E17-6. Glendower Corporation has earnings of $3.00 per Class A share for the year just ended. Its tax rate is 50%, and its expected earnings on assets is 8% before tax. In each case below, indicate whether the described outstanding security is dilutive or antidilutive. Show all calculations.

   a. 12% debentures convertible at three shares per $100 debenture

   b. 12% debentures convertible at two shares per $100 debenture

   c. 12% debentures convertible at one share per $100 debenture

   d. Preferred shares that have annual dividends of $4 and are convertible at one Class A share for each preference share

   e. Preferred shares as in (d) above, but with an annual dividend of $2

   f. Options with an exercise price of $100

   g. Options with an exercise price of $75

   h. Options with an exercise price of $60

E17-7. The following data are applicable to Bechtold Business Forms Inc. as at 31 December 19X4:

Share capital, 40,000 common shares	$ 705,000
Dividends on common shares	34,000
Prior-period adjustment, income tax recovery	17,800
After-tax extraordinary gain: sale of division	24,200
Sales revenue	439,000
Cost of goods sold	274,000
General, selling, and administrative expenses	133,500
Tax rate	45%

On 1 October, Bechtold Business Forms Inc. issued 5,000 new shares.

Required: What is the earnings per share for 19X4? Show all calculations.

E17-8. The following information pertains to B.G. Co. for the operating year 31 December, 19X1:

   (i) 200,000 new common shares were issued on 1 April 19X1. As a result, 800,000 common shares were outstanding in total.

   (ii) On 1 July, 19X1, long-term convertible bonds were issued at par with a face value of $1,000,000. The bonds were 10% bonds with interest paid twice annually, on 31 December and 1 July. The first interest payment is to be on 31 December 19X1. Each $1,000 bond is convertible into 200 common shares. As of 31 December 19X1, none had been converted.

   (iii) Earnings before taxes was $700,000 for the year ended 31 December 19X1.

   (iv) The applicable tax rate is 50%.

   Required:

   a. What is the basic earnings per share?

   b. What is the fully diluted earnings per share?

E17-9. Turner Automotive issued 1,200 options to key employees as part of their remuneration package on 31 December 19X5. Each right gave the employee the option to buy one share of common stock for $15 each after 31 December 19X6, provided the employee was still with the company. On 1 September 19X7, 300 options were exercised. The imputed interest rate is 15%. The following data pertain to the 19X7 fiscal year:

Revenue	$ 215,000
Cost of goods sold	108,000
Operating expenses	81,500
After-tax extraordinary loss: sales of division	6,000
Share capital, 9,000 common shares at year-end	209,000
Tax rate	50%

Required: Calculate the earnings per share for 19X7.

E17-10. Indicate the impact of each of the following unrelated events on (i) basic earnings per share and (ii) fully-diluted earnings per share. If you think you require more information to decide, then state what additional information is needed and why.

   a. The company issued a stock dividend of two common shares for each common share now held.

   b. The company thought that its depreciation policy was inappropriate. The company decided to revise it to reflect the view that the function life of a significant group of plant assets would be twenty years instead of the ten years originally chosen.

   c. The holders of 500 B shares elected to convert their holdings to 500 A shares. The B shares have the same dividend rights as the A shares, but no voting rights. They are convertible into A shares on a one-for-one basis until the end of the current year, at which time they become non-convertible.

   d. Convertible bonds were issued at par with a coupon rate of 11%. The bonds may be converted at the rate of 20 shares for each $1,000 face value bond. Prior to the issue of the bonds the basic and fully-diluted earnings per share were $2.50. The company's tax rate is 30%.

   e. The company had not paid any dividends on cumulative preferred shares for the past two years. At its regular directors' meeting today, they declared a dividend on the preference shares sufficient to eliminate any accumulated arrears in dividends.

PROBLEMS

P17-1. Sharpton Limited had a net income for 19X2 of $4,500, with no extraordinary items. At the beginning of 19X2 there were 500 common shares outstanding, and in the middle of the company's financial year it issued an additional 500.

   Required: Calculate the earnings per share.

(CICA adapted)

P17-2. You are given the following information for Garden Island Mfg. Ltd. for 19X0. The company's year-end is 31 December.

Preferred stock: 100 non-convertible 5% cumulative shares of $10 each.

Common stock: number of shares outstanding 1 January	1,000
Additional shares sold during year:	
1 March	120
1 July	50
1 September	45
Income: Net income before extraordinary items	$ 3,470
Extraordinary losses net of tax	530
Net income	$ 2,940

Required: Calculate the earnings per share for the year.

P17-3. On 1 January 19X1 MFG Ltd. issued $50,000 face value of convertible bonds with a coupon rate of 16%. Each $100 of bonds was convertible into one common share. No bonds were converted during 19X1. The company has a tax rate of 55%. A total of 1,000 common shares was outstanding all year. The following information is also available:

Net income before extraordinary items	$ 4,560
Extraordinary gain, net of tax	350
Net income	$ 4,910

Required: Calculate the fully diluted earnings per share for 19X1.

P17-4. On 1 January 19X2 Bonham Mfg. Ltd. issued stock rights to its existing shareholders — one right for each share then held. One right gave each existing shareholder the option to purchase one common share for $3. One thousand rights were exercised on 30 September 19X2. The company's imputed interest rate is 20% and its tax rate is 55%. The company's net income was $6,600, and there were no extraordinary items. A total of 1,500 shares was outstanding on 1 January 19X2.

Required: Calculate the earnings per share for 19X2.

P17-5. The income statement for Hepworth Enterprises Limited for the year ended 31 December shows the following:

Income before income tax	$ 330,000
Income tax	145,000
Income before extraordinary items	185,000
Add: Extraordinary loss (net of income tax)	90,000
Net income	$ 95,000

Required: Compute the earnings per share for the year for each of the assumptions shown below.

a. The company has only one class of shares, and 150,000 are outstanding.

b. The company has the following outstanding shares: (i) 10,000 6% cumulative preferred shares, $50 par value, and (ii) 150,000 common shares, no par value. The dividends for the current year are unpaid.

P17-6. You are given the following fragmentary information about Johnson Limited. Its fully diluted earnings per share after extraordinary items is $2.60. At the start of the year it had 1,500 common shares outstanding. During the year it issued common shares as follows: 1 April — 200, 1 June — 240, and 1 October — 80.

Johnson also has cumulative convertible preference shares. It issued and has outstanding 200 of these shares. The par value of the preference shares is $25 and the dividend rate is 5%. The shares are convertible into common shares in the ratio of two common shares for each preference share.

Required:

a. What is the number of common shares outstanding for purposes of calculating the basic earnings per share?

b. What is the company's total net income for the year (*not* earnings per share) after extraordinary item? Show your calculations.

P17-7. Balderston Corporation had the following shares outstanding at 1 July 19X6: 6,000 Class A (common) shares; 5,000 Class B cumulative redeemable shares with an annual dividend of $3.75 paid on 1 July; and 6,000 Class C non-cumulative convertible shares with an annual dividend of $2.90 paid on 1 June and declared as of 1 May. One Class C share was convertible into two A shares, and the directors had declared the dividend on both B and C shares for the year. The net income before extraordinary items was $60,000, and the net income after extraordinary items was $50,000.

The following events regarding the Class A shares took place in the company's fiscal year ending 30 June 19X7:

1 September	— sold for cash	600
1 January	— issued for converted C shares	2,000
1 March	— purchased and cancelled	300
1 June	— issued in return for equipment	3,000

Required:

a. What is the average weighted number of A shares outstanding for the year?

b. What is the income attributable to common shareholders?

c. What is the earnings per share, both basic and fully diluted?

P17-8. Optimistic Corporation (OC) tended to make accounting judgements that looked on the bright side, and Pessimistic Corporation (PC) tended to do the reverse. Both had a net income of $300,000 before the following items, and both had 500,000 common shares outstanding throughout the year.

(i) Both incurred organizing expenses of $100,000. OC felt that these represented a permanent benefit to the company and did not propose to amortize them, whereas PC felt that prudent accounting policy indicated an immediate write-off.

(ii) Both purchased computer equipment costing $350,000. OC chose a straight-line depreciation over eight years, saying that the function it had purchased the equipment for would be in place at least that length of time, and it was sure the equipment would continue to be cost-effective for that period. PC chose a three-year straight-line policy on the grounds that innovation in this area was so swift that it was appropriate to use a relatively short functional life.

(iii) Both owned shares in similar companies that totalled 20% of the voting shares in each case. These other companies had reported a profit for the year of $150,000. No dividends were actually declared. OC considered that it had significant influence and therefore used the equity method. PC used the cost method.

(iv) PC (despite its negative view of the economic situation) paid its executives a bonus of $69,000, whereas OC gave its executives stock options that had an estimated market value of the same amount.

(v) At the end of the prior year OC and PC each had a wholly owned subsidiary company. Each subsidiary had a loss in the current year of $300,000. However, at the end of the prior year OC had declared a special dividend equal to all its shares in this subsidiary.

Required:

a. What is the earnings per share for OC and for PC? Show your calculations.

b. How many of the above differences in practice are acceptable under generally accepted accounting principles? Explain.

P17-9. Roslin Limited had 2,500 common Class A shares outstanding at the start of its fiscal year, which was 1 January. It also had outstanding 3,500 $4.12 cumulative redeemable Class B shares with a dividend date of 28 February plus 6,000 non-cumulative $4.12 convertible Class C shares with a dividend date of 28 February. No dividends were declared during the year. Class C shares are convertible to Class A shares on a 1:1 basis. The following activity took place with the A shares:

1 February	— issued shares for cash	360
15 April	— converted C shares to A shares	1,500
1 October	— purchased and cancelled	400
1 October	— issued for cash	2,000

Required:

a. What is the income attributable to the A shares?

b. What is the weighted average number of A shares outstanding for the year?

c. The company's net income is $50,000. What are the basic and fully diluted earnings per share? Show all calculations.

P17-10. Marlbank Limited has 3,500 common shares outstanding at the beginning of its fiscal year. It also has outstanding 50 Class B shares with a cumulative preference as to dividend for $4.00 and no right to participate in dividends beyond that amount. Three years ago it issued $10,000 11% convertible debentures that can be converted into common shares on the basis of four common shares for each $100 debenture surrendered for conversion. The applicable tax rate is 48%. The company's net income is $3,400 before extraordinary items and $2,980 after extraordinary items.

Required:

a. Calculate the basic earnings per share.

b. Calculate the fully diluted earnings per share. Show all calculations.

P17-11. Burnstown Corporation has financial results and share capital identical with those of Marlbank Limited (in P17-10 above). However, Burnstown's convertible debentures have an interest rate of 12% and a face amount of $55,000; and each $100 debenture can be converted into ten common shares. Burnstown's tax rate is 50%.

Required:

a. Calculate the basic earnings per share.

b. Calculate the fully diluted earnings per share. Show all calculations.

c. At what conversion rate for each $100 debenture would the conversion privilege on the debentures be neither dilutive nor antidilutive?

P17-12. Lanark Corporation had a net income before extraordinary items of $3,400 and a net income after extraordinary items of $2,980. Its tax rate was 50%, and it expected to earn 12% on its assets. At the beginning of the year it had the following: (i) share capital of 3,500 Class A shares, with no preference as to dividend and voting rights; (ii) 50 cumulative preference shares paying a fixed dividend of $4 per annum; (iii) 100 non-cumulative preference shares with a fixed dividend of $2.25 per annum that had been declared; and (iv) 100 options giving the holder the right to purchase Class A shares at $35 each for the next two years.

Required:

a. What is the basic earnings per share.

b. What is the fully diluted earnings per share? Show your calculations.

P17-13. Consider the same scenario as in P17-12, but assume that the options give the right to purchase A shares at $10 each.

Required:

a. Calculate the basic earnings per share.

b. Calculate the fully diluted earnings per share. Show all calculations.

c. At what exercise price would the option be neither dilutive nor antidilutive?

P17-14. Almonte Limited had 3,500 common shares outstanding. It had a net income of $3,400 before extraordinary items and $2,980 after extraordinary items. Its tax rate was 50%. It also had outstanding 50 cumulative Class B preference shares that paid a dividend of $4 per annum, and 600 Class C non-cumulative preference shares that paid a dividend of $2.25 per annum and were convertible on the basis of five common shares for each Class C share. Dividends on the Class C share had been declared and paid for the year.

Required:

a. Calculate the basic earnings per share.

b. Calculate the fully diluted earnings per share. Show all calculations.

c. At what conversion rate would the convertible shares be neither dilutive nor antidilutive?

d. Does the rate at which the convertible shares become dilutive depend on the income earned that year? Explain.

P17-15. Consider the same scenario as in P17-14, but assume that the dividend on the Class C shares had not been declared.

Required:

a. Calculate the basic net income per share.

b. Calculate the fully diluted earnings per share. Show all calculations.

c. What disclosure, if any, is recommended by the *CICA Handbook?*

P17-16. Tricolor Corporation had a net income before extraordinary items of $3,400 and a net income after extraordinary items of $2,980. Its tax rate was 45%, and it expected to earn 12% on its assets. At the beginning of the year it had the following: (i) share capital of 3,500 Class A shares, with no preference as to dividend and voting rights; (ii) 50 cumulative preference shares paying a fixed dividend of $4 per annum; (iii) 100 non-cumulative preference shares with a fixed dividend of $2.25 per annum that had been declared; (iv) 100 options giving the holder the right to purchase Class A shares any time during the next two years.

Required:

a. What is the basic earnings per share?

b. What is the fully diluted earnings per share? Show your calculations.

c. Indicate the section(s) of the financial statement in which this information would be disclosed.

d. What conversion price for each option would be needed to allow a conversion that is neither dilutive nor antidilutive?

(By Jane Craighead)

P17-17. The net income of Godfrey Inc. for the year 1988 was $2,800,000. On 3 January 1988 the equity structure of the firm was as follows:

Current liabilities	$ 6,200,000
Long-term debt:	
Notes payable — 11%	300,000
20-year 9% bonds due 1997 and convertible into common stock at the rate of three shares per $100; issue price — $100.	12,000,000
Shareholders' equity:	
Preferred shares: issued 1 January 1970; cumulative as to dividends of 7%	5,000,000
Common shares: issued and outstanding — 500,000 shares	2,000,000

During your investigation of the records you discovered the following additional information:

(i) On 1 July 1988, non-cumulative preference shares paying an annual fixed dividend of $8 were issued at $100 in the amount of $6,000,000. Each preference share is convertible into five common shares.

(ii) Dividends of $4 per share were declared and paid on the 8% preferred shares in 1988.

(iii) There are outstanding warrants to purchase 10,000 common shares. The warrants are exercisable at $10 plus one warrant for each share. The expiry date on the warrants is July 1995.

Required:

a. Prepare all the necessary earnings per share figures that the company will require for its 1988 financial statements. The company is subject to a 50% tax rate and invests all excess cash at 5% after tax. Show all your calculations *and label them.*

b. Explain what must be disclosed for this company with respect to earnings per share and specify where that information should be shown.

(CMA adapted)

P17-18. On 15 January 19X8 the Senior Management Committee of Johnson Inc. asked you to develop data about its earnings over the past two years. Your working papers include the following information:

(i) Net income for each of the respective fiscal years is as follows:

19X6 — $3,420,000
19X7 — 3,280,000

(There are no extraordinary transactions in either year.)

(ii) On 1 January 19X6, 300,000 shares of common stock as well as 35,000 shares of 12% $50 cumulative convertible preferred were outstanding. Conversion terms on the preferred stock provides for three shares of common stock for each preferred share, to be adjusted for any stock dividends and stock splits.

(iii) On 31 December 19X6 the common stock was split 2 for 1.

(iv) On 31 July 19X7 the Board of Directors declared and distributed a 25% stock dividend to its common shareholders. On that day the stock traded at $16 per share.

(v) Preferred stock cash dividends are paid promptly on 31 December of each year. To date, no preferred stock has been converted.

(vi) The company's tax rate is 45%.

Required:

a. Prepare a schedule to illustrate in detail the number of common shares outstanding at the end of each of the two years 19X6 and 19X7.

b. For 19X7 calculate the basic earnings per share and the fully diluted earnings per share. Show all calculations. If necessary, round all decimals to two places.

(CMA adapted)

P17-19. Tamworth Limited has heard that it is a requirement that earnings per share (EPS) be disclosed on financial statements. The management is in the process of preparing the financial statements for the year just finished. The company's year end is 31 December, and the applicable tax rate is 40%.

In late January the accountant comes to you for advice about what EPS data must be shown in the annual report. She provides you with the following summary of events:

Bonds payable, 12%, due six years from the last fiscal year-end	
(1,000 bonds issued, convertible at 15 shares each)	$ 1,000,000
Preferred shares (authorized, issued, and outstanding — 10,000	
shares, 10% non-cumulative, redeemable at 115)	1,000,000
Common shares (no-par-value, issued 100,000)	200,000

Additional details:
No share transactions took place during the year just past. The net income for the year was $2,500,000. All dividend payments are up to date.

You discover during your discussions with the accountant that in mid-January of the current year the company issued 10,000 shares of common stock and used this cash to redeem 2,000 shares of preferred. The accountant did not know how to treat these transactions and wondered if this information should be disclosed in last year's financial statements.

Required: As a consultant to the company, prepare all of the required EPS disclosure(s) that are necessary for the company's financial statements. Give your reasons for the disclosure recommendations you make. Specify where the EPS information should appear in the statements. (The *CICA Handbook* states that the "material" events subsequent to the date of the financial statements or dilution of EPS by possible conversions should be disclosed. Part of your task here is to calculate these effects and decide on materiality.)

(CMA adapted)

P17-20. Madon Ltd. is a manufacturer of light fixtures. The accountant is preparing the financial statements for the year ended 31 December 19X3. Selected financial information necessary for earnings per share (EPS) calculations is summarized as follows:

Bonds payable, 9.5% non-convertible	$ 90,000
Common stock, no par: authorized — 100,000 shares; issued and outstanding throughout the year, 50,000 shares.	600,000
Preferred stock, 6%, par $10, convertible, cumulative: authorized — 25,000 shares; issued and outstanding throughout the year, 10,000 shares.	100,000
Contributed capital in excess of par, preferred stock.	30,000
Retained earnings (no dividends declared through the year)	290,000
Income before extraordinary items	85,000
Extraordinary loss (net of tax)	15,000
Net income after taxes	70,000
Average income tax rate	40%

The preferred shares are convertible into common at one preferred for one common.

Required:

a. Prepare all necessary EPS figures. Assume all amounts are material. Show your calculations.

b. Assume that 5,000 preferred shares are converted to common. Give the appropriate journal entry.

(CGA adapted)

P17-21. You are given the following information about Hepworth Inc.:

(i) For the year ended 31 December 19X5 income before extraordinary items was $2,500,000 and net income was $3,000,000.

(ii) At the beginning of 19X5 there were 2,000,000 common shares outstanding. On 30 September of that year an additional 120,000 common shares were issued.

(iii) An issue of 10% convertible bonds with a principal amount of $2,000,000 was outstanding during the year. Each $1,000 bond is convertible into forty common shares.

(iv) An issue of 5% convertible preferred shares, par $100, in the amount of $1,000,000 is also outstanding. Each preferred share is convertible into five common shares.

(v) The income tax rate is 40%.

(vi) The required dividends were paid to the preferred shareholders, and $100,000 was paid to the common shareholders.

Required:

a. Without regard to materiality, present the earnings per share figures required for presentation in the financial statements. Round to three decimal places.

b. Does the concept of materiality change your answer to part (a)? Explain.

(CGA adapted)

BIBLIOGRAPHY

ACCOUNTING PRINCIPLES BOARD. *Opinion No. 15: Earnings per Share.* New York: American Institute of Certified Public Accountants, 1969. An influential pronouncement of the predecessor body to the FASB.

CHERRY, DONALD C., and CONROD, JOAN E.D. "EPS — A Financial Ratio in Question." *CA Magazine* (June 1983). A discussion of the merits of using ROI in place of EPS.

PARKER J.R.E. "Income Reporting and the Canada-U.S. Gap in GAAP." *CA Magazine* (May 1974). A distinguished Canadian academic discusses the significant reporting differences between Canada and the U.S with regard to EPS.

SKINNER, ROSS. *Accounting Standards in Evolution.* Toronto: Holt, Rinehart, and Winston of Canada Ltd., 1987. The best single source for an extended discussion of the issues raised by the use of EPS as a measure of performance.

CHAPTER 18

Statement of Changes in Financial Position

Introduction

The **statement of changes in financial position (SCFP)** can be developed in a variety of forms, but the basic purpose of them all is to explain the change in an organization's liquidity over some period of time, such as a year. It is a required financial statement in both Canada and the United States.

Definitions of "Funds"

Cash is used here to refer to cash on hand or in the bank. The liquidity of a company is its ability to pay its bills as they come due, usually by payment in cash. One definition of the **funds** used in the SCFP would therefore be cash on hand and in the bank. However, other assets are so readily converted into cash that they are referred to as **cash equivalents**. Examples are short-term notes that trade in active markets (such as government treasury bills) and short-term notes payable of large corporations (such as those of IBM). A second definition of *funds*, therefore, would be cash, plus cash equivalents less current bank loans and short-term notes payable.

Since a current asset is normally one that will be converted into cash within a year, there is an argument that a third definition of funds should be net current assets, often referred to as **working capital**. A banker may well be prepared to make a loan on the basis of working capital other than cash (particularly accounts receivable and inventory). Such a banker would thus be interested in the changes in working capital over the period and the amounts of each. For that reason, the banker would prefer an SCFP drawn up using working capital as the definition of funds.

Thus it is possible to draw up different statements of changes in financial position for the same company using different definitions of funds. In this chapter the term *funds* will refer to whatever measure of liquidity is being used at that time.

In 1985 a revised *Handbook* section [*CICA* 1540] was issued that resulted in some significant changes in the way the statement should be prepared when included in audited financial statements. Although the title *Statement of changes in financial position* is retained, the definition of funds is now specified as cash and other liquid resources termed "cash equivalents" [*CICA* 1540.04]. The revised section also calls for important changes in the recommended format of presentation. Thus, the former widespread use of a definition of funds as "working capital" has been ruled out. It should be noted that cash and cash equivalents includes cash on hand and on deposit plus temporary investments in liquid marketable securities, with short-term borrowing deducted. The components of cash and cash equivalents must be disclosed [*CICA* 1540.06].

The result is an SCFP based on a fairly "hard" measure of liquidity that is more difficult to manipulate than, say, working capital. In the period prior to the adoption of cash and cash equivalents as the definition of funds, there had been growing uneasiness over the use of working capital as the measure of funds. The period was difficult economically, and some felt that on occasion companies were classifying assets as current (and hence treatable as working capital) even though their liquidity was quite doubtful. For example, a faltering company might decide to sell off a division to raise cash and reduce losses. The decision to divest would, technically, convert that division's assets from plant assets to current assets.

While the adoption of cash and cash equivalents as the definition of funds will mean that public financial statements will no longer use working capital, the use of working capital for some analyses will still be useful. Hence the method for converting from a cash-equivalents basis to a working-capital basis can be usefully studied. We will explain the method later. The adoption of cash equivalents was done in a period of economic upheaval, and many professional accountants think that in trying to adopt a "safe" method they threw the baby out with the bath water. The thrust of this text is that there are a variety of acceptable definitions of funds for analytical purposes, but that only one is acceptable for financial statements that must have an unqualified audit opinion.

Throughout most of this chapter *cash* and *cash equivalents* will be used as the measure of funds. These will be generally referred to as *cash equivalents*, but occasionally as *cash* if the context makes the meaning clear.

Basic Methodology

The basic approach of the SCFP can be seen in Table 18-1 below. It shows the balance sheets at the beginning and end of the period in the left-hand and right-hand columns respectively. The balance-sheet items have been grouped so that cash-equivalent assets and liabilities are shown as one net amount. The SCFP is prepared by analysing the changes between the beginning and end of the year, as will be explained later. This example will use cash and cash equivalents as the definition of funds, as required by the *CICA Handbook*. However, if funds are redefined to mean working capital, for instance, the same basic methodology can still be applied.

TABLE 18-1:   ANALYSIS OF CHANGES IN BALANCE-SHEET ITEMS

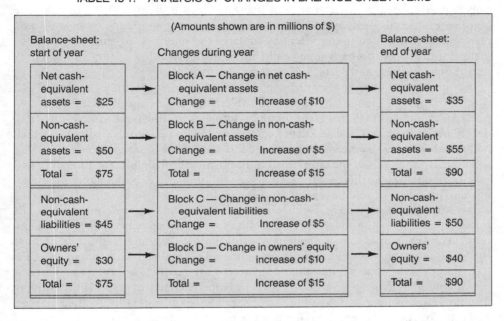

Table 18-1 shows that we can analyse *which* cash-equivalent items changed by examining the changes in cash-equivalent items in Block A.

Furthermore, from the basic accounting equation (Total assets = Total liabilities + Owners' equity) we can derive the following relationship.

Change in Block A = Change in Block C + Change in Block D − Change in Block B

Changes in Block B will arise from (i) changes in non-cash current assets; (ii) purchases of non- current assets; and (iii) the sale of non-current assets and the removal of their historic cost and accumulated depreciation from the accounts. Changes in Block C will arise from (i) changes in current liabilities that are not cash equivalents, such as accounts payable; (ii) the issue and/or redemption of long-term debt; (iii) the amortization of a bond debt premium; and (iv) changes in deferred income taxes. Changes in Block D will arise from (i) the issue and/or redemption of share capital; (ii) payment of dividends; and (iii) net income for the period. Some of these accounting changes arise from a flow of funds, and some do not. The basic methodology for preparing the SCFP requires that the two types of changes be separated.

In analysing the accounts of a real company the large number of accounts to be dealt with would make the analysis confusing if a systematic methodology were not used.

The **worksheet method** and **T-account method**, to be introduced later in this chapter, are simply orderly ways of analysing these changes to produce the SCFP.

The basic methodology for preparing the SCFP, as Table 18-1 shows, is to analyse the changes in the balance sheet between two dates, and to recognize a flow of funds only if it arises because of a change in items in Block B, C, and D. Thus, a change between cash equivalents would not be regarded as a flow of funds, but only as a restructuring within cash equivalents. Similarly the purchase of short-term investments for cash or with a bank loan would not be treated as a flow of funds since it only results in an increase and decrease within cash equivalents.

In contrast, certain changes within non-cash-equivalent assets might be treated as a flow of funds even though no net cash-equivalent assets were involved in the transaction. An example is the repayment of a long-term debt by the issue of new long-term debt. This is treated as if the new debt had been issued for cash-equivalent assets which had then been used to redeem the existing debt.

The reason for this is the emphasis on disclosure of all significant financing and investing activities. In this case the refinancing of long-term debt is a material financing activity, and it should be reported as such on the SCFP.

It is worth noting that an SCFP that uses cash equivalents as the definition of funds is less dependent on how the assets and liabilities are classified between the current and non-current categories than is a statement using working capital. In addition, because the SCFP is an analysis of liquidity, a reader would naturally assume that in an SCFP based on working capital, the valuation placed on the current assets and liabilities is reasonably close to their current market value. Note that if a firm used LIFO in valuing inventory, for instance, it is possible that cost might be substantially less than market, and therefore liquidity might be significantly understated.

Format of the Statement

In the format required by the 1985 *Handbook* revision [1540.18], flows of cash and cash equivalents are reported under three categories: (i) **Operating activities**, (ii) **Financing activities**, and (iii) **Investing activities**.

Operating activities include fund flows generated by the ordinary business activities of the company. Usually net income after tax is used as the starting point for calculating it. Operating activities might include extraordinary items if they are of an operating nature. The purchase and sale of plant assets might also be included if they are part of a regular replacement program.

Financing activities include activities that "result in changes in the size and composition of the capital structure of the enterprise." This category includes the issue and redemption of both long-term debt and shares.

Investing activities include the purchase and sale of long-term assets not included in operating activities as part of a regular replacement program.

Dividends may be included under operating or under financing or they may be presented as a separate category. The format of the SCFP is illustrated by the example below:

STATEMENT OF CHANGES IN FINANCIAL POSITION

	19X1	19X0
Operating activities:		
Income before extraordinary items	$251	$(43)
Add: Charges and credits to operations not		
requiring a current cash payment or receipt	25	25
	276	(18)
Net change in non-cash working capital balances		
related to operations	(21)	(16)
	255	(34)
Financing activities:		
Issue of long-term debt	25	15
Issue of capital	12	10
Redemption of long-term debt	(25)	(26)
Redemption of capital	(5)	
	7	(1)
Investment activities:		
Sale of non-current assets	89	125
Purchase of non-current assets	(211)	(125)
	(122)	0
Dividends	(25)	(25)
Net increase (decrease) in cash equivalents	115	(60)
Cash and cash equivalents, beginning of year	65	125
Cash and cash equivalents, end of year	$180	$ 65

Note that the flow of cash equivalents from operations is shown *net*. The details of cash inflow and outflow due to sales and purchases is not shown. However, cash from operations should be reconciled to the income statement, or the components of cash from operations should be disclosed [*CICA* 1540.12.a]. In addition, certain changes in owners' equity and non-current assets and liabilities are treated *as if* cash had been used as a medium of exchange, even if no flow of cash was involved in the transaction. This is because the *Handbook* emphasizes disclosure of all material transactions of an operations, investing, or financing nature.

Note too that there is an item under *Operating activities* for changes in working capital items other than cash equivalents. This would be for changes in such things as accounts receivable and inventories. If, however, there were a change in such an item that was caused by a financing or investing activity, it should be shown under one of those two headings. The SCFP prepared on a cash-equivalents basis can be converted to one prepared on a working-capital basis by omitting such changes in non-cash working capital balances.

Non-cash transactions such as the following should be reported on the SCFP:

1. retirement of long-term debt by issuing of new long-term debt

2. conversion of long-term bonds or preferred shares into common shares

3. purchase of plant assets by issuing a long-term mortgage to the vendor.

However, if a plant asset is traded in on the purchase of a new one, it is customary to show only the net amount paid for the new asset.

Net Income and Disposal of Assets as a Source of Funds

Two elements in the preparation of this statement are usually confusing and need further explanation. These are (i) funds generated by operating activities and (ii) proceeds on sale of non-current assets.

Income measurement has been purposely designed by accountants to match the revenue and its related expenses to the accounting period in which the revenue is deemed to be recognized regardless of when the item was paid for or when the expenditure was made for the expense items. For the statement of changes in financial position this needs to be modified to exclude those revenues and expenses that do not represent a flow of funds. In order to calculate the funds generated by operations, it is necessary to adjust the reported income for any revenues and expenses which did not give rise to a flow of cash equivalents in the current period.

Sales revenue is usually matched by an inflow of working capital because a sale results either in a cash inflow or the recording of an accounts receivable. If the SCFP is to be prepared on a cash-equivalents basis, the change in accounts receivable needs to be recognized in the computation of funds generated by operations.

Most expenses on the income statement represent an outflow of working capital in the current period, but there are some notable exceptions. Usually these exceptions are non-current assets, acquired prior to the current period, whose costs are being allocated (through depreciation or amortization) to the periods that benefit from their use. These allocated expenses should be excluded in calculating the flow of their use. These allocated expenses should be excluded in calculating the flow of funds. This can be done either by excluding them directly or by starting with the net income reported on the income statement and adding back those items that should have been excluded in the first place. The second method is more commonly used, but it has had the unintended effect of convincing some people that by adding back these expenses an inflow of funds has been created.

For example, suppose the following is the condensed income statement for a city parking garage:

Parking charges (all cash)		$580,000
Salaries	$ 83,000	
Mortgage interest	268,000	
Municipal taxes	68,000	
Depreciation on parking garage	89,000	508,000
		$ 72,000

Assume that all expenses other than depreciation have been paid in cash except the municipal taxes, which are still owing. If funds are defined as cash equivalents, then all the expenses except the depreciation and municipal taxes represent an outflow of funds. The taxes are not an outflow because only a short-term liability has been incurred. No cash payment has been made. The taxes can be either omitted or cancelled later by adding back the change in accounts payable. The **direct** method of presentation is as follows:

Operating activities:		
Revenues		$580,000
Expenses resulting in an outflow of funds:		
Salaries	$83,000	
Mortgage interest	268,000	351,000
Funds generated by operating activities		$229,000

The **indirect method** is as follows:

Operating activities:	
Net income	$ 72,000
Add: Expense which did not result in an outflow of cash	
— depreciation	89,000
— increase in accounts payable	68,000
Funds generated by operating activities	$229,000

The second source of confusion is the treatment of gains or losses on disposal of non-current assets. For the income statement, the correct treatment is to match the net book value of the asset at the time of sale with the proceeds received from the sale, and to show the net amount as a gain or loss on disposal. However, for the SCFP the treatment must be different. The flow of funds arises from the amount actually received as proceeds of the sale, not from the gain or loss on disposal. The net book value of the asset disposed of does not affect the flow of funds in the current period since it is connected with a payment in an earlier period. As a result, we remove from reported income any gain or loss on the sale of non-current assets and report the proceeds as a funds inflow. The accounting relationship is as follows:

Loss or gain on sale = Proceeds − Net book value of assets disposed of

In effect, the loss or gain on sale is removed from the income statement, and the net book value of assets disposed of is removed from the changes in non-current assets. Then, proceeds from sale, the numerical equivalent, is substituted. In addition, the proceeds from sale are usually excluded from operating activities and reported instead under investing activities.

Care must be taken not to treat as a flow of funds the decrease in non-current assets and their related depreciation accounts that arises from writing the assets out of the books at the time of disposal. This will be illustrated below.

Worksheet and T-Account Methods

We explained above how the SCFP is prepared by analyzing the changes between the balance sheets at the beginning and end of the period. However, analyzing and recording the effect of these changes for even the smallest company is likely to be confusing and lead to errors unless a consistent and clear methodology is used. The one to be illustrated here is the **worksheet method**. An alternative, the **T-account method**, will be sketched and illustrated in Appendix 18-1. Both methods have one objective in common — to make sure that all balance-sheet changes are accounted for in the preparation of the SCFP.

First, however, let us briefly review the basic steps in preparing the SCFP that were introduced in Chapter 3.

1. The balance sheets for the start and end of the period are arranged in columnar form beside each other.

2. The changes in all accounts between the start and end of the year are calculated.

3. All changes for funds are identified and segregated into a separate column. Funds are defined here as cash equivalents, but could be defined differently for special-purpose statements.

4. All changes for non-funds are segregated into another column, and the reason for the change is investigated. It would normally be one of the following: (i) purchase or sale of a non-current asset; (ii) retirement or issue of long-term debt or share capital or both; (iii) net income less dividends declared; or (iv) a change in net current assets other than cash equivalents.

5. The statement of changes in financial position is prepared using (4).

Under the worksheet approach, steps (1) to (3) are used to produce the information at the top of the worksheet. Then as step (4) is done, journal entries are used to transfer each of the changes in the non-funds column to its appropriate place in the columnar SCFP, which is set out at the bottom of the worksheet. A highly condensed worksheet format is set out in Table 18-2.

The T-account approach sets up T-accounts for each of the non-fund changes in column D of the worksheet set out in Table 2 18-2. As each adjusting journal entry is made, the amounts are posted to the appropriate T-account or to the draft SCFP,

TABLE 18–2:   CONDENSED WORKSHEET

	Trial balances End of year (A)	Trial balances Start of year (B)	Change in: Funds (C)	Change in: Non-funds (D)	Adjustments (E)	Final balance (F)
Cash equivalents, net	16	1	15			15
Other net current assets	14	14		0	xxx	0
Plant assets	30	20		10	xxx	0
Non-current liabilities	(10)	(15)		5	xxx	0
Owner's equity	(50)	(20)		(30)	xxx	0
	0	0	15	(15)		
Sources of funds						15
Operating						
					xxx	xxx
					xxx	xxx
Financing					xxx	xxx
Investing	Changes in non-cash items from here are analysed under the categories shown to the left and entered here				xxx	xxx
					xxx	xxx
					xxx	xxx
					xxx	xxx
Net change in funds						(15)
Totals					0	0

instead of to column E of the worksheet. When each T- account balances, this is an indication that each change in a non-fund account has been fully accounted for, as does a zero balance for non-fund accounts in column F of the worksheet. These two approaches are conceptually the same.

The basic reasoning behind the adjusting journal entries and the methodologies have now been explained. The next step is to work through an extended example.

Extended Example of SCFP

It is helpful in understanding the statement of change of financial position if one works through a detailed example. We will use the worksheet method here. (In Appendix 18-1 we will work through the same example using the T-account method.) We begin by considering the following scenario about Food Limited, a mythical company based on a real Canadian one.

BASIC INFORMATION

Here is a summary of the available information about Food Limited.

1. The company reported an income of $10,300 for the year 19X1. An examination of its income statement reveals the following items:

	Expense	Income
Depreciation	$10,100	
Amortization of goodwill	1,400	
Profit on sale of plant assets		$2,200
Income of subsidiary recorded using the equity method (no cash dividends were received)		2,000
Amortization of premium on bond payable		300

2. The company paid a cash dividend of $4,000.

3. The tax expense reported on the income statement exceeded the tax payable with respect to 19X1 by $2,900, giving rise to an increase in deferred income tax by that amount.

4. Holders of 200 redeemable convertible preference shares exercised their purchase option and converted their shares with a book value of $10 each into a total of 200 common shares.

5. A bond with a par value of $7,000 was issued at par.

6. During the year, land and buildings were sold for $3,100, of which $1,250 was regarded as payment for the land and $1,850 for the building. The land had originally cost $700 and the building $2,000. There was accumulated depreciation of $1,800 on the building at the time of disposal. The company purchased a new building site for $22,000. It was estimated that the land cost $2,000 and the remaining $20,000 was for the building. These transactions are summarized as follows:

	Balance start of year	Depreciation for year	Book value of disposals	Purchases	Change for year	Balance end of year	Proceeds of disposal	Gain on disposal
Land	$ 22,100		$ (700)	$ 2,000	$ 1,300	$ 23,400	$(1,250)	$ 550
Buildings								
Cost	162,000		(2,000)	20,000	18,000	180,000		
Depreciation	(36,200)	(10,100)	1,800		(8,300)	(44,500)		
Net	125,800	(10,100)	(200)	20,000	9,700	135,500	(1,850)	1,650
Total			$ (900)	$22,000	$11,000	$158,900	$(3,100)	$2,200

7. An analysis of the current assets and liabilities that were not cash equivalents indicates that all the changes that took place in them during the year were due to operations, with one exception. A building had been sold with payments due over the next twelve months, and $700 was unpaid at the end of the year. It had been included in accounts receivable. The accounts receivable at the beginning of the year were entirely due to operating items.

The trial balance at the beginning and end of 19X1 is shown below, together with the changes in the account balances. Credit balances are shown in parentheses. In preparation for the worksheet analysis, the changes have been split into changes in funds (column C) and changes in non-fund accounts (column D). We can see immediately that the cash equivalents have increased by $6,000 for the year, but we need to analyze column D in order to find out the reasons for this change.

FOOD LIMITED
TRIAL BALANCE

| | Year | | Increase or (decrease) in assets | |
	19X1 A	19X0 B	Cash and cash equivalents C	Other assets and liabilities D
Cash and short-term investments	$ 43,000	$ 35,000	$8,000	
Accounts receivable	12,600	7,900		$ 4,700
Inventories	156,800	146,100		10,700
Prepaid expenses	11,500	8,600		2,900
Land	23,400	22,100		1,300
Buildings	180,000	162,000		18,000
Depreciation	(44,500)	(36,200)		(8,300)
Long-term investment	25,000	23,000		2,000
Goodwill	7,300	8,700		(1,400)
Bank loan	(25,000)	(23,000)	(2,000)	
Accounts payable	(120,000)	(100,000)		(20,000)
Bond payable — face amount	(220,000)	(213,000)		(7,000)
— premium	(4,700)	(5,000)		300
Deferred income tax	(19,600)	(16,700)		(2,900)
Redeemable preferred shares	(2,900)	(4,900)		2,000
Common shares	(9,000)	(7,000)		(2,000)
Retained earnings	(13,900)	(7,600)		(6,300)
Total	$ 0	$ 0	$6,000	$(6,000)

ANALYSING THE CHANGES

To prepare the statement of changes in financial position we now analyze the changes in column D. The preparation can be broken down into five distinct steps, as set out below. The general pattern is that each change in a non-fund account represents either (i) a funds inflow or outflow, which needs to be reflected in the SCFP on the worksheet; or (ii) a non-fund entry (such as depreciation), which requires an equivalent adjustment somewhere else on the worksheet (usually in the funds generated from operations).

As the analysis of each item is done, it is used to prepare an adjusting journal entry which accounts for each change in a non- fund item. The items in each journal entry affecting the statement of changes in financial position will be shown in italics. When every item has been accounted for by journal entry, the SCFP on the worksheet will be completed. It can then be drawn up in the more normal format. Let us now work through the five preparatory steps.

1. Calculate the funds generated from operations

We are told in the notes that the net income for 19X1 was $10,300 and that the company paid $4,000 in dividends. These two items account for the net increase of $6,300 in retained earnings (see column D above).

It has already been explained why expenses arising from the allocation of expenditures of earlier periods means that the net income for the current period rarely measures the net funds flow for the period. We have been given these non-funds expenditures in the introductory notes, and they should be added back to the net income to calculate the total amount of funds inflow arising from operations. This will be done as we analyze each of the non-fund changes. The adjusting journal entry for the worksheet is as follows:

```
Entry (a)
Net income                                          10,300
        Operating: net income                                 10,300
To record funds generated from operations: all
   expense and income items that did not arise
   from a flow of funds in this period will be
   added back to net income when analysing the
   related non-fund change.
```

2. Analyse each non-cash asset

The net change in each non-cash asset is also shown on the worksheet. This net change in a non-cash asset is often the result of a mixture of (i) sales or other disposals of assets; (ii) purchases of new assets; (iii) amortization and/or depreciation of part of the expenditure of an earlier period against income of the current period; and (iv) changes in current assets and/or liabilities other than cash or cash equivalents. These all have different effects on funds flow and need to be shown to the reader separately.

First, let us consider the land increase of $1,300, from column D of the Trial Balance. From the additional information given at the beginning of the example, we can analyse this figure as follows:

Proceeds on disposal of land on hand	$(1,250)	(b)
Gain on disposal	550	(c)
Net	(700)	
Purchases of additional land	2,000	(a)
Net change in book value	$1,300	(d)

Items (a) and (b) will appear on the statement of changes in financial position. Item (c) affects net income, but does not create a flow of funds and needs to be deducted from net income in order to arrive at the funds provided by operations. Item (d) offsets the difference in the balance for land between balance-sheet dates. Thus, the adjusting journal entry is as follows:

Entry (b)		
Investing: purchase of land	2,000	
Operating: gain on disposal	550	
Investing: proceeds of disposal of land		1,250
Land		1,300
To record funds flow arising from sale of land and remove gain on disposal from operating income.		

Second, let us turn to the buildings increase of $18,000 and the depreciation increase of $8,300, from column D of the Trial Balance. We can analyse these figures as we did the land increase:

Proceeds of sale	$(1,850)	(b)
Gain on disposal	1,650	(c)
Net	(200)	
Depreciation charged to current period	(10,100)	(d)
Purchases	20,000	(a)
Net change in plant assets and depreciation	$ 9,700	
Being:		
Change in plant assets	$18,000	
Change in accumulated depreciation	(8,300)	
	$ 9,700	

Once again, items (a) and (b) will appear on the SCFP as investing activities, whereas items (c) and (d) will be found in the operating activities section of the statement showing funds arising from operations. This can be summarized in a journal entry as follows:

Entry (c)		
Investing: purchase of plant assets	20,000	
Operating: eliminate gain on disposal	1,650	
Buildings: depreciation	8,300	
Investing: proceeds of sale of building		1,850
Operating: add back depreciation		10,100
Buildings: asset		18,000
To record funds-flow effects of purchase and sale of buildings as well as add back the non-funds entries.		

Third, let us consider the decrease of $2,000 in long-term investment, from column D of the Trial Balance. We are told that the company, using the equity method, had entered $2,000 income from a subsidiary in its books, although it had not received any cash dividends. This means that the net income includes $2,000 from this source that does not represent an inflow of funds. Therefore, it should be removed, and the following entry should be made:

Entry (d)
Operating: remove income of subsidiary   2,000
           Long-term investment   2,000
To remove income recorded under the equity
  method that does not represent a flow of
  funds.

Next, let us analyse the goodwill decrease of $1,400, from column D of the Trial Balance. We are told that $1,400 of goodwill has been amortized as a charge against income in the current period. Once again, this does not represent a flow of funds and should be removed, as follows:

Entry (e)
Goodwill   1,400
          Operating: add back goodwill amortization   1,400
To reverse entry for goodwill — does not involve
  a flow of funds.

Finally, let us analyse the increases in accounts receivable ($4,700), in inventories ($10,700), and in prepaid expenses ($2,900), all from column D of the Trial Balance. These are changes in current assets other than cash and cash equivalents. The usual practice is to show only the net change in these items, provided the changes arose through the normal operations of the company. One would normally expect that most of the changes in these assets would be attributed to the operating segment of the statement. But the opening and closing balance should be reviewed to detect any changes that were due to financing or investing activities. In our example a change of $700 in accounts receivable is caused by the sale of plant assets, and this would be shown separately. The journal entry should be as follows:

Entry (f)
Operating: increase in non-cash current assets   17,600
Investing: increase in non-cash current assets   700
          Accounts receivable   4,700
          Inventories   10,700
          Prepaid expenses   2,900
To record net change in non-cash current
  assets.

3. Analyse liabilities that are not cash equivalents

First, let us analyse the increase of $7,000 in the face amount of bonds payable, from column D of the Trial Balance. The supplementary notes supplied above indicate that the company issued bonds at par. The journal entry should therefore be as follows:

Entry (g)
Bonds payable   7,000
       Financing: issue of bond payable   7,000
To record funds inflow from bond issue.

Second, let us consider the decrease of $300 in the premium of bonds payable, from column D of the Trial Balance. The premium on bonds payable of $300 has been amortized during the year. This does not involve an inflow of funds, and the funds derived from operations should be reduced accordingly. The following journal entry should be made:

Entry (h)
Operating: remove bond premium amortization   300
       Bond payable — premium   300
To eliminate entry for bond premium
   amortization.

Third, let us turn to the increase of $2,900 in deferred income taxes, from column D of the Trial Balance. The change in deferred income taxes arises from the difference between the tax expense calculated as the appropriate amount to match to the period and the actual amount of the payment required by Revenue Canada and the provincial equivalent. This does not involve a flow of funds, and net income should be increased accordingly through the following entry.

Entry (i)
Deferred income tax   2,900
       Operating: add back deferred income tax   2,900
To eliminate entry for deferred income tax.

Finally, let us analyse the increase of $20,000 in accounts payable, from column D of the Trial Balance. Current liabilities that are not cash equivalents are treated similarly to the comparable assets. They are analysed to see what changes are operating, financing, or investing. The net change is then shown as an item on the statement. In this case all the change is due to operating. The journal entry is as follows:

Entry (j)
Accounts payable   20,000
       Operating: change in non-cash current liabilities   20,000
To transfer change in non-cash current liabilities
   to operating.

In our example the change in accounts payable was due entirely to operations. In other cases it is quite possible that a major change in accounts payable might arise from the purchase of a plant asset (e.g., a payment due on a building under construction). Under such circumstances change in accounts payable due to this purchase would be shown under investing activities.

4. Analyse the changes in owners' equity

First, let us consider the decrease of $2,000 in redeemable preferred shares and the increase of $2,000 in common shares, from column D of the Trial Balance. The supplementary information indicates that $2,000 in redeemable preference shares were exchanged for the equivalent in common stock. Although no cash probably changed hands, it is the purpose of the statement of changes in financial position to account for all major changes in the financial position of the company. Therefore "non-cash" transactions of this type are shown on the statement as offsetting inflows and outflows. The journal entry is as follows:

Entry (k)		
Financing: conversion of preference shares	2,000	
Common share capital	2,000	
Preferred share capital		2,000
Financing: issue of common shares		2,000
To record conversion of preference shares to		
common shares. This is shown as a source		
and use of funds even though no actual flow		
of funds took place.		

Finally, let us analyse the increase of $6,300 in retained earnings, from column D of the Trial Balance. The figure can be broken down as follows:

Net income	$10,300
Dividends paid — to appear as a funds outflow on the statement	4,000
Net change	$ 6,300

The net income has already been reflected in journal entry (a) above. Therefore the dividends should be accounted for by means of the following journal entry:

Entry (l)		
Financing: dividend	4,000	
Retained earnings		4,000
To record dividend as a use of funds.		

Posting the Entries to the SCFP Worksheet

Now that the changes in the non-current items have been analyzed and the journal entries prepared, the final step is to post the entries to the worksheet. This will be shown below starting at column C from Table 18-2. Note that the letters identifying the journal entries are given here as well.

	Increase or (Decrease)				
	Cash and cash equivalents C	Other assets and liabilities D	Journal entry	Adjustments E	Total
Cash and short-term investments	$ 8,000				
Accounts receivable		$ 4,700	f	$ (4,700)	
Inventories		10,700	f	(10,700)	
Prepaid expenses		2,900	f	(2,900)	
Land		1,300	b	(1,300)	
Buildings		18,000	c	(18,000)	
Depreciation		(8,300)	c	8,300	
Long-term investments		2,000	d	(2,000)	
Goodwill		(1,400)	e	1,400	
Bank loan	(2,000)	0			
Accounts payable		(20,000)	j	20,000	
Bonds payable — face amount		(7,000)	g	7,000	
— premium		300	h	(300)	
Deferred income tax		(2,900)	i	2,900	
Redeemable preferred shares		2,000	k	(2,000)	
Common shares		(2,000)	k	2,000	
Retained earnings		(6,300)	a	10,300	
			l	(4,000)	
	$ 6,000	$ (6,000)		$ 6,000	0
Operating activities					
Net income per income statement			a	$(10,300)	$(10,300)
Depreciation			c	(10,100)	(10,100)
Amortization of goodwill			e	(1,400)	(1,400)
Deferred income tax increase			i	(2,900)	(2,900)
Gain on disposal of land			b	550	550
Gain on disposal of building			c	1,650	1,650
Income arising from use of equity method			d	2,000	2,000
Amortization of bond premium			h	300	300
Net increase in non-cash current assets			f	17,600	17,600
Net increase in non-cash current liabilities			j	(20,000)	(20,000)
Financing activities					
Proceeds of bond issue			g	(7,000)	(7,000)
Issue of common stock			k	(2,000)	(2,000)
Dividends			l	4,000	4,000
Redemption of preferred shares			k	2,000	2,000
Investing activities					
Purchase of land			b	2,000	2,000
Purchase of building			c	20,000	20,000
Sale of building			c	(1,850)	(1,850)
Sale of land			b	(1,250)	(1,250)
Increase in accounts receivable			f	700	700
				(6,000)	(6,000)
Total change in cash and cash equivalents				$ 0	$ (6,000)

PREPARING THE STATEMENT

The worksheet provides all the information needed to prepare the SCFP. We can now proceed using the proposed format, as follows:

FOOD LIMITED
CASH FLOW INFORMATION
For the year ending 31 December 19X1

Operating activities		
Net income per income statement		$10,300
Add (subtract) items that did not involve a cash		
inflow or outflow		
Depreciation	$10,100	
Amortization of goodwill	1,400	
Deferred income tax increase	2,900	
Gain on disposal of land	(550)	
Gain on disposal of building	(1,650)	
Income arising from use of equity method	(2,000)	
Amortization of bond premium	(300)	
Change in current assets other than cash	(17,600)	
Change in accounts payable	20,000	12,300
Cash and cash equivalents from operations		22,600
Financing activities		
Proceeds of bond issue	7,000	
Issue of common stock	2,000	
Redemption of preferred shares	(2,000)	
Dividends	(4,000)	3,000
Investing activities		
Sale of building	1,850	
Sale of land: cash receipts to date	550	
Purchase of land	(2,000)	
Purchase of building	(20,000)	(19,600)
Net increase in cash		6,000
Balance, start of year		12,000
Balance, end of year		$18,000
Changes in cash components		
Cash		$ 8,000
Bank loan (increase)		(2,000)
Net		$ 6,000

Disclosure Requirements

The *CICA Handbook* [1540] sets out the following requirements:

1. The statement of changes in financial position must use cash and cash equivalents as *funds* [*CICA* 1540.04]. The use of working capital as funds is no longer acceptable.

2. The components of cash and cash equivalents should be disclosed [*CICA* 1540.06]. They would normally include cash, net of short-term borrowings, and temporary investments. The *Handbook* also notes that the components "may, in some cases, include certain other elements of working capital when they are equivalent to cash."

3. The SCFP should disclose at least the following items:
   (i) cash flows from operations, with a reconciliation to the income statement, or disclosure of the cash components
   (ii) cash flows from extraordinary items
   (iii) outlays for acquisition and proceeds on disposal of assets by major category (i.e., operating, financing, and investing activities) if not included in (i) and (ii) above
   (iv) the issue, assumption, redemption, and repayment of debt not included in (i) and (ii) above
   (v) the issue, redemption, and acquisition of share capital
   (vi) payment of dividends, with those paid by subsidiaries to minority interests identified separately [*CICA* 1540.12].

4. The items listed in (3) above should normally be classified as operating, investing, and financing activities [*CICA* 1540.18]. Item (i) is classed as operating, as is (ii) when it relates to operations. Item (iii) is normally classed as investing, although regular replacement of plant assets may be classed as operating. Items (iv) and (v) are classed as financing. The treatment of item (vi), dividends, is left vague; one can choose to class it as operating, as financing, or as a separate category altogether [*CICA* 1540.17].

Skinner [1987] points out that the shift from a statement whose categories are the sources and uses of funds to a statement that has the three-part division of operating, financing, and investing activities is a potential source of non-comparability between statements. It is relatively easy to decide whether an item is a "source" or "use" of funds, but it is more difficult to decide whether it should be shown as operating, financing, or investing. For example, the purchase of a fixed asset required for the company's normal business activities could be considered as similar in nature to the purchase of inventory; hence it could be classed as an operating activity, rather than an investing activity. Similarly, strictly speaking the investment income and interest expense on the income statement should probably be considered as financing activities, although the *Handbook* doesn't appear to require this.

Examples from Published Reports

Thomson Newspapers Limited

Excerpts from the financial statements of Thomson Newspapers have been given above in Chapters 5 and 13.

	1986	1985
	(in thousands of $)	
Cash provided by (used in) operating activities		
Income before extraordinary items	$200,695	$175,617
Charges to operations not requiring a current cash payment		
Depreciation	27,761	26,120
Deferred income taxes	27,664	34,203
Amortization of goodwill	3,187	3,037
Equity in pre-tax (income) loss of Augusta Newspaper Company	(40)	5,455
Other (net)	711	(459)
	259,978	243,973
Net change in non-cash working capital balances related to operations	(15,368)	18,994
	244,610	262,967
Cash provided by (used in) investment activities		
Acquisition of subsidiary companies less cash of $3,130,000	(80,325)	(98,117)
Purchase of property, plant and equipment	(25,679)	(26,913)
Investment in Augusta Newsprint Company	—	(12,192)
Proceeds on disposal of investments and property, plant and equipment	5,511	19,136
	(100,493)	(118,086)
Cash provided by (used in) financing activities		
Dividends	(80,016)	(68,643)
Reduction in long-term debt	(147,076)	(33,165)
Preference shares purchased for cancellation	(213)	(565)
Extraordinary items	20,577	—
Proceeds from long-term debt	11,044	52,812
Other (net)	4,599	(471)
	(191,085)	(50,032)
Net increase (decrease) in cash during year	(46,968)	94,849
Cash position at beginning of year	114,357	19,508
Cash position at end of year	$ 67,389	$114,357

Observe the significant cash inflow generated by operations. The company was able to make a significant reduction in its debt and make additional acquisitions; and yet it was still able to have a significant positive cash position at the end of the year.

Summary

The statement of changes in financial position is one of the four financial statements that are required of companies under GAAP. Its objective is to provide information about how the activities of the enterprise have been financed and how its financial resources have been used during the period covered by the statement. The statement shows the changes in the *funds* of the enterprise over the period. In the past, *funds* usually meant *working capital*, but now funds must mean *cash and cash equivalents*. The SCFP is prepared by (i) calculating the changes in all balance sheet accounts over the period, (ii) adjusting for changes that did not incur a flow of funds, and (iii) identifying the activities that account for the flow of funds in the remaining balances.

QUESTIONS

Q18-1. Review and be sure you understand the following terms:

  a. working capital

  b. funds

  c. cash

  d. cash equivalents

  e. worksheet method *versus* T-account method

  f. operating activities

  g. financing activities

  h. investing activities

  i. direct *versus* indirect presentation of funds from operating activities

Q18-2. Describe the similarities and differences between the worksheet and T-account approaches to preparing the SCFP. (See Appendix 18-1 for details on the T-account approach.)

Q18-3. A worksheet has been used to prepare financial statements in such diverse situations as (i) preparing a balance sheet and income statement from a trial balance, (ii) preparing consolidated financial statements, and (iii) preparing the statement of changes in financial position. Do all worksheets start from a trial balance? What are the similarities and differences in objectives of the adjusting journal entries?

Q18-4. Explain whether each of the following would be (i) added to net income, (ii) deducted from it, or (iii) left out for the purpose of calculating "net income provided from operating activities." In each case explain why the item is included as an adjustment and whether there is any related item appearing elsewhere on the SCFP.

  a. loss on sale of truck

  b. amortization of patent

  c. profit on sale of land

d. extraordinary write-down of inventory

e. loss on redemption of bonds

f. amortization of bond premium

g. $35,000 of income from an associated company (using equity method) — actual dividend was $25,000

h. tax recovery with respect to a prior year

Q18-5. Shortly before the *CICA* revision a major firm of chartered accountants wrote the following: "Traditionally, the statement of changes in financial position has been prepared in terms of working capital. However, in recent years the usefulness of the working capital format has been challenged as more enterprises reporting positive working capital funds flow experience severe liquidity problems." Explain how it could happen that a firm could show an inflow of net working capital and yet experience severe liquidity problems. How would you test for this possibility if you were analysing a firm's financial statements in which working capital use was used as the definition of funds.

Q18-6. Publicly listed companies have been required to provide balance sheets and income statements in most countries for over a century. Yet it is only fairly recently we have seen a widespread demand that the statement of changes in financial position should be a required part of the financial statements provided to shareholders. Set out below are some possible reasons. Discuss each and evaluate its relative importance. Can you think of other reasons?

a. more sophisticated readers of financial statements

b. more arbitrary allocation of accounting costs

c. insolvency is a bigger concern

d. trend to greater disclosure of financial results

e. less confidence in accuracy of income measurement

f. greater emphasis on cash flow from finance

Q18-7. State whether each of the following independent circumstances affects the flow of (i) cash and (ii) net working capital.

a. A customer mails in payment of $1,250 on his accounts receivable.

b. Convertible bonds payable totalling $15,000 are converted into common shares in accordance with their conversion privilege.

c. Peter Limited has $100,000 in bonds outstanding. Each year, starting in 19X2, $10,000 of the total outstanding must be repaid. On the balance sheet for 19X1, $90,000 of the bonds are shown as a long-term liability, but the remaining $10,000 are shifted up to current liabilities because they are due for payment within one year.

d. Gina Corporation has revised its depreciation policy since a review of it has convinced management that it has been writing off excessive amounts. As a result of the reduced depreciation charges, the net income for this year will be $18,000 higher than it would have been under the old policy.

e. Assunta Limited had sold airtight stoves with a two-year warranty and provided $30 per stove at the time of sale as the estimated cost of providing this warranty service. At the end of 19X0 it had an estimated liability for warranties of $68,000. However, experience showed that the stoves were so reliable that only $10 per stove was needed for estimated warranty costs. As a result, in 19X1 it was able to make a one-time write-down of its estimated liability for warranties of $23,000.

Q18-8. A widely used investment advisory service, "The Value Line Investment Survey," plays down the importance of income measurement and instead computes what it terms the "cash flow," which is the net income with depreciation and amortization added back. Value Line calculates the "cash flow per share" and compares it to the price of the company's stock over a time period. Value Line argues that "this approach makes for a truer appraisal of the direction and level of cash income for a period of years." Evaluate Value Line's approach. Do you agree with their argument?

Q18-9. State in each of the situations below whether you would prepare to have a statement of changes in cash or the equivalent statement of changes in working capital. (Disregard here the *CICA Handbook* requirements for audited statements.) Explain your reasoning.

   a. You are the owner of a thriving new firm of consultants. Your services are much sought after by various levels of government. These clients are regarded as very good credit risks, although they tend to take about three months to pay a bill once it is submitted. Your bank manager is uneasy at being asked to lend the money you need to finance your staff wages between the time the work is done and when it is paid for.

   b. You plan to purchase a franchise for painting houses during the summer. The terms of the franchise require you to pay an initial fee of $1,000 and 5% of the gross billings. You plan to hire college students on a combined salary/incentive basis, and payments will be made at the end of each month. A local paint store will give you thirty days' credit at no interest charge and 24% for accounts unpaid after thirty days. You think you have enough money to get started, but you want to work out a budget to make sure you can get through the season. Would it be a cash or working capital budget?

   c. Pan American World Airways has had some uneasy creditors. Would it have preferred to present a projected-cash forecast or a working-capital forecast to its creditor banks?

Q18-10. "Unlike an income statement, an analysis of changes of 'funds' can be presented in such a way that its content is independent of methods of cost allocation." Do you agree? Discuss.

Q18-11. In this chapter we stated that for published financial statements *funds* must consist of cash and cash equivalents, not working capital. What do you think are the relative merits of using working capital instead of cash equivalents? Using a neighborhood lumberyard as an example, indicate under what conditions you would prefer to have funds defined as (i) working capital (ii) cash and cash equivalents.

Q18-12. Note that from a methodological point of view the SCFP is prepared by defining some group of assets and/or liabilities as the items of interest to be the funds and then using the change in all other balance-sheet items to explain the changes in these funds. Could the same methodology usefully be applied to explain the changes in the following balance-sheet items:

   a. owners' equity

   b. long-term debt

   c. "quick" current assets (cash and accounts receivable)

   d. retained earnings

Q18-13. "An SCFP that is based on current assets is a prisoner of the methods used to value the current assets. This is potentially very troublesome with respect to inventory." Evaluate this statement.

Q18-14. As usually presented, the SCFP shows information about the issue and redemption of long-term debt and the purchase and sale of plant assets, even when the transactions do not involve the payment or receipt of funds. At the same time, the statement does not show one of the major sources of funds flow, namely, the sale of the company's product and the payment of staff and suppliers. Can you justify this uneven disclosure pattern? Explain.

Q18-15. Readers of a business publication were advised that "if the cash-flow trend goes south when earnings are going north, watch out. Something is wrong." This implies that cash flow is a better indicator of the company's health than earnings. Explain under what circumstances this might be (i) true (ii) untrue.

Q18-16. An executive in the beer industry was quoted as saying that his company was interested in acquiring companies not involved with beer because the beer market was mature and "the heavy capital investment in brewing means a lot of depreciation expense, hence a lovely cash inflow." Is his reasoning about the source of cash inflow correct? Explain.

Q18-17. *Forbes* magazine related that one of the favourite stories of those who believe in the importance of watching cash flow instead of reported income is "of a giant retailer whose cash flow turned negative even as earnings soared ever higher. Most investors ignored the cash flow, to their later dismay." The company referred to was W.T. Grant, a major U.S. retailer, similar to Woolco or K-Mart, that went bankrupt in the mid-1960s. Is it possible for cash flow to be negative while earnings soar? Explain. If you were the manager of Grant's and thought there might be an error in the accounting system that produced such results, where would you first look for errors? Explain.

Q18-18. A security analyst made a name for himself through his ability to identify companies that were likely to suffer a bad enough loss of liquidity to force them to apply to the courts for protection from creditors. He did it mainly by converting the SCFP from a working-capital basis to a cash basis. A critic of this approach said "Cash flow can, of course, be hyped just like earnings." What are some of the ways in which cash flow can be "hyped"?

Q18-19. In 19X0 Stirling Ltd. had a $10 million issue of serial bonds outstanding. The first series of these bonds in the amount of $1 million was to mature in August 19X1. The controller prepared the statement of changes in financial position for the 19X0 fiscal year on a working-capital basis. In her preparations, the controller showed a use of working capital of $1 million relating to these bonds. Was this treatment correct? Explain fully. Would your answer have been different if the statement had been prepared on a cash-equivalents basis? Explain.

(CMA adapted)

Q18-20. Business transactions may be classified into one of the following three categories:
  (i) transactions that affect only current asset or current liability accounts
  (ii) transactions that affect both current and non-current accounts
  (iii) transactions that affect only non-current accounts.
Explain the effect of each category on working capital when the statement of changes in financial position is prepared using the working-capital definition of *funds*.

Q18-21. How do changes in the allowance for doubtful accounts affect the statement of changes in financial position prepared on a working-capital basis? Explain.

Q18-22. How would a stock dividend be reported, if at all, on the statement of changes in financial position? Explain.

Q18-23. It has been suggested that there could be a variety of statements focusing on asset flows in addition to the statement of changes in financial position (based on either cash and cash equivalents or working capital). What use, if any, might be found in a statement that concentrates on the flow of other short-term assets such as accounts receivable? inventory? Discuss.

Q18-24. One of the reasons given for the rise in popularity of the statement of changes in financial position is that people mistrust accrual accounting because "it is too flexible in its assumptions and requires too much judgement in its application to be reliable." Do you think this is a fair appraisal of accrual accounting? Discuss.

Q18-25. To what extent is a statement of changes in financial position simply recombining information already available in the other financial statements, such as the balance sheet and income statement? What new information does it usually provide?

Q18-26. It has been said that the SCFP avoids the allocation problems inherent in the income statement but "only at the expense of creating another problem — that of presenting information whose usefulness is limited because its proper interpretation is not clear." What is meant by this? Do you agree? Discuss.

Q18-27. "A *cash flow* within the context of the statement of changes in financial position means something different from the *flow of cash*." What does this mean? Do you agree? Explain.

EXERCISES

E18-1. A company was considering preparing a statement of changes in financial position under one of the following definitions of "funds": (i) net current assets; (ii) cash and short-term investments less bank debt; (iii) net current assets less inventory. In each of the unrelated cases below, explain whether the event outlined would affect funds in each of the three cases above, and whether it would be an increase or a decrease.

   a. A review of the company's finished goods inventory indicates that a major write-down of $400,000 is required because of technological obsolescence.

   b. Short-term investments have declined in market value by $150,000.

   c. Land and a building were purchased for $2,300,000 and then sold immediately on a long-term capital leaseback.

   d. Accounts receivable were written down by $83,000 because of the bankruptcy of a major customer. This had not been previously provided for through the allowance for doubtful accounts.

E18-2. Show the adjusting journal entry, if any, that would be required in the worksheet for the statement of changes in financial position for each of the following unrelated events. Funds are defined here as cash and cash equivalents.

   a. A truck with a historic cost of $22,000 and accumulated depreciation of $14,000 was sold for $10,000 cash.

   b. Bonds with a face value of $25,000 were redeemed at a cost of $22,000. They had originally been sold at par.

   c. A patent was purchased for $350,000 two years ago. It is now being depreciated on a straight-line basis at the rate of 20% per year.

    d. A dividend of $90,000 was paid in cash.

    e. A dividend of $90,000 was paid by transferring to the shareholders the shares of a subsidiary company. Both the approximate market value and the historic cost of the shares transferred was $90,000 as of the date the dividend was declared.

    f. Depreciation charges for the year were $123,000.

    g. The company's income tax provision (expense) for the year was $890,000, but the taxes actually payable with respect to that year were $700,000. The difference was deferred income tax.

E18-3. Show the journal entry, if any, that would be required in the worksheet for the SCFP for each of the following unrelated cases of disposal of old assets and acquisition of new ones:

	Payment	Receipt	Old asset: historic cost	Net book value	Market value	New asset: market value
a.	$300		$ 900	$600	$350	$ 650
b.	250		850	500	800	1,050
c.		$600	1,020	720	800	200
d.	850		800	620	400	1,250
e.		350	950	0	400	50
f.	430		450	150	0	430

E18-4. During the past fiscal year Petra Ltd. experienced the following events. In each case explain whether the event (i) represents an inflow of working capital, (ii) represents an outflow of working capital, or (iii) has no overall effect on working capital.

    a. In return for allowing another company the use of a small warehouse for two years, Petra got the free use of a delivery truck.

    b. Petra purchased an existing business by an outright purchase of the assets and the right to do business under the original company's name. The value of the tangible assets was $350,000; but $500,000 was paid to get the business outright, including the name. Petra decided to treat the purchase difference of $150,000 as goodwill and to expense it immediately. It was paid for in cash.

    c. Petra acquired a building under a long-term capital lease.

E18-5. For each of the transactions below, indicate the item(s) on the SCFP that would be affected under each of the following assumptions: (i) funds are defined as net working capital; (ii) funds are defined as cash and short-term investments. Ignore income-tax effects.

    a. Issue of common shares for plant assets.

    b. Extraordinary write-off of inventory on instructions of board of directors.

    c. Revision upwards of estimate for short-term liability warranty.

    d. Change of policy to cost inventory at LIFO instead of FIFO. This resulted in reduction of stated value of inventory on balance sheet.

    e. Abandonment of plans to expand geographically as a result of heavy losses. Land and buildings in the area to be abandoned were put up for sale and classified as current assets.

    f. Land purchased for new plant site. The vendor agreed to help finance the purchase by accepting a mortgage as part payment. As a result the company paid $80,000 cash and gave a mortgage for the difference, $300,000.

g. Income of $35,000 recognized from an unconsolidated associated company that was accounted for using the equity method. No dividends were paid in the year.

h. Shipment of parts costing $25,000 received from a supplier on credit.

E18-6. Would each of the following events affect a statement of changes in financial position based on funds equal to cash and equivalents? Would it increase or decrease net funds? Explain.

a. Borrowing money from the bank on a short-term loan.

b. Reclassifying $100,000 of total long-term debt of $800,000 as short term.

c. Buying a delivery truck by trading another piece of equipment owned by the firm.

d. Buying a delivery truck for cash.

e. Buying a delivery truck by giving a note payable due in two years.

f. Buying a delivery truck by issuing common shares.

g. Paying a supplier's account by cheque.

h. Writing off obsolete inventory.

i. Declaring a dividend payable in shares of another company held as a long-term investment.

E18-7. A company had transactions recorded in the journal entries below. What effect would each have on the change of funds reported on the SCFP under each of the following assumptions: (i) funds are defined as working capital; (ii) funds are defined as cash and equivalents.

a. Asset (old) — accumulated depreciation	25,000.00	
Asset (new) — historic cost	33,500.00	
Asset (old) — historic cost		35,000.00
Accounts payable		15,000.00
Bank		8,500.00

To record disposal of old asset and acquisition of new one.

b. Assets for immediate disposal	1.00	
Accumulated depreciation — plant asset	8,339.00	
Plant asset (at cost)		8,340.00

To record decision to dispose of equipment by sale.

c. Bank	5,000.00	
Note receivable	35,000.00	
Asset for immediate disposal		1.00
Gain on disposal		34,999.00

To record disposal of asset above.

d. Work-in-process inventory	35,670.00	
Income from construction in progress		35,670.00

To record estimated income for period under the percentage-of-completion method.

e. Tax provision (expense)	34,680.00	
Deferred income tax — long term		25,470.00
Taxes payable		9,210.00

To record tax provision and tax liability under the deferred income tax method.

E18-8. A young lawyer financed part of the start-up of her practice by a loan from her bank. To convince her bank that she was a good long-term credit risk, she presented a statement of changes in financial position to them at the end of the year that showed that she had been able to increase her working capital. She also submitted an income statement that showed she was starting to earn a reasonable net professional income. At the same time she wanted to keep her bank loan within reasonable limits. For each of the following events indicate: (i) if it would increase or decrease her cash position (net of the bank loan); (ii) if it would affect her reported income during the current period; and (iii) if it would increase or decrease her net working capital. Give your reasons.

a. January: She did some professional work for a client. She has not yet billed the client, but believes that the work she has done to date can be billed for $350.00.

b. February: She invoices the client for $350.00 and receives payment a week later.

c. March: The volume of the work justifies the purchase of a small word processor to help with routine typing. The cost is $5,000: $500 is due on delivery with the balance due in equal installments over the next eighteen months.

d. April: One of the accounts billed in February for $1,300 has not been paid, and it seems likely that only $500 of it will ever be collected. It is not written down to $500, but is definitely a factor in assessing the adequacy of the provision for doubtful accounts.

e. July: A client who came in for help in January retains the lawyer on a retainer basis. The agreement is that $3,000 will be paid immediately, and this will go toward the first $3,000 of legal work done in the next twelve months. By the end of the fiscal year six months later, it is estimated that only $1,200 of legal work has been done to date.

f. At the end of the fiscal year it is estimated that the inventory of stationery and legal forms is $800. This had been charged to expense as purchased.

E18-9. A friend who operates a small woodworking shop that makes special-purpose desks for microcomputers tells you that he believes his working capital has increased by $30,000 for the year. He asks you to check this for him. In discussion and examination of his records you discover the following:

   (i) He purchased a power saw for $500 in the last month of the year, intending to pay for it the following month. No entry has yet been made in his accounts.

  (ii) A customer gave him a deposit of $100 on a job. He forgot to deposit the funds and gave them to his wife to buy groceries instead.

 (iii) In counting the inventory some semi-finished work with a material content of $890 and $350 of his labour was overlooked.

 (iv) A customer payment of $870 in December was mislaid and not deposited into the bank or credited to the customer's account until after the end of the fiscal year.

Required: Show the changes, if any, you would make to your friend's estimated increase in working capital of $30,000.

E18-10. The net income for Melville Ltd. in the year just past was $2,100,000. The following information is taken from the company's records relating to the same year:

Capital expenditures during the year	$6,200,000
Depreciation expense	2,400,000
Decrease in non-current deferred tax liability	200,000
Dividends declared on common shares	700,000
Patent amortization expense	75,000
Increase in non-cash current liabilities	35,000
Decrease in non-cash current assets	50,000

Required: Calculate the cash equivalents provided by operations. Show all your calculations.

(CMA adapted)

E18-11. The following items relate to the statement of changes in financial position of Chantry Limited for the year ended 31 December 19X0.

(i) Declared a stock dividend of 150 shares of $5 market-value common to the holders of common shares.

(ii) Purchased $25,000 worth of machinery by paying $5,000 in cash and signing a note for the balance. Repayment terms are $5,000 on 31 December of each year.

(iii) Set up an appropriation of retained earnings for expansion in the amount of $15,000.

(iv) Wrote off an accounts receivable in the amount of $375 after the customer declared bankruptcy.

(v) Amortized bond premium of $175 and recorded patent amortization of $340.

(vi) Reported an extraordinary gain of $12,000 (net of $4,000 tax) on the sale of investments. The book value of the investments was $22,000.

Required: Indicate how each item should be shown on the statement of changes of financial position if funds are defined as cash and cash equivalents. If an item would not appear on the statement, explain why.

(CMA adapted)

E18-12. Frankford Limited showed net income of $250,000 for the year ended 31 December 19X7. The following items relate to the company's activities during the year:

(i) Sales included a $16,000 transaction for which a five-year 16% note was received. Interest is payable annually.

(ii) Depreciation expense amounted to $40,000.

(iii) A loss of $7,000 on the sale of machinery was incurred. Payment was $3,000 cash and a promissory note for $8,000 due on 1 December. The company's year end was 31 December.

(iv) Premium on bonds payable was amortized in the amount of $1,500.

(v) The deferred tax credit increased by $23,000.

(vi) Fixed assets in the amount of $65,000 were purchased for cash during the year.

(vii) Non-cash current assets increased by $15,000, and non-cash current liabilities increased by $23,000.

Required: Calculate the amount of cash and equivalents provided by operations. Show all your calculations.

(CMA adapted)

E18-13. Here are some criticisms directed against the format of the SCFP prepared according to GAAP:

(i) The purchase of a plant asset to carry on the business is no different from the purchase of inventory to do the same thing. Yet one is classed as an investment, and the other is classed as an operating item.

(ii) Income from investments should be a financing item, not an operating item. Similarly, interest expense should be an investment item, not an operating item.

(iii) Short-term borrowings are often used to finance inventory or accounts receivable or both. However, they are treated as a cash equivalent. Thus a company that borrows to finance accounts receivable or inventory would appear to be suffering a negative cash flow. This would look the same if they were borrowing to do something that did not involve the acquisition of liquid assets, such as borrowing to pay a dividend.

(iv) An increase in accounts payable is treated as an outflow of operating funds. However, payables may have increased as the result of acquiring a plant asset. Thus the resulting increase would better be treated as an investment item instead of an operating item.

Required:

a. Are each of these criticisms justified? Discuss.

b. Explain how the scenarios outlined in each criticism might mislead the casual reader of financial statements.

E18-14. In each unrelated case below, give the adjusting journal entry needed on the worksheet to produce an SCFP based on cash and equivalents:

a. The company experienced the following changes for the year: non-cash current assets, $45,678 decrease; non-cash current liabilities, $32,000 decrease.

b. Depreciation expense for the year was $35,000, and amortization of intangible assets was $18,000.

c. Securities with a net book value of $35,000 were sold for $29,000.

d. Three plant assets that cost $1,000 each were sold under the following unrelated conditions:

   (i) Asset A had never been depreciated and was sold for $1,000.

   (ii) Asset B had accumulated $500 depreciation and was sold for $1,000.

   (iii) Asset C was purchased this year, had been depreciated already to the extent of $500, and was sold for $1,000.

e. Plant assets were purchased at a cost of $35,000.

f. The company used the equity method to account for the income of a related company. It reported an income from that source of $85,000. Actual dividends received were $39,000.

g. Holders of $500,000 convertible bonds had elected to use the conversion option and had acquired 50,000 newly issued common shares.

PROBLEMS

P18-1. Set out below is the trial balance of Portsmouth Limited at the beginning and end of 19X5.

	End of 19X5	Start of 19X5	Difference
Cash	$ 12,560	$ 28,310	$(15,750)
Accounts receivable	61,640	55,120	6,520
Inventory	125,240	110,560	14,680
Land, buildings and equipment	762,987	824,908	(61,921)
Accumulated depreciation	(485,260)	(481,478)	(3,782)
Goodwill	15,000	18,000	(3,000)
Bank loan	(15,000)	(150,000)	135,000
Accounts payable	(64,125)	(90,420)	26,295
Bond payable	(100,000)	(140,000)	40,000
Mortgage payable	(50,000)	(50,000)	0
Preferred shares	(46,000)	(50,000)	4,000
Common shares	(25,000)	(25,000)	0
Retained earnings	(192,042)	(50,000)	(142,042)
	$ 0	$ 0	$ 0

You are also given the following additional information:
(i) An abbreviated income statement for the year:

Sales		$624,120
Cost of goods sold	$367,860	
Selling and administrative	85,000	
Depreciation	56,218	
Amortization of goodwill	3,000	512,078
		112,042
Gain on sale of land and buildings		45,000
		$157,042

(ii) The proceeds from the sale of land and buildings were $54,485. The accumulated depreciation on the buildings disposed of was $52,436, and their original cost was $61,921.

(iii) Goodwill is being amortized at the rate of $3,000 per year.

(iv) Under the terms of its trust indenture the company retired bonds payable with a face value of $40,000. They had originally been issued at par.

(v) The company elected to retire redeemable preferred shares with a book value of $4,000.

(vi) A dividend of $15,000 was paid during the year.

Required: Prepare a statement of changes in financial position for the year 19X5 using a worksheet and showing your adjusting journal entries. Index your journal entries to the worksheet entries. Use working capital for *funds*.

P18-2. Here are the balance sheets for 19X4 and 19X5 for Ashworth Corporation, and its income statement for 19X5.

BALANCE SHEET

	19X5	19X4	Net change
Assets			
Current assets	$ 30,000	$20,000	$10,000
Plant assets — net	80,000	60,000	20,000
Patents	3,000	3,200	(200)
Total assets	$113,000	$83,200	$29,800
Liabilities			
Current liabilities	$18,000	$ 9,000	$ 9,000
Deferred income taxes	2,000	1,000	1,000
Long-term liabilities — bonds	60,000	50,000	10,000
	$80,000	$60,000	$20,000
Owners' Equity			
Common stock	$ 12,000	$10,000	$ 2,000
Retained earnings	21,000	13,200	7,800
	$33,000	$23,200	$ 9,800
Total liabilities and owners' equity	$113,000	$83,200	$29,800

INCOME STATEMENT

Sales	$265,000
Cost of goods sold	117,800
Gross margin	$147,200
Selling administrative	23,000
Depreciation	15,000
Amortization	200
Net income — before tax	$109,000
Income tax	54,800
	$54,200

Required: Set up a worksheet to see how far you could go in creating the SCFP. What significant parts are missing? How important are these omissions? Can any of them be estimated?

P18-3. In 1981 Golden & Gale Ltd. published an annual report that includes the following financial statements:

GOLDEN & GALE LTD.
STATEMENT OF CHANGES IN FINANCIAL POSITION
For the year ended 31 December 1981

Sources of working capital			
1. Depreciation		$15,000	
2. Deferred income tax		8,250	
3. Par value of 10-year 12% bonds issued 2 January 1981		50,000	
4. Reduction in book value of machinery sold (see note 1)		21,000	
5. Profit for the year, per income statement	$18,000		
Add back: amortization on bond discount	250		
Working capital provided by the year's normal business operations		18,250	
6. Total sources of funds			$112,500
Uses of working capital			
1. Purchase of delivery equipment (note 2)		$80,000	
2. Dividends declared		12,000	
3. Sinking fund instalment		3,000	
4. Discount on bonds issued 2 January 1981		2,500	
5. Total use of funds			97,500
Increase in working capital			$15,000

GOLDEN & GALE LTD.
INCOME STATEMENT
For the year ended 31 December 1981

Sales revenue		$154,615
Gain on sale of machinery		5,000
Deduct expenses:		
Cost of goods sold	$75,000	
Depreciation	15,000	
Other operating expenses	12,300	
Bond interest	6,250	
Rent (note 3)	16,450	
		125,000
Income before tax		$34,615
Deduct income tax expense		
(note 4)		16,615
Net income		$18,000

GOLDEN & GALE LTD.
SCHEDULE OF CHANGES IN FUNDS

	As at 31 December		Funds increase (decrease)
	19X1	19X0	
Quick assets			
Cash	$19,000	$17,000	$ 2,000
Accounts receivable	24,000	27,000	(3,000)
Marketable securities	16,000	10,000	6,000
Total quick assets	$59,000	$54,000	$ 5,000
Current liabilities			
Accounts payable for merchandise	$ 6,000	$ 8,000	$ 2,000
Income tax payable	1,500	2,000	500
Dividends payable	3,000	3,000	—
Total current liabilities	$10,500	$13,000	$ 2,500
Net quick assets	$48,500	$41,000	$ 7,500
Add: Unexpired costs reported as current assets:			
Inventories	$32,000	$24,000	$ 8,000
Prepaid operating expenses and supplies	3,000	3,500	(500)
	$35,000	$27,500	$ 7,500
Working capital	$83,500	$68,500	$15,000

Notes to the Financial Statements:
1. Machinery sold during the year had an original cost of $48,000 against which depreciation of $27,000 had been recorded. It was sold for $26,000.

2. The total cost of the new delivery equipment purchased during the year was $100,000 of which $50,000 was paid in cash at the time of purchase, $30,000 was paid by a 90-day note (paid before the year-end) and $20,000 was paid in common shares of the company.
3. The rent is payable under a long-term lease that expires 31 December 1987.
4. The company uses the tax allocation method to report its income tax expense. Income tax of $8,365 is currently payable at the rate of 48% on the company's taxable income for the year. The balance of income tax, $8,250, has been deferred as a result of timing differences between the company's reported expenses and their availability as deductions for tax purposes.

Required: Reconstruct the company's SCFP on a more logical, understandable, and accurate basis. (Retain working capital as the definition of funds.)

(Written by J.E. Smyth)

P18-4. A lawyer friend who has had his own practice for about four years asks for your advice about the reasons for his shortage of cash. He gives you the following trial balance as of the start and end of his most recent year:

	End	Start	Difference
Cash	$ 1,200.00	$ 5,800.00	$–4,600.00
Accounts receivable	32,000.00	32,580.00	–580.00
Leasehold improvements	18,000.00	15,920.00	2,080.00
Office equipment	7,800.00	4,500.00	3,300.00
Accumulated depreciation	–1,560.00	–1,120.00	–440.00
Goodwill		17,000.00	–17,000.00
Bank loan	–9,280.00	–10,440.00	1,160.00
Family loan	–40,000.00	–57,000.00	17,000.00
Original equity	–5,000.00	–5,000.00	0.00
Retained earnings	–3,160.00	–2,240.00	–920.00
	$ 0.00	$ 0.00	$ 0.00

"I wouldn't be so worried about the drop in my bank balance," he said, "if it weren't for the fact that my overall liquidity seems to have dropped, despite a net income of (i) $57,920 before writing off the goodwill of (ii) $17,000. Of course, I moved during the year and had to pay (iii) $16,080 for leasehold improvements in the new office. But I was able to get (iv) $12,000 for the existing leasehold improvements in my old office out of the new tenant who moved in. They had only cost me (v) $14,000 originally and I had depreciated them by (vi) $1,890 this year, so I didn't come out too badly. The same tenant also bought some of my equipment that had not been depreciated for original cost of (vii) $5,800, and this helped to pay for a lot of the new equipment, which cost (viii) $9,100. I only took (ix) $40,000 of the firm's income out in personal drawings, and this made it possible to retire (x) $17,000 of the loan from my wife's family."

Required:

a. Prepare an SCFP for the year, using net working capital as the definition for funds. Index your entries to the items (i) to (x) above.

b. If funds were defined as "cash net of bank loan," what would be the change in funds for the year? Reconcile the amount of that change with the net change in working capital calculated in part (a).

c. Does your friend's liquidity position appear to be serious? Briefly, what advice would you give him?

P18-5. Armstrong Co. was formed three years ago and has been very successful. Its current president and majority shareholder (51%), Roberta Armstrong, has undertaken an ambitious plant expansion program. The expansion is forecast to take three years and to cost $500,000. It was started at the beginning of the last fiscal year. Armstrong wants to maintain control; thus expansion is to be financed by internally generated funds. The company is experiencing cash flow difficulties in the current year, 19X6. There is a note payable to Eastern Bank in the amount of $125,000 due on April 30, 19X6 for which a 24-month extension is requested. Eastern Bank has financial statements for the last two years on its files and is evaluating the loan extension request. The fiscal year for Armstrong Co. coincides with the calendar year.

INCOME STATEMENTS

	19X4	19X5
Sales	$1,500,000	$2,100,000
Cost of goods sold	850,000	1,310,000
Gross margin	650,000	790,000
Operating expenses	415,000	509,000
Earnings before tax	235,000	281,000
Income tax (50%)	117,500	140,500
Net income	$117,500	$140,500

BALANCE SHEETS

	19X4	19X5
Cash	$ 54,000	$ 41,000
Accounts receivable	78,400	92,000
Inventory	107,000	112,000
Plant and equipment	433,000	590,000
Less: Depreciation	(81,700)	(102,800)
Total assets	$590,700	$732,200
Accounts payable	$ 42,300	$ 55,000
Notes payable	125,000	125,000
Accrued liabilities	5,600	17,000
Common stock	160,000	160,000
Retained earnings	257,800	375,200
Total	$590,700	$732,200

Required:

a. If you were the loan officer at Eastern, how would you assess the loan extension request? (Show all your calculations and make your assumptions explicit.) What else might you want to look at?

b. Would you grant the extension if sales were expected to grow at the same rate in 19X6 as the year before with cost of goods sold at the same percentage of sales? Is it realistic for Armstrong to expand using internally generated funds?

P18-6. Shown below are some of the financial statements of Watts Equipment Rental. Part of the balance sheet for 19X2 was run over by a tractor and destroyed. The surviving portion is shown below. The rest of the surviving information is also presented.

BALANCE SHEETS

	19X1	19X2
Current assets	$107,850	$138,970
Land, buildings, and equipment	878,900	
Accumulated depreciation	(481,500)	
Goodwill	30,000	
Total assets	$535,250	
Current liabilities	$145,250	$106,310
Bond payable	180,000	
Mortgage payable	50,000	
Preferred shares	70,000	
Common shares	40,000	
Retained earnings	50,000	
Total liabilities and equity	$535,250	

PARTIAL INCOME STATEMENT
Year Ended 31 December 1982

Gross profit, less expenses	$310,960
Selling and administrative	127,960
Depreciation	38,000
Goodwill	5,000
Net income	$140,000

Other information:
  (i) During 1982, equipment which had cost $35,300 some time ago was sold for $33,860. There was accumulated depreciation of $34,240 on the equipment.
  (ii) Bonds worth $80,000, which had been issued at par, were redeemed during the year.
  (iii) Goodwill is amortized at a rate of $5,000 per year.
  (iv) Preferred shares with a book value of $34,000 were redeemed during the year.
  (v) A dividend of $15,000 was paid during the year.
  (vi) Included in the current assets were cash and cash equivalents of $35,000 at the end of 19X1 and $50,000 at the end of 19X2.

Required: Complete the balance sheet for 19X2 and prepare a statement of changes in financial position based on cash equivalents.

P18-7.   (i) "Emphasizing earnings while ignoring cash flow actually rewards companies for putting off needed capital investment. The smaller the depreciation charge, the higher the earnings. In turn, higher earnings produce better stock prices. Finally, the stock price is often reflected in a fatter pay cheque for the chief executive officer. Is that one important reason for the notoriously low level of capital spending in the U.S.? Chief executives are only human."

   (ii) "Of course, total reliance on cash-flow information could be equally dangerous. Any capital investment turns cash into plant and hurts cash flow in the short term. Cash-flow figures are only valuable when looked at over a number of quarters or years. As an FASB expert on cash flow says, "Asking which one is better, cash flow or earnings, is like asking which you should cut out, your heart or your lungs."

Required: Write an essay (500 words maximum) criticizing each of the above passages in depth. Evaluate their strengths and weaknesses.

P18-8. Here is the trial balance of Shultz Inc. at the end of 19X3.

TRIAL BALANCE
(millions of $)

	19X3
Cash	23
Marketable securities	917
Accounts receivable (net)	865
Inventories	1,409
Machinery and equipment	6,210
Accumulated depreciation	(1,770)
Patents	481
Accounts payable	(1,027)
Other current liabilities	(550)
Taxes payable	(275)
Current portion of bonds payable	(226)
Long-term debt	(783)
Deferred income taxes	(673)
Common shares	(181)
Retained earnings	(4,420)
	0

The company's statement of changes in financial position for the year ending 19X4 is shown below:

SCFP
(millions of $)

	19X4
Operating activities:	
Net earnings	$519
Depreciation and depletion	330
Deferred income taxes	141
Gain on sale of plant	(63)
Net from earnings	927
Increase in other current liabilities	275
Increase in inventories	(131)
Increase in accounts receivable	(193)
Other items, net	(110)
Net from operating activities	768
Investing activities:	
Sale of plant assets	94
Capital expenditures	(906)
Purchase of patent	(93)
Net from investing activities	(905)
Financing activities:	
Increase in long-term debt	165
Increase in debt due within one year	131
Issuing of common shares	20
Dividends to shareholders	(60)
Reduction in long-term debt	(318)
Net from financing activities	(62)
Net increase (decrease) in cash equivalents	(199)
Cash and cash equivalents, beginning of year	940
Net increase (decrease)	(199)
Cash and cash equivalents, end of year	$741

In addition you are informed that machinery and equipment with a historical cost of $153 million was disposed of during 19X4 for $94 million.

Required: Prepare a balance sheet as of the end of 19X4. Show all your calculations.

P18-9.   A company has listed the following information about its events and transactions.

(i) Depreciation in the amount of $240,000 was included in the determination of net income.

(ii) At the beginning of the fiscal year, the company's capital structure included 20,000 authorized common shares, 10,000 of which were issued and outstanding. During the period the company declared a 3 for 1 stock split.

(iii) Machinery costing $100,000 with a carrying value of $45,000 was sold for $52,000.

(iv) Bonds which were originally issued at face value in the amount of $200,000 were converted into $40,000 par-value common shares.

(v) During the year equipment with a fair market value of $18,000 was acquired for 2,000 no-par-value common shares.

(vi) Income for the year was $350,000. This amount included a deduction for an extraordinary loss net of taxes in the amount of $32,000.

(vii) Toward the year-end, a two-year 12% note was issued for inventory valued at $50,000.

(viii) The allowance for doubtful accounts was increased by $28,000.

Required: For each of the above, explain whether it represents an inflow or outflow of cash and equivalents, and explain how each should be classified in the statement of changes in financial position. If any item is neither a source nor a use of cash and equivalents, explain why it is not and indicate the disclosure, if any, that should be made of the item in the SCFP.

(CMA adapted)

P18-10.   Shown below are some of the financial information and statements of Standard Equipment Co.
Information:

(i) During 19X2, equipment that had cost $35,300 some time ago was sold for $33,860. There was accumulated depreciation of $34,240 on the equipment, and depreciation provided for the year was $38,000.

(ii) Long-term bonds worth $80,000, which had been issued at par, were redeemed during the year.

(iii) Goodwill is amortized at a rate of $5,000 per year.

(iv) Preferred shares with a book value of $34,000 were redeemed during the year.

(v) A dividend of $15,000 was paid during the year.

BALANCE SHEETS

	19X1	1982	Change
Cash	$ 5,650	$ 12,970	$ 7,320
Accounts receivable	43,200	48,000	4,800
Inventory	59,000	63,000	4,000
Land, buildings, and equipment	784,200	748,900	(35,300)
Accumulated depreciation	(462,800)	(466,560)	(3,760)
Goodwill	26,000	21,000	(5,000)
Total Assets	$455,250	$427,310	$(27,940)
Bank loan	$ 49,250	$ 3,310	$(45,940)
Accounts payable	86,000	93,000	7,000
Current portion of mortgage payable	10,000	10,000	0
Bond payable	135,000	55,000	(80,000)
Mortgage payable	40,000	40,000	0
Preferred shares	70,000	36,000	(34,000)
Common shares	45,000	45,000	0
Retained earnings	20,000	145,000	125,000
Total Liabilities and Equity	$455,250	$427,310	$(27,940)

Required: Prepare a statement of changes in financial position using cash and cash equivalents as *funds*.

P18-11. A friend recently approached you to ask for help in preparing a balance sheet and statement of changes in financial position for her bank. She had just had an argument with her bookkeeper who had quit on the spot, leaving behind the financial statements shown below. Your friend says: "I could only get the balance sheet for the start of the year. The statement of changes in financial position uses working capital, instead of cash and cash equivalents as I promised my bank I'd deliver."

BALANCE SHEETS

	19X4	19X5
Cash	$ 65	
Marketable securities	136	
Accounts receivable, net	78,897	
Inventory	23,561	
Machinery and equipment	58,916	
Accumulated depreciation	(1,256)	
Buildings	2,359	
Accumulated depreciation	(589)	
Goodwill	560	
Bank loan	(563)	
Short-term commercial loan	(2,561)	
Accounts payable	(5,682)	
Current part of long-term debt	(251)	
Other current liabilities	(635)	
Taxes payable	(2,542)	
Long-term debt	(50,000)	
Preferred shares	(12,000)	
Common stock	(56,000)	
Retained earnings	(32,415)	
	$ 0	0

STATEMENT OF CHANGES IN FINANCIAL POSITION
For the year ended 30 September 19X5

Sources of funds

Operations	$32,568
Depreciation: building	163
machinery and equipment	1,000
Amortize goodwill	60
Total sources	33,791

Uses of funds

Purchase equipment	3,229
Retire long-term debt	10,000
Retired preferred shares	4,000
Dividends	4,070
Total uses	21,299
Net increase in funds	$12,492

Represented by increases (decreases) in:

Assets			Liabilities	
Cash	$ 18		Bank loan	$(563)
Marketable securities	22		Short-term commercial paper	999
Accounts receivable	10,066		Accounts payable	549
Inventory	2,313		Other current liabilities	(100)
			Taxes payable	(958)
	$12,419			$ (73)

Required: Using the information provided, prepare the SCFP and balance sheet for 30 September 19X5. Use cash and cash equivalents (including marketable securities) for *funds.*

P18-12. Terrence Nervous is the new owner and president of a clothing chain trying to capture the student market. Terrence is particularly concerned about the income for the year just ended. The chief accountant for the firm, however, has argued that the cash flow, not the profits, should be the greatest concern for a young firm. Although Terrence is not convinced by the accountant's argument, he is willing to listen. To help prove her point, the chief accountant has asked you to prepare an SCFP in approved format using the information given below.

TRIAL BALANCES FOR 19X5

	End 19X5	Start 19X5
Cash	$ 63,948	$ 57,844
Accounts receivable	51,000	48,938
Inventory	124,000	128,750
Land, buildings, and equipment	970,780	952,780
Depreciation	(369,650)	(364,000)
Goodwill	18,000	21,000
Bank loan	(55,000)	(35,000)
Accounts payable	(79,830)	(84,685)
Bond payable — face	(100,000)	(100,000)
Bond payable — premium	5,000	6,000
Mortgage payable	(130,000)	(130,000)
Deferred income taxes		
Common shares	(150,000)	(120,000)
Retained earnings	(348,248)	(381,627)
Total	$ 0	$ 0

Additional information:

(i) The firm experienced a net loss of $16,379 for the year. Included in the loss was a gain of $19,000 on the sale of a building.

(ii) A total of $17,000 in dividends was paid out during the year.

(iii) During the year the company sold a building it had acquired when Terrence, the new owner, took over. Proceeds from the sale of the building were $139,000. Accumulated depreciation at the time of the sale was $27,000. In addition new equipment was purchased for $165,000. No other changes occurred in the land, buildings, and equipment account during the year.

(iv) Most of the financing that was required for the purchases of new equipment was provided by the issue of common stock and funds generated by sales. There is, however, an outstanding account payable of $5,000 arising from the purchase of new equipment.

(v) Goodwill is amortized at the rate of $3,000 per year.

(vi) The bond premium is amortized at the rate of $1,000 per year.

Required:

a. Prepare the statement of changes in financial position in approved format for the year.

b. Discuss the relative importance of net income and cash flow in assessing the financial health of the firm. Do you think that cash flow could be of special concern to newly established firms? If so, why?

P18-13. The Racquet Shop is a local sports shop that specializes in racquet sports. The firm has been following a strategy of steady growth, and future prospects appear good. Management plans to finance their growth for the coming year by obtaining short-term and long-term debt. The bank is interested in examining the cash-flow position. Therefore management asks you to prepare a statement of changes in financial position using cash and cash equivalents as *funds*. They provide you with the following financial statements and information.

TRIAL BALANCES FOR 19X3

	End 19X3	Start 19X3
Cash	$ 12,560	$ 28,310
Marketable securities	25,000	0
Accounts receivable	61,640	55,120
Inventory	85,933	99,485
Land and buildings	1,075,844	905,344
Depreciation	(736,984)	(701,034)
Long-term investments	245,000	275,000
Bank loan	(75,000)	(100,000)
Accounts payable	(56,870)	(49,238)
Bond payable	(100,000)	(100,000)
Mortgage payable	(50,000)	(50,000)
Deferred income taxes	(47,000)	0
Preferred shares	(40,000)	(50,000)
Common shares	(70,000)	(60,000)
Retained earnings	(330,123)	(252,987)
Total	$ 0	$ 0

Additional information:

(i) 500 preferred shares valued at $20 per share were converted for common stock of the same total value.

(ii) Dividends paid during the year amounted to $35,000.

(iii) Land and buildings with a book value of $118,370 were sold, resulting in a loss of $13,370. The only other change in the Land and buildings account during the year resulted from the purchase of a new building for $320,500. The purchase was financed through internally generated funds and the sale of long-term investments totalling $30,000.

Required:

a. Prepare the statement of changes in financial position for the year. Make any assumptions you deem necessary and state them clearly.

b. How would the cash-flow position differ in appearance if a working-capital definition for *funds* were used?

P18-14. Shown below are the financial statements of Johannes Storage Limited. The company has a computerized accounting system. Unfortunately a new trainee hit the wrong key and much of the financial data was lost before any hard copy had been made. All surviving information is presented below:

TRIAL BALANCE

	End 19X5	End 19X4
Cash	$ 42,766	$ 47,023
Other current assets	127,569	117,900
Land and buildings		125,500
Depreciation		(27,800)
Goodwill		29,500
Bank loan	(70,000)	(80,000)
Accounts payable	(27,565)	(30,498)
Bond payable — face		(65,000)
Mortgage payable		(50,000)
Common shares		(25,000)
Retained earnings		(41,625)
Total		$ 0

PARTIAL INCOME STATEMENT
Year ended 31 December 19X5

Gross profit less expenses	$127,690
Selling and administrative	78,015
Amortization of goodwill	2,500
Depreciation	15,380
Gain on sale of Building	10,000
Net income	$ 41,795

Additional information:

(i) New buildings were purchased at a total cost of $88,900. These acquisitions were mostly financed through funds generated from the sale of an existing building and a bond issue of $35,000.

(ii) Dividends paid during the year totaled $15,000.

(iii) A building with a historical cost of $35,000 was sold during the year. At the time of the sale the book value of the building was $27,570.

Required:

a. Complete the balance sheet for 19X5.

b. Prepare a statement of changes in financial position for 19X5. Use cash and cash equivalents for *funds.*

P18-15. Shown below are the financial statements of Chan and Tien Consulting Service, a small business consulting service started by two business school graduates and recently taken over by a large public consulting corporation. Much of their accounting data was lost during a recent flood in their basement office. All the salvaged information is given below:

TRIAL BALANCE

	End 19X9	End 19X8
Cash	$ 74,857	$ 70,241
Other current assets	149,873	164,562
Land and buildings		125,500
Depreciation — buildings		(70,439)
Equipment		81,476
Depreciation — equipment		(28,985)
Goodwill		9,000
Bank loan	(75,000)	(60,000)
Accounts payable	(24,678)	(30,498)
Mortgage payable		(50,000)
Common shares		(45,000)
Retained earnings		(165,857)
Total		$ 0

PARTIAL INCOME STATEMENT
Year ended 31 December 19X9

Gross profit less expenses	$118,311
Selling and administrative	91,793
Amortization of goodwill	1,500
Depreciation	10,343
Depreciation — buildings	5,157
Loss on sale of equipment	750
Net income	$ 8,768

Additional information:
(i) New equipment was purchased at a total cost of $8,769.
(ii) Dividends paid during the year totaled $7,500.
(iii) Some old equipment damaged in the flood was sold, resulting in a loss of $750. At the time of the sale the equipment, which had originally cost $17,000, had a book value of $1,250.
(iv) During the year $20,000 in common shares were issued.
(v) The mortgage on their principal building was paid off near the end of the year.

Required:

a. Complete the balance sheet for 19X9.

b. Prepare the statement of changes in financial position for 19X9. Make any assumptions you feel are appropriate and state them at the bottom of the summary.

P18-16. Reliable Motors Limited is a well-established car dealership that specializes in the sale of imported sports cars. The owner of the company is considering opening up another dealership elsewhere in the city. Naturally he is concerned about the risk of borrowing too much money. Thus he wants to use internal funds to as great an extent as possible to finance the new operation. A clerk at his garage has drawn up a statement of changes in financial position and a summary of selected accounts, both shown below.

STATEMENT OF CHANGES IN FINANCIAL POSITION
Year ended 31 December 19X5

Sources of Funds		
From operations:		
Net income		$ 358,570
Items not affecting cash:		
Depreciation	$57,595	
Amortization of goodwill	3,902	
Gain on sale of equipment	(32,180)	
Increase in deferred income tax	(27,310)	2,007
Total from operations		360,577
Disposal of equipment	61,000	
Common share issue	75,000	
Decrease in long-term notes receivable	38,934	174,934
Total sources		535,511
Uses of Funds		
Purchase of building	257,000	
Payment of mortgage	22,098	
Dividends	75,000	
Retirement of bonds	50,000	
Total uses		404,098
Increase (decrease) in working capital		131,413
Working capital, beginning of year		1,510,247
Working capital, end of year		$1,641,660

BEGINNING AND ENDING BALANCES
FOR SELECTED ACCOUNTS

	End 19X5	Start 19X5
Cash	$ 98,756	$ 88,234
Short-term notes receivable	235,465	204,589
Accounts receivable	73,495	53,268
Inventory	1,567,363	1,488,934
Bank loan	189,434	137,432
Accounts payable	143,985	187,346

The owner has noticed that the SCFP above uses working capital as the definition for funds. Given that the financial statements will be used by banks and other creditors to evaluate whether to arrange loans to the company, and given the nature of his business in terms of liquidity of assets, the owner has decided that an SCFP using cash and cash equivalents as a definition of funds would be more appropriate.

Required:

a. Using the information given above, prepare a new statement of changes in financial position based on cash and cash equivalents.

b. Evaluate the relative merits of an SCFP that uses working capital as the definition for funds and an SCFP that uses cash and cash equivalents as the definition for funds. Discuss this issue in the context of a company such as Reliable Motors engaged in the retail car trade. How could financial statements be improved by employing the advantages of each format?

c. To what extent are the nature of the given business and the nature of the financing decision to be made important in determining which definition of funds is more appropriate? Discuss some of the factors that you think are most important.

APPENDIX 18-1
Preparing a Statement of Changes Using The T-Account Method

The T-account method is the same in principle as the worksheet method used in the text. Some people may find it easier to grasp the principles of preparing the SCFP through using the T-account method. It might also be preferable to use the T-account method when preparing the statement for a small enterprise or when a computer spreadsheet program is not available.

The basic steps in preparing an SCFP using the T-account method are as follows:

1. The changes in balance-sheet items during the period are calculated, as in the worksheet method.

2. These changes are posted to the top line of simple T-accounts, usually with one account for each balance-sheet item. If funds are defined as cash and cash equivalents, then a single account might be used to accumulate all non-cash current assets and another account might be used for all non-cash current liabilities. (The postings are shown boldface in the accounts of our example below.)

3. The balance in each account is broken down into items that are relevant for preparing the SCFP. (These items are shown in italics in the accounts of our example below.) The purpose of this analysis is to explain the net change in the account in terms of funds flow.

4. The items analyzed in (3) above are posted to a roughly formatted statement of changes or, in very small organizations, to a finished-format statement of changes. When all the changes in each account are accounted for, that account is flagged in some manner to indicate that all items have been posted to the SCFP. In the accounts of our example below, these postings are shown in ordinary type with a reference letter indicating the journal entry in the text to which each refers.

5. The statement of changes in financial position is prepared in good form.

We will now illustrate the T-account method by applying it to the same extended example that we used in this chapter to demonstrate the worksheet method. For convenience, we repeat below the trial balance for Food Limited.

FOOD LIMITED
TRIAL BALANCE

| | Year | | Increase or (decrease) in assets | |
	19X1	19X0	Cash equiva- lents	Other assets and liabilities
	A	B	C	D
Cash and short-term investments	$ 43,000	$ 35,000	$8,000	
Accounts receivable	12,600	7,900		$ 4,700
Inventories	156,800	146,100		10,700
Prepaid expenses	11,500	8,600		2,900
Land	23,400	22,100		1,300
Buildings	180,000	162,000		18,000
Depreciation	(44,500)	(36,200)		(8,300)
Long-term investment	25,000	23,000		2,000
Goodwill	7,300	8,700		(1,400)
Bank loan	(25,000)	(23,000)	(2,000)	
Accounts payable	(120,000)	(100,000)		(20,000)
Bond payable — face amount	(220,000)	(213,000)		(7,000)
— premium	(4,700)	(5,000)		300
Deferred income tax	(19,600)	(16,700)		(2,900)
Redeemable preferred shares	(2,900)	(4,900)		2,000
Common shares	(9,000)	(7,000)		(2,000)
Retained earnings	(13,900)	(7,600)		(6,300)
Total	$ 0	$ 0	$6,000	$(6,000)

The Changes in column D above are posted to simple T-accounts, usually with one account for each balance sheet item. The only exceptions are non-cash current assets and liabilities which can be grouped into two accounts for posting.

The T-accounts are shown below. The most straightforward ones will be shown first, then the more difficult ones. The journal entries are the same ones used in the chapter and are not repeated here to save space.

Non-cash Current Assets			
Accounts receivable	**4,700**		
Inventory	**10,700**		
Prepaid expenses	**2,900**		
Net change	**18,300**		
Net current assets	*18,300*	Investing	700 (f)
		Operating	17,600 (f)

The above account is for the total of the changes in non-cash working capital. Therefore, it includes accounts receivable, $4,700; inventory, $10,700; and Prepaid expenses, $2,900. Because $700 of the increase is due to an unpaid account arising from the sale of the building, that amount is classified as Investing, and the balance is considered an Operating item.

Non-cash Current Liabilities			
		Net change	**20,000**
Operating	20,000 (j)	*Accounts payable*	*20,000*

A number of the changes in the balance-sheet accounts arise from amortization and depreciation. Since they do not create a flow of cash, they are added back to net income. Hence, we make the following postings:

Long-term investments			
Net change	**2,000**		
Income of subsidiary	*2,000*	Operating: reduce profit	2,000 (d)

Goodwill			
		Net change	**1,400**
Operating: add back	1,400 (e)	*Amortization*	*1,400*

Bond payable — premium			
Net change	**300**		
Amortization	*300*	Operating: eliminate	300 (h)

Deferred income tax			
		Net change	**2,900**
Operating: eliminate	2,900 (i)	*Charged to net income*	*2,900*

The change in bonds payable arose from a straightforward issuing of more bonds.

Bond payable — face amount			
		Net change	7,000
Capital: proceeds	7,000 (g)	*Issue at par*	*7,000*

The next two T-accounts arise from the application of the principle that all material changes should be disclosed. Although the preferred shares were surrendered for common shares, the two transactions are treated as if the preferred and common shares were redeemed and issued for cash.

Redeemable preferred shares			
Net change	2,000		
Converted to common	*2,000*	Financing: conversion	2,000 (k)

Common shares			
		Net change	2,000
Financing: issue	2,000 (k)	*Issued on conversion*	*2,000*

Retained earnings are factored out into dividends and net income. Then each is transferred to the appropriate part of the SCFP.

Retained earnings			
		Net change	6,300
Dividends	*4,000*	*Net operating income*	*10,300*
Operating: net income	10,300 (a)	Dividends	4,000 (l)

We now come to the more difficult accounts. The land-account change arose from a purchase of $2,000 and the elimination of the cost of $700 of the land that was sold. Whereas the $2,000 purchase is a satisfactory explanation for the SCFP, the $700 is not. Instead the $700 must be factored out into two items: (i) the proceeds of sale of $1,250 and (ii) the profit of $550 on the sale. Item (i) is then usable as an explanation of a cash inflow, and item (ii) is eliminated against net income (as all income items not creating a cash flow are eliminated).

Land

Net change	**1,300**		

Purchase of land	2,000	Cost of land	700
Restate cost of land	700		
Gain on sale	550	Proceeds of sale	1,250
Investing: proceeds	1,250 (b)	Operating: eliminate gain	550 (b)
		Investing: purchase	2,000 (b)

A complication also arises with the buildings and depreciation accounts. The sale of a building affects the two accounts because both the historic cost and the accumulated depreciation must be eliminated. The technique used here is to explain as much as possible of the change in each of the depreciation and building accounts before dealing with the sale; and then to transfer the balance into one account (in this case, the Building account) to handle the building sale.

Depreciation

		Net change	**8,300**

Accumulated depreciation		Depreciation expense	
of building sold	1,800	for year	10,100
Operating: depreciation expense	10,100 (b)	Transfer to Building account	1,800

The change in the depreciation account arose from the annual depreciation charge of $10,100 and the write-off of accumulated depreciation of $1,800 of the building sold. The depreciation expense is transferred to the Operating section of the SCFP to be added back to net income. The remaining amount, $1,800, is transferred to the Building account.

Buildings

Net change	**18,000**		
Transferred from above	1,800		
Total	**19,800**		

Purchase of building	20,000	Proceeds of disposal	1,850
Gain on disposal	1,650		
Investing: proceeds	1,850 (c)	Operating: eliminate	1,650 (c)
		Investing: purchase	20,000 (c)

The only straightforward item here is the purchase of the building, which can be transferred to the Investment portion of the SCFP. The remaining $200 in the balance to be analyzed can be factored into Proceeds of disposal, $1,850, and Profit on disposal, $1,650. The first is an

Investment item, and the second is an Operating item. Because Profit on disposal is deducted from net income, it does not give rise to a cash flow.

Once these postings have been done, we arrive at the roughly formatted SCFP produced below. When put into good form, it will be the same as the one produced with the worksheet method, as shown in the body of this chapter.

SCFP — ROUGH FORMAT

	Decrease	Increase	Net
Operating activities:			
(f) Change in current assets	$17,600		
(j) Change in current liabilities		$20,000	
(d) Income from using equity method	2,000		
(e) Goodwill amortized		1,400	
(h) Bond premium amortization	300		
(i) Deferred income tax increase		2,900	
(a) Net income		10,300	
(b) Gain on sale of land	550		
(b) Depreciation expense		10,100	
(c) Gain on sale of building	1,650		
	22,100	45,700	$22,600
Financing activities:			
(g) Bond issue		7,000	
(k) Conversion of preferred shares	2,000		
(k) Issue of common shares		2,000	
(l) Dividend	4,000		
	6,000	9,000	3,000
Investing activities:			
(f) Increase in accounts receivable	700		
(b) Sale of land		1,250	
(b) Purchase land	2,000		
(c) Sale of building		1,850	
(c) Purchase building	20,000		
	22,700	3,100	(19,600)
			$ 6,000

BIBLIOGRAPHY

CLARK, RICHARD S. "Statement of Changes: In Need of a Change?" *CA Magazine* (February 1983). A critique of the use of working capital. The authors anticipate the *CICA Handbook* changes of 1985.

MALLOUK, BRENDA. "Statement of Changes in Financial Position: Switching from Working Capital to Cash Base." *CGA Magazine* (January 1988). A good exposition of the preparation of the SCFP in the approved format.

MANN, HARVEY. "A Worksheet for Demonstrating the Articulation of Financial Statements." *The Accounting Review* (October 1984).

SKINNER, ROSS. *Accounting Standards in Evolution.* Toronto: Holt, Rinehart, and Winston of Canada Ltd., 1987. This book provides an excellent and thoughtful critique of the accounting standard on the statement of financial changes.

CHAPTER 19
Consolidated Financial Statements

Introduction

The financial statements of a **parent company** and **subsidiary** are described as **consolidated financial statements** when they are combined together with the intention of showing the affairs of both legal entities as if they were a single economic unit. They are produced by adding the financial statements of parent and subsidiary companies line by line (e.g., adding together like assets and liabilities), eliminating any intercompany or reciprocal items, and providing for minority interest [or reciprocal items, *CICA* 1600.03]. Consolidated statements should be contrasted with **combined financial statements**, which are sometimes prepared to present the financial statements of companies under common management (e.g., the subsidiaries of a parent company).

In Chapter 10 we discussed the **equity method** and **cost method** of accounting for the investment in shares of other companies, and there we mentioned consolidated financial statements briefly. The equity method of accounting for subsidiaries and the consolidation approach are two forms of presentation. In appropriate circumstances, statements may be prepared under either method. In this chapter we assume that the parent controls the majority of the shares entitled to vote, which is the normal basis for preparing consolidated statements.

Because it is easy to confuse the equity method of accounting and the preparation of consolidated financial statements, let us consider differences and similarities between the two. First, under the **equity method** the entity being reported on is the parent company. The assets on the balance sheet, for example, are those of the parent only, and the income statement shows sales and other items for the parent only. The income of the investee is reported as a single item, usually under *other income*, on the income statement of the parent. The investment in the investee is included on the balance sheet as part of long-term investments. By contrast, with *consolidated financial statements* the entity being reported on is the group of companies composed of the parent and its subsidiaries. In effect, the boundaries of the entity are expanded to include the financial operations of all the companies. Thus, for instance, sales are total sales of the enlarged entity, but sales from one company to another within the enlarged entity are eliminated. Furthermore, the interest of minority shareholders is disclosed.

Second, the **equity method** may be used within the accounting system of the parent company. The results would then be reflected in the financial statements of the parent.

By contrast, for reasons to be explained below, the consolidation of financial statements has no effect on the books of account of the parent or any subsidiary.

In the following diagram we outline the steps in preparing the financial statements of a parent and subsidiary company. Assume for this example that the journals have been posted to the general ledger.

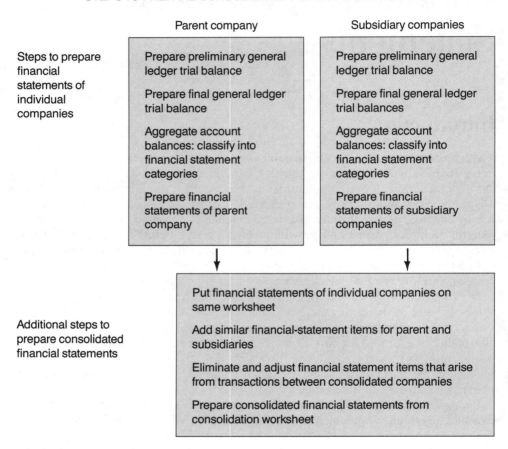

STEPS TO PREPARE CONSOLIDATED FINANCIAL STATEMENTS

	Parent company	Subsidiary companies
Steps to prepare financial statements of individual companies	Prepare preliminary general ledger trial balance Prepare final general ledger trial balance Aggregate account balances: classify into financial statement categories Prepare financial statements of parent company	Prepare preliminary general ledger trial balance Prepare final general ledger trial balances Aggregate account balances: classify into financial statement categories Prepare financial statements of subsidiary companies
Additional steps to prepare consolidated financial statements	Put financial statements of individual companies on same worksheet Add similar financial-statement items for parent and subsidiaries Eliminate and adjust financial statement items that arise from transactions between consolidated companies Prepare consolidated financial statements from consolidation worksheet	

The diagram above illustrates that the accounting process of preparing consolidated financial statements takes place outside the books of the companies after the financial statements of the individual entities have been prepared. Both the cost and equity methods of accounting for a subsidiary require entries within the books of account, but only in the books of the parent. In preparing the financial statements of the parent company above, either the equity or cost method could be used to record the investment in the books of the investor or parent company. It is usually simpler to use financial statements of the parent where the *cost method* has been used (and we will use the cost method in this chapter for that reason). Nevertheless, if the equity method has been used, it can be adjusted for use in the consolidation worksheet.

In this chapter we will develop an explanation of consolidated financial statements sufficient to explain the concept. The financial statements of most public companies are published in consolidated form because companies find it convenient to carry on business activities through subsidiary corporations. Given the widespread use of subsidiaries, it is important to understand the differences between consolidated and unconsolidated statements. It will become apparent that the technical problems of consolidating financial statements can assume great complexity, and anyone wishing to prepare such statements should go beyond the introductory material given in this chapter. For the average user of such statements, however, the material given here should provide an adequate introduction.

Basic Example

Here is a very basic example. Stella Furniture Limited (SFL) made a line of pine furniture that had sold well in Ontario. Since they were close to Quebec, they decided to establish a manufacturing organization there. This involved hiring staff, renting a building, and buying some equipment. They considered the relative merits of operating the Quebec operation as a branch of SFL, but ultimately decided that they would be better off operating under a distinctly Quebec name. They formed a company, Stella Quebec Inc. (SQI), and SQI then issued common shares to SFL for $80,000 and used the funds received to purchase the assets it needed. Immediately after incorporation of SQI, the condensed trial balances of the two companies looked as follows:

	SFL	SQI	Total
Net assets	$ 150,000	$ 80,000	$ 230,000
Investment in SQI	80,000		80,000
Share capital — SFL	(100,000)		(100,000)
—SQI		(80,000)	(80,000)
Retained earnings — SFL	(130,000)		(130,000)
—SQI		0	0
Total	$ 0	$ 0	$ 0

Note that the shares of SQI are on SFL's trial balance as a long-term investment of $80,000. This exactly equals the issued share capital in SQI's books.

Suppose that the Quebec operations run by SQI are an integral part of the total SFL operation. The shareholders of SFL would then want to know how the combined SFL-SQI operation was prospering. They might be given the financial statements of both companies separately, but shrewder readers would try to fit them together to see what the total Stella operation looked like. Consolidated statements are simply a way of doing this — they fit statements together to report on the larger economic entity. This is consistent with other developments in accounting: the trend is away from **legal** criteria and towards **economic** ones instead (e.g., as in the recognition convention).

It can be seen from examining the example above that simply adding the two statements together is not enough. SFL's ownership of shares in SQI is a means of indirectly owning assets in Quebec. The amount of the investment in SQI in SFL's statement needs to be eliminated so that these assets are not counted twice. Similarly, the owner's equity in SQI's statement needs to be eliminated to avoid double counting and to ensure that only the parent company's share capital is shown on the consolidated balance sheet. This could be done as follows:

	Total	Eliminations	Consolidated
Net assets	$ 230,000		$ 230,000
Investment in SQI	80,000	(80,000)	0
Share capital — SFL	(100,000)		(100,000)
—SQI	(80,000)	80,000	0
Retained earnings — SFL	(130,000)		(130,000)
— SQI	0		0
Total	$ 0	$ 0	$ 0

The eliminating entry on the consolidation worksheet would be as follows:

Share capital — SQI	80,000	
Investment in SQI		80,000

To eliminate SFL's investment in SQI against SQI's owners' equity.

In the chart above, the column on the far right is the **consolidated trial balance** of SFL and its wholly owned subsidiary SQI. Note that it is exactly the same as SFL's trial balance would have been had it owned the assets in Quebec directly and not created a separate corporation. We have thus achieved the objective of reporting on the economic unit while looking through the legal form of separate incorporations. The circumstances are rarely as simple as the ones given in this instance (as subsequent examples will show), but the basic intent of consolidated financial statements remains unchanged.

The elimination entry above is not made in the books of either the parent or the subsidiary, but only on the worksheet that combines the financial statements of the two companies into a consolidated financial statement.

When to Consolidate

The basic premise is that the financial statements are more informative when they report on the larger economic entity than on each of the individual companies. If this does not hold true in a particular instance, then the individual statements should be supplied instead.

There is a presumption that a parent company should provide consolidated financial statements that include itself and all its subsidiaries. Therefore, to supply non-consolidated statements to the public would be the rare exception. The *CICA Handbook* [3050.03] defines a **subsidiary** as "a company in which another company owns, directly and/or indirectly through other subsidiaries, a majority of shares carrying the right to elect at least a majority of the members of the board of directors."

The exceptions to this rule, according to the *Handbook*, are those cases where the basic assumptions behind consolidations are not met. These cases are summarized below.

1. The changes in equity in the subsidiary will not accrue to the parent (e.g., it is in bankruptcy), or the parent's control over the subsidiary is seriously impaired (e.g., the subsidiary is in a foreign country and there are significant restrictions on the transfer of funds). In such cases the cost method should be used instead [*CICA* 3050.08].

2. A formal plan exists for the parent to divest itself of the subsidiary. In this case the amount of the investment should be shown on the balance sheet at the lower of net realizable value or at the amount produced by using the equity method [*CICA* 3050.10].

3. The subsidiary is a bank, and the financial statements are not prepared in accordance with generally accepted accounting principles. In this case the equity method should be used, but without adjusting the results of the subsidiary to conform to generally accepted accounting principles [*CICA* 3050.12].

4. Consolidation would fail to provide a more informative presentation to the shareholder. In this case the financial statements of the parent company should include either (i) separate financial statements of the subsidiary (or combined financial statements of the subsidiaries) or (ii) condensed financial statements of the subsidiary (subsidiaries) with notes, provided all information significant to the other appropriate consolidated statements is disclosed. In addition, an explanation should be provided of any adjustments of the net income or loss of the excluded subsidiary to arrive at the amount of income included in the parent's income statement. [*CICA* 3050.14].

For such cases where consolidation is not used, the reasons for excluding a subsidiary company should be stated.

The Purchase Method of Accounting

The Stella Furniture example, presented earlier, involves a self-established subsidiary, Stella Quebec Inc.. While many subsidiaries are established by their parent corporations, other parent-subsidiaries result from business combinations in which one company (the investor or parent company) acquires sufficient voting shares of another company (the investee or subsidiary company) to obtain control of it. Under Canadian accounting standards most business combinations are accounted for by the **purchase method** [*CICA* 1580]. In rare circumstances Section 1580 requires that the combination be accounted for by the **pooling-of-interests method**. Under the purchase method, the assets of the subsidiary are valued on the consolidated balance sheet at the *new* historic cost price implied by the amount the parent paid for the subsidiary's shares. Although this appears to be a departure from the cost principle in accounting, it really is not because the valuation placed on the assets is the actual cost to the parent.

Under the pooling-of-interests method, the assets are valued on the consolidated balance sheet at their *original* historic cost to the subsidiary. This method is used when both companies are considered to have come together as equals, and rare circumstances preclude identifying either as the purchaser or acquirer.

In the example above, Stella Furniture Limited established Stella Quebec Inc. and paid an amount for SQI's shares that was exactly equal to the cost of the underlying assets acquired. But suppose that SQI had been in existence before SFL became interested in operating in Quebec and that SFL had to purchase the SQI shares from other owners. Under such circumstances it is probable that SFL would have paid a price for the shares that was different from their book value. Let us change our original example slightly and assume SFL purchased the shares of SQI from an owner who had operated SQI for one year. SFL paid $110,000 for 100% ownership in SQI. At the time of purchase SQI had retained earnings of $10,000.

If the financial statements of the two companies were added together, they would look as follows:

	SFL	SQI	Total
Net assets	$ 120,000	$ 90,000	$ 210,000
Investment in SQI	110,000		110,000
Share capital — SFL	(100,000)		(100,000)
— SQI		(80,000)	(80,000)
Retained earnings — SFL	(130,000)		(130,000)
— SQI		(10,000)	(10,000)
Total	$ 0	$ 0	$ 0

The technical problem in preparing this consolidation is that the investment in SQI of $110,000 no longer neatly cancels out against the owners' equity of $90,000 (i.e., $80,000 + $10,000) of SQI. However, the substantive issue is that SFL has effectively purchased the assets of SQI for $110,000 by purchasing 100% of the shares; yet on the books of SQI these assets are stated at their historic cost to SQI of $90,000, not their purchase cost to SFL of $110,000. Under the cost convention it is appropriate for SQI to report its assets at a valuation of $90,000. Nevertheless, it can be argued that for consolidation purposes they should be treated as "sold" to SFL and restated at the value implied by the price of $110,000 that SFL paid for the shares of SQI.

The accountant's response to this is to revalue the assets of SQi to their effective purchase cost to SFL for purposes of consolidation only (except in the rare case of *push-down* accounting, to be discussed later.) To this end, the tangible assets are valued at their market price as of the date of acquisition of the shares, and the remainder is considered to be goodwill. This puts the consolidated balance sheet of SFL in the same accounting position as if the company had purchased the assets directly instead of buying SQI's shares. The purchase difference that is attributable to tangible assets is depreciated at the same rate as those assets. Any amount attributed to goodwill is amortized by the straight-line method over its estimated life, which cannot exceed forty years [*CICA* 1580.58].

In practice, it is possible to have negative goodwill (i.e. the market value of the tangible assets is greater than the purchase price of the company's shares). It seems irrational behaviour for someone to sell a company for less than the market value of its tangible assets, but on occasion it happens. The *CICA Handbook* [1580.44] recommends that this difference should be assigned to the non-monetary assets using "judgement," rather than some predetermined rule such as pro rata allocation.

In our modified example let us assume that SFL paid the extra $20,000 for SQI because it thought (i) the building had gone up in value by $10,000 and (ii) the former owners had built up general business goodwill for SQI that was worth another $10,000. SFL depreciates its own similar buildings at 5% and has decided to amortize the goodwill over forty years. The elimination and adjusting entries on the consolidation worksheet at the date of acquisition would be as follows:

	Total	Adjustments and eliminations	Consolidated
Net assets	$ 210,000	$ 10,000	$ 220,000
Investment in SQI	110,000	(110,000)	0
Goodwill		10,000	10,000
Share capital — SFL	(100,000)		(100,000)
— SQI	(80,000)	80,000	0
Retained earnings — SFL	(130,000)		(130,000)
—SQI	(10,000)	10,000	0
Total	$ 0	$ 0	$ 0

Net assets	10,000	
Goodwill	10,000	
Share capital — SQI	80,000	
Retained earnings — SQI	10,000	
Investment in SQI		110,000

To eliminate the investment in SQI against the owners' equity of SQI and allocate the purchase difference of $20,000 against plant assets and goodwill.

Note that the retained earnings of the subsidiary up to the time of acquisition have been eliminated. This means that the consolidated retained earnings include only the earnings of the subsidiary *after* the date of acquisition and the earnings of the parent since its own formation.

PUSH-DOWN ACCOUNTING

The price that an acquiring company pays for the acquired company's shares implies a valuation for the assets of the acquired company. This is recognized in the consolidations process when the *purchase difference* between the book value of an acquired company's assets and the value implied by the price paid for its shares is attributed to the underlying assets for consolidations purposes.

In **push-down accounting** the new value implied by the price paid for the shares of the acquired company is actually used to revalue the assets in the acquired company's books. In the U.S. the SEC has indicated that it will *require* push-down accounting when the purchase of shares means that the subsidiary is substantially wholly owned by one party. It will encourage (but not require) push-down accounting when there is a substantial minority interest, outstanding debt, or preferred stock.

In an *Accounting Guideline* issued in 1987 the Steering Committee of the Accounting Standards Committee was lukewarm to the idea of push-down accounting on the grounds that it raised "a number of fundamental matters of principle relating to the basis on which assets and liabilities are measured in financial statements." For example, the basis of valuation is being changed as the result of a transaction in which the entity did not participate. It concluded that push-down accounting was only acceptable when (i) virtually all of the subsidiary's voting shares had been acquired; and (ii) there is no significant public interest remaining in its debt securities, preferred shares, non-voting common shares, or other securities.

The Pooling-of-Interest Method of Accounting

The pooling of interest method is to be used, in theory, when there is a business combination where none of the parties can be identified as the acquirer. Because the payment of cash for shares identifies an acquirer, pooling is restricted to certain share exchanges between companies of approximately equal size. For instance, under the pooling method Company A issues new shares of its own and exchanges them for shares in Company B. Instead of valuing the shares at their market value (or at the market value of the assets indirectly acquired) as in the purchase method, Company A assigns a value in its accounts to the newly acquired shares of Company B that is equal to their book value as shown on Company B's books. This avoids any recognition of the probable difference between the book value of the assets acquired and the price paid for them by the issue of shares. This means that no assets have to be revalued for purposes of consolidation and no goodwill appears that has to be amortized. Furthermore, income is reported from the inception of all companies in the consolidation, not just from the date of acquisition for each subsidiary.

Let us modify our Stella Furniture example so that it meets the criteria for pooling. Suppose that Stella Furniture Limited purchased the shares of Stella Quebec Inc. by issuing its own shares to the existing owner of SQI. Let us continue to assume that SFL calculated the value of SQI to be $110,000 and that the existing owner was agreeable to selling its shares of SQI for shares of SFL worth $110,000. The journal entry on the books of SFL would be as follows:

Investment in SQI	80,000.00	
Share capital		80,000.00

To record purchase of shares of SQI estimated to be worth $110,000 by the issue of SFL stock estimated to be of the same value. Because this is being recorded under the pooling-of-interest method, the shares issued are valued above at the book value at date of acquisition of the SQI assets.

Note that the assets of SQI would, on consolidation, be valued at their book value at acquisition. As a result there would be no entry to record the additional depreciation of $500 (i.e., 5% of $10,000) and amortization of goodwill of $250 (i.e., 1/40 x 10,000), as under the purchase method. Thus, under the pooling method the reported consolidated income would be higher by $500 + $250 = $750. A critic of this method would say that both the owners' equity and the value of the assets have been understated, and that depreciation and amortization have been understated accordingly. In addition, all the earnings prior to the pooling of both companies would be included as part of the combined company profits, even if the merger took place on the last day of the year.

It should be noted as well that the basic consolidation approach is similar whether one uses the purchase approach or the pooling-of-interest approach. The difference lies only in the value assigned to the share capital issued, the assets acquired, and the earnings.

The pooling method was fashionable in the 1950s and 1960s, and it was used to window-dress consolidated income statements by eliminating any additional charges for depreciation or amortization. It also made it possible (i) to recognize "instant profits" by selling off assets whose original book value was recorded at an amount that was less than their market value and (ii) to record earnings achieved by the acquired company prior to the date of acquisition. In 1970, the Accounting Principles Board reduced the use of this practice by AICPA Opinion 16, and it is now used much less in the U.S. Pooling had been widely condemned by financial writers, as was the APB's slowness in dealing with it [Briloff, 1972]. In 1974 a section was added to the *CICA Handbook* [1580.21] saying: "The pooling-of-interest method should be used to account for those rare business combinations in which it is not possible to identify one of the parties as the acquirer." This is reported to have substantially eliminated the use of the method in Canada.

Joint Ventures — Proportionate Consolidation

The *CICA Handbook* [3055.03] defines a **joint venture** as "an arrangement whereby two or more parties (the venturers) jointly control a specific business undertaking and contribute resources towards its accomplishment. The life of the joint venture is limited to that of the undertaking which may be of short or long-term duration depending on the circumstances." A joint venture differs from the usual parent-subsidiary relationship in that there is joint control of it by the two or more corporations that own it, instead of one dominant shareholder having control. A joint venture may be a legal partnership between the venturing corporations, or it may be in the form of a separate corporation in which the joint control is exercised by explicit agreement between the shareholding corporations. An example would be the joint ventures that Cadillac-Fairview enters into with its major tenants, such as the Eaton Centre in Toronto.

Under proportionate consolidation each venturer would proceed in the same manner as with a conventional consolidation, except that the amounts brought on to the consolidations worksheet would not be the full amounts on the trial balance of the joint venture, but only the venturer's proportionate share in the venture. Thus, if Cadillac-Fairview owns 49% of a joint real-estate venture, then it would bring on to the consolidations worksheet 49% of the assets, liabilities, revenues, and expenses of that joint venture.

Accounting Procedures for Consolidation

BALANCE SHEETS

For purposes of illustration we will assume that the parent company uses the cost method of reporting the income of the subsidiary in its own books and the purchase method for consolidation purposes. This is the most common and simplest situation to explain. We used it in the first example in this chapter.

The basic steps for preparing a consolidated balance sheet are as follows:

1. Accounting policies for all companies are brought into conformity (e.g., with respect to capitalization of development costs).

2. Any gains or losses on intercompany transactions are eliminated so that the entity will report intercompany asset acquisitions at their cost to the consolidated group.

3. Any debts between consolidated companies are eliminated.

4. The investment of the parent company in shares of the subsidiary is eliminated against the subsidiary's owners' equity account (as was done in the examples above).

5. Assets of subsidiaries are adjusted to their acquisition price, and depreciation expense is adjusted similarly.

6. Like accounts for the parent and subsidiary are added together line by line (as was done in the examples above).

The sixth step above, adding like accounts, is easy to understand but may be hard to put into practice if the subsidiary's books have not previously been aligned with the parent's books. Most large companies have a standardized chart of accounts that subsidiaries are expected to adopt to facilitate consolidation. In addition, it is necessary to make sure that all companies being consolidated coordinated their accounting treatment for intercompany transactions, so that a sale by one, for instance, was also recorded as a purchase by the other within the same time period.

The second step above, elimination of intercompany gains or losses, would make it impossible for the related companies to increase their consolidated net income by marking goods up and selling them to one another. All inventories within the consolidated entity are written down to their cost to the first selling company. If the gain or loss arises on the sale from a parent to a subsidiary (termed a **downstream sale**), then all the gain or loss is eliminated against retained earnings. If the gain or loss arises from the sale from a subsidiary to a parent (an **upstream sale**), then the gain or loss elimination is split between retained earnings and minority interest (a balance-sheet category to be explained shortly) in proportion to their holdings [*CICA* 1600.32].

For example, if the parent has finished goods in its inventory at $300 and sells them to its subsidiary at $500, then the intercompany gain of $200 would be eliminated against the retained earnings of the parent, provided that the goods were still in the inventory of one of the companies. One reason for this is that otherwise the parent could report profits by forcing the subsidiary to purchase the goods. If the sale had been from subsidiary to parent, then the $200 would have been split between minority interest and retained earnings in proportion to their ownership interests. Note that this elimination takes place even if $500 is the parent's normal selling price. Of course, if they had been sold outside the consolidated entity and were no longer in inventory, then the gain on the intercompany sale would have been realized and would not be eliminated. This is because the sale would have taken place at arm's length between a company in the entity and outsiders.

The third step above, elimination of intercompany debts, is designed to prevent double counting on the consolidated statements. Hence accounts such as the following are eliminated between consolidated companies:

a. accounts receivable against accounts payable

b. dividends receivable against dividends payable

c. sales against purchases

d. bonds receivable against bonds payable

The fourth step above, elimination of the parent's investment in subsidiary shares against the owner's equity in the subsidiary, has already been illustrated in simple form. In our previous example the parent owned 100% of the subsidiary's shares. When less than 100% is owned, the owners' equity identified with the remaining minority shareholders is shown on the consolidated balance sheet as a new item, **minority interest**.

In our Stella Furniture example, the parent owned 100% of the subsidiary's shares. Let us now suppose instead that the parent purchased only 75% of the shares, and paid 75% of the amount shown in the first example, or $60,000. The resulting combined trial balance is shown below, with the new eliminating entry reflecting the different circumstances.

	SFL	SQI	Total	Eliminations	Consolidated
Net assets	$ 170,000	$ 80,000	$ 250,000	$ (60,000)	$ 190,000
Investment in SQI	60,000		60,000		60,000
Minority interest				(20,000)	(20,000)
Share capital — SFL	(100,00)		(100,000)		(100,000)
Share capital — SQI		(80,000)	(80,000)	80,000	0
Retained earnings — SFL	(130,000)		(130,000)		(130,000)
Retained earnings — SQI		0	0		0
	$ 0	$ 0	$ 0	$ 0	$ 0

Share capital — SQI	80,000.00	
Investment in SQI		60,000.00
Minority interest		20,000.00

To eliminate SFL's investment in shares of SQI ($60,000) and set up a minority interest account equal to 25% of the owners' equity of SQI.

In this example SQI has just begun operations; hence there are no retained earnings. If SQI had had retained earnings, 25% of them would have been added to the minority interest along with 25% of the capital share of SQI.

The amount of the minority interest on the consolidated balance sheet is made up of two components: (i) the minority interest at the time the subsidiary was acquired by the parent and (ii) the minority interest in earnings, less dividends, subsequent to the time of acquisition by the parent. The calculation of the minority interest at the date of acquisition is something that many find the most difficult part. The important thing to remember is that, once calculated, this amount never changes in later years regardless of the subsequent fortunes of the subsidiary (unless of course there are further share sales or purchases). The thing that does change is the minority interest subsequent to acquisition, which will be illustrated next.

Suppose that circumstances are unchanged from the above example except that one year has passed and SQI has a net income of $16,000 and $16,000 more assets. The revised example would then look as follows:

	Total		Eliminations	Consolidated
Net assets	$ 266,000			$ 266,000
Investment in SQI	60,000	(a)	$ (60,000)	0
Minority Interest		(b)	(20,000)	
		(c)	(4,000)	(24,000)
Share capital — SFL	(100,000)			(100,000)
— SQI	(80,000)	(a)	60,000	
		(b)	20,000	0
Retained earnings — SFL	(130,000)	(c)	(12,000)	(142,000)
— SQI	(16,000)	(c)	16,000	0
	$ 0		$ 0	$ 0

(a) Share capital — SQI   60,000
         Investment in SQI   60,000
     Elimination of investment in SQI against the owners' equity
         of SQI.

(b) Share capital — SQI   20,000
         Minority interest   20,000
     Transfer minority interest in owners' equity at time of
         acquisition to separate minority interest account.

(c) Retained earnings — SQI   16,000
         Minority interest   4,000
         Retained earnings — SFL   12,000
     Transfer 25% of earnings since acquisition to minority
         interest and 75% to consolidated retained earnings.

Note that the retained earnings of SQI have been split into two parts: (i) the amount at the date of acquisition and (ii) the subsequent change. The amount at the date of acquisition does not increase consolidated retained earnings—it is eliminated against the investment in subsidiary account. By contrast, the subsequent change does indeed increase consolidated retained earnings, but only to the extent of the parent company's interest (which in this case is 75% of $16,000, or $12,000).

Consolidated financial statements are the only type where the term "minority interest" appears, and it is customary to place it on the balance sheet between the liabilities and owners' equity, in a place of isolation. As a category, it represents the interest of those shareholders of the subsidiary companies included in the consolidation. We have explained how the amount is arrived at; but—as with the owners' equity account itself in a system based on historic costs—it is much more difficult to say what that amount is supposed to measure. The *CICA Handbook* does not try.

The closing balance in the consolidated retained earnings is exactly the same as SFL's would be if it had used the equity method of accounting. This is not surprising. Equity accounting entries are intended to pick up the parent's share of the reported income of the subsidiary, as does the consolidation process.

An Extended Example

The examples to date have been intended to illustrate single, but important, points. We will now work through a detailed example to illustrate the following:

1. Elimination of intercompany gains or losses on sales between companies in the consolidated entity.
2. Elimination of intercompany debt within the consolidated entity.
3. Purchase of shares at a price different from net book value.
4. Purchase of less than 100% of the shares, creating a minority interest.

Suppose Parent bought 60% of the shares of Subsidiary for $16,000. The trial balances of the two companies as of the date of acquisition are given below:

	Parent	Subsidiary	Combined
Accounts receivable	$ 4,000	$ 4,000	$ 8,000
Inventory	3,000	1,000	4,000
Plant assets (net)	150,000	50,000	200,000
Investment in bonds	25,000		25,000
Investment in subsidiary	16,000		16,000
Accounts payable	(35,000)	(10,000)	(45,000)
Bonds payable		(35,000)	(35,000)
Share capital — Parent	(50,000)		(50,000)
— Subsidiary		(5,000)	(5,000)
Retained earnings — Parent	(113,000)		(113,000)
— Subsidiary		(5,000)	(5,000)
Total	$ 0	$ 0	$ 0

One year later their trial balances were as follows:

	Parent	Subsidiary	Combined
Accounts receivable	$ 31,000	$ 20,000	$ 51,000
Inventory	17,000	9,000	26,000
Plant assets (net)	130,000	70,000	200,000
Investment in bonds	25,000		25,000
Investment in subsidiary	16,000		16,000
Accounts payable	(45,000)	(30,000)	(75,000)
Bonds payable		(49,000	(49,000)
Share capital — Parent	(50,000)		(50,000)
— Subsidiary		(5,000)	(5,000)
Retained earnings — Parent	(124,000)		(124,000)
— Subsidiary		(15,000)	(15,000)
Total	$ 0	$ 0	$ 0

In addition, the following information is available.

a. Parent has purchased goods totalling $35,000 from Subsidiary. The goods cost Subsidiary $25,000. Parent has sold all of them, but has still not paid $20,000 of the bill.

b. Subsidiary has purchased merchandise for $18,000 that cost Parent $11,000. Of the $18,000, $9,000 is still on hand at the year-end. The entire bill is unpaid.

c. The bonds on the books of Parent are due from Subsidiary.

d. Parent originally bought 60% of the shares of Subsidiary for $16,000. Of the purchase difference $5,000 was attributed to the buildings (10% depreciation rate), $3,000 to land, and the balance of $2,000 to goodwill (5% amortization rate).

The consolidation is shown below. The eliminations are indexed by letter to the information above and to the consolidation adjustments and eliminations below.

	Combined		Eliminations	Consolidated
Accounts receivable	$ 51,000	(a)	$ (20,000)	
		(b)	(18,000)	$ 13,000
Inventory	26,000	(b)	(3,500)	22,500
Plant assets (net)	200,000	(d)	5,000	
		(e)	(500)	
		(d)	3,000	207,500
Investment in bonds	25,000	(c)	(25,000)	0
Investment in subsidiary	16,000	(d)	(16,000)	0
Goodwill on consolidation		(d)	2,000	
		(e)	(100)	1,900
Accounts payable	(75,000)	(a)	20,000	
		(b)	(18,000)	(37,000)
Bonds payable	(49,000)	(c)	25,000	(24,000)
Minority interest		(d)	(4,000)	
		(f)	(4,000)	(8,000)
Share capital — Parent	(50,000)			(50,000)
— Subsidiary	(5,000)	(d)	5,000	0
Retained earnings — Parent	(124,000)	(b)	3,500	
		(f)	(6,000)	9
		(e)	600	(125,900)
— Subsidiary	(15,000)	(d)	5,000	
		(f)	10,000	0
Total	$ 0		$ 0	$ 0

(a) Accounts payable	20,000	
Accounts receivable		20,000

Eliminate intercompany debt of $20,000. (There is no intercompany profit to eliminate because the goods have been sold outside the entity.)

(b) Accounts payable   18,000
   Retained earnings   3,500
      Accounts receivable   18,000
      Inventory   3,500

Eliminate intercompany debt of $18,000. Also eliminate
  downstream intercompany profit of 7,000 × 9,000/18,000
  = 3,500 (taxes are ignored int his example).

(c) Investment in bonds   25,000
      Bonds receivable   25,000

Eliminate portion of subsidiary bonds payable held by
  Parent.

(d) Plant assets — buildings   5,000
   Plant assets — land   3,000
   Goodwill on consolidation   2,000
   Share capital   5,000
   Retained earnings   5,000
      Investment in subsidiary   16,000
      Minority interest   4,000

Investment elimination at date of acquisition, as follows:

	Subsidiary total	Minority 40%	Parent 60%
Share capital	$ 5,000	$ 2,000	$ 3,000
Retained earnings	5,000	2,000	3,000
Total book value - owners' equity	$ 10,000	$ 4,000	$ 6,000
Purchase difference allocated to:			
— Buildings (10% depreciation)		$ 5,000	
— Land (no depreciation)		3,000	
— Goodwill (5% amortization)		2,000	10,000
Total purchase price			$ 16,000

(e) Retained earnings   600
      Plant assets — building   500
      Goodwill on consolidation   100

Depreciation and amortization on assets with respect to the
  purchase difference:
        Buildings = 10% on 5,000 = 500
        Goodwill   = 5% on 2,000 = <u>100</u>
                           <u>600</u>

(f) Retained earnings — Subsidiary   10,000
        Minority interest   4,000
        Retained earnings   6,000
   To allocate earnings since time of purchase of shares:

	Subsidiary total	Minority 40%	Parent 60%
Retained earnings: balance - sheet date	$ 15,000	$ 6,000	$ 9,000
Retained earnings: date of purchase	5,000	2,000	3,000
Increase (earnings since purchase)	$ 10,000	$ 4,000	$ 6,000

INCOME STATEMENTS

In the example given above for Parent and Subsidiary, the retained earnings of Parent increased during the first year from $113,000 to $124,000, or $11,000. Let us suppose that Parent paid no dividends and the increase is due entirely to net income. Similarly, suppose that Subsidiary's increase of $10,000 is also due entirely to net income. Assume that the interest on Subsidiary's bond payable is 10%. Further assume that the applicable tax rate is 50%. Here are the trial balances for the income statements for the same year.

	Parent	Subsidiary	Combined
Sales	$ 150,000	$ 100,000	$ 250,000
Opening inventory	3,000	1,000	4,000
Purchases	112,500	46,000	158,500
Subtotal	115,500	47,000	162,500
Closing inventory	7,000	13,000	20,000
Cost of goods sold	108,500	34,000	142,500
Administrative and selling costs	22,000	37,500	59,500
Interest costs		3,500	3,500
Total costs	130,500	75,000	205,500
Net operating income	19,500	25,000	44,500
Interest income	2,500		2,500
Net income before income taxes	22,000	25,000	47,000
Provision for income tax	11,000	15,000	26,000
Net income after income taxes	$ 11,000	$ 10,000	$ 21,000

The consolidation and eliminating entries are made in a manner similar to those for the balance sheet. As before, we have indexed by letter the adjustments and eliminations.

	Combined		Eliminations	Consolidated
Sales	($ 250,000)	(a)	$ 53,000	(197,000)
Opening inventory	20,000			20,000
Purchases	142,500	(a)	(53,000)	89,500
Subtotal	162,500		(53,000)	109,500
Closing inventory	(20,000)	(b)	3,500	(16,500)
Cost of good sold	142,500		(49,500)	93,000
Administrative and selling				
expenses	59,500	(e)	600	60,100
Interest costs	3,500	(c)	(2,500)	1,000
Total costs	205,500		(51,400)	154,100
Net operating income	(44,500)		1,600	(42,900)
Interest income	(2,500)	(c)	2,500	
Net income before income				
tax	(47,000)		4,100	(42,900)
Provision for income tax	26,000		0	26,000
Minority interest		(d)	4,000	4,000
Net income after income tax	$ (21,000)		$ 8,100	$ (12,900)

(a) Sales 53,000

   Purchases   53,000

To eliminate sales of $35,000 from Subsidiary to Parent and
$18,000 in sales from Parent to Subsidiary.

(b) Closing inventory 3,500

   (Balance sheet: inventory   3,500)

To eliminate intercompany profit of 9,000/18,000 × (18,000
 − 11,000) = 3,500 on unsold merchandise bought from
 Parent.
(Note that one side of the entry is used to write down the
inventory on the consolidated balance sheet.)

(c) Interest income 2,500

   Interest costs   2,500

To eliminate 10% interest on bonds of Subsidiary held by
 Parent.

(d) Minority interest 4,000

   (Balance sheet: minority interest   4,000)

To eliminate minority interest in income of Subsidiary: 40%
 of $10,000 $ $4,000.
(Note that one side of this entry is a credit to the *minority
interest* item on the consolidated balance sheet.)

(e) Administrative and selling expenses 600

   (Balance sheet: purchase difference   600)

To amortize a portion of the purchase difference.
 (Note that one side of the entry is a credit to the
 consolidated balance sheet.)

Notice that in the consolidated income statement above, the Eliminations column totals to a reduction in combined incomes of $8,100 due to the elimination of inventory profits ($3,500), amortization of the purchase difference ($600), and minority interest ($4,000). Since the net income flows into the retained earnings one would expect to find a similar reduction in retained earnings on the consolidated balance sheet. This can be demonstrated as follows:

Retained earnings — Parent		$124,000
— Subsidiary		15,000
		139,000
Deduct:		
Purchased retained earnings	5,000	
Consolidation adjustments and eliminations		
(as above)	8,100	13,100
Consolidated retained earnings		$ 125,900

Alternatively, as reported on a consolidated statement of retained earnings, the flow of net income into retained earnings would be as presented below. Observe that at the date of acquisition the consolidated retained earnings equal the retained earnings of Parent.

Notice that the consolidated net income is exactly equal to the income that Parent would report if it had used the equity method of accounting. The closing balance in consolidated retained earnings is also the same as if the equity method had been used. This is demonstrated as follows:

EQUITY METHOD

Net income — Subsidiary	$ 10,000
Parent's share — 60%	$6,000
Unrealized gain — inventories	(3,500)
Depreciation — buildings	(500)
Amortization — goodwill	(100)
Equity pick-up	$ 1,900

At this point Parent would record the following entry in its separate entity accounts:

Investment in subsidiary	1,900.00	
Equity in earnings of subsidiary		1,900.00
To record income under the equity method.		

The credit in this entry would increase Parent's reported net income to $12,900 (i.e., 11,000 + 1,900). Note that this equals the consolidated net income determined earlier.

OTHER FINANCIAL STATEMENTS

In the preceding sections we have illustrated the consolidation of balance sheets and income statements. The same principles apply in consolidating the statement of changes in financial position and the statement of retained earnings.

Where Consolidation is not Appropriate

The purpose of consolidation is to aid the shareholder of the parent company to get a view of the entire economic entity by looking through the legal form. There are some readers of financial statements who do not find this a useful approach and prefer to have unconsolidated financial statements. It is possible that in particular instances non-consolidated statements are the most useful. The purpose of this section is to discuss some of these special circumstances.

First, Revenue Canada collects income tax on the individual corporation, not on the consolidated entity. Therefore, statements for each individual legal entity must be prepared on a non-consolidated basis for this purpose alone.

Second, one may look at financial statements for the purpose of deciding whether the company should be given a loan. The collateral available as security for a loan is an arrangement between the lender and the legal entity, the borrowing corporation—not the consolidated economic entity. It is therefore important to examine the financial statements of the individual companies within the consolidation to make sure that the collateral on the proposed loan can be, and is, pledged by the appropriate companies of the group. In addition, loan covenants (such as the number of times interest must be covered by earnings) are usually stated in terms of the financial position of the legal entity to which the loan is made. Hence, to establish whether these covenants are being adhered to, it is necessary to look at the unconsolidated financial statements. It is possible for consolidated statements to hide detail that is important to some readers.

Finally, most jurisdictions have restrictions on the payment of dividends if such payments would make the company insolvent or reduce the value of the assets below the combined value of the liabilities and the owners' equity. This restriction applies to the individual company. Consequently, directors contemplating a dividend should examine the unconsolidated financial statements of the company.

Examples from Published Reports

In Chapter 2 above, we presented the entire financial statements of Consolidated-Bathurst Inc. (1987). For the following examples we will focus on notes to the financial statements, as they give the consolidation policies followed.

Thomson Newspapers Limited

Excerpts from the financial statements of Thomson Newspapers have been given above in Chapters 5, 13, and 18.

Note 1.   Accounting Policies
(a) Basis of consolidation
   The consolidated financial statements include the accounts of all subsidiary companies. Subsidiary companies acquired during the year have been accounted for using the purchase method. Earnings have been included from the respective dates of acquisition.

This company published 154 newspapers at the end of 1986. They are held through Thomson Newspapers Limited in Canada and Thomson Newspapers Inc. in the United States. If each newspaper were held by a separate operating company, the consolidating worksheet might stretch from one side of the room to the other! More likely, the newspapers would be consolidated by regional groupings before a final consolidation was done.

Loblaw Companies Limited

Excerpts from the financial statements of Loblaw Companies have been given above in Chapter 12.

Note 1.   Summary of Significant Accounting Policies
(a) Basis of consolidation: The consolidated financial statements include the accounts of the Company and all subsidiaries. The effective interest of the Loblaw Companies Limited in the equity share capital of principal subsidiaries is 100%, except for Kelly, Douglas & Company, Limited which is 85% owned.

Eastman Kodak Company

Excerpts from the financial statements of Eastman Kodak have been given above in Chapters 8 and 14.

Notes to Financial Statements
Major Accounting Policies
Basis of consolidation: The consolidated financial statements include the accounts of Eastman Kodak Company and its majority-owned subsidiary companies except the Eastman Kodak Credit Corporation which is accounted for under the equity method. Intercompany transactions are eliminated and net earnings are reduced by the portion of the earnings of subsidiaries applicable to minority shareholders. The excess of the cost of investments in subsidiaries over the value ascribed to the equity in such subsidiaries at the time of acquisition is amortized generally over the succeeding 15-year period.

Summary

Consolidation is the process of taking the separate financial statements of two or more legal entities and combining them into one statement for the combined economic entity. It is most likely that the legal entity will produce its own financial statements for purposes such as tax payment, but usually the financial statements of subsidiaries are not shown separately from the consolidated statement. An exception would be those subsidiaries whose operations are fundamentally different from those of the parent.

A consolidated balance sheet shows the assets of the entire entity, with the interest of minority shareholders explicitly given. A similar treatment is accorded the other financial statements of the entity. By contrast, in a joint venture only the company's share of assets, sales, purchases, etc., is included in the statement.

QUESTIONS

Q19-1. Review and be sure you understand the following terms:

    a. consolidated financial statements

    b. joint venture

    c. equity method *versus* consolidation

    d. equity method *versus* cost method

    e. consolidation worksheet

    f. consolidated trial balance

    g. legal entity *versus* economic entity as the basis for reporting

    h. subsidiary company

    i. parent company

    j. purchase method *versus* pooling-of-interest method of valuation

    k. minority interest on balance sheet

    l. minority interest on income statement

    m. proportionate consolidation

    n. upstream versus downstream sales

    o. combined financial statements

    p. push-down accounting

Q19-2. Specify the differences and similarities between consolidating financial statements and using the equity method of accounting for shares.

Q19-3. The equity method has been described as "one-line consolidation." To what extent is this true?

Q19-4. If the management of a company were worried about "improving the bottom line" on their consolidated statements, how would they be tempted to distribute the positive purchase difference of a newly acquired subsidiary over the assets? (*Hint:* Consider goodwill.) Explain.

Q19-5. Indicate whether you think each of the following companies should issue consolidated statements. Explain your reasons.

    a. Bolinda Limited, a Canadian company, has 100% ownership in a South American subsidiary, Bolinda S.A. The subsidiary pays dividends regularly. However, because of the laws of its country, the subsidiary can send only 10% of the invested capital to Canada.

b. Fermoy Corporation has a 20% voting interest in Bolingbroke Limited, which in turn has a 20% interest in Burridge Limited. Fermoy owns a 40% interest in Burridge Limited directly. Fermoy has one member on the board of Bolingbroke, with which it has close business interests, but it does not consider itself to have "significant influence" on Bolingbroke.

c. Crown Realty Ltd., a Canadian company, has purchased 75% of the shares of Eagle Shores Corporation, a southern U.S. realty corporation. The management of Eagle regard this as an unfriendly takeover. They are seeking help from politicians in their state to pass legislation to the effect that only U.S. citizens can sit on the board of realty companies.

d. Diversified Products Limited is a holding company for a variety of small companies. Their only common characteristics are that they were founded by owner-managers and are now 100% owned by Diversified.

Q19-6. Explain in non-technical language what the purchase difference between the net book value of shares and the amount paid for them represents. What scope, if any, does this offer for window-dressing?

Q19-7. Explain in non-technical language how the pooling and purchase methods differ. Under the method, what else besides the assets could be regarded as being understated?

Q19-8. *Business Week* once reported that a number of U.S. companies are creating "foreign clones." They incorporate a second company in a foreign jurisdiction such as Bermuda and then distribute the clone's shares to its existing shareholders in exact proportion to their present holdings. The clones are then free of U.S. income taxes and other restrictions that U.S. companies have to face. They conduct all their business outside the United States. For purposes of reporting to shareholders, should the clone and the U.S. company be consolidated? combined? neither? Give your reasons.

Q19-9. Explain why it is not usually satisfactory to prepare consolidated statements by simply adding together the financial statements of the companies. Under what circumstances, if any, would this be appropriate?

Q19-10. Under what circumstances should a company not issue consolidated financial statements? Are there any circumstances under which it would be appropriate to issue non-consolidated statements to one set of readers and consolidated statements to another set? Explain.

Q19-11. Parent purchased 100% of the shares of Subsidiary under "fire sale" conditions for $1,300,000 because it was the only company interested in buying them. It later had the tangible assets of Subsidiary appraised. The net market value of the assets was given as $1,800,000. What are the various plausible accounting treatments that might be given to this negative purchase difference of $500,000? Evaluate the merits of each.

Q19-12. If you knew the amount for each of the following on the consolidated financial statement, would you also know the amount on the unconsolidated financial statements of the parent? Explain.

a. share capital

b. retained earnings

c. goodwill on consolidation

d. accounts payable

e. minority interest

f. deferred income tax

g. net income after tax

Q19-13. Is the purchase method of consolidation a violation of the historic-cost convention? Explain.

Q19-14. The U.S. corporation Borg-Warner issued as a dividend to its shareholders all the shares it owned in York International Corporation, a company that manufactures air conditioners. After this "spinoff" the shareholders held exactly the same assets as before, except that they now owned York directly instead of through Borg Warner. What do you speculate the affect of this spinoff was on Borg-Warner's consolidated net income? consolidated balance sheet?

EXERCISES

Note: Unless otherwise indicated, the following assumptions hold for all the Exercises:
(1) the purchase method of valuation is used
(2) the parent company uses the cost method of accounting for its investment in the subsidiary
(3) the fair market value of the assets and liabilities acquired is the same as the book value
(4) goodwill is amortized over forty years

E19-1. The balance sheets of Parent Inc. and Subsidiary Inc. as of 31 December 19X1 are as follows:

	Parent Inc.	Subsidiary Inc.
Cash	$ 5,000	$ 400
Receivables	2,250	800
Inventories	1,500	1,600
Property assets (net)	9,000	4,000
Total assets	$ 17,750	$ 6,800
Accounts payable	$ 3,050	$ 2,800
Share capital	12,000	2,400
Retained earnings	2,700	1,600
	$ 17,750	$ 6,800

Required:
On 1 January 19X2, Parent Inc. acquired controlling interest in Subsidiary Inc. under one of the different conditions described below. In each case, show the consolidated balance sheet as well as the adjusting and eliminating entries that would be appropriate (all transactions are for cash):

a. Parent acquired 100% of the shares of Subsidiary for $4,000.

b. Parent bought 100% of the shares of Subsidiary for $4,800.

c. Parent bought 100% of the shares of Subsidiary for $3,600, which was estimated to be the net market value of Subsidiary's assets and liabilities.

d. Parent bought 90% of the shares of Subsidiary for $3,600.

e. Parent bought 90% of the shares of Subsidiary for $4,000.

E19-2. Consider the same scenarios as outlined in E19-1 above. Here are the balance sheets for Parent Inc. and Subsidiary Inc. as of 31 December 19X2, one year after acquisition.

	Parent Inc.	Subsidiary Inc.
Cash	$ 1,500	$ 400
Receivables	3,600	2,000
Inventories	2,400	1,800
Long-term investment	4,000*	
Property assets (net)	6,000	6,000
Total assets	$ 17,500	$ 10,200
Accounts payable	$ 3,000	$ 2,800
Share capital	12,000	2,400
Retained earnings	2,500	5,000
	$ 17,500	$ 10,200

* This is only true for assumptions (a) and (e). In other situations the investment and cash accounts will be different. You should be able to work out by how much.

Required: Consolidate these balance sheets under each of the five assumptions given in E19-1.

E19-3. In each case below, explain whether the terms are incompatible with each other (in the sense that a company would not use both at the same time).

a. cost method versus pooling-of-interest method

b. equity method versus consolidated financial statements

c. equity method versus cost method

d. upstream sale versus downstream sale

e. joint venture versus full consolidation

E19-4. The income statements of Parent Co. and Sub Ld. for the year ended 31 December 19X5 appear as follows:

	Parent Co.	Sub Ltd	Total
Sales	$ (324,500)	$ (123,485)	$ (447,985)
Opening inventory	23,402	2,385	25,787
Purchases	203,948	83,555	287,503
Subtotal	227,350	85,940	313,290
Closing inventory	34,693	13,895	48,588
Cost of goods sold	192,657	72,045	264,702
Selling and administrative including depreciation	66,409	39,586	105,995
Interest costs	0	7,500	7,500
Total costs	259,066	119,131	378,197
Net operating income	(65,434)	(4,354)	(69,788)
Interest income	(5,000)	0	(5,000)
Net income	$ (70,434)	$ (4,354)	$ (74,788)

Required: For each situation below, show the impact on the total column above if it were to be adjusted to produce the consolidated income statement. (Remember that we are assuming that Parent uses the cost method of accounting for the income of Sub.) Specify which components of net income are changed (e.g. sales, cost of goods sold). Consider each situation independently.

% Owned by Parent Co.	Item
a. 40	Dividends paid from Sub Ltd. to Parent Co. totalled $20,000.
b. 35	Sales from Sub Ltd. to Parent Co. amounted to $23,494 for the year.

c.	65	Sales from Parent Co. to Sub Ltd. amounted to $43,578 for the year.
d.	20	The upstream closing inventory profit was $3,750.
e.	80	The downstream closing inventory profit for the year was $3,750.
f.	50	The purchase difference (attributed to goodwill) was $10,000, to be amortized over ten years.
g.	100	Sub Ltd. borrowed $10,000 from Parent Co. on 1 January 19X5. The interest rate is 11%.

E19-5. Using the information provided in E19-4 above, show the impact on the income of the consolidated company for each of the cases shown below. Specify which components of income are changed (e.g. sales, cost of goods sold). Consider each situation independently. Assume that Parent Co. owns 50% of Sub Ltd. in all cases.

a. Assume items (a), (b), and (f) from E19-4 exist.

b. Assume items (a), (b), (c), and (d) from E19-4 exist.

c. Assume items (c), (e), and (g) from E19-4 exist.

d. Assume items (b), (d), and (f) from E19-4 exist.

e. Assume items (a), (b), (c), (d), and (e) from E19-4 exist.

f. Assume items (b), (c), (f), and (g) from E19-4 exist.

g. Assume items (a), (b), (c) and (e) from Exercise 19-4 exist.

E19-6. Provided below are the 19X5 income statements, balance sheets, and other financial information for Growth Inc. and its new subsidiary Swift Investments Ltd. (Remember that we are assuming that Growth accounts for its investment in Swift on a cost basis.)

INCOME STATEMENTS

	Growth	Swift	Total
Sales	$ (483,579)	$ (138,304)	$ (621,883)
Cost of goods sold	198,345	78,522	276,867
Selling and administrative, including depreciation	145,582	33,452	179,034
Total costs	343,927	111,974	455,901
Income from operations	(139,652)	(26,330)	(165,982)
Interest costs	0	4,000	4,000
Interest income	(4,000)	0	(4,000)
Net income	$ (143,652)	$ (22,330)	$ (165,982)

BALANCE SHEETS

	Growth	Swift	Total
Cash	$ 98,353	$ 54,443	$ 152,796
Accounts receivable	109,490	53,948	163,438
Inventory	153,939	72,420	226,359
Due from associated company	50,000		50,000
Plant assets (net)	318,875	163,636	482,511
Investment in Swift	80,075		80,075
Accounts payable	(24,604)	(26,967)	(51,571)
Bank loan	(150,000)	(105,000)	(255,000)
Bonds payable		(50,000)	(50,000)
Share capital	(350,000)	(125,000)	(475,000)
Retained earnings	(286,128)	(37,480)	(323,608)
	$ 0	$ 0	$ 0

Additional financial information:

(i) Sales from Growth to Swift during the year totalled $7,823. There was an inventory profit of $825 on goods not yet resold at year-end.

(ii) Sales from Swift to Growth amounted to $3,213 for the year. All of the goods were sold by year-end.

(iii) Growth acquired 50% of Swift on 2 January 19X5 for $80,075. Retained earnings of Swift at the time were $15,150, and its share capital was $125,000. The purchase difference is to be amortized over ten years.

(iv) Swift issued $50,000 in bonds bearing an interest rate of 8%. The entire issue is held by Growth.

(v) Included in Swift's accounts receivable is $3,949 owed by Growth. Included in Swift's accounts payable is $185 owed to Growth.

Required: Prepare both a consolidated income statement and a consolidated balance sheet for Growth Inc. for 19X5. Show all calculations.

E19-7.   Give the adjusting entry, if any, that would be required in the consolidation worksheet for the balance sheet and income statement for each of the unrelated items below.

a. In the current year Sub had an after-tax income of $65,000 and paid no dividends. Parent owns 80% of Sub.

b. Sub had a net income of $80,000 and paid a $50,000 dividend, of which Parent received 80%. Parent used the cost method of accounting for Sub and credited the dividends to investment income.

c. The same item exists as in (c) above, but here Parent used the equity method of accounting for Sub.

d. Parent sold merchandise with a value of $53,000 to Sub at a markup of 30% to Parent. Sub had $12,000 of this merchandise still in inventory at the year-end.

e. Parent has just purchased 80% of Sub at a price of $450,000. At the time of purchase, the market value of Sub's net tangible assets was $500,000, and its owners' equity was $400,000.

PROBLEMS

Note: Unless otherwise specified, the following assumptions hold for all the Problems:

    (1) the purchase method of valuation is used

    (2) the parent company uses the cost method of accounting for its investment in the subsidiary

    (3) the fair market value of the assets and liabilities acquired is the same as the book value

    (4) goodwill is amortized over forty years

P19-1. Set out below is the balance sheet of A Company Ltd. and the consolidated balance sheet of A Company Ltd. and its subsidiary, B Company Ltd.

	A. Co. Ltd. Balance sheet 31 Dec. 19X8	A Co. Ltd. Consolidated balance sheet 31 Dec. 19X8
Current assets	$ 1,500	$ 1,800
Tangible fixed assets (net)	2,500	4,500
Investment in B Ltd. (at cost)	1,800	
Goodwill (net)		*
Total	$ 5,800	$ *
Current liabilities	$ 800	$ 1,500
Minority interest	—	360
Retained earnings	*	600
Share capital	*	4,000
Total	$ *	$ 6,460

* You should be able to calculate these numbers from your knowledge of consolidation accounting.

You are also given the following additional information:

(i) A Company Ltd. bought 80% of B Company Ltd on 1 January 19X8. On this date B Company Ltd. had a share capital account of $1,600 and retained earnings of $400. The difference between A Company Ltd.'s investments and 80% of the book value of B Company Ltd. was goodwill. This goodwill is being amortized over five years on a straight-line basis.

(ii) During 19X8 A Company Ltd.'s sales to B Company Ltd. amounted to $1,000. A Company Ltd.'s gross profit margin is 40% of sales. One half of these goods are still in B Company Ltd.'s inventory at 31 December 19X8.

(iii) On 31 December 19X8 A Company Ltd. owes B Company Ltd. $300.

Required: Prepare a balance sheet for B Company Limited as at 31 December 19X8. Show all your calculations to explain your answer.

P19-2. Shown below is a condensed trial balance of Parent Company and Sub Company as of 31 December 19X9.

	Parent	Sub
Cash	$ 1,260	$ 320
Accounts receivable	8,920	1,690
Inventories	12,460	2,310
Dividends receivable	250	
Notes recievable	1,000	
Investments	3,000	
Property assets (net)	8,410	3,630
Accounts payable	(9,420)	(2,360)
Dividends payable		(250)
Taxes payable	(1,063)	(530)
Notes payable		(1,000)
Preferred stock	(5,000)	
Common stock	(15,000)	(2,000)
Retained earnings	(4,817)	(1,810)
Total	$ 0	$ 0

You are also given the following additional information:

(i) Of the Parent Company's accounts receivable, $1,450 is due from Sub Company.

(ii) The inventories of the Sub Company include products purchased from Parent for $1,250. The products cost Parent $950 to produce.

(iii) The $1,000 notes receivable on Parent's trial balance is a five-year note owed by Sub Company.

(iv) The $250 dividends receivable on Parent's trial balance is from Sub's stock.

(v) Parent Company purchased 90% of the common stock of the Sub Company on 1 January 19X7 for $3,000. At the date of acquisition Sub Company's stock was on the books at $2,000 and retained earnings equalled $1,000. The purchase difference is being amortized over five years.

Required:

a. Prepare a consolidated trial balance for Parent Company. Show your worksheet and adjusting entries, indexing the latter to the additional information above.

b. Calculate what the balance would be in the investments account of Parent Company at 31 December 19X9 if it had been keeping this account using the equity method instead of the cost method.

P19-3. On 1 January 19X9, A Company bought 60% of the outstanding shares of B Company for $10,000. On this date the shareholders' equity portion of the balance sheets of the two companies was as follows:

	A Company	B Company
Retained earnings	$ 40,000	$ 12,000
Share capital	25,000	8,000
	$ 65,000	$ 20,000

The difference between the purchase price paid by A Company and the book value of B Company was attributed to fixed assets with an expected life of five years. The results of the 19X9 operations for the companies was as follows:

	A Company	B Company
Net income in A's case, (excluding its share of B's net income)	$ 10,000	$ 2,000
Dividends	2,000	1,000

The following noteworthy events also occurred in 19X9:

(i) A Company's sales to B Company amounted to $800. At year-end one-quarter of these goods were still in B Company's inventory. The original cost of the remaining goods to A Company was $80.

(ii) On 15 July B Company's common shares split two for one.

Required:

a. Assume A Company prepares consolidated financial statements that include B Company. (i) Calculate the minority interest and consolidated retained earnings as they would appear on the consolidated balance sheet of A Company at 31 December 19X9. Be sure to show how you arrived at your answer. (ii) Is minority interest a liability or owners' equity (or something else)? Explain briefly.

b. Assume that A Company accounts on its own books for its investment in B Company using the equity method. (i) Determine the balance in A Company's investment account and A's retained earnings at 31 December 19X9. Be sure to show clearly how you arrived at your answer. (ii) Did dividends paid by B Company to A Company increase, decrease, or leave unchanged A Company's investment in B Company as per the equity method? Explain briefly the rationale for this treatment of dividends.

P19-4. Shown below is a condensed trial balance of Parent Limited and the consolidated trial balance as of 31 December 19X0 for Parent Limited and its subsidiary Sub Limited.

	Parent Limited only	Consolidated Parent and subsidiary only
Cash	$ 890	$ 1,340
Accounts receivable	6,850	8,140
Inventories	13,150	18,380
Notes receivable	2,300	1,000
Investments	4,000	0
Property assets (net)	9,610	14,472
Copyrights and patents	3,704	3,704
Goodwill on consolidation	*	1,040
Accounts payable	(8,930)	(11,467)
Taxes payable	(2,320)	(3,215)
Notes payable	(2,489)	(2,489)
Minority interest	*	(656)
Preferred stock	(6,500)	(7,500)
Common stock	*	(15,000)
Retained earnings	(5,265)	(7,749)
	$ 0	$ 0

* You should be able to fill in these missing accounts from your knowledge of consolidation accounting.

You are also given the following additional information:

(i) Of Parent Limited's accounts receivable, $300 is due from Sub Limited.

(ii) The inventories of Sub Limited include products purchased from Parent Limited for $1,310. The products cost Parent Limited $850 to produce.

(iii) $1,300 of the notes receivable on Parent Limited's trial balance is a five-year note owned by Sub Limited.

(iv) During the year Parent Limited bought goods for $30,000 from Sub Limited. They cost Sub Limited $18,000 to produce. All were sold by year-end.

(v) Parent Limited purchased 90% of the common stock of Sub Limited one year earlier for $4,000. At the date of acquisition Sub Limited's stock was on the books at $2,000 and its retained earnings equalled $1,000. The purchase difference is being amortized over five years.

(vi) Sub Limited paid Parent Limited $3,000 in dividends in 19X0.

Required:

a. Prepare the consolidating worksheet and final trial balance for Sub Limited. Index your eliminating and adjusting entries to the additional information above.

b. Calculate what the balance would be in the investments account of Parent Limited at 31 December 19X0 if it had been keeping this account using the equity method instead of the cost method.

P19-5. Listed below are the income statements for Elgin Limited (in Ontario) and its subsidiary Clayton Corporation (in New York) for the year ending 30 June 19X1. (All figures are in Canadian dollars.)

	Elgin Limited	Clayton Corporation
Sales	$ 190,880	$ 39,580
Cost of sales	124,700	28,350
Gross margin	$ 66,180	$ 11,230
Selling expenses	21,880	4,580
Administrative expenses	11,260	3,310
Net operating profit	$ 33,040	$ 3,340
Interest expense		1,100
Interest income	2,200	
Income before taxes	$ 35,240	$ 2,240
Income taxes	17,800	1,100
Income after taxes	$ 17,440	$ 1,140

You are also given the following additional information:

(i) Of the interest expense of $1,100 of Clayton Corporation, $600 was paid to Elgin Limited.

(ii) Elgin Limited sold $51,000 worth of goods to Clayton Corporation. Of this amount, $19,000 worth are still in the inventory of Clayton Corporation. These remaining goods cost Elgin $17,000 to produce.

(iii) Elgin Limited owns 80% of the shares of Clayton.

Required: Prepare the consolidated income statement.

P19-6. **a.** At the beginning of 19X0, P Company acquired 90% of the voting shares of S Company in a corporate combination accounted for as a purchase. On its books, P Company adopted the equity method of accounting for its investment in S Company. During 19X0, there were no transactions between the companies involving intercompany gains or losses, and the year-end audit established that P Company had properly applied the equity method of accounting. The 19X0 separate entity income statements for P Company and S Company showed net incomes of $55,000 and $10,000 respectively. Which of the following represents the consolidated net income for P Company and its only subsidiary, S Company, for 19X0? (Show your calculations.)

(i) $55,000

(ii) $58,500

(iii) $64,000

(iv) $65,000

(v) None of the above or not determinable from the above facts.

b. On 1 January 19X1 Investor Limited purchased for $50,000 a 40% common-stock interest in Investee Limited, whose net identifiable assets had a fair and a book value of $100,000. The investment is to be accounted for by the equity method. Investee's net income for 19X1 is $30,000, and investor receives dividends of $13,333 from

Investee. Which of the following represents the single maximum amount that Investor Limited could report in 19X1 as income from this investment? (Show your calculations.)

(i) $13,333

(ii) $13,083

(iii) $12,000

(iv) $11,750

(v) None of the above or not determinable from the above facts

c. The investment described in item (b) above appears as a long-term investment in Investor's balance sheet at 31 December 19X1. Which of the following represents the correct amount? (Show your calculations.)

(i) $63,083

(ii) $50,000

(iii) $48,667

(iv) $48,417

(v) None of the above or not determinable from the above facts

P19-7. Punk Rock Corporation (PRC) acquired an interest in Disco Corporation (D) on 1 January, Year 1, for $188,600 and carries its investment at cost. The consolidated balance sheet at the end of Year 5 included a $5,100 asset called "Unamortized excess of purchase price over fair value of net identifiable assets acquired." A footnote explained that the original excess had been amortized in the consolidated statements at the rate of 12.5% per year. The book value and market value of D's net assets were $200,000 at the beginning of Year 1.

At the end of Year 5, PRC's retained earnings were $232,000 and D's net assets equalled $242,000. Included in PRC's inventory at the end of Year 5 were goods purchased from D that had been marked up $10,000.

Required:

a. Determine the percentage of D's common stock owned by PRC.

b. Compute the amount of consolidated retained earnings at the end of Year 5.

c. Compute minority interest at the end of Year 5.

P19-8. A few years ago, Jim Morrison, President of Morrison Hotel Ltd., decided to purchase 18,000 of the 20,000 outstanding shares of stock of Krieger Door Co. Since that time, Morrison Hotel Ltd. has debited the investment account for its share of Krieger's earnings and has credited that account for its share of the dividends. Balance sheets for the two firms as at December 31, 19X5 are shown below. Data indicates that there is a short-term note outstanding in the amount of $10,000 which Krieger owes to Morrison. There is accrued interest of $800 on this note. As well, Krieger owes Morrison $15,000 for managerial services used by Krieger. This amount has been recorded in the books of both firms. The purchase price discrepancy is attributable to over-valuation of the land that Krieger owns.

BALANCE SHEETS

	Morrison	Krieger
Cash	$ 53,800	$ 31,000
Receivables	168,400	74,500
Interest receivable	700	1,900
Inventories	202,200	52,100
Prepaid expenses	5,500	1,300
Investment in Krieger Door co.	267,770	0
Equipment and buildings	401,600	231,500
Accumulated depreciation	(120,000)	(40,000)
Land	55,000	30,000
Total assets	$ 1,034,970	$ 382,300
Payables	$ 186,000	$ 67,700
Tax payable	31,000	9,300
Interest payable	3,100	0
Common shares	500,000	170,000
Retained earnings	314,870	135,300
Total liabilities and equity	$ 1,034,970	$ 382,300

Required: Prepare a consolidated balance sheet as at 31 December 19X5.

P19-9. On 1 January 19X0, Johnson Investment Corp. bought 80% of Harrison Exercise Co. The shares were purchased from McKinnon Holding Co., which still held the other 20% of the voting shares as at 31 December 19X1. In 19X0, Harrison Exercise Co. made $75,000 and paid dividends of $15,000. In 19X1, there was a loss of $25,000, and dividends were $10,000. The balance in the minority interest account was $170,000 on 31 December 19X1. The excess of purchase price over the net book value of assets of Harrison Exercise Co. on 1 January 19X0 was $40,000. This amount was attributed to land.

Required: What is the balance of the investment in Harrison account on Johnson's books on 31 December 19X1 using each of the following methods? Show all your calculations.

a. the cost method
b. the equity method

P19-10. A few years ago, Sergeant Motor Corp. acquired control of Johnson Marine Ltd. for $490,000 in cash. On that date, the book values of the net assets of Johnson Marine Ltd. approximated market. The transaction took place long enough ago that section 1580 of the *CICA Handbook* (requiring the amortization of goodwill) was not in effect. The following data are for the current year-end.

	Sergeant	Johnson	Consolidated
Investment in Johnson	$ 670	$ 0	$ 0
Other assets	1,700	1,030	2,500
Goodwill	0	0	40
Total assets	$ 2,370	$ 1,030	$ 2,540
Bonds payable	$ 500	$ 0	$ 350
Other liabilities	280	330	530
Minority interest	0	0	70
Share capital	600	200	600
Retained earnings	990	500	990
Total liabilities and equity	$ 2,370	$ 1,030	$ 2,540

Required:

a. What method was used to account for the purchase in the books of Sergeant Motor Corp.? Explain.

b. What percentage of shares of Johnson Marine Ltd. are held by Sergeant Motor Corp.? State your assumptions and show your calculations.

c. What is the face value of bonds now held by Johnson Marine? Explain.

d. Johnson Marine owes Sergeant Motors $70. How much does Sergeant Motors owe Johnson Marine? Explain.

e. What was the balance in Johnson Marine's retained earnings account when Sergeant Motors bought control? Show your calculations.

f. How much of the retained earnings of $500 for Johnson Marine is included in the $990 on the balance sheet? Explain.

g. Prepare the investment elimination entry as of the date of the balance sheet given above.

P19-11. Set out below are the final trial balances of Parent Limited and its subsidiary Sub Limited.

TRIAL BALANCES

	Unconsolidated trial balance Parent Limited	Unconsolidated trial balance Sub Limited	Adjustments	Consolidated trial balance
Current assets	$ 10,000	$ 3,000		
Plant assets (net)	71,600	43,000		
Long-term investment in Sub (at cost)	18,900			
Goodwill				
Current liabilities	(5,600)	(4,500)		
Bonds payable	(14,400)	(10,000)		
Minority interest				
Share capital	(5,500)	(4,000)		
Retained earnings	(32,000)	(4,000		
Sales	(120,000)	(64,000)		
Cost of goods sold	65,000	32,000		
Other expenses	12,000	8,500		
	$ 0	$ 0		

You are also given the following additional information:

(i) Parent purchased 80% of the shares of Sub at the beginning of the current year, paying $8,900 for its common shares and purchasing $10,000 of Subs bonds at par. At the date of purchase, Sub's share capital was $4,000 and it had retained earnings of $5,000. Sub's assets were believed to be worth approximately their book value. The purchase difference was to be amortized over the first five years. Parent accounts for its investment using the cost method for reporting income.

(ii) During the current year Sub paid no dividends, but there was a prior-period adjustment of $1,000.

(iii) Parent's sales to Sub during the year totalled $32,000. Of this amount, $890 remained in Sub's inventory at the year-end. The cost to Parent of this remaining inventory was $354.

(iv) A review of the accounts receivable of Parent revealed that $1,500 was owing from Sub at the year-end. It is not considered to be a bad debt.

Required:

a. Complete the consolidating worksheet given above. Then, fill out the consolidated balance sheet and income statement shown below.

CONSOLIDATED BALANCE SHEET

Current assets
Plant assets (net)
Goodwill   _____
                                            ==========

Current liabilities
Minority interest
Share capital
Retained earnings   _____
                                            ==========

CONSOLIDATED INCOME STATEMENT

Sales
Cost of goods sold
Other expenses   _____
Net Income   ==========

b. Calculate the balance that would be in Parent's "Long-term investment in Sub" account at the end of the year if it had used the equity method of accounting for income instead of the cost method.

c. In general, does an increase in the minority interest from the beginning to the end of a year equal the amount shown for minority interest on the income statement? If not, what would be the usual reason for any discrepancy?

P19-12. The trial balances of Parent Inc. and its subsidiary, Sub Inc., as of 30 November 19X5 are shown below.

TRIAL BALANCES

	Parent	Subsidiary	Total
Cash	$ 15,364	$ 7,521	$ 22,885
Marketable securities	75,000	75,000	150,000
Accounts receivable	157,465	196,391	353,856
Due from associated company	75,000	0	75,000
Inventory	851,264	362,134	1,213,398
Prepaid expenses	21,365	10,000	31,365
Investment in subsidiary	354,000		354,000
Land and buildings	1,254,879	685,291	1,940,170
— depreciation	(376,463)	(352,461)	(728,924)
Equipment	589,476	235,891	825,367
— depreciation	(176,843)	(120,560)	(297,403)
Patents — net	25,124	0	25,124
Bank loan	(125,879)	(137,889)	(263,768)
Accounts payable	(835,000)	(462,300)	(1,297,300)

(Continued)

Bonds payable	(80,000)	(75,000)	(155,000)
Share capital	(358,000)	(380,000)	(738,000)
Opening balance, retained earnings	(1,416,533)		(1,416,533)
Dividends	65,000	12,000	77,000
Sales	(580,251)	(258,146)	(838,397)
Cost of goods sold	214,650	85,124	299,774
Selling and administrative	148,564	51,236	199,800
Investment income	(23,000)		(23,000)
Interest expense	9,600	9,750	19,350
Income taxes	115,218	56,018	171,236
	$ 0	$ 0	$ 0

Your research indicates the following additional information about the two companies:

  (i) Parent has purchased all of Sub's outstanding bond issue, which has a coupon rate of 13%.

 (ii) Sub has bought about $150,000 in merchandise from Parent, and about $65,000 is still in inventory. It was sold to Sub at a mark-up of 40% on its selling price. Sub has not paid for $34,000 of these purchases, and the trial balance of Parent includes the amount owing under ordinary accounts receivable.

(iii) Parent owns 80% of Sub. Parent purchased the shares on 1 December 19X4, when the share capital of Sub was $380,000 and its retained earnings were nil. Parent accounts for Sub in its books using the cost method. Any purchase difference is amortized at 5% straight-line.

(iv) Sub has paid dividends of $12,000 during the year.

Required: Prepare the consolidated balance sheet and consolidated income statement for 19X5. Show all your calculations.

P19-13. Shown below are the condensed trial balances of Parent Ltd. and its subsidiary, Sub Ltd., as of 31 December 19X5.

TRIAL BALANCES

	Parent Ltd.	Sub Ltd.
Cash	$ 56,273	$ 25,359
Accounts receivable	48,392	32,932
Inventory	18,579	5,222
Plant assets	234,763	123,945
Investment	120,000	
Accounts payable	(25,823)	(12,458)
Share capital	(225,000)	(75,000)
Retained earnings	(227,184)	(100,000)
Total	$ 0	$ 0

You are also given the following additional information:

(i) Of Parent's accounts receivable, $1,750 is due from Sub Ltd.

(ii) Of Sub's accounts receivable, $1,000 is due from Parent Ltd.

(iii) The inventory of Sub includes products purchased from Parent for $1,700. The products were manufactured by Parent at a cost of $1,400.

(iv) Parent purchased 60% of Sub for $120,000 on 1 January 19X5. At the date of purchase the share capital of Sub Ltd. was $75,000, and its retained earnings totalled $82,540. The purchase difference was attributed to goodwill to be amortized over 40 years.

Required:

a. Prepare a consolidated trial balance for Parent Ltd. Show your worksheet and adjusting entries, indexing the entries to the additional information above.

b. Calculate what the balance would have been in the investments account of Parent Ltd. at 31 December 19X5 if Parent had been keeping the account on the equity basis instead of the cost basis.

P19-14. Provided below are the 19X6 income statement for John's Industries Ltd. and the 19X6 consolidated income statement for Warner Limited, which owns 80% of John's.

INCOME STATEMENTS

	John's Industries	Warner Consolidated
Sales	$ (148,022)	$ (457,349)
Cost of goods sold	82,141	227,156
Selling and administrative	70,000	205,000
Amortization of goodwill		*
Total costs	152,141	*
Income from operations	4,119	*
Interest costs	9,000	6,500
Interest income	(3,000)	(3,000)
Net income before minority interest	10,119	*
Net income	$ 10,119	*

* You should be able to fill in these missing accounts from your knowledge of consolidation accounting. Round to the nearest dollar if necessary.

You are also given the following additional information:

(i) Warner acquired its share of John's Industries five years ago for $205,000, when John's share capital was at $125,000 and its retained earnings totalled $93,750. The purchase difference is being amortized over 10 years.

(ii) Over the course of the year Warner made sales of $13,953 to John's. The cost to Warner to produce the goods was $7,001. At year-end John's inventory still includes $7,972 worth of these goods.

(iii) John's sales to Warner totalled $3,615, all of which Warner resold by year-end.

(iv) Warner has loaned John's $62,500 at an annual interest rate of 12%.

Required: Prepare the income statement for Warner Limited for 19X6. Show all calculations to explain your work.

P19-15. Provided below are the 19X6 income statements and trial balances for Conglomerate Inc. and its subsidiary Simcoe Ltd.

INCOME STATEMENTS

	Conglomerate Inc.	Simcoe Ltd.	Total
Sales	$ (532,533)	$ (245,642)	$ (778,175)
Cost of goods sold	320,674	153,234	473,908
Selling and administrative including depreciation	167,348	68,465	235,813
Total costs	488,022	221,699	709,721
Income from operations	(44,511)	(23,943)	(68,454)
Interest costs	12,000	6,500	18,500
Interest income	(8,500)	(3,000)	(11,500
Net income	$ (41,011)	$ (20,443)	$ (61,454)

TRIAL BALANCES

	Conglomerate Inc.	Simcoe Ltd.	Total
Cash	$ 113,944	$ 64,953	$178,897
Accounts receivable	109,234	49,449	158,683
Dividends receivable	1,300		1,350
Inventory	153,939	72,420	226,359
Notes receivable	55,000	23,000	78,000
Plant assets (net)	234,763	145,742	380,505
Investment in Simcoe	135,000		135,000
Accounts payable	(24,604)	(26,967)	(51,571)
Dividends payable		(2,000)	(2,000)
Bank loan	(150,000)	(107,000)	(257,000)
Notes payable	(85,000)	(55,000)	(140,000)
Share capital	(400,000)	(125,000)	(525,000)
Retained earnings	(143,576)	(39,597)	(183,223)
	$ 0	$ 0	$ 0

You are also given the following additional information:

(i) Conglomerate purchased 65% of Simcoe on 1 January 19X6. Conglomerate paid $135,000 for its share of the firm. At the time of the acquisition Simcoe had common stock totalling $125,000 and retained earnings of $21,154. Of the purchase difference $13,000 was attributed to plant assets and will be amortized over 20 years. The remainder of the purchase difference was attributed to goodwill and will be amortized over 10 years.

(ii) Sales from Conglomerate to Simcoe totalled $35,000 for the year. At year-end $15,000 of the goods remained in Simcoe's inventory. These goods had cost Conglomerate $7,200 to produce.

(iii) Sales from Simcoe to Conglomerate totalled $17,000 for the year. None of the goods remained in Conglomerate's inventory at year-end.

(iv) Included in Conglomerate's accounts receivable at year-end was $4,560 owed by Simcoe. Conglomerate owes Simcoe $15,332 on its account.

(v) Simcoe has declared, but not paid, a dividend of $2,000.

(vi) Simcoe borrowed $55,000 from Conglomerate and signed a promissory note for the funds. The interest rate on the note is 10%.

Required: Prepare both a consolidated income statement and a consolidated balance sheet for Conglomerate Inc. Show all calculations.

P19-16. Show below is the trial balance of Parent Inc. as well as the consolidated trial balance of Parent Inc. and its 60% owned subsidiary, Sub Inc.

TRIAL BALANCES

	Parent	Consolidated
Cash	$ 12,358	$ 21,000
Marketable securities	64,500	132,020
Accounts recievable	186,452	223,322
Bonds receivable: associated company	63,200	0
Inventory	372,904	435,912
Prepaid expenses	19,250	31,601
Investment in subsidiary	280,000	0
Land and buildings	854,352	1,435,616
— depreciation	(258,470)	(432,849)
Equipment	48,560	268,560
— depreciation	(32,000)	(152,560)
Development costs	18,000	18,000
Goodwill		53,960
Bank loan	(130,000)	(267,889)
Accounts payable	(55,936)	(56,315)
Bonds payable	(75,000)	(76,300)
Minority interest		(204,939)
Share capital	(358,000)	(358,000)
Retained earnings*	(706,546)	(745,765)
Dividends	65,000	65,000
Sales**	(1,491,616)	(1,762,406)
Cost of goods sold	671,227	733,045
Selling and administrative	141,244	192,480
Interest and investment income	(15,680)	(264)
Interest expense	24,600	40,671
Income taxes	301,601	370,833
Amortization of goodwill		1,420
Minority interest in net income of Sub		33,847
	$ 0	$ 0

* Retained earnings are as of the beginning of the year *before* the current year's income and *before* the current year's dividends.

** To save you time calculating, it may help to know that the net income of Parent is $368,624, and the consolidated net income is $390,374.

You are also given the following additional information:

(i) Parent uses the cost method to account for its investment in Sub.

(ii) In order to finance the purchase of equipment, Parent bought $100,000 in bonds issued by Sub. As of the balance-sheet date $63,200 are still outstanding, which is the same amount that was outstanding one year earlier. The bonds bear interest at 13%.

(iii) Parent owes Sub $10,350 in trade accounts payable, and Sub owes Parent $4,910. Total sales from Parent to Sub were $146,250, of which $40,800 are still in inventory at an average mark-up of 50% of selling price. There were no sales from Sub to Parent during the year.

(iv) Parent bought all its shares in Sub two years prior to the balance-sheet date for $280,000. This represented 60% of the outstanding shares of Sub. At the date of acquisition, Sub's share capital was $220,000 and its retained earnings were $152,000. The purchase difference was to be amortized over forty years.

(v) During the current year Sub paid dividends of $12,000.

Required:

a. Using the trial balances and supplementary information above, construct the same sort of trial balance for Sub. Inc.

b. Suppose Parent had used the equity method rather than the cost method in accounting for Sub.

(i) What would the balance have been in the "Investment in Sub" account at the *end* of the year on Parent's books? Show your calculations.

(ii) What would the balance have been in retained earnings of Parent at the *end* of the first year?

BIBLIOGRAPHY

AMERICAN INSTITUTE OF CERTIFIED PUBLIC ACCOUNTANTS. *Opinion No. 16: Business Combinations.* New York: AICPA, 1970.

BRILOFF, A.J. *Unaccountable Accounting.* New York: Harper and Row, 1972. Briloff was an accounting professor at New York University who wrote a series of popular articles attacking financial disclosure practices of his time.

LUDWICK, A.M. and SIMPSON, K.W. "The Case of the Missing Property or When Does 50% = 1/2?" *CA Magazine* (April 1973). An argument in favour of proportional consolidation.

CHAPTER 20
Price-Change Accounting

Introduction

Price-change accounting is a general term that includes (i) general-price-level accounting and (ii) current-value accounting.

General-price-level (GPL) accounting is a form of historic-cost accounting in which amounts are stated in terms of a unit of constant purchasing power. It is also called **constant-dollar accounting** or **current-purchasing-power accounting**. Those who support it point out that by stating all financial-statement items in units of the same purchasing power it becomes possible to overcome the distorting effect of inflation. It thus enables one to measure and report explicitly on the gain or loss experienced by the company through holding assets and liabilities with a fixed monetary value in a period of changing general price levels. It is based on a concept of maintaining the financial capital of the firm after adjustment for inflation. The concept of (real) **financial capital maintenance** holds that a firm's income for a period should be measured by the change in the firm's monetary amount of net resources after adjustments for such things as dividends and capital contributions.

Current-value (CV) accounting departs from the historic-cost approach and states assets at their current value instead of their historic cost. It is intended to compensate for the problems that arise when historic costs — even when adjusted for general price-level changes — depart significantly from current values. It is based on a concept of maintaining either the financial or the physical capital of the firm. The concept of **physical capital maintenance** holds that a firm's income for a period should be measured in terms of *real assets* rather than their monetary value. As an example, suppose a young couple bought a house or condominium unit that went up in value by 10% over the next three years. According to the concept of *financial* capital maintenance, the couple are better off because they could now sell their house and get back more than they put in. By contrast, according to the concept of *physical* capital maintenance, the couple are no better off because they started with the house and still have (and presumably still need) a house. Obviously there is no "right" concept here. The one chosen depends on what the decision-maker wants to measure.

An accounting system may be based on either historic cost or current values. Furthermore, it may or may not reflect the changing purchasing power of the unit of currency on which it is based. On this basis we can categorize four approaches, as shown below.

Valuation Method	Is the Changing Purchasing Power of Currency Reflected in Accounts?	
	No	Yes
Historic cost	Conventional accounting systems using GAAP	General-price-level (GPL) systems
Current value	Physical capital maintenance approach	Financial capital maintenance approach

Inflation became a serious problem in most countries in the late 1960s. It improved somewhat by the mid 1980s. Public and professional interest in introducing price-change accounting has risen and fallen roughly according to the severity of inflation. In the United States the S.E.C. pressured the Financial Accounting Standards Board to develop standards for price-change accounting. Similar activity took place in England and Canada. The Canadian standard, Section 4510 of the *CICA Handbook*, was issued in December 1982. The standards in Section 4510 are merely recommended, not required. Moreover they apply to larger companies only. The opposition to price-change accounting in Canada was fairly significant, and some companies refused to publish any such information. In 1986 the requirement for publication of price-change information was dropped in both the U.S. and Britain. By the end of 1986 only a small proportion of companies in the U.S. were reporting price-change information, and the number in Canada had dropped to about a dozen.

Although the popularity of price-change accounting is presently on a downward path, the basic ideas behind it are nevertheless worth understanding for three important reasons. First, price-change accounting helps to put into perspective the criticisms made of accounting systems based on historic cost with no adjustment for (i) the changing purchasing power of the unit of currency and (ii) the changing market values of assets and liabilities. Second, it raises the fundamental problems of income measurement in interesting and insightful ways. Third, because price-change accounting is likely to continue to be around in some form, it is important to understand its strengths and limitations.

General-Price-Level Accounting

General-price-level (GPL) accounting differs from traditional historic-cost (HC) accounting in one way only: GPL accounting states the historic cost of financial-statement items in a unit of purchasing power that is the same for all the items being reported on. By contrast under traditional historic-cost accounting, assets and liabilities are recorded in the books of account in the unit of currency as of the date of the original transaction. The units of currency used in traditional historic-cost accounting are almost certainly different from one another in their purchasing power.

For example, suppose that at the start of a fiscal year a company purchased a piece of machinery for $1,000 with an expected functional life of two years. At the time of the purchase the general price index was 100. The company decided to use straight-line depreciation. Suppose by the end of the first fiscal year the general price-level index was 110, and by the end of the second year it was 120.

Under HC accounting the asset would be shown throughout at its historic cost of $1,000, with depreciation of $500 charged each year. Under GPL accounting the cost would be reported in units of purchasing power. For example, the company might decide to use the dollar as of the end of the second year as the unit of purchasing power. Then the asset would be restated as costing $1,200 (i.e., 1,000 x 120/100), which is its historic cost of $1,000 in units of currency of two years earlier restated to its cost in units of currency at the end of the second year. A summary of the cost in various units of purchasing power is given below:

Year	Price index	Units of purchasing power	Cost
Start of 1	100	Start-of-year-1 dollars	$1,000
End of 1	110	End-of-year-1 dollars	$1,100
End of 2	120	End-of-year-2 dollars	$1,200

Another way of stating the difference between HC accounting and GPL accounting is to say that *GPL uses a constant unit of purchasing power to report its results, whereas HC uses a mixture of units without disclosing which are being used*. GPL does not revalue the assets; it restates their historic cost.

FEATURES OF GPL ACCOUNTING

The single dominant feature of GPL accounting has already been identified: reporting in units of constant purchasing power. As a result, we can further focus on three other characteristics. First, a numeraire is used to represent a unit of constant purchasing power. Second, a choice has to be made of which numeraire to use. Third, a distinction must be made between monetary and non-monetary items on the balance sheet.

The Numeraire

The **numeraire** is the brief name for the unit of purchasing power that will be used in the GPL statements. It is the standard against which all other prices are measured. It could be a constant unit of purchasing power, such as the 1989 dollar, or it could be one that is created anew for every financial statement year-end. The only basic requirement is that it should represent a constant unit of purchasing power.

Although it is the objective of GPL accounting to use a numeraire whose purchasing power is constant over time, it is difficult conceptually to develop a measure that guarantees this result. The usual approach is to identify a bundle of commodities and services that would be purchased by a typical consumer over a week, and then to say that a unit of currency has constant purchasing power over time if it would buy the same bundle as time passes. If the unit of currency does not buy a constant bundle, then one measures the change in its purchasing power by means of a ratio called the **consumer price index (CPI)**. This ratio consists of the amount of currency required to buy the defined bundle compared to the amount required in the base period.

This approach, and its conceptual problems, will be familiar to those students who have taken an economics course that touches on the subject of price indices. The core problem is measuring the consumer's "well offness" as conditions change. For example, suppose prices are generally drifting in one direction (e.g., upward), but changing at different rates. Consumers may then prefer to consume more of the relatively cheaper items and less of the expensive ones. Their "well offness" may, therefore, not have declined in proportion to the increase in price of the original bundle. Thus here the price index would overstate the amount they would have to receive to be as "well off" as they were before. Another difficulty arises when new products come on the market in place of old ones. There may be no satisfactory way to measure how the bundle should be redefined to measure the same amount of consumer satisfaction. For example, the car used in computing a 1970 bundle of consumer items is a quite different product from the one sold today.

The usual meaning attached to *returning the real financial capital* of the shareholder is returning an amount that will have the same purchasing power as that originally invested. The usual approach is to multiply the original capital investment by the change in the consumer price index since that time. The conceptual problem posed by index numbers is ignored in order to achieve another purpose. For example, is $100 of share capital contributed when the consumer price index was 145 still the "real financial capital" three years later when the price index is 183? Because prices have risen, the capital would have to be more — but how much more? The relationship between the price levels is calculated as $(183/145)(100) = 126.21$. Whether individual shareholders would be as well off with $126.21 as they were with $100 three years previously is something that is not directly measurable; but we assume this is true through the use of the price index.

Choice of Numeraire

The main criterion influencing the choice of the numeraire is that its meaning should be clear to the reader of the financial statements.

One approach is to start with some numeraire, such as the Canadian dollar at the end of 1970, and use it consistently thereafter. This has the advantage that the financial statements of previous years are directly comparable with the current statements. The disadvantage is that over time the reader may lose an intuitive grasp of what the purchasing power of the numeraire is, and hence the usefulness of the statements is lessened.

A second approach is to use a numeraire that is easily understandable by the reader, even if it must be replaced regularly. This has the disadvantage that prior financial statements must be restated in the new numeraire. Readers who are not familiar with financial statements in units of purchasing power may well be confused if they try to compare current financial statements with those of prior years having a different numeraire. The advantage is that the current year's dollar can be used as the unit of purchasing power.

The second approach is the one universally adopted, and it will be the one used in this text. To reduce the confusion, we will refer to the financial statements and the numeraire specifically; e.g., 1989 financial results expressed in 1984 $'s".

Monetary and Non-Monetary Items

A **monetary item** is any asset (or liability) whose value (liability) is exactly equal to the amount of currency contracted for, with no adjustment for the change in the general purchasing power of that currency. Examples of *monetary assets* are Canadian currency, accounts receivable, and mortgages receivable. Examples of *monetary liabilities* are accounts payable, bonds payable, and mortgages payable. An example of a *non-monetary asset* is inventory. An example of a *non-monetary liability* is an automobile warranty because the company giving the warranty cannot be sure what the labour and parts costs will be at the time of repair.

Monetary Assets

The essential characteristic of a **monetary asset** is that its value is stated in terms of a fixed amount of currency, so that its real (purchasing power) value shrinks during a period of inflation and rises during a period of deflation. Since GPL accounting concerns itself with the real value of capital, it measures the change in the purchasing power of monetary assets, termed a **monetary loss** or **gain**, and includes it as part of the year's income. This gain or loss is not reported by historic-cost accounting.

For example, investors put $100,000 into a company whose sole function was to purchase and hold mortgages. With the proceeds, mortgages were bought with a yield of 12%, to be paid at the end of each financial year. Interest income was paid out to the shareholders at the end of each year. At the end of three years the company still had the mortgage portfolio, and all the mortgages were considered current and well protected by underlying property values. When the mortgages were purchased, the general consumer price index was 123. At the end of the first year it was 135.3; at the end of the second, 148.83; and at the end of the third, 163.71.

Under HC accounting the income per year would be reported as $12,000, and the owners' equity (or share capital) at all year-ends would be $100,000. This is consistent with the assumption that "well offness" should be measured in terms of financial capital, measured in currency, disregarding any change in purchasing power.

By contrast, under GPL accounting the monetary change would be calculated each year, and the results would be reported using units of the same purchasing power. Let us assume the numeraire is dollars at the end of Year 3. Then the transactions of the earlier periods could be translated using the price index, as follows:

Transaction	At time of transaction Amount	At time of transaction Index	Conversion factor	In Year 3 $'s
Year 1				
Capital contributed	$ 100,000	123.00	163.71/123.00	$ 133,098
Interest and dividends	12,000	135.30	163.71/135.30	14,520
Year2				
Interest and dividends	12,000	148.83	163.71/148.83	13,200
Year 3				
Interest and dividends	12,000	163.71	163.71/163.71	12,000

The three-year experience would be summarized in Year 3 $'s in the following manner:

Original capital contributed (restated)			$ 133,098
Interest income — Year 1:	$ 14,520		
— Year 2:	13,200		
— Year 3:	12,000	$ 39,720	
Cost of mortgages (restated)	133,098		
Value at end of period (in current $'s)	100,000		
Monetary loss		33,098	
Net income after monetary loss		6,622	
Paid in dividends		39,720	
Excess of dividends over income			33,098
Owners' equity, end of period			$ 100,00

This indicates dividends were greater than income; and part of them were in reality a return of capital.

The difference between HC and GPL accounting in this example can be seen clearly if we suppose that the company were wound up at the end of the third year. HC accounting would indicate, "Here is your original capital back". By contrast, GPL accounting would indicate, "You put in $100,000 three years ago. Because prices have gone up over that time, you would have to get $133,098 in present-day dollars now in order to be as well off. But in fact you are getting only $100,000."

Monetary Liabilities

A **monetary liability** is one where the debtor's obligation is stated in fixed monetary terms, and there is no adjustment for changes in the value of that monetary unit. Most liabilities are fixed and hence monetary, although a few (e.g., a commitment to keep a product repaired) are not.

A debtor owing a monetary liability during a period of inflation experiences a monetary gain because the sum returned to the creditor has less purchasing power than the sum originally received. It would at first appear that a company would benefit from having its monetary liabilities as large as possible. On the other side, there is the question whether the party holding the debt is able to obtain a yield on it sufficient to offset the impact of inflation. Note that, taxes aside, if the non-inflationary rate of interest is 2%, then the total rate of interest will have a tendency to be 2% plus the expected inflation rate for the period of the debt. In other words, the inflationary component of the interest rate will tend to balance out the monetary gain or loss.

Using our mortgage company example above, we could calculate the net income per year as the difference between the gross income and the monetary loss. In Year 3 $'s, this would be as follows:

	Gross interest	Principle of mortgage — start of year		Principle of mortgage — end of year		Monetary loss	Net income after monetary loss
Year 1	$ 14,520	$ 133,098	(a)	$ 120,998	(b)	$ 12,100	$ 2,420
Year 2	13,244	120,998		109,998	(c)	11,000	2,244
Year 3	12,000	109,998		100,000	(d)	9,998	2,002
	$ 39,764					$ 33,098	$ 6,666

All figures are in Year 3 $'s. Those indexed by letter are determined as follows:
(a) 163.71/123.00 × 100,000 = 133,098
(b) 163.71/135.30 × 100,000 = 120,998
(c) 163.71/148.83 × 100,000 = 109,998
(d) 163.71/163.71 × 100,000 = 100,000

Supporters of GPL accounting would point out that experience tends to support the assertion that creditors usually are able to obtain this inflationary component, and that GPL accounting makes it possible to indicate to the reader what the monetary loss is. With HC accounting, the monetary gain or loss is ignored, and the reader is simply told the gross interest cost or income. In a period of rising prices the historic-cost statements tend to overestimate the real revenue of monetary assets and the real interest cost of monetary liabilities.

Monetary Gain as Income

There is general agreement that a loss or gain on a monetary asset should be considered part of the income of the period and included in retained earnings. The argument is that the gain or loss is *real* in the sense that there has been a decline in the purchasing power of each dollar of monetary assets.

There is less agreement over recognizing a monetary gain on a debt during a period of inflation, although the weight of opinion appears to favour doing so. The counter-argument is that the proceeds of the debt may have been used to purchase plant assets whose real value has declined more sharply than originally anticipated when the depreciation policy was established. Since it is not accounting practice to write down plant assets to market, except under unusual circumstances, this decline in value would not be recorded and hence not offset against the monetary gain.

For example, Tankers Limited was established to borrow funds on a ten-year mort-gage bond and invest it in an oil tanker that would then be leased to a large oil company. The tanker cost $50 million, and the full amount was borrowed at 12%. The credit of the lessee was considered good, even through the owners' equity in the company was minimal. At the start of the first fiscal year the consumer price index was 100, and at the end of the year the index was 115.

If the company used GPL accounting, it would restate the cost of the tanker to $57.5 million and show a monetary gain of $7.5 million to offset the interest costs of $6 million. However, the tanker market may suffer a general decline, and the company may have a potential loss if it is resold. If the rental rates on the tanker reflected world rental rates, then this market decline would show itself later in a drop in rental revenues. (For example, after OPEC price hikes, tanker rental rates in terms of real prices tend to drop because the demand for crude oil, and hence for tankers to carry it, tends to drop.)

Unusual Features of GPL Accounting

The monetary losses and gains reported under GPL accounting are a natural by-product of using a numeraire with a fixed purchasing power; once this is done, then a monetary gain or loss must be reported in some manner. By the same token, since neither historic-cost nor current-value accounting based on preservation of physical capital use a numeraire with constant purchasing power, they do not report a monetary loss or gain.

Another unusual feature of GPL accounting is the importance of recording the acquisition date of all assets so that their historic cost can be restated in terms of the numeraire. This **vintaging** of assets would be a start-up cost of introducing GPL accounting, but would only need to be done once. Thereafter, the GPL financial statements at the start of the year would be restated in the units of purchasing power as of the end of the year, and only the current year's transactions would then have to be restated and included. It should be noted that this means it is not sufficient to produce a GPL statement by taking *one* year's historic-cost balance sheet and adjusting it for the change in the price index over the year. The individual items in it must be GPL-adjusted from the date of acquisition.

Because the numeraire is usually changed annually to the current value of the unit of currency, the financial statements of the previous year are not comparable unless they are changed to the same numeraire. This would not be technically difficult if all the statements are published in GPL form because the same conversion factor would apply throughout.

IMPLEMENTATION OF GPL ACCOUNTING

The steps in converting an HC statement to a GPL-adjusted one can be summarized as follows:

1. Choose the numeraire. Usually this is the unit of currency of the most recent financial statement.

2. Choose the price index to be used to convert all other years' currency into the numeraire. The *CICA Handbook* [4510.49] recommends either the consumer price index (CPI) or the gross national expenditure implicit price deflator, both published by Statistics Canada.

3. Identify the monetary items and the non-monetary items.

4. Convert the opening trial balance into amounts measured in terms of the numeraire. To do this, determine the date of acquisition of all non-monetary assets and liabilities. Then convert their historic cost values to GPL values by multiplying their original HC-accounting amounts by the ratio of the numeraire price index divided by the price index at the date of acquisition. For example, a piece of equipment was purchased for $5,000 when the CPI was 130. It was 180 as of the date chosen for the numeraire. The restated cost would therefore be 5,000 (180/130) = 6923.

The usual rules of accounting are applied to test the new amounts to see whether they are above current market values. Those accounts usually written down to market values under HC systems (e.g., inventories) are also written down to market under GPL accounting. Plant assets would not usually be written down to market.

Convert share capital the same way as non-monetary liabilities.

It is not necessary to vintage monetary assets since their value at any time is the unit of currency in which they are payable. They are restated in terms of the numeraire by multiplying them by the ratio of the price index at the end of the year over the index at the start of the year. For example, a monetary asset, cash, was $100 at the start of the year when the price index was 150. It would be restated in terms of the numeraire as 100 (180/150) = 120. Note what this means: the $100 on hand at the beginning of the year has the equivalent purchasing power of $120 in current dollars. It should *not* be interpreted to mean that the company had $120 in the bank at the start of the year.

5. Restate all transactions during the current year in terms of the numeraire, using price indices published through the year by Statistics Canada. To reduce the clerical work, it is acceptable to use averages for operating items such as purchases and sales. However, material individual transactions such as purchases of large non-monetary assets should be treated individually.

Monetary assets and liabilities at the end of the current year are as shown in the HC balance sheet. Non-monetary assets and liabilities must be calculated by starting with the opening GPL trial balance and then adding all items calculated above.

6. The amount needed to balance the statements is the monetary gain or loss for the year. This could be calculated individually for each of the monetary items, but the process is so laborious that it is customary to assume the balancing figure is the gain or loss. The major monetary gain or loss in the major transactions would be identified, and the remainder would be assumed to be smaller items.

AN EXTENDED EXAMPLE

In this example the steps set out above will be followed. Although the major elements of GPL accounting will be present, it will be kept simple enough that the monetary gain or loss can be derived directly.

M. Ltd. is a company that started life at the end of Year 1. To keep the illustration simple all transactions take place at the end of each fiscal year (31 December), except for the final one. All dollar figures in this example represent thousands of dollars.

On 31 December Year 1, M Ltd. started business. At that time the CPI was 100. The owners raised $200 by sale of shares and used the proceeds to purchase two units of inventory costing $50 each. The remaining funds of $100 were put in the bank. There was no other activity. Thus Year 2 was the first year of active operations.

On 31 December Year 2, M Ltd. sold one unit of inventory for $75 on credit and charged cost of goods for half the acquisition cost. At that time the CPI stood at 110. On that date M Ltd. also purchased a plant asset for $150. A $100 ten-year 12% bond (with interest payable each 31 December) was issued to raise part of the funds. The balance was paid out of available cash.

On 31 December Year 3, M Ltd. sold the remaining unit of inventory for $90 on credit. It charged one-tenth of the cost of plant assets as depreciation expense. M Ltd. also paid interest of $12 in cash on the bond. Consumer prices had risen 5% during the year, and the CPI stood at 115.50.

On 1 January Year 4, M Ltd. sold all its plant assets for $180. Its accounts receivable were paid in cash, and its long-term debt was retired. Prices had not risen from Year 3.

A summary of the above transactions using HC accounting is given below. Credit balances are shown in parentheses.

SUMMARY OF TRANSACTIONS — HISTORIC-COST BASIS

Item	CPI = 100 Trial balance Year 1	Trans- actions Year 2	CPI = 110 Trial balance Year 2	Trans- actions Year 3	CPI = 115.5 Trial balance Year 3	Trans- actions Year 4	CPI = 115.5 Trial balance Year 4
Cash	$ 100	(50)	50	(12)	38	180 165 (100)	
							283
Accounts receivable		75	75	90	165	(165)	0
Inventory	100	(50)	50	(50)	0		0
Plant assets							
Cost		150	150		150	(150)	0
Depreciation				(15)	(15)	15	0
Total assets	200	125	325	13	338	(55)	283
Long-term debt		(100)	(100)		(100)	100	0
Share capital	(200)		(200)		(200)		(200)
Income Yr. 2		(25)	(25)		(25)		(25)
Income Yr. 3				(13)	(13)		(13)
Income Yr. 4						(45)	(45)
Owners' equity	(200)	(25)	(225)	(13)	(238)	(45)	(283)
Total liability + owners' equity	(200)	(125)	(325)	(13)	(338)	55	(283)
Sales		(75)		(90)			
Cost of sales		50		50			
Depreciation				15			
Interest				12			
Gain on sale						(45)	
Net income		(25)		(13)		(45)	

The implementation steps will now be followed to convert the Year 3 financial statements onto a GPL basis, with comparative figures for Year 2. Year 3 is chosen for this example because it represents the greatest challenge. Year 4 will be left to illustrate another point later.

1. *Choose the numeraire.*
   Following convention, we will choose the numeraire to be the unit of currency as of the end of Year 3.

2. *Choose the price index.*
   We will use the given CPI of 115.5.

3. *Identify the monetary items and the non-monetary items.*
   The monetary items are the cash, accounts receivable, and long-term debt. The non-monetary items are the inventory and the plant assets.

4. *Convert the opening trial balance for Year 3 (i.e., the trial balance for the end of Year 2) as well as all subsequent non-monetary items into the numeraire.*
   The monetary items are restated from the *start* of Year 2. This is done by multiplying their historic-cost amounts by the change in the purchasing power of the unit of currency, or 115.5/110. Non-monetary items are restated by expressing their original transaction values in terms of the numeraire. Thus we have the following:

GPL BALANCING AMOUNT — END OF YEAR 2 IN YEAR 3 $'s
Numeraire = 115.5

Item	Date of acquisition	Index at time	Historic cost	Conversion factor	Balancing amount
Cash	End of Year 2	110	$ 50.00	115.5/110	$ 52.50
Accounts receivable	End of Year 2	110	75.00	115.5/110	78.75
Inventory	End of Year 1	100	50.00	115.5/100	57.75
Plant assets	End of Year 2	110	150.00	115.5/110	157.50
Long-term debt	End of Year 2	110	(100.00)	115.5/110	(105.00)
Share capital	End of Year 1	100	(200.00)	115.5/100	(231.00)
Balancing amount					$ 10.50

The balancing amount above is the balance in retained earnings at the start of Year 3, measured in terms of the numeraire and using GPL accounting to measure income. This can be demonstrated by stating the Year 2 income statement in terms of the numeraire, as follows:

GPL INCOME CALCULATION — YEAR 2 IN YEAR 3 $'s
Numeraire = 155.5

Item	Time of transaction	Index	Historic cost	Conversion factor	Balancing amount
Sales	End of Year 2	110	$ 75.00	115.5/110	$ (78.75)
Cost of sales	End of Year 1	100	50.00	115.5/100	57.75
					21.00

Monetary loss in holding cash (acquired end of Year 1)				
Purchasing power in terms of the numeraire				
— Start of company		$ 100 (115.5/100)	115.50	
— End of Year 2		100 (115.5/110)	105.00	10.50
Net income after monetary loss — Year 2				$ 10.50

5. *Restate all transactions through the year in terms of the numeraire.*

All sales took place at the end of the year. Hence they are already stated in terms of the numeraire. Interest was also paid at the end of the year. However, the inventory was purchased in an earlier period. Therefore its cost must be restated, and depreciation must be recalculated using the restated cost of the plant asset. This is shown below:

GPL INCOME CALCULATION — YEAR 3 IN YEAR 3 $'s

Item	Time of transaction	Index	Historic cost	Conversion factor	Numeraire (@115.5)
Sales	End of Year 3	115.5	$ 90.00	115.5/115.5	$ (90.00)
Cost of sales	End of Year 1	100.0	50.00	115.5/100.0	57.75
					(32.25)
Interest					12.00
Depreciation — 10% of $150 (115.5/110)					15.75

Monetary loss:

	Opening balance	Trans-actions	Closing balance	Actual balance	Loss	
Cash	$ 52.50	$ (12.00)	$ 40.50	$ 38.00	$ 2.50	
Receivables	78.75	90.00	168.75	165.00	3.75	
Long-term debt	(105.00)		(105.00)	(100.00)	(5.00)	1.25
Net income — Year 3						$ (3.25)

6. *Balance the statements by means of the monetary gain or loss.*

Since every item except the monetary loss is calculated directly, the loss can be derived as the balancing figure. In practice this is what is done to avoid the tedious calculations that would otherwise arise. However, the major sources of monetary gain or loss can be, and should be, identified (as was done above).

TRIAL BALANCE — YEAR 3 IN YEAR 3 $'s

Cash	$ 38.00
Accounts receivable	165.00
Plant assets — cost	157.50
Accumulated depreciation	(15.75)
Long-term debt	(100.00)
Share capital	(231.00)
Net income — Year 2	(10.50)
— Year 3	(3.25)
	$ 0

This concludes the example for GPL accounting, but we will return to it later when the examples for current-value accounting have been developed. For the moment let us emphasize the following characteristics of GPL accounting illustrated by this example: (i) it is essentially cost-based accounting with an adjustment for price-level changes; (ii) the monetary loss is measured as a by-product of the price-level restatements; (iii) vintaging of assets is done; and (iv) the introduction of the monetary loss and the use of the numeraire introduce a complexity in the statement beyond that of traditional GAAP-based accounting.

Current-Value Accounting

Current-value (CV) accounting is a term used to describe accounting reports that show the contemporary value of the company's assets instead of their historic cost (whether measured in dollars or units of purchasing power). The use of asset values instead of costs represents a major departure from both historic-cost and general-price-level accounting.

Although financial statements that show current asset values are intuitively appealing, they do pose problems. Different current values can be calculated for a given asset. Moreover, valuation frequently relies heavily on estimates of future events whose outcome is neither known nor knowable. Accountants have traditionally been reluctant to depart from the "objectivity" of historic-cost systems. Nevertheless value-based systems have had greater public appeal than GPL-adjusted systems, and in Canada, the United States, and England we have seen serious attempts to introduce a version of current value.

VALUATION AND THE REALIZATION PRINCIPLE

If one is going to state an asset at its value instead of its cost, then the recognition convention immediately raises the issue of realization. An asset held for several periods will be stated at different values at different financial statement dates, and the amount of the change will be reported in the accounts. This increase (or decrease) in asset values is frequently referred to as a **holding gain** (or **loss**) because it arises from ownership of the asset over time, rather than from the trading or manufacturing activities of the company.

Under cost-based accounting, asset values would not be restated until the point of realization. Recall that the *point of realization* is defined as the point at which the major portion of the economic activity has taken place, and the risks are substantially over. If assets are to be restated to their current value at each financial year-end, then the gain or loss will have to be recognized at the time of each revaluation, not just at the point of realization.

How one interprets these changes in asset values depends on the concept of *capital maintenance* that one chooses to use. There are two choices. First, one can define capital maintenance as the maintenance of (real) financial capital (i.e., the general purchasing power of capital). Here a gain is represented by asset values in excess of the original contributed capital, adjusted for changes in the purchasing power of money. Second, one can define capital maintenance as the maintenance of physical capital. Here a gain is represented by assets in excess of those required to maintain a productive capacity equal to that originally provided by the contributed capital.

We will discuss later what part of this gain should be treated as part of the income available for distribution to shareholders.

Asset Valuation

The asset valuation performed in CV accounting is necessarily limited, and it is important to understand what this limitation is. Its basic approach is to take each asset one by one and assign a value to each that represents its current value according to some criterion, such as its current replacement cost or selling price. This process does not measure the value of these assets to the company as a group. Hence it does not measure the total value of the company's assets; it only provides the total of the individual assets it measures.

The reason for this limitation is that one would otherwise have to arrive at a value for the whole company, which involves even more difficult problems of measurement and forecasting than the already serious ones of CV accounting. The difference between the value of the total company and the valuation arrived at using current value is usually referred to as **goodwill**. The valuation of this goodwill is left to the investor. The objective of CV accounting is to aid in that assessment, not to make it. We will discuss asset valuation in more detail below.

Liability Valuation

The treatment of liabilities under most current-value systems is not consistent with the treatment of assets. Long-term debt (e.g., bonds payable) is not shown at the price assigned to it by the market. Instead it is valued using customary historic-cost rules. This is the treatment recommended, for instance, in the *CICA Handbook* [4510].

The reason for this inconsistency appears to be the paradoxical situation that a company whose debt is regarded by the market as increasingly risky would as a result show a gain because of the decrease in market value of its long-term liabilities. If it valued the bond liability on its balance sheet at its current market value, then it would report a gain each time its situation got worse and the bonds dropped in price.

On the other hand, even when the market perceives no change in a company's riskiness, its bonds may drop in price because the market rate of interest has risen. The fall in price may represent the present value of the gain the company has made by issuing its bonds at a time when interest rates were lower. If at the same time the company had assets consisting of a bond portfolio it would, under CV accounting, record any gains or losses arising from a change in market value. Hence, the treatment between the two is not symmetrical.

It could be argued that it might be possible to break down a change in bond price into two components: the market effect due to changing interest rates overall and the risk effect due to changing perceptions of the company's riskiness to the investor. The change due to the market effect might then be included in income, and the risk effect might be excluded to avoid the inconsistency described above. However, this has not been done.

Owners' Equity

Since the total assets under current value do not equal the sum of their individual market values, the total for owners' equity does not represent the value of the business to the owners.

Under the concept of maintenance of real financial capital, the share capital is shown at its original amounts adjusted for general price-level changes, as in GPL-adjusted accounting. Under the concept of maintenance of physical capital, the share capital is shown at the original amounts contributed, in the same manner as historic-cost statements.

Operating income for the period under both concepts is calculated by deducting from revenue the *current* cost of the expenses, instead of their *historic* cost. The general intent is to show the operating profit that would have been earned had the company had to pay current costs to carry on its activities. Gain or losses that arise from holding assets from an earlier period would be identified as such and shown separately. For example, depreciation might be calculated by applying the depreciation formula (e.g., straight line over ten years) to the current cost of the asset instead of to its historic cost. Opening inventory was valued at its current value at the beginning of the year, and hence cost of goods sold includes it at that cost. Any change between the current cost of these assets and their purchase cost is termed a *holding gain* (or *loss*). The amount of this holding gain or loss will differ between the physical and financial capital concepts because the purchase cost for the latter is restated to reflect general purchasing power changes. We will show later that the choice of capital maintenance concept helps to determine whether holding gains are (i) income that could be distributed to shareholders; or (ii) part of owners' equity that needs to be retained within the business.

We will first examine CV accounting using the *physical capital* concept, in which the usual test is whether the physical capital is maintained (not the financial capital). This means that at the end of the year, (i) the physical assets (inventory, plant assets, etc.) must be as productive physically as those at the beginning of the year; and (ii) the net monetary assets (e.g., cash, accounts receivable and payable) must be sufficient to permit the company to carry on its normal operations.

A company's assets are constantly being used or traded. Hence there is no possibility that they could be physically the same at the beginning and end of the year. Therefore a surrogate is needed for physical capital maintenance. The surrogate is the market value of the non-monetary assets at each point in time. If the company is able to maintain the net market value of its physical assets, then we infer that it is as well off as before.

Monetary assets are part of the buffer stock of the company. They are a necessary part of its operations that are generally related to buying, making, and selling the company's product. If the input price of the product rises, the company presumably will be able to gain a higher selling price, and the value of the monetary assets needed to support this activity will have to go up. As a result, there will be less cash available for dividends, and some have argued that this represents a decrease in the income available for distribution to owners. The amount that should be taken out of income available to owners and retained within the business to finance monetary assets is termed a **monetary working-capital adjustment**.

VALUATION OF ASSETS

The general principle in CV accounting is that assets should be shown at their current value. If a well-defined market exists there is a presumption that it will give the "current market value." Usually, however, most physical assets of a firm cannot be bought and sold readily. Thus their current market value is not readily determined and must be approximated. We will now discuss the most common methods of approximation.

Realizable Value

In general, the **realizable value** of an asset is the estimated net amount (after completion and disposal costs) that would be paid for it in an efficiently operating market under ordinary selling conditions.

The net realizable value of inventory is the same as that calculated in Chapter 6 when applying the lower-of-cost-and-market test.

The net realizable value of a plant asset is the estimated receipts if it were sold. If it has to be dismantled and transported to a new location, these estimated costs would be deducted. For plant assets at remote sites (e.g., mine plants), the transportation costs may reduce the realizable value to zero. Alternatively, an estimate might be made of the net realizable value if sold as a working operation in the present site. However, in effect one would be trying to estimate the total value of the operation, and this would involve the familiar problems of subjectivity.

A large asset such as an oil refinery consists of many separate items including motors, pressure chambers, pumps, and gauges. It is quite possible to get two different estimates of realizable value by valuing it either as an entity or as a collection of individual items. Presumably one would use the higher estimate on the grounds that the company would act in its best interests by getting the highest price possible.

Some assets of the firm may not have a meaningful realizable value. We have already referred to assets in remote sites which may be very valuable to the company in that site, but too remote to resell. Some intangible assets (e.g., subscription lists for newspapers) may have a well-defined realizable value; but for others (e.g., organization expenses or purchased goodwill), the concept of realizable value may not be meaningful.

Current Costs

The **current cost** of an asset is "the amount of cash or other consideration that would be needed currently to acquire an asset having the same service potential as embodied by the asset owned and, depending on the extent of technological change, would be determined by reference to either current reproduction cost or current replacement cost" [*CICA* 4510.15 (a)].

The **current reproduction cost** is the amount "that would be needed to acquire a used asset of the same age, in the same location and in the same condition as that owned or the amount of cash or other consideration that would be needed currently to acquire a new asset that has the same service potential as the existing asset had when it was new, adjusted for depreciation and amortization" [*CICA* 4510.15 (b)].

The current reproduction cost refers to the "service potential" of the asset, which implies such attributes as production capacity, service life, and quality of output. This cost is therefore the cost of something that will have operating characteristics that are similar to, but not necessarily identical with, those of the asset being valued.

For example, a company has a car to operate an internal courier service. The car is two years old, originally cost $10,000, and is depreciated at 30% a year on a declining-balance basis. Its net book value at this point is therefore $0.7 (0.7) 10,000 = \$4,900$. Suppose, a new car of the same type would cost $12,000. The current reproduction costs of the car would be the price of equivalent new cars adjusted for depreciation, or

0.7 (0.7) 12,000 = \$5,880. If an equivalent used car could be found, then the current reproduction cost would be its purchase price. Defining this cost in terms of the depreciated cost of a new item is an attempt to approximate the price of a used-car market if one does not exist.

Current replacement cost is the amount that "would be needed currently to acquire the best available asset to undertake the function of the asset owned, adjusted for depreciation or amortization if appropriate" [*CICA* 4510.15 (c)].

The emphasis in this definition is on the function performed by the original asset, not its physical attributes. This is a more difficult concept to deal with because it is often debatable whether the same function is being performed by the second asset. Also, the second asset may perform additional functions, and an estimate has to be made of the split between the cost of the two functions.

In our car example above, it may be argued that a courier service is unnecessary, and that the same results could be achieved by using electronic mail. Suppose most, but not all, of the company people involved have computer terminals. Then the additional cost of electronic mail would be minimal. Further suppose that the productivity of some, but not all, of those without terminals would benefit if they were given a terminal because they could use it for other purposes. The debatable point is whether electronic mail performs the same function, or substantially so, as a courier service. If it was decided that it did, then the current replacement cost would be the marginal cost of adding the electronic mail service to the computer network, including a part of the cost of the additional terminals. This would be taken as the current cost, even though the company continued with the car-based courier service. In other words, management cannot veto the use of current replacement cost by refusing to use the new function. However, they can argue that the functions are not really functional replacements.

Value in Use

The **value in use** of an asset is "the present value of future cash flows expected to result from the use of an asset by the enterprise and from its ultimate disposition" [*CICA* 4510.15 (f)].

In a smoothly functioning market envisioned by the economist, it is the expected value in use that would set the current price that people would be willing to pay for an asset. Hence realizable value, current replacement cost of an equivalent asset, and value in use would all be about the same in an efficient market.

Value in use is dependent on being able to estimate the cash flows that arise from the use of an asset (either net cash income or cash savings from the use of the asset). In most real situations it is not possible to attribute the cash flow to individual assets unless one aggregates assets together into some organizational units such as a self-contained factory or operating division. Despite this difficulty, value in use may provide an alternative test at times for the credibility of current values arrived at by other means.

Conceptual Issues in Asset Valuation

It is difficult to choose between alternative measures of current value without reconsidering the main objective for doing CV accounting in the first place; namely, to provide a measure of capital maintenance that is based on either (i) real financial capital (i.e., the general purchasing power of capital) or (ii) physical capital (i.e., productive capacity). If there were a well-organized market for all assets, the valuation problem would disappear as long as one accepted that maintaining the market value of the asset is equivalent to maintaining its operative productivity.

It is when one no longer has reliable market prices as a referrent that the difficulty starts. We then find the problem commonly found in accounting, that the measurements that appear the most relevant are also the most subjective. We can list the valuation methods in ascending order of relevance (and ascending order of subjectivity) as follows:

1. *Realizable value* is only highly relevant if there is a well-organized market for the assets. This is rare. If one arrives at realizable value by valuing each individual asset (which makes it easier to find market values), then one has to make assumptions about disposition costs, and one ignores the value of goodwill. If realizable value is applied literally in such cases, it is difficult to see how the result would be a meaningful proxy for maintaining physical capital.

2. *Current reproduction cost* recognizes changes in the technology of doing essentially the same thing, but does not recognize different ways of doing the same function. If one used this method consistently, then the physical capital would be maintained for doing things in the same way, but radically new ways for achieving the same objective would be ignored. For example, railways would have recognized the replacement of the steam engine with diesel, but not the growth of air transportation as an alternative method for moving passengers and high-value cargo.

3. *Current replacement cost* recognizes new ways of accomplishing the same purpose through quite different assets. If this were used consistently, it would provide a measure of capital maintenance that accommodates major technological change. For example, the copper long-distance telephone cables owned by the telephone companies would not be priced at their own replacement cost if satellite communications provided a functionally equivalent alternative.

   Current replacement cost may not reflect a major economic change, however. For example, if traffic on long-distance lines fell off because of general economic decline, their earning power would decline. In the event there were an organized market for the purchase and sale of such long-distance lines, their market price would fall as a result. Does that mean that the owners' physical capital has declined? Probably not, if we think of their capital as being the capacity to send messages over long distances. The apparent paradox arises here because we have defined the proxy of physical capital to be market value, and in this example the physical capital has remained the same while the market value has dropped.

4. *Value in use* is conceptually the best proxy for current market value, but its calculation depends on identifying and estimating the present value of future cash flows. Its use can also lead to the same paradox as that described above when market values are used as a proxy for physical capital.

If a market value for all assets were freely available, then the depreciation of plant assets could be established as the decline in market value over the period. When other valuation methods such as replacement cost are used, a problem arises known as *backlog depreciation*. Consider the following example.

A piece of equipment was purchased for $100 at the start of Year 1. It was estimated to have a service life of two years with no salvage value. It was to be depreciated at 50% a year. At the end of Year 1 the cost of a similar new item was $120, and at the end of Year 2 it was $140.

Following the rules of CV accounting, the asset was depreciated at 50% of $120 = $60 the first year, and 50% of $140 = $70 the second year. Just after the end of the second year the asset was scrapped. On the balance sheet at the end of Year 2 the account appeared as follows:

Equipment — replacement cost (new) of old asset	$140
— depreciation charged to income	130
	$ 10

The $10 difference is **backlog depreciation**, or **catch-up depreciation**, the amount by which annual depreciation charges have failed to equal the replacement cost of the asset. Suppose in this example that the equipment was the only item in the company and that it had been leased annually for a cash payment equal to its annual depreciation charge. At the end of two years the company would have $130 cash, which would not be sufficient to buy a replacement. Because it did not know at the end of Year 1 what the replacement cost would be at the end of Year 2, it based its annual depreciation on the then replacement cost of $120. It could be argued that the Year 1 results should be restated and that the $10 ought to be charged back to it.

The backlog depreciation problem is not serious if the company has a number of assets that have to be replaced regularly over time. Suppose in the example above that the company had two items of equipment, each with a functional life of two years, and that it replaced one each year and disposed of the old machine for nil value. To start the example, assume at the beginning of the first year it had one half-used machine valued at $50 and that it purchased a new one for $100. At the end of the first year it disposes of the older machine at the start of the year, buys a new one for $120, and records depreciation of 2 x $60 = $120. The machine disposed of would have been restated at the end of the year to $60 and would have accumulated depreciation of $60. Assuming it was disposed of at nil value, there would be no gain or loss on the sale.

At the end of the second year depreciation of 2 x $70 = $140 would be recorded. The machine bought at the start of the first year would be disposed of for nil value and would have accumulated depreciation of 60 + 70 = $130. If it had been restated to $140 at the end of the second year, there would be a loss on disposal of 140 − 130 = $10, representing the backlog depreciation. Because the example assumes there is a machine disposal each year, there would be a steady recognition of backlog depreciation.

HOLDING GAINS AND LOSSES

A holding gain or loss is a change in the value of an asset or liability that arises from external market forces rather than the operating activities of the company. Examples would be changes in the realizable value of finished goods inventory; the realizable value of copper held in raw materials inventory; the replacement cost of plant assets; and the market value of outstanding debt caused by interest rate changes in the market.

A **realized holding gain** is one where the gain has met the usual accounting tests of revenue realization. With inventory this would usually be after a sale. For example, an item of inventory was purchased for $30 at the end of 19X5. It was held during 19X6 and was worth $35 at the end of the year. During 19X7 it was sold for $48. The holding gain of $5 at the end of 19X6 would be unrealized, but would be realized the following year because of the sale. The holding gain of $13 during 19X7 would be realized in the same year because of the sale. In the case of plant assets, a realized holding gain would be proportionate to their depreciation.

An **unrealized holding gain** is one that arises because of an increase in market value over historic cost, but where the usual accounting tests of realization have not been met. Thus in the preceding example, it occurred in 19X5 when inventory had increased in market value but had not yet been sold.

Should holding gains be treated as income available for distribution or as part of the owners' equity that needs to be retained to maintain the physical capital? There seems to be general consensus that *unrealized* holding gains should not be available for distribution regardless of the capital maintenance concept used. Whether one regards *realized* holding gains as available for distribution depends on whether one uses the physical or financial concept of capital maintenance. An example will help to illustrate the issue.

A company's sole activity during a year was to purchase one item of inventory for $30 at the beginning of the year and sell it at the end of the year for $50 cash. The holding gain was, therefore, a realized one. By the end of the fiscal year the same item cost $40. During the year, there was a change of 10% in the general price level. We can calculate the income under each of the two concepts of capital maintenance as follows:

CV INCOME STATEMENTS

		Capital concept	
		Real financial	Physical
Sales		$ 50	$ 50
Cost of sales at current cost		40	40
Operating income		10	10
Value of inventory at time of disposal	40		
Adjusted historic cost (30 × 1.10)	33		
Realized holding gain		7	
Net income		$ 17	$ 10

Thus we can draw up two balance sheets:

CV BALANCE SHEETS

	Capital concept	
	Real financial	Physical
Cash	$ 50	$ 50
Contributed capital	$ 33	$ 30
Holding gain		10
Needed to maintain financial/physical capital	$ 33	$ 40
Retained earnings	17	10
Total	$ 50	$ 50

If one wished to maintain the physical capital of the company — to be able to repurchase another item of inventory — then only $10 could be distributed to the owners, and the holding gain would not be regarded as income. This would leave $40, which is just sufficient to replace the inventory. On the other hand, the real financial capital concept indicates that anything in excess of $33 (i.e., 30 x 1.10, the original capital contribution restated in current dollars) is available for distribution.

There is a further issue with maintenance of physical capital that needs to be pointed out. It is argued that some of the holding gain should be recognized as income if part of the financing of that inventory is provided by debt. In the above situation, for example, suppose that $15 had been provided by the owners and $15 had been borrowed from the bank. It could be argued that although $40 is needed to maintain the company's physical capital, the owner's physical capital is the equivalent of a half-interest in the inventory, or $20, because the rest is financed by the bank. The other half of the holding gain was created by a fortunate investment of the bank's money (in which the shareholders bore the ultimate risk), and now accrues to the shareholders and should be available for dividends. When the time comes to buy another unit of inventory at $40, the bank will be asked to lend $20 instead of $15. This difference in viewpoint, within the physical capital maintenance concept, over whether the holding gain on debt accrues to the owner is essentially the difference between the entity and proprietorship views of the firm (explained in Chapter 3). The *CICA Handbook* [4510.15 (i)] has accepted the proprietorship view and recommends a **financing adjustment**, which recognizes as income the portion of the holding gain financed by net monetary liabilities. This will be illustrated later.

INCOME TAX UNDER CURRENT-VALUE ACCOUNTING

Under historic-cost accounting systems the matching principle indicates that the tax expense for a period should be based on the reported accounting income, not on the taxable income. As a result, it is common to have deferred income taxes representing the timing differences between accounting and taxable income. The adoption of current value will likely result in another shifting of income between periods. This immediately raises the question whether tax expenses should be based on income as calculated using generally accepted accounting principles or on current value.

In principle, it seems clear that the adoption of current value for income reporting indicates that current-value income should be used for the calculating of annual tax expense. Deferred income tax accounting is itself a controversial (and often misunderstood) issue, however, and to base it on current value income runs the danger of making it even more controversial by adding a new technique that is still experimental. As a practical matter, it has seemed prudent to keep tax accounting unchanged until current value accounting has been better accepted. As a result the *CICA Handbook* [4510.40] has proposed that tax accounting should remain the same as on the historic-cost financial statements.

AN EXTENDED EXAMPLE USING
PHYSICAL CAPITAL MAINTENANCE (PC)

To illustrate CV accounting we will adapt our example about M Ltd. discussed in the section on GPL accounting above. We will retain the original scenario and add the following new data. In Year 2, inventory had a replacement cost of $57.50. In Year 3, inventory had a replacement cost of $80.00. In Year 3, plant assets had a replacement cost of $160.00 and a resale value of $135.00. Their value in use was estimated in Year 3 to be $180.00. Let us now apply current-value accounting with the maintenance of physical capital (CV-PC).

Recall that at the end of Year 2, inventory was sold for $75.00. Each unit of inventory has a historic cost of $50.00 and a current (replacement) cost of $57.50. The realized holding gain would therefore be $7.50 (i.e., 57.50 − 50.00), and the unrealized holding gain on the unsold inventory would be the same. The total holding gain would be $15.00 (i.e., 2 x 7.50). Because all the assets had been financed by the owners, any holding gain would be excluded from income. Since the outstanding debt had just been acquired and there was no gain due to investments arising from debt, there would be no financing adjustment. The income for Year 2 would be calculated as follows:

CV-PC INCOME STATEMENT — YEAR 2

Sales	$ 75.00
Cost of goods sold	57.50
	$ 17.50

The balance sheet for Year 2 would therefore read as follows:

CV-PC BALANCE SHEET — YEAR 2

Cash	$ 50.00
Accounts receivable	75.00
Inventory — at replacement cost	57.50
	182.50
Plant assets — cost and replacement value	150.00
Total assets	$ 332.50
Long-term debt	$ 100.00
Owners' equity — contributed capital	200.00
— holding gain (inventory)	15.00
Required to maintain physical capital	215.00
Retained earnings	17.50
	232.50
Total liabilities and owners' equity	$ 332.50

Note that the cost of goods sold is stated at the cost of the inventory as of the end of the year. The fixed assets are valued at their replacement cost instead of their resale value of $135 or net realizable value of $180. This is based on the assumption that the replacement cost should be used if it is lower than the expected value so as not to anticipate the additional income over market that the firm can earn through the use of this asset. Because it is the firm's intention to use this plant asset in a productive capacity, it should use the resale value of $135 only if the asset is to be sold.

By treating holding gains as a part of owners' equity and not available for dividends, the physical capital approach ensures that assets with a market value of $215 remain in business. This is sufficient to purchase two new units of inventory costing $115 with $100 cash left on hand, which is exactly the physical capital that the company started with.

Let us now calculate the income for Year 3. The holding gains for Year 3 are as follows:

CV-PC HOLDING GAINS — YEAR 3

	Current cost: end of year	Current cost: start of year	Holding gain
Increase in inventory	$ 80.00	$ 57.50	$ 22.50
Increase in plant assets	160.00	150.00	10.00
Total holding gain for year 3			$ 32.50

The financing adjustment is calculated by finding the proportion of the assets giving rise to a holding gain that were financed by debt, which is the ratio of debt to the total of debt and owners' equity (calculated on Year 2 current cost). Thus we have the following:

Financing adjustment = 32.50 x 100.00/(100.00 + 232.50) = 9.77

The income statement would then read as follows:

CV-PC INCOME STATEMENT — YEAR 3

Sales	$ (90.00)
Costs of goods sold	80.00
Gross profit	(10.00)
Depreciation — 10% of $160	16.00
Interest	12.00
Financing adjustment	(9.77)
Loss	8.23

Note that the cost of goods sold is stated at the replacement cost of the inventory as of the end of the year, and the depreciation is based on the current value of the asset($160).

The balance sheet for Year 3 would be drawn up as follows:

CV-PC BALANCE SHEET — YEAR 3

Cash		$ 38.00
Accounts receivable		165.00
		203.00
Plant assets — replacement value	$ 160.00	
— depreciation	16.00	144.00
Total assets		$ 347.00
Long-term debt		$ 100.00
Owners' equity — contributed capital		200.00
— holding gain — Year 2		15.00
— Year 3	32.50	
less: financing adjustment	(9.77)	22.73
Required to maintain physical capital		237.73
Retained earnings: Year 2 net income	17.50	
Year 3 (loss)	(8.23)	9.27
Total		247.00
Total liabilities and owners' equity		$ 347.00

This concludes the example of CV accounting with maintenance of physical capital. Note that the holding gains of $15.00 and $22.73 are included as part of the amount required to maintain physical capital, and that only $9.27 is available for distribution to shareholders. The amount of $237.73 is deemed to be sufficient to retain the physical capital under the following assumptions:

Cash on hand at incorporation		$ 100.00
Inventory at hand at incorporation — 2 units		
value of first unit when sold	$57.50	
value of second unit when sold	80.00	
	137.50	
Plant assets purchased subsequent to incorporation:		
increase in value	10.00	
Financing adjustment	(9.77)	137.73
		$ 237.73

This seems a rather convoluted way to try to apply the concept of physical capital maintenance. The inventory is included at its value at the time of disposition rather than the present time, and assets purchased since the beginning of the company have to be dealt with by their increase in value since acquisition. If anything, this simply demonstrates the difficulty in developing a workable concept of physical capital maintenance.

AN EXTENDED EXAMPLE USING FINANCIAL CAPITAL MAINTENANCE (FC)

To apply the concept of (real) financial capital maintenance, one selects current cost as the attribute to be measured. A *real* dollar (i.e., one adjusted for price-level changes) is used as the scale of measurement. The similarity to GPL accounting is particularly evident in three ways:

1. The share capital is shown in units of purchasing power.

2. Monetary gains and losses are shown.

3. The opening trial balance in current values is restated to current dollars, and any holding gain for the year is recalculated in terms of these restated values.

Let us now illustrate current-value accounting with the maintenance of real financial capital (CV-FC) by reworking our M Ltd. example. We will not need any additional given data. In the course of our calculations we will make comparisons with the results produced by general-price-level accounting (GPL), current-value-accounting with physical capital maintenance (CV-PC), and historic-cost accounting (HC).

In Year 2 the opening trial balance for Year 1 would be restated in Year 2 $'s as follows:

CV-FC TRIAL BALANCE — YEAR 1

	In Year 1 $'s	In Year 2 $'s
Cash	$ 100.00	$ 110.00
Inventory	100.00	110.00
Share capital	(200.00)	(220.00)
	$ 0.00	$ 0.00

Because the inventory was purchased at the end of Year 1, the $100 is both its cost and market value.

Let us now draw up the income statement for Year 2, giving the equivalent in GPL, CV-PC, and HC for comparison. The GPL income statement and balancing amount have already been shown for Year 2 in Year 3 $'s. We now give them again for Year 2 but in Year 2 $'s. Note that one set can be converted into the other by multiplying by the ratio of their respective indices of 110 and 115.5.

GPL INCOME CALCULATION — YEAR 2 IN YEAR 2 $'s
Numeraire = 115.5

Item	Time of transaction	Index	Historic cost	Conversion factor	Balancing amount
Sales	End of Year 2	110	$ 75.00	110.0/110	$ (75.00)
Cost of sales	End of Year 1	100	50.00	110.0/100	55.00
					20.00

Monetary loss in holding cash (acquired
end of Year 1)
 Purchasing power in terms of the
  numeraire

— Start of company		$ 100 (110.0/100)	110.00	
— End of Year 2		100 (110.0/110)	100.00	10.00
Net income after monetary loss — Year 2				$ 10.00

GPL BALANCING AMOUNT — END OF YEAR 2 IN YEAR 2 $'s
Numeraire = 115.5

Item	Date of acquisition	Index at time	Historic cost	Conversion factor	Balancing amount
Cash	End of Year 2	110	$ 50.00	110/110	$ 50.00
Accounts receivable	End of Year 2	110	75.00	110,110	75.00
Inventory	End of Year 1	100	50.00	110/100	55.00
Plant assets	End of Year 2	110	150.00	110/110	150.00
Long-term debt	End of Year 2	110	(100.00)	110/110	(100.00)
Share capital	End of Year 1	100	(200.00)	110/100	(220.00)
Balancing amount					$ 10.00

Holding gains are calculated as shown below. Note how CV-FC differs from CV-PC here. Under CV-FC, the historic cost is adjusted for purchasing power changes. Moreover, under CV-FC, realized holding gains are included in income, whereas unrealized holding gains are included as part of equity not available for distribution until realized.

HOLDING GAINS — YEAR 2

	CV-FC	CV-PC
Replacement cost of goods on hand	$ 57.50	$ 57.50
Historic cost of goods on hand	55.00	50.00
Unrealized holding gains	2.50	7.50
Replacement cost of goods sold in year	$ 57.50	$ 57.50
Historic cost of goods on hand	55.00	50.00
Realized holding gains	2.50	7.50
Total holding gains	$ 5.00	$ 15.00

INCOME STATEMENTS — YEAR 2
(in Year 2 $'s for CV-FC and GPL)

	CV-FC	GPL	CV-PC	HC
Sales	$ (75.00)	$ (75.00)	$ (75.00)	$ (75.00)
Cost of goods sold	57.50	55.00	57.50	50.00
	(17.50)	(20.00)	(17.50)	(25.00)
Monetary loss	10.00	10.00		
Realized holding				
(gain)	(2.50)			
Net income	$ (10.00)	$ (10.00)	$ (17.50)	$ (25.00)

TRIAL BALANCES — YEAR 2
(in Year 2 $'s for CV-FC and GPL)

	CV-FC	GPL	CV-PC	HC
Cash	$ 50.00	$ 50.00	$ 50.00	$ 50.00
Accounts receivable	75.00	75.00	75.00	75.00
Inventory	57.50	55.00	57.50	50.00
Plant assets	150.00	150.00	150.00	150.00
Long-term debt	(100.00)	(100.00)	(100.00)	(100.00)
Share capital	(220.00)	(220.00)	(200.00)	(200.00)
Holding gains — realized			(7.50)	
— unrealized	(2.50)		(7.50)	
Retained earnings	(10.00)	(10.00)	(17.50)	(25.00)
	$ 0.00	$ 0.00	$ 0.00	$ 0.00

Note that the results for CV-FC and CV-PC are identical on the asset side; the difference lies in owners' equity because of the differing interpretation of capital maintenance. The CV-FC interpretation is that (i) the monetary loss must be recognized and deducted from income and (ii) part of the holding gain on inventory is due to a change in the purchasing power of money, and this should be reflected. Once this has been done, the portion of the holding gain that has been realized may be taken into income.

Let us now produce the Year 3 statements. First, the Year 2 trial balances would be restated in Year 3 dollars by multiplying each value above by $115.5/110 = 1.05$. The income would be calculated as shown below. Under CV-FC there is a monetary loss of $1.25, just as there is under GPL. (The method of calculating it was shown above in the section on GPL accounting.) The calculation of the financing adjustment for CV-PC ($9.77) was already shown above. There is no financing adjustment under CV-FC because all holding gains above the restated cost are considered to be available for distribution to shareholders. The holding gain is calculated below. Note that all of the inventory gain is considered to be realized because the inventory has been sold by the end of Year 3. However, only 10% of the holding gain on the plant assets has been realized because only 10% of the cost of the asset has been charged against revenue.

CV-FC HOLDING GAINS — YEAR 3

Asset	Cost in Year 2 $'s	Restated in Year 3 $'s	Market value	Holding gain Total	Holding gain Realized	Holding gain Unrealized
Inventory	$ 55.00	$ 57.75	$ 80.00	$ 22.25	$ 22.25	
Plant assets	150.00	157.50	160.00	2.50	.25	2.25
Holding gain				$ 24.75	$ 22.50	$ 2.25

CALCULATION OF INCOME — YEAR 3
(in Year 3 $'s for CV-FC and GPL)

	CV-FC	GPL	CV-PC	HC
Sales	$ 90.00	$ 90.00	$ 90.00	$ 90.00
Cost of goods sold	80.00	57.75	80.00	50.00
Gross profit	10.00	32.25	10.00	40.00
Depreciation	16.00	15.75	16.00	15.00
Interest	12.00	12.00	12.00	12.00
Monetary loss	1.25	1.25		
Financing adjustment			(9.77)	
Holding gain realized	(22.50)			
Net income (loss)	$ 3.25	$ 3.25	$ (8.23)	$ 13.00

The net incomes for both CV-FC and GPL are the same because of the simple assumptions of our example. Normally one would expect them to be different. The Year 3 trial balances would be as follows:

TRIAL BALANCES — YEAR 3
(in Year 3 $'s for CV-FC and GPL)

	CV-FC	GPL	CV-PC	HC
Cash	$ 38.00	$ 38.00	$ 38.00	$ 38.00
Accounts receivable	165.00	165.00	165.00	165.00
Inventory	0.00	0.00	0.00	0.00
Plant assets	160.00	157.50	160.00	150.00
— accumulated depreciation	(16.00)	(15.75)	(16.00)	(15.00)
Long-term debt	(100.00)	(100.00)	(100.00)	(100.00)
Share capital	(231.00)	(231.00)	(200.00)	(200.00)
Holding gains — Year 2			(15.00)	
— Year 3			(22.73)	
Unrealized holding gains	(2.25)			
Retained earnings — Year 2	(10.50)	(10.50)	(17.50)	(25.00)
— Year 3	(3.25)	(3.25)	8.23	(13.00)
	$ 0.00	$ 0.00	$ 0.00	$ 0.00

We turn now to Year 4 in which nothing happened except that all assets were converted into cash (preparatory to winding up the company). Recall that Year 3 $'s and Year 4 $'s are equivalent. The income statements would read as follows:

CALCULATION OF GAIN ON DISPOSAL — YEAR 4
(in Year 3 $'s for CV-FC and GPL)

	CV-FC	GPL	CV-PC	HC
Proceeds from sale of plant assets	$ 180.00	$ 180.00	$ 180.00	$ 180.00
Cost of asset disposed of	160.00	157.50	160.00	150.00
Accumulated depreciation	16.00	15.75	16.00	15.00
Net book value	144.00	141.75	144.00	135.00
Net gain	36.00	38.25	36.00	45.00
Holding gain now realized	2.25			
Gain on disposal recognized	$ 38.25	$ 38.25	$ 36.00	$ 45.00

The trial balances would look as follows:

TRIAL BALANCES — YEAR 4
(in Year 3 $'s for CV-FC and GPL)

	CV-FC	GPL	CV-PC	HC
Cash	$ 283.00	$ 283.00	$ 283.00	$ 283.00
Share capital	(231.00)	(231.00)	(200.00)	(200.00)
Holding gains — Year 2			(15.00)	
— Year 3			(22.73)	
— Year 4			(36.00)	
Retained earnings — Year 2	(10.50)	(10.50)	(17.50)	(25.00)
— Year 3	(3.25)	(3.25)	8.23	(13.00)
— Year 4	(38.25)	(38.25)		(45.00)
	$ 0.00	$ 0.00	$ 0.00	$ 0.00

We have now applied four different accounting methods to the same scenario. The assets being converted are the same in each case. Therefore the difference between the accounting methods lies in how the success of the firm is interpreted under the various capital maintenance concepts when the same $283.00 is returned to the shareholders. Let us summarize the interpretations of each method.

Historic cost (HC)
The original contribution was $200. This is now being returned with profits as follows:

Original contribution	$ 200.00
Profit on trading operations	38.00
Profit on sale of plant assets after charging trading operations for its share of use	45.00
Total assets	$ 283.00

General price level (GPL)

Anything in excess of $231 (the real value of the original capital) represents a gain for the company. The sources of this gain of $52 are analysed as follows:

Original capital in Year 1 $'s		$200.00
Restated to Year 4 $'s		$ 231.00
Earnings stated in Year 4 $'s — Year 2	10.50	
— Year 3	3.25	
— Year 4	38.25	52.00
Total assets		$ 283.00

Current value with financial capital maintenance (CV-FC)

Anything in excess of $231 (the real value of the original capital), represents a gain for the company. Although the gain, $52, is the same as under GPL accounting, the explanation for it is different. This can be seen by examining the income statement of each year.

Original capital in Year 1 $'s		$200.00
Restated to Year 4 $'s		$ 231.00
Earnings stated in Year 4 $'s — Year 2	10.50	
— Year 3	3.25	
— Year 4	38.25	52.00
Total assets		$ 283.00

Current value with physical capital maintenance (CV-PC)

The interpretation of this accounting method seems the most difficult of all because the amounts are represented in dollars, but the basic objective is directed at maintaining the same amount of physical capital (inventory, cash, and plant assets), not dollars. The company started with $100 and two units of inventory. It is this real physical capital at which the maintenance concept is directed. Every time the inventory and plant assets increased in value this did not represent a profit to the shareholders. If they spent such profits they would be unable to replace the inventory and other assets that they owned. Hence, all holding gains must be identified as part of the capital that must be retained within the firm to maintain productive capacity. The capital that must be retained within the firm is shown in the following calculation:

Original capital		$ 200.00
Holding gains: — Year 2	$ 15.00	
— Year 3	22.73	
— Year 4	36.00	73.73
Needed to maintain productive capacity		$ 273.73
Assets on hand		283.00
Available for distribution to owners		$ 9.27

The amount left over (i.e., $9.27) was already reflected by the annual net incomes, which were measuring how much would be available to shareholders while still leaving productive capacity intact. From our previous calculations we have the following:

Year 2	$ 17.50
Year 3 (Loss)	(8.23)
Net income	$ 9.27

CICA Handbook Disclosure Recommendations

The *CICA Handbook* has approached price-change accounting in a tentative manner. It is not required of any company, and for larger ones whose shares are publicly traded it is only "recommended" as supplementary information to be supplied to the reader. The recommendation does not apply to producing real estate assets, banks, or trust and insurance companies. Moreover, price-change accounting is not to replace the conventional cost-based financial statements.

The *Handbook* states that the index used to make constant-dollar restatements should normally be either the Consumer Price Index for Canada or the Gross National Expenditure Implicit Price Deflator. However, if the historic-cost financial statements are presented in a currency other than Canadian, then an appropriate foreign index corresponding to one of the above two should be used [*CICA* 4510.49].

When using price-change accounting, the *Handbook* recommends that the following be disclosed:

1. The current cost of
    (a) cost of goods sold [*CICA* 4510.38 (a)]
    (b) depreciation, depletion, and amortization of property, plant, and equipment [*CICA* 4510.38 (b)]
    (c) inventory [*CICA* 4510.42]
    (d) property, plant and equipment [*CICA* 4510.42]

2. Current and deferred amounts of income tax expense [*CICA* 4510.17]

3. Income before extraordinary items after reflecting the changes from the historic cost basis to the current cost basis. [*CICA* 4510.17]

4. The amount of changes in the current cost amounts of
    (a) inventory [*CICA* 4510.18]
    (b) property, plant, and equipment [*CICA* 4510.18]

5. Net assets after restating inventory and property, plant, and equipment on a current-cost basis [*CICA* 4510.18 (c)]

6. The financing adjustment [*CICA* 4510.21]

7. The effect of GPL changes on holdings gains with respect to:
   (a) inventory [*CICA* 4510.24]
   (b) property, plant, and equipment [*CICA* 4510.24]
   (c) monetary gains and losses [*CICA* 4510.24]

It will be apparent that the authors of this *Handbook* section wanted to include both GPL and CV accounting, but stopped short of recommending that a full set of statements should be produced. An earlier proposal that an adjustment should be made to income to reflect the gain or loss on monetary items was dropped.

Examples from Published Reports

Consolidated-Bathurst Inc.

Excerpts from the financial statements of Consolidated-Bathurst have been given above in Chapters 2 and 19. By 1986 the company had ceased providing information based on price-change accounting, as had the vast majority of public Canadian companies.

Here is the segment on price-change accounting from the 1983 financial statements of Consolidated-Bathurst.

REPORTING THE EFFECTS OF CHANGING PRICES

	Historical as reported	Current cost	Adjustment
	(millions of $)		
Consolidated earnings for the year ended December 31, 1983			
Depreciation	$ 60	$ 97	$ 37
Cost of sales	1,148	1,161	13
Income taxes	21	21	11
Earnings (loss) before extraordinary charge	43	(7)	(50)
Selected consolidated assets as at December 31, 1983			
Property and plant — net	911	1,274	363
Inventory	306	310	4
Common shareholders' equity	522	889	367

The Corporation has prepared the inflation accounting data shown above substantially in accordance with the recent recommendations of the Canadian Institute of Chartered Accountants (CICA) for reporting the effects of changing prices. The current replacement cost amounts for the Corporation's property and plant were determined, in most cases, by using appropriate specific indices. This method assumes that these assets would have the same useful lives as presently used in the historical-cost statements and would be replaced with similar technology although this, in fact, might not be the case. The current replacement cost of inventory and the adjustment to cost of sales were determined by using estimated specific price changes with occurred during 1983. The purpose of such accounting is to give information about the effects of both past and present inflation on the Corporation.

The effect of past inflation is measured through calculations of the current replacement cost of property and plant. The significant difference between the current replacement cost and historical cost of these assets reflects, on the one hand, the large understatement of the net property and plant ($1,274 against $911) and, on the other hand, the increased annual cost of maintaining these assets which would result in a higher depreciation charge to earnings ($97 against $60).

The effect of present inflation on the Corporation is reflected through adjustments to the cost of goods consumed in 1983 as it was charged to cost of sales and to inventory values as they were stated on the balance sheet at year-end. These adjustments reflect several factors: the length of time the inventory has been held; the use of average cost for inventory valuation; and the rate of inflation during the year. In the pulp and paper industry, inventory — especially wood — can be in stock for a considerable period of time. The cost of that inventory when consumed and as charged to cost of sales will usually be lower than the cost of replacing the inventory at that moment. In 1983, however, the curent replacement cost of inventory was only marginally higher than the historical cost. The current replacment cost of the inventory as at December 31, 1983, was calculated to be $310 as against $306 in the historicqal accounts. The adjustment to cost of sales for 1983 was estimated to be $13. The total adjustment for the effects of inflation would have been an increase of $367 in shareholders' equity and a charge of $50 to consolidated earnings.

Supplementary Information

In addition to giving information about the direct effect of inflation on costs and on selected asset values, the CICA requires the disclosure of sufficient additional information to enable readers to make an assessment of income on a current-cost basis under both an operating capability and financial concept of capital maintenance.

The operating capability concept is concerned with the fact that sufficient capital (inventory and property and plant) is maintained in the Corporation to continue previous levels of output of goods and services. The financial concept is concerned with the fact that the current cost dollar value of inventory and property and plant does not decrease. To allow calculation of these concepts, the following information is given:

i. Increase in current cost amounts of property and plant and inventory based on:

General inflation	$56
Specific prices	$33

ii. Adjustment to recognize the level of debt in the Corporation:

On specific price increases of property and plant and inventory amounting to $33	$14
On current cost adjustments made to earnings during the year and amounting to $50	$21

iii. General purchasing power gain on net monetary liabilities $29

Comparing these 1983 excerpts with those from 1946 (given in Chapter 2), we find that the more recent ones represent a much higher level of disclosure and assume a much greater sophistication on the part of the reader. (The same holds true for the 1987 excerpts given in Chapter 2.) Observe that in accordance with the format recommended in the *CICA Handbook*, the company does not give a complete price-change financial statement, but only information about items likely to be of special interest (such as plant assets and inventory).

Summary

The two main approaches to price-change accounting have very different objectives. General-price-level accounting creates financial statements that are adjusted for changes in the general level of prices. They typically show what the financial statements would have looked like if the unit of currency had remained unchanged throughout the year. GPL accounting is an attempt to keep cost-based accounting useful in a time of changing price levels, and it identifies monetary gains and losses through holding monetary assets.

In contrast, current-value accounting drops historic-cost valuation in favour of using current market values. It seeks to identify and separate holding gains from income earned from operations.

This chapter illustrates how the two methods can be combined to identify both monetary losses and holding gains. In addition, together the methods show assets and liabilities at their current market value for the current year and at their market values of prior years adjusted for inflation.

QUESTIONS

Q20-1. Review and be sure you understand the following terms:

    a. GPL accounting *versus* CV accounting

    b. constant-dollar accounting

    c. financial capital maintenance *versus* physical capital maintenance

    d. numeraire

    e. consumer price index

    f. monetary item

    g. monetary gain

    h. monetary loss

    i. monetary asset

    j. monetary liability

    k. vintaging

    l. holding gain (or loss)

    m. realizable *versus* unrealizable holding gain

n. monetary working-capital adjustment

o. realizable value *versus* current cost *versus* current reproduction cost *versus* current replacement cost *versus* value in use.

p. backlog depreciation

q. financing adjustment under physical capital maintenance

Q20-2. "If this is constant-dollar accounting, why does the same net income for our previous financial year get stated as one amount in last year's statements and as another amount in the current year's statements?" Explain.

Q20-3. It has been half-seriously suggested that since people find it confusing to use a newly revalued dollar in each succeeding year, we should instead agree to take the dollar of some arbitrary year — say 1983 — and use that one from now on. What would be the merits of this approach? The problems?

Q20-4. A company started business on 1 January 19X6 with one bond it purchased for $100. The general level of prices increased 10% over the next twelve months, and the market price of the bond went up to $105.

   a. Show the calculation of owners' equity at 31 December 19X6 using each of the following methods:
   (i) historic-cost accounting;
   (ii) GPL accounting;
   (iii) CV accounting with maintenance of physical capital; and
   (iv) CV accounting with maintenance of financial capital.

   b. Assume instead that the stock was sold on December 31, 19X6 for $105. What would now be your answers to (a) above?

   c. Discuss the merits of each accounting method as applied in (b) above.

Q20-5. Do you agree or disagree with the following statements? Explain why.

   a. "If monetary liabilities are larger than monetary assets, the company will experience a monetary loss in a period of falling prices."

   b. "If monetary liabilities are smaller than monetary assets, the company will experience a monetary loss in a period of rising prices."

   c. If the general price level rises faster than the actual market value of inventory, then the company will report a holding loss under CV accounting with maintenance of physical capital.

   d. If the general price level rises faster than the actual market value of inventory, then the company will report a realized holding loss under CV accounting with maintenance of physical capital.

Q20-6. Indicate whether each of the following are monetary or non-monetary assets or liabilities, or something else. Explain your decision.

   a. work in process

   b. land held for resale

   c. patents and copyrights

   d. bank loan

   e. deferred income tax

   f. short-term investments

   g. advance payments received from customers

   h. income taxes payable

i. preferred stock issued with a fixed date and price for redemption

j. prepaid insurance

Q20-7. Does the choice between FIFO and LIFO to value inventory have any impact on reported operating income under each of the following accounting methods? Explain.

    a. historic-cost

    b. current-value with maintenance of physical capital

    c. general-price-level

Q20-8. Because its shareholders complained that they found the financial statements confusing, a company that used GPL adjustment decided to freeze the dollar value as of 19X0 and thereafter always show the financial statements in 19X0 dollars. During 19X1, general prices increased 10%.

    a. Assuming that the monetary assets were greater than the monetary laibilities, would the company show a monetary gain or loss in 19X1?

    b. Does the fact that the company used 19X0 dollars in its statements have any impact on the size of the reported 19X1 monetary gain or loss? Explain.

    c. The company referred to this policy of freezing on 19X0 dollars as "true constant dollar accounting." Were they correct? Explain.

    d. What difficulties, if any, would you expect the company to have because of this freeze policy?

Q20-9. Explain the difference between a realized and unrealized holding gain. What, if anything, is a company implying if they simply combine both types into one account?

Q20-10. In each of the following unrelated circumstances, explain if the shift from historic-cost accounting to current-value accounting with financial capital maintenance would

    (i) increase reported net income

    (ii) decrease reported net income or

    (iii) have no effect. (Assume that realized holding gains are included in income.)

    a. The opening inventory at historic cost was $8,000, but its market value was $10,000. The market value and cost of the closing inventory was the same at $13,000.

    b. Closing inventory had a historic cost of $89,000 and a market value of $95,000.

    c. Plant assets had a replacement value of $500,000 at the start of the year and $600,000 at the end. The equivalent historic costs were $400,000 and $450,000 respectively. There had been no disposals, and the above amounts do not include accumulated depreciation.

    d. Net monetary assets were $60,000 at the start of the year and $80,000 at the end of the year.

    e. Salaries of $350,000 were paid during the year.

Q20-11. For each case listed in Q20-10, explain if the shift from historic-cost-based accounting to GPL accounting would (i) increase reported net income, (ii) decrease reported net income, or (iii) have no effect. Assume that the price index was 189 at the start of the year and 150 at the end.

Q20-12. "GPL accounting is just historic-cost accounting in a new disguise. It has all the virtues and all the weaknesses of its parent." Do you agree? Explain.

Q20-13. What new financial-statement terms are introduced with the adoption of GPL accounting? CV accounting? Explain each of them in non-technical language.

Q20-14. "The conceptual problem posed by index numbers has been ignored in order to achieve another purpose." Explain briefly what "the conceptual problem" of index numbers is. Is it solvable? Explain. What is the "other purpose" to be achieved? How well do you think we have achieved the other purpose in light of our problem with index numbers?

Q20-15. It has been said that GPL accounting is historic-cost accounting with one change only. What is that change? Why does one of the two methods measure and report on monetary gains and losses whereas the other does not? Are both capable of reporting such gains or losses if required? Explain.

Q20-16. It is often regarded as a good business strategy in a period of inflation to own tangible assets such as inventory or land and buildings that are financed with monetary liabilities. What assumption is implicit in this strategy about the rate of increase in the value of the assets versus the rate of interest on the debt?

Suppose a company adopted the above strategy and profitably held a portfolio of debt-financed assets over a five-year period. How would each of the major accounting systems evaluated in this chapter report on the company's annual success? Explain. Assume the asset was purchased for $500,000 and sold for $800,000. During the five-year period, the general price level rose 20%. The debt cost was 10% of $500,000 per year.

Q20-17. Explain whether each of the concepts listed below are an *integral* part or *ever* a part of (i) GPL accounting and (ii) CV accounting.

a. monetary gain or loss

b. holding gain or loss

Q20-18. Explain how a company that used CV accounting for its liability valuation could show a holding gain on its debt as it slid toward bankruptcy. Suppose at the point immediately before bankruptcy its long-term debt with a face value of $100 million was only 30% of its face value in the bond markets. Who has "gained" the other 70%? How should this be shown properly in the income statement?

Q20-19. "In a period of rising prices the historic-cost statements will tend to overestimate the real revenue of monetary assets and the real interest cost of monetary liabilities." Explain in your own words.

Q20-20. A company prepared a 19X3 financial report using GPL accounting methods. The company showed in its comparative balance sheet that it had $300,000 cash on hand at the end of 19X3 and $250,000 on hand at the end of 19X2.

a. Did it really have $250,000 on hand at the end of 19X2? If not, then what interpretation do you put on the $250,000?

b. Is this a useful way of portraying the company's cash position as at the end of 19X2?

Q20-21. Suppose you purchased an imported car a year ago for $10,000. Shortly afterwards the government imposed voluntary import quotas on imported cars, and a year later the same car sold for $12,000 on the used-car market. During that same period the consumer price index had increased by 4%. A friend advised you to sell your car and "make a profit of $2,000."

a. What concept of capital maintenance is your friend implicitly using?

b. What other concepts could be used, and what gain on disposal would they report?

c. Which concept would make the most sense to you as a car owner?

Q20-22. One justification for producing price-adjusted financial statements is that they reflect the "real" economic factors better than historic-cost statements, even though the current values used are of necessity approximations. A major accounting firm has objected that "incorporating such 'soft' data into historical financial statements blurs the picture and causes confusion. We end up with financial statements which are neither a record of past transactions nor a forecast of the future, but something in between — neither fish nor fowl." Evaluate the merits of this objection.

Q20-23. The stated objective of financial reporting is often said to be to provide information that is *useful to the decision-maker who will use it.* Potentially there are many different users, such as the owners of the company, creditors, outside investors, and government. In order to serve the needs of each, it has been suggested that one should prepare columnar financial statements on five or six bases, with one for each user. Presumably price-adjusted financial statements would provide several of these columns. However, some critics of this proposal claim that with multi-column financial statements one would inevitably be asked: "But which one is the real financial statement?" What would your answer be? Explain.

Q20-24. Some accountants assert that current-value (current-cost) accounting is subjective whereas historical-cost accounting is objective.

Required:

a. Discuss briefly the validity of this assertion.

b. Identify and explain three considerations involved in deciding whether to replace financial reporting information based on historical-cost with information based on current values.

c. How would the amount(s) reported on the balance sheet for a fixed asset, such as an office building held for rental purposes, be determined under historical-cost accounting and under current-value accounting? Explain.

d. With respect to *two* of the considerations identified in part (b), evaluate the information conveyed by the amount(s) determined in part (c).

(CMA adapted)

EXERCISES

E20-1. Mehta Ltd. decided to prepare financial statements every quarter. You are given the following information about the company.

Quarter	Opening inventory	Purchases	Closing inventory	Sales	Price index	Market value of inventory
Prior					182.5	$ 12,000
First	$ 10,000	$ 125,000	$ 8,000	$ 228,600	183.8	9,000
Second	8,000	180,000	25,000	293,400	185.2	26,800
Third	25,000	120,000	50,000	171,000	189.3	62,300
Fourth	50,000	3,000	5,000	135,000	199.2	6,400
				$ 828,000		

The company wants to present quarterly results showing sales, cost of sales, and gross margin.

Required:

a. Calculate the sales, cost of sales and gross margin under each of the following accounting methods: (i) historic-cost, (ii) current-value with maintenance of physical capital, (iii) current-value with maintenance of financial capital, and (iv) general-price-level. Use the end of the fourth quarter for the numeraire wherever applicable and assume all purchases and sales took place at the end of each quarter.

b. What is the difference between the gross margin reported on a historic-cost basis and that reported on a current-value basis? Explain why this difference exists.

c. What is the difference between gross margin reported on a historic-cost basis and that reported on a general-price-level basis? Explain why this difference exists.

d. Which accounting method do you think would be of most use to internal management? Outside investors? Explain.

E20-2. In each of the following independent situations, indicate whether there is a (i) monetary gain or loss or (ii) a holding gain or loss. Calculate how much it is for the financial year.

a. Accounts receivable were valued at $120,000 as of the end of the financial year, but on further inspection they were found to be worth only $112,000. Prices had risen 10% over the period.

b. One hundred shares purchased for $35.00 each on the first of the year had risen to $45.00 each after six months. At the end of the year, however, they were down to $30.00 each.

c. Long-term mortgage receivable was $100,000 all during the year, but the general price index went from 180 at the start of the year to 195 at the end of the year.

d. Y Company started on 1 January with capital of $100,000 Canadian, which was transferred to a foreign bank and converted into the local currency in anticipation of starting up operations in that country. The other country encountered severe financial difficulties and Y Company decided to repatriate its money back to Canada. It had done so by the end of the year, but due to devaluation of the foreign currency the amount that was returned to Canada amounted to only $35,000 Canadian.

e. A company issued long-term bonds for $800,000 and was able to redeem them within the same fiscal year for $750,000 because interest rates had gone up. During the same period the general price level rose by 10%.

E20-3. For each of the following situations, show the GPL balance sheet for Year 2. Prices went up 10% during Year 2. The company undertook no activity and had the same assets on hand at the end of Year 2 as it had at the end of Year 1.

a. A Company had a policy of holding monetary assets. At the end of Year 1 it had the following: cash, $10,000; accounts receivable, $20,000; and mortgages receivable, $30,000. The company was entirely financed with owners' equity.

b. B Company had a policy of holding only non-monetary assets. At the end of Year 1 it had the following: inventory, $10,000; plant assets, $20,000; and land for investment purposes, $30,000. It financed these assets in part with a mortgage payable of $40,000. The rest was financed with owners' equity. The market values of all non-monetary assets exceeded their restated costs as of the end of Year 2.

c. C Company had a policy of mixing monetary assets and liabilities with non-monetary ones. At the end of Year 1 it had the following assets: inventory, $10,000;

plant assets, $20,000; and mortgage receivable, $30,000. Its long-term debt was $40,000, and the rest was financed with owners' equity. The market values of all non-monetary assets exceeded their restated costs as of the end of Year 2.

d. D Company had the same assets as B Company, but was less fortunate in the choice of assets purchased. At the end of Year 2 the market values of the assets were as follows: inventory, $8,500; plant assets, $18,000; and land, $20,000. The management agreed to revalue the inventory to market for financial-statement purposes. However, they left the other assets at their restated costs on the grounds that these were long-term investments and a "write-down would only be appropriate if it became evident that this decline in value was of a long-term nature."

e. E company had the same results as D Company, but the management felt that the decline in value of all assets should be recognized immediately.

E20-4. Of the two valuation policies used by management in E20-3(d) and (e) above, which is more appropriate when reporting to the company's shareholders? To prospective purchasers of a majority share in the company? Would a version of current-value accounting be more appropriate? Explain.

E20-5. For each of the following independent cases, calculate the holding gain or loss for the year under the assumptions of (i) physical capital maintenance and (ii) financial capital maintenance. Assume in each case that the GPL increase for each year was 10% and that for the last half of the current year the increase was 5%.

a. Inventory was purchased for $3,500 at the start of the year. At the end of the year its replacement cost is $4,000.

b. Inventory was purchased for $3,500 at the start of the year. At the end of the year its replacement cost is $3,000.

c. Inventory was purchased for $3,500 at the start of the year. At the end of the year its replacement cost is $3,500.

d. Inventory was purchased two years ago for $2,000. At the beginning of the current year, a year later, it had a replacement cost of $2,500. At the end of the current year its replacement cost is $2,200.

e. Land was purchased halfway through the current year for $90,000. An appraisal at the end of the year indicates that its current selling price is $100,000.

f. Land was purchased halfway through the current year for $90,000. An appraisal at the end of the year indicates that its current selling price is $90,000.

E20-6. In each of the following examples, explain the different valuation approaches that might be used. In each case, use at least two of the following terms: (i) realizable value, (ii) current cost, (iii) current reproduction cost, (iv) current replacement cost, (v) value in use.

a. A salesman's two-year-old car would cost $13,400 in the current used-car market. However, it is a more expensive model than the company now purchases. A new model of the car it would now purchase costs $15,000, and a two-year-old equivalent model would cost $9,500.

b. A firm has an electric typewriter that uses a "golfball" typing element that is controlled from the keyboard by electrical-mechanical linkages. The typewriter cost $950 new, and its equivalent can be purchased on the used office equipment market for about $250. It is being replaced with an electronic typewriter that cost $1,400, which is preferred to the golfball model because it is faster and has a memory that will automatically type frequently used phrases and check spelling. It is estimated that four of the firm's typists using the electronic typewriters can produce as much work as five typists using the older machines.

c. Immediately after Christmas a merchant surveyed her stock of unsold electronic toys. She estimates that they cost her $3,000, but that she could buy them in the after-Christmas market for $1,200. She further estimates that she can get rid of them at a January sale, but only after heavy mark-downs, and that after normal selling costs she can net $1,400. If she fails to sell them in January, she is certain that newer models will make them unsalable by April.

d. A specialized scrap merchant buys old computers and salvages the precious metals used in them. He has just bought one in perfect working order that originally cost $850,000. If he used it in his office instead of scrapping it, he estimates that he could save $10,000 per year over the next five years after investing $20,000 in adapting existing software to his needs. He decided not to do so because he could buy a new computer for $14,000 whose software can be adapted to his needs for about $2,000. It would give him the same annual savings. If he takes apart the old computer and sells it for scrap, he will receive about $1,500.

E20-7. It is generally agreed that long-term liabilities should be shown at their present (discounted) values. Suppose that in a period where inflation averages 6%, the market interest rate is 8%. Assume it is generally agreed that 2% of this is the "real" interest rate and the remaining 6% reflects the inflationary expectations. Suppose that in this setting a company has a warranty liability that is expected to come due in 36 months. At present prices this warranty is expected to cost $1,000; but if prices increase at 6% compounded annually, the cost at the point when it comes due is expected to be $1,191. Which of the following policies would you recommend for recording the initial liability? Justify your answer.

a. Record it at its expected cost of $1,191 discounted at the market interest rate of 8%, or $945.85.

b. Record it at its present-day cost of $1,000 discounted by the real interest rate of 2% or $942.32.

c. Record it at its present-day cost of $1,000 discounted by the market rate of interest of 8%, or $793.83.

d. Record it at its expected cost of $1,191 discounted at the real interest rate of 2%, or $1,122.

E20-8. Provided below are the purchase and sales records for the year for one line of goods sold by Reeve's Hardware.

	Units	Price	Total	Replacement cost	Price level
Purchases:					
5 January	20	$ 50	$ 1,000		110
15 July	25	65	1,625		130
Sales:					
12 March	10	85	850	55	115
5 June	5	90	450	55	125
15 July	5	90	450	65	130
31 December	18	100	1,800	70	135

Required: Calculate the sales and cost of goods sold, assuming FIFO, for each of the accounting methods below. Round all figures to the nearest dollar.

a. the historic-cost method

b. the GPL adjusted method (in $'s of 31 December)

c. the current-cost method with physical capital maintenance

d. the current-cost method with real financial capital maintenance (in $'s of 31 December)

E20-9. Provided below are the historical-cost financial statements for selected years for Cray Paper Supplies.

BALANCE SHEET

	19X0 year-end	19X1 year-end	19X2 year-end
Cash	$ 65,000	$ 45,800	$ 45,800
Accounts receivable	0	27,000	27,000
Inventory	35,700	41,700	41,700
Plant assets	135,000	135,000	135,000
Accumulated depreciation		(13,500)	(13,500)
Accounts payable	(35,700)	(25,000)	(25,000)
Bonds payable	(75,000)	(75,000)	(75,000)
Common stock	(125,000)	(125,000)	(125,000)
Retained earnings	0	(11,000)	(11,000)
	$ 0	$ 0	$ 0

INCOME STATEMENT, 19X2

Sales	$ 53,500
Cost of goods sold	19,000
Operating income	34,500
Expenses:	
Depreciation	13,500
Salary	10,000
Net income	$ 11,000

You are also given the following additional information:

(i) Cray Paper Supplies was founded on 31 December 19X0. In each year all transactions took place on the last day of the year.

(ii) The company uses FIFO to cost its inventory. All the inventory as of the end of 19X2 was purchased as of the end of 19X1.

(iii) The company suspended operations for a year during 19X2 as a legal problem was cleared up. They expect to continue operations in 19X3.

(iv) No dividends have ever been paid by Cray Paper Supplies.

(v) The Price index was at 100 when the company was founded. The index rose to 115 by the end of 19X1 and to 125 by the end of 19X2.

Required:

a. Prepare the general-price-level comparative financial statements for the years 19X1 and 19X2 using each of the following:

(i) a current-dollar numeraire (state each year's results in end of 19X2 dollars)

(ii) a constant-dollar numeraire (state each year's results in end of 19X0 dollars)

b. What was the gain or loss as calculated in part (a)(i) above? Justify the amount by referring to monetary assets and liabilities on hand.

E20-10. The following are among the assets held by Apprentice-Hull, a publisher of newspapers and magazines, as of 31 December 19X6.

(i) A new printing press was bought for $275,000 on 1 January 19X1. The press is being depreciated on a straight-line basis over a period of 10 years.

(ii) Raw materials costing $74,000 were purchased on 30 June 19X6 and were turned into goods. Of these goods, an amount with a historical cost of $53,000 was sold during the year, and the remainder was left in inventory at year-end. (Calculate the cost of goods sold and the carrying value of the ending inventory.)

(iii) Finished goods inventory, in the form of unsold magazines and books, cost $125,000 under GPL accounting as of 31 December 19X5. Of these, goods at a GPL cost of $64,000 remained in inventory at the end of 19X6.

(iv) The company issued $100,000 worth of bonds on 31 June 19X3.

(v) On 1 November 19X3 three cars and two vans were added to the company's fleet of delivery vehicles. The vehicles are expected to last for four years and are depreciated on a straight-line basis. The total cost of the vehicles was $82,000.

(vi) On 31 December 19X2 Apprentice-Hull issued $200,000 worth of preferred shares. The shares had a five-year term, and the holder was entitled to a guaranteed dividend of 10%. The shares are redeemable at the holder's option five years from the issue date.

(vii) On 30 July 19X3 the president purchased his favorite painting for his office. The painting cost $13,000 at the time, but it is now said to be worth $27,000.

Provided below are the price level indices for selected dates.

Date	Index
1 January 19X1	105
30 June 19X1	112
31 December 19X2	114
30 June 19X3	121
1 November 19X3	127
31 December 19X5	142
20 June 19X6	154
31 December 19X6	159

Required: For each item listed above, calculate the value it would have on the GPL balance sheet of 31 December 19X6. Round all figures to the nearest dollar. If there is room to doubt whether any of the above items are monetary in nature, defend your choice.

E20-11. The owner of a successful, small office-supply business is considering selling her operation to generate funds for a new venture. In attempting to establish a reasonable asking price for her firm, she sought the advice of some close friends in the business community. Some of the comments she received are shown below:

Friend #1: "You should take the net selling price of your assets as the asking price for your firm. After all, no one is likely to pay much more than what the assets are worth on the market."

Friend #2: "I think you should consider using the current replacement cost of your assets as a proxy for the value of your firm. By that I mean that you should investigate how much it would cost you to replace all of your assets with ones that would be capable of providing the same function. This would lead to a fair price, because any potential buyer would have to spend that sum to purchase the productive assets elsewhere."

Friend #3: "Your business has developed into a secure and profitable operation. The true value of the firm is the expected present value of all future cash flows. The firm is really worth the future profits to be generated over the remaining life of your productive assets."

Required: Discuss the relative merits of each of the valuations outlined by the owner's friends. Be sure to discuss the advantages and disadvantages of each. Pay special attention to the information that would be needed to provide fairly accurate figures for each method of valuation.

E20-12. Uneda Taxi Ltd. has decided to prepare current-value financial statements for the fiscal year just ended. In attempting to find the current value for the fleet of 20 cars, the accountant is faced with a dilemma of what figures to use. As outlined below, the accountant has arrived at different numbers using four different valuation methods.

> Realizable value: the estimated net market value of the twenty-car fleet is $215,000 − $75,000 = $140,000.
>
> Current reproduction cost: The cost to acquire similar assets of the same age and condition and have them delivered to their location would be $160,000.
>
> Current replacement cost: The cost of acquiring the best available cars to provide the same service would be $200,000 (after adjustments for depreciation).
>
> Value in use: The fleet is expected to generate cash flows of $215,000 during the remainder of its useful life.

Required: For each situation below, describe which of the above valuation methods would be most appropriate. Give your reasons.

a. New propane-fueled cars have been developed. They are more expensive to purchase but can be operated at much lower cost. In addition there is a new taxi company in the city, and its effect on Uneda Taxi is uncertain.

b. The market is stable, with no new competition expected and no change in customer-usage trends expected.

c. Business is largely dependent on the weather. There is a well-established trading market for used automobiles, and technology has changed little.

d. There is a new taxi company in the city, but its expected effect on Uneda is minimal, as the new firm will operate in a different area of the city. No new technological advances are expected for some time.

E20-13. Company A purchased a piece of equipment for $100, which was expected to last three years and have no residual value. Using current-value accounting, the company charged as depreciation at the end of each year one-third of the current replacement cost at that time. The replacement cost was $120 at the end of Year 1, $150 at Year 2, and $180 at the end of Year 3.

Required:

a. Calculate the annual depreciation charge for the three years, and the accumulated depreciation at the end of Year 3.

b. When the asset was disposed of early in Year 4, it was found that the replacement cost had risen to $195. What is the amount of the backlog depreciation?

c. The accounting-policy staff started to argue about the correct treatment of this backlog depreciation. Elda asserted: "It's the amount we should have charged against income in Years 1 and 2 if only we had known what the ultimate replacement cost would be. The annual depreciation should have been one-third of $195, or $65 per year, and we charged something less. Therefore we should charge backlog depreciation against income of this year, just as we do for any change of accounting estimates." Hon disagreed: "Why single out plant assets as the place where we recognize that our charge against income has been insufficient? The same thing happens with inventory, for instance, because we charge cost of sales with its replacement cost at the moment of sale, but we may have to replace it later with an item of higher cost." Elda and Hon then turn to you to ask for your opinion. Give a well-reasoned response.

PROBLEMS

P20-1.   On 1 January 19X3 a firm of consultants started into business, and the partners put $5,000 into it. Suppose that their only expense was rent. It was partly paid on 31 December 19X3. On that same date they withdrew $22,000, billed all their customers, and collected part in cash. The trial balance on 31 December 19X3 is shown below.

Cash	$ 15,000
Accounts receivable	9,000
Accounts payable	(11,000)
Owners' equity — original contribution	(5,000)
Sales	(45,000)
Drawings	22,000
Rent	15,000
	$ 0

During 19X4 the partners followed the same pattern of doing all their paying and billing on 31 December as they had in 19X3. Their trial balance at the end of 19X4 looked as follows:

Cash	$ 25,000
Accounts receivable	8,000
Accounts payable	(10,000)
Owners' equity — original contribution	(13,000)
Sales	(50,000)
Drawings	25,000
Rent	15,000
	$ 0

At the beginning of 19X3 the consumer price index was 100. It increased to 105 by 31 December 19X3 and to 115.5 by 31 December 19X4.

Required:

a. Prepare the 19X3 financial statement as of 31 December 19X3 on a GPL basis. Use end-of-19X3 dollars as the numeraire.

b. Restate the 19X3 financial statement as of 31 December 19X4 on a GPL basis, by using end-of-19X4 dollars as the numeraire.

c. Prepare the 19X4 financial statement as of 31 December 19X4 on a GPL basis, by using end-of-19X4 dollars as the numeraire.

d. What would the monetary gain or loss have been in 19X4 if the trial historic-cost balance was unchanged, but you knew that the customers had been billed evenly through the year. Assume the average consumer price index for 19X4 was 110. Explain in plain English what this change in the monetary gain or loss, if any, represents.

P20-2. The charter of a student-housing co-operative requires its members to pay an annual rent that "covers its annual costs." They have been using historic-cost accounting. Their main assets are eight four-bedroom to six-bedroom houses that they use as residences for their members and two additional houses that are used for food services. The houses are financed almost entirely by mortgages taken out when they were purchased. They are depreciated on a straight-line basis at 5% per annum, which is considered adequate.

Since the houses were bought three years ago for $500,000 they have been appraised periodically with the following results:

End of first year:	$600,000
End of second year:	650,000
End of third year:	630,000

When the co-operative purchased the houses, the consumer price index was 100. It was 110 at the end of the first year, 120 at the end of the second, and 135 at the end of the third.

There is no dispute among the members about the general principle that they should cover their costs, but there is dispute about how this should be interpreted. One proposal is that depreciation should be charged on a historic-cost basis, as at present, since the most objectively determined cost is what was paid for the houses. A second proposal is that the cost should be based on current market values since the intent of the agreement was that the members should cover current economic costs and not benefit from the price appreciation created by the wise investment decision three years before. A third proposal is that the intent was that the members should cover depreciation based on the historic cost of the houses, but adjusted for price changes.

Required:

a. They know of your interest in price-change accounting and ask you to write them a two-page memo evaluating the fairness to the members of the three proposed methods.

b. One of the members has a different argument. He asserts that the real intent of the agreement was that the original capital invested in the project should be preserved. Because the houses were virtually entirely financed by debt, he claims that there was no original capital to start with, and hence the historic-cost method is the only appropriate one. Do you agree? Explain.

P20-3. You are chief accountant of a small firm. The owner asks you to transform financial statements as of 31 December 19X3 traditionally prepared using historic cost (HC) into statements based on (i) general price level (GPL) and (ii) current value with maintenance of physical capital (CV-PC). You decide to start with the easier part first. You ask the bookkeeper to take the trial balance for 31 December 19X2 and modify it to make it appropriate to include with the statements of 31 December 19X3. After some time she presents you with the following:

TRIAL BALANCES
31 December 19X2

	HC as of 31 December 19X2	GPL in $'s of 31 December 19X3	CV-PC, market values as of 31 December 19X2
Cash	$ 12,000.00	$ 12,000.00	$ 12,000.00
Accounts receivable	25,000.00	25,000.00	25,000.00
Inventory	40,000.00	44,000.00	45,000.00
Plant assets	85,000.00	93,500.00	95,000.00
Accumulated depreciation	(45,000.00)	(49,500.00)	(45,000.00)
Bank loan	(25,000.00)	(25,000.00)	(25,000.00)
Accounts payable	(36,000.00)	(36,000.00)	(36,000.00)
Long-term debt	(30,000.00)	(30,000.00)	(30,000.00)
Capital stock	(30,000.00)	(33,000.00)	(30,000.00)
Retained earnings	4,000.00	4,400.00	4,400.00
	$ 0.00	$ 5,400.00	$ 15,400.00

As she handed the trial balance to you, she said: "I have done about as much as I know how. The inflation rate was 10% during 19X3. I have adjusted the monetary assets and liabilities, and estimated the market values; so it's not surprising that the GPL and CV-PC trial balances don't balance. Exactly what the balance at the bottom of the GPL and CV-PC trial balances means is something you will have to figure out."

Required:

a. Explain why the GPL trial balance above does not balance.

b. Calculate the owners' equity section of the balance sheet for 31 December 19X2 using CV-PC.

c. Assume there was no activity in the company whatever during all of 19X3. Calculate the owners' equity portion of the balance sheet in comparative form for 31 December 19X2 and 19X3, all in $'s of 31 December 19X3.

d. On 31 December 19X3 the company sold all the inventory on hand (since 31 December 19X2) for $80,000. Calculate the profit on the sale before holding or monetary gains or losses under (i) HC, (ii) GPL, and (iii) CV-PC.

e. Give a general explanation (i) why the net income under GPL, CV-PC, and under HC differ from one another and (ii) why someone might prefer to calculate the net income under GPL or CV-PC rather than HC.

P20-4. An investor purchased on rented land a parking garage for $100,000 that had to be torn down at the beginning of Year 3 when the land rent was finished. He decided to rent the garage to a near relative for an annual rent of $50,000 payable in advance at the beginning of each of the two years. The relative was to pay all costs except depreciation.

When the investor purchased the garage, the price index was 145.00. At the end of Year 1 it was 152.50, and at the end of Year 2 it was 162.40. The investor planned to put the rent into a bank account (no interest payable) and purchase another garage at the start of Year 3.

Required:

a. Show the income statements and balance sheets for Year 1 and Year 2 using the historic-cost accounting system. Assume straight-line depreciation.

b. Complete the following GPL statements:

	Year 1 results in Year 1 $'s	Year 1 results in Year 2 $'s	Year 2 results in Year 2 $'s
Year-end index	152.25		162.40
% price increase for year			
% price increase from start of Year 1			
Income Statement			
Rental income			
Depreciation			
Monetary loss			
Loss for year			
Balance Sheet			
Cash on hand			
Building — at cost			
Accumulated depreciation			
Owners' capital			
Retained earnings:			
Loss — Year 1			
Loss — Year 2			

c. Would the investor get his $100,000 back intact? Explain. Assuming that the price of garages increased at the same rate as the general price level, would he be able to buy a garage? How well does the GPL accounting approach inform him of what is really going on?

P20-5. At the time the investor in P20-4 above purchased the garage for $100,000, he paid the market price for it. Suppose that at the end of Year 1 the garage had a market value of $115,000, and at the end of Year 2 it had a market value of $120,000. Assume that the depreciation expense for Year 2 is the amount required to make the net book value nil. The investor sold the garage at the start of Year 3.

Required:

a. Prepare CV income statements and balance sheets for Year 1 and Year 2 using the concept of physical capital maintenance.

b. What would be the amount available for distribution to shareholders at the end of the second year according to these financial statements? Explain what the numbers mean.

c. Do these financial statements have any advantages or disadvantages compared to GPL financial statements? Explain.

P20-6. Reconsider the scenario presented in P20-5.

    a. Prepare CV financial statements using the concept of financial capital maintenance. Use a columnar format similar to that in P20-4 changing the items described in the left-hand column where necessary.

    b. Evaluate the usefulness of this form of statement, especially in comparison to the form of the CV-PC statement.

    c. Compare this financial statement to the GPL statement. Are they similar? Why? Would this normally happen? Which do you think is more useful? Explain.

P20-7. Provided below are the historic-cost financial statements of Home Software Ltd., whose year-end is 31 December.

BALANCE SHEETS

	19X0	19X1
Cash	$ 54,000	$ 64,780
Accounts receivable	0	37,500
Inventory	45,000	32,200
Plant assets	234,000	234,000
Accumulated depreciation	0	(23,400)
Accounts payable	(53,000)	(55,750)
Bonds payable	(110,000)	(110,000)
Common stock	(170,000)	(170,000)
Retained earnings	0	
Income for year		(9,330)
	$ 0	$ 0

INCOME STATEMENT, 19X1

Sales	$ 168,000
Cost of goods sold	93,300
Gross profit	74,700
Expenses	
Selling and administrative	28,770
Interest	13,200
Depreciation	23,400
Net income	$ 9,330

You are also given the following additional information:

(i) The company was established on 31 December 19X0, with all founding transactions occurring on that date. The price index at the time was 100. The price index rose to 111 by the end of 19X1.

(ii) The opening inventory in 19X1 consisted of 300 units. Purchases for the year totalled 500 units. Six hundred units were sold during the year.

(iii) Transactions occurred throughout the year. Assume that, on average, the price index was 107 in 19X1. The annual average replacement cost for each unit of the goods was $161, and the year-end replacement cost was $172. The company employs FIFO to value inventory.

(iv) The replacement cost of all of the plant assets was $262,000 on 31 December 19X1. All plant assets are depreciated on a straight-line basis over a ten-year period. There were no additions during 19X1.

(v) The bond issue bears an interest rate of 12%. The interest is payable on 31 December of each year until the issue on 31 December 19X8.

Required: Prepare the current-value balance sheets and income statements for 19X1 using each of the following concepts:

a. maintenance of physical capital (for simplicity, assume the financing adjustment is based on year-end amounts)

b. maintenance of real financial capital

P20-8. Provided below are the 19X2 current-value financial statements of Shades Ltd., a sunglass lens maker and retailer. The statements were prepared under the assumption of physical capital maintenance.

TRIAL BALANCE — CV-PC
31 December 19X2

Cash	$ 75,600
Accounts receivable	58,350
Inventory	76,800
Plant assets	256,000
Accumulated depreciation	(25,600)
Accounts payable	(48,750)
Bonds payable	(100,000)
Common stock	(200,000)
Holding gains:	
Inventory	(4,800)
Cost of goods sold	(8,440)
Plant assets — realized	(3,100)
— unrealized	(27,900)
Financing adjustment	11,813
Retained earnings	0
Income for year	(59,973)
	$ 0

INCOME STATEMENT — CV-PC
31 December 19X2

Sales		$ 305,200
Cost of goods sold	180,840	
Expenses:		
Selling and administrative	38,600	
Depreciation	25,600	
Interest	12,000	
Financing adjustment	(11,813)	245,227
Net income		$ 59,973

You are also given the following additional information:

(i) The company was established on 1 January 19X2. The price index at the time their assets were acquired was 107. It rose to 118 by the end of 19X2. The financing adjustment was based on the year-end balance.

(ii) The opening inventory in 19X2 consisted of 1,710 units, each worth $40. During the year 4,110 units were sold. Purchase for the year totalled 4,000 units. Each unit of ending inventory was purchased at a cost of $45.

(iii) Transactions occurred throughout the year. Assume that, on average, the price index was 112 in 19X2. The annual average replacement cost for each unit of the goods was $44, and the year-end replacement cost was $48. The company employs FIFO to value inventory.

(iv) The historic cost of the plant assets was $225,000. All plant assets are depreciated on a straight-line basis over a ten-year period.

(v) The bond issue bears an interest rate of 12%. The interest is payable on 31 December of each year until the issue matures on 31 December 19X8.

Required: Prepare the 19X2 current-value balance sheet and income statement where real financial capital maintenance is desired. Round all figures to the nearest dollar.

P20-9. Here are the historic-cost financial statements of Sinclair Products Ltd. for 19X2. Their year-end is 31 December.

BALANCE SHEET — HC
31 December 19X2

Cash	$ 93,300
Accounts receivable	46,500
Inventory	50,000
Plant assets	240,000
Accumulated depreciation	(72,000)
Accounts payable	(51,000)
Bonds payable	(75,000)
Common stock	(180,000)
Income for year	(24,250)
Retained earnings, start of year	(27,550)
	$ 0

INCOME STATEMENT — HC
31 December 19X2

Sales	$ (182,500)
Cost of goods sold	94,000
Gross profit	(88,500)
Expenses:	
Selling and administrative	32,000
Depreciation	24,000
Interest	8,250
Operating profit	(24,250)
Net income	$ (24,250)

You are also given the following additional information:

(i) Transactions occurred throughout the year. Assume that, on average, the price index was 108 in 19X2. The annual average replacement cost for each item of the inventory was $23, and the year-end replacement cost was $25. The company employs FIFO to value inventory.

(ii) The company was established in January 19X0. The price index at the time their assets were acquired was 104. There was no change in the price index between the time of acquisition and the end of 19X1. The price index rose to 113 by the end of 19X2. The company experienced no holding gains prior to 19X2.

(iii) The bond issue bears an interest rate of 11%. The interest is payable on 31 December of each year until the issue matures on 31 December 19X6.

(iv) The opening inventory in 19X2 consisted of 2,100 units. During 19X2 4,384 units were sold. There were 2,500 units in inventory at the end of 19X2.

(v) The replacement cost of all of the plant assets was $265,000 on 31 December 19X2. All plant assets are depreciated on a straight-line basis over a ten-year period.

Required: Prepare the current-value balance sheets and income statements for 19X2 using each of the following concepts:

a. maintenance of physical capital (for simplicity, calculate the financing adjustment on the basis of the year-end balances)

b. maintenance of real financial capital (round your answers to the nearest dollar)

P20-10. Provided below are the 19X2 current-value financial statements of Timeless Watches. The statements were prepared under the concept of maintenance of real financial capital. The company's year-end is 31 December.

TRIAL BALANCE — CV-FC
31 December 19X2

Cash	$ 76,930
Accounts receivable	61,292
Inventory	62,000
Plant assets	264,000
Accumulated depreciation	(26,400)
Accounts payable	(59,852)
Bonds payable	(85,000)
Common stock	(237,981)
Holding gains	
Inventory	(318)
Plant assets — unrealized	(3,405)
Retained earnings	0
Income for year	(51,266)
	$ 0

INCOME STATEMENT — CV-FC
31 December 19X2

Sales		$ 292,991
Cost of goods sold	178,879	
Expenses:		
Selling and administrative	35,550	
Depreciation	26,400	
Interest	11,050	
Realized holding gains		
— Cost of goods sold	(8,224)	
— Plant assets	(1,460)	
Monetary loss (gain)	(470)	241,725
Net income		$ 51,266

You are also given the following additional information:

(i) The company was established on 1 January 19X2. The price index at the time their assets were acquired was 104. It rose to 110 by the end of 19X2.

(ii) The opening inventory in 19X2 consisted of 3,000 units worth $27 each. During the year 6,000 units were sold. Purchases for the year totalled 5,000 units. Each unit of ending inventory was purchased at a cost of $30.

(iii) Transactions occurred throughout the year. Assume that, on average, the Price Index was 107 in 19X2. The annual average replacement cost for each item of the inventory was $29, and the year-end replacement cost was $31. The company employs FIFO to value inventory.

(iv) The historic cost of the plant assets was $245,000. All plant assets are depreciated on a straight-line basis over a ten-year period.

(v) The bond issue bears an interest rate of 13%. The interest is payable on 31 December of each year until the issue matures on 31 December 19X8.

(vi) The cost of goods sold, as it would appear on a historical-cost income statement, was $166,000.

Required: Prepare the 19X2 current-value balance sheet and income statement where physical capital maintenance is desired. Round all figures to the nearest dollar.

P20-11. Disclosure of supplementary information with respect to the effects of changing prices is recommended in Section 4510 of the *CICA Handbook*, as discussed in this chapter.

The concept of preferred capital maintenance is not specified by the Accounting Standards Committee because, in their view, different capital-maintenance concepts might be relevant to different users in different circumstances. However, the committee does call for disclosure of current-cost income after maintenance of operating capability. In addition, they call for sufficient supplementary information to allow calculation of (i) current-cost income attributable to shareholders based on maintenance of operating capability financed by shareholders and (ii) current-cost income after maintenance of financial capital. The latter income measurement can be computed in nominal dollars or in constant dollars.

Consider the following financial statement.

THE CANADIAN COMPANY
BALANCE SHEET
30 June 19X1
(in thousands of $)

	19X1	19X0
Assets:		
Cash	$ 10,000	$ 5,000
Marketable securities	10,000	
Accounts receivable (net)	30,000	25,000
Inventory	100,000	80,000
Property, plant, and equipment (net)	500,000	490,000
Total Assets	$ 650,000	$ 600,000
Liabilities and shareholders' equity:		
Current liabilities	$ 100,000	$ 80,000
15% bonds payable, due 2 July 19X9	150,000	150,000
Deferred income taxes	100,000	90,000
Preferred shares, $6 par-value	100,000	100,000
Common stock	150,000	150,000
Retained earnings	50,000	30,000
Total liabilities and shareholders' equity	$ 650,000	$ 600.00

Notes:

	19X1	19X0
Increase in current cost of inventory and property, plant, and equipment	$ 75,000	
Effect of general price changes	50,000	
Excess of increase in current costs over increase in general prices	$ 25,000	
Purchasing power gain on net monetary liabilities	$ 20,000	
Current costs:		
Cost of sales	$ 440,000	
Depreciation	70,000	
Inventory	110,000	$ 85,000
Property, plant, and equipment (net)	575,000	560,000
Historical costs:		
Cost of sales	$ 400,000	
Depreciation	60,000	

Required:

a. Explain the essential difference between maintenance of financial capital and maintenance of operating capability (productive capacity).

b. (i) What is the difference between maintenance of operating capability and maintenance of operating capability financed by shareholders?

(ii) What must be included if income after maintenance of operating capability is to be reconciled to income after maintenance of operating capability financed by shareholders?

c. What are the major differences between maintenance of financial capital measured in nominal dollars and maintenance of financial capital measured in constant dollars?

d. Based on the above balance sheet information, calculate and identify the preferred financing adjustment discussed in Section 4510 of the *CICA Handbook*.

*(*CMA adapted)

BIBLIOGRAPHY

CANADIAN INSTITUTE OF CHARTERED ACCOUNTANTS. *Estimating Current Values: Some Techniques, Problems and Experiences*. Toronto, 1979. A report by a task force commissioned by the CICA to look at some of the practical issues in arriving at current values. Required reading for anyone who assumes it is a simple task.

CHASTEEN, LANNY. "A Taxonomy of Price Change Models." *The Accounting Review* (July 1984). Sets out twelve possible price-change accounting models.

DRUMMOND, CHRISTINA S.R., and STICKLER A.D. *Current Cost Accounting*. Toronto: Methuen Publications, 1983. Intended as an introduction and practical guide. The two authors are from Price Waterhouse.

HOBB, PETER. "Reporting the Effects of Changing Prices." *CA Magazine* (December 1982). An assessment of Section 4510 from the viewpoint of a CICA research manager.

IJIRI, YUJI and NOEL, JAMES. "A Reliability Comparison of the Measurement of Wealth, Income and Force." *The Accounting Review* (January 1984) An examination of the relative merits of current and historical cost against such criteria as reliability.

LEHARI, REIN A., "The Best Way to Value a Real Estate Company," *CA Magazine* (July 1983). The author, a partner of Price Waterhouse, advocates using the present value of cash flows of individual properties as the basis of valuation.

MCDONALD, BILL and MORRIS, MICHAEL H. "The Relevance of SFAS 33 — Inflation Accounting Disclosures in the Adjustment of Stock Prices to Inflation." *The Accounting Review* (July 1984). A study that tests the reaction of security returns to anticipated and unanticipated inflation in order to assess the relevance of Statement of Financial Accounting Standard No. 33.

PRICE WATERHOUSE. *Current Cost Accounting: Reporting the Effects of Changing Prices.* Toronto, 1982. Price Waterhouse has been an advocate of GPL accounting rather than CV accounting. This monograph helps to explain its views.

————. *The Mechanics of Price Level Accounting.* Toronto, 1974. An illustration of how GPL accounting works.

SWANSON, EDWARD P. "Accounting for Changing Prices: Some Mid-Course Corrections." *Journal of Accountancy* (April 1984). An evaluation of the FASB's position on price-change accounting.

CHAPTER 21
Financial-Statement Analysis

Introduction

Our approach so far in this text has been to examine individual items in the financial statements, ask what the accounting treatment of each item was, and consider whether this treatment was appropriate. This might be characterized as a *micro* approach because we have tended to take a close-up view of accounting issues. We now look at financial statements from a greater distance — more of a *macro* approach. These two approaches reinforce each other. By taking a broader view we have an easier time seeing the interrelationships and relative importance of items on the financial statements. The micro approach that we have used to date has given us the background to ask perceptive questions about individual items that go to make up the larger picture behind the financial statements.

A **financial-statement ratio** is a number produced by dividing one number on the financial statement by another. For example, the current assets might be divided by the current liabilities to produce a number such as 2. Usually, the ratio is expressed in the form "2:1," although there are exceptions, such as earnings per share where it is assumed the reader knows the income given is for one share. In this chapter we review some of the commonly used ratios and evaluate the strengths and weaknesses of the overall technique. Our understanding of the nature of financial-statement analysis has increased over the past two decades because of closer integration with statistical analysis and with research on the nature of stock-market behaviour. This will be reflected in our approach to this topic.

The Nature of Financial-Statement Analysis

Traditionally the analysis of financial statements has been based on computing ratios of numbers found in the financial statements and using these ratios as overall indicators of some aspect of the company. For instance, the ratio of current assets to current liabilities, the so-called **current ratio**, has been a traditional test of the liquidity of companies. The general belief was that the ratio should be 2:1 or higher.

Financial-statement analysis might be thought of as the culmination of the study of financial accounting. In other words, one first studies the individual items making up the financial statements to understand their meaning and why they are grouped as they are. Then one moves to fitting them all together, using ratio analysis as one of the techniques for evaluation.

The objectives of analysing financial statements might be any of the following:

1. To seek companies that are particularly successful in their operations, so that the investor can make an above-average rate of return by buying their shares. This would be of particular interest to a prospective investor.

2. To evaluate the riskiness of a company if the intention is to lend it money. This would be of particular interest to a prospective lender.

3. To evaluate the quality of the management by their ability to make good use of the resources entrusted to them. This would be of particular interest to either a prospective or present investor or lender.

These are ambitious objectives. Usually the financial statements offer only a partial view into a company's operations. Nevertheless, that view is an important one. Financial-statement analysis is one of the few analytical tools that can be applied systematically across a wide number of companies.

A ratio analysis is termed **cross-sectional** if it uses several ratios that are all as of the same date. Typically, this would be a comparison of several companies at one point in time. A ratio analysis is termed **longitudinal** or **time-series** if it uses ratios over a series of time periods. Typically, it will be for the same company over a period of years. It is also possible to analyse just one company at just one time period or several companies over many time periods. Such analyses will be explored below.

Implications of Efficient Market Research

There is a growing body of evidence [Foster, 1986] that investors in a large and well-organized capital market, such as the New York Stock Exchange or the Toronto Stock Exchange, react swiftly (say, within a day) to published information about a company. There is every reason to think they react swiftly to information published in companies' financial reports. The implication of this is that as an investor, one should not expect to make above-average stock-market profits through analysing published financial reports of widely traded companies.

While it is important to keep this attribute of the **efficient capital market** in mind, it is essential to avoid the common belief that reading financial statements is pointless for the investor. Financial-statement analysis is still useful — even to the investor — for the following reasons:

1. Many companies are too small to attract wide market interest, and hence there is no efficient market for trading their shares. Others are closely held, and the owners do not wish to have the company's shares publicly traded. One large firm of chartered accountants estimated that 80% of its clients were companies whose shares were not traded on a public stock exchange. Assisting the management of such companies to analyse the significance of their financial statements was one of their most important services. Analysis is also useful to those outside the firm, such as those purchasing shares in a closely held company or those lending money to a company (e.g., a bank or a lender purchasing a private placement of bonds).

2. Being familiar with a company through financial-statement analysis and other means may make it easier to see the significance of new information and to react to it more quickly than others. The "industry specialist" within large investment firms may be seen as an example of this.

3. Assessing the riskiness of a security through financial-statement analysis is consistent with the concept of efficient capital markets because the investor should be interested in the riskiness of a stock.

For more information about the implications of efficient markets research for the financial-statement analyst, the texts by Lev [1974], Dyckman [1975], and Foster [1986] provide good basic coverage.

Implications of Statistical Evaluation

A financial-statement ratio is a *statistic*, or a number that is created by combining other numbers according to a rule. Those with a background in statistics who have studied financial-statement ratios caution us against their careless use as follows:

1. If we calculate the same ratio, such as the current ratio, for different companies or for different dates of the same company, we would expect to find some variations. In fact it is the expectation of differences that leads us to make the calculation. However, we have very little knowledge about how much variation to expect and what variations might be significant. Unfortunately, there is good reason to expect that most ratios will *not* form a statistically normal distribution. Hence the usual tests of statistical significance cannot be applied.

2. We would expect to find — and indeed do find — that most financial-statement ratios are highly correlated. The implication for the statistical results is that computing a lot of different ratios that test for similar characteristics (e.g., liquidity) does not lead to much greater certainty about the findings.

3. Many ratios fail to account for any changes in the underlying factors that heavily influence the statistical results. For example, showing the trend of earnings per share over a ten-year period may be misleading unless the changing value of the dollar is adjusted for. In a period of heavy inflation there will be a strong upward bias on earnings per share because of the falling value of the unit of currency.

A fuller discussion of the statistical properties of financial-statement ratios and their limitations can be found in Lev [1974] and in Foster [1986].

Types of Financial-Statement Ratios

Ratios are commonly classified into the following main types:

1. Tests of short-term solvency — the sort of test that would be of interest to a bank or supplier.

2. Tests of profitability — whether the reported profit is reasonable in the light of certain tests. This is a test that would be of interest to the long-run equity investor.

3. Tests of long-run solvency — of interest to a bondholder.

4. Industry — specific tests — useful in making comparisons between companies in the same industry.

We will now examine each of these types of tests and give examples.

Tests of Short-Term Solvency

Tests of short-term solvency are typically intended for use by the creditor, such as a bank or supplier, who is interested in the riskiness of a short-term loan. Not surprisingly, these tests concentrate on current liabilities and current assets. The most common ratios are shown below.

CURRENT RATIO

The **current ratio** is defined as follows:

Current ratio = Current assets / Current liabilities

The current ratio is a traditional test of a company's ability to meet its current liabilities. The common belief used to be that this ratio should not drop below 2:0, but there is no systematic evidence to support this belief.

Note that in this context the manner in which a company classifies its current liabilities and current assets can become significant. For example, in an industry that has an operating cycle longer than one year, it is common to classify inventory as current even if it will not be sold within the next twelve months. In such a case, one would want to be sure that the payables were classified similarly. If they were not, it would be appropriate to revise the acceptable minimum level for the ratio upwards.

It is also useful to note that any ratio will converge on 1.0 as the same constant is added to the numerator and denominator. Similarly, the ratios will diverge further from 1.0 as a constant is subtracted. Consider the following examples:

	Original ratio	Constants added or subtracted	Revised ratio	More or less favourable?
(a)	3:2 = 1.5	(3 + 2):(2 + 2)	5:4 = 1.250	Less
(b)	3:2 = 1.5	(3 − 1):(2 − 1)	2:1 = 2.000	More
(c)	2:3 = 0.667	(2 + 2):(3 + 2)	4:5 = 0.800	More
(d)	2:3 = 0.667	(2 − 1):(3 − 1)	1:2 = 0.500	Less

Note that in case (a) a favourable current ratio of 1.5 has become less favourable, whereas in case (c) the reverse has happened. In both cases, however, the ratio has converged toward 1.0 from its original amount. Similarly, the ratio became more favourable when a constant was subtracted in (b) and less favourable when it was subtracted in (d).

The significance of this is that it is often possible for companies to arrange their affairs to add or subtract constant amounts from both current assets and current liabilities. For example, delaying payment to suppliers results in adding the same amount to both the bank balance (assuming it is not in overdraft) and accounts payable. Similarly, paying suppliers sooner than normal would result in the same amount being deducted from both cash and accounts payable. There may be practical limits to the company's abilities to do this, but the analyst needs to keep in mind that the possibility exists.

Recall from Chapter 6 on inventory that the choice of inventory valuation method may have a significant impact on the value assigned to inventory. In addition, inventory is valued on the assumption that the firm is a going concern. A short-term creditor's worry is over the protection to be offered if the firm's ability to operate is jeopardized — that is, if the "going concern" assumption is not valid. This has led to the use of the ratio discussed below.

QUICK RATIO

The **quick ratio** is defined as follows:

Quick ratio = Current assets readily convertible into cash / Current liabilities

It is also referred to as the **acid test ratio**. It might be used by a creditor who had doubts about how long a company might survive and wanted to see how easily the current liabilities could be paid out of those current assets that were most readily converted into cash.

Here is an example of how the current and quick ratios might be calculated for Schlumberger Limited, a company that operates world-wide. It manufactures and operates sophisticated equipment for detecting oil deposits. At the time of preparing its 1986 statements, the company had suffered a loss for the first time since it was listed in 1962.

SCHLUMBERGER LIMITED

	1986	1985
	(thousands of $ U.S.)	
Current Assets:		
Cash	$ 45,247	$ 41,339
Short-term investments	3,765,128	4,548,785
Receivables less allowance for doubtful accounts		
(1986 — $55,663: 1985 — $29,597)	974,681	1,272,968
Inventories	560,032	699,961
Other current assets	66,909	77,144
Total current assets (A)	5,411,997	6,640,197
Deduct: Inventories	560,032	699,961
Total quick assets (B)	4,851,965	5,940,236
Current Liabilities:		
Accounts payable and accrued liabilities	$1,338,758	$1,188,271
Estimated liability for taxes on income	826,894	948,409
Bank loans	1,034,615	1,046,780
Dividend payable	84,787	89,357
Long-term debt due within one year	8,155	18,516
Total current liabilities (C)	3,293,209	3,291,333
Current ratio (A/C)	1.64	2.02
Quick ratio (B/C)	1.47	1.80

Given the poor operating results, it is not surprising that the current and quick ratios dropped from 1985 to 1986. Only inventories have been deducted to calculate the quick ratio. It is often worthwhile to examine the other current assets to see if any others look "soft" enough to be deducted. In this case the other current assets are relatively small, and hence not material. However, in other cases one may find receivables denominated in a currency whose continued value is doubtful, or receivables from a related company.

It was pointed out in previous chapters that assets are often specifically pledged to certain creditors, and other creditors such as Revenue Canada have a preferred position to most unsecured creditors. Specifically secured creditors have the right to seize and sell the pledged assets until their debts are completely satisfied. Preferred creditors have the right to be paid ahead of general creditors. For this reason, care must be taken in the use of the quick ratio. As an alternative, budgets of the statement of changes in financial position might be constructed for cash or net current assets, although this would require more information and calculation than would be required for the ratios discussed here.

One should be careful not to assume that large current and quick ratios are always a good signal about a company. Such large ratios are achieved by building up current assets and running down current liabilities. Recall from earlier chapters that net current assets are simply a form of safety margin and are not usually in themselves revenue producing. Therefore, a high current or quick ratio could also be interpreted negatively as an indicator of management's inability to operate within a smaller safety margin, causing a build-up of non-productive assets.

ACCOUNTS RECEIVABLE TURNOVER RATIO

The **accounts receivable turnover ratio** is defined as follows:

Accounts receivable turnover ratio = Sales/Accounts receivable

It has many similarities to the inventory turnover ratio. In fact, similar ratios can be used to indicate the "turnover" in any group of assets, such as plant assets.

A related measure for accounts receivable is the **number of days' sales in receivables**. It is defined as follows:

Days' sales in receivables = Accounts receivables/Average sales per day

This ratio can be thought of as the average number of days before a customer pays for a purchase. If the days' sales in receivables ratio creeps up for a company, it may be an indication of one or more of the following:

(i) offering easier credit terms as a means of maintaining sales, (ii) declining management expertise over credit control and the collection of outstanding accounts, or (iii) less favourable overall economic conditions. Note that the days' sales in receivables ratio rises (drops) as the accounts receivable turnover ratio drops (rises).

Let us calculate the days' sales in receivables for Schlumberger Limited for three consecutive years.

SCHLUMBERGER LIMITED

| | 31 December | | |
	1986	1985	1984
	(thousands of $ U.S.)		
Operating revenue	$4,568,395	$5,585,060	$5,246,429
Average revenue per day (A)	12,516	15,302	14,374
Accounts receivable (B)	974,681	1,272,968	1,103,100
Average days' sales in receivables (B/A)	78	83	77

The shift in the average days' sales in receivables ratio from 77 to 83 to 78 does not appear to indicate any particular trend. As business fell off in 1986, the company seems to have tightened its receivables policy and got the term of receivables back to where it had been in 1984. The calculations show that, on average, receivables were outstanding for over two months.

INVENTORY TURNOVER RATIO

The **inventory turnover ratio** is defined as follows:

Inventory turnover ratio = Sales / Average inventory, or
Cost of goods sold / Average inventory

In either form this ratio can be interpreted as a measure of a company's ability to dispose of its inventory quickly if it needs to raise money. If, for instance, the ratio of cost of goods sold to average inventory is 4.00, this implies that the inventory turns over four times a year, or every three months.

If one is going to use this ratio to make statements about the turnover within a given time period (e.g., turnover per year), then the *cost of goods sold* should be used in the numerator since it is based on the same valuation method as inventory. However, if the ratio is just used as an index to compare how rapidly the inventory turnover varies from period to period, then the use of *sales* in the numerator would also be appropriate since *sales* and *cost of sales* are usually highly correlated. Recall that in Canada information about the cost of goods sold is not required, but it is considered "desirable" by the *Handbook*.

One can also measure inventory turnover by the **days' sales in inventory**. It is defined as follows:

Days' sales in inventory = Inventory on hand / Average daily cost of goods sold

This ratio can be thought of intuitively as the average number of days the company's inventory would last if no restocking took place. Obviously, the company would not run out of all items of inventory at the same time. Seasonal variations in sales and inventory levels are important influences to consider when using this ratio.

Inventory turnover for Loblaws Companies Limited is shown below. The days' sales in receivables is also shown so that it can be compared to that of Schlumberger Limited given above.

LOBLAWS COMPANIES LIMITED

	1986	1985	1984
		(millions of $)	
Sales	$7,838.9	$6,931.1	$6,419.4
Average sales per day (A)	21.5	19.0	17.6
Accounts receivable (B)	219.8	207.9	152.8
Inventory (C)	599.3	523.5	443.4
Average days' sales in receivables			
(B/A)	10.2	10.9	8.7
Inventory turnover (C/A)	27.9	27.6	25.2

The inventory appears to turn over on average about every twenty-seven days (using *average sales per day* as the numerator — the company does not provide the *cost of sales*). By contrast, the average days' sales in receivables is about every ten days.

Although one would expect the inventory turnover to be high in a grocery chain, the days' sales in receivables appears puzzling since the public normally pays cash at the checkout counter. Initially one might well suspect that the days' sales in receivables should be nil. However, the company also operates a wholesale division with sales of $3,409 out of the total of $7,838.9 reported above. If one assumes that the credit sales were only out of the wholesale division, then the days' sales in receivables for 1986 should be calculated as follows:

Days' sales in receivables = 219.8/(3,409/365) = 23.53 days (instead of 10.2 days)

This example illustrates the potentially misleading results that can arise from the uncritical use of averages. If one is calculating the accounts receivable turnover, then it is worth searching out how much of the sales are for cash and then deducting them from the denominator. Similarly, when calculating inventory turnover, one should ask whether the sales amounts apply to all of the inventory or just the finished goods, and then one should modify the calculations appropriately.

EVALUATION OF SHORT-TERM RATIOS

It is important to remember that the purpose of measures of short-term liquidity is to provide the user with an indicator of a company's ability to meet its creditors' demands over the short term by quickly converting non-cash current assets into cash. Simplistic uses of these ratios have been criticized by such analysts as Lev [1974] and Foster [1986] on the grounds that the accepted threshold levels for each ratio (such as the 2:1 ratio often quoted as desirable for the current ratio) have been given too much importance in the light of available evidence. The reader should be prepared to use these measures as warning signals to look deeper into particular aspects of a company's financial position, rather than as definitive indicators of the degree of solvency.

Tests of Profitability

Tests of profitability are designed to answer such questions as the following:

1. If I know the dollar amount of the net income, how can I judge whether it is good or bad in comparison with
   (a) other companies in the same industry?
   (b) the same company's results in prior years?
   (c) what I could earn on this money in another investment?

2. If I have decided that the net income is unacceptably low, how can I analyse why it is low?
We will now examine ratios that can be used to help answer these questions.

RATE OF RETURN ON ASSETS

The **rate of return on assets** can be defined as follows:

> Rate of return on assets = "Income"/Total assets employed,
> where "Income" = Net income after tax + Net after-tax interest expense
> + Minority interest in earnings

Investors evaluating their portfolios of investments might go through each item in their portfolios to see what the yield of each item is compared to its market price. To do this an investor would form the following ratio:

> Annual yield of a given security / Current market price

The investor might then decide to keep or sell each security on the basis of the attractiveness of its yield in the light of other factors, such as riskiness and alternative investment opportunities.

In a similar manner one could form the rate-of-return-on-assets ratio for an individual company, namely:

Rate of return on assets = "Income"/Total assets employed,
where "Income" = Net income after tax + Net after-tax interest expense
+ Minority interest in earnings

The numerator ("Income") consists of the after-tax earnings on the three sources of capital: (i) shareholders (both common and preferred), (ii) creditors, and (iii) minority shareholders of subsidiary companies when the results are consolidated. The denominator consists of the total asset base that provides the means of earning the income. This ratio measures the return on invested capital for a given company. Therefore this ratio is also called **return on investment (ROI)**.

Because it is often difficult to obtain the *market value* of the assets, it is common to use the *book value* of the assets instead. If this is done, then all the figures needed can usually be found on conventional financial statements, although occasionally on some statements the numbers may have been combined with others.

Let us use Imasco Limited to illustrate the rate of return on assets. Imasco is a large Canadian company that had its origins in Imperial Tobacco. It subsequently expanded into the consumer-marketing field with Shoppers Drug Mart, Peoples Drug Stores (in the U.S.), and the UCS stores that sell such items as cigarettes, newspapers, and magazines. In 1986 Imasco acquired Canada Trust, through purchase of the holding company Genstar Corporation, and incorporated the assets it wished to keep in the subsidiary Imasco Enterprises Inc. (hereafter "Enterprises"). Imasco does not include the Enterprise subsidiary in its consolidated financial statements. Because the nature of the Enterprises operations is felt to be different enough, Imasco has decided to use the equity method instead.

If one begins the analysis by calculating the ratio of net earnings to total reported assets, the results are as follows:

IMASCO LIMITED
(thousands of $)

	1987	1986	1985
Net earnings	$ 183,567	$ 261,745	$ 234,108
Total assets	5,399,951	2,986,644	2,741,572
Return on investment	3.40%	8.76%	8.54%

There is clearly a sharp drop in 1987. This could be due to a decline in overall profitability or to a change in the mix of the operations with the less profitable ones playing a more dominant role. Ideally, one would like to be able to divide the balance sheet and income statement into each of the operating segments to calculate the ROI for each. It is instructive to see how much this can be done from the information provided. The brief summaries given below have been prepared by taking the figures from the published balance sheet and income statement and then breaking them down as much as possible from the information provided in the notes to the financial statements. Some condensing has been done from the original to save space.

IMASCO LIMITED
BALANCE-SHEET DATA, 1987
(thousands of $)

	Total	Unspecified	Enterprises	Tobacco	Restaurant	Drug store	Sundry
Current Assets:							
Cash and short-terms	$ 40,229	$ 40,229					
Accounts and notes receivable	264,773	264,773					
Inventories	970,888	0		$420,152	$60,513	$442,109	$48,114
Prepaid expenses	29,481	29,481					
	1,305,371	334,483	0	420,152	60,513	442,109	48,114
Other Assets:							
Investments and receivables	101,505	101,505					
Deferred charges	63,885	63,885					
Fixed assets	970,763	0	0	108,694	551,791	294,607	15,671
Goodwill	237,358	237,358					
Investment in Imasco Enterprises	2,721,069	0	2,721,069				
	4,094,580	402,748	2,721,069	108,694	551,791	294,607	15,671
Total assets	5,399,951	737,231	2,721,069	528,846	612,304	736,716	63,785
Capital employed	4,779,820	0	2,721,069	548,779	620,224	851,027	38,721
Difference	$ (620,131)	$ (737,231)	$ 0	$ 19,933	$ 7,920	$114,311	$(25,064)

IMASCO LIMITED
INCOME-STATEMENT DATA, 1987
(thousands of $)

	Total	Unspecified	Enterprises	Tobacco	Restaurant	Drug store	Sundry
Revenues	$(5,625,074)	$(5,625,074)					
Sales and excise tax	1,058,867	1,058,867					
Operating costs	(4,566,207)	(4,566,207)					
	4,206,667	4,206,667					
Equity in net earnings of Imasco Enterprises Inc.	(88,620)	0	$(88,620)				
Operating earnings	(448,160)	0	(88,620)	$(210,009)	$(128,316)	$(14,765)	$(6,450)
Corporate expenses	23,425	23,425					
Interest — net	156,788	156,788					
Earnings before income taxes	(267,947)	(267,947)					
Income taxes	55,301	55,301					
Earnings before extraordinary items	(212,646)	(212,646)					
Extraordinary items	29,079	29,079					
Net earnings	$ (183,567)	$ (183,567)					

Observe that of the current assets, only inventories have been identified by segment; and of the long-term assets, only fixed assets have been identified by segment. However, for each segment Imasco uses a term called *capital employed* that includes (i) directly identifiable assets at net book value; and (ii) current liabilities, excluding income taxes payable, bank debt, and other debt. The capital employed per segment is shown in our summary of balance-sheet data. Observe that it corresponds reasonably closely with the amount of the total assets per segment, as shown in the same summary. In the income-statement data, only *revenue* and *operating earnings* are segmented. The operating earnings appear to be earnings prior to common corporate costs.

For the purpose of computing a proxy for ROI, let us use *operating earnings* for income and *capital employed* for assets. A three-year summary of this proxy for ROI is shown below for each operating segment of the company.

IMASCO LIMITED
OPERATING EARNINGS / CAPITAL EMPLOYED

Year	Enterprises	Tobacco	Restaurant	Drug store	Sundry
1987	3.25%	38.27%	20.69%	1.73%	16.66%
1986	n/a	46.33%	20.91%	9.94%	22.85%
1985	n/a	41.93%	19.50%	12.33%	8.48%

There is a marked difference between the segments in the rate of contribution per dollar of capital invested. Tobacco contributed the most, and restaurants were in second. Imasco Enterprises seems low in comparison with most of the others. In 1987, the company had net assets of roughly $5 billion, and Enterprises represented about half of the total. Therefore this new investment would have played a very significant role in affecting the trend in ROI shown above. We will return later to an examination of Imasco's financial statements.

The ratio of rate of return on assets seems to be a very useful one, in part because it invites comparison with the yield that can be obtained by other companies on their assets. However, a little reflection will make one aware that this ratio needs to be handled even more carefully than most of the other ratios. The numerator's major component is net income, but the reported income of any given year is the end product of an imperfect matching process. It is also influenced to some extent by accounting-policy decisions on such matters as depreciation and inventory valuation. One should therefore be prepared to examine the income statement to decide how "soft" the income measurement might be because of such factors.

It is also worthwhile to consider whether the income used in the ratio should include extraordinary items. Generally, income *before* extraordinary items is thought to produce more meaningful ratios.

The denominator, total assets, is measured at historic cost. Further, we know that it is quite possible for some important assets (in an economic sense) to be excluded from accounting measurement. This might be particularly important in a high-technology company that does much of its own research and development. Such technological know-how would not be shown explicitly on the balance sheet, and yet it might be a very important factor in the company's earnings. On the other hand, if a company's assets have been recently purchased and most of the assets are on the balance sheet, then the book value might be a reasonably good proxy for the value of the underlying assets.

The problems noted above have been raised already in this text. They are raised here again to increase awareness of the care that needs to be exercised in using comprehensive ratios of this sort. In general, the more powerful the potential use of an accounting ratio is, the more it uses highly aggregated accounting measures; thus, the more careful one has to be to understand what these measures are and what their weaknesses might be in each given instance. In brief, there is no substitute for understanding and evaluating the accounting issues that lie behind the process generating the accounting numbers on financial statements.

For convenience, let us use "Income" to stand for the numerator of the rate of return on assets ratio, as given near the beginning of this section. If we divide both numerator and denominator by *Sales*, then we have the following:

Rate of return on assets = ("Income"/Sales) × (Sales/Total Assets)

We have thus broken the rate of return into two components: (i) the profit on sales, or profit margin ratio, and (ii) the asset turnover ratio. (This approach was used for years by the du Pont Company in the United States as a means of evaluating its divisions.) We will now examine each of these components individually.

PROFIT MARGIN RATIO

The profit margin ratio is defined as follows:

Profit margin *ratio* = "Income"/Sales,
where "Income" = Net income after tax + Net after-tax interest expense
+ Minority interest in earnings

To illustrate the profit margin ratio, let us return to Imasco Limited. We will remove the revenues and expenses of Imasco Enterprises Inc. in order to examine the rest of the company, which is essentially a manufacturing and retailing operation.

IMASCO LIMITED
(thousands of $)

	1987	1986	1985
Sales, net of excise and sales tax	$4,566,207	$4,310,780	$3,625,973
Net earnings	183,567	261,745	234,108
Interest expense — pre tax	156,788	38,658	49,300
— tax effect	(74,474)	(18,363)	(23,418)
"Income"	$ 265,881	$ 282,040	$ 259,990
"Income" from Imasco Enterprises	88,620		
"Income" without Imasco Enterprises	$177,261	$282,040	$259,990
Profit margin ratio:			
Including Enterprises	5.82%	6.54%	7.17%
Excluding Enterprises	3.88%	6.54%	7.17%

Notice how the profit margin ratio has been slipping over the three-year period.

The return on investment has been slipping as well, as the following analysis shows:

IMASCO LIMITED
(thousands of $)

A. *With Imasco Enterprises*

Year	Rate of return on assets ("Income" / Total assets)	= =	Profit margin ratio ("Income" / Sales)	× ×	Asset turnover ratio (Sales / Assets)
1985	259,992 / 2,741,572 = 9.48%		259,992 / 3,625,973 = 7.17%		3,625,973 / 2,741,572 = 132.26%
1986	282,040 / 2,986,644 = 9.44%		282,040 / 4,310,780 = 6.54%		4,310,780 / 2,986,644 = 144.34%
1987	265,881 / 5,399,951 = 4.92%		265,881 / 4,566,207 = 5.82%		4,566,207 / 5,399,951 = 84.56%

B. *Without Imasco Enterprises*

1985	259,992 / 2,741,572 = 9.48%		259,992 / 3,625,973 = 7.17%		3,625,973 / 2,741,572 = 132.26%
1986	282,040 / 2,986,644 = 9.44%		282,040 / 4,310,780 = 6.54%		4,310,780 / 2,986,644 = 144.34%
1987	177,261 / 2,678,882 = 6.62%		177,261 / 4,566,207 = 3.88%		4,566,207 / 2,678,882 = 170.45%

Although the asset turnover has been steadily rising from 1.32 times per year to 1.70, it is insufficient to offset the declining profit margin ratios. One can get a partial insight into the reason for this decline by expressing costs as a percentage of sales, as follows:

IMASCO LIMITED

	1987 dollars	1987 percent	1986 dollars	1986 percent	1985 dollars	1985 percent
Net sales	4,566,207	100.00	4,310,780	100.00	3,625,973	100.00
Operating costs	4,206,667	92.13	3,844,910	89.19	3,193,941	88.09
Operating earnings	359,540	7.87	465,870	10.81	432,032	11.91
Corporate expenses	23,425	0.51	20,020	0.46	17,308	0.48
Interest	156,788	3.43	38,658	0.90	49,300	1.36
Earnings before income tax	267,947	5.87	407,192	9.45	365,424	10.08
Income taxes	55,301	1.21	145,447	3.37	131,316	3.62

Focusing on *operating earnings* as a percentage of sales, we see that there has been a drop from 11.91% in 1985 to 7.87% in 1987. The segmented information provided in the notes allows us to analyse this factor by industry segment, as shown below.

IMASCO LIMITED
Excluding Imasco Enterprises
(thousands of $)

	1987	1986	1985
Tobacco: Earnings percentage	58.41%	33.23%	33.33%
Revenues	$1,787,614	$1,769,776	$1,451,130
Operating earnings	$210,009 = 11.75%	$246,015 = 13.90%	$222,024 = 15.30%
Restaurant: Earnings percentage	35.69%	26.82%	23.49%
Revenues	$1,656,350	$1,508,710	$1,321,248
Operating earnings	$128,316 = 7.75%	$118,768 = 7.87%	$108,289 = 8.02%
Drug store: Earnings percentage	4.11%	35.86%	32.74%
Revenues	$2,019,540	$1,909,631	$1,425,407
Operating earnings	$14,765 = 0.73%	$92,999 = 4.87%	$93,590 = 6.57%

(Continued)

	1987		1986		1985	
Other: Earnings percentage	1.79%		3.59%		4.04%	
Revenues	$213,335		$191,146		$176,088	
Operating earnings	$6,450 =	3.02%	$8,088 =	4.23%	$7,192 =	4.08%
Total: Earnings percentage	100%		100%		100%	
Revenues	$5,625,074		$5,325,134		$4,353,254	
Operating earnings	$359,540 $	6.39%	$465,870 $	8.75%	$432,032 $	9.92%

This analysis allows us to draw some important conclusions. The major segment in terms of contribution to total operating earnings has been tobacco. In 1987 tobacco, with earnings of $210,009, contributed 58.41% of total earnings. However, in terms of profitability, tobacco has fallen from a ratio of operating earnings to revenues of 15.30% in 1985 to 11.75% in 1987. Even so, the ratio of earnings to revenues for tobacco has been significantly higher than the other segments that Imasco has tried to develop. The margin for restaurants has been falling slowly from 8.20% in 1985 to 7.75% in 1987. The margin for drugstores started from an even lower ratio of 6.57% in 1985 and has fallen dramatically to 0.73% in 1987. Thus, it appears that the poor prospects for the tobacco segment has encouraged Imasco to find other non-tobacco industries to invest in, but it has been unable to find ones with operating margins as attractive as that of tobacco.

ASSET TURNOVER RATIO

The **asset turnover ratio** is defined as follows:

Asset turnover ratio = Sales/Total assets

The asset turnover ratio can be interpreted as a measure of how intensively the firm's assets are being used in its operations. The higher the ratio of Sales/Assets is, the more intensively the assets are being used. In the case of Imasco Limited we are unable to trace the assets directly to segments by type, but we are given an overall measure, *capital employed*, that we will use as a proxy for assets. The calculation for each segment is shown below.

IMASCO LIMITED
Excluding Imasco Enterprises
(thousands of $)

	Tobacco	Restaurant	Drug store	Sundry
Sales:				
1987	$1,787,614	$1,656,350	$2,019,540	$161,570
1986	1,769,776	1,508,710	1,909,631	137,017
1985	1,451,130	1,321,248	1,425,407	155,469
Capital employed:				
1987	$548,779	$620,224	$851,027	$38,721
1986	531,017	568,097	935,362	35,389
1985	534,300	555,458	759,290	72,243
Sales/Capital employed:				
1987	3.26	2.67	2.37	4.17
1986	3.33	2.66	2.04	3.87
1985	2.72	2.38	1.88	2.15

This analysis indicates that tobacco has the highest ratio of sales to capital employed, whereas restaurants and drug stores are significantly lower in their use of assets. We have already shown that tobacco has a higher (but falling) ratio of operating revenue to sales. Thus the fact it also has the highest ratio of sales to capital employed makes it doubly attractive. If only the health problems associated with it would disappear!

We are unable to compute an accounts receivable turnover ratio because accounts receivable are not identified by segment. However, we are able to compute the inventory turnover ratio:

IMASCO LIMITED
Excluding Imasco Enterprises
(thousands of $)

	Tobacco	Restaurant	Drug store	Sundry
Sales:				
1987	$1,787,614	$1,656,350	$2,019,540	$161,570
1986	1,769,776	1,508,710	1,909,631	137,017
1985	1,451,130	1,321,248	1,425,407	155,469
Inventory:				
1987	$420,152	$60,513	$457,801	$32,422
1986	403,580	49,914	543,033	30,354
1985	443,769	51,969	375,740	38,226
Sales/Inventory:				
1987	4.25	27.37	4.41	4.98
1986	4.39	30.23	3.52	4.51
1985	3.27	25.42	3.79	4.07

The inventory turnover ratios have been generally rising, which is usually considered an indicator of more efficient use of inventory. Note the vast difference in inventory turnover between the restaurant segment and the others. This is a good example of the need to look at segment results when there are widely differing "industries" within the same company.

It should be apparent by now that ratio analysis is a technique that enables one to start asking fruitful questions, but by itself it rarely gives definite answers. For instance, in the case of Imasco, one would want to know more about trends in the tobacco, restaurant, and drug-store industries in order to judge whether Imasco was leading or lagging behind its competitors. Even more importantly, one would also want to be able to judge whether the low return that the company is apparently willing to accept on its investment in Canada Trust and related companies (i.e., Imasco Enterprises) will ultimately pay off.

RETURN AND RISK
FOR COMMON SHAREHOLDERS

Although measures of the overall return on assets are helpful, more specific questions would probably be of greater concern to the common shareholders. What is the return to the common shareholders? How much risk are the common shareholders undertaking to earn that return? The following ratios address these questions.

Rate of Return on Common Shareholders' Equity

A measure that is similar to the rate of return on assets is the **rate of return on common shareholders' equity**. It is defined as follows:

$$\text{Rate of return on shareholders' equity} = \frac{\text{Earnings available to common shareholders}}{\text{Common shareholders' equity (weighted average)}}$$

where Earnings available to common shareholders
= Net income after tax − Dividends payable to preferred shareholders

We will see below that this numerator is also the numerator of the earnings per share ratio.

Let us calculate the rate of return on common shareholders' equity for Imasco Limited.

IMASCO LIMITED
RETURN TO COMMON SHAREHOLDERS
(thousands of $)

	1987	1986	1985
Net income after tax	$183,567	$261,745	$234,108
Payable to preferred shareholders	10,754	348	348
Earnings available to common shareholders	172,813	261,397	233,760
Shareholders' equity:			
— Start of year	447,958	447,645	447,332
— End of year	797,057	447,958	447,645
— Average	622,508	447,802	447,489
Return on common equity	27.76%	58.37%	52.24%

Observe that shareholders' equity has risen over these three years while earnings available to common shareholders has dropped. As a result, there has been a steep decline in return on common equity.

The rate of return on common shareholders' equity is a ratio that is often reported in the financial press, where it is usually used to compare different companies. However, in many cases the usefulness of this ratio is very limited and even questionable for two main reasons. First, the numerator (Earnings available to common shareholders) is based on *reported income*, and we have already given numerous caveats about the careless use of this number (e.g., see Chapter 4). Second, the denominator (Common shareholders' equity) is the residual of *assets* minus *liabilities*, each of which are valued at historic cost plus adjustments. We have already discussed these items individually and pointed out the dangers of uncritically relying on their numbers. The same dangers apply when these numbers are aggregated.

In general, one should understand and be aware of this ratio. At the same time, however, one should exercise great care in using it.

Earnings per Share

The **earnings per share** ratio is usually defined as follows:

$$\text{The earnings per share} = \frac{\text{Earnings available to common shareholders}}{\text{Weighted average number of common shares outstanding}}$$

where Earnings available to common shareholders
  = Net income after tax − Dividends payable to preferred shareholders

As mentioned earlier, the numerator is also the numerator of the rate of return on common shareholders' equity.

We have already discussed earnings per share in Chapter 17, where we explained how the numerator and denominator are calculated. This ratio is used to evaluate the earnings of the same company over a period of years. It should *not* be used to make comparisons between companies because the number of shares outstanding is not comparable between them.

Price Earnings Ratio

The **price earnings ratio**, as its name suggests, relates earning per share to the price at which the company's stock is traded. It is defined as follows:

$$\text{Price earnings ratio} = \frac{\text{Current market price per share}}{\text{Current earnings per share}}$$

A high multiple usually means that the reason the stock is in high demand is that investors see potential in the company other than that indicated by its current earnings.

Funds Flow per Share

The **funds flow per share** can be defined as follows:

$$\text{Funds flow per share} = \frac{\begin{array}{c}\text{Earnings available to common shareholders}\\ \text{+ Depreciation + Amortization}\end{array}}{\text{Weighted average number of common shares outstanding}}$$

where Earnings available to common shareholders
  = Net income after tax − Dividends payable to preferred shareholders

From this equation we can see that funds flow per share resembles earnings per share except that depreciation and amortization have been added back into the numerator. Because these somewhat arbitrary charges do not now affect the ratio, some people claim that the funds flow per share is a more reliable indicator of company perform-ance than earnings per share. Funds flow per share has been charted over time as the *value line* of a given stock, which has given its name to the Value Line Investment Survey, a well-known U.S. investment survey service.

Common Shareholder Leverage

One of the basic ideas of investment theory is that one should look not only at the return to the investor, but also at the risk undertaken to earn the return. In general, the higher the return one seeks, the higher the risk one must expect to accept. One way in which the return to common shareholders may be increased is to borrow part of the capital needed in the hope of obtaining a rate that will turn out to be less than the overall yield of the company's assets. Consider the following example. The assets in Company A and Company B each earn 10%, but Company B has borrowed half its capital at 8%.

	Company A	Company B
Debt at 8% interest	0	$ 50,000
Common shareholder equity	$100,000	$ 50,000
Total assets	$100,000	$100,000
Return on assets before tax	10%	10%
Annual return on assets	$ 10,000	$ 10,000
Interest cost at 8%	0	4,000
Net income before tax	10,000	6,000
Income tax at 50%	5,000	3,000
Net income after tax	$ 5,000	$ 3,000
Return on shareholder equity	5%	6%

The common shareholders in Company B have increased their return by borrowing half the capital needed. This is an example of **common shareholder leverage**. As long as the pre-tax cost of borrowing capital is less than the pre-tax yield from the assets, then the common shareholders can increase their percentage yield by this borrowing. Such a technique is known as **trading on the equity** or, in Britain, **gearing**.

Trading on the equity has its risks, however. If the company is less profitable than expected, then the yield on assets may fall below the level anticipated when the borrowing was done. Another risk is that the interest rate on the debt may rise above the level expected when the debt was first incurred. Should the cost of borrowing rise above the yield on the assets, then the yield to the shareholders will be decreased and may even become negative. The company may also suffer a funds outflow to service its debt, with resulting problems of solvency. In the section on measures of long-run solvency below, we will discuss tests for this possibility.

BREAK-EVEN ANALYSIS

Break-even analysis assumes that the costs of operating can be approximated by splitting these costs into (i) those that do not vary with the volume of operations and (ii) those that do vary. From these components, one then calculates the volume at which the company will earn enough revenue just to cover its costs, or break even. For example, suppose a company's fixed costs are $3,000,000 and its variable costs are approximately 40% of sales. Then the profit for any volume of sales can be estimated as follows:

Profit = Sales − 3,000,000 − 40% of Sales

From this equation, it follows that the break-even sales for the company would be $5,000,000.

Tests of Long-Run Solvency

The short-term tests of solvency, discussed earlier, examine the availability of net current assets to meet debts. By contrast, long-run tests of solvency look at more permanent structural factors that may impair the company's abilities to meet its debts.

DEBT TO EQUITY RATIO

The **debt to equity ratio** is a measure of the risk run by the company in providing part of its capital in the form of debt instead of shareholder equity. In its simplest form the right-hand side of the balance sheet is divided into debt and equity components, and the ratio is formed as follows:

Debt to equity ratio = Debt / Equity

Most forms of debt require that interest be paid and the principal repaid according to the terms of the contract, regardless of any financial difficulty experienced by the company. If the company fails to make the payments, it can be declared in default. Sometimes redeemable preferred shares are included as debt, rather than equity, because the option for redemption may lie with the shareholder, and other terms of the issue may make it unlikely that the company would refuse. In general, companies with a low debt to equity ratio are less risky than those with a high ratio.

Consider the following example about Company T, adapted from the financial statements of an actual Canadian company:

COMPANY T
(thousands of $)

	19X7	19X6
Current liabilities	$ 176,527	$ 293,275
Long-term liabilities	430,401	372,760
Deferred income tax	332,200	308,800
Total	$ 939,128	$ 974,835
Shareholders' equity		
Preferred shares — cumulative redeemable	$ 225,332	$ 226,717
Common shares	108,248	106,542
Retained earnings	747,980	743,460
Total equity	$1,081,560	$1,076,719
Total liabilities and equity	$2,020,688	$2,051,554

The notes to the financial statements indicate that the company is obligated to redeem 2% of the outstanding preferred shares each year or face unspecified penalties. Suppose the penalty is that the owners of preferred shares have the effective right to put the company into bankruptcy. The preferred shares have a variable dividend rate of 1% plus one-half the average prime bank rate. Thus, if the bank prime rate is 12%, then the dividend on the preferred shares must be $(12/2) + 1 = 7\%$.

How should the debt to equity ratio be calculated? One approach would be to form the ratio as follows:

COMPANY T
(thousands of $)

	19X7	19X6
Total debt	$ 939,128	$ 974,835
Total equity	1,081,560	1,076,719
Debt to equity ratio	0.87	0.91

However, even a brief examination of the financial statement above should make one suspect that perhaps this approach is too simplistic. The main purpose of the debt to equity ratio is to estimate the risk of default by comparing borrowed capital with the capital contributed by the risk-taking equity owners. With this in mind, should we treat the deferred income tax as a liability? Recall from Chapter 13 that there is no attempt under the present rules of the *CICA Handbook* to treat deferred income taxes as a liability. In particular, there is no attempt to discount it. Thus, the ratios in our example probably overstate the liability component of the deferred income taxes. Let us assume that if we did discount the deferred income taxes, half of them would be liabilities and the other half would be essentially a form of owners' equity. (If you find this unclear, refer back to our discussion of deferred income taxes in Chapter 13.)

How should we treat the redeemable preferred shares? In our example they appear to have been issued in a period in which the Canadian banks were willing, for reasons of tax advantages, to purchase preferred shares of this type instead of giving outright bank loans.

However, the terms under which the shares were purchased were virtually as stringent as the terms of an ordinary bank loan. In other words, the power of the bank to compel redemption of the shares was just as compelling as its power to force repayment of a loan. Therefore, looking through the legal form to get at the economic substance, there is good reason to treat these outstanding shares as the equivalent of a bank loan, and hence to reclassify them as a liability.

If the proposed reclassification of the deferred income tax and preferred shares were made, the calculation of the debt-equity would be as follows:

COMPANY T
(thousands of $)

	19X7	19X6
Total debt as previously calculated	$ 939,128	$ 974,835
Deduct: 50% of deferred income tax	(166,100)	(154,400)
Add: redeemable preferred shares	225,332	226,717
Revised total debt	$ 998,360	$1,047,152
Total equity as previously calculated	$1,081,560	$1,076,719
Add: 50% of deferred income tax	166,100	154,400
Deduct: redeemable preferred shares	(225,332)	(226,717)
Revised total equity	$1,022,328	$1,004,402
Total liabilities and equity as previously calculated	$2,020,688	$2,051,554
Revised debt equity ratio	0.98	1.04

The revised ratios have been raised from the previous ones by the reclassification of the preferred shares, and they have been reduced by the treatment of the deferred income tax. The higher ratios imply that there is more riskiness in the capital structure of the company than originally indicated. This example illustrates once again the importance of understanding what the numbers on the financial statements mean.

INTEREST COVERAGE

The **interest coverage** is the number of times fixed financing costs (such as interest) are capable of being covered by annual income, or perhaps operating cash flows. The ratio can be defined as follows:

$$\text{Interest coverage} = \frac{\text{Income before income taxes} + \text{Fixed financing costs}}{\text{Fixed financing costs}}$$

The main purpose of this ratio is to show how much cushion the company has in covering its fixed financial commitments. The higher the ratio is, the better the fixed charges are covered. It is usual to include only income before extraordinary items because we are testing the company's ability to cover its fixed charges from regular income. This ratio originally concentrated on the ratio of net income to *interest costs* (hence its name); but with the rise of leasing as a means of asset acquisition, other forms of fixed financing commitment also become relevant.

This ratio has been criticized on the grounds that net income is not a good proxy for liquidity. It has been suggested that cash flow generated by operations would be a better measure of liquidity. In that case, the numerator would be as follows:

Cash flow generated by operations + Fixed financing costs

Let us use Imasco Limited to illustrate the interest coverage ratio. Keep in mind that in the 1987 fiscal year Imasco issued long-term debt to cover its purchase of Genstar Corporation (to get Canada Trust). Thus it raised its long-term debt from $685 million at the end of 1986 to $2,480 million at the end of 1987.

IMASCO LIMITED
INTEREST COVERAGE
(thousands of $)

	1987	1986	1985
Net income — before tax and extraordinary items (A)	$267,947	$407,192	$365,424
Interest: on long-term debt	143,404	52,088	53,693
on capital leases	3,987	4,585	4,616
Total fixed financing costs (B)	147,391	56,673	58,309
Total of A and B (i.e., C)	$415,338	$463,865	$423,733
Depreciation and amortization D	$145,216	$135,465	$111,703
Interest coverage:			
— after depreciation and amortization (C/B)	2.82	8.18	7.27
— before deducting depreciation and amortization (C + D)/B	3.80	10.58	9.18

It is possible to calculate a variety of ratios to measure the extent of coverage of fixed financing costs. Two of them for Imasco Limited are shown above. They both indicate that the coverage looks ample, but that it dropped sharply in 1987 after the acquisition of Canada Trust.

The two main criticisms of such interest coverage ratios will sound familiar by now. First, they use accounting numbers, such as net income, whose "hardness" needs to be examined carefully in each case. It is possible for net income to vary widely for some companies depending on the assumptions made. Second, by focusing the readers' attention on the financial statistics of just one year, they divert attention away from the dynamic nature of business operations. For example, the coverage of fixed charges may be excellent for the year under examination, but the reader may miss the fact that the debt of the company is coming up for renewal in a period when interest rates are likely to be much higher (or lower) than the debt now maturing. Another possibility is that the company may have high fixed manufacturing costs, and hence its net income may be subject to wide variation, depending on the firm's sales volume.

In preparing the interest coverage ratio, one must be careful to see if any interest payments have been capitalized. Disclosure of capitalized interest is required by the *CICA Handbook* [3850].

Other Analytical Ratios

The ratios presented so far are general ones in that they are suitable for application to most companies and industries. In addition, many industries have developed ratios specifically suited to their operations. Such ratios are particularly useful for making comparisons between companies in the same industry. Some examples are shown below.

SOME RATIOS FOR PARTICULAR INDUSTRIES

Industry	Ratios
Airlines	Cost of operation per seat-mile flown
	Revenue per seat-mile flown
Electrical power generators	Capital cost per kilowatt installed
Trucking	Operating cost per ton-mile
	Revenue per ton-mile
Oil exploration	Cost of drilling per foot
Retail stores	Sales per employee
	Sales per square foot of display space

Approaches to Financial-Statement Analysis

There is no single approach to financial-statement analysis that can be considered the best. Nevertheless, one may well find that the following steps are a useful way to begin.

1. Read the financial statements and the whole financial report thoroughly, including the disclosure of accounting policies. Look for unusual items that need to be kept in mind and for general financial attributes of the company that might later be tested for. For example, is there an auditor's report? Is the audit opinion unqualified? What kind of business does the company appear to be in? Does the type of business lead you to anticipate any problems to test for, such as rapid inventory obsolescence? Are important assets and liabilities (in an economic sense) not shown or undervalued (e.g., real estate valued at original purchase cost) in the financial statements of this company? What issues are highlighted in the report to the shareholders? It is important to examine closely the summary of accounting policies.

2. To understand the financial statements better, do some background reading on the company and the industry. Try looking them up in some general index, such as

InfoGlobe, or a specialized index, such as that for the *Wall Street Journal*. An investment service such as *Moody's* or *Value Line* will often give helpful information on the industry and the company. Research reports from brokerage firms are also frequently helpful.

3. Consider what important financial information is not shown in the financial statements because of the very nature of how accounting works. For example, in a closely held business the owner-managers may not be paying themselves a salary that is competitive with the market, and as a result the operating results may be overstated or understated. It is also possible that transactions have taken place between related parties, on terms that are more or less favourable than they would have been at arm's length. In a large public company the present financial results may be the result of good or bad strategic decisions made years ago, and a high return on investment may or may not continue.

4. Be clear what decision needs to be made when the analysis is over. Then, tailor the approach to be as efficient as possible. For example, if the decision is whether to make a short-term loan, then attention should be directed to the company's ability to repay it, using tests of short-term solvency and comparing the results to a cash budget. If the quick ratio yields a clearly favourable result, then additional time should not be spent on other ratios of short-term solvency.

5. See if it is possible to develop industry-specific tests to permit comparisons with similar companies. Sometimes a standard reference service like Statistics Canada can provide industry statistics.

Financial-statement analysis is a field where there is no substitute for common sense. A clear realization of the inherent weaknesses of financial reporting is crucial. If done carefully, financial-statement analysis can give insights into the nature of a company's operation that cannot be obtained anywhere else.

Summary

The main tests that can be developed with financial-statement ratios are those of profitability and solvency. In this chapter we introduced some of the most common ones and showed how they could be applied to real companies. These tests rarely provide conclusive answers to questions about solvency and profitability. The results of the tests should be treated instead as a means of formulating perceptive questions about a company.

There is an extensive body of evidence that the stock market reacts quickly to available information, such as that given in financial statements. This means that relying entirely on published financial statements to find undervalued companies whose shares are publicly traded is not likely to be successful. Nevertheless, financial-statement analysis can be very productive when used for other purposes, such as internal management decisions, the analysis of privately held companies, and as a preliminary step in the analysis of publicly held companies.

QUESTIONS

Q21-1. Review and make sure you understand the following terms:

   a. current ratio

   b. efficient capital market

   c. quick ratio

   d. accounts receivable turnover ratio

   e. inventory turnover ratio

   f. rate of return on assets

   g. profit margin ratio

   h. asset turnover ratio

   i. rate of return on common shareholders' equity

   j. earnings per share

   k. price earning ratio

   l. funds flow per share

   m. common shareholder leverage

   n. break-even analysis

   o. debt to equity ratio

   p. interest coverage

Q21-2. "Since the stock market knows everything, there is no point in analysing a company's financial statements." Do you agree? Discuss.

Q21-3. "To be a good financial-statement analyst, one must first become a good financial accountant." Do you agree? Why or why not?

Q21-4. Imagine that you could subscribe to a phone-in service that would on request immediately feed in key financial ratios to your personal computer, which would be programmed to pick out the same five ratios for every company.

   a. Which five ratios would you pick? What are your reasons?

   b. For each of the above five ratios, what amount would you pick as the critical value that your computer program would draw special attention to? Explain how you arrived at the amounts.

   c. What decisions would you want to make with the help of these ratios?

Q21-5. Explain why the high correlation between various financial-statement ratios limits the usefulness of computing many different ratios to test for short-term solvency.

Q21-6. What aspects of a company's financial situation (i.e., profitability, short-term solvency, or long-term solvency) are each of the following ratios intended to test? Explain.

   a. acid-test

   b. asset turnover

   c. interest coverage

   d. number of days' sales in receivables

   e. earnings per share

   f. rate of return on assets

    g. funds flow per share

    h. debt to equity ratio

Q21-7. In each of the following unrelated cases, explain whether the proposed attempt to manipulate the financial ratio would work.

    a. In an attempt to make the current ratio of 2:1 more favourable, the controller arranged to have the company's suppliers paid before the company year-end. They would normally have been paid after the year-end. The company has no bank loans and would not incur any in making the payment early.

    b. Would your answer to (a) be different if the company had to finance the early payments with an increase in their bank loan?

    c. In an attempt to increase the rate of return on assets, the company decreased its asset base by selling equipment and renting it back under an operating lease.

    d. Would your answer to (c) be different if the company leased the equipment back under a capital lease?

    e. Wishing to increase its earnings per share, a company repurchased and cancelled half of its outstanding shares.

    f. A company changed its year-end from 31 December to 30 June. The controller explained to the financial press that this new date was a low point in the annual cycle; and because of the lower inventory at that date, the ratio of inventory turnover would be higher, "something this company has always wanted to achieve."

    g. In shifting from historic-cost accounting to current-value accounting the company noted that "although depreciation charges will be higher because of higher value assigned to the plant assets, this means that the funds flow per share will be higher as well."

Q21-8. Are the following pairs of ratio changes possible? If possible, are they likely? Explain.

    a. The current ratio goes up while the acid test goes down.

    b. The debt to equity ratio goes up while the interest coverage drops.

    c. The rate of return on assets drops while the profit margin and asset turnover ratios go up.

    d. The earnings per share drop, but the cash flow per share goes up.

    e. The current ratio goes up, while the inventory turnover ratio falls.

Q21-9. "The rate of return on assets is a good analytical tool. But accountants have blunted it badly by using historic costs of assets instead of market values." Evaluate this statement.

Q21-10. In calculating the rate of return on assets, should one use the gross cost of the asset (i.e., the cost before deducting the accumulated depreciation) or the net cost? Is your answer any different if one used replacement cost instead of historic cost? (*Hint:* What is your reason for calculating this ratio?)

Q21-11. "The rate of return on investment is a ratio that needs to be handled even more carefully than most of the other ratios." Give reasons to support this statement and evaluate them.

Q21-12. "In general, the more powerful the potential use of an accounting ratio is, the more it uses highly aggregated measures; and thus, the more careful one has to be to understand what these measures are, and what their weaknesses might be in each given instance." Give examples of five ratios that use "highly aggregated measures" and evaluate the appropriateness of the above quotation for each of them.

Q21-13. Some analysts prefer *funds flow per share* to *earnings per share* because the former is less subject to arbitrary charges such as depreciation. Assume in each of the cases below that the company had the same reported annual net income for a period of ten years. During that same period would the funds flow per share rise, fall, or stay the same? Explain.

    a. The company is gradually moving from a labour-intensive production mode to one that makes heavy use of robots.

    b. The company rents all its plant assets on operating leases.

    c. The company is reducing its clerical staff by 50% with a new computer system it is leasing.

    d. The company is reducing its clerical staff by 50% with a new computer system it has purchased.

Q21-14. Is it possible for the short-term and long-term tests of solvency to give off contrary signals? Explain.

Q21-15. Here are some industry-specific ratios. How well do you think they measure the efficiency of that industry?

    a. Bus line: cost per passenger-mile paid for

    b. University: student/staff ratio

    c. University: percentage of available classroom seats filled

    d. Retail store: Sales per available square foot

Q21-16. The *Value Line Investment Survey* has this to say about the usefulness of net income as a measure of company success: "In order to present a consistent income series to relate to price (of a stock) — one that is less distorted by periodic changes in the rate of depreciation — we add depreciation back to reported earnings. This makes for a *truer appraisal of the direction and level of income* over a period of years." Do you agree or disagree? Explain why.

Q21-17. A test that is sometimes applied is to compare the rate of return on shareholders' equity with the rate of return on all assets "to see if the shareholders are getting as good a return as the debt holders." Is this a useful test? Explain.

Q21-18. The inventory turnover ratio might be calculated using one of the following for the inventory amount: (i) closing inventory; (ii) average of opening and closing inventories; and (iii) monthly weighted average. Discuss the relative merits of each with respect to the following:

    a. probable accuracy of the figure

    b. sensitivity to distorting factors such as seasonal variations

    c. cost

    d. the types of decisions that might be based on the results of this measure

Q21-19. Two companies are roughly the same size and are in the same industry. How appropriate would it be to compare the following ratios between the two companies? Explain.

    a. earnings per share

    b. current ratio

c. days' sales in receivables

d. inventory turnover

e. return on investment

f. debt to equity ratio

g. cash flow per share

h. profit margin

Q21-20. In comparing the same company's results two years apart, how appropriate would it be to use each of the ratios listed in Q21-19 above?

Q21-21. For many years the du Pont company used return on investment as its prime measuring tool for evaluating the performance of divisional managers. Critics said it focused too much attention on the short-term results that could be measured by the accounting system, and neglected important but hard-to-measure attributes. (du Pont ultimately dropped the system.) Do you think this criticism is valid? Explain.

Q21-22. It has been suggested that the groups that are most interested in using the results of ratio analysis are (i) common-stock investors, (ii) management, (iii) lenders, (iv) labour unions, and (v) regulatory agencies.

a. What use might each of the above groups make of such ratios?

b. If each group was allowed to use just one ratio, which one do you think it would be? Defend your choice.

Q21-23. What is the difference between a cross-sectional and a longitudinal ratio analysis? What general purpose does each best serve?

Q21-24. How does the rate of return on assets differ from the rate of return on shareholders' equity? What factors can make it higher? lower?

Q21-25. Financial-statement ratios have been criticized as being *static* and incapable of reflecting the dynamic changes within the company. Some critics suggest that forecasted income statements and cash flow summaries are more useful than ratios for deciding on the attractiveness of a company. How well founded do you think this suggestion is?

Q21-26. The owner-manager of a business wanted to expand and needed bank financing. The bank manager gave her the loan, but made her agree to maintain a certain minimum current ratio. The owner-manager complained that as a result, her firm had become "fat and sloppy." What did she mean by this remark? What other tests might be used to see if she was right? Assuming that she was correct, what do you deduce about the bank manager's preferences with respect to company policy?

Q21-27. In the early days of the Ford Motor Company, Henry Ford was forced by the creditors of the company to increase the shareholders' equity. To Ford's own dismay, he could only do so by selling shares to outsiders. Consequently, the company was no longer family-owned. Assuming that all participants were acting rationally, explain what other personal objectives might have led Ford to sell shares to outsiders when he really didn't want to share control of the company with anyone else.

Q21-28. An important factor in most financial-statement analyses is *comparability;* that is, the means to compare the given company with (i) some other company during the same period of time or (ii) the same company at some other point in time. Give examples of practical problems that would make comparability difficult.

EXERCISES

E21-1. Company F used FIFO in valuing its inventory. Its condensed balance sheet is shown below.

COMPANY F
(thousands of $)

	Assets			Liabilities and Equity	
	19X5	19X4		19X5	19X4
Cash	$ 12,000	$ 10,000	Current liabilities	$ 48,000	$ 31,000
Accounts receivable	24,000	20,000	Long-term debt	63,000	48,000
Inventory	36,000	31,000	Common share		
Plant assets			capital	30,000	30,000
— cost	148,000	121,000	Preferred shares		
— depreciation	(59,000)	(45,000)	(10% cumulative)	10,000	10,000
			Retained earnings	10,000	18,000
	$ 161,000	$ 137,000		$ 161,000	$ 137,000

You are also given the following additional information:

	19X5	19X4	19X3
Retained earnings	$ 10,000	$ 18,000	$ 15,000
Sales	192,000	180,000	170,000
Net income before tax	18,000	21,000	17,000
Income tax expense	10,000	9,000	8,000
Provision for depreciation	14,000	12,000	13,000
Interest expense (before tax)	6,500	4,500	4,000
Common shares outstanding	10,000	10,000	10,000
Total assets	161,000	137,000	130,000
Inventory	36,000	31,000	30,000

Assume the after-tax interest is 50% of before-tax interest.

Required: For both 19X5 and 19X4 calculate each of the following ratios:

a. current

b. quick

c. accounts receivable turnover

d. days' sales in receivables

e. inventory turnover

f. days' sales in inventory

g. rate of return on assets

h. profit margin

i. rate of return on common shareholders' equity

j. earnings per common share

k. funds flow per share

l. debt to equity

m. interest coverage (using income)

n. interest coverage (using funds flow)

E21-2. Company G used FIFO in valuing its inventory. Its condensed balance sheet is shown below.

COMPANY G
(thousands of $)

Assets	19X8	19X7	Liabilities and Equity	19X8	19X7
Cash	$ 16,568	$ 14,589	Accounts payable $	89,521	$ 71,256
Accounts receivable	25,897	14,562	Accrued liabilities	1,546	1,580
Inventory	254,785	212,630	Bonds payable	125,000	135,000
Land	112,589	112,589	Deferred taxes	59,421	42,563
Buildings	589,452	550,436	Preferred shares	12,000	12,000
Equipment	125,893	110,582	(5% cumulative)		
Accumulated			Common shares		
depreciation	(125,894)	(110,112)	(500,000 issued)	589,125	589,125
Goodwill	50,000	50,000	Retained earnings	172,677	103,752
	$ 1,049,290	$ 955,276		$ 1,049,290	$ 955,276

You are also given the following additional information:

	19X8	19X7	19X6
Sales	$ 207,176	$ 131,058	$ 124,000
Cost of goods sold	82,870	52,423	53,000
Administrative costs	25,489	15,486	12,000
Interest expense	13,251	12,584	10,000
Depreciation	25,483	24,136	15,000
	60,083	26,429	34,000
Income taxes	27,037	11,893	15,300
Net income	$ 33,046	$ 14,536	$ 18,700

Retained earnings at the start of 19X7 were $98,560. Assume the after-tax interest cost is 55% of before-tax interest cost. At the end of 19X6 the accounts receivable were $13,000 and the inventory was $186,000.

Required: For both 19X8 and 19X7 calculate each of the following ratios:

a. current
b. quick
c. accounts receivable turnover
d. days' sales in receivables
e. inventory turnover
f. days' sales in inventory
g. rate of return on assets
h. profit margin
i. rate of return on common shareholders' equity
j. earnings per common share
k. funds flow per share
l. debt to equity
m. interest coverage (using income)
n. interest covering (using funds flow)

E21-3. Company H used FIFO in valuing its inventory. Its condensed balance sheet is shown below.

COMPANY H
(thousands of $)

Assets				Liabilities and Equity		
	19X4	19X3			19X4	19X3
Cash	$ 8,520	$ 4,892	Accounts payable		$ 58,421	$ 65,148
Accounts receivable	15,874	18,542	Customer deposits		45,213	40,123
Inventory	127,392	135,480	Mortgage payable		85,000	90,000
Land	85,214	77,125	Preferred shares		25,000	35,000
Buildings	451,286	400,186	(5% cumulative)			
Equipment	86,254	145,760	Common shares			
Accumulated			(500,000 issued)		450,000	450,000
depreciation	(85,120)	(81,256)	Retained earnings		25,786	20,458
	$ 689,420	$ 700,729			$ 689,420	$ 700,729

You are also given the following additional information:

	19X4	19X3
Sales	$ 126,992	$ 166,878
Cost of goods sold	82,870	52,423
Administrative costs	8,360	15,486
Interest expense	3,782	12,584
Depreciation	11,879	24,136
	20,101	62,249
Income taxes	9,045	28,012
Net income	$ 11,056	$ 34,237

Assume the after-tax interest cost is 50%.

Required: For both 19X4 and 19X3 calculate each of the following ratios:
a. current
b. quick
c. accounts receivable turnover
d. days' sales in receivables
e. inventory turnover
f. days' sales in inventory
g. rate of return on assets
h. profit margin
i. rate of return on common shareholders' equity
j. earnings per common share
k. funds flow per share
l. debt to equity ratio
m. interest coverage (using income)
n. interest coverage (using funds flow)

E21-4. Set out below are some common ratios for a particular company. If you complete them in order, you should be able to supply any missing numbers from the ratios already worked out. The company had no long-term debt. The marginal tax rate is 50%.

    a. Current ratio = 1.99. Current assets = $25,000

   ·**b.** Quick assets = $14,893. Quick ratio = ?

    c. Sales = $125,687. Accounts receivable turnover = 10.18.

    d. Number of days' sales in receivables = ?

    e. Number of days' sales in inventory = 125.6. Inventory = ?

    f. Return on assets = 9%. Total assets = $282,927.90. Net income = ?

    g. Profit margin = ?

    h. Common shareholders' equity = $135,269.00. Rate of return on common equity = ?

E21-5. In its published analyses of over 1,600 stocks, the *Value Line Investment Survey* makes use of some of the ratios discussed in this chapter. Moreover, *Value Line* also employs some other ratios, shown below. For each of these ratios, state what aspect of company operations or financial health it is probably intended to measure. How reliable an indicator do you think each is?

    a. Sales/Number of common shares

    b. Dividends per share

    c. Capital spending per share

    d. Owners' equity / Shares outstanding

E21-6. How would the following financial-statement ratios be affected by the change from historic-cost accounting to general-price-level accounting if the general price level rose? Be sure to explain your reasoning.

    a. Net income/Total assets

    b. Current ratio

    c. Debt to equity

    d. Number of days' sales in accounts receivable

E21-7. Shown below are grouped sets of ratios. Assume in each case that the value of the ratio(s) in (i) decreases. Indicate in what direction, if any, the value of the ratio in (ii) would likely go as a result. Explain your reasoning.

    a. (i) Current ratio; (ii) Quick ratio

    b. (i) Inventory turnover; (ii) Number of days' sales in inventory

    c. (i) Asset turnover ratio, profit margin ratio; (ii) Return on investment

    d. (i) Accounts receivable turnover, inventory turnover; (ii) Current ratio

    e. (i) Earnings per share; (ii) Return on investment

E21-8. In each of the following cases, which item is likely to increase reported income on the financial statements the most in the period indicated? Explain.

    a. Percentage-of-completion method *or* completed-project method of recognizing income during the early stages of construction of a plant asset.

    b. Annuity method *or* straight-line method of depreciation toward the end of an asset's functional life.

    c. Successful efforts method *or* full costing method of allocating costs during the first half of the exploration program for an oil field.

    d. FIFO method *or* LIFO method *or* average cost method of costing inventory during a period of rising inventory prices. (Assume steady inventory levels.)

    e. The redemption of a bond payable selling at a discount and replacement with a bond yielding market interest *or* retaining the original bond. In year of redemption? The next year?

f. An operating type of lease *or* a capital type of lease for an asset during the middle period of its functional life.

g. Accrued benefit method *or* projected benefit method of pension funding immediately after the start of the plan.

E21-9. Explain what effect, if any, each of the following independent transactions will have on (i) a quick ratio that is 1:1 or better, (ii) a pre-tax return on investment of 11%, and (iii) the long-term interest coverage ratio. In all cases assume the tax rate is 50%.

a. A bank loan is paid off. The rate was 12%.

b. Inventory was sold on credit at a profit.

c. Fixed assets were purchased by assuming a mortgage of 13%.

d. 6% cumulative redeemable preference shares were issued at par.

e. Short-term marketable securities were sold, and the proceeds were put in the company's bank to cover general financing needs. The securities had yielded 10%.

E21-10. Compute the rate of return on common shareholders' equity in each of the independent cases below. Identify those cases where leverage is working to the advantage of the shareholders and explain why.

Company	Total assets	Interest-bearing debt	Common equity	Return on assets	After-tax cost of debt
A	$ 300,000	$ 100,000	$ 200,000	8.00%	5.00%
B	300,000	150,000	150,000	8.00%	5.00%
C	300,000	150,000	150,000	5.00%	8.00%
D	300,000	175,000	125,000	7.00%	7.00%
E	300,000	100,000	150,000	6.00%	8.00%
F	300,000	180,000	120,000	8.00%	5.00%

E21-11. In each of the independent situations below, calculate the requested ratio. Round all answers to the second decimal place. Show all calculations and state any assumptions employed.

a. Simkowic Ltd. had a profit margin ratio of 6.1%. Sales for the year were $245,000. The firm averaged $190,000 in total assets for the year. Calculate the rate of return on assets for the year.

b. Warner Manufacturing had a quick ratio of 0.9:1 at the end of 19X4. Here are the balances in selected accounts: cash, $65,000; accounts receivable, $44,000; inventory, $90,000; and temporary investments, $26,000. Calculate the current ratio.

c. Net sales on account for Tunes Limited for the year were $425,000. The average days' sales in receivables figure was 32.2 days. Calculate the accounts receivable turnover ratio and the average balance in accounts receivable.

d. Orpheus Ltd. had a debt to equity ratio of 0.625:1. Total assets for the company were $360,000. All of its liabilities, $32,500 were current. Calculate the long-term debt to equity ratio.

e. A mid-size chain store performed well enough to achieve a net income of $75,000 after preferred dividends. The $75,000 represented an earning of $3.4091 per common share. The book value of the weighted average number of shares was $27 per share. Calculate the return on common shareholders' equity for the year.

E21-12. Explain the effect (i.e., an increase, a decrease, or no effect) that each of the independent transactions below has on (i) earnings per share, (ii) working capital, and (iii) the quick ratio. State any assumptions that you make.

a. Inventory costing $200,000 is sold on account for $265,000.

b. A milling machine, which had cost $110,000 and was 90% depreciated, was sold for $10,000.

c. Tal Ltd. issued 20,000 shares of common stock at $12 per share. Tal used the assets to purchase the assets of another firm, Geller Ltd., which consisted of the following: accounts receivable, $35,000; inventory, $85,000; and plant assets, $160,000. Tal Ltd., the acquiring firm, also agreed to assume current liabilities of $40,000 of Geller. Tal had been earning 12% on its assets and expected to earn 13% on the net assets it had just purchased.

d. Amoeba Inc. deems that $4,000 of its accounts receivable are uncollectible and writes them off. The loss had been provided for in the allowance for doubtful accounts the previous year.

e. Temporary investments which had cost $25,000 are sold for $19,500. At the previous year-end they had been valued at $17,000 and a loss on temporary investments of $8,000 had been provided for.

f. Some merchandise costing $4,000 that Largo Ltd. sold for $8,000 is returned because of defects. Customers receive a total of $7,500 in cash refunds.

g. Fad Inc. purchases $125,000 in merchandise inventory on account.

h. Gesualdo Ltd. declares dividends of $60,000. The dividends will be paid during the next accounting period.

E21-13. It has been said that GAAP requires certain items to be put on the balance sheet that *according to the definitions of GAAP* should not be considered liabilities. Examples would include the following three items: (i) deferred income tax credits, (ii) credits created when prices on items under long-term purchase commitments decline and, (iii) deferred gain from a sale-and-leaseback contract where the lease is an operating lease.

Required:

a. Evaluate whether each of the 3 items cited above should be considered (i) a liability under GAAP or (ii) a liability under the general definition of what constitutes a liability.

b. How should an analyst of a financial statement treat each of the 3 items above when evaluating the affairs of the company? Explain.

E21-14. Explain what effect each of the unrelated events below would have on the following ratios: (i) asset turnover, (ii) return on investment, and (iii) current ratio? If you think that more information is needed to determine the effect, indicate what is needed and make an assumption about it.

a. A freak storm at the end of the fiscal year meant that goods costing $85,000 and invoiced at $102,000 could not be shipped until after the start of the next fiscal year.

b. A heavy-duty truck was bought for cash for $85,000 five years ago and has been fully depreciated on a straight-line basis. The company replaces it with a new truck that is identical to the original one and that also costs $85,000 cash. The company intends to use the same depreciation policy for the new truck.

c. On reviewing its depreciation practices, the company decided that the allocation method it used was proper but that the functional life of its plant was significantly less than first thought. As a result of this change of estimate, there was an additional charge for depreciation for this year of $183,000.

d. On reviewing its year-end inventory count, the company discovered a cut-off error. Goods costing $125,000 that had been included in the inventory count as being on consignment with a customer had in fact been sold to that customer, and an invoice for $148,000 had been issued prior to the year-end. The invoice was unpaid.

e. A service department that had an annual cash cost of $258,000 and allocated costs of $56,000 for office space was closed down. Its work was contracted out to another firm for an expected annual cost of $265,000. The vacant office space was occupied by an existing department that had been using rented space at an annual cost of $14,000.

f. A piece of equipment had been rented for the past three years on what the company considered an operating lease. This year the lessee insisted on additional lease terms that have the effect of turning it into a capital lease. The payments remain the same as before.

PROBLEMS

P21-1. *Business Week* Magazine reports the availability of a service that predicts a given company's likelihood of having financial difficulties. It does so by combining on a weighted basis the following ratios: (i) retained earnings/total assets, (ii) debt/equity, (iii) earnings volatility over the past ten years, (iv) return on total assets, (v) fixed charge coverage, (vi) "liquidity," and (vii) asset size. The service boasts that its predictions to date have been quite accurate.

Required: In the light of the critique made of various ratio approaches in this chapter, what issues would you be concerned about if you were asked to evaluate this service by your employer who was thinking of subscribing to it?

P21-2. *The Wall Street Journal* ran an article about a technical default by Korean Air Lines on a syndicated loan. It reported that bankers were unwilling to comment on the actual terms of the technical default. However, the article did say that loan agreements typically contained the following types of provisions about the maintenance of financial ratios:

 (i) current assets must be a certain percentage of current liabilities

 (ii) total liabilities must be a certain percentage of net worth

 (iii) long-term debt must not exceed an agreed percentage of total equity in the company

 (iv) cash on hand must cover an agreed percentage of the expected cost of paying off interest and principal on the loan outstanding

 (v) dividends cannot be declared in excess of 50% of net income without approval from those making the loan.

The lead banker for the loan to Korean Air Lines was Bank of Montreal Asia Ltd.

Required:

a. How effective do you think each of the above provisions would be in protecting the interests of those holding long-term debt? What prospects would the creditors have if the airline was unable to maintain the ratios?

b. What alternative approaches besides ratios would you suggest as appropriate provisions for such loans? Justify your choices.

c. How many of the ratios mentioned above are open to manipulation? Explain how.

P21-3. A friend asks you confidentially for advice about whether she should pursue her interest in a local business that might be for sale. The present owner will not allow her to tell you the name of the firm or the kind of business it is in. Nevertheless, the owner has permitted her to give you the following unaudited trial balance.

TRIAL BALANCE

		Debts
Cash		$ 15,000
Accounts receivable		35,000
Inventory		43,128
Subtotal		93,128

	Cost	Depreciation	
Building	$ 164,288	$ 83,000	81,288
Equipment	18,642	12,560	6,082
Subtotal			87,370
Total assets			$180,498

	Credits
Accounts payable	$ (25,241)
Taxes payable	(1,245)
Accrued wages	(584)
	(27,070)
Mortgage payable	(56,481)
Owners' equity at beginning of year	(86,128)
Drawings	25,000)
Sales	(186,143)
Opening inventory	25,148
Closing inventory	(43,128)
Purchases	117,270
	(86,853)
Wages	28,562
Rentals	1,589
Office expenses	4,712
Utilities	3,512
Licences	562
Delivery expenses	1,856
Heating costs	4,859
City taxes	4,526
Telephone	856
Net	(35,819)
Total credits	$ (180,498)

Required:

a. On the basis only of the above trial balance, what advice would you give your friend about the attractiveness of this business? What are your reasons?

b. What are the three most important additional pieces of financial information you would advise your friend to ask the present owner? Justify your choices.

P21-4. You are simply given the following information about a company:

CONDENSED BALANCE SHEET

Assets

Cash		$ 1,200
Accounts receivable		85,000
Inventory		107,035
		$ 193,235
Building and equipment — cost	$ 395,714	
— accumulated depreciation	261,580	134,134
		$ 327,369

Liabilities and Equities

Accounts payable	$ 86,124
Taxes payable	25,410
	111,534
Mortgage payable	241,000
Owners' equity:	
Beginning of year	12,000
Drawings	(65,000)
Net income	27,835
Closing balance (overdrawn)	(25,165)
	$ 327,369)

CONDENSED INCOME STATEMENT

Sales	$ 258,124
Cost of goods sold	98,041
Wages	28,562
Rentals	45,169
Office expenses	21,458
Utilities	125
Licences	55
Delivery expenses	18,547
Heating costs	1,258
City taxes	4,526
Telephone	12,548
Net income	$ 27,835

Required: Assess each of the following aspects of the company and explain your reasoning:

a. short-term and long-term solvency

b. profitability

c. performance of management

P21-5. A friend shows you the following ratios of a company he is thinking of buying. The only other information he has is that the company has no long-term debt and he thinks its sales are in the order of $250,000.

Current ratio	1.73
Quick ratio	0.77
Accounts receivable turnover	3.04
Days' sales in receivables	120.19
Inventory turnover	2.41
Days' sales in inventory	151.35
Rate of return on assets	8.50%
Profit margin	11%
Asset turnover	1.92

Required: Deduce as much as you can about the company. In particular, what is your assessment of its (i) solvency, (ii) profitability, and (iii) management performance?

P21-6. In the early 1980s, in an article titled "Fairyland Revisited," *The Economist* Magazine made highly critical comments about the financial reporting practices of Britain's nationalized industries. Regarding the National Coal Board's financial report, it emphasized the following points:

(i) Gain on the sale of miner's houses used to be treated as an extraordinary item, but was now included in normal operating income. If the Board had not made this accounting change, it would have reported an operating loss instead of a small profit.

(ii) The Board normally includes in inventory only those supplies "where there is a recurring demand" and charges the other purchased supplies directly to expense. However, it had decided to revive a former practice of physically counting and valuing those supplies that until then had not been included in inventory. The value was 14.4 million pounds sterling, and the reported profit for the year was 5.5 million pounds.

(iii) The Board intended to make another policy change in which underground mine roadways would all be capitalized. Until now it had only capitalized those whose life was longer than twenty years.

Required:

a. Assuming that full disclosure of the above items was made in the notes to the financial statements, how many of the above items are likely to mislead the sophisticated investor?

b. If the reader's attention was not directed to each of these items through a note in the financial statements, which of them would nevertheless be detected by an alert reader?

c. How significant a change do you think these items would make on the balance sheet of the National Coal Board? Explain your reasoning.

d. What significant financial ratios, if any, would be affected by the changes discussed in *The Economist?*

P21-7. Here are abbreviated financial statements for M Ltd., a developer of high-technology communications equipment.

BALANCE SHEET

Cash and short-term investments	$ 166,976
Accounts receivable	76,412
Inventories	119,242
Plant assets (net)	244,973
	$ 607,603
Notes payable	$ 95,965
Accounts payable and accrued liabilities	48,071
Current portion of long-term debt	2,974
Long-term debt	183,655
Share capital	217,707
Retained earnings	58,631
	$ 607,003

INCOME STATEMENT

Sales	$ 255,085
Opening inventory	99,757
Purchases	144,615
	244,372
Closing inventory	118,272
Cost of goods sold	126,100
Other expenses	120,285
Interest on long-term debt	5,912
Income taxes (recovery)	(12,009)
Net income for year after taxes	$ 14,797

Required:

a. Compute the following ratios:

(i) current ratio

(ii) quick ratio

(iii) accounts receivable turnover

(iv) inventory turnover

(v) profit margin ratio (assume a 50% marginal tax rate)

(vi) asset turnover ratio

(vii) debt/equity

(viii) interest coverage

b. On the basis of the ratios you have calculated, evaluate the financial soundness of the company in the eyes of a holder of long-term bonds.

P21-8. Here is some information taken from the financial report of a Canadian forest-products company. (Throughout this question all dollar figures represent thousands of $.) The marginal tax rate is 50%. The pre-tax interest expense is $3,000.

Sales	$ 439,209
Return on investment	3.019%
Profit margin	4.979%
Ratio of all debt to all equity	1.175
Long-term debt	$ 288,474
Interest on long-term debt	$ 6,630
Current ratio	1.477
Quick ratio	0.714
Days' sales in receivables	40
Asset turnover	0.60655

Required: Calculate each of the following:

a. Total assets

b. Net income after taxes

c. Current liabilities

d. Inventory

e. Accounts receivable

f. Cash

g. Net fixed assets

h. Rate of return on shareholders' equity

P21-9. Here is some information taken from the financial report of a Canadian manufacturing company. (Throughout this question all dollar figures represent thousands of $.) The marginal tax rate is 50%. The pre-tax interest expense is $3,000.

Sales	$ 200,000
Return on investment	1.472%
Profit margin	2.551%
Ratio of all debt to all equity	1.242
Long-term debt	$ 141,516
Current ratio	1.517
Quick ratio	0.826
Days' sales in receivables	73
Asset turnover	0.577

Required: Calculate each of the following:

a. Total assets

b. Net income after taxes

c. Current liabilities

d. Inventory

e. Accounts receivable

f. Cash

g. Net fixed assets

h. Rate of return on shareholders' equity

P21-10. *The Globe and Mail* reported that ever since "staid old Dominion Bridge Co. Ltd." was transformed into Amca International Ltd., it has been the darling of some investors and the object of criticism for its accounting methods. In 1984 one of its critics raised the following issues:

(i) Amca had calculated the equity per share in its 1983 statements by dividing shareholders' equity by the number of common shares, something it had been doing "for the past 100 years." Many outsiders argued that the new issue of retractible preferred shares should have been subtracted first. Management said that the CICA had not issued any formal guidelines on this matter. One commentator in the investment community said that it was sometimes permissible to exclude preference shares if they were convertible and if the conversion price had already been passed.

(ii) In one of its 1983 quarterly reports, Amca had included a "$9.8 million pension-surplus refund" when calculating its earnings per share.

(iii) In 1978 Amca had decided to adopt the percentage-of-completion method for recognizing income. This allowed it to include some "anticipated but unbilled receivables" in its working capital, thus making its debt-to-equity ratio "appear healthier than it was." The company defended the practice as common among large construction companies in the United States.

Required: Comment on the propriety of the three practices described above. In particular, for each practice, show the following:

a. Determine whether it affects the balance-sheet ratios (regardless of its propriety).

b. Evaluate the effect of each item on reported income per common share. Discuss whether you think each of the practices *ought* to be regarded as acceptable. (Disregard here the CICA guidelines.)

P21-11. Provided below is information from the annual reports of three companies.

	Firm 1	Firm 2	Firm 3
Sales	$ 1,600,000	$ 1,600,000	$ 1,600,000
Expenses:			
Cost of product sold	676,800	873,600	1,184,000
Salary and wages	177,600	127,200	144,000
Employee benefits	10,800	6,000	7,200
Depreciation	0	18,000	18,000
All other	494,800	377,200	192,800
Total expenses	1,360,000	1,402,000	1,546,000
Net profit	240,000	198,000	54,000
Average total assets	$ 450,000	$ 1,300,000	$ 450,000

Required: One firm operates movie theatres, one is a food wholesaler, and one is a jewellery retailer. From the data given above, determine which firm is in which industry. Give your reasons.

P21-12. The sales of Sam Pull Enterprises were $2,000,000 for the year. A financial analyst computed the following ratios based on the year-end in the balance sheet.

Debt to equity ratio (all liabilities to all equities)	52%
Rate of return on assets	9.6%
Net income as a percentage of revenue	15%
Tax expense as a percentage of pretax income	40%
Rate of return on shareholders' equity	12.5%

Required: Calculate each of the following:
a. Interest expense
b. Income tax expense
c. Total expenses
d. Net income
e. Total assets
f. Total liabilities

P21-13. The income statements and balance sheets of Taurus Inc. and Aries Inc. are provided below. Assume that the year-end balances approximate the annual average. The income tax rate is 40%.

INCOME STATEMENTS

	Taurus Inc.	Aries Inc.
Sales	$ 1,700,000	$ 1,500,000
Less cost of sales	950,000	660,000
Gross profit	750,000	840,000
Less selling and administrative expense	215,000	325,000
Operating income	535,000	515,000
Interest expense	37,500	100,000
Net income before tax	497,500	415,000
Income tax	199,000	166,000
Net income	$ 298,500	$ 249,000

BALANCE SHEETS

	Taurus Inc.	Aries Inc.
Cash	$ 85,000	$ 45,000
Accounts receivable	525,000	395,000
Merchandise inventory	1,000,000	700,000
Plant and equipment	3,200,000	3,670,000
Total assets	$ 4,810,000	$ 4,810,000
Accounts payable	$ 471,000	$ 279,000
Income taxes payable	199,000	166,000
Long-term bonds payable	375,000	1,000,000
Share capital	2,015,000	2,015,000
Retained earnings	1,750,000	1,350,000
Total liabilities and equities	$ 4,810,000	$ 4,810,000

Required: Analyse the given data to determine the following. Use any financial ratios you deem appropriate.
a. Which company is more profitable?
b. Which company is more liquid?
c. Which company is in a more secure position in terms of long-run solvency?

P21-14. As an employee of a bank you are asked by the assistant manager to analyse the financial statements of two loan applicants shown below.

BALANCE SHEETS
31 December 19X9

	Fast-track Inc.	Quick-slick Ltd.
Cash	$ 28,875	$ 54,250
Accounts receivable	101,500	52,500
Inventories	149,625	53,375
	280,000	160,125
Fixed assets	210,000	224,875
Accumulated depreciation	(140,000)	(35,000)
	70,000	189,875
	$ 350,000	$ 350,000
Current liabilities	$ 140,000	$ 106,750
Long-term debt: 14%	87,500	8,750
Common stock	35,000	65,000
Retained earnings	87,500	169,500
	$ 350,000	$ 350,000

INCOME STATEMENTS
For the year ended 31 December 19X9

	Fast-track Inc.		Quick-Slick Limited	
Sales		$ 626,500		$ 638,750
Inventory at 1/1/X9	$ 138,700		$ 50,209	
Purchases	462,075		437,516	
	600,775		487,725	
Inventory at 31/12/X9	149,625		53,375	
Cost of goods sold		451,150		434,350
Gross profit		175,350		204,400
Operating expenses:				
Selling	96,481		92,615	
Administrative	41,340		41,610	
Interest	12,250	150,071	1,225	135,450
Net income before taxes		25,279		68,950
Income taxes		9,100		21,000
Net income		16,179		47,950

You are also given the following additional information:

(i) Both companies are in the same industry.

(ii) No extraordinary transactions took place during the year.

(iii) Neither company had cash sales during the year.

(iv) The accounts receivable balances at 31 December approximated the average for the year for each company.

(v) The operating expenses included depreciation of $17,500 for Fast-track and $35,000 for Quick-slick.

Required: Fast-track and Quick-slick have each applied for a long-term loan of $75,000. Evaluate the financial soundness of each company. Indicate which company is the better credit risk for the loan.

(CMA adapted)

P21-15. Alpha Limited and Beta Limited are both medium-sized companies involved in the servicing of farm equipment in Saskatchewan. Here is some selected information from their accounts.

	Alpha Limited	Beta Limited
Retained earnings	$ 60,000	$ 30,000
Common stock, 16 par	340,000	70,000
Current liabilities	30,000	100,000
Long-term liabilities	70,000	300,000
Total assets	500,000	500,000

You are also given the following additional data.

(i) Alpha has 68,000 common shares outstanding; Beta has 14,000 common shares outstanding.

(ii) The income tax rate for each company is 45%.

(iii) The retained earnings shown above include a net after-tax income of $49,500 for Alpha and $13,000 for Beta.

(iv) For each company, interest expense equals 10% of total liabilities.

Required:

a. For each company compute *three* ratios that measure equity position (i.e., the adequacy of equity or the economic return on equity or both.) Also compute the leverage factor for each company. (Round to the nearest dollar.)

b. Interpret and evaluate each situation indicated by your computations in part (a) above.

c. Suppose Alpha was in the fishing industry in British Columbia instead of in the servicing of farm equipment in Saskatchewan. How would this affect your analysis? Explain.

(CGA adapted)

P21-16. The unclassified comparative balance sheets for Isabella Ltd. read as follows.

COMPARATIVE BALANCE SHEETS
As at 31 December 19X4

	19X4	19X3
Cash	$ 100,000	$ 103,000
Accounts receivable	35,000	37,000
Allowance for bad debts	(2,000)	(5,000)
Inventory	25,000	30,000
Plant and equipment	300,000	270,000
Accumulated depreciaiton	(70,000)	(60,000)
Investments	75,000	86,000
Total assets	$ 463,000	$ 461,000
Accounts payable	$ 10,000	$ 13,000
Dividends payable		5,000
Current portion of long-term debt	10,000	10,000
Mortgage payable	90,000	100,000
Common shares	170,000	170,000
Retained earnings	183,000	163,000
Total liabilities and equities	$ 463,000	$ 461,000

In 19X4, sales were $150,000 and cost of sales was $75,000. On 15 January 19X5 the company split its shares and issued two new shares for every old share outstanding (i.e., a two-for-one split).

Required:

a. Calculate each of the following for 31 December 19X4:

(i) acid test ratio

(ii) receivables turnover ratio

(iii) inventory turnover ratio

(iv) average collection period (i.e., days' sales in receivables)

b. How would the split on 15 January 19X5 affect the 19X5 balance sheet? Explain fully.

c. How does the accounting treatment of a stock split differ from that of a stock dividend? Be specific.

(CGA adapted)

P21-17. The Last Hurrah Company is a manufacturer of dairy products. The following information was extracted from a recent financial report.

	19X1	19X2	19X3
Sales	$ 14,000,000	$ 13,000,000	$ 12,000,000
Net income	100,000	140,000	160,000
Interest expense, net of income tax	10,000	2,000	9,000
Shareholders' equity	1,400,000	1,450,000	1,460,000
Shares of common stock outstanding*	20,000	20,000	24,000
Total assets	3,500,000	3,500,000	3,700,000
Market value per share	$ 66.00	$ 72.00	$ 45.00

* On 31 December 19X3, 4,000 common shares were issued as a stock dividend.

Required:

a. Compute the following for 19X2 and 19X3. (Round off to three decimal places.)

(i) profit margin ratio

(ii) return on investment ratio

(iii) earnings per share

(iv) price-earnings ratio

b. Which of the above ratios would you prefer as a measure of profitability? Why?

(CGA adapted)

BIBLIOGRAPHY

BALDWIN, BRUCE A. "Segment Earnings Disclosure and the Ability of Security Analysts to Forecast Earnings Per Share." *The Accounting Review* (July 1984). A test of the proposition that using financial results by segments permits better financial forecasts.

BOOCOCK, KEITH, and DROZD, F. ANNE. "Forecasting Corporate Collapse." *CA Magazine* (November 1982). A survey of reasons why companies fail.

DEITRICK, JAMES W., and HARRISON, WALTER T. JR., "EMH, CMR, and the Accounting Profession." *Journal of Accountancy* (February 1984) A discussion of the implications of the efficient markets hypothesis (EMH) and capital markets research (CMR).

DYCKMAN, THOMAS R.; DOWNES, DAVID H.; and MAGEE, ROBERT P. *Efficient Capital Markets and Accounting: A Critical Analysis.* Englewood Cliffs, N.J.: Prentice-Hall, Inc., 1975. A readable assessment of the efficient markets hypothesis.

FOSTER, GEORGE. *Financial Statement Analysis*. 2nd edition. Englewood Cliffs, N.J.: Prentice-Hall, Inc., 1986. Similar in approach to Lev (see below), but with more extensive coverage of the statistical techniques.

HURTUBISE, ANDRE, and SYLPH, JAMES M. "Financial Forecasts and Projections: Engagements on Two Levels." *CA Magazine* (January 1985). An evaluation of a 1983 CICA Guideline entitled "Auditor Review of Financial Forecasts."

LEV, BARUCH. *Financial Statement Analysis: A New Approach*. Englewood Cliffs, N.J.: Prentice-Hall, Inc., 1974. Good coverage and critique of the conventional financial-statement ratios. Also reviews and evaluates the implications of research.

WILLIAMSON, ROBERT W. "Evidence on the Selective Reporting of Financial Ratios." *The Accounting Review* (April 1984). An examination of the annual reports of some Fortune 500 companies to see if they reported selectively by using those ratios most favourable to themselves.

WYATT, ARTHUR. "Efficient Market Theory." *Journal of Accountancy* (February 1983). Describes some business activities that appear to deny the validity of the efficient markets hypothesis.

APPENDIX 1

Present Value Tables

TABLE 1.   PRESENT VALUE FACTORS

Periods Hence	1%	2%	3%	4%	5%	6%	7%	8%	9%	10%
1	.9901	.9804	.9709	.9615	.9524	.9434	.9346	.9259	.9174	.9091
2	.9803	.9612	.9426	.9246	.9070	.8900	.8734	.8573	.8417	.8264
3	.9706	.9423	.9151	.8890	.8638	.8396	.8163	.7938	.7722	.7513
4	.9610	.9238	.8885	.8548	.8227	.7921	.7629	.7350	.7084	.6830
5	.9515	.9057	.8626	.8219	.7835	.7473	.7130	.6806	.6499	.6209
6	.9420	.8880	.8375	.7903	.7462	.7050	.6663	.6302	.5963	.5645
7	.9327	.8706	.8131	.7599	.7107	.6651	.6227	.5835	.5470	.5132
8	.9235	.8535	.7894	.7307	.6768	.6274	.5820	.5403	.5019	.4665
9	.9143	.8368	.7664	.7026	.6446	.5919	.5439	.5002	.4604	.4241
10	.9053	.8203	.7441	.6756	.6139	.5584	.5083	.4632	.4224	.3855
11	.8963	.8043	.7224	.6496	.5847	.5268	.4751	.4289	.3875	.3505
12	.8874	.7885	.7014	.6246	.5568	.4970	.4440	.3971	.3555	.3186
13	.8787	.7730	.6810	.6006	.5303	.4688	.4150	.3677	.3262	.2897
14	.8700	.7579	.6611	.5775	.5051	.4423	.3878	.3405	.2992	.2633
15	.8613	.7430	.6419	.5553	.4810	.4173	.3624	.3152	.2745	.2394
16	.8528	.7284	.6232	.5339	.4581	.3936	.3387	.2919	.2519	.2176
17	.8444	.7142	.6050	.5134	.4363	.3714	.3166	.2703	.2311	.1978
18	.8360	.7002	.5874	.4936	.4155	.3503	.2959	.2502	.2120	.1799
19	.8277	.6864	.5703	.4746	.3957	.3305	.2765	.2317	.1945	.1635
20	.8195	.6730	.5537	.4564	.3769	.3118	.2584	.2145	.1784	.1486
21	.8114	.6598	.5375	.4388	.3589	.2942	.2415	.1987	.1637	.1351
22	.8034	.6468	.5219	.4220	.3418	.2775	.2257	.1839	.1502	.1228
23	.7954	.6342	.5067	.4057	.3256	.2618	.2109	.1703	.1378	.1117
24	.7876	.6217	.4919	.3901	.3101	.2470	.1971	.1577	.1264	.1015
25	.7798	.6095	.4776	.3751	.2953	.2330	.1842	.1460	.1160	.0923
26	.7720	.5976	.4637	.3607	.2812	.2198	.1722	.1352	.1064	.0839
27	.7644	.5859	.4502	.3468	.2678	.2074	.1609	.1252	.0976	.0763
28	.7568	.5744	.4371	.3335	.2551	.1956	.1504	.1159	.0895	.0693
29	.7493	.5631	.4243	.3207	.2429	.1846	.1406	.1073	.0822	.0630
30	.7419	.5521	.4120	.3083	.2314	.1741	.1314	.0994	.0754	.0573
31	.7346	.5412	.4000	.2965	.2204	.1643	.1228	.0920	.0691	.0521
32	.7273	.5306	.3883	.2851	.2099	.1550	.1147	.0852	.0634	.0474
33	.7201	.5202	.3770	.2741	.1999	.1462	.1072	.0789	.0582	.0431
34	.7130	.5100	.3660	.2636	.1904	.1379	.1002	.0730	.0534	.0391
35	.7059	.5000	.3554	.2534	.1813	.1301	.0937	.0676	.0490	.0356
36	.6989	.4902	.3450	.2437	.1727	.1227	.0875	.0626	.0449	.0323
37	.6920	.4806	.3350	.2343	.1644	.1158	.0818	.0580	.0412	.0294
38	.6852	.4712	.3252	.2253	.1566	.1092	.0765	.0537	.0378	.0267
39	.6784	.4619	.3158	.2166	.1491	.1031	.0715	.0497	.0347	.0243
40	.6717	.4529	.3066	.2083	.1420	.0972	.0668	.0460	.0318	.0221
41	.6650	.4440	.2976	.2003	.1353	.0917	.0624	.0426	.0292	.0201
42	.6584	.4353	.2890	.1926	.1288	.0865	.0583	.0395	.0268	.0183
43	.6519	.4268	.2805	.1852	.1227	.0816	.0545	.0365	.0246	.0166
44	.6454	.4184	.2724	.1780	.1169	.0770	.0509	.0338	.0226	.0151
45	.6391	.4102	.2644	.1712	.1113	.0727	.0476	.0313	.0207	.0137
46	.6327	.4022	.2567	.1646	.1060	.0685	.0445	.0290	.0190	.0125
47	.6265	.3943	.2493	.1583	.1009	.0647	.0416	.0269	.0174	.0113
48	.6203	.3865	.2420	.1522	.0961	.0610	.0389	.0249	.0160	.0103
49	.6141	.3790	.2350	.1463	.0916	.0575	.0363	.0230	.0147	.0094
50	.6080	.3715	.2281	.1407	.0872	.0543	.0339	.0213	.0134	.0085

(Continued)

TABLE 1. PRESENT VALUE FACTORS (Continued)

Periods Hence	11%	12%	13%	14%	15%	16%	17%	18%	19%	20%
1	.9009	.8929	.8850	.8772	.8696	.8621	.8547	.8475	.8403	.8333
2	.8116	.7972	.7831	.7695	.7561	.7432	.7305	.7182	.7062	.6944
3	.7312	.7118	.6931	.6750	.6575	.6407	.6244	.6086	.5934	.5787
4	.6587	.6355	.6133	.5921	.5718	.5523	.5337	.5158	.4987	.4823
5	.5935	.5674	.5428	.5194	.4972	.4761	.4561	.4371	.4190	.4019
6	.5346	.5066	.4803	.4556	.4323	.4104	.3898	.3704	.3521	.3349
7	.4817	.4523	.4251	.3996	.3759	.3538	.3332	.3139	.2959	.2791
8	.4339	.4039	.3762	.3506	.3269	.3050	.2848	.2660	.2487	.2326
9	.3909	.3606	.3329	.3075	.2843	.2630	.2434	.2255	.2090	.1938
10	.3522	.3220	.2946	.2697	.2472	.2267	.2080	1911	.1756	.1615
11	.3173	.2875	.2607	.2366	.2149	.1954	.1778	.1619	.1476	.1346
12	.2858	.2567	.2307	.2076	.1869	.1685	.1520	.1372	.1240	.1122
13	.2575	.2292	.2042	.1821	.1625	.1452	.1299	.1163	.1042	.0935
14	.2320	.2046	.1807	.1597	.1413	.1252	.1110	.0985	.0876	.0779
15	.2090	.1827	.1599	.1401	.1229	.1079	.0949	.0835	.0736	.0649
16	.1883	.1631	.1415	.1229	.1069	.0930	.0818	.0708	.0618	.0541
17	.1696	.1456	.1252	.1078	.0929	.0802	.0693	.0600	.0520	.0451
18	1528	.1300	.1108	.0946	.0808	.0691	.0592	.0508	.0437	.0376
19	.1377	.1161	.0981	.0829	.0703	.0596	.0506	.0431	.0367	.0313
20	.1240	.1037	.0868	.0728	.0611	.0514	.0433	.0365	.0303	.0261
21	.1117	.0926	.0768	.0638	.0531	.0443	.0370	.0309	.0259	.0217
22	.1007	.0826	.0680	.0560	.0462	.0382	.0316	.0262	.0218	.0181
23	.0907	.0738	.0601	.0491	.0402	.0329	.0270	.0222	.0183	.0151
24	.0817	.0659	.0532	.0431	.0349	.0284	.0231	.0188	.0154	.0126
25	.0736	.0588	.0471	.0378	.0304	.0245	.0197	.0160	.0129	.0105
26	.0663	.0525	.0417	.0331	.0264	.0211	.0169	.0135	.0109	.0087
27	.0597	.0469	.0369	.0291	.0230	.0182	.0144	.0115	.0091	.0073
28	.0538	.0419	.0326	.0255	.0200	.0157	.0123	.0097	.0077	.0061
29	.0485	.0374	.0289	.0224	.0174	.0135	.0105	.0082	.0064	.0051
30	.0437	.0334	.0256	.0196	.0151	.0116	.0090	.0070	.0054	.0042
31	.0394	.0298	.0226	.0172	.0131	.0100	.0077	.0059	.0046	.0035
32	.0355	.0266	.0200	.0151	.0114	.0087	.0066	.0050	.0038	.0029
33	.0319	.0238	.0177	.0132	.0099	.0075	.0056	.0042	.0032	.0024
34	.0288	.0212	.0157	.0116	.0086	.0064	.0048	.0036	.0027	.0020
35	.0259	.0189	.0139	.0102	.0075	.0055	.0041	.0030	.0023	.0017
36	.0234	.0169	.0123	.0089	.0065	.0048	.0035	.0026	.0019	.0014
37	.0210	.0151	.0109	.0078	.0057	.0041	.0030	.0022	.0016	.0012
38	.0190	.0135	.0096	.0069	.0049	.0036	.0026	.0019	.0013	.0010
39	.0171	.0120	.0085	.0060	.0043	.0031	.0022	.0016	.0011	.0008
40	.0154	.0107	.0075	.0053	.0037	.0026	.0019	.0013	.0010	.0007
41	.0139	.0096	.0067	.0046	.0032	.0023	.0016	.0011	.0008	.0006
42	.0125	.0086	.0059	.0041	.0028	.0020	.0014	.0010	.0007	.0005
43	.0112	.0076	.0052	.0036	.0025	.0017	.0012	.0008	.0006	.0004
44	.0101	.0068	.0046	.0031	.0021	.0015	.0010	.0007	.0005	.0003
45	.0091	.0061	.0041	.0027	.0019	.0013	.0009	.0006	.0004	.0003
46	.0082	.0054	.0036	.0024	.0016	.0011	.0007	.0005	.0003	.0002
47	.0074	.0049	.0032	.0021	.0014	.0009	.0006	.0004	.0003	.0002
48	.0067	.0043	.0028	.0019	.0012	.0008	.0005	.0004	.0002	.0002
49	.0060	.0039	.0025	.0016	.0011	.0007	.0005	.0003	.0002	.0001
50	.0054	.0035	.0022	.0014	.0009	.0006	.0004	.0003	.0002	.0001

(Continued)

TABLE 1.   PRESENT VALUE FACTORS (Continued)

Periods Hence	21%	22%	23%	24%	25%	26%	27%	28%	29%	30%
1	.8264	.8197	.8130	.8065	.8000	.7937	.7874	.7813	.7752	.7692
2	.6830	.6719	.6610	.6504	.6400	.6299	.6200	.6104	.6009	.5917
3	.5645	.5507	.5374	.5245	.5120	.4999	.4882	.4768	.4658	.4552
4	.4665	.4514	.4369	.4230	.4096	.3968	.3844	.3725	.3611	.3501
5	.3855	.3700	.3552	.3411	.3277	.3149	.3027	.2910	.2799	.2693
6	.3186	.3033	.2888	.2751	.2621	.2499	.2383	.2274	.2170	.2072
7	.2633	.2486	.2348	.2218	.2096	.1983	.1877	.1776	.1682	.1594
8	.2176	.2038	.1909	.1789	.1678	.1574	.1478	.1388	.1304	.1226
9	.1799	.1670	.1552	.1443	.1342	.1249	.1164	.1084	.1011	.0943
10	.1486	.1369	.1262	.1164	.1074	.0992	.0916	.0847	.0784	.0725
11	.1228	.1122	.1026	.0938	.0859	.0787	.0721	.0662	.0607	.0558
12	.1015	.0920	.0834	.0757	.0687	.0625	.0568	.0517	.0471	.0429
13	.0839	.0754	.0678	.0610	.0550	.0496	.0447	.0404	.0365	.0330
14	.0693	.0618	.0551	.0492	.0440	.0393	.0352	.0316	.0283	.0254
15	.0573	.0507	.0448	.0397	.0352	.0312	.0277	.0247	.0219	.0195
16	.0474	.0415	.0364	.0320	.0281	.0248	.0218	.0193	.0170	.0150
17	.0391	.0340	.0296	.0258	.0225	.0197	.0172	.0150	.0132	.0116
18	.0323	.0279	.0241	.0208	.0180	.0156	.0135	.0118	.0102	.0089
19	.0267	.0229	.0196	.0168	.0144	.0124	.0107	.0092	.0079	.0068
20	.0221	.0187	.0159	.0135	.0115	.0098	.0084	.0072	.0061	.0053
21	.0183	.0154	.0129	.0109	.0092	.0078	.0066	.0056	.0048	.0040
22	.0151	.0126	.0105	.0088	.0074	.0062	.0052	.0044	.0037	.0031
23	.0125	.0103	.0086	.0071	.0059	.0049	.0041	.0034	.0029	.0024
24	.0103	.0085	.0070	.0057	.0047	.0039	.0032	.0027	.0022	.0018
25	.0085	.0069	.0057	.0046	.0038	.0031	.0025	.0021	.0017	.0014
26	.0070	.0057	.0046	.0037	.0030	.0025	.0020	.0016	.0013	.0011
27	.0058	.0047	.0037	.0030	.0024	.0019	.0016	.0013	.0010	.0008
28	.0048	.0038	.0030	.0024	.0019	.0015	.0012	.0010	.0008	.0006
29	.0040	.0031	.0025	.0020	.0015	.0012	.0010	.0008	.0006	.0005
30	.0033	.0026	.0020	.0016	.0012	.0010	.0008	.0006	.0005	.0004
31	.0027	.0021	.0016	.0013	.0010	.0008	.0006	.0005	.0004	.0003
32	.0022	.0017	.0013	.0010	.0008	.0006	.0005	.0004	.0003	.0002
33	.0019	.0014	.0011	.0008	.0006	.0005	.0004	.0003	.0002	.0002
34	.0015	.0012	.0009	.0007	.0005	.0004	.0003	.0002	.0002	.0001
35	.0013	.0009	.0007	.0005	.0004	.0003	.0002	.0002	.0001	.0001
36	.0010	.0008	.0006	.0004	.0003	.0002	.0002	.0001	.0001	.0001
37	.0009	.0006	.0005	.0003	.0003	.0002	.0001	.0001	.0001	.0001
38	.0007	.0005	.0004	.0003	.0002	.0002	.0001	.0001	.0001	.0000
39	.0006	.0004	.0003	.0002	.0002	.0001	.0001	.0001	.0000	
40	.0005	.0004	.0003	.0002	.0001	.0001	.0001	.0001		
41	.0004	.0003	.0002	.0001	.0001	.0001	.0001	.0000		
42	.0003	.0002	.0002	.0001	.0001	.0001	.0000			
43	.0003	.0002	.0001	.0001	.0001	.0000				
44	.0002	.0002	.0001	.0001	.0001					
45	.0002	.0001	.0001	.0001	.0000					
46	.0002	.0001	.0001	.0001						
47	.0001	.0001	.0001	.0000						
48	.0001	.0001	.0000							
49	.0001	.0001								
50	.0001	.0000								

(Continued)

TABLE 1.   PRESENT VALUE FACTORS (Continued)

Periods Hence	31%	32%	33%	34%	35%	36%	37%	38%	39%	40%
1	.7634	.7576	.7519	.7463	.7407	.7353	.7299	.7246	.7194	.7143
2	.5827	.5739	.5653	.5569	.5487	.5407	.5328	.5251	.5176	.5102
3	.4448	.4348	.4251	.4156	.4064	.3975	.3889	.3805	.3724	.3644
4	.3396	.3294	.3196	.3102	.3011	.2923	.2839	.2757	.2679	.2603
5	.2592	.2495	.2403	.2315	.2230	.2149	.2072	.1998	.1927	.1859
6	.1979	.1890	.1807	.1727	.1652	.1580	.1512	.1448	.1386	.1328
7	.1510	.1432	.1358	.1289	.1224	.1162	.1104	.1049	.0997	.0949
8	.1153	.1085	.1021	.0962	.0906	.0854	.0806	.0760	.0718	.0678
9	.0880	.0822	.0768	.0718	.0671	.0628	.0588	.0551	.0516	.0484
10	.0672	.0623	.0577	.0536	.0497	.0462	.0429	.0399	.0371	.0346
11	.0513	.0472	.0434	.0400	.0368	.0340	.0313	.0289	.0267	.0247
12	.0392	.0357	.0326	.0298	.0273	.0250	.0229	.0210	.0192	.0176
13	.0299	.0271	.0245	.0223	.0202	.0184	.0167	.0152	.0138	.0126
14	.0228	.0205	.0185	.0166	.0150	.0135	.0122	.0110	.0099	.0090
15	.0174	.0155	.0139	.0124	.0111	.0099	.0089	.0080	.0072	.0064
16	.0133	.0118	.0104	.0093	.0082	.0073	.0065	.0058	.0051	.0046
17	.0101	.0089	.0078	.0069	.0061	.0054	.0047	.0042	.0037	.0033
18	.0077	.0068	.0059	.0052	.0045	.0039	.0035	.0030	.0027	.0023
19	.0059	.0051	.0044	.0038	.0033	.0029	.0025	.0022	.0019	.0017
20	.0045	.0039	.0033	.0029	.0025	.0021	.0018	.0016	.0014	.0012
21	.0034	.0029	.0025	.0021	.0018	.0016	.0013	.0012	.0010	.0009
22	.0026	.0022	.0019	.0016	.0014	.0012	.0010	.0008	.0007	.0006
23	.0020	.0017	.0014	.0012	.0010	.0008	.0007	.0006	.0005	.0004
24	.0015	.0013	.0011	.0009	.0007	.0006	.0005	.0004	.0004	.0003
25	.0012	.0010	.0008	.0007	.0006	.0005	.0004	.0003	.0003	.0002
26	.0009	.0007	.0006	.0005	.0004	.0003	.0003	.0002	.0002	.0002
27	.0007	.0006	.0005	.0004	.0003	.0002	.0002	.0002	.0001	.0001
28	.0005	.0004	.0003	.0003	.0002	.0002	.0001	.0001	.0001	.0001
29	.0004	.0003	.0003	.0002	.0002	.0001	.0001	.0001	.0001	.0001
30	.0003	.0002	.0002	.0002	.0001	.0001	.0001	.0001	.0001	.0000
31	.0002	.0002	.0001	.0001	.0001	.0001	.0001	.0000	.0000	
32	.0002	.0001	.0001	.0001	.0001	.0001	.0000			
33	.0001	.0001	.0001	.0001	.0001	.0000				
34	.0001	.0001	.0001	.0000	.0000					
35	.0001	.0001	.0000							
36	.0001	.0000	.0000							
37	.0000									

(Continued)

TABLE 1. PRESENT VALUE FACTORS (Continued)

Periods Hence	41%	42%	43%	44%	45%	46%	47%	48%	49%	50%
1	.7092	.7042	.6993	.6944	.6897	.6849	.6803	.6757	.6711	.6667
2	.5030	.4959	.4890	.4823	.4756	.4691	.4628	.4565	.4504	.4444
3	.3567	.3492	.3420	.3349	.3280	.3213	.3148	.3085	.3023	.2963
4	.2530	.2459	.2391	.2326	.2262	.2201	.2142	.2084	.2029	.1975
5	.1794	.1732	.1672	.1615	.1560	.1507	.1457	.1408	.1362	.1317
6	.1273	.1220	.1169	.1122	.1076	.1032	.0991	.0952	.0914	.0878
7	.0903	.0859	.0818	.0779	.0742	.0707	.0674	.0643	.0613	.0585
8	.0640	.0605	.0572	.0541	.0512	.0484	.0459	.0434	.0412	.0390
9	.0454	.0426	.0400	.0376	.0353	.0332	.0312	.0294	.0276	.0260
10	.0322	.0300	.0280	.0261	.0243	.0227	.0212	.0198	.0185	.0173
11	.0228	.0211	.0196	.0181	.0168	.0156	.0144	.0134	.0125	.0116
12	.0162	.0149	.0137	.0126	.0116	.0107	.0098	.0091	.0084	.0077
13	.0115	.0105	.0096	.0087	.0080	.0073	.0067	.0061	.0056	.0051
14	.0081	.0074	.0067	.0061	.0055	.0050	.0045	.0041	.0038	.0034
15	.0058	.0052	.0047	.0042	.0038	.0034	.0031	.0028	.0025	.0023
16	.0041	.0037	.0033	.0029	.0026	.0023	.0021	.0019	.0017	.0015
17	.0029	.0026	.0023	.0020	.0018	.0016	.0014	.0013	.0011	.0010
18	.0021	.0018	.0016	.0014	.0012	.0011	.0010	.0009	.0008	.0007
19	.0015	.0013	.0011	.0010	.0009	.0008	.0007	.0006	.0005	.0005
20	.0010	.0009	.0008	.0007	.0006	.0005	.0005	.0004	.0003	.0003
21	.0007	.0006	.0005	.0005	.0004	.0004	.0003	.0003	.0002	.0002
22	.0005	.0004	.0004	.0003	.0003	.0002	.0002	.0002	.0002	.0001
23	.0004	.0003	.0003	.0002	.0002	.0002	.0001	.0001	.0001	.0001
24	.0003	.0002	.0002	.0002	.0001	.0001	.0001	.0001	.0001	.0001
25	.0002	.0002	.0001	.0001	.0001	.0001	.0001	.0001	.0000	.0000
26	.0001	.0001	.0001	.0001	.0001	.0001	.0000	.0000		
27	.0001	.0001	.0001	.0001	.0000	.0000				
28	.0001	.0001	.0000	.0000						
29	.0000	.0000								

TABLE 2. CUMULATIVE PRESENT VALUE FACTORS

Periods 0 to:	1%	2%	3%	4%	5%	6%	7%	8%	9%	10%
1	.990	.980	.971	.962	.952	.943	.935	.926	.917	.909
2	1.970	1.942	1.913	1.886	1.859	1.833	1.808	1.783	1.759	1.736
3	2.941	2.884	2.829	2.775	2.723	2.673	2.624	2.577	2.531	2.487
4	3.902	3.808	3.717	3.630	3.546	3.465	3.387	3.312	3.240	3.170
5	4.853	4.713	4.580	4.452	4.329	4.212	4.100	3.993	3.890	3.791
6	5.795	5.601	5.417	5.242	5.076	4.917	4.767	4.623	4.486	4.355
7	6.728	6.472	6.230	6.002	5.786	5.582	5.389	5.206	5.033	4.868
8	7.652	7.325	7.020	6.733	6.463	6.210	5.971	5.747	5.535	5.335
9	8.566	8.162	7.786	7.435	7.108	6.802	6.515	6.247	5.995	5.759
10	9.471	8.983	8.530	8.111	7.722	7.360	7.024	6.710	6.418	6.145
11	10.378	9.787	9.253	8.760	8.306	7.887	7.499	7.139	6.805	6.495
12	11.255	10.575	9.954	9.385	8.863	8.384	7.943	7.536	7.161	6.814
13	12.134	11.348	10.635	9.986	9.394	8.853	8.358	7.904	7.487	7.103
14	13.004	12.106	11.296	10.563	9.899	9.295	8.745	8.244	7.786	7.367
15	13.865	12.849	11.938	11.118	10.380	9.712	9.108	8.559	8.061	7.606
16	14.718	13.578	12.561	11.652	10.838	10.106	9.447	8.851	8.313	7.824
17	15.562	14.292	13.166	12.166	11.274	10.477	9.763	9.122	8.544	8.022
18	16.398	14.992	13.754	12.659	11.690	10.828	10.059	9.372	8.756	8.201
19	17.226	15.678	14.324	13.134	12.085	11.158	10.336	9.604	8.950	8.365
20	18.046	16.351	14.877	13.590	12.462	11.470	10.594	9.818	9.129	8.514
21	18.857	17.011	15.415	14.029	12.821	11.764	10.836	10.017	9.292	8.649
22	19.660	17.658	15.937	14.451	13.163	12.042	11.061	10.201	9.442	8.772
23	20.456	18.292	16.444	14.857	13.489	12.303	11.272	10.371	9.580	8.883
24	21.243	18.914	16.936	15.247	13.799	12.550	11.469	10.529	9.707	8.985
25	22.023	19.523	17.413	15.622	14.094	12.783	11.654	10.675	9.823	9.077
26	22.795	20.121	17.877	15.983	14.375	13.003	11.826	10.810	9.929	9.161
27	23.560	20.707	18.327	16.330	14.643	13.211	11.987	10.935	10.027	9.237
28	24.316	21.281	18.764	16.663	14.898	13.406	12.137	11.051	10.116	9.307
29	25.066	21.844	19.188	16.984	15.141	13.591	12.278	11.158	10.198	9.370
30	25.808	22.396	19.600	17.292	15.372	13.765	12.409	11.258	10.274	9.427
31	26.542	22.938	20.000	17.588	15.593	13.929	12.532	11.350	10.343	9.479
32	27.270	23.468	20.389	17.874	15.803	14.084	12.647	11.435	10.406	9.526
33	27.990	23.989	20.766	18.148	16.003	14.230	12.754	11.514	10.464	9.569
34	28.703	24.499	21.132	18.411	16.193	14.368	12.854	11.587	10.518	9.609
35	29.409	24.999	21.487	18.665	16.374	14.498	12.948	11.655	10.567	9.644
36	30.108	25.489	21.832	18.908	16.547	14.621	13.035	11.717	10.612	9.677
37	30.780	25.969	22.167	19.143	16.711	14.737	13.117	11.775	10.653	9.706
38	31.485	26.441	22.492	19.368	16.868	14.846	13.193	11.829	10.691	9.733
39	32.163	26.903	22.808	19.584	17.017	14.949	13.265	11.879	10.726	9.757
40	32.835	27.355	23.115	19.793	17.159	15.046	13.332	11.925	10.757	9.779

(Continued)

TABLE 2. CUMULATIVE PRESENT VALUE FACTORS (Continued)

Periods 0 to:	11%	12%	13%	14%	15%	16%	17%	18%	19%	20%
1	.901	.893	.885	.877	.870	.862	.855	.848	.840	.833
2	1.712	1.690	1.668	1.647	1.626	1.605	1.585	1.566	1.546	1.528
3	2.444	2.402	2.361	2.322	2.283	2.246	2.210	2.174	2.140	2.106
4	3.102	3.037	2.974	2.914	2.855	2.798	2.743	2.690	2.639	2.589
5	3.696	3.605	3.517	3.433	3.352	3.274	3.199	3.127	3.058	2.991
6	4.230	4.111	3.998	3.889	3.784	3.685	3.589	3.498	3.410	3.326
7	4.712	4.564	4.423	4.288	4.160	4.039	3.922	3.812	3.706	3.605
8	5.146	4.968	4.799	4.639	4.487	4.344	4.207	4.078	3.954	3.837
9	5.537	5.328	5.132	4.946	4.772	4.607	4.451	4.303	4.163	4.031
10	5.889	5.650	5.426	5.216	5.019	4.833	4.659	4.494	4.339	4.192
11	6.206	5.938	5.687	5.453	5.234	5.029	4.836	4.656	4.486	4.327
12	6.492	6.194	5.918	5.660	5.420	5.197	4.988	4.793	4.610	4.439
13	6.750	6.424	6.122	5.842	5.583	5.342	5.118	4.910	4.715	4.533
14	6.982	6.628	6.303	6.002	5.724	5.468	5.229	5.008	4.802	4.611
15	7.191	6.811	6.463	6.142	5.847	5.576	5.324	5.092	4.876	4.676
16	7.379	6.974	6.604	6.265	5.954	5.668	5.405	5.162	4.938	4.730
17	7.549	7.120	6.729	6.373	6.047	5.749	5.475	5.222	4.990	4.775
18	7.702	7.250	6.840	6.468	6.128	5.818	5.534	5.273	5.033	4.812
19	7.839	7.366	6.938	6.550	6.198	5.877	5.584	5.316	5.070	4.844
20	7.963	7.469	7.025	6.623	6.259	5.929	5.628	5.353	5.101	4.870
21	8.075	7.562	7.102	6.687	6.312	5.973	5.665	5.384	5.127	4.892
22	8.176	7.645	7.170	6.743	6.358	6.011	5.696	5.410	5.149	4.910
23	8.266	7.718	7.230	6.792	6.399	6.044	5.723	5.432	5.167	4.925
24	8.348	7.784	7.283	6.835	6.434	6.073	5.746	5.451	5.182	4.937
25	8.422	7.843	7.330	6.873	6.464	6.097	5.766	5.467	5.195	4.948
26	8.488	7.896	7.372	6.906	6.490	6.118	5.783	5.480	5.206	4.956
27	8.548	7.942	7.409	6.935	6.513	6.136	5.797	5.492	5.215	4.964
28	8.601	7.984	7.441	6.961	6.533	6.152	5.810	5.502	5.223	4.970
29	8.650	8.022	7.470	6.983	6.551	6.166	5.820	5.510	5.229	4.975
30	8.694	8.055	7.496	7.003	6.566	6.177	5.829	5.517	5.235	4.979
31	8.733	8.085	7.518	7.020	6.579	6.187	5.837	5.523	5.239	4.983
32	8.768	8.112	7.538	7.035	6.590	6.196	5.844	5.528	5.243	4.986
33	8.800	8.135	7.556	7.048	6.600	6.203	5.849	5.532	5.246	4.988
34	8.829	8.157	7.572	7.060	6.609	6.210	5.854	5.535	5.249	4.990
35	8.855	8.176	7.586	7.070	6.616	6.215	5.858	5.538	5.251	4.992
36	8.878	8.192	7.598	7.079	6.623	6.220	5.862	5.541	5.253	4.993
37	8.900	8.208	7.609	7.087	6.629	6.224	5.864	5.543	5.255	4.994
38	8.918	8.221	7.619	7.094	6.634	6.228	5.867	5.545	5.256	4.995
39	8.936	8.233	7.627	7.100	6.638	6.231	5.869	5.547	5.257	4.996
40	8.951	8.244	7.635	7.105	6.642	6.234	5.871	5.548	5.258	4.997

(Continued)

TABLE 2.   CUMULATIVE PRESENT VALUE FACTORS (Continued)

Periods 0 to:	21%	22%	23%	24%	25%	26%	27%	28%	29%	30%
1	.826	.820	.813	.806	.800	.794	.787	.781	.775	.769
2	1.509	1.492	1.474	1.457	1.440	1.424	1.407	1.392	1.376	1.361
3	2.074	2.042	2.011	1.981	1.952	1.924	1.896	1.868	1.842	1.816
4	2.540	2.494	2.448	2.404	2.362	2.320	2.280	2.241	2.203	2.166
5	2.926	2.864	2.804	2.746	2.689	2.635	2.583	2.532	2.483	2.436
6	3.244	3.167	3.092	3.021	2.951	2.885	2.821	2.759	2.670	2.643
7	3.508	3.416	3.327	3.242	3.161	3.083	3.009	2.937	2.868	2.802
8	3.725	3.619	3.518	3.421	3.329	3.241	3.156	3.076	2.998	2.925
9	3.905	3.786	3.673	3.566	3.463	3.366	3.273	3.184	3.100	3.019
10	4.054	3.923	3.799	3.682	3.570	3.465	3.364	3.269	3.178	3.092
11	4.177	4.036	3.902	3.776	3.656	3.544	3.437	3.335	3.239	3.147
12	4.278	4.128	3.985	3.852	3.725	3.606	3.493	3.387	3.286	3.190
13	4.362	4.203	4.053	3.912	3.780	3.656	3.538	3.427	3.322	3.223
14	4.431	4.265	4.108	3.962	3.824	3.695	3.573	3.459	3.351	3.249
15	4.489	4.315	4.153	4.001	3.859	3.726	3.601	3.483	3.372	3.268
16	4.536	4.357	4.190	4.033	3.887	3.751	3.623	3.503	3.390	3.283
17	4.575	4.391	4.219	4.059	3.910	3.771	3.640	3.518	3.403	3.295
18	4.608	4.419	4.243	4.080	3.928	3.786	3.654	3.530	3.413	3.304
19	4.634	4.442	4.263	4.097	3.942	3.799	3.664	3.539	3.421	3.310
20	4.656	4.460	4.279	4.110	3.954	3.808	3.673	3.546	3.427	3.316
21	4.675	4.476	4.292	4.121	3.963	3.816	3.679	3.552	3.432	3.320
22	4.690	4.488	4.302	4.130	3.970	3.822	3.684	3.556	3.435	3.323
23	4.702	4.499	4.311	4.137	3.976	3.827	3.688	3.559	3.438	3.325
24	4.712	4.507	4.318	4.143	3.981	3.831	3.692	3.562	3.440	3.327
25	4.721	4.514	4.323	4.147	3.985	3.834	3.694	3.564	3.442	3.328
26	4.728	4.520	4.328	4.151	3.988	3.837	3.696	3.566	3.443	3.329
27	4.734	4.524	4.332	4.154	3.990	3.839	3.698	3.567	3.444	3.330
28	4.739	4.528	4.335	4.156	3.992	3.840	3.699	3.568	3.445	3.331
29	4.743	4.531	4.337	4.158	3.994	3.841	3.700	3.569	3.446	3.331
30	4.746	4.534	4.339	4.160	3.995	3.842	3.701	3.570	3.446	3.332
31	4.749	4.536	4.341	4.161	3.996	3.843	3.701	3.570	3.447	3.332
32	4.751	4.538	4.342	4.162	3.997	3.844	3.702	3.571	3.447	3.332
33	4.753	4.539	4.343	4.163	3.997	3.844	3.702	3.571	3.447	3.332
34	4.754	4.540	4.344	4.164	3.998	3.845	3.703	3.571	3.448	3.333
35	4.756	4.541	4.345	4.164	3.998	3.845	3.703	3.571	3.448	3.333
36	4.756	4.542	4.345	4.165	3.998	3.845	3.703	3.571	3.448	3.333
37	4.757	4.543	4.346	4.165	3.999	3.846	3.703	3.571	3.448	3.333
38	4.758	4.543	4.346	4.165	3.999	3.846	3.703	3.571	3.448	3.333
39	4.759	4.544	4.347	4.166	3.999	3.846	3.703	3.571	3.448	3.333
40	4.759	4.544	4.347	4.166	3.999	3.846	3.703	3.572	3.448	3.333

(Continued)

TABLE 2. CUMULATIVE PRESENT VALUE FACTORS (Continued)

Periods 0 to:	31%	32%	33%	34%	35%	36%	37%	38%	39%	40%
1	.763	.758	.752	.746	.741	.735	.730	.725	.719	.714
2	1.346	1.332	1.317	1.303	1.289	1.276	1.263	1.250	1.237	1.224
3	1.791	1.766	1.742	1.719	1.696	1.674	1.652	1.630	1.609	1.589
4	2.130	2.096	2.062	2.029	1.997	1.966	1.936	1.906	1.877	1.849
5	2.390	2.345	2.302	2.260	2.220	2.181	2.143	2.106	2.070	2.035
6	2.588	2.534	2.483	2.433	2.385	2.339	2.294	2.250	2.209	2.168
7	2.739	2.677	2.619	2.562	2.508	2.455	2.404	2.355	2.308	2.263
8	2.845	2.786	2.721	2.658	2.598	2.540	2.485	2.431	2.380	2.331
9	2.942	2.868	2.798	2.730	2.665	2.603	2.544	2.486	2.432	2.379
10	3.009	2.930	2.855	2.784	2.715	2.649	2.587	2.526	2.469	2.414
11	3.060	2.978	2.899	2.824	2.752	2.683	2.618	2.555	2.496	2.438
12	3.100	3.013	2.931	2.854	2.779	2.708	2.641	2.576	2.515	2.456
13	3.130	3.040	2.956	2.876	2.799	2.727	2.658	2.592	2.528	2.468
14	3.152	3.061	2.974	2.892	2.814	2.740	2.670	2.602	2.538	2.478
15	3.170	3.076	2.988	2.905	2.825	2.750	2.679	2.610	2.546	2.484
16	3.183	3.088	2.999	2.914	2.834	2.757	2.685	2.616	2.551	2.488
17	3.193	3.097	3.006	2.921	2.840	2.763	2.690	2.620	2.554	2.492
18	3.201	3.104	3.012	2.926	2.844	2.767	2.693	2.624	2.557	2.494
19	3.207	3.109	3.017	2.930	2.847	2.770	2.696	2.626	2.559	2.496
20	3.211	3.113	3.020	2.933	2.850	2.772	2.698	2.627	2.560	2.497
21	3.215	3.116	3.022	2.935	2.852	2.773	2.699	2.628	2.561	2.498
22	3.217	3.118	3.024	2.937	2.853	2.774	2.700	2.629	2.562	2.498
23	3.219	3.120	3.026	2.938	2.854	2.775	2.701	2.630	2.563	2.499
24	3.221	3.121	3.027	2.939	2.855	2.776	2.701	2.630	2.563	2.499
25	3.222	3.122	3.028	2.939	2.855	2.776	2.702	2.631	2.563	2.499
26	3.223	3.123	3.028	2.940	2.856	2.777	2.702	2.631	2.564	2.500
27	3.224	3.123	3.029	2.940	2.856	2.777	2.702			
28	3.224	3.124	3.029	2.941	2.856	2.777	2.702			
29	3.224	3.124	3.029	2.941	2.856	2.777	2.702			
30	3.225	3.124	3.030	2.941	2.857	2.777	2.702	2.631	2.564	2.500
31	3.225	3.124	3.030	2.941	2.857	2.778	2.703			
32	3.225	3.124								
33	3.225	3.125								
34	3.225	3.125								
35	3.225	3.125	3.030	2.941	2.857	2.778	2.703			
36	3.226	3.125								
37	3.226									
38	3.226									
39	3.226									
40	3.226	3.125								

(Continued)

TABLE 2.　CUMULATIVE PRESENT VALUE FACTORS (Continued)

Periods 0 to:	41%	42%	43%	44%	45%	46%	47%	48%	49%	50%
1	.709	.704	.699	.694	.690	.685	.680	.676	.671	.667
2	1.212	1.200	1.188	1.177	1.165	1.154	1.143	1.132	1.122	1.111
3	1.569	1.549	1.530	1.512	1.493	1.475	1.458	1.441	1.424	1.407
4	1.822	1.795	1.769	1.744	1.720	1.695	1.672	1.649	1.627	1.605
5	2.001	1.968	1.937	1.906	1.876	1.846	1.818	1.790	1.763	1.737
6	2.129	2.090	2.054	2.018	1.983	1.949	1.917	1.885	1.854	1.824
7	2.219	2.176	2.135	2.096	2.057	2.020	1.984	1.949	1.916	1.883
8	2.283	2.237	2.192	2.150	2.108	2.068	2.030	1.993	1.957	1.922
9	2.328	2.279	2.232	2.188	2.144	2.102	2.061	2.022	1.984	1.948
10	2.360	2.309	2.260	2.214	2.168	2.124	2.083	2.042	2.003	1.965
11	2.383	2.330	2.280	2.232	2.185	2.140	2.097	2.055	2.015	1.977
12	2.400	2.345	2.294	2.244	2.196	2.151	2.107	2.064	2.024	1.984
13	2.411	2.356	2.303	2.253	2.204	2.158	2.114	2.071	2.029	1.990
14	2.419	2.363	2.310	2.259	2.210	2.163	2.118	2.075	2.033	1.993
15	2.425	2.368	2.315	2.263	2.214	2.166	2.121	2.078	2.036	1.995
16	2.429	2.372	2.318	2.266	2.216	2.169	2.123	2.079	2.037	1.996
17	2.432	2.375	2.320	2.268	2.218	2.170	2.125	2.081	2.038	1.998
18	2.434	2.377	2.322	2.270	2.219	2.171	2.126	2.082	2.039	1.998
19	2.436	2.378	2.323	2.271	2.220	2.172	2.126	2.082	2.040	1.999
20	2.437	2.379	2.324	2.271	2.221	2.173	2.127	2.083	2.040	1.999
21	2.437	2.379	2.324	2.272	2.221	2.173	2.127	2.083	2.040	2.000
22	2.438	2.380	2.325	2.272	2.222	2.173	2.127			
23	2.438	2.380	2.325	2.272	2.222	2.173	1.127			
24	2.438	2.380	2.325	2.273	2.222	2.174	2.128			
25	2.439	2.380	2.325	2.273	2.222	2.174	2.128	2.083	2.040	2.000
26	2.439	2.381	2.326	2.273	2.222	2.174	2.128			
27										
28										
29										
30	2.439	2.381	2.326	2.273	2.222	2.174	2.128			

APPENDIX 2
References to the CICA Handbook

The locations of the references in the *CICA Handbook* are shown in square brackets. The excerpts have been reprinted with permission, © The Canadian Institute of Chartered Accountants, Toronto, Canada.

Income tax
> disclosure on income statement: [1520], 144
> liability, re-estimating a prior-period adjustment: [1506.25], 432
> incorrect provision discovered subsequently: [3290.22], 432
> loss carryforward: [3470.44] and [3470.56], 507
> reasonable assurance and: [3470.52], 508

Instalment accounts: [3020.02], 183

Intangible assets
> amortization disclosure: [3080.03], 376
> basis of valuation: [3080.02], 376
> separate disclosure for items: [3080.01], 376

Interest capitalization: [3850.03], 302
> disclosure requirements: [3850], 850

Interest expense, disclosure: [1520], 144

Interest income, timing of recognition: [3400.09], 141

Interperiod tax allocation, required: [3470.13] and [3470.20], 491

Inventory valuation
> absorption costing: [3030.06], 241
> basis: [3030.10], 250
> change: [3030.13], 251
> lower-of-cost-and-market rule: [3030.11], 242
> methods: [3010.10]. 237
> overhead costs included: [3050.06], 251

Investment
> in affiliated company: [3010.03], 173
> tax credit, cost-reduction approach: [3805.12], 509
> *See also* Long-term investment; Passive investment; Temporary investment

J

Joint venture, definition: [3055.03], 741

L

Lease
> amortization rate and method to be shown: [3065.25], 556
> capital. *See* Capital lease
> disclosure obligations due within one year: [3065.22], 556
> disclosure of amortization costs: [3065.21], 556
> disclosure of future minimum lease payments: [3065.32], 556
> disclosure of interest expense: [3065.26], 556
> disclosure of minimum lease payments for next five years: [3065.23], 556
> financing, up front costs: [3065.40], 547
> general disclosure provisions: [3065], 535
> lease obligation shown separately: [3065.22], 546

> net investment and income, lessor to show separately: [3065.24], 556
> separate disclosure on balance sheet: [3065.21], 546
> treatment of land: [3065.73], 551
> uncertainty re lessor's ability to collect: [3065.07], 542
> *See also* Sale-and-leaseback

Liabilities
> definition: [1000.25], 424
> treatment under current-value accounting: [4510], 785
> *See also* Income tax

Long-term debt: [3210], 473

Long-term investment
> decline in market value: [3050.33], 399
> with market value, disclosure of: [3050.44], 399
> without market value, disclosure of: [3050.41], 399

Lower-of-cost-and-market rule. *See* Inventory valuation; Temporary investment

M

Minority interest in income or loss: [1520], 144

N

Negative goodwill on consolidation: [1580.44], 738

O

Operating rental expense, disclosure: [1520], 144

P

Passive investment, cost method re revenue recognition: [3050.28], 396

Pension
> adjustments to be amortized: [3460.43], 601
> amortization of past service costs: [3460.71], 601
> annual expense for defined contribution plans: [3460.65], 601
> disclosure for defined benefit plans: [3460.60], 601
> disclosure of past service liability for defined benefit plans: [3460.60], 601
> disclosure of past service liability for defined contribution plans: [3460.74], 601
> experience gains and losses to be amortized: [3460.52], 601
> gains or losses in period of termination: [3460.54], 601
> management responsibility: [3460.17], 601
> plan, defined: [3460.03(a)], 581
> plan, accrued benefit method to be used: [3460.22] and [3460.28], 600

Check Figures for Selected Exercises and Problems

CHAPTER 1

E1-3.	Six of the items are on the balance sheet, and three of them are credits.
E1-5.	Three of the items are found on the income statement.
E1-9.	Two are liabilities.
E1-10.	One is classified as owners' equity.
E1-13.	Assets at the end of the period were $111,610
E1-15.	Gain on exchange = $1,500
E1-16.	Warranty expense = $3,000 in 19X1.

P1-2.	Net income = $7,600.
P1-3.	Retained earnings = $13,830.
P1-5.	Retained earnings = $876.
P1-6.	Total assets = $784,620
P1-7.	Net income = $60,726.
P1-8.	Net income = $15,840.
P1-9.	Net income after tax = $66,428.
P1-10.	Net income = $70
P1-11.	Owners' equity = $101,608.

CHAPTER 2

P2-19.	**b.**(ii.) $4.50 is a discount.

CHAPTER 3

E3-3.	Four are assets.
E3-4.	Two are owners' equity.
E3-9.	**a.** Debit retained earnings $50,000.

P3-1.	Assets > $7,000.
P3-2.	**a.** Working capital increase = $35,000.
P3-3.	Cash provided during year = $23,000.
P3-4.	Total assets = $490,436 and $445,152.
P3-5.	Total assets = $260,838 and $260,320.
P3-6.	**a.** Net income = $492.02.
P3-7.	Funds changed by $21,400.
P3-8.	Funds increase = $16,150.
P3-9.	Let x = the proceeds of the building, then construct the usual SCFP and solve for x.

P3-10.   Net change in working capital > $50,000.
P3-11.   Total assets = $1,741,251.
P3-12.   Net income = $4,920.

CHAPTER 4

E4-6.   Net income for 19X8 = $38,200.
E4-7.   **a.** Net income for January = $30,775.
E4-8.   **a.** Answer is between $4,500 and $5,500.
E4-9.   Debit depreciation expense for between $6,500 and $7,000.

P4-4.   The revised net income is between $225,000 and $240,000.
P4-6.   The total income over the three years is $249,450. The income from one of the years for each of the methods is $37,050; $90,520; and $93,780.
P4-10.   Net income is between $4,500 and $5,000 overstated.
P4-11.   Net income is between $20,000 and $23,000 in 19X2.

CHAPTER 5

E5-1.   At least two are cash items.
E5-2.   At least two are timing matters.
E5-4.   LCM aggregate in one of the years = $6,620.
E5-5.   Corrected balance is between $50 and $100.
E5-10.   **a.** The least profitable month yields a profit of $760.
E5-18.   **a.** Cost > Market.
    b. LCM yields highest net income.
E5-19.   Net current assets between $30,000 and $80,000.
E5-20.   Net current assets between $30,000 and $80,000.
E5-23.   Debit cash for $34,600.
E5-25.   Overstated by between $1,700 and $2,000 in 19X3.

P5-2.   Adjusted bank balance = 1,639.10.
P5-4.   Only one of the entries affects the cost of goods sold.
P5-5.   Present value of four payments of $100,000 = $316,986 at 10%.
P5-8.   The company could expect to get $38,604.48 cash when the charge slips were deposited.
P5-10.   Reconciliated bank balance > $4,000.
P5-11.   **b.** (ii) Market = $8,348.75.
P5-14.   Beginning balance after reconciliation in 1985 — $6,005.
P5-17.   Unrealized loss of between $3,500 and $4,700.
P5-18.   Cash is between 6,500 and 7,100.

CHAPTER 6

E6-4.   **a.** FIFO has the lowest valued inventory. Why?
    b. Use the latest purchase for "market."
E6-5.   **e.** The inventory was overstated by $400 because the consignment goods should not have been included. Therefore total assets at the end of Year 1 were overstated by $400. At the end of Year 2 we are entitled to assume that inventory was counted properly, so there would be no effect on total assets at that time. The income for Year 1 would be overstated (because closing inventory was overstated, thus cost of goods sold would be understated, and hence net income is oversta-ted).
E6-6.   **a.** Income for Year 2 is for Job 1, between $80,000 and $85,000; for Job 2, between $13,000 and $15,000; and for Job 3, between ($400,000) and ($425,000).
E6-7.   **a.** Loss for Year 2 is between $30,000 and $33,500.
    b. *Hint:* Use the annual gains or losses provided to calculate the cumulative losses to date. Then assume the contract price remains unchanged and derive the cost.
    c. Loss recorded for Year 2 is between $280,000 and $290,000.
E6-8.   Income in Year 5 for Scylla = $5,000.
E6-10.   **a.** Ending inventory at cost = $7,667.11.
    b. Cost of goods sold = $11,625.00
E6-11.   Ending inventory at LCM is between $82,000 and $87,000.
E6-12.   Expenses > $20,000.
E6-13.   Inventory < $75,000.

P6-1. Cost percentage is about 69%.
P6-2. Cost percentage is about 73%.
P6-3. Purchasing agent's plan requires about $37,000 less cash.
P6-6. **a.** LIFO = $2,500.
P6-8. Purchases are approximately $282,500.
P6-9. Estimated loss is between $65,000 and $70,000.
P6-10. Insurance claim is between $80,000 and $90,000.
P6-13. Inventory is between $20,000 and $22,000.
P6-14. Purchases are between $117,000 and $125,000.
P6-15. Inventory at LCM is between $8,000 and $10,000.
P6-16. Inventory is between $55,000 and $60,000.
P6-18. LCM estimate < $5,000.
P6-19. Purchases < $50,000.
P6-20. **a.** $3,093.00.
P6-22. **b.** Income in Year 2 = $10,000.
P6-23. Division Y's income in Year 2 = $11,857.71.
P6-24. Wilson Inc., Year 2 income to date = $420,000.
P6-25. LCM estimate for one of the years = $3,438.96.
P6-26. **a.** In one year the margin = $1,203.85.
   b. In one year the margin = $496.60.
   c. In one year the COGS = $1,577.76.
P6-27. NPV = $275,814.89.
P6-31. **c.** Gross margin percentage = 51%.
P6-32. Correct inventory is between $38,000 and $40,000.
P6-33. **b.** $165,000 to $170,000.
P6-34. **a.** LIFO is $35,000 to $38,000.
P6-35. Loss is less than $80,000.
P6-36. A = $1.75.
P6-37. Ending inventory at retail is over $25,000 and less than $28,300.
P6-38. Inventory for 1984 is over $33,000.
P6-39. **c.** Gross margin is $7,285,000.

CHAPTER 7

E7-1. **d.** The cost of the maintenance would not normally be capitalized. The challenge will be to figure out how to approximate the split of the puchase price between car and maintenance costs.
E7-4. At least one is expensed.
E7-5. Less than four are plant assets.
E7-9. Interest cost < $3,000.
E7-22. Annual depreciation is between $4,000 and $4,500.
E7-24. **a.** *Hint:* use normal selling price.
E7-25. **a.** Debit equipment $12,667.68.
E7-26. Purchase price of machine is between $43,000 and $44,000.
E7-27. **a.** (i) $13,000 to $13,500.
E7-28. **a.** Effective, but efficient?

P7-3. New taxi goes on the books at $10,700.
P7-4. Credit to cash is $1,500.
P7-6. (iii) or (iv).
P7-7. Leasehold improvements should be amortized.
P7-8. **a.** Explain why the decision whether to capitalize would not change, but the amount capitalized might.
P7-12. **a.** Total assets for all common shares = $1,000,005.
P7-13. **b.** Debit equipment $20,000.
P7-14. 31 Dec. 19X0: debit depreciation expense $615.

CHAPTER 8

E8-3. **c.** (iii) Depreciation is between $9,000 and $9,500.
E8-5. **d.** NBV at start of year < $12,000.
   g. Initial cost is between $10,000 and $20,000.

E8-6.   **c.** Depreciation > $20,000.
E8-7.   Year 5: successful efforts = $104,533.
E8-8.   Depreciation expense falls.
E8-10.   New rate = 25.33%.
E8-11.   Charge per ton is between $2.00 and $3.00.
E8-12.   Declining balance = $7,714.
E8-13.   **b.** (i) Change in estimate.
E8-14.   **a.** Debit plant and equipment $24,000.
E8-16.   Net income understated by $7,500 in 19X1.

P8-3.   **d.** Usage method is lowest, but by a fluke. What would you normally expect would be lower?
P8-7.   Net amount to amortize = $2,000,000.
P8-8.   Income decreases by > $25,000.
P8-9.   Revised income > $105,000.
P8-12.   Net income of East Co. = $1,586,273.00.
P8-13.   **b.** Accumulated depreciation (31 Dec. 19X7) = $72,000.
P8-14.   **a.** Depreciation expense = $675.
P8-15.   **b.** Depreciation expense is around $935.

CHAPTER 9

P9-2.   The value of the business as a going concern appears to exceed the break-up value by $3,670; so the purchaser would normally be prepared to pay an amount equal to the market value of the assets he is acquiring plus the value of the goodwill, provided he gets the business as a going concern.
P9-3.   The value of the goodwill is $1,047 at 10% discount rate, and the present value of the earnings at 15% is around $10,300.
P9-5.   The value of the goodwill in each case is Franchise 1 — negative; Franchise 2 — between $11,000 and $12,000; and Franchise 3 — between $20,000 and $21,000.
P9-9.   Total capitalized = $500,000.
P9-21.   Excess earnings expected are from $12,000 to $13,000.

CHAPTER 10

E10-1.   **a.** *Hint:* Accrue the interest for the elapsed period.
           b. Net income for the period is around $43.00.
           c. The liability should be accrued because the dividend was declared in the current year.
           e. *Hint:* If a shareholder receives a dividend to which he is not entitled, he will receive a letter from his broker asking him to pay it over so it can be sent to the new shareholder entitled to the dividend.
E10-3.   **d.** Cost = $35,000.
E10-5.   **d.** Net income under equity method is between $61,000 and $62,000.
E10-7.   Purchase price difference amortization = $675.00.
E10-8.   **a.** Between $15,500 and $17,000.
           b. Between $19,500 and $21,000.
           c. Between $55,000 and $65,000.
           d. Between $49,000 and $52,000.
E10-12.   Initial investment in Riverview = $60,000.
E10-13.   Investment account balance is between $81,000 and $83,000.
E10-14.   Goodwill = $2,000.

P10-2.   **a.** Webster owns 20% of Soperton.
           c. Income would be less by $300,000.
P10-7.   **a.** Implied goodwill = $14,100.
P10-9.   **f.** Loss on sale is between $35,000 and $40,000.
           h. Discount needed > $50,000.
P10-10.   There was a net loss in 19X1.
P10-11.   Loss on disposal > $50,000,000.
P10-12.   Purchase difference amortization is from $3,600 to $3,700.
P10-13.   Purchase difference amortization is from $600 to $700.
P10-14.   **a.** 31 January: unrealized loss is between $700 and $800.

CHAPTER 11

E11-3. Estimated cost of goods sold exceeds the sales revenue.

P11-1. **d.** Adjustment required is $45,000.
P11-2. **c.** Adjustment required is $5,600.
P11-3. Adjustment required is $3,675.
P11-4. **c.** Warranty expense is between $17,000 and $18,000.
P11-6. **c.** Adjustment needed is between $600 and $700.
P11-9. **a.** Adjustment needed = 400 containers.
P11-10. Debit loss on damages $250,000.

CHAPTER 12

E12-1. **b.** Answer is between $1,000,000 and $1,100,000.
E12-3. Assuming straight-line amortization, the bond discount written off at the time of redemption is $480, and deferred charges for bond issue costs are $720.
E12-4. **b.** Gain on redemption would be $10,000.
E12-5. Column G has 4 yeses. Column H has 5 gains. Column I has 3 nos.
E12-7. **b.** Guaranteed rate may be greater than market rate.
E12-8. **b.** Year-end adjustment = $1,754.40.

P12-1. **c.** Mortgage issue costs are $360.
P12-2. Total market value of package = $1,018.58.
P12-3. **b.** Bond interest expense is $15,188.
P12-4. **b.** Gain on redemption of bonds is $51,000.
P12-5. **c.** Gain on redemption of bonds is $16,500.
P12-7. **a.** In the first year, interest method gives $8,771, and straight-line method gives 9,228.93.
P12-8. Bonds priced to yield 8% would be sold for $43,917.00.
P12-9. **b.** Excess earnings of $5,671.83 would be transferred to general bank account.
P12-15. Debit equipment $78,862.
P12-16. **a.** Amount of bond discount is around $380.
P12-17. **b.** Debit investment in bonds $2,000.
P12-18. **b.** Debit investment in bonds $140,000.

CHAPTER 13

E13-3. Six are timing differences. Three result in credits.
E13-5. **a.** Tax expense under the accrual method is $10,509.
E13-6. **a.** The tax recovery in the fifth year is $480, and there is a current tax expense with respect to that year of $3,840.
E13-7. **c.** In Year 3 there is a tax recovery of $3,300 with respect to the current year and $225 with respect to a prior year.
E13-8. **a.** $8,000.
E13-10. **a.** Credit tax recovery $2,250.
E13-11. **a.** Recovery for Company A from 19X1 to 19X5 = $1,350.
E13-13. **a.** In year 19X1 tax recovery = $450 for situation (ii).

P13-1. The tax payable is $177,265.
P13-2. Deferred income tax decreases by $4,500 in the third year, and reduces the balance in the account to nil.
P13-3. Total taxable income is $2,750,000.
P13-4. **c.** Income tax expense is approximately $107,000, and the credit to taxes payable is approximately $101,000.
P13-6. **d.** Balance in deferred income taxes at the end of Year 4 is $6,600.
P13-7. Balance in deferred income tax account at the end of 19X5 is about $86,000.
P13-8. Taxable loss = $38,000.
P13-10. Tax provision = $26,100.
P13-11. **b.** Net income before extraordinary items is $132,750.
P13-12. UCC for Year 8 = $23,082.
P13-13. **a.** Tax payable is approximately $8,300.
P13-14. **a.** Taxable income = $67,000.

P13-15. **c.** Balance is between $65,000 and $70,000.
P13-17. **a.** (i) Total tax expense = $8,000 for all years together.
P13-18. **a.** Total net income for Preston = $2,500.
P13-19. **a.** Long-term deferred income tax in 19X1 = ($1,575).
P13-20. **a.** Total tax expense = $12,002.
P13-21. Tax liability for 19X2 = $4,243.
P13-22. **a.** Company A: Debit deferred income tax $550 in both (i) and (ii).
P13-23. Net income before tax raises $50,000 after adjustments.
P13-24. **b.** Year-end balance in long-term deferred income tax for 19X3 = ($1,878).

CHAPTER 14

E14-1. This is an operating lease, and the customary matching rules apply.
E14-3. **b.** Rate is between 10% and 13%. If you don't have a calculator that computes this directly, try picking an amount such as 11% and seeing if your result is too high or too low. This will tell you the direction to go in making your next guess. The correct answer is a round amount.
E14-4. *Hint:* Make some reasonable assumptions to test whether the company should write down the asset before putting it into rental inventory.
E14-5. **a.** Net loss = $215,489.80.
E14-6. **c.** 1.22.
E14-7. **b.** Long-term portion is around $1,225,000

P14-1. Difference in fifth year is $693.11.
P14-2. The lease in (iii) is an operating lease.
P14-3. **a.** First year's difference is $16,000.
　　　　　b. Tasty's debt/equity ratio = 10.87 at end of Year 2.
P14-5. **b.** The interest expense for the lease in Year 1 = $17,893.05.
P14-6. Present values at 10% are as follows:
　　　　　Oxnard—$280,947.60;
　　　　　Fofar—$281,424.94;
　　　　　Sunbury—$252,106.60; and
　　　　　Battersea—$282,751.09.
P14-7. The number of machines is between 5 and 10.
P14-8. *Hint:* In evaluating whether the lease is capital or operating, look at the economic incentives at the end of 15 years as well as the legal requirements.
P14-9. **a.** The gain on the sale is $37,500.
P14-10. *Hint:* Since the gross revenues are identical in all cases, all you have to do it concentrate on the comparative expenses.
P14-11. **a.** (i) Financing type.
P14-13. Lessee's interest expense = Lessor's interest expense.
P14-14. **c.** Interest income = $416.67.
P14-15. **c.** Interest income = $367.41.
P14-16. **c.** Interest income = $956.67.
P14-17. Interest income = $1,955.23.
P14-18. **b.** Difference is approximately $7,000.
P14-19. **c.** Annual depreciation = $8,000.

CHAPTER 15

E15-1. **e.** (i) Accounting liability would go up because some of the retirement benefits that have been increased 5% are with respect to past service, and they are an expense that up to now has not been recognized.
　　　　　e. (ii) Gross actuarial liability would go up because the present value of pension benefits is now higher.
　　　　　e. (iii) Accounting pension expense would go up starting immediately.
　　　　　e. (iv) Market value of pension fund investments would be unchanged.
　　　　　e. (v) Unfunded actuarial liability would go up because the gross actuarial liability has increased and the value of the pension investments has not changed.
E15-3. *Hint:* This is a defined contribution plan. Therefore the employee gets any of the "experience" gains or losses such as higher yield on the pension investments.
E15-4. **b.** The adjustment is $400.
E15-5. **b.** The "appropriate" amount is not a single figure, but one that falls within a range. Can you figure out what the range should be?

E15-7. *Hint:* One of the important things here is to recognize that under the proposed plan the employees could lose both their job and their pension benefits at the same time.
E15-8. The present value of past service costs is approximately $245,000.
E15-9. Amortization of past service costs is about $35,000 per year.
E15-10. Pension expense in Year 1 is approximately $100,700.

P15-3. Investment income would only be recorded on the books of the trustee.
P15-4. Since this is a defined benefit plan, any fund "surplus" goes to the employer.
P15-7. The expected present value of the pension benefits at the point of retirement is $270,473.
P15-8. **b.** (ii) $14,757.97.
P15-9. **b.** (ii) $26,316.44.
P15-10. **a.** Around $3.68 million
P15-11. *Hint:* Be sure not to confuse funding issues with accounting issues.
P15-12. **b.** (i) Around $52,000.

CHAPTER 16

E16-2. In three of the cases the stated capital would be increased.
E16-8. A dilutive situaiton exists in only one of the cases cited.

P16-2. **a.** A switch would be sensible only at two of the year-ends.
P16-3. 500 new shares were issued.
P16-11. Value of warrants <$5,000.
P16-18. **b.** Basic EPS = $1.88.
P16-19. **b.** Around $550,000.

CHAPTER 17

E17-2. The basic EPS for net income is $5.00 in two cases and $2.00 in three other cases.
E17-3. The fully-diluted EPS in each case is different, but all are approximately $5.00.
E17-4. Approximately 27,000.
E17-5. Approximately 12,500 fully diluted.
E17-6. Three are dilutive.
E17-7. EPS after extraordinary items is between $1.10 and $1.17.
E17-8. **b.** Approximately $0.45.
E17-9. Fully-diluted EPS is between $0.75 and $0.82.

P17-1. Around $6.00
P17-2. EPS after extraordinary items is around $2.50.
P17-3. EPS after extraordinary items is aorund $5.65.
P17-4. EPS after extraordinary items is around $3.00.
P17-5. EPS after extraordinary items is around $0.45.
P17-6. **b.** Around $5,700.
P17-7. **c.** EPS after extraordinary items is around $1.70.
P17-8. Optimistic had an EPS of around $0.80, and Pessimistic had a loss of around $0.60.
P17-9. **b.** Around 4,700.
P17-10. **b.** EPS after extraordinary items is around $0.80.
P17-11. **b.** EPS after extraordinary items is around $0.40.
P17-12. **a.** EPS after extraordinary items is around $0.75.
P17-13. **c.** Around $14.00.
P17-14. **a.** EPS after extraordinary items is around $0.40.
P17-15. **a.** EPS after extraordinary items is around $0.80.
P17-16. **b.** EPS before extraordinary item = $0.89.
P17-17. Fully diluted EPS is about $2.60.
P17-18. Fully diluted EPS is about $3.25.
P17-20. Basic EPS after extraordinary item is about $1.30.
P17-21. Basic EPS after extraordinary item is about $1.45.

CHAPTER 18

E18-1. **d.** The effect on (i) net current assets and (ii) cash would be different.
E18-9. Actual working capital > $30,000.
E18-10. Working capital from operations is about $4,400,000.
E18-12. Working capital from operations is abut $300,000.

P18-1.   Total funds from operations = $171,260.
P18-3.   Total funds from operations is around $36,000.
P18-4.   Net change in working capital = $4,020.
P18-5.   *Hint*: This requires estimation of the 19X6 results. There is no "right" answer.
P18-6.   Working capital at the end of year 19X2 = $17,660.
P18-8.   Total assets = $8,898.
P18-10. Net cash inflow of about $54,000.
P18-11. Change in cash equivalents is about $400.
P18-12. Net cash outflow of $14,000.
P18-13. Change in cash and cash equivalents is about $34,000.
P18-14. Net increase in cash is about $5,800.
P18-15. Net cash outflow of about $10,000.
P18-16. Net cash outflow of about $11,000.

CHAPTER 19

E19-1.   **e.** The purchase difference is $400.
E19-2.   **e.** Retained earnings = $5,500.
E19-3.   Three are incompatible.
E19-5.   **a.** Under (b), debit sales and debit cost of goods sold for $23,494.
E19-6.   Total consolidated assets = $1,029,145.

P19-1.   Retained earnings of subsidiary is $200.
P19-2.   Consolidated retained earnings are $5,126.
P19-3.   **b.**(i) Balance in investment account is $10,880.
P19-4.   Consolidated retained earnings are around $7,800.
P19-5.   Consolidated income after taxes is $16,300.
P19-7.   **b.** Around $251,000.
P19-8.   Consolidated retained earnings are around $315,000.
P19-9.   **a.** Between $690,000 and $705,000.
             b. Between $715,000 and $723,000.
P19-10. *Hint:* Find the percentage minority ownership by calculating the $70 minority interest as a function of the changing retained earnings. Assume that the capital stock of $200 is unchanged over the period.
P19-11. **b.** Balance at end of period is about $36,000.
P19-12. End-of-year consolidated retained earnings is about $1,470,000.
P19-13. **b.** Investments balance under equity method is about $130,000.
P19-14. Consolidated income is about $17,000.
P19-15. Consolidated income is about $43,000.
P19-16. **b.** Balance of investment in Sub. is about $319,000.

CHAPTER 20

E20-1.   **a.** Gross margin is (i) $395,000, (ii) $394,000, (iii) $413,222, and (iv) $414,005.
E20-2.   **a.** There would be a monetary loss but no holding loss.
E20-3.   **b.** Monetary gain is $4,000.
E20-5.   **f.** There is no gain or loss under the physical capital maintenance concept, but there is a loss of around $4,500 under the financial capital maintenance concept.
E20-8.   GPL adjusted gross margin is about $1,300.
E20-9.   **b.** Gain of about $2,400.
E20-10. Net book value of press is about $166,600.

P20-1.   **c.** Owners' equity at 31 Dec. 19X4 in dollars of the same date is a deficit of $23,000.
P20-2.   At the end of Year 1, GPL = $26,250.00.
P20-3.   **d.** The correct answers (not necessarily in the right order) are $35,000, $36,000, and $40,000.
P20-4.   **b.** The total retained earnings for Year 2 in Year 2 $'s is $6,667, which consists of a loss in one year and a gain in the other.
P20-5.   Net loss in Year 1 is around $7,000.
P20-8.   Financing adjustment is about $8,900.
P20-9.   Financing adjustment is about $2,500.
P20-10. Financing adjustment is about $711.
P20-11. Financing adjustment is about $26,000.

CHAPTER 21

E21-1.	**j.** For 19X4, EPS = $1.10.
E21-2.	**f.** For 19X7, day sales in inventory = 555.
E21-3.	**a.** current ratio = 1.51.
E21-4.	**h.** Return on shareholders' equity is around 9%.
E21-7.	**a.** If the current ratio goes down, then (1) current assets go down or (2) current liabilities go up or (3) both. If (1) holds, then the quick ratio will be unaffected if the decrease is only in inventory; otherwise it will decrease. If (2) holds, then the quick ratio will decrease. If (3) holds, then the answer cannot be determined.
E21-9.	**a.** (i) Up, because subtracting the bank loan from current liabilities, and the payment from current assets will increase the ratio (since it is already greater than 1). (ii) Up, since the general return on assets is 11%. (iii) Up, since net income is higher and the amount of long-term interest is unchanged.
E21-11.	**a.** Profit margin = 0.0612.
P21-7.	**a.** (vi) Asset turnover ratio = 42.
E21-8.	**c.** Current liabilities = $102,710.
E21-9.	**h.** Return on equity = .02
E21-12.	**c.** $1,700,000.
E21-17.	**a.** (iii) EPS for 19X3 is about $6.70.

Subject Index

A

Absorption costing in inventory, 241
Account form of balance sheet, 109
Accounting
    compared with bookkeeping, 8
    ultimate test of, 8
Accounting and Auditing Guidelines, 57
Accounting conventions, 9
Accounting equation, 2
Accounting errors, accounting treatment of, 152
Accounting estimates
    disclosure of "rare or unusual" items, 152
    nature of, 152
    retroactive adjustment not normally used,
        152
Accounting Guideline
    re push-down accounting, 739
    re full costing, 347
Accounting income
    for tax accounting purposes, 490
    versus taxable income, 20
Accounting model, compared with economic
    model, 26
Accounting principles
    compared with deductive logic methods, 9
    definition, 9
Accounting Principles by Ross Skinner, origin of,
    56
Accounting Principles Board (APB)
    Opinion No. 11 (*Accounting for Income
        Taxes*), 501
    Opinion No. 15, 658
    Opinion No. 16, 741
    Opinion No. 21, 180, 231, 464
    Predecessor to FASB, 59
Accounting Research Advisory Board (ARAB),
    nature of, 56
Accounting standard setters, fundamental prob-
    lems faced by, 63
Accounting standards, development in U.S., 58
Accounting Standards Committee (AcSC)
    how topics are chosen for study, 56
    role of, 52
    role within CICA, 56
Accounts payable, 427

Accounts receivable
    ageing, 228
    assignment, 184
    collectability, 178
    control and subsidiary ledgers, 226
    credit cards and, 230
    credit management, 228
    definition, 102
    deferred interest, 180
    direct-write-off method, 179
    disclosure requirements, 181
    discounting, 179
    factoring, 184
    instalments over one year, treatment of,
        183
    justified assumptions, 185
    long-term, 223
    management of, 226
    nature of, 174
    pledged as collateral, 183
    related party transactions, 182
    returns and allowances, 184
    subsidiary ledger, 226
    unusual items, 182
    valuation, 177
Accounts receivable turnover ratio, 833
Accrued benefit cost method, 584
Accrued liability, 107, 429
Accrued wages, as a current liability, 429
Acquisition by company of own shares
    accounting for, 633
    restrictions on, 631
Acquisition cost, re depreciation, 335
AcSC. *See* Accounting Standards Committee
Actuarial cost
    definition, 584
    nature of, 596
Actuarial liability
    definition, 585, 596
    unfunded, 597
Actuary
    definition, 583
    role in pension plan, 596
Adjusted basic earnings per share, 666

Author Index

Key Term Index

The following key terms are also included in the Subject Index above.